W9-CNC-655

PAGES PACKED WITH ESSENTIAL INFORMATION

"Value-packed, unbeatable, accurate, and comprehensive."

—*The Los Angeles Times*

"The guides are aimed not only at young budget travelers but at the independent traveler; a sort of streetwise cookbook for traveling alone."

—*The New York Times*

"Unbeatable; good sight-seeing advice; up-to-date info on restaurants, hotels, and inns; a commitment to money-saving travel; and a wry style that brightens nearly every page."

—*The Washington Post*

THE BEST TRAVEL BARGAINS IN YOUR BUDGET

"All the dirt, dirt cheap."

—*People*

"Let's Go follows the creed that you don't have to throw your life's savings to the wind to travel—unless you want to."

—*The Salt Lake Tribune*

PURCHASED FROM
MULTNOMAH COUNTY LIBRARY
TITLE WAVE BOOKSTORE

REAL ADVICE FOR REAL EXPERIENCES

"The writers seem to have experienced every rooster-packed bus and lunar-surfaced mattress about which they write."

—*The New York Times*

"[Let's Go's] devoted updaters really walk the walk (and thumb the ride, and trek the trail). Learn how to fish, haggle, find work—anywhere."

—*Food & Wine*

"A world-wise traveling companion—always ready with friendly advice and helpful hints, all sprinkled with a bit of wit."

—*The Philadelphia Inquirer*

A GUIDE WITH A SPIRIT AND A SOCIAL CONSCIENCE

"Lighthearted and sophisticated, informative and fun to read. [Let's Go] helps the novice traveler navigate like a knowledgeable old hand."

—*Atlanta Journal-Constitution*

"The serious mission at the book's core reveals itself in exhortations to respect the culture and the environment—and, if possible, to visit as a volunteer, a student, or a teacher rather than a tourist."

—*San Francisco Chronicle*

LET'S GO PUBLICATIONS

TRAVEL GUIDES
Australia
Austria & Switzerland
Brazil
Britain
California
Central America
Chile
China
Costa Rica
Costa Rica, Nicaragua & Panama
Eastern Europe
Ecuador
Egypt
Europe
France
Germany
Greece
Guatemala & Belize
Hawaii
India & Nepal
Ireland
Israel
Italy
Japan
Mexico
New Zealand
Peru
Puerto Rico
Southeast Asia
Spain & Portugal with Morocco
Thailand
USA
Vietnam
Western Europe
Yucatan Peninsula

ROADTRIP GUIDE
Roadtripping USA

ADVENTURE GUIDES
Alaska
Pacific Northwest
Southwest USA

CITY GUIDES
Amsterdam
Barcelona
Berlin, Prague & Budapest
Boston
Buenos Aires
Florence
London
London, Oxford, Cambridge & Edinburgh
New York City
Paris
Rome
San Francisco
Washington, DC

POCKET CITY GUIDES
Amsterdam
Berlin
Boston
Chicago
London
New York City
Paris
San Francisco
Venice
Washington, DC

PURCHASED FROM
MULTNOMAH COUNTY LIBRARY
TITLE WAVE BOOKSTORE

LET'S GO

GREECE

RESEARCHERS

CHARLOTTE ALTER   SARAH MORTAZAVI
JILLIAN GOODMAN   ANSLEY RUBINSTEIN
PHOEBE STONE

IYA MEGRE MANAGING EDITOR
ANDREW FINE RESEARCH MANAGER

EDITORS

COURTNEY A. FISKE   CHARLIE E. RIGGS
SARA PLANA   RUSSELL FORD RENNIE
OLGA I. ZHULINA

HOW TO USE THIS BOOK

COVERAGE LAYOUT. *Let's Go Greece* begins in **Athens**, the heart of the country and a natural jumping off point. From there, coverage extends through mountainous **Central Greece** and into the multicultural expanse of **Northern Greece**. Mainland coverage ends in the **Peloponnese**, home to many of Greece's most important ancient sites. We then embark on a tour of Greece's legendary islands, starting with the **Cyclades**, where backpackers have island hopped since the invention of the backpack. We then travel to the Cyclades' neighbors—the **Dodecanese Islands**, **Northeast Aegean Islands**, **Evia**, and **the Sporades**—before heading west to the final island group, the **Ionian Islands**. The trip ends in **Crete**, Greece's largest island, and still, in many places, an undiscovered treasure. The **suggested itineraries** at the beginning of each chapter point to the best spots in each region and can help structure either a long or a short trip.

TRANSPORTATION INFO. For making connections between destinations, information is generally listed under both the arrival and departure cities. Parentheticals usually provide the trip duration followed by its frequency and price, which is for one-way trips unless otherwise stated. For more general information on travel, consult **Essentials** (p. 8).

COVERING THE BASICS. Before departing, consult the **Discover Greece** chapter (p. 1) for recommendations on when to go and for country-wide suggested itineraries (p. 4). Logistical and practical questions are answered in the **Essentials** chapter (p. 8.), and **Life and Times** (p. 39) gives an overview of Greek history, culture, and customs. **Beyond Tourism** (p. 60), suggests volunteer, study abroad, and temporary work opportunities to enrich your travel experience. The **Appendix** (p. 506) lists Greek phrases, pronunciations, and other quick and helpful resource info.

PRICE DIVERSITY. Our researchers list establishments in order of value from best to worst, with absolute favorites denoted by the Let's Go thumbs-up (⛶). Since the cheapest price does not always mean the best value, we have incorporated a system of price ranges for food and accommodations; see p. IX.

PHONE CODES AND TELEPHONE NUMBERS. Area codes for each region appear opposite the name of the region and are denoted by the ☎ icon. Phone numbers in text are also preceded by the ☎ icon.

LANGUAGE AND OTHER QUIRKS. The Greek name of each city and town is printed after its English name. Transliterations give syllabic pronunciation, with the stressed syllables capitalized. For a guide to the Greek alphabet, see the **Appendix** (p. 506).

A NOTE TO OUR READERS. The information for this book was gathered by Let's Go researchers from May through August of 2009. Each listing is based on one researcher's opinion, formed during his or her visit at a particular time. Those traveling at other times may have different experiences since prices, dates, hours, and conditions are always subject to change. You are urged to check the facts presented in this book beforehand to avoid inconvenience and surprises.

CONTENTS

RESEARCHERS

Charlotte Alter   *The Dodecanese, Northeast Aegean, Aegina*

Sponges, weddings, swim teams, communists, and old men—Charlotte had a way of attracting the best of Greece as she ferried from Karpathos to Limnos, deftly dealing with the ferries' notoriously inconsistent schedules. Charlotte uses her shrewd eye and even shrewder pen to describe the high- (and low-) lights of these diverse, underappreciated islands.

Jillian Goodman   *Athens and the Cyclades*

Jillian battled the smog of Athens and the crowds of Mykonos and won: she found standouts in Exarhia and the best beaches in Milos. With a bottle of citron in one hand and a chunk of local cheese in the other, Jillian mastered the Cycladic island-hop.

Sarah Mortazavi   *Northern and Central Greece, Ionian Islands*

From the peaks of Mount Olympus to the valleys of Vikos Gorge, Sarah walked, trekked, hiked, and crawled up and down Northern and Central Greece. With a twinkle in her eye and a shot of humor in her writing, Sarah took down overpriced hostels and enjoyed some of the most pristine scenery in Greece.

RESEARCHERS

Ansley Rubinstein   *Crete, the Cyclades, Evia and the Sporades*

Ansley "Extreme Island-Hopper" Rubinstein went from the biggest (Crete) to the smallest (The Little Cyclades), and traveled on three ferries, two buses, and a plane in one day. After spending last summer in Sydney, Greece's small island towns were a cinch for this LG-alum.

Phoebe Stone   *The Peloponnese and the Ionian Islands*

With sunglasses securely fastened to her head, Phoebe faced the Peloponnese's treacherous bus schedules with aplomb. Traveling from one ancient site to another, she often spent more time talking to columns than she did to people. Not even a lack of tourists and Anglophones could stop this world traveler from making her way from Olympia to Kithera.

STAFF WRITERS

Julia Cain

Megan Popkin

Madeleine M. Schwartz

Anna Kathryn Kendrick

Harker Rhodes

Alexandra Perloff-Giles

Ansley Rubinstein

ACKNOWLEDGMENTS

ANDREW THANKS: Team Greece, for putting up with my emails, gchats, skypes, twits, fbook messages. Iya, for cupcakes. Lots of them. Russell, for SummerUnFun (and Olga, our MVP). RM Pod, for SummerFun. The waitresses at Noir for wearing black. Joe, for smoking. Mamram, for the photo shoot. David, for his left leg. And Lily Allen.

THE EDITORS THANK: First and foremost our lord (Jay-C) and savior (Starbucks, Terry's Chocolate Orange). We also owe gratitude to Barack Obama (peace be upon Him), the Oxford comma, the water cooler, bagel/pay-day Fridays, the HSA "SummerFun" team for being so inclusive, Rotio (wherefore art thou Rotio?), the real Robinson Crusoe, the Cambridge weather and defective umbrellas, Bolt-Bus, Henry Louis Gates, Jr. (sorry 'bout the phone call), the office blog, gratuitous nudity, the 20-20-20 rule and bananas (no more eye twitches), the Portuguese flag, trips to the beach (ha!), sunbathing recently-married Mormon final club alums, non-existent free food in the square, dog-star puns, and last but not least, America. The local time in Tehran is 1:21am.

But seriously, the MEs and RMs, our researchers (and all their wisdom on table-cloths and hipsters), LGHQ, HSA, our significant others (future, Canadian, and otherwise), and families (thanks Mom).

Publishing Director
Laura M. Gordon
Editorial Director
Dwight Livingstone Curtis
Publicity and Marketing Director
Vanessa J. Dube
Production and Design Director
Rebecca Lieberman
Cartography Director
Anthony Rotio
Website Director
Lukáš Tóth
Managing Editors
Ashley Laporte, Iya Megre,
Mary Potter, Nathaniel Rakich
Technology Project Manager
C. Alexander Tremblay
Director of IT & E-Commerce
David Fulton-Howard
Financial Associates
Catherine Humphreville, Jun Li

Managing Editor
Iya Megre
Research Manager
Andrew Fine
Editors
Courtney A. Fiske, Sara Plana, Russell Ford Rennie, Charlie E. Riggs, Olga I. Zhulina
Typesetter
C. Alexander Tremblay

President
Daniel Lee
General Manager
Jim McKellar

PRICE RANGES
GREECE

Our researchers list establishments in order of value from best to worst, honoring our favorites with the Let's Go thumbs-up (✋). Because the best *value* is not always the cheapest *price*, we have incorporated a system of price ranges based on a rough expectation of what you will spend. For **accommodations,** we base our range on the cheapest price for which a single traveler can stay for one night. For **restaurants,** we estimate the average amount one traveler will spend in one sitting. The table below tells you what you'll *typically* find in Barcelona at the corresponding price range, but keep in mind that no system can allow for the quirks of individual establishments.

ACCOMMODATIONS	RANGE	WHAT YOU'RE *LIKELY* TO FIND
❶	under €22	Campgrounds, HI hostels, basic dorm rooms. Expect bunk beds and a communal bath; you may have to provide or rent towels, sheets, or tents at campgrounds. Ah, to commune with nature.
❷	€22-33	Domatia, upper-end hostels, or lower-end hotels. You may have a private bathroom, or there may be a sink in your room and a communal shower in the hall. Ah, to commune with fellow travelers.
❸	€34-45	A small room with a private bath, probably in a budget hotel. Should have decent amenities, like a phone and TV. Breakfast may be included. Ah, to commune with buttered toast.
❹	€46-60	Similar to ❸, but should have more amenities or be in a more highly touristed or conveniently located area. Breakfast is often included in the price of your room. More communing with toast.
❺	over €60	Large hotels and upscale chains. If it's a ❺ and it doesn't have the perks or service you're looking for, you've probably paid too much and should have better communed with your wallet.

FOOD	RANGE	WHAT YOU'RE *LIKELY* TO FIND
❶	under €6	Probably a street-corner stand, gyro or souvlaki hut, bakery, or fast-food joint. For the traveler on the go.
❷	€6-12	Sandwich shops, pizzerias, and lower-end tavernas. May be takeout or sit-down, sometimes with a server. Like a ❶, minus some grease and plus some health benefits.
❸	€13-19	Typically sit-down. Mid-priced entrees, seafood, and pasta dishes. More upscale ethnic eateries. Shelling out that extra euro for tip.
❹	€20-25	A somewhat fancy restaurant or taverna. Few restaurants in this price range have a dress code, but some may look down on T-shirts and jeans; basically, don't dress for duress.
❺	over €25	Your meal might cost more than your hostel, but here's hoping it's something fabulous—or else involves a lot of good wine.

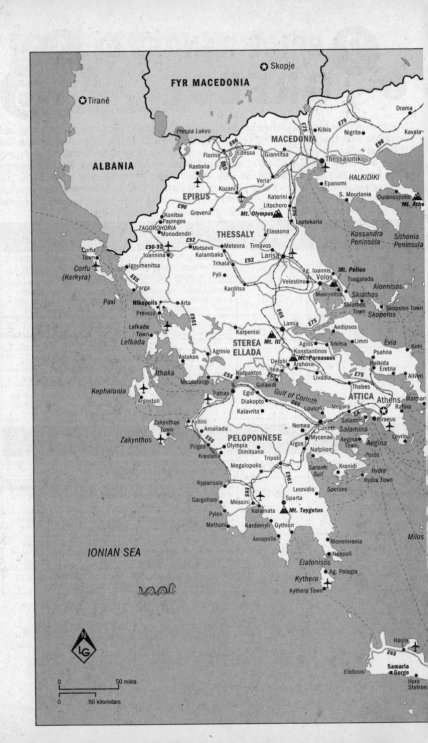

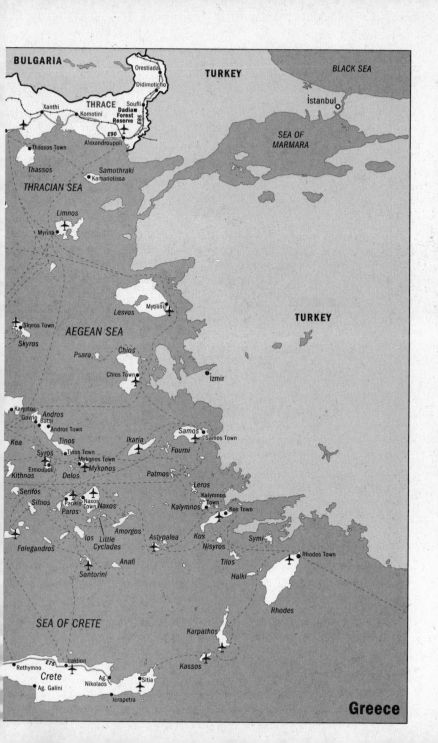

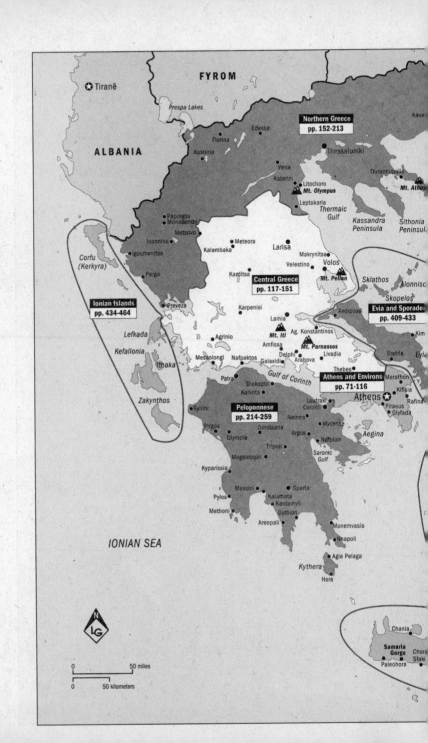

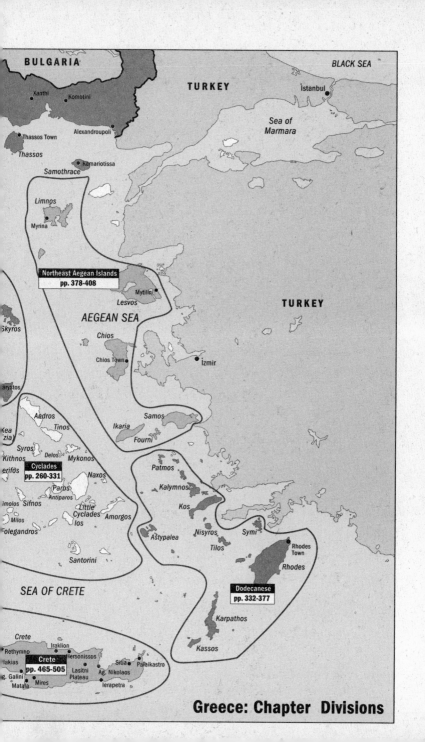

Greece: Chapter Divisions

DISCOVER GREECE

Greece (Ελλάδα) is a land where monasteries are mountainside fixtures, lei-surely siestas are standard issue, and circle-dancing and drinking until day-break are summer rites. The ancient Greeks sprung to prominence millennia ago, and visitors today explore evidence of magnificent past civilizations, as well as Greece's island beaches, spectacular gorges, and rustic village life. The all-encompassing Greek lifestyle is a fascinating mix of high-speed chaos and sun-inspired lounging, as old men hold lively debates in town *plateias*, teen-agers zoom on mopeds around the clock, and unpredictable schedules force tourists to adopt the natives' go-with-the-flow attitude.

FACTS AND FIGURES

OFFICIAL NAME: Hellenic Republic.

POPULATION: 10,737,428

CAPITAL: Athens

AVERAGE BAR CLOSING TIME: Sun-rise or when the *ouzo* runs out

YEARS OF CIVILIZATION: About 5200

DAYS OF SUNSHINE PER YEAR: 300

LENGTH OF COASTLINE PER GREEK CITIZEN: 1.37m

RATIO OF FOREIGNERS TO LOCALS: 9:10

PERCENTAGE OF ISLANDS INHAB-ITED: 12%

NUMBER OF OLIVE TREES PER GREEK CITIZEN: 12

NUMBER OF GODS IN THE ANCIENT GREEK PANTHEON: 12

NUMBER OF GODS IN THE GREEK ORTHODOX CHURCH: 1

WHEN TO GO

Late June through August is high season in Greece. Hotels, *domatia*, and night-life are in full swing as the 38°C (100°F) sun blazes over ancient cities and young sun bathers. If the crowds and frantic pace of summer travel aren't your style, consider visiting with the lighter crowds in May, early June, or Septem-ber, when avid hikers can take advantage of the pleasant weather and unsullied trails in Northern and Central Greece. In ski areas like Kalavrita (p. 231) and Karpenisi (p. 129), winter brings another high season. Accommodations and food are cheaper in the low season, but many sights, restaurants, and nightlife options have shorter hours or close altogether. Ferries, buses, and trains are particularly inconsistent during the low season.

WHAT TO DO

THE ROAD TO RUINS

In Greece, it's harder to avoid ruins than to find them. Since they survive in a broad spectrum of importance, quality of preservation, and overall impressive-ness, you may find yourself bored unless you're a Classicist or an archaeologist. Some ancient sights, however, are not to be missed. The perfectly proportioned columns of Athens' **Parthenon** (p. 92) haven't looked so good in years, thanks to

TOP TEN PLACES TO MEET A GREEK GOD

The first god you should befriend is Hermes, the traveler god. Once he's on your side, you can concentrate on wooing the many other ancient deities whose legends live on in Greece.

1. Visit the volcanoes of **Nisyros** (p. 360) and **Santorini** (p. 319) to see the forge of Hephaestus, god of fire.

2. Partying on **Mykonos** (p. 267) or **Ios** (p. 311) will put you in an alcoholic stupor and connect you with the god of wine and revelry, Dionysus.

3. Seek the guidance of Athena, goddess of war and wisdom, at her patron city, **Athens** (p. 71).

4. Do Ares, god of bloodlust, proud by visiting **Thessaloniki's** War Museum (p. 164).

5. A hike through Crete's **Valley of Death** (p. 505) might lead you to Hades.

6. Reach for the sun on **Ikaria** (p. 383), in honor of fallen Icarus.

7. You may run into Apollo at his oracle at **Delphi** (p. 117) or sanctuary at **Delos** (p. 269).

8. **Lesvos** (p. 393), home of the 10th Muse, Sappho, is a good place to seek the other nine.

9. Find Poseidon at his temple on **Cape Sounion** (p. 103), if you don't run into him on a ferry.

10. Mount Olympus (p. 192). Duh.

the views from the top floor of the new, $200 million **Acropolis Museum** (p. 92). Near Athens is Cape Sounion, where the seaside **Temple of Poseidon** (p. 103) sits on a 60m promontory overlooking the Aegean. If you can spare a day from partying on Mykonos, head to the floating island of **Delos** (p. 269), birthplace of Apollo and Artemis, where you will find an island-wide archaeological site. A voyage through the Peloponnese will take you back to the era of nymphs, satyrs, and gods in disguise. Sprint across the well-preserved stadium on the way to the original Olympic fields at **Ancient Olympia** (p. 237); wander through watery, fresco-covered tunnels at **Ancient Corinth** (p. 217); peer into Agamemnon's tomb at **Mycenae** (p. 222); or witness Byzantine times standing still at **Mystras** (p. 248), the former center of Constantinople's rule in the Peloponnese. After traversing mountain roads, visitors can seek wisdom at the ancient **Delphic Oracle** (p. 120) or learn about endurance at **Marathon** (p. 105). The Minoan palaces of **Knossos** (p. 487) and **Phaistos** (p. 491) on Crete come straight out of mythology. Finally, heal all of your aches and pains at the **Asclepion** (p. 367) on Kos, the ancient home of Hippocrates and the world's first medical school.

ISLANDS IN THE SUN

The islands have long been a sun-worshipper's paradise, drawing those who follow Helios and Apollo and those who follow tanning oil. Beachside days melt through spectacular sunsets into starry, disco-filled nights and back again, in a continuum of ▓hedonistic delight. In addition to the heavenly sands and turquoise waters, the islands offer ancient sites, intriguing museums, and peaceful small-town life. A favorite of international vacationers, **Skiathos** (p. 416), in the Sporades, harbors the piney Biotrope of Koukounaries beach and lovely Lalaria. In the Aegean Sea, the black-sand beaches on **Santorini** (p. 311) soak up the sun's hot rays, while the hills of **Kia** are the perfect place to watch the sun set. The wide variety of beaches and multi-colored rocks on **Milos** (p. 320) are a rainbow-splashed paradise. Sea caves once ransacked by pirates on the coast of **Skyros** (p. 431) now welcome swimmers. After basking on the shores of **Lesvos** (p. 393), visitors can stop to pay homage to Sappho at the eclectic and hospitable village of **Skala Eressou** (p. 402). Stumble out of all those pesky clothes at wild Paradise Beach on **Mykonos** (p. 260), and take back a shot of ouzo on **Ios** (p. 307) and **Kos** (p. 361). Snorkeling, water-skiing, or just loafing in the sun fill the days on **Naxos** (p. 282), and the undisturbed beauty of **Therma** on Samothrace is the perfect way to relax after hiking the mountains of Northern Greece. **Vai** (p. 504) and **Ierapetra** (p. 499) in Crete and castle-crowned Haraki Beach on **Rhodes** (p. 332) beg travelers to drop their packs in the languid sun.

☑LET'S GO PICKS

BEST PLACE TO DINE WITH THE GODS: Reaching the peak of **Mount Olympus** (p. 192) is an other worldly 2-day adventure, best broken up by a meal and a night's rest at the Zolotas Refuge (p. 194).

BEST PLACE TO READ KARL MARX: Explore the history of Greece's Communist Party on **Ikaria** (p. 383). 15,000 of its members were exiled to the island after World War II, and some are still alive to talk about the most recent Civil War.

BEST PLACE TO STIR UP REBELLION: The neighborhood of **Exarhia** in Athens (p. 75) is home to thousands of students, many of whom led protests in 1973 against the military junta. More recently, in 2008, country-wide protests against unemployment began in this Mediterranean-meets-New York neighborhood.

BEST PLACE TO BE A KID AGAIN: Ride the kiddie train through the Old Town in **Kavala** (p. 167) and hunt for sweets at Athens's unbeatabale **Matsoukas.**

BEST BATTLEGROUNDS: Each October, a 1571 naval battle is recreated at the Old Port of **Nafpaktos** (p. 126), complete with pyrotechnics.

BEST BATHS: You can bathe nude in the springs at **Therma,** a daytrip from Kamariotissa, or relax in the naturally radioactive waters at **Agios Kirykos** (p. 384), renowned for their healing powers.

BEST OBJECTS M.I.A.: Greeks have been longing for their Colossus of **Rhodes** (p. 332) since it tumbled into the Aegean in 226 BC. The celebrated Winged Victory of **Samothrace** resides in the Louvre in Paris. Ever since Lord Elgin shipped its marble reliefs to the British Museum in London, the **Acropolis** (p. 90) in Athens has been missing some key parts.

BEST PLACE TO BE A LOCAVORE: Eat locally-made cheese, locally-grown meat, and locally-fermented wine on the locally proud island of **Naxos** (p. 282).

BEST-PRESERVED BODIES: Mary Magdalene's hand is kept in Simonos Petra monastery on **Mount Athos** (p. 184). **Osios Loukas** monastery (p. 123) keeps its namesake saint's body in a Snow White-esque glass coffin. If you peek through the reliquary at Agio Andreas cathedral in **Petra,** you may see the top of Saint Andrew's head.

BEST PLACE TO PRETEND YOU'RE AN OLYMPIC ATHLETE: At **Ancient Olympia** (p. 237), you can take a lap around the stadium where Greek athletes competed 2300 years ago.

BEST PLACE TO THINK DEEP THOUGHTS: Take your most profound questions to the Philopappos Hill in **Athens** (p. 95), where Socrates was imprisoned. In **Vikos Gorge** (p. 212), any thought can be considered deep.

TAKE A HIKE

Take out your walking stick and rev up your engines. Hiking or motorbiking—or a combination of the two—lets you cruise among rural villages independent of sporadic bus schedules. On foot, you'll cross through graceful hills, passing mountain goats and wildflowers along the way. To the delight of climbers, 80% of the Greek landscape is mountainous. Clamber to the abode of the gods at **Mount Olympus** (p. 192), ascending over 2900 steep, stunning meters to one of its eight peaks. During the summer, Dionysus's old watering hole, **Mount Parnassos** (p. 122), makes a great hiking and mountain biking trip. The traditional villages of the **Zagorohoria** (p. 211) and their surrounding wilderness turn mere walking into an enticing adventure. On **Mount Athos** (p. 184), trails verge on sublime, as the paths from monastery to monastery scramble over grass-carpeted crags and yield divine views of the sea below. Neighboring **Vikos Gorge** (p. 212), the world's steepest canyon, challenges hikers with a 6hr. trek, while the western coast of **Kalymnos** (p. 367) provides some of the best climbs—and pubs—in Greece. **Samaria Gorge** (p. 474) and the quieter **Valley of Death** (p. 505) in Crete plunge you below eagles' nests and around trees that cling to the steep canyon sides. The trails around Zakros wind up to Zeus's childhood hiding place, **Kamares Cave** (p. 326).

SUGGESTED ITINERARIES

The following itineraries are designed to lead you to the highlights of Greece's distinct regions, from cosmopolitan hubs to sleepy villages. While these itineraries are intended for those who haven't traveled around Greece very much, even seasoned Hellenophiles can use them as a template for additional daytrips and excursions. Still, there are many ways to explore the country, not all of which we can cover. For more ideas, especially on less touristy spots that you might otherwise skip over, see the regional chapter introductions. Don't be afraid to plot out your own route: the famous Greek hospitality will make you feel welcome wherever you go.

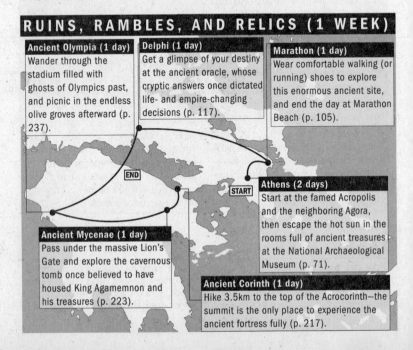

RUINS, RAMBLES, AND RELICS (1 WEEK)

Ancient Olympia (1 day)
Wander through the stadium filled with ghosts of Olympics past, and picnic in the endless olive groves afterward (p. 237).

Delphi (1 day)
Get a glimpse of your destiny at the ancient oracle, whose cryptic answers once dictated life- and empire-changing decisions (p. 117).

Marathon (1 day)
Wear comfortable walking (or running) shoes to explore this enormous ancient site, and end the day at Marathon Beach (p. 105).

END

START

Athens (2 days)
Start at the famed Acropolis and the neighboring Agora, then escape the hot sun in the rooms full of ancient treasures at the National Archaeological Museum (p. 71).

Ancient Mycenae (1 day)
Pass under the massive Lion's Gate and explore the cavernous tomb once believed to have housed King Agamemnon and his treasures (p. 223).

Ancient Corinth (1 day)
Hike 3.5km to the top of the Acrocorinth—the summit is the only place to experience the ancient fortress fully (p. 217).

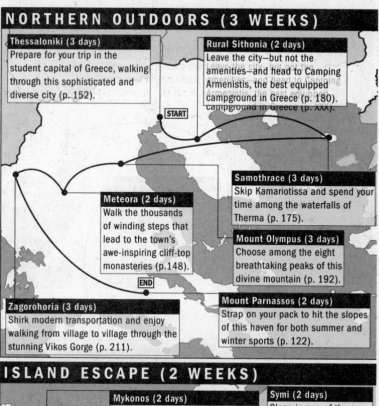

NORTHERN OUTDOORS (3 WEEKS)

Thessaloniki (3 days)
Prepare for your trip in the student capital of Greece, walking through this sophisticated and diverse city (p. 152).

Rural Sithonia (2 days)
Leave the city—but not the amenities, and head to Camping Armenistis, the best equipped campground in Greece (p. 180).

START

Meteora (2 days)
Walk the thousands of winding steps that lead to the town's awe-inspiring cliff-top monasteries (p.148).

Samothrace (3 days)
Skip Kamariotissa and spend your time among the waterfalls of Therma (p. 175).

Mount Olympus (3 days)
Choose among the eight breathtaking peaks of this divine mountain (p. 192).

END

Zagorohoria (3 days)
Shirk modern transportation and enjoy walking from village to village through the stunning Vikos Gorge (p. 211).

Mount Parnassos (2 days)
Strap on your pack to hit the slopes of this haven for both summer and winter sports (p. 122).

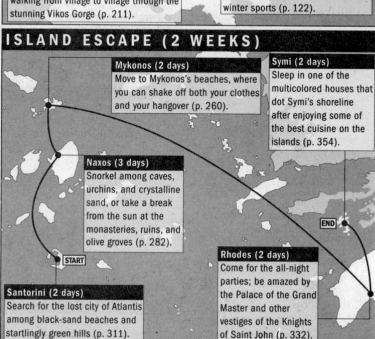

ISLAND ESCAPE (2 WEEKS)

Mykonos (2 days)
Move to Mykonos's beaches, where you can shake off both your clothes and your hangover (p. 260).

Symi (2 days)
Sleep in one of the multicolored houses that dot Symi's shoreline after enjoying some of the best cuisine on the islands (p. 354).

Naxos (3 days)
Snorkel among caves, urchins, and crystalline sand, or take a break from the sun at the monasteries, ruins, and olive groves (p. 282).

END

START

Rhodes (2 days)
Come for the all-night parties; be amazed by the Palace of the Grand Master and other vestiges of the Knights of Saint John (p. 332).

Santorini (2 days)
Search for the lost city of Atlantis among black-sand beaches and startlingly green hills (p. 311).

GREEK TO ME (1 MONTH)

Zagorohoria (1 day)
Ramble through petite towns that stick to traditional folk ways (p. 211).

Corfu (2 days)
Explore beaches, hikes, ancient sites, and laid-back villages on this endlessly diverse island (p. 434).

Mount Olympus (2 days)
Challenge yourself to reach the cloud-top home of the gods (p. 192).

Delphi (1 day)
Seek the advice of the legendary oracle or get inspired by the mesmerizing panoramic views (p. 117).

START

Athens (3 days)
Live the big-city life. Don't forget to visit the National Archaeological Museum, the Acropolis, the Agora, and more for a refresher course in Greek history (p. 71).

Ancient Olympia (1 day)
Pay a visit to the home of international (or inter-city-state) athletic competition (p. 237).

Monemvasia (1 day)
Don't fall off the cliffs next to this ancient city as you gaze in awe at the Old Town's monumental fortress (p. 253).

Kythera (2 days)
Enjoy this tranquil island with untouched beaches, Venetian castles, and crystal-clear waters (p. 256).

Hania (2 days)
Stroll along the port then head south to hike Samaria Gorge (p. 474).

Iraklion (1 day)
Skip the city and head to the nearby Minoan ruins of Knossos and Phaistos (p. 481).

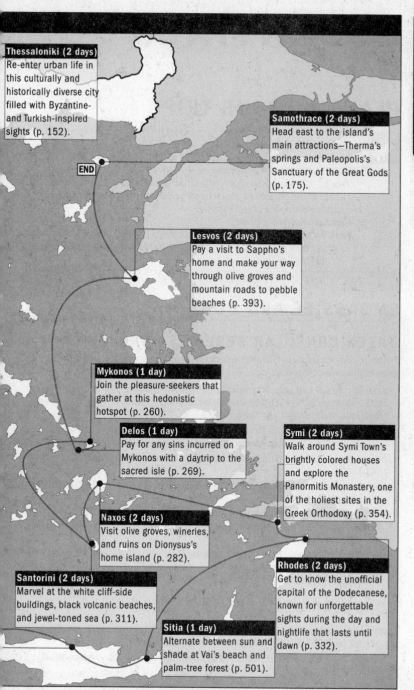

Thessaloniki (2 days)
Re-enter urban life in this culturally and historically diverse city filled with Byzantine- and Turkish-inspired sights (p. 152).

Samothrace (2 days)
Head east to the island's main attractions—Therma's springs and Paleopolis's Sanctuary of the Great Gods (p. 175).

END

Lesvos (2 days)
Pay a visit to Sappho's home and make your way through olive groves and mountain roads to pebble beaches (p. 393).

Mykonos (1 day)
Join the pleasure-seekers that gather at this hedonistic hotspot (p. 260).

Delos (1 day)
Pay for any sins incurred on Mykonos with a daytrip to the sacred isle (p. 269).

Symi (2 days)
Walk around Symi Town's brightly colored houses and explore the Panormitis Monastery, one of the holiest sites in the Greek Orthodoxy (p. 354).

Naxos (2 days)
Visit olive groves, wineries, and ruins on Dionysus's home island (p. 282).

Santorini (2 days)
Marvel at the white cliff-side buildings, black volcanic beaches, and jewel-toned sea (p. 311).

Rhodes (2 days)
Get to know the unofficial capital of the Dodecanese, known for unforgettable sights during the day and nightlife that lasts until dawn (p. 332).

Sitia (1 day)
Alternate between sun and shade at Vai's beach and palm-tree forest (p. 501).

ESSENTIALS

PLANNING YOUR TRIP

> **ENTRANCE REQUIREMENTS**
> **Passport** (p. 9). Required for citizens of all nations. Must be valid for 90 days after the period of intended stay.
> **Visa** (p. 10). Not required for citizens on Australia, Canada, Ireland, New Zealand, the UK, the US, and numerous other countries. For specific information, check www.projectvisa.com.
> **Inoculations**. None required.
> **Work Permit** (p. 11). Required for all EU citizens planning to work in Greece for over three months and all other foreigners planning to work in Greece for any length of time.

EMBASSIES AND CONSULATES

GREEK CONSULAR SERVICES ABROAD

For more information on Greek consulates abroad, see www.embassiesabroad.com/embassies-of/Greece.

Australia: Greek Embassy, 9 Turrana St., Yarralumla, Canberra, ACT 2600 (☎+61 02 6273 3011; fax 02 6273 2620). **Consulates** in Adelaide, Brisbane, Darwin, Melbourne, Newcastle, Perth, Sydney, and Tasmania.

Canada: Greek Embassy, 80 MacLaren St., Ottawa, ON K2P 0K6 (☎+1-613-238-6271; www.greekembassy.ca). **Consulates** in Montreal, Toronto, and Vancouver.

Ireland: Greek Embassy, 1 Upper Pembroke St., Dublin 2 (☎+353 1 676 7254; fax 1 661 8892).

New Zealand: Greek Embassy, 38-42 Waring Taylor, Petherick Tower, Box 24066, Wellington (☎+64 4 473 7775; fax 4 473 7441).

UK: Greek Embassy, 1A Holland Park, London W11 3TP (☎+44 20 72 29 38 50; www.greekembassy.org.uk). **Consulates** in Belfast, Birmingham, Edinburgh, Gibraltar, Glasgow, Leeds, and Southampton.

US: Greek Embassy, 2217 Massachusetts Ave. NW, Washington, D.C. 20008 (☎202-939-1300; www.mfa.gr/washington). **Consulates** in Atlanta, Boston, Chicago, Houston, Los Angeles, New York, San Franscisco, and Washington, D.C.

CONSULAR SERVICES IN GREECE

Australia: Level 6, Thon Building, Corner Kifisias and Alexandras., Ambelokipi, Athens 115 23 (☎21087 04 000; www.greece.embassy.gov.au/).

Canada: 4 Ioannou Gennadiou, Athens 11521 (☎21072 73 400; http://greece.gc.ca).

European Community: 2 Vas. Sofias, Athens 10674 (☎21072 51 000; fax 44 620).

Ireland: 7 Vas. Konstantinou, Athens 10674 (☎21072 32 771; fax 40 217).

New Zealand: 76 Kifissias, Ambelokipi, Athens 11526 (☎21069 24 136; fax 24 821).

UK: 1 Ploutarhou, Athens 10675 (☎21072 72 600; http://ukingreece.fco.gov.uk/en/).

US: 91 Vas.Sofias, Athens 10160 (☎21072 12 951; http://athens.usembassy.gov/).

TOURIST OFFICES

Start early when trying to contact tourist offices—like most things Greek, they run on their own schedule. Polite persistence coupled with genuine excitement works wonders. Two national organizations oversee tourism: the **Greek National Tourist Organization (GNTO),** known as the "EOT" in Greece, and the **tourist police.** The GNTO can supply general information about sights and accommodations throughout the country. The main office is in Athens at Tsoha 7 (☎210 870 7000; www.gnto.gr); another information desk is located at Eletherios Venizelos Airport (☎210 353 0445). Tourist police deal with local travel issues like finding a room or bus schedules. Although their English may be limited, officers tend to be quite willing to help, and serve as an important resource for travelers who have been swindled. Let's Go lists locations and contact information for tourist offices and the tourist police in the **Practical Information** section of each city. There are also official Greek tourism boards in several countries:

Australia and New Zealand: 37-49 Pitt St., Sydney, NSW 2000 (☎+61 612 9241 1663; fax 612 9241 2499).

Canada: 1500 Don Mills Road, Suite 102, Toronto, ON M3B 3K4 (☎+1-416-968-2220; fax 416-968-6533).

UK and Ireland: 4 Conduit St., London, W1S 2DJ (☎+44 207 495 9300; fax 207 495 4057; www.gnto.co.uk).

US: Olympic Tower, 645 5th Ave., Suite 903, New York, NY 10022 (☎+1-212-421-5777; www.greektourism.com).

DOCUMENTS AND FORMALITIES

PASSPORTS

REQUIREMENTS

Citizens of Australia, Canada, Ireland, New Zealand, the UK, and the US need valid passports to enter Greece and to re-enter their home countries. Greece does not allow entrance if the holder's passport expires in under 90 days after the period of intended stay; returning home with an expired passport is illegal and may result in a fine.

PASSPORT MAINTENANCE

Photocopy the page of your passport with your photo as well as your visas, traveler's check serial numbers, and any other important documents. Carry one set of copies in a safe place, apart from the originals, and leave another set at home. Consulates also recommend that you carry an expired passport or an official copy of your birth certificate in a part of your baggage separate from other documents.

If you lose your passport, immediately notify the local police and your home country's nearest embassy or consulate. To expedite its replacement, you must show ID and proof of citizenship; it also helps to know all information previously recorded in the passport. In some cases, a replacement may take weeks to process, and it may be valid only for a limited time. Any visas stamped in your old passport will be lost forever. In an emergency, ask for immediate temporary traveling papers that will permit you to re-enter your home country.

ESSENTIALS

> ⚔ **ONE EUROPE.** European unity has come a long way since 1957, when the **European Economic Community (EEC)** was created to promote European solidarity and cooperation. Since then, the EEC has become the **European Union (EU),** a mighty political, legal, and economic institution. On May 1, 2004, 10 South, Central, and Eastern European countries—Cyprus, the Czech Republic, Estonia, Hungary, Latvia, Lithuania, Malta, Poland, Slovakia, and Slovenia—were admitted into the EU, joining 15 other member states: Austria, Belgium, Denmark, Finland, France, Germany, Greece, Ireland, Italy, Luxembourg, the Netherlands, Portugal, Spain, Sweden, and the UK. On January 1, 2007, two others, Bulgaria and Romania, came into the fold, bringing the tally of member states to 27.
>
> What does this have to do with the average non-EU tourist? The EU's policy of freedom of movement means that most border controls have been abolished and visa policies harmonized. Under this treaty, formally known as the **Schengen Agreement,** you're still required to carry a passport (or government-issued ID card for EU citizens) when crossing an internal border, but, once you've been admitted into one country, you're free to travel to other participating states. Most EU states are already members of Schengen (minus Cyprus) as are Iceland and Norway. EU newcomers Bulgaria and Romania are still in the process of implementing the free travel agreement. The UK and Ireland have opted out of the agreement, but have created their own Common Travel Area, whose regulations match those of Schengen.
>
> For more important consequences of the EU for travelers, see **The Euro** (p. 12) and **Customs** (p. 11).

VISAS, INVITATIONS, AND WORK PERMITS

VISAS

EU citizens do not need a visa to enter Greece. Citizens of Australia, Canada, New Zealand, and the US do not need a visa for stays of up to 90 days, but this three-month period begins upon entry into any of the countries that belong to the EU's **freedom of movement** zone. For more information, see **One Europe** (p. 10). Those staying longer than 90 days may purchase a visa from the Greek embassy or consulate in the area of your permanent residence. A visa costs €60 and allows the holder to spend six months in Greece.

Double-check entrance requirements at the nearest embassy or consulate of Greece (listed on p. 8) for up-to-date info before departure. US citizens can also consult http://travel.state.gov.

Entering Greece to study requires a special visa. For more information, see the **Beyond Tourism** chapter (p. 60).

WORK PERMITS

Admittance to a country as a traveler does not include the right to work, which is authorized only by a **work permit**. For more information, see the **Beyond Tourism** chapter (p. 60).

IDENTIFICATION

When you travel, always carry at least two forms of identification on your person, including a photo ID. A passport and a driver's license will usually suffice. Never carry all of your IDs together; split them up in case of theft or loss and keep photocopies in your luggage and at home.

STUDENT AND YOUTH IDENTIFICATION

The **International Student Identity Card (ISIC),** the most widely accepted form of student ID, provides discounts on some sights, accommodations, food, and transportation, access to a 24hr. emergency help line, and insurance benefits for US cardholders. Admission to national archaeology sites and museums is either free or 50% off for students, while tickets on the Greek National Railway (OSE in Greece) are 25% off. Applicants must be full-time secondary or post-secondary school students at least 12 years old. Because of the proliferation of fake ISICs, some services require additional proof of student identity. For travelers who are under 26 years old but are not students, the **International Youth Travel Card (IYTC)** also offers many of the same benefits as the ISIC.

Each of these identity cards costs US$22. ISICs and IYTCs are valid for one year from the date of issue. To learn more about ISICs and IYTCs, check out www.myisic.com. Many student travel agencies (p. 20) issue the cards; for a list of issuing agencies or more information, see the **International Student Travel Confederation (ISTC)** website (www.istc.org).

The **International Student Exchange Card (ISE Card)** is a similar identification card available to students, faculty, and children aged 12 to 26. The card provides discounts, medical benefits, access to a 24hr. emergency help line, and the ability to purchase student airfares. An ISE Card costs US$25; visit www.isecard.com for more info.

CUSTOMS

Upon entering Greece, you must declare certain items from abroad and pay a duty on the value of those articles if they exceed the allowance established by Greece's customs service. Goods and gifts purchased at duty-free shops abroad are not exempt from duty or sales tax; "**duty-free**" means that you won't pay tax in the country of purchase. Duty-free allowances were abolished for travel between EU member states on June 30, 1999, but still exist for those arriving from outside the EU. Upon returning home, you must likewise declare all articles acquired abroad and pay a duty on the value of articles in excess of your home country's allowance. Jot down a list of any valuables brought from home and register them with customs before traveling abroad. It's a good idea to keep receipts for all goods acquired abroad.

Greece imposes a **value added tax** (VAT) on sales, which is included in the retail price—19% on purchases made on the mainland, 13% on purchases made in the Aegean islands. Travelers from non-EU countries who spend more than €120 in one shop in one day are entitled to claim some of their VAT on these items when leaving Greece, as long as they take the items out of Greece within three months of their purchase. Claiming your VAT refund can involve complicated paperwork; try to ask about VAT at any shops where you make substantial purchases, or contact **Global Refund** (☎+1-866-706-6090; www.globalrefund. com) for more information.

MONEY

CURRENCY AND EXCHANGE

The currency chart below is based on August 2009 exchange rates. Check the currency converter on websites like www.xe.com or www.bloomberg.com for the latest exchange rates.

EUROS (€)		
AUS$1 = €0.58	€1 = AUS$1.71
CDN$1 = €0.64	€1 = CDN$1.56
NZ$1 = €0.48	€1 = NZ$2.10
UK£1 = €1.17	€1 = UK£0.85
US$1 = €0.71	€1 = US$1.41

As a general rule, it's cheaper to convert money in Greece than at home. While currency exchange will probably be available in your arrival airport, it's wise to bring enough foreign currency to last for at least 24-72hr.

When changing money abroad, try to go only to a bank (τράπεζα, TRAH-peh-za) that has at most a 5% margin between its buy and sell prices. Since you lose money with every transaction, convert large sums at one time.

THE EURO. As of January 1, 2009, the official currency of 16 members of the European Union—Austria, Belgium, Cyprus, Finland, France, Germany, Greece, Ireland, Italy, Luxembourg, Malta, the Netherlands, Portugal, Slovakia, Slovenia, and Spain—has become the euro.

The currency has some important—and positive—consequences for travelers hitting more than one eurozone country. For one thing, money-changers across the eurozone are obliged to exchange money at the official, fixed rate (below) and at no commission (though they may still charge a service fee). Second, euro-denominated traveler's checks allow you to pay for goods and services across the eurozone, again at the official rate and commission-free.

TRAVELER'S CHECKS

Traveler's checks are one of the safest and most convenient means of carrying funds. **American Express** (www.americanexpress.com) and **Visa** (http://usa. visa.com/personal/using_visa/travel_with_visa.html) are the best-recognized brands. Many banks and agencies sell them for a small commission. Check issuers provide refunds if the checks are lost or stolen, and many provide additional services, such as toll-free refund hotlines abroad, emergency message services, and assistance with lost and stolen credit cards or passports. **Traveler's checks** are widely accepted in Greece, except in remote rural areas where cash is the preferred and occasionally only form of payment accepted. Ask about toll-free refund hotlines and the location of refund centers when purchasing checks. Remember, too, always to carry emergency cash.

CREDIT, DEBIT, AND ATM CARDS

Where they are accepted, credit cards often offer superior exchange rates—up to 5% better than the retail rate used by banks and other currency-exchange establishments. Credit cards may also offer services such as insurance or emergency help and are sometimes required to reserve hotel rooms or rental cars. **MasterCard** (a.k.a. EuroCard in Europe) and **Visa** are the most frequently accepted; **American Express** cards work at some ATMs and at AmEx offices and major airports.

The use of **ATM cards** is widespread in Greece. Armed with a MasterCard or Visa, you can withdraw money in any place large enough to justify a bank, and certainly in all of the touristed areas. Debit cards are as convenient as credit cards and can be used wherever its associated credit card is accepted.

The two major international money networks are **MasterCard/Maestro/ Cirrus** (for ATM locations ☎+1-800-424-7787; www.mastercard.com) and **Visa/PLUS** (for ATM locations visit http://visa.via.infonow.net/locator/ global/). Users of either of these two cards should be set almost anywhere in country. Most ATMs charge a transaction fee that is paid to the bank that owns the ATM. It is a good idea to contact your bank or credit card company before going abroad; frequent charges in a foreign country can sometimes prompt a fraud alert, which will freeze your account.

PINS AND ATMS. To use a cash or credit card to withdraw money from a cash machine (ATM) in Europe, you must have a four-digit Personal Identification Number (PIN). If your PIN is longer than four digits, ask your bank whether you can just use the first four or whether you'll need a new one. Credit cards don't usually come with PINs, so, if you intend to hit up ATMs in Europe with a credit card to get cash advances, call your credit card company before leaving to request one.

Travelers with alphabetic, rather than numerical, PINs may also be thrown off by the lack of letters on European cash machines. The following are the corresponding numbers to use: 1 = QZ; 2 = ABC; 3 = DEF; 4 = GHI; 5 = JKL; 6 = MNO; 7 = PRS; 8 = TUV; 9 = WXY. Note that if you mistakenly punch the wrong code into the machine three times, it will swallow your card for good.

GETTING MONEY FROM HOME

If you run out of money while traveling, the easiest and cheapest solution is to have someone back home make a deposit to your bank account. Otherwise, consider one of the following options.

WIRING MONEY

It is possible to arrange a **bank money transfer**, which means asking a bank back home to wire money to a bank in Greece. This is the cheapest way to transfer cash, but it's also the slowest, usually taking several days or more. Note that some banks may only release your funds in local currency, potentially sticking you with a poor exchange rate; inquire about this in advance. Theoretically, a bank-to-bank transfer should take only a few hours; most often, it takes significantly longer—up to seven days. Money transfer services like **Western Union** are faster and more convenient than bank transfers—but also much pricier. Western Union has many locations worldwide. To find one, visit www.westernunion.com Money transfer services are also available to **American Express** cardholders and at selected **Thomas Cook** offices.

ESSENTIALS

US STATE DEPARTMENT (US CITIZENS ONLY)

In serious emergencies only, the US State Department will forward money within hours to the nearest consular office, which will then disburse it according to instructions for a US$30 fee. If you wish to use this service, you must contact the Overseas Citizens Services division of the US State Department (☎ +1-202-501-4444, from US 888-407-4747).

COSTS

The cost of your trip will vary considerably, depending on where you visit, how you travel, and where you stay. The most significant expenses will probably be your round-trip (return) airfare to Greece (see **Getting to Greece: By Plane,** p. 19) and a railpass or bus pass.

STAYING ON A BUDGET

To give you a general idea, a bare-bones day in Greece (camping or sleeping in hostels/guesthouses, buying food at supermarkets) would cost about US$60-80 (€40-50); a slightly more comfortable day (sleeping in hostels/guesthouses and the occasional budget hotel, eating one meal per day at a restaurant, going out at night) would cost US$130-160 (€90-110); and, for a luxurious day, the sky's the limit. Don't forget to factor in emergency reserve funds (at least US$200) when planning how much money you'll need.

TIPS FOR SAVING MONEY

Some simpler ways include looking for free entertainment, splitting accommodation and food costs with trustworthy fellow travelers, and buying food in supermarkets rather than eating out. Bring a **sleepsack** (folding a large sheet in half length-wise and sewing the seam will work) to avoid charges for linens in hostels and do your **laundry** in the sink (unless you're explicitly prohibited from doing so). Museums often have certain days once a month or once a week when admission is free; plan accordingly. If you are eligible, consider getting an **ISIC** or an **IYTC** (p. 11); many sights and museums offer reduced admission to students and youths. For getting around quickly, **bikes** are the most economical option. Renting a bike is cheaper than renting a moped or scooter. Drinking at bars and clubs quickly becomes expensive; it's cheaper to buy alcohol at a supermarket and imbibe before going out. That said, don't go overboard to save money. Though staying within your budget is important, don't do so at the expense of your health or a great travel experience.

TIPPING AND BARGAINING

Greek law requires that restaurant and cafe prices include a 13% gratuity surcharge. You do not need to leave a tip unless you want to show your appreciation for a particularly good server (around 5%), but it is common to round up your check to the nearest euro. Similar rounding rules apply to taxi rides.

Bargaining skills won't get you as far as they would have even five years ago, but you can try your luck when appropriate. Paying the asked price for street wares might leave the seller marveling at your naïveté, while bargaining at the shop of a master craftsman would be disrespectful. The price tends to be more flexible in informal venues. If it's unclear whether bargaining is appropriate in a situation, hang back and watch someone else buy. Also, if you seem unsure, merchants might start the negotiations themselves. Merchants with any pride in their wares will refuse to sell to someone who has offended them in the negotiations. *Domatia* (private room) prices rise in summer and drop in winter (unless you're visiting a mountain town known for winter activities).

You'll likely have success bargaining in *domatia* and other small hotels. If your taxi trip won't be metered or ticketed—though you should generally seek out metered rides—bargain before you get going.

PACKING

Pack lightly: lay out only what you absolutely need, then take half the clothes and twice the money. The **Travelite FAQ** (www.travelite.org) is a good resource for tips on traveling light. The online **Universal Packing List** (http://upl.codeq.info) will generate a customized list of suggested items based on your trip length, the expected climate, your planned activities, and other factors. If you plan to do a lot of hiking, also consult **The Great Outdoors**, p. 34.

> **Converters and adapters:** In Greece, electricity is 230 volts AC, enough to fry any 120V North American appliance. 220/240V electrical appliances won't work with a 120V current, either. Americans and Canadians should buy an adapter (which changes the shape of the plug; US$5) and a converter (which changes the voltage; US$10-30). Don't make the mistake of using only an adapter (unless appliance instructions explicitly state otherwise). Australians, Brits, and New Zealanders (who use 230V at home) won't need a converter but will need a set of adapters to use anything electrical. For more on all things adaptable, check out http://kropla.com/electric.htm.

SAFETY AND HEALTH

GENERAL ADVICE

In any type of crisis, the most important thing to do is **stay calm.** Your country's embassy abroad (p. 8) is usually your best resource in an emergency; registering with that embassy upon arrival in the country is a good idea. The government offices listed in the **Travel Advisories** box (p. 16) can provide information on the services they offer their citizens in case of emergencies abroad.

LOCAL LAWS AND POLICE

Greek police are used to having foreigners around, but that does not mean they allow them to break the law. Photographs and notes cannot be taken near military establishments (including docks). The purchase of pirated goods (including CDs) is illegal; keep your receipts for proof of purchase. Taking objects or rocks from ancient sites is forbidden and can lead to fines or prison sentences. Drunk driving and indecent behavior also can result in arrest, heavy fines, and imprisonment. A passport or photo ID should be carried with you at all times.

DRUGS AND ALCOHOL

Visitors of all ages generally have little difficulty obtaining alcohol in Greece. Drugs laws are very strict. Conviction for possession, use, or trafficking of drugs, including marijuana, will result in imprisonment and fines. If you use prescription drugs, have a copy of the prescriptions themselves and a note from a doctor available, especially at border crossings. Keep all medication with you in your carry-on luggage. Authorities are particularly vigilant at the Turkish and Albanian borders.

ESSENTIALS

ESSENTIALS

SPECIFIC CONCERNS

NATURAL DISASTERS

One of the world's most seismically active countries, Greece experiences frequent and occasionally large **earthquakes**. The most recent in Athens in 1999 wreaked an estimated US$3 billion worth of damage and caused nearly 1,800 casualties. Earthquakes are unpredictable and can occur at any time of day. If a strong earthquake does occur, it will probably only last one or two minutes. Protect yourself by moving underneath a sturdy doorway, table, or desk, and open a doorway to provide an escape route. In mountainous regions, landslides may follow quakes.

DEMONSTRATIONS AND POLITICAL GATHERINGS

Strikes and demonstrations occur frequently in Greece. Although generally orderly and lawful, they can spiral out of control: most recently, in December 2008, riots and violent demonstrations, involving destructive vandalism and forceful clashes between civilians and the police, rocked Athens and other major cities across the country. Disruption of public services, such as public transportation and air traffic control, can occur unexpectedly due to union strikes. Common areas for protest include the Polytechnic University area, Exarcheia, Omonoia, Syntagma Square and Mavili Square (near the US embassy) in Athens, and near Aristotle University in Thessaloniki.

TERRORISM

Spearheaded by domestic terrorist groups with Marxist-anarchist leanings, and anti-globalization agendas, terrorist activity against both domestic and foreign targets has been on the rise in Greece over the past decade. **Revolutionary Struggle**, an extreme leftist paramilitary organization, launched a rocket at the US embassy in Athens in early 2007. Its successor organization, **Revolutionary Nuclei**, has claimed responsibility for numerous attacks since, involving the use of Molotov cocktails, small arms, and homemade explosive devices. The best thing you can do to be safe is to be aware of your surroundings, especially in crowded areas and tourist sites. The box below on travel advisories lists offices to contact and webpages to visit for the most updated list of your home country's government's advisories about travel.

TRAVEL ADVISORIES. The following government offices provide travel information and advisories by telephone, by fax, or via the web:

Australian Department of Foreign Affairs and Trade: ☎+61 2 6261 1111; www.dfat.gov.au.

Canadian Department of Foreign Affairs and International Trade (DFAIT): ☎+1-800-267-8376; www.dfait-maeci.gc.ca. Call or visit the website for the free booklet *Bon Voyage...But.*

New Zealand Ministry of Foreign Affairs: ☎+64 4 439 8000; www.mfat.govt.nz.

United Kingdom Foreign and Commonwealth Office: ☎+44 20 7008 1500; www.fco.gov.uk.

US Department of State: ☎+1-888-407-4747, 202-501-4444 from abroad; http://travel.state.gov.

PERSONAL SAFETY

EXPLORING AND TRAVELING

To avoid unwanted attention, try to blend in as much as possible. Respecting local customs (in many cases, dressing more conservatively than you would at home) may ward off would-be hecklers. Familiarize yourself with your surroundings before setting out and carry yourself with confidence. Check maps in shops and restaurants rather than on the street. If you are traveling alone, be sure someone at home knows your itinerary and never tell anyone you meet that you're by yourself. When walking at night, stick to busy, well-lit streets and avoid dark alleyways. If you ever feel uncomfortable, leave the area as quickly and directly as you can. There is no sure-fire way to avoid all the threatening situations that you might encounter while traveling, but a good **self-defense course** will give you concrete ways to react to unwanted advances. **Impact, Prepare**, and **Model Mugging** (www.modelmugging.org) can refer you to local self-defense courses in Australia, Canada, Switzerland, and the US.

If you are using a **car**, learn local driving signals and wear a seat belt. Children under 40lb. should ride only in specially designed car seats, available for a small fee from most car-rental agencies. Study route maps before you hit the road and, if you plan on spending a lot of time driving, consider bringing spare parts. For long drives in desolate areas, invest in a cell phone and a roadside assistance program. Park your vehicle in a garage or well-traveled area and use a steering-wheel locking device in larger cities. Sleeping in your car is the most dangerous way to get your rest, and it's also illegal in many countries.

POSSESSIONS AND VALUABLES

Never leave your belongings unattended; crime can occur in even the safest-looking hostel or hotel. Bring your own padlock for hostel lockers and don't ever store valuables in a locker. Be particularly careful on **buses** and **trains;** horror stories abound about determined thieves who wait for travelers to fall asleep. Carry your bag or purse in front of you where you can see it. When traveling with others, sleep in alternate shifts. When alone, be careful in selecting a train compartment: never stay in an empty one and always use a lock to secure your pack to the luggage rack. Use extra caution if traveling at night or on overnight trains.

There are a few steps you can take to minimize the financial risk associated with traveling. First, **bring as little with you as possible.** Second, buy a few combination **padlocks** to secure your belongings either in your pack or in a hostel or train-station locker. Third, **carry as little cash as possible.** Keep your traveler's checks and ATM/credit cards in a **money belt**—not a "fanny pack"—along with your passport and ID cards. Fourth, **keep a small cash reserve separate from your primary stash.** This should be about US$50 (US dollars or euro are best) sewn into or stored in the depths of your pack, along with your traveler's check numbers and photocopies of your important documents.

PRE-DEPARTURE HEALTH

In your passport, write the names of any people you wish to be contacted in case of a medical emergency and list any allergies or medical conditions. Matching a prescription to a foreign equivalent is not always easy, safe, or possible, so, if you take **prescription drugs,** carry up-to-date prescriptions or a statement from your doctor stating the medications' trade names, manufacturers, chemical names, and dosages. While traveling, be sure to keep all medication with you in your carry-on luggage.

The names in Greece for common drugs are: **Depon** and **Panadol** (acetaminophen), **Algoflex** and **Nurofen** (ibuprofen), and **Ospen** and **Penadur** (penicillin).

USEFUL ORGANIZATIONS AND PUBLICATIONS

The American **Centers for Disease Control and Prevention** (**CDC**; ☎+1-800-CDC-INFO/232-4636; www.cdc.gov/travel) maintains an international travelers' hotline and an informative website. Consult the appropriate government agency of your home country for consular information sheets on health, entry requirements, and other issues for various countries (see the listings in the box on **Travel Advisories,** p. 16). For quick information on health and other travel warnings, call the **Overseas Citizens Services** (☎+1-202-647-5225) or contact a passport agency, embassy, or consulate abroad. For information on medical evacuation services and travel insurance firms, see the US government's website at http://travel.state.gov/travel/abroad_health.html or the **British Foreign and Commonwealth Office** (www.fco.gov.uk). For general health information, contact the **American Red Cross** (☎+1-202-303-5000; www.redcross.org).

STAYING HEALTHY

Common sense is the simplest prescription for good health while you travel. Drink lots of fluids to prevent dehydration and constipation and wear sturdy, broken-in shoes and clean socks. The Greek sun can be especially brutal in the summer, so also be sure to bring a hat and sunscreen.

ONCE IN GREECE

ENVIRONMENTAL HAZARDS

High altitude: Allow your body a couple of days to adjust to less oxygen before exerting yourself. Note that alcohol is more potent and UV rays are stronger at high elevations.

Hypothermia and frostbite: A rapid drop in body temperature is the clearest sign of overexposure to cold. Victims may also shiver, feel exhausted, have poor coordination or slurred speech, hallucinate, or suffer amnesia. Do not let hypothermia victims fall asleep. To avoid hypothermia, keep dry, wear layers, and stay out of the wind. When the temperature is below freezing, watch out for frostbite. If skin turns white or blue, waxy, and cold, do not rub the area. Drink warm beverages, stay dry, and slowly warm the area with dry fabric or steady body contact until a doctor can be found.

Sunburn: Always wear sunscreen (SPF 30 or higher) when spending significant amounts of time outdoors. If you get sunburned, drink more fluids than usual and apply an aloe-based lotion. Severe sunburns can lead to sun poisoning, a condition that can cause fever, chills, nausea, and vomiting. Sun poisoning should always be treated by a doctor.

INSECT-BORNE DISEASES

Many diseases are transmitted by insects—mainly mosquitoes, fleas, and lice. Be aware of insects in wet or forested areas, especially while hiking and camping. Wear long pants and long sleeves, tuck your pants into your socks, and use a mosquito net. Use insect repellents such as DEET and soak or spray your gear with permethrin (licensed in the US only for use on clothing).

FOOD- AND WATERBORNE DISEASES

Prevention is the best cure: be sure that your food is properly cooked and that the water you drink is clean. Watch out for food from markets or street vendors that may have been cooked in unhygienic conditions. Other culprits are raw shellfish, unpasteurized milk, and sauces containing raw eggs. Buy bottled water or purify your own water by bringing it to a rolling boil or treating it with **iodine tablets** (boiling is more reliable). Always wash your hands before eating or bring a quick-drying liquid hand cleaner.

OTHER HEALTH CONCERNS

MEDICAL CARE ON THE ROAD

All travelers from the European Economic Area and Switzerland receive health care in Greece for free or at a reduced cost with the presentation of a **European Health Insurance Card.** While Greece offers outstanding medical training, the healthcare system is vastly under-funded. Public hospitals are overcrowded; in some locations, their hygiene may be questionable and English may not be spoken. Private hospitals, especially those in Athens and Thessaloniki, generally provide better care, but they cost more; to use them you will need good health insurance. If your regular policy does not cover travel abroad, you may wish to buy additional coverage.

Pharmacies (φαρμακείο, far-mah-KEE-ah), labeled by green or red equal-armed crosses, are common. In most towns and cities, at least one pharmacy is open at all hours—most post listings of available 24hr. pharmacies in their windows. To reach a pharmacy, dial ☎107 from any phone; for hospitals, dial 106; and for an ambulance, dial 166. The person at the end of the line may answer in Greek, but they will likely know English or transfer you to someone who does.

If you are concerned about obtaining medical assistance while traveling, you may wish to employ special support services. The **International Association for Medical Assistance to Travelers (IAMAT;** US ☎+1-716-754-4883, Canada +1-416-652-0137; www.iamat.org) has free membership, lists English-speaking doctors worldwide, and offers details on immunization requirements and sanitation. For those whose insurance doesn't apply abroad, you can purchase additional coverage.

GETTING TO GREECE

BY PLANE

When it comes to airfare, a little effort can save you a bundle. Courier fares are the cheapest for those whose plans are flexible enough to deal with the restrictions. For those with flexibility *and* patience, **standby flights** are one way to save; be prepared to spend all day at the airport for a week or more before finally boarding a plane. Call major airline companies for details (see **Commercial Airlines,** p. 21). Tickets sold by consolidators are also good deals, but last-minute specials, airfare wars, and charter flights often beat these fares. The key is to hunt around, be flexible, and ask about discounts. Students, seniors, and those under 26 should never pay full price for a ticket.

ESSENTIALS

AIRFARES

Airfares to Greece **peak between June and August;** holidays are also expensive. The cheapest times to travel are October and late March. Midweek (M-Th morning) round-trip flights run cheaper than weekend flights, but they are generally more crowded and less likely to permit frequent-flier upgrades. Not fixing a return date ("open return") or arriving in and departing from different cities ("open-jaw") can be pricier than round-trip flights. Patching one-way flights together is the most expensive way to travel. Flights between Greece's capitals or regional hubs—Athens and Thessaloniki—will tend to be cheaper.

Fares for round-trip flights to Athens and Thessaloniki from the US or Canadian east coast cost US$800-1300 in the high season (June-Aug.), US$600-850 in the low season (Oct.-Mar.); from the US or Canadian west coast US$1200-2000/600-1200; from the UK, UK£190-250/120-220; from Australia AUS$2700-4200/1700-3800; from New Zealand NZ$3200-5000/2600-4800.

BUDGET AND STUDENT TRAVEL AGENCIES

While knowledgeable agents specializing in flights to Greece can make your life easy, they may not spend the time to find you the lowest possible fare—they get paid on commission. Travelers holding ISICs and IYTCs (p. 11) qualify for big discounts from student travel agencies. Most flights from budget agencies are on major airlines, but in high season some may sell seats on less reliable chartered aircrafts.

The Adventure Travel Company, 124 MacDougal St., New York City, NY 10021, USA (☎+1-212-674-2887; www.theadventuretravelcompany.com). Offices across Canada and the US including New York City, San Diego, San Francisco, and Seattle.

STA Travel, 2871 Broadway, New York City, NY 10025, USA (24hr. reservations and info ☎+1-800-781-4040; www.statravel.com). A student and youth travel organization with offices worldwide, including US offices in Los Angeles, New York City, Seattle, Washington, DC and a number of other college towns. Ticket booking, travel insurance, railpasses, and more. Walk-in offices are located throughout Australia (☎+61 134 782), New Zealand (☎+0800 474 400), and the UK (☎+44 8712 230 0040).

FLIGHT PLANNING ON THE INTERNET. The internet may be the budget traveler's dream when it comes to finding and booking bargain fares, but the array of options can be overwhelming.

STA (www.statravel.com) and **StudentUniverse** (www.studentuniverse.com) provide quotes on student tickets, while **Orbitz** (www.orbitz.com), **Expedia** (www.expedia.com), and **Travelocity** (www.travelocity.com) offer full travel services. **Priceline** (www.priceline.com) lets you specify a price and obligates you to buy any ticket that meets or beats it; **Hotwire** (www.hotwire.com) offers bargain fares but won't reveal the airline or flight times until you buy. Other sites that compile deals include www.bestfares.com, www.flights.com, www.lowestfare.com, www.onetravel.com, and www.travelzoo.com.

Cheapflights (www.cheapflights.co.uk) is a useful search engine for finding—you guessed it—cheap flights. **Booking Buddy** (www.bookingbuddy.com), **Kayak** (www.kayak.com), and **SideStep** (www.sidestep.com) are online tools that let you enter your trip information and search multiple sites at once. *Let's Go* does not endorse any of these websites. As always, be cautious and research companies before you hand over your credit card number.

COMMERCIAL AIRLINES

TRAVELING FROM NORTH AMERICA

Crossing the pond? Standard commercial carriers like **American** (☎+1-800-433-7300; www.aa.com), **United** (☎+1-800-538-2929; www.ual.com), and **Northwest** (☎+1-800-225-2525; www.nwa.com) will probably offer the most convenient flights, but they may not be the cheapest. Check **Air France** (☎+1-800-237-2747; www.airfrance.us), **Alitalia** (☎+1-800-223-5730; www.alitaliausa.com), **British Airways** (☎+1-800-247-9297; www.britishairways.com), and **Lufthansa** (☎+1-800-399-5838; www.lufthansa.com) for cheap tickets from destinations throughout the US to all over Europe. You might find an even better deal on one of the following airlines, if any of their limited departure points is convenient for you.

Aer Lingus (☎+1-888-474-7424; www.aerlingus.ie). Affordable flights to Athens from Boston, Chicago, Orlando, New York City, San Francisco, and Washington, D.C.

SWISS (☎+1-877-359-7947; www.swiss.com). Inexpensive flights to Athens and Thessaloniki from Boston, Chicago, Orlando, New York City, and San Francisco; usually connects through Zurich.

TRAVELING FROM IRELAND AND THE UK

British Airways (☎+44 0844 493 0787; www.britishairways.com). Flights from London to Athens.

easyJet (☎+44 0871 288 2236; www.easyjet.com). London to Athens and Thessaloniki.

KLM (☎+44 0871 222 7740; www.klmuk.com). Cheap tickets to Athens from London and Dublin.

TRAVELING FROM AUSTRALIA AND NEW ZEALAND

Qantas Air (in Australia ☎+61 13 13 13; www.qantas.com.au). Flights from Brisbane, Melbourne, Perth and Sydney to Athens.

Singapore Air (in Australia ☎+61 29 262 7285, in New Zealand ☎+64 9 379 3209; www.singaporeair.com). Flights from Auckland, Christchurch, Melbourne, Perth, and Sydney to Athens.

Thai Airways (in Australia ☎+61 13 00 651 960, New Zealand ☎+64 9256 8518; www.thaiair.com). Flights from Melbourne, Perth, and Sydney to Athens.

BUDGET AIRLINES

For travelers who don't place a premium on convenience, we recommend ✇**budget airlines** (p. 21) as the best way to jet around Europe. Travelers can often snag these tickets for illogically low prices (i.e., less than the price of a meal in the airport food court), but you get what you pay for: namely, minimalist service and no frills. In addition, many budget airlines fly out of smaller regional airports several kilometers out of town. You'll have to buy shuttle tickets to reach the airports of many of these airlines, so plan on adding an hour or so to your travel time. After round-trip shuttle tickets and fees for services that might come standard on other airlines, that €1 sale fare can suddenly jump to €20-100. Still, it's possible to save money even if you live outside the continent by hopping a cheap flight to anywhere in Europe and using budget airlines to reach your final destination. Prices vary dramatically; shop around, book months ahead, pack light, and stay flexible to nab the best fares. For a more detailed list of these airlines by country, check out www.whichbudget.com.

easyJet (☎+44 871 244 2366; www.easyjet.com). Flights from London to Athens and Thessaloniki.

Aegean Air (☎+30 210 626 1000; www.aegeanair.com). Flights from Amsterdam, Barcelona, Berlin, Lisbon, London, Paris, Rome, and other European cities to Athens and Thessaloniki.

Sky Europe (☎+421 23 301 7301; www.skyeurope.com). Flights from Amsterdam, Prague, Venice, and Vienna to Athens and Thessaloniki.

BY FERRY OR BUS

BY FERRY. Ferries are a popular way to get to and travel within Greece; finding a boat agency to facilitate your trip should not be difficult. Be warned that ferries run on irregular schedules. A few websites, such as www.ferries.gr, have tried to keep updated schedules online but often are incomplete. Try to look at a schedule as close to your departure date as possible; you usually can find one at a tourist office or posted at the dock. That said, you also should make reservations and check in at least 2hr. in advance; late boarders may find their seats gone. If you sleep on the deck, bring warm clothes and a sleeping bag. Bicycles travel free, but motorcycles cost extra.

The major ports of departure from Italy to Greece are **Ancona** and **Brindisi** in the southeast. Bari, Otranto, Trieste, and Venice also have a few connections. For Greece-Italy schedules, see **Patra** (p. 226), **Kefallonia** (p. 452), **Corfu** (p. 434), or **Igoumenitsa** (p. 208). Ferries also run from **Samos, Chios,** and **Kos** to various Turkish ports.

BY BUS. There are very few buses running directly from any European city to Greece. **Eurolines,** Via Mercadante 2/b, Firenze 50144, Italy (☎+39 055 35 71 10; www.eurolines.it) and **Busabout,** 258 Vauxhall Bridge Road, London SW1V 1BS, UK (☎+44 020 7950 1661; www.busabout.com), transport travelers to Italian ports including Ancona, Brindisi, and Venice on their own buses, then arrange ferry transport to locations in Greece. From there, travelers can catch connections to locations throughout Greece.

BORDER CROSSINGS

Greece shares its borders in the north with Albania, Bulgaria, Macedonia, and Turkey. Overland transportation between Greece and its northern neighbors is limited to buses and some trains to all bordering countries except Albania. Thessaloniki is the transportation hub between Greece and these countries.

GETTING AROUND GREECE

BY PLANE

COMMERCIAL AIRLINES

For small-scale travel on the continent, *Let's Go* suggests ☐**budget airlines** (p. 21) for budget travelers, but more traditional carriers have made efforts to keep up with the revolution. The **Star Alliance Europe Airpass** offers low economy-class fares for travel within Europe to 220 destinations in 45 countries. The pass is available to non-European passengers on Star Alliance carriers, including Air China, Egypt Air, Lufthansa, Scandinavian Airlines, Singapore Airlines, SWISS International Airlines, TAP Portugal, Thai Airways International, and Turkish Airlines. See www.staralliance.com for more information. In addition, a number of European airlines offer discount coupon packets. Most are only available as tack-ons for transatlantic passengers, but some are standalone offers. Most must be purchased before departure, so research in advance.

EuropeByAir (☎+1-888-321-4737; www.europebyair.com). FlightPass allows you to hop between hundreds of cities in Europe and North Africa. Most flights US$99.

oneworld (www.oneworld.com). A coalition of 10 major international airlines. Offers deals and cheap connections all over the world, including within Europe.

BUDGET AIRLINES

The recent emergence of no-frills airlines has made hopscotching around Europe by air increasingly affordable. Though these flights often feature inconvenient hours or serve less popular regional airports, with ticket prices often dipping into single digits, it's never been faster or easier to jet across the continent. The following resources will be useful not only for crisscrossing Greece but also for those ever-popular weekend trips to nearby international destinations.

SWISS (☎+1-877-359-7947; www.swiss.com). Inexpensive flights to Athens and Thessaloniki from the continental US (Boston, Chicago, Orlando, New York City, and San Francisco), as well as from Barcelona, Berlin, Dublin, Istanbul, London, Madrid, Montreal, Paris, and Toronto; nearly all connect through Zurich.

BY TRAIN

Although trains in Greece are cheap, they run less frequently than buses and don't cover as wide a geographic area. They are generally slower than other European trains and can get pretty gritty. If you're lucky, you may come across a new, air-conditioned, intercity train, which is worth the price.

The **Hellenic Railways Association** or **OSE** (www.osenet.gr), connects Athens to major Greek cities like Thessaloniki, Patra, and Volos. Lines do not yet go to the mainland's west coast (although plans are in progress to extend the railway to Ioannina), and they are rarely useful for remote areas or archaeological sites. Bring food and water, because on-board cafes are pricey. Second-class compartments, which seat two to six, are great places to meet fellow travelers. Trains, however, are not always safe; for safety tips, see p. 17. Make sure you are on the correct car, as trains sometimes split at crossroads. Towns listed in

ESSENTIALS

parentheses on European train schedules require a train switch at the town listed immediately before the parentheses.

You can either buy a **railpass,** which allows you unlimited travel within a particular region for a given period of time, or rely on buying individual **point-to-point** tickets as you go. Almost all countries give students or youths (under 26, usually) direct discounts on regular domestic rail tickets, and many also sell a student or youth card that provides 20-50% off all fares for up to a year.

DOMESTIC RAILPASSES

If you are planning to spend much time within Greece, a national pass—valid on all rail lines in Greece—may be more cost-effective than a multinational pass.

NATIONAL RAILPASSES. The domestic analog of the Eurailpass, the **Greece Pass,** offers from three to ten days of unlimited first-class travel in one month on railways throughout Greece, as well as free ferry crossings and ferry discounts on certain lines. This pass must be purchased from a travel agent or **Rail Europe** before you leave for Europe. You need to get your pass validated before you use it on the train; just bring the pass and your passport to an official in the train station prior to use so that he or she can record the first and last day of the eligibility of the pass. For more information, check out www.eurail.com/eurail-greece-pass.

INTERRAIL. InterRail offers passes that allow travel throughout 30 European countries (including Greece), as well as passes limited to one country. To be eligible, you must have been living in one of the 30 participating countries for at least six months. For more info, visit www.railpassshop.com.

MULTINATIONAL RAILPASSES

EURAIL PASSES. Eurail is valid in much of Europe: Austria, Belgium, Bulgaria, Croatia, Czech Republic, Denmark, Finland, France, Germany, Greece, Hungary, Ireland, Italy, Luxembourg, Montenegro, the Netherlands, Norway, Poland, Portugal, Romania, Serbia, Slovenia, Spain, Sweden, and Switzerland. It is not valid in the UK. **Eurail Global Passes,** valid for a consecutive given number of days, are best for those planning on spending extensive time on trains every few days. Global passes valid for 10+ predetermined (not necessarily consecutive) days within a certain period are more cost-effective for those traveling longer distances less frequently. **Eurail Saver Passes** provide first-class travel for travelers in groups of two to five. **Eurail Youth Passes** provide parallel second-class perks for those under 26. Check online for complete rates and discounts (www.raileurope.com). **Eurail Flexi Passes** offer the same service as Global Passes but with flexible dates within a given period.

FURTHER RESOURCES FOR TRAIN TRAVEL
Info on rail travel and railpasses: www.raileurope.com.
Point-to-point fares and schedules: www.raileurope.com/us/rail/fares_
schedules/index.htm. Allows you to calculate whether buying a railpass
would save you money.
Railsaver: www.railsaver.com. Uses your itinerary to calculate the best railpass for your trip.
European Railway Server: www.railfaneurope.net. Links to rail servers
throughout Europe.

BY BUS

Buses are an essential part of travel in Greece. Service is more extensive, more
efficient, and often more comfortable than on trains, and fares are cheap.
Unless you're sticking close to train routes, **KTEL bus service** should be sufficient
for longer bus trips. Always check with an official source about scheduled
departures. Posted schedules are often outdated and all services are curtailed
significantly on Saturday and Sunday; bus schedules on major holidays run
according to Sunday schedules. Unless they are going longer distances, buses
rarely run at night. The English-language weekly newspaper **Athens News** prints
Athens bus schedules; they are also available online (www.ktel.org). Try to
arrive at least 10min. ahead of time, as Greek buses have a habit of leaving
early. In major cities KTEL bus lines may have different stations for different
destinations, and schedules generally refer to endpoints (e.g., "the bus leaves
Kalloni at 3pm and arrives in Mytilini at 4pm") with no mention of the numerous stops in between.

Ask the conductor before entering the bus whether it's going to your
destination (the signs on the front can be misleading), and ask to be
warned when you get there. If you're stowing bags underneath, make sure
they're in the compartment for your destination (conductors take great
pride in packing the bus for easy unloading, and may refuse to open the
"final destination" compartment at the "halfway" stop). If the bus passes
your stop, stand up and yell "STAH-see" (σταση). On the road, stand near
a sign reading σταση to pick up an intercity bus. KTEL buses are green or
occasionally orange or yellow, while intercity buses are usually blue. For
long-distance rides, buy your ticket beforehand in the office (otherwise,
you may have to stand for the entire journey). For shorter trips, pay the
conductor after you have boarded; reasonably close change is expected.

Often cheaper than railpasses, **international bus passes** allow unlimited travel
on a hop-on, hop-off basis between major European cities. The prices below
are based on high-season travel.

Busabout (☎+44 8450 267 514; www.busabout.com). Offers 3 interconnecting bus circuits
covering 29 of Europe's best bus hubs. Prices start at $579 (students $549) for 1 circuit.

BY CAR

Cars offer speed, freedom, access to the countryside, and an escape from the
town-to-town mentality of trains. Although a single traveler won't save by renting a car, four usually will.

Cars are a good choice in Greece, a country where public transportation is generally nonexistent at night; they are especially useful in regions like Crete, where buses between nearby small towns often follow maddeningly indirect routes. Ferries will take you and your car island-hopping if you pay a transport fee for the car. Drivers in Greece must be comfortable with a standard transmission, winding mountain roads, and the Greek alphabet—signs in Greek appear roughly 100m before the transliterated versions. Driving is especially useful for exploring remote villages in northern Greece.

With a fatal accident rate that tops that of most countries in Europe, driving in Greece can be a dangerous enterprise. Drivers are notoriously reckless and aggressive (especially in Athens), often driving on sidewalks and expecting pedestrians to move out of the way. Over the past several years, the Greek government has mounted a campaign to expand and improve the nation's highway infrastructure—an initiative that has resulted in nicer roads and considerably higher tolls. As a result, roads in Greece are generally well maintained. The country's mountainous terrain, however, forces them to take sharp twists and turns, and when venturing into smaller towns and villages, travelers accustomed to driving in North America find roads uncomfortably narrow.

You must be 18 years old to drive, and both front-seat passengers are required by law to wear seatbelts; common sense says that all passengers should be strapped in. As in the US and most of Europe, cars drive on the right side of the road. For an informal primer on European road signs and conventions, check out www.travlang.com/signs. The **Association for Safe International Road Travel** (**ASIRT; ☎**+1-301-983-5252; www.asirt.org) can provide more specific information about road conditions. ASIRT considers road travel (by car or bus) to be relatively safe in Greece, although notes that drivers often drive on sidewalks or while intoxicated, and fail to signal when making turns.

DRIVING PERMITS AND CAR INSURANCE

INTERNATIONAL DRIVING PERMIT (IDP)

If you plan to drive a car while in Greece, you must be over 18 and have an **International Driving Permit (IDP)**, accompanied by a valid driver's license from your home country.

Your IDP, valid for one year, must be issued in your own country before you depart. An application for an IDP usually requires one or two photos, a current local license, an additional form of identification, and a fee. To apply, contact your home country's automobile association. Be vigilant when purchasing an IDP online or anywhere other than your home automobile association; many vendors sell permits of questionable legitimacy for higher prices.

CAR INSURANCE

Most credit cards cover standard insurance. If you rent, lease, or borrow a car, you will need a **green card,** or **International Insurance Certificate,** to certify that you have liability insurance and that it applies abroad. Green cards can be obtained at car-rental agencies, car dealers (for those leasing cars), some travel agents, and some border crossings. Rental agencies may require you to purchase theft insurance in countries that they consider to have a high risk of auto theft.

RENTING A CAR

You can rent a car from a US-based firm (Alamo, Avis, Budget, or Hertz) with European offices, from a European-based company with local representatives (Europcar), or from a tour operator (Auto Europe, Europe By Car, and Kemwel

Holiday Autos) that will arrange a rental for you from a European company at its own rates. Multinationals offer greater flexibility, but tour operators often strike better deals. It is always significantly less expensive to rent a car from the US than from Europe. Ask airlines about special fly-and-drive packages; you may get up to a week of free or discounted rental.

Expect to pay US$40-100 per day plus tax (5-25%) for a tiny car, and more for larger cars and for four-wheel-drive. Take note that smaller rental cars might have difficulty getting up some of Greece's mountainous roads with numerous people in the car. Standard transmission is usually your only option when renting cars in Greece. Most rental packages offer unlimited kilometers. Return the car with a full tank of petrol (gasoline) to avoid high fuel charges. National car rental chains often allow one-way rentals, allowing you to pick up the car in one city and drop it off in another. There is usually a minimum hire period and sometimes an extra drop-off charge of several hundred euro. Reserve ahead and pay in advance if at all possible. Always check if prices quoted include tax and collision insurance; some credit card companies provide insurance, allowing their customers to decline the collision damage waiver. Ask about discounts and check the terms of insurance, particularly the size of the deductible.

To rent a car in Greece, you need to be at least 21 years old. Some agencies require renters to be 23 or 25. Policies and prices vary from agency to agency. Small local operations occasionally rent to people under 21, but be sure to ask about the insurance coverage and deductible and always check the fine print. For more specific information about car rental in Greece, contact the Panhellenic Federation of Offices for Car & Motorbike Rentals (☎281 028 0914). Rental agencies with operations in Greece include **Alamo** (www.alamo.com), **Avis** (www.avis.com), **Budget** (www.budgetrentalcar.com), **Europcar International** (www.europcar.com), **Hertz** (www.hertz.com), and more.

ON THE ROAD

Speed limits in Greece range from 50km/hr. in developed areas to 100-120km/hr. on highways. There are four major national highways in Greece: the E65 runs from Patra to Athens via Corinth; the new E65 runs from Corinth to Tripoli; the E75 runs from Athens to Thessaloniki via Larisa, and the Egnatia Odos highway runs from Igoumenitsa to the Turkish border in Evros via Thessaloniki. Petrol prices vary but average about US$6.89 per gallon in Athens.

DRIVING PRECAUTIONS. When traveling in the summer, make sure to bring substantial amounts of water (a suggested 5L of water per person per day) for drinking and for the radiator. You should always carry a spare tire and jack, jumper cables, extra oil, flares, a flashlight, and heavy blankets (in case your car breaks down at night or in the winter). If you don't know how to change a tire, learn before heading out, especially if you are planning on traveling in deserted areas. If your car breaks down, stay in your vehicle.

DANGERS

Large sections of the highways in Greece have only one lane in each direction, so Greek drivers tend to use the hard shoulder as a second, slower lane. This means there is no emergency lane in these areas, so avoid driving in the slower lane when going around blind corners to avoid a collision with a stopped vehicle. Likewise, if you break down, don't pull over to the hard shoulder on roads where it could be used as an extra lane. Roads are often windy and

ESSENTIALS

uncomfortably narrow. Custom dictates that when two cars come headlight to headlight on a narrow road, one driver must pull over and let the other pass; this often involves tricky maneuvering in reverse.

BY BOAT

If you spend any time on Greece's many islands, you will get to know the widespread, unpredictable system of ferries and other aquatic transport very, very well. Much to travelers' chagrin, no centralized schedule exists for Greece's myriad ferries: individual ferry companies maintain their own websites and set separate schedules, some of which purport to be comprehensive. Ticket offices in departure ports post daily schedules for confused visitors. Arrive at the dock 1-2hr. before departure for a decent seat, though ferries could depart at any point, from 5min. early to 3hr. late. Bring a windbreaker if you want to wander the deck when at sea. For short distances, indoor seats fill up quickly.

FERRIES

MAKING SENSE OF FERRIES. Ferries are absolutely essential for reaching the Greek islands, but with schedules that sometimes change week to week (or day to day), they can leave travelers baffled. The key to making good use of ferries is understanding ferry routes and planning your trip accordingly. The ferry service in Greece is sparse during low-season months, but begins to pick up as summer approaches and brings waves of island-seeking tourists. Most ferries, rather than shuttling back and forth between two destinations, trace a four- or five-port route. Many ferry companies will allow you to buy your round-trip ticket "split," meaning that you can ride the Piraeus-Syros-Tinos-Mykonos ferry from Piraeus to Syros, get off, get back on when the same ferry passes Syros several days later, proceed to Tinos, and so on. Remember that geographic proximity is no guarantee that you'll be able to get to one island from another. Many ferry companies lump islands into groups (such as the Western Cyclades—Serifos, Sifnos, and Milos—and the Central Cyclades—Naxos, Paros, and Mykonos), and while traveling among islands within one group is generally hassle-free, shuttling between adjacent groups can cause headaches.

Also note that there is very little service from the Cyclades to the Dodecanese. Understanding the routes also will help you make sense of discrepancies in ticket prices and travel times.

MAJOR PORTS AND SCHEDULES. As the millennia-old port of Athens, **Piraeus** is the heart of the ferry routes through the Aegean Sea. Routes run to most major islands in the Cyclades, as well as Crete, the Saronic Gulf Islands, several major islands in the Dodecanese and Northeast Aegean Islands, and Turkey. **Rafina**, Athens's smaller, eastern port, sends ferries to Evia, some of the northernmost Cyclades, and many of the Northeast Aegean Islands. Most ferries depart for the Ionian Islands from **Patra** or **Kyllini** on the Peloponnese or **Igoumenitsa** in Epirus. **Agios Konstantinos** and **Volos** handle most ferries to the Sporades and Evia.

Available from ferry companies or posted at the port police, regional schedules with the departure times, routes, and names of each departing ferry are published weekly. Make sure to look at the most updated version of the ferry schedules or call the agency on the island from which you want to leave. As particular ferries, even within companies, vary widely in quality, local travelers should pay close attention to the model of the ferry that they will be riding. Ask around or check on the web (www.ferries.gr) for tips, schedules, and prices.

HYDROFOILS AND CATAMARANS

Hellenic Seaways (☎+30 210 419 9100; www.hellenicseaways.gr) runs most of the hydrofoils and catamarans in Greece.

DOLPHIN RIDES. Flying Dolphins, the standard name for hydrofoils in Greece, go twice as fast and look twice as cool, but cost twice as much. If you have cash to spare and want to minimize travel time, these crafts provide extensive, standardized, and sanitized transport between islands; offices and services are listed in the **Transportation** sections of all cities and towns.

Keep in mind that traveling by Dolphin is like traveling by seaborne airplane: passengers are assigned seats and are required to stay in the climate-controlled cabin for the duration of the trip, which may be less than ideal for the easily seasick; there's also something tragic about sailing the Aegean in a craft that won't let you get salt on your fingers and wind in your hair.

CATAMARANS. These high-speed double-hulled boats are similar to hydrofoils in speed and cost, but are generally more reliable. They are also very popular with tourists, so don't expect to be able to buy a same-day ticket.

BY MOPED AND MOTORCYCLE

Mopeds and motorized bikes don't use much gas, can be put on trains and ferries, and are a good compromise between costly car travel and the limited range of bicycles. Indeed, motorbiking is a popular way of touring Greece's winding roads. Although renting wheels is the most cost-efficient way to avoid unreliable public transportation, they can be uncomfortable for long distances, dangerous in the rain, and unpredictable on rough roads. On many islands, roads suddenly turn into tiny trails that must be walked. Moped (μηχανάκι, mee-hah-NAH-kee) rental shop owners often loosen the front brakes on the bikes to discourage riders from using them (relying on the front brakes makes accidents more likely), so use the back brakes. If you've never driven a moped before, a cliffside road is not the place to learn.

 UNSAFE AT ANY SPEED. A word of caution: a disproportionate number of tourist-related accidents occur on mopeds, and the majority of the deaths of US tourists in Greece involve mopeds. Regardless of your level of experience, winding, poorly-maintained roads and reckless drivers make using a moped hazardous. Always wear a helmet and never ride with a backpack.

RENTING. Moped rentals are everywhere. Although a law passed in 2000 mandates that mopeds can only be rented to those licensed to operate such a vehicle, this is rarely, if ever, enforced. Bike quality, speed of service in case of breakdown, and prices for longer periods vary drastically, but expect to pay at least US$15 per day for a 50cc scooter, the cheapest bike that still has the power to tackle mountain roads. More high-tech bikes cost 20-30% more and usually require a Greek motorcycle license. Ask before renting if the price quote includes tax, insurance, and a full tank of gas, or you may be hit with an unexpected fee. Avoid handing your passport over as a deposit; if you have an accident or mechanical failure, you may not get it back until you cover all repairs. Information on local moped rentals is in the **Practical Information** section for individual cities and towns.

ESSENTIALS

KEEPING IN TOUCH

BY EMAIL AND INTERNET

The internet becomes more accessible each year in Greece. Although in some places it's possible to forge a remote link with your home server, in most cases this is a much slower (and thus more expensive) option than taking advantage of free **web-based email accounts** (e.g., www.gmail.com). **Internet cafes** and the occasional free internet terminal at a public library or university are listed in the **Practical Information** sections of major cities. For lists of additional cybercafes in Greece, check out www.cybercaptive.com and www.netcafeguide.com.

Taking a **laptop** on the road can be a convenient option for staying connected. Laptop users can occasionally find internet cafes that will allow them to connect their laptops to the internet. Travelers with wireless-enabled computers may be able to take advantage of an increasing number of internet "hot spots," where they can get online for free or for a small fee. Newer computers can detect these hot spots automatically; otherwise, websites like www.wififreespot.com and www.wi-fihotspotlist.com can help you find them.

BY TELEPHONE

CALLING HOME FROM GREECE

Prepaid phone cards are a common and relatively inexpensive means of calling abroad. Each one comes with a Personal Identification Number (PIN) and a toll-free access number. You call the access number and then follow the directions for dialing your PIN. To purchase prepaid phone cards, check online for the best rates; www.callingcards.com is a good place to start. Online providers generally send your access number and PIN via email, with no actual "card" involved. You can also call home with prepaid phone cards purchased in Greece (see **Calling Within Greece,** p. 31).

PLACING INTERNATIONAL CALLS. To call Greece from home or to call home from Greece, dial:

1. The **international dialing prefix.** From **Australia,** dial ☎0011; **Canada** or the **US,** ☎011; **Ireland, New Zealand,** or the **UK,** ☎00; **Greece,** ☎00.
2. The **country code** of the country you want to call. To call **Australia,** dial ☎61; **Canada** or the **US,** ☎1; **Ireland,** ☎353; **New Zealand,** ☎64; the **UK,** ☎44; **Greece,** ☎30.
3. The **city/area code.** *Let's Go* lists the city/area codes for cities and towns in Greece opposite the city or town name, next to a ☎, as well as in every phone number. If the first digit is a zero (e.g., ☎0210 for Athens), omit the zero when calling from abroad (e.g., dial ☎210 from Canada to Athens).
4. The **local number.**

Another option is to purchase a **calling card,** linked to a major national telecommunications service in your home country. Calls are billed collect or to your account. Cards generally come with instructions for dialing both domestically and internationally.

CALLING WITHIN GREECE

The simplest way to call within the country is to use a prepaid phone card issued by Greece's **Organization of Telecommunications (OTE)** available at kiosks and OTEs. There are local OTE offices in most towns and cardphones are often outside. Swipe your card in the payphone and the computerized phone will tell you how much time, in units, it has left. Another kind of prepaid telephone card comes with a PIN and a toll-free access number. Instead of inserting the card into the phone, you call the access number and follow the directions on the card. These cards can be used to make international as well as domestic calls. Phone rates typically tend to be highest in the morning, lower in the evening, and lowest on Sunday and late at night.

CELLULAR PHONES

Greece has very good cell phone coverage, and as all incoming calls are free, a cell phone might be a good investment. Buying an international cell phone that can be used in Greece, however, can be extremely expensive. Stick to a Greek cell phone; a bare-bones model will probably cost around US$70. Several small companies offer Greek cell phones for rent, at prices ranging from US$50-100 for two-weeks. The international standard for cell phones is **Global System for Mobile Communication (GSM).** To make and receive calls in Greece, you will need a GSM-compatible phone and a **SIM (Subscriber Identity Module) card,** a country-specific, thumbnail-size chip that gives you a local phone number and plugs you into the local network. Many SIM cards are prepaid, and incoming calls are frequently free. For more information on GSM phones, check out www.telestial.com. Companies like **Cellular Abroad** (www.cellularabroad.com) rent cell phones that work in a variety of destinations around the world.

 GSM PHONES. Having a GSM phone doesn't mean you're necessarily good to go when you travel abroad. The majority of GSM phones sold in the US operate on a different frequency (1900) than international phones (900/1800) and will not work abroad. Tri-band phones work on all three frequencies (900/1800/1900) and will operate through most of the world. Additionally, some GSM phones are SIM-locked and will only accept SIM cards from a single carrier. You'll need a SIM-unlocked phone to use a SIM card from a local carrier when you travel. Greece operates on the 900 frequency.

TIME DIFFERENCES

Greece is two hours ahead of Greenwich Mean Time (GMT), seven hours ahead of New York, ten hours ahead of San Francisco and Vancouver, and eight hours behind Sydney. Greece observes daylight saving time, though it may be at a different time than your country. More info is at www.worldtimeserver.com.

BY MAIL

SENDING MAIL HOME FROM GREECE

Airmail is the best way to send mail home from Greece. **Aerogrammes,** printed sheets that fold into envelopes and travel via airmail, are available at post offices. Write "airmail," *"par avion,"* or "αεροπορικό" on the front. Most post offices will charge exorbitant fees or simply refuse to send aero-grammes with enclosures. Surface mail is by far the cheapest and slowest way to send mail. It takes one to two months to cross the Atlantic and one to three to cross the Pacific—good for heavy items you won't need for a while, like souvenirs that you've acquired along the way.

SENDING MAIL TO GREECE

To ensure timely delivery, mark envelopes "airmail," "*par avion*," or "αεροπορικό." In addition to the standard postage system whose rates are listed below, **Federal Express** (☎+1-800-463-3339; www.fedex.com) handles express mail services from most countries to Greece. Sending a postcard or letter (up to one oz. and 16.5cm by 24.5cm) within Greece costs US$0.98.

There are several ways to arrange pickup of letters sent to you while you are abroad. Mail can be sent via **Poste Restante (General Delivery)** to almost any city or town in Greece with a post office, and it is generally reliable. Address Poste Restante letters like so:

Napoleon BONAPARTE
Poste Restante
Chania, Greece 73100

The mail will go to a special desk in the central post office, unless you specify a post office by street address or postal code. It's best to use the largest post office, since mail may be sent there regardless. It is usually safer and quicker, though more expensive, to send mail express or registered. Bring your passport for pickup; there may be a small fee. If the clerks insist that there is nothing for you, ask them to check under your first name as well. *Let's Go* lists post offices in the **Practical Information** section for each city and most towns.

ACCOMMODATIONS

DOMATIA (ROOMS TO LET)

Private homes all over Greece put up signs offering *domatia* (rooms to let). *Domatia* are perhaps the ideal accommodations: they are cheap and let you absorb some local culture by staying in a Greek home. Always negotiate with owners before settling on a price. You may be greeted by *domatia* owners as you step out at a bus stop or port; though this is illegal in many areas, it is still common. Many rooms offered at the bus stop or port are inexpensive; since proprietors are in direct competition with other owners, good deals abound. Make owners pinpoint the location of their house and don't pay until you've seen the room.

While *domatia* may be run like small hotels in tourist towns, in out-of-the-way places they can provide warm coffee at night and friendly conversation. Prices vary depending on region and season. You can expect to pay about €15-25 for a single in the more remote areas of Northern and Central Greece and €20-35 for a single (€25-45 for a double) on heavily traveled islands. Never pay more for a *domatio* than you would for a hotel in town, and remember that *domatia* owners often can be bargained down, especially when the house is not full. If in doubt, ask the tourist police: they may be able to set you up with a room and conduct the negotiations. Most private rooms operate only in high season and are the best option for those arriving without reservations.

HOSTELS

Many hostels are laid out dorm-style, often with large single-sex rooms and bunk beds, although private rooms that sleep from two to four are becoming more common. They sometimes have kitchens and utensils for your use, breakfast and other meals, storage areas, laundry facilities, internet, transportation to airports, and bike or moped rentals. However, there can be drawbacks: some hostels impose a maximum stay, close during certain daytime "lockout" hours, have a curfew, don't accept reservations, or, less frequently, require that you do chores. In Greece, a dorm bed in a hostel will average around €15-30.

 A HOSTELER'S BILL OF RIGHTS. There are certain standard features that we do not include in our hostel listings. Unless we state otherwise, you can expect that every hostel has no lockout, no curfew, a kitchen, free hot showers, some system of secure luggage storage, and no key deposit.

Hostels are not as prevalent in Greece as they are throughout the rest of Europe. Those that exist (usually in the most popular tourist destinations) are almost never affiliated with an international hosteling organization, so a hosteling membership won't do you much good. Hostels are not regulated so don't be surprised if some are less than clean or don't offer sheets and towels. Some Greek hostels offer private rooms for families and couples, and others have a maximum stay of five days. Greek youth hostels generally have fewer restrictions than those farther north in Europe. Many are open year-round and few have early curfews (some curfews, however, are strictly enforced—you might be left in the streets if you come back too late). In summer they usually stay open 6-10am and 1pm-midnight, with shorter hours in winter. It's advisable to book in advance in the summer at some of the more popular hostels in Athens, Santorini, Crete, or Nafplion.

HOTELS

Hotel singles in Greece start at €20 per night, doubles €30. You'll typically share a hall bath; a private bath will cost extra, as may hot showers. Smaller guesthouses and pensions often are cheaper than hotels. If you make reservations in writing, indicate your night of arrival and the number of nights you plan to stay. The hotel will send you a confirmation and may request payment for the first night. Often it is easiest to make reservations over the phone or online with a credit card.

The government oversees the construction and classification of most hotels, which are grouped into six classes: "L," "luxury," is followed by "A" through "E," in descending order of amenities. Greece gradually is transitioning to the star-based classification system used by many other European nations. Assume hotels do not have amenities such as A/C and TV unless they are specified. More information is available from the **Hellenic Chamber of Hotels**, Stadiou 24, Athens 10564 (☎+30 210 331 0022; www.grhotels.gr). Late at night, in low season, or in a large town, it's a buyer's market and bargaining is appropriate. Hotels often ask for your passport as a security deposit, but don't give it to them—suggest that they take down your passport number or offer to pay up front. Sleazy hotel owners might offer you only their most expensive rooms, compel you to buy breakfast, squeeze three people into a hostel-size triple and charge each for a single, or quote a price for a room that includes breakfast and private shower and then charge extra for both. Don't pay until you've seen the room. If a room seems unreasonably expensive, stress that you don't want luxuries and they might give you a cheaper option. If you think you've been exploited, threaten to file a report with the tourist police; the threat alone often resolves "misunderstandings."

LONG-TERM ACCOMMODATIONS

Travelers planning to stay in Greece for extended periods of time may find it most cost-effective to rent an apartment. A basic one-bedroom (or studio) apartment in Athens will range €600-1000 per month. Besides the rent itself, prospective tenants usually are also required to front a security deposit (frequently one month's rent and the last month's rent). Newspapers like **Athens News** (www.athensnews.gr) and websites like **www.expatriates.com** and **Craigslist** (athens.craigslist.org/apa/) can be useful in finding an apartment or house. Other sites such as www.apartmentsgr.com, www.apartmentsgreece.com, and www.sublet.com provide extensive listings of apartments, sublets, and subleases tailored to foreigners.

CAMPING

Camping in Greece not only saves you money, but provides refuge from the regulations of hostels and the monotony of hotel rooms. The **Greek National Tourist Organization** (**GNTO**) is primarily responsible for campgrounds. All GNTO campgrounds have a special operating license; most have drinking water, lavatories, and electricity. To find these, contact the **Panhellenic Camping Association,** 9 Mavromichali St., Athens, Greece 106-7 (☎+30 210 362 1560); also, check out sites like www.camping-in-greece.gr and www.greecetravel.com/campsites, which list many of the official camping sites in the country. Ask at local tourist offices for more info on the **Hellenic Touring Club,** which runs a number of campgrounds, especially in Northern Greece. Greece also has many private campgrounds, which may include pools, mini-marts, and tavernas. Prices depend on the facilities; you'll likely pay €4-8 per person and €2-3 per tent. Be aware that parking and camping outside the authorized campsites is illegal and punishable by hefty fines under Greek law.

THE GREAT OUTDOORS

The **Great Outdoor Recreation Page** (www.gorp.com) provides excellent general information for travelers planning on camping or enjoying the outdoors.

NATIONAL PARKS

Although the environment and wildlife in Greece have been largely ignored in the past, the situation has been improving greatly. The EU required that Greece set up a managed wildlife preserve on Zakynthos in 2000, and further designated 274 areas—which, combined, cover 18% of Greece—as protected.

In addition to protected sites, there are 10 National Parks in Greece, covering 169,709 acres. Most offer well-maintained trials perfect for walking and hiking. There are two protected marine parks, around Alonissos and Zakynthos. Dolphins and monk seals make their home near Alonissos, while Zakynthos's Laganas Bay is home to the loggerhead turtle, an endangered species.

WILDERNESS SAFETY

Staying **warm, dry,** and **well hydrated** is key to a happy and safe wilderness experience. For any hike, prepare yourself for an emergency by packing a first-aid kit, a reflector, a whistle, high-energy food, extra water, rain gear, a hat, mittens, and extra socks. For warmth, wear wool or insulating synthetic materials designed for the outdoors. Check weather forecasts often and pay attention to the skies when hiking, as weather patterns can change suddenly. Always let someone—a friend, your hostel, a park ranger—know when and where you are going. See **Safety and Health,** p. 15, for info on outdoor medical concerns.

ORGANIZED ADVENTURE TRIPS

Organized adventure tours offer another way of exploring the wild. Activities include archaeological digs, biking, canoeing, climbing, hiking, kayaking, photo safaris, rafting, and skiing. Tourism bureaus often can suggest parks, trails, and outfitters. Organizations that specialize in camping and outdoor equipment like REI and EMS also are good sources for info.

> **Specialty Travel Index,** P.O. Box 458, San Anselmo, CA 94979, USA (in the US ☎+1-888-624-4030, elsewhere +1-415-455-1643; www.specialtytravel.com).

SPECIFIC CONCERNS

SUSTAINABLE TRAVEL

As the number of travelers on the road rises, the detrimental effect they can have on natural environments is an increasing concern. With this in mind, *Let's Go* promotes the philosophy of sustainable travel. Through sensitivity to issues of ecology and sustainability, today's travelers can be a powerful force in preserving and restoring the places they visit.

Ecotourism, a rising trend in sustainable travel, focuses on the conservation of natural habitats—mainly, on how to use them to build up the economy without exploitation or overdevelopment. Travelers can make a difference by doing advance research, by supporting organizations and establishments that pay attention to their carbon "footprint," and by patronizing establishments that strive to be environmentally friendly.

Greece is the perfect locale to expand and explore your ecotourist sensibilities: with more than 16,000 km of coastline and over 2,000 islands, as well as wonderful diversity in flora and fauna alike, Greece presents abundant opportunities for travelers to apply their knowledge about the environment. Because so much of the country is undeveloped, backpackers play an important role in keeping the environment pristine. Small actions, like packing up excess waste when leaving a campground, using environmentally-friendly shampoo when bathing in the outdoors, and picking up trash on a beach go a long way. You also can promote ecotourism by supporting organizations that synthesize tourism and conservation. The **Ecotourist Centre of Dadia** (http://ecoclub.com/dadia/lodge.html), for example, supports conservation efforts in the Dadia Forest. See this book's **Beyond Tourism** chapter (p. 60) for opportunities to volunteer for environmental causes in Greece.

ESSENTIALS

ESSENTIALS

In addition to ecotourism, **agrotourism** has become a buzzword in recent years. It typically involves no physical exertion—visitors are meant to sit, observe, and relax, although can pitch in if they are so inclined—and denotes an escape from the comforts of the city more than anything else. Staying in a guesthouse in the countryside on a working farm, travelers can familiarize themselves with agricultural occupations and lifestyles, experience local cuisine, and immerse themselves in local culture. The Greek-based company **Agrotouristiki**, 2 Nikis St., Syntagma, Athens 1056 (☎+30 210 331 4117) works with GNTO to develop agrotourist infrastructure and promote agrotourist excursions.

ECOTOURISM RESOURCES. For more information on environmentally responsible tourism, contact one of the organizations below:

Conservation International, 2011 Crystal Dr., Ste. 500, Arlington, VA 22202, USA (☎+1-800-429-5660 or 703-341-2400; www.conservation.org).

Green Globe 21, Green Globe vof, Verbenalaan 1, 2111 ZL Aerdenhout, the Netherlands (☎+31 23 544 0306; www.greenglobe.com).

International Ecotourism Society, 1301 Clifton St. NW, Ste. 200, Washington, DC 20009, USA (☎+1-202-506-5033; www.ecotourism.org).

United Nations Environment Program (UNEP; www.unep.org).

WOMEN TRAVELERS

Anecdotes about overly aggressive male suitors are common from women travelers in the Mediterranean. Indeed, women exploring on their own inevitably face some additional safety concerns. Single women can consider staying in hostels that offer single rooms that lock from the inside or in religious organizations with single-sex rooms. It's a good idea to stick to centrally located accommodations and to avoid solitary late-night treks or metro rides. Always carry extra cash for a phone call, bus, or taxi. **Hitchhiking** is never safe for lone women or even for two women traveling together. Look as if you know where you're going and approach older women or couples for directions if you're lost. Generally, the less you look like a tourist, the better off you'll be. Dress conservatively, especially in rural areas. Wearing a conspicuous wedding band might helps to prevent unwanted advances.

Your best answer to verbal harassment is no answer at all; feigning deafness, sitting motionless, and staring straight ahead at nothing in particular will usually do the trick. The extremely persistent can sometimes be dissuaded by a firm, loud, and very public "Go away!" (FEE-ghe!). Don't hesitate to seek out a police officer or a passerby if you are being harassed. Memorize the emergency numbers in places you visit and consider carrying a whistle on your keychain. A self-defense course will both prepare you for a potential attack and raise your level of awareness of your surroundings (see **Personal Safety,** p. 17).

GLBT TRAVELERS

Though legal in Greece since 1951, homosexuality is still frowned upon socially—especially in more conservative villages—and gay, lesbian, bisexual, and transgendered (GLBT) individuals are not legally protected from discrimination. That said, cosmopolitan regions like Athens and Thessaloniki offer some gay bars and clubs. The islands of Hydra, Lesvos, Rhodes, Ios, and

Mykonos (arguably the most gay-friendly destination in Europe) offer gay and lesbian hotels, bars, and clubs.

To avoid hassles at airports and border crossings, transgendered travelers should make sure that all their travel documents consistently report the same gender. Many countries (including Australia, Canada, Ireland, New Zealand, the UK, and the US) will amend the passports of post-operative transsexuals to reflect their gender, although governments are generally less willing to amend documents for pre-operative transsexuals and other transgendered individuals. Listed below are contact organizations, mail-order catalogs, and publishers that offer materials addressing some specific concerns. **Out and About** (www. planetout.com) offers a weekly newsletter addressing travel concerns and a comprehensive site addressing gay travel concerns. The online newspaper **365gay.com** also has a travel section (www.365gay.com/travel/travelchannel. htm). The website **www.purpleroofs.com** provides an international gay and lesbian travel directory.

International Lesbian and Gay Association (ILGA), 17 Rue de la Charité, 1210 Brussels, Belgium (☎+32 2 502 2471; www.ilga.org). Provides political information, such as homosexuality laws of individual countries.

Damron Travel Guides, (☎+1-415-255-0404; www.damron.com). Publishes *Damron Men's Travel Guide, Damron Women's Traveller, Damron Accommodations Guide, Damron City Guide,* and *Damron Women's Traveller* annually.

TRAVELERS WITH DISABILITIES

The Paralympic Games, which took place in Athens in September 2004, inspired Greece to begin improving its facilities for disabled people. Hotels, train stations, cruise ships, and airports are increasingly installing facilities for the disabled, and special air transportation to many of the larger islands is available aboard Olympic Airways. Still, Greece's mountainous terrain and winding, uneven streets can prove difficult for travelers with disabilities, and few of the archaeological sites or smaller towns are wheelchair-accessible. Those with disabilities should inform airlines and hotels when making reservations; time may be needed to prepare special accommodations. Call ahead to restaurants, museums, and other facilities to find out if they are handicapped-accessible. Guide dog owners should note that there is no quarantine for taking dogs in and out of Greece. While rail is probably the best form of travel for disabled travelers in Europe, the railway systems of Greece have limited wheelchair accessibility. For those who wish to rent cars, some major car rental agencies (e.g., Hertz) offer hand-controlled vehicles.

Accessible Journeys, 35 W. Sellers Ave., Ridley Park, PA 19078, USA (☎+1-800-846-4537; www.disabilitytravel.com). Designs tours for wheelchair users and slow walkers. The site has tips and forums for all travelers.

Flying Wheels Travel, 143 W. Bridge St., Owatonna, MN 55060, USA (☎+1-877-451-5006; www.flyingwheelstravel.com). Specializes in escorted trips to Europe for people with physical disabilities; plans custom trips worldwide.

Mobility International USA (MIUSA), 132 E. Broadway, Ste. 343, Eugene, OR 97401, USA (☎+1-541-343-1284; www.miusa.org). Provides a variety of books and other publications containing information for travelers with disabilities.

Society for Accessible Travel and Hospitality (SATH), 347 5th Ave., Ste. 605, New York City, NY 10016, USA (☎+1-212-447-7284; www.sath.org). An advocacy group

ESSENTIALS

that publishes free online travel information. Annual membership US$49, students and seniors US$29.

MINORITY TRAVELERS

Greeks stare, point, and whisper as a daily pastime. If you're not obviously Greek, everyone will want to know who you are. While Greeks tend to hold stereotypes about every group of people imaginable, they place a great value on individualism; you may be asked (out of curiosity, not malice) all manner of questions or referred to continually as "the [insert your nationality here]," "the [insert religion here]," or simply "the foreigner."

Greece presents two strong and entirely different views about foreigners, and travelers should expect to encounter both. On the one hand, the Greek tradition of hospitality is unmatched. Greeks consider it almost a sacred duty to help travelers, providing them with advice and homemade food. On the other hand, it's important to remember Greece's historical position: most European nations have at one time or another invaded, betrayed, or colonized part of Greece, forging an "us-versus-them" mentality. Greeks are proud of their heritage and nationality, and often tend to view racial, religious, and cultural diversity as detrimental to society. That said, it is rare that minority travelers ever face any overt discrimination or violence. Non-white travelers admittedly will have more trouble blending in and will be at the receiving end of more stares, questions, and comments. Once the locals' curiosity is satisfied, however, you should be welcomed.

DIETARY CONCERNS

Vegetarians can make do in Greece if they don't mind making a meal of appetizers—green beans (Φασολάκια, fah-so-LAH-kia), Greek salad (χοριάτικη, ho-ree-AH-tee-kee), spinach pie (σπανοκόπιτα, spa-no-KO-pee-ta), and boiled greens (χορτα, HOR-tah). Ask before you order; many seemingly vegetarian entrees (like stuffed vegetables) can contain meat. **Vegans** should be aware that it is virtually impossible to avoid all animal products in Greek food. One exception occurs during Lent, when meat and meat stock disappear from many dishes. There are almost no Greek vegetarians, so if questioned your best bet is to argue weather ("It's so hot I only want vegetables") or allergies ("I'm allergic to lamb and goat"), as opposed to ideology. This book has made an effort to list some of the few vegetarian restaurants in Greece. The travel section of the **The Vegetarian Resource Group's** website, at www.vrg.org/travel, has a comprehensive list of organizations and websites that are geared toward helping vegetarians and vegans traveling abroad. Other helpful internet resources include www.vegdining.com, www.happycow.net, and www.vegetariansabroad.com.

Travelers who keep **kosher** likely will run into difficulty in Greece. There are few kosher establishments. Observant travelers should contact synagogues in larger Greek cities where they still exist, such as Thessaloniki, for information on kosher restaurants. Your own synagogue should have access to lists of Jewish institutions across the nation. If you are strict in your observance, you might have to prepare your own food on the road. A good resource is the **Jewish Travel Guide**, edited by Michael Zaidner (Vallentine Mitchell; US$18). Travelers looking for **halal** restaurants likely will find them in areas with large Muslim populations in Northern Greece; in other regions you might have to make your own meals. The website www.zabihah.com is helpful for finding restaurants.

LIFE AND TIMES

Greece is a hodgepodge of cultures and influences, the nexus of east and west, of ancient and modern times, the birthplace of proud emperors and of freedom fighters. It's hardly surprising that this land at the center of it all, renowned for its hospitality, has been host to a succession of towering civilizations. From Egyptian and Babylonian trade with Crete's Minoan civilization to the Orthodox Christian customs developed during the Byzantine era, to the pointed arches and spices that linger after 400 years of Turkish rule, each visiting power left its mark on Greece. In 1829, Greece won its independence from the Ottoman Empire. Since then, the country has worked to build a modern democracy along the sparkling shores of the Mediterranean.

HISTORY AND POLITICS

ANCIENT GREECE (7000 BC-AD 324)

The **Neolithic period** in Greece began around 7000 BC with the birth of agriculture. Influenced by Middle Eastern immigrants and traders, Greece progressed over the next few millennia from a succession of farming and fishing communities to the grand societies of the Minoan and Mycenaean civilizations. Over the course of just a few generations, the Greeks produced a dazzling, enduring body of literature and philosophy that served for a legacy of Western thought that flourishes to this day.

THE BRONZE AGE (3000-1100 BC)

NICE MINOAN YOU

Though the Greeks had long worked with copper, the advent of bronze metallurgy kicked off a rapid expansion of Greek power. By 2000 BC, the Crete-based **Minoans** had constructed huge palaces as centers of government, religion, and trade like Knossos, Malia (p. 489), and Phaistos (p. 491). Around 1500 BC, however, Minoan civilization mysteriously ended. One explanation is that a 1645 BC volcanic eruption on the island of Thera, now Santorini, caused a devastating tsunami. This disaster is thought to have had lasting cultural repercussions that reduced the Minoans' once magnificent empire to burned-out ruins and broken pots. Their writing system, Linear A, which remains indecipherable to this day, also faded into the debris.

THE MIGHTY MYCENAEANS

After Minoan civilization went out with a bang, the Aegean fell under the control of a mainland people called the **Mycenaeans.** Mycenaean rule extended throughout the southern mainland, Crete, the Cyclades, and the Dodecanese as far as Cyprus, but power was isolated in large cities. It centered on grand palaces at Tiryns, Pylos, Thebes, and Mycenae. In Mycenae and Tiryns, inhabitants built citadels surrounded by "Cyclopean" walls, so-called because later Greeks thought only a Cyclops could lift such massive stones (and perhaps because the crooked structure implied that the builders lacked depth

LIFE AND TIMES

perception). The Linear B writing system inscribed on tablets found at these sites mystified linguists for years until Michael Ventris, an architect-turned-linguist, cracked the code in 1954. Ventris found that the scratched characters simply represented early phonetic syllables of Greek. The Mycenaeans' written legacy, however, extends far beyond those stone tablets into the pages of Homer, the eighth century BC poet. Some hypothesize that Mycenaean military expeditions to Troy in Asia Minor ignited the **Trojan War,** described in Homer's *Iliad.* The famed war began when Paris, prince of Troy and the handsomest man in the world, abducted Helen from her husband Menelaus, king of Sparta. Enraged, Menelaus launched a war against Troy and its supporting regions that lasted 10 years. Finally, Odysseus clinched a victory by using the much-famed Trojan Horse; thinking it was a gift of surrender, the Trojans let the huge wooden creature into their city walls, only to be attacked that night by the Greek soldiers hiding inside it. Epic.

A SHOT IN THE DARK AGE (1100-800 BC)

Bronze Age civilizations in the Aegean met an abrupt end in the 12th century BC, when an invasion of **Dorians** from the Balkan highlands to the north scattered the Mycenaeans, relocating Greeks to Asia Minor and the coast of the Black Sea. This break-up marked the onset of the **Dark Age,** so-called because modern-day historians know very little about it. Though seaborne trade flourished in Athens, the rest of what we now know as the country of Greece suffered as trade declined. The desperate population emigrated in large numbers to the Dodecanese islands, Asia Minor, and Cyprus. By the end of the eighth century, however, the development of the city-state began to put the Greeks back on the map.

WE BUILT THIS CITY-STATE ON ROCK AND ROLL (800-500 BC)

The **Archaic Period's** advances forged a cohesive Greek identity. The development of the Greek alphabet, the first coinage, the first Panathenaic festival, the beginning of colonial expansion, and the first Olympic Games all appeared during this time. Joined by a shared language, the residents of city-states began to see themselves as Greeks, not just Athenians or Spartans, as they had in the past. In a testament to this rising communal identity, the Eleusinian Mysteries, the most sacred of religious celebrations in ancient Greece, were opened to anybody who spoke Greek. Foreigners, however, were scorned and ridiculed—they were called *barbaroi* (barbarians), a word intended to mock their non-Greek languages, which to Greek ears sounded like a nonsensical "bar-bar-bar."

During this time, the **polis,** or city-state, rose as the major Greek political unit. A typical polis was ruled in this period by an aristocracy and encompassed the city proper and surrounding areas. Within any town, the strategically placed **acropolis,** or citadel, and **agora,** or marketplace, formed the two major cultural landmarks. Thinkers pondered philosophy and traders hawked their wares amid the agora's *stoas* (colonnaded administrative buildings). Outside the city center, amphitheaters and stadiums hosted major public events, from dramatic and athletic exhibitions to political and religious gatherings.

SITTIN' ON TOP OF THE WORLD (500-399 BC)

The **Classical Period** began amid a series of attacks on the Greek city-states from the east. From roughly 500-477 BC, mighty king **Darius** and his son **Xerxes** sought to expand the Persian empire by force. Led by Athens and Sparta, the Greeks defied overwhelming odds to defeat the Persians in legendary battles at Marathon, Plataea, and Salamis. The hoplite phalanx, a novel battle formation designed to both intimidate and protect, clinched victory for the Greeks.

Prosperity ensued, and victorious Athens rose to prominence as the wealthiest and most influential polis in all of Greece. Equipped with a strong navy—built for use in the Persian Wars on the advice of famed statesman and general Themistocles—Athens made waves in the Mediterranean. Early on, Athens established itself as the powerful head of the **Delian League,** an organization of city-states that, though formed to defend against Persian aggression, soon became the Athenian empire. Proudly adhering to its system of direct democracy, Athens ushered in an era of extraordinary achievement in art, literature, and philosophy. Its subject city-states, however, were growing frustrated with what they saw as Athens' greed.

In the Peloponnese, meanwhile, Sparta devoted itself to an autocratic dual monarchy and a rigorous, militaristic lifestyle. Male Spartans spent their lives from age seven to 60 in military training, conquest, or defense; women trained to become fit mothers and proper models for their military sons. Rising competition between Athens and Sparta eventually dragged the rest of Greece into the violent **Peloponnesian War** (431-404 BC), sparked in part by rapid Athenian expansion under **Pericles.** The war ended in defeat for Athens, as Spartan soldiers captured the city and established an oligarchy there. Athenians soon revolted, restoring their democracy in 403 BC, but the formerly dominant city-state soon plunged into unrest. It was this revived democracy that executed the great philosopher Socrates for questioning the sanctioned pantheon of gods and "corrupting the youth."

PHILIP AND HIS PHALANX (399-336 BC)

The period after the Peloponnesian War witnessed a gradual devolution of city-state power. First Sparta and later Thebes tried to lead and maintain a unified Greek alliance, but both ultimately succumbed to Persian political influence. A new force in Macedonia soon capitalized on the weakness of the rest of Greece and seized control. **King Philip II,** with his improved phalanx (a closely formed group of infantry with overlapping spears and joined shields), conquered the Greek city-states in 338 BC at the **Battle of Chaeronea.** Though many Greeks saw him as a foreign barbarian, Philip did his best to prove that he wanted to unify Greek society—subject, of course, to his monarchy—and not to destroy it.

ALEXANDER THE AVERAGE (336-323 BC)

Alexander took the throne after his father Philip was assassinated in 336 BC. The charismatic 21-year-old had been tutored by the great Athenian thinker Aristotle. Greece's new lord was quite the fan of Homer's epics—he is said to have slept with a copy of the Iliad under his pillow—and, perhaps inspired by those mythic battles, he ruled with an iron fist. In 335 BC Alexander mercilessly razed Thebes, leaving intact only the house of the poet Pindar. Once in control of Greece, he expanded his domain and ultimately would reach as far as India and Egypt. While taking control of the Persian capital of Persepolis, Alexander gained the loyalty and respect of his followers by leading and participating in the most dangerous battles himself. By the time of his sudden death at 33, Alexander's rule had spread Greek culture and language throughout the eastern Mediterranean. During the **Hellenistic Era** that followed, Classical learning continued to diffuse to distant realms throughout the former empire.

The Macedonian Empire quickly crumbled after Alexander's death in 323 BC, restoring some independence to the Greek city-states. At that point, three Greek dynasties ruled simultaneously, each convinced of its right to sole power: the **Antigonid** in Macedonia, the **Seleucid** in Syria and Asia Minor, and the **Ptolemaic** in Egypt. Greek self-rule, however, would not last: the Romans began invading in 201 BC; by 146 BC Greece had been conquered and was part of the Roman Empire.

MAGNA GRAECIA TO MAGNA ROMA (201 BC-AD 324)

The Romans wanted desperately both to emulate and to control Greece. As they defeated the Seleucids of Asia Minor and conquered Macedonia in the First and Second Macedonian Wars, the Romans filled the power vacuum left by Alexander. At the end of the second war in 197 BC, Greece gained nominal "independence," but was still treated as a territory. Greek cities began to support their former enemies against Rome, and the **Achaean League,** a confederation made primarily of northern Peloponnese towns, openly rebelled in 146 BC. Rome flexed its muscles in response, destroying Corinth and asserting itself more harshly than ever.

Though Roman treatment of its Greek province varied widely over the following centuries, Hellenic culture seeped steadily into Roman society. Roman authors modeled their work after Greek classics, Greek sculpture was brought into Roman homes, and Roman architects adopted Greek styles. As the Roman poet Horace wrote, *"Graecia capta ferum victorem cepit"* ("Captive Greece captured its brutish conqueror"), and a Greco-Roman culture spread throughout the Roman Empire. Gradually, the Roman Empire declined; historians have filled whole libraries with speculation as to why, blaming everything from disease to overextension of the military.

BYZANTINE ERA (AD 324-1453)

Unlike other lands, which were ruined by the decline of the Roman Empire, Greece emerged into a period of cultural rebirth and prosperity. Power stretched from the Balkans through Greece to Asia Minor and Egypt, lands which would soon be referred to as Byzantium.

NEW ROME, NEW RELIGION: THE RISE OF CONSTANTINOPLE

As Rome slowly weakened, its empire split into lopsided halves. The stronger Eastern Empire was centered in Greece and the Middle East, and the destabilized Western Empire was based in Rome. Each had its own set of rulers. As a result of this unusual political arrangement, the two empires began to compete for power. Western Emperor **Constantine** converted to Christianity and plunged Greece into civil war, defeating Eastern Emperor **Licinius** in 324 and establishing himself as sole Roman Emperor. Constantine soon founded a Nova Roma (New Rome) on the site of **Byzantium,** a Greek colony at the northern tip of Asia Minor. The capital, dubbed Constantinople after the emperor's death and later renamed Istanbul by Ottoman rulers, gave Constantine's Christian empire a strategic location between the Black Sea and the Aegean Sea. Christianity flourished in Greece under Constantine and his successors: **Theodosius I** banned paganism in 391, and in 395 the Olympic Games were outlawed because nudity was considered pagan. What came to be known as the Byzantine Empire made Greece a center of learning, trade, and culture unrivaled in its time.

LIFE AND TIMES

During the sixth century, Emperor **Justinian's** battles against the Sassanians of Persia and the western Vandals (who had sacked Rome) overextended the empire's strength. Justinian did score points in domestic politics—he codified Roman law and undertook massive building projects, such as the awe-inspiring Church of Hagia Sophia, an architectural masterpiece that still stands in Istanbul. But, under constant attacks by Avars, Mongols, and Slavs, the empire began to weaken.

IT'S NOT YOU, IT'S ME: THE GREAT SCHISM

The **Arabs** began military forays into Byzantium soon after, demanding imperial attention in the early eighth century. So did iconoclasm, a religious movement involving a good deal of icon-smashing. Greek Christians believed that visual representations of God violated the commandment against idolatry, and some interpreted their losses against the Arabs as punishment for this violation. By the mid-700s, Church doctrine demanded that all images be demolished. Iconoclasm itself eventually was crushed in 843, much to the delight of modern-day art historians.

The crowning of **Charlemagne,** King of the Franks, as Holy Roman Emperor in 800 fed growing tensions between East and West in the so-called Byzantine Commonwealth; the creation of a Holy Roman Empire in the West served only to further divide the two factions. The **Great Schism** of 1054 resulted in a mutual excommunication of the Orthodox and Roman Catholic Churches' leaders— each church declared the other a false church, and the two factions developed into the distinct denominations they are today.

THE CURSE OF CRUSADERS

Even as they protected themselves from invaders, the Byzantine Greeks continued to spread Christianity. Missionaries reached out into the Slavic kingdoms and Russia, sowing the seeds of Orthodox Christianity throughout Eastern Europe. In 1071 the Byzantines lost control of eastern Anatolia to the **Seljuk Turks,** and Greek monasteries in the Aegean and Black Sea areas were transformed into armed fortresses to ward off Turkish pirates. From 1200 to 1400, Norman and Venetian crusaders invaded the Byzantine Empire. During the **Fourth Crusade,** they looted and desecrated Constantinople and tried to impose western Catholic culture on the city. Despite having strong leaders, Byzantine nobles needed to ally with Latin, Slavic, and even Turkish rulers through marriage for their realm to survive. Finally, the once-indomitable Byzantine Empire, the longest-lasting empire in history, was reduced to Constantinople and its environs. On May 29, 1453 (a day still considered cursed by Greeks), the Ottoman Turks at last overran the fading city.

OTTOMAN RULE (1453-1821)

ISTANBUL, NOT CONSTANTINOPLE

As soon as the Turks moved in, they renamed Constantine's capital Istanbul, making the city the seat of their own empire. The **Ottoman Empire** prospered at first, but eventually its diverse regions grew apart. The Muslim Turkish rulers treated their Greek subjects as a *millet*—a semi-autonomous community ruled by its own religious leaders—though Greeks could choose to integrate themselves into Ottoman society. The head of the Orthodox *millet*, the Ecumenical Patriarch of Constantinople, was ultimately accountable to the Sultan, the

LIFE AND TIMES

empire's divine ruler. For centuries, Turkish dominance was threatened only by the hardy Venetian navy, which continued to raid the Sultan's Greek territory. Meanwhile, the Orthodox Church's strong tradition became the foundation of Greek autonomy. Fueled by religious tension and the harsh taxes levied by the Ottomans, nationalist sentiment began to build against the Turks.

THE GREAT IDEA (1821-1900)

UP IN ARMS: THE GREEK NATIONALIST REVOLT (1821-1829)

On March 25, 1821, **Bishop Germanos of Patra** raised a Greek flag at the monastery of Agia Lavra, sparking an empire-wide rebellion. Middle-class rebels hoped the Orthodox Russian czar and Greek peasants would join the revolt; when they didn't, the rebels met with a crushing defeat. Disorganized but devoted guerrillas in the Peloponnese waged sporadic war on the Turkish government for the next decade. Under the leadership of rebel heroes **Botsaris, Koundouritis, Mavrokordatos, Miaoulis,** and **Ypsilanti,** the Greeks slowly chipped away at Ottoman control. The Greek passion for independence stirred up a feeling of Philhellenism in Europe, which eventually convinced Britain, France, and Russia to take up the Greek cause. The Romantic poet Lord Byron wrote flowery prose about Greek heroism and even took up arms alongside the revolutionaries. In 1829, with military support from other European powers, Greece finally won its independence. But, to the Greeks' dismay, the narrow borders of the new monarchical state included only a fraction of the six million Greeks living under Ottoman rule. For the next century, Greek politics centered on achieving the **"Megali Idea"** (the Great Idea): freeing Istanbul from the Turks and uniting all Greeks, even those in Asia Minor, into one sovereign state. Although Greece gained back some territory over the next century, including Thessaloniki and the island of Crete, it never realized these ambitious goals.

NEW BEGINNINGS (1829-1900)

After the War of Independence, joy melted into disappointment. Puny and poor, the Greek state was divided by an agrarian problem that plagued it for the entire century: landowners clung to their traditional privileges while peasants demanded the land redistribution that they had been promised in exchange for fighting.

The first president of Greece, **Ioannis Kapodistrias,** was elected in 1827 and made an earnest—if autocratic—attempt to create a strong government. His assassination in 1831 thwarted plans to establish a democracy and prompted a European political intervention. Britain, France, and Germany declared Greece a monarchy, and in 1833 gave the crown to German **Prince Otto,** a rich, powerful teenager who angered Greeks by appointing his German cronies to high-ranking positions. He moved the capital from its provisional site in Nafplion to Athens and created a parliamentary system. Though he embraced the Megali Idea, Otto's opposition to Italian unification led to an upsurge in latent resentments against his leadership. In 1862, the Athens garrison staged a coup, removing Otto from power. In need of a leader, the Greeks accepted the British choice of the Danish prince, **George I,** as king; the Brits gave the Greeks control of the Ionian Islands as an extra perk. George's rule brought general stability, Greece's first railways, and a new constitution that emphasized the importance of the elected prime minister. Problems of land distribution, however, remained unsolved.

LIFE AND TIMES

TWENTIETH CENTURY

COHESION AND CATASTROPHE (1900-1932)

The Prime Minister elected in 1910, **Eleftherios Venizelos** (since immortalized in street names throughout modern Greece) made extensive progress in stabilizing the country. In the aftermath of the Balkan Wars, Venizelos successfully worked to reunify Crete with Greece. Later, savvy Balkan alliances nearly doubled Greek territory. With the momentum that followed the additions of Macedonia and Epirus to Greece, Venizelos set up an Allied revolutionary government in Thessaloniki. After WWI, Venizelos learned that Greece would not be receiving land in Asia Minor, and in 1919 he ordered an outright invasion of Turkey. The young Turkish general (and de facto leader of the country) **Mustafa Kemal,** later known as Atatürk, crushed the Greek army. As it retreated, Turkish forces ordered the slaughter of Greek and Armenian citizens along the Turkish coast. Putting an end to the violence, the 1923 **Treaty of Lausanne** enacted a massive population exchange that sent one million Greeks living in Asia Minor to Greece and 400,000 Turkish Muslims from Greece to Turkey. Called the **Katastrofí,** or Catastrophe, this exchange drew the curtain on Greece's Megali Idea.

THE EMERGING STATE AND THE SECOND WORLD WAR (1932-1945)

Political and economic turmoil rocked the 1930s. Greece lived through brief intervals of democracy, monarchy, and military rule. King George II lost power through a series of coups that reinstated a democracy; Venizelos, the former prime minister, headed the new government for five years until royalists forced his exile. When George II resumed the throne in 1936, he personally appointed extreme nationalist General **Ioannis Metaxas** as prime minister. Metaxas presided over an oppressive military state, but his leadership during the early stages of WWII earned him lasting respect. In 1940, Metaxas is said to have rejected Mussolini's demand that Italy occupy Greece during WWII with a resounding "Ohi!" ("No!"); the Greeks now celebrate **Ohi Day** as a national holiday. Although it held off the Italian forces, Greece fell to Germany in 1941 and endured four years of bloody and brutal Axis occupation. During this time, communist-led resistance received broad support from the Greek populace, but Western powers, wary of a Communist Greece, hesitated to fund anti-Nazi resistance forces that also opposed monarchy. Over one million Greek Jews perished in Nazi concentration camps during the war.

BREAK UP AND MAKE UP: CIVIL WAR AND RECONSTRUCTION (1944-75)

The devastating Greek Civil War, marked by purges and widespread starvation, broke out in 1944 between Greek loyalists and Communists. With economic support from the US under the **Truman Doctrine,** the anti-Communist coalition government eventually defeated the Soviet-backed Democratic Army of Greece in 1949. Keeping a visible hand in Greek politics, the US helped bring **General Papagos, Constantine Karamanlis,** and the right-wing **Greek Rally Party** to power. During this time, Greece found its place among Western democracies, becoming a member of NATO in 1952. When Karamanlis resigned after the assassination of a Communist official in 1963, left-wing **George Papandreou** came to power.

LIFE AND TIMES

On April 21, 1967, a group of unknown colonels staged a coup that resulted in a military junta that lasted seven years. Using torture, censorship, and arbitrary arrest to repress Communist forces, the junta enjoyed official US support and funding at the height of the Cold War. Yet in 1974, after helping to incite a Turkish invasion of Cyprus that led to a nationwide student uprising that left 20 dead, the junta lost power. Former president Karamanlis returned to power with a newly-formed conservative party, **New Democracy (ND)**. He instituted parliamentary elections and organized a referendum on the system of government. A two-thirds vote knocked out the monarchy, and Parliament approved a new constitution on June 19, 1975.

GIVE GREECE A CHANCE (1975–PRESENT)

The constitution of 1975 established Greece as a presidential parliamentary republic modeled more or less on the democracies of other Western European nations. The Parliament is elected based on a system of proportional representation, and the leader of the party with the majority in Parliament becomes the Prime Minister. Parliament in turn elects a ceremonial president to a five-year term, but the Prime Minister and the cabinet play the most influential roles in the political process.

Guided by founder **Andreas Papandreou**, the leftist **Panhellenic Socialist Movement (PASOK)** won landslide electoral victories in 1981 and 1985. Appealing to voters with the simple slogan *"Allaghi"* ("Change"), Prime Minister Papandreou promised a radical break with the past. In office he steered Greece into the European Community (EC), now the EU, and made women's rights a legislative issue. Papandreou managed to anger his constituents in short order, and after three general elections in 10 months, **Constantine Mitsotakis** of the more conservative **New Democracy** party became Prime Minister by a slim majority.

Attempting to solve Greece's economic and diplomatic problems and bring the country into the European political fold, Mitsotakis imposed an austere economic program, limiting wage increases and authorizing the sale of state enterprises. This policy became vastly unpopular when it threatened many jobs in the public sector, and in 1993 a resurgent Papandreou defeated Mitsotakis in an emergency election. Two years later, poor health forced Papandreou to leave his post.

Fellow socialist **Costas Simitis** took control of the party in 1996 and pursued aggressive economic reforms, privatizing banks and previously state-owned companies in spite of opposition from perpetually striking labor unions. PASOK also made strides in international relations by becoming more friendly to NATO and opening talks with Turkey. The administration slashed Greece's budget deficit, brought inflation down, and reduced the national debt.

GREECE TODAY

In the 2004 elections, power went back to New Democracy, elevating Kostas Karamanlis to Prime Minister and relegating former Foreign Minister George Papandreou's PASOK to the minority party. Karamanlis was elected to a second term in September of 2007. Karamanlis's administration has focused its efforts on the economic development of northern Greece, and promised to alleviate the strain on farmers, and hopes to reform Albanian immigration policy.

THE KKE

The Greek **Communist Party**, or **KKE**, is the third-strongest political party in Greece, but still far behind ND and PASOK. Suspicious of NATO and the West,

KKE members resent American cultural influence and are responsible for much of the visible anti-American sentiment in Greece.

GREECE AND TURKEY: BREAKING THE ICE

One of Greece's continuing projects is normalizing relations with nearby Turkey. The two nations have been on less-than-friendly terms in the past, but, in part through mutual displays of support after both countries suffered devastating earthquakes in 1999, they have begun to patch up their differences. In January 2001, Foreign Minister George Papandreou traveled to Turkey, the first such visit in 37 years. There he signed cooperation agreements concerning tourism, the environment, the protection of investments, and terrorism.

A big obstacle straining Greco-Turkish relations is the little island of **Cyprus.** The **Republic of Cyprus,** internationally recognized by the UN and all foreign governments aside from Turkey, is a member of the EU. **Turkish Cyprus,** in the northern part of the Island, is recognized only by Turkey. A unification plan proposed by the United Nations came to a vote in April 2004, and though it passed in the Turkish half of Cyprus, it did not come close to gaining the necessary votes in the Republic of Cyprus. In March 2007, the demolition of the wall on Ledra Street in Nicosia, Cyprus's capital, marked an important step in the relationship by facilitating border crossings between the two sides of the divided city. But optimism quickly faded. Since the fall of the wall, negotiation talks have slowed. The victory of Turkish nationalists in the northern part of the island in the April 2009 parliamentary elections threatens to hinder the unification process even further.

PEOPLE

DEMOGRAPHICS

About 11 million people live in Greece. The extremely homogeneous population is 93% ethnically Greek and 98% Greek Orthodox (p. 49), but the annual influx of foreigners travelers in Greece each year makes the country seem more diverse.

MINORITIES

Greece is peppered with small but distinct ethnic and religious minorities. Currently some 500,000 to 1 million **Albanians** live in Greece, making it the country's largest minority population. Despite general denials of racism by the Greek people and government, concerns remain about prejudice toward the expanding immigrant population. In past years, reports of violence against illegal Albanian immigrants by the Greek border patrol have cropped up with increasing frequency.

The over 100,000 **Slavic** and **Turkish Muslims** in Thrace constitute the country's largest religious minority group. Though the older generation of Muslims remains distinct from Orthodox Greeks in language and culture, younger generations have largely assimilated into mainstream Greek society. **Gypsies,** or Roma, make up another significant minority group. They have remained on the fringes of Greek society for centuries and are now concentrated in Athens and Thessaloniki. The status of the Roma population, plagued by devastating poverty, is viewed as one of the country's largest social problems. **Jewish** communities have been present in Greece since the AD first century, but about

LIFE AND TIMES

90 percent of Jews were deported to concentration camps during the Nazi occupation in WWII (p. 45), despite the efforts of the Greek Orthodox Church and many individuals to shelter them. Only about 5000 Jews live in Greece today. Other official minorities include the **Vlachs** and the **Sarakatsanis,** groups of nomadic shepherds descended from Latin speakers who settled in Greece. The region of Macedonia is home to some 60,000 **Slavs,** who are still unrecognized as a minority by the Greek government.

LIFE AND TIMES

LANGUAGE

Aside from being a medium for communication, the Greek language, **Ellinika** (Ellhnik1, eh-lee-nee-KAH) is a link to Greece's past and a key to its continued prominence in the future. During the Golden Age, Greek flourished as the language of democracy, philosophy, and power; with Alexander the Great's campaigns abroad, it became the *lingua franca* in much of the Near East. Now, barely 12 million people speak Greek around the world. Each speaker is seen as essential to the continuation of the language and every word key to the preservation of the Greek alphabet, the oldest in the world.

To the non-speaker, the nuanced levels of idiom, irony, and poetry in Greek can present a seemingly impenetrable barrier to understanding. Although mastering Greek is a daunting task, learning enough to order a meal or get to the airport is surprisingly easy. The Greek language is phonetic and all multisyllabic Greek words come with a handy accent called a *tonos*, which marks the stressed syllable. Most sentences are simple, with a structure similar to that of English. Fortunately, many Greeks—and certainly most working in the tourist industry—understand English.

MYTHOLOGY

Greek myths simmer with spicy, titillating scandal. The adventures of the gods and their mortal counterparts have inspired artists, writers, musicians, and psychoanalysts for centuries (hello, Freud!). Moreover, Greek mythology is inextricably intertwined with the nation's religion, history, and literature.

In ancient times, worship centered on prayer and offerings to the gods. Temples and rites were at the heart of religious practice, and pilgrimages were often undertaken to consult oracles or to appease angered gods. Foreign deities were welcomed into the Greek pantheon, the canon of gods, to make sure no god was ignored or offended. There was even an altar to the unknown god, just to keep all the bases covered.

The Greek gods behaved like soap-opera characters—the immortal all-stars lacked morals and were slaves to lust, greed, and jealousy. The Greeks knew that these divine passions were not to be trifled with: mythology is full of ugly examples of what happens to mortals who challenge or disrespect gods. The weaver Arachne was turned into a spider because she dared to declare herself more skilled than Athena. Tantalus, after serving the gods human flesh at a feast, was condemned to stand in a pool in Hades, forever tormented by hunger and thirst with "tantalizing" food and water just beyond his reach. Though the worship of Greek gods faded with the advent of Christianity, the pantheon's legacy is visible in Greece's plentiful ancient ruins, and the influence of the myths is felt even today.

RELIGION

THE ORTHODOX CHURCH

Christianity in Greece dates to the AD first century. The Apostle Paul and other missionaries were the first to spread Christianity and establish Christian communities in cities in Greece and Asia Minor. Five of Paul's epistles, which eventually formed part of the New Testament, were addressed to these new Christian communities. By the fourth century, persecution of the Christians had ended and the Church was well established throughout the Mediterranean. After the 11th-century Great Schism (p. 43), Greek churches evolved into what is now Eastern Christianity, centered at the **Patriarchate of Constantinople.** A member of the family of Orthodox Churches, the **Church of Greece** received a measure of autonomy in 1850; its head bishop would no longer be required to report to any higher-ranking official. The Church is still under the spiritual guidance of the **Ecumenical Patriarch in Constantinople.**

The Orthodox Church of Greece is the preeminent religious body in the country today. The Church is protected by the state, which pays for the maintenance of churches and for the salaries of the clergymen. Over 98% of the population of Greece is baptized and hundreds of monastic communities are scattered throughout the land, the most prominent of which are found on the Mount Athos Peninsula. Orthodox Christianity, which takes its name from the Greek *orthos* ("true") and *doxa* ("belief"), affirms a loving God who entered into this life in the person of Jesus. Honored as Lord and Savior, Christ revealed the one God as Father, Son, and Holy Spirit—the Holy Trinity. The Church celebrates these beliefs in worship during the service of the **Divine Liturgy.** Faith is also expressed in scripture and tradition, which includes the veneration of icons, prayers, a rich history of rituals and customs, and the Ecumenical Councils. Because of their religious example, the **saints** are greatly revered.

TURF WARS

For nearly two centuries, the structural arrangement between the Church of Greece and the Patriarchate of Constantinople has remained peaceful but tense. The Church of Greece's boundaries do not match those of the Greek state, and many believe that the Church of Greece should encompass the country's internationally recognized borders. Such sentiment crystallized in the spring of 2004, when territorial tension surfaced between the Archbishop of the Greek Church and the Ecumenical Patriarch. When three vacancies for sees (bishop seats) opened in northern Greece, an area under the Patriarchate's control, 35 bishops in the Hierarchy (the full body of the Church of Greece) affirmed the Archbishop's motion to elect new bishops for the sees. This violation of jurisdiction was not welcomed by the Ecumenical Patriarch, who threatened to excommunicate the Archbishop. Though both sides eventually compromised, the eruption underscored an uneasy relationship between the independent Greek Church and the central branch of Orthodox Christianity.

OTHER RELIGIOUS TRADITIONS

While Orthodox Christianity reigns in Greek society and the government grants certain advantages and support to the Church of Greece, the Greek Constitution guarantees freedom of religion and repudiates proselytizing. There are a few small **Armenian Orthodox, Roman Catholic,** and **Muslim** communities. Before WWII, Greece had a thriving **Jewish** population, but only a few organized Jewish communities remain today.

LIFE AND TIMES

FOOD AND DRINK

Greek food is a product of the country's location on the Mediterranean. Medical studies have highlighted the Greek diet as a good model for healthy eating; its reliance on unsaturated olive oil, fresh fish, and vegetables has prevented high rates of heart disease and obesity in the population. Though the prevalence of cheap and greasy foods has caused some recent health concerns, penny-pinching carnivores will thank Zeus for lamb, chicken, or beef **souvlaki** and hot-off-the-spit **gyros**—pronounced "GHEE-ro"—stuffed into pitas. Vegetarians can eat their fill on the cheap, though this might mean putting together a meal of several *mezedes* (small snack dishes). **Toast** refers to a panini-like grilled sandwich, not to be confused with plain bread out of the toaster. **Tzatziki,** a garlicky cucumber yogurt dip served with bread, is a good way to start off a meal (or ripen your breath enough to ward off amorous overtures). Try the feta-piled **horiatiki** (Greek salad), savory pastries like **tiropita** (flaky, tissue-thin layers of pastry—called *phyllo*—full of feta), **spanikopita** (spinach and feta *phyllo* pastry), and the cheeses, produce, and vegetables found at markets in cities. **Baklava,** a dessert made of *phyllo*, nuts, and honey, is a sweet way to round off your meal.

Caffeine addicts can get their fix with several varieties of brew, including the strong, sweet sludge that is Greek coffee, the instant coffee referred to as "Nes" (as in "Nescafé"), or the frothy, iced-coffee frappes that take an edge off the heat in the summer. Potent *raki* and *tsipouro*, moonshine produced from the dregs of wine, are popular on the mainland and Crete. **Wine,** important enough in ancient Greece to monopolize the attention of the god Dionysus, is plentiful and widely varied. **Ouzo,** a powerful, licorice-flavored Greek spirit, is served before meals with a glass of water—when you pour the ouzo into the water, the mixture turns white. Before drinking, say, *"Geia maV!"* ("YAH-mas"), the Greek equivalent of "Cheers!"

Breakfast, served only in the early morning, generally consists of coffee and a simple piece of toast with *marmelada* (jam), a pastry, or thick Greek yogurt with honey. Lunch, a hearty and leisurely meal, is usually eaten sometime between 2 and 5pm. Dinner is a drawn-out, relaxed affair, served late, often between 10pm and midnight. A Greek restaurant is known as a **taverna** or *estiatorio* (often the more expensive of the two), and a grille is a *psistaria*. *Kafeneios* are traditional coffee shops frequented primarily by groups of older Greek men; women may feel uncomfortable among the bros. Many restaurants don't offer printed menus, so waiters will ask you if you want salad, appetizers, or the works. Be careful not to wind up with mountains of food—Greek portions tend to be large. Restaurants often put bread and water on the table; an added charge for the bread and sometimes the water may or may not be listed or mentioned. Most Greeks pay with cash when they dine out, so don't expect to be able to eat your way through the country with a credit card. While service is always included in the check, it is customary to round the bill up or leave some coins as an extra tip.

CUSTOMS AND ETIQUETTE

HOME HOSPITALITY

Greek hospitality is legendary, literally: Zeus is the god of guests and hospitality. From your first days in the country, you may be invited to drop by a stranger's home for coffee, share a meal at a local *taverna*, or attend an engagement party or baptism. The invitations are genuine; it's impossible to spend any length of time in the country and not have some friendly interaction with locals. Greet new acquaintances with *"kalimera"* ("good morning") or *"kalispera"* ("good evening"). Personal questions are ordinary and expected in Greece; people you've just met will ask about family, career, salary, and other information. Returning questions in kind is expected and appreciated, so don't be shy!

TABLE MANNERS

Offering food and drink to guests is how the Greeks say hello. When offered, take it—it's almost always considered rude to refuse. Hosts usually will offer coffee upon a guest's arrival. Visiting and gossiping over coffee, either at a cafe or at someone's home, is how many Greeks spend their nights. Wine drinkers should note that glasses are filled only halfway but are constantly replenished; it's considered bad manners to empty your glass. There's no going Dutch in Greece—when out to eat, the bill usually is paid by the host rather than split among the diners. Even though it's understood that the host will foot the bill, dramatic (but fruitless) attempts to throw in money are common. Never offer money in return for an invitation to dine at someone's home. A small gift, such as a toy for the host's children, is a welcome token of gratitude.

R-E-S-P-E-C-T!

Be deferential to elders. This may mean offering a seat on a bus or helping someone cross the street. Visitors to churches are expected to dress conservatively; both men and women always should cover their shoulders and knees. Take signs forbidding photography seriously. Even if photography isn't specifically forbidden in a particular church or monastery, it is still rude, as is photographing the military. Even if you're hoping that a tiny rock from Delphi will become your own personal oracle if you take it home with you, refrain from pocketing "souvenirs" from ancient sites. Not only is it disrespectful, but it could be considered looting and is a possible cause for arrest.

ART AND ARCHITECTURE

A heritage of craftsmanship many centuries old lives on in Greece. The number and quality of carefully wrought works that have survived to the present day attest to the importance of art in the ancient and modern Greek worlds. Classical Greeks used diverse materials to represent the faces of the mighty gods, the deeds of mythical heroes, and the natural beauty they saw in the human body. Although modern audiences admire ancient Greek statues and pottery in museums, it is important to remember that the Greeks produced art not just to marvel at its beauty but also for use in everyday life. Pottery was the Tupperware® of the time, used as daily dishware and for storage and trade. Architecture developed through the functional construction of stadiums, commercial buildings, and religious temples. Today, Greece's double legacy of form and function lives on in the centuries of art and architecture that it influenced.

LIFE AND TIMES

CYCLADIC/MINOAN PERIOD (3000-1500 BC)

"Less is more" was the motto for the Bronze Age Cycladic civilizations and their minimalist sculpture, which survives mostly in small marble statuettes. These miniature pieces gracefully simplified the human form; a nude goddess, arms folded straight across her body, is a typical figure. The Minoans of Crete also created scores of miniature votive statuettes, like the two earthenware snake goddesses, decorated with opaque colored glazes, that reside in Iraklion's Archaeological Museum (p. 485). It was architecture, however, that brought the Minoans glory, with formidable palaces like the one at Knossos. The palaces were cities unto themselves, and their labyrinthine design echoed the complex administrative and religious roles of Minoan priest-kings. The massive pillars, ceremonial stairways, and decorative stucco reflect Near Eastern aesthetic and structural influences resulting from trade with Egypt and Mesopotamia.

Minoan artists adorned plaster with bull-leaping ceremonies, gardens, and jumping dolphins in vibrant frescoes. Though a little dusty, several Minoan frescoes were preserved in the ash of the epic volcanic eruption that destroyed much of Thira (modern Santorini) around 1500 BC; this style of fresco can be seen at the National Archaeological Museum in Athens (p. 98), at Knossos, or in Iraklion's Archaeological Museum. The Minoans were also renowned throughout the Aegean for their multicolored Kamares-style pottery, which consisted of red and white ornamentation on a dark background. Kamares-style designs include curvy abstract patterns and stylized ocean and plant motifs.

MYCENAEAN PERIOD (1500-1100 BC)

The Mycenaean palaces at Mycenae, Pylos, Thebes, and Tiryns emphasized symmetry more so than earlier architecture and centered on the *megaron*, a Near East-inspired reception room. Decorative frescoes revamped the fanciful Minoan model according to Mycenaean warrior taste.

Trailblazers in their own right, the Mycenaeans were the first Europeans to produce monumental sculpture. By 1500 BC Mycenaean royal graves had evolved into *tholoi*, beehive-shaped stone structures covered in packed earth. While the relief work on these tombs shows Minoan influence, the larger-than-life masonry is distinctly Mycenaean. The royal tombs and triangular 13th-century BC Lion's Gate sculpture at Mycenae (p. 223) also display this aesthetic.

IT'S HIP TO BE SQUARE: GEOMETRIC PERIOD (1100-700 BC)

A new art form based on ceramics evolved out of the collapse of Mycenaean civilization and the Dark Age that followed. There to pick up the pieces were the Athenians, who stood at the center of the new movement. The pottery of the **Proto-Geometric Period** (1100-900 BC) was decorated with Mycenaean-inspired spirals, arcs, patterned lines, and concentric circles. These patterns became more intricate in the **Geometric Period,** as artists covered clay figurines and pottery with abstract angular motifs that resembled woven baskets. Identically posed stick-figure humans and grazing animals began to appear among the continuous, patterned bands and tight rows of thick black lines. Signs of Near Eastern contact with Greece showed up again as Syrian and Phoenician floral and animal designs crept into the adornment of Greek cooking vessels. Architects of the Geometric Period focused on the development of one-room temples with columned porches. These temples were regarded as the houses of the gods or goddesses they honored, and each *oikos* (house) came complete with a sculpture of its inhabitant.

ARCHAIC PERIOD (700-480 BC)

During the **Archaic Period,** Greek art and architecture gradually traded stylized lines for the curving human realism that would come to characterize the later Classical Period. It was in this period that structures such as the acropolis, agora, amphitheater, and gymnasium were perfected.

The **Doric** and **Ionic orders**—whose columns have lined many an art history student's nightmares—diverged during these years. The Doric order breathed new life into temples' one-room inner sanctums and outer colonnades with arrow-straight marble columns. Around the sixth century BC, however, the Greek colonies along the coast of Asia Minor branched off into the exotic Ionic order. Austere Doric designs just wouldn't do for the Ionian architects, who conjured slender, fluted columns, often topping them with twin curlicued volutes. Ornate Ionic temples boasted forests of columns: the Temple of Hera on Samos (p. 382) had 134.

The depiction of the human body became a central concern during the Archaic period, with sculptors crafting large-scale male figures called *kouroi.* Each *kouros* was a naked young man in a rigid pose lifted from Egyptian statues—one leg forward with both feet planted firmly, hands clenched at sides—and grinning the famous Archaic smile. The female equivalent of the *kouros,* the *kore,* sported the latest fashions instead of her birthday suit; sculptors suggested the female form through folds and hemlines of the *kore*'s clothing. By the fifth century BC, sculpture had turned toward realistic depiction, reaching its height soon afterward in the Classical Period. The relaxed posture of the free-standing **Kritios Boy** (490 BC), now in the Acropolis Museum (p. 92), broke the stiff, symmetrical mold of its Archaic model: the Kritios Boy's weight is shifted onto one leg and his hips and torso tilt naturally.

Though sculptors focused on realism, two-dimensional art remained abstract. Athenian vase painters depicted humans using Corinth's black figure technique, drawing black silhouettes with carved features. Human figures appeared in the half-profile of Egyptian art: moving figures' chests faced forward, and each person stared straight out with both eyes. Figures conveyed emotion with gestures rather than facial expressions, pulling their hair in grief or flailing their limbs in joy.

CLASSICAL PERIOD (480-323 BC)

The arts flourished during the Classical Period as Athens reached the peak of its political and economic power under Pericles and his successors. As Greek architects perfected the Doric and Ionic orders, Classical temples became more spacious and fluid than the stocky temples of the Archaic Period. The majestic Athenian **Acropolis** (p. 90) gazed down over Athens, crowned by its star attraction, the ▒**Parthenon.** Built as a temple for Athena, protectress of Athens, the Parthenon once held the huge statue of Athena Parthenos, literally, "Athena the Virgin." Created by **Phidias,** the same sculptor who worked on the Temple of Zeus at Olympia (p. 237), this monumental work of perfect proportion was over 40 ft. tall and was made of ivory and gold.

LIFE AND TIMES

Sculptors mastered the natural representation of the human form during the Classical Period. The sculptures of the Temple of Zeus at Olympia reveal meticulous attention to detail. Sculptures from the Classical Period include the **Charioteer** (470 BC) at Delphi, now immortalized in the Delphi Museum, and a statue of Zeus or Poseidon (465 BC), arms outstretched, now housed in the National Archaeological Museum (p. 98). By the middle of the fifth century BC Classical sculptors had adopted a detailed humanism, but the sculpted faces lacked personalized expression. Sculptors pursued a universal perfection of the human form, suppressing all imperfections in service of the impersonal, idealized style, which remained in vogue through the beginning of the fourth century BC.

Classical potters swooned over the red figure technique that had been gaining steam since 540 BC. Red figure vase painting featured a black painted background, allowing the naturally reddish clay to show through as the drawn figures. Vase-makers then painted on details with a fine brush. Inspired by the growing realism in sculpture, early Classical masters used this technique to indicate emotion on the faces of humans and animals.

HELLENISTIC PERIOD (323-46 BC)

The death of Alexander the Great marked the beginning of the Hellenistic Period, a prodigious era for art and architecture. During this time, two of the Seven Wonders of the Ancient World were created: the **Colossus of Rhodes**, a gigantic statue of the sun god Helios, and the **Pharos**, a monumental lighthouse on the harbor in Alexandria. Architectural innovations, like the **Corinthian order** of columns (based on the Ionic column but topped with a capital of acanthus leaves), enhanced temples and public buildings. Astoundingly precise acoustics graced the amphitheaters at Argos and Epidavros (p. 225); a coin dropped on stage is audible in the most distant seat in the theaters over two millennia after their construction. Hellenistic sculpture exuded passion and tested the aesthetic value of ugliness, displaying all the technical mastery and twice the human emotion of Classical works.

BYZANTINE AND OTTOMAN PERIODS (AD 324-1829)

The art and architecture in Greece under Byzantine and Ottoman rule was limited by the often-strict cultural dictates of these imperial societies. Though Byzantine artistry developed within a set of religious conventions that discouraged creative experimentation, artists throughout the era still created magnificent mosaics, iconography, and church architecture. Early Byzantine churches were based on the layout of Roman basilicas, with long buildings featuring a semicircular apse at one end and windows lining a wooden ceiling. The floor and lower parts of the walls were usually covered in marble while the upper parts were reserved for mosaics and frescoes.

Byzantine artists transformed almost any flat surface they found into glittering art. By illuminating manuscripts, carving ivory panels, embossing bronze doors, and covering *cloisonné* enamels with jewels, they made sure to let it shine. Byzantine iconography aimed for religious authenticity; artists underwent years of spiritual and technical training before gaining permission to portray sacred subjects. Each figure stares out with a soulful gaze, and the determined frontal pose against a gold background in the church's dim light creates the illusion of the figure floating between the iconostasis (icon screen separating the altar from the people) and the viewer. In Byzantine mosaics, a unique shimmering effect adds to the brilliance, as contrasting gold and silver *tesserae* (the small cubes of stone or ceramic covered in glass or metallic foil) reflect the light at sharp angles. Sparkling examples can be seen in churches in Thessaloniki (p. 161), at the Monastery of Osios Loukas (p. 123), on Mount Athos (p. 184), and at Meteora (p. 147).

MODERN ART (1829-PRESENT)

Nationalist sentiment after Greek independence led the government to subsidize local art. King Otto encouraged young artists to study their craft in Munich. The **Polytechneion,** Greece's first modern art school, was established in 1838. The first wave of post-independence Greek painters showed strong German influence, while sculptors looked to Classical Greece for inspiration. Modern Greek painters have experimented with various European trends, including Impressionism, Expressionism, and Surrealism. Other painters rejected foreign influence, among them the much adored **Theophilos Chatzimichael** (1873-1934). The contemporary paintings of **Yiannis Psychopedis** (b. 1945) combine social and aesthetic criticism. Painter **Opy Zouni** (b. 1941) has won international acclaim for her geometric art.

LITERATURE

EARLY MASTERS

EPIC TALES. The Greek literary tradition began with rich oral poetry, delivered long before written Greek appeared. The most famous storyteller is the blind bard **Homer,** who may or may not have composed the **Iliad** and the **Odyssey** in the eighth century BC. Details of the legendary poet's life range from sparse to nonexistent. It remains unclear precisely who pulled folktales about the Trojan War and its aftermath into the two epics. Regardless of their author's true identity, the *Iliad*'s mythic military struggle is still revered for its account of heroism's human costs, while the *Odyssey* has inspired many of the journeys, physical and otherwise, that have made their way into the canon of Western literature.

SING IN ME, O MUSE. Homer's contemporary **Hesiod** chronicled the five Ages of Man in **Works and Days,** offering advice on farming, rural life, and other human experiences. In the **Theogony,** he gave an account of the creation of the world and the genealogy of the gods. **Archilochus of Paros** wrote biting satirical and erotic poetry; legend holds that members of an entire family hanged themselves after they were ridiculed in his verse.

On Lesbos in the seventh century BC, lyric poet **Sappho,** ancient Greece's only known female poet, earned herself the title of the 10th Muse for her verse. **Pindar** of Thebes (518-438 BC), acclaimed by the ancients as the greatest of poets, wrote odes commissioned by sports-obsessed nobles to commemorate athletic victories. **Callimachus** (305-240 BC), who lived in Alexandria, wrote elegies in Hellenistic Greek. His personal tone and wit greatly influenced Roman poetry. **Apollonius** of Rhodes also worked from Alexandria and invented the popular form of the mini-epic.

STORY BECOMES HISTORY. Herodotus (484-425 BC) chronicled the epic battles and personalities of the Persian Wars—plus centuries' worth of melodramatic

LIFE AND TIMES

context and rumor—in his monumental (and rather sensationalist) *Histories*, earning him the title "Father of History." Herodotus's detailed account of the wars must have come from interviews with old men with sharp memories, as the battles in question took place during his childhood. Hard-headed **Thucydides** (c. 460-400 BC) immortalized the Peloponnesian War, chronicling Athens's conflict with Sparta and examining the effects of war on nations and people. The genre of pseudo-historical romance took Greece by storm in the AD first century, generating personal love poems and erotic novels. **Plutarch**, writing around AD 100, constructed biographies of famous Greeks and Romans in **Parallel Lives.**

EMPERORS AND INTRIGUE: BYZANTINE LITERATURE

The Byzantine Era produced the most-read work of literature ever: the Greek-language **New Testament** of the Bible. After Emperor Constantine converted to Christianity in the AD fourth century, most literature was written by monastery-bound theologians or court historians. In the sixth century, **Procopius**, one of Emperor Justinian's generals, reported on all aspects of his boss's reign. He wrote two conventional tracts for publication, Procopius's *History of His Own Time and On the Buildings*, and left behind a *Secret History*—an insider's account of the intrigues and debauchery common in the court of Justinian and his wife Theodora. **Photius** (820-893), twice appointed Patriarch of Constantinople, admired the "pagan" works of Homer and encouraged their study. This avid reader was a writer as well; his massive *Bibliotheca* chronicled Greek works in over 270 articles.

FACING THE PAST: MODERN LITERATURE

The advent of Greek independence in 1829 (p. 44) gave rise to the Ionian School of modern literature, which dealt with the political and personal issues of the Greek revolution. **Dionysios Solomos** (1798-1857), whose **Hymn to Liberty** became the Greek national anthem, is still referred to as the "national poet." **Constantine P. Cavafy** (1863-1933) played a key role in the revival and recognition of Greek poetry. Twentieth-century poets would infuse their own odes with Modernism, alternately denouncing and celebrating nationalism and politics. **George Seferis** (1900-1971), known for his imbuing his works with symbolism and mythology, became the first Greek to win a Nobel Prize for Literature in 1963. In 1979, **Odysseas Elytis** (1911-1996), who looked at politics in a different light and incorporated French Surrealism into his work in an effort toward national redemption, was awarded the Nobel Prize for Literature as well. The many novels of **Nikos Kazantzakis** (1883-1957), perhaps the best known modern Greek author, include *Odyssey*, a modern sequel to the Homer's epic (1958), *Report to Greco* (1965), *Zorba the Greek* (1946), and *The Last Temptation of Christ* (1951); the last two were made into successful films. *Freedom or Death* (1956), his homage to Greek revolts against the Ottomans on his home island of Crete, analyzes the Greek-Turkish conflict and explores the concept of masculinity. More recently, social critic and author **Nikos Dimou** has risen to fame as the acclaimed, but often controversial, Greek writer of *On the Misery of Being Greek* and numerous anthologies of poems.

SCIENCE AND PHILOSOPHY

The philosophical and scientific writings of the ancient Greeks awed even the hardnosed Romans. According to Hellenic tradition, the first philosopher was the sixth-century BC thinker **Thales of Miletus**, who believed that the universe had an ordered structure and that everything moved toward a predetermined end. This teleology, or end-oriented world-view, contributed to every major Greek philosophy. **Pythagoras,** a math whiz and purported student of Thales, came up with theorems that still make regular appearances in high school math homework.

Early philosophical works, which survive on fragments of papyrus and in the reports of later writers, paved the road for **Socrates** (469-399 BC). Although Socrates refused to commit his words to untrustworthy paper, his legacy was preserved and carried on by his pupil **Plato** (428-348 BC). Socrates described himself as a gadfly, nipping at the ass of the horse that was Classical Athens. He brought philosophy down from the stars and into the agora, where he spent his days picking over the morals and beliefs of anyone who would stop for a chat. This style of asking questions is still called the Socratic method. Socrates's radical lifestyle and constant questioning eventually angered influential Athenians, generally because he had proven them fools. In 399 BC, he was tried for impiety, introducing new gods, and corrupting the youth; he was sentenced to death by hemlock poisoning.

Plato became the new master philosopher of ancient Greece, primarily by writing up the sharp conversations that he and Socrates had had with other thinkers over bowls of wine. In **The Republic,** his most famous work, Plato muses about the components of an ideal state and the definition of a just individual. He believed that knowledge acquired through the senses is impure, and that only the soul can know the essence of things; the objects seen in life are only shadows of true Forms. Plato's pupil, **Aristotle** (384-322 BC), diverged from his mentor's teachings and took a more empirical approach to philosophy, placing value on knowledge gained from experience as well as from abstract reason. Aristotle's quest for knowledge reached into the realms of physics, biology, and mechanics. A few years later, **Euclid** wrote **The Elements,** the source of the principles of geometry that we know and love today. **Archimedes** created complex mathematical formulas with circles and cylinders, inventing the Archimedes screw, a device to move water, and conceiving of the principles of density and buoyancy during a particularly enlightening bath.

Greeks experimented in medicine as well. In the fifth century BC, before he became famous for his oath, **Hippocrates** suggested that disease might not be the result of divine punishment. A combination of speculation and observation yielded the idea of "four humors" flowing through the body (yellow bile, black bile, phlegm, and blood), which corresponded to personality traits and the four elements; an imbalance caused illness. Research in Alexandria, Egypt in the third century BC pushed medical knowledge further. Work on animal brains, hearts, and organs inspired **Galen of Pergamum** to try the art of human dissection, expanding knowledge about human anatomy.

Under Roman rule, the natural sciences wilted in Greece. The Romans were impressed by the body of knowledge the Greeks had acquired, but they were confused by the concept of "knowledge for knowledge's sake." During the Middle Ages, advancements in European medicine evaporated entirely. Fortunately, Greek scientists had written about their findings, which have thus survived through the ages.

THE PERFORMING ARTS

THEATER

The precise origins of Greek theater are uncertain. Tragedy is sometimes said to have grown out of competitions in which the winner received a goat, thus

LIFE AND TIMES

earning the name *tragodoi* (goat songs). Comedy, on the other hand, probably developed out of songs written out of the ever-appealing pastime of making fun of people. Greek drama played a major part in religious festivals in honor of Dionysus, where all attendants were performers in the chorus as well as audience members. **Thespis,** who was bold enough to step out of the chorus and deliver lines, is credited as the first actor (hence "thespian"). **Aeschylus** (525-456 BC) wrote the first dialogue between characters, and is best known for the *Oresteia,* his trilogy recounting an intergenerational revenge cycle. **Sophocles** (496-406 BC) followed with the cathartic Oedipus plays, which detail the ruinous tale of a man who becomes king of Thebes by unwittingly killing his father and marrying his mother. **Euripides** (485-406 BC), Sophocles's contemporary, added the biting observations of *Medea* and *The Bacchae* to the tradition. **Aristophanes** (450-385 BC) proved that puns and sexual innuendoes always get laughs. His smash-hit comedies poked fun at prominent citizens like Socrates or wartime policies: in the play *Lysistrata,* peace-loving Greek women withhold sex from their husbands until the end of the Peloponnesian War. **Menander** (342-291 BC), following in Aristophanes's footsteps, brought along "New Comedy," which was loved and copied by the Romans.

Though the heyday of Greek theater ended with the fall of Classical Greece, theater still holds a strong cultural presence today. Contemporary playwrights like **Iakovos Kambanellis** (b. 1922), who incorporated his experiences in a WWII concentration camp into his socially conscious plays, have wooed audiences with portrayals of 20th-century Greek life. The **Athens Festival,** held from May to October, features Classical drama at the ancient Theater of Herod Atticus, as well as concerts, opera, choruses, ballet, and modern dance. At the **Epidavros Theater Festival,** held each year from June to August, even a language barrier won't detract from the ominous chorus that, in Aeschylus's time, made "boys die of fright and women have miscarriages." Tickets for the festivals are available at the Athens Festival Box Office, 39 Panepistimiou, inside the arcade. (☎21032 72 000. Open M-F 8:30am-4pm, Sa 9am-2:30pm.)

OPA! MUSIC

Greek music reflects Greek passion for life and tradition. Greeks have been making music since the Bronze Age and early musical instruments from this period have been found on Crete. Although Greeks had no system of musical notation before the fifth century BC, they devised a theory of **harmonics.** It was necessary for early poets to remember musical formulas, since poems were sung or chanted. During the Classical Period, appreciation of music came to be considered an essential part of education, and the mark of a good musician became the ability to convey virtue through his music. An integral part of Greek drama, music also graced most other social gatherings and interactions. This tradition carried on through the ages in folk music, and in many areas today it is common to see a wide circle of locals and tourists, hands joined, dancing. The dance steps for the followers are comfortably repetitive, so don't hesitate to join in—enjoy yourself!

Though its earliest origins are disputed, a new musical style emerged from Turkey's western coast during the population exchange with Greece in the 1920s that unsettled established notions of poetic music. The Turkish influences merged with new types of music emanating from *tekedes* (hashish dens) and *amanedes* (Middle Eastern cafes). Gritty, urban **rembetika,** which may have gotten its name from the Turkish word *rembet* ("outlaw"), used traditional Greek instruments to sing about the stark side of modern life, focusing on drugs, prison, and alienation. *Rembetika* emerged as the cry of the lower class, as newly transplanted refugees living in urban shantytowns embraced its sorrowful expressiveness. Interest in traditional *rembetika* has recently resurfaced, and musicians strumming the ubiquitous *bouzouki* (a traditional Greek stringed instrument) can be found in restaurants, clubs, and cafes. Pop music in Greece combines traditional folk rhythms, Middle Eastern influences, and European club beats. Greece's hottest pop stars today, including Anna Vissi, Sakis Rouvas, and Elena Paparizou, mix traditional styles with contemporary sounds.

HOLIDAYS AND FESTIVALS

DATE	FESTIVAL	DESCRIPTION
January 1	Feast of St. Basil/New Year's Day	Commemorates the new year. Greeks traditionally cut a sweet bread *(vassilopita)* baked with a lucky coin inside.
January 6	Epiphany	Celebrates Jesus's baptism.
January 8	Gynecocracy	Switches gender roles in Thracian villages; women sit in cafes and men do housework. Literally means "rule of women."
Late January or Early February	Carnival	Three weeks of feasting and dancing that precede Lenten fasting. Patra, Skyros, and Kefallonia host the best celebrations.
Early March	Clean Monday	Starts Lent (fasting period of about 40 days before Easter). Revelers go outside and fly kites.
March 25	Greek Independence Day/Feast of the Annunciation	Commemorates the 1821 struggle against the Ottoman Empire and celebrates Archangel Gabriel's visit to Mary.
Late April or early May	Easter	Celebrates Jesus's resurrection from the dead. The single holiest day in the Greek calendar is marked by countless traditions and all-day celebrations.
Late April or early May	St. George's Day	Honors the dragon-slaying knight with rowdy festivals.
May 1	Labor Day	Celebrates workers.
Early June	Ascension	Commemorates Jesus's ascension into heaven. Celebrated 40 days after Easter with different rituals in each region.
Mid June	Pentecost	The day of the Holy Spirit, celebrated 50 days after Easter.
August 15	Feast of the Assumption of the Virgin Mary	Honors Mary's ascent into heaven. Village and city celebrations abound.
September 8	The Virgin Mary's Birthday	Celebrates Mary's birthday; some villages finance a feast by auctioning off the honor of carrying the Virgin's icon.
October 26	Feast of St. Demetrius	Observed along with the opening of a new stock of wine. Celebrated enthusiastically in Thessaloniki.
October 28	Ohi Day	Commemorates Metaxas's supposed response of "€ci!" (OH-hee; "No!") to Mussolini's demand to occupy Greece in October of 1940.
December 25	Christmas	Remembers Jesus's birth. Greeks celebrate both Christmas Eve and Christmas day, when children make the rounds singing *kalanda* (carols).

BEYOND TOURISM

A PHILOSOPHY FOR TRAVELERS

HIGHLIGHTS OF BEYOND TOURISM IN GREECE

STUDY classics, language, and theater at the **Athens Centre** (p. 65).

RESCUE endangered sea turtles on the beaches of Zakynthos (p. 61).

TEACH English to students of all ages in Crete (p. 63).

FLIP to our "Giving Back" sidebar features for even more regional Beyond Tourism opportunities.

As a tourist, you are always a foreigner. Sure, hostel-hopping and sightseeing can be great fun, but connecting with a foreign country through studying, volunteering, or working can extend your travels beyond tourist traps. We don't like to brag, but this is what's different about a *Let's Go* traveler. Instead of feeling like a stranger in a strange land, you can understand Greece like a local. Instead of asking for directions, you can be the one who gives them (and correctly!). All the while, you get the satisfaction of leaving Greece in better shape than you found it. It's not wishful thinking—it's Beyond Tourism.

As a **volunteer** in Greece, you can roll up your sleeves, cinch down your Captain Planet belt, and get your hands dirty doing anything from saving sea turtles to digging for lost ruins. This chapter is chock-full of ideas to get involved, whether you're looking to pitch in for a day or run away from home for a whole new life in Greek activism.

Ahh, to **study** abroad! It's a student's dream, and when you find yourself reading Homer where he wrote his epics, it actually makes you feel sorry for those poor tourists who don't get to do any homework while they're here. No place can compete with the diversity of Greek's archaeological sites and the multitude of classical civilizations that exist in bits and pieces throughout the country.

Working abroad is one of the best ways to immerse yourself in a new culture, meet locals, and learn to appreciate a non-US currency. Yes, we know you're on vacation, but we're not talking about normal desk jobs—we're talking about leading tour groups through the Vikos Gorge and recruiting club-goers for nightspots on Kos, all in the name of funding another month of globe-trotting. Popular tourist destinations like Athens and many of the Cyclades and Ionian Islands are great places to look for jobs. Still, it is important to note that you must get a **work permit** to work legally in Greece (p. 11), and that a recent spike in unemployment may make finding a job much more difficult.

SHARE YOUR EXPERIENCE. Have you had a particularly enjoyable volunteer, study, or work experience that you'd like to share with other travelers? Post it to our website, www.letsgo.com!

VOLUNTEERING

Feel like saving the world this week? Volunteering can be a powerful and fulfilling experience, especially when combined with the thrill of traveling in a new place. Though Greece is considered wealthy by international standards, there is no shortage of aid organizations. From providing medical care to refugees to ensuring the survival of wildlife species for the future, Greece has plenty of opportunities to give back.

Most people who volunteer in Greece do so on a short-term basis at organizations that make use of drop-in or summer volunteers. These are referenced both in this section and in the town and city listings. The best way to find opportunities that match your interests and schedule may be to search online at websites like **ww.volunteerabroad.com, www.servenet.org,** and **www.idealist.org**; most programs have contact information and many provide detailed descriptions and instructions on the Internet. Those looking for longer, more intensive volunteer opportunities usually choose to go through a parent organization that takes care of logistical details and often provides a group environment and support system—for a fee.

I HAVE TO PAY TO VOLUNTEER? Many volunteers are surprised to learn that some organizations require large fees or "donations," but don't go calling them scams just yet. While such fees may seem ridiculous at first, they often keep the organization afloat, covering airfare, room, board, and administrative expenses for the volunteers. (Other organizations must rely on private donations and government subsidies.) If you're concerned about how a program spends its fees, request an annual report or finance account. A reputable organization won't refuse to inform you of how volunteer money is spent. Pay-to-volunteer programs might be a good idea for young travelers who are looking for more support and structure (such as pre-arranged transportation and housing) or anyone who would rather not deal with the uncertainty of creating a volunteer experience from scratch.

BEYOND TOURISM

WILDLIFE CONSERVATION

Greece's loggerhead turtles are some of the country's most famous residents. Since the mid-1970s, enviromentalists have created a host of organizations to protect the endangered turtles and their habitats near Greece's beaches.

SEA TURTLES

Archelon Sea Turtle Protection Society, 3h Marina Glyfadas, 16675, Glyfada (☎21089 82 600; www.archelon.gr). Non-profit group devoted to studying and protecting sea turtles on the beaches of Zakynthos, Crete, and the Peloponnese. Opportunities for seasonal field work and year-round work at the rehabilitation center. €150-€250 participation fee for 6 weeks includes lodgings for those who work at the center. Field volunteers are put up at private campgrounds, but must provide their own camping equipment.

Earth, Sea, and Sky Ionian Nature Conservation, P.O. Box 1063, Saxilby, Lincoln LN1 2TN, UK (www.earthseasky.org). Promotes awareness of sustainable tourism and conservation. Although particularly concerned with sea turtles, they organize a variety of volunteer programs and preservation activities. Centered on Zakynthos.

GIVING BACK

LET FLY, TILOS!

Big falcons fan? No, not Atlanta's NFL team, but one of the over 150 bird species that can be found on Tilos' mountainous coasts, where at least 10% of the world's population of Eleonora's Falcons make their nests.

Hikers scaling Tilos' heights will find themselves climbing alongside bird-enthusiasts who get their dose of extreme from spotting a blue-cheeked bee-eater along the mountain path. Unfortunately, an increase in the numbers of hikers and bird-watchers alike has caused more visitor traffic. The growing number of tourists has prompted the formation of the **Tilos Park Association (TPA)**, which monitors seal, turtle, falcon, and orchid populations on Tilos and its 16 uninhabited islets. Founded in 2004 by Konstantinos Mentzelopoulos, the Livadia-based TPA has mounted an aggressive campaign to ensure the protection of Tilos's natural treasures.

With the support of over one third of the island's residents, the TPA organizes regular seminars on conservation and operates an information booth in Livadia. Volunteers can help with clean-up efforts on the beaches and paths, species monitoring, building a new nature appreciation trail, and more. The TPA also welcomes volunteers in their clean-up campaigns or to complete ecology field work for academic credit.

Contact Konstantinos Mentzelopoulos. (☎22460 70 880; www.tilos-park.org.gr/; email tilospark@otenet.gr.)

The Katelios Group for the Research and Protection of Marine and Terrestrial Life, Kefallonia 28086 (☎26710 81 009; www.kateliosgroup.org). Organizes volunteer efforts to protect hatchling sea turtles and promote sustainable development on Kefallonia. Volunteers pay €150-200 per month to participate in the summer, though the fee includes accommodations at their campsite.

The Mediterranean Association to Save the Sea Turtles (MEDASSET), Likavitou 1c, Athens 10672 (☎21036 40 389; www.medasset.org). Assesses the condition of sea turtles throughout the Mediterranean, with sites at Zakynthos and Kefallonia. Volunteers can receive free lodging for at least 3 weeks of work at the Athens office.

OTHER FAUNA

Fiskardo's Nautical & Environmental Club (FNEC) and Ionian Sea Research Centre, Fiskardo, Kefallonia 28084 (☎26740 41 081; www.fnec.gr). Conducts marine research, promotes environmental awareness, and engages volunteers in conservation efforts. Volunteers patrol the region on horseback to aid in forest fire protection, run an educational museum and radio station, participate in local community service projects, catalog marine mammals, and help with other environmental research.

Hellenic Ornithological Society, Vas. Irakleiou 24, Athens 10682 (☎/fax 21082 27 937; www.ornithologiki.gr/en/enmain.htm) and Kastritsiou 8, Thessaloniki 54623 (☎/fax 23102 44 245). Organizes volunteer field work to protect endangered species of birds. Also seeks volunteers to help with office work and educational presentations.

Hellenic Society for the Study and Protection of the Monk Seal (MOm), 18 Solomou, Athens 10682 (☎21052 22 888; www.mom.gr). Runs a rehabilitation center on Alonnisos for the highly endangered Mediterranean monk seal. Also conducts information sessions for local fishermen and the general public about how to further conservation efforts. Volunteers should have a basic knowledge of Greek.

Lesbian Wildlife Hospital, O. Christofa I Chatzigianni, Agia Paraskevi, Lesvos 81102 (☎22530 32 006; www.wildlifeonlesvos.org). Provides medical aid for needy wildlife on the northeast Aegean island.

Rhodes Animal Welfare Society (RAWS), Tsairi, Rhodes 85100 (☎/fax 22410 69 224; http://home19.inet.tele.dk/rita1/raw1.htm). A non-profit organization that cares for stray animals and finds them new homes. Founded in 1990, RAWS has helped with nearly 5000 adoptions and has neutered 3000 animals.

Tilos Park Association, Livadia 85002 (☎22460 70 892; www.tilos-park.org.gr). Monitors seal, turtle, falcon, and orchid populations on Tilos and its 16 uninhabited islets. Volunteers can help with clean-up efforts on the beaches and paths, species monitoring, building a new nature appreciation trail, and island surveillance for illegal activities.

SOCIAL WELFARE

Global Volunteers, 375 E. Little Canada Rd., St. Paul, MN 55117, USA (☎+1-800-487-1074; www.globalvolunteers.org/1main/greece/volunteer_in_greece. htm). Sends volunteers to locations in Crete to teach English to students or provide care for and teach computer skills to physically and mentally handicapped individuals.

Médecins du Monde-Greece, Sapfous 12, Athens 10553 (☎21032 13 150; www.mdmgreece.gr). A member of the international Médecins du Monde, the Greek branch brings together doctors, nurses, and non-medical personnel to provide medical care for refugees and victims of war, natural disasters, and other catastrophes in Greece and developing countries.

Multi-Functional Centre of Social Support and Integration of Refugees (www.redcross.gr). An initiative of the Hellenic Red Cross that provides social support to refugees and asylum seekers and helps integrate them into Greek society. The 1-week training program usually takes place in June.

OTHER OPPORTUNITIES

The American Farm School, Office of the Trustees and Greek Summer, 1133 Broadway, Ste. 1625, New York, NY 10010, USA (☎+1-212-463-8434; www.afs.edu.gr) and P.O. Box 23, Thessaloniki 551 02 (☎23104 92 700). Runs community service projects in villages. 6-week summer program for high school students in Thessaloniki US$6000, not including airfare.

Conservation Volunteers Greece, Omirou 15, Athens 14562 (☎21038 25 506; www. conservationvolunteers.com.au/volunteer/Greece.htm). Volunteers ages 18-30 participate in 2- to 3-week community programs in various areas of Greece. Projects range from reforestation to preserving archaeological sites. Accommodations provided.

Service Civil International Voluntary Service (SCI-IVS), 5474 Walnut Level Rd., Crozet, VA 22932, USA (☎+1-206-350-6585; www.sci-ivs.org). Arranges placement in a wide variety of volunteer work camps in Greece for those over 18. Membership US$35.

Volunteers for Peace, 1034 Tiffany Rd., Belmont, VT 05730, USA (☎+1-802-259-2759; www.vfp.org). Arranges placement in work camps in many countries, including Greece. Membership (US$30) required for registration. Programs US$300 for 2-3 weeks.

Youth Action for Peace UK (YAP UK), P.O. Box 43670, London SE22 OXX, UK (☎+44 08 7016 57927; www.yap-uk.org). Opportunities such as volunteering at health institutions and renovating buildings in villages in Greece. Work camp placement fee £80-180.

STUDYING

It's completely natural to want to play hookey on the first day of school when it's raining and first period Trigonometry is meeting in the old cafeteria, but when your campus is in Thessaloniki and your meal plan revolves around perfectly-seasoned gyros, what could be better than the student life?

A growing number of students report that studying abroad is the highlight of their learning careers. If you've never studied abroad, you don't know what you're missing—and, if you have studied abroad, you do know what you're missing. Study-abroad programs range from basic language and culture courses to university-level classes, often for college credit (sweet, right?). In order to choose a program that best fits your needs, research as much as you can before making your decision—determine costs and duration as well as what kinds of students participate in the program and what sorts of accommodations are provided.

In programs that have large groups of students who speak the same language, you may feel more comfortable, but you will not have the same opportunity to practice a foreign language or to befriend other international students. Traditionally, Greek college students live in apartments as opposed to dorms, so you will be hard-pressed to experience dorm life studying abroad in Greece. A more likely scenario is that the study abroad program will place you in an apartment with other students in the program. If you live with a Greek family, there is a potential to build friendships with natives and to experience day-to-day life in more depth, but conditions can vary greatly from family to family and from region to region.

VISA INFORMATION. Passport-bearing citizens of Australia, Canada, the EU, Iceland, Israel, Japan, New Zealand, Norway, Switzerland, and the US are allowed a 3-month stay in Greece without a visa, though they are not eligible for employment during that time. Apply for visa extensions at least 20 days prior to the 3-month expiration date. If you plan to study in Greece for longer than 3 months, a **student visa** is necessary. To get one, you must first obtain admission into an academic or language program in Greece. Then apply to your embassy for a student visa (US$20-45) for however long you want to study. Be sure to obtain a visa well before you leave.

UNIVERSITIES

Most university-level study-abroad programs are conducted in Greek, although many programs offer lower-level language courses and classes in English. Those relatively fluent in Greek may find it cheaper to enroll directly in a university abroad, though getting college credit may be more difficult. You can search www.studyabroad.com for various semester-abroad programs that meet your criteria, including your desired location and focus of study. Most of the study programs based in Greece are located in highly traveled areas, especially in Athens, on Crete, and in the Cyclades. Programs vary tremendously in expense, academic quality, living conditions, and exposure to local culture and languages. The following is a sampling of organizations that can help place students in university programs abroad or that have their own branch in Greece.

AHA International, 221 NW Second Ave., Ste. 200, Portland, OR 97209, USA (☎+1-800-654-2051; http://www.ahastudyabroad.org/). 12-week terms in the fall and spring or 4-week terms in the summer. Summer term from US$3453; includes separate art and language programs. Fall or spring term from US$10,350.

American College of Thessaloniki (ACT), P.O. Box 21021, Pylea, Thessaloniki 55510 (☎23103 98 238 or 98 239; www.act.edu); study abroad admissions at Anatolia College Trustees Office, 130 Bowdoin, Ste. 1201-1202, Boston, MA 02108, USA (☎+1-617-742-7992). The opportunity to study in Greece in a predominately Greek student environment. Foreign students choose to enroll either for a term abroad or as an exchange student. Study abroad student fee from US$9470.

Arcadia University for Education Abroad, 450 S. Easton Rd., Glenside, PA 19038, USA (☎+1-866-927-2234; www.arcadia.edu/cea). Operates programs in Greece. Fall or spring term US$13,990; full year US$23,990.

The Athens Centre, Archimidous 48, Athens 11636 (☎21070 12 268; www.athenscentre.gr). Language, classics, poetry, and theater classes. Many universities also are affiliated with the Athens Centre. Semester courses €180-640; summer €1800-2200.

College Year in Athens, P.O. Box 390890, Cambridge, MA 02139 (☎+1-617-868-8200 in the US, 21075 60 749 in Greece; www.cyathens.org). Runs semester-long, full-year, and summer programs that focus on ancient Greek civilization, East Mediterranean area studies, and modern Greek language for undergraduates. All courses taught in English. Summer programs include intensive modern Greek instruction on Paros and a 3-week archaeology program on Crete or Santorini. Fall or spring term US$17,210; summer term from US$2500-3600; full year US$31,150.

Deree College, The American College of Greece, Gravias 6, Agia Paraskevi 15342 (☎21060 09 800; www.acg.gr/deree). Bachelor's degrees granted in a wide variety of subjects. Classes taught in English. Open to students of all international backgrounds.

University of Indianapolis Athens Campus, Pl. Syntagma, Athens 10557 (☎21032 37 077; www.uindy.gr). Fall and spring semesters at the University of Indianapolis's Athens branch. Residential hall housing in Plaka provided. Organizes summer study programs.

Rutgers Study Abroad, 102 College Ave., New Brunswick, NJ 08901, USA (☎+1-732-932-7787; studyabroad.rutgers.edu/program_greece.html). A 6-week program in Athens, the Peloponnese, Macedonia, and Crete focuses on material culture and history. NJ residents US$5195; non-NJ residents US$6195.

LANGUAGE SCHOOLS

Old lady making snarky comments to you in the *plateia?* Cute moped girl that is totally into you? To communicate is to be human, and without the local language in your toolbelt, you're up a creek without a κοντό. Fear not! Language schools are here to help.

While language school courses rarely count for college credit, they do offer a unique way to get acquainted with the culture and language of Greece. Schools can be independently run or university affiliated, local or international, youth-oriented or full of old people—the opportunities are endless. Some worthwhile organizations include:

Greek Language Institute, National Registration Center for Study Abroad, P.O. Box 1393, Milwaukee, WI 53201, USA (☎+1-414-278-0631; www.nrcsa.com/country/greece.html). Branches in Athens, Thessaloniki, and Chania, Crete offer immersion-based classes. 2-week courses from US$1660; 4-week US$3205.

Kentro Ellinikou Politsmou (Hellenic Culture Center), Tilemahou 14, Athens 11472 (☎/fax 21052 38 149; www.hcc.edu.gr) and Arethoussa, Ikaria 85302 (☎22750 61 140). Seminars in modern Greek language in Athens and on Ikaria from €440.

Lexis Centre of Greek Language and Culture, 48 Daskalogianni, Chania, Crete 73100 (☎2821 055673; www.lexis.edu.gr). 2- to 10-week courses, with extra activities and excursions available. €205-980.

Omilo, Tsaldari 13, Marousi 15122 (☎21061 22 896; www.omilo.com). Language courses for a range of proficiency levels offered in Athens, Nea Makri, Limni, and Nafplion. 1-week course €300; 2-week €550; 8-week €380-475.

School of Modern Greek Language, Aristotle University of Thessaloniki, Thessaloniki 54124 (☎23109 97 576; www.auth.gr/smg). Year-long and seasonal intensive programs offered. Limited scholarships available; consult website. Courses from €300.

ART STUDY

Aegean Center for the Fine Arts, Paros 84400 (☎22840 23 287; www.aegeancenter. org). Spring session in Paros and fall session in both Paros and Tuscany, Italy. Singing, painting, drawing, photography, sculpture, print-making, literature, creative writing, and art history classes. Studio apartment housing in Greece; villa accommodations in Italy. University credit and financial aid available. Fall term €8800; spring term €7500.

Art Research Tours and International Studios (☎+1-800-232-6893; www.artis-tours. org/greece.html). A 24-day drawing program in Athens and the Peloponnese.

Art School of the Aegean, P.O. Box 1375, Sarasota, FL 34230, USA (☎+1-941-351-5597; www.greecetravel.com/schools/aegeanartschool). 18+. 1- to 3-week summer programs in painting, ceramics, and writing on Samos US$950-2050.

Cycladic School, Folegandros 84011 (☎/fax 22860 41 472; cycladicschool.cndo.dk). 6- to 12-day classes on the history and culture of Greece, particularly of Folegandros. Features drawing and painting instruction.

Dellatolas Marble Sculpture Studio, Spitalia, Tinos 84200 (☎/fax 22830 23 664; www.tinosmarble.com). Artists' workshops in a functioning marble studio. Classes run May-Oct. 2-week course €1000, each additional week €500.

Hellenic International Studies in the Arts (☎69460 87 430; www.hellenicinternational. org). Courses in painting and drawing, photography, writing, sculpture, and Cycladic culture, among other arts. Semester courses US$10,850; summer US$2450-3550.

Island Center for the Arts, Skopelos 37003 (☎24240 24 036; www.islandcenter.org). Runs painting and photography classes from Skopelos.

ARCHAEOLOGICAL DIGS

Students who find their way to Greece to study abroad are often interested in classics and archaeology—they're in the right place for it, after all. **The Archaeologic Institute of America,** 656 Beacon St., Boston, MA 02215, USA (☎+1-617 353 9361; www.archaeological.org), puts out the annual **Archaeological Fieldwork Opportunities Bulletin,** which lists sites in Greece and is available online at http://www.archaeological.org/webinfo.php?page=10015. The **Hellenic Ministry of Culture** (www.culture.gr) maintains a complete list of archaeological sites in Greece. Below is a list of organizations that can help you find an archaeological dig with participation opportunities.

The American School of Classical Studies at Athens, Souidias 54, Athens 10676 (☎+1-609-683-0800 in the US, 21072 36 313 in Greece; www.ascsa.edu.gr). Since 1881, American graduate students and professors have flocked here to participate in ongoing excavations of ancient sites, including Corinth and the ancient Athenian agora. 6-week summer program (US$3675) allows undergraduates to work at its sites and others. Visit the website to find a list of publications and links to archaeological programs.

Archaeology Abroad, 31-34 Gordon Sq., London WC1H OPY, UK (☎+44 20 8537 0849; www.britarch.ac.uk/archabroad). A magazine about archaeology that contains biannual bulletins with fieldwork opportunities. Subscriptions £22-26.

British School in Athens, O. Souidias 52, Athens 10676 (☎21072 10 974 or 92 146 in Greece, +44 20 7862 8732 in the UK; www.bsa.gla.ac.uk). Conducts fieldwork annu-

BEYOND TOURISM

ally. Courses for undergraduates, postgraduates, and teachers also available. Recent work has been conducted at Athens, Delphi, and Pylos.

Canadian Institute in Greece, Dion. Aiginitou 7, Athens 11528 (☎21072 232 01; www.cig-icg.gr). Archaeological fieldwork and research at various sites throughout Greece.

German Archaeological Institute, Fidiou 1, Athens 10678 (☎21033 07 400; www.dainst.org). This research center offers an extensive archaeological library, publishes an annual journal, hosts lectures and forums, and assists in excavations.

OTHER INSTRUCTION

Athens Institute of Sailing, Alimos Marina, Athens (www.sailingcoursesingreece.com). Runs basic and intermediate sailing and yachting classes out of an Athens marina. Taught in English. Classes from €400.

Dora Stratou Dance, Scholiou 8, Plaka, Athens 10558 (☎21032 44 395; www.grdance.org). Offers folk dance and culture classes. 1-week workshop €120.

The Glorious Greek Kitchen (☎21437 31 161; www.cuisineinternational.com; www.dianekochilas.com/glorious_1.asp). Cooking classes are held on Ikaria, where instructor Diane Kochilas used to own a restaurant. 6-day class and housing, US$1850.

Ionian Village, 83 St. Basil Rd., Garrison, NY 10524, USA (☎+1-646-519-6190; www.ionianvillage.org). The Greek Orthodox Archdiocese of America runs this religious and cultural summer camp for teens and young adults up to the age of 30, most of whom are Greek Orthodox or of Greek descent. Programs are based at a resort-like facility west of Patra. Full registration including travel US$3990.

Skyros, 92 Prince of Wales Rd., London NW5 3NE, UK (☎+44 20 7267 4424; www.skyros.com). 1- to 2-week sessions in the Sporades on various topics ranging from writing to yoga. Courses from £545-925.

WORKING

We haven't yet found money growing on trees, but we do have a team of dedicated Researchers looking high and low. Some travelers want long-term jobs that allow them to integrate into a community, while others seek out short-term jobs to finance the next leg of their travels. Those who can teach English will find many job openings in Greece.

Many popular youth hostels have bulletin boards with both long- and short-term employment opportunities. **City News** (http://athens.citynews.com/Employment.html) lists updated opportunities for work in Athens. Websites like www.jobs-in-europe.net and www.jobsabroad.com also can be helpful. EU citizens will have a much easier time finding work and will generally make better money than those from outside the EU. Note: working abroad often requires a special work visa **Transitions Abroad** (www.transitionsabroad.com) also offers updated online listings for work over any time period.

VISA INFORMATION. For legal employment in Greece, foreigners must apply for a **work permit** from the Ministry of Labor, Pireos 40, Athens 101 82. Permits can be difficult to acquire, so apply well in advance. EU residents can work in Greece for up to 3 months without a work permit, but one is required for longer stays.

BEYOND TOURISM

LONG-TERM WORK

If you're planning on spending a substantial amount of time (more than 3 months) working in Greece, search for a job well in advance. International placement agencies are often the easiest way to find employment abroad, especially for those interested in teaching. Although they are often only available to college students, **internships** are a good way to ease into working abroad. Many students say the interning experience is well worth it, despite low pay (if you're lucky enough to get paid at all). Be wary of advertisements for companies offering to get you a job abroad for a fee—often times, these same listings are available online or in newspapers. Some reputable organizations include:

International Association for the Exchange of Students for Technical Experience (IAESTE), 9 Iroon Polytechniou Street, Athens 15780 (☎21077 21 946; www.iaeste. org). Chances are that your home country has a local office, too; contact it to apply for hands-on technical internships in Greece. You must be a college student studying science, technology, engineering, agriculture, or applied arts (check their website for a list of accepted fields of study). "Cost of living allowance" covers most non-travel expenses. Most programs last 8-12 weeks.

Council on International Educational Exchange (CIEE), 300 Fore St., Portland, ME 04101, USA (☎+1-207-553-4000 or 800-40-STUDY/407-8839; www.ciee.org). Assists in both study abroad and teaching abroad. Tucked into its study abroad listings is a resource for international internships.

Trekking Hellas, Filellinon 7, Athens 10557. (☎21033 10 323; www.treeking.gr). Hires experienced travelers to guide others on various expeditions throughout Greece, including mountain treks and sea kayaking. Applicants, who are generally between 22 and 35 and are fluent in more than 1 language, must go through extensive training to demonstrate their abilities in the outdoors.

TEACHING ENGLISH

Suffice it to say that teaching jobs abroad pay more in personal satisfaction and emotional fulfillment than in actual cash. Nevertheless, even volunteer teachers often receive some sort of a daily stipend to help with living expenses. In almost all cases, you must have at least a bachelor's degree to be a full-fledged teacher, although college undergraduates can often get summer positions teaching or tutoring.

The Greek-language impaired don't have to give up their dream of teaching, either. Private schools usually hire native English speakers for English-immersion classrooms where no Greek is spoken. (Teachers in public schools will more likely work in both English and Greek.) Those who wish to teach English in Greece should have a university degree—preferably in English literature or history—and a solid command of English. To obtain a teaching license in Greece, you must present your diploma and your passport translated into Greek, among other things; for current requirements contact the **Hellenic Ministry of Education,** Mitropoleos 15, Athens 10185. (www.ypepth.gr.) Greek schools rarely require teachers to have a **Teaching English as a Foreign Language (TEFL)** certificate, but certified teachers often find higher-paying jobs. Placement agencies or university fellowship programs are the best resources for finding teaching jobs in Greece. The alternative is to make contacts directly with schools or just to try your luck once you get there. If you are going with the latter, the best time to look is several weeks before the start of the school year in September. The following organizations are helpful in placing teachers in Greece.

BEYOND TOURISM

International Schools Services (ISS), 15 Roszel Rd., P.O. Box 5910, Princeton, NJ 08543, USA (☎+1-609-452-0990; www.iss.edu). Hires teachers for more than 200 overseas schools, including in Greece. Candidates should have teaching experience and a bachelor's degree. 2-year commitment is the norm.

GoAbroad.com, 8 E. First Ave., Ste. 102, Denver, CO 80203, USA (☎+1-720-570-1702; www.goabroad.edu). Its 'Teach Abroad' section has useful listings for various teaching opportunities in a number of countries, including Greece.

Office of Overseas Schools, US Department of State, Room H328, SA-1, Washington, D.C. 20522, USA (☎+1-202-261-8200; www.state.gov/m/a/os). Keeps a comprehensive list of both schools abroad and agencies that arrange for Americans to teach abroad.

AU PAIR WORK

Au pairs are typically women in their late teens or twenties who work as live-in nannies, caring for children and doing light housework in foreign countries in exchange for room, board, and a small spending allowance or stipend. One perk of the job is that it allows you to really get to know the country without the high expenses of traveling. Drawbacks, however, often include mediocre pay and long hours. Au pairs in Greece generally work 30-45 hr. per week, including a few evenings, for €45-70 per week, depending on the number of children, duties, and qualifications. Much of the au pair experience depends on the family with whom you're placed. The agencies below are a good starting point for looking for employment as an au pair.

InterExchange, 161 6th Ave., New York, NY 10013, USA (☎+1-212-924-0446 or 800-AU-PAIRS/287-2477; www.interexchange.org).

MEMBER OF
EUROPE'S FAMOUS HOSTELS.COM

www.**ThePink Palace**.com
CORFU ISLAND, GREECE

WORLD FAMOUS BACKPACKERS DESTINATION HOSTEL / RESORT
OPEN ALL YEAR AROUND
LIVE THE LIFE!

Included in the Price from 19 to 30 Euros per Person per Night:
* Free Pick-Up on Arrival
* Private or shared ensuite rooms - A/C & beach view balcony
* Cooked Breakfast & 3 Course Greek Dinner Included
* Famous Toga Parties, Greek Dancing & Theme Nights
* 24 Hour Bar with Long Happy Hours / 24 Hour Reception
* Private Beach & Jacuzzi
* Boat Excursions, Island Tours and 4-Wheeler & Kayak Safaris
* Scuba Diving, Cliff Jumping and All Sorts of Water Sports
* Free Wi-Fi Internet, Internet Cafe and Free Luggage Room
* Discount Bus Service to / from Athens

(+30) 26610 53103 OR 53104 - MOBILE (+30) 69452 30727

info@thepinkpalace.com

WWW.THEPINKPALACE.COM

Childcare International, Trafalgar House, Grenville Pl., London NW7 3SA, UK (☎+44 20 8906 3116; www.childint.co.uk).

Nine Muses, El. Venizelou 4B, P.O. Box 76080, Nea Smimi, Athens 17110 (www.nine-muses.gr). An agency with online applications that places au pairs who are EU nationals with families in Greece.

SHORT-TERM WORK

If you're more of a dishwasher than an au pair, or if you'd just like to work an odd job for a few weeks to fund another month of traveling, short-term work might be right up your alley. For citizens of Greece or other EU countries, getting a job in Greece is relatively simple. For all others, finding work in Greece can be difficult, as the government tries to restrict employment to citizens and visitors from the EU. If your parents were born in an EU country, you may be able to claim dual citizenship or at least the right to a work permit.

Arrive in the spring and early summer to search for hotel jobs (bartending, cleaning, etc.). Most nightspots don't require much paperwork, but offer meager pay. Head to the islands of Kos or Rhodes for some of the best nightclub opportunities. Check the bulletin boards of hostels and the classified ads of local newspapers, such as the Athens News.

Another popular option is to work several hours a day at a hostel in exchange for free or discounted room and/or board. Most often, these short-term jobs are found by word of mouth or by expressing interest to the owner of a hostel or restaurant. Due to high turnover in the tourism industry, many places are eager for help, even if it is only temporary. *Let's Go* lists temporary jobs of this nature whenever possible; look in the Practical Information sections of larger cities.

ATHENS Αθήνα AND ENVIRONS

More than many ancient cities in Greece, modern Athens is tied to its illustrious past. Thousands of years' worth of ghosts gaze down from every hilltop and peek around each alleyway. Athens, however, is also a daring and modern place; its fiercely patriotic citizens pushed their capital into the 21st century with massive building projects and clean-up efforts before the 2004 Olympic Games. Contemporary art galleries flourish in the literal shadow of their older counterparts. Scores of outdoor theaters with views of the Acropolis play domestic and foreign films. Hipster bars and large warehouses converted into performance spaces crowd the streets among Byzantine churches, traditional *tavernas*, and toppled columns. Whether making your home here or passing through on your way to the islands, don't miss the chance to explore a city that, against all odds, is more energetic and exciting than ever.

HIGHLIGHTS OF ATHENS

STICK your nose to the windows on the top floor of the new **Acropolis Museum** (p. 92) to see the Parthenon in its full majesty.

EXPLORE Exarhia's inexpensive and hip restaurants and cafes (p. 86).

DEVOUR cheap, delicious candies at **Matsoukas** (p. 87).

HISTORY

If you reach back far enough, Athens's history blurs into myth. In the first of what would be many epic struggles over this capital, **Poseidon** and **Athena** were said to have fought for the right to be the city's patron god. Poseidon struck the Acropolis with his trident and water gushed forth, but it was Athena's gift, an olive tree, that won the city's admiration and worship. Moving forward to the age of mortals, ancient Athenians believed that their *polis* had been united under the sword of **Theseus,** the Minotaur-slayer, as early as the 16th century BC. Capturing both the artistic and the political world by the 8th century BC, Athens's initial fame for **Geometric pottery** foreshadowed a bright future. Two hundred years later, law-giver **Solon** ended the servitude of native citizens and established democratic law. Thus began Athens's long, often-tortured relationship with popular government.

Victory over Persia in the 5th century BC brought a golden age of democracy and art to the new Athenian empire. Philosophers like **Socrates, Plato,** and **Aristotle,** joined by playwrights like **Aeschylus, Aristophanes, Euripides,** and **Sophocles** gave Athens its legendary status as the birthplace of Western thought. Athens, however, didn't remain the center of the world for long. Militaristic **Sparta** (p. 41) crushed it in the bloody, drawn-out **Peloponnesian War** (431-404 BC), and power shifted northward when **Philip II** and **Alexander the Great** of Macedonia (p. 41) conquered Athens and the rest of the known world. By the AD second century, the Roman Empire ruled the city, and in AD 324 **Constantine** simply ignored it, establishing his grand imperial capital in Constantinople. **Justinian** delivered

71

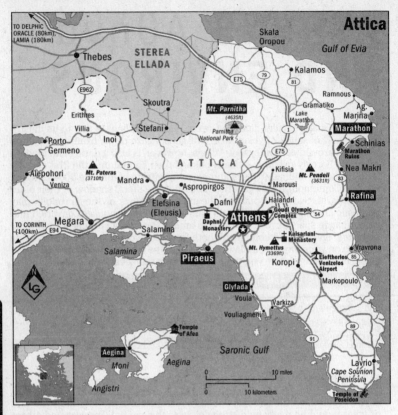

a further blow to Athens in 529, banning the teaching of Classical philosophy and allowing the once-great city to fall into ruin.

Five hundred years later, Byzantine emperor **Basil II** ordered Athens's glory restored; in the coming centuries, it passed (along with much of Greece) through the hands of the **Franks,** the **Catalans,** and **Venetian** merchants. In 1456, the **Ottoman Turks** began their 400-year regime, leaving Athens a backwater. The success of the **Greek independence** effort in 1829 ushered in a new era of extensive restoration and passionate nationalism. Today, Athens's *plateias*, wide boulevards, and National Gardens follow the plan of architects hired by modern Greece's first king, the unpopular German prince **Otto.**

The 1923 **Treaty of Lausanne** and population exchange with Turkey brought Athens an influx of ethnic Greeks who had been living in Asia Minor. Rural workers then flocked to Athens, further swelling its ranks. In the past 100 years, the city's population has exploded from a paltry 169 families to almost half of Greece's 11 million residents. Preparations for the 2004 Olympic Games fueled another age of urban renewal in Athens; the transit authority fought the sinister *nefos* (smog) by banning cars from historic Plaka and by further restricting drivers' access to downtown areas. With its magnificent new public transportation system, Athens no longer suffers from the confounding urban sprawl produced by years of turnover. The new **Eleftherios Venizelos Airport,** which lies to the city's southeast, has been consistently rated among the world's best airports since its 2001 opening.

◼ INTERCITY TRANSPORTATION

Flights: Eleftherios Venizelos (ATH ☎21035 30 000; www.aia.gr). Greece's international airport has 1 massive but navigable terminal. Arrivals are on the ground fl., departures on the 2nd. Metro Line 3 (blue), connects the airport to Syntagma station in the Athens city center (€6). **Suburban Rail,** which serves the airport and runs along the Attiki Odos highway, connects with Line 1 (green) at Neratziotissa and with the blue line at Doukissis Plakentias—the most central stations in Omonia and Syntagma, respectively (about 30min.). 6 OASA public bus lines run to and from the airport from Athens, Piraeus, Dafni, and Kifisia. To get from Plateia Syntagma in the city center to the airport, take the X95 (40-90min. depending on traffic, every 10-15min., €3.40), which runs 24hr. Pick it up on Amalias, near the top right corner of Pl. Syndagma. From Ⓜ Ethniki Amyna, take the X94 (every 15min. 7:30am-9:55pm, €3; wait by the exit) or the X95, and from Ⓜ Dafni take the X97 (every 30-55min., €3). From Piraeus, take the X96 (every 15-30min., €3), which runs 24hr. Catch the bus in Pl. Karaiskaki on the waterfront, on Akti Tzelepi, across from Philippis Tours. From Kifisia, catch the X92 from Pl. Platanos (every 45-60min., €3). If your travels have taken you to Kifisos Intercity Bus Station, take the X93 (every 20-45min, €3). 2 **KTEL regional bus** lines serve the airport, as well. From Rafina, the bus (€3) leaves every 30min. from the stop midway up the ramp from the waterfront, and stops at Loutsa (Artemis) along the way. Buses drop off at 1 of the 4 departure entrances and wait outside the 5 arrival exits. You can catch the bus from Lavrio at Keratea, Kalivia Thorikou, and Markopoulo, as well. **Taxis** from the airport to Pl. Omonia runs around €32, including the extra €0.35 charge for each piece of luggage over 10kg and a €3.40 surcharge from the airport. Watch drivers carefully; they often rig the meters.

Trains: Hellenic Railways (OSE), Sina 6 (☎21036 24 402, reservations 21052 97 777, timetables in Greek 1440; www.ose.gr). Contact the railway offices to confirm schedules before your trip.

Larisis Station (☎21052 98 829). Ticket office open daily 5am-midnight. Trains go to Northern Greece. Take trolley #1 from El. Venizelou (Panepistimiou) in Pl. Syndagma (every 10min. 5am-midnight, €0.45) or take the metro to Sepolia. Trains depart for **Thessaloniki** (regular: 7hr., 5 per day, €14; express: 5hr., 6 per day, €28). To get to **Bratislava, Bucharest, Budapest, Istanbul, Prague, Sofia,** and other international destinations, take a train from Larisis Station to Thessaloniki and change there.

Peloponnese Train Station (☎21052 98 735) for buses to **Albania, Bulgaria,** and **Turkey.** Ticket office open daily 5:45am-9pm. From Diligani, easiest entry is through Larisis Station; exit to your right and go over the footbridge. From El. Venizelou (Panepistimiou) in Syndagma, take blue bus #057 (every 15min. 5am-11:30pm, €0.45). To: **Kalamata** (6hr., 3 per day, €7), **Nafplion** (3hr., 2 per day, €5), and **Patra** (regular: 4hr., 3 per day, €5.30; express: 3hr., 5 per day, €10). **Luggage storage** available (€2-3 per piece per day).

Buses: Athens has 4 bus terminals, 2 of which serve the regional bus line and 2 of which serve the suburban bus lines. Check regional schedules by calling ☎21051 14 505 (from within Athens; schedules listed in Greek only), or suburban schedules at www.ktelattikis.gr.

Terminal A: Kifissou 100 (☎21051 249 104). Take blue bus #051 (every 15min. 5am-12am, €1) from the corner of Zinonos and Menandrou near Pl. Omonia. Don't mistake the private travel agency at Terminal A for an information booth. Buses to: Alexandroupoli, Arta, Astros, Dimitsana, Epidavros, Florina, Githio, Igoumenitsa, Ioanina, Ithaki, Kalamata, Kalavrita, Kastoria, Kavala, Kefallonia, Kerkira, Korinthos, Lefkada, Loutraki, Messolongi, Monemvassia, Nafpaktos, Nafplio/Argos/ Mikines, Neapoli, Olympia, Parga, Patra, Pilos/Methoni, Pirgos, Preveza, Sparti, Thessaloniki, Tripoli, Veria, Xanthi, Xilokastro, and Zakonthos).

Terminal B: Liossion 260 (☎21083 17 153). Take blue bus #024 from Pl. Syntagma on the National Gardens side of Amalias, or from Panepistimiou (45min., every 20min. 5:10am-11:40, €1). Buses to: Agios Konstantinos, Amfissa, Delphi, Distomo/Ossios Loukas, Edipsos, Galaxidi, Chalkida, Kamena Vourla, Karditsa, Karpenissi, Katerini/Litohoro, Kimi, Lamia, Larissa, Livadia, Thiva, Trikala/Meteora, Volos/Pilio.

Mavromateon 29: ☎21082 10 872. In Exarhia. Walk up Patission from the National Archaeological Museum and turn right on Enianos (Alexandras Av.); it's on the corner of Areos Park. Take trolley #2, 5, 9, 11 or 18. Buses to: Agia Marina (from which ferries depart for Evia), Kalamos, Lavrio, Marathon, Nea Makri, Oropos, Porto Rafti, Rafina, Sounion via Coast Road, and Sounion via Lavvio. Tickets are sold at 2 stands 50m apart.

Plateia Eleftherias: From Pl. Syndagma, go west on Ermou, turn right on Athinas, turn left on Evripidou, and walk to the end of the street. Buses A16 or B16 go to Daphni Monastery and Eleusis (10-20min., 5am-11pm, €1).

Ferries: Check schedules at the tourist office, in the *Athens News*, with the Port Authority of Piraeus (☎21042 26 000), over the phone (☎185, from Athens only), or at any travel agency. Most ferries dock at Piraeus, others at nearby Rafina. Those headed for the **Sporades** leave from Agios Konstantinos or Volos, and those going to the **Ionian Islands** leave from Patra, Kyllini, or Igoumenitsa.

Piraeus: Take M1 (green) south to its end or take bus #040 from Filellinon and Mitropoleos right off Plateia Syndagma (every 15min.). To nearly all Greek islands other than the Sporades and Ionians: Siros, Tions, Mykonos; Paros, Naxos, Ios, Santorini; Kithnos, Serifos, Sifnos, Milos; Serifos, Sifnos, Milos; Paros, Ios, Santorini; Chios, Mytillini; Paros, Naxos, Donousa, Amorgos, Astipalea; Siros, Ikaria, Samos, Astipalea, Kalimnos, Kos, Nisiros, Tilos, Rodos; Siros, Kos, Rodos; Kalimnos, Kos Rodos; Syros, Patmos, Leros, Los, Rodos; Heraklio; Chania; Rethymno; Paros, Naxos, Ios, Sikinos, Folegandros, Santorini, Anafi; Kithnow, Serifos, Sifnos, Kimolos, Milos, Folegandros, Sikinos, Ios, Santorini, Anafi; Patmos, Leros, Kos Rodos. See Piraeus (p. 112) for prices, frequencies, and durations.

Rafina: From Athens, buses leave for Rafina from Mavromateon 29, 2 blocks up along Areos Park or a 15min. walk from Pl. Syndagma (1hr., every 30min. 5:40am-10:30pm, €2). Ferries to: Andros, Evia, Marmari, Mykonos, Naxos, Paros, and Tinos. Flying Dolphins sail to: Andros, Mykonos, Naxos, Paros, Syros, and Tinos. See Rafina (p. 115) for prices, frequencies, and durations.

✦ ORIENTATION

Athenian geography can mystify newcomers. When you're trying to figure out the city, check out the detailed free maps available at the **tourist office** (p. 81; www.gnto.gr). While this information is available at several locations throughout the city, including the Rafina and Piraeus ports, the most convenient place to get a map (along with current ferry schedules) is in the arrivals hall at the airport terminal building. The city map includes suburban rail, tram, and metro routes. *Now in Athens* magazine has a more detailed street plan. If you lose your bearings, ask for directions back to **Syntagma**, the city's transportation hub. The **Acropolis**, which stands at the center of the city, is a good reference point. Athenian streets often have multiple spellings or names, so check the map again before you panic. Several English-language publications can help you navigate Athens. The weekly *Athens News* gives addresses, hours, and phone numbers for weekly happenings, as well as news and ferry information (€2.50; available at the airport and at kiosks around the city).

Athens and its suburbs occupy seven hills on the periphery of Attica. **Syntagma**, the central *plateia*, is encircled by the other major neighborhoods. Clockwise, they are: **Exarhia** at 12 o'clock, **Kolonaki, Pagrati, Plaka, Monastiraki, Psiri,** and **Omonia.** The three major squares—**Syntagma, Monastiraki,** and **Omonia**—are connected by three major streets: **Ermou, Athinas,** and **Stadiou.**

A 30min. car, bus, or taxi ride south takes you to the seaside suburb of **Glyfada. Piraeus,** the primary port, lies to the southwest of central Athens. In a wider clockwise circle, **Kifisia** and **Marousi** lie outside Athens to the north; the port of **Rafina** to the northeast; and **Lavrio** to the southeast. The airport, **Elefthe-rios Venizelos,** is on the road to Lavrio.

SYNTAGMA. P. Syntagma (S7ndagma) is the center of Athens. The stately, Neo-classical **Parliament building** and the **Tomb of the Unknown Soldier** mark the foot of the **National Gardens;** looking in the opposite direction, the long stretch of **Ermou** teems with trend-seeking teenagers and street performers. Airport-bound buses leave from the southern edge of the square, and the main metro entrance is across from the Parliament on **Amalias.** Banks, luxurious hotels, and enor-mous department stores crowd the square and its surrounding streets, **Georgiou, Filellinon,** and **Othonos. Nikis** and **Voulis,** behind Filellinon, are lined with cheap eats, tourist offices, and stores. **Mitropoleos,** Ermou, and **Karageorgi Servias** (later becoming Perikleous, then Athinados) start here and extend far into Monas-tiraki and Psiri. The occasional public concert, the changing of the guard at the Parliament building, and the abundance of unlicensed vendors around the square, add to Syntagma's status as an energetic hub of human activity.

PLAKA. Plaka (Pl1ka), the busy maze of small roads on the hill beneath the Acropolis, is bounded by the **Temple of Olympian Zeus** and the *plateia* of the **Mitropoli Cathedral.** Many of its streets are pedestrian-only, and vendors take full advantage of the extra sidewalk space. While **Kydatheneon** and **Adrianou** have scores of tourist-oriented *tavernas* and souvenir shops, the smaller, quieter streets have retained some antique charm. With lots of student-friendly accom-modations, appealing eateries, and proximity to the most famous of Athens' ancient sights—including the **Acropolis**—Plaka is an excellent place to stay.

MONASTIRAKI. Monastiraki (Monasthr1ki; Little Monastery) hosts a fantasti-cally frenetic **flea market.** Stop by on Sunday and wade through stalls heaping with handcrafted rugs, antique lamps, and stacks of jewelry of varying authen-ticity and price. The cries of fruit sellers and souvlaki vendors ring through the square from dawn to dusk, while crowded *tavernas* and the nearby colony of trendy bars in Psiri keep pedestrian traffic flowing late into the night. Monasti-raki's main *plateia,* just off the main thoroughfare of **Ermous,** has a large metro station as well as several fast-food joints. Byzantine churches and ancient ruins, including the **Roman Agora** and **Hadrian's Library,** crowd this area, and the Ancient Agora and Acropolis are just beyond the neighborhood's northern border. **Psiri,** north of Ermou, and the major thoroughfares of **Miaouli** and **Aristofanous,** are bounded by **Evripidou** to the north and **Athinas** to the east.

OMONIA. This is almost unavoidable due to its well-trafficked metro station and proximity to the KTEL Attiki bus station: visitors should be wary of pick-pockets and hustlers. Just north of the square, **Central Polytechnic University** and the **National Library** are both on **Panepistimiou,** with the **National Archaeological Museum** just beyond. **Larisis Station,** serving northern Greece, and **Peloponnese Station,** serving the south, are both located on **Konstantinoupoleos,** northeast of P. Karaiskaki, and are accessible from Deligiani.

 LET'S NOT GO. The burned-out buildings and hefty police presence around Omonia Square are clues to its reputation as a locus of violent crime, and it should especially be avoided after dark.

EXARHIA. In 1973, progressive Exarhia (Ex1rcia) was the site of a massive demonstration against the right-wing dictatorship. Today, students from the

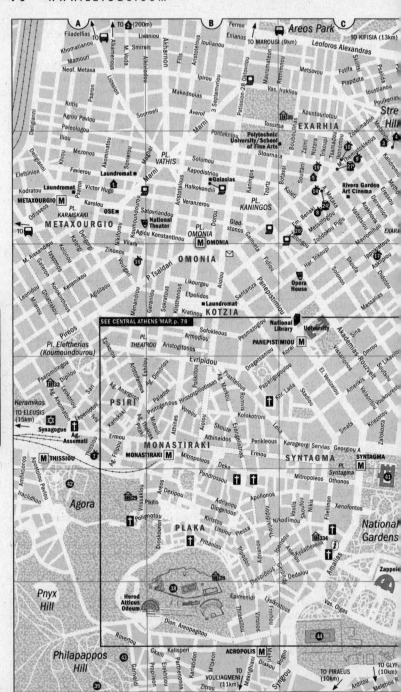

ATHENS AND ENVIRONS

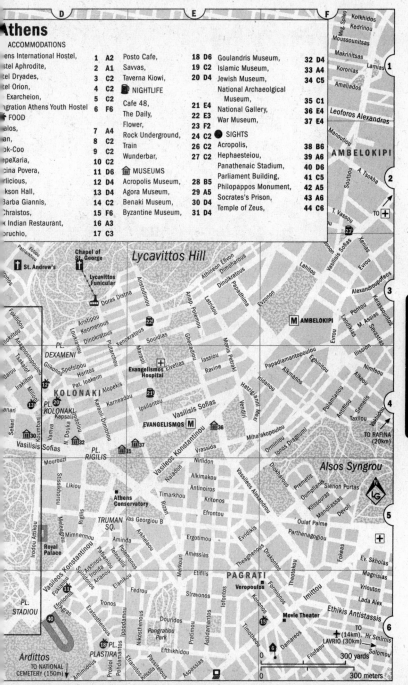

ATHENS AND ENVIRONS

ATHENS AND ENVIRONS

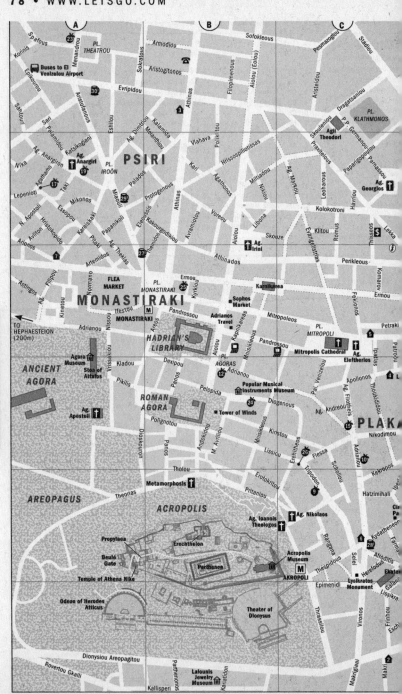

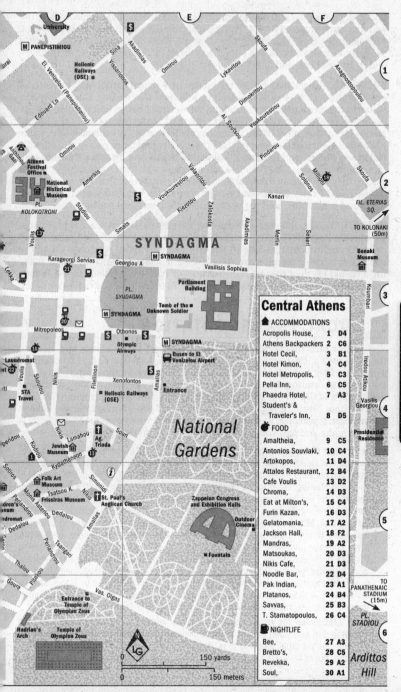

Central Athens

🏠 **ACCOMMODATIONS**

Acropolis House,	1	D4
Athens Backpackers	2	C6
Hotel Cecil,	3	B1
Hotel Kimon,	4	C4
Hotel Metropolis,	5	C3
Pella Inn,	6	C5
Phaedra Hotel,	7	A3
Student's & Traveler's Inn,	8	D5

🍴 **FOOD**

Amaltheia,	9	C5
Antonios Souvlaki,	10	C4
Artokopos,	11	D4
Attalos Restaurant,	12	B4
Cafe Voulis	13	D2
Chroma,	14	D3
Eat at Milton's,	15	C4
Furin Kazan,	16	D3
Gelatomania,	17	A2
Jackson Hall,	18	F2
Mandras,	19	A2
Matsoukas,	20	D3
Nikis Cafe,	21	D3
Noodle Bar,	22	D4
Pak Indian,	23	A1
Platanos,	24	B4
Savvas,	25	B3
T. Stamatopoulos,	26	C4

🍷 **NIGHTLIFE**

Bee,	27	A3
Bretto's,	28	C5
Revekka,	29	A2
Soul,	30	A1

bordering university still fill the graffiti-covered streets, and occasionally erupt with the same youthful fervor. These days, their demands include hip products, for sale at the thrift shops and record stores that pack this anarchist enclave turned bohemian mecca. It's a long way from Pl. Syntagma, both in distance and in atmosphere, and definitely worth the trip.

KOLONAKI. Athens may be the birthplace of Western democracy, but a modern-day plutocracy is alive and well in Kolonaki (Kolwn1ki). Euros flow like water in this posh district, nourishing the designer shops and upscale restaurants that line its sidewalks. Kolonaki lies uphill from Syntagma, at the foot of Mount Lycavittos; most of its commerce centers on glitzy **Patriarhi Ioakim,** while restaurants, bars, and cafes populate the smaller and more pedestrian-friendly **Plutarchou, Haritos,** and **Loukianou.** Kolonaki's **Benaki** and **Byzantine Museums** contain sizable collections of priceless artifacts, and with their reasonable entrance prices, they are far more palatable to the budget traveler than the nearby boutiques. Every Friday, **Xenokratous** is overtaken by the humbler pleasures of fresh fruits and vegetables, sold in the crowded *laiki* (farmer's market).

PAGRATI. Youths and yuppies chat over Fanta® or iced coffee and play backgammon in Pagrati (Pagr1ti), southeast of Syntagma, beyond the National Gardens. Though relatively close to the city center, Pagrati stretches far to the south and is less oriented toward tourists. The many cafes along **Imittou** make for a casual evening sipping mixed drinks or coffee after visits to the **Panathenaic Stadium** and the **First National Cemetery. Pagratiou Park** is a reminder of the days before the area's gentrification.

⌐ LOCAL TRANSPORTATION

Buy yellow bus/trolley/tram/metro tickets at most street kiosks and validate them yourself at the purple machine on board. Tickets cost €1 and are good for 1½hr. after they're validated. There are several options for those who plan to use public transportation frequently. You can buy many tickets at once, or opt for a 24hr. ticket (€3), which grants unlimited travel on city bus, trolley, tram, and metro within 24hr. of its validation. A weekly card (€10) is also available. **Hold on to your ticket.** If you drop it or don't validate it, even when it seems like nobody is there to make you pay, you can be fined up to €72 on the spot by police.

Metro: Most of the Athens metro was rebuilt for the 2004 Olympics. It is now fast, convenient, and gleaming. The underground network consists of 3 lines. **M1,** the green line, runs from northern Kifisia to the port of Piraeus. Neratziotissa, between the stations of Eirini and Marousi, close to the northern end of the line, intersects with the Suburban Rail. **M2,** the red line, currently runs from Ag. Antonios to Ag. Dimitrios. It eventually will continue from Ag. Antonios to Anthoupoli and from Ag. Dimitrios to Helliniko toward the Saronic Gulf. **M3,** the blue line, runs from Egaleo, west of the city center, to Doukissis Plakentias (where it intersects the Suburban Rail) and the airport. After renovations, it will continue northwest from Egaleo to Haidari, and ultimately may be extended to Port Zea in Piraeus. A new metro line is planned to run from Alsos Veikou to Maroussi, looping across both the red and blue lines. A €1 ticket allows for travel along any of the lines (with transfers permitted) and on any bus, trolley, or tram for up to 1½hrs. after its validation. Buy tickets at metro stations or from one of the many automatic machines. Trains run 5am-midnight. Hold on to your ticket to avoid a fine.

Buses: KTEL buses (the yellow ones) leave from Terminals A and B, Mavromateon 29, and Pl. Eleftherias, and travel all over the Attic peninsula. Unlike much of Greek transportation, they are punctual, so be on time. Buy KTEL bus tickets on board or in the terminal. The other buses frequently visible around Athens and its suburbs are blue, designated by 3-digit numbers. Both are good for travel throughout the city and ideal for daytrips to **Daphni** and **Kesariani,** the northern suburbs, **Glyfada** and the coast, and other destinations in the greater Athens area. The Metro stations' and tourist offices' maps of Athens label all of the most frequented routes. Buses run M-Sa 5am-11:30pm, Su and public holidays 5:30am-11:30pm. The X95 from Syntagma to El. Venizelou airport, X96 from Piraeus to El. Venizelou airport, and #040 from Piraeus to Syndagma all run 24hr. Check KTEL bus schedules by calling Terminal A (☎21051 24 910) or B (☎21083 17 153).

> **EASY RIDER.** Unlimited weeklong passes for travel on any mode of public transportation are available for €10 where bus, metro, and tram tickets are sold. If you're in Athens for a week or more, it's a bargain: 6 daily round-trip journeys plus one more ride, and you break even.

Trolleys: Yellow and crowded, trolleys are distinguished from buses by their electrical antennae. Buy a bus/trolley ticket ahead of time at a kiosk (€0.80). Service is frequent and convenient for short hops within town. See the detailed Metro and tourist office map for routes and stops. Trolleys operate M-Sa 5am-midnight, Su and public holidays 5:30am-midnight.

Trams: Noiseless and electrically powered, 2 new tram lines opened in July 2004, right before the Olympics. **Line 1** runs from Pl. Syndagma, in the city center, down to the coast and continues south to Helliniko. It connects with the M2 (red) in Neos Kosmos. **Line 2** begins in Neo Faliro, where it connects with the M1 (green). From there it continues along the Apollo Coast to Glyfada.

Taxis: Meter rates start at €1.05, with an additional €0.48 per km within city limits and €0.84 outside city limits. Midnight-5am everything beyond the start price is €0.68 per km. There's a €3.40 surcharge for trips from the airport, and a €0.95 surcharge for trips from port, bus, and railway terminals; add €0.35 extra for each piece of luggage over 10kg. Pay what the meter shows, rounding it up to the next €0.20 as a tip. Hail your taxi by shouting your destination—not the street address, but the area (e.g., "Pangrati"). The driver will pick you up if he feels like heading that way. Get in the cab and tell the driver the exact address or site. Many drivers don't speak English, so write your destination down (in Greek if possible); include the area of the city, since streets in different parts of the city may share the same name. It's common to ride with other passengers going in the same direction. For an extra €1.70-5 you can schedule a pickup—call a radio taxi: **Acropolis** (☎21086 95 000 or 21086 68 692); **Ikaros** (☎21051 52 800); **Ermis** (☎21041 15 200); **Kosmos** (☎21052 18 300).

> **EYES ON THE METER.** If a cab already carrying passengers picks you up, be sure to check the meter when you get in. Don't get tricked into paying for more than the distance you traveled in the cab.

Car Rental: Try the places on Syngrou. €35-50 per day for a small car with 100km mileage (including tax and insurance); about €200-350 per week. Student discounts up to 50%. Prices rise in summer.

⚟ PRACTICAL INFORMATION

TOURIST AND FINANCIAL SERVICES

Tourist Office:Information Office, Amalias 26 (☎21033 10 392; www.gnto.gr). Brochures on travel throughout Greece and an indispensable Athens map (the same offered in larger metro stations). The most up-to-date bus, train, and ferry schedules and prices,

ATHENS AND ENVIRONS

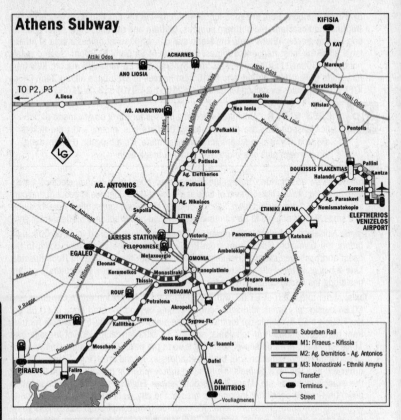

Athens Subway

Suburban Rail
M1: Piraeus - Kifissia
M2: Ag. Demitrios - Ag. Antonios
M3: Monastiraki - Ethniki Amyna
Transfer
Terminus
Street

as well as lists of museums, embassies, and banks. The staff can be impatient, however, so try to prepare specific questions, if possible. Their website is also a good source of information. Open M-F 9am-7pm, Sa-Su 10am-4pm.

Budget Travel: Academy Travel, Iperidou 5 (☎21032 45 071; www.academytravelgreece. com). Specializes in custom island-hopping routes and discount hotels. Open M-F 9am-8pm. **STA Travel,** Voulis 43 (☎21032 11 188). Open M-F 9am-5pm, Sa 10am-2pm. **Consolas Travel,** Aiolou 100 (☎21032 54 932 or 41 751; www.consolas.gr), on the 9th fl. above the post office. Open M and Sa 9am-2pm, Tu-F 9am-5pm. **Adrianos Travel, Ltd.,** Pandrossou 28 (☎21032 31 015; www.adrianostravel.gr), near Mitropoli Cathedral in Plaka, on the 2nd fl. Open M-F 9am-6pm, Sa 9am-1pm.

Banks: National Bank, Karageorgi Servias 2 (☎21033 40 500), in Pl. Syndagma. Open M-Th 8am-2:30pm, F 8am-2pm. Open for **currency exchange** M-F 3:30-5pm, Sa 9am-2pm, Su 9am-1pm. **American Express,** the post office, some hotels, and other banks (list available at tourist office) offer **currency exchange.** Commission about 5%. 24hr. currency exchange at the airport, but with exorbitant commissions.

LOCAL SERVICES

Luggage Storage: Pacific Ltd. (☎21035 30 160; www.pacifictravel.gr), in El. Venizelos Airport's arrivals terminal, across from the large cafe. Open 24hr. Main branch at Nikis

26 (☎21032 41 007), in Syndagma. €2 per day, €30 per month. Open M-Sa 8am-8pm. Many hotels have free or inexpensive luggage storage. Lockers are also available at Ⓜ Monastiraki, Ⓜ Piraeus, and Ⓜ Omonia.

Bookstores: Around Syntagma, there are 2 ▧ **Eleftheroudakis (Book-lover's) Book Stores,** Panepistimiou 17 (☎21032 58 440) and Nikis 20 (☎21032 29 388). The air-conditioned, 8-fl. Panepistimiou location has a Food Company cafe. It is a mecca for English-, French-, and German-speakers nostalgic for fiction, reference, and travel books in their native tongue. Open M-F 9am-9pm, Sa 9am-6pm. AmEx/MC/V. **Compendium Bookshop,** Nikodimou 5 (☎21032 21 248), just off Nikis on the left. Has new and used books, large fiction and poetry sections, poetry readings, and a children's book room. Open M, W, Sa 9am-5pm; Tu and Th-F 9am-8pm. Zoodochou Pigis, off Akademias in Exarhia, is lined with bookstores frequented by students, selling old, new, and foreign books, magazines, and newspapers.

Libraries: The British Council Library, Pl. Kolonaki 17 (☎21036 71 300 or 21036 33 211). Offers books on English literature and language. Open July-Aug. M-F 9am-2pm; Sept.-June M-Sa 10am-7pm. **Hellenic American Union Library,** Massalias 22 (☎21036 80 000), on the 4th fl. of the Hellenic American Union, 4 1/2 blocks east of Ⓜ Panepistimio. Has a wide variety of English books on Greece. Open M and F 9am-8pm; Tu, W, Th 9am-8:30pm; Sa 9am-3pm. Non-Greek students restricted to use within the library; general public must fill out a form at the circulation desk.

Laundromats: Most *plintirias* (launderers) have signs reading "Laundry." Be sure to specify if you don't mind mixing colors. **National,** Apollonos 17 (☎21032 32 226), in Syntagma. Wash, dry, and fold €4.50 per kg. Open M and W 8am-4pm, Tu and Th-F 8am-8pm. **Zenith,** Apollonos 12 and Pentelis 1 (☎21032 38 533). Wash and dry €4 per kg. Open M and W 8am-4pm, Tu and Th-F 8am-8pm.

EMERGENCY AND COMMUNICATIONS

Emergency: Athens Police (☎100). **Ambulance** ☎166 or 21077 00 273. **SOS Doctors** ☎1016. **Poison control** ☎21077 93 777. **AIDS Help Line** ☎21072 22 222. Dial ☎14944 from within Athens for 24hr. hospital information. *Athens News* lists hospitals. Free emergency health care for tourists.

Tourist Police: Dimitrakopoulou 77 (☎171). Great for information, assistance, and emergencies. English spoken. Open 24hr.

Pharmacies: Marked by a green cross. About 1 every 4 blocks is open 24hr.; they rotate. Once a pharmacy closes, it will list on its door the nearest ones that are open 24hr.; the "Useful Information" section of *Athens News* also lists the day's emergency pharmacies.

Hospitals: Emergency hospitals or clinics on duty can be reached at ☎106. **KAT,** Nikis 2 (☎21080 14 411), is located between Marousi and Kifisia. **Geniko Kratiko Nosokomio** (Y. Gennimatas; Public State Hospital), Mesogion 154 (☎21077 78 901). A state hospital, **Aeginitio,** Vas. Sofias 72 (☎21072 20 811) and Vas. Sofias 80 (☎21077 70 501), is closer to Athens's center. Near Kolonaki is the public hospital **Evangelismos,** Ypsilantou 45-47 (☎21072 01 000).

Telephones: OTE, Patission 85 (☎21082 14 449), Athinas 45 (☎21032 16 699), or Stadiou 15. Has phone books for most European and Anglophone countries. Overseas collect calls can only be made at Patission location. For information on overseas calls, dial ☎161 from any landline phone; for directory assistance in and outside of Athens, dial ☎131. Most phone booths in the city operate by phone cards (€3, €6, €12, or €24), available at OTE offices, kiosks, and tourist shops. For rates and general OTE info, call ☎134 (English spoken); for a domestic English-speaking operator, call ☎151. Open M-F 8am-2pm.

Internet Access: Free Wi-Fi is now available through the **athenswifi** network in Pl. Syntagma, Pl. Kotzia, and Thissio. Athens also teems with Internet cafes. Expect to pay €3-6 per hr.

Bits'n Bytes Internet, Kapnikareas 19 (☎21038 22 545; www.bnb.gr), in Plaka, and Akadamias 78 (☎21052 27 717), in Exarhia. This mother of new-age internet cafes has fast connections in a spacious, black-lit joint with A/C. Internet 9am-midnight €5 per hr., midnight-9am €3 per hr. Vending machines sell coffee, juice (€1), and sandwiches (€1-2). Open 24hr.

Lobby Internet Cafe, Imittou 113 (☎21070 14 607), by Pl. Pangratiou, in Pagrati. Mainly a cafe with a few computers and a printer (€0.25 per page). Internet €4 per hr. Open daily 9am-1am.

Quicknet Cafe, Glathstonos 4 (☎21038 03 771), just off of Patission, in Exarhia. Extremely fancy with large, new flatscreen PCs, fast connections, A/C, and comfortable swivel chairs. Internet €2.50 per hr. Cappuccino €1.50. Open 24hr.

Rendez-Vous Cafe, Voulis 18 (☎21032 23 158), in Syndagma. Sip coffee or snack on fresh white chocolate chip cookies (€0.40). Internet €3 per hr. Open M-F 7:30am-9pm, Sa 7:30am-6pm.

Post Offices: For customer service inquiries call the **Greek National Post Office** (ELTA) at ☎210 3243311. For shipping abroad, try parcel post at the Syntagma ELTA branch at Mitropoleos 60 (☎21032 42 489). Open M-F 7:30am-8pm. Stamps for postcards and letters up to 20g. €0.70, plus €3.20 for registered mail and €2.90 for express.

Acropolis/Plaka branch (☎21092 18 076). Exchanges currency and accepts Poste Restante. Sends packages up to 2kg abroad. Open M-F 7:30am-6pm. **Postal Code:** 11702.

Exarhia branch, at the corner of Zaimi and K. Deligiani. Exchanges currency and accepts Poste Restante. Open M-F 7:30am-2pm. **Postal Code:** 10022.

Omonia branch, Aiolou 100 (☎21032 53 586). Machine distributes stamps 24hr.; credit card required. Poste Restante. Accepts parcels up to 2kg abroad. Open M-F 7:30am-8pm, Sa 7:30am-2pm. **Postal Code:** 10200.

Syntagma branch (☎21062 26 253), on the corner of Mitropoleos. Sells stamps, exchanges currency, and accepts Poste Restante. **Postal Code:** 10300.

⌂ ACCOMMODATIONS

The reception desk at **Youth Hostel #5** (otherwise known as Pagration Youth Hostel), Damareos 75 in Pagrati, acts as the Athens branch of the **Greek Youth Hostel Association,** which has 10 other affiliated hostels in Thessaloniki, Patra, and Olympia as well as on Santorini and Crete that share common (and very reasonable) rates. (☎21075 19 530. Open M-F 9am-3pm.) The **Hellenic Chamber of Hotels,** Stadiou 24, provides info and reservations for hotels throughout Greece. Reservations require cash deposit, length of stay, and number of people; contact them one month in advance. (☎21033 10 022; www.grhotels.gr. Open May-Nov. M-F 8:30am-1:30pm.)

SYNTAGMA

Tourist services are easy to find in the heart of Athens, but cheap, quality accommodations are difficult to come across. Though it can be noisy, Syntagma is centrally located; just be wary of overpriced and underwhelming tourist traps.

Hotel John's Plaza, Patrou 5 (☎21032 29 719). The lobby smells like cigarette smoke, but the rooms are clean and spacious and the prices are reasonable. Stop in at the taverna next door for an inexpensive meal before venturing out to the more pleasant parts of town. Singles €35; doubles €50; triples €60. Cash only. ❸

Hotel Kimon, Apollonos 27 (☎21033 14 658), near Agias Filotheis. Though not the cheapest option in Athens, this hotel's immaculately kept rooms and spectacular rooftop view of the Acropolis make it well worth the price. Modest rooms with iron bedsteads and colorful light fixtures. Here's a tip: triples have a trundle, so bring three friends or lovers and turn it into a quad for only €30 each. Rooms have TV, A/C, and baths; some have balconies. Doubles €80; triples €120; quads €144. Lower prices available for longer stays. Cash only. ❺

Hotel Metropolis, Mitropoleos 46 (☎21032 17 871; www.hotelmetropolis.gr). Balconies with views of the square or the Acropolis and friendly staff distinguish this otherwise simple hotel. A/C, TV, and phone in each room. Free luggage storage. Free Wi-Fi. Singles €70; doubles €80; triples €90; quads €120. AmEx/MC/V. ❺

PLAKA

Plaka is the Greek word for "plain," but the area's accommodations are full of highs and lows. If you're lucky and book ahead, you should be able to find something low in price and high in quality in this excellently located neighborhood.

▨ Athens Backpackers, Makri 12 (☎21092 24 044; www.backpackers.gr). ⓂAcropolis; walk down Ath. Diakou away from the Acropolis and take the 1st left onto Makri. While its proximity to the city's major sights is a huge plus, the real draw here is the spectacular view of the Acropolis from the rooftop, where cold beer (€1.50), cheap cocktails (€3), and karaoke flow nightly during summer. Plenty of space between bunks in tidy, spacious rooms. Breakfast, luggage storage, A/C, and the friendly Aussies at the front desk sweeten the deal. Some rooms have bath and patio. Also offers weekend daytrips to sites near Athens, complete with tours and lunch (€40-50). Laundry €5. Free Wi-Fi. 6- or 8-bed dorms €18-25. AmEx/MC/V. ❶

▨ Hotel Acropolis House, 6-8 Kodrou (☎21032 22 344 or 26 241; www.acropolishouse.gr), across from Adonis Hotel. This 19th-century mansion-turned-guesthouse has been run by the same family since 1965. While the rooms are a tad small and very basic—bed, desk, TV, and not much else—the high ceilings, Neoclassical architectural detailing, and floor-to-ceiling art collection add charm. A/C. Some rooms have bath, others have a bathroom on the hall. Breakfast included. Doubles €60-79. Reservations recommended in the high season. ❹

Phaedra Hotel,Cherefondos 16 (☎21032 38 461 or 23 321; www.hotelphaedra.com). Follow Vas. Adrianou until it ends at Lyssikratous; Phaedra is on the left. A superb location and plain rooms made spiffy with dark wooden bedsteads and crisp white sheets draw you in, but it's the enormous rooftop garden with views of the nearby Acropolis that sets this 21-room hotel apart. Singles €50-60; doubles €60-70; triples €75-85. ❹

Student's and Traveler's Inn (HI), Kydatheneon 16 (☎21032 44 808; www.studenttravellersinn.com). ⓂSyndagma. Follow Filellinon in same direction as traffic, Kydatheneon is the 4th left. Basic, bright, and clean rooms with A/C make this hostel one of the best deals in Plaka. A backpackers' delight, with balconies and a garden bar open daily until midnight. Travel agents on duty to help you organize the rest of your trip. Breakfast €4-5.50. Storage free for 1 day, €7 per week, €15 per month. Free Wi-Fi. Reception 24hr. Reservations recommended. Dorms €25-27; doubles €55-65, with bath €60-70; triples €75-85; quads €88-100. For the cheapest digs, request the "dungeon" downstairs, a windowless dorm (€12). V. ❶

MONASTIRAKI

With its nearby markets, Monastiraki is noisy at all hours, but the neighborhood's activity and central location make it an appealing place to set up camp. Straddled between hip Psiri and the Ancient Agora, all the city has to offer is just a few steps away.

Hotel Arion, Agiou Dimitriou 18, Psiri (☎21032 40 415; www.arionhotel.gr). Look for the signs around the corner from Hotel Cecil to lead you to Hotel Arion, hidden on a quiet church square just off busy Athinas. Sleek and swank rooms with clean modern lines and glass-walled bathrooms. Try to get one of the 6th fl. rooms with a view of the Acropolis and the church below; Acropolis views are a dime a dozen in this area, but this is one you won't soon forget. Roof garden. TV and A/C in all rooms. Breakfast included. Free Wi-Fi. Singles €110; doubles €130; triples €150; breakfast included. AmEx/MC/V. ❺

Pella Inn, Karaiskaki 1 (☎21032 50 598). From ⓂMonastiraki, walk 2 blocks down Ermou, away from Pl. Syndagma. Rooms are small but tidy, and the views are way better than the modest rates would suggest. On the dividing line between Monastiraki and Psiri, you'll be well situated to enjoy the area's best attractions. All rooms have A/C and hot water. Breakfast included. Free luggage storage. Dorms €15; doubles with private bath €60; triples with shared bath €60; quads with shared bath €80. Prices negotiable, especially during low season. Cash only, unless reserving online. ❶

Hotel Cecil, Athinas 39 (☎21032 17 079; www.cecil.gr), on the border of Psiri, just a few blocks down from the Varvakia market and 4 blocks from ⓂMonastiraki. Wood-floored, high-ceilinged rooms with spotless baths, A/C, and TVs. Roof bar with Acropolis view. Breakfast included. Free luggage storage. Reserve at least 1 week in advance. Singles €50-70; doubles €79-99; triples €120-140; quads €145. AmEx/MC/V. ❹

EXARHIA

Though far from the city center, Exarhia teems with its own brand of activity. Whether you'd rather wander the Archaeological Museum or spend all your time in a local bar, you're sure to find it just a few steps away from your hotel.

▨ **Hotel Orion,** Em. Benaki 105 (☎21033 02 387; www.orion-dryades.com). Walk up Em. Benaki toward the Strefi Hill, or take bus #230 from Pl. Syntagma. Orion's rooms might charitably be described as "cozy," but its array of amenities and funky 70s decor more than make up for the small size. All rooms have A/C and TVs. Exquisite rooftop canopy, kitchen, and killer view of the Acropolis. Breakfast €6, but the bakery around the corner has great pastries for less. Internet €1 per day. Singles €30; doubles with private baths €40-45. MC/V. ❷

Hotel Dryades, Dryadon 4 (☎21038 27 116). Next door to Hotel Orion, at the base of the Strefi Hill. Orion's up-market sister is one of Athens's nicest mid-level accommodations, with large stylish rooms and baths, and an organic Frank Lloyd Wright feel. Full kitchen and TV lounge. Breakfast €6. Internet €1 per day. Rooms with park views €55; doubles with Acropolis views €65. MC/V. ❹

The Exarcheion, Themistokleous 55 (☎21038 00 731). Right at the center of the bustling neighborhood, near a string of restaurants and *tavernas;* 5min. from ⓂOmonia. Sparse rooms have a funky appeal. Balcony, rooftop garden bar, and A/C. Breakfast €5. Bar in lobby. Reservations recommended. Singles €50; doubles €60-65; triples €80; quads €100. 10% discount for Let's Go readers. €5-10 discount for reserving online. MC/V. ❹

PAGRATI

Kolonaki's high prices may scare off budget travelers, but Pagrati has a few affordable accommodations. Pagrati is relatively far from the city center, so if you're looking for something to do at night, try one of the many (over-priced) cafes lining **Imittou,** the neighborhood's main drag.

▨ **Pagration Athens Youth Hostel,** Damareos 75 (☎21075 19 530). From Omonia or Pl. Syndagma, take trolley #2 or 11 to Filolaou (past Imittou) or walk through the National Garden, down Eratosthenous, then 3 blocks down Efthidiou to Frinis and down Frinis until you come to Damareos; it's on your right. There's no sign for this cheery, family-owned hostel—just the number 75 and a green door. The charming common spaces and ultra-helpful staff make this out-of-the-way hostel worth the 20-25min. walk to the city center. TV lounge and full kitchen. Hot showers €0.50. Laundry €4 to wash, with dryer €7; or line-dry on the roof for free. Quiet hours 2:30-5pm and 11pm-7am. High-season dorms €12. When the hostel fills up, the owner opens the roof (€10 per person) to travelers; bring a sleeping bag. Cash only. ❶

◖ FOOD

SYNTAGMA

Thanks to its proximity to two luxury shopping malls and one transportation hub, Syntagma's dining options are primarily bland and expensive. Try one of these places if you are famished in the neighborhood, or buy some bread, cheese, fruit, and wine from one of the many markets on **Apollonos** and take them to the nearby National Gardens for a picnic.

▨ **Matsoukas,** Karageorgi Servias 3 (☎21032 52 054). Shelves packed floor to ceiling with delicious sugary treats. Dried fruit, chocolate, cookies, and colorful marzipan abound. Try a chunk of nougat (€12 per kilo) or a ball of marzipan rolled in pistachios (€15 per kilo). Ouzo and *metaxa* €9-15. Open daily 8am-midnight. MC/V.❶

Chroma, Lekka 8 (☎21033 17 793). Join trendy diners on the red and green leather couches at this upscale cafe for mozzarella sticks with bacon sauce (€8), or enjoy a mixed drink at the bright orange bar. Fresh pastas €10-12. Open M-F and Su 8am-2am, Sa 8am-10pm. MC/V. ❷

Apostolis and Takis, Petraki 7 (☎21032 25 172). Souvlaki (€1.70) on the go, served with a smile. Open daily 8am-6pm. Cash only.❶

Cafe 21, Voulis 21 (☎21032 23 651). The already affordable prices at this little eatery shrink by around 25% when you take it to go. Espresso *freddo* €3.10, to go €2. Club sandwich €8/6. Open daily 7am-10pm. Cash only. ❷

Caré Caré, Voulis 22, at Petraki (☎21032 37 071). If you're coming in from a late flight and looking for a relaxing bite to eat, stop at this piano bar to unwind with a brew and some live music. Small cheese plate €2. Beer €5. Piano Th-Sa. Open daily 9am-late. Cash only.❶

Cafe Voulis, (☎21032 34 33), on Voulis, just off Ermou. Look for it behind the forest of parked motorcycles. Unlike its neighbors, which extend aggressive awnings practically into the street, Cafe Voulis takes it nice and easy. Perch on a molded wood stool and sample from a brief menu of sandwiches and salads. Caprese sandwich €2.60. Cold chicken pasta €5. Open daily 10am-10pm. Cash Only. ❶

PLAKA

Plaka teems with lively dining options, particularly the main drag, **Kydatheneon,** where proprietors are aggressively friendly. During the day, ubiquitous mini-marts sell yogurt, spanakopita, and fresh fruit. Vendors roast souvlaki by the bushel and gelaterias open their doors for icy treats. After nightfall, the old district's crowded streets fill with glowing lights and live music radiating from nearby *tavernas*. Get away from Kydatheneon, though, and you'll have your pick of the many spots with uninterrupted views of the Roman Agora, Mt. Lycavittos, or the Acropolis.

▨ **Taverna Platanos,** Diogenous 4 (☎21032 20 666), near the Popular Musical Instruments Museum and Roman Agora. An oasis of cool and quiet minutes away from Plaka's most crowded streets. Fresh, traditional Greek fare. Stuffed grape leaves, grilled dishes, and foods cooked with ample amounts of olive oil, as well as a selection of fruit, cheese, and a few desserts. Enjoy it on the outdoor patio, or inside the cozy *taverna*. Spinach pie €3.80. Greek salad €6.30. Moussaka €7.40. Open M-Sa noon-4:30pm and 7:30pm-midnight, Su noon-4:30pm. Cash only. ❷

▨ **Beneth,** Adrianou 97 (☎21032 38 822). Beneth's quiet elegance sets it apart from the eclectic souvenir vendors and *tavernas* of Adrianou. Pre-made sandwiches (€2.50) and impeccable French tarts. Bounty of traditional Greek breads and pastries. Cookies €6-12 per kilo. Baklava €2 per piece. Open daily 7am-10pm. Cash only. ❶

▨ **Stamatopoulos,** Lissiou 26 (☎21032 28 722). Walking north on Adrianou, turn left at Eat at Milton's. Family-owned since 1882, this popular restaurant tucked in a corner just off 1 of Plaka's busiest streets has a bright outdoor terrace, lively Greek music, and dancing every night. Grilled *haloumi* cheese with tomatoes €5. Veal in a clay pot with white sauce €10. Open M and W-Su 7pm-3am. Cash only. ❷

Scholarhio Ouzeri Kouklis, Tripodon 14 (☎21032 47 605; www.scholario.gr). The folks at Scholarhio proudly proclaim their establishment "The Most Traditional Family Restaurant," and it's hard to argue. They serve you a platter with 18 traditional Greek dishes, including Greek salad and stuffed tomatoes, which you can choose from individually (€3-6), or as one of their many special meals. Open daily 11am-2am. MC/V. ❷

Eat at Milton's, Adrianou 91 (☎21032 49 129; www.eatatmiltons.gr). Look for the nut vendor on the corner. A blip of modern hipsterdom among Plaka's ancient ruins and traditional *tavernas*. You won't find much Greek food here; instead, try classy-cool dishes like beef cheeks with mashed potatoes and truffle oil or sea bass with leek, celery, and mussels (both €19). If that's too pricey for dinner, opt for a daytime dessert (lemon soufflé €6) or coffee (€2-3.50) break. If that's not pricey enough, complement your meal with a bottle of Dom Perignon (price not listed, but if you have to ask, it's too expensive for you). Open daily 8am-1am. Cash only. ❹

Antonis Souvlaki, Adrianou 118 (☎21032 46 838). The great deals at this tiny storefront would be easy to miss if not for the crowds of locals at its door. Vegetarian options. Pork or chicken gyros and souvlaki €1.90. Mythos beer €1.40. Open daily whenever the owners feel like it, but usually 10:30am-10:30pm. Cash only. ❶

MONASTIRAKI

Skip the *tavernas* and takeout just outside the metro for the bounty of fresh, friendly food available on the side streets of Monastiraki and nearby Psiri. You'll find everything from traditional Greek *estiatorios* with views of the Acropolis to exotic gelaterias on trendy plazas.

Mandras, Ag. Anargiron 8 (☎21032 13 765), at Taki. Live, modern Greek music plays every night at 9 in this attractive brick building in the heart of Psiri. Try 1 of the lunch specials: Greek salad, meatballs, fruit, and a coke €12. Ouzo shrimp €15. Music daily 9pm-4am. Open daily 8am-4am. Cash only. ❸

Zidoron, Ag. Anargiron 17 (☎21032 15 368). A Greek restaurant that takes its Greekness lightly. Classics like grilled *haloumi* (€4.50) alongside creative pasta and grilled dishes. Try the Santorini salad with capers and "sour cheese" (€6) and the grilled sardines (€6.50) for a light and refreshing meal. Dining room open daily 10am-8pm. Bar open daily 4pm-2am. Cash only. ❷

Attalos Restaurant, Adrianou 9 (☎21032 19 520), near the Thisseon area, on the edge of the Agora and the Temple of Hephaestus. Excellent views from outdoor tables and a welcoming *taverna* atmosphere inside. No matter where you sit, the staff is eager to please. Offerings range from mussels *saganaki* (€6.20) to a vegetarian's dream plate of zucchini, eggplant, and tomato croquettes (serves 2-4; €8). Pumpkin balls €5.50. Open daily 10am-1am. AmEx/MC/V. ❷

Savvas, Mitropoleos 86 (☎21032 45 048). Cab drivers and kiosk vendors recommend this famous souvlaki joint as the best in town. Restaurant prices for gyros (€6-9) shrink to €1.80 for takeout orders. Open daily 10am-3am. Cash only. ❶

ATHENS AND ENVIRONS

Pagotomania, Taki 21 (☎21032 30 001), at Aisopou. This hip gelateria is head and shoulders cooler than its competitors in Pl. Monastiraki. Over 30 flavors of gelato made on the premises, including wild cherry, choco-banana, and yogurt with honey, orange and peach. The parlor's glass walls, which open onto the street in warm weather, let you to enjoy your frozen treat on a red banquet under the trees. Scoops €1.70. Waffle with ice cream €5.50. Open daily 10am-4am. Cash only. ❶

EXARHIA

Hungry 20-somethings demand cheap food around Exarhia, and many of the options are basic but tasty.

📷 **0 Barba Giannis,**Em. Benaki 94 (☎21038 24 138). From Exarhia, take Metaxa to Benaki and walk 3 blocks toward the Strefi Hill; it's the yellow building on the corner with tall green doors. "Uncle John's" is informal, and that's how the locals like it—at 3pm, when other cafes sit empty, Giannis is bustling. The Provençal color scheme and iron work above the long windows give the place a French feel, but the food is pure Greek. So is the staff: only Tony speaks English. Stewed veal with pasta €7. Open M-Sa noon-1:30am. Cash only. ❷

📷 **Cook-cou Food,** Themistokleous 66 (☎21038 31 955). This cafe's zebra-print booths and pulsing techno-pop might feel out of place in other neighborhoods, but in Exarhia it fits right in. The kitchen fashions typical Greek ingredients into creative treasures, such as lentils with mango (€5.50) and chicken breast stuffed with *manouri* cheese (€7). The menu changes daily, but the house wine (€1 per glass) is always a steal. Vegetarian entrees €4.50-€6. Meat entrees €6.80-€7.50. Open in summer M-Sa 7am-7pm, in winter M-Sa 1pm-1am. Cash only. ❷

Pobruchio,Asklipiou 53 (☎21036 14 296). If you're approaching Exarhia from posh and polished Kolonaki, take a minute at this coffee shop to acquaint yourself with your new surroundings. The entrance is plastered with posters for rock bands and art openings. Brochures and maps inside help you find the hippest events in Exarhia. Relax on one of the mod barstools with a coffee or a beer from the locally brewery Craft. Open M-Sa 11am-late. Cash only. ❶

CrepeXaria, (☎21038 40 773), on the corner of Ikonomou and M. Themistokleous on Pl. Exarhia. Smack at the top of the square, CrepeXaria is a fun and convenient place to cool your heels and fill your belly. Choose from a variety of savory and sweet crepes, including the super-duper chocolate-banana-nut-coconut-Grand Marnier concoction (€4.40). Craft your own combinations, or try one of the many pizzas, salads, or "Arabian bread" sandwiches on the menu. Open daily noon-5am. Cash only. ❶

FROM THE ROAD

VA, VA, VARNAKIOS

I really love food. What's more, I love small food. But Athens doesn't do anything small. So I found myself in a food funk. My summer diet of Greek salad and souvlaki had lost its novelty. I was getting seriously gloomy, but then I discovered Varnakios, on Athinas between Armodiou and Aristogeitonos—Athens's largest open-air food market.

There were young squashes crying to be stuffed with bread crumbs and oregano and fried in olive oil. There were cherries waiting to be flambéed with ouzo and served over ice cream. There were lemons asking to be slid under the skin of the chickens across the street, who were in turn asking to be oven-roasted to a crisp golden brown.

It was too much, so I left. I planned. I went back.

My itinerary included four weeks of island-hopping, which meant snacks. So on my second trip, I restricted myself to grub that would keep: dried apricots, almonds, roasted peanuts coated with honey and sesame seeds. And then—oh, I couldn't help myself—a couple of stone fruits, a bag of olives, and a chunk of feta. I threw the nuts and fruits together for a killer trail mix and ate the olives and feta for dinner with a loaf of bread from the bakery down the street and a bottle of wine from the corner market. Stone fruits for desert. Small and delightful, no kitchen necessary.

—Jillian Goodman

Bean, Em. Benaki 45 (☎21033 00 010). Modern decor belies the menu's *taverna* flavor. Hanging lamps and small white lights illuminate this simple indoor-outdoor space. Array of Italian-influenced pastas, salads, and entrees, plus a full case of daily specials. Appetizers €5-6. Grilled pork €9.50. Open M-Sa 1pm-midnight. Cash only. ❷

KOLONAKI

The **market** in Pl. Dexamani every Friday, with an array of vendors selling everything from souvlaki to fresh olives, is your best bet if you're on a budget. In general, though, Kolonaki caters to those who can splurge on fine dining.

▨ **Derlicious,** Tsakalof 14 (☎21036 30 284), tucked between boutiques on the southernmost block of Tsakalof. The sign is written idn Greek letters, but you'll know it by the open coals just behind the counter. Such low-priced fare is rare in Kolonaki, and although the staff might be brisk, the cheap and "derlicious" food is worth every penny. Try the *flaouto* (big tortilla) with chicken (€3.22). Open M-W and Su 1pm-4am, Th 1pm-5am, F-Sa 1pm-6am. Cash only. ❶

▨ **Taverna Kiouri,**Filikis Eterias 4 (☎21036 14 033). Look for it below street level. A bastion of homespun simplicity in slick Pl. Kolonaki, Kiouri sells traditional Greek food for modest prices. Try meatballs with egg and lemon sauce (€8) or daily specials like sardines cooked with tomatoes and vegetables (€8). No matter what you choose, you'll be taken care of by the welcoming staff. M-Sa 8am-10pm. Cash only. ❷

Jackson Hall, Milioni 4 (☎21036 16 546). An outpost of a Kansas City burger bar makes an obvious play to the American tourist. A New York classic burger will set you back €15—but for the homesick traveler, it might just be worth it. Apple pie with ice cream €7. Open daily 10am-3am. MC/V. ❸

PAGRATI

Imitou, the main drag, is lined with Euro-style cafes that will try to tempt you with overpriced—€2.80 for a basic Greek coffee—but don't be fooled. The surprisingly big **Spar supermarket,** Formionos 23 (open M-F 8am-9pm, Sa 8am-8pm) is a frugal standby, and cheap eats hide here and there.

▨ **Cucina Povera,** Eforionos 13 (☎21075 66 008; www.cucinapovera.gr). Walk east from the Panathenaic Stadium (away from the Acropolis) on Vas. Konstandinou, then turn right on Eratosthenous and left onto Eforionos. Cucina Povera whips up elegant dishes from simple ingredients, such as *aubergine millefeuille* with creamy cheese (€8.50) and stuffed rooster with vegetables and Gruyère (€12.50). The menu changes daily, but the house burger stuffed with olives, *metsovone* cheese, and potatoes is always on the menu for €12. Open M-Sa noon-3pm and 8-11pm, Su noon-3pm. Cash only. ❷

O Chraistos, Imittou 129 (☎21075 62 400 or 210 752 4677). Near Frynis. Souvlaki is never the healthiest option, but this little joint takes it to a whole new level. Pork souvlaki €3 to stay, to go €2.20. Open 2pm-12:30am. Cash only.❶

Posto Cafe, Pl. Plastira 2 (☎210 751 0210). Just to the right once you reach Pl. Plastira from Eratosthenous. In a small storefront almost behind a white awning (look for the Illy coffee sign), Posto is a relaxed place to sit with the gentlemen of the neighborhood and enjoy a Greek coffee (€1.20) or a quick bite to eat. Try the spanakopita (€1.50) or a fresh crepe (€3-5). ❶

◔ SIGHTS

ACROPOLIS

Reach the entrance on the west side by walking north from Areopagitou, by following the signs from Plaka, or by exiting the Agora to the south and following the path uphill. The well-worn marble can be slippery, so wear shoes with good traction. ☎ 21032 10 219. Open daily in summer 8am-7:30pm, in winter 8am-2:30pm. €12, students and EU citizens over 65 €6, under 19 free. Admission includes entrance to the Acropolis, the Agora, the Roman Agora, the Olympian Temple of Zeus, and the Theater of Dionysos, within a 48hr. period. Tickets can be purchased at any of the sights.

As the most well-known symbol of Athens, the profile of the Acropolis is a common sight around the world. Upon climbing the steps up to the **Propylaia,** even the most jaded traveler will be awed by the majesty of the immense structures arrayed on the plateau. The **Parthenon,** built in the 5th century BC, towers over the Aegean, featuring a panoramic view of the city. Although a visit to the Acropolis seems to be *de rigeur* for those spending time in Athens, it really is the best way to experience firsthand the majesty of ancient Greek civilization. Visit as early in the day as possible to avoid massive crowds and the intense midday sun.

HISTORY

BEGINNINGS. The area of the Acropolis was originally the tiny city of Athens, inhabited by **Mycenaeans** worshipping a nature goddess. As the fledgling *polis* (city-state) grew into a sprawling military power, the strategic hilltop site was fortified into a refuge for Athenians in times of war. Wealthy *aristoi,* noblemen who considered themselves closer to God than commoners, took control of Athens in the 12th century BC, moving power downhill to the Agora and leaving the Acropolis as a purely religious site. A wooden shrine went up to **Athena Polias,** defender of crops and fertility, and her alter ego Pallas Athena, the city's virgin protectress.

PERICLEAN PROJECT. The Acropolis as it stands today owes much to the determination of **Pericles** (c. 495-429 BC). After Athens's victory against Persia left it in control of a growing empire, this Classical leader commissioned a series of grand architectural displays. Basking in post-Marathon glory, Pericles convinced members of the Delian League to donate great sums to the *polis's* beautification campaign. This imperial fund-raising footed the bill to secure legendary artists, including **Iktinos, Kallikrates,** and **Phidias,** for the site's new design. In 447 BC, only ten years after construction commenced, they unveiled the completed Parthenon, dedicated to Athena. Work on the **Propylaea,** the **Temple of Athena Nike,** and the **Erechtheion** soon followed. Even in the Golden Age of Athens, however, citizens were quick to complain that Pericles's Acropolis project was too extravagant. Plutarch memorably blasted the leader for "gilding and bedizening" Athens like a "wanton woman adding precious stones to her wardrobe." Luckily for modern viewers, Pericles persisted, commissioning more temples on the Acropolis, the **Hephaesteion** in the Agora, and the **Temple of Poseidon** at Sounion.

THE TEST OF TIME. Almost as soon as the Acropolis was completed, it fell to Sparta in 404 BC. Ever since, its function has shifted every time it has changed hands. Byzantine Christians renamed it the **Church of Agia Sophia,** worshipping there (and defacing the pagan sculptures) until **Frankish Crusaders** made the building a fortified palace for the Dukes de la Roche in 1205. Catholics came to use the space as a church again, dedicating it to **Notre Dame d'Athènes,** and by the 15th century Ottoman rulers had re-cast it as a mosque.

The Acropolis's buildings themselves remained remarkably intact until a Venetian siege in 1687, when the attackers' shells accidentally blew up a Turkish supply of gunpowder stored under the Parthenon's roof. Its structure has deteriorated since then. By the dawn of the 19th century, the Englishman Lord Elgin was chiseling the most stunning marble reliefs off of the Parthenon and carting them to London, where they remain, displayed in the British Museum despite pleas by the Greek government for their return. Large-scale restoration efforts on the Acropolis are still underway, and much of the Parthenon statuary that Elgin didn't make off with has been recently relocated to the Acropolis Museum to shelter it from acid rain.

RUINS

The first structure within the site's gate is the **Temple of Athena Nike,** on the upper right platform as you walk up the stairs. Along the path where a Classical ramp once lay, visitors walk through the Roman **Beulé Gate,** named for the French archaeologist who unearthed it, and past the imposing **Propylaea,** the unfinished entrance attributed to Mnesikles. Famous for its ambitious multi-story design, the Propylaea combines Ionic columns with a Doric exterior.

◪PARTHENON. The ancient architect Iktinos overlooked nothing in the design of the **Temple of Athena Parthenos,** more commonly known as the Parthenon. He placed eight columns instead of the typical six at the front of the temple. Fearing that perspective would make them look spindly from a low vantage point, Iktinos made each column bulge slightly to create an optical illusion of perfect symmetry. In plotting the temple's dimensions, he followed a meticulous four-to-nine ratio, a variation on the aesthetically ideal Golden Mean. Iktinos's obsession with proportion and order, traits that came to epitomize Classical architecture, pushed the Parthenon past traditional Doric boxiness into the sublime.

The **metopes** (scenes in the open spaces above the columns) that once bordered the sides of the Parthenon celebrated Athens's rise to such greatness. On the far right of the southern side, the Lapiths battled the Centaurs, while on the east the Olympian gods triumphed over the Titans. The north side depicted the victory of the Greeks over the Trojans, and the western facade reveled in Athens's triumph over the Amazons. The **pediments** at either end marked the zenith of Classical decorative sculpture. The east pediment once depicted Athena's birth, while the west pediment showed Athena and Poseidon's contest for the city's devotion. Many of these celebratory pieces, damaged over the centuries, are now in London's British Museum or in the Acropolis Museum.

Inside the temple, in front of a pool of water, stood Phidias's greatest sculptural feat: a 12m gold and ivory statue of Athena. Although the statue has since been destroyed, the National Museum houses an AD second-century Roman copy, which is fearsomely grand even at its significantly reduced size.

◪ACROPOLIS MUSEUM. Although the Acropolis Museum currently is undergoing extensive renovations, it still is arguably the most striking part of the entire complex, with a collection composed exclusively of masterpieces. Five of the original Erechtheion **Caryatids** appear monumentally huge in their small glass casement. The carvings of a lion devouring a bull and of a wrestling match between Herakles and a sea monster display the Ancient Greeks' mastery of anatomical detail and emotional expression. Notice the empty space where room has been left for the British to return the missing Elgin marbles. (*Open daily 8am-7:30pm; hours are shortened in the low season. No flash photography or posing with the statues. English labels. Avoid going 10am-1pm, when it is most crowded.*)

TEMPLE OF ATHENA NIKE. This tiny temple, on the right as you first enter the Propylaia, is undergoing a renovation process that has involved rebuilding it from the ground up. It was first constructed in the middle of the Peloponnesian War, during a brief respite known as the "Peace of Nikias" (421-415 BC). Ringed by eight miniature Ionic columns, it housed a statue of winged **Nike,** the goddess of victory. When the Athenians were seized by a paranoid fear that Nike would flee and take with her any chance of victory in the renewed war, they

ATHENS AND ENVIRONS

The Acropolis

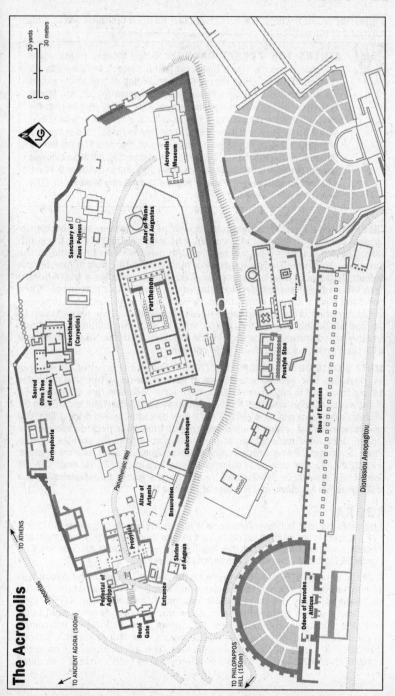

TO ATHENS

TO ANCIENT AGORA (500m)

Theorias

Beulé
Gate

Pedestal of
Agrippa

Propylaia

Entrance

Shrine
of Aegeus

Altar of
Artemis

Brauronion

Panathenaic Way

Arrhephoria

Sacred
Olive Tree
of Athena

Erechtheion
(Caryatids)

Sanctuary of
Zeus Polieus

'Parthenon'

Altar of Rome
and Augustus

Acropolis
Museum

Chalcotheque

Prostyle Stoa

Stoa of Eumenes

Dionissiou Areopagitou

Odeon of Herodes
Atticus

TO PHILOPAPPOS
HILL (150m)

0   30 yards
0   30 meters

N

ATHENS AND ENVIRONS

clipped the statue's wings. The remains of the 5m thick **Cyclopean wall** that once surrounded the entire Acropolis now lie below this temple.

 ATHENS FOR POCKET CHANGE. Budget travelers, rejoice: you're in Athens, where the wine is cheap, the food is cheaper, and the sights are (almost) free. Most of the ruins are outdoors, letting visitors ramble around the **Rock of Saint Paul,** the **Philopappos Monument** (p. 95), and **Mount Lycavittos** (p. 97) without dropping a euro. After leaving your bags at the Student's and Traveler's Inn (p. 85), pick up local wine, beer, or juice (€1-3) from a corner kiosk and a gyro (€1-2) from Savvas (p. 88), and picnic at 1 of these ancient sights with great Acropolis views. Also note that the **Benaki Museum of Islamic Art** (p. 99) is free on Wednesday, the **Ilias Lalounis Jewelry Museum** is free on Wednesday after 3pm and on Saturday 9-11am, and the **War Museum** and **Popular Musical Instruments Museum** (p. 100) never have admission fees.

ERECHTHEION. The Erechtheion, to the left of the Parthenon, contains the famous **Caryatid** sculptures, six women who support the roof on the south side. They're actually replicas; most of the originals can be found in the Acropolis Museum. The structure was built in 406 BC, just before Sparta defeated Athens in the Peloponnesian War. It is named after a snake-bodied hero whom Poseidon speared in a dispute over the city's patronage. When Poseidon struck a truce with Athena, he was allowed to share her temple—the eastern half is devoted to the goddess of wisdom and the western part to the god of the sea. The eastern porch, with its six Ionic columns, contained an olive-wood statue of Athena; like the Temple of Athena Nike, it contrasts with the Parthenon's dignified Doric columns.

OTHER SIGHTS ON THE ACROPOLIS. The southwestern corner of the Acropolis overlooks the reconstructed **Odeon of Herodes Atticus,** a functional theater dating from the Roman period (AD 160). *(Open M-Sa 8am-7pm. €2, students €1, visitors with an Acropolis ticket free. MC/V. For performance information head to the Odeon box office on Dionysiou Areopagitou. ☎21032 32 771. Open daily 9am-2pm and 6-9pm.)* The Athens **Hellenic Festival** occurs every summer, with numerous performances in the Odeon; schedules are available at the booth across from the theater. *(Panepistimiou 39. Contact the Athens Festival Office for more information about summertime shows. ☎21032 72 000. Most shows start at 9pm and tickets cost around €30, but range €20-500. Open M-F 8:30am-4pm, Sa 9am-2:30pm.)* Nearby are the ruins of the **Classical Theater of Dionysus, the Asclepion,** and the **Stoa of Eumenes II.**

AGORA

Enter the Agora off Pl. Thission or Adrianou, or as you descend from the Acropolis. ☎21032 10 185. Map kiosks and informational placards are plentiful throughout the park, but it might be helpful to bring extra material. Open daily 8am-8pm. €4, non-EU students and EU seniors €2, under 19, EU students, and visitors with an Acropolis ticket free.

If the Acropolis was the showpiece of the ancient capital, the Agora was its heart and soul, serving as the city's marketplace, administrative center, and focus of daily life from the 6th century BC through the AD 6th century. Many of the great debates of Athenian democracy were held here; Socrates, Aristotle, Demosthenes, Xenophon, and St. Paul all instructed in its stalls. Following its heyday, the Agora, like the Acropolis, passed through the hands of various conquerors. The ancient market emerged again in the 19th century, when a residential area built above it was razed for excavations. Today, the Agora is a peaceful respite from the bustling commerce that surrounds it. As you explore the ruins, you're likely to hear the sounds of nature overpowering the low buzz of traffic.

HEPHAESTEION. The Hephaesteion, built in 415 BC on a hill in the north-western corner of the Agora, is the best-preserved Classical temple in Greece. The detailed original friezes are still easily visible covering the ceiling of the temple's inner chamber. They depict the battle between Athenian hero Theseus and the Pallantids. The temple was put to various uses until 1834, when it served as the welcoming pavilion for King Otto.

ODEON OF AGRIPPA. This concert hall, built for Roman Emperor Augustus's son-in-law and right-hand man, now stands in ruins on the left of the Agora as you walk from the museum to the Hephaesteion. When the roof collapsed in AD 150, the Odeon was rebuilt at half its former size. Later, a recreational building with a colonnade of tritons was built over the ruins of the Odeon and parts of the Middle Stoa, which they called the Palace of Giants.

STOA OF ATTALOS. This multi-purpose building was filled with shops and was home to informal philosophers' gatherings. Attalos II, King of Pergamon, built the Stoa in the 2nd century BC as a gift to Athens. Reconstructed between 1953 and 1956, it now houses the Agora Museum, which contains relics from the site. The stars of the collection are the black figure paintings by Exekias and a calyx krater (a vase used to mix wine, with a form resembling the sepals of a flower), depicting Trojans and Greeks quarreling over the body of Patroclus, Achilles's closest companion and possible lover. (☎21032 10 185. Open M 11am-8pm; Tu-Su 8am-8pm.)

MIDDLE STOA. Extending most of the way between the Stoa of Attalos and the Hephaesteion, the Middle Stoa was the largest building in the Agora and was used for a wide variety of organizational and religious purposes. Although it was destroyed by a fire in AD 267, you can ascertain its immense size by the numerous column bases that remain.

OTHER ANCIENT SITES

PHILOPAPPOS HILL. The Philopappos Hill, a lush respite from park-deprived Athens, is southwest of the Acropolis and accessible from Apostolou Pavlou. Abundant trails, sheltered picnic areas, and a postcard-perfect view of the Parthenon make this a great place for afternoon exploration. A marble road weaves past **Agios Dimitrious,** where you're likely to stumble upon a church service in progress. According to legend, Dimitrious persuaded God to smite 17th-century Turkish invaders with lightning before they could harm the worshippers in this small, icon-filled church. Just before Ag. Dimitrious, a narrow path veers off to the left, toward a stone cave with iron bars. This nondescript opening was once, as a sign indicates, **Socrates's Prison;** a series of rooms was carved into the cliff face and later used to house treasures from the Acropolis during World War II. Farther up, toward the Acropolis, are the ruins of **Pnyx Hill,** where the Athenian Assembly once met, and the **Hill of the Nymphs,** which looks out on an ancient observatory.

The peak, where the marble Monument of Philopappos stands, has Athens's best view of the Acropolis. The angles and distance that render the view so breathtaking also made the Acropolis an easy target for the Venetians in 1687; it was from this peak that they shot the disastrous volley that accidentally detonated the Parthenon's gunpowder stores. The monument was erected between AD 114-116 in memory of Julius Antiochus Philopappos, a Roman dignitary who settled on the hill after being exiled from his home in the Near Eastern kingdom of Commagene.

ROMAN AGORA. The Roman Agora was built between 19 and 11 BC with donations from Julius and Octavian Caesar. The columns of the two surviving **prophylae** (halls), a nearly intact entrance gate, and the **gate of Athena Archgetis** stand as testaments to what was once a major meeting place for Athenians. Proving that people take interest in anything as long as it's old, the AD first-century **vespasianae,** or public toilets, are a popular site. A **mosque** dating from 1456 sits nearby. By far the Agora's most intriguing structure is the well-preserved (and restored) **Tower of the Winds.** This octagonal stone tower, built in the first century BC by the astronomer Andronikos, was initially crowned with a weathervane. The top of each side of the tower has a carving of the personification of each of the eight winds. On the walls are markings that allowed the structure to be used as a sundial from the outside and a water-clock from the inside. Since its construction, the tower also has functioned as a church and as a Dervish monastery. (☎ 21032 45 220. Open daily 8am-7pm. €2; students €1; EU students, under 19, and visitors with an Acropolis ticket free.)

TEMPLE OF ZEUS AND HADRIAN'S ARCH. Fifteen majestic Corinthian columns—the remnants of the largest temple ever built in Greece, dedicated to Zeus—rise out of a barren field on the edge of the National Gardens, the centerpiece of a complex of ancient ruins. A map at the entrance will show you the way to the **Basilica of Olympeion,** the **Lawcourt at Delphinion,** and the **Temples of Kronos and Rhea** among others, although good luck finding them—that's the only map, and its orientation makes it difficult to read. At the outer edge stands Hadrian's arch, which was built to commemorate his visits and gifts to the city. Facing the Acropolis, the arch reads "This is Athens, the ancient city of Theseus," referring to the city's mythical founder. On the other side, facing the emperor's addition, it proclaims, "This is the city of Hadrian and not of Theseus." Nearby, at Vas. Olgas and Amalias, is a memorial to a man whose ambitions were a bit less worldly, though no less grand: the English Romantic poet Lord Byron, who lost his life fighting for Greek independence. (Entrance on Vas. Olgas near Amalias, across from the entrance to the National Garden. ☎ 21092 26 330. Open daily 8:30am-8pm. Temple admission €2, students €1, under 19 free. Arch free. A ticket gives access to the Acropolis, the Theater of Dionysus, the Ancient and Roman Agorae, the Keramikos, and Hadrian's Library; €12, students €6.)

KERAMIKOS. Most sites in the Agora are more dead than alive, but the Keramikos is especially so: it includes a large cemetery built around a segment of the Sacred Way, the road to Eleusis. The **Sacred Gate** arched over this road, lined with **public tombs** for state leaders, famous authors, and battle victims. Worshippers began the annual Panathenaic procession along its path. Also within the site is a section of the 40m wide boulevard that ran through the Agora and Diplyon Gate and ended at the sanctuary of Akademes, where Plato founded his Academy in the 4th century BC. The **Oberlaender Museum** displays finds from the burial sites; its pottery and sculpture are highlights. (Northwest of the Agora; the archaeological site begins where Ermou and Pireos intersect. From Syndagma, walk toward Monastiraki on Ermou for 1km. ☎ 21034 63 552. Open M 11am-7:30pm, Tu-Su 8am-7:30pm. €2; non-EU students and EU seniors €1; EU students, under 19, and visitors with an Acropolis ticket free.)

HADRIAN'S LIBRARY. Just north of the Roman Agora, by the Monastiraki metro station, Hadrian's Library is situated around a large central courtyard. The library, originally built in AD 132, was damaged by a Herulian invasion in 267, then rebuilt from 407 to 412. The ruins of a 5th-century church, a 7th-century church, and a 12th-century cathedral sit on the same site. (☎21032 49 350. Open M-F 8am-2pm. €2, students €1, EU students free.)

BYZANTINE ATHENS

Hours vary. The best time to visit is 9-11am. Modest dress required.

Places of worship hide in plain sight all over Athens. Sanctuaries sit on tiny, crumbling streets, squeeze between modern buildings, and squat resignedly behind porticos, their modest facades almost overwhelmed by modern architecture. Inside their doors, however, ornate, icon-filled rooms unfold, dimly lit and smelling of incense. If no service is in session (services usually Su morning and 6pm every evening), a recording of chanting may be playing.

Many historians see Constantine's establishment of a Christian empire in 324 as the death-knell for Classical culture. But the 11th- and 12th-century golden age of Byzantine art has left behind its own share of masterpieces—devotional mosaics, delicate icons, and cross-shaped domed buildings—many of which can be found on the streets of Athens. **Kapnikaria Church,** just below ground-level on Ermou and Kalamiotou, has typical Byzantine architecture; the frescoes inside are by a 20th-century painter, Photis Koruglou. Dedicated to the Virgin Mary, this church was built above the ruins of a temple to a female goddess, probably Athena or Demeter. (☎21032 24 462. Open M and W 8am-2pm, Tu and Th-F 8am-12:30pm and 5-7pm, Su 8-11:30am.)

Down Mitropoleos from Syndagma, where the street intersects with Evangelistras and Pandrossou, are **Agios Eleftherios** and the **Mitropoli Cathedral,** still under construction after a recent earthquake. A frieze with the Attic calendar of feast days adorns the front facade, and a statue in the courtyard honors Archbishop Damaskinos Papandreou, one of the first to stand up for Greece's Jewish population during the Nazi occupation. **Agia Apostoli,** which stands at the eastern edge of the Ancient Agora but is visible from Vrisakiou near Dioskouron, dates from the early 11th century, making it one of Athens's oldest churches. White-walled **Metamorphosis,** tucked near Panos on Pritanou, a backstreet circling the base of the Acropolis, was also built in the 11th century and restored in 1956. Another **Church of the Metamorphosis,** at Monis Asteriou and Kidatheneion in Plaka, is capped by a majestic dome and once had gorgeous illuminated wall paintings, but is now a tragic example of what time and the Mediterranean weather will do if left unchecked. Eleventh-century Russian Orthodox **Agia Triada,** a few blocks from Pl. Syndagma at Filellinon 21, is filled with silver angel icons. Farther on Filellinon is the **Sotira Lykodimou,** the largest medieval building in Athens, dating from 1031. Built as part of a Roman Catholic monastery, it is now a Russian Orthodox church. The **Chapel of Saint George,** another small but elaborate structure, looms over Athens from the peak of Mt. Lycavittos on top of a ruined temple to Zeus.

MODERN ATHENS

MOUNT LYCAVITTOS. From the peak of Mt. Lycavittos, the tallest of Athens's seven hills, visitors can see every inch of the city. A **funicular rail** travels to the top. Your ticket entitles you to 15% off the cafe and shop at the mountain's peak, as well as 20% off at the gift shop at the bottom. Once you get to the top, peek into the quaint **Chapel of Saint George,** whose walls are adorned with intricate religious murals, and where baptisms and services are still performed on Sunday. Take your time appreciating the astounding 360° view that spans from the mountains over the Acropolis to the water. The colorful stadium seating of the **Lycavittos Theater** is 180° from the Acropolis. Using the Acropolis as a point of reference, the neighborhoods of Monastiraki, Omonia, and Exarhia are on your right. Continuing clockwise, you will see Areos Park behind the small circular patch of green that is Strefi, another of the seven hills. The eastern view gazes down onto more parks and Mt. Hymettus, and offers a glimpse of the Panathenaic Stadium, the National Garden, and the Temple of Olympian Zeus. *(Funicular 2min., every 10-30min. 9am-3am, roundtrip €6. A path from the end of Loukianou in Kolonaki takes 15-20min. Hikers should bring water, watch out for cacti and slippery rocks. Do not climb alone, especially at night.)*

PANATHENAIC STADIUM. Also known as the **Kallimarmaro** ("Pretty Marble"), the horseshoe-shaped Panathenaic Stadium is wedged between the National Gardens and the neighborhood of Pangrati, carved into a hill. The Byzantines destroyed the Classical stadium, but its gleaming white marble was restored in 1895. The stadium was the site of the first modern Olympic Games in 1896 and was refurbished once again for the 2004 games, where it served as the finish line for a marathon that matched Phidippides's 490 BC route (see **Marathon,** p. 105). Marble steles near the front honor Greece's gold and silver Olympic medalists. The stadium's history and sheer size make it worth a trip.*(On Vas. Konstantinou. From Syndagma, walk down Amalias 10min. to Vas Olgas and follow it to the left. Or take trolley #2, 4, or 11 from Syndagma. Free.)*

PARLIAMENT BUILDING. Every hour on the hour on the hour, a small crowd of tourists assembles in front of the Parliament building to witness the ▨**changing of the guard.**The guards *(evzones)* on duty execute a series of marionette moves in perfect unison, as the new guard arrives to take their place. Both sets pause for a presentation of arms and a uniform inspection before the new guards take their place. Longer, more elaborate ceremonies take place on Sundays at 11am. ▨**The National Gardens** sprawl serenely behind the Parliament building. Broad stripes of white gravel meander past beds of plant life, artificial ponds, and the occasional fallen column. A quiet refuge in the middle of Athens's busiest center, the gardens have shade and plenty of places to sit. Skip the Spanish Fountain and the meager zoo and make for the Central Lake: it's no more than a pond, but there's a nice turtle pond nearby, a pretty trellis with climbing vines, and some great flora as you get closer to the Parliament.

OUTDOOR MARKETS. Athens's markets attract bargain-hunters, browsers, award-winning chefs, and a lot of *yiayias* (grandmothers dressed in widows' black). The ▨**Flea Market,** adjacent to Pl. Monastiraki, explodes on Sunday into a festive garage sale where old forks and teapots are sold alongside family heirlooms. The antiques bazaar on Avyssinias St. is particularly lively. *(Open M, W and Sa-Su 8am-8pm.)* **Varnakios,** the biggest outdoor food market in Athens, is on Athinas between Armodiou and Aristogeitonos. *(Open M-Th 6am-7pm, F-Sa 5am-8pm.)* Not for the faint of heart, the meat market, which closes at 3pm, overwhelms with the sights and smells of livers, kidneys, and skinned rabbits. Early risers can jostle with Athenian cooks for choice meats, fish, fruits, vegetables, breads, and cheeses. Roving **farmers' markets,** or *laikes,* pervade central Athens, stopping every morning to take over a *stenodthromos* (narrow street) in one particular neighborhood of the city. Other than following a trail of corn shucks and peanut shells, the best way to track them is to call the Athens office of **Laikes Agores,** Zoödochou Pigis 2-4 *(☎21038 07 560; www.laikesagores.gr).*

🏛 MUSEUMS

▨**NATIONAL ARCHAEOLOGICAL MUSEUM.** The National Archaeological Museum's collection consists almost exclusively of masterpieces. Countless spectacular objects trace the development of Greek art through its many periods.

ATHENS AND ENVIRONS

Heinrich Schliemann's golden **Mask of Agamemnon** shines brilliantly, though it actually belonged to a king who lived at least 300 years before the mythic Mycenaean leader. A female **Cycladic statue** stands as not only the most intact but the largest such sculpture to survive, topping 1.5m. Abundant *kouroi* (young male figurines that constitute the primary subject of archaic Greek art) from the 8th century BC onward lead toward the Classical bronze spear-thrower who represents either Poseidon or Zeus. In the museum's lovely basement garden, mosaics and more sculptures line a cafe. *(Patission 44. Walk 20min. from Pl. Syndagma down Stadiou to Aiolou. Turn right onto Patission; or, take trolley #2, 4, 5, 9, 11, 15, or 18 from the uphill side of Syndagma or trolley #3 or 13 from the north side of Vas. Sofias. From ⓂVictoria, walk straight to the 1st street, 28 Oktovriou; turn right and walk 5 blocks. ☎ 21082 17 717. Open Apr.-Oct. Tu-Su 8:30am-3pm; Nov.-Mar. M 10:30am-5pm, Tu-Su 8:30am-3pm. €7, students and EU seniors €3, EU students and under 19 free.)*

▓BENAKI MUSEUM. Over the course of his travels, philanthropist Antonis Benakis assembled a formidable collection of artwork and artifacts. He donated everything to the state in 1926, along with his former home—a looming, white Neoclassical structure that is something of a masterpiece itself—where his and other artifacts are on display. Among the media represented are Neolithic, Classical, and Roman Period sculpture, Geometric pottery, and an extensive collection of artifacts from the Byzantine and Ottomon periods, including intricate costumes and wonderfully recreated Byzantine period rooms. The museum also exhibits metalwork, jewelry, and paintings, which focus primarily on the Greek War of Independence. Check out the impressive and extensive gift shop before you leave. *(Koumbari 1 at Vas. Sofias in Kolonaki. ☎ 21036 71 000; www. benaki.gr. Open M, W, F-Sa 9am-5pm; Th 9am-midnight; Su 9am-3pm. €6; seniors and adults with children €3; students with ISIC or university ID free. Temporary exhibitions €3.)*

▓BENAKI MUSEUM OF ISLAMIC ART. Opened in 2005 to showcase the Benaki Museum's collection of Islamic art, this immaculate building stands out from its crumbling surroundings. Organized chronologically, the museum documents the history of the Islamic world from the 12th to the 18th centuries through displays of brilliantly colored, well-preserved tiles, metalwork, and tapestries. The exhibit includes many examples of pottery and text with elegant Kufic inscriptions, as well as a marble reception room transported from a 17th-century Cairo mansion. The basement exhibits ruins as exciting as they are out of place: during the construction of the museum, builders discovered parts of the famed **Themistoclean Wall,** which the Greeks built in 478 BC to defend against Persian invaders. And be sure to check out the roof deck and cafe, with an incredible view of the nearby Ancient Agora and the Keramikos necropolis. *(Ag. Asomaton 22 on Dipylou, in Psiri near ⓂThissiou. ☎ 21032 51 311; www.benaki.gr. Open Tu and Th-Su 9am-3pm, W 9am-9pm. €5, students and seniors €3, W free.)*

▓NUMISMATIC MUSEUM If you can't figure out how many *akche* it took buy a goat in the Ottoman empire, this fascinating museum is the place to visit: it tells the story of Greece, from ancient to modern times, through its coins. Its extensive collection of currency, plus seals and stamps, molds and metals, has been housed in the handsome home of Heinrich Schlieman, the "father of Mycenaean archeology" and numismatic enthusiast, since 1983. On your way out, stop for an *espresso fredo* at the shaded garden cafe in the museum's courtyard. *(Panepistimiou (El. Venizelou) 12. From ⓂSyntagma, turn left onto Amalias, which becomes Panepistimious once it passes Vas. Sofias; look for it on the right. ☎ 21036 12 519; www.nma.gr. Open Tu-Su 8:30am-3pm. "Coins of the Ancient World" program for groups of up to 25 children aged 9-18 with chaperone; 1½hr.; call ☎ 21036 12 519 to arrange. €3; students €2. Free audio tour. Cash only.)*

TOP TEN LIST

TOP TEN SIGNS YOU'VE BEEN IN GREECE FOR A WHILE

While backpacking around Greece and mingling with locals, you're sure to absorb some native behaviors. Here are some telltale signs that it's all Greek to you—and you get it.

1. You find yourself considering traffic signs to be mere "caution advisories."
2. Every time you meet an old woman you expect her to offer you a room to rent.
3. You find yourself calling every food store, no matter how diminutive or limited its offerings, a supermarket.
4. You've taken to calling both friends and hated enemies *"malaka."*
5. You believe that the olive (and its by-products) is a key ingredient to healthy living, rather than an optional salad/martini additive.
6. You refer to the time period since 1600 as "recent times."
7. You refuse to call Istanbul anything but "Constantinoupoli."
8. You think that the food pyramid must be some sort of conical meat dish composed of souvlaki.
9. You've started taking sides in regard to the Peloponnesian War of the 5th century BC.
10. You've resolved to name your first-born child Panos.

POPULAR MUSICAL INSTRUMENTS MUSEUM. This interactive museum is no place for silent contemplation. Audio headsets reproduce the music of the *kementzes* (bottle-shaped lyres) and *tsambouras* (goat-skin bagpipes) on display. Exhibits showcase antique instruments from the 18th, 19th, and 20th centuries. *(Diogenous 1-2 in Plaka. Going uphill on Pelopida, it's the door on your left just after you pass the Roman Agora. ☎21032 50 198. Open Tu and Th-Su 10am-2pm, W noon-6pm. Free.)*

BYZANTINE AND CHRISTIAN MUSEUM. Within its newly renovated glass and marble interior, this well-organized museum documents the day-to-day, religious, and political aspects of life under the Byzantine Empire. Its collection of metalware, mosaics, sculpture, and painted icons presents Christianity in its earliest stages. Example-oriented exhibits explain the area's conversion from a polytheistic to a monotheistic society, including a display describing the conversion of the Parthenon into the **Church of Agia Sofia.** Videos and photographs of the artifacts' original locations put them in context. *(Vas. Sofias 22. ☎210 7211 027; www.byzantinemuseum.gr. Open Tu-Su 8:30am-3pm. €4; non-EU students and seniors €2; EU students, under 18, disabled persons, families with 3 or more children, military, and classicists free.)*

GOULANDRIS MUSEUM OF CYCLADIC AND ANCIENT GREEK ART. This museum's main building houses an extensive collection of artifacts from the Cyclades islands, as well as from Cyprus and the ancient mainland, ranging from 3000 BC to AD 300, while the recently annexed mansion next door holds temporary exhibitions. The celebrated marble Cycladic figurines, one of them almost life-size, are prized possessions, and the top floor is an immersive exhibition on life in Ancient Greece. On your way in between the two buildings, stop for tea at the charming courtyard cafe. *(Neophytou Douka 4. Walk 10-15min. toward Kolonaki from Syndagma on Vas. Sofias; turn left on Neophytou Douka. Handicapped accessible entrance at the main building. ☎21072 28 321. Open M and W-F 10am-4pm, Su 10am-3pm. Admission M €3.50, Tu-Su €7; seniors €3.50, ages 19-26 €2.50, under 18 and archaeologists and archaeology students with university pass free.)*

NATIONAL GALLERY. The Gallery, also known as the "Alexander Soutzos Museum," traces Greek artists' experiments with Orientalism, Impressionism, Symbolism, Cubism, and more, from the 18th to the 21st centuries. Greece's War of Independence is memorialized in the ground floor's 19th-century portraits and other images. This floor also houses a handful of older paintings by masters from Italy,

France, the Netherlands, and Spain. The second floor shows more conceptual contemporary works and has space for temporary exhibitions. *(Vas. Konstantinou 50, where Vas. Konstantinou meets Vas. Sofias by the Hilton. ☎ 21072 35 857 or 35 937. Open M and W-Sa 9am-3pm, Su 10am-2pm. €6.50, students and seniors €3, under 12 free.)*

FOLK ART MUSEUM. For a peek at rural Greek culture, visit this collection of traditional costumes, metalwork, ceramics, embroidery, and other art created outside the academy. One room, covered in murals by folk artist Theophilos Chatzimichael, has been transported intact from its original house. *(Kydatheneon 17, in Plaka. ☎ 21032 13 018. Open Tu-Su 10am-2pm. €2; students and EU seniors €1; EU students, children, and Classicists free.)*

JEWISH MUSEUM. This collection documents over two millennia of Jewish life in Greece with letters, costumes, photographs, religious items, and reconstructed spaces arranged around a central staircase. Of special note are the fourth floor, which memorializes the tens of thousands of Greek Jews murdered by the Nazis and the resistance groups who fought to save them, and the fifth floor, which houses a reproduction of an Ottoman Jewish living room, hand-painted by the museum's founder. *(Nikis 39, in Plaka. ☎/fax 21032 25 582; www. jewishmuseum.gr. Open M-F 9am-2:30pm, Su 10am-2pm. €5, students and seniors €3.)*

▓ NIGHTLIFE

Many already exciting neighborhoods burst with life after dark. Quiet cafes become festive bars, restaurants vibrate with chatter and live music, outdoor theaters unlock their doors, people swarm around brilliantly illuminated ruins, and late-night club-goers get the parties started. Athens offers an abundant array of unique entertainment, ranging from movie screenings in the National Gardens to live performances at the **Odeon of Herod Atticus** (☎21092 82 900). The English-language monthly magazine *Inside Out* offers valuable information on events and festivals in Athens.

PLAKA

Locals avoid joining Acropolis-bound tourists during the day, but they flock to ancient sights at night. Enormous outdoor lights make most of the city's famous ruins visible from any modest hill. Before hitting the inviting bars below, join young Athenians wandering about the Odeon theater, hanging out in the Acropolis, or playing guitar and sharing beers on Saint Paul's Rock. You might catch the views from one of Athens's several outdoor rooftop movie theaters. **Cine Paris,** Kydatheneon 22 (☎21032 25 482), plays Hollywood films with Greek subtitles and sells movie posters. (Shows 8:45 and 11:10pm. Tickets €8.)

> **Brettos,** Kydatheneon 41 (☎21032 32 110). Serves its own ouzos (€3-4) straight from the barrel. Offers over 90 different varieties of Greek wine. Backlit shelves of colorful glass bottles line the walls from from counter to ceiling, converting Brettos into a cathedral of liquor for its devout clientele. Red wine €2 per glass. Ouzo €2.50-€19 per bottle. Open daily 10am-midnight. Cash only.

MONASTIRAKI AND PSIRI

The district's two neighborhoods follow opposite clocks. Just when the frenetic market roads of Monastiraki shut down for the day and silence finally reigns, the bar-heavy streets of Psiri awaken to prove their reputation as some of Athens's hippest and loudest. Many of Psiri's pounding nightclubs have closed in the last couple of years, but there is still plenty of spirit to be found in the neighborhood.

■ **Psira,** Miaouli 19 (☎21032 44046), half a block from Pl. Iroön. On a street full of relaxed and funky pubs, Psira is the most relaxed and funkiest. Its tiny interior is wall-papered with images of the South Seas and hung with photos of James Dean and lots of tinsel. There's room for all on the sidewalk outside. Beer €4. Mixed drinks €6. Open daily noon-4am or later. Cash only.

Atitaso, Miaouli 18 (☎21032 12 624), just across from Psira, A relaxed and funky pub of a different stripe. This one pumps rock music into the street, and has a subdued vibe that'll make you want to linger. Check out the multi-colored lanterns and Christmas lights over the bar. Beer €4. Mixed drinks €6. Open daily 2pm-4am. Cash only.

& Style, Ag. Anargyron 12. Your basic neighborhood bar, complete with intimate wooden tables and plenty of floor space to mix and mingle. Mixed drinks €8. Open daily 2pm-2am. Cash only.

Revekka, Miaouli 22 (☎21032 11 174), in Pl. Iroön, in the center of Psiri. This 2-fl. eclectic cafe-bar blossoms at night, when its dozens of sidewalk tables fill with happy patrons. Beer €2. Open daily 11am-3am.

EXARHIA

As the sun goes down on Exarhia, bars spill out into the streets, blasting tunes which range from jazz to death metal. Athens News has lists of movies played at the outdoor **Riviera Garden Art Cinema,** Valtetsiou 46, which has its own accompanying bar (€8, students €6).

Wunderbar, Themistokleous 80 (☎21038 18 577), on Pl. Exarhia. A pop oasis in Exar-hia's alternative desert. Late-night revelers lounge under large umbrellas outside, enjoying one of Wunderbar's signature specialty chocolate drinks (€5). Mixed drinks €8. Champagne €9. Open M-Th 9am-3am, F-Su 9am-dawn. Cash only.

Rock Underground, Metaxa 21 (☎21038 22 019). The long-haired and bearded crowd enjoy the immortal pairing of heavy-metal headbanging and backgammon at this smoky, brick-walled hangout. The sign out front mimics the logo of London's Tube system, hinting at the slightly British flavor of this cafe-bar. Th-Su the club becomes **MetalGround,** with live music and plenty of thrash. Beer €2-5. Mixed drinks €6. Open daily 10am-3am. Cash only.

Train Cafe, Em. Benaki 72 (☎21038 44 355). High ceilings, bright walls, and scrumptious apple pie (€5) make this inviting cafe-bar a favorite with the locals. Classic rock, pop, and reggae. Mixed drinks €7. Open daily 10am-2am. Cash only.

KOLONAKI

Milioni and the eastern end of Haritos are the hottest spots for summertime action as long as you're prepared to shell out euro. Performances are staged in **Lycavittos Theater** as part of the Athens Festival, which has hosted acts from the Greek Orchestra to Pavarotti to the Talking Heads. In summer, open-air **Dexameni "CineFrame"** cinema, in the center of Pl. Dexameni at the foot of Mt. Lycavittos, plays Greek and American movies with surround sound. (☎21036 02 363. Shows daily 8:45 and 11pm. €7, students €5, children under 5 free.) Athinaia "Refresh" cinemas, Haritos 50, is another nearby movie theater. (☎21072 15 717. Shows 9pm and 11pm. €6.50.) At **City, Azul, Baila,** and **Le Souk,** all at Haritos 43, patrons drink beer (€5-6) and mixed drinks (€8-10) on tables that spill into the pedestrian-only street. You'll find another pocket of chic lounges slightly above Pl. Kolonaki, on **Skoufa** between Omirou and Lykavittou.

Flower, Dorylaou 2 (☎21064 32 111), in Pl. Mavili. An intimate little dive, Flower offers drinks and snacks in a casual, mellow setting. Additional seating outside in the square. Shots €4. Mixed drinks €7. Open daily 7pm-late. Cash only.

The Daily, Xenokratous 47 (☎21072 23 430), under a trellis at the foot of Mt. Lycavittos. TVs show sports games at this cozy cafe-bar. Open-air seating in summer. Pints of Heineken €4, ½L €6. Mixed drinks €6-10. Open daily 8am-2am. Cash only.

Cafe 48, Karneadou 48 (☎21072 52 434), 3 blocks down Ploutarchou from Haritos. Take a left on Karneadou and walk to the end of the block. This pink-walled, diner-like cafe-bar plays American music. Beer €3-4. Open daily 7am-midnight. Cash only.

Showroom, Iroklitou 4 (☎2103546460). Has a partnership with the Missoni design studio's home division, so its interior is predictably plush. Come for people-watching and pumping Euro-pop. Cocktails €9-12. Open M-F 8:30am-2am, Sa-Su 8:30am-4am. AmEx/MC/V.

Tribeca, Skoufa 46 (☎21036 23 451). Creative mixed drinks and an innovative DJ set. Cash only.

▶ DAYTRIPS FROM ATHENS

◼CAPE SOUNION PENINSULA Ακρωτήριο Σούνιο

Orange-striped KTEL buses go to Cape Sounion from Athens. 1 leaves from the Mavromateon 14 bus stop (near Areos Park, on Alexandras and 28 Oktovriou-Patission) and stops at all points on the Apollo Coast (2hr., every hr. 6:30am-6pm, €5). The other follows a less scenic inland route that also stops at the port of Lavrio (2hr., every hr. 6am-6pm, €4). The last coastal bus leaves Sounion at 9pm, the last inland at 9:30pm.

A tiny tourist colony rests atop the sharp cliff of Cape Sounion, where in 600 BC ancient Greeks built the enormous ◼**Temple of Poseidon** in gleaming white marble. Legend holds that King Aegeus of Athens leapt to his death from these cliffs when he saw his son Theseus's ship sporting a black sail, a sign of his son's demise. Unfortunately for Aegeus, Theseus was on board getting drunk with his sailing buddies and had forgotten to raise the victorious sail. Today, visitors flock to the area to see the 16 Doric temples that remain from Pericles's reconstruction in 440 BC. Hundreds of names are scribbled into the monumental structure; look closely for Lord Byron's on the square column as you face away from the cafeteria. Across the street 500m below is the somewhat deteriorated **Temple of Athena Sounias.** (Both temples ☎39 363. Open daily from 10am to sunset except on Christmas, Easter, and May 1. €4; students and seniors over 65 €2; EU students, and under 18 free. Nov.-Mar. Su free.)

The cape has a handful of attractive **beaches** and hotels down the inland side of the temple. Teeming with vacationing families, the beaches along the Apollo Coast between Piraeus and Cape Sounion have a carnival atmosphere on summer weekends. Towns often have free public beaches and, despite the area's crowds, some seaside stretches along the bus route remain uncrowded. Drivers will let you off almost anywhere if you ask. If you stay here, **Camping Bacchus ❶**, 50m toward Lavrio from Saron, is a decent option. Ask to stay by the entrance to avoid loud family caravans. The site has a bar, restaurant, laundry, and mini-mart. (☎22920 39 572. €7.50 per person; €6.50 per tent. Tent rental €10.) Next to the bus station, **Cafe Naos ❶** more than compensates for its unspectacular food with one of the best views in Attica. While eating, diners can gaze at the temple and over the Aegean. (Salami sandwich €2.80. Open daily 9am-after sunset.)

MOUNT PARNITHA Πάρνηθα

Bus #714 (Sa-Su 6:30am, 2:30pm; €0.65) leaves from Acharnon off Stounari, in a parking lot near Pl. Vathis. It's best to buy a ticket at a metro station or kiosk in advance; few places in the vicinity sell them, especially in the morning.

When the bus lets you off at the majestic peak of Mt. Parnitha, about 1hr. outside Athens, you will see, of all things, the tastelessly glitzy **Mont Parnes casino** (☎21024 69 111; open daily at 9am) and the cable car (every 30min.

ATHENS AND ENVIRONS

8:30am-3pm, every 10min. after 3pm; €1.20) that takes you there. Luckily, this decidedly unnatural wonder is a lone intrusion, and there is still a vast national park to explore. Its many trails feel a world away from the city, though few are far from public transportation and well-equipped rest stops. The **19th Parnitha station,** a few meters from Hotel-Chalet Kyklaminia and the Tradia Chapel, is a good place for hikers to begin; several trails start behind the kiosk. At the fork in the road toward Athens, a map with Greek labels marks paths uphill away from Mont Parnes. Hikes of varying levels of difficulty will lead you along paved roads, gravel paths, and narrow trails to **Skipiza Spring,** the **Caves of Pan,** and **Bafi Refuge ❶,** a hostel and cafeteria with a beautiful lookout point and detailed trail maps. (☎21021 69 050. Beds €12.) To reach Bafi, turn uphill away from the casino at the fork in the road 0.5km below the casino. Follow signs to the white gravel path until trails diverge at a quarry-like ravine. From there, follow red markings past a small patch of steep rock after about 15min. and continue for another 10min. It's a fairly easy **hike** of about 3km. The bugs are particularly audacious, so insect repellent is necessary.

GLYFADA AND THE COAST Γλυφάδα

Buses A2, A3, and B2 leave from Vas. Amalias and travel along the coastline on Poseidonos (30-40min., €0.80). The spotless, air-conditioned tram (€1) leaves from the same spot every 8min. until midnight and is uninterrupted by traffic. Take the #5 from Syntagma, and the #3 to go up and down the coast.

From Faliro to Sounion, the towns along the Saronic Gulf coast have become synonymous with swanky clubs and crowded beaches. Glyfada Town is the commercial hub, densely packed with shopping malls and aggressively chic cafes. Both **tram** and bus hug the sea as they head from Athens to Glyfada, so you can scope out the beaches just beyond the stops named after them. The closest—**Edem, Batis,** and **Kalamaki**—are less than pristine, but they charge no admission. Kalamaki in particular is known for its loud music and drunken, dancing masses. For a slightly quieter but still well-attended shore, head to Batis, or follow the crowds of suburban teenagers to Zefyros further south. Beyond Platas Glyfadas toward suburbs **Vouliagmeni** and **Varkiza,** beaches are cleaner and more secluded. Entrance fees of €5-10 often include use of pools and bungalows.

On the Third Marina (toward the beach from tram stop Paleo Demarhio, follow the marina around to the right) is a **Sea Turtle Rescue Center,** where visitors can walk around pools that contain injured turtles rescued in Greece. Located inside old train cars, the center is Athens's only turtle hospital. The staff is eager to offer information and readily accepts volunteers. (☎21089 82 600. Open Sa-Su 11am-5pm; M-F for groups by appointment)

If you feel like shopping, hop back on the tram and head into **Glyfada Town,** where most daytime activity is confined to **Lazaraki,** which runs parallel to the seaside streets Diadohou Pavlou and Posidonos Avenue, and **Metaxa,** which arcs above Lazaraki starting at the Platia Katraki tram stop. This is no luxury village—graffiti and dumpsters are common sights—so unless you're planning on buying a new Greek wardrobe, stick to the beach during the day. Don't expect much from Glyfada's dining options—most are designed to wring the most money from shoppers with the least effort. **Zisimopolou** is lined with expensive cafes, such as the palatial **Lis Cafe,** at the corner of Metaxa, and the popular **Marquise,** where the street intersects with Lazaraki. You're better off getting a sandwich and a Greek coffee from one of the smaller cafes wedged between stores on Metaxa, such as **Magnolia ❶** (☎210 8948 522; www.magnoliacafe.gr. Small sandwiches such as ham and cheese €3. Cash only). **Garden of Eden ❷,** Zerva 12, is a block from Hotel Ilion away from the center. Lebanese dishes like *makdous* (baby eggplant stuffed with walnuts and spices; €3.50) and *kas-kas* (meatballs in spicy tomato sauce; €8) are accented by stained-glass windows and hookahs. (Open daily 8:30pm-midnight. MC/V.)

With beach views and hipster crowds, the clubs of Glyfada have earned their hot rep. They tend to be expensive, but cabs of trendy Athenians still flock here nightly. **Balux,** Posidonos 58 in Glyfada (☎21089 41 620), **Mao** (☎21089 44 048; pool open during the day €8), on Diadohou Paulou in Glyfada, and **Akrotiri** (☎21089 59147), on Vas. Georgiou B5 at Ag. Kosmas, are three colorful, beachside options. Also look for **Acanthus** and **Envy.** Cover is usually €10-15, and clubwear is expected (no shorts). Drinks typically range €6-12 but can go as high as €100 for a bottle of vodka and mixers for your table. Envy and Mao are accessible by tram, but the best bet for most clubs is to call a taxi (☎21096 05 600). A cab to Glyfada should cost about €10, but traffic and nighttime charges can make rates swell to €13-17. Ask the price in advance; if your cab is packed with more than just your party, don't be swindled into a set price per individual.

MARATHON Μαραθώνας

The bus from the Mavromateon 29 station in Athens goes to Marathon (1-2hr., every hr. 5:30am-10:30pm, €3.40). Look for the "Marathon" label and remind the driver of your destination (it's a local bus and makes many stops). When returning to Athens, look for an orange-striped bus among scores of tour buses, and flag it down. A car or taxi (☎66 277) is the best way to see the sights; they are spread out and there is often no public transportation.

Near the end of the Persian Wars in 490 BC, an overjoyed messenger ran 42km (26 mi.) from here to bring his fellow Athenians two words: "(N4kh 3min)!" ("Victory to us!"). Though **Phidippides** collapsed and died of fatigue immediately afterward (this last 42km followed a grueling 450km the week before), his feat of endurance has made the town of Marathon's name a household word. In addition to the countless marathon races across the globe, runners today trace Phidippides's famous route twice annually here, where it all started.

Marathon today is a vast plain full of archaeological sites to explore. Get an early start, as most of the museums and visitor centers in the area close at 3pm. Best to bring a car, though if you must take the bus, get off first at **Marathon Town** where you can catch a cab to explore the sites (the bus will stop first at Marathon Beach, where you can catch a glimpse of the cerulean sea, but stay on and come back later). Use Marathon Town as a jumping-off point to explore the area's many ancient sites. With luck you'll find a taxi waiting on **Marathon Avenue**—make friends with your driver, since you'll want to stick with him the whole morning—and set out for **Ramnous,** 15km northeast of the town. Here are the ruins of the **Temple of Nemesis,** goddess of divine retribution, and **Thetis,** goddess of justice. (☎22940 63 477. Open Tu-Su 8:30am-3pm. Tu-Sa €3, Su free.) East of the town are the cave of the demigod **Pan** and the medieval **Tower of Oinoi.** The **Archaeological Museum of Marathonas** is near the settlement of **Vranas,** and though its collection is small it is rich with treasures. As you might expect, the museum highlights the pivotal battle against Persia that occurred here. An atrium displays the Athenian trophy, as well as gifts and slabs from tombs of the 192 Athenians who died in battle. The exhibits also include a collection of Egyptian-style statues, which wear Pharaoh costumes and symbols of control over Lower and Upper Egypt, excavated from the coastal area of Brexiza. Also on the museum grounds is a burial site, uncovered by archaeologist Spyros Marinatos in 1969. A wooden walkway surrounds the spooky mound of rocks, where visitors can peer through glass planks to see the remains of ancient skeletons buried there from 2000-1600 BC. Back toward Marathon Beach is the grassy **Tomb of the Fallen,** where the war victims from 490 BC are buried. (☎22940 55 155. Open

MARATHON MADNESS

Lace up your Nikes for an event that draws thousands to Greece every winter: the Athens Classic Marathon. Circa 490 BC, messenger Phidippides cemented his place in posterity when he highailed it all the way from Marathon to Athens on foot—approximately 42.195 km, or 26¼ mi.—to proclaim the demise of the Persian forces with his last breath. The race, which includes everyone from schoolgirls to senior citizens, starts in Marathon and culminates in Athens' palatial Panathenaic Stadium—the place where the first modern Olympics were held. The stadium, which seats over 60,000, was built during Lykourgos's reign, around 330 BC. It was then thrice restored, most recently by Georgios Averof, who dished out 4 million drachmas in gold to renovate the grand area for the Olympic Games on April 5, 1896.

Fear not, all ye faint of form: if your calves aren't quite up to the arduous 26 mi., you can join the hordes who gather to cheer contestants toward a triumphant finish. The event, held in October or November each year, is open to participants of all ages and fitness levels.

For information on entry fees, the date of this year's race, and online registration, call ☎21093 31 113 or 21093 15 886 or visit www. athensclassicmarathon.gr. Email info@athensclassicmarathon.

Tu-Su 8:30am-3pm. €3; students €2; EU students, children under 18, classicists, and archaeologists free.)

Say goodbye to your taxi and spend the rest of the afternoon and evening at **Marathon Beach,** a delightfully hectic seaside town. If you decide to stay the night, **Marathon Hotel,** Ag. Pantalimonos 25, 50m before the *plateia* on the road coming from Athens, has rooms with air-conditioning, TV, fridge, balcony, and bath. (☎22940 55 222. Breakfast included. Singles €40; doubles €55; triples €65; quads €75. Cash only.) Grab breakfast before you leave, and something sweet for later, from **Papaioannou Bakery,** just across the street at Panteleimonos 36. (☎22940 55 231. Open 6am-7pm. Cash only).

Culinary options include an array of *tavernas* that open right onto the beach. **Taverna Limanaki ❸** is the first to the left of the small *plateia,* and serves plates heaped with grilled and fried seafood. (☎22940 55 306. Fried anchovies €8. Fresh fish €25-60 per kg. Open daily noon-1am.) **O Varhas ❷,** Poseidonos 7, on the beach, is a few doors down to the left of the *plateia* as you face the sea. (☎22940 56 300. Ask for an English menu. Squash fries €4. Marinated small fish €8.50.) If you would rather picnic on the beach, this tiny area has two **supermarkets,** one just before you reach the *plateia* at 3 Ag. Panteleimonas (plastic 1.5L bottle of wine €2.70, watermelon €0.58), and another inland on Dimosthenous (open daily 8:30am-10pm). Once evening rolls around, visit the town's multiplex movie theater, **Village Cool Cinema,** 1-3 Tymbos, off Eleftherias. It plays mainstream English-language films with Greek subtitles nightly at 9 and 11:15pm (☎22940 55 603, tickets €7.) There's also **Way Out** internet cafe and billiards right next door, Dimosthenous 8, which comes highly recommended by Marathon residents (☎22940 55 431, open 8am-late).

AEGINA Αίγινα

Athenians make haste to the whitewashed shores of Aegina, where the big city's bustle is transported on summer weekends. Now best known as a weekend getaway and major pistachio supplier, ancient Aegina was once an important political presence. Relations with the mainland were more strained back then than they are today, as the little island repeatedly betrayed its Athenian neighbor in ancient wars. Aegina first sided against their Hellenic brethren, Sparta, in 491 BC when Xerxes's army laid siege to Athens, kicking off the Persian Wars. Though returning humbly to the Greek side in 480 BC and even winning the praise of the Delphic Oracle for having the swiftest navy on the seas, Aegina turned against Athens in Sparta's 459 BC insurgency against the mainland. Aegina soon sank into geopolitical obscurity, only emerging over 2000 years later, in 1827, as the temporary capital of a partially liberated Greece. Travelers to Aegina will find that its attractions are as rich as its legacy, including gorgeous beaches, wild nightlife, and the well-preserved remains of the Temple of Aphaia, not to mention the endless flood of pistachio-flavored treats.

AEGINA TOWN

☎ **22970**

As soon as your ferry docks in Aegina Town, you'll know that you've entered "the pistachio capital of the world." With preserved, jellied, flavored, red, flaked, shelled, and regular varieties, there are as many ways to eat pistachios here as there are weekend visitors from Athens. Those looking for a carefree beachside romp will do well to stay in town. For a more substantive experience, rent a moped and delve deeper into the forested, church-crowned terrain.

▐ TRANSPORTATION

Ferries: Kiosks on the docks sell tickets to neighboring islands; check the windows for the latest schedules. **ANES** (☎22970 25 635; open 8am-9pm), **Nova** (☎22970 24 200; open 8am-9pm), **Aegean** (☎22970 25 800; open 6:30am-9pm), and **Hellenic Seaways** (☎22970 22 945; open 6am-9pm) cover most destinations. Ferries to **Agistri** (20min., 1-3 per day, €3), **Piraeus** (1hr., at least 11 per day, €8-9), and **Poros** (1hr., 2-3 per day, €8.60) via **Methana** (35min., 2-3 per day, €5.70).

Flying Dolphins: Hellas Flying Dolphins (☎22970 27 462) has a ticket stand on the quay and goes to **Piraeus** (35min., 15 per day, €14). Aegean flying dolphins also go to **Piraeus** (11 per day, €9.80).

Buses: (☎22970 22 787), in Ethnegarcias Park, at the corner of the waterfront; schedules are taped to the kiosk. Buses run to **Agia Marina** via the **Temple of Aphaia** (30min., 9 per day 6:30am-8pm, €1.70), **Perdika** (15min., 9 per day 6:30am-7:30pm, €1) via **Marathonas,** and **Souvalda** (25min., 8 per day 6:30am-8pm, €1.30).

Taxis: The station (☎22970 22 635) is to the left of the quay on the waterfront. €3 to Marathonas.

Moped Rental: €7-20 per day from any of Aegina's many rental agencies.

▐ ✚ ORIENTATION AND PRACTICAL INFORMATION

The central quay is expensive, but *tavernas* and hotels get cheaper toward either end of the waterfront street. Street signs are scarce so navigation can be difficult, but the town is small enough that you'll never be more than a block or so from the waterfront. Running parallel and one block inland, **Pan Irioti** is lined with small shops, markets, *tavernas*, and the occasional moped rental shop. **Aphaias** runs on a tangent curve to Pan Irioti, and both are bisected perpendicularly by **Aiakou,** which takes you back to the waterfront and is home to upscale bars, shops, and the cinema.

Budget Travel: Karagiannis Travel, Kanari 2 (☎22970 25 664), 1 block inland opposite the ticket kiosks. Ask the congenial staff for info about the island, free maps, free luggage storage, flight tickets, and help with accommodations. Cars from €30 per day. Mopeds from €12 per day. Bikes €6 per day. Open daily 8:30am-8pm, later in summer.

Bank: National Bank (☎22970 26 930), to the right of the waterfront quay, past the port police. **Currency exchange** and **24hr. ATM.** Open M-Th 8am-2:30pm and F 8am-2pm. **ATE** and **Emporiki,** also on the waterfront.

Police: Leonardou Lada 11 (☎22970 22 100). **Tourist Police** (☎22970 27 777), in the same building. Open daily 8am-8pm.

Pharmacy: 3 are along Aiakou. 1 is on the corner of Aikou and Spiro Rodi (☎22970 22 404). Open 7:30am-1:30pm, 5-8:30pm.

Medical Center: (☎22970 22 222), 1.5km along the waterfront to the left of the ferries when facing inland. Open 24hr.

Telephones: OTE, Paleas Choras 6 (☎22970 22 399), up Aiakou to the right, near Pension Giakas. Open M-Th 7:30am-1:30pm and F 7:30am-1pm.

Internet Access: e-Global (☎22970 27 819), 1 block inland, across from the basketball courts to the far right of the waterfront past the church. Wi-Fi and dozens of computers. €2.50 per hr. for non-members, €2 per hour for members. Membership €0.50. Open daily 9am-4am. **Avli** (☎22970 26 438), on Aikaou. Restaurant with free Wi-Fi. Open daily 9am-3am.

Post Office: Kanari 6 (☎22970 22 398), in Pl. Ethnegersias, behind the bus station. **Poste Restante** and **Western Union**. Open M-F 7:30am-2pm. **Postal Code:**18010.

ACCOMMODATIONS

It's hard to find a room for under €30, since the island is such a popular destination for Athenian weekenders. Unlike most islands, heading inland does not afford better deals; the cheapest *domatia* can be found on either extreme of the waterfront. Arriving midweek to avoid the weekend Athenian flood will give you some bargaining power.

Pension Giakas, Agios Nikolaos 8 (☎22970 23 072), in the green-doored building behind the inland church. Spacious studios have kitchenette alcoves, baths, A/C, and TVs; ask at Karagiannis Travel for reservations or directions. Singles €25-40; doubles €30-45. Cash only. ❷

Hotel Avra (☎22970 22 303), on the waterfront, near the beach to the far left facing inland. Rooms have A/C, TVs, fridges, new baths, and narrow balconies overlooking narrow streets. Singles €30; doubles €50. Cash only. ❷

Hotel Pavlou, Aeginitou 21 (☎22970 22 795), behind the church on the far right of the quay, facing inland. Classy rooms have A/C, TVs, fans, balconies, fridges, and some dried flowers to spice things up. Some have separate baths. The family also runs the slightly cheaper Hotel Athina a few blocks inland. Singles €30-40; doubles €45-60. Cheaper rates for longer stays. Cash only. ❸

Hotel Plaza, Kazatzaki 4 (☎22970 25 600), at the left end of the waterfront, 2 doors down from Hotel Avra. Nautically-themed hotel with modestly furnished, shell-pink rooms that come with baths, A/C, and fridges. Some have a balconies overlooking the water. Reception 24hr. Singles from €35 without sea view; prices negotiable. Cash only. ❸

FOOD

Tavernas line the right side of the harbor, though it can be hard to distinguish between the authentic and the tourist-centric. For a combination of the two, head to the strip of *ouzeria* at the far left of the harbor, past the bus stop. In general, the farther you stray from the ferry dock, the better the food will be. On Dimokratious, between the church and the bus station, the **aromatic fish market** is worth a visit; you can even see your dinner still flapping in buckets. *Tavernas* around the fish market on **Dimokratious** (to the right when facing inland) are also a good bet.

Taverna Ta Karafakia (☎22970 28 637), 1 block in from the water, near the fish market. Simple, affordable food, with the fish taken from the market next door. Appetizers €3-7. Entrees €5-10. Open daily 10am-11pm. MC/V. ❷

Lekkas, Kazntzaki 14 (☎22970 22 527), on the waterfront just past the bus station. Pick among your home-made favorites. The souvlaki (€7) is served on sand-top tables where your feet can get lapped by the waves. Appetizers €3-5. Entrees €5-7. Open daily 10am-late. Cash only. ❶

Avli (☎22970 26 438). Head up Aikaou and take the 1st left for 2 blocks. In Avli's courtyard, diners can escape the foot traffic while tasting the variety of spaghetti dishes (€4-7) and enjoying the free Wi-Fi. Entrees €4-8. Open daily 9am-3am. Cash only. ❷

Yacht Club Panagakis, Dimokratious 20 (☎22970 26 654). Accessible from both the waterfront and the street behind it. Massive crepes (€4.70-10) come with fillings that range from turkey and mayo to chocolate and walnuts. Open daily 7am-late. MC/V. ❷

SIGHTS AND BEACHES

Aeginian citizens gather for theater, songs, fireworks, and feasting during the yearly **Aegina Festival** in mid-August. At the chlorinated splendor of **Faros Water-park,** 1km to the right of the waterfront, facing inland, you can find a network of pools and slides. (☎22970 22 540. Open daily 10:30am-7:30pm. €3.) The two **beaches** in town are remarkably shallow and fairly warm. The best and most popular is on the far left end of the waterfront, facing inland; the sand isn't amazing, but the clear, temperate water is worth a dip.

TEMPLE OF APOLLO. Aegina Town's archaeological fame teeters on the last half-column of the Temple of Apollo. The 8m Doric column dates to 460 BC and stands on **Kolonna Hill,** ancient Aegina's acropolis. Excavation of the site, home to 10 consecutive early Bronze Age communities, is ongoing. Today Byzan-tine-era cisterns and the foundations of prehistoric homes sit in stony silence alongside the monolithic column. Fortunately, the on-site **archaeological museum** speaks for them, detailing the growth of the town and its fortifications from 2500-1400 BC. Highlights include a magnificent early-Classical ◪**sphinx** (460 BC), artifacts from the Temple of Aphaia, and an extensive collection of Neo-lithic pottery. *(To the far left of the waterfront when facing inland; turn left past the playground.* ☎22970 22 248. *Museum and site open Tu-Su 8:30am-3pm. €3, EU students with ID €2.)*

CHURCH OF FANEROMENI. The underground church of Faneromeni contains a rare icon of the Virgin Mary. Locals say that the night before construction was to begin on a site above Faneromeni, the architect in charge had a vision instructing him to dig instead of build. Doing just that, he unearthed the icon. Call the monastery Moni Kimisis Theotokou to set up an appointment. *(A 15min. walk inland south of the town.* ☎22970 62 000. *Modest dress required. Free.)*

CHURCH OMORFI ELISSIA. The church is accessible by appointment with the archaeology museum and boasts a number of well-preserved frescoes. *(2km out of town.* ☎22970 22 637. *Modest dress required. Free.)*

Aegina

TO PIRAEÜS

Souvala
Vathi
Bathi
Vaia
Livadi
Temple of Apollo
Kipseli
Pallahora
Temple of Aphaia
Ag. Nektarios
Mesagros
Ag. Marina
Faneromeni
Kondos
Aegina Town
Alones
TO PIRAEÜS
Faros
Marathonas
Pahia Rahi
Portes
Aiginitisa
Mount Oros (531m)
Anitseo
Perdika
Sfedari
Moni
Cape Tourlos

TO AGISTRI, POROS (VIA METHANA), HYDRA, SPETSES (VIA POROS)

0   2 miles
0   2 kilometers

🎵 🎬 ENTERTAINMENT AND NIGHTLIFE

Check out open-air **Cinema Anesis,** featuring nightly showings of Greek and American new releases; pick up a schedule at the ticket office a few blocks inland on Aiakou. (☎22970 26 331. Tickets €8. Showings 9 and 11pm.)

Inn on the Beach (☎22970 25 116; www.innonthebeach.gr), past the church on the waterfront. Waves crash up against the blue-lit patio with palm trees and billowy curtains. A chic crowd circulates the bar and private tables, sipping creamy frozen drinks (€10) made from fresh fruit amid the loud dance tracks. Strawberry mojito €9. Open daily 11am-3am. Cash only.

Ellinikon, Toti Chatzi 10 (☎69361 11 213; www.ellinikon.net), 50m down from Inn on the Beach. Aegina's main and oldest dance club is a Gordian knot of writhing limbs and swiveling hips that threatens to spill over the street and into the sea. Mixed drinks €10. W Greek night. Cover €10; includes 1 drink. Open daily midnight-dawn. AmEx/MC/V.

🏛 DAYTRIPS FROM AEGINA TOWN

TEMPLE OF APHAIA. The well-preserved Doric Temple of Aphaia is the main archaeological draw on the island. Legend has it that this is where the nymph **Aphaia,** daughter of Zeus and Karme, was rendered invisible in a narrow escape from King Minos's unwelcome advances. Built in the fifth century BC, her temple still boasts a spectacular set of double-tiered columns that provided inspiration for the Parthenon; more details can be found in the on-site museum. Evening visitors may be joined by peacocks from the surrounding hills. *(10km from Aegina Town, and 2km from Agia Marina on the eastern coast of the island. Take the Agia Marina bus from Aegina Town and ask the driver to stop at the temple, or take the 30min. hike up the steep, gravel shortcut. Daily buses from Aegina Town to Agia Marina stop at the temple. Buses run from Aegina Town to Agia Marina (40min., 9 per day 7am-8:30pm, €1.70); for nearby sites, tell the driver your destination. You can buy bus tickets in Agia Marina at the kiosk in the plateia where the bus lets you off. ☎ 22970 32 398. Museum open Tu-Su 8am-2:15pm. Temple open daily 8am-2:15pm. Museum and temple €4, students €2.)*

AGIOS NEKTARIOS AND PALIOHORA. The compound of the massive, marble and bronze church at Agios Nektarios is the second-largest place of worship in the Balkans. Though unfinished, the church allows visitors to admire the three-tiered interior and glorious gold-foiled wall paintings. In the compound near the church, nuns tend to the different chapels dedicated to saints, and pilgrims light candles in worship.

The turn-off just after Agios Nektarios leads 1km up to Paliohora, the "town of 300 churches" and a former refuge from pirate invasions. Built in 1462, the town was destroyed by the Turkish invaders under Barbossa. It later regaining its glory, only to be abandoned in the 1750s. The only remnants are the 33 churches sprinkled on the hillside. Narrow footpaths interconnect the churches, and many of the small, whitewashed buildings are left open; some churches house icons amid open-roofed rubble. Visit either early in the day or near dusk, because the trek between the churches can get very hot. Bring water—there's nowhere to buy it nearby—and wear comfortable shoes. *(A 15min. bus from Aegina Town; ask to be let off at Agios Nektarios. Modest dress required. Free.)*

ATHENS AND ENVIRONS

KEA Κέα (Τζία)

The lushness of this verdant island is a sharp contrast to the smog of Athens. The island's crowds, which predominantly consist of Greeks who return regularly, come to bask in the well-kept secret that is Kea. Escape the main port to discover the island's preserved beauty. Oak-covered mountains harbor the twisting streets of Ioulida, the island's capital. *Ammouthitses* (little coves) speckle the island's perimeter.

KORISSIA Κορισσία   ☎22880

The island's main port runs along a short waterfront. While Korissia exudes a friendly, relaxed atmosphere, it still provides all the services under the sun.

▐ TRANSPORTATION

Ferries: Depart from Kea for **Lavrio** (1hr.; M-F 3 per day, Sa-Su 5 per day; €6). Ticket office next to the ferry landing and Yiannis Rent a Car.

Catamarans: To **Kithnos** or **Lavrio** (1 per day). **Flying Dolphin ticket office** (☎22880 21 435), directly across from the ferry landing, connected to the Stegathi Bookshop.

Buses: To: **Ioulida** (12min., 5 per day); **Katomeria** (3 per day); **Otzias** beach (3 per day); **Pisses** beach (3 per day); **Vourkari** (7min., 5 per day). All €1.60-3.20. Schedules for times and stops posted at the main stop in front of the landing dock in Korissia. These do not run regularly until mid-June, before which they serve as school buses.

Taxis: (☎69730 12 813, 69373 82 702, or 69773 31 431), line up at the ferry landing; call them individually. €7 to Ioulida; €6 to Vourkari.

Car Rental: Yiannis Rent a Car (☎22880 21 898), on the right before the ticket office, away from the dock. €35-45 per day. AmEx/MC/V.

▌ PRACTICAL INFORMATION

Bank: Alpha Bank (☎22880 22 702), 1 block past the ATM on the left. Open M-Th 8am-2:30pm, F 8am-2pm. **24hr. ATMs** at the Flying Dolphin ticket office (p. 111) and on the corner of the harbor, to the right of the Karthea Hotel.

Laundromat: Tzia Laundromat (☎22880 21 154). Walk from Piraeus Bank along the bay, make a right at the far side of the river, and turn left after 100m. Dry cleaning available. Open M-Sa 8am-1pm and 6-8pm.

Tourist Police: (☎22880 21 100), a few blocks back from the waterfront.

Pharmacy: (☎22880 22 277; fax 69455 47 567), in Ioulida. Open M and W 9am-2pm, Tu and Th-F 9am-2pm and 5:30-8:30pm, Sa 10am-1pm.

Medical Services: Clinic (☎22880 22 200), in Ioulida.

Internet Access: Art Cafe (☎22880 21 181), on the waterfront next to the National Bank ATM. €2 per 30min., less for longer increments.

Postal Code: 84002.

▐▐ ACCOMMODATIONS AND CAMPING

▨ **Palagia Kastriani** (☎22880 24 348). If you're up for an adventure, this monastery, perched high in the hills of Kastriani on Kea's northeastern shore, is the place to stay. It's a €16 cab ride from the port, but the jaw-dropping vistas of rolling hills and rocky cliffs along the way make it well-worth the cost. Dinner included. Doubles €30. Reserve in advance. ❷

Kostis Rooms (☎22880 21 483), on a plot of farmland overlooking the port. Atmosphere and beach proximity make up for unadored rooms with TVs, fridges, and verandas. Min. stay 1 week in summer. Doubles €30-50. ❸

Hotel Karthea (☎22880 21 204) on the corner of the bay. Clean rooms have baths, A/C, and TVs; some have bay views. Breakfast included. Singles €70; doubles €90. ❺

Camping Kea (☎22880 31 302), 50m from Pisses beach; 30min. by bus from Korissia. Mini-market, laundry facilities, and bathrooms. €5.50 per person; €5.50 per tent. ❶

▐ FOOD

Akri (☎22880 21 196; fax 69775 74 957), after the supermarkets by the beachside road. Serves delicious homemade food like *strapatsiata* (tomato, egg, and cheese casserole; €5). Open daily noon-midnight. ❶

Cafe Ezaharoplasteio (☎22880 21 493). Perfect for a milkshake (€3) or ice cream. Also serves breakfast. Open daily 9am-11pm. ❶

PIRAEUS Πειραιάς   ☎21041

Unlike Aegina and Kea, Piraeus and Rafina are not places to spend the night: visitors head here to reach Greece's beloved islands. The natural harbor of Piraeus has been Athens's port since 493 BC, when Themistocles created a naval base for the growing Athenian fleet. A hilly peninsula studded with big apartment buildings, Piraeus is one of the busiest ports in the world. Though its charms may not be immediately apparent to those arriving at the port, Piraeus does have trendy shops, orange trees, and plenty of outdoor park space.

▐ TRANSPORTATION

Ferries: Most ferries circling Greece run from Piraeus. Unfortunately, the ferry schedule changes on a daily basis; the following listings are only approximate. Be flexible with your plans. Check *Athens News* and the back of the *Kathimerini* English edition or stop by a travel agency for updated schedules. Ferries sail directly to nearly all major Greek islands, except for the Sporades and Ionians. Until recently, there were five gates, organized by letter; now, gates are organized by number, all preceded by the prefix "E". Ferries for the Dodecanese leave from gate **E1.** For Chios and Lesvos, ferries depart from gate **E2.** For Crete, go to **E3.** Ferries for the Cyclades leave from gate **E7,** and ferries for the Saronic Gulf leave from **E8.** For Ikaria and Samos, ferries leave from **E9.** International ferries (2 per day, around €30) head to destinations in Turkey. To: Aegina, Amorgos, Anafi, Astypalea, Chios, Donousa, Folegandros, Chania, Crete, Hydra, Ikaria, Ios, Iraklia, Iraklion (Crete), Kalymnos, Kimolos, Kithnos, Kos, Koufonisia, Leros, Lesvos, Limnos, Milos, Mykonos, Naxos, Paros, Patmos, Poros, Rethymno (Crete), Rhodes, Samos, Santorini, Schinousa, Serifos, Sifnos, Sikinos, Spetses, Syros, and Tinos.

Hydrofoils: Leave from the port of Zea and go to: **Aegina** (every hr.); **Amorgos** (1 per week); **Hydra** (6 per day); **Ikaria** (3 per week); **Ios** (6 per week); **Kithnos** (5 per day); **Milos** (1-2 per day); **Mykonos** (2-4 per day); **Naxos** (1-3 per day); **Paros** (1-4 per day); **Poros** (6 per day); **Samos** (2 per week); **Santorini** (daily); **Serifos** (6 per week); **Sifnos** (1-2 per day); **Spetses** (6 per day); **Syros** (2-4 per day); **Tinos** (2-4 per day).

Buses: The **#96** shuttles to and from the airport every 30min. (€3). Pick it up across from Fillipis Tours on Akti Tzelepi. The **#40** goes between Syndagma and Piraeus (every 15min. 5am-12:45am, €0.45).

Metro: To get to Piraeus from Athens by **metro,** take the **M1** (green) line **Kifisia/Piraeus** to the last stop (20min., €0.70). The metro station is on Akti Poseidonos.

🔲 🔃 ORIENTATION AND PRACTICAL INFORMATION

Piraeus can seem chaotic and confusing, but there is method to the madness. A free shuttle takes travelers from the metro to gate **E1** every 15min. The large, busy street running alongside **Akti Miaouli** and **Akti Kondyli** is **Akti Poseidonos.** The hydrofoil port is on the other side of the peninsula, a 10min. walk along any of the streets running inland off Akti Miaouli.

Budget Travel: 🔳**Fillipis Tours,** Akti Tzelepi 3 (☎21041 17 787 or 33 182). From the metro, go left and walk 200m until you come to Pl. Karaiskaki. Walk toward the water; it's on the left side of the cluster of offices, near ferry departure gate E8. This extremely helpful office sells ferry and plane tickets, helps with accommodations, has free **luggage storage,** and **rents cars.** Open daily 5:30am-11pm. Other ticket agencies can be found on Akti Tzelepi and Akti Poseidonos.

Laundromat: Hionati Laundry, Bouboulinas 50 (☎21042 97 356), in Zea. €4 per kg. Open M-F 8am-2pm and 5-9pm, Sa 8am-3pm.

Emergency: Call the **Athens police** at ☎100 or an **ambulance** at ☎166. The **port police** (☎21042 26 000) are on Akti Tzelepi in the mirrored building. **Zea** has separate port police (☎21045 93 144) on the water. The **tourist police** can be reached at ☎171.

Internet Access: LaserNet (☎21041 29 905), in Pl. Kenari on Port Zea. A large dim room with a bar brimming with cyber junkies. €1 per hr. Open 24hr.

Post Office: The main branch (☎21041 71 5184) is on Tsamadou, a few blocks from Polytechniou. Open M-F 7:30am-8pm. **Postal Code:** 18501.

🔾 ACCOMMODATIONS

Inexpensive, quality accommodations are much more difficult to find in Piraeus than in Athens.

Pireaus Dream, Notara St. (☎21042 96 160), a few blocks over from the E9 and E10 ferry gates. Stylishly decorated rooms, some of which overlook the bay. Breakfast included. Free Wi-Fi. Singles €55; doubles €65; triples €80. ❹

Hotel Ideal, Notara St. Immaculate rooms with bath, TV, and A/C. Singles €50; doubles €65; triples €70. ❹

Hotel Glaros (☎21042 94 050), just off Akti Miaouli. A less glamorous option than Hotel Ideal for the same price. ❹

Hotel Phidias, Koundouriotou 189 (☎21042 96 160), between Bouboulinas and 2 Merarhias. Spacious rooms with large baths, TV, and A/C. Breakfast €7.50. Singles €50; doubles €60; triples €70; quads €80. MC/V. ❹

🔾 FOOD

Inviting but pricey restaurants line the waterfront around **Microlimano,** the small bay to the south of the main port. **Bakeries** and **breadshops** are a tasty, thrifty, and speedy dining alternative. Several **supermarkets** also are available, including one at 2 Merarhias and Karaiskou. (Open M-F 8am-9pm, Sa 8am-6pm.)

Creta, Ag. Dimitrou (☎21041 24 417). Walk left from the E3 ferry gates; after 200m, turn right at the church. A souvlaki spot still undiscovered by tourists. The beef kebab (€7) and the meatless gyros (€2.50) are among the best choices. Open daily 10am-3am. ❷

Jimmy and the Fish, Akti Koumoundorou 46 (☎21041 24 417). Head here if you're looking to splurge. Mussels with tomato sauce and parmesan €13. Saffron risotto with porcini mushrooms €19. Strawberry soup with ice cream €7. Open daily 12:30pm-1am. AmEx/MC/V. ❹

READY. SET.

LET'S GO

www.letsgo.com

THE STUDENT TRAVEL GUIDE

👁 SIGHTS

ARCHAEOLOGICAL MUSEUM. This museum's prized possession is the second floor's *Piraeus Apollo*, a hulking hollow bronze figure with outstretched arms. An enormous grave monument consisting of three statues—the deceased, his father, and his slave—dated to about 330 BC, is across the hall as you walk in. Found on the Black Sea coast, the monument once was painted in full color. Three other bronze statues of Athena and Artemis were found near the port in 1959; they had been shelved in a storeroom for safekeeping when Sulla besieged Piraeus in 86 BC. The strange spots of color in their eyes are precious stones. *(H. Trikoupi 31. ☎ 210 4521 598. Open Tu-Su 8:30am-3pm. €4, students €2, under 16 free.)*

HELLENIC MARITIME MUSUEM. This museum traces naval history using detailed ship models. Inside its main entrance, the building includes part of the 5th-century Themistoclean wall, which protected the three ancient ports of Kantharos, Munychia, and Zea. Of particular note is a model of an Athenian trireme used in the Persian Wars; it is on display in Room B. The courtyard holds torpedo tubes, naval weapons, and part of a WWII submarine. *(At Zea; follow the ramp to the dock at Akti Themistokleous and Botassi. ☎ 210 4516 264. Open Tu-Sa 9am-2pm. €3, children and students €1.50.).*

RAFINA Ραφήνα ☎22940

Attica's second-most prominent port, Rafina is a smaller, quieter version of Piraeus. Though ferry service from Rafina is not as frequent as service from Piraeus, it is increasing and prices can be as much as 10% cheaper. Compared to its larger counterpart, there's less to do in Rafina, but it's easier on the eyes, ears, and lungs.

🚍 TRANSPORTATION

Ferries, Hydrofoils, and Catamarans: From Rafina to: **Andros** (2hr., 5-6 per day, €10.50); **Marmari, Evia** (50min., 5-8 per day, €9); **Mykonos** (5hr., 4-6 per day, €16); **Paros** (1-2 per day, €21); **Syros** (2 per week, €14.10); **Tinos** (4hr., 5-6 per day, €15.50). Flying Dolphins zip daily to: **Mykonos** (1hr., €30); **Paros** (€34); **Syros** (€23.40); **Tinos** (€27). The **port authority** (☎22940 22 300) supplies info on ferry times, which fluctuate weekly and even daily, especially during high season. Along the waterfront, **Blue Star Ferries** (☎22940 23 561), **Rafina Tours** (☎22940 22 700), and **Hellas Flying Dolphins**(☎22940 22 292) sell tickets. All open daily 6am-9pm.

Taxis: (☎22940 23 101), in front of the *plateia.*

ℹ PRACTICAL INFORMATION

Bank: Alpha Bank (☎22940 24 159), on the left once you reach the end of the *plateia.* **24hr. ATM.** Open M-Th 8am-2:30pm, F 8am-2pm. **Commercial Bank** (☎22940 25 184), next to Alpha Bank. **24hr. ATM.** Open M-Th 8am-2:30pm, F 8am-2pm. 24hr. ATMs. Additional **ATMs** are clustered across from Hotel Avra near the waterfront.

Police: ☎22940 22 100. **Port police:** ☎22940 28 888.

Pharmacy: (☎22940 23 456), just off Vas. Georgiou, which forms the right border of the *plateia.* Open M-F 8:30am-2pm, Tu and Th-F 8:30am-2pm and 5:30-9pm.

Medical Services: For a doctor, call ☎22940 22 633 or 28 428. In a medical emergency, dial ☎166.

Post Office: (☎22940 25 182), on El. Venizelou. Follow the inland road hugging the marina 1 street beyond Vas. Georgiou. Look for the OTE shop on your right on the inland end of the *plateia,* beside the church. Open M-F 7:30am-3pm. **Postal Code:** 19009.

Internet Access: Lanarena, Kiprou (☎22940 26 692). €1.50 per hr., min. €1. Open daily 9am-3am.

ACCOMMODATIONS

Avra Hotel (☎22940 22 780), at the top of the curving street surrounding the marina, Akti Andrea Pandreou, on the left. The largest of the hotels around the *plateia*, with the luxury to back it up. Features a restaurant and a bar, large meeting and banquet rooms, and satellite TV in each room. Breakfast included. Internet access. Book 1 week in advance. Singles, doubles, and triples €85-140. AmEx/MC/V. ❺

Hotel Akti (☎22940 29 370), across the street from the Avra Hotel. Reasonably-sized doubles and triples are much less expensive than those at nearby Avra Hotel, but you sacrifice the beachfront view. Restaurant and bar, plus roof bar. Singles €55; doubles €65; triples €85. ❹

FOOD

The **mini-mart,** on Kiprou, sells fruits, vegetables, and toiletries. (Open daily 8am-2pm and 5-10pm.)

Pallinis (☎22940 23 356), at the end of the marina. Selection of fried seafood and excellent service. Hake with garlic €8. Open daily 11am-midnight. ❷

Eon Grill House (☎21060 38 164), at the end of the marina. Pork souvlaki €7 eat in, €1.80 for take out. ❶

CENTRAL GREECE

Situated at the crossroads of the country, the expansive region of Central Greece is rugged and authentic, offering lush mountains and rural charm that are not to be missed. Stretching from the foothills of Mount Olympus in the north to the peaceful seaside villages that dot the shore of the Gulf of Corinth, Central Greece's Alpine summits give way to lively cities that make this region as diverse as it is charming. Walk the monasteries teetering on the cliffs of Meteora; they have to be seen to be believed. Visit the ruins of the renowned oracle at Delphi or kick back at the perfectly preserved small town of Metsovo. The idyllic Makrynitsa in the Mt. Pelion peninsula is the perfect vantage-point for seeing the twinkling lights of the popular seaside getaway of Volos.

HIGHLIGHTS OF CENTRAL GREECE

HANG in suspense at the mid-air monasteries of **Meteora** (p. 148).

FIND your way by consulting the oracle at **Delphi** (p. 117).

TAKE A BREAK from your break at the popular seaside getaway of **Volos** (p. 136).

STEREA ELLADA Στερεά Ελλάδα

For centuries, advice-seeking pilgrims from across the ancient world gravitated to Sterea Ellada to inquire at the Oracle of Delphi. Many years later, 10th-century Orthodox saint Osios Loukas built a Byzantine monastery nearby, which ailing believers continue to visit today in search of a sacred cure. For more action-oriented visitors, the small mountain villages offer thrilling ski slopes, the western coast is covered in deep forest, and the monumental ruins shed light on tales of history. As it has over the course of history, Sterea Ellada caters to both the minds and the bodies of those that traverse its mountain paths and seaside villages.

DELPHI Δελφοί   ☎ 22650

The sign along the road that marks the entrance to Delphi proclaims, "Every intellectual human being of free will deserves to be regarded as a citizen of the town of Delphi." Locals take this mentality to heart as they host the countless travelers who come to marvel at Delphi's wonders. This town of 2500 was once so significant that Greeks felt it was the *omphalos* (navel) of the earth. The age of the Olympian gods started here, when Apollo defeated Gaia's son; soon after Zeus released two eagles, one toward the east and one toward the west. They collided directly over Delphi—a sacred stone still marks the spot. Ever since pilgrims from far and wide have flocked here to the oracle, seeking the cryptic guidance of Apollo's priestess. Although an earthquake in the

Central Greece

AD seventh century caused significant damage to the town, Delphi remains a place of pilgrimage for tourists, and the entire city is built around it. Hotels are ubiquitous, as are overpriced restaurants and trinket shops. Despite the crowds of tourists, the ancient site and the stunning panoramic views make it a memorable visit.

◳ TRANSPORTATION

Buses: Station (☎22650 82 317), on Pavlou, on the western end of town, Open daily 8am-10:10pm. To: **Amphissa** (30min., 8 per day 6:30am-10.15pm, €2.40); **Athens** (3hr.; M-Sa 6 per day 5:30am-6pm, Su 7 per day 5:30am-9pm; €13.60) via **Arahova** (20min. €1.40) and **Livadia** (50min., €3.80); **Itea** (30min., 7 per day 6:30am-10:15pm, €1.70); **Lamia** (2hr., 5 per day 10am-6pm, €8.40); **Nafpaktos** (2hr.; M-Sa 4 per day 10:15am-8:15pm, Su 3 per day 3:45pm-10:15am; €9.70) via **Galaxidi** (1hr., €3.20); **Patra** (3hr.; M-Th and Sa 1:15pm, F-Su 1:15 and 3:45pm; €12.10); **Thessaloniki** (5hr.; M-Th and Sa 10:15am, F and Su 3:15pm; €31.40) via **Katerini** (€26), **Larisa** (€19.60), and **Velestino** (€16.10).

Taxis: (☎22650 82 000). Wait on the eastern end of Pavlou, toward the archaeological site outside Cafe Delfikon.

✦ 🛈 ORIENTATION AND PRACTICAL INFORMATION

Delphi's main street, **Friderikis-Pavlou** (referred to as "Pavlou"), runs east-west through town. At the western end is the bus station. Facing the city from the bus station, **Apollonas** snakes uphill to the left, and Pavlou veers to the right. The oracle and museum are on Pavlou at the eastern end, a few hundred meters past the town, toward Athens.

Tourist Office: Pavlou 12 (☎22650 82 900), in the town hall. From Pavlou, head toward Athens; the office is up a flight of stairs on your left, in a stucco courtyard. The friendly English-speaking staff can assist with buses and accommodations or provide maps, information, and guidebooks. Open M-F 8am-2:30pm. If the office is closed, the bus station can help you out.

Bank: National Bank, Pavlou 16 (☎22650 82 791). **24hr. ATM.** Open M-Th 8am-2:30pm, F 8am-2pm.

Police: Sygrou 3 (☎22650 82 222), directly behind the church that sits at the peak of Apollonas.

Medical Services: There is no hospital, but if you need a doctor you can call the **Medical Center** (☎22650 82 307).

Telephones: OTE, Pavlou 10, past the steps to the information office. Open M-Sa 7:30am-3:10pm, Su 9am-2pm.

Internet Access: The cafe (☎22650 82 321) on the ground level of Hotel Parnassos, on Pavlou, across from the Down Town Club, has internet and Wi-Fi (€4 per hr). Open daily 7:30am-midnight. **Cafe Delfikon,** Pavlou (☎22650 83 212), past Hotel Sibylla. €3 per hr. Open daily 7:30am-1am.

Post office: Pavlou 28 (☎22650 82 376). **Poste Restante.** Open M-F 7:30am-2pm. **Postal Code:** 33054.

🏠 🏕 ACCOMMODATIONS AND CAMPING

Almost every other building in Delphi is a hotel, but budget accommodations are still hard to come by. The stiff competition makes proprietors open to negotiation, so try your luck at bargaining. The tourist office has a comprehensive list of hotels by price range.

Hotel Artemis, Pavlou 60 (☎22650 82 294; www.panartemis.gr), 100m from the bus station. Hospitable owner Ioannis Lefas rents spotless tiled rooms with A/C, TVs, and baths. Breakfast included. Singles €35; doubles €45; triples €60; 5-person room €95-105. 10% discount for *Let's Go* readers. MC/V. ❸

Hotel Pan, Pavlou 53 (☎22650 82 294; www.panartemis.gr), 100m from the bus station. Run by the owner of Hotel Artemis. Clean rooms with A/C, TVs, and baths. Breakfast included. Singles €35; doubles €45; triples €60; quints €95-105. 10% discount for *Let's Go* readers. MC/V. ❸

Hotel Sibylla, Pavlou 9 (☎22650 82 335; www.sibylla-hotel.gr). 8 simple rooms with wonderful views of the mountainside. Each room comes with TV, fan, and attractive bath. Attentive owner can help orient you in Delphi, provides restaurant recommendations, and exchanges currency. Singles €26-30; doubles €32-36; triples €40-50. Discount for *Let's Go* readers. Prices vary seasonally. ❷

Hotel Olympic, Pavlou 59 (☎22650 82 793; www.olympic-hotel.gr). Modern and stylish rooms with few amenities. Breakfast €5. Singles €25; doubles €30; triples €40. ❷

Camping Apollon (☎22650 82 762; www.apolloncamping.gr), 1.5km out of town. Buses heading west out of Delphi can drop you off. Swimming pool, laundry (€5 per 5kg), mini-mart, restaurant, and great views. €8 per person; €4 per tent. Tent rental €6. Electricity €4. ❶

📷 FOOD

Delphi's many restaurants cater to tourists and most are highly (read: over-) priced. Prix-fixe menus, however, drop costs and are available at most places.

▨ **Vakchos,** Apollonas 31 (☎22650 83 186), just below the church. The most delicious food in town with views to match. Salads €4-6. Entrees €5-10. Open daily 8-10:30am, noon-4pm, and 6:30-11pm. ❷

▨ **O Dionysis,** Apollonas 28 (☎22650 82 442), just a few doors to the east of Vakchos. A meal for savvy travelers that won't break the bank. The small menu includes classic Greek dishes. Combo meal of souvlaki and Greek salad €6. Gyro €2. Entrees €2-6. Beer €2.50. Open daily 11am-midnight. ❶

Melopoleio, Pavlou 14 (☎22650 83 247), near the town hall. The name, which translates to "honey shop," alludes to the delicious pastries they serve alongside their famous coffee. Coffee €3. Pastries €2-3. Free Wi-Fi. Open daily 7am-midnight. ❶

👁 SIGHTS

THE DELPHIC ORACLE

A sacred site from 1500 BC or earlier, the Oracle of Delphi was the most important source of sacred wisdom in the ancient world from around the seventh century BC until the advent of Orthodox Christianity. When the oracle answered a pilgrim's pressing question, usually with just a few ambiguous words, its authority was accepted almost universally. After all, it was the Delphic oracle that foretold Cadmus's founding of Thebes and prophesied Oedipus's horrific fate. But the oracle held sway over more than religious matters and personal fortune-telling; Delphic approval sanctioned many political decisions, including the reforms that led to democracy in Athens. Hoping to make powerful friends and receive positive forecasts, city-states from all over the Greek world erected treasuries and donated immense sums to the oracle.

The Pythian Games, in which athletes, musicians, and poets were judged by Apollo's golden rule of harmony and balance, were held on the steps every four years from before the fifth century BC to the AD fourth century. Legend says that when the great Greek poet Homer participated in the Pythian Games, he lost because his musicianship could not match his unrivaled poetic talent. From Delphi, head out of town on the road toward Athens and follow the highway to a paved path on the left, which leads to the ruins and museum.

ARCHAEOLOGICAL SITE. The inscription "Know thyself" (γνωθι σεαυτον) has crumbled from the portal of the ancient temple, but it still governs the meditative atmosphere of peaceful, windswept Delphi. Cut into the steep mountainside, the ancient sanctuary reigns over the brush-dotted valley below. The sheer scale of the constructions are compelling enough, but couple that with the diversity of the buildings, and the site more than merits its status as one of Greece's top archaeological sites. Now, as in the past, the **Temple of Apollo** is the centerpiece of the oracle site. A largely wooden incarnation of the temple was burned in 548 BC, was demolished again by an earthquake in 373 BC, and still lies in ruin today. Ancient proclamations etched along the stone base are still visible. To reach the Temple of Apollo, follow the **Sacred Way,** which winds up the site in the footsteps of ancient pilgrims. To the left are the treasuries of supplicant cities, including the reconstructed **Treasury of the Athenians,** excavated in the early 20th century. Past the Temple of Apollo, the theater, a picture of geometric perfection and amazing acoustics, is no less impressive. After one glance at the view, you will understand why performances held here

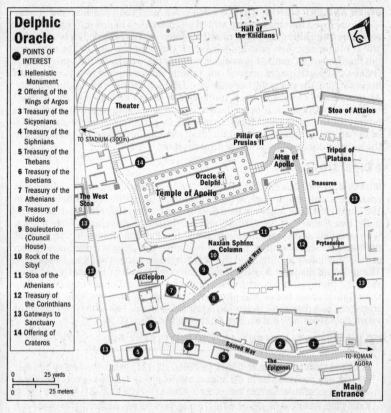

Delphic Oracle

● POINTS OF INTEREST

1 Hellenistic Monument
2 Offering of the Kings of Argos
3 Treasury of the Sicyonians
4 Treasury of the Siphnians
5 Treasury of the Thebans
6 Treasury of the Boetians
7 Treasury of the Athenians
8 Treasury of Knidos
9 Bouleuterion (Council House)
10 Rock of the Sibyl
11 Stoa of the Athenians
12 Treasury of the Corinthians
13 Gateways to Sanctuary
14 Offering of Crateros

Hall of the Knidians
Theater
TO STADIUM (300m)
Stoa of Attalos
The West Stoa
Pillar of Prusias II
Altar of Apollo
Tripod of Plataea
Treasures
Oracle of Delphi
Temple of Apollo
Naxian Sphinx Column
Sacred Way
Prytaneion
Asclepion
Sacred Way
The Epigonoi
TO ROMAN AGORA
Main Entrance

0   25 yards
0   25 meters

never used backdrops. For a glimpse of ancient Delphi as an athletic arena, make your way up the winding trail to the **stadium** at the very top of the hill. The site is most pleasant in the late afternoon, when there are fewer tour groups and cooler weather. The site is staffed by knowledgeable guides who lead the groups from tour buses. They won't mind if you tag along and will be happy to answer your questions, especially if you give them a tip. *(Open daily 8am-8pm. €6, students €3. Site and museum €9/5. Guidebooks and maps (€3-15) are sold at the entrance, but the tourist office in town can provide similar materials for free.)*

■**ARCHAEOLOGY MUSEUM.** The museum, before the ruins on the left as you head out of town, houses artifacts exclusively from the ancient city. The well-organized exhibition has stunning relics far beyond the standard fare of ceramics and pottery. Among the notable collection are the Twins of Argos—the oldest monumental votive offering, the marble frieze of the Siphnian Treasury, the altar from the temple of Athena Pronaia, a Naxian sphinx, the haunting bronze Charioteer of Delphi, and many of the impressive gifts presented as offerings to the oracle. The excavations that yielded these treasures began in 1892 and were completed in 1935 by the Ecole Française d'Athens. *(☎ 22650 82 312. Open M 1:30-8pm, Tu-Su 8am-8pm. €6, students €3. Site and museum €9/5.)*

OTHER ANCIENT SIGHTS. On the main road, past the museum, you'll pass the now-closed **Kastalian Spring,** which pilgrims used in order to clean themselves before calling upon the oracle because it was believed to bestow the gift of eloquence. Just past the spring, on the opposite side of the road, are the remains of an ancient **gymnasium** where athletes trained for the Pythian Games. All participants arrived one month before the competition to train here so that they would become accustomed to the thin mountain air. Another 200m down the road, the **Temple of Athena Pronaia** was the ancient entrance to Delphi and served as a lounge and campground for pilgrims bound for the sanctuary. Three remaining Doric columns of the original 20 of the stunning *tholos*, a round building used for an unknown purpose, are the sole evidence of its architectural mastery.

OTHER SIGHTS

MUSEUM OF THE DELPHIC FESTIVALS. While in Delphi, consider visiting this small, fascinating museum, which chronicles the celebrations held here in 1927 and 1930. The museum is in the former house of Eva Sikelianos (originally Eva Palmer of New York) and her husband Angelos, a Greek poet, who planned and staged recreations of the Pythian Games in the ancient theater and stadium. The productions were the first performances in an archaeological site and paved the way for other venues such as Epidavros. The museum displays a collection of the costumes that Eva designed from studying pictures on ancient vases and wove by hand on a loom, as well as the original sheet music and photographs from the two festivals. *(At the peak of Apollonos, walk uphill to the church. Turn right onto Sygrou, then walk uphill to the museum on the left. Open M and Th-Su 8:30am-3pm. €1, students and groups €0.35.)*

🎵 🎭 ENTERTAINMENT AND NIGHTLIFE

European Cultural Center of Delphi (☎22650 82 731). Hosts the Festival of Greek Drama with performances in the ancient theater in July. Also has temporary international art exhibitions. Contact their office in Athens (☎21033 12 781) for more info.

Katoi Club, Pavlou (☎69325 26 578), 75m up from the bus station. Red-lit dance club has moving lights suspended above the dance floor, private tables, and a DJ that plays American and international pop. Beer €5. Mixed drinks €7-10. Open 9:30pm-late.

Down Town Club, Pavlou 33 (☎69465 02 043). Popular among locals. Grab a drink at the bar or take advantage of the large dance floor. Beer €3. Mixed drinks €7. Check the door for special drink deals. Cover €5; includes 1 drink. Open 9:30pm-late.

🥾 HIKING

Delphi is a perfect access point for some of the best hiking in the area; there are several trails with amazing views. At the steps on the eastern end of Apollonos where it meets Pavlou, you will find a posted map of the trails that you can follow up Mt. Parnassos and the surrounding peaks.

Corycian Cave. For those who want a route less-traveled, take a trip to the magnificent Corycian Cave. Buy a trail map in advance, bring plenty of water, and hike with a partner. The cave, at the top of the mountain, was an ancient sanctuary of Pan and the woodland nymphs. Its dusky, enormous interior is a welcome escape from the heat, and the dark interior houses impressive stalagmites. You can have a taxi (20min., €25) drop you off at the trailhead that leads to the Corycian Cave—it is marked by a red triangle blaze—and hike up (30min.), then hike back to Delphi (2½hr.). You can also hike to the caves from Delphi (3hr.) and back down (2½hr.). From Delphi, walk east until you hit the

CENTRAL GREECE

edge of town, marked by a panoramic overlook. Take the stairs to your left until you hit Sikelanios St. at the top, follow it up to the Museum of Delphic Festivals, walking past it on the dirt road. Just before the paved road turns into a dirt road there is an unmarked trail on the hill to your left. Follow it as it climbs uphill and provides amazing panoramic views of the city. After 2hr. you will pass a farmhouse on your left and soon after see a spring. Climb the hill behind the spring to the wide dirt road, leaving the E4 trail. Continue to follow the road (you will see intermittent white signs pointing to "Korikon"). About an hour later you will pass a forest ranger station and a sign pointing to the cave. After 10min. you will see the trailhead to the caves on your left off the road, marked by a red triangle. To hike back down return downhill and take a right on the dirt road. When the road forks after 1km, take a left and head toward the "Delphi Panorama" and "Kroki." Walk for about 2km past fir trees and farmland, staying on the dirt road. When you spot a stone spring a few feet from a sign pointing to Delphi, cut to the spring and resume the E4 dirt trail in front of it.

E4. The E4 trail, an easy day-hike running north-south up the side of the mountain, begins here. Climb the steps up to Sygrou and follow the road to the right, past the Museum of the Delphic Festivals, until it becomes a dirt road. Look for the metal pole and stone beach on the right that marks the continuation of E4 on the hill to your left, and follow the trail markers (red squares and yellow lines). The trail is relatively well-marked at the beginning but be sure to bring a trail map and plan your route in advance to avoid getting lost. The initial hill on the edge of town offers panoramic views of Delphi town and the stadium. From the top of the hill, you can trek to the peak of Eptalofas (800m)—a lengthy 7hr. trek over 18km—where there is a refuge if you plan on staying the night. For a shorter day hike (around 6hr.), hike the Eptalofas trail for 3hr. until you reach a small hilltop that has incredible views of the surrounding countryside and coast. There are blocks of rocks in a wheat field perfect for a picnic lunch.

DAYTRIP FROM DELPHI

OSIOS LOUKAS Όσιος Λουκάς

The lack of bus service from Delphi or Arahova forces visitors to take a car or taxi (☎ 22650 31 566; 25min. each way). When negotiating the price, ask the taxi driver either to wait 1hr. at the monastery (€35) or to return to town and pick you up later (€50). ☎ 22650 22 797. Open daily from May 3 to Sept. 15 8am-2pm and 4-7pm, from Sept. 16 to May 2 8am-5pm. Modest dress required. €3, seniors and students €2, EU students and children free.

Stunning Byzantine architecture, gilt mosaics, vibrant frescoes, and intricate brick and stonework adorn the monastery of Osios Loukas. Built in the 10th and 11th centuries and still in use today, this exquisite complex on the green slopes of Mt. Elikon, over 500m above sea level, overlooks the orchards and vineyards of Boeotia and Phokis. Christian saint Osios Loukas was born in AD 896 in Delphi, a center formerly dedicated to the Olympian gods and polytheistic worship, and became a monk at the age of 14. In 946, Osios Loukas settled at the lush and enchanting site of the monastery that now bears his name, building a cell, a small church, and a garden. Rumors that his church's relic worked miracles brought believers, leading to an expansion of the grounds and the establishment of a monastery. With aid from fellow hermits and money from admirers, Osios Loukas began construction of two larger churches. The first, the **Church of the Panagia** (Church of the Virgin Mary), was finished soon after his death in 953. The larger and more ornate **Katholikon of Osios Loukas,** built in 1011, became the site of his reliquary. The monastery, which is undergoing minor restoration, is scarred from 13th-century Frankish occupation and German bombing during WWII. The complex consists of the two churches, a crypt, and monks' cells.

CENTRAL GREECE

The **Archaeology Museum,** on the right after the arched stone gate, sells guidebooks (€2.50-4) and tickets for entrance into the monastery. The one-room museum, formerly a workplace and refectory, has remnants and carvings from Osios Loukas's architectural past and merits only a glance. The Katholikon of Osios Loukas, past the museum on the right, is the monastery's most impressive area. Built on the Greek cross basilica plan, the church has resplendent mosaics made of stone, enamel, and gold. Frescoes depict scenes from Christianity, including an especially impressive one of Jesus on the upper dome. A small passageway in the Katholikon's northwestern corner, at the front of the sanctuary on the left, links it to the Church of the Panagia. In this passageway is the monastery's most prized relic—the desiccated body of the saint himself, lying in a transparent glass coffin. Pilgrims come to pray at Osios Loukas's velvet-slippered feet, and thousands have said that his tomb cured them of various ailments. Some have been even bolder—Loukas's left hand, protruding from his habit, has lost a few fingers to relic-seekers. The **crypt** is between the museum and the churches, accessible by an entrance in the exterior of the Katholikon. Protected from the elements, its stunning frescoes have retained their original splendor. Past the crypt entrance is a small **courtyard;** walk in and to the left to peek at the luxuries enjoyed by medieval monks. Climbing the tower at the far end of the courtyard yields a beautiful view.

THEBES (THIVA) Θήβα   ☎ 22620

Buried beneath the low-rise apartment buildings and lazy *tavernas* of modern Thebes lies its claim to fame: its history, both illustrious and notorious. History has surfaced—literally—in spots throughout the city, as attempts at construction have revealed the edifices of ancient Thebes. Theban buildings grace the avenues of Cadmus (the city's legendary first king), Oedipus (exiled king and namesake of Freud's complex), and Epaminonda (the general who ended Spartan dominance). Rising to prominence during the height of the Greek city-state, 600-400 BC, Thebes capitalized on its fertile plains and strategic location between Northern Greece and the Peloponnese to become a cultural center and the inspiration for great works by Sophocles, Euripides, and Aeschylus. Alexander the Great's army cut short this prosperity around 335 BC by setting fire to the city, reducing it to rubble; only temples and Pindar's ancestral home were spared. Modern Thebes, a tiny, unremarkable city, doesn't quite live up to its reputation. To be fair, it's not really trying; the city focuses on family and community, encouraging vibrant evenings on the main street. The unique combination of archaeological sites and inviting cafes makes Thebes an interesting daytrip.

⌐ TRANSPORTATION

Buses: Station (☎ 22620 27 512) is below Thebes at Estias 10. Buses to: **Asopia/ Kallithea/Neohoraki** (2:30pm); **Athens** (1½hr., every hr. 6am-6pm, 7:15pm, 8:15pm; €7.20); **Lamia/Laprisa/Katerini/Thes/Niki** (11am); **Mairomati** (8pm); **Panagia/ Neohori** (8pm); **Prodromo/Thisbi/Domraina/Xironomi/Ellopia** (10:30am, 1:55pm, 4pm); **Tanagra/Schimatari** (2:30pm); and **Vagia** (10:30am, 1:55pm, 4pm, 8pm). Regular buses run to **Livadia**(45min., every hr. 7:40am-9:40pm, €3.20) from a stop about 2km out of town; walk all the way down Pindarou past the Archaeological Museum and go down the steps. Take the left fork then the right onto Laiou. Take a left onto St. Athanasiou and follow the blue signs to Livadia to the small bus shelter before the gas station on your right. Buy your ticket on board.

Taxis: (☎ 22620 27 077). Visit Pindarou 45, where they wait in front of the garden 24hr.

⚙️ 🛈 ORIENTATION AND PRACTICAL INFORMATION

Two parallel main streets, **Epaminonda** and **Pindarou**, run from the top of the hill into the valley below. Epaminonda hosts a variety of cafes and shops; Pindarou is lined with small retail stores and businesses. From the bus station, with your back to the terminal and the dirt parking lot on your left, follow the road in front of you to the right and take the first right as it enters the roundabout. Follow Eteokleous up the hill to a *plateia* where first Pindarou and then Epaminonda veer to the right. Turn right onto Epaminonda to find hotels, *tavernas*, and other sights.

Bank: National Bank, Pindarou 94 (☎22620 23 331). **24hr. ATM.** Open M-F 8am-2:30pm. Just uphill on the other side of the street, there is an **Alpha Bank** (open M-Th 8am-2:30pm, F 8am-2pm), along with many others on the downhill end of Pindarou.

Pharmacy: Numerous pharmacies line Epaminonda and Pindarou; there is 1 just downhill from Hotel Meletiou.

Hospital: (☎22620 24 444). Out of town; best reached by taxi (€3-5). The

Telephones: OTE, Vourdouba 20 (☎22620 27 799), between Epaminonda and Pindarou. Open M-F 7:30am-3pm, Sa 9am-2pm.

Internet Access: Central Internet Cafe, Antigonis 39 (☎22620 24 111), in an alcove pushed back from the street; to get there, turn left at the downhill end of Pl. Epaminonda. Internet €2 per hr. Also has bowling, pool tables, foosball, and a bar. Open daily 10am-3am.

Post Office, Drakou 17 (☎22620 27 810), on a side street between Pindarou and Epaminonda. Poste Restante available. Open M-F 7:30am-2pm. **Postal Code:** 32200.

🛏️ ACCOMMODATIONS

Hotel Niovi, Epaminonda 63 (☎22620 29 888; www.hotelniovi.gr). Friendly English-speaking staff and stylish rooms with A/C, TVs, and tiled private baths. Singles €45, with breakfast €48; doubles €50/55; triples €60/70. MC/V. ❸

Hotel Meletiou, Epaminonda 58 (☎22620 27 333), across the street from Hotel Niovi. Could use refurbishing. Rooms with A/C, TVs, fridges, and baths in graceful, spacious surroundings. Breakfast €7. Singles €60; doubles €90; triples €120. Cash only. ❹

Hotel Dionysion, Dimokritou 5 (☎22620 89 253), walk downhill on Epaminonda and turn left.. Luxurious lobby with a bar and cafe, but somewhat claustrophobic rooms. Breakfast included. Wi-Fi. Parking available. Singles €60; doubles €85; triples €110; quads €130. AmEx/MC/V. ❹

🍴 FOOD

By evening, people fill the pedestrian-only sections of Thebes as cafes and *tavernas* move tables into the street. Bakeries, fruit stands, and gyro and souvlaki restaurants provide inexpensive options (€1-3). Most restaurants from Epaminonda to Pindarou offer similar fare at similar prices. If you prefer to make your own meals, try a supermarket like **Dia,** Epaminonda 63. It's directly underneath Hotel Niovi, across the street from Hotel Meletiou. (Open M-F 8:30am-9pm, Sa 8am-8pm.) There are two **Champion markets,** one on Pindarou 108 and another on Epaminonda 36, uphill from the hotels. (Both open M-F 8am-9pm, Sa 8am-4pm, Su 8am-2:30pm.). There are a few smaller markets and mini-marts along Epaminonda and the side streets, but these close around 2:30pm.

🍽️ Pouros, Pl. Kadmias (☎22620 28 455). Turn left on Antigonis from Epaminonda; you'll see the large sign at the end of the street. The view of the plains beyond Thebes from the enchanting courtyard is a picturesque backdrop for the generous portions of

CENTRAL GREECE

classic Greek food. A truly standout restaurant. Meat sampler €4. Entrees €5-8. Open daily 8am-midnight. Cash only. ❷

Dionysos, Epimanonda 88 (☎22620 24 445), just past the *plateia.* Opened in 1922, this restaurant has been cooking traditional fare longer than the rest. Entrees €5-6.50. Veal with lemon €6.50. Open daily 8am-4:30pm and 6:30pm-2am. V. ❷

Cafe Nuevo, on the 3rd floor of a shopping mall at Epaminonda 2 and Eteokleous. A favorite daytime hangout of Theban teenagers. If you're lucky, you'll catch a live performance by one of Greece's teenybopper heartthrobs. ❷

🕶 ⬛ SIGHTS AND NIGHTLIFE

Thebes's antiquities traditionally have been its main attraction. The **Archaeological Museum,** Threpsiadou 1, at the end of Pindarou, houses an extensive collection of art and artifacts from roughly four millennia of history (3000 BC-AD 1500). To get an equivalent archaeological experience, you can peer into the open excavation pits—the source of the museum's collection—sprinkled among buildings throughout the city. Segments of a Mycenaean palace and acropolis (c. 1400 BC) are visible. The largest of these, the **House of Cadmus,** is on the left along the way to the museum, a block after the taxis, behind an iron fence. Also nearby are the ancient **Mycenaean Chamber Tombs,** which are closed to the public, but whose entrances are still visible. Take Vourdouba downhill from Pindarou all the way to the bottom, then turn left on Avlidos (beyond the island), and right up the stone stairs and up the hill.

Chic Cafe Theatro, Epaminonda 79. The square's most lively venue, with a DJ spinning pop for a young crowd that congregates outside on posh couches. Tea and coffee €1.50-2.50. Mixed drinks €4. Open daily 8am-late. ❷

NAFPAKTOS Ναυπακτος ☎26340

When in Patra, visit Nafpaktos. Vacationing urbanites and Greek children sunbathe side by side on some of the most attractive pebble beaches in central Greece, which extend from the picturesque Venetian fort in the Old Port. This historic town has been in the hands of the Turks, Venetians, and, since 1829, the Greeks. The residents of Nafpaktos celebrate this history through the careful preservation of the Old Port and by hosting festivals to commemorate significant events such as the Naval Battle of Nafpaktos (1571) and the end of Turkish rule (April 18, 1829). The tree-lined, pedestrian-only waterfront avenues are packed with cafes, *tavernas,* and playgrounds, creating the ideal atmosphere for bike riding or an evening stroll.

▐ TRANSPORTATION

Buses: Nafpaktos has 2 bus stations. Check for bus times at **Tourist Information** in the town square. Both stations are close to street corners, and the signposted times and other useful info might be difficult to find.

The 1st is on the corner of Athinon and Asklipiou. Buses go to **Delphi** (M-F 5 per day, Sa 2 per day, Su 1 per day) and then continue on to points throughout central Greece. Check the station for specific times.

The 2nd station is on Manassi, which runs perpandicular to Athinon and the sea. Buses go to **Athens** and **Patra** (M-F 8 per day, Sa 2 per day, Su 1 per day), **Thessaloniki,** and the **Peloponnese.**

Taxis: (☎26340 251 11). In front of the main *plateia* and near the harbor in the Old Port.

❖ ⚡ ORIENTATION AND PRACTICAL INFORMATION

Coming from the east, Athinon leads into the town's central **plateia**, where it becomes Ilarchou Tzavela; it then becomes G. Ath. Nova as it continues past the **Old Port**. One block toward the water from Athinon, Noti Botsari leads east. If you arrive on the bus from points eastward, such as Galaxidi, you'll likely be let off at the Asklipiou bus station. Walk in a general westerly direction—all roads lead to the Old Port.

Tourist Office: (☎26340 38 533), on the southeastern corner of the Old Port's central *plateia*. The staff can orient you and answer questions. Open daily July-Aug. 10am-2pm and 6-9pm, Sept.-June 10am-2pm and 5-8pm.

Bank: National Bank, Il. Tzavela 86 (☎26340 20 184), and **Alpha Bank,** Il. Tzavela 81 (☎26340 29 313), both just off the main *plateia*. **Currency exchange** and **24hr. ATMs.** Both open M-Th 8am-2:30pm, F 8am-2pm.

Police: (☎26340 27 258), off G. Ath. Nova, about 6 blocks west of the Old Port.

Pharmacy: Around the *plateia* and down Athinon. Late-night pharmacies posted.

Hospital: (☎26340 23 690), on the eastern end of town. Call the police or a taxi to arrange transportation to the hospital. Small **medical clinic** on Maypomath (☎26340 36 000). If you need serious medical attention, the hospital in Patra will be more helpful.

Internet: In the town **library** (☎26340 27 388), 2 blocks up the hill from the National Bank. Free internet and a small selection of English books. Open M-Tu and Th-F 8am-2:30pm, W 8am-7pm. **Hobby Club** (☎26340 22 288), on Navmachias. €2 per hr. Open M-Sa 9am-10pm. Wi-Fi at a few of the cafes along the Old Port, like **Gala Cafe & Bar.** Open daily 9am-2am.

Post Office: Tzavela 33 (☎26340 27 232), a few blocks down from the banks, on the right. Open M-F 7:30am-2pm. **Postal Code:** 30300.

▓ ▓ ACCOMMODATIONS AND CAMPING

Accommodations in Nafpaktos range from rather mediocre hotels along G. Ath. Nova to more expensive options by Gribovo beach. That said, there are a few affordable gems close to the old town.

▓ **Hotel Diethnes** (☎26340 27 342), on the right on the road entering town before reaching the Old Port. Justifiably very popular among travelers. Wonderful hospitality, great location, and bright, colorful rooms with hardwood floors, A/C, baths, TVs, and balconies. English-speaking owner will happily take care of you during your stay. Book ahead if visiting in the summer months. Singles €30-35; doubles €40. Extra bed €5. MC/V. ❷

Hotel Nafpaktos (☎26106 23 788), set on the Old Port end of Gribovo Beach. Even though the hotel is 1 block from the water, almost every balcony has a lovely bay view. All rooms have A/C, TVs, and Wi-Fi. Breakfast €5. Wheelchair-accessible. Singles €35; doubles €45; suites from €90. MC/V. ❸

Pension Aphrodite (☎26340 27 230), just steps away from Club Cinema on Apokafkou. Head 1 block east from the main *plateia* on Athinon, then turn right on Arvanti and walk to the beach; the pension is on the right. Decent white rooms with A/C, TVs, and balconies. Ask about getting an extra bed. Singles €30-40; doubles €40-50. Cash only. ❷

Platanitis Beach Camping (☎26340 31 555), 4km out of town on G. Ath. Nova. Has its own mini-mart, restaurant, and wooded campsites that extend to the pebbly beach. €4.50 per person; €3.50-4 per tent. Tent rentals €6. Electricity €3.50. ❶

CENTRAL GREECE

FOOD

Bakeries, souvlaki stands, and fast-food restaurants clutter the central *plateia* area and Old Port. For exhausted beach gods and castle-goers, a few excellent restaurants are tucked away within easy walking distance.

Papoulis (☎26740 21 578). Head to the Old Port's central *plateia* and turn toward the water onto a cobblestone road; the tavern is straight ahead. The locals' pick for tastiest meal in town. The owner's mother grew up in the building, adding to the homey feel. Flavorful dishes like spicy country sausage with green peppers. Entrees €6-10. Open daily noon-1am. Cash only. ❷

Ev Oivos (☎26740 28 266), on the inland side of the port at the Gribovo Beach side of the pedestrian road. Similar fare to any traditional Greek tavern, but the chef has a knack for bringing a contemporary flair to each dish. Entrees are flavored by a novel combination of spices. Try the chicken with mushroom and cream sauce. Entrees and salads €6-10. Open daily 6pm-1am. Cash only. ❷

Payoto Mania, 27 Botsari (☎26340 24 833). More than 40 flavors of homemade gelato. Scoop €1.70. Open M-Sa 4pm-2am. Cash only. ❶

SIGHTS AND BEACHES

VENETIAN CASTLE. One of the best examples of fortress architecture in Greece, the impressive castle dominates the picturesque town from 200m above sea level. Besides boasting the best vista around, the citadel also contains the tiny **Church of the Prophet Elias,** the remains of a Byzantine bath and church, and a large cistern to help the fortress weather sieges. Its walls, which reach down to the port, formed five zones of fortification, and now are woven into the construction of modern houses on the hill. Footpaths wind around the walls, past fountains, and through century-old gates; one begins off Il. Tzavela just past the post office. A leisurely walk up to the base of the fortress takes about an hour if starting at the port. *(Look for the cobblestone steps and the sign that says "KASTRO/Castle" on the right. Well-posted road signs will guide your way to the castle directing from G. Ath. Nova to Thermou. Just look aup—the fortress sticks out.)*

OLD PORT. Enclosed by low walls and watchtowers, the port is a romantic backdrop for the town's hottest cafes. Plaques on the walls commemorate the October 7, 1571 **Battle of Lepanto,** in which the united Christian fleet defeated the Ottomans, bringing an end to their naval superiority. A statue also honors battle hero **Miguel de Cervantes Saavedra,** who wrote of his experiences in Don Quixote. At night both the fortress and the port are spectacularly illuminated.

BEACHES. During the day, a lively crowd of children and teens, young and old, all frolic in the water and sunbathe on the beaches. The town straddles two beaches, which together form a crescent on either side of the handsome Old Port. Both have jungle gyms, swing sets, and an ample selection of cafes and taverns. *(When facing the water at the Old Port, Gribovo beach will be to the left. Psani beach is on the right. The public showers and toilets are on Psani beach.)*

ENTERTAINMENT AND FESTIVALS

Nafpaktos's week-long **Carnival,** held annually during the week before Lent, features music, dancing, free wine, and souvlaki. During the rest of the year, cafes and *ouzeria* along Psani beach and in the Old Port are filled with customers from around 8:30 to 11:30pm, when those who don't hit the hay hit the clubs.

CENTRAL GREECE

Na Blue, at the end of the Old Port along Psani beach. A water park with a pool, water-slides, bar, and free lounge chairs and umbrellas that line the beach. Pool and water-slides €5-8. Open daily 11am-8pm.

Club Cinema, Apokafkou 12 (☎26340 26 026), past Pension Aphrodite away from Gribovo. One of the town's classiest nightlife destinations. An imposing front door conceals a large dance floor that spills out onto a beachfront patio. Cover €5. Open F-Sa 11pm-late.

KARPENISI Καρπενήσι ☎22370

The alpine resort town of Karpenisi is Evritania's relaxed capital and the perfect base for exploring the nearby countryside and villages, but outside of the winter months, the town itself has little to offer by way of entertainment. Founded when five agrarian settlements in the foothills of Mt. Timfristos merged early in the era of Ottoman rule, Karpenisi suffered for years as an economic backwater, weakened by emigration and unemployment. In recent years, a thriving tourism industry has breathed new life into the city, bringing increased prosperity as outdoor enthusiasts discover the region's extraordinary beauty. Winter marks the peak tourist season, when Mt. Velouchi opens its six lifts to skiers and snowboarders. South of Karpenisi, streets give way to rolling pastures and the Karpenisiotis River gorge.

▐ TRANSPORTATION

Buses: Char. Trikoupi (☎22370 80 013), a 20min. walk southeast of the *plateia*. Bus schedules change frequently, so be sure to confirm times. To: **Agrinio** (3½hr.; M-Sa 8:45am, Su 1:15pm; €9.70); **Athens** (4hr.; 9am, noon, 4:15pm; €22.50); **Lamia** (1hr., 4 per day 6:40am-4:15pm, €6.40); **Megalo Chorio** and **Mikro Chorio** (20min., daily 6:50am and 1pm, €1.40); **Proussos** (1hr., F 5:45am and 1pm, €2.90). Ask at the station about service to smaller villages. In winter, buses to the **Velouchi Ski Center** (12km) can be arranged for large groups.

Taxis: (☎22370 22 666). Available 24hr. at the stand at the high end of the *plateia*.

▐▐ ORIENTATION AND PRACTICAL INFORMATION

Karpenisi is at the foot of Mt. Velouchi, about 75km west of Lamia. To get to the main *plateia* from the bus station, follow **Charilaou Trikoupi** downhill as it forks right, then make a right up steep **Karpenisioti**—there is no street sign, but you will know it when you see the path of grass and a white wall with child-like paintings, which leads to the square. The bus often drops people off by the main *plateia* next to the church instead. **Zinopoulou** borders the *plateia*'s eastern side—you will know it by the large Alpha Bank; Karpenisioti branches off from it as the two streets head downhill. The other main road, **Ethnikis Antistasis,** runs roughly parallel to Zinopoulou at the other end of the *plateia* just behind the church, beginning with the OTE office. At the corner where Eth. Antistasis meets the corner of the *plateia*, **Grigoriou Tsitsara** runs downhill to the left, between the church and the OTE. The largest church and the town hall are on the northern end of the *plateia*, near a monument to soldiers who died in 20th-century wars.

Tourist Office: (☎22370 21 016), on a street that leads out from the top of the *plateia* next to the church. With your back to the Alpha Bank, the street is on your left. The staff, some of whom speak English, offer maps and brochures and can help with out-door excursions, but their hours can be unreliable. Open M-F 9am-2pm and 5-8pm, Sa

10am-2pm and 5-8pm, Su 10am-2pm. **Hellenic Alpine Club (EOS)** (Karpenisi office ☎22370 23 051, Lamia office 26 786). Runs mountain refuge huts in Evritania.

Bank: Alpha Bank, Zinopoulou 7 (☎22370 25 608), in the *plateia*. **24hr. ATM.** Open M-Th 8am-2:30pm, F 8am-2pm.

Laundry: Ariston, Karpenisioti 30 (☎22370 22 887). €3-10 per load. Open M-Sa 8am-2pm and 7-9pm.

Police: Eth. Antistasis 9 (☎22370 89 160).

Hospital: P. Bakogianni (☎22370 80 680), a long walk past the police station; signs point the way.

Telephones: OTE, Eth. Antistasis 3. Open M-F 7:30am-1:30pm.

Internet Access: Library (☎22370 80 269). Take the 1st left after the police station and keep along the street, passing a park; the library is on your left before the road turns. Free internet access. Open M-Tu 9am-2pm, W 9am-7pm, Th-F 9am-2pm.

Post office: Ag. Nikolaou 3 (☎22370 23 542), off Karpenisioti to the left. **Poste Restante.** Open M-F 7:30am-2pm. **Postal Code:** 36100.

ACCOMMODATIONS

Hotels in Karpenisi aren't budget-friendly, particularly on weekends and during the winter high season. The cheapest option is a room at one of the local *domatia*. The tourist office lists rooms and prices.

Hotel Galini, Riga Fereou 3 (☎22370 22 914). Follow G. Tsitsara downhill and take the 2nd right. The plain and fluorescent-lit aged rooms may not be the most comfortable, but with fridges, TVs, and baths, they're still the best deal in town. Singles €20; doubles €30; triples €40. Longer stays may be discounted. Cash only. ❶

Hotel Elvetia, Zinopoulou 17 (☎22370 22 465; www.elvetiahotel.gr). Attentive staff and luxurious ski lodge-style lounge, and rooms with TVs and baths; some with balconies. Breakfast included. Doubles €40-55; triples €50-65. Cash only. ❸

City Hotel Apollonion, Karpenisioti 4 (☎22370 25 002), off the *plateia*. Stylish carpeted rooms with TVs, balconies, phones, and gleaming tiled baths. Breakfast included. Singles €40-45; doubles €50-55; triples €60-65. Cash only. ❸

FOOD

Karpenisi has a wide variety of dining options, all within a short walk of the central *plateia*.

Folia (☎22370 24 405), in a small alley to the left of the 1st street off Karpenisiotihas. Small menu of excellently-prepared Greek meals. Live Greek music. Salads €2-6. Entrees €6-9. Open daily 3pm-midnight. Cash only. ❷

Taverna Panorama, Riga Fereou 18 (☎22370 25 976), just beyond Hotel Galini away from the *plateia*. Family-friendly *taverna* serves meat dishes *tisoras*, including veal cooked in a clay bowl (€7) under a thick canopy of vines over a romantically low-lit patio. Entrees €7-9. Open daily 1-6pm and 7pm-midnight. Cash only. ❷

ENTERTAINMENT AND NIGHTLIFE

The afternoon shifts into the evening as the small cafes where Karpenisians chat over iced coffee slowly evolve into crowded bars. Just down the street from the *plateia*, **Zinopoulou** has all the main cafes and bars. If you're in town in summer, **Ylortes Dassous (Celebrations of the Forest),** in the end of July and continuing for about 25 days, is replete with theatrical performances, dances, food, and music.

Senso (☎22370 23 887), past the police station—be on your best behavior. Beer €3. Mixed drinks €5. Open daily 8am-3am.

Cinema Cafe, Eth. Antistasis (☎69737 35 872). Take a left after the police station and it's on the right. This pastel-colored cafe boasts an expansive outdoor patio. Coffee €2-3. Beer €3-5. Mixed drinks €5-6. Open M-F 8am-3am, Sa-Su 9am-3am.

Karpenisi Ski Center (☎22370 21 111), 11km up Mt. Velouchi from the town. Comes alive when the snowflakes start to fall. The mountain has 6 lifts and 12 slopes that weave down 2000m of powdery bliss. The slopes at the top of the mountain are best reached by car; follow the signs to the ski center. Ask at the information office for any buses headed to the slopes. Ski season Nov.-Mar.

◪ DAYTRIP FROM KARPENISI

PROSSOS Προυσσάς

15km beyond Megalo Chorio and 32km beyond Karpenisi. Buses run sporadically, usually 1 per week (€2.90) from Karpenisi; ask at the bus station for times. If there is a bus, you can catch it as it heads by Megalo or Mikro Chorio; walk down to the main road or to the hamlet of Gavros. Ask to be let off at the monastery, on the left side of the road before you enter the village. Verify the return time as you exit the bus, but be prepared to take a taxi back to Karpenisi. If you can't make the weekly bus, a return trip by taxi should cost about €40.

The area surrounding Karpenisi is like something out of a story book: old-fashioned stone houses rest on mountainsides while herds of goats snooze in nearby pastures. Actually getting to these places takes some initiative, though, as public transportation is sparse. The trip to the small village of Proussos is an adventure in itself; unless you catch the bus, which runs only once per week, enjoy the utterly spectacular roadside scenery and admire your taxi driver's uncanny ability to maintain control of his vehicle as it swerves alongside steep ravines and past flimsy, intermittent guardrails. The ◪**Monastery of the Virgin of Proussiotissa** here is well worth the trip. Inside is an icon of the Madonna said to have been painted by St. Luke the Evangelist and believed to work miracles. The monastery has an abundant stock of heavenly *loukoumi* (Turkish jellied candy covered in powdered sugar), which the hospitable monks offer to visitors. In the evenings, the monks' chanting mingles with the sound of rushing water from the Karpenisiotis River and echoes through the ravine. (Open daily dawn to dusk. Modest dress required. Free.)

Proussos's **clock tower** belts out the hour from a precarious hilltop overlooking the monastery. The dark **Black Cave,** a rumored ancient oracle and a hideout for Greek women and children during the War of Independence, is along a trail that begins on the far side of the village near a bridge; bring a flashlight to explore. The village is a 20min. walk beyond the monastery on the main road. There are no hotels in Proussos, but as in most Evritanian villages, many homes offer fairly inexpensive *domatia*, marked by signs in the center of town. As for food, ◪**Ellinon Geuseis ❷**, just before the plateia on the left, is worth the trek from the monastery. The house specialty, *stamnas* (locally grown meat with feta cheese and tomato sauce; €7.50), is served on a porch with panoramic views of the gorge. (☎22370 80 198. Open daily 8am-2am.)

LAMIA Λαμία   ☎22310

A crossroad for other major cities with almost no sights to its name, Lamia is mainly a jumping-off point for travelers bound for Northern or Central Greece. Though most visitors only stay in Lamia long enough to see the inside of a bus station, the downtown area is lined with stores and cafes, and is pleasant enough to entertain those looking to take a break from their packed itineraries, particularly with a day at Mt. Iti National Park.

▮ TRANSPORTATION

Trains: There are 2 train stations in Lamia.

The local train station, Konstantinopoulos 1 (☎22310 44 883), down the street from the local bus station. To **Athens** (3hr., 6:15am and 6:15pm, €6.60).

Lionokladi train station (☎22310 61 061), 10km west of Lamia. This main rail stop is along the Athens-Thessaloniki line. To reach the station, catch the bus marked "Stavros" at the local bus station (15 min.; 10am, 12:40, 1:30pm) or the corner of Drosopolou and Hatzopolou at Pl. Parkou (15min., every hr. 6:05am-9:05pm, €0.70), but give yourself at least 30min. to make it there. Purchase train tickets at the **OSE office**, Averof 34 (☎22310 23 201), the 3rd right down El. Venizelou from the southwestern corner of Pl. Parkou. Open M-F 8am-9pm, Sa 8am-3pm. Intercity trains run to **Athens** (3hr., 8 per day 6am-9pm, €6.70) via **Thebes** (1hr., €3.20), **Livadia** (1hr., 5 per day, 6am-3:50pm, €3), and **Thessaloniki** (3hr., 4 per day 9am-7:35pm, €9.10). Express trains are available at higher prices; call the station for information.

Buses: There are 4 intercity bus stations. Beginning from the northernmost to the south-ernmost station:

Rosaki Angeli 69 (☎22310 22 627), east of the center. To **Agia Marina** (20min., every hr. 6:30am-9:15pm, €1.40), **Raches** (50min., 8 per day 5:45am-8pm, €2.90), and **Volos** (2hr.; M-F 9am and 3pm, Sa 9am; €9.30).

Papakiriazi 27 (☎22310 51 345). Head downhill from Pl. Parkou, walk down Satovriandou, and turn left; the station is on the corner. To **Athens** (3hr.; every 1-1½hr. 5am-9:15pm; €18.40). Take the Athens bus and ask to be let off at Agios Kostantinos (45min., €4.30) for ferries to the Sporades.

Botsari 5 (☎22310 28 955), is to the right of Satovriandou on the same street as the Athens bus station. To **Karpenisi** (1hr.; M-F 6 per day 7am-9pm, Sa-Su 5 per day 7am-9pm; €6.40) and the **Evritania** region.

The main intercity bus station, Agrafon 41 (☎22310 22 802) is a 20-30min. walk from the city center. From Pl. Parkou, follow Satovriandou south until the railroad tracks. Make a left, follow-ing the tracks for a few blocks until you hit Leonidou (which becomes Athinon after the tracks). Follow Athinon downhill then make a left at Agrafon (the street just before the red gas station). A 5min. walk will bring you to the bus station. To: **Agrinio** (4hr.; 2:30, 7pm; €20.80); **Delphi** (2hr.; 10:30am, 12:30, 7pm; €8.20) via **Amfissa** (1hr., €5); **Chalkida** (2hr.; 11am, 6:15pm; €13.80); **Karditsa** (7 per day 8am-7pm, €7.40); **Patra** (4hr.; 4 per day 11:15am-midnight; €16.90); **Thessaloniki** (4hr., 4 per day 11am-6pm, €23.30) via **Larisa** (2hr., €12.20); **Trikala** (2hr., 6 per day 8:45am-8:15pm, €8.60).

Local Transportations: Buses leave from Konstantinopoulos 2 (☎22310 51 348), below the city, near the railroad tracks. Follow Satovriandou south and take a right when you reach the tracks. Several buses per day go to small towns and villages around Lamia. A bus runs to **Lionokladi** train station (15min.; 10am, 12:40, 1:30pm; €1).

Taxis: (☎22310 34 555). Wait at stands in each of the 4 main *plateias*. 24hr.

◀▪ ▮ ORIENTATION AND PRACTICAL INFORMATION

Inland off the Maliakos Gulf and 160km north of Athens, Lamia climbs gently to a northwesterly ridge, crowned by the **kastro**. The city extends outward from the roughly rectangular arrangement of its four central *plateias*. South-eastern **Plateia Parkou** is crowded and lined with banks. From the southeast-ern corner **Satovriandou** heads downhill to three bus stations and the local rail station. **Kapodostriou** heads eastward and is the main shopping district and the route to the main bus station. From Pl. Parkou's northeastern corner, above the National Bank, **Kolokotroni** leads north to the leafy **Plateia Laou**, passing **Rosaki Angeli** on the way. West from Pl. Parkou head up **Apostoli Kounoupi** to reach **Plateia Eleftherias**, full of cafes and home to Lamia's trendiest night-life. From here, **Riga Fereou** connects Pl. Eleftherias to the northwest corner

CENTRAL GREECE

of Pl. Parkou. Pl. Eleftherias connects with sleepy Pl. Diakou via **Diakou** on its southern side. A network of small pedestrian-only streets interlaces the squares and houses small cafes, book stores, and boutiques.

Bank: National Bank, Kapodistriou 1 (☎22310 57 607), at the corner of Kolokotroni. **24hr. ATM.** Open M-Th 8am-2:30pm, F 8am-2pm.

Police: (☎22310 56 845), 2km out of town. Take a taxi or follow Leonidou out of the city onto Athinon; it's on the right, about a block past Kavafi. Limited English spoken.

Hospital: Karaiskaki (☎22310 56 100 or 56 200), 1km north of the city. Open 24hr.

Telephones: OTE, Skilvaniotou 1, on the western side of Pl. Eleftherias. Open M, W, Sa 7:30am-2pm; Tu and Th-F 7:30am-2pm and 5:30-9pm.

Internet Access: Free Wi-Fi available at Pl. Eleftherias. **Escape,** Ipsilandou 6 (☎22310 20 240), north of Pl. Eleftherias. €2 per hr. Open 24hr. **Spot,** Ipsilandou 17 (☎22310 27 056). €2 per hr. Open 24hr.

Post office: Pl. Diakou (☎22310 47 718). **Poste Restante.** Open M-F 7:30am-2pm. **Postal Code:** 35100.

ACCOMMODATIONS

Those who choose to spend the night in Lamia can stay at any number of moderately priced hotels in the heart of the city, though the area is bustling and noisy all night long.

Hotel Athena, Rosaki Angeli 41 (☎22310 20 700), 1 block south and 2 blocks east of Pl. Laou. Attractively-furnished rooms, renovated in 2008, with soft beds. Each room comes with bath, hair dryer, TV, fridge, A/C, phone, and huge balcony. Breakfast €5. Free Wi-Fi. Singles €35; doubles €45; triples €55; quads €65. ❸

Thermopyles Hotel, Rosaki Angeli 36 (☎22310 21 366). Plain rooms with linoleum floors. Each has TV, phone, A/C, small balcony, and bath. Singles €30; doubles €40; triples €50. ❸

Hotel Neon Astron, Pl. Laou 5 (☎22310 26 245). The cheapest rooms in town. Though the plain white rooms have seen better days, they all come with TVs, A/C, phones, and baths; some have balconies. The hotel cat will probably greet you as you enter. Singles €28; doubles €30; triples €40. ❷

FOOD

▨ **Ouzo Melathron,** Aristoteli 3 (☎22310 31 502; www.ouzomelathron.gr), off Pl. Laou. Take the stairs on the northern side. 5 ft. long tongue-in-cheek menu brims with creative takes on traditional dishes and a few inventions. If you're feeling adventurous, try the "unnamed salad" (too good to find a name that matches; €5.24), the "transsexual lamb" (it's actually chicken; €4.40), or "viagra" (don't ask). The food is beautifully prepared with generous portions and served in a green lantern-lit courtyard. Vegetarian options available. Entrees €5-10. Open daily 11am-1am. ❷

Elisia (Hlusia), Kalyva Bakogianni 10 (☎22310 27 006), just off Pl. Laou, the pedestrian street left of Hotel Neon Astron. Traditional Greek cuisine. Try the moussaka (€6) or any number of grilled meats. Entrees €4-8. Open daily 5pm-midnight. ❷

Tsiatsos Konnos, Pl. Laou 6 (☎22310 34 616). Windows filled with mouth-watering heaps of *loukoumi* that are hard to resist. *Loukoumi* (€3) and baklava (€2) are also sold by the kg (€9-11). Open daily 8am-10pm. ❶

CENTRAL GREECE

⚙ SIGHTS

KASTRO. The imposing remains of the *kastro* (castle) loom over the city. Built in the Classical period, it has undergone renovations under the Romans, Franks, Catalans, and Ottomans. Before Greece's 1884 annexation of Thessaly and Domokos, Lamia's *kastro* served as the core of the country's border defenses. The barracks, built by King Otto in 1880, were used until WWII. It now serves as a well-organized **Archaeological Museum** that displays items from the Neolithic to Roman periods found in tombs outside Lamia. Aside from the standard ceramic figurines and bronze and gold jewelry, highlights include the earliest preserved vase depicting a naval battle and a reconstructed floor mosaic. *(Head east out of Pl. Parkou on Kapodistriou and take the second left onto Amalias. Walk up the hill and cross Eklision when Amalias ends to go up a stone stairway. Turn right and follow the road at the top of the stairs, keeping the kastro on your left. After a 5min. walk, you'll see a marked path leading up to the museum entrance, inside the kastro's walls. ☎ 22310 29 992. Open Tu-Su 8:30am-3pm. €2, students €1, EU students and under 18 free.)*

FOLKLORE MUSEUM. For an interesting, albeit brief, look at local history, check out the two-room Folklore Museum. Its small but well-displayed collection is worth a quick look and includes traditional clothing, cooking utensils and farm equipment, and a vintage ouzo press. *(Kalyva Bakogianni 6. ☎ 22310 37 832. Open M-F 8am-2:30pm. Free.)*

GARDENS OF AGIOS LOUKAS. If the museums and shops in the center aren't for you, you may consider spending some time looking down on the city—literally. The quiet Gardens of Agios Loukas on Ag. Loukas hill begins at the top of Pl. Diakou behind a striking Statue of Athanasios Diakos. A hero in the War of Independence, Diakos was burned to death by the Turks in 1821. Take the steps up to the top, then go right to reach the gardens.

🎵 🎭 ENTERTAINMENT AND NIGHTLIFE

▨ **Agora,** Othonos 28 (☎22310 51 451), 2 blocks east of Pl. Laou on the right and down the steps. Has been entertaining crowds in its outdoor courtyard for over 2 decades. The cabana-like bar has palm trees and multiple bars in a relaxed setting. Beer €5. Mixed drinks €7-9. Open May-Sept. daily 8am-3am.

   Central, Pl. Eleftherias 10 (☎22310 44 877). Has so many trendy patrons they spill out onto the streets. Open daily 8:30am-3am.

   Sketch, Riga Fereou (☎22310 51 350), just off Pl. Eleftherias. Red awnings and tasteful chandeliers. Serves drinks all day and night—it's noon somewhere. Beer €4-6. Mixed drinks €6.50-7.50. Open daily 9pm-4am.

▶ DAYTRIP FROM LAMIA

MOUNT ITI NATIONAL PARK

The mountain and its villages are best reached by car, but the local bus station in Lamia has service to many of the small villages. Buses leave from Lamia's local station for Loutra Ipatis and nearby Ipati (40-50min.; 10:30am, 1:15, 3pm; €1.50). Ask for the return schedule at the bus station before you depart. For more hiking information, contact the Hellenic Alpine Club of Lamia (☎ 22310 26 786), which can suggest routes and provide directions to mountain refuges.

Hiking and outdoor enthusiasts will enjoy the impressive gorges, scenic hiking trails, and small mountainside villages of Mt. Iti National Park, located 35km

CENTRAL GREECE

southwest of Lamia. The walk up to the mountain leads through different conditions, from exposed rocky terrain to thick forest, to open pastures, and is an idyllic and easy **hike.** The boundaries of the national park extend to the base of the mountain, and the best access points are the small villages at the mountain's base. Ipati is the most convenient base for a hike to the summit (3-3½hr.) and back (2½hr.) A 6km trail begins on the western end of town by the bus stop; the trail is clearly marked at all points with red blazes and red squares on a white background. From the bus stop in the center of town, follow the road uphill until it turns into the trail. After an hour, the trail leads to a wire fence; follow it across an open field and stream until it ends where a road begins. Follow the road and you will shortly see the continuation of the trail marked on an uphill turn on your right. After 2½hr. there is a spring where you can fill your water bottle, and a second spring 20min. from the top. The actual peaks themselves are not accessible from the trail, but there is a beautiful view next to a closed refuge; signs point the way to the left of the road.

For those who prefer to stay closer to sea level, **Ipati** is home to a waterfall and the ruins of a *kastro*. The village of **Loutra Ipatis,** 5km closer to Lamia, has a beautiful public garden and an array of cafes and *tavernas*. To reach the 8km trail to the summit of Mt. Iti, walk south through town toward the mountain; at the southernmost end of town, you'll find a dirt road leading to the mountainside. The town's tree-shaded main intersection is populated with dining establishments, and the gardens are on the northeast side. Check out the mysterious covered pit in the gardens, with a bubbling hot spring barely visible at the bottom.

AGIOS KONSTANTINO Άγιος Κωνσταντίνος ☎22350

Directly at the foot of an imposing mountain range, Agios Konstantinos is the closest port to Athens with ferries to the Sporades; it thus functions as a portal between the mainland and the Aegean Sea. Most travelers will experience it as a layover during a longer journey, and for good reason: aside from a small beach and the peaceful central *plateia*, there is little else to do while waiting for your ferry.

Due to its status as a transportation hub, Agios Konstantinos has a good variety of accommodations for a town of its size. Friendly ◼**Hotel Olga ❸**, Evoikou 11, is the first in the strip of hotels along the waterfront to the right of the *plateia*. Spacious, white-tiled rooms have cheery blue curtains and bedspreads. Each room has A/C, phone, fridge, TV, bath, and a balcony with a harbor view. (☎22350 32 266. Breakfast €5. Singles €30; doubles €40; triples €50.) **Hotel Poulia ❷**, Thermopylon 4, is in the center of town off the right side of the *plateia* when facing inland (there are signs from the bus station). Small rooms come with varying levels of amenities: some doubles have TVs, A/C, and baths. The cheapest rooms come with fans, sinks, and communal baths. (☎22350 31 663. Singles €20-30; doubles €24, with bath €35-44; triples €30-40. Group rates available.) The main *plateia* is surrounded by inexpensive *tavernas* and bars; after dark, children play soccer on the grass while the rest of the community relaxes at the outdoor tables. The undeniable local favorite is **To Parco ❷**, on the edge of the *plateia* farthest from the water. Try their oven meatballs (€5.50), as you watch local families congregate at the adjacent playground. (☎22350 33 360. Open daily 8am-2am. Entrees €4-8.) **Kaltsas Grill House ❷**, on the right side of the *plateia*, serves generous portions of meat. (☎22350 33 323. Seafood €6.50-14. Entrees €5-8. Open daily 9am-midnight.) For something sweet to tide you over until the next meal, **Artopoeia ❶**, Thermopylon 3, by Hotel Poulia, sells bread and pastries (€0.50-2.50) heaping with powdered sugar. (☎22350 31 684. Open daily 6am-10:30pm.)

CENTRAL GREECE

The bus stop is to the left of the *plateia* (when facing inland) a few meters away from the church that forms the border of the *plateia* (☎22350 32 223). **Buses** go to Athens (2hr., M-F every hr. 5:45am-10pm, €14.20), Lamia (1hr., every hr. 6am-11:30pm, €4.30), and Thessaloniki (4hr., 7:15am and 2:15pm, €27.50). **Ferries** and **Flying Dolphins** (☎22350 31 874) come to the pier, immediately seaward of the *plateia*. Buy your tickets from one of two offices on the right side of the *plateia*. Ferries leave for Alonnisos (4hr., M-Th 9:30, 11am, and 3pm; T-W 9:30am and 11am; F 9:30am, 3, 5, 8pm; Sa 9:30am, 1, 3pm; Su 3:30pm, €37), via Skiathos (3hr., €29.70) and Skopelos (4hr., €37). Check departure times posted outside the ticket offices; often it's best to call ahead to your destination to confirm times. (Alonnisos ticket office ☎24240 65 220; Skiathos 24270 22 204; Skopelos 24240 22 767.) Flying Dolphins go to Alonnisos (2hr.; M-Th and Sa 9:30am, F 9:30am and 7:45pm, Su 3pm; €44), via Skiathos (1hr., €32.50) and Skopelos (1hr., €44). **Taxis** (☎22350 31 850) line up behind the church. The **port police** (☎22350 31 920) is above the ticket offices. There are **24hr. ATMs** in front of the Galaxias supermarket and next to the **OTE**, which is to the right of the *plateia*, around the corner and on the waterfront. (☎22350 31 699. Open M-F 7:30am-3pm.) The **post office**, 5 Riga Feraiou, 20m inland, is one block past the OTE toward Hotel Olga. (☎22350 31 855. Open M-F 7:30am-2pm.) **Postal Code:** 35006.

THESSALY Θεσσαλία

From the urban bustle of Volos and Larisa to the peaceful villages of the Mt. Pelion Peninsula, Thessaly runs the gamut of lifestyles and attractions. The larger cities are home to some of the wildest nightlife on mainland Greece, while the otherworldly monasteries at Meteora define themselves by spiritual simplicity. Thessaly's plains are home to farmers who tend sheep and goats in the summer before returning home to fish from the waters of the Pinios River. In this out-of-the-way region, you'll find a wealth of genuine hospitality but very little English.

VOLOS Βόλος   ☎24210

Volos has the commercial appeal of a large city with the added draw of a nearby beach. Unsurprisingly, hotels quickly book up on weekends in July and August. In Greek mythology, Jason and the Argonauts launched their quest for the Golden Fleece from Volos. Today, most tourists are content to stay in the city and browse the stores on Ermou or lounge in a cafe by the port. The small bottles of distilled grape liquor served here, known as *tsipouro*, have brought the city national fame. Volos's orderly network of wide avenues contains a complete array of modern conveniences. Yet for a city of its size, Volos is refreshingly clean and safe. Come nightfall, strolling couples fill the harborside, and dozens of cafes and seafood restaurants push tables up to the water.

▐ TRANSPORTATION

Trains: (☎24210 24 056). Take Lambraki out of town and turn right at the flags at the end of the park. Walk 2-3min. down the road parallel to the track. Trains go to **Larisa** (1hr.; M-F 16 per day 5:40am-11:45pm, Sa-Su reduced; €2.10). Change trains in Larisa for **Athens** and **Thessaloniki**.

Ferries: To **Alonnisos** (4hr., daily Tu-Th and Sa-Su, €24), **Skiathos** (2hr., daily, €18.50), and **Skopelos** (3hr., daily, €24). **Sporades Travel,** Argonafton 33 (☎24210 23 400). English-speaking staff sells tickets. Open daily 6am-9pm.

CENTRAL GREECE

Flying Dolphins: The agencies near the pier all sell tickets. Check with **Falcon Tours,** Argonafton 34 (☎24210 39 299; www.hellenicseaways.gr). Open daily 7am-10pm. 2 per day go to **Alonnisos** (2hr.; 12:30, 6:30pm; €40) via **Skiathos** (1hr., €31), **Glossa** (1hr., €34), and **Skopelos** (1hr., €40). A 3rd ferry goes to **Skiathos** and **Skopelos** at 9am.

Buses: (☎24210 33 254), in the Old Town, about a 10min. walk up Lambraki. To: **Agios Ioannis** (2½hr., 3 per day 8:30am-6pm, €6); **Athens** (4hr., 12 per day 5am-1am, €17-24); **Larisa** (1hr., 12 per day 5:45am-9:30pm, €5); **Makrynitsa** (45min., 10 per day 6:15am-9:30pm, €1.40) via **Portaria** (40min., €1.14); **Milies** (1hr., 5 per day 6am-7pm, €4.10); **Thessaloniki** (3hr., 9 per day 4:30am-8:30pm, €16.60); **Trikala** (2hr., 2 per day 4:30am and 2:30pm, €10.10); **Tsagarada** (2hr., 4 per day 5am-3:30pm, €4). Service reduced Sa-Su and in winter.

Taxis: (☎24210 27 777). Line up in front of Pl. Ag. Konstantinou. Available 24hr.

Car Rental: Prices fluctuate depending on season and type of vehicle. **Avis,** Argonafton 41 (☎24210 20 849). Cars from €60 per day. Mopeds from €20 per day. Open M-Sa 8:30am-9:30pm, Su 9:30am-1pm and 6-9pm. **Hertz Car Rental,** Iasonos 90 (☎24210 22 544). Cars from €30-55 per day. Open M-F 9am-2pm and 5-9pm, Sa 9am-2pm and 6-8:30pm, Su 10am-2pm.

◼🗗 ORIENTATION AND PRACTICAL INFORMATION

Volos's bus station and tourist office are on **Lambraki,** a 10min. walk west from the city and the waterfront. On its way east into town, the road runs past the train station and **Riga Fereou Park** before coming to an end at a fountain. **Argonafton** is the waterfront walkway, home to lively *tavernas* and cafes. Moving inland, **Iasonos** and **Dimitriados** are the next streets parallel to the water; both are packed with banks, bakeries, and fast-food joints. After Dimitriados and also parallel to Argonafton, **Ermou,** a pedestrian-only street, contains boutiques that sell women's clothes and shoes. Near the center of the city, it leads into an open *plateia* with the **Church of Agios Nikolaos.** The point at which Ermou becomes **Polymeri** marks the start of the long seaside park. The **Church of Agios Konstantinos,** easily visible from the docks jutting out into the harbor, sits at the end of the park. Here, Argonafton and Dimitriados join to become **Nikolaou Plastira.** This quieter street heads past a few bars and *ouzeria* to the hospital and the Archaeological Museum before ending at Volos's popular **Anavrou Beach** in the residential section of town.

Tourist Office: (☎24210 30 931 or 30 940). Across the street from the bus station up Lambraki, in the large brick building with the glass front. Helpful English-speaking staff has maps, transportation timetables, and info about Volos and the Pelion Peninsula. Open M-F 8am-8pm, Sa-Su 9am-4:30pm.

Banks: There are several major banks with **currency exchange** and **ATMs** on Iasonos and Dimitriados. **National Bank,** Iasonos 50 and 91 (☎24210 90 800 or 34 811). Open M-Th 8am-2:30pm, F 8am-2pm. **Citibank,** Argonafton 27 (☎24210 76 380), on the corner of El. Venizelou, has a **24hr. ATM.** Open M-Th 8am-2:30pm, F 8am-2pm.

Bookstore: Newsstand, Iasonos 78 (☎24210 23 000), 1 block inland from the meeting point of the port and Argonafton. Sells a small collection of English novels, magazines, and history books. Open M-Sa 8am-10pm, Su 9am-9pm.

Police: (☎24210 39 061). On the corner of Ath. Gazi and Ath. Rozou. A 2nd police station also contains a small **tourist police** unit, 28 Oktovriou 179 (☎24210 39 063).

Hospital: Polymeri 134 (☎24210 39 225 or 27 531), next to the museum. Open 24hr.

Telephones: OTE, El. Venizelou 22 (☎24210 95 936), on the corner of El. Venizelou and Sokratous. Open daily 7:30am-2pm.

CENTRAL GREECE

- **Internet Access: Diavlos Youth Center,** Topali 14 (☎24210 25 363), off Dimitriados. The best rates in town and an atmosphere blessedly free of cigarette smoke. €1.20 per hr. Open M-F 10am-10pm. **The Web,** Iasonos 141 (☎24210 30 260), at the corner with Ogl. A gamer's paradise, lined with flatscreen computers. €2.40 per hr. Open 24hr.

Post Office: Dimitriados 209 (☎24210 90 602). At the intersection of Dimitriados and Ag. Nikolaou. **Poste Restante** available. Open M-F 7:30am-8pm. **Postal Code:** 38001.

🏠 ACCOMMODATIONS

Volos's hotels vary little in location and amenities and are almost never cheap. Most of the budget options are clustered in alleys along the waterfront or on the small streets leading away from the harbor. As usual, negotiating can slash prices. If you are coming into Volos on a weekend, book early and expect a price hike.

Hotel Jason, P. Mela 1 (☎24210 26 075), on the waterfront across from the ferry dock. Some of the simple but comfortable rooms have A/C with high ceilings, and most boast balconies overlooking the water. All have phones, baths, fans, and TVs. Singles €30-35; doubles €40; triples €60. Cash only. ❷

Hotel Santi, Topali 13 (☎24210 33 341), off Argonafton. Basic rooms, each with bath, TV, phone, A/C, and small balcony. Unbeatable location just 1 block from the waterfront. Singles €35-40; doubles €50-60; triples €60-70. Bargain for lower prices for longer stays. Cash only. ❸

Hotel Iolkos, Dimitriados 25 (☎24210 23 416), at a large roundabout where Leof. Labraki splits into Dimitriados and Iasonos. An excess of plastic flowers mark the entrance to this budget option. Bare rooms with fans, sinks, TVs, and communal baths. A useful last-minute resort; this is one of the few hotels that isn't usually booked through the weekend. Reception 24hr. Singles €25-30; doubles €40. Be sure to bargain. Cash only. ❷

Hotel Roussas, Iatrou Tzanou 1 (☎24210 21 732), on the corner of Nik. Plastira; look for the purple balconies. Though a bit removed from the main waterfront (about 20min. away), Roussa—whose attractive rooms have baths, fridges, phones, A/C, TVs, and balconies—is ideal for those looking to spend time relaxing on the beach. Singles €30; doubles €40; triples €50. Lower prices in winter. Cash only. ❷

🍴 FOOD

Stock up on provisions for a beachside picnic at **Asteras Supermarket,** Iasonos 34-38. (☎24210 31 524. Open M-F 8am-9pm, Sa 8am-8pm.) Fast food is available at countless locations in the three parallel streets inland from the docks. Most of the restaurants in Volos are clustered along the main waterfront area. Splurging on ouzo and *tsipouro* at one of Volos's signature waterfront *ouzeria* is a memorable experience. Each has a wide selection of *mezedes*, including seafood plates with prawns and octopus.

Tzafoplas, Argonafton 40 (☎24210 27 721). This seafood restaurant boasts a loyal clientele that packs the place at all hours. Fish and seafood sold per kg. Entrees €6-9. Open daily 10am-3am. Cash only. ❷

Noodle Bar, Iasanos 105 (☎24210 23 040), on the corner of K. Glavani. You can't miss the stark white chairs, tables, and bottles of Kikkoman; you'll also inevitably hear the club music blaring at this Asian restaurant. The food ranges from the surprising mango salad tossed with carrots and onions (€4.90) to the traditional chow mein (€5.70). Vegetarian options available. Entrees €5.70-9.10. Open daily noon-1am. Cash only. ❷

Evelin, Argonafton 47 (☎24210 30 481). For an Italian take on the freshest seafood, check out the diverse menu at this waterfront favorite. From pizzas and calzones (€8.60-11) to meat on the grill and fresh seafood, you are sure to find something delectable. Try the *Skopelos* (oven-baked fish with white wine, tomatoes, and herbs; €10). Open daily noon-midnight. Cash only. ❷

Poseidon, Argonafton 31 (☎24210 36 629). Don't let the cartoon sign of King Triton fool you—the seafood here is first class, offering the day's freshest catches. 2-person seafood platter €22. Fish and seafood €35-60 per kg. Open daily noon-3am. Cash only. ❷

👁 SIGHTS

ARCHAEOLOGICAL MUSEUM. Situated in an Neoclassical mansion, this museum displays reconstructed tombs and *stelae* (upright stones) from Demetrias. The collection of miniature Neolithic objects includes seals, spindle whorls, tools of bone and stone, a set of beautiful inscribed pottery, and ornate painted gravestones. The human remains in graves from the Middle Bronze Age are of particular interest, and English pamphlets make the museum a worthwhile visit. *(Athanasaki 1. A 30min. walk along the water from the ferry docks. ☎ 24210 25 285. Open M 1:30-8pm, Tu-Su 8:30am-8pm. €2, seniors €1, students free.)*

ARCHAEOLOGICAL SITES AT DIMINI AND SESKLO. Dimini dates back to 4000 BC and contains two major sites. The main site was constructed sometime at the end of the fifth millennium BC, and the more recent of the two, southwest of the main site, was built during the Mycenaean period. Both sites have ruins of houses and evidence of early city planning. Sesklo is the oldest known settlement in Thessaly and has the oldest acropolis in all of Greece, dating from 6500 BC. *(Dimini is 4km west of the city center and Sesklo is 5.5km farther along the connecting road. ☎24210 85 960. Both open Tu-Su 8am-8pm. €2, seniors €1, students free. Tickets cover both sites.)*

THE ART CENTER OF GIORGIO DE CHIRICO. Four rooms showcase temporary exhibits of Greek modern art as well as a permanent collection of 19th- and 20th-century pieces. Also of interest is a small display featuring miniature replicas of Princess Diana's dresses, designed by Volos's native Christina Stambolian. Displays are in Greek, but the English-speaking curator is eager to provide information. *(Metamorphoseos 3, behind the conservatory, which is at the beginning of Dimitriados, on the corner of the street with Hotel Iolkos. ☎24210 31 701. Open M-F 10am-1pm and 6-9pm, Sa 10am-1pm. Free.)*

🎭 NIGHTLIFE

The waterfront between the docks and Ag. Konstantinos becomes a hive of activity at night. Each of the cafes has its own character—there's enough variety to satisfy every taste.

Reef, Argonafton (☎24210 24 168). Blue phosphorescent glow emanates from a full-sized fish tank in the middle of the floor. Beer €3.50-5. Mixed drinks €6-7.50. Open daily 10am-4am.

Breeze, Nik. Plastira 4B (☎24210 36 178). Plays house and pop. Open daily 10am-3am.

Lioyerma (☎24210 36 178). Overlooking the harbor, Lioyerma rocks an outdoor bar and a sprawling network of couches and tables. Beer €3.50-5. Mixed drinks €6.50-7. Open daily 9am-6am.

Blaze (☎24210 88 332), by the train station. Mixed drinks €8. Cover €8; includes 1 drink. Open M-Th and Su until 3:30am, F-Sa until 6am.

Astra (☎24210 62 182), in Alykes. A popular traditional *bouzouki* haven. Cover €10; includes 1 drink. Open F-Sa midnight-4am.

Fengaria (☎24210 88 733), in Alykes. Head over here if you want to dance to *rembetika* tunes. Cab to Alykes €4. Cover €8-9; includes 1 drink. Open W-Sa midnight-4am.

Noa, in Alykes. A restaurant and bar that switches gears to become a *discothèque* around 1am. Mixed drinks €8-9. Open M-Th and Su until 3:30am, F-Sa until 6am.

TSAGARADA Τσαγαράδα ☎24260

Stunning Tsagarada isn't a town surrounded by wilderness—it is wilderness that happens to have a few stores and houses. The colorful flower gardens cascade downhill into bluffs with the peaceful Sporades as a distant backdrop. Tsagarada has succumbed to some tourism of the particularly expensive variety, but its sprawling layout preserves the village's charm. Spread across a wide area on the slope just below the highway, Tsagarada is comprised of four hamlets: **Agios Kyriaki, Agios Paraskevi, Agios Stefanou,** and **Agios Taxiarhon.** In the main *plateia*, where the bus stops, you will find the church of the hamlet's name and a massive, 1000-year-old plane tree. The tree's gnarled branches shade the cafe tables below and make it perfect for climbing. From the *plateia*, a well-marked path leads 1hr. down to the blue-green waters and pearlwhite stones of local favorite ☒**Milopotamos beach.**

Though hotel prices here are exorbitant, by the bus stop there is a list of *domatia* in the area where you can negotiate a night's stay. The tourist office, on the street connecting Ag. Paraskevi and the main *plateia*, has a computer kiosk outside where you can search for housing. Between Ag. Paraskevi and the main *plateia*, a stone path leads off the main road to the charming **Villa Ton Rodon ❹**, whose rooms have baths and TVs. Shuttered doors open onto porches overlooking brilliant rose bushes and a panoramic view of the sea. (☎24260 49 340; villatonrodon.gr. Breakfast included. Doubles €60-70.) Overlooking the main *plateia*, **Anatoli ❷** serves delicious traditional Greek food. The leaf-covered outdoor patio offers a serene view of the Aegean over the treetops. (☎24260 49 201. Rabbit with onions €9. Open daily noon-midnight.)

Though Tsagarada is reachable from Agios Ioannis by a 2hr. hike over difficult terrain, it's more convenient to take the **bus** from Volos on the Agios Ioannis route (2hr., 4 per day 5am-3:30pm, €4). Return schedules are posted in the bus stop, but it's best to ask for a schedule at the Volos bus station. Most visitors will enter at Ag. Paraskevi, where a **tourist office** is visible from the main road. (☎24260 48 993. Open M-F 9am-3pm.) A **24hr. ATM**, the **post office** (☎24260 49 215; open M-F 7:30am-2pm), and a covered bus stop are near the main road.

MOUNT PELION Όρος Πήλιο

The cool, moist peninsula is an anomaly in mostly sun-scorched Greece. With seemingly untouched greenery and ideal weather, nothing short of its incredible mountainside could protect the area from invasion. While the rest of Greece groaned under Ottoman rule, the peninsula was an autonomous center of Greek nationalism. Thankfully, even the mountains can't keep tourists away from the natural beauty of this peninsula.

MAKRYNITSA Μακρυνίτσα ☎24280

High in the Pelion mountain range, serene Makrynitsa soars over the Pagasitic Gulf. The town's breathtaking views of the Volos metropolitan area have earned it the apt nickname "balcony of Pelion." The small town extends only a few hundred meters in three directions from the main *plateia*, and cars are forbidden due to its designation as a protected traditional settlement. In the early evening, the setting sun illuminates the gulf with deep red and orange hues.

Come nightfall, Makrynitsa looks down onto the indigo- and white-speckled valley like the best box seat in a giant opera house.

■? TRANSPORTATION AND PRACTICAL INFORMATION. Makrynitsa is accessible by daily **buses** from Volos (¾hr., 10 per day 6:15am-9:30pm, €1.40) via the neighboring village of Portaria (40min., €1). From the bus turnaround, a short walk uphill hugging the mountainside takes you to the parking lot. Here, the left-most road, **17 Martiou,** leads to the *plateia.* Don't rush past the old houses renting *domatia* or the stores selling herbs and souvenirs—the buildings themselves are worth a look before entering the main *plateia,* which houses the town's central church, shaded by immense oak trees and overlooking the mountainside below.

Portaria, 2km away, is a 20min. walk from Makrynitsa's parking lot. From there, you can catch buses to other Pelion destinations, including the beaches at Agios Yiannis and Milopotamos. **24hr. ATMs, a police station** (☎24280 99 105 or 85 401; open 8am-2pm), and a **post office** (☎24280 99 104; open M-F 7:30am-10:30am) can be found in Portaria. There are **pay phones** and a **mailbox** in Markrynitsa's *plateia.* **Postal Code:** 37011.

? ACCOMMODATIONS. Because of its protected status, staying in Makrynitsa during the winter high season costs a fortune (singles around €65). Luckily, nearby Portaria has several exceptionally cheap *domatia* (singles around €20; doubles €30) and during the summer upscale rooms go for cheap prices. As nearly every building in Makrynitsa seems to be a hotel or *domatia,* there's plenty of options. On 17 Martiou headed into Makrynitsa's *plateia,* you'll pass a series of *domatia* and hotels on the right. **Hotel Theodora ❷** exudes luxury in its gorgeous, old-fashioned rooms, each with wooden furniture, satin comforters, furry rugs, TV, bath, and amazing views of the Pagasitic Gulf. The warm proprietress and inexpensive prices seal the deal. (☎24280 99 179. Breakfast €5. Singles €25; doubles €30; triples €35. Higher prices in winter. MC/V.) Farther down 17 Martiou, just before the *plateia,* is **Hotel Achilleus ❷,** whose rooms have TVs and baths; some have beautiful balconies. (☎24280 99 969. Singles €25-50; doubles €50-70; triples €70-90. Cash only.) Just next door, **Hotel Kentavros ❸** has well-decorated rooms complete with a loose canopies over the beds, wooden shutters, TVs, phones, and baths. (☎24280 99 075. Doubles €40-80. Cash only.) One of the many *domatia* is the delightful **Theofipos ❷,** just a few stores down from the main parking lot. Comfortable rooms open into a shared living room and dining area. Some rooms have fireplaces and couches. (☎24280 99 435. Doubles €30. Cash only.)

❏ FOOD. Several small restaurants have outdoor seating and spectacular views from elevated verandas. Most affordable is local *ouzeri* **A+B ❶,** past the *plateia* on the small trail that runs behind the church. From the porch, patrons have a superb view of Makrynitsa, Volos, and the gulf. (☎24280 99 355. Entrees €5-6.50. Open daily 11am-midnight. Cash only.) Right before A+B, near the end of the row of shops, is **Leonidas ❷.** Try the flavorful *spetzofei* (sausage and peppers; €8), a local specialty. Top off your meal with homegrown figs drenched in honey. (☎24280 99 533. Entrees €7-8. Open daily noon-6pm and 8pm-late. Cash only.) In the *plateia,* **Pantheon ❷** monopolizes the spectacular vista of the Pagasitic Gulf, with tables that sit against the railing. The fresh mountain air is sure to work up a hearty appetite, so treat yourself to the *moschari kokkonisto* (braised veal; €9) or rabbit with tomato sauce (€9). (☎24280 99 143. Entrees €7-9. Open daily 10am-midnight. Cash only.)

CENTRAL GREECE

◙ **SIGHTS.** To reach the **Museum of Folk Art and the History of Pelion,** take the downhill path that begins to the left of the church in the *plateia* and follow the signs. On all three stories of a converted 1844 mansion, the museum has recreations of 18th-century Greek rooms—which look cutting-edge in the midst of the antiquated village—and old paintings including works by Volos painter Hristopoulos. (☎24280 99 505. Open Tu-F 10am-4:30pm, Sa-Su 10am-5pm. €2, students free.) The town's remarkable churches include the 400-year-old **Church of Agios Yiannis the Baptist** in the main *plateia*, where you can answer that burning question of what it's like to be inside a tree; the hollowed-out trunk of a tall, leafy tree looms by the entrance. The peaceful church of **Kimisi Theotokou** once housed a *krifto scholio*, a secret school that taught the forbidden Greek language during Ottoman rule. The bell tower with the clock that overlook the *plateia* are a distinct marker of the church. (Churches open at the whim of their caretakers; early to mid-morning and evening are the best times to visit. Take the uphill path behind the church in the main *plateia*.) From the main parking lot, a road leads steeply uphill to the **Monastery of Agios Gerasimos** (20min.), which has a beautiful view. (Open daily 7am-noon and 4-6pm.) Makrynitsa's old houses are a sight in themselves. Stained-glass lanterns, false painted windows, and symbols to protect against evil spirits adorn outer walls.

LARISA Λάρισα ☎2410

As the fifth-largest city in Greece, the capital of Thessaly, and the location of a regional NATO office, Larisa has the hustle and bustle of a major city, but it is by no means a tourist hot spot. Lacking notable sights and inherent charm, Larisa, whose name means "stronghold" in Ancient Greek, likely will be no more than a stop on the way to more exciting destinations. Those who do end up staying the night, though, will find a large university community that supports some of the best nightlife in mainland Greece.

▐ TRANSPORTATION

Trains: (☎24102 36 250). Head south on Panagouli and bear slightly left onto Paleologou at the 5-way intersection; it's on the southern side of the small park. Regular and intercity express trains run to **Athens** (4-5hr.; 12 per day 7:07am-3:11am; regular €10.70, express €20-33), **Thessaloniki** (1hr., 4 per day 7:30am-9:26pm, €10-18), and **Volos** (45min., 16 per day 5:26am-8:47pm, €2.10).

Buses: (☎24105 37 777 or 567 600). 150m north of Pl. Laou at Olympou and Georgiadou. To: **Athens** (4hr., 8 per day 4am-midnight, €7); **Ioannina** (4hr.; 9am, 3pm; €16.50); **Kastoria** (4hr., 3 per day noon-12:30am, €16.40); **Thessaloniki** (2hr.; M-F 13 per day 6am-7:30pm, Sa-Su reduced; €13.50); **Volos** (1hr., 12 per day 5:45am-9:30pm, €5). There is a smaller **branch station** at Iroön Polytechniou 14 (☎24106 10 124). Walk south on Olympou to Pl. Laou, where Panagouli begins, continue south on Panagouli, turn right at the 5-way intersection, and walk about 600m to the gas station-bus stop on the left. Buses to **Karditsa** (1hr., 11 per day 6am-8:30pm, €6) and **Trikala** (1hr., 16 per day 6am-9pm, €5.70).

Taxis: (☎24106 61 414). Line up around the Pl. Tahydromiou. Available 24hr.

◣◪ ORIENTATION AND PRACTICAL INFORMATION

Surrounded by fertile corn and wheat fields, Larisa is just southeast of the **Pineios River,** in the middle of eastern Thessaly. The bus station in the north and the train station in the south mark the boundaries of the city's main commercial district, which forms a grid of confusing, labyrinthine streets. A map is essential in Larisa for basic orientation, but asking around is still necessary because of constant construction and road closings. From the bus station, **Olympou** heads south to **Plateia Laou,** one of Larisa's three main squares. Here, the broad avenue **Panagouli** (which continues south) runs perpendicular to **Kyprou,** which runs east-west at the bottom of Pl. Laou, leading westward to **Plateia Mikhali Sagika.** Panagouli continues to the bottom of the commercial grid where it crosses **Iroön Polytechniou** at a five-way intersection. Heading west brings you to the small bus station, heading east to the train station. Below Pl. Laou, Panagouli marks the eastern border of **Plateia Ethnarhou Makariou,** the town center, often called **Plateia Tahydromiou** ("Post Office Square"). The northern edge of this *plateia* is formed by **Panepistemio,** which turns into **Papakyriazi;** this can be taken west three blocks to **Papanastasiou,** which runs parallel to Panagouli. From here, Papanastasiou runs north to Pl. Mikhali Sagika where it meets Kyprou, and even further north to ancient ruins. Papanastasiou heads south past the post office and police station, passing **Mandilara,** which runs east-west, two blocks south from the post office, and Ipirou two blocks down.

Tourist Office: Ipirou 58 (☎24106 70 437), on Ipirou in between Papanastasiou and Botsari. Maps, pamphlets, and advice, though few resources about Larisa itself. Limited English spoken. Open M-F 7am-2:30pm.

Bookstore: The Press, Papakyriazi 53 (☎24105 33 583). Follow Papakyriazi west 2 blocks past Papanastasiou. Maps of the city (€8) as well as newspapers and magazines. Open daily 7am-midnight.

Police: Papanastasiou 86 (☎24106 83 137 or 83 146). 7 blocks south of Papakiriazi and 1 block down from the tourist office, close to Ag. Nikolaos church.

Hospital: Georgiadou (☎24105 34 471), east of the main bus station. Open 24hr.

Telephones: OTE, Fillelinon 22 (☎24109 95 327), just north of Pl. Mikhali Sagika on the road that begins from the center of the *plateia.* Open M, W, F 7:30am-9pm; Tu and Th 7:30am-3pm.

Internet Access: Traffic, Patroklou 14 (☎24102 50 210), at Rousvelt. This chic cafe has computers with high-speed internet. €2 per hr. Open 10am-3am.

Post Office: Papanastasiou 52 (☎24102 56 144), at Diakou. Open M-F 7:30am-8pm. **Poste Restante** and **currency exchange. Postal Code:** 41001.

▐ ACCOMMODATIONS

Mid-range to upper-level hotels can be found along the side streets that connect the three main *plateias.* The cheapest options are near the train station and the smaller bus station, but they're an hour hike south from the main bus station. In town, it's difficult to find a room under €40.

Hotel Diethnes, Paleologou 8 (☎24102 34 210), on the left after exiting the train station. Modern hotel with cool, elegantly decorated rooms with bath. Bar in hotel. Reception 24hr. Singles €30; doubles €38; triples €45. Cash only. ❷

Hotel Pantheon, Paleologou 10 (☎24102 34 810). Most of its orange, yellow, and bright green rooms have TVs, sinks, phones, and A/C. Some have balconies and small baths. Bare-bones singles are the cheapest in the city, but after a night you may consider spending extra cash for an upgrade. Singles €22, with bath €30; doubles €30/35; triples €30/45. Cash only. ❷

Hotel Doma, Skarlatou Soutsou 1 (☎24105 35 025), at the intersection with Kyprou. Each spacious room has a TV, phone, and A/C. Non-smoking rooms available. Helpful English-speaking staff. Bar and room service. Singles €30, with breakfast €37; doubles €45/65; triples €60/80. Cash only. ❷

FOOD

Most of Larisa's cafes, bars, and *tavernas* are on Pl. Tahydromiou and its surrounding streets, where they blend into an uninterrupted river of chairs, tables, and blasting music. During the day, you'll perfect your pronunciation of *"signomi"* (excuse me) as you navigate this busy area. Tempting scents draw crowds into the *psistarias* (grills) on Panos, where lamb and whole chickens slowly turn on spits in the window of each establishment. Cheap food is no problem here—almost every other store serves fast food, from pasta to sandwiches and souvlaki.

Kafodeio, Olympou 3 (☎24105 34 362). This alternative hole-in-the-wall *taverna* with exposed brick walls ironically blasts loud classical music for a student crowd. Appetizers €3-5. Entrees €7-11. Open noon-1am. Cash only. ❷

To Pidari, Asklipiou 40 (☎24106 26 508), on the corner of Kapadistriou, this cozy *taverna* draws in crowds even late into the night with its classic and simply-prepared Greek food. Appetizers €3-5. Entrees €7-8. Open until late. Cash only. ❷

Estro, Panagouli 27 (☎24105 52 442), on the eastern side of Pl. Ethnarhou Makariou. If the cheap eateries aren't for you, treat yourself to the dimly-lit courtyard and generous portions of this classy Italian eatery. Pizzas €9.70-11.50. Pastas €6.20-8. Open 7pm-midnight. ❷

To Sidrivani, Protopapadaki 8 (☎24105 35 933), on the southern side of Pl. Tahydromiou. Claims to be the oldest restaurant in Larisa, and any existing doubts are quieted by the bubbling pots full of delicious homemade Greek cuisine. Vegetarian entrees available. Lamb with vegetables €7. Open noon-midnight. Cash only. ❷

◉ SIGHTS

LARISSA'S MUNICIPAL ART GALLERY. One of the best 20th-century art collections in Greece displays works by almost all of Greece's renowned modern artists. One of the many highlights is a tri-panel painting of Larissa by Agenor Asteriadis. *(Papandreou 2, in the district of Neapoli. A 40min. walk from the center, Papanastasiou turns into Karditsis, which can be taken to Papandreou. Bus # 4 also goes down Karditsis, just ask for the closest stop. ☎24106 16 266. Open M-W and F 10am-2:30pm and 7-10pm. €1, EU students free.)*

RUINS. Larisa's disappointing archaeological sites are clustered on the city's northern hill. Two ancient theaters have been uncovered in the last century. One of them, **Ancient Theater A,** is now available for viewing after over a decade of restoration. Theater A dates from the late third century BC to the beginning of the Roman period. In a field above Ancient Theater A are a couple of sections of columns from the ancient **acropolis,** which is no longer standing. The whole area is fenced off for construction, so all you can do is take a quick peek. Beyond the remnants of the acropolis is the **Byzantine fortress,** where an equally tiny section of the ruins is visible. *(Pl. Miteras, which begins at the corner of El. Venizelou and Papanastasiou and continues northward. Open 24hr. Free.)*

ALKAZAR PARK AND ARCHAEOLOGICAL MUSEUM. Down the opposite side of the hill is the Peneios River. Crossing the river on Ag. Haralabous and turning right, you'll find the shade-filled Alkazar Park. The park is without a doubt the most serene spot in the city—even the graffiti here seems decorative. At the intersection of El. Venizelou and 31 Augustou is a small yellow mosque with a single minaret that now serves as the Archaeological Museum. Showcasing Neolithic and Classical statues and ruins from the province, the collection's primary highlight is a mosaic floor that depicts Nike crowning Atton. (☎ 24102 88 515. Open Tu-Su 8am-3pm. Free.)

🞠 NIGHTLIFE

At night, the area around **Plateia Tahydromiou** becomes one large outdoor cafe. Dense with students, the indistinguishable bars and clubs generally have reasonably priced drinks (beer €3-4) and the students take part in a wild club scene. Larisa's impressive discos generally have a €5-10 cover, which includes one drink.

Ermes, Rousvelt 41 (☎24106 21 022), on Rousvelt and Mandilara in Pl. Trigoni. This bar is hip, young, and fills up before the other bars. Though it's the least expensive of Larisa's bars, the Art Deco decor and blue lights make cheap feel swanky. Mixed drinks €6.50. Open 10am-3am. Cash only.

Arco, Papakiriazi 20 (☎24105 36 798). Swarming with people and playing music late into the night, this popular bar's signature quote, "Every Day is Like Sunday," makes you want to spend your Sundays here. The packed tables spiral out into the *plateia* as English-speaking bartenders serve from the giant bar that dominates the middle of the cafe. Frappes €3. Beer €4. Mixed drinks €6. Open 10am-3am. Cash only.

Blow (☎24105 36 798), corner of Papakiriazi and Megalou Alexandrou. For a change of pace from the trendy bars in the main *plateias,* come to this quirky rock hangout where students lay back and listen to loud house beats. Open 10am-5am. Cash only.

Xilia Xeilia (☎24102 88 977 or 88 475). This club, whose name means "a thousand lips," is a €3 taxi ride from Pl. Tahydromiou. The sweeping entrance, complete with curtains and Corinthian columns, opens into an all-white interior with towering fountains and a narrow stage. Live Greek music every night, often featuring performances by the best *bouzouki* players in the country. Drinks €9. Bottles of whiskey €30-110. Open M-Th and Su 11:30pm-3:30am, F-Sa 11:30pm-6am. Cash only.

Red, about a €5-6 cab ride away. Considered the hottest dance club in Larisa. On especially wild nights, you may catch the bartenders diving into the indoor pool, while the masses grind scandalously to Greek pop. Beer €5. Mixed drinks €7. Open in summer 10pm-7am. Cash only.

KALAMBAKA Καλαμπάκα ☎24320

East of the North Pindhos mountain range lies small, comfortable Kalambaka. Chances are you'll stay in Kalambaka if you plan on seeing Meteora in more than one day. The tourist-friendly town remains fairly inexpensive, despite the volume of people passing through. Kalambaka's un-paralleled hospitality, stunning scenery, and high-quality budget accommodations might make you think twice about leaving.

🞠 TRANSPORTATION

Trains: The distinctive yellow train station (☎24320 22 451) is on the corner of Pindou and Kondyli. To **Athens** (4hr., 4 per day 6:33am-5:35pm, €10.90-20.30) and **Palaio-farsalos** (1hr., 5 per day 8:53am-5:36pm, €8.90), where you can change trains to reach **Thessaloniki** (3hr., 4 per day 7:42am-5:36pm, €8.90).

Buses: Averof 2 (☎24320 22 432), downhill from Pl. Dimarhiou on Rodou. Open 6:15am-9pm. To: **Athens** (5hr., 7 per day 7am-1am, €25) via **Lamia** (3hr., €10.50); **Ioannina** (3hr.; 8:50, 11:50am, 3:20pm; €11.20) via **Metsovo** (2hr., €6.20); **Kastraki** (5min., every hr. 7:45am-10pm, €1); **Meteora** (15min.; M-F 9am, 1, 5pm; Sa-Su 8:30am,

CENTRAL GREECE

12:30pm; €1); **Patra** (5hr.; Th 10am, F and Su 3pm; €27.50); **Thessaloniki** (3hr., 6 per day 5:15am-7pm, €17.50); **Trikala** (30min., every 30min. 6:10am-11pm, €2).

Taxis: (☎24320 22 310), on Rodou below the town hall square. 24hr.

⬛🔢 ORIENTATION AND PRACTICAL INFORMATION

There are two squares in Kalambaka: **Plateia Dimarhiou** (Town Hall Square) and **Plateia Riga Fereou** (Central Square). Pl. Dimarhiou has a large fountain and stands on an incline, whereas Pl Riga Fereou is completely flat though it also has a smaller fountain. In Pl. Dimarhiou, standing with your back to the fountain and the Meteora cliffs, **Vlachava** cuts diagonally behind you, in the upper left of the square, and leads to the **Old City** and **Kanari.** Going clockwise, to your immediate left is **Trikalon,** which leads to Pl. Riga Fereou, **Rodou** is in front, slightly to the right, and heads to the bus station, and **Ioanninon,** the road to Ioannina, downhill to the right. **Patriarhou Dimitriou** is farthest right on a slight uphill, intersecting with Vlachava at the tourist information office at the corner. From Pl. Riga Fereou, many cafes and bars, open at all hours, congregate on the pedestrian street **Dimoula,** two blocks down Trikalon from the *plateia.* With the cliffs on your left, **Kondyli** branches off to the right at the end of Pl. Riga Fereou and leads to the train station.

Tourist Office: Pl. Dimarhiou (☎24320 75 306), on the corner where Vlachava and Dimitriou intersect. Provides maps, bus and train schedules, and monastery hours. Helpful pamphlets are available after hours in a box on the door. Open M-F 8am-9pm, Sa 9am-5pm, Su 10am-4pm.

Bank: National Bank, Sidirodromou 1 (☎24320 23 334), in Pl. Riga Fereou. **24hr. ATM.** Open M-Th 8am-2:30pm, F 8am-2pm.

Laundry: The Green Wash, Trikala 81 (☎24320 23 970), several blocks past Pl. Riga Fereou. Wash and dry €8. Open 8am-8:30pm.

Police: (☎24320 76 100), 10min. from the center of town down Ioanninon at the intersection with Pindou. Open 24hr. **Tourist Police** in the same building. Open 24hr.

Medical Services: Health Center (☎24320 22 222), 1km from town, on the road to Ioannina.

Internet Access: Arena, Dimoula 21 (☎24320 77 999), 1 block down Dimoula off Trikalon past Pl. Riga Fereou. €2 per hr., €1.20 from 11pm-5:30am. Open 10am-5:30am. **Boca...rs,** Dimoula 3 (☎24320 77 200). Wi-Fi and computer terminals. €2 per hr. Open 10am-2am.

Post Office: Trikalon 23 (☎24320 22 466), between the two *plateias.* **Poste Restante.** Open M-F 7:30am-2pm. **Postal Code:** 42200.

🏠📷 ACCOMMODATIONS AND CAMPING

Hawks offering *domatia* here are infamous for luring travelers with promises of good prices, then hitting them with exorbitant surcharges. Make sure you know the details before agreeing to anything. The accommodations with the best views, comfort, and hospitality are in the quiet, highrise-free Old Town near the foot trail to Meteora. From Pl. Dimarhiou, take Vlachava uphill, which turns into Sopotou at the intersection with 25 Martiou. Continue along the road and you will see winding **Kanari,** where all the accommodations listed below are located.

🏠 **Alsos House,** Kanari 5 (☎24320 24 097; www.alsoshouse.gr), in the Old Town at the base of Meteora. Spacious rooms, each with bath, A/C, and balcony with breathtaking view of Meteora. Amiable English-speaking proprietor Yiannis will pick guests up from the bus or train station, take them for walks on the hidden paths once used by monks,

CENTRAL GREECE

and enlighten them with deep conversation. Breakfast included. Shared kitchen. Free Wi-Fi. Reservations recommended. Singles €30-35; doubles €50; triples €75; quads €80; 2-room apartment with kitchen €70-80. MC/V. ❷

Koka Roka, Kanari 21 (☎24320 24 554). Large rooms draw backpackers from around the world. The warm proprietress offers advice, while Aussie Arthur serves his guests a tasty meal every night at the adjacent *taverna* of the same name. Internet €3 per hr. Reception 24hr. Singles €25; doubles €35-40; triples €50-60. Cash only. ❷

Vrachos Camping (☎24320 22 293), 1km out of town toward Kastraki and the monasteries. Most popular campgrounds, with a pool, restaurant, and great views. Curfew midnight. €8 per person with tent, €10 per person with car. Caravans with bed but no bath €11. Discounts available. Cash only. ❶

🔧 FOOD

To save some cash or to slap together a picnic for a day at the monasteries, visit the **Carrefour supermarket,** Rammidi 14, just off Trikalon past Pl. Riga Fereou. (☎24320 78 543. Open M-F 8am-9pm, Sa 8am-8pm. Cash only.) Each Friday, Vlachava and its main cross street, Kondyli, turn into a full-scale marketplace (open 7am-2pm), which sells fresh produce and household goods.

Taverna Paramithy, Dimitriou 14 (☎24320 24 441), a few blocks from Pl. Dimarhiou on Dimitriou. This restaurant's name means "Fairy Tale Tavern." A look at the canopy of grape leaves shading the porch and you'll agree that the name is well-deserved. With cheap and delectable traditional cuisine, the *taverna* offers meat or fish dishes, slow-cooked to perfection. Appetizers €2-3.50. Entrees €5-7. Open daily 11am-midnight. Cash only. ❷

Koka Roka Taverna, Kanari 21 (☎24320 24 554), inside its namesake hotel near the beginning of the Meteora footpath in the heart of the Old City. The souvlaki and lamb chops have been described in the restaurant's guest book as a "religious experience," while the Greek salad has been called "the best in Greece." Koka Roka is also the cheapest place to enjoy a beer, with large €1.50 bottles. Entrees €4-8. Open daily 10am-1am. Cash only. ❷

Arhondariki, Trikalon 9 (☎24320 22 449), just off Pl. Riga Fereou on the way to Pl. Dimarhiou. Overlooking the *plateia*, Arhondariki is the perfect spot to enjoy hearty dishes and people-watch. Classic dishes like the signature moussaka (€7), cooked with pure olive oil. Entrees €4.40-8.50. Open daily noon-midnight. ❷

📷 SIGHTS

BYZANTINE CHURCH OF THE ASSUMPTION OF THE VIRGIN. The church was built in the seventh century atop a Classical temple whose pagan mosaics now are entombed beneath the floor. Though the main structure was remodeled in 1573, the original baptism basin remains at the entrance. *(Follow signs in the plateia; after several blocks that wind up to the foot of the slopes, you'll spy its stone bell tower. It is also reachable from the Old Town by a path starting from behind the Koka Roka hotel and taverna that passes right by the church. Open 8am-1pm and 4-9pm. €1.50. Modest dress required.)*

METEORA CLIFFS. The only thing more stunning than seeing the Meteora cliffs is seeing them at night. The street closest to the cliffs (the street just above the Church of the Assumption of the Virgin) has benches facing the up-lit mountains and a view of the city below. In late July, the town honors its patron saint with a celebration complete with music, dance, and food. Nearby Kastraki holds a three-day wine festival with free samples in late August.

NIGHTLIFE

Crystal, Dimoula 4 (☎24320 77 577). The last bar on the corner is packed late into the night. Drinks €4-8. Open daily 10am-2am.

Boca...rs, Dimoula 3 (☎24320 77 200). Bustling bar at night. Open daily 10am-2am.

Bloo, Trikalon 100. A younger crowd congregates here for the loud pop and (surprise) blue lights. Open daily 10am-1am.

METEORA Μετέορα

The monastic community of Meteora (meh-TEH-o-rah), whose name means "hanging in the air" or "in suspense," rests atop awe-inspiring peaks that ascend to the sky. Believed to have been inhabited by hermits as early as the 11th century, the summits were chosen as the location of a series of 21 gravity-defying, frescoed Byzantine monasteries in the 14th century. Six of the monasteries are still in use and open to the public; the largest and most popular of which are Grand Meteoro and Varlaam. The other four monasteries are less celebrated, and thus refreshingly more quiet, charming, and intimate. Still, Meteora is hardly an undiscovered treasure, and gift shops and tourists are as common as the frescoes.

TRANSPORTATION AND PRACTICAL INFORMATION

Most monasteries close one day per week. Though most monasteries run on a 9am-5pm schedule, opening and closing hours vary from monastery to monastery and change often; consult the tourist office in Kalambaka for times. Even if a monastery is closed, it is still worth checking out, as the outside is often as spectacular as what's inside. Photography is forbidden in certain areas, and modest dress is required. Generally this means no sleeveless tops for men or women. Women are required to wear a long skirt (though wraps are provided at the monasteries), while men should wear long shorts or pants. Most of the monasteries close midday, so many people decide to pack picnics, though there are food stands by Varlaam and Grand Meteora. (€2 per monastery, under 12 free.)

Buses: Leave for Meteora from the bus station on Rodou. (20min.; M-F 9am, 1, 5pm; Sa-Su 8:30am and 12:30pm; €1.40.) Buy tickets on board or at the bus station.

Taxis: A taxi from Kalambaka is about €5.

WALKING THE MONASTERIES

The origins of the settlements on the Meteora rocks are unknown: one story claims that the first recluse was **Barnabas,** a monk who founded the *skite* (a small, remote monastic cell) of the Holy Ghost in the mid-10th century. By the 11th century, hermits and ascetics followed his example, moving to the pinnacles and crevices of Meteora and worshipping in a church dedicated to the **Theotokos** (Mother of God), which still can be seen below the Ag. Nikolaos monastery. As persecution at the hands of Turkish and Frankish marauders increased in the 12th century, Orthodox Christians fled to the summits of these impregnable columns of rock. In 1344, the region's first monastic community was founded when the monk **Athanasios,** his spiritual father **Gregorios,** and 14 fellow monks began to build Grand Meteoro. Athanasios was a well-educated monk whose journeys brought him to Constantinople, Crete, and finally Mt. Athos, to which he fled to avoid Turkish invasions. He occupied his time weaving baskets in a nearby cave, and referred to women as "the sling" (that vault the stones of sin into men's hearts) or as "the affliction" (addicting men to the sinful pleasures of the flesh). He displayed this penchant for description slightly more constructively when he gave Meteora its name. Later, the Greek-Serbian king of Thessaly and Epirus, Ioannis Versis Angelos Komininos Palaeologos, traded regal comforts for Meteora's rugged rocks and built many of its later monasteries.

When the Ottomans ruled most of Greece, Meteora served as an outpost of Christianity. In the 16th century, it grew into a community of 21 monasteries, which amassed large libraries of both religious and secular books and created dazzling icons and frescoes. However, when donations tapered off in the late 1700s and the popularity of monastic life waned, many of these manuscripts and books were sold for a fraction of their actual worth. Small brotherhoods still exist at Grand Meteoro, Varlaam, Ag. Triada, and Ag. Nikolaos, while Ag. Stephanos and Roussanou are now convents.

The first ascetics scaled Meteora's cliffs by wedging timbers into the rock crevices to build small platforms; traces of these steps still can be seen in the walls. After the monasteries were completed, visitors arrived by means of extremely long rope ladders. Those who were too weak or too timid to climb were hoisted up in baskets. Once these devices were pulled up, though, the summits became inaccessible. Today, motorized winches have replaced the rope-spool cranes, and only provisions are yanked up by rope. In 1922, in the ultimate facilitation of a quicker rise to heaven, bridges were built between the pillars, and steps were carved into the rocks.

Begin your tour of Meteora at **Grand Meteoro,** the largest and most famous monastery and the location of the bus stop. You then can work your way down through its neighbors, **Varlaam, Roussanou,** and **Agios Nikolaos.** A sign on the highway between Varlaam and Roussanou marked "Ag. Triada" points into the bush to a short trail to Triada (20min.). The last monastery, **Agios Stephanos,** is about 800m from Ag. Triada. Though it's probably a good idea to get a regional map before leaving Kalambaka, the monasteries are all within walking distance and are connected by a single road. To head back down to Kalambaka from Ag. Triada, there is a trail off the road connecting the monastery with the highway. Consider making your way to one of the smaller monasteries first thing in the morning to experience the (short-lived) serenity of the monasteries before the crowds show up.

Before heading out, stop by Alsos Rooms to speak with Yiannis; he is happy to provide his accurate, handwritten hiking map. The general advice given to tourists, however, is to stay on the roads at all times. If possible, split the Meteora hikes between two days, covering the two eastern monasteries one day and the remaining four in the west on another. Doing the entire circuit in a day could take as long as 6hr. if you plan on hiking up to and down from the monasteries. Walking from Grand Meteoro to Ag. Stephanos (including the detour to Ag. Nikolaos) takes about 2hr. All monasteries have water fountains, but always bring your own bottle.

GRAND METEORO. The **Monastery of the Transfiguration,** known as "Grand Meteoro," is the site at which St. Athanasios began his imitation of the community at Mt. Athos in the 14th century. Looming 475m above Thessaly's plain, the complex, known in its entirety as **Platys Lithos,** reached its peak in the 16th century, when it was visited by the reigning patriarch and accorded the same privileges as the autonomous Mt. Athos. Around this time, the **Church of the Transfiguration** was built and was capped by an exalted dome with a *pantokrator* (a central image of Christ). The *katholikon* (nave) stands 24m high, and is constructed

FROM THE ROAD

NGUAGE'S LABOR'S LOST

As a visitor in Greece, having never experienced the language or culture beyond the odd piece of baklava, I had to tackle the Greek alphabet. The ρ is an 'r'? Why does that 'o' have a line through it? I remember the first few days, as I stubbornly struggled with my map and alphabet guide, determined to read the street name and match it up with some semblance of an English transliteration. I'd spend 10 minutes at each street simply trying to figure out where I was. Ordering at restaurants was a feat, as I bypassed places without English menus for fear of looking stupid.

Finally, I had had enough, so I started to ask for directions. The first time I did, an old man insisted on walking me to the correct street and pointing me in the right direction. In another instance, an elderly woman flagged down two college girls and a deliveryman, all of whom stayed with me until I found my way. A third time, a cab driver refused to take me in his cab and gave me walking directions instead ("because it is so close!").

It took me a while, but I finally decided that the steep learning curve was a blessing in disguise. It wasn't really a signal to try harder to master Greek, but rather an obvious reminder that the best parts of traveling are the people and the little acts of kindness that strangers show daily. In the end, asking for directions in broken Greek doesn't make you look stupid—but staring at a street sign for 15 minutes might.

—Sarah Mortazavi

in Byzantine style with a 12-sided dome. Murals created by the mid-16th century Cretan painter Theophanes Bathas-Strelitzas cover the walls. If you manage to get past all of the tourists you will find a former carpenter's workshop, a small, haunting catacomb, the old kitchen, and a small **museum**. The museum's collections of early printed texts of Plato and Aristotle and old gospel parchments attest to the monastery's past preeminence as an intellectual center. (☎24320 22 278. Open M and W-Su 9am-5pm. €2.)

VARLAAM. The second-largest monastery is about 800m downhill from Grand Meteoro. The complex was founded in the 14th century by one of Athanasios's contemporaries who, in a display of true humility, named it after himself. It went into disrepair until the 16th century when two brothers from a prominent family in Ioannina and their two disciples moved to the "Rock of Varlaam," beginning construction on the church in its present form in 1542. The *katholikon's* 16th-century frescoes depict hermits, martyrs, an apocalyptic sea serpent swallowing doomed sinners, and St. Sisoes looking pitifully upon Alexander the Great's skeleton. The monastery's **library** contains 290 manuscripts, including a miniature Bible from 959 that belonged to Emperor Constantine Porfyrogenitos. (☎24320 22 277. Open M-W and F-Su 9am-4pm. €2.)

ROUSSANOU. Bear right at the fork on the highway to reach Roussanou. Visible from most of the valley, it is one of Meteora's most spectacularly situated monasteries. With steep sides, three of which overlook the drop to the valley below, Roussanou seems to sprout from the steep cliff as a natural continuation of the boulders. Unfortunately, the magnificent exterior is not matched by the interior—as the church is now home to a group of nuns, only the *katholikon* is open for viewing and it hardly distinguishes itself among its more glamorous neighbors. The heavenly exterior can be enjoyed even by those without a ticket. Still, the history of Roussanou might compel you to visit anyway—the church proudly housed Greek refugees fleeing the Turks in 1757 and 1897. (☎24320 22 649. Open daily 9am-6pm. €2.)

AGIOS NIKOLAOS. Farther down the road (a 20min. downhill detour from Roussanou) is the 16th-century monastery of Agios Nikolaos Anapafsas, only 2.5km from Kastraki. Built on the ruins of an older monastery, it is situated on the summit of a very narrow boulder. Construction constraints meant that Agios Nikolaos had to be built vertically rather than horizontally, making it the second-tallest monastery, next to Grand Meteoro. Standing at the top of the bell tower gives the impression that you're hanging in mid-air over mind-boggling depths. (☎ *24320 22 375. Open M-Th and Sa-Su 9am-2:30pm. €2.)*

AGIA TRIADA. From the steps of Roussanou, just before you pass through the gates with the listed hours and climb the last set of steps to the metal bridge, take the (mostly) paved path uphill to your left. When it hits the road, bear right and continue to find Agia Triada; movie buffs will recognize it from the James Bond flick *For Your Eyes Only.* As you head down the stairs that lead to the bathroom, enjoy the panoramic view of the Pindos Mountains in the distance with Kalambaka's traditional red-roofed houses immediately below. Ambitious monk Dometius built the monastery in 1438, but many of the **wall paintings** weren't added until the 18th century. Unfortunately, most of the monastery's prized manuscripts and heirlooms were lost in WWII, but the beautiful church walls are enough to entertain any visitor. (☎ *24320 22 220. Open M-W and F-Su 9am-5pm. €2.)*

AGIOS STEPHANOS. Originally a convent, Agios Stephanos became a monastery in the early 15th century. Today it is once again home to an active community of nuns. Of its two churches, the newer **Agios Haralambos,** built in 1798, is the more prominent, larger, and featuring restored frescoes. The older church, **Protomartia Stephanou,** built in 1350, contains naturally faded and cracked walls that serve as a reminder of the true age and character of the church. The **museum** displays icons, manuscripts, liturgical vestments, and crosses. Its intricate wooden *iconostasis* is carved into figures of birds, animals, and people. The gargoyle fountain at the top is a great place to fill up a water bottle, as the Ag. Stephanos's proximity to a spring makes the water here the purest and coldest on Meteora. (☎ *24320 22 279. Open Tu-Su 9am-1:30pm and 3:30-5:30pm. €2.)*

NORTHERN GREECE

Northern Greece does not experience the same mass tourism found in the other Greek provinces, and visitors reap the benefits. You'll barely remember—let alone miss—the beaches as you move inland amid soaring mountains and beautiful small towns, whose architecture, food, and population represent the influences of Greece's northern neighbors. With its proximity to Albania, the Former Yugoslavian Republic Of Macedonia, Bulgaria, and Turkey, the region is starkly more Balkan than the remainder of Greece. Northern Greece has all the sights any traveler would want: from the multicultural urban experience of Thessaloniki to the internationally-renowned campgrounds of Arministis; from the heights of Mount Olympus—Greece's highest summit—to the depths of the Vikos Gorge—the steepest in the world. For travelers seeking distance from Athens and the islands, Northern Greece offers an idyllic alternative.

HIGHLIGHTS OF NORTHERN GREECE

AIN'T no mountain high like **Mount Olympus,** Greece's tallest peak (p. 192).
AIN'T no valley low like the world's steepest gorge, the **Vikos Gorge** (p. 212).

MACEDONIA Μακεδονία

Macedonia earned itself a place in history when its native son Alexander forged a massive empire stretching to Egypt and India by 323 BC. A few centuries later, the region served as the geographical entry point for St. Paul, who brought Christianity to Europe. The historical boundaries of Greek Macedonia under the Byzantine Empire were much greater than the modern province's current territory; pieces of the historical region of Macedonia lie within Albania, Bulgaria, and the Former Yugoslav Republic of Macedonia. In recent decades, Macedonia has become the focal point of tensions between northern Greece and the Balkan states as Greeks have demanded exclusive use of the name "Macedonia" and even the return of formerly Hellenic lands. Despite its identity struggle, Macedonia is one of Greece's most multidimensional provinces. Offering a range of attractions—excellent archaeological sites, peaceful beaches, and beautiful and burgeoning urban areas—Macedonia keeps its visitors intrigued with endless surprises and historical flavor.

THESSALONIKI Θεσσαλονίκη ☎ 2310

Thessaloniki (also called "Salonica") is one of the most historically diverse and cosmopolitan cities in Greece. Forget nature—Thessaloniki is definitely an urban experience that is as modern or historical as you make it. With its charming *plateias*, old churches and mosques, and ubiquitous ruins, Thessaloniki dazzles travelers as an evolving monument to European history. Kassandros,

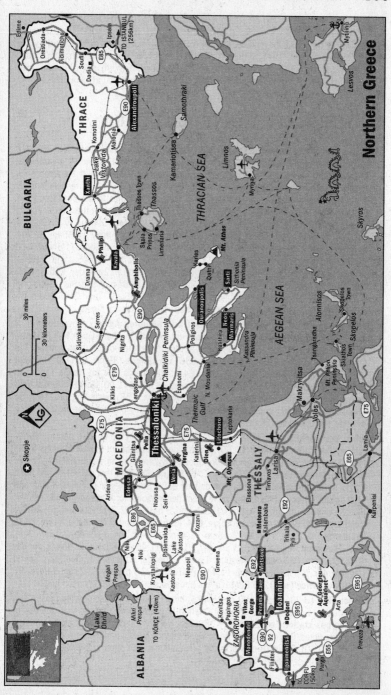

King of Macedonia in 315 BC, founded and named the city after his wife—or so he told her; the city's name also means "Victory in Thessaly." Thessaloniki became part of the modern Greek state in 1913 but soon was devastated by the Great Fire in August 1917, which destroyed much of the city's infrastructure. Conquered by three empires, home to Muslim and Jewish populations, and now the largest city in Greece after Athens, urban sophistication is the key in this cultural capital of Greece.

◪ INTERCITY TRANSPORTATION

Flights: Macedonia Airport (SKG; ☎23109 85 000), 16km east of town. Take bus #78 (€0.60), which runs every 40min. from both the KTEL bus station and Pl. Aristotelous, or by taxi (50min., €15). There's an **EOT** branch (☎23109 85 215) at the airport. For tickets, head to **Olympic Airways,** Kountouriotou 3 (☎23103 68 200, reservations 68 666; olympicairlines.com), across the street from the entrance to the port. Open M-F 8:30am-4pm. **Aegean Airlines** (☎23104 76 470). Has a branch at the airport. Flights to: **Athens** (50min., 10-16 per day 6am-11pm, €77); **Chios** (50min.; Tu 5:10am, W 7:25pm, Th 6am, F and Su 10:05am; €66); **Chania** (1½hr., daily 11:35am, €133); **Kerkyra** (1hr.; M, Th, Sa 3:35pm, Tu 4:15pm, F 9:30pm; €69); **Iraklion** (1½hr.; M and Th 6:45am, Tu-W, F, Su 7:25pm; €128); **Limnos** (50min.; M and W 6:45am, Tu 5:10am, Th 6am, F 6:40pm, Sa 5:55am; €93); **Mytilini** (1hr. 50min., 12 per day, €105); **Rhodes** (2hr.; M and W 6:45am, Tu 5:10am and 7:25pm, Th 6am, F and Su 1:50pm, Sa 5:55am; €133); **Samos** (1hr. 20min.; Tu 5:10am, W 2:45pm, F and Su 5:20am, Sa 5:55am; €77). Subject to change; double-check before booking flights.

Ferries: Buy tickets at **Karacharisis Travel and Shipping Agency,** Kountouriotou 8 (☎23105 13 005), 1 block from the main entrance to the port. Open M-F 8:30am-8:30pm, Sa 8:30am-2:30pm. There are several ferry lines during high season. The Chios line to: **Chios** (20hr., Tu 2:30pm, €36) via **Limnos** (8½hr., €23-30), **Mytilini** (14hr., €35), and **Santorini** (17-18hr., €41). The Naxos line to: **Naxos** (14hr., Tu 7pm, €39) via **Syros** (12hr., €38) and **Mykonos** (13hr., €41.50). Buy **Flying Cat** tickets at **Karacharisis.** Fast boats go to **Skiathos** (4hr., €58) beginning Jan. 19th via **Skopelos** (5hr., €59) and **Alonnisos** (5¾hr., €59). They usually leave at least once per day, but schedules change weekly.

Trains: Main terminal (☎23105 17 517), on Monastiriou in the western part of the city. Take any bus down Egnatia (€0.60). Tickets are sold at the International Trains booth (☎2310 5 99 033) at the train station. Open daily 7am-9pm. International trains go to: **Istanbul, Turkey** (14hr., daily 7:17am, €14); **Skopje, FYROM** (4hr.; daily 9am and 6pm; €11); **Sofia, Bulgaria** (7hr., daily midnight, €50). Both regular domestic trains and **high-speed intercity (IC) trains** serve most destinations. To: **Alexandroupoli** (regular: 8hr., 3 per day 7:35am-11:44pm, €10. IC: 5hr., 3 per day 12:21pm-2am, €25); **Athens** (regular: 7hr., 5 per day 8am-11:45pm, €14. IC: 5hr., 6 per day 7:24am-1:51am, €33); **Drama** (regular: 3hr., 3 per day 7:18am-11:44pm, €6. IC: 2hr., 3 per day 7:18am-2am, €16); **Komotini** (regular: 5hr., 3 per day 7:18am-11:44pm, €8.20. IC: 4hr., 3 per day 12:21pm-2am, €20); **Larisa** (regular: 1½hr., 13 per day 5:08am-10:09pm, €5); **Xanthi** (regular: 4hr., 3 per day 7:18am-11:44pm, €7. IC: 3hr., 3 per day 12:21pm-2am, €19). The **Travel Office** (☎23105 98 110) has updated schedules and prices in English

Buses: KTEL (☎23109 81 100 or 95 423) buses connect Thessaloniki to most major Greek cities. Except for buses to the **Chalkidiki prefecture,** all leave from the dome-shaped **bus station** (☎23105 95 406), 3km west of the city center. Call for updated departure times. Bus #1 is a shuttle between the bus station and the train station (every 10min., €0.60). Bus #78 connects the bus station to the airport, passing through the waterfront corridor (every 40min., €0.60).

International Buses: leave from the main train station (☎23105 99 100) on Monastiriou in the city's western part; take any bus down Egnatia to get there (€0.60). Buses to: **Istanbul, Turkey** (12hr., Tu-Su 10am and 10pm, €45); **Sofia, Bulgaria** (6hr., 5 per day 7:30am-10pm, €19). The dome holds offices for each of the KTEL district booths.

Domestic Buses: To the Chalkidiki prefecture leave from the **Chalkidiki Station** (☎2310 3 16 575), in the eastern outskirts of the city. Allow at least 1hr. to get there. Take bus #31 eastbound down Egnatia from the bus terminal. When bus #31 reaches its final stop, get off, and take the #36 KTEL Chalkidiki bus to the station. Your initial bus ticket will allow you to get on the #36 bus for no extra charge. Buses to: **Armenistis** (3hr., 3 per day 11:15am-6:30pm, €12.30); **Ierissos** (1hr., 7 per day 6:15am-6:30pm, €9.70); **Kalithea** (1hr., 14 per day 5:45am-9pm, €8); **Nea Marmaras** (2hr., 3 per day 9:15am-5:15pm, €11.70); **Ouranoupolis** (2hr., 8 per day 5:30am-6:30pm, €11.20); **Sarti** (3hr., 3 per day 9am-5pm, €17).

DESTINATION	LENGTH	FREQUENCY	PRICE	TELEPHONE
Alexandroupoli	5hr.	8 per day 7:30am-11:30pm	€24	☎23105 95 439
Athens	6hr.	11 per day 7am-11:45pm	€35	☎23105 95 413
Corinth	7hr.	11:30am	€37	☎23105 95 405
Drama	2hr.	13 per day, every hr. 7:30am-9pm	€11.50	☎23105 95 420
Edessa	1hr.	Every hr. 6am-8pm	€7.50	☎23105 95 435
Florina	3hr.	6 per day 7:30am-p8m	€11.30	☎23105 95 418
Grevena	2hr.	5 per day 8:30am-8pm	€12	☎23105 95 485
Igoumenitsa	8hr.	1pm	€36.80	☎23105 95 416
Ioannina	6hr.	6 per day 7:30am-10pm	€27.10	☎23105 95 442
Karditsa	3hr.	4 per day 10am-9:30pm	€15	☎23105 95 440
Kastoria	3hr.	7 per day 8:30am-9:30pm	€15	☎23105 95 440
Katerini	50min.	Every 30min. 6:30am-10:30pm	€8	☎23105 95 428
Kavala	2hr.	Every hr. 6am-10pm	€13.50	☎23105 95 422
Komotini	4hr.	7 per day 8:30am-11:30pm	€28	☎23105 95 419
Kozani	1hr.	Every hr. 6am-10pm	€10.30	☎23105 95 484
Lamia	4hr.	11 per day 7:30am-12:15am	€21.10	☎23105 95 416
Larisa	2hr.	Every hr. 8am-10pm	€10.50	☎23105 95 430
Metsovo	4hr.	6 per day 7:30am-9:30pm	€23	☎23105 95 442
Parga	9hr.	10am, 9:30pm	€33	☎23105 95 406
Patra	7hr.	4 per day 8:15am-9pm	€39.40	☎23105 95 425
Ancient Pella	50 min.	Every 40min. 6:30am-10:30pm	€3	☎23105 95 435
Pirgos	10hr.	M-Th and Sa-Su 9:45am, F 2:30pm	€46.30	☎23105 95 409
Preveza	8hr.	Daily 3pm	€37.20	☎23105 95 406
Serres	1hr.	Every 30min. 6am-10pm	€7.40	☎23105 95 464
Trikala	3hr.	6 per day 8:30am-10pm	€15	☎23105 95 405
Veria	1hr.	Every hr. 6:15am-8:45pm	€6	☎23105 95 432
Xanthi	3hr.	8 per day 8am-11:30pm	€17	☎23105 95 423

NORTHERN GREECE

NORTHERN GREECE

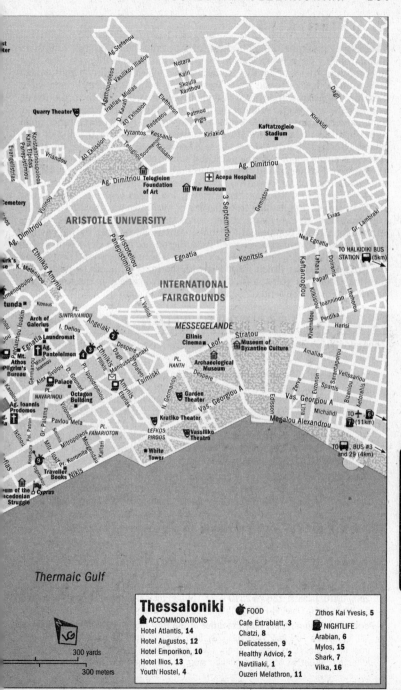

NORTHERN GREECE

Thessaloniki

🏠 ACCOMMODATIONS
Hotel Atlantis, **14**
Hotel Augustos, **12**
Hotel Emporikon, **10**
Hotel Ilios, **13**
Youth Hostel, **4**

🍴 FOOD
Cafe Extrablatt, **3**
Chatzi, **8**
Delicatessen, **9**
Healthy Advice, **2**
Navtiliaki, **1**
Ouzeri Melathron, **11**

Zithos Kai Yvesis, **5**
🍷 NIGHTLIFE
Arabian, **6**
Mylos, **15**
Shark, **7**
Vilka, **16**

Thermaic Gulf

⚏ ORIENTATION

Thessaloniki stretches along the waterfront of the Thermaic Gulf's northern shore from the iconic **White Tower** in the east to the **harbor** in the west. The most important arteries run parallel to the water. Closest to shore is **Nikis,** which runs from the harbor to the White Tower and is home to the city's main cafes. Next are **Mitropoleos,** the traffic of which runs from the harbor to the tower, and **Tsimiski,** with traffic running the other direction. At the White Tower end, Tsimiski terminates in **Plateia Hanth.** The *plateia* is a common reference point and a bus stop. Next comes store-lined **Ermou,** named after the god of merchants (Hermes). Farthest from shore is **Egnatia,** a six-lane avenue; the **Arch of Galerius** is also a major meeting point and stands at Egnatia's intersection with D. Gounari. Farther inland from Egnatia are **Agios Dimitriou** and the **Old City.** The roads north of Ag. Dimitriou grow increasingly tiny and steep toward the Old City's ancient walls, panoramic views, and cheap *tavernas.* Intersecting all these streets and leading from the water into town are, in order from the western harbor to the eastern tower: Ionos Dragoumi, Eleftherios Venizelou, Aristotelous, Agias Sophias, and Ethnikis Aminis. **Aristotelous,** a wide pavilion where breezes sweep unobstructed from the ocean, is the city's center, with a bevy of restaurants, businesses, and banks. The area between Tsimiski and the Arch of Galerius, **Plateia Navarinou,** with the ruins of Galerius's palace, is a meeting ground for young locals. The older crowd gathers in the *tavernas* of **Ladadika,** at the harbor end of Tsimiski and Mitropoleos.

⊟ LOCAL TRANSPORTATION

Thessaloniki and its suburbs are connected by an extensive public transportation network.

Local buses: Run throughout the city. An office opposite the train station provides schedules. Maps posted at some of the bus stops show the city routes. The depot most frequently visited by travelers is at the train station and is the starting point for **bus #1,** which runs to the **KTEL** dome, **bus #8,** which goes to the **White Tower** stop, and **bus #73.** At the small depot at Pl. Eleftherias by the harbor you can catch **buses #5, 6,**and **33,** which navigate the waterfront on **Tsimiski** and **Mitropoleos,** and **bus #24,** which goes to the **Old City.** Buses #10, 11, and 31 run down **Egnatia.** €0.50 at newsstands, €0.60 on the bus, €2 for a 24hr. pass.

Taxis: (☎2310 5 51 525). Run down Egnatia, Tsimiski, and Mitropoleos. Stands are at Ag. Sophia and the intersection of Mitropoleos and Aristotelous. Rides within the city should not exceed €4, though ordering a taxi by phone adds €1.50 to the fare.

⚇ PRACTICAL INFORMATION

TOURIST AND FINANCIAL SERVICES

Tourist Offices: EOT (☎23109 85 215), at the airport. Open M-F 8am-8pm, Sa 8am-2pm. **GNTO,** Tsimiski 136 (☎2310 2 21 100), at the eastern end of Tsimiski, north of the White Tower. Open M-F 8am-2:50pm, Sa 8:30am-2pm.

Permits for Mount Athos: Holy Executive of the Holy Mount Athos Pilgrims' Bureau, 1st fl., Egnatia 109 (☎23102 52 578). Take bus #10 from the train station, bus #31 from the intercity bus station, or any bus along Egnatia, and ask for #109 or the Mt. Athos office. Get off at the Lasonithou stop. All men need permits to visit Mt. Athos.

NORTHERN GREECE

Passports required; pick up permit in person. Women are not allowed to visit the mountain. English spoken. Open M-F 9am-2pm, Sa 10am-2pm.

Consulates: See **Consular Services in Greece** (p. 8).

Banks: Citi Bank, Tsimiski 21 (☎23103 73 300). Open M-Th 8am-2:30pm, F 8am-2pm. **HSBC,** Tsimiski 8 (☎23102 86 044). Open M-Sa 8am-2:30pm, Su 8am-2pm. No bank accepts Bulgarian or Albanian currencies; travelers coming from these countries must head to the exchange booths at El. Venizelou's intersection with Ermou. All the above banks have **24hr. ATMS.**

LOCAL SERVICES

Bookstores: Malliaris, D. Gounari 39 (☎23102 77 113). Large selection of English travel and leisure reading, computer equipment, magazines, and newspapers. Open M-F 9am-9pm, Sa 9am-5pm. MC/V. **Newsstand,** Ag. Sophias 37 (☎23102 87 072). Wide selection of international newspapers and magazines. Open daily 7am-10pm. Cash Only. **Traveller Books,** Proxenou Koromila 41 (☎23102 75 215), 1 block inland from Nikis east of Aristotelous. Has English travel guides. Open M, W, Sa 9:30am-3pm; Tu, Th, F 9:30am-9pm.MC/V.

Laundromat: Homestyle Laundry, Manolaki Kyriakou (☎23102 13 026), just north of the rotunda. Wash and dry €6.50. Open M-F 9am-7pm, Sa 9am-3pm.

EMERGENCY AND COMMUNICATIONS

Police: (☎23105 53 800). **Tourist police,** 5th fl., Dodekanisou 4 (☎23105 54 871). Free maps and brochures. Open daily 8am-10pm.

Hospital: Acepa Hospital, Kiriakidi 1 (☎23109 93 111). **Hippokratio General Hospital,** A. Papanastassiou 50 (☎23108 92 000). Some doctors speak English. On weekends and at night call ☎1434 to find which hospital has emergency care.

Telephones: OTE, Karolou Diehl 33 (☎23102 41 999), at the corner of Ermou and Karolou Diehl, 1 block east of Aristotelous. Near the Ag. Sophia church between Ag. Sophia and Aristotelous. Open M and W 8:30am-2pm, Tu and Th-F 8:30am-2pm and 5:30-8:30pm. Another location (☎23105 51 599), by the intersection of 26 Oktovriou 1 and Pl. Dimokratias, at the west end of Egnatia near the city court. Open M-F 8:30am-2pm.

Internet Access: E-Global, Vas. Irakliou 40 (☎23102 52 780; www.e-global.gr), behind the shopping complex housing the American Consulate. Internet €2.20 per hr., min. €1. Open 24hr. Another location at Egnatia 17 (☎23109 68 404), 1 block east of the Arch of Galerius. **Meganet,** Pl. Navarinou 5 (☎23102 50 331; www.meganet.gr). Overlooks Galerius's Palace and a charming fountain of a boy relieving himself. Internet noon-midnight €2 per hr., midnight-noon €1 per hr. Open 24hr. **Bits and Bytes,** Vas. Irakliou 43 (☎23102 57 812). With 250 computers, it's a gamer's paradise. Internet noon-midnight €2 per hr., midnight-noon €1 per hr. Open 24hr.

Post Office: Aristotelous 26 (☎2310 2 68 954), just below Egnatia. Open M-F 7:30am-8pm, Sa 7:30am-2pm, Su 9am-1:30pm. A branch office (☎2310 2 27 604), on the corner of Eth. Aminis and Manosi near the White Tower, is in charge of parcels. Open M-F 7am-8pm. Both offer Poste Restante; to make sure your mail gets to the Aristotelous branch, specify "Kentriko." **Postal Code:** 54101.

⌂ ACCOMMODATIONS

Welcome to the big city—don't expect to find comfort and cleanliness at a low price. Thessaloniki's cheaper hotels are clustered along the western end of **Egnatia,** between Pl. Dimokratias and Aristotelous. Most are a bit gritty, ranging from ramshackle sleaze to mere cheerlessness, but all are easy to locate—just look for the neon signs. Egnatia is loud at all hours; rooms on the street have balconies, while quieter back rooms may have just one window. If your room doesn't have air-conditioning, get a room behind Egnatia; it is almost impossible to sleep with the window open and equally hard to sleep through the street noise. Some mid-level hotels are farther away from the noise, set a few blocks behind Egnatia on **Dragoumi** around **Plateia Dikastiriou.** For more luxurious options, head toward the **waterfront** area two blocks west of Aristotelous. The closer you get to the water, the more you'll pay.

Hotel Augustos, El. Svoronou 4 (☎23105 22 550; www.augustos.gr). Follow Egnatia toward Pl. Dimokratias and take a right onto El. Svoronou—you can't miss the large gold and green sign. Clean Rooms with wooden floors and high ceilings. Some have A/C and TVs. Free Wi-Fi. Reception 24hr. Singles €25, with bath €30; doubles €40/50; triples €50/60. Cash only. ❷

Hotel Kastoria, Egnatia 24 and L. Sofou 17 (☎23105 36 280). Most buses stop right outside at the Kolombou stop on Egnatia. With the closure of Thessaloniki's only youth hostel, getting a room here is the cheapest available option. Though sporting cracked linoleum floors and water-stained ceilings, the hotel is a budget alternative to some of its pricier neighbors. Rooms have sinks, and each fl. has a communal bathroom. Reception 24hr. Singles €20; doubles €30; triples €40. Prices go up €10 in Sept. Cash only. ❶

Hotel Atlantis, Egnatia 14 (☎2310 5 40 131; www.atlantishotel.com.gr), by the Kolombou bus stop. The hotel underwent renovations last year, and the rooms show it. Clean and stylish, the standard rooms have sinks and bedding. Shared baths are well-maintained. A comfortable stay, but only the pricier rooms have A/C and fridges. Hospitable English-speaking staff. Breakfast €4. Free Wi-Fi. Reception and bar 24hr. Singles €27, with bath €33; doubles €40; triples €50. AmEx/MC/V. ❷

Hotel Olympic, Egnatia 25 (☎23105 66 870). Simple but comfortable rooms, each with A/C, TV, phone, fridge, and bath. Plenty of inviting couches on the 1st fl. are great for a group hang-out after a long day. Blissfully soundproof windows. Breakfast €5. Reception 24hr. Singles €30; doubles €45; triples €60. €5 discount for *Let's Go* readers all year except Sept. AmEx/MC/V. ❷

Hotel Emporikon, Sygrou 14 (☎2310 5 14 431), on Sygrou and Egnatia, about halfway between Aristotelous and Pl. Dimokratias. Frequented by an older tourist crowd, the rooms are quieter than others on Egnatia. Breakfast included. Free Wi-Fi. Singles €45; doubles €55; triples €70. Weekend discounts. Cash only. ❸

Hotel Ilios, Egnatia 27 (☎23105 12 620). Each no-frills, clean room comes with A/C, TV, fridge, and bath. The embroidered pillowcases add a touch of class to a pleasant stay. Breakfast €3. Singles €30; doubles €40; triples €52. Cash only. ❷

🍴 FOOD

Most sidewalks in Thessaloniki are lined with restaurants' comfortable chairs and umbrellas. Even the most tightly-packed alleys have outdoor seating, and at any given time you will see a group of locals lingering over savory meals or sipping iced coffee. In a city that places such an emphasis on a good meal, it won't be hard to have a memorable dining experience. Upscale **Ladadiki** just behind the port, is frequented by an older crowd. Between **Egnatia** and **Aristotelous,** alleyways house *ouzeria*, where roaming musicians squeeze their way through tightly packed tables on cobblestone roads. Continuing eastward, Plateia Athonos is a student favorite, while **Plateia Navarinou** acts as a porch for the tables of well-priced *ouzeria* that overlook Galerius's Palace. Behind the Rotunda and before the White Tower, find some ostentatiously positioned (and priced) but nevertheless tasty *ouzeria*. The **Old City** brims with *tavernas* and restaurants that have sweeping views of the gulf. Thessaloniki's restaurants have a delightful custom of giving patrons watermelon or sweets gratis after a meal. The local syrup-drenched cake, *revani*, a gift of the many refugees from Asia Minor, is especially good.

🖾 **Ouzeri Melathron,** Karypi 21-34 (☎23102 75 016). From El. Venizelou, walking toward Egnatia take the 1st right after Ermou into the cobblestone passageway; there is no street sign, but Melathron's chairs and signs are visible. The cheeky menu at this secluded gem features a little of everything and a lot of chicken. Try the Transvestite Lamb (actually chicken; €5.94) or Maria's Tits (smoked pork chop in mild mustard sauce; €6.16). Numerous salads €2-7. Seafood €6-21. Entrees €6-21. Free round of drinks with ISIC. Open daily 12:30pm-2:30am. MC/V. ❷

🖾 **Healthy Advice,** Al. Svolou 54 (☎23102 83 255). Already missing your ecofriendly-health-food fix? The friendly French-Canadian owner will personally serve you innovative sandwiches and salads, even concocting unique creations (€3.50-7) using the freshest ingredients. Ask for Theo's salad (blue cheese with corn, jalapenos, arugula, hot sauce, and a homemade mustard dressing). Open daily 11:30am-2am. Cash Only. ❶

🖾 **Delicatessen,** Kouskoura 7 (☎23102 36 367), just off the Tsimiski and Iktinou intersection. Hands down the most popular place to eat souvlaki (€2), and for good reason: after tasting it here, you won't want to eat the Greek staple anywhere else. Try lamb, chicken, or even mushroom and cheese souvlaki. Open M-W noon-4am, Th-Sa noon-5:30am. Cash only. ❶

Navtiliaki, Pl. Ag. Georgiou 8 (☎23102 47 583; www.nautiliaki.gr), just behind the Rotunda. This *ouzeri,* known for its excellent seafood, also has meat and vegetarian options as well as a sizeable selection of prepared cheeses. Squid souvlaki €6.80. Eggplant with feta and tomato sauce €3.50. Squid stuffed with cheese €6.80. Entrees €5.50-12.50. Open daily 1pm-2am. Cash only. ❷

🖸 SIGHTS

🖾**ARCH OF GALERIUS AND THE ROTUNDA.** At D. Gounari and Egnatia stands the striking Arch of Galerius, known to locals as "Kamara" ("Arch"), and just above it is the large Rotunda (now known as Agios Georgios), both of which formed part of the palace built by Caesar Galerius AD 297-306. Caesar Galerius erected the arch to commemorate his victory over the Persian Shah Narses in 297, covering it with relief sculptures detailing his triumphs. According to a legend, Christians, who suffered greatly under Galerius's persecutions, rubbed out his face in every panel—but one still can make out the Persians, with their distinctive headgear, in the upper panels. The Rotunda, once connected to the Arch, was originally a temple to Jupiter at the head of Galerius's palace. With the dominance of Christianity, the rotunda was re-appropriated into a church in the fifth century, filled with mosaics of saints martyred at the hands of Galerius and Diocletian. Under the Ottomans, the Rotunda served as a mosque from 1590 to 1912. An estimated 36 million *tesserae* (small sea pebbles) were assembled to represent gilded facades, birds, and saints, though today they are barely visible due to damage from age and an earthquake in 1978. Sadly, the building is more impressive in theory than in reality—scaffolding covers every inch of the interior as it is being reconstructed indefinitely. (☎23109 68 860. Arch open 24 hr. Free. Rotunda open in summer Tu-F 8am-7pm, Sa-Su 8:30am-3pm; in winter Tu-Su 8:30am-3pm.)

WHITE TOWER. The White Tower looms over the eastern part of the seafront like an oversized chess piece, a symbol of the city and a common nighttime rendezvous point where booksellers line the port starting from the White Tower and stretching east. Originally part of the 15th-century Ottoman seawall, the tower became the Ottoman death row where Janissaries—members of an elite corps of Ottoman soldiers—carried out notoriously gruesome executions. Blood was seen seeping from the tower's stone walls so often that locals began calling it the "Bloody" or "Red" Tower. One prisoner, Nathan Gueledi, whitewashed the tower in 1890 in exchange for his release, thus inaugurating its current name. Today, a walk to the top of the tower no longer means inevitable death, but instead offers a chance to see a marvelous view of the city and its shoreline. Multimedia presentations on each of the six floors dramatically details Thessaloniki's history. *(At the eastern end of Nikis. Take bus #3, 5, 6, 33, or 39.* ☎ *23102 67 832. Open Tu-Su 8:30am-3pm. €3, students €2, EU students free.)*

ROMAN AGORA. The second-century odeon and covered market still stand at the top of Aristotelous. The agora's lower square once held eight caryatids, which since have been sent to the Louvre. Known in Ladino, the language of the Sephardic Jews, as "las Incantadas" ("the enchanted women"), they were thought to have been magically petrified. The site has undergone major renovations, and although they're often overtaken by children playing soccer, the agora and market are the best places in the city to feel the influential Roman presence in Thessaloniki. *(From Egnatia, go inland up Aristotelous; the agora is at the end. Open daily 8am-8pm. Free.)*

THE PALACE OF GALERIUS. A tiny section of the once 150 sq. km royal complex is open for viewing in Pl. Navarino, two blocks south of the arch. The southeastern section of the mighty palace, which used to extend from the Rotunda to the sea, was unearthed in excavations in the 1950s and 60s. The weathered, geometric mosaic floors and partially preserved octagonal hall—believed to have housed Galerius's throne—are highlights. *(Open daily 8am-5:30pm. Free.)*

BEY HAMAMI. The Ottomans ruled Thessaloniki for almost 500 years and left an indelible imprint on its landscape: Turkish buildings and baths still dominate the streets. Bey Hamami, built in 1444, was the first bathhouse of its kind in Thessaloniki and was in use until 1968. Its labyrinthine interior has surprisingly cool antechambers that unfold as you explore, leading to a tepid room and the immense domed sauna beyond. Today these decorated domes and colorful marble-tiled floors house various modern art exhibitions. *(On Egnatia, east of Aristotelous. Open M-Su 11am-8pm. Free.)*

BEDESTEN. A late 15th-century covered marketplace and craftsmen's workshop, the Ottoman Bedesten is said to have emitted delicious perfumes of musk and amber. Inscriptions carved into the domes in French, Greek, South Slavic, and Turkish evoke the varied ethnicities of Thessaloniki in its cosmopolitan heyday. *(On El. Venizelou, 1 block south of Egnatia.)*

HAMZA BEY CAMI. Built by a bey's daughter from 1467-68 as a *mesçid* (a hall of worship minus the minaret), Hamza Bey Cami gained both a minaret and official mosque status in the late 16th century. Although it was an active mosque for Thessaloniki's growing Muslim population for over three centuries and was the largest mosque in Greece, it is being renovated for an indefinite period of time and is closed to the public. *(On Egnatia, just past El. Venizelou.)*

🏛 MUSEUMS

▮ARCHAEOLOGICAL MUSEUM. This fantastic collection includes some of the area's most prized artifacts. The treasures from Vergina's royal Macedonian tombs, once the highlight of Thessaloniki's collection, were returned to Vergina in 1998, but the museum still displays plenty of jewels, as well as Macedonian coins, prehistoric pottery, and several coffins. The **Derveni krater** from the late fourth century BC is the most important piece in the collection. This ornate vessel, made of an alloy of tin and bronze, depicts Ariadne and Dionysus's wedding. Initially used as a means of mixing water and wine, the Derveni krater was later used as a depository urn for funerary ashes. It is the only intact bronze vessel with relief decorations preserved from the time period. Sculptures of a famously erotic Aphrodite and parts of an enormous statue of Athena share space with a grand mosaic depicting Dionysus with Ariadne, Apollo stalking Daphne, and Ganymede in Zeus's eagle talons. *(M. Andronikou 6. At the eastern end of Tsimiski. Bus #12 or 39. ☎ 23108 30 538; pistekp@cultur.gr. Open M 1:30-8pm, Tu-Su 8am-8pm; reduced hours in winter. €6, students and seniors €3, EU students and children free. Combined ticket with the Museum of Byzantine Culture €8.)*

MUSEUM OF BYZANTINE CULTURE. This museum, exhibiting the largest collection of early Christian wall paintings outside of the Vatican, illuminates Byzantine life. In keeping with Thessaloniki's position as the second-most important city in the Byzantine Empire, the huge museum leads visitors from the rise to the fall of the empire. Through well-organized displays on daily life, economics, engineering, and imperial dynasties, visitors learn that the Byzantine Empire was more than the oft-depicted monocultural theocracy. The painted funerary art and tenth-century metal vessels that held holy myrrh from the graves of Thessaloniki's protector saints are particular highlights. Impressive Christian iconography dominate the tombs and walls in the exhibit's first half, giving way to 15th- and 17th-century religious paintings in the second half. *(Stratou 2. Behind the Archaeological Museum, across from 3 Septemvriou. Bus #12 or 39. ☎ 2310 8 68 570; www.mbp.gr. Open M 10:30am-5pm, Tu-Su 8:30am-3pm; reduced hours in winter. Wheelchair-accessible. €4, students and seniors €2, EU students and children free. Combined ticket with the Archeological Museum €8. Guided tour €15)*

JEWISH MUSEUM OF THESSALONIKI. A sign at the entrance to the museum proclaims, "Thessaloniki: The Metropolis of Sephardism." Inside, exhibits tell the tragic story of that metropolis's height and demise. Waves of Jewish refugees fleeing 15th-century Reconquista Spain were invited by the Ottoman Sultan to settle in his lands. The museum's ground floor uses pictures, gravestones, and folk artifacts to show the subsequent 500-year history of Thessaloniki's Jewish community, once the largest in Europe. At its height, the Jewish population comprised more than half of the city. The second floor features an extensive timeline of Jews in Thessaloniki, including mini-biographies of notable Jews of Thessaloniki. The last room memorializes the Holocaust, during which 96.5% of the city's Jewish members were murdered in concentration camps. The role of Thessaloniki Jews in momentous uprisings against the Nazis during the Holocaust is also highlighted, noting that many sang the Greek national anthem as they were being put to their deaths. This thorough and detailed account is worth the visit. Exhibits and brochures are in English and Greek. *(Aghiou Mina 13. Easy to miss, when walking toward Egnatia from El. Venizelou it is the first right after Tsimiski. ☎ 2310 2 50 406; www.jct.gr. Groups should call in advance. Open Tu-F and Su 11am-2pm, W-Th 5-8pm. €3, students free.)*

MUSEUM OF THE MACEDONIAN STRUGGLE. Once the Greek consulate to Turkish Thessaloniki (1892-1912), this house now contains memorabilia from the wars that made Macedonia officially Greek, focusing on the Balkan Wars (1912-1913). The exhibits include the personal artifacts of rebel leader Pavlou Melas, along with captured war booty. The models and reproduced photographs shed light on the scope of this nationalistic struggle and its role as one of the triggers of WWII. Although a bit disorganized at times, the museum provides English pamphlets with facts about the collection and a historical overview of the Macedonian War. *(Prox. Koromila 23. The entrance is innocuously hidden right on the corner of Prox. Koromila and Ag. Sofia, next to an elementary school. 1 block from the water. Take bus #3, 5, 6, 12, or 39. ☎2310 2 29 778. Open Tu-F 9am-2pm, Sa-Su 11am-2pm. Wheelchair-accessible. Free.)*

WAR MUSEUM. This haven for gun lovers and war buffs features military paraphernalia used from the War of Independence through the Civil War. Also on display are some Ottoman military artifacts and weapons captured from Greece's enemies. The basement is devoted to females who aided in war and resistance efforts. *(G. Labraki 4. Located opposite the southern entrance to Macedonia University, just east of 3 Septemvriou. ☎23102 66 195. Open Tu-F 9am-2pm, Sa-Su 10am-2pm. Free.)*

📷🌿 ENTERTAINMENT AND FESTIVALS

Alpha Odeon, Tsimiski 43 (☎23102 90 100), in the same mall as the US Embassy. Indoor movie theater that shows a variety of American films (€8) and draws students from the nearby Aristotle University.

Dhasos "Forest" Theater (☎23102 18 092), uptown in the forest near the acropolis, adjacent to the zoo. You can't miss the posters plastered all over town for the theater, music, and dance performances at this venue.

Ellinis (☎2310 2 92 304), at Pl. Hanth, across from the Archaeological Museum. Films show shortly after 9pm and at 11:10pm. €6.

Iyoklima, Voutira 2 (☎23105 21 892), south of Nikis near the port, or Palios Stathmos. Perfect for summer visitors looking for *rembetika* music.

Natali Cinema, Vas. Olgas 3 (☎23102 92 304). American movies with Greek subtitles play at the waterfront under the stars.

International Fairgrounds, across from the Archaeological and Byzantine museums. Holds festivals throughout the year. The **International Trade Fair and Song Festival** (Sept.; www.helexpo.gr); the **Dimitria Festival** (Oct.; celebrates the city's patron saint with a number of theater productions, films, and dance performances); the internationally revered **Thessaloniki Film Festival** (Nov.; www.filmfestival.gr); and the new **Documentary Festival** (Mar.)

Thessaloniki's Wine Festival, at which different wineries offer tastings, is celebrated at Nea Elvetia park in Sept.

🎵 NIGHTLIFE

There are several main hubs for late-night fun in Thessaloniki. The **Ladadika** district, which served as the city's red-light strip until the 1980s, is now a sea of dance clubs playing everything from American R&B to Greek contemporary music (on Katouni, just off Tsimiski). Roads become sidewalks in Ladadika where the alleys south of Egnatia have all-night bars packed so tightly that it feels like an after-hours block party. Most of the bars are huddled around the Viara St. and Sigrou St. The bustling waterfront on **Nikis,** stretching from the port to the White Tower, is filled with *ouzeria* that are so packed the crowds overflow onto the streets. The **airport** area has a smattering of open-air discos featuring live, modern or traditional Greek music, but if you are planning on club-hopping it's safest to go with a group.

To get into many of the chic establishments, you'll have to dress to impress and, if you're not one yourself, have an attractive woman on your arm. Though

the clubs boom until dawn, the summer nightlife isn't much by Salonican standards—most partiers head to the mega-beach clubs of Kalithea on Kassandra,
Chalkidiki. From May to the end of September, three **pirate boats** transform
themselves into floating clubs. One of the boats blasts reggae, another Greek
and alternative music, and the third combines disco with Latin beats. The
30min. trips depart from behind the White Tower and continue on past sunrise. (Beer €6. Mixed drinks €8-9. No cover. Cash only.) The following clubs are
popular year-round, but call in advance for special events during low season.

Kafotheio Ellenico, Iounstinou 3 (☎23102 37 016). With your back to Egnatia, the
street is to the left of Venizelou. Brimming with personality, this German-owned bar has
a 1920s-style interior where every wall and shelf is covered with bric-a-brac from the
bygone era. 107 different types of beer (€5-21) from all over the world. Couple that with
a collection of board games and it will be hard to tear yourself away. Mixed drinks €6-7.
Open daily 8am-2am. Cash only.

Shark, Themistokli Sofouli and Argonavton 2 (☎23104 16 855; www.shark.gr), in
Kalamaria around the gulf. Take Bus #5 to Stadium Kalamarya. A foundation of Thessaloniki's nightlife for 11 years, this trendy bar-restaurant attracts Greece's young,
chic professionals. As the night progresses, Shark clears out its tables, turns up the
music, and becomes a full-fledged club. Waterfront views of the city's skyline from the
balcony (open only in summer) thrill the dancing masses. Beer €7. Mixed drinks €9.
Open daily 8pm-6am. Cash Only.

Idolls, Maria Callas 9 (☎23108 19 595), in the airport area. Packed with a lively crowd,
this bar maintains a cool—though unpretentious—rocker vibe. A DJ mixes both Greek
and American tracks, while a big screen tucked in the corner plays music videos. Beer
€5. Mixed drinks €8. Open daily 9:30am-4am. Cash only.

Vilka, Octovriou 26, to the west of the port on the road closest to the water. Take Bus #31
and ask for the Vilka stop—you can't miss the huge neon sign. Play Russian Roulette
with your night by heading here for rotating nightly events. Located in an old factory, this
huge complex is a venue for bar and club events. Open-air seating, surrounded by palm
trees. Sophisticated ambience. Unfortunately, you must check with organizing clubs and
bars to find out events, or just show up and prepare to be entertained. Cover charge
varies for each show. Drinks €10. Open daily 10pm-6am. Cash only.

⚏ DAYTRIPS FROM THESSALONIKI

ANCIENT VERGINA Αρχαία Βέργινα

*Buses (☎23105 95 432) run from Thessaloniki to Veria (1hr., every hr. 6:15am-8:45pm,
€6). From Veria take the bus to Vergina (20min., 9 per day 6:50am-8:15pm, €1.30). Ask to
be let off at the Vergina archaeological sites. Follow the signs for the Royal Tombs. Buses
run from Vergina back to Veria (20min., 10 per day 6:30am-8:15pm, €1.30) but are less
reliable. Open M 1:30-7:30pm, Tu-Su 8am-7:30pm; in winter Tu-Su 8am-7:30pm. €8, students and seniors €4, EU students and under 19 free.*

Unearthing the ruins of Vergina, once the capital of ancient Macedonia, was an
archaeological watershed. Among the finds were Greek inscriptions on Macedonian tombstones that bore Greek names, proving that the ancient Macedo-
nians were in fact a Greek tribe. Scholars believe that the objects found in the
tombs could have belonged only to the royal Macedonian family of Philip II,
father of Alexander the Great (p. 41). This assumption was verified by the fact
that the tombs date to 350-325 BC, the years of Philip's rule. The excavations
began in 1856, when Macedonia was still under the Ottoman Empire. A French
archaeologist uncovered a Macedonian tomb and other stones, but it was not

until over 60 years later that the site underwent heavy excavation. In 1937, a professor from the University of Thessaloniki held classes at the site, and the university was given excavation rights during WWII. The most impressive treasures, however—including the royal tombs and the acropolis—were not found until the late 1970s.

At once morbid and dazzlingly beautiful, Vergina's **museum** is the highlight of the site. The museum is actually within the **Great Tumulus,** the largest burial mound in Greece at over 12m tall and 110m in diameter. It was built in the early fourth century BC and housed the graves of Vergina's common citizens that were buried atop massive royal tombs. Your eyes will need a few minutes to adjust to the darkness of the museum, only penetrated by overhead lights illuminating the artifacts found in the Great Tumulus. These include Attic vases, clay and ivory figurines, gold jewelry, and carved funerary *stelae* (inscribed columns) of commoners' graves. Throughout the museum you can walk alongside four of the **royal tombs,** which lie in their original locations, each containing an anterior Ionic or Doric colonnade decorated with mythological scenes. The large room behind the colonnade contains the deceased's remains and items intended to accompany him or her into the afterlife, though they are not available for viewing. The next tomb, nicknamed the **Tomb of Persephone,** lies at the edge of the Tumulus along with a *heroon* (shrine). Excavators discovered well-preserved frescoes, the most intact of which depicts Hades abducting Persephone. The **Tomb of the Prince** probably belongs to Alexander IV, son of Alexander the Great. Born shortly after his father's death, the prince was murdered at the age of 13 by Cassander, one of his father's generals. The silver hydra containing his bones and his spectacular gold myrtle wreath are on display, along with other artifacts. The most impressive of the tombs is that of Philip II, the conqueror who paved the way for his son Alexander's expansions. Visitors descend down steps and come face to face with the imposing entrance. Dating from 336 BC, the marble and porcelain gates stand at almost 10m tall. **Philip's tomb** holds a number of treasures now on display, including a magnificent gold chest that held his remains, a gold wreath that sat on his head when he was placed on the funerary pyre, and his complete gold-lined suit of armor with a massive shield depicting a soldier conquering an Amazon.

Ancient Vergina's ruins are currently closed for renovation and scheduled to reopen in 2010. To get to the **Palace of Palatitsa,** turn right as you exit the museum and make a left at the intersection. Follow the road uphill and you will get reach the ruins in about 10min. On the walk up to Palatitsa lies the **Macedonian Tomb,** believed to be that of Philip II's mother, **Queen Evridiki.** A downhill path leads to the **ancient theater** where Philip II was assassinated in 336 BC while celebrating the marriage of his daughter. Legend has it that he was punished for committing hubris by declaring himself a god.

ANCIENT PELLA Αρχαία Πέλλα

Ancient Pella is on the main Thessaloniki-Edessa highway, 38km west of Thessaloniki. Take the bus on the Giannitsa-Edessa Line (50 min., every 40min. 6:30am-10:30pm, €3) and make sure you're let off at "Ancient Pella," not "New Pella." The site is a 15min. walk from the bus station; continue along the road following the sign for the Archaeological Museum. The same bus stop has a return bus (every 40min.). €6; students €3; seniors, EU students, and under 18 free. Museum entrance fee subject to change with the opening of the new museum in Sept. 2009.

Pella was the center of the world for over a century. When King Archelaus chose to move the capital of his Macedonian state here in 400 BC, the site, situated on what was then the shore of the Theramaic Gulf, fostered eastern trade and developed a rapport with southern Greece. In the fourth century

BC, as Philip II became a powerful leader, Pella prospered and grew to be the greatest city in Macedonia. The splendid new palace built here was home to intellectual and artistic talents from the Hellenic world; Aristotle was born in Pella in 356 BC. Alexander the Great, Philip's son, inherited the kingdom after his father's assassination in 336 BC. As he conquered eastward to present-day India, Pella remained the capital. The city's glory days ended in 168 BC when it was ransacked by Roman general Aemilius Paulus, who carried away most of the city's riches. In the first century BC a massive earthquake hit the city, but even that did not deter residents. After all that, for reasons still unknown today, many years later all the residents abandoned the city. This once-vibrant capital remained a ghost town for 200 years until Macedonian chieftains chose the swamps of Pella to launch their guerrilla warfare against the ruling Turks in the early 19th century.

The Pella **ruins** take only an hour to see, as most of the archaeological site is being excavated by students from the University of Thessaloniki. As you enter the site from the right, there is the **House of Dionysus,** where several floor mosaics have been lifted and are on display at the museum. As you walk closer to the center you can see the houses of rich men. At the heart of the site are the remains of the **agora,** the commercial center of the ancient city, with the three wells from which much of the pottery in the museum was collected. To the left, the **House of the Abduction of Helen** has well-preserved mosaic floors with beautifully executed scenes from 325-200 BC of Helen being abducted by Theseus. The **House of Plaster** displays a splendid rectangular Ionic colonnade. North of the houses and the agora are the **acropolis** and **palace,** which are off-limits to visitors. Built in ten stages, the palace is a blend of architectural styles. Expanded by Philip, it fell with the rest of Pella at the hands of Aemilius Paulus. The exposed pipes throughout the site show the state of the art drainage system that is one component of Pella's then-cutting-edge Hippodamian system of construction.

Directly across the highway, the **museum** houses gold-leaf jewelry, terra-cotta figurines, and a white marble bust of Alexander the Great. Exquisite mosaics taken from the ruins show Dionysus riding a panther, a female centaur preparing libations in the cave of the nymphs, and a lion hunt, traditionally featured in men's apartments. The mosaics, composed of *tesserae* outlined with thin lead strips, are the earliest-known mosaics to mimic a three-dimensional look. The museum is changing locations (in the north end of the ruins) in September 2009, and at the time of writing many pieces had been removed to prepare for the transfer, to be returned by 2010. *(Museum ☎ 23820 31 160 or 33 050. Open Apr.-Oct. M 1:30pm-8pm, Tu-Su 8am-8pm; Nov.-Mar. Tu-Su 8am-3pm.)*

KAVALA Καβάλα ☎2510

The gateway to eastern Macedonia and one of Greece's major port cities, Kavala exudes a charm that far surpasses its commercial importance. Originally built by Thassian colonists in the seventh century BC, it was named "Neapoli" ("new city") to signify its centrality in the islanders' mainland expansion. During the Byzantine period, Kavala was the place where the apostle Paul first set foot in Europe, dubbing it "Christopolis" ("city of Christ"). Kavala was given its current name under the Ottoman Empire, which conquered the city in the 14th century. On the eastern hill of the city, the Byzantine district of Panagia shadows the modern city and the port with its meandering cobblestone streets, *kastro,* and Ottoman *imaret.* The palm-lined port and Rapsani beach draw travelers seeking a more modern pace than on nearby islands.

▣ TRANSPORTATION

Flights: The **M. Alexandrou airport** (☎25910 53 273) is 32km outside the city. Take the bus to Chrissoupolis (every 30min. 6am-9pm, €3) and then a taxi (€3). You also can take a taxi (€25) directly from the city center; ask at the Tourist Information Office for a discount. **Olympic Airways,** at the airport (☎2510 53 270), has daily flights to **Athens** (1hr.; 7am, 9:40pm; €75-100).

Ferries: Ferries leave from the east end of the port in front of several restaurants and ticket ferry booths. Call or visit the Tourist Information Office for updated information. To: **Chios** (15hr., 2 per week, €32); **Lesvos** (11hr., 2 per week, €27); **Piraeus** (32hr., 2 per week, €40) via **Limnos** (4hr., 2 per week, €16); **Samos** (19hr., W 8pm, €39). Student tickets ½-price. Buy tickets to **Thassos** (1hr.; 10 per day 8am-10pm; €3, students and children €1.50) at the white ticket kiosks on the Thassos dock.

Flying Dolphins: Leave for **Thassos** (40min., 4 per day, €10) from the eastern dock.

Buses: The station (☎25108 37 176) is at the corner of Filikis Eterias and M. Chrisostomou, between the waterfront and the post office. Buses to: **Athens** (9hr., daily 8:45am and 8:30pm, €52); **Drama** (1hr., every 30min. 6am-9:15pm, €3.60) via **Philippi** (20min., €1.70); **Thessaloniki** (2hr., 15 per day 6am-8:40pm, €13.50); **Xanthi** (1hr., 17 per day 6:30am-8pm, €5). To get to **Alexandroupoli** (2hr., 6 per day 9:30am-1am, €13.50), go to Seven-Eleven, M. Chrisostomou 4 (☎25108 37 176), directly opposite the main entrance of the bus station, where you'll find schedules, tickets, and the bus itself. Open daily 9am-midnight.

Taxis: (☎25102 32 001 or 22 424), just behind the port behind Pl. Eleftherias, on the corner of Venizelou and Averof. 24hr.

▣ ORIENTATION AND PRACTICAL INFORMATION

The road on the waterfront is **Ethnikis Antistasis,** until it is cut off by **Averof** to the east. One block farther east of this intersection, hotel-lined **Erithrou Stavrou** becomes the closest street to the waterfront. Parallel to E. Stavrou is **Eleftherios Venizelou,** which leads into the **Old City** (called **Panagia**), Kavala's most historically interesting area. Located on a peninsula jutting into the Aegean northeast of the port, it is hemmed in by ancient walls under the turrets of the Byzantine fortress. A detailed map of Kavala can be found next to the small port police kiosk at the Thassos ferry dock and at most hotels.

Tourist Information Office (☎25102 31 011), off El. Venizelou at Pl. Eleftherias in a large, windowed kiosk. An English-language oasis of information with helpful staff. Maps (€3), brochures, ferry schedules, bus schedules, and accommodations information are available. A ticket window on the side of the kiosk allows you to purchase tickets to the many performances in town. 1 computer with internet (€2 per hr.) available. Open M-Sa 8am-9pm.

Tours: Next to the Tourist Information Office in front of the National Bank, a blue train gives a free tour (15min., every hr.) through the Old Town—a great way to get oriented and avoid the uphill walk.

Banks: Alpha Bank, El. Venizelou 28 (☎25102 29 084), on the corner of Mitropoleos and El. Venizelou across from the public park. **Currency exchange.** Open M-Th 8am-2:30pm. Pl. Eleftherias, on El. Venizelou by the tourist office directly behind the port, is surrounded by banks with **ATMs,** including the **National Bank** adjacent to the ticket office. Most open M-Th 8am-2:30pm, F 8am-2pm.

Police: Omonias 119 (☎25106 22 273), 4 blocks north of the port. Follow Averof to the OTE, then bear left. Open 24hr.

NORTHERN GREECE

Hospital: Stavrou 113 (☎25102 92 000), 4 blocks inland past Panagia. Open 24hr.

Telephones: OTE (☎25105 61 160), on Kyprou and Averof, 1 block east and 2 blocks inland of the post office. Open M and W 7:30am-3pm, Tu and Th-F 7:30am-8:30pm, Sa 8:30am-2:30pm.

Internet Access: Most are located on El Venizelou west of the bus terminal. **The Web,** El. Venizelou 32 (☎25108 36 660). €2.20 per hr., €3 per 2hr. Open 24hr.

Post Office: The main branch (☎25108 33 330) at Kavalas and Stavrou, 1 block north of the bus station. **Currency exchange.** Open M-F 7:30am-8pm. **Postal Code:** 65110.

ACCOMMODATIONS AND CAMPING

Domatia are scarce and hotels aren't cheap in Kavala, making it difficult to find a good place to crash. Camping in Kavala's natural setting is a popular option. A few indoor budget accommodations also exist.

- **George Alvanos Rented Rooms,** Anthemiou 35 (☎25102 21 781). Enter the Panagia District on Poulidou at the *imaret,* turn left at the fork in the street going up Mehmet Ali, and follow the road straight (keep left at the bright red mosque). The road should take you to Anthemiou; the house has a sign outside and is on your left. If you time it right, you can take the blue kiddie train (every hr.) from the tourist office up to the house. One of the only budget accommodations in the city, this centuries-old house has beautifully furnished, wood-floored, spotless rooms with fridge and fan. Be prepared for some of the idiosyncrasies of an old house. Shared kitchen and baths. Singles €20; doubles €30. Cash only. ❷

- **Batis Beach Campground** (☎25102 43 975; www.batis-sa.gr). The beach is 4km outside of Kavala. Blue bus #8 (€1) leaves from in front of the post office, at M. Chrisostomou and Erithrou Stavrou (every 20min. 6am-8pm), and stops right outside. Mini-mart and outdoor cinema. Campers must provide their own tents. €6 per person; €6 per tent. Electricity €4. MC/V. ❶

- **Hotel Galaxy,** El. Venizelou 27 (☎25102 24 521). Among the cheaper accommodations in the area. Retro hotel with furniture that belongs in the 70s, but the location is ideal (right by Pl. Eleftherias). Carpeted rooms have fridges, fans, and TVs. Some rooms with balconies. Breakfast €5. Singles €40; doubles €55; triples €65. Cash only. ❸

- **Hotel Acropolis,** El. Venizelou 29 (☎25102 23 543). From the bus station, walk 2 blocks away from the water and turn right on El. Venizelou; it's 1 block on your right. Open since 1935, this historic hotel has been renovated and has spacious rooms with high ceilings, TV, fridge, and A/C. Some rooms have amazing views of the waterfront; those that don't go for lower prices. Be sure to negotiate the rates. Singles €40, with shared bath €45; doubles €70/85; triples €90/110. Reduced prices from Nov-March. MC/V. ❸

FOOD

Tavernas line **Poulidou** in Panagia and the area near the waterfront. On Saturdays a **public market** opens up on the waterfront, west of Dagli on E. Antistasis, selling everything from fresh fruit to dishware.

- **Mikros Mylos Bakery,** Dagli 8 (☎25102 28 132), on the corner of El. Venizelou and Dagli, 1 block inland from Hotel Oceanis. The bakery you wish you had grown up with. Whimsical displays feature freshly baked pastries and breads, chocolate truffles, Greek sweets, and candy. *Kurabies,* a local specialty with whole almonds and powdered sugar (€4.30 per box), are not to be missed. Open daily 6:30am-10pm. Cash only. ❶

- **Al Xalili,** Theodorou Poulidou 43 (☎25108 35 051). Hookah pipes and chalices tastefully displayed on the warm, brick walls. Diners can sip their wine and bask in the peaceful aura of this quiet corner of the Old City. Appetizers €3-5. Entrees €5-9. Open daily noon-1am. Cash only. ❷

Orea Mitilini (☎25102 24 749), on eastern end of the port where the ferries dock. Despite the ample seating, this seafood joint is still usually packed with locals in search of simple, fresh fish. Mussels with rice €7.60. Appetizers €3-6. Entrees €5-9. Open daily 11am-1am. Cash only. ❷

👁 🏖 SIGHTS AND BEACHES

Once home to the Thassian colony of Neapoli, the **Old Town** is now known as the **Panagia District.** This web of steep streets and Ottoman-style houses unfolds atop the promontory beside the port.

BYZANTINE KASTRO. The current citadel was constructed in 1425 by the Venetians and was later renovated and enlarged by the Turks. Underneath it are the remains of Byzantine walls dating from the fifth century BC. Known by the locals as *Srourio*, the *kastro* is divided into two fields separated by a tower and wall. You can climb up and walk the walls that were once used to connect the three watchtowers for a stunning view of the port and the city. Children now play in the inner field where there was once an early Byzantine cistern used as a prison, food storehouse, and guardhouse. In the outer field, a small **amphitheater** has a coffee shop and a stage that showcases musical and cultural performances. In the **Eleftheria Festival** in late June, students celebrate Kavala's liberation from the Ottomans by performing dances at the castle. In July, the international festival of Cosmopolis highlights various cultures through dance, theater, and photography exhibitions from all corners of the world. (*Follow the signs from Panagia's entrance on Poulidou. Open daily 8am-9pm. €2, students €1.50.*)

KAMARES AQUEDUCT. The Kamares aqueduct, erected in 1550 under Sultan Süleyman the Magnificent, connects the Old City with the New City and completes the circuit of Panagia. This colossal construction initially doubled as a defensive wall: the Ottoman city's guards would patrol its top, while water from nearby springs flowed through it. Tracing the path of the aqueduct through the Old City is a great walking tour of the major historical sites. (*To trace the aqueduct's path, follow the uphill road Mehmet Ali, take a left onto Navarinou, and another left on Issidorou, taking you right past the Kastro. Follow Issodorou and make a right at the end of the road.*)

OTTOMAN IMARET. This beautiful specimen of Islamic architecture was built in 1817 by native Kavalian Mehmet Ali, Pasha of Egypt, and completed in 1954. Originally a donation to fulfill the Islamic principle of charity, it served as a seminary, poor house, and boarding school to benefit the public. Ironically, it is now an exclusive hotel, and while its protected status doesn't permit tourists to view the interior, if you win the lottery you can look into staying the night. (*On the right as you enter Panagia at Poulidou 38, where the street forks and ascends to the kastro. Visible from the intersection of Poulidou and Mehmet Ali roads.*)

MEHMET ALI'S HOUSE. In 1769, the founder of the last Egyptian dynasty, Mehmet Ali, was born in this house on the tip of the promintory. Ali was recognized as the Pasha of Egypt in 1807 and given the island of Thassos as a gift. Another present from the Greeks of Egypt, a bronze statue of Ali mounted on a horse, still stands there. From the house, there are splendid views of the sea and of Kavala. (*Continue from Poulidou 3 blocks from the imaret, to where the cliff comes to an end.*)

ARCHAEOLOGICAL MUSEUM. The Archaeological Museum nicely complements any trip to Amphibolis or to the sights of Thassos. Many of its artifacts were plundered by the Bulgarians during WWII, but the museum was reorganized and restored in 1952. The gold jewelry and wreaths, elaborate

Hellenistic funeral painting, and the reconstruction of a Macedonian burial chamber are all worth checking out. *(In the park on the waterfront, between Ethnikis Antistasis and Erithrou Stavrou, by Farilou Park.* ☎ *25102 22 335. Open Tu-Su 8am-3:30pm. €2, students €1, EU students free.)*

BEACHES. There are 46km of beaches west of Kavala. **Rapsani,** in the western part of Kavala, at the end of Eth. Antistasis, has been improved in recent years and currently attracts the most sunbathers. The sandy beach of **Kalamitsa,** 2km past Rapsani, has *tavernas,* showers, and three bars, and it is slightly less touristy than Rapsani. **Batis** is next, 1km down the shoreline, followed by pebble-covered **Tosca,** renowned for its clean water. The city's main resort beaches, with hot summer nightlife and long strips of sand, are **Palio,** 10km southwest of Kavala, **Nea Iraklitsa,** another 2km, and **Nea Peramos,** 16km from Kavala. *(Buses leave from the post office near the bus station every 20-30min. Take blue bus #8 to the beaches before Batis (20 per day 6am-8pm). To get to the farther beaches, take the green bus (30 per day 6am-10pm; Palio €1, Nea Iraklitsa €1.10, Nea Peramos €1.50). Bus times are flexible. Ask at the bus station for hours. Alternatively, taxis to the beaches range from €3 to Kalamitsa to €10 to Nea Peramos.)*

NIGHTLIFE

There are many nightlife options in Kavala, especially near **Platela Karaoli Dimitrou** and the waterfront street of **Athnikis Antistassis.** Many tourists head to the beaches of Palio or Aspri Amos, a €7 cab ride away, but if you prefer to stay in Kavala, check out the options below.

Cafe Briki, Poulidou 76 (☎69443 33 220). Classy stone interior with wooden rafters—looks a little like a ski lodge. The only thing that can overshadow the upscale decor is the stunning view of the port and the city from the balcony. Beer €3.50-5. Mixed drinks €6-7. Open daily 9am-2am. Cash only.

Old Town Bar, Poulidou 19-21 (☎25102 26 044). The preferred student hang-out both day and night. Adjacent to a lookout point, with a warm, brick interior and a friendly staff. Beer €3. Mixed drinks €6. Open 11am-2am. Cash only.

Anapsekterio, (☎69470 25 607), at the northwest corner of Municipal Iroon Park, under Kyprou. Green lights illuminate the brick background to the bar. Outdoor seating on the grass, under the shadow of the impressive town hall. Open daily noon-2am. Cash only.

DAYTRIPS FROM KAVALA

PHILIPPI Φίλιπποι
Take the bus from Kavala to Drama (every 30min. 6am-9:15pm, €1.70). Make sure to specify that you want the archaeological site of Philippi. The bus drops you off at the western section of the site, where the museum is. ☎ *2510 5 16 470. Site open daily 8am-7pm. €3, students and seniors €2, EU students free. The museum has been undergoing renovations for the last decade but is scheduled to reopen in September 2009.*

About 15km north of Kavala, the city of Philippi lies in splendid ruin. Philip II of Macedon conquered the city, originally called Crenides, in 356 BC. Unsurprisingly, he named it after himself and the name stuck, even after being conquered by the Romans in 148 BC. In 42 BC, the Battle of Philippi between the combined armies of Brutus and Cassius and those of Octavian and Mark Antony was fought at the outskirts of the city. The defeat of the former, who had conspired in the death of Julius Caesar, opened the path for Octavian, later called "Augustus Caesar," to become Roman Emperor in 27 BC.

A new phase in the city's history began in AD 49 with the visit of St. Paul. In the Bible's book of Acts, Philippi is referred to as "a leading city of the district of Macedonia and a Roman colony," as well as the place where Paul baptized Lydia, the first European Christian. In the mid-fourth century, the first Christian church in Europe was built here, and in the fifth and sixth centuries, the city prospered as a religious center, inspiring devouts from across Europe to make the pilgrimage. After the Ottoman conquest, Philippi was left to decay.

The site, which can be appreciated even by non-history buffs, contains the remains of 20 buildings of interest and a **museum**. The Kavala-Drama highway divides Philippi, leaving the central **Roman ruins**—the forum, the agora, the Via Egnatia (the important trade route which passed though the city), and the baths—on your left as you exit the bus from Kavala. Across the street, in the western section, lie the Classical and Roman theaters, the museum, and the prison that held St. Paul. In the far northwestern corner is the city's acropolis, built between the fifth and fourth centuries BC and reconstructed during Byzantine control. You can still see parts of the mosaic floors and columns that signal the city's importance.

THRACE Θράκη

The province that forms present-day Thrace, in the northeastern pocket of Greece, historically has been home to a people not considered ethnically Greek. In Roman times, Indo-European, non-Hellenic Thracians inhabited the mountainous region until they were subdued by Roman conquest in AD 46. The region then became an imperial trading card, passed from the Byzantine Empire to the Bulgarian Empire, back to the Byzantine Empire, and finally to the Ottoman Empire where it remained for 530 years. Only at the close of WWI in 1919, 90 years after Greece achieved independence, was the region completely returned to Greece. Thrace's mixed population of Greeks, Thracian Muslims, Bulgarians, and Albanians and the equally eclectic food, architecture, and traditions allow visitors to live and breathe a part of Greece's complex and rich history.

ALEXANDROUPOLI Αλεξανδρούπολη ☎25510

Travelers often rush through Alexandroupoli on their way to Turkey, the Northeast Aegean Islands, or the hinterlands of Thrace, overlooking the hidden charms this port city has to offer. The long-standing military presence in Alexandroupoli has stripped it of the Muslim influence found in other Thracian cities. After dark it transforms into a veritable festival, making it one of the better places in Greece to get stranded.

▐▀ TRANSPORTATION

Flights: Dimokritos Airport (AXD; ☎25510 45 198) is 6km east of town and only reachable by taxi (€4). Flights to **Athens** (1hr., 2-4 per day, €77) and **Sitia** (2hr., 3 per week, €90). Buy tickets at **Sever Travel** (☎25510 22 555) on Dikastarion and Karaiskaki. Walking inland from the lighthouse, it faces the water at the corner of the 1st intersection on your left. Open M, Th, Sa 9am-2:30pm and T, W, F 9am-2;30 and 6pm-9pm.

Ferries: Saos Ferries, Kyprou 15 (☎25510 23 306 or 23 307). Look for the flags in between the lighthouse and the train station and walk down. Open M-F 9am-5:30pm and 6:30pm-9pm, Sa 9am-5pm, Su 10:30am-4pm.) To **Samothrace** (3hr.), **Limnos** (5hr.), and **Lesvos** (12hr.). **Kikon Tours,** El. Venizelou 68 (☎25510 25 455). Open M and W 8:30am-2:30pm, T and Th-F 8:30am-2pm and 6pm-9pm, Sa 9am-2pm. To: **Kavala** via **Chios** (12hr., 2 per week, €31); **Lesvos** (10 hr., 2 per week, €26); **Limnos**

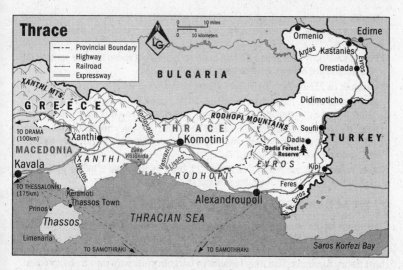

Thrace

- - - Provincial Boundary
───── Highway
──┼── Railroad
═════ Expressway

0   10 miles
0   10 kilometers

BULGARIA

GREECE

XANTHI MTS

TO DRAMA (100km)

MACEDONIA

Kavala

TO THESSALONIKI (175km)

Keramoti
Thassos Town
Prinos

Thassos

Limenaria

Xanthi
XANTHI
Nestos
Lake Vistonida
Kompsatos

THRACE
Komotini

Vasvazis
Lissos

RODHOPI

THRACIAN SEA

RODHOPI MOUNTAINS

Ormenio
Ardas
Orestiada

Didimoticho

Soufli
Dadia
Dadia Forest Reserve

EVROS

Kipi

Feres

Alexandroupoli

TO SAMOTHRAKI   TO SAMOTHRAKI

Edirne
Kastanies
Evros

TURKEY

R. Evros

Saros Korfezi Bay

(4hr., daily, €15); **Samos** (16hr., 2 per week, €38). Ferry tickets are also available at **Sever Travel** (see **Flights**, p. 172).

Flying Dolphins: Run from June 20 to September 20. To **Samothrace** (1hr.).

Trains: Station, M. Alexandrou 1 (☎25510 26 395), 400m east of the lighthouse, in front of Pl. Eleftherias. Trains to: **Athens** (regular: 14½hr., daily 3:22pm, €24.80; express: 10hr., 2 per day 6:40am and 8:30pm, €51.50); **Komotini** (regular: 1hr., 2 per day 8:30am and 3:20pm, €1.90; express: 50min., 3 per day 6:40am-8:30pm, €4.50); **Thessaloniki** (regular: 5hr. 30min., 2 per day 8:29am and 3:22pm, €9.70; express: 5hr., 3 per day 6:42am-8:32pm, €16.20); **Xanthi** (regular: 1hr., 2 per day 8:30am and 3:20pm, €2.60; express: 50min., 3 per day 6:40am-8:30pm, €6.60); **Istanbul, Turkey** (9hr., 1am, €45).

Buses: Station, El. Venizelou 36 (☎25510 26 479), off Maiou, 500m inland from the docks. Buses to: **Athens** (11hr., daily 6:45pm, €61); **Didimotiho** (1hr., every hr. 4:15am-8:45pm, €7.80) via **Feres** (30min., €2.40) and **Soufli** (1hr., €4.20); **Kipi** (45min., 5 per day 6:50am-7:30pm, €3.50); **Komotini** (1hr., every hr. 6:10am-8:10pm, €5.70); **Thessaloniki** (regular: 5hr., 15 per day 5:15am-10pm, €26.50; express: 4hr., daily 10am and 5pm, €26.50) via **Xanthi** (1hr., 9 per day, €9.50) and **Kavala** (2hr., 9 per day, €12.50).

Taxis: (☎25510 33 500) on Megalou Alexandrou. Fares inside the city cost up to €4. Available 24hr.

▓ 🛈 ORIENTATION AND PRACTICAL INFORMATION

Everything a traveler could need is within 10min. of the waterfront center, which is marked by a **lighthouse**. Standing at the lighthouse facing inland, **Megalou Alexandrou** is the road right on the water, stretching left toward a row of cafes (west) and right toward the train station (east). Halfway between the lighthouse and the train station, **Kyprou** leads inland to small **Plateia Kyprou**. The three main streets running parallel to Alexandrou (**Dimokratias, E. Venizelou,** and **Paleologou**) are about three blocks inland, linked by narrow by-streets.

NORTHERN GREECE

Banks: Dimokratias is 1 long string of banks with **24hr. ATMs,** including the **National Bank of Greece,** Dimokratias 240 (☎25510 64 612). Open M-Th 8am-2:30pm, F 8am-2pm.

Police: Karaiskaki 6 (☎25510 66 300 or 66 100), 2 blocks inland from the water at the intersection just before the lighthouse. Open 24hr.

Hospital: (☎25510 74 000), in the suburb of Hilli. Open 24hr.

Telephones: OTE, I. Kavyri 5 (☎25510 56 171), just off Venizelou, a block toward the water from the bus station. Open M, W, Sa 7:20am-3pm, T and Th 7:20am-9pm.

Internet: Meganet, Dikastirion 55 (☎25510 31 902), on the waterfront in the narrow road directly opposite the restaurant Mylos. Internet noon-6pm €1.80, 6pm-midnight €2, midnight-noon €1.20. Open 24hr.

Post Office: M. Alexandrou 42 (☎25510 23 122), on the water 2 blocks west of the lighthouse. Open M-F 7:30am-2pm. **Postal Code: 68100.**

ACCOMMODATIONS AND CAMPING

Like most of its neighbors, Alexandroupoli has pricey lodgings. The best options are the ones closest to the train and bus stations. You'll find signs for *domatia* in roads a few blocks inland from the water—look up to second- and third floors for signs. You may be able to bargain your way into a cheap room.

Hotel Vergina, Karaoli 74, directly across the street from the train station at the point where M. Alexandrou becomes Karaoli. 10 basic rooms with baths, TVs, A/C, and phones. 3 of the rooms have beautiful sea views but what you gain from the view you lose with space; the less glamorous rooms are much bigger. Unfortunately, the owner does not speak English. Singles €30; doubles €40; triples €50. Cash Only. ❷

Hotel Marianna, Malogaron 11 (☎25510 81 456), 2 streets east of Vergina toward Dimokratias. Rooms outfitted with fridges, A/C, and TVs. The aqua-themed curtains and linens provide splashes of cheer. Singles €40; doubles €50; triples €60. Cash Only. ❸

Camping Alexandroupolis (☎25510 28 735; camping@ditea.gr), 1km west of the town center on the water. Campers must bring their own tent. €4.80 per person; €3.55 per tent; €2.56 per car. Electricity €3. Cash only. ❶

FOOD

Fast food joints and a number of cafes line the waterfront and the area around Dimokratias and M. Alexandrou.

Taverna Archipelagos, Apolloniathos 20, a 5min. walk west of the post office. Popular for both lunch and dinner. Try the seafood pasta (€8.50) or the fried mussels (€6) while sitting right at the waterfront. Entrees €5.50-12. Open daily noon-3am. Cash only. ❷

Seaside Taverna Mylos, M. Alexandrou 2 (☎25510 35 519), across from the post office; look for the windmill. Delicious fresh seafood brought in every morning by Samothracian fisherman. Ask for the celebrated crab salad served in a giant shell (€6), the octopus salad (€8), or any of the many selections of fresh fish and ouzos available. Entrees €6-8. Open daily until midnight. Cash only. ❷

Dodoin, M. Alexandrou/Kanari 2 (☎25510 33 882), across the street from the lighthouse. What's a day by the sea without some ice cream? This place serves nothing but, with seating right next to the lighthouse. Their mouth-watering selection includes over 20 flavors (€2 per scoop) and sundaes like the Frutopia (3 scoops of ice cream with fruit topping and strawberry syrup; €6.50) or their Greek pastry with ice cream filling (€6.50). Open daily 5am-1am. Cash only. ❶

🔍 SIGHTS

CATHEDRAL OF AGIOS NIKOLAOS. The walls of the beautiful 19th-century Cathedral of Agios Nikolaos, one block inland and one block east of the bus station, house unique artifacts like the Byzantine **Virgin Trifotissa**, a 13th-century icon of Mary and the baby Jesus from Aenos. Because Mary's eyes are so prominent in the depiction, the icon was worshipped for protection against bad eyesight. The altar is adorned with magnificent stained glass windows. *(Services daily 7-9am and 6:40-7pm.)*

ECCLESIASTIC ART MUSEUM. Inside the cathedral is Alexandroupoli's Ecclesiastic Art Museum, whose ornaments and paintings are housed in eight rooms, each devoted to a different aspect of religious art. Don't miss the display of priest's vestments in room three, or the workshop that demonstrates the process of painting an icon. An English guidebook translating the captions is available upon request. *(☎25510 82 282. Open Tu-F 9am-2pm, Sa 9:30am-1:30pm. €3, students €2.)*

🎵 NIGHTLIFE

The sound of a trumpet marks the end of the day as the carnival rides at the port light up, traffic is banished from M. Alexandrou, and families and young locals wander the streets well into the night. Xanthi truly transforms at night, where the chairs normally facing the water are turned to face the streets; everyone watches the kids play in the streets, singles drink at the waterfront bars, and village elders argue over cups of coffee. At night, cafes and trendy bars along the shore on M. Alexandrou play a mix of Mediterranean and American music all night.

Soho, Dimokratias 300 (☎25510 88 134). Oh-so trendy. Blue neon lights draw in party-goers like moths to a flame. Or like moths to a blue neon light. Open daily 8am-3am.

Peree Anemon ke Idatom, Nikeeforou Foka 2 (☎25510 83 043). With your back to Mylos' windmill, the side street is directly in front of you. Meaning "About Winds and Water," this low-key cafe-bar is named after a Greek idiom meaning trivialities. Student, bohemian vibe. Open daily 10am-late.

SAMOTHRACE Σαμοθράκη

Samothrace was famous as the Delphi of the South for housing a centuries-old religious cult that worshipped the Anatolian gods. Modern-day Samothrace, too, appears to be touched by the divine: its remote wilderness and picturesque landscape have eluded the mass tourism of other Greek islands. The local population is laid-back, even by Greek standards. Samos, meaning "height by the coast," does not do justice to the mountain vistas and sparkling ocean that Samothrace is famous for.

KAMARIOTISSA Καμαριώτισσα ☎25510

This transportation hub is the main starting point for exploring Samothrace's many charms. If you can, head out from Kamariotissa to the island's highlight, Therma, sooner rather than later. With variable bus and ferry schedules that are as elusive as they are infrequent, Kamariotissa is an instant reminder that you are now on island time.

TRANSPORTATION

Ferries: Dock on the southern edge of town. To: **Alexandroupoli** (2½hr., 1-2 per day, €11-13.50); **Kavala** (3hr., 2 per week, €16); **Lesvos** (7hr., Sa 5:15pm, €28); **Limnos** (3hr., 5 per week, €15). For tickets and schedules to Alexandroupoli, ask the port police or **Saos Tours** (☎25510 23 512). Open daily 9am-1pm and 6-9pm. For schedules to Kavala, call ☎25102 23 716; for Limnos ☎22540 22 225; for Lesvos ☎22510 40 827.

Buses: Stop on the waterfront across from Saos Tours. To **Chora** (8 per day, 7:45am-8pm, €1), **Profitis Ilias** (5 per day, 6:45am-8:15pm, €1.50) via **Alonia** and **Lakoma,** and **Therma** (daily 7am and 2pm, €2). Schedules and prices fluctuate often, especially during the low season; consult the bus drivers and stands for more information.

Taxis: (☎25510 41 733). Queue on the waterfront. 24hr.

Car Rental: A car or moped is the best way to get around the island. **Kyrkos Rentals,** (☎25510 41 620), on the waterfront where you disembark from the ferry. Cars €30-60 per day. Mopeds and bikes €20 per day including helmet and insurance. Open daily 8am-midnight, depending on ferry schedule.

ORIENTATION AND PRACTICAL INFORMATION

Everything in Kamariotissa is located on one street along the waterfront. This road runs out of town to the northeast and the road to Chora runs east out of town just past the bus stop (at the stop sign).

Banks: National Bank, (☎25510 41 750), near the point of disembarkment along the main road. **24hr. ATM** and **currency exchange.** Open M-Th 8am-2:30pm, F 8am-2pm.)

Police: (☎25510 41 203). **Port Police,** (☎25510 41 305), 5 shops to the left of the bank and marked by a Greek flag.

Medical Clinic: (☎25510 41 217), in Chora. Open 24hr.

Internet Access: Cafe Aktaion, (☎25510 41 056), on the waterfront across from the ferry docks. €3 per hr. Open daily 8am-2am.

Post Office: (☎25510 41 244), at the end of the main port road. Facing the ferries, go left for about 100m. Open M-F 7:30am-2pm. **Postal Code:** 68002.

ACCOMMODATIONS AND CAMPING

Many travelers breeze through Kamariotissa on their way to Therma and the campgrounds. Some camp in the surrounding area, but there's no reason to avoid the established campgrounds. There are few hotels by the main waterfront area (most are on the road leading to Therma and Chora), so *domatia* are your best bet. *Domatia* signs are scattered around the waterfront road and prices for a single range €25-35. In a pinch, try the **SAOS ferry office** for modern housing that's more like an apartment than a hotel room, with full kitchen, air-conditioning, and bathroom (singles €25-30).

Hotel Kyma, (☎25510 41 263 or 41 336), on the waterfront on the outskirts of Kamariotissa at the beginning of the road to Therma. Clean, simple rooms close to a stone beach. Rooms have small private baths, fridges, and A/C; only some rooms have a view, and it's worth putting in a request. Doubles €50; triples €65. Prices reduced May-June. Cash only. ❸

Kaviros Hotel (☎25510 98 277 or 41 774; kavirshotel@gmail.gr), in Therma, to the left of the grocery store 3 Amigos. Among the few hotels in the area. Friendly management and rooms with A/C, TVs, fridges, and baths. Singles and doubles €30-40. Cash only. ❸

NORTHERN GREECE

Camping Platia (☎25510 98 244), 15km from Kamariotissa and 2km beyond Therma on the coast. Bounded by wilderness on one side and a spectacular view of the Aegean on the other. Showers, baths, a mini-mart, and phones. Check in advance for openings as they may only accept campers in the high season (July-Aug.). €3 per person; €2 per child under 13 . €3 per tent. Cash only. ❶

Camping Varades (☎25510 98 291), 5km from Therma on the coastal road. Similar amenities to Camping Platia, plus a cafe, except more concrete and less greenery. Open from late June to Sept. €3 per person; children under 15 €2; €3 per tent. Cash only. ❶

FOOD

Waterfront *tavernas* in Kamariotissa specialize in fresh seafood, while Therma is known for its olives, feta cheese, and honey.

Yi Garides (☎69458 94 107), on the waterfront next to the Saos ferries office. Try the mussels (€6.50) or, if you're with a group, the specialty is lobster with spaghetti (market price). The owner will happily buy fresh fish by request. Entrees €5-9.50. Cash Only. ❷

At Klimataria (☎25510 41 535), 1 door down from Hotel Kyma. Enticing home-cooked dishes behind a glass counter in the kitchen. Try the Klimataria Specialty (chicken filet stuffed with feta and tomato; €8). Pasta, meat, and seafood dishes €6.50-8. Open daily noon-5pm and 7pm-1am. Cash only. ❷

NIGHTLIFE

Kamariotissa's *tavernas* often stay open late, bringing young crowds to their dance floors.

Isalos, on the waterfront across from the ferry docks. Draws in the locals with its cheap beer (€2.50) and Greek hits. Open daily 9am-3am.

Energy (☎697 40 96 640), to the right of the docks. Walk for about 10min. and look for the sign pointing to the left; the sign will be visisble. Locals inevitably end up at the town's only dance club. You will most likely spot at least one familiar face in the disco-lit greenery. Open June-Sept. 11:30pm-6am.

HIKES AND BEACHES

The island's only sand beach is the soft arc of **Pahia Ammo** on the southern coast, whose radiant blue water could have splashed off a postcard. The best way to get to Pahia Ammo is to rent a car or moped, as buses are infrequent. Stony black beaches ring the rest of the island. Ask a bus driver to drop you off anywhere along the coast, then hunt down an isolated stretch of shore. At the end of the line along the northern coast is popular **Kypos**, whose main attraction is a cave that looks out at the rocky beach. Three white buses per day go to Kypos. Schedules change frequently; ask bus drivers in Kamariotissa for schedules.

The verdant island of Kamariotissa holds a wealth of hiking trails leading to cascading waterfalls, mountain vistas, and the summit of the steep mountain **Fengari.** Trails are generally unmarked; the best way to explore them is to rent a vehicle in Kamariotissa and head to the coast or interior. Hiring a local tour guide, available for a negotiable fee at some of the trailheads, is also a good idea, as trekkers who attempt to ascend alone can get lost or injured in the wild terrain. Ask locals from the villages that dot the mountain's flanks for directions to trailheads.

NORTHERN GREECE

🔀 DAYTRIPS FROM KAMARIOTISSA

🏛 THERMA Θέρμα

Buses (daily 7am and 2pm, €2) from Kamariotissa stop at the base of town next to the thermal springs. Open daily 7am-noon. Baths €2.

The most convenient hub for outdoor activities is the small town of Therma, about 13km from Kamariotissa. The natural environment and tiny population make this an intimate environment to explore the wilderness. The loyal free spirits who migrate to Therma for the summer swear by its unending delights; it seems that no matter how much time you spend in Therma, its thrills are never exhausted. Thermal water bursts from the refreshing **thermal springs** at a scorching 92°C and is cooled down to 42°C for public use. Public baths are nude, with men and women separated. To take a dip in your own private hot spring, walk right at the parking lot before Cafe Therma up a wide dirt path for 100m. Take the first downhill path at your right, which has been paved with rocks, and walk into the white house that is not far from the initial dirt path.

The **hiking** trail to the summit of **Fengari** ("Moon") mountain takes about 4hr. (according to locals, it can take twice as long for inexperienced hikers) and is one of Therma's highlights. You can either walk up from the trail next to the thermal springs or walk up the main road in town until you hit a crossroads; a private home is to your left, the trail to Fengari is on your right, on a path through the forest. Both end up on a plateau with electrical towers; the path to Fengari lies just behind them and has trail markings on the trees. Enchanting 🏛 **Foias** ("Killer") waterfalls, 17km from Kamariotissa and 5km past Therma, are infamous for their beauty. Follow the main road that goes around the island away from Kamoriotissa for 5km; you'll reach a large parking lot from which the well-marked path will lead you to the first of seven waterfalls in about an hour. The easy 2km hike meanders alongside a gurgling stream and beneath twisted trees. Watch your step; the trail can be slippery since it ends at a waterfall. The first three waterfalls don't require a guide or superb hiking skills, but if you are interested in continuing on, it is best to hire or ask a local to go with you. For a less visited option, try the waterfalls closer to Therma. While the hike is easy, trails are unmarked, so ask the workers at Cafe Therma, right by the bus station, for information about hiring a local guide. To reach the path to the waterfalls, take the left fork through town from the bus stop. Take the first right after a mini-mart and follow this road past tavernas and a bakery. When the road ends, turn left and follow the unpaved road; when it meets an asphalt-paved road, turn right. The road ends again at Taverna Yefiris; turn right and head up the shaded road. The dirt trail follows the stream on the right side of the road; head right or left 20m before the Marina Hotel. There is also a second route via the Gina Vathra River. Follow the street leading left off the main road connecting Therma and the coastal road—there is a sign for Gina Vathra. Follow the road past the bridge until you hit a wire fence, with a dirt road to your right. Follow the path and it will take you directly to a waterfall.

PALEOPOLIS Παλαιόπολις

Take the bus to Therma and ask to be let off at the ruins. Site open Tu-Sa 8:30am-8:30pm. €3, students €2, EU students free. Paleopolis Museum ☎ 25510 41 474. Open Tu-Su 8:30am-3pm. Museum admission included in Sanctuary of the Great Gods entrance fee.

Paleopolis and its **Sanctuary of the Great Gods** lie 6km east of Kamariotissa (half-way between Kamariotissa and Therma) and are Samothrace's premier archae-ological attractions. This destination was once the center of a centuries-old religious cult that predated Christ, and stubbornly persisted 400 years after the

NORTHERN GREECE

spread of Christianity. Before being colonized and disbanded by the Aeolians in the AD fourth century, pre-Olympian gods ruled over Samothrace: the Great Mother goddess Axieros and her cronies Axiokersa, Axiokersos, and Kasmilos. The ruins were once home to a secret cult, whose rituals are shrouded in mystery (revealing them was punishable by death). What is known is that initiates had to confess their worst deed and wear two items: a purple fillet around their stomach and an iron ring, many of which have been excavated and can be found in the museum. People would go on pilgrimages to the island, and buildings were constructed so that returning initiates could watch newcomers' initiations in secret ceremonies.

It is reported that Philip II of Macedon, Alexander the Great's father, first met his wife Olympias at their initiation into this cult. The enormous cylindrical **Arsinoëin Rotunda,** given to Samothrace by Queen Arsinoë II of Egypt (288-270 BC), demonstrates the continued patronage of the site by Alexander's successors, the Ptolemys. Candidates for initiation were purified in the rotunda, and the center held pits for sacrifices, an altar for libations, and seats for the audience. The sacrificial site's walls (now in the museum) are decorated with rosettes and ox heads.

The **Winged Victory** (or **Nike**) **of Samothrace,** the statue that is the pride of the island, once stood upon a marble base here before it took a mid-19th-century trip to Paris, where it is currently a defining focal point of the Louvre. It was perched at a height overlooking all the buildings as well as a clear view of the coast. Above the sanctuary are the remains of the ancient town of Samothrace where the apostle Paul stopped in AD 49-50 on his way from Asia Minor to Phillipi. It is believed that the first-century **Christian Basilica,** whose ruins lie at the eastern edge of the ancient harbor, was built in commemoration of Paul's visit. The walls of the **Old City** (called the **Cyclopic Walls**) are visible from the site, but are closed to visitors. Beside the ruins, the **Paleopolis Museum** houses many of the site's artifacts such as libation vessels and a terra-cotta sarcophagus. Of note are the giant entablatures from the Arsinoëin Rotunda, the **Hieron** 9a bust of the blind Samothracean prophet Tiresias), and a cast of the missing-in-action Nike. Other highlights include the beautiful winged and draped Akroterial statue of victory from the Hieron, an inscription from the Anaktoron in Greek and Latin forbidding the uninitiated from entering the inner sanctum (AD 200), and the erotic scenes depicted on a first-century BC pot.

CHALKIDIKI Χαλκιδική

The three fingers of Chalkidiki peninsula—Mt. Athos, Sithonia, and Kassandra—point southeast into the Aegean, boasting spectacular scenery and amazing beaches. Central and Eastern Europeans and urban Thessalonians spread their bodies out on Sithonia and Kassandra to sunbathe with the backdrop of Agion Oros, "The Holy Mountain," which continues its thousand-year tradition of Orthodox asceticism. Visits to Mt. Athos are strictly regulated, and reservations for pilgrimages should be made a few months in advance. Visitors to Sithonia and Kassandra will find no barriers of entry, other than the Chalkidiki public transportation system. Frequent buses run between the Chalkidiki station in Thessaloniki (☎23103 16 575) and the three peninsulas, but bus service does not run from finger to finger; you have to return to Thessaloniki. Kassandra is the most developed; some of the largest nightclubs in Greece are located there in Kalithea. Sithonia, still heavily forested and rural in atmosphere, has managed to resist most of the deleterious effects of tourism and offers visitors plenty of relatively unchartered territory perfect for relaxing and exploring.

SITHONIA PENINSULA Σιθωνιά

It is hard to believe the turquoise coasts and tranquil mountains of this Peninsula aren't carefully staged. Despite its increasingly high-profile status, there is plenty of land (and sea) that is exhilaratingly untouched and waiting to be explored. Sithonia is the middle peninsula sandwiched between nightclub-infested Kassandra and hermetic Mt. Athos. Its remote beaches and rolling mountains have to be seen to be believed. Terrific camping sites dot the coves off the single road that loops around the coast, providing an affordable window to the supreme nature of the peninsula. Its isolation and the infrequency of internal transportation make it hard to blow through in a day or two—give yourself plenty of time to enjoy and relax.

NEOS MARMARAS Νέος Μαρμαράς ☎23750

Neos Marmaras is the kind of place where everyone could know your name if you just stuck around long enough. Though there are many tourists from Eastern Europe and, in the high season, Greek students on summer vacation, Neos Marmaras still maintains its small-town feel. Most people speak English, and you can experience famous Greek hospitality when you stay at one of the many *domatias*. Vacationers flock for the gorgeous sunsets and surrounding beaches. The town, which is a single strip with restaurants and hotels on one side and water on the other, makes a great hub for exploring the peninsula.

⬛ TRANSPORTATION

Buses: (☎23710 22 309 or 3 16 555) run to **Thessaloniki** (2½hr., 4 per day 6am-6:30pm, €11.70) via nearby small towns, including **Nea Moudania** (1hr., €6). The bus coming from Thessaloniki continues to **Sarti** (1hr., 4 per day 11:30-8:50pm, €4).

Taxis: (☎23750 71 500) sit by the beach and by Dionysios.

Moped Rentals: Because Sithonia's public transportation can be frustrating, renting a moped or car is probably the best way to see the peninsula. **Moto Rental,** (☎69369 86 111) 2 doors up from Filippos, a short 3min. walk to your right when facing the ocean from the first plateia. Moped €15 per day; bike €7 per day. License required. Open daily 9am-10pm).

✈🛈 ORIENTATION AND PRACTICAL INFORMATION

The **first bus stop** is where the road running along the shoreline begins. From here, the bus turns left and goes toward the sea. The **second stop** is at Dionysios restaurant. Immediately ahead is the taxi stand, followed by the docks, and the police station and National Bank on the opposite side of the street; this is the **first plateia.** The road then angles left, following the shore, and descends until it arrives at the **second plateia,** which has a *periptero*, a map listing accommodations, and the **third bus stop.** The **fourth bus stop,** the last in Neo Marmaras, is 300m along the same road by the soccer stadium.

Tourist Office: For help getting oriented, go to English-speaking **Antica** (☎23710 21 120 or 23750 72 120), with 1 location next to the National Bank and 3 others scattered throughout the *plateias*. This traditional jewelry and gift shop sells detailed maps of the peninsula and books with hiking routes throughout Chalkidiki. Open daily 10am-1am. **Meli Tours** (☎23710 72 113), behind the church. Recommends rooms, books excursions, and offers an all-day boat tour of Mt. Athos (€30-45) daily. Open daily 8am-11pm.

Bank: National Bank (☎23710 72 794), just after the police station on the main street in the middle of the 1st *plateia*. **24hr. ATM** and **currency exchange.** Open M-Th 8am-2:30pm, F 8am-2pm.

Police Station: (☎23710 71 111), 2 doors up from the National Bank. Open daily 7am-5pm.

Medical Services: There is no hospital in Neos Marmaras, but the town doctor, Serhan Chehade, sees patients and has 24hr. service in case of emergencies. His office, **Chalkidiki Health Services** (☎23710 72 233 or 77 0895), is next to the National Bank. Office hours daily 8am-9pm.)

Internet Access: Stadium (☎23710 72 826), in front of the church, 2 stores down from Meli Tours. Internet €2 per hr. Pool tables €6 per hr. Beer €3. Open daily 9am-1am.

Post Office: (☎23710 71 334), in the 1st **plateia** across the street from the city map. **Poste Restante.** Open M-F 7:30am-2pm. **Postal Code:** 63081.

ACCOMMODATIONS AND CAMPING

Vacancies are scarce on summer weekends. Along the waterfront, signs with maps of the village list *domatia;* most singles run around €30. You'll have to haggle to find anything below €20, but, as you will soon find, prices are negotiable, and the longer you stay, the less you pay. For something cheaper and closer to Sithonia's breathtaking wilderness, try one of the numerous campgrounds.

> **TIP**
>
> **THE TRUTH ABOUT TENTS.** Campgrounds in Sithonia—and many places in Greece—do not rent one-person tents. You must bring them yourself, or plan to buy.

▨ **Marmaras**(☎23750 71 901)**,** a 20 min. walk from the town in nearby Paradissos. Pine trees, a private sand beach, and an amphitheater-like setting that gives every tent its own level and view of the beach and environs. Large group tents, provided by the campground, come with tables, mosquito nets, fridges, lamps, and mattresses (€30; price can be negotiated for a single camper). Campers are expected to bring their own tents. Laundry €6. €6 per person; €5.50 per site and tent; €2 per car. Electricity €3. ❶

House Filippos (☎23750 71 963), 20m down from Moto Rental on the main drag. Slightly removed from the waterfront's swarms of tourists. Large, pristine rooms have slate floors, TVs, A/C, baths, and semi-private balconies—you can see into other people's homes, presumably they are looking back. Each room comes with a full kitchen. Singles €25; doubles €40; triples €50. ❷

Elena Rooms (☎23750 71 848). At the other end of the main *plateia* on the way to the 3rd bus stop; you'll see the sign. Individual rooms are available along with an apartment-style two bedroom suite with a large balcony. All rooms come with TVs, A/C, baths, and kitchens. Singles €30; doubles €40; quads €70. ❷

FOOD

▨ **Nora Natura** (☎23750 71 046), at the 2nd bus stop just as the road bends. Natural local products including spices, olive oils, olives, soaps, and *halva*. Try free samples of their *raki*, honey, and *loukoumi* (Greek delights). Open daily 9am-1am. ❶

Ladi ke Rigani (☎23750 71 234), 20m from the Bank of Greece toward the 1st bus stop. This local favorite offers the best meat dishes in Neos Marmaras. Souvlaki and most dishes under €3. Open daily 11am-2am. ❶

NORTHERN GREECE

Dionysios (☎23750 71 201), in the 1st *plateia,* right in front of the 2nd bus stop. Greek classics, with many seafood and Italian dishes and seats available on the water. Entrees €6.50-14.50. Open daily 8:30am-3am. AmEx/MC/V. ❷

🎵 NIGHTLIFE

Neos Marmaras's nightlife centers on the strip of bars between the two *plateias* and a series of discos on the beach.

Molos (☎23750 71 331), 300m from Dionysios on the waterfront, Greeks and foreigners mingle and watch the surf on crisp, white couches. Beer €6. Mixed drinks €4.50-10. Open daily 10pm-5am.

Nuovo Cafe (☎23750 72 177), on the 2nd floor above a desserterie ,directly across from the map listing the *domatia.* The people in-the-know head to Cosmo Guide's 2009 pick for bar-cafe of the year, with techno beats and a young clientele.

Senso Cafe (☎23750 645 826 886). Even in the low season, locals swarm here.

Villa (☎23750 72 900), 2km away, on the road that goes around the peninsula. Accessible by taxi (€3.50). This big disco blares Greek music.

RURAL SITHONIA   ☎23750

Explore more of Sithonia by renting a moped or taking the **bus** that goes around the peninsula. Swim to a small island off the long, white beach of **Kalogrias,** or head to **Linerake** on the eastern coast for turquoise, shallow water and a lush landscape. **Kavotripias,** also on the east coast, is a secret paradise of heavenly beaches with mermaids and other figures carved out of the rocks. For water sports head to **Lagomendra,** a beach 10km before Neos Marmaras coming from Thessaloniki. Another worthwhile trip is to the interior of Sithonia, specifically up the mountain to the traditional village of **Parthenon.**

For a longer stay, over the mountain to the eastern side is the famous **🏕Camping Armenistis ❶,** which is also accessible from Thessaloniki by bus (3hr.; 11:15am, 2:30, 6:30pm; €12.30). There is no direct bus between here and Neo Marmaras so plan ahead if you want to see both. King among campgrounds, it has every amenity imaginable (including laundry, supermarket, cafe, bar, creperia, as well as sports facilities and an on-site doctor). This isolated site is a favorite for families and students alike; lined with golden sands, crystal water, and coves, it is the perfect spot for a weekend trip, though some campers end up staying for weeks (at a discounted rate). The campground also hosts numerous music festivals every summer that feature local rock bands, including **Crashfest**—a long-weekend festival with DJs and extreme sports, held in July. Check the website for events. You can also purchase tickets here for a tour around the Mt. Athos peninsula leaving (M-W and F-Su 9am) from Ouranoupolis for €30 (☎23710 91 487; www.armenistis. com.gr. Free movie screenings W and Su at 9pm. Reception 8am-midnight. Campers must provide their own tents. Open from mid-June to late Aug., depending on weather. €7.20 per person; and €6.30 per tent; €8.50 per RV. Mobile home rental €55-80. Electricity €3.70. MC/V.)

MOUNT ATHOS PENINSULA

OURANOUPOLIS Ουρανούπολις   ☎23770

The last secular settlement on monastic Athos, Ouranoupolis is at the top of Chalkidiki's easternmost finger, 148km southeast of Thessaloniki. This gateway to the cradle of Orthodoxy lies just beyond a trans-peninsular depression

NORTHERN GREECE

dug by Xerxes as a canal for his invading fleet. There isn't much to see in Ouranoupolis beyond the beaches, and even nicer beaches are plentiful on the other peninsulas, particularly Sithonia; if you're not visiting Athos's monasteries, Ouranoupolis is probably not worth the trip. Tickets for the **cruise** around Athos, which traces the western side of the peninsula, can be purchased from the offices near the tower. (☎23770 71 370. Daily 10:30am and 1:30pm, €16.) You can also purchase tickets at **Camping Armenistis,** and a shuttle to Ouranoupolis is provided in the high season. (☎23770 91 487; www.armenistis.gr.) Also interesting are the mostly uninhabited **off-shore isles,** many of which are recovering from recent devastating fires.

Many people spend the night in Ouranopolis in order to head to Mt. Athos in the morning. There are several reasonably affordable choices. Dozens of private houses offer *domatia* (around €25-30), but make sure to see the room before committing to anything, as some can be run-down and even unpleasant. **Camping Ouranoupoli ❶** lies on a beach 1.5km outside of town along the highway (taxi €2.50) and has showers, a supermarket, and a restaurant. Call in advance to make sure it is open. (☎23770 71 171. Laundry €5. €5 per person; €7 per tent.) The rooms in **Hotel Athos ❷,** which is one street back from the waterfront, are small but elegant, with a nice view of the beach. (☎23770 71 368. Singles €25; doubles €32; triples €40.) Those looking for a last supper before entering Mt. Athos—or a triumphant reward after the monks' spartan cuisine—should avoid the pushy waiters from the row of *tavernas* on the waterfront. Most of these eateries are tourist traps, serving mediocre food at high prices. Instead, try **Kentpikon ❸,** on the main road that leads to the tower, next to the police station. The friendly, English-speaking waitress serves reasonably priced, tasty dishes, and her elderly mother is always there to welcome guests. (☎23770 71 204. Entrees €5-9. Open daily 9am-10pm.)

Facing town with your back to the tower, both the main *taverna* strip and the Athos ferry office are on your left. **Ferries** (€5) run only to Mt. Athos. (☎23770 21 041. Call to reserve tickets and receive information. Open daily 8:30am-7pm.) The **bus stop** is in front of the tower in the parking lot. Updated times are posted by the restaurant behind the tower. Buses synchronized with the ferry from Athos go to Athens (7hr., 2:15pm, €30) and Thessaloniki (3hr., 6 per day 5:30am-5:30pm, €10). On the Thessaloniki-Ouranoupolis bus, ask the driver to let you off at the beach resort of **Tripiti,** 10km from Ouranoupolis. From there you can take a ferry (10am, noon, 3pm; €4) to **Amouliani,** a small village on an island known to the locals as the "donkey's island." From Amouliani's small port, renting a boat or hiking along the water are the best ways to explore the nearby untouched coves. The town of Ouranoupolis centers around the distinctive, medieval **Fosfori Tower** by the sea. This beautiful tower has the best views in town, and the museum inside, still a work in progress, represents Mt. Athos's history with Greek and English labels and displays small models of the different monasteries. (☎23770 71 389. Open daily 8am-3pm. €2.) The road out of town extends parallel to the waterfront. To reach the **Holy Executive of the Holy Mount Athos Pilgrims' Bureau,** which issues permits for Athos, walk down the path that runs between the waterfront tavernas behind the tower; when you reach the end of the path, take a right and walk up the street for two blocks. Arrive well ahead of your ferry time since lines tend to be long. (☎23770 71 422. Open daily 7:30am-2:30pm.) On a right side street two blocks down is an **Agricultural Bank** with a **24hr. ATM.** (Open M and Th 9am-2:30pm, F 9am-2pm.) Three blocks down, **Mamounia Internet Cafe** (☎23770 71 577) offers **internet** access and Wi-Fi on three computers. (€3 per hr. Open daily 10am-2am.)

MOUNT ATHOS Ὄρος Ἄθως ☎ 23770

The monasteries on Mt. Athos have been the paradigm of Orthodox asceticism for over a millennium. Originally settled by five Hellenic cities, Athos, along with the rest of Greece, was conquered first by the Macedonian Empire and then by the Romans. The then-secular settlements thrived under Byzantine control until pirate attacks in the seventh century left the peninsula uninhabited. Athos's current status as a religious community began in AD 963 when Agios Athanasios Athonitis, a friend of the Byzantine emperor, created the first communal monastery on the peninsula; this monastery, known as **Megistes Lavra,** still stands today. For much of the Byzantine and Ottoman periods, Mt. Athos formed the bedrock of Greek Orthodoxy, most notably speaking out against a unification with Western Christendom in the 15th century. Today, the Holy Community of Mount Athos is a semi-autonomous state comprised of 20 Orthodox monasteries, many *skites* (hamlets), some 1800 monks, and at least as many full-time workers. The verdant peninsula's only non-green surface, the jagged limestone peak of Mt. Athos itself, soars 2027m above the waves. Eagles and jackals roam the area, and natural springs deliver a wealth of water into the sea. The monks sequester themselves against the background of this lush sanctuary, shunning material pleasures to pursue a spiritual life. Emperor Constantine's edict of 1060 **forbids women and female domestic animals from setting foot on the peninsula,** with the exception of the female hens that provide the monks' eggs. Though this rule officially is considered to have come about out of respect for the Virgin Mary, it likely was enacted to end the scandalous relationships between the monks and Vlach shepherdesses who had settled on the mountain. Long pants are mandatory on Mt. Athos and swimming is forbidden.

HISTORY. Named after a Thracian giant buried by Poseidon beneath the mountain, Athos predates Christianity. The Christian tradition began here when, according to tradition, the **Virgin Mary** came to the mountain. After Jesus's death, when the apostles divided up areas to visit to preach the "good news," Mary asked for a region as well and was given Iberia in Asia Minor. On her way there, however, the archangel Gabriel directed her to Athos. Before Mary's time, many had tried to tame the rowdy peninsula, from Alexander the Great to Xerxes. Though the peninsula, then known as **"Akte,"** had been a center of paganism, Orthodox Christians believe that the moment Mary's foot graced its soil, the false idols disintegrated in realization of their own worthlessness.

Legend claims that the first monastic settlements were founded by Constantine the Great and his mother, Helen, but monkish habitation was not recorded before the 10th century. Over the following centuries, Athos flourished periodically—at one point it contained 40 settlements and 40,000 monks—but its low points ached with natural disasters, pirate invasions, internal squabbling, and a lack of attraction to monastic ideals. Mt. Athos retained some degree of autonomy during the Turkish occupation by surrendering promptly to the Ottomans, accepting their rule, and sending heavy taxes to Istanbul. During the centuries preceding the Greek liberation of 1821, Mt. Athos was supported and populated by Serbs, Bulgarians, Romanians, and Russians, who still have affiliations with particular monasteries. At the height of imperial Russia's expansionist policies at the end of the 19th century, some 3000 Russian monks inhabited Agios Panteleimonos. After WWI, the Treaty of Lausanne made Mt. Athos an official part of Greece while still allowing it to retain much autonomy; a body of monks, elected from each of the 20 monasteries, was set up to legislate and to govern the peninsula. Dwindling vocations through the 1950s threatened the stability of Mt. Athos, and it soon became a target for real estate developers; the end of its 1000-year tradition of monastic asceticism seemed imminent. Fortunately, Athos has been rejuvenated by hundreds of young men, many from Australia and Cyprus, inspired to take vows of Orthodox monasticism.

Starting in the 14th century, financial difficulties brought on the practice of **idiorrythimico**, which allowed monks to keep their own money and eat and pray individually. Today, all the monasteries follow the cenobitic system: they are run like communes, with shared money and duties. Athos retains an unsurpassed wealth of Paleologian and late Byzantine art, manuscripts, treasure, and architecture. Each monastery houses *lipsana*, remains of dead saints that only Orthodox men are supposed to be allowed to see. Especially impressive are the **Hand of Mary Magdalene**, which is said to remain (skin intact) in **Simonos Petra**, and the **belt of the Theotokos**, also known as **"Agia Zoni"** ("the holy girdle"), the only relic of the Virgin Mary, in **Vatopediou**. Several monasteries possess fragments of the **True Cross**. The **Gifts of the Magi**, presented to Jesus at his birth, are said to be housed in **Agios Pavlou**; five of the 28 pieces are displayed for nightly veneration.

TRANSPORTATION

With **permit** in hand, arrive at the western port of **Ouranoupolis** the night before your entry date to Athos. Given the unpredictable nature of Greece's public transportation, arriving in Ouranoupolis that morning if you plan to take the 9:45am ferry is risky.

Buses: Run to Ouranoupolis from **Athens** (7hr., 11pm, €30) and from **Thessaloniki**'s Chalkidiki station (2hr., 3 per day 5:15am-5pm, €10).

Ferries: From Ouranoupolis, the scheduled boats go to **Dafni** (2hr.; 9:45am, noon, 12:10pm; €5). A ferry called Agia Anna, which runs twice daily, continues from Dafni to the skiti community of **Kafsokalivia** at the peninsula's tip, stopping briefly at the monasteries of Simonos Petras, Grigoriou, and Dionysiou, and returning to Dafni before going back to Ouranopoulis. Schedules for Agia Anna change frequently and tickets are bought on board; ask at the boat ticket booth for updated information (Ouranoupolis-Dafni €5, round-trip €10). To reach the peninsula's eastern monasteries, take the **bus**, synchronized with the ferry arrivals, from Dafni to **Karyes** (30min., €2.50). Get off the boat quickly, as the 2 buses fill up in a matter of seconds.

Local Transportation: You can hike or take the minivan taxis (☎23770 23 267) between monasteries. When the buses arrive in Karyes, about 10 minivans wait to take visitors to their respective monasteries. Ask the drivers which minivans go where. The cost of the ride is divided among passengers, so travel with a group to save money. You should not pay more than €7, unless you are going to Megistis Lavra (€10-15).

PRACTICAL INFORMATION

Because Athos's hikes can be long, arduous, and often are unmarked, a topographical map of the peninsula will be invaluable. Pick up a green **Mount Athos Tourist Map** (€7.50) or buy a **guidebook** with a map (€4-10) in Ouranoupolis or Karyes. If you stay overnight in Ouranoupolis, consider leaving your pack at your hotel or *domatia* in order to avoid hiking with unnecessary weight. Those arriving on the early bus will be able to leave their packs at the hotel in Karyes or at any monastery.

Karyes, the capital of Mt. Athos, has an **OTE** next to the Athonite Holy Council Building and a **hotel** ❹ (€45 for up to 3 people). To find the **post office**, continue straight ahead after disembarking from the bus and make a left after the large scaffolded church. (☎23770 23 212. Open M-F 8am-2:30pm.) In **Dafni,** you also can find a **convenience store,** a **police station,** and a **cafe. Postal Codes:** Karyes 63086, Dafni 63087.

OBTAINING A PERMIT. Men who wish to see Mt. Athos must secure a permit in advance; call the **Holy Executive of the Holy Mount Athos Pilgrims' Bureau,** Egnatia 109 (☎23102 52 578; piligrimsbureau@c-lab.gr; open M-F 9am-2pm, Sa 10am-2pm), in Thessaloniki (p. 158). You must call six months in advance if you want to visit the community during Easter week or in the peak summer months if you are not of the Orthodox faith; in the winter, next-day permits are available. Even if you forget to reserve a spot far in advance, it is worth calling to see if there is an opening. You are more likely to get a short-term permit if you are flexible as to the exact day you want to visit Mt. Athos. One hundred daily permits are reserved for Orthodox applicants, including a significant number set aside for Greeks living out of the country, but there are only 10 available for non-Orthodox men. Mail (don't fax) a copy of your passport to the office at Egnatia 109, Thessaloniki 54638. Call two weeks ahead of your visit to confirm the reservation, and visit the office with your passport to pick up the permit. Though this process can be frustrating, the bureau will deny entry to anyone who fails to complete it. Passes cost €30 for foreigners and €10 for students.

You must strictly observe the date of arrival on your permit, but there is a one-day grace period if you can't make the exact date. You will not be admitted without your **passport.** The regular permit is valid for a **4-day stay.** Official extensions are limited to 3 days and can only be applied for once in Mt. Athos—to request one you must go to the peninsula's capital Karyes—but unofficial extensions are easier to come by, as monks often allow considerate, interested visitors to stay longer. If heading to Mt. Athos from Ouranoupolis, **bring your permit and passport** to the Athos office (☎23102 71 422; open 7:30am-2pm) by 7:30am on the day your visit begins. With your back to the entrance of the tower, take a right at the end of the waterfront strip, and walk two blocks uphill. At the office, you will receive your entrance pass, called the **"Diamonitirion,"** complete with the blue seal of the monastic community; you must present this before boarding the ferry to Mt. Athos. Arrive early, as lines are long. Visitors taking the 9:45am ferry must be in Ouranoupolis no later than 9am; if you miss the boat, you will not be able to visit Athos. Taking the first bus leaving from Chalkidiki bus station at 5:15am will allow time to pick up your pass and make the boat connection. The agency will supply you with a list of monasteries to arrange for accommodations.

◉ SIGHTS

MONASTERIES

MEGISTIS LAVRAS. On the southeastern tip of the peninsula, Megistis Lavras is the oldest, largest, and wealthiest of the 20 monasteries on Mt. Athos. Its monks are known to be stern and conservative. Though it is one of the more frequently visited monasteries, it's also the most isolated: to get there you will need to get a ride (€10-20 per person depending on the number of visitors) from Karyes, or embark on a long, tiring hike from either Iviron (6hr) or Agia Anna (4hr). (*☎23770 23 754.*)

NORTHERN GREECE

KARAKALOU. With thickly forested hills to the north and the ocean to the south, picturesque Karakalou has the beautiful brotherly kiss icon depicting Peter and Paul. Karakalou's rules for non-Orthodox visitors are very strict. (☎23770 23 225.)

PHILOTHEOU. Philotheou, Greek for "God-loving," is one of Mt. Athos's most stunningly located monasteries, on a plateau over the northern coast. The abbey is surrounded by orchards, gardens, and lush chestnut forests. Philotheou, founded by monks from Megistis Lavra in 1015, is one of the stricter monasteries: non-Orthodox guests must eat after the others and are not allowed to enter the church, though many do. (☎23770 23 256.)

IVIRON. Beautifully situated near a meadow overlooking the northeastern coast, Iviron, founded by Georgian monks in 980, was the second monastery on Mt. Athos; it is currently among the most popular and friendly. Father Jeremiah, a monk originally from Australia, answers all historical and spiritual questions clearly and patiently. Iviron is home to one of the most important icons in the Orthodox Christian world: the **Panagia Portaiatissa,** a depiction of Mary believed to have performed many miracles. (☎23770 23 643. Reservations noon-2pm.)

PANDOKRATOROS AND STAVRONIKITA. Pandokratoros and nearby Stavronikita are on the northern coast, close to Karyes and about 5km north of Iviron, accessible by bus. Home to a small community of friendly monks, Pandokratoros was the last monastery to become communal in 1992, and is one of the few that imposes no special restrictions on its non-Orthodox visitors. Stavronikita is the smallest and "youngest" monastery, completed in 1536; it's also one of the friendliest, most peaceful, and most popular; book months in advance. Don't miss the wonderful **mosaic of Saint Nicholas,** known as *Sterdas* ("the one with the oysters"), as it supposedly was found at sea with an oyster stuck to the saint's head. (*Pandokratoros* ☎23770 23 880. *Stavronikita* ☎23770 23 255. Reservations noon-2pm.)

VATOPEDIOU. Moated and turreted like a medieval castle, Vatopediou lies on the northern coast in a secluded bay and is now populated largely by Greek-Cypriot monks. Though tradition claims it was founded by Constantine the Great, the monastery more likely was erected by three brothers from Andrianoupolis in the late 10th century. Historically favored by emperors and princes, Vatopediou is the most visited monastery on Athos, including recent visits by former U.S. president George H.W.

THE BIG SPLURGE

ATHOS BY SEA

The 20 monasteries of Mt. Athos, preserved since the Byzantine era, form one of the most breathtaking sights in all of Greece. Unfortunately, it's not easy for tourists to visit them. Only males are allowed to enter the Holy Mountain, and they are required to obtain a special entrance permit, with preference given to Orthodox Christians. Those who can't enter the holy peninsula that the monks call the "Garden of the Virgin" can still see the monasteries by boat.

An all-day boat tour originating from Sithonia visits both the eastern and western coasts of Mt. Athos, stopping in Ouranoupolis for lunch. Meli Tours in Neos Marmaras offers this package deal for €45. The cruise, which starts at 9:30am, takes you to the monasteries by way of the scenic route to the port of Ormos Panagias, on the eastern coast of Sithonia.

From there, a boat takes you around the Mt. Athos peninsula. Alternatively, you can jump aboard at the port of Ouranoupoli at 10:30am, and the 3hr. trip will cost you only €25. You'll be back in Neos Marmaras by 5pm with enough time to enjoy a few hours of daylight before experiencing one of the region's famous sunsets.

☎23750 72 113. Meli Tours open 9am-11pm. Tours offered daily Apr.-Oct.

Bush and England's Prince Harry; call at least two months ahead for a reservation. (☎ 23770 23 219. Reservations 9am-1pm.)

SIMONOS PETRA. On the edge of a sheer cliff on the southern coast, the breathtaking complex of Simonos Petra only has room for 10 guests. The extremely kind and hospitable monks invite travelers to relax in the roomy guest quarters, which extend out on a balcony overlooking the cliff to the sea. Under constant renovation, this monastery is frequently booked; you'll need to call at least two months in advance to get a bed. (☎ 23770 23 254. Reservations 1-3pm.)

GRIGORIOU. In a secluded bay just southeast of Simonos Petra, Grigoriou is one of the more liberal monasteries. Though the guesthouses are under construction, visitors are treated to large amounts of complimentary *raki* (anise-flavored spirit). (☎ 23770 23 668.)

DIONYSIOU. An hour and a half from Grigoriou, Dionysiou, one of Athos's biggest monasteries, rests on a rocky bluff over the Aegean. The monks here are welcoming, English is prevalent, and guest quarters are luxurious. Most rooms are singles, and showers (rare on Athos) with hot water (still rarer) are available. (☎ 23770 23 687.)

AGIOS PAVLOU. One hour southward along a shoreline path, Agios Pavlou serves as the starting point for visitors hoping to make it to the top of Mt. Athos. A new path makes it possible to spend the night at Ag. Pavlou. (☎ 23770 23 741. Reservations 10:30am-1:30pm.)

XEROPOTAMOU. The recently renovated Xeropotamou houses an American monk and, only a 40min. hike from Dafni, is the easiest monastery to access. (☎ 23770 23 251. Reservations 12:30pm-2:30pm.)

OTHER SIGHTS

SLAVIC MONASTERIES. In addition to the Greek monasteries, Slavs, not to be outdone, inhabit several abbeys. The great migration of Slavs to the peninsula began in the 19th century with the emergence of the Pan-Slavic movement in the Balkans. Both political and religious ambitions converged to give the Slavs and Russians a piece of the monastic action. At one time, there were nearly equal numbers of Greek and Slavic monks on the mountain. However, political turmoil—notably the 1917 Russian Revolution—cut off the supply of funds and novices at the source, ending the Russian government's official role in the area. Today, three Slavic monasteries remain: onion-domed Russian **Agios Panteleiomonos** (guest quarters closed for construction), Bulgarian **Zografou** (☎ 23770 23 247), and Serbian **Hiliandariou** (☎ 23770 23 797). All Slavic monasteries welcome visitors, but are challenging to reach by foot.

SKITES AND HERMITAGES. Only a handful of Athos's monks still choose to live as ascetic hermits, eschewing material comforts and the "fast-paced" mainstream-monastic lifestyle in favor of caves and huts on the peak's harsh slopes. Monks who have given their lives to meditation and the contemplation of God in isolation inhabit the huts, cells, and tiny churches that dot the southernmost end of the island, between Megistis Lavras and Ag. Pavlou. These small communities are known as *"skites,"* and each is affiliated with one of the larger monasteries. Many hermits will allow you to stay with them, but you must bring your own food and sleeping bag and be careful not to disturb their meditations. The barren southeastern slope of Athos, called *"Karoulia"* after the pulleys the monks use to bring food to their caves, is home to some of the most extreme ascetics and some of the biggest *skites*. **Agia Anna** (☎ 23770 23 320), at

NORTHERN GREECE

the foot of Mt. Athos, is a *skiti* run by a brotherhood of nine warm, welcoming monks who offer pilgrims rooms and meals.

⛰ HIKING

Hikes through Mt. Athos's winding mountain paths, high above emerald coves and speckled by fluorescent blue and yellow butterflies, rival any in Greece. All paths are marked with footprints and occasional signs in Greek. The trail from Megistis Lavras to Agia Anna is one of the wildest and most scenic among the Holy Mountain's family of trekking superlatives. The lack of auto accessibility and the breathtaking bluffs plunging into the Aegean beside rocky peninsulas make this region a favorite among the most reclusive hermits. The 8hr. hike can be shortened to 6hr. by stopping at **Kafsokalivia** (☎23770 23 319) and taking the ferry to Agia Anna or by using the new path that starts from Ag. Pavlou.

Other popular hikes include the ascent of Athos's peak, a hot, dry eight-hour trek from **Agia Anna** (☎23770 23 320). A 6hr. climb will take you to the Church of the Panagia, which has mattresses for overnight stays and a small well to refill your water bottle, just 2hr. from the summit. An easier trail (2hr.) that traverses the Athos mountainside runs from Iviron monastery to Koutloumousiou (☎23770 23 226), near Karyes. Catch a ride from Karyes back to Iviron or continue to another monastery in the vicinity.

For any hike, it is advisable to take along a copy of the green Mt. Athos Road Editions Map (available in stores in Karyes and Ouranoupolis; €7.50) or another Athos guide. Paths can be narrow and poorly marked, and those on the map might have been swallowed by brush. Stop frequently to verify directions and never hike alone; starting at one of the more popular monasteries will ensure company. Be sure to bring lots of water and bear in mind the lay of the peninsula: western shore hikers will enjoy Athos's shadow until 11am, while the eastern shore is perfect for late afternoon rambles. Make sure to be back from your excursion by sunset or you will be locked out of a meal and bed. The light monastic fare is insufficient for a long hike, so try to bring some nourishment of your own. If you tell the monks in your monastery that you are going to miss a meal, they might give you a modest amount of bread and vegetables. Alternatively, you can hop into a monk-driven minibus for a bumpy ride back to Karyes. Buses gather at most monasteries at about 8:30am, after the morning meal, to transport people back to Dafni via Karyes. From Karyes, ask around for another bus traveling in your direction or ask the minivan driver to let you off at your monastery of choice. Keep in mind that any special request, especially with fewer people in tow, will cost you extra. At no point, however, should you pay more than €20.

LITOCHORO Λιτόχωρο ☎23520

With Mt. Olympus towering above the city, the quintessential small-town atmosphere of Litochoro is charged by its location at the foot of the gods. The town's twisting back alleys lead across the mountainside to the *plateia* known as *kentro* (center), where locals relax in the shadow of Olympus. Litochoro provides information about the mountain and its trails. Though it's possible to ascend the mountain from its western side, beginning in Kokkinopilos village, this treeless route can't match the lush canyon trails that originate in Litochoro. Litochoro's proximity to the archaeological site Dion also makes it a perfect location for a daytrip if scaling the mountain is not on your itinerary.

TRANSPORTATION

Buses: (☎23520 81 271). Depart from the KTEL station, Ag. Nikolaou 20, opposite the tourist office. To **Athens** (5hr., 3 per day 9:30am-midnight, €30), **Plaka** (15min., Sa-Su every hr. 1-7:15pm, €2.50), and **Katerini** (30min., 12 per day 6am-10pm, €3). To reach **Larisa,** switch buses at crossroads (2hr., 3 per day 6am-5:15pm, €6.40).

Taxis (☎23520 82 333). Wait in the main *plateia.*

ORIENTATION AND PRACTICAL INFORMATION

Agiou Nikolaou, Litochoro's main street, runs east-west leading up to a fountain at **Plateia Agiou Nikolaou,** the central *plateia.*

Tourist Office: (☎23520 83 100 or 23523 50 103), down Ag. Nikolaou, past the police station right next to the fire department and the town hall. Provides information in English, free maps of the town, and a €5 map of the mountain. Open July-Aug. daily 8am-2pm and 3-9pm. The **town hall,** just next door to the fire department, also provides information. Open M-F 9am-2pm. **Greek Alpine Club (EOS)** (☎23520 82 444), a small stone building in the parking lot below Litochoro, off Ithakisiou.

Bank: National Bank (☎23520 81 025), in Pl. Ag. Nikolaou. **24hr. ATM.** Open M-Th 8am-2:30pm, F 8am-2pm.

Police: Ag. Nikolaou 20 (☎23520 81 100 or 81 111), just below the *plateia,* on the left as you walk downhill.

Hospital: Health Center (☎23520 22 222), 5km out of town toward Plaka. 24hr. emergency facilities.

Telephones: OTE, Ag. Nikolaou 36 (☎23520 84 099), on the right as you walk downhill, right next to the post office. Open M-F 7:20am-2pm.

Internet Access: Battleground, 48 Ag. Nikolaou. €2.60 per hr. Open daily 10am-2am. **C4 Internet Station,** right in front of Hotel Park on Ag. Nikolaou. €2.60 per hr. Open daily 11am-2am.

Post Office: 38 Nikolaou (☎23520 84 222). Open M-F 7:30am-2pm. **Postal Code:** 60200.

ACCOMMODATIONS AND CAMPING

Accommodations prices in Litochoro are fairly constant, and any price discrepancies can be eliminated by negotiating. Lodging is more expensive during Litochoro's famous annual Olympus Marathon in late June. The town is liveliest during this time of year and makes for a worthwhile experience, but remember to make reservations well in advance. Though the cheapest options are the out-of-town campgrounds, there are some affordable indoor options. The beach, 5km from town, is chock-full of campgrounds with the cheapest possible housing.

Papanikolau, Niko. Espik. Kitaus 1 (☎23520 81 236), behind the *plateia* on a road that veers off to the left. Picturesque residence that perfectly suits its mountain surroundings with a fireplace in the sitting room and a stone entrance covered in ivy. Open since 1987 but renovated in 2006, the rooms are modern and stylish, in a comfortable setting that evokes Litochoro's small-town charm. Each room has a kitchenette, TV, fridge, glassed-in veranda, and A/C. Breakfast buffet €4. Singles €40; doubles €45; triples €55. Room rates rise €5 July-Aug. Reservations recommended 1 day in advance. ❸

Hotel Park, Ag. Nikolaou 23 (☎23520 81 252), on 19th Fevrouariou down from the *plateia.* You may be welcomed by the owner's dog next to the shrine of Greek kitsch at the reception. Each simple room comes with bath, TV, fridge, A/C, and balcony, making this a comfortable (and reasonably priced) option. Reception 24hr. Singles €25; doubles €35; triples €45. ❷

Hotel Enipeas (☎23520 84 328), just off the main *plateia*. Clean, tiled rooms have TVs, fridges, and A/C. Fills up quickly in the high season. Breakfast €5. Singles €40; doubles €50; triples €60. ❸

Olympus Zeus (☎23520 22 115; www.olympios-zeus.gr). Rents bungalows that resemble small houses, each with fridge, bath, and phone. Less crowded than nearby Olympus Beach, this mix between a campground and a resort has 2 restaurants, a bar, and a beach volleyball net. Campground €6.50 per person; €4 per tent; €3.40 per car; electricity €3.80. Singles €70; doubles €80; triples €90; quads €100. Prices significantly lower in the low season. Book 1 week in advance for private rooms. ❶ / ❺

Olympus Beach (☎23520 22 112; www.olympos-beach.gr.). Simple bungalows for 1 to 4 people with baths, beds, and fridges. The area is like its own small town, with a supermarket, nightclub, 24hr. bar, and beach. The owners also offer a nice campsite adjacent to the bungalows. Reception 24hr. Campground €7.50 per person; €7.50 per tent; €3.50 per car. Bungalows €47. MC/V. ❶ / ❹

☕ FOOD

Those wisely seeking water and trail snacks for the arduous hike up Olympus should stay away from the expensive supermarkets just above the *plateia*. Instead, try **Arvanitides**, Perikliko Torba 14, at the end of short, winding Ermi, the road right between the post office and the OTE office. (☎23520 21 195. Open 8am-9pm. Cash only.)

Gastrodromio En Olympojust (☎23520 21 300), off the *plateia* by the church. Enjoy a remarkable view of the mountain and choose from a menu straight out of a hunting lodge: lamb with olives and rosemary (€11) is featured alongside wild boar (€14.50), and deer with chocolate sauce (€19.50). The wine menu is equally varied, with 308 options. Entrees €8-13.50. 3-course fixed *menùs* €12.50-19.50. Open daily noon-midnight. MC/V. ❸

Ta Mezedakia, Vas. Ithakisiou 3 (☎23520 84 574.). Specializes in "little appetizers," as its name suggests. Eat tasty Greek classics while you watch people start or finish their Olympus trek from the porch. Entrees €6-10. Open 5pm-midnight. Cash only. ❷

🎵 NIGHTLIFE

If you want to party, start your evening in the bars around the bottom of Ag. Nikolaou, just below the park. The action moves over to Plaka by midnight and continues toward the beach as the night goes on. Locals fill two bar-cafes adjacent to each other: **Destiny** and **Cafe Artio**. Partying in Plaka can get expensive: a taxi from Litochoro costs around €6, cover is around €8, and the price of drinks can add up quickly. Fueling up on *retsina* and *ouzo* at one of the tiki-torch-lit *psistarias* (grills) before hitting the clubs is a cheaper way to enchance your experience.

Destiny, Ag. Nikolaou 82, across from Hotel Park. More about cut-off jeans than cutting-edge fashion; a laid-back staff and owner share drinks with lounging clientele. Open 10am-1am.

Cafe Artio, Ag. Nikolaou 82 (☎23520 21 051). Trendy clients drink into the night. Open 9am-2am.

Bolero, Ag. Nikolaou 98 (☎23520 82 702), just above Abbia. Caters to an older, after-work crowd. Mixed drinks €5. Open 8am-4am.

Baraki, on the road to Plaka, on the left side of Olympus Beach facing the water. One of the few bars that is open on a weekday and is packed on weekend nights. Voted one of the top 30 beach bars in Greece, Baraki (meaning "little bar") has personalized decor that changes every year and lounge chairs just short of the shore. Try the "blowjob" or any number of creative mixed drinks. Open 10am-5am.

◪ DAYTRIP FROM LITOCHORO

ANCIENT DION Αρχαία Λίον

A taxi to Dion from Litochoro costs about €10. The walk to Dion takes about 2hr., but it's pleasant, with a constant view of Mt. Olympus. Follow the E4 road that leads downhill right beside the police station and continue straight; turn left at the T-intersection after about 1hr.; the way to Dion is clearly signposted. ☎ 23510 53 206. Site open daily 8am-8pm. Museum open M 1:30pm-8pm, Tu-Su 8am-8pm. Site €4, over 65 €2, EU students free. Museum €3/2/free. Joint ticket €6/€3/free.

In Dion, at the foot of Mt. Olympus and the ancient Baphyras River, Roman appropriations of a Hellenistic city give these ruins twice as much historical value, making it one of Greece's biggest and most fascinating archaeological sites. The Greek **theater** where Alexander the Great made sacrifices the night before beginning his 334 BC campaign into Asia is but one example of the site's historic holiness; Macedonian kings traveled great distances to the city to make sacrifices to Zeus. "Dion," in fact, is derived from a form of Zeus's name. The city was also home to a number of cults worshipping various gods—temples to Artemis, Demeter, Zeus; even the Egyptian goddess Isis, admired by Alexander the Great—were constructed at this site. At the **Sanctuary of Zeus,** you can look for the god's image and see if you can find his trademark thunderbolt clasped in his hand. Dion later fell to the Romans, who built elaborate **public baths.** In the Temple of Isis a stretch of water was created to resemble the Nile in honor of her Egyptian origins.

Destroyed by a combination of earthquakes, fires, and the Visigoths in the AD fourth century, the city (or what remained of it) was preserved by subsequent mudslides. Underneath the wreckage, Christian basilicas lived in harmony with temples of the empire's old religions. Thessaloniki University has been excavating Dion since the 1930s and has uncovered some spectacular artifacts. You may even catch some excavation work in progress as you walk through the ruins. Almost every winter, however, some of the site, only 5m above sea level, fills with water, and most excavations have to begin anew in the spring. The three-story **museum,** just a 5min. walk into town, displays many of the treasures that have been recovered, such as the statue of Zeus, marble cult statues, impressive funeral monuments, and a beautiful mosaic floor from the **Villa of Dionysos** depicting Medusa. The museum also displays a first-century BC **hydravlis,** a forerunner to the pipe organ, the first of its kind found in Greece and the oldest in the world. English explanations make the displays easily accessible.

MOUNT OLYMPUS Ολύμπος Όρος ☎ 23520

Mount Olympus, the highest mountain in Greece standing at 2917m, mesmerized the ancients so much that they believed it to be the dwelling of their immortal pantheon. The sharp peaks saw no successful mortal ascent until 1913, when Christos Kakalos, a Litochorian shepherd, guided two Swiss photographers up to Mytikas's zenith. The group took the first photos of Mt. Olympus, and rumor has it that Kakalos became so famous that he never paid for a meal again. For a few months in the summer, thanks to a number of well-maintained trails, the summit is accessible to just about anyone with a head for heights, a taste for adventure, and about two days to spare; the climb is strenuous but not technically difficult. The mountain and its surrounding region became Greece's first national park in 1938. More than 1700 plant species and 23 different types of flowers grow only on the mountain, and its tea leaves are well known throughout the country.

AT A GLANCE

CLIMATE: The mountain and its surrounding region are said to feature all the climates of Europe, from Litochoro's Mediterranean weather to the summit's snowy tundra.

FEATURES: The Plateau of the Muses (p. 196), Mavrologos Gorge (p. 195), and Kazania, "the cauldron" (p. 196).

HIGHLIGHTS: Drinking from the spring at the Chapel of Agios Spileo (p. 195), tackling Kaka Skala, "the evil staircase" (p. 196), writing your name in the book underneath the Greek flag at the summit of Mytikas (p. 196).

GATEWAY: Litochoro.

CAMPING: Camp at any of the refuges listed under **Accommodations** (p. 194).

ORIENTATION

As you ascend, you'll pass the three zones of flora on the peak: the lowest has leafy, green oak, chestnut, and arbutus trees. From 800-1800m you'll find shadowy birch and fir forests before emerging above the tree line to views of the summit and surrounding blue sea. Mt. Olympus has eight peaks: **Agios Andonios** (2817m), **Kalogeros** (2701m), **Mytikas** ("The Needle," 2917m), **Profitis Ilias** (2803m), **Skala** (2866m), **Skolio** (2911m), **Stefani** ("The Throne of Zeus"; 2909m), and **Toumba** (2801m).

PRACTICAL INFORMATION

WHEN TO GO. Each winter, well over 7m of snow buries Mt. Olympus, and even in late July, snowfields linger in the ravines. Unless you're handy with an ice pick and crampoons, you'll want to climb between May and October. Mytikas, the tallest peak, is not accessible without special equipment until June, and returns to the domain of professionals around September. Weather conditions can change rapidly near the summits; even in mid-summer, be prepared for anything from chilly clouds and rain to unrelenting sun.

Road Conditions: Trails are well-marked and well-maintained but straying from them can be dangerous; most of the rescue team's calls are from lost climbers. Do not climb alone—even if you are traveling alone, try to find someone to hike with at a refuge. Also **beware of belladonna berries,** small, grape-like black fruit that grow on purple flowers. They are poisonous and just touching them, much less eating them, can cause unconsciousness. Though the climb is not recommended for those at risk of altitude sickness, the hike itself is accessible to people of any (or no) hiking experience.

Refuges: EOS refuge **Zolotas "Spilios Agapitos"** (☎23520 81 800). Reliable resources for all aspects of hiking—updates on weather and trail conditions, advice on itineraries and routes, and reservations for any of the Greek Alpine Club (EOS) refuges. The staff has years of experience and is happy to give info over the phone in English. As the refuge is 2100m up the mountain, it's best to call from Litochoro before embarking on the climb. Open for calls 6am-10pm. The **EOS office** (☎23520 82 444) is the small stone building in the parking lot below Litochoro off Ithakisiou. The parking lot is just below Gastrodromio En Olympo and the *plateia*. It's worth stopping by even if the office is closed—many of the members of the Mt. Olympus search-and-rescue team hang out there, and are glad to help hikers. Open M-Th 10am-2pm, F 10am-2pm and 7pm-9pm.

Gear: If you're climbing between June and Sept., you'll need equipment: sturdy ankle-high shoes, sunscreen, a head covering, some snacks, at least 2L of water, light walking clothes, a wool or synthetic fleece sweater or jacket (the summit is 8-15˚C/46-59˚F in the summer), and an extra shirt and waterproof windbreaker. You also might want to purchase a light, portable emergency kit. Some hikers swear by trekking poles for maintaining balance and climbing steep terrain. Either bring your own or purchase them at the Zolotas refuge for €35. To avoid carrying unnecessary weight, take a small day pack and leave your luggage in Litochoro; the EOS office stores bags for free.

Guides: You can buy a colorful bilingual fold-out map with contour lines and all the major trails at most local shops, kiosks, and bookstores for €3-5. A *Road Editions* map, produced with data from the Greek Army Geographical Service, is the best and most expensive map (€8).

ACCOMMODATIONS

Reaching Mytikas in one day is only recommended for experienced hikers up for an 8km, 8hr. ascent and a strenuous 6hr. hike back down. For those who want to savor the summit trails or are concerned about the possibility of altitude sickness from leaping from the Aegean to 3000m and back in one day, an overnight stay in one of the refuges is a good idea. Keep in mind that they provide beds, blankets, meals, and water, but no sheets or towels. Three refuges are near the summits, accessible from different trails with varying difficulties. All of them, particularly Zolotas, tend to fill up on weekends between June and October. Call at least one week in advance for reservations. At the refuges, breakfasts tend to run €4, soups and salads €4-5, and pasta and meat dishes €3-5. Snacks are also available for purchase. Bring a flashlight to navigate your way to the bathroom after the generator is shut down. The refuges' managers are prepared to embark on emergency rescues if need be.

Zolotas Refuge (☎23520 81 800; elev. 2100m), also called "Spilios Agapitos" or "Refuge A." Named after owner Constantine Zolotas, it's about 800m below Skala and Mytikas peaks and can be reached by a very easy walk from the Prionia trailhead. The 90 beds, telephone, and very cold showers make this refuge the largest and cushiest, though also the most crowded—reservations are recommended. Curfew 10pm. Open from mid-May to Oct. 6am-10pm. €12, with any Greek mountain club membership €10. You also can set up a tent nearby and use the refuge's facilities for €4.90. ●

Kakalos (☎69373 61 689; elev. 2650m), called "Refuge C." Much closer to the summit than Zolotas, on the other side of the mountain in the Plateau of Muses. Accessible by a trail of intermediate difficulty, Diastavrosi. The small refuge has 18 beds. Reception 24hr. Open from June to mid-Sept. F-Su only to groups (though stranded hikers are not turned away). €12, with any Greek mountain club membership €10. ●

G. Apostolidis (☎23102 44 710; elev. 2760m), better known as "SEO Refuge," 15min. from Kakalos, beneath Stefani and Profitis Ilias. Accessible by the Diastavrosi trail. Has extraordinary sunrise views. Sleeps 100 and can accommodate extras and late-comers in its glass-walled porch or living room. Meals served 9am-9:30pm. Reception 24hr. Open June-Sept. €10, with any Greek mountain club membership €8. ●

HIKING

The two trailheads that reach the top of Mount Olympus are **Prionia** and the intermediate trail **Diastavrosi**. You can reach Prionia two ways: via the main road from Litochoro (5hr. walk, 1hr. drive, €25 taxi), or you can hike to Prionia through the scenic trail along the **Enipeas Canyon.** Start in Litochoro and after an easy and beautiful hike along the river (5hr.), you will arrive at the Prionia trailhead. To reach Diastavrosi, you must either walk (4hr.), drive (40min.), or take a taxi (€20) from Litochoro.

PRIONIA. The most popular and easiest route begins at Prionia (elev. 1100m). At the trailhead, you'll find drinking-water taps, toilets, and a small restaurant. From here, a manageable walk (3hr., 4km) takes you to the **Zolotas refuge** (p. 194). The well-marked trail is part of the European **E4** path from Spain to Greece. There's one last chance for water before the refuge, about 45min. from Prionia. After another 15min. you will be able to see the refuge, but it will be another 2hr. before you reach it. As you approach the tree line, you'll be encouraged by bright clumps of wildflowers.

ENIPEAS CANYON. The low-key, beautiful trail from Litochoro to Prionia runs along an E4 trail by the Enipeas River through the **Mavrologos Gorge,** whose name means "black mountain," since the trees are so dense that you can't see the sun. The parts of the trail that go up through Enipeas Gorge are not difficult in themselves, but they add about 5hr. to the ascent from Prionia, making it a total climb of 8-9hr. Gorgeous stretches punctuate the 18km climb, but it's a long hike with many ups and downs on multiple bridges, so be sure to bring water. To find the trailhead, walk uphill from Litochoro's main *plateia* past the Hotel Aphrodite, and follow signs to **Mili**, past the town cemetery, to the Restaurant Mili. There is drinking water at the trailhead. Continue past with the restaurant to your right. When you reach the walkway, make a right and walk along it for a short distance. At the fork, follow the yellow diamond markers reading "E4" up the left side of the Mavrologos Gorge. Keep following yellow diamonds, red blazes, spray-painted numbers, and orange and white plastic strips tied on trees, crossing over the river at the new bridges. Parts of the trail have views down into the gorge. When the trail descends to the river, you will see several lovely, clear green pools; though they couldn't be more tempting, swimming is forbidden. After 3hr. you'll reach the tiny **Chapel of Agios Spileo,** built at the source of a small spring inside a gaping cave. About 20min. farther, after a bridge crossing, you will see a signpost with three routes: the route to your far right (labeled **Monastery**) takes you to the **Monastery of Agios Dionysios,** which was a refuge for Greek partisans during WWII until it was bombed by the Nazis. The middle route (labeled **Prionia**) continues along the E4 path and also offers a chance to visit the Monastery from the opposite side. Taking the Prionia route, follow the dirt road for 60m before turning left up the hill to see the charred shell of the Monastery of Agios Dionysios. According to locals, when Agios Dionysiou built the church in the 15th century, he was aided by a bear. After a short dispute that followed the church's completion, however, the saint petrified the bear, which can still be seen standing across the ridge from the church. You can fill your water bottle here and leave a small donation for the restoration of the large and beautifully-situated monastery. Follow the outside wall of the monastery to a fork in the road and continue straight. You'll reach another fork after 15min. Take the left branch to go to the **Falls of Perivoli** and the right branch to reach Prionia after another hour. There are free **camping** zones between Ag. Dionysios and the Prionia trail.

DIASTAVROSI. The second trailhead is at Diastavrosi (also called Gortsia; elev. 1300m), 14km away, leading up to **Kakalos** and the SEO refuges. This longer (11km) trail includes a stunning ridge walk with views of the Aegean, the Macedonian plain, and Thessaloniki's smog. On cloudless days you may also be able to spy Mt. Athos and Thassos. As you climb higher, the difference in altitude is noticeable as the amount of vegetation dwindles. The well-marked trail reaches the SEO and Kakalos refuges in about 6-8hr. Begin at Diastavrosi's parking lot—to reach it, turn right off the gravel road halfway between Litochoro and Prionia. Then take the uphill path on the left and follow the red blazes, striped plastic strips on trees, and signs of the mule caravan that uses this route. In about 1hr., you'll pass through the **Barba Meadow,** which has a water tap. An hour later, you'll reach a cement water tank with an unhelpful painted map off to the left. Go straight here, not left, and the path leads up to **Petrostrounga** (elev. 1800m), about 3hr. from the trailhead. Four hours from the trailhead you'll begin approaching the tree line, reaching **Skourta Hill** in another 30min. or so. Here the trees will turn into small grassy fields with goat pens. The beautiful **Lemos Ridge** leads you gently toward the peaks, beginning with the **Skourta summit** (elev. 2485). About 5hr. from the beginning of the hike you'll hit the **Plateau of the Muses** (or-eh-PEH-thio moos-ON), a sweeping expanse of green under the Stefani, Toumba, and Profitis Ilias peaks. Take the clearly marked fork left for the Kakalos refuge (elev. 2650m) or right for the SEO refuge (elev. 2760m). A trail also goes up to the top of Profitis Ilias, where you'll see a tiny stone church, built in 1925. It's about half an hour to Profitis Ilias from either refuge. You usually can find water in two places along the Diastavrosi trail: at the turn-off between Barba and Spilla (1hr. from the trailhead, marked on the trail) and at Stragos spring. It's best not to depend on the springs, though, as they run dry in warm weather.

MYTIKAS. From the refuges, the next step is conquering the top. Once you get there and meet the gods, make sure to write your name in the book underneath the Greek flag at the summit. There are only two trails, both classified as intermediate, to the top: **Louki,** "steep gorge," and **Kaka Skala,** "the evil staircase." Despite its ominous name, Skala is the easier of the two, though both have sheer drops and require some scrambling. Slightly longer, Kaka Skala climbs the ridge behind Zolotas on a broad but steep path to the Skala peak (2861m). Although it is possible to go up Skala from the Kakalos or SEO refuges via the **Zonaria** trail, which connects to the Kaka Skala route, it is not recommended, as doing so adds almost 2hr. to the ascent, making it a total of 4-5hr. to reach Mytikas. To take the more direct route from Zolotas, walk uphill. After about 45min. (1.2km), you'll find a signpost at a fork in the road. The left option takes you along the E4 trail to Skala and Skolio peaks; the right is the Zonaria trail, which leads to the Louki trail fork and the SEO and Kakalos refuge paths. If you're going to Mytikas via Skala, 50m beyond the signpost you'll find an unmarked fork. Take the right leg and continue ascending for about 1hr. along exposed terrain until you reach Skala peak. From here, hikers can turn left up to the Skolio peak (2904m) for a sweeping view of Mytikas and Profitis Ilias, or grab handholds on the mostly vertical "path" plummeting down to the sharp saddle point between Skala and Mytikas and then back up "The Needle." Those distracted by rocks loosed from climbers above should glance to their left—the 500m drop into **Kazania** ("The Cauldron"), named for the clouds of mist that steam up from it, will brush away all extraneous concerns. From Zolotas reaching Mytikas takes about 3hr., from the SEO and Kakalos refuges, it takes about 5hr.

The Louki trail should be used only for ascent; only serious climbers should attempt it for the descent. Louki branches off Zonaria about halfway (45min., 700m) between its endpoint on the Skala trail and SEO path respectively. After balancing along the precipitous Zonaria trail, hikers must turn straight up Louki's red-blazed gorge. During a pause in the shower of dust from climbers above, those with particularly good grips can peruse the plaques commemorating

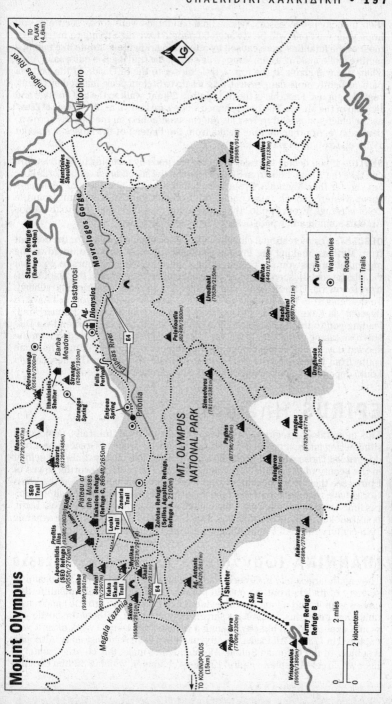

Mount Olympus

NORTHERN GREECE

their unlucky predecessors, whose final handholds were not as secure as you hope your next one will be. Though 50 people have died trying to meet Zeus, most of the fatalities were caused by attempting ridiculous stunts like taking a picture while making a 50m jump (true story); the trail itself is quite safe. After 300m you will arrive at the top. A little closer to the SEO side of the Zonaria path, a slightly more dangerous trail goes up to Stefani peak, marked by a bent, rusted signpost. Past this is the SEO path, a 20min. walk to the SEO refuge and Plateau of the Muses. The bowl-shaped slopes are known as the **"Throne of Zeus,"** as the chief god is said to rest his enormous cranium on the *Stefani* (crown) peak above. Approaching the peaks from the Plateau of the Muses, it's about 1½hr. up to Mytikas via Louki.

SKOLIO. If you decide to resist tempting the gods by climbing to Mytikas, you can take the 20min. hike from Skala to Skolio, the second-highest peak (2911m; 7m shorter than Mytikas). From here, you'll have the best view of Olympus's sheer western face. It takes about 2hr. to reach the Skolio summit from the Zolotas refuge. From Skolio, 1hr. south along the ridge takes you to the Agios Antonis summit and a path descending back to Zolotas.

DESCENT. For recreational climbers Kaka Skala should be used for the descent from Mytikas, making the Prionia trailhead the most direct route down the mountain, unless you are prepared for a detour of several hours to go down via Diastavrosi. Descending via Kaka Skala takes 2hr. to reach the Zolotas refuge (follow the E4 trail signs) and another 2hr. to reach the Prionia trailhead. To descend from Mytikas and go down the Diastavrosi trail, you will have to descent via Kaka Skala and then divert from the trail along the Zounari trail, leading you to the Kakalos and SEO refuges where you can descend via Diastavrosi, taking about 8hr. If you are going up Mytikas and back down on the second day from Zolotas refuge, it will amount to 7hr. of hiking. The same route from Kakalos or the SEO refuge will take about 9hr. The descent via Louki depends on your speed of hiking with climbing equipment.

EPIRUS Ήπειρος

This mountainous region is world-famous for its beautiful trails, peaks, and shimmering lakes; it draws international hikers for some of Greece's best outdoor treks. Those who enjoy exhilarating fresh air and quality trails will delight in the beauty of the Pindos Mountains region. The postcard-worthy towns of Epirus see their share of tourism, but the Zagorohoria villages near the Vikos Gorge have retained a timeless feeling, despite a recent influx of visitors. Epirus links itself to a living past—the old dialect of Vlach, descended from Latin, is still spoken in some of the towns, and the preserved mosques of the dynamic 19th-century ruler Ali Pasha still grace the city of Ioannina.

IOANNINA Ιωάννινα   ☎ 26510

The eighth-largest city in Greece, Ioannina has a little bit of a lot: the beautiful scenery of its lakefront, a youthful population and the vibrant nightlife that comes with it, and a long history evident in the Old City (Frourio) and museums. Despite all this, Ioannina is surprisingly laid-back, without the bustle you would expect from a big city. Ioannina reached its political peak after it was captured in 1788 by Ali Pasha, an Albanian-born leader and visionary. Although a subject of the Ottoman Sultan, Ali intended to make this city the capital of his own Greek-Albanian empire. His fiery character, which won him the title

Ioannina

Lake Pamvotis

TO NISI

0   200 yards
0   200 meters

TO ✈
KTEL KASTORIAS (1km)
PERAMA CAVES (4km)

TO KONITSA (75km)

TO ✚ (5km),
IGOUMENITSA (88km)

Asian Camii and Municipal Museum

FROURIO

Ali Pasha's Hamam

Silverworks Gallery

Its Kale

Fethiye Camii

Byzantine Museum

Tomb of Ali Pasha

G. Papandreou

Main Bus Terminal

Shrine to St. George the Neomartyr

Sports Stadium

City Hall

Venetian Clock Tower

PL. KING PIRUS

Archaeological Museum

PL. 25 MARTIOU

Litharitsia Park

ANDREA PAPANDREAU SQ.

Prefecture of Ioannina

PL. PARGAS

PIROU SQ.

Olympic Airways

TO ℹ (300m),
✚ (5km),
DODONI (45km)

Preveza Station

Ioannina

ACCOMMODATIONS
Hotel Elpis, **14**
Hotel King Pyrros, **7**
Hotel Tourist, **9**

FOOD
Brettania, **5**
Diethnes, **4**
Feesa Roifa, **10**
Filippas, **18**
To Rembetiko, **15**

NIGHTLIFE
Fuego, **16**
N-Club, **12**
Skala, **11**

MUSEUMS AND SIGHTS
Byzantine Museum, **13**
Municipal Museum, **17**

"Lion of Ioannina," eventually caused the Sultan to view him as a threat, and he was executed in 1822. Present-day Ioannina is a charming, modern city, with easy access to notable sights, such as Dodoni, the Perama caves, and the Vikos Gorge, earning Ioannina its status as the hub and capital of Epirus.

▐ TRANSPORTATION

Flights: Ioannina National Airport (IOA; ☎26510 26 218). Take bus #2 or 7 (€0.90) from the stop in front of the clock in the central *plateia*, or get a taxi (€10). Bus tickets cannot be bought on board; they must be purchased at 1 of the many snack kiosks all over town. **Olympic Airways** (☎26510 39 131) flights go daily to **Athens** (1hr.; M-Th and Sa 10:35am-8:35pm; F 10:30am, 5:25pm, 9pm; Su 10:35am, 4:10pm, 8:35pm; €52-90) and **Thessaloniki** (55min.; M-Th and Sa 10:35pm and 8:35pm; F 10:35am, 5:25pm, 9pm; Su 10:35,am, 4:10pm, 8:35pm; €86-105).

Buses: G. Papandreou 58 (☎26510 26 286). To: **Agrinio** (3hr., 6 per day 8:30am-7pm, €13.10); **Arta** (1hr., 8 per day 6:30am-8pm, €6.40); **Athens** (6hr., 9 per day 7:15am-midnight, €35.20); **Dodoni** (30min., M and F 7am and 2:45pm, €1.90); **Igoumenitsa** (2hr., 9 per day 6am-8pm, €8.30); **Kastoria** (3hr., daily 10:30am and 2:15pm, €17.70); **Konitsa** (1hr., 7 per day 5am-7pm, €5.60); **Metsovo** (1hr.; 4 per day 5am-2pm; Sa 6:50am and 2pm; Su 4:30pm; €5.30); **Monodendri** (55min.; M, W, F 6:15am and

NORTHERN GREECE

2pm; €3.40); **Papingo** (1hr., F 5:30am and 2:30pm, €4); **Parga** (1hr., 8:30am, €11); **Patra** (4hr., 9:30am and 2:30pm, €21); **Preveza** (1hr.; 8 per day 6:30am-8:15pm, Sa-Su reduced service; €9.30); **Thessaloniki** (4hr., 6 per day 7am-10:30pm, €28.70); **Volos** (3hr., 3 per day 10:45am-7pm, €14) via **Larisa** (5hr., €17.50).

Ferries: Dock outside the Frourio and go to **Nisi** (every 30min. 6:30am-11pm, €1.80).

Taxis: (☎26510 46 777). Line up 24hr. around the corner from the bus station and outside the Frourio, before the gates that lead to the Municipal Museum. Prices double after 1am. €1.50 surcharge when you call for a pick-up.

✦ ✚ ORIENTATION AND PRACTICAL INFORMATION

Ioannina is at the center of Epirus, at the edge of **Lake Pamvotis,** and surrounded by the peaks of Pindos. Not far into the lake is a small, hilly island called "Nissaki" or simply **"Nisi"** ("the islet" or "the island"). The **Old Ciy,** known as Frourio, is on the waterfront, while **Plateia King Pirus,** the city center, is inland across from **Litharitsia Park;** a signature Venetian clock tower marks the adjacent *plateia,* **Andrea Papandreou,** which is closer to the water. **Georgios Averof** is a broad avenue that runs from the main gate of the Old City uphill to the city center. After the *plateia,* G. Averof becomes **Dodonis,** the city's primary artery, full of shops, restaurants, bars, and cafes. **28 Oktovriou** intersects G. Averof between the two *plateias,* and contains many stores, as well as the post office, police station, and OTE office. The main bus station is 1km outside of the city on G. Papandreou St., which runs parallel to the waterfront. To reach the city center from the main bus station, with your back to the station, turn left and walk along the street. The road will become **Kountourioti** and curve right, bisecting Averof as it begins, just a block away from the walls of the Old City. One block closer to the Old City from Kountourioti, **Karamanli** passes the main gate of the Frourio to the waterfront on a road that eventually leads to Panagou. From the same intersection of Averof and Karamanli, **Ethnikis Antistaseos** runs in the opposite direction along the side of the Frourio. Most of Ioannina's nightlife and a long line of outdoor cafes are located down Karamanli and Eth. Antistaseos.

Tourist Office: EOT, Dodonis 39 (☎26510 46 662), about 500m down Dodonis on the left, just past the playground. Friendly, English-speaking staff provide info for the province. Open July-Aug. M-F 9am-1pm and 5pm-8pm, Sa 9am-1pm; Sept.-June M-F 7:30am-3pm.

Banks: Dodonis and Averof are full of banks with **24hr. ATMs. National Bank,** G. Averof 4 (☎26510 54 735), on the right just before Pl. King Pirus, walking uphill from the waterfront. Open M-Th 8am-2:30pm, F 8am-2pm.

Police: 28 Oktovriou 11 (☎26510 91 290 or 65 934), across from the post office. **Tourist Police** (☎26510 65 917; www.uoi.gr/tourist_police), in the same building. Open daily 8am-10pm.

Hospital: 2 hospitals, each about 5km from the center of town. **Hatzikosta** (☎26510 80 111), on Makriani on the way to Igoumenitsa, handles emergencies on even dates. **University Hospital** (☎26510 99 111), on Universal, 5km from the end of Dodonis toward Dodoni, does so on odd dates.

Telephones: OTE, 28 Oktovriou 2-4 (☎26510 715 99). Open M and W 7:30am-2pm, Tu and Th-F 7:30am-6pm.

Internet Access: Free Wi-Fi can be picked up on many of Ioannina's streets. **The Web,** Pirsinella 21 (☎26510 26813), on the 1st street on the right along Dodonis after Pl. King Pirus walking away from the waterfront. €2 per hr. Open 24hr.

Post Office: 28 Oktovriou 1 (☎26510 28 698), at the intersection with Botsari. Open M-F 7:30am-8pm. **Postal Code:** 45110.

NORTHERN GREECE

ACCOMMODATIONS AND CAMPING

You get what you pay for in Ioannina. This isn't a bad place to consider camping. Otherwise, hotels range from cheap, noisy, and slightly uncomfortable to expensive and luxurious.

King Pyrros Hotel, I. Gounari 3, (☎26510 27 652; www.kingpyrros.gr), across the street from Pl. Andrea Papandreou. Surprisingly peaceful considering its central location by the main *plateia*. Large, stylish rooms, an attentive staff, and all the amenities. Each room has A/C, TV, phone, fridge, bath, and free Wi-Fi. Singles €45; doubles €56; triples €65; quads €70. MC/V. ❸

Hotel Tourist, Kolleti 18 (☎26510 25 070). Follow the signs for the hotel on Averof and take a right on Kristali. Maybe the best value for your money. Quiet, well-decorated rooms are far from Averof's incessant racket. Rooms have A/C, baths, phones, and TVs. Reception 24hr. Singles €30; doubles €40; triples €50. Cash only. ❷

Hotel Elpis, Neoptolemou 10 (☎26510 26 209 or 69755 21 573). The street is a side road directly opposite the pedestrian entrance to the Frourio, off Kountouriatou. This small, family-run hotel has cheap, no-frills rooms. A/C costs extra. Singles €25-30; doubles €40. Cash only. ❷

Limnopoula, Kanari 10 (☎26510 25 265), a few blocks from the bus station en route to Perama. This unspectacular but well-priced campground has a lake, restaurant, and bar. Despite the lack of English, the friendly staff is patient and accommodating. Reception 7am-midnight. €8 per person; €4 per tent; €5 per car. Cash only. ❶

FOOD

Georgios Averof is saturated with joints selling souvlaki, gyros, and hamburgers, all decent and similarly priced. Some inviting *tavernas* on the waterfront combine sit-down meals, lake views, and live music. At almost any of the ubiquitous sweet shops, you can sample the delicious local baklava. Try Ioannina's speciality, *kaimaki*, a tasty Turkish ice cream made from sheep's milk.

To Rembetiko, Neo Georgiou 14 (☎26510 75 535). Decent portions of well-known dishes that keep their tables busy all day. Open daily noon-2am. Entrees €4.80-7. ❶

Feesa Roifa, G. Averof 55 (☎26510 45 330). Simple, delectable Greek dishes like grilled chicken (€5.50) and the more exotic lamb tongues (€6.80), as well as a selection of pies (€2.90-4.50). Entrees €5.50-7. ❷

Filippas, Panagou 4 (☎26510 31 170). Look for the yellow signs on the waterfront. The menu is an eclectic combination of different cultural cuisines, all prepared with a distinctly Greek spin. Entrees €6-12. ❷

Brettania Cafe, Pl. King Pirus (☎26510 30 600), before Diethnes, below the Hotel Brettania. A classy patisserie with French decor and style. A wide variety of local baklava (€10.50 per kg., €1.90 per piece) as well as mouth-watering French pastries. Open daily 8am-1:30am. ❶

Diethnes, G. Averof (☎26510 74 366), just before 28 Oktovriou, heading away from the waterfront. Doubling as a cafe, this shop has been keeping local dentists in business since 1950 by carrying every sweet imaginable. Pick up a scoop of top-notch *kaimaki* (€1 per scoop) to go or stay to savor a piece of fresh baklava (€2) with a cup of coffee. 6 other locations in Ioannina, but this is where it all began. Open 7am-2am. ❶

NORTHERN GREECE

👁 SIGHTS

🏛 THE FROURIO

Ioannina's signature landmark, the Frourio (a.k.a. the **kastro** or the **Old City**) presides regally over the shore, with a slender minaret at each end. Most of the castle was built in the 13th century by Thomas Preljubovic, the Serbian ruler of Ioannina who also was known as "Albanitoktonos" ("Albanian-killer"). To secure a bloodless surrender in their conquest of 1430, the Turks assured Ioanninans that they could remain in their houses within the fortress walls. After a failed 1611 Greek insurrection, the Turks changed their minds and cracked down. One Sunday, when all the Greeks were in church, the Turks seized their houses. At many points throughout the *kastro*'s history, however, Jews, Turkish Muslims, and Christians lived peacefully side by side; even when the great Ali Pasha came to power and rebuilt the walls in 1795, the communities flourished together in peace. The approximately 4000 Jews dwindled to the 100 that reside there today when the Nazis sent the Jewish community to death camps, and the fortress hasn't seen the same diversity since then. The Frourio is now home to placid neighborhoods with narrow streets, old Turkish-style homes, several museums, and all of Ioannina's major sights. Though its several entrances are all open 24hr, the main entrance, like that of any self-respecting fortress, has several sharp turns to make invasion slow and tricky. Just outside this entrance is an unmarked shrine to **Saint George the Neomartyr.** Ioannina's patron saint, he was tortured and hanged in 1838 by Turkish overlords for marrying a Christian.

THE ITŞ KALE. This strategic remove, the inner citadel was made the city's primary fortress in 1205 and later became Ali Pasha's headquarters, where he lived, built a mosque, and was buried. Though it once was enveloped in turmoil, the Itş Kale is now a peaceful area surrounded by the Pindos Mountains and Pamvotis Lake. The small ruined buildings on both sides as you enter the walls were guard posts, and the cafe on the left was originally a kitchen. To the immediate right along the wall are the remnants of Ali Pasha's **hammam** (baths), and around what is now the Silverworks Gallery of the Byzantine Museum is the **serai** (residence) that once housed Ali, his harem, and his ornately decorated audience chambers. Though it's hard to imagine in the serenity of today's site, Ali Pasha held most of his tortures and executions at the plane tree near the *serai*, running the gory gamut from skinning to impaling to suspending on hooks hung from the tree's branches. **Katsandonis,** a famed fighter in the War of Independence, is said to have sung patriotic hymns while being brutally hammered to death here, a scene reenacted frequently in Greek shadow-puppet theater.

Though a **circular tower** is all that is left from the original Byzantine fortification, the **Byzantine Museum** has a small collection from the period that includes intricate wooden sanctuary doors, stone carvings, calligraphic manuscripts, and post-Byzantine icons. Helpful plaques in the first part of the museum chronicle the history of Epirus and Ioannina in English. (☎ 26510 27 761. Open Tu-Su 8am-5pm. €3, students €2.) The **Fethiye Camii** (Victory Mosque) to the right of the museum is the third mosque in its location, a space once occupied by a 13th-century church. The current mosque was rebuilt in 1795 by Ali Pasha himself. In front of the mosque, weeds and rubble obscure the **Tomb of Ali Pasha,** a sarcophagus that contains his headless body; his head and neck are buried in Istanbul. The gilded cage that originally decorated the tomb was looted by Nazis in 1943, and it was recently replaced with a green iron replica. Ioannina

NORTHERN GREECE

is the silver capital of Greece, and at the impressive **Silverworks Gallery** you'll find snuffboxes, tea services, and belt buckles to prove it. An etching beside the desk depicts the Frourio as it looked in its glory days. *(From the Frourio's main entrance, follow the path to the right and then take the first left; continue until you reach the long ramp that heads up to the site.* ☎ *26510 25 989. Site and museum open 8am-10pm. Show your Byzantine Museum ticket for admission.)*

MUNICIPAL MUSEUM. The smaller of the Frourio's walled inner areas is a little farther to the left, of the Itş Kale from the main entrance—follow signs to the museum housed in the lovely **Aslan Pasha Camii,** whose rusting piles of cannon balls attest to the citadel's former prominence. On the left as you enter is the long, rectangular former **medrasa** (school for Qur'anic study). In front of it, the tombstones engraved in Arabic are the remains of an **Ottoman cemetery.** The small building behind the mosque is Aslan Pasha's **mausoleum.** Following the 1611 rebellion, the Turks replaced the former church with an elegant mosque. The Municipal Museum, in the former mosque, has a beautiful interior prayer room, displaying a colorful *mimbar,* the pulpit from which the Imam reads from the Qur'an. The small but fascinating collection focuses on Ioannina's diverse ethnic past, and is divided into Jewish, Greek, and Muslim exhibits, displaying sacramental pieces, costumes, and silverworks. *(*☎ *26510 26 356. Open daily 9am-4pm; May-Oct. 8am-8pm. €4.50, EU students and seniors €2.50.)*

Across from the Municipal Museum and down a set of stairs is the private collection of **Fotis Rapakousis,** displaying Greek weapons from the 15th century through the Balkan Wars. *(Open M-F. Show your Municipal Museum ticket for admission.)*

OTHER SIGHTS

NISI. Getting to the small island of Nisi on the taxi boat may be the most exciting part of the pedestrian-only island—the sights in Nisi hardly compare to those of Ioannina. Ali Pasha met his death after being betrayed by his Greek wife (a perennially unsatisfied bunch) in this now-peaceful town chock full of souvenir shops and whitewashed houses. The underwhelming two-room **Ali Pasha Museum** displays his enormous bronze hookah, which he is shown happily puffing in nearly every portrait. *(*☎ *26510 81 791. Open daily 9am-9:30pm. €0.80.)* Signs point the way to **Saint Pantaleimon** and four other monasteries. A short walk from the museum, the **frescoes** of St. Nicholas Philanthropinos, painted by Katelanou in 1542, depict saints, the life of Jesus, and seven ancient sages, including Plato, Aristotle, and Plutarch, who were said to have foretold the coming of Christ. If the monastery is locked, ask next door for a tour.

◐ NIGHTLIFE

You don't have to look far to find nightlife in this happening city. Most of Ioannina's late-night action takes place on the waterfront along the base of the Frourio walls. Cafes and discos line the waterfront on Papagou, and bars sit parallel to the main entrance to the Frourio. To reach a string of relaxed after-hours cafes, walk past the main *plateia* away from the Frourio walls to Soutsi and Mavili, or walk to the beginning of Dodonis. More options are on the other side of the peninsula; head back to Diethnes and walk along the perimeter of the walls for 400m or take Karamanli, which begins soon after the **Ferris wheel,** to Eth. Antistasios. Bars and clubs await across from the park.

N-Club, Garivaldi 1 (☎26510 28 028), on the corner of Garivaldi and Eth. Antistaseos adjacent to the Frourio walls. This super-modern club packs in the young and trendy youth of Ioannina day and night. Beer €3. Mixed drinks €7. Open daily 10am-3am.

Fuego, Papagou 5 (☎ 1228 33 988). Follow the main road along the waterfront past a few bar patios; it's on the corner as the street bends. The spacious interior of this trendy hangout has lounges, a patio, and even a playground, but don't get too excited—it's for the kids. Grown-up amusements like board games (bilingual Scrabble, anyone?) and Wi-Fi help pass the time. Drinks €6-9. Open daily 10am-2am.

Skala (☎ 26510 37 676), behind N-Club. Locals come to this low-key hangout to listen to pop and Greek tunes before hitting up the clubs. Beer €3. Mixed drinks €6. Open daily 9pm-3am.

◆ DAYTRIPS FROM IOANNINA

◆ PERAMA CAVES Σπήλαιον Περάματος

Take local bus #16 or 8 from 28 Oktovriou off the main plateia heading away from the city center (20min., every 20min. 7am-10pm, €0.90). Bus tickets can't be purchased on board; buy them in advance at one of the many snack kiosks in town. At Perama, follow the signs to the cave. ☎ 26510 81 650. Open daily 9am-5pm. €7, students €3, under 7 free. Tours every 15min.

You may lose your sense of time and space in the spectrally-lit, glimmering Perama Caves, which are among the largest in the Balkans. A 500-step stairway over 1.1km long leads from narrow passageways to immense caverns filled with eerily hanging rock formations. Created over the course of 1.5 million years, the cave has 19 different stalactites and stalagmites—three times as many as typical caves—some of which are unique to Perama. The huge cavities were discovered accidentally by two locals who were seeking shelter from Nazi bombs during WWII. Subsequent excavations have uncovered the teeth and bones of a unique species of bear, which are now on display in Athens. Certain formations are named after landmarks they vaguely resemble, such as the "Tower of Pisa," the "Egyptian Sphinx," and "The Statue of Liberty" while unique formations (such as the "Cross") can be found nowhere else. The 45min. Greek and English guided tours give general facts about the caves and their creation. The formations alone make it worth a visit, but factor in the cool temperature—a steady 17°C/62°F—and the cave is a must-see, if only as a break from the scorching heat.

DODONI Δωδώνη

The interior of the theater is currently under construction, but the site and exterior of the theater can be viewed. Buses to Dodoni (30min.; M and F 7am, 2:45pm; €1.90) are infrequent, and they return to Ioannina immediately. Ask to be let off at the theater. You can take a taxi (at least €20) and take the return bus in the afternoon (passes by daily around 3:15pm). If you're stranded, call a taxi (☎ 26510 46 777), but expect to pay a €2-3 surcharge. ☎ 26510 82 287. Open daily 8am-7pm. €2, students and seniors €1, EU students free.

Ancient Dodoni, the site of mainland Greece's oldest oracle, lies at the base of a mountain 23km southwest of Ioannina. An oracle of Zeus and his consort Dione Naia, Dodoni's sacred oak tree was thought to be a portal of the divine wisdom of the king of the gods. From the earliest recorded ceremony as far back as 2000BC, such worthy figures as Odysseus and Achilles sought advice under its leafy shade until the site was all but demolished by the Romans in 167 BC. At its height, Dodoni was the second greatest oracle in the ancient world, surpassed only by Delphi. Unlike Delphi, however, this oracle was consulted mostly on personal rather than political matters. Unlike the complicated hexameters that served as answers at Delphi, Dodoni's replies were either "yes" or "no," expressed through the doves nestling in the tree, the rustling of its branches, or nature's sounds heard reverberating in the many cauldrons surrounding the oracle. According to Herodotus, an Egyptian priestess who was kidnapped by Phoenician sea traders transformed herself into a dove to escape captivity. She settled at Dodoni and convinced Zeus to establish his oracle at the serene spot. A clan of priests called the **Hellopes, Helloi,** or **Selloi** guarded the heavenly site, but eventually they were replaced by three priestesses called **Doves.** The **Naia Festival,** an Olympic-like series of pan-Hellenic athletic and dramatic contests, was held here every four years in Zeus's honor.

The enormous **amphitheater** near the entrance to the site was built in the early third century BC. The original design seated 17,000 before the Romans replaced the lowest rows with a retaining wall and improved the still-visible drainage system to accommodate their blood sports. Every seat in the vast complex has an amazing view of the stage, and it is easy to picture the drama and violence that once occurred here. The acoustics are so good that whispers made on stage can be heard clearly even by those in the nosebleed seats. Sometimes the theater is used in the summers for music and dance performances. Beyond the amphitheater are the ruins of the oracle itself, where a new sacred oak recently has been planted. Little remains today of the original building that housed the tree and its pilgrims. A fifth-century BC temple and the 350 BC **bouleuterion** and **prytaneion,** now almost totally vanished, once surrounded the oracle. Following the Aetolian sack in 219 BC, a larger Ionic temple to Zeus was built in 167 BC. Later, in the AD fifth century, the site was home to some of the largest early Christian basilicas.

AGIOS GEORGIOS AQUEDUCT Άγιος Γεώργιος

Take the bus to Preveza (1hr., 8 per day 6am-8pm, €6) and ask the driver to let you off at Agios Georgios. Once you get off, cross the highway and take the road leading downhill for about 1km. To return, go back up the road to take the bus back to Ioannina (1hr., 10 per day 6am-7:30pm, €6).

The location of the remains of Nikopolis's Roman aqueduct, high in the mountains, is gorgeous, but the well-preserved structure crossing the Louros rapids has a beauty of its own. Construction of the aqueduct at such an altitude was a major feat of classical engineering. Over 50 years later, the aqueduct was connected to the city's **nymphaion fountain.** Although the site has no signs or explanations, the area is serene and beautiful, and it's still fascinating to watch the stream flow under the ancient construction.

METSOVO Μέτσοβο ☎ 26560

On the western slope of the Katara Pass lies the alpine town of Metsovo. An instantly endearing hamlet built into the side of a mountain, the town itself is a piece of art, kept in near-perfect condition by the fortune left by Metsovite-turned-Swiss-banker Baron Tositsas. The self-proclaimed "Vlach capital" contains some of the last speakers of that Romance dialect, which is currently on the verge of extinction. Its position in the North Pindos mountains makes it a gold mine of exquisite hikes, but be forewarned: the weather is schizophrenic. Even in summertime there's a mix of thunderstorms, sunny days, and frigid nights. The intricate local costumes and rugs, along with the festivals and traditional weddings that turn the town into one continuous celebration in July, showcase Metsovite culture in full form.

⌐ TRANSPORTATION

Buses: From the main *plateia*, buses go to **Ioannina** (1hr., 4 per day 6:15am-4:30pm, €5.30) and **Thessaloniki** (5hr., 5 per day 7am-10:30pm, €20). You can check the bus schedule on the placard across from the white building with the Eurobank at the beginning of the road to Ioannina. The Thessaloniki bus passes by on the main highway 6km away, but won't stop unless you flag it down.

Taxis: (☎6945200 820), in the *plateia*. 24hr.

✈ 🅿 ORIENTATION AND PRACTICAL INFORMATION

Navigating through Metsovo is easy: all roads in Metsovo lead to the main *plateia*. The bus drops off in front of a sign for **Hotel Egnatia information** (not the hotel but a small souvenir shop bearing the same name). With your back to the sign and the park in front of you, there are two roads to your left. The road heading uphill is the main road that leads to Ioannina and Trikala after passing the Tositsas Museum. The road beside it, on an even plane to the left, leads to John Xaralabapoulos's Rooms and Hotel Olympic, passing the police station. The road dead ahead wraps around the park in a circle leading back to the souvenir shop, and connecting to the road on your right from the same spot. The street to your right has many of the town's restaurants and leads to Hotel Filoxenia and the Evangelos Averof contemporary art gallery.

Tourist Office: Stop by Hotel Filoxenia to speak with British-educated Yiannis at the beginning of your stay. Assuming the role of a tourist office, he has prepared binders filled with information about hiking paths, maps, museum hours, and just about anything you would ever want to know about the town. **Town Hall** (☎26560 41 207), on the 2nd fl. of the large building that houses the Eurobank, where the main road to Ioannina meets the *plateia*. Brochures are available; most are in Greek. Open M-F 8am-2:30pm.

Bank: National Bank (☎26560 41 296), on the road that wraps around the *plateia* and the park. Open M-Th 8am-2:30pm and F 8am-2pm. **Agricultural Bank** (☎26560 41 160), on the same road. Open M-Th 8am-2:30pm and F 8am-2pm. Both have **24hr. ATMs.**

Police: (☎26560 41 233). From the souvenir shop, take the even road to your left beside the main road and keep to your right; the station is right around the corner.

Hospital: (☎26560 41 112), at the top of the town, along the road to Ioannina. Open 24hr.

Telephones: OTE (☎26560 42 199), on the 2nd fl. of the building across the street from the hospital. Open M-F 8am-2pm.

Internet Access: Super Star (☎26560 41 696). The 2nd road to the right from the souvenir shop runs downhill to the Agios Nikolaos monastery; the road heading uphill beside it leads to Super Star. €2 per hr. Open daily 10am-1am. **Metsovo Cafe** (☎26560 42 661), on the road to Ioannina beside Sergio Cafe. Terminals and Wi-Fi €2 per hr. Open daily 10am-1am.

Post Office: (☎26560 41 245), on the road toward Ioannina and Trikala. **Poste Restante.** Open M-F 7:30am-2pm. **Postal Code:** 44200.

🏠 ACCOMMODATIONS

Room prices spike outrageously during Metsovo's two high seasons (from mid-July to Sept. and Dec.-Mar.). During these times, the town is best visited as a daytrip. In low season, however, the rooms are more reasonably priced. You can find *domatia* by taking the even road to your left on the way to Hotel Olympic; most offer simple rooms for about €25-30.

🏨 **Hotel Filoxenia** (☎26560 41 021), behind the *plateia*'s park on the circular road surrounding it. The name ("hospitality") says it all. British-educated proprietor Yiannis is a 1-stop source for all things Metsovo, even if you don't decide to stay at his cozy ski-lodge-like hotel. Full of wisdom, humor, and experience traversing the mountainous area, he has helpful info, arranges hikes in the nearby Valia Skalda National Park, and stores gear. Breakfast €4. Singles €25-30; doubles €35-45; triples €50. Cash only. ❷

NORTHERN GREECE

John Xaralabapoulos's Rooms (☎26560 42 086). A handpainted sign reading "Domatia Rooms" marks the entrance, just past the basketball court. Large, comfy rooms with understated charm. Singles €25-30; doubles €30-35; triples €35-45. Cash only. ❷

Hotel Olympic (☎26560 41 337), behind John Xaralabapoulos's Room. Well-kept wood-paneled rooms, each with bath, TV, and phone. Breakfast €5. Singles €30; doubles €45; triples €50. AmEx/MC/V. ❷

🍴 FOOD

A stop at Metsovo would not be complete without sampling the local food, especially the Metsovo cheese, which is sold throughout the region.

Galaxias (☎26560 41 202; www.metsovo.com/galaxyhotel). With your back to the entrance of the town hall, take a left and walk past the small park; you'll see the huge sign for the hotel and restaurant. Though the mansion is appealing at 1st glance, be sure to explore the sunny, green-garden eating area with its more relaxed, summertime feel. Homemade local specialties like Metsovo village pasta (€5.80). Entrees €5-8. Open 11am-11pm. MC/V. ❷

Koutouki Tou Nikola (☎26560 41 732), on the street toward the post office. With your back to the Hotel Egnatia bus stop, you'll see the large sign if you look left. Rub elbows with local families at this restaurant in Nikola's basement. Trout from Lake Metsovo €5.50. Acclaimed vegetable pies (€3). Entrees €5-7. Open 12:30pm-1am. ❷

Kryfi Folia (☎26560 41 628), in the *plateia*, 1 shop down from the Agricultural Bank. At this local favorite, you can watch the meat slow-roasting on a spit as you tuck into dishes like the *kokoretsi* (lamb intestines; €6.50) and *kontosoufli* (pork and lamb souvlaki; €6). Entrees €6-10. Open 11am-midnight. Cash only. ❷

👁 SIGHTS

THE EVANGELOS AVEROF GALLERY OF CONTEMPORARY ART. Thanks to the Baron Tositsas and his nephew, Evangelos Averof-Tositsas, Metsovo has far more sights than you'd expect in a 5000-person town. This museum exhibits 19th- and 20th-century Greek paintings, including Averof-Tositsas's private collection, in a surprisingly large series of rooms. *(Off the main plateia, next to the Hotel Filoxenia. Follow the road after the 2 banks; it's on your right after the bend around the park. ☎26560 41 210. Open from mid-July to mid-Sept. M and W-Su 10am-6:30pm; from mid-Sept. to mid-July 10am-4pm. €3, students €2.)*

THE TOSSIZZA MUSEUM. Also known as the folk art museum, Tossizza displays traditional costumes, silverware, and wood carvings, along with recreations of traditional rooms. The apartment on top of the museum, which belongs to the former Foreign Minister, has photos of Averof with political heavyweights like JFK. *(Up the hill 50m on the main road in a mansion to the left of the main road, opposite the Shell gas station. ☎26560 41 084. Open M-W and F-Su from mid-July to mid-Sept. 9am-1:30pm and 4-6pm; from mid-Sept. to mid-July 9am-1:30pm and 3-4pm. €3, students €2. Visitors are only admitted in small groups; wait at the door for the guide who appears every 30min.)*

AGIOS NIKOLAOS MONASTERY AND CHURCH OF PANAGLA. For a short trip, pack a picnic lunch and walk to this monastery. Built in the 14th century, it was originally one of the most important monasteries in the area, undergoing cycles of disrepair and restoration until 1950 when Averof-Tositsas restored the frescoes painted in 1702. These frescoes had been perfectly preserved by smoke from the fires of squatting shepards. Today, you can see the formerly covered icons and the famous moss-covered bell tower overlooking the picturesque valley below the town. After visiting the church, walk through the vineyard to the main road. Stay to the left, and soon after passing the less-than-romantic sewage station, you'll see a path leading downhill on your right just before the road goes uphill, and a small sign leading you to the Church of the Panagia by passing a water mill. The Church of the Panagia is not open to visitors, though the secluded, lush gardens are worth a look. *(30min. walk from the plateia down the hillside; signs point the way. Open dawn-dusk.)*

The ⬛Hellenic Mountaineering Club (EOS), based in Ioannina, supplies information and leads weekend trips throughout the region. (☎26510 22 138. Open M-Sa 7-9pm.) The Paddler Kayaking and Rafting School (☎26550 23 777 or 26550 23 101), with offices in Konitsa and Megalo Papingo, gives lessons and oversees outings to local rivers. A major local outfitter is Alpine Zone, Josef Eligia 16 (☎26560 23 222; www.alpinesone.gr), located off Averof in Ioannina, specializing in rafting equipment and outings. For more information, contact Marios at Pension Monodendri (☎26530 71 300) or Nikos at Koulis Restaurant (☎26530 41 115), in Monodendri and Papingo respectively. The best time to see alpine flowers is between April and June. Colored foliage flares brilliantly in the dry autumns. The best season for rafting is April through May, when the full rivers start to warm up.

VALIA KALDA NATIONAL PARK. Valia Kalda (Vlach for "warm valley") is home to 80 species of birds and a number of endangered animals such as the brown bear, the wild cat, and the wild goat. Its dramatic landscape and gushing rivers are rich enough to occupy any outdoors enthusiast for weeks. *(For more information on Valia Kalda and other outdoor activities in Metsovo, contact the town hall (☎26560 41 207) or Yiannis of Hotel Filoxenia (p. 206).)*

🎭🎆 NIGHTLIFE AND FESTIVALS

What used to be Vlach courting day is now **Yiorti,** a festival celebrated on July 26. All women and most men dress in traditional bright costumes for the modern festivities, splashing the entire town with color. At some point between July 20 and July 26, depending on the weather, the residents embark on a hike up the park to celebrate in honor of the Greek gods. Baron himself was a believer in the Olympian pantheon, and as part of the donation deal, mandated the yearly visit. Reserve rooms at least three weeks in advance if you'll be there during the festival.

Sergio, on the road to Ioannina. Metsovo doesn't offer much in the way of nightlife, but if you're itching to go out, drop by Sergio. The orange glow and cozy seats add to the laid-back atmosphere. Mixed drinks €6. Open daily 10am-2am.

IGOUMENITSA Ηγουμενίτσα ☎26650

A connection point between Italy and Greece, Igoumenitsa (ee-goo-men-IT-sa) is often a traveler's first or last glimpse of the Greek mainland. The town's enormous port, the third-largest in Greece, sends boats to four cities in Italy and to Corfu. Tourist agencies seem to outnumber people, harried backpackers scramble in search of their ships, and it appears as if life never stands still in this small, somewhat unsettling town.

⬛ TRANSPORTATION

Buses: Station (☎26650 22 309) on the corner of Apriloxou and Minermou, just 1 block up from the waterfront. From the ports, walk south along the waterfront away from the Old Port and just a few blocks from Corfu Port; take a left on Minermou. Open daily

5:30am-8:30pm. Buses to: **Athens** (7hr., 4 per day 7:30am-8:30pm, €37); **Ioannina** (2hr., 8 per day 6:30am-8pm, €8.20); **Parga** (1hr., 4 per day 6am-5:15pm, €4.50); **Preveza** (2hr., 11:45am and 3:30pm, €8.60); **Thessaloniki** (8hr., 10:30am, €34).

Ferries: Igoumenitsa's long port has 4 subdivisions from which ferries leave. The **Old Port,** on the waterfront's northern edge (follow the signs) is in the center of town and mostly sends boats to Italy. **Corfu Port** is south of the Old Port. Beyond Corfu Port, about a 20-30min. walk from the Old Port is the **New Port,** whose boats go to both Italy and Corfu. The **Fourth Port,** at the southernmost point of the harbor, sends ships to Italy. Tickets to **Corfu** (1hr.; 6 per day 2:30am-8:30pm; €8, students €3.20, children €2.60) can be purchased at Corfu Port in one of several white kiosks. They also can be bought on the ferries, but without discounts. For tickets to Italy, shop around at the waterfront agencies, as some have student rates and some accept Eurail and InterRail passes; bargain before you buy, and be sure to ask if the €5 port tax is included. Destinations in Italy include: **Ancona** (14hr.; Tu, Th, Sa-Su 8pm and 11:30pm; M, W, F 8pm and midnight; €53-78); **Bari** (9hr., daily 9pm and midnight, €36-68); **Brindisi** (7hr., daily 6am and 11:30pm, €36-62); **Venice** (19hr., M-Tu and F-Sa 8:30am, €49-69). Most boats depart before noon or late in the evening. Contact **Giogiakas Travel,** Ethnikis Antistasis 44 (☎26650 26 778 or 28 259), farther north from the entrance to the Old Port, for additional information on ferry schedules and fares. Open 8am-10pm.

Taxis: (☎26650 25 000). Line up on Eth. Antistasis, especially by Corfu Port. 24hr.

Car Rentals: Europcar, Pargas 5 (☎26650 23 477), facing the police station between the Old Port and Corfu Port. Cars from €45 per day. Mopeds €15 per day. Open daily 9am-11pm.

ORIENTATION AND PRACTICAL INFORMATION

Igoumenitsa is on the westernmost corner of mainland Greece, about 20km from the Albanian border. **Ethnikis Antistasis,** which becomes **Agion Apostolon** south of Corfu Port connecting it to the New Port, runs along the waterfront and overflows with travel agencies and banks. To the north after it's divided by a lane barrier, the inland side of the street is bordered by cafes and bars, marking the edge of the nightlife district. Igoumenitsa's main shopping area is on **Lamprari Grigariou,** the first pedestrian street parallel to the waterfront. To reach the central *plateia*, walk two blocks inland on **Eleftheriou Venizelou,** which begins across from the Old Port just north of **8 Dekembriou** and marks the beginning of Lamprari Grigariou.

Tourist Office: (☎26650 22 227), 20-30min. away from the center of town at the New Port. Supplies free maps. Open daily 8am-2pm.

Bank: National Bank, Eth. Antistasis 16A (☎26650 22 415), across the road from the Old Port. Open M-Th 8am-2:30pm and F 8am-2pm. Many banks on the same road have **currency exchange** and **ATMs.**

Police: Ag. Apostolon 5 (☎26650 22 100), on the continuation of Eth. Antistasis, across from Corfu Port. **Tourist Police** (☎26650 29 647), in the same building. Open daily 8:30am-1:30pm. **Port Police,** in a Corfu Port booth, near customs.

Medical Services: Though there are general practitioners in town, the only **hospital** (☎26640 22 203) is 15min. away, in Filiates.

Telephones: OTE, Grigariou Labraki 35, (☎26650 23 499), at the end of Grigariou. Open M and W 7:30am-3pm, Tu and Th-F 7:30am-8pm, Sa 8am-3pm.

Internet Access: Sports Cafe, 18 Dagli (☎26650 225 13), just behind the cafe-bar Dali. Terminals and Wi-Fi €1.50 per hr. Open daily 10am-3pm and 6pm-midnight.

Post Office: Tzavelenas 2 (☎26650 46 100), 1km north along the waterfront on the corner of a playground. **Poste Restante.** Open M-F 7:30am-2pm. **Postal Code:** 46100.

ACCOMMODATIONS

Accommodations in Igoumenitsa can be misleading. Often long-established hotels are higher-priced than their newer and nicer counterparts. The hotels are surprisingly underdeveloped and some are overpriced.

Hotel Acropolis, Eth. Antistasis 14 (☎26650 28 346 or 28 063). The English-speaking owner is eager to please, and the cheerful rooms provide the best bang for your buck. Right on the waterfront, each stylish, ocean-inspired rooms has a balcony, A/C, bath, fridge, TV, and Wi-Fi. Singles €25-40; doubles €45; triples €65. AmEx/MC/V. ❷

Hotel Oscar, Ag. Apostolon 149 (☎26650 23 338). With your back to Corfu Port, look left for the fluorescent lights. The location is perfect for catching an early-morning bus or ferry to Corfu, but the aged rooms leave much to be desired. The rooms are simple but a bit worn with fridges and balconies; some have A/C. Reception 24hr. Singles €30-40; doubles €50; triples €60. Cash only. ❸

Hotel Egnatia, Eleftherias 2 (☎26650 23 455), in the far right corner of the central *plateia*. The bright wallpaper patterns and tiled floors may be a bit disconcerting, but the amenities are available without the waterfront price. Rooms have TVs, A/C, baths, and some have balconies. To avoid being woken up by morning traffic, ask for a room facing the quiet wooded area behind the hotel. Tell the receptionist what time you plan on returning if you don't want to be locked out. Singles €25; doubles €35; triples €50. Cash only. ❸

FOOD

The best of the city's restaurants are on the northern edge of the waterfront, past the ports and, as expected, provide quality seafood. Dozens of bakeries and markets line the pedestrian street just inland from the harbor.

Alekos, Eth. Antistasis 84 (☎26650 23 708), north of the ports. An eclectic menu with something for everyone, including pasta, pizza, and Greek dishes. Specializes in seafood caught in the harbor waters. Entrees €5.80-7. Open daily noon-12:30am. ❷

Oinomaiereio, El. Venizelou 6 (☎26650 26 086). A chance to people-watch while enjoying reasonably priced seafood and meat dishes. Try the octopus (€8) or souvlaki (€5.50). Entrees €5-8. Open daily noon-midnight. ❷

ENTERTAINMENT AND NIGHTLIFE

Igoumenitsa's bland nightlife centers on a strip of bars along the waterfront. A short distance from the city, dance clubs **Soho** and **Ostria** attract a trendy local crowd peppered with stranded tourists. (Beer €2. Mixed drinks €5-6. Cover €8; includes 1 drink.) Buses (€1) run every hour from the center of town until midnight. To return later, catch a taxi (€5).

Privilege (☎26650 23 505), a few doors down from Taverna Alekos. Young tourists and locals chatter at this stylish and popular cafe, entertained by American and Greek tunes. Beer €3. Mixed drinks €4. Open daily 10am-5am.

Cafe Dalí, Antistasis 124 (☎26650 28 057). Removed from the center but well worth the walk. Packed with the most stylish young Greeks, the bar's gold-tinted decor and chandeliers are loosely inspired by the artist himself. Open daily 10am-2am.

ZAGOROHORIA Ζαγοροχώρια

Between the Albanian border and the North Pindos mountain range, a string of 46 *choria* (hamlets) quietly coexist, showing few signs of interference from modern-day society. A trip to Zagorohoria immerses visitors in the blissful relaxation of simple village life. The tiny towns are chock-a-block with cobblestone roads and slate-tiled rooftops that give the area a picture-book atmosphere. Also home to Vikos Gorge, the deepest canyon in the world, Zagorohoria provides opportunities for nature enthusiasts to hike around rough-riding rivers, stark peaks, and dark caves. These natural treasures, in addition to the surrounding Vikos-Aoös National Park, entice all who venture out here with gorgeous scenery and unbeatable sites. While hiking and trekking are the major tourist attractions of the area, the romantic draw of traveling back in time and exploring the traditional villages is enough of a reason to go.

MONODENDRI Μονοδένδρι ☎26530

Monodendri is almost impossibly small, consisting of a few hotels and *tavernas*, despite the regular flow of hikers bearing cameras and sunburns. There are buses to nearby Ioannina only three days a week, but the friendly locals and cozy hotels will make you not want to return to the bustle of a big city. The village, located at the top of **Vikos Gorge,** (p. 212), is an unrivaled base for hikers looking for daytime adventure and nighttime comfort. The must-see natural overlook, **Oxia Point,** has breathtaking views of the entire Vikos Gorge and is an easy 1hr. walk from the village and . The panorama is best reached by following a red-blazed trail that begins behind the Monodendri Hotel. As the harsh winters often leave the markers unclear, ask Marios at the hotel to show you the footpath. The view is also accessible by car; Oxia Point lies at the end of the main road 6km past the town. Another equally easy hike (20min.) goes beyond the abandoned **Monastery of Agia Paraskevi,** which is 1km from Monodendri's lower *plateia;* many signs point the way. The monastery houses an operating icon-painter's workshop. A small terrace has stunning views of the beginning of the gorge trail, and an edgeless, meter-wide path is cut straight into the sheer rock wall. The treacherous path leads to a small cave once used by monks to hide from raiders. Signs from the *plateia* point along the slightly difficult trail to **Megali Spilia** (30min.), another nearby cave where Zagorohorians used to hide from marauders.

On the road to Ioannina just as the street starts to curve, **Monodendri Hotel** ❸ has cozy and stylish rooms, and the welcoming owners seek to make their guests as comfortable as possible. The owner's English-speaking son, Marios, provides information about trekking in the area and picks up passengers from Vikos Village (€50) or Megalo Papingo (€35) after their hikes. Marios's wealth of knowledge and patience with visitors has been aiding *Let's Go* readers, even those not staying the night, for over a decade. (☎26530 71 300; www.monodendrihotel.com. Breakfast included. Bagged lunch for the trail €3.50. Reception 8am-11pm. Singles €35; doubles €45; triples €60. MC/V.) **Arhondiko Zarkada Hotel** ❷, on the left as you walk up from the bus station, has large, comfortable rooms, each with bath, TV, phone, internet, and gorgeous stone balcony. Some rooms even have jacuzzis. (☎26530 71 305. Breakfast included. Singles €25; doubles €40; triples €60. AmEx/MC/V.) On the lower road, a few minutes from the main *plateia*, **Arktouros Hotel** ❸ has basic rooms, each with TV and water-massage in the bath, perfect after a long day of hiking the Vikos Gorge. (☎26530 71 455. Singles €25; doubles €50. Cash only.) A few *tavernas* are scattered along the main road. The friendliest is **Katerina's** ❷, on the porch of Monodendri Hotel, where Marios's mother, Mrs. Daskalopoulou, prepares the food—only after learning your name. Every dish is lovingly prepared with the customer in mind, and requests are welcome. Finish off your hearty meal with a big slice of milk pie (€3.50), which is not to be missed.

The bus stop, all the hotels, and most of the restaurants are on Monodendri's one paved road. **Buses** go to Ioannina (1hr.; M, W, and F 7:30am, 2:45pm; €3.40). **Taxis** can take you to Ioannina or Konitsa (€35). Monodendri's lower *plateia* is accessible by a footpath that descends to the left a few stores up from the last taverna on the street and is marked by a sign; follow the path downhill and turn left at the fork. The *plateia* is home to a cafe, a **phone**, a **mail box**, and signposts for all the trailheads; it also serves as the starting point for all the lookouts and hikes in Vikos Gorge. There is no bank; the closest are in Kalpaki and Konitsa. Monodendri Hotel **exchanges currency** for guests of the establishment and *Let's Go* readers. The nearest **hospital** is in Ioannina. Both the town kiosk, across from Arhondiko Zarkada Hotel, and Monodendri Hotel have good trail maps (around €7.50). **Postal Code:** 44007.

VIKOS GORGE Φοράγγι Βίκου ☎ 26530

Vikos Gorge, whose walls are 900m deep and only 1100m apart, is the steepest on earth. In spring time, the river that has taken millions of years to form the gorge rushes along the 15km stretch of canyon floor. By summer, all that is left is the occasional puddle hidden among white boulders in the riverbed. Vikos Gorge is splashed with a faded mix of colors that change as the sunlight moves over them. Rusted iron deposits in the gorge's rock leave an orange-pink tint that drips over the gray walls, complemented as the seasons pass with the brilliant hues of spring wildflowers, summer butterflies, autumn foliage, and views of the green waters running below Vikos Village. When night falls, listen for the shrill chirping of crickets and watch fireflies dance in the trees, blending into the star-studded sky.

People have walked through the gorge's deep ravine since the 12th century BC, when early settlers took shelter in its craggy caves. Today, hikers follow its path, which stretches from the village of Kipi in the south to Megalo Papingo at its northernmost tip, and winds its way through the center of the Zagorohoria. The **hiking** trail through the gorge is the **O3** domestic trail section of the Greek National E4 route, running from the Aoös River near Konitsa all the way to Kipi. Before you go, be sure to get a map (€7.50), sold at the *periptero* (kiosk) on the main road through Monodendri, the Monodendri Hotel (p. 211), and No Limits in Papingo. If you get confused, just look for the red diamonds on white, square backgrounds with "O3" stenciled on them or for red spray paint, which inconsistently marks the path, so keep your wits about you to avoid getting lost. Most hikers enter the gorge from **Monodendri,** but it also can be accessed from **Kipi,** the **Papingo** villages, and **Vikos Village.** It is a 5hr. walk from Vikos Village to Monodendri and 6hr. from the Papingos to Monodendri. The trail often descends into the rocky bottom of the gorge before re-ascending to the trail through the forest, and the entry point is often unmarked; keep to the left and watch for an opportunity to return to the trail.

To reach the gorge from Monodendri, take the marked path from the lower *plateia.* After about 700m (40min.) along the steep, winding descent, you'll reach a fork in the path. Go left to enter the canyon's dry riverbed of smooth rocks, and head toward the far-off villages of the Papingos and Vikos. After about 4km (1hr.), the right fork will bring you to the village of Kipi, with its trademark stone bridges. To descend into the gorge, take the left fork as it climbs above the left bank of the riverbed. The path is fairly level and pleasant for some time, continuing through a shady woodland along the riverbank with opportunities to descend to the very bottom of the gorge. About 2hr. into the hike, you'll have a chance to fill your water bottle at a drinking water tap. On the way, you'll pass open groves mowed clean by grazing horses. About 9km (4-5hr.) from Monodendri, you'll reach the crossroads that lead up to Vikos Village. The trail suddenly becomes a more orderly stone path, which, after about 20m, makes a 90° turn up and to the left toward Vikos (300m; about 45min.). Before you go up to Vikos, don't miss the chance to cool off at the river to your left—the unbelievably frigid waters are a great spot for a picnic lunch or (if you can stand the cold) a refreshing swim. If you're Papingo-bound, maintain the course that descends to the right, hugging the riverbanks into the grassy pasture. Be warned, the trail is not well marked in this area and it is easy to get lost—be sure to bring a map along with you. About halfway through the grassy clearing, a frenzy of red arrows on the boulders on the stream's opposite bank marks the ford and the continuation of O3 to Papingo. Another hour out of the gorge brings you to the Megalo Papingo-Mikro Papingo split. From here, it's 30min. to either village.

Hikers entering from the Papingo villages should follow signs from the *plateias*. Stone stairways lead you most of the way. The trailhead in **Vikos Village** is slightly outside town, but clearly marked signs and willing villagers are available for help. This intermediate-level trail (1hr.) descends to **Voidhomatis springs**, the radiant source of the Vikos river. In Vikos Village, home to fewer than 30 people, there are few *tavernas* and steep room rates. **Sotiris Karpouzis** ❹ has a multilingual staff that offers food and *domatia* as well as rides back to Monodendri (€35). (☎26530 411 76. Reception open until 1am. Triples €50. Cash only.) A second hotel, **Ioanni Dinoli** ❹, is right by the trailhead, but the rooms are no cheaper. (☎26530 421 12. Rooms €50. Meals €10. Cash only.) The obliging owner of the second *taverna*, **Foris** (☎26530 42 170), in the *plateia*, provides rides (€30) to Monodendri.

PELOPONNESE
Πελοπόννησος

Voyage into the Peloponnese for the awesome landscapes, small mountain towns, and unparalleled ancient sites, including Olympia, Mycenae, Corinth, Mystras, and Epidavros. Breathtaking scenery, from the barren slopes of Mani to the forested peaks and flower-blanketed pastures of Arcadia, imbues the land with ageless natural beauty. More goats than buses and more farmers than financiers, getting around the craggy Peloponnese can be difficult but it's all the more charming because of it. Away from large, urban transportation hubs, the serene, sparsely populated mountain and seaside villages welcome visitors to traditional Greek living at its best.

HIGHLIGHTS OF THE PELOPONNESE

HEAR acoustic perfection at the ancient theater of **Epidavros** (p. 225).

RUN in ancient paths at the original Olympic Stadium in **Olympia** (p. 235).

EXPLORE the beaches and canyons on the endless coastlines of **Kithera** (p. 256).

CORINTHIA Κορινθία AND ARGOLIS Αργολίδα

Legend holds that Argos, a monster endowed with 100 unblinking eyes, once stalked the northern Peloponnese, subduing unruly satyrs and burly bulls. While these creatures have left no tangible remains behind, the region's ruins of stone temples and fortresses reveal the spirit of the great ancient cities—Mycenae, Corinth, and Argos—that once competed for control of land and sea. The bustling ports hearken back to a day when merchants peddled simpler wares, while secluded mountain villages preserve a more traditional, relaxed way of life.

NEW CORINTH Κόρινθος ☎27410

Modern Corinth may be very different from its ancient predecessor, but it still relies on its strategic location on the crossroads of Greece's agricultural and industrial commerce for its economic success. The city's focus on business comes at the expense of the tourism industry, resulting in few hotels, English menus, and information centers. But fear not—locals will happily assist you with menus, and the trendy coffee shops, retail stores, 24hr. internet cafes and groceries easily meet most traveler's needs.

TRANSPORTATION

Buses: There are 3 bus stations in and around Corinth, 2 of which are useful. The other, located at the closed suburban rail station, should be avoided.

KTEL Station A (☎27410 75 424), in the center of town. Walking inland on Eth. Antistasis, turn right on Koliatsou halfway through the park; the station terminal is outside a bakery, on the corner

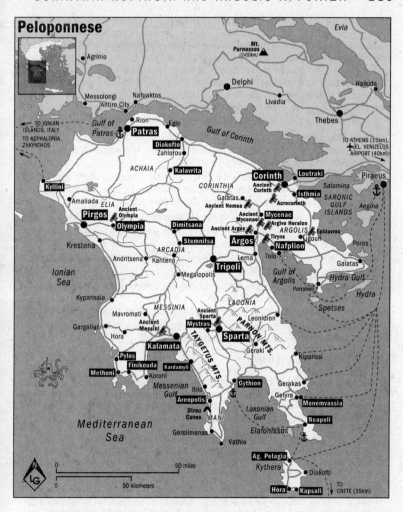

Peloponnese

of Koliatsou and Kolokotroni. To **Ancient Corinth** (20min., every hr. 8am-9pm, €1.40), **Ancient Nemea** (45min., 3 per day, €4), and **Loutraki** (20min, 2 per hr. 5am-10pm, €2). Buses also run to the larger KTEL station near the canal (15min, every 30min., €1.40).

KTEL—Isthmos Station, near the canal. The station is 10km from Corinth. €1.40 for a bus from KTEL Station in the center of town, or €3 for a taxi. To: **Argos** (1hr.); **Nafplion** (1½hr.); **Patra** (2hr.); **Sparta** (2½hr.); **Tripoli** (2hr.). Buses usually run around 8am and 2pm. Consult the **tourist office** in Corinth (see p. 216) or ask your hotel for schedules.

Taxis: (☎27410 73 000), along Eth. Antistaseos, in front of the park and the Court of Justice.

🔲 🔢 ORIENTATION AND PRACTICAL INFORMATION

New Corinth is nestled into the coast; its two main beaches are **Ieratiki** and **Kalamia.** The streets are organized in a grid pattern. The main street, **Ethnikis**

Antistaseos, runs inland from the marina. **Ermou,** the central walkway, and **Kolokotroni** run parallel to Eth. Antistaseos, on the left and right respectively as you look away from the waterfront. All three intersect **Damaskinou,** which runs along the harbor. Most of the town's shops, restaurants, and hotels are found on these four streets. Two blocks inland from the shore, between Eth. Antistaseos and Ermou, is the city's central **park.** Opposite the park on Eth. Antistaseos stands the **Court of Justice,** where taxis line up. Bus station A and the train station are a few blocks southeast of the marina down Damaskinou. To find the harbor from the train station, turn left onto Dimokratias and take the first right.

Tourist Information and Police: Ermou 51 (☎27410 23 282). Provides maps, brochures, and assistance in English. Open daily 8am-2pm. Also a small information desk at Kolokotroni 6 (☎27410 72 662).

Banks: Citi Bank, Eth. Antistaseos 7 (☎27410 23 934), 1 block up from the waterfront. **Currency exchange** and a **24hr. ATM.** Open M-Th 8am-2:30pm, F 8am-2pm. More banks, located in the city's center, offer similar services.

Public Toilets: Across from the park on Eth. Antistaseos. Open daily 7am-10pm.

Pharmacies: ☎31207 31 480. Many on Eth. Antistaseos, Koliatsou, and Ermou. Typically open M-F 8am-2pm and 5-8pm, Sa 8am-2pm.

Hospital: Athinon (☎27511 20 188). Found on the far side of town toward Athens. **Ambulance:** ☎166. Open 24hr.

Internet Access: Internet spots throughout the city, particularly along the walkway on Pilarinou. **Bites and Bytes** (☎27410 99 311), on Koliatsou 2 blocks from intersection with Eth. Antistaseos. Satellite TV, drinks, and snacks. Internet €2 per hr. Open 24hr.

Post Office: Adimantou 35 (☎80050 24 122), facing the park, between Eth. Antistaseos and Ermou. Open M-F 7:30am-5pm. **Postal Code:** 20100.

ACCOMMODATIONS

Corinth has a handful of hotels located around the center common, easy to find since the city is so small. Cost does not vary much between hotels. The biggest campground in the area sits a few kilometers outside the city, so without personal transportation, reaching the site can be tricky and expensive.

Hotel Korinthos, Damaskinou 26 (☎27410 26 701). Low prices for rooms with private baths, A/C, TVs, and Wi-Fi. Although it's set on the wharf, don't expect any waterfront views. Owner speaks excellent English and is willing to help with any concerns. Likely the best hotel in town. Breakfast €5. Singles €35; doubles €45; triples €55. AmEx/MC/V. ❸

Hotel Ephira, Eth. Antistaseos 52 (☎27410 24 514; www.ephirahotel.gr), in the center of town close to Kalamia Beach. Recently renovated, the hotel has a garden, a large dining room, and a helpful staff. Each room includes bath, TV, A/C, phone, and Wi-Fi. Breakfast €5. Wheelchair-accessible. Singles €40; doubles €65; triples €75; suites €150. MC/V. ❸

FOOD

After 9pm, the harbor perks up with workers in search of dinner. For a leisurely meal, head toward the wharf and walk along behind the university. Pricier restaurants line the waterfront. If you're only looking for a drink and a quick snack, walk along Pilout, the pedestrian road parallel to the shore.

Mediterane, Nikolaou 29 (☎27410 73 232). From the park on the wharf, walk with the sea on your right. The chef revamps the menu daily based on the catch of the day. Features the lowest prices and some of the best dishes found in Corinth. Large screen projects big sporting events and football matches. Most waiters speak English and help translate the menu. Wheelchair-accessible. Open daily noon-1am or last customer. Cash only. ❷

Number 1, Eth. Antistaseos 1 (☎27410 85 335). All the Greek fast food imaginable, served in a modern diner setting. The latest jams play on a robust sound system. If you're looking for a trendy atmosphere to go with your fries, then the extra dollars are worth it. Wheelchair-accessible. Open daily 9:30am-noon and 2:30pm-2am. MC/V. ❷

Il Corso Cafe, Ermou48, on the water end of the park in Corinth center. Just 1 of the 5 cafes situated on the park, this joint has the best espresso—according to the Corinthians (not the Biblical kind). Whether you're craving an iced cappuccino or a stronger drink to get the edge off, this cafe's offerings really hit the spot. Snacks come with all the drinks. Wheelchair-accessible. Open daily 8am-10pm. MC/V. ❷

█ NIGHTLIFE

Much of New Corinth's nightlife centers on **Kalamia beach.** To reach it, walk along downtown's other main street, **Koliatsou** (perpendicular to Eth. Antistaseos on either side of the park) from the left of the Court of Justice to Ap. Pavlou, the third street parallel and to the right of Eth. Antistaseos as you look inland. Take Ap. Pavlou inland, then make a right on Notara after the beautiful St. Paul Cathedral to reach the beach.

In the past few years, the wild nightlife has migrated to Loutraki, where clubs, gambling, and a multitude of other sins have taken over the city. Corinthians rave about **Casino,** a palace of games and booze, but watch out for the steep prices. If you are short of time or cash, stake out a calmer night in Corinth. Locals gather along the pedestrian path on Pilarinou Street during the earlier evening hours. Most cafes open and close around the same times and the menus have comparable prices. If you're looking for slightly later hours and a more relaxing feel, head to the park in Corinth center, where cafes and bars like **Il Corso** spread out onto the green

Half Note Jazz Club. A stylish cafe-bars and lounge, perfect for a drink while people-watching. The action peaks here around 10pm. Beer and wine €2-4. Mixed drinks €4-7. Open M-F 8am-1am.

█ DAYTRIPS FROM CORINTH

ANCIENT CORINTH Αρχαία Κόρινθος
Ancient Corinth is 7km southwest of New Corinth. Buses leave from center of modern Corinth (20min.; 1 per hr. 7am-9pm, €1.20). ☎27410 31 207; www.ancientcorinth.net. Open daily in summer 8:45am-7pm, in winter 8:45am-5pm.

Ancient Corinth's opulent wealth and risqué delights were anything but old-fashioned. Prosperous merchants stopped by here to line their pockets and mingle with **hetairai,** famously clever courtesans in the service of Aphrodite. But don't go looking for their pleasure palaces: what remains of the Classical world's Sin City is buried beneath the ruins of the settlement the Romans built after sacking Corinth. Today, remnants of the Greek and Roman cities stand side by side.

The remains of the ancient Roman city stand with the older Greek ruins at the base of the Acrocorinth against a scenic mountain-and-ocean backdrop. As you enter, on the left you will notice the **Fountain of Glauke,** named after Jason the Argonaut's second wife, the daughter of Creon, King of Corinth. After Medea, Jason's seriously bitter ex, gave her a poisoned cloak, Glauke jumped into the fountain, trying in vain to stop the burning. Beyond you will notice the

PELOPENNESE

seven breathtaking original columns from the **Temple of Apollo** that have defiantly endured the trials of time since the sixth century BC. A walk around the side of the temple reveals that these remains are but a small portion of a long building that was supported by 38 columns. Standing on the other side of the temple, the **forum,** the center of Roman civil life, opens before you. Without a guidebook, it might be difficult to gain anything from these remains other than an impression of simply how skilled ancient Corinthian and Roman artisans and craftsmen were. A plaque in the forum indicates the **Julian Basilica,** which served as a court-house and once held statues of the family of Julius Caesar.

The **Acrocorinth** is located a steep 3.5km uphill from the museum. Emerging from the crags and ridges of the massif is the ▓fortress built in the tenth cen-tury; its walls encircle the ruins of buildings from the 14th to 18th centuries. Those who want to experience the entire fortress should head past the first three gates and toward the summit. Here, where sacred *hetairai* once initiated disciples into the "mysteries of love" (read: ▓crazy sex acts) at Aphrodite's altar, and where Jason's flying horse, Pegasus, quenched its thirst, only a small chapel to St. Dimitrios remains. The dazzling view of Corinth, however, makes a trip to the Acrocorinth wholly satisfying, even for the less historically inclined. Venture around the rest of the relatively empty fortress, which contains acres of tow-ers, mosques, gates, and walls. Don't forget sturdy shoes, sunscreen, and water (bottles available at the cafe by the parking lot for €0.50); be careful on the rocks—they're slippery even when dry. (The easiest way up to Acrocorinth is by taxi from the center of the village of Ancient Corinth (€7); taxis will wait at the top of the acrocorinth to drive you back down (€15). The walk up the hill takes a little over an hour and can be confusing at times. Open daily 8:45am-7pm.)

ANCIENT NEMEA Αρχαία Νεμέα

The ancient site is 5km from modern Nemea. Take the bus from center of Corinth (45min.-1hr., 5 per day 8am-4pm, €4). Make sure to watch for signs for Ancient Nemea and ask to be let out at the sign reading "Ancient Nemea." ☎27410 22 739; www.nemea.org. Site and stadium open Tu-Su 8:30am-7pm. Museum open Tu-Su in summer 8:30am-7pm, in winter 8:30am-3pm. Site and stadium €4, students and seniors €2, EU students and under 18 free.

The remoteness of Ancient Nemea keeps away many of the tourists who visit Ancient Corinth. The site, excavated in the 1880s by a team of French engineers, was cleaned up and revamped by Professor Steven G. Miller's team 35 years ago. A highlight is exploring the stadium that housed one of the four Panhellenic games.

NAFPLION Νάφπλιον ☎27520

Nafplion's Old Town fully earns its reputation as one of the most attractive getaways in Greece. The flawless urban design of the Venetians conveniently places everything within a few minutes walk from the central square. With two breathtaking hilltop fortresses, romantic winding streets, and a buzzing water-front to explore, visitors can spend days uncovering the secrets of Nafplion, one of the Peloponnese's treasures.

▐ TRANSPORTATION

Buses: KTEL, Syngrou 8 (☎27520 27 423). To: **Argos** (20min., 2 per hr., €2); **Athens** (3hr., 1 per hr. 5:10am-8pm, €11); **Epidavros** (1hr.; 10:15am, noon, 2:30pm; €3); **Mycenae** (45min., 10am and 2pm, €3); **Tolo** (30min., 14 per day 7am-8pm, €2); **Tripoli** (1½hr.; M-Sa 8:30am, 4:30, and 6:30pm, Su 8:30am; €7).

Taxis: (☎27520 24 120). Line up on Syngrou near the bus station.

Nafplion

FOOD
Agnanti Restaurant, 5
Elatos, 3
Elias, 9
Gelateria dii Roma, 7
Mary's Corner, 6

ACCOMMODATIONS
Amymon E Pension, 4
Hotel Pack, 1
Dafni Pension, 8
Pension Marianna, 10
Tirins Hotel, 2

Bourtzi Castle

Gulf of Argos

TO TOLO (10km), EPIDAVROS (27km)
TO TOLO (10km), EPIDAVROS (27km)
Agiou Adrhianou
Vizandiou
Argonafton
Charmanda
Kokinopoulou Panagia
Rue Martignas
Asklipiou
Kolokotroni
Niklara
TO KARATHONA BEACH
Kyprou
25 Martiou

TO TIRYNS (4km), ARGOS (12km)
Eglou
Argous
Thisseos
Stadium
Swimming Pool
TO LERNA (50km), TRIPOLI (100km)

Bouboulinas
Vas. Georgiou
Irakleous
Kilkis
National Gallery
Navarinou
Sidiras Merarchias
Atlantic Supermarket
Vas. Pavlou
Old Train Station

New Train Station
Dhervenakion
Motor Traffic Rent-a-Moto
PL. KAPODISTRIAS
Player V. Player
Polizoidhou
Statue of Kapodistrias
NEW TOWN
Breeze
Syngrou
Palamidi Fortress

Staikos Travel
Avis Rent A Car
Miaouli
Sofroni
Folklore Museum
Military Museum
Amalias
Ag. Terzaki
PL. TRION
Vas. Konstandinou
Komboloi Museum
Cathedral
Papanikolaou
 Plapouta
TAXI
Polizoidhou

Vas. Othonos
Riga Fereou
Vas. Alexandrou
Kotsobopoulou
Ipsilandou
Siokou
Archaeological Museum
SYNDAGMA
Odyssey Bookstore
Staikopoulou
Farmakopoulou
Kapodistriou
Kokkinou
Ag. Spiridon
Fotomara
Genadiou
Avrantia Beach

Polizoidhou
Zigomala
Anstdou
Nafplia Palace Elevator
ACRONAFPLIA
Fortress
TO KARATHONA (3km)

200 yards
200 meters
0

PELOPENNESE

Rent-A-Moto, Sidiras 15 (☎27520 22 702), 1 block past the post office. Mopeds €10-85. Bicycles €10 per day. Prices include helmets, taxes, and insurance. Open daily 8am-9pm.

⚓ 🛈 ORIENTATION AND PRACTICAL INFORMATION

Nafplion's Old Town is little more than half a kilometer long. The main road along the water is **Miaouli,** which continues as a footpath along the perimeter of the town. Two small **parks** separate the new and old parts of town. The cobblestone Venetian section is full of squares and pedestrian walkways with high-end clothing boutiques, tourist shops, art galleries, and jewelers, while the new town's traffic speeds along pavement lined with pharmacies, supermarkets, fast-food chains, cheap Greek outlets, and gas stations.

Tourist Office: 25 Martiou (☎27520 24 444), across from the OTE. Free maps and brochures of Nafplion and the surrounding area. Open daily 9am-1pm and 4-8pm.

Banks: There are 2 branches of the **National Bank of Greece,** both with **24hr. ATMs.** Pl. Syndagma (☎27520 70 001); the other (☎27520 21 355) is on the corner across the street from the National Gallery on Sidiras Merarchias. Both open M-Th 8am-2:30pm, F 8am-2pm.

Bookstore: Odyssey (☎27520 23 430), in Pl. Syndagma. Sells stamps, newspapers, maps, guidebooks, and English-language paperbacks. Open M-Sa 9am-2am.

Police: Pavlou Kountourioti (☎27520 21 100). Open 24hr. **Tourist police** (☎27520 98 729) in same building. Open daily 8am-2am.

Medical Services: Nafplion Hospital (☎27520 27 309). Walk east on Sidiras Merarchias for 15min., then take a left onto Asklipiou. Hospital is on the right; the main entrance is on the opposite side of the block.

Telephones: OTE, Polizoidhou 2 (☎27520 22 139). On the left side of 25 Martiou as you walk toward the New Town. Open M, W, Sa 7:30am-3pm; Tu and Th-F 7:30am-9pm, Su 8am-3pm. **Payphones** in front of the OTE and next to the National Bank in Pl. Syndagma.

Internet Access: Numerous options throughout Nafplion. **Player V. Player (PVP),** Bouboulinas 36 (☎27520 21 418). €2 per hr. Open 24hr.

Post Office: (☎27520 24 855), on the corner of Syngrou and Sidiras Merarchias. **Western Union** available. Open M-F 7:30am-2pm. **Postal Code:** 21100.

🏠 ACCOMMODATIONS

Romantic pensions are scattered in the blocks of the Old Town. Larger hotels with cheaper rates line the edge of the New Town along the park across the street from the bus station. Looking for a good bargain in the old quarters could take hours, but finding the right pension is well worth the effort.

Pension Marianna, Potamianou 9 (☎27520 24 256; www.pensionmarianna.gr). Tucked quietly into the mountainside, this gem has jaw-dropping views of the city and handsomely adorned rooms, each with A/C, TV, phone, minibar, and bath. Worth the price. Singles €65, with breakfast €75; doubles €75/80; triples €85/100. MC/V. ❺

Tirins Hotel, Othonos 41 (☎27520 21 020), 1 block from the port. Rooms with balconies and all the standard amenities. Singles from €40; doubles from €60. Bargain for lower prices on longer stays. Cash only. ❸

Amymone Pension (☎27520 99477). This well-run boutique pension has rooms themed by color and decked out with flatscreen TVs, dust-free corners, and an incredible breakfast served at its sister hotel, Adiandi. Breakfast included. Singles from €60; doubles from €70. Cash only. ❺

Hotel Park (☎27520 27 428), on the newer side of town right on the park. Significantly lower prices for larger rooms. If you're willing to forego the romantic Venetian part of town, this is the place to do it. Rooms have A/C and TVs. Breakfast €5. Free Wi-Fi. Wheelchair-accessible. Singles from €35; doubles €60. ❸

Dafni Pension, Fotomara 10 (☎27520 29 856). Smaller rooms include A/C, TVs, phones, and private baths; some have balconies. Breakfast included. Free Wi-Fi. Singles €40-70; doubles €60-90. Cash only. ❹

🍴 FOOD

The Old Town's intimate alleyways house countless lantern-lit *tavernas* underneath overhanging flowers and balconies. The most popular restaurants sprawl onto the open squares and along the harbor, but many other options are hidden in the narrowest roads between the water and the squares.

Ellas (☎27520 27 278), in Pl. Syndagma. Refreshingly inexpensive considering its central location, with a cheerful staff and outdoor seating. The friendly owner, Costas, will probably lure you in as you stroll by. Chicken with rice €5. Salads €2.50. Entrees €5-7. Open daily noon-4pm and 7-11pm. MC/V. ❷

Agnanti, Akti Miaouli (☎27520 29 332), along the water. Sits above the water at the very end of the road before it changes into a foot path wrapping around the point. If you're looking for a romantic evening with an alternative to Greek cuisine, this is the place. House specialty is wonderfully fresh pasta with excellent cream sauce. Starters €4-12. Entrees €14-22. MC/V. ❹

Elatos (☎27520 27 704), along the 1st blocks of restaurants along the water in the Old Town. Enjoy some of the town's best seafood along with water views. Entrees €11-17. Ask about the group rate, which often includes wine and beer. Open daily 10am-10pm. Cash only. ❸

Mary's Corner, Sidiras Mirarchias 11 (☎27520 23 803). This neighborhood staple is a fresh, cheap alternative to the standard sit-down restaurant, with delicious souvlaki (€1.70), cheeseburgers (€3), and other entrees made in front of you. Open 24hr. Cash only. ❶

SandwichLand Canteen, Sid. Mirarchias 6 (☎27520 25 654), 2 doors down from Mary's Corner. Run by Mary's son and his wife. It serves a similar menu at slightly cheaper prices. Open daily noon-1am. Cash only. ❶

Antica Gelateria di Roma, 3 Farmakopoulon (☎27520 23 520). Mouth-watering Italian gelato—good luck deciding which flavor to order. 1 scoop €2, 2 scoops €3.50. Open past midnight. Cash only. ❶

👁 SIGHTS AND BEACHES

Towering over the rooftops, the Palamidi Fortress and the Acronapflia immediately grab visitors' attention. But the Old Town itself, with its spectacular architectural diversity, is a display of living history. Pl. Syndagma boasts a Venetian mansion, a Turkish mosque, and a Byzantine church, while Ottoman fountains, cannons, monuments, and statues sit in the alleyways. After passing from the Venetians to the Ottomans and back again, Nafplion served as headquarters for the Greek revolutionary government in 1821 and as Greece's first capital (1821-1834). President John Kapodistrias was assassinated here in Ag. Spiridon Church; the bullet hole is still visible in the church wall.

⊠PALAMIDI FORTRESS. The supposed 999 steps (travelers attest that there are fewer—around 860) that once provided the only access to the 18th-century fort since have been supplemented by a 3km road (taxis €3.50-5; "This Car Climbed Palamidi Fortress" bumper stickers not available). The steps begin from Polizoidhou past the park, marked by two cannonballs. The fort's spectacular views of the town, gulf, and much of the Argolid make the climb well worth it. The fortress itself is extensive, well preserved, and fun to explore (at your own risk if you leave the marked areas); be extremely cautious of drop-offs and ledges. Follow the signs to the **"Prison of Kolokotrones,"** the tiny subterranean cell in which the famous Greek general was imprisoned by King Otto. For two weeks in June, coinciding with the full moon, there is a **classical music festival** with concerts every night. *(Bring water and try to go in the morning, when the steps are shaded. ☎ 27520 28 036. Open daily 8am-7pm; reduced hours in low season. €4, students and seniors €2, EU students and under 19 free.)*

ACRONAFPLIA. The fortress walls of the Acronafplia, the acropolis of Nafplion, were fortified by three successive generations of conquerors—Byzantines, Franks, and Venetians. The views of the Palamidi Fortress, the gulf, and the Old Town are fantastic. *(Take the tunnel that runs into the hill at the end of Zygomala to the Nafplia Palace elevator, or follow the signs from the bus station.)*

MUSEUMS. Nafplion has a wealth of modest but well-run museums. Opened in 2004, the **National Gallery-Nafplion Annex** is a must-see for the art lover or history buff. The museum houses a wide array of 19th-century oil paintings that depict the 1821 Greek Revolution, and has a section for temporary art exhibits. *(Sidiras Merarchias 23. Open M, Th, Sa 10am-3pm; W and F 10am-3pm and 5-8pm; Su 10am-2pm. €3, students and seniors €1.50, M and under 13 free.)* Nafplion's **Folklore Museum** is an award-winning collection featuring rotating themes based around Greek textiles, clothing, and furniture. *(Vas. Alexandrou 1, 4 blocks from the water at Sofrani. ☎ 27520 28 379. Open M and W-Sa 9am-3pm and 6-9pm, Su 9am-3pm. €4, students and children €2, groups €3.)* The **War Museum** displays a collection of historic firearms. *(Amalias 22, toward the New Town from Pl. Syndagma. ☎ 27520 25 591. Open Tu-Su 9am-2pm. Free.)*

BEACHES. Arvanitia, Nafplion's secluded pebble beach, is on Polizoidhou past where the steps of Palamidi begin. On hot days, pop music blares over the noise of the sun-soaked crowd. For a cleaner, more serene alternative, take the foot-path that runs along the water from the Arvanitia parking lot. The 45min. walk will reveal three quiet, rocky coves. If you're dying for a long, sandy beach, try the mostly undeveloped **Karathona** beach, a 3km hike along the coast from Arvanitia (taxi €3), or head to **Tolo,** where you can rent water sports equipment (€8-15). Buses (€1) head there from Nafplion every hour.

NIGHTLIFE

Nightlife in Nafplion often involves enjoying a relaxing drink in one of the many bars on the waterfront near Pl. Syndagma or on Vas. Konstandinou or Staikopolou. At night, the trendy cafe-bars along the waterfront, such as **Pantheon, Ekplous,** and **Serio,** surge with young heartthrobs and pounding beats. They offer beer (€3-5) and mixed drinks (€5.50-6.50). The search for alternative nightlife might land you in a taxi for the 15min. ride to **Tolo,** a tourist-packed beach resort. Check with waiters at **Abaka,** Bouboulinas 63 (☎ 27520 25 131) for the most happening clubs of the season.

Agora Music Café, Vas. Konstandinou 17 (☎ 27520 26 016). International and Greek pop music pumps all night, but the frappes and espressos are the real reason to come here. Open daily 8am-3am.

MYCENAE Μυκήνες

The spectacular remains of ancient Mycenae, which according to legend was founded by Perseus, are on a rocky knoll between Mt. Ag. Elia to the north and Mt. Zara to the south. Enough of the ancient citadel remains for visitors to imagine how magnificent it must have been in its heyday. Gargantuan **Cyclopean walls**, 13m high and 10m thick, surround the palace and its accompanying structures, which blanket most of the hill. Outside the central fortified city, down the road toward town, several impeccably preserved *tholoi* tombs—most notably the so-called **"Treasury of Atreus"**—clearly show the architectural expertise of the Mycenaeans. Most of the ruins date from around 1280 BC, when the city was the center of a vast Mycenaean Empire. The relics unearthed here are among the most celebrated archaeological discoveries in modern history, including countless jewels and the famous Mask of Agamemnon. As a result, many have been taken to the National Archaeological Museum in Athens (p. 98).

Mycenae's origins, interactions with other Near Eastern civilizations, and subsequent decline have long puzzled historians. Thought to have been settled as early as 2700 BC by a tribe from the Cyclades, Mycenae, along with other nearby cities, remained under the shadow of the Minoans for centuries. It wasn't until the collapse of the Minoan civilization in the mid-15th century BC that Mycenae rose to the top of the Greek world (p. 39). Mycenaean culture flourished for centuries until the 12th century BC, when the Dorians attacked from the north. The Dorians successfully conquered Greece, and Mycenae lost its grasp on the culture it had helped to create. The city remained inhabited through the Roman period, but by Byzantine times it had been swallowed by the earth and forgotten.

In 1874, German businessman, Classicist, and amateur archaeologist Heinrich Schliemann arrived on the scene. Fresh from his lucrative dig at Troy and eager to further establish the historical validity of Homeric epics, he began a quest to uncover the city of Agamemnon, the king who (according to Homer) led the Greek forces in the Trojan War. It was impossible to overlook the probable connection between these finds and Homer's description of a "well-built citadel... rich in gold." Schliemann began his dig just inside the citadel walls at the spot where several ancient authors described royal graves. He found massive walls that surrounded elaborate tombs laden with dazzling artifacts. Discovering 15 skeletons, which he believed to be those of Agamemnon and his cohorts, Schliemann sent a telegram to the Greek king that read, "Have gazed on face of Agamemnon." Moments after he removed its mask, however, the "face" underneath disintegrated. Modern archaeologists, who still cringe at the thought of such reckless excavation, date the tombs and mask to four centuries before the Trojan War.

⌨ TRANSPORTATION. Buses go to Mycenae from Nafplion (45min., 10am and 2pm, €3). Take the bus to its final stop at the end of the asphalt road in the parking lot. Be careful not to get off at Argos, mistaking the fortress on the hill for Mycenae.

▥ RUINS. The two sights after the entrance booth are two impressive but oft-overlooked *tholoi*: the **Tomb of Aegisthus** and the **Tomb of Clytemnestra,** both with expansive burial chambers you can enter. When you return to the main path, you'll pass through the imposing **Lion's Gate,** the portal into the ancient city, with two lions carved in relief above the lintel (estimated to weigh 20 tons). On the right after the gate is **Grave Circle A,** where Schliemann found most of his artifacts. This area contains six 16th-century BC **shaft graves** that have yielded 14kg worth of gold.

The path winds back and forth up the hillside, passing remnants of homes, businesses, and shrines from the formerly bustling complex. The **palace** and **royal apartments** are at the highest part of the citadel on the right. The open spaces include

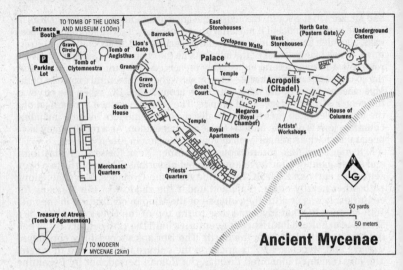

Ancient Mycenae

guard rooms, private areas, and an impressive staircase; look for the **megaron,** or royal chamber, with its round hearth framed by the bases of four pillars. To the left of the citadel are the remaining stones of the ancient **temples,** thought to have been dedicated to Athena or Hera. The farthest end of the city, past the **Artisan Workshops,** is the best place to get a sense of the immensity of the complex's walls. For non-claustrophobics, the **underground cistern** offers a chance for exploration at your own risk. This tunnel, which bores 18m underground to what used to be a spring, guaranteed water during sieges. It's pitch black and the steps are uneven and slippery; use your flashlight, travel in a group, and watch your step.

Follow the asphalt 400m back toward the town of Mycenae to the **Tomb of Agamemnon** (a.k.a. the "Treasury of Atreus"), the largest and most impressive *tholos*, named by Schliemann for the king he so desperately wanted to discover here. The tomb is similar in design to the two *tholoi* near the entrance booth, but significantly larger and perfectly preserved. A 40m passage cut into the hillside leads through an immense doorway and into the grave itself. Inside, glance up to see the 120-ton lintel stones above you, arranged in concentric circles. The dim interior of the *tholos* conveys a ghostly majesty, but to the dismay of both archaeologists and tourists, the tomb was found empty, having lost its valuables to robbers.

To reach the **museum,** follow the signs from the entrance booth, bearing left from the acropolis. The museum displays an extensive collection of pottery and ceramics, which show evidence of trade with areas as far as Spain and Afghanistan, as well as a detailed history of the ancient city and its excavations. While the most important artifacts found at the site are in the National Archaeological Museum in Athens, the museum offers gorgeous views of the neighboring hills. (Open daily June-Oct. 8am-7:30pm; Nov.-May 8am-3pm. Museum open M noon-7pm, Tu-Su 8am-7pm. Site, museum, and Agamemnon's Tomb €8, students and seniors €4, EU students and children free. Guidebooks €3.50-6.50. Bags larger than book-size are not allowed in the acropolis. Wear sturdy shoes and bring water.)

EPIDAVROS Επίδαυρος ☎27530

Epidavros was once both a town and a sanctuary, sacred first to the ancient deity Maleatas, then to Apollo, who assumed aspects of the former patron's identity. Eventually, the sanctuary came to be devoted to Apollo's son, the medically gifted demigod Asclepius. When the good doctor got a little overzealous and began to raise people from the dead, Zeus laid the smack down with a thunderbolt. Asclepius, however, continued to guard over Epidavros, which became famous across the ancient world as a center of medicine. The prestige of the ancient health center reached its peak in the early fourth century BC, when people traveled across the Mediterranean for medical and mystical cures to a disastrous onslaught of plagues. Asclepius made diagnoses in dream visitations; recent finds indicate that surgeries took place here as well. Over the centuries, the complex grew to include temples dedicated to Aphrodite, Artemis, and Themis. The sanctuary complex was closed along with all other non-Christian sanctuaries by Emperor Theodosius II in AD 426. With the notable exception of the theater, the ruins are not as well preserved as those at Mycenae, though restoration efforts have been underway for the past few years.

🖪🔁 TRANSPORTATION AND PRACTICAL INFORMATION. Buses run from Nafplion (1hr.; 10:15am, noon, 2:30pm; €3). Buses return from Epidavros to Nafplion at 7:15am and 11:30am. A snack bar and restaurant serve the site but visitors might want to pack a lunch.

◙ SIGHTS. Built into a hillside in the third century BC, the ◙**Theater of Epidavros** is without a doubt the site's most splendid structure. Initially constructed to accommodate 6000 people, its capacity was expanded to 12,300 in the next century. The theater's 55 tiers face half-forested, half-flaxen mountains so awe-striking they distract from the tragedies played out on the stage. However, the theater itself is just as spectacular. Attempt to grasp its vastness by standing on the top balcony and surveying the carefully constructed rows of seats below you. Though it often is said that the theater was designed by Polykleitos the Younger, architect of an even larger theater at Argos, it is not old enough to have been his work. The theater's acoustics defy belief, as yelling, singing, coin-dropping, whispering, and even match-lighting tourists from all nations enthusiastically demonstrate from the stage area—every sound made there can be heard even in the last row of seats. The secret to the theater's acoustic perfection is its symmetrical architecture; the entire amphitheater was built in proportion to the Fibonacci sequence.

The theater recently has come alive after centuries of silence: during July and August it hosts the ◙**Epidavros Theater Festival.** During the festival, the National Theater of Greece and visiting companies perform Classical Greek plays translated into modern Greek. In recent years, the schedule has expanded to include eclectic music and dance programs. (☎21092 82 900. Performances begin in the evening after the site closes. Tickets can be purchased in advance online or by phone; last minute tickets may be available at the site's box office. On performance nights, KTEL buses make a round-trip trek from Nafplion (7:30pm, €6), leaving 20min. after the performance ends.)

The **Archaeological Museum** lies between the theater and the ruins. While much of the museum is closed to visitors because of restoration efforts, the three open rooms display a cramped but fascinating collection. The room closest to the entrance holds an array of ancient medical instruments, as well as a series of engraved stone tablets, some of which describe Asclepius's miraculous cures in detail. Make sure to check out the vast collection of marble statues in the middle room. The room farthest from the entrance is filled with intricate **entablatures** from the Temple of Asclepius and the *tholos*. Most impressive, however, is the perfectly preserved Corinthian capital, regarded as the architect's prototype for all the capitals of the Temple of Asclepius. ((Museum and ticket office ☎27530 22 009.)

The extensive ruins of the **Sanctuary of Asclepius** have undergone restoration efforts that use brand-new stone, rather than attempting to blend in with the past. Still, the ruins easily convey a sense of the complex's massive size. Walking from the museum, you'll first pass the **Xenon,** an ancient hotel that now consists of little more than a maze of foundations. The **gymnasium** containing the remains of a Roman odeon is the first structure of the more concentrated complex of ruins. To the left is a **stadium,** of which only a few tiers of seats and the athletes' starting blocks survive. Two of the most important structures of the ancient sanctuary, the **Temple of Asclepius** and the famous **tholos,** are in front and to the left as you approach the ruins from the museum area. The *tholos*, thought to have been built by Polykleitos the Younger in the mid-fourth century BC, contains a stone labyrinth that was intended to recreate trials in Hades—however, you must read about this on the information plaque, as visitors are not allowed to look into the vertical recesses of the *tholos*. Beside the *tholos* are the remains of the **abaton,** where ailing patients would wait for Asclepius to reveal the proper treatment. Farther along the path on the eastern edge of the site lie the ruins of second-century **Roman baths.** (Site open in high season M noon-7:30pm, Tu-Su 8am-7:30pm; in low season M noon-5pm, Tu-Su 8am-5pm; festival season F-Sa 8am-9pm. €6, students and seniors €3, EU students and under 18 free. Guidebook €2-10.)

ELIA Ἠλιδα AND ACHAIA Αχαία

In rural Elia and Achaia, pebble beaches near coastal plain port cities are as much a regional attraction as the jagged mountains rising dramatically inland. Summers bring locals and travelers alike to the inviting shores of the Mediterranean, while in winter Greeks and tourists head to higher ground to ski. The mountainous region was first settled by Achaians from the Argolid, and later ruled by Romans. Afterward, Franks, Ottomans, and Venetians all violently disputed this land, leaving a visible wake in the occasional ruins that crop up across the area's terrain.

PATRA Πάτρας   ☎26106

Greece's third-largest city spreads from ancient hilltop ruins to a modern, heavily-trafficked harbor below, with an eclectic mix of boutiques, businesses, and restaurants that quite literally rests on ancient foundations. Local Patrans, proud of their city, are quick to challenge the idea that most incoming tourists view the city as nothing more than a stopover on the way to Athens or an Italian ferry destination. Stretching between storefronts throughout the city are stone pedestrian streets, picturesque alleys, and large, impressive *plateias*, perfect for exploring on foot. The populations of nearby universities, meanwhile, assure that Patra stays alive well into the late hours. Aside from festivals and shows held throughout the year, the city is well-known for its Carnival celebrations. From mid-January to the start of Lent, Patra breaks out into Carnival madness—music, food, and all-night revelry.

P E L O P E N N E S E

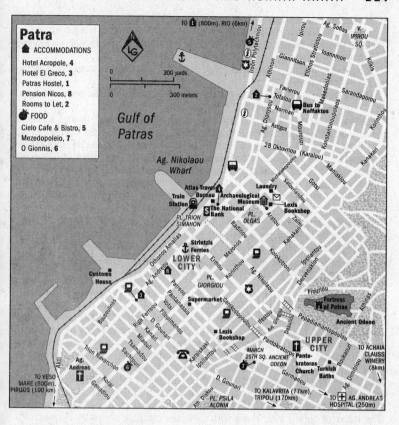

TRANSPORTATION

If you're coming from Athens by car, choose between the **New National Road**, which runs inland along the Gulf of Corinth, and the slower, scenic **Old National Road**, which hugs the coast. From central Greece, take the new **Rio Antirrio** bridge to Rio on the Peloponnese. From Rio, the #6 bus stops at **Kanakari** and **Aratou** (30min., €1.10), four blocks uphill from the main station.

Trains: Oth. Amalias 27 (☎26106 39 108), in the center of town. Ticket booth open daily 7am-2:30am. To: **Athens** (Regular: 4hr. with transfer in Korinthos; 7 per day 2:30am-5:57pm. €9.40. Express 3hr.; 5 per day 5:55am-5:55pm; €12.40); **Egio** (35min., 7 per day 2:30am-5:55pm, €1.20-3.60); **Kalamata** (5hr.; M-F 6am, 1:30, 9:44pm, 2:30am; €8). Construction projects sometimes stop train travel entirely—check to see they're running before making travel plans. The trains to Athens tend to be packed, so reserve seats even if you have a railpass. Cash only.

Buses: KTEL is the bus operator in Patra. It operates out of 4 stations:

Central Station: Zaimi 2 & Oth. Amalias (☎26106 23 886). To: **Athens** (3hr., 21 per day 2:30am-9:45pm, €14); **Egio** (M-F 16 per day 7am-9pm, Sa-Su and holidays 7am-10:15pm; €3.60); **Kalamata** (8am and 2:30pm, €20); **Kalavrita** (M-F 5:30, 7:15am, 1:10, 4pm; Sa-Su 7:15am and

4pm. €8); **Thessaloniki** (daily 8:15am, noon, 3:15, 9pm; €40); **Tripoli** (daily 7:15am and 2pm, €16). More destinations in Achaia Region; check the station for departure information.

Etoloakarnanias Station: Norman 5 (☎26104 21 205). Buses to **Delphi** (2½hr.) via **Itea** and **Nafpaktos** (20min.; M-F 7 per day 7:15am-8:35pm, Sa 1:30pm; €4-7).

Zakynthos Station: Oth. Amalias 48 (☎26102 20 993). Buses to **Zante** via **Killini** (3hr., 4 per day 8:40am-7:30pm, €7).

Trikala Station: Oth. Amalias 58 (☎26102 74 938). Buses to and **Chania, Iraklio, Kefalinias, Kefallonia,** and **Lefkada.** Check the station for times.

Ferries: To buy tickets and find departure gates, go to the ticket counters scattered around Oth. Amalias. Domestic ferries to: **Corfu** (6¾hr.; M, W, Th, Sa midnight; €33); **Ithaka** (3½hr., 12:30pm and 8:30pm, €16) via **Sami** on Kefallonia (3hr., €8); **Zakynthos** (1½-3hr., €14). International ferries go to Italy and Turkey; check at Gate 6 for schedule and rates. For more information on ferry travel, call **Port Authority** (☎26103 41 002), at the start of Gounari, or contact the **Info Center**, Oth. Amalias 6 (☎26104 61 740). Another great resource for ferry travel is **Altas Travel** (☎26102 24 439), on Oth. Amalias, opposite the train station. Open M-F 9am-1pm and 3:30-6pm.

Car Rental: Many along Ag. Andreou. **Hertz Rent-A-Car**, Karalou 2 (☎26102 20 990). Turn right between the train station and the information center. Cars from €60 per day. Open M-Sa 8am-2pm and 5-8:30pm, Su 9:30am-1pm and 5:30-8pm. AmEx/MC/V.

Taxis: Line up in *plateias* and by the bus station. 24hr. **Radio Express** ☎26104 50 000 or 18 300.

⚜ 🛈 ORIENTATION AND PRACTICAL INFORMATION

Patra is divided into an upper and a lower city, both of which are arranged in a grid. Most hotels, restaurants, and shops are in the heart of the lower city. **Othonas Amalias** (called **Iroön Polytechniou** past the new port) runs parallel to the waterfront. There are three main squares downtown. One block from the train station along Oth. Amalias is **Plateia Trion Simahon**, with palm trees, cafes, and kiosks. **Agios Nikolaou** runs inland from the *plateia* and intersects the city's major east-west streets. From the corner of Ag. Nikolaou and Mezonos, walk three blocks south on Mezonos to find **Plateia Giorgiou**, with sculpted fountains. The heart of New Patra, lined with designer clothing shops, is between Pl. Giorgiou and **Plateia Olgas**, three blocks to the left with your back to the water. Access the upper city by walking away from the water on Ag. Nikolaou.

Tourist Office: Info Center, 6 Oth. Amalias (☎26104 61 740; www.infocenterPatra.gr). Provides festival schedules, transportation info, museum info, maps, brochures, **internet** (20min. max) and bicycles to explore the area (all free). Offers information on Greece in English, French, German, Italian, and Spanish. Open daily 8am-8pm.

Banks: National Bank (☎26106 37 400), in Pl. Trion Simahon on the waterfront. **24hr. ATM** and **currency exchange.** Open M-F 8am-2:30pm. Ag. Andreou is lined with banks, ATMs, and currency exchange locations. All have the same hours as the National Bank.

Luggage Storage: (☎26103 41 002), at Gate 6 in the ferry port. €2. Open 8am-10pm. Also at the train station (☎26106 39 108). €1.60. Open 7am-10pm.

International Bookstore: Eleftheroudakis Bookstore, Ermou 42 and Pl. Georgiou (☎26106 62 180). Great collection of books in English including travel guides and new releases.

Laundromat: All-Star Laundry, 21 Zaïmi (☎26102 78 189). Wash and dry €8. Open M, W, Sa 9am-2pm, Tu and Th-F 9am-2pm and 6-9pm. Many along Zaïmi.

Police: Achaia Headquarters are at Ermou 95 (☎26102 26 150). **Tourist Police**, Gounari 52 (☎26106 95 191).

PELOPENNESE

Hospital: Ag. Andreas Hospital (☎26102 27 000), on Patron-Class past the church and on the left.

Telephones: OTE, at the corner of D. Gounari and Kanakari. Open M, W, Sa 7:30am-2:30pm, Tu and Th-F 7:30am-8:30pm.

Internet Access: Plug 'n Play (☎26103 61 492), on Trion Navarchon. €1.50 per hr. Printing €0.10 per sheet. Open daily 8am-2am.

Post Office: Zaïmi St. (☎26106 20 644), on the corner of Mezonos. **Western Union.** Open M-F 7:30am-2pm. **Postal Code:** 26001.

ACCOMMODATIONS

Most hotels in Patra are on or near **Agios Andreou** to the left of Pl. Trion Simahon facing inland, or on **Agios Nikolaou.** Many look budget but cost more than you'd expect; there are, however, a few good finds.

Hotel Acropole, 32 Ag. Andreou St. (☎26102 79 809). Great location compensates for the small rooms. Rooms have internet, TVs, A/C, and private baths. Breakfast included. Wheelchair-accessible. Singles €35; doubles €45-55. Extra beds upon request. MC/V. ❸

Pension Nicos, Patreos 3 (☎26106 23 757), 2 blocks off the waterfront. Low prices and a prime location make the hike up to the 3rd fl. entirely worth it. Rooms all have A/C and TVs; some have private baths. The roof deck is a definite bonus. The wood-paneling and close neighbors make the rooms a little dark. Singles €30-35; doubles €40-50; triples €45-55. Cash only. ❷

Rooms to Let Spyros Vazouras, Tofalou 2 (☎26104 52 152; www.patrasrooms.gr), 2 blocks up from the harbor, across from the new port entrance. These large, brightly tiled rooms are equipped with A/C, TVs, and baths. Other perks include a communal fridge and a rooftop deck with ocean views. If the door is locked, press the intercom to contact Spyros and he'll come let you in. Singles €30; doubles €40; extra bed €10. ❷

Hotel El Greco, Ag. Andreou 145 (☎26102 72 931). Walking along Andreou with the water on your right, it's 4 blocks past Pl. Trion Simahon on the left. Plants flourish in the modern lounge and lobby of this family-run establishment. Each clean room has bath, TV, fridge, hairdryer, and A/C; some have balconies. Breakfast €6. Check-out noon. Singles €45; doubles €55; triples €65-70. ❸

Patra Youth Hostel, Iroön Polytechniou 68 (☎26104 27 278). From the port, walk away from town with the water on your left for about 1km. This creaky, turn-of-the-century mansion sat empty for 43 years after being occupied by Germans in WWII. If you're looking for the bare-bones, this might be the place to crash. Leave valuables at reception desk. Sheets €1. Check-out 10:30am. Dorms €12. ❶

FOOD

Walk along the waterfront and through any of the main *plateias* for options ranging from gyro stands to fancy Italian restaurants to quiet creperies. Higher-quality restaurants can be found by walking to the top of **Kolokotroni** from Pl. Olgas. Every square offers cafes with shaded outdoor seating where visitors can take time to cool down on hot summer afternoons. A walk through the old Roman streets of the upper city, by the Odeion and Fortress, reveals *tavernas* where locals sit back and enjoy late dinners. **Dia Discount Supermarket,** on Andreou near the bridge, has cheap groceries. (☎21098 94 414. Open M-F 8:30am-9pm, Sa 8am-8pm. Cash only.)

Mezedopoleio, Germanou 2 (☎26102 24 834), on the edge of 25 Martiou Sq. down from the Odeion. Enormous trees in the *plateia* provide wonderful natural shade. Extensive menu adds appeal to a restaurant whose main attraction is the outdoor seating in the square. An extensive array of salads (€4) and main dishes (€5-12). ❷

O Gionnis Restaurant, 2nd restaurant on the left after the intersection of Rig. Fereou and Navarhon. Reasonable prices and homemade no-fluff Greek cuisine mean it's usually mobbed with locals. Energetic young waiters (purr) bustle from table to table, making for fresh (and steaming hot) food. Salads €3-4. Entrees €5-8. Open daily noon-1am. Cash only. ❷

Cielo Cafe & Bistro (☎26104 22 222), on Iroön Polytechniou just before Gate 6 on the water. White walls and pastel cushions welcome the summer. Stop in here for a casual drink and watch the wharf. Frozen hot chocolates and coffees (€4-6) are their specialty. Pasta €8. Salads €6. Sandwiches €4. Open daily 9am-3am. Cash only. ❷

🔍 SIGHTS

AGIOS ANDREAS. The largest Orthodox cathedral in Greece, with a dome that soars to 46m and a capacity of 5500 people, is dedicated to St. Andrew. The saint was martyred here in the first century on an X-shaped crucifix (he felt unworthy of dying on a cross like Jesus's). A decade ago, the Catholic Church returned St. Andrew's holy head to his place of martyrdom. The top of the head is visible through its reliquary, an ornate silver replica of the cathedral itself, in front of the remains of the crucifix on the right of the church. The cathedral's frescoes, gold mosaics, and delicately latticed windows are both religiously significant and artistic masterpieces in their own right. One highlight is the large, intricately carved wooden chandelier in the center. Behind the cathedral on Eth. Korai is the beautiful Church of Saint Andrew, the original church built between 1836 and 1843. This building has bright frescoes, chandeliers, and a small well allegedly built by the saint himself. Legend holds that anyone who drinks from the well will return to Patra. (About 2km from the port. Walk along the waterfront or Ag. Andreou with the water to your right until you reach the cathedral; it will be on your left. ☎26103 30 644. Open daily 7am-8:30pm. Modest dress required.)

ACHAIA CLAUSS WINERY. A narrow road meanders uphill through grapevines and shaded countryside to this castle-like, internationally renowned winery 8km southeast of Patra. Founded in 1861 by German-born Baron Gustav von Clauss, its weathered stone buildings have aged as well as its wine. Try a complimentary sample of its famous Mavrodaphne, a superb and sweet dessert wine reputedly named for the black eyes of Clauss's lost love, Daphne. The wine is renowned in the international community—numerous awards, diplomas, and letters from grateful ambassadors adorn the walls—and the staff is friendly and incredibly knowledgeable. Be sure to take a tour of the old wine cellars to see the Imperial Cellar, where images of Dionysus rowing wine to shore grace the beautifully carved barrels. The oldest wine, a €1250 Mavrodaphne from 1873, is bottled for special occasions, most recently the 2004 Olympics in Athens. Visitors can buy other wines (€2.20-28) on the spot. Before you leave, wander around the main house to catch a breathtaking view of the ocean and Patra. (Take bus #7 (every 30min., €0.70). The stop is between Maizonos and Riga Ferraiou. ☎26103 68 100. Vineyard open daily 11am-8pm. Tours in English 10am-4pm. Free.)

THE FORTRESS OF PATRA. Overlooking the modern hustle and bustle of the city is this ancient fortress. Built over the ruins of an ancient acropolis using many of the same materials, Patra's fortress remains surprisingly intact considering its continuous, turbulent use from the AD sixth century to WWII. Controlled at times by the Byzantines, Franks, Turks, Venetians, and even the Vatican, the fortress serves as a tribute to the city below and the various influences that have helped shape it. More than just a monument to ages past, the fortress hosts occasional

P E L O P E N N E S E

concerts in the courtyard. The castle's high location makes it a perfect spot to get a bird's-eye view of the city. *(Walk to the upper city from Ag. Nikolaou. Then walk about 10min., following the fortress wall on Papadiamandopoulou, to the main entrance at the opposite side of the castle along Athinas. ☎ 26102 23 390. Open Tu-Su 8:30am-3pm. Free.)*

ANCIENT ODEION. Southwest of the castle in the upper city, this Roman theater, built before AD 160 and used until the third century, once held an audience of 2500. Ancient travel writer Pausanias described it as the second most impressive theater in Greece, after Athens's Theater of Herodes Atticus. Excavated in 1889, the theater was restored after WWII. Visitors now can make out the ancient *cavea*, where spectators sat, and *proskenion*, the wall at the back of the stage. In the summer, the theater hosts the **Patra International Festival,** which features nightly music. *(☎ 26102 76 207. Open Tu-Su 8:30am-3pm. Free. Festival takes place mid-June to Sept. Check at Info Center for performance times and prices.)*

TURKISH BATHS (HAMMAM). These baths in the old, upper part of Patra reputedly have been in continued use since 1500, although they received a renovation in 1987. *(Boukaouri 29 ☎ 26102 74 267. Open for women M and F 9am-9pm; Tu, Th, and Sa 2:30-5pm; W 9am-2:30pm and 5:30-9pm. Open for men Tu, Th, and Sa 9am-2:30pm and 5:30-9pm; W 2:30-5pm.)*

🎵 🎭 ENTERTAINMENT AND NIGHTLIFE

Walking out of the city's center on **Agios Dionysiou** along the water, a row of cafes attract the major night life of Patra. The clubs in Patra usually open in the winter, when school is in session and university students are in the city for the weekend. During the summer they close as people flock to the beaches. There are, however, still plenty of trendy lounge-type nightspots. To find the most popular, head out of Patra along Dionysiou and toward the bridge until you reach Politechniou. About 1km from the train station is a row of clubs. **Dose,** along with **It: the bar** and **W.,** are the best. Choose according to scene and theme, because all the cafes and bars have dockside seating and offer similar menus. (Mixed drinks €6-8. Espresso €3-6. Snacks and appetizers €2-15. Desserts €5-7. All open 8:30am-2am.)

For a relaxed night out, head along the waterfront on the National Road with the water on your right.

Veso, Akti Dymaion 17, about a 20min. walk out of the city center past Ag. Andreas Cathedral. An outdoor mall with restaurants, cafes, an 8-screen cinema, and Mondo Bowling. Most films (€7.50) screened in English with Greek subtitles. Open daily 9am-2am.

Mondo Bowling (☎26103 61 888; www.mondo.gr). Most crowds show up around midnight Tu-Th. €5 per game. Prices vary during the week, with special rates for students, women, and children (€3). Open daily 9am-2am.

KALAVRITA Καλάβρυτα ☎26920

Although most famous for its ski resort, which comes alive in winter, the town of Kalavrita ("good springs" in Greek) remains a worthwhile year-round destination. The modern town, founded in 1835, was built on the ancient city of Kynaitha and the fresh mountain springs of the area that give the town its name. During WWII, the Nazis executed all the town's men, who fought in the resistance. Kalavrita has built a museum and memorial for the victims in the school where the women and children were held hostage. Because of its beauty and historical significance, Kalavrita is not to be missed. Try to visit

PELOPENNESE

during the summer months—the low season—where the normally expensive rooms run for a little bit less.

⊏ TRANSPORTATION

Trains: At the time of writing, renovations were underway on the train line from Kalavrita to Diakofto.

Buses: Station (☎26920 22 224) uphill on Eth. Antistasios. Take the first right onto Kapota; it's 1 block down on your left at the intersection of 3 roads. Heavily reduced service Sa-Su. Call or visit the station ahead of time to confirm schedules and prices. M-F to: **Aigio** (1¼hr., 5 per day, €10); **Athens** (3hr., 2 per day, €15); **Diakofto** (45min., 2 per day, €3); **Patra** (2hr., 5 per day, €8).

Taxis: (☎26920 22 127). Line up along the side of the *plateia*, as well as by the bus and train stations.

✴ ？ ORIENTATION AND PRACTICAL INFORMATION

Navigating Kalavrita involves three main roads, each running perpendicular to the train station and tracks on the uphill side. Facing uphill, the street to the left is **Konstantinou**, which becomes **Agios Alexiou** a few blocks later. The pedestrian walk to the center is **Syngrou**, which becomes **25 Martiou.** The road to the right is **Kallimanti**, which becomes **Ethnikis Antistasios.** Uphill about 100m is the central *plateia.* Most of the town's accommodations, shops, and service centers are found on these three roads or connecting streets between.

Bank: National Bank, 25 Martiou 4 (☎26920 22 212), 100m downhill from the central *plateia.* **Currency exchange** and **24hr. ATM.** Open M-Th 8am-2:30pm, F 8am-2pm. ATMs also found on all main roads.

Police: Fotina 7, 2nd fl. (☎26920 22 213). To the right off Ag. Alexiou, 4 blocks beyond the central *plateia.*

Pharmacies: 4 in town. The one across from the hospital (☎26920 23 047) has the longest hours. Open M-Sa 8am-2pm and 5-9pm.

Telephones: In the central *plateia* and by the train station.

Internet Access: Plug 'n Play (☎26920 24 218), across from Hotel Filoxenia on Antistaseos. €2 per hr. Open daily 9am-midnight.

Post Office: Ag. Alexiou 17 (☎26920 22 225). Open M-F 7:30am-2pm. **Postal Code:** 25001.

⌂ ACCOMMODATIONS

The few hotels in Kalavrita are expensive for those traveling on a budget, even during the low season in the summer. Nevertheless, most hotels have few guests and might compromise on the price. Many hotels open for the bustling winter season and close for the summer. Book ahead in winter; no need to in summer.

Hotel Filoxenia (☎26920 22 422; www.hotelfiloxenia.gr), 1 block from the bus station as you head toward town. Convenient location, especially if carrying luggage. Rooms are small but all have balconies, A/C, satellite TV, bath, and Wi-Fi. Breakfast €5. Wheelchair-accessible. In winter singles €92; doubles €110. In summer singles €40; doubles €49. MC/V. ❻

Hotel Maria (☎26920 22 296; www.kalavrita.biz/maria.htm), 1 block uphill from the train station on the right side of Syngrou. Bright, clean rooms with TVs in a central location. Try to snag a balcony. Breakfast €5. From Dec. 15 to Mar. doubles €70; triples €90; quads €110. Apr.-June and from Sept. to mid-Dec. singles €30; doubles €50; triples €50-60. July-Aug. prices 10% higher. Cash only. ❸

PELOPENNESE

Hotel Anesis (☎26920 23 070; www.anesishotel.gr). This stone hotel offers security and a wintry feel. Carpeted rooms have phones, TVs, bathtubs, and tiny minibars. Wheelchair-accessible. In winter singles €75-85; doubles €85-100; triples €95-110. In summer singles €35-45; doubles €55-56; triples €65-76. MC/V. ❸

🗲 FOOD

Indistinguishable *tavernas* and fast-food joints line Ag. Alexiou and Syngrou. Most serve Greek staples (€5-7). Across the street from the bus station there is a **supermarket**. (Open M-Sa 8am-10pm.) There are other supermarkets scattered about the town, offering a good alternative to the sometimes expensive tavernas. Cafes are abundant, especially around the church. Look near the bus station for local favorites.

◪ **Spitiko** (☎26920 24 260), near the supermarket across from the bus station. A local favorite with wonderfully delicious lamb *fricace* (€8). Open most days 9am-1am. Cash only. ❷

Aroma, Martiou (☎26920 24 843). Uphill from the churchyard on the right. Something of a *nouveau* Greek restaurant. Come if you crave something lighter. English menu. Salads €4. Entrees €6-12. Open daily noon-1am. Cash only. ❷

👁 🏔 SIGHTS AND OUTDOOR ACTIVITIES

KALAVRITA SKI CENTER. 14km from downtown Kalavrita, the Kalavrita Ski Center operates 8 lifts on 13 ski slopes of varying difficulty. With ski schools, restaurants, and Saturday-night skiing, the center caters to the needs of skiers (and non-skiers) of all ages and skill levels. (☎26920 24 241; www.kalavrita-ski.com. Taxis ☎26920 22 127; €20. Buses run from the town to the mountain during winter. Open Dec.-Apr. 8:30am-4pm.)

MUNICIPAL MUSEUM OF THE KALAVRITA HOLOCAUST. The museum resides in the school where the women and children were locked as the men of the town were arrested and executed by the Nazis. The Site of Sacrifice, where the men were shot en masse in 1943, lies above the town. The museum follows the organization of the Holocaust museums of Washington, D.C. and Jerusalem. (☎26920 23 646. Open Sept.-May Tu-Su 9am-4pm, June-Aug. 10am-5pm. €3, groups €2, EU students and under 18 free. The Site of Sacrifice is about 2km past the post office and the current school. Ask at the museum for directions.)

🍸 NIGHTLIFE

The most happening place in the winter is, unsurprisingly, the ski center, where people gather for evening drinks. In other seasons and on weekdays, nightlife centers around cafes on Syngrou and the central *plateia*.

Portokali, at the end of the train tracks. This club plays Greek pop and light traditional music (get your folk dance on) all night long.

Diadromes, on Syngrou. Caters to a younger crowd. Has a small bar and crowded dance space where rock tunes are blasted. Drinks €5.

Skiniko, 25 Martiou 59, a few blocks up from the *plateia*. Those in the mood for classic rock from Greece and the US will enjoy the vinyl stylings here. Mixed drinks €5. Open Sept.-May.

Slalom, in the central *plateia* next to the church. Serves drinks and snacks late into the night. Dim lamps strung through trees make for some of the best outdoor seating in town. Coffee €1.50-3. Mixed drinks €5. Open daily 8am-1am.

Bresler's Cafe, Ag. Alexiou 1 (☎24 459). Plays mainly American club hits. Snacks €1-1.70. Beer €2.40. Mixed drinks €5-6. Open daily 6:30am-1am.

◪ DAYTRIPS FROM KALAVRITA

VOURAIKOS RIVER RAVINE . Perfect for summer hikes, the ravine is a celebration of Greece's mountainous beauty. Its wild cliff sides, waterfalls, caves, and untouched flora and fauna are so treasured by the town that every May, Kalavrita's town hall organizes a communal ravine hike. Among the natural wonders is the River Styx, where the Olympian gods took their most sacred oaths. Explore the ravine by train or foot. If going by foot, it's recommended that you begin your trek at Zachlorou, halfway from Diakofto to Kalavrita. *(☎26910 43 206 in Diakofto, 26920 22 245 in Kalavrita.)*

GREAT CAVE MONASTERY. Sixteen centuries of religious history lie 950m above sea level, hidden in a monumental cave near Kalavrita. Built in AD 362, the Great Cave Monastery is the oldest monastery in Greece. It is home to a wax icon of the Virgin Mary, sculpted by St. Luke (the multi-talented, apparently) 2000 years ago. According to the friendly monks, the icon was discovered by a local saint, St. Efrosini, in the cave itself and has performed wondrous miracles ever since. Check out the church's ancient mosaic floors, frescoes, and bronze door. As you walk in, head toward the staircase that lies just right of the small gift shop—four cannons point the way to the **museum.** Captions in both English and Greek describe the communion cups, clerical vestments, and religious manuscripts from the 11th to the 13th centuries. Especially noteworthy is the group of 400-year-old handmade crosses on the left wall. Follow a footpath uphill from the monastery and reach the "hole in the rock," a rock formation with (surprise!) a hole in it, through which a mysterious whistle sometimes is heard. *(Unless you are driving, transportation is fairly difficult. Buses from Kalavrita to Egio run twice per day, 15min. Ask to be let off at the monastery. Look for the signs reading (M6nh Meg1lou Sphlaio7). Taxis also are available; €22 round-trip. For a particularly scenic route, take the rail to Diakopto, get off at Zachlorou, and climb an ancient and well-marked footpath for 45min. Monastery open daily 7am-1pm and 2-7pm. Museum €2.)*

KYLLINI Κυλλήνη ☎26230

For a port town that handles almost all the tourist traffic to Zakynthos, Kyllini is surprisingly undeveloped; the town has almost no bus service, few accommodations, and only a handful of cafes. This otherwise disappointing town's highlights are the ruins of a hilltop fortress (signs in town point the way) and its sandy, isolated beach. Since most travelers don't spend much time here, the beach is splendidly undisturbed but still offers free lounge chairs under reed-woven umbrellas.

Ferries go to Argostoli (2hr., 1-2 per day, €12.50), Poros (1hr., 6-9 per day, €8.50), and Zakynthos (1hr., 7 per day 8am-10pm, €6.50); check for updated schedules at the docks. Buy tickets from one of the three kiosks on the dock; the kiosk on the right, facing the port entrance, sells tickets to Zakynthos, and the two on the left sell tickets to Kefallonia. To leave Kyllini by land, take the **bus,** from the stop across from the port gate, to Pirgos (1hr., 2 per day, €4.60). Ask for times in cafes or police station. The last bus usually leaves in the early afternoon. If you miss the last bus from Pirgos, you'll have to take a **taxi** (☎26230 71 764) to Lehena and from their catch a bus to Pirgos. From Pirgos, buses leave for most destinations in the Peloponnese and Athens. The **post office** is a block past the pharmacy. (Open M-F 7:30am-2pm.) **Postal Code:** 27068.

PIRGOS Πύργος ☎ 26210

Pirgos lacks both sights and cheap accommodations. However, its rail and road connections to southwestern Greece and Athens mean you might have to pass through. With more beautiful and intellectually stimulating cities nearby, there's no need to go out of your way for a visit.

TRANSPORTATION. Trains in the Peloponnese are both unreliable and slow. If you have to make your way using public transportation, stick to buses. Fortunately, **buses** in Pirgos tend to run on a regular schedule, facilitating a relatively painless escape. The **KTEL Bus Station,** 6 Eithrou Staurou (☎ 26210 20 604) sends buses to: Athens (5hr., M-Sa 11 per day 5am-12:30am, €25); Delphi (5hr., M-F 8:45am and 3pm, €24); Kalamata (2hr., 10am and 5:15pm, €12); Patra (2hr., M-F 11 per day 5:30am-12:30am, €9); Kyllini (1½hr., M-F 10:30am and 2:25pm, €6); Olympia (1hr., 16 per da 5:15am-9:45pm, €4.30); Tripoli (3hr., M-F 7:30am and 3:30pm, €9). On Saturdays, there is generally only morning service, even less on Sunday. Make sure to call the station for the schedule.

OLYMPIA Ολυμπία ☎ 26240

Set among quiet meadows of cypress and olive trees, modern Olympia bears little evidence of its cosmopolitan past. Though it is most famous as the home of the ancient Olympic Games, Olympia also boasts pristine natural beauty. The city teems with tourist shops and hotels but keeps a relaxed pace of life that makes visiting its ancient sites and stunning surroundings a pleasure.

TRANSPORTATION

All buses and trains to and from Olympia go through Pirgos. At the bus and train stations you can find connections to destinations beyond Pirgos.

Trains: Go to Pirgos (45min., 5 per day 7:20am-3:40pm, €1.20).

Buses: Head to Pirgos (35min., 16 per day 6:30am-9:45pm, €3.40) and **Tripoli** (3½hr.; M-F 8:45am, 12:30, 5:30pm, Sa-Su 8:45am and 5:30pm; €12).

Taxis: Line up along the main street and down by the train station.

ORIENTATION AND PRACTICAL INFORMATION

Olympia consists primarily of one main avenue, **Kondili.** Not much enters or leaves Olympia without traveling along this road. The train station is one block down from the main road, on your left walking into Olympia. Take a left onto the road across the Hotel Ilis. If you still manage to get lost, there are signs on almost every corner.

Tourist Office: Kondili (☎ 26240 23 173), next to the National Bank. Helpful staff provides bus schedules, information, and free maps. Open daily 9am-3pm.

Bank: National Bank (☎ 26240 22 501). Numerous others in town. Open M-Th 8am-2:30pm, F 8am-2pm. Most banks have **currency exchange** and **24hr. ATMs.**

Police: Em. Kountsa 1 (☎ 26240 22 100), 1 block up from Kondili, behind the tourist office. Also function as the **tourist police.**

Pharmacy: (☎ 69776 68 806), on your left in the 1st block with stores as you enter the town. Open M-F 8am-2:30pm and 4-9:30pm, Sa 8:30am-2:30pm and 4-9:30pm, Su 10am-1pm and 5-9:30pm.

Medical Services: (☎26240 22 222). Walk from the ruins to the other end of Kondili and turn left before the church. Continue straight as the road winds to the right, then turn right. 24hr. health center. Nearest large hospital is in Pirgos.

Telephones: Along Kondili and lining the road to the ancient site.

Internet Access: Most of the hotels have public Wi-Fi. Cafes next to the train station are also Wi-Fi hotspots. There are no internet cafes in town. Try **Hotel Kronio;** they have computer for guests and may let you use it.

Post Office: Pierre de Coubertain (☎26240 22 578), on the side street past the tourist office on the right. Open M-F 7:30am-2pm. **Postal Code:** 27065.

ACCOMMODATIONS AND CAMPING

The hotels in Olympia are all pretty similar, which offer standard rooms and amenities. Nevertheless, there are a few hidden gems among the bunch; call ahead. Because of Olympia's steady stream of tourists, bargaining for room rates does not work as well here as in other parts of the Peloponnese.

Hotel Pelops, Barela 2 (☎26240 22 542). Turn right onto the street before the church upon entering town and walk up a block; the hotel is to your right. Run by a Greek-Australian family. The best Olympia has to offer. Along with the Olympic standard (A/C, TV, balcony and private bath), Pelops treats you with access to the pool of the grand Europa Hotel, the option of a home-cooked dinner, and the low-down on Olympia. Reservations recommended. Singles €45; doubles €55. Rates rise July-Aug. Cash only. ❹

Hotel Kronion, Tsoureka 1 (☎26240 22 188), the 1st hotel on your left as you enter town. The reception isn't as dolled up as the neighbors', but it more than holds its own. Many of the rooms have full baths. The owner is always ready to give advice and answer questions about Olympia, modern and ancient. Full-service breakfast included. Singles €40; doubles €50. Rates rise July-Aug. Cash only. ❸

Camping Alfios (☎26240 22 951), up the hill behind the town, next to Hotel Europa. Wonderful views from the campsites as well as a pool and restaurant. Breakfast €7. Free electricity and Wi-Fi. €8 per person; €4 per tent. Campers €12. MC/V. ❶

Hotel Ilis (☎26240 22 547), along Kondili just beyond the church. The basic amenities (TV, A/C, and bath), plus 1 of the most plentiful breakfast buffets in the town. Internet. Singles €40; doubles €50; triples €60. Reservations recommended. MC/V. ❸

FOOD

Restaurants are aggressive in Olympia: servers will call out and beckon you to sit at one of their tables. Even the side streets are wallpapered with photographic menus. The restaurants are all comparable in quality—not the best you'll taste in Greece, but far from the worst. Due to intense competition, prices are the same everywhere. At night, locals and tourists mingle in the *tavernas* and bars along Kohili.

Aegean (☎26240 22 540), along the road to the train station on your right. Don't judge its plastic appearance—despite the touristy flair, this *taverna* actually has some of the freshest food in town. Recommended by all the locals and passed over by many of the tourists. Moussaka plate €4. Souvlaki plate €7. ❷

Praxitelis Taverna, Spiliopouloy 3 (☎26240 23 570), just past the police station walking toward the ruins. The multilingual menu offers grilled pasta and meat from along with other options. Try one of the 7 "menu" options (€9-13), featuring combinations of Greek specialties and sides. Entrees €4-16. 10% discount to students with ID. Also lets rooms upstairs as Pension Leonideon. ❸

🅖 SIGHTS

Olympia has several museums that examine the town's ancient legacy and sur-roundings. Beyond these, the natural beauty of the area is a sight in itself. Orga-nized walks, river parties, rafting, and kayaking are just a few of the activities available in the summer months. Participation is free, but early reservation is absolutely necessary. For more information, visit the tourist office, which can provide both info and schedules.

ANCIENT OLYMPIA ARCHAEOLOGICAL MUSEUM

Through the parking lot opposite the ancient site. ☎ *26240 22 529. Open Apr.-Oct. 12:30-7:30pm, Nov.-Mar. 8:30am-3pm. €6, with ancient site €9; seniors and students with ID €3; EU students and under 18 free. Flash cameras prohibited.*

Many find ancient Olympia's gleaming new museum a greater attraction than the ancient site itself. A team of French archaeologists began unearthing the site from 1400 years of accumulated silt in 1829. The organized excavations that continue today started in 1875, and most of what has been extracted resides in the museum. Since military victors from across the Greek world sent spoils and pieces of their own equipment to Olympia as offerings to the gods, the museum doubles as a display of Greek military history, with entire rooms filled with helmets, cuirasses, greaves, swords, spear points, and other military paraphernalia. The most spectacular military offering is a common **Corinthian helmet** (490 BC), partially destroyed by oxidation. While richer, better preserved headgear can be found elsewhere in the museum, this helmet has a faint inscription on the chin guard that reads "Miltiades dedicated this to Zeus." Miltiades led the outnumbered Greeks to victory over the Persians at Marathon in 479 BC; he may have worn this helmet in the battle. Beside it is another head-piece, whose inscription reveals it to be from the Persian side.

The museum's array of sculpture includes some of the greatest extant pieces in the world. One stunning centerpiece is the large western pediment from the Temple of Zeus, depicting the myth about a group of centaurs who attended the wedding of the king of Lapiths. After having a few too many drinks, the horse-men made the mistake of trying to abduct the Lapith women, a move they surely regretted in the morning (along with the hangover) after the vicious battle that ensued. A three meter tall Apollo stands in the center of the scene, imposing peace and order on the group. The pediment's fragments have been reassembled along one wall of the main room. Even the overlooked objects here astound—every case holds pieces that would be highlights of a lesser col-lection. Don't miss the room dedicated to Phidias, including some of his tools and shards of a plain drinking cup that, when they were cleaned and mended, bore the inscription "I belong to Phidias."

ANCIENT OLYMPIA

☎ *26240 22 517. Open daily 8:30am-7:30pm. €6, seniors and students €3, EU students and children under 18 free; museum and site €9. The ruins are practically unmarked. Sev-eral guides are available at the museum shop—try those by A. and N. Yalouris (€8), Monolis Andronicos (€5.50), or the Ministry of Culture (€9).*

Before there were photo finishes, drug tests, and aerodymanic unisuits, there were the games of Olympia. A green tract between the rivers Kladeo and Alphios, the city was one of the ancient world's most important cultural centers for a millennium. Participants from Asia Minor, Greece, Macedo-nia, North Africa, and Sicily convened here to worship, compete, and learn among masterpieces of art and architecture and the most cultured poets and musicians. Every four years for 1169 years, warring city-states would

PELOPENNESE

call a sacred truce and travel to Olympia for the most splendid Panhellenic assembly of the ancient world.

HISTORICAL OVERVIEW. Olympia was settled in the third millennium BC, when it was dedicated to **Gaia,** the Earth Mother, who had an oracle at the site. The first athletic contests commenced in Zeus's honor, only to be forgotten again until 884 BC. The first Olympic revival took place on the Oracle of Delphi's orders to Iphtos, King of Elia; prophecy told that the Games would save Greece from civil war and plague. The first recorded Olympiad was in 776 BC, which must have been a peaceful, disease-free year. Initially, the most athletic men, naked as jaybirds, competed in a simple *stadion*, or foot-race, lasting 192m (the stadium's length). As the Games's popularity broadened, longer races, wrestling, boxing, the pentathlon (long jump, discus, javelin, running, and wrestling), the hoplite race (in full bronze armor), and equestrian events joined the slate of events. The Olympics were celebrated through the AD fourth century, until Emperor Theodosius concluded that the sanctuary (and thus the Games themselves) violated his anti-pagan laws. Soon thereafter, earthquakes in AD 522 and 551 destroyed much of the Olympic site.

ARCHAEOLOGICAL SITE. The central sanctuary of the Olympic complex, eventually walled and dedicated to Zeus, was called the **Altis.** Over the centuries, it held temples, treasuries, and a number of monuments to the gods. The complex was surrounded by various facilities for participants and administrators, including the stadium on the far eastern side. Pausanias, a traveler-historian in the AD second century, noted a whopping 69 monuments built by victors to thank the gods. A few sections are roped off, but you can climb up the steps of the Temple of Zeus and walk along its perimeter.

As you enter the site, facing south, veer slightly to the left to reach the **training grounds.** Here you'll find the remains of the second-century BC **gymnasium.** This open-air quadrangle surrounded by Doric columns was reserved for athletes like runners and javelin throwers who needed space to practice. If you continue straight through the gymnasium, you will reach the re-erected columns of the square **Palaestra,** or wrestling school, built in the third century BC. More than a mere athletic facility, the Palaestra ensured that competitors wouldn't become one-dimensional, uncivilized brutes. The young men wrestled one moment and studied metaphysics the next in nearby rooms.

As you continue south and slightly west, the next group of structures includes a reddish, surprisingly intact, walled-in building: the **workshop of Phidias,** the sculptor. For the Temple of Olympian Zeus, Phidias produced an ivory and gold statue of the god so magnificent that it became one of the ■**Seven Wonders of the Ancient World.** It stood 12.4m tall and portrayed the god seated on his throne with an expression revealing benevolence and glory. In tune with the themes of the Olympic Games, Zeus cupped a statue of Nike, the goddess of victory, in his right palm. When the Games were abolished in the fourth century, the statue was moved to Constantinople, where it was destroyed in a fire in AD 475. Adding insult to injury, the Byzantines built a church on top of the workshop in the AD fifth century, constructing new walls but leaving the foundation intact. As a result, the identity of the site was debated for years. The traditional sources were affirmed by recent excavations that have uncovered molds, sculpting tools, and the famous cup bearing the inscription "I belong to Phidias." These finds are currently in the museum. Just past the workshop and slightly to the left is the huge **Leonidaion,** built in 330 BC by a wealthy man from Naxos named Leonidas. Though the building officially was dedicated to Zeus some time after 350 BC, it served a primarily secular role, often hosting officials and other VIPs.

PELOPENNESE

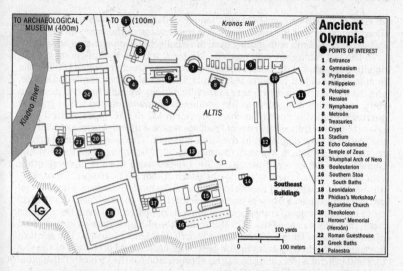

Ancient Olympia

● POINTS OF INTEREST

1 Entrance
2 Gymnasium
3 Prytaneion
4 Philippeion
5 Pelopion
6 Heraion
7 Nymphaeum
8 Metroön
9 Treasuries
10 Crypt
11 Stadium
12 Echo Colonnade
13 Temple of Zeus
14 Triumphal Arch of Nero
15 Bouleuterion
16 Southern Stoa
17 South Baths
18 Leonidaion
19 Phidias's Workshop/Byzantine Church
20 Theokoleon
21 Heroes' Memorial (Heroön)
22 Roman Guesthouse
23 Greek Baths
24 Palaestra

At the **Bouleuterion,** to the right as you face the entrance, lie the remains of the South Processional Gate to the Altis. The procession of athletes and trainers entered the sacred area on their way to the Bouleuterion (to the right of the gate), where the ancient Olympic council met. Each athlete was required to make a sacrifice to Zeus and take the sacred oath, swearing his eligibility and intent to abide by the rules of the Games.

North of the Bouleuterion (toward the entrance) are the ruins of the once-gigantic **Temple of Olympian Zeus,** the centerpiece of the Altis after its completion in 456 BC. Home to Phidias's awe-inspiring statue, the 27m long sanctuary was the largest temple completed on the Greek mainland before the Parthenon. The temple's elegant facade, impressive Doric columns, and accurately modeled pedimental sculpture exemplified the Classical design that evolved before the Persians invaded Greece. Today only a half-column stands, while the rest of these tremendous pillars, toppled in segments, lie as they fell after a sixth-century earthquake.

Past the temple, to the right as you face the entrance, lie the remains of the **Echo Stoa,** which was used for competitions between trumpeters and heralds. The musical prowess of the competitors was no doubt enhanced by the colonnade's rumored seven-fold echo. At the northern edge of the colonnade, stone blocks that once supported statues of victorious athletes lead to the **Crypt,** the official entrance to the stadium used by athletes and judges. This domed passageway (of which only one arch survives) and the stadium as it stands today are products of the Hellenistic period, built over the remains of the earlier, similarly positioned stadium. Having survived the effects of powerful earthquakes, the stadium appears much as it did 2300 years ago. The judges' stand and the start and finish lines are still in place, and the stadium's grassy banks still can seat nearly 40,000 spectators; you may feel inspired to take a lap or two to bond with Olympians of millennia past. As you leave the passageway to the stadium, the remains of **treasuries** erected by distant states to house votive offerings sit in a row on the northern hillside to your right. Continuing left as you face the hill, you'll see the space that once held the small-scale temples donated by individual cities. Beyond the treasuries are the remains of the **Nymphaeum** and the **Metroon,** an elegant fourth-century BC Doric temple dedicated to Zeus's mother, Rhea. Along the terrace of the treasuries stand the remains of the bases of 16 bronze statues of Zeus, built with money from fines collected from cheating athletes.

To the left facing the hill, past the Metroon and the Nymphaeum, are the dignified remains of the **Temple of Hera,** or Heraion. Erected around 600 BC, the temple is the oldest building at Olympia, the oldest Doric temple in Greece, and the best-preserved structure at the site. Originally built for both Zeus and Hera, it was devoted solely to the goddess when Zeus moved to his grander quarters (ironically now in far worse shape) in 457 BC. The *cella* of the temple is where the magnificent **Hermes of Praxiteles** was unearthed during excavations; the statue is now displayed in the site's museum. This temple figured prominently in the Heraia, a women's footrace as old, if not older, than the Olympic Games, also held every four years. Today's ◙**Olympic flame** is lit every other year at the Altar of Hera, at the northeastern corner of the temple. From here, it is borne by a variety of means to the site of the modern Games. This trip can involve thousands of runners passing the torch hand-to-hand, also drawing on more current forms of transportation like boats, planes, and even laser beams (as in the unique case of the 1976 Montreal Games). The **Prytaneion** is northwest of the Temple of Hera and contains a hearth, the Altar of Hestia. The spirit of the Games reached its culmination here with feasts, held on behalf of the victors and official guests, expressing an appreciation for the virtues of discipline and honor embodied by the athletes.

OTHER SIGHTS

MUSEUM OF THE HISTORY OF THE OLYMPIC GAMES IN ANTIQUITY. This museum is jam-packed with info about the ancient Olympic Games, with multilingual explanations of the different events and antiquity's various other athletic festivals. Beyond a historical outline, specific artifacts dating back to the ninth century BC are arranged by event, from bronze tripod cauldrons, to portions of the original wreaths given as prizes, to intact shields and even a wheel from an iron chariot used in races. One highlight is a remarkably well-preserved mosaic floor from a Roman house in Patra that depicts Olympic events. Although the explanations of the Games are very thorough, many specific objects have little or no explanation; ask a friendly staff member for further information. *(At the end of Kondili, before the incline toward the ancient site; look for the signs. ☎ 26240 29 119. Open Apr.-Oct. M 12:30-7:30pm, Tu-Su 8:30am-7:30pm; Nov.-Mar. M 12:30-3pm, Tu-Su 8:30am-3pm. Free.)*

MUSEUM OF THE HISTORY OF EXCAVATIONS IN OLYMPIA. The one small room that houses this museum presents a brief, nostalgic glance at the long process of excavation in Olympia, dating back to 1829. Beyond newspaper clippings from the 1800s and the official documents that allowed for excavations, the smaller objects on display—like a box filled with tickets to the old museum, inventory lists from the daily excavations, and pages from excavation diaries and manuscripts from 1908—add depth to the story of discovery. The museum also has a large collection of instruments used in the original excavation. Though small, this museum is valuable for understanding the practical side of the site's archaeology. *(Next to the Museum of the History of the Olympic Games in Antiquity. If it is locked, ask a staff member at the Olympic Games museum to open it.)*

MUSEUM OF THE OLYMPIC GAMES. Tracing the modern Games from 1896 to 2004, this museum displays pins, stamps, photographs, posters from each Olympiad, and biographies of prominent athletes. Notice how the shape and style of the Olympic Torch has changed over the past century, and don't miss the silver medal from the 1996 Games in Atlanta, donated by

Niki Bakoyianni, the women's high-jump medalist. (☎26240 22 544. 2 blocks from Kondili, on Avgerinou. Turn next to Hotel Ilis; it's the large white building at the end of the street. Open Tu-Su 8am-3:30pm. €2. Guidebook €6.)

ARCADIA Αρκαδία

Beyond the noisy bustle of urban Tripoli, mountainous and heavily forested Arcadia is speckled with red-roofed villages and monasteries. Introduced into mythology and literature for its serene landscape, "Arcadia" became synonymous with pastoral paradise. Well past ancient times, an archetypal image lingered of a green idyll inhabited by Pan, Dionysus, nymphs, satyrs, and the lucky mortals who cavorted with them. While few foreign tourists venture as far as Arcadia's outer reaches, those who do can enjoy the rare company of mountain goats on the isolated slopes.

TRIPOLI Τρίπολη   ☎27102

Visitors don't come to Tripoli in search of museums, old ruins, or any of the typical Greek stuff. The capital of Arcadia, Tripoli is a breath of fresh air, perfect as a detour from the heavily-touristed towns. Along with a lack of touristy T-shirts, Tripoli remains a strong base for the Greek military, holding on to the city's proud history of leadership during the War of Independence in 1821. During the day, uniformed soldiers walk the streets. At night, the garrison goes to sleep, and the streets come alive with some of the best nightlife around, a pleasant change from most of the small villages of the Peloponnese.

TRANSPORTATION

Trains: The station and lines are being renovated through 2009.

Buses: KTEL Arcadias station, Nafpliou 50 (☎27102 22 560 or 30 140). Walk along Venizelou (which becomes Nafpliou), the street across from the Arcadia Hotel with the arrow pointing down it toward the police station; it's on the right. Taxis from town €4. Newly renovated with restaurant, large convenience store, and free internet terminals. To: **Athens** (2hr., 17 per day 5am-10pm, €13); **Kalamata** (1hr., 8:30am and 12:45pm, €7); **Nafplio** (1hr.; 10am, 2:05, 5pm; €6); **Patra** (3hr., 4 per day 8:30am-4pm, €16); **Pirgos** (3½hr., 5 per day 8:30am-6:30pm, €15); **Thessaloniki** (9hr., 11:15am and 3:15pm, €40).

Taxis: (☎27102 33 010). Line up in Pl. Ag. Vasiliou.

ORIENTATION AND PRACTICAL INFORMATION

Tripoli is shaped like a cross, with **Plateia Agiou Vasiliou**, marked by the **Church of Agiou Vasiliou**, at the central joint. Four other *plateias* form the ends of the cross, at the ends of the four roads that branch out from Ag. Vasiliou. From **Plateia Kolokotronis, Vasiliou Giorgiou**, to the left as you face the National Bank, takes you to Pl. Ag. Vasiliou. Facing the church in Pl. Ag. Vasiliou, turn left and head north onto **Ethnikis Antistasis** to reach **Plateia Petrinou**, recognizable by the large, Neoclassical Maliaropouli Theater. Continue on Eth. Antistasis past pedestrian-only **Deligianni**, which runs perpendicular to Eth. Antistasis. Farther up, the city **park** will be on your right. At the center of the park, to the left of Eth. Antistasis as you face Pl. Ag. Vasiliou, is **Plateia Areus**, with a 5m tall statue of war hero Kolokotronis.

PELOPONNESE

Bank: National Bank (☎27102 71 110), in Pl. Kolokotronis. **Currency exchange** and a **24hr. ATM.** Open M-Th 8am-2:30pm, F 8am-2pm.

Police: Spetseropoulou 20 (☎27102 22 229), 1km from Pl. Kolokotronis. Walk toward the train station and go right at the traffic light; it's another 150m.

Hospital: (☎27102 38 542), at the end of Erithrou Stavrou. Walk straight ahead with your back to the church from Pl. Ag. Vasiliou; the road becomes E. Stavrou, which intersects with Panargadon after 500m. At the intersection, turn left. After 300m, look right, and you'll see the hospital.

Telephones: OTE, 280 Ktovriou 29 (☎27102 22 999). From Pl. Ag. Vasiliou, take Eth. Antistasis and go left on 28 Oktovriou at the National Bank branch. Offices are upstairs. Open M, W, Sa 7:30am-3pm; Tu and Th-F 7:30am-8:30pm.

Internet Access: At most cafes and at the bus station (p. 241). **Cinema Billiards Club,** 45 Kennedy or 2 Deligianni (☎27102 38 010), to the right off Eth. Antistasis walking from Kolokotronis. 10am-4pm €1 per hr.; 4pm-midnight €2 per hr.; midnight-2am €2.50 per hr. Open daily 10am-2am.

Post Office: Pl. Ag. Vasiliou (☎27102 22 565), behind Galaxy Hotel. Turn right 1 block past the war museum onto Nikitara. Open M-F 7:30am-8pm. **Postal Code:** 22100.

ACCOMMODATIONS

All of Tripoli's hotels are in or near the *plateias*. As a transportation hub with some of the best nightlife in the region, the city draws village youth looking for weekend clubs, businessmen attending conventions, and a diverse mix of international travelers stuck for the night, but it still lacks budget accommodations.

Hotel Alex, Georgiou 26 (☎27102 23 465). The leather and marble lobby and shiny silver elevator give way to spotless white rooms, each with big bath, A/C, TV, phone, and balcony. Breakfast €7. Free Wi-Fi. Wheelchair-accessible. Singles €50; doubles €80; triples €90; suites €100. MC/V. ❹

Arcadia Hotel, Pl. Kolokotroni 1 (☎27102 25 551). Recently redesigned with modern decor, this hotel has raised the standard in comfort, style, and unfortunately price. Each room has flatscreen TV, A/C, internet, and carpeted floors. Breakfast included. Wheelchair-accessible. Singles €60; doubles €90. MC/V. ❺

Hotel Anaktorikon, 48 Eth. Antistassis (☎27102 25 545), between Deligiannis and the city park. Old-world elegance and perks at decent prices. The plush red carpeting leads to sitting areas with artwork, luxurious red brocade couches, and a piano. Each room has A/C, TV, phone, minibar, balcony, and a large bath with tub. Singles €50; doubles €70-80. MC/V. ❹

FOOD

Tripoli's restaurants offer a few surprises for the well-seasoned traveler in Greece: spicy curries, beef filets, and whole grain breads. Many dining options are tucked away on unnamed side streets that abut churches and are covered by a canopy of overhanging branches. This romantic atmosphere provides a quiet escape from the traffic of the squares. Unlike the rooms in Tripoli, the restaurants generally provide a good value.

Yades, Malliaropou 9 (☎27102 37 643). Pasta dishes are the local favorite. The entrees are made with local products, but seasoned with international flavors. Always attracts a crowd. Entrees €6-14. MC/V. ❸

Faces Bar and Restaurant, Deligianni 15 (☎27102 27 750), on the corner of Eth. Antistasis. This aptly-named establishment's walls are decorated with the pictures of many famous 20th-century icons. Although the eatery is Chicago-themed—its owner is a former Windy City bookie—its food retains a Hellenic flair. Salads €2.90-8.90. Vegetarian linguini €7.90. Entrees €6-29. Open daily 9am-2am Cash only. ❷

Hungry?, on the corner of Deligianni and Tasou. Large portions of delicious pizza (€2.80 per slice) leave no doubt as to why Tripoli's youth stop here regularly before going out. Burgers €2.20. Open 24hr. Cash only. ❶

ENTERTAINMENT AND NIGHTLIFE

The exuberant nightlife scene is difficult to summarize: very similar (and enjoyable) bars and cafes line the streets surrounding the main square, most of which fill up at night. Local high school students crowd the cafe-bars in the narrow pedestrian-only area around Deligianni and Eth. Antistasis. In the summer, posters advertise dance groups, choirs, and plays performed in the city's main *plateias* and nearby villages. The side roads branching off of and parallel to Deligianni are home to some clubs. Cover is generally €10. The **Tegea Panigyris** is a theater and dance festival in nearby Tegea, kicked off each year on August 14. During the festival, public transportation shuttles Greeks out to the town, but for a regular schedule of local bus routes, check out the large sign in front of the Arcadia Hotel.

Cova. Pop music plays in a retro 19th-century bar, with high ceilings, tiles, stained glass, chandeliers, and lots of color. Beer €4. Mixed drinks €6. Open daily 8am-3am.

Prince, across the street from Hungry? Decorated in a modern Middle Eastern theme with bright paintings on the walls. Beer €5. Mixed drinks €7. Open daily 9am-3am.

PYLOS Πύλος ☎27230

Cradled in the Messina hills, Pylos rests on the bay of Navarino. It enjoys spectacular summer sunsets that paint the sky shades of orange and purple as the sun disappears behind Sfaktiria, the island that shelters the bay. With little in the way of museums or activities, you may find yourself restless within the town walls. Nearby towns along the coast, however, are just as idyllic and well worth exploring.

TRANSPORTATION

Buses: Station (☎27230 22 230), in the back of the *plateia* on the right when facing inland. Buses go to: **Athens** (6hr., 9am and 4:30pm, €10); **Finikouda** (20min., 4 per day 6am-7:15pm, €1.40); **Kalamata** (1hr.; M-F 8 per day 6:35am-8:20pm, Sa 7 per day, Su 4 per day 9am-8:20pm; €4.30); **Methoni** (15min.; M-Sa 5 per day 6am-9pm, Su 8am, 2:15, 9pm; €1.20).

Taxis: (☎27230 22 555). Line the left side of the *plateia*.

PRACTICAL INFORMATION

Most of the town's businesses line the *plateia*, the waterfront, and the roads leading to Methoni and Chora.

Bank: National Bank (☎27230 22 202), in the *plateia*. **24hr. ATM.** Open M-Th 8am-2:30pm, F 8am-2pm.

Police: (☎27230 22 316), in a building on the left side of the waterfront. **Tourist Police** (☎27230 23 733) also located here.

Medical Services: Health Center (☎27230 22 315), on the road heading right from the *plateia*. Open 24hr.

PELOPENNESE

Internet Access: The town of Pylos has Wi-Fi. Cards providing service may be purchased in Pylos at **Pandigital** (☎27230 28 201), 1 block from the town square heading toward Kalamata. €10 per 10hr. Computers with internet also available at Pandigital. €2.50 per hr.

Post Office: (☎27230 22 247). Facing inland at the bus station, turn right and walk up a block; it's on the left. Open M-F 7:30am-2pm. **Postal Code:** 24001.

ACCOMMODATIONS AND CAMPING

You'll spot "rooms to let" signs as the bus gets into town from Kalamata.

Hotel Miremare (☎27230 22 751), on the waterfront. Open since 1945. Bright, colorful rooms with arts-and-crafts posters and decorations, TVs, fridges, baths, and balconies facing the sea. Breakfast included. Singles €40-50; doubles €50-60; triples €60-70. Cash only. ❹

Hotel Nilefs, 4 Rene Pyot (☎27230 22 518), behind the Archaeological Museum. Dino-sized rooms with colorful baths, A/C, TVs; some have balconies. Singles €30-40; doubles €40-60; triples €60-72. Cash only. ❸

Camping Erodios (☎27230 28 240; www.erodioss.gr), about 10km north of Pylos. The best of the beach camping in the area. Laundry facilities, beach volleyball, a self-service restaurant, mini market, and rooms and bungalows with A/C and TVs. Camping €4-7; bungalows €40-60. Prices vary seasonally. Cash only. ❶

FOOD

Many waterfront restaurants serve *taverna* staples alongside fabulous sunset views.

Gregoris (☎27230 22 621). Signs lead the way to the restaurant up the hill on the road leading to Kalamata. The best of Pylos cuisine. Eat dishes made from the catch of the day, often stewed according to old family recipes, in a backyard filled with flowers and grape vines. Try the succulent stuffed tomatoes. Salads and starters €3-5. Entrees €5-7. Cash only. ❷

Koykos (☎27230 22 950), also up the road to Kalamata, a bit past Gregoris, has seating on the water's edge. Although slightly overdone in its homage to Greek interior design (think marble floors, brick columns, and stone arches), the classic Greek *taverna* dishes are delicious. Salads €2.50-4. Entrees €5-7.50. Cash only. ❷

SIGHTS AND BEACHES

FORTRESSES. Defensive edifices guard both sides of Navarino Bay. **Neocastro,** to the south, is easily accessible from the town; walk up the road to Methoni and turn right at the sign reading "Frourio" (Frourio). Built by the Turks in the 16th century, the fortress was won by the Greeks during the War of Independence. The well-preserved walls enclose 19 acres of land. Boasting a magnificent view of the bay, inside are a citadel and graceful church, which was originally a mosque. If you find the explanations lacking, ask a friendly staff member. The **Museum of the Rene Puaux Collection,** to the left as you enter the site, contains artistic works celebrating Greek triumph in the War of Independence from the personal collection of French journalist Rene Puaux. Prior to the museum's creation, the building was a maximum-security prison and occupied by Germans. (☎27230 22 010. Site and museum open Tu-Su 8:30am-3pm. €3, seniors and students €2, EU students and children free.)

SFAKTERIA. Just offshore, this isle is famed as the site of a rare Spartan defeat during the Peloponnesian War and home to the remains of a defensive wall built during that period. Sfaktiria has a number of war memorials and a

PELOPENNESE

wooden church built by Russian soldiers without the use of a single nail. Aging aristocrats desperate for an heir may want to make use of the island's natural arch; legend has it that any pregnant woman who walks under it will bear a male child. *(To see the islands up close, you can take a boat tour from the port. Inquire at the small booth across from the port police. ☎ 27230 23 115. 2hr. €8-10 per person. 11am-9pm.)*

BEACHES. If the tiny plots of sand that locals call "the beach" in Pylos don't do it for you, comparatively sizable beaches surround the town. Buses to Athens and Kyparissia pass by sandy, shallow, and much wider **Yialova beach**, 6km north of town, where sunken ships poke out from the waters. Just ask the bus driver to let you off. The **Navarino Fortress** lies at the end of the beach, between Yialova and the more famous, seemingly never-ending **Xrisi Ammos** (Golden Sand) beach. *(Buses to Kyparissia can drop you off on a side road, and the beach is 3km away. Because of the infrequency of public transportation, especially on weekends, you may want to use private transportation. The motorboat tour booth will take tourists to the Golden beach for an extra €2 per person and stay for 3hr. to allow for swimming.)*

LACONIA Λακωνία

Visitors to Laconia, most famous as the home to ancient Greece's most formidable city-state, Sparta, will find the terrain surprisingly un-spartan in its offerings. With some of the Peloponnese's highest peaks, the region features craggy mountains. Ancient olive groves and ruins hint at the long history that has unfolded in Laconia over the centuries. While Sparta's name may attract you to the region, the cities are not where you will find the true essence of Laconia. Head on the roads winding between orchards and hike the surrounding peaks. There you will discover plenty of accommodations and campgrounds hidden in the web between the urban centers.

SPARTA Σπάρτη ☎27310

This—is—Sparta. Built on top of the ancient city, modern Sparta's gritty urban sprawl barely hints at its historic military past other than in the names of its streets. Most unfortunately, the modern city leaves only a few of the ancient ruins explosed for the curious traveler. Unless you have a burning desire to see the Spartan battle fields, explore the city's well-advertised Museum of the Olive, or wrestle with wolves, don't bother wasting time in Sparta; the time is better used by heading to nearby Mystras, a magnificent archaeological site.

TRANSPORTATION

Buses: The station (☎27310 26 441) is downhill on Lykourgou toward the Archaeological Museum. Continue past a small forested area on your right; it's on the right, 10 blocks from the town center. The bus station is often crowded and not particularly tourist-friendly, as there often are confusing transfers on the bus routes. To: **Areopoli** (1hr., 4 per day 9am-5:45pm, €6); **Athens** (3hr., 11 per day 5:45am-8pm, €18) via **Tripoli** (1hr., €4) and **Corinth** (2hr., €12); **Gythion** (45min., 6 per day 9am-9pm, €4); **Kalamata** (1hr., 9am and 2:30pm, €4); **Monemvasia** (2½hr., 3 per day 11:45am-8:30pm, €8.70); **Mystras** (20min., hourly 9am-7pm, €2); **Neapoli** (3hr., 4 per day 7am-7:30pm, €16).

ORIENTATION AND PRACTICAL INFORMATION

Sparta's main streets, **Paleologou** and **Lykourgou**, have most of the city's services. They intersect in the center at the town hall. From there, the *plateia* is one block uphill along Lykourgou away from the bus station. Walking uphill toward the *plateia* along Paleologou will bring you to Ancient Sparta. To reach the center of town from the bus station, go about 10 blocks slightly uphill on Lykourgou.

Tourist Office: (☎27310 26 771), on the 3rd fl. of the town hall, in the glass building in the far left corner of the *plateia* facing away from Paleologou. English spoken. Info about Sparta and some hotel info available. Open M-F 8am-2pm.

Bank: National Bank, Paleologou 106 (☎27310 23 845), 3 blocks toward Ancient Sparta from Lykourgou and the town center. Has a **24hr. ATM, currency exchange,** and long lines. Open M-Th 8am-2:30pm, F 8am-2pm.

Police: ☎27310 24 852, on Ep. Vresthenis, off Lykourgou, 1 block past the bus station toward the *plateia*. Open 24hr. The **tourist police** (☎27310 20 492) is in the same building. Open daily 8am-9pm.

Hospital: Nosokomeio (☎27310 28 671), 1km north of Sparta. 7 buses per day (€1) go there. Open 24hr.

Internet Access: Many cafes have free Wi-Fi. **Public Library** (☎27310 21 180) on Lykourgou, 4 blocks from town hall heading toward Mystras. Free internet, plus a small selection of English books. Open M-Sa 9am-7pm.

Post Office: Archidamou 84 (☎27310 26 565), off Lykourgou, halfway between the bus station and the center. Open M-F 7:30am-2pm. **Postal Code:** 23100.

ACCOMMODATIONS

It's hard to find a bargain among the numerous mid-range hotels grouped on Paleologou. There are really no stand-out choices in the city, and you may find the accommodations lacking in quality and hospitality, not a traditional Spartan virtue.

Sparti Inn, Thermopylon 109 (☎27310 21 021), on the corner of Gortsologou. The best choice in town. Clean and spacious rooms with large windows. Rates are negotiable, so don't hesitate to bargain when checking in. Wheelchair-accessible. Singles from €40; doubles €50. Extra beds available. MC/V. ❸

Hotel Cecil, Paleologou 125 (☎27310 24 980), 5 blocks north of Lykourgou toward Ancient Sparta, on the corner of Paleologou and Thermopylon. Singles €30; doubles €45; triples €55. Cash only. ❷

Hotel Dioscouri, Lykourgou 182 (☎27310 28 484), at the intersection with Atridon. Decent rooms in good condition because of recent renovations. Singles €40; doubles €50; triples €55. Cash only. ❸

FOOD

Sparta's restaurants serve standard menus at reasonable prices. Supermarkets and bakeries fill the side streets of Paleologou, while cheap fast-food joints surround the main *plateia*.

Zeus, in the Maniatis Hotel. The city's best offering has the crowds to prove it. A less than Spartan menu features international and Greek dishes, with a range of spices adding a little flair to their mains. Appetizers €4-9. Entrees €12-20. Open daily noon-midnight. Reservations recommended for dinner. MC/V. ❸

Diethnes (☎27310 28 636), on Paleologou, a few blocks to the right of the main intersection with Lykorgou facing the *plateia*. An intimate garden with orange trees may lead you to forget you're in the middle of a busy city. Tasty Greek food with a few vegetarian options (€4.50). Lamb entrees (€7), paired with all types of sides, are the specialty. Salads €2.50-4.50. Entrees €5-8. Open daily 8am-midnight. Cash only. ❷

Elyssé Restaurant, Paleologou 113 (☎27310 29 896), across from the National Bank. Busy at all times, Elyssé offers a large, fresh selection of local specialties and traditional Greek dishes. The staff recommends 1 of the many vegetable entrees (€2.80-6) or the *bardouniobiko* (chicken in tomato sauce, onions, and feta; €6.90). Open daily 11am-midnight. Cash only. ❷

📷 SIGHTS

ANCIENT SPARTA. The few remains of the ancient city lie in an olive grove 1km north of town. An enormous statue of buff **Leonidas,** the famous warrior king who fell at the Battle of Thermopylae in 480 BC—and strangely resembles actor Gerard Butler—looms over the northern end of Paleologou. The Spartans built a large tomb for their leader, but his body was never found. The tomb, therefore, still lays empty in a public park to the left of the road heading up to the ruins. To reach the ruins, turn left at the statue, then make your first right and follow the signs. The otherwise unimpressive site is highlighted by a few fragments of the acropolis and the remains of the ancient theater. To reach the theater, turn left at the sign to the first path branching off the main cobbled road.

ARCHAEOLOGICAL MUSEUM. A beautiful, well-kept park hides a fountain, assorted ancient statuary, and the museum. Headless statues usher visitors into the museum, which features a large collection of everything from beautiful mosaics to haunting votive masks used in ritual dances at the sanctuary of Artemis Orthia. The rooms to the right, facing inward, display various representations of the Dioscuri—the twins Castor and Pollux—locally revered as symbols of brotherly love and honor, as well as larger-than-life third-century BC marble heads of Hercules and Hera. One room is devoted to prehistoric pottery, weaponry, and jewelry. English captions accompany all the artifacts. (*On Lykourgou, across from the OTE. ☎27310 28 575. Open Tu-Su 8am-7:30pm. €2, seniors and students €1, EU students and children free.*)

COUMANTAROS ART GALLERY. This collection has a small permanent collection of 19th-century Dutch and French paintings, including one by Gustave Courbet. Upstairs, the gallery hosts temporary exhibits from the National Gallery in Athens. (*Paleologou 123, next to Hotel Cecil. ☎27310 81 557. Open M-Sa 9am-3pm,Su 10am-2pm. Free.*)

MUSEUM OF THE OLIVE AND GREEK OLIVE OIL. This refreshing non-Spartan site, housed in a

IN RECENT NEWS

JAILBREAK DÉJÀ VU

Many criminals daydream abou daring jailbreaks; few, howeve manage to turn these dreams into reality. Two Greek robbers defied all odds and managed to pull i off... twice.

In 2006, Vassilis Paleokostas and Alket Rizaj were doing time in the Korydallos Prison, a high security facility near Athens. During their daily exercise time, a helicop ter landed in the prison's centra yard. In hopped Paleokostas and Rizaj, and off they went—leaving behind the astonished guards who assumed the helicopter was simply bringing a visit by prison inspectors. Both men were eventu ally recaptured, and (perhaps fool ishly) returned to Korydallos.

In February of 2009—one da before Paleokostas and Rizaj had been scheduled to appear in cour over their first escape—anothe helicopter swung low over Kory dallos at exercise time, dropping down a rope ladder into the waiting hands of the two convicts. Guards firing up at the escape attemp had to take cover when a woman with an automatic rifle blazed back, and the chopper managed to get away with both men on board. Police found the aban doned aircraft later, its pilot bound and gagged inside. A couple pos ing as vacationers had chartered his helicopter, and then hijacked i to use for the prison break.

The aftermath? Resignations from the secretary of the ministry of justice, the inspector-general o prisons, and the head of Korydal los—and two more Greek crooks back at large.

beautiful building, stands out among the ubiquitous concrete apartment complexes. Three floors of exhibits explain the economic, technological, and cultural significance of the olive. (*Othonos Amalias 129. Walk 3 blocks to the left of Lykourgou facing the plateia and 4 blocks to the right; it's on the left as the road ends. ☎ 27310 89 315. Open M and W-Su 10am-6pm. €3, students and seniors €1.50, EU students free.*)

OTHER RUINS. Many of the ruins surrounding Sparta are reachable by foot, though a few require a car. From the northeastern corner of town, near Hotel Apollon, a 10min. walk east along Ton 118 toward Tripoli leads to the **Sanctuary of Artemis Orthia,** where Spartan youths proved their courage by enduring repeated floggings. Three remaining platforms of the **Shrine to Menelaus and Helen** are 5km away in the same direction. Take the road to Tripoli, past the bridge, and turn at the sign for "Menelaus Palace." The ruins of a **Shrine to Apollo** are 5km south on the road to Gythion in the town of Amiklai.

◤ NIGHTLIFE

At night, the side streets off Paleologou swell with young people, while the *plateia* draws families and an older crowd that drinks away the hours at outdoor cafes. Due to the literally Spartan laws, nightlife ends earlier on weekdays than in many other Greek cities (3:30am).

Ministry Music Hall, on Paleologou 1 block north of the intersection with Lykourgou. Brimming with energy, people, and, of course, loud music, the Ministry is the place where Sparta's hipsters go to see and be seen. The interior is adorned with unicycles and mandolins, and the atmosphere is comfortable and welcoming. Beer €2-3.50. Mixed drinks from €6. Open daily 8am-2am.

Leghi Spartis, in the beautiful Old Town Hall in the *plateia.* Caters to those seeking a slightly calmer scene. Popular with families, it offers coffee (€2-3.50), mixed drinks (€5-6), snacks, desserts, and sandwiches. Open daily 9am-3am.

Caprice, in the back of the *plateia.* A deceptively large, popular club tucked behind neon green lights and small palm trees with a large indoor space past the outdoor lounge. White leather-backed chairs support Sparta's most chic as they stiffly sip their drinks of choice. Beer €3-5. Mixed drinks €6-7. Open daily 9pm-5am.

◤ DAYTRIP FROM SPARTA

▒MYSTRAS Μύστρας
Buses leaving Sparta's main station and the corner of Lykourgou and Leonidou (20min., 9 per day 7:20am-8:20pm, €1.20) stop at the restaurant Xenia near the main entrance at the bottom of the hill. It gets hot and requires scrambling around, so go early, bring water, and wear comfortable shoes. Consider getting another resource like Guidebook Mystras, by Manolis Chatzidakis (€6.50), to supplement your exploration. Free maps are available. ☎ 27310 83 377. Open daily 8am-7:30pm. €5, students and children €3, EU students free.

Once the religious center of all Byzantium and the locus of Constantinople's rule over the Peloponnese, Mystras lays dormant, a magnificent fortified city saturated with remains of Byzantine churches, chapels, and monasteries. The city was founded by French Crusader **Guillaume de Villeharduin** in 1249 with the construction of a central castle at the top of the hill. It first changed hands in 1262 when the Venetians took over. Under Byzantine rule, the town flourished; in the following centuries it grew into a city, draining Sparta of its inhabitants as they sought protection in Mystras's fortress. By the early 15th century, Mystras was an intellectual and cultural center with a thriving silk industry. The golden era collapsed when the city fell to the Turks in 1460. Aside from the brief recapture of the city by the Venetians (1687-1715), the Turks maintained control of the city until the Greek War of Independence. When King Otto founded modern Sparta in 1834, Mystras was ignored in favor of a new, modern city. The churches, frescoes, and ruins of Mystras now overlook the sprawling city.

An intricate network of paths traces through three tiers of ruins, descending from royalty to nobility to commoners. Although not as well-preserved as many of the religious edifices that encircle it—they're almost completely intact, if a bit faded at the frescoes—the dramatic **castle** gives a breathtaking view of the site and the surrounding countryside. Most people climb to the castle first and work their way down. The **palaces,** which date from the AD 13th to 15th centuries, are downhill from the castle, and feature a large throne room among their pointed arches and dressed stone walls. Next to them is **Agia Sophia,** built by Manuel Katakouzenos, the first despot of Morea. This is where the city's royalty were buried, among the striking, still-visible frescoes. Farther downhill lies the magnificent **Pantanassa,** a convent with an elaborately ornamented facade, frescoes, and an icon of Mary said to work miracles. The ground floor displays many wall-paintings from the 17th and 18th centuries. On the lower tier you can find the **Metropolis of Agios Demetrios,** with detailed frescoes, flowery courtyard, and a small museum of architectural fragments, clothing, and jewelry. Its air-conditioned room holds everything from 14th-century manuscripts to marble sculptures to a reconstruction of a Byzantine woman's shoe. Also on the lower tier are the two churches that comprise the fortified monastery of **Brontochion.** The first, **Aphentiko** (a.k.a. **"Hodigitria"**), glows with two-story frescoes depicting saints; **Agios Theodoros** is its neighbor. In the far corner of the lower tier, every centimeter of the awe-inspiring **Church of Peribleptos** is bathed in colorful, exquisitely detailed religious paintings.

Though hotels are scarce, spending the night in Mystras is possible and, if you're looking for peace and quiet, preferable to staying in Sparta. The cheapest option is *domatia.* Owners will post signs outside their doors if rooms are available. One option are the **rooms ❷** above the Ellinas Restaurant on the main square. (☎27310 20 047. Doubles €25-35. Cash only.) The **Byzantine Hotel ❷,** also on the main square, offers reasonably priced and spacious rooms full of sunlight; many overlook the pool in the backyard. (☎27310 83 309. Wheelchair-accessible. Singles €30; doubles €50. MC/V.) Eateries are also clustered around the main square, the best of which is **Mistras Bistrot ❸.** Although the live music and art exhibitions are wonderful additions, the real focus is the exceptionally fresh food. (☎27310 29 350. Appetizers €5. Entrees €6-12.)

MANI Μάνη

Mani gets its name from the Greek word manis, which means "wrath" or "fury." Sparsely settled and encircling the intimidating Taygetus Mountains, the region juts out vulnerably into the surrounding sea. During Roman times, Mani founded the league of Free Laconians and threw off Spartan domination. Ever since, Maniots have resisted foreign rule, boasting even today that not one Ottoman set foot on their soil. While historically fierce and proud of it, Maniots are warm hosts to those who visit their well-preserved villages and unique, gray stone tower houses. Home to Byzantine ruins, small fishing villages, world-class beaches, and the famous Caretta sea turtle, Mani continues to surprise visitors with its diversity. The landscape follows suit: the lush north gives way to stark southern mountains, which stand out against the piercing blue oceans and endless stretches of sand and pebbles.

GYTHION Γύθειο   ☎27330

Gythion unfolds along a long stretch of waterfront, spreading inland where the steep hill pressing against the sea turns away from the coast. It is the southern part of town that distinguishes this pleasant seaside village from its neighbors. Here, a narrow causeway connects the offshore island of Marathonisi to the mainland. From town, the sight of the wooded isle stretching out into the bay adds character to an already gorgeous view, though the town sadly doesn't radiate the same beauty.

⌨ TRANSPORTATION

Ferries: To **Antikithera; Kissamos; Kithera;** and **Pireus.** Inquire at **Rozakis Travel** (☎27330 22 207), on the waterfront by the police station. Car and motorbike rentals are also available at Rozakis.

Buses: The bus station (☎27330 22 228) is on the northern end of the waterfront, opposite a park in the fast food restaurant Top Tzante. Buses go **Areopoli** (1hr., 4 per day 10:15am-6:45pm, €2.40) and **Sparta** (1hr., 6 per day 7:30am-7pm, €8.90) and continue from there on to other destinations.

Taxis: (☎27330 23 423). Line up outside the bus station.

✈ 🛈 ORIENTATION AND PRACTICAL INFORMATION

Going south from the bus station along the main harbor road, **Vasileos Pavlou,** you'll find most hotels on your right. Stores and offices crowd around the inland *plateia* by the bus station. The small **Plateia Mavromichali** appears as the road curves and continues to the dock. Vas. Pavlou turns into Proth. Genataki after the *plateia*; Proth. Genataki ends at the causeway to Marathonissi.

Bank: National Bank (☎27330 22 313), next to the bus station. **Currency exchange** and a **24hr. ATM.** Open M-Th 8am-2pm, F 8am-1:30pm.

Police: Vas. Pavlou (☎27330 22 100), halfway between the bus station and Pl. Mavromichali.

Pharmacy: Scattered throughout town; one (☎27330 22 036) is across from the bus station. Open M-F 8am-2pm and 5-9pm.

Medical Services: Health Clinic Proth. Genataki (☎27330 22 003), heading toward the causeway. The nearest hospital is in Sparta (p. 245).

Internet Access: Mystery Cafe (☎27330 25 177), on Kapsali, around the corner from the National Bank and down the street about 50m. €3 per hr. Open daily 11am-1am.

Post Office: Ermou 18 (☎27330 22 285). Facing the bus station, go around the left corner and trace the *plateia* to Archaiou Theatrou; follow it to the right for 2 blocks. Open M-F 7:30am-2:30pm. **Postal Code:** 23200.

⌂ ⌂ ACCOMMODATIONS AND CAMPING

Gythion has an overabundance of seaside *domatia* and hotels, so prices are low and negotiable. With the same modern amenities and more hospitality, these *domatia* are the best way to go if staying by the port. Many of the rooms are wonderfully refurbished. The best ones are found slightly beyond the center of the port. Head toward Marathonisi while keeping the water on your left and you will find signs for rooms to let.

▨ **Xenia Karlaftis Rooms** (☎27330 22 719), to the very left of the waterfront facing inland. Now run by Xenia's daughter, who offers juice and homemade desserts to her guests upon arrival, this 25-year-old establishment offers clean rooms with baths and

PELOPENNESE

views of Marathonissi; most have balconies and TVs. Kitchens available. Singles €25; doubles €30; triples €40; quads €45; apartments €60. ❷

Enoikiazomena Domatia (☎27330 25 000), next to Xenia's rooms. Clean and bright rooms overlooking the water. All the same amenities as Xena's, but slightly higher rates. Free internet. Singles €30, doubles €40. Cash only. ❷

Meltemi Camping (☎27330 22 833), on Mavrovouni beach, 4km out of town toward Areopoli. Overwhelming number of amenities for a campground, including showers, cooking area, washing machines (€4), market, restaurant, cinema, and pool. Electricity €3.50. €5 per person; €4 per child; €5 per tent; €4 per car. 2- to 5-person bungalows €30-55. ❶

FOOD

Gythion's dining options are no different from any other visitor-friendly Greek town. A bakery is across the street from Masouleri Kokkalis, and many supermarkets and fruit stores cluster around the bus station. (Most open 7:30am-2pm and 6-9pm.)

Isalos Restaurant (☎27330 24 024), in the center of the main wharf strip. Try the steam oysters or any of the fresh, daily-changing fish options. Appetizers €4-8. Greek grill €10. Entrees €7-20. Cash only. ❸

To Nisaki (☎27330 23 830), on Marathonissi. An airy, calm setting for anyone looking to escape the waterfront *tavernas'* noisy crowds. Great views of the town during the day and at night, when the lights reflect of the gently rippling waters of the bay. Large windows keep the summer view intact during winter months. Salads €2.50-4.80. Tzatziki €3.20. Fish from €46 per kg. Grilled entrees €5.50-12. Open daily 10am-1am. ❷

Saga (☎27330 21 358), on Genataki just between the causeway and the *plateia*. Prides itself on its fresh fare and excellent service. Salads €3-7. Entrees €7.50-14. Fish from €15. Open daily 8am-1am. MC/V. ❸

◎ ⌐ SIGHTS AND BEACHES

MARATHONISSI. Gythion's must-see site is a small wooded island laden with mythology and history. Here, Paris and Helen are said to have consummated their love. Lovebirds still flock to the island's small chapel for frequent weddings. Also on the island is the **Museum of Mani,** which features pictures and stories detailing the unique region. The masterfully built **ancient theater** of Gythion, spanning 240°, has endured the centuries remarkably well. Its class divisions remain—note the differences between the seats for dignitaries in front and the simpler seats farther back. Though the ruins themselves are well-preserved, the current use of the surrounding field as a parking lot somewhat spoils the effect. The crumbling remains of ancient Roman walls that were destroyed by an earthquake lay scattered on the nearby hill. *(Heading away from the bus station, walk past the post office on Archaiou Theatrou until it ends at the theater entrance.)*

BEACHES. There is a disappointing **public beach** north of the bus station (walk with the water on your right); the better beaches are outside of town. **Mavrovouni,** home to the campgrounds, is 2km from Gythion toward Areopoli. Winds and deep waters make it a popular surfing spot. Plenty of beachgoers also hang out at one of the nearby bars along the 4.5km long beach, where beer runs €3-4 and mixed drinks are usually €5. Home to the endangered Loggerhead sea turtle *(Caretta caretta)*, Mavrovouni is also the site of a great deal of scientific research regarding the species. Visitors should ask the local tour agencies about precautions necessary to protect the turtles. *(From Gytheion, take one of the four*

PELOPENNESE

daily buses, a taxi (€3.50), or walk 30-40min.) Three kilometers north is rocky **Selinitsa,** known for its incredibly clear water and outstanding views of Gythion at night. *(Take a taxi (€5) or walk, following the signs that point the way.)* **Vathy,** a well-known and well-loved spot among locals, 10km along the road to Areopoli, has a mix of sun and shade that appeals to both the sun worshippers and the sunburned. *(Taxis €11.)*

AREOPOLI Αρεόπολη ☎27330

A unique combination of mountain scruff and romantic Byzantine architecture, Areopoli has a shaggy natural charm that lures travelers to its cobbled, winding streets and traditionally designed stone buildings. Just a ten minute walk from the main *plateia* is the sea, adding to the town's elemental beauty.

TRANSPORTATION. The bus station (☎27330 51 229) is a corner counter in Xasero Taverna, across from the small chapel in the corner cafe of the *plateia.* **Buses** from Areopoli go to Athens (5hr., 4 per day 8am-6pm, €22.70) via Gythion (35min., €2.30) and Sparta (1hr., €6) and to Itilo (20min.; M-Sa 6:30, 9am, 1:45pm; €1.20). From Itilo, you can catch a bus to Kalamata (4 per day). A bus running into Mani goes to the **Dirou Caves** (leaves 11am, returns 12:45pm; €1.20), Gerolimenas (40min., 3 per day 11:45am-7:30pm, €2.90), and Vatheia (1hr.; M, W, F 1:45pm; €3.60), with limited service on Sunday and holidays. If you need a **taxi** and do not see one idling on the square, call ☎69727 28 72.

ORIENTATION AND PRACTICAL INFORMATION. All services can be found in the *plateia* or off Kapetan Matapa, the main road running into the Old Town from the *plateia.* To find the **National Bank,** with a **24hr. ATM,** walk on the main road away from Pirgos Dirou and make a left on the street closest to the gas station. (☎27330 51 293. Open M-F 9am-1pm.) The **police** are 500m out of town on the main road toward Pirgos Dirou. (☎27330 52 300.) As you walk facing the sea, a **pharmacy** is two doors down from the post office. (☎27330 29 510. Open M 8am-2pm, Tu-F 8am-2pm and 5-9pm.) A **health center** is 50m down a street that starts in the main *plateia* and runs away from the ocean, next to the first church; signs point the way. (☎27330 51 259. 24hr.) Opposite the health center is the **OTE.** (☎27330 51 299. Open daily 8am-1pm.) The **post office** is on the street with the National Bank, across from Hotel Mani. It **exchanges currency** and traveler's checks, and offers **Poste Restante.** (☎27330 51 230. Open M-F 7:30am-2pm.) **Postal Code:** 23062.

ACCOMMODATIONS. Though you won't find much variety in price, Areopoli's rooms range from century-old tower houses to modern hotels. Follow Kapetan Matapa and turn left at the end to get to **Tsimova's Rooms ❷,** behind the church in the Old Town. A haven for history buffs, this 300-year-old house supposedly once hosted Kolokotronis, the famed general of the War of Independence. A small garden sits between the reception room and the spacious, uniquely appointed rooms, which have air-conditioning, TVs, mini-fridges, and baths. (☎27330 51 301. Reservations recommended. Singles €25-40; doubles €35-60; triples €40-60.) On the same road as the National Bank, **Hotel Trapela ❺** might take the cake for highest rates, but prices are negotiable in low season. Homemade pastries at breakfast, romantic stone-walled rooms with aged woodbeam ceilings, and a private garden enveloped in flowers are just part of the experience. (☎27330 52 690. Singles €60; doubles and triples €60-80; quads €120. MC/V.) **Kouris Hotel ❷,** situated on the town's square, has 11 rooms with standard amenities and wonderful hospitality. (☎27330 51 340. Singles €35; doubles €40. Cash only.)

PELOPENNESE

☐ **FOOD.** Restaurants line the square. A local favorite is **Nikola's Place ❷**. The menu shifts on a nightly basis depending upon what ingredients are fresh. (☎27330 51 366. Entrees €6-10. Open daily 8am-1am Cash only.) **Mparmpa Petros Taverna ❷** is along Kapetan Matapa to the left when you walk from the small square toward the large church of the Old Town. The specialty dishes use pork raised on the owners' family farm. Before settling into the romantic garden seating area, you can take the friendly staff's tour of the kitchen. (☎27330 51 205. Pork with wine sauce €8. Entrees €6.50-9. Open daily 1pm-late. Cash only.) Across from the church in the Old Town, quiet **Lithostroto ❷** has an extensive menu and outdoor seating on the cobblestone street right under a tree. (☎27330 54 240. Stuffed vine leaves €6.50. Starters and salads €3-5. Grilled meats €6-9. Cash only.)

🗺 **DAYTRIP FROM AREOPOLI: DIROU CAVES** (Σπήλαια Δυρού). Part of a subterranean river, the unusual ⬛**Dirou Caves** (**Spilia Dirou** or **Vlihada Cave**) are a cool and quiet escape. The caverns are strung with tiny crystalline stalactites, while vermillion stalagmites slice the water's surface. Discovered at the end of the 19th century and opened to the public in 1971, the caves have yet to be fully explored. Experts speculate that they are 70km long and may extend all the way to Sparta. The 1.3km boat ride through the freshwater cave lasts about 30min., followed by a 10min. walk out of the caves. The tiny boats, guided only by a small oar, rock their way through the narrow, incredibly low channels. Passengers often have to duck and lean to avoid the stalactites, which change from brilliant orange to green in the various small enclosures. Floating lights illuminate the tour, but unlit recesses branch off on each side. On your way out, you can also visit the small **Neolithic Museum,** which displays findings from Alepotrypa Cave at Dirou. The unique olive leaves have remained relatively intact from Neolithic times, and the complete skeleton of a young woman is morbid but intriguing. A small pebble beach, popular with local children, sits to the side of the caves' exit.

MONEMVASIA Μονεμβασία ☎27320

Byzantine enthusiasts on their way to Monemvasia's sights may be puzzled when the bus drops them off in a modern town. The New Town of Monemvasia (a.k.a. "Gefyra") is a logical starting point for entry onto the island that contains the famed historical city. Below the monumental fortress built into precipitous cliffs, Old Town Monemvasia's winding cobblestone paths, low archways, and narrow flights of stairs accentuate the town's medieval origins. A week could easily be spent in the Old Town and its environs, which are all within striking distance of dozens of beaches, excellent hiking trails, and a few vineyards.

▣ TRANSPORTATION

Monemvasia's remote location makes getting around difficult; rental car or moped will considerably improve your travels.

Buses: Station inside **Malavsia Travel Agency,** on Spartis. Check Malavisa for schedules. All buses go through **Molai** (30min.; 7:15 am, 2:15, 5:15 pm; €3). From Molai they continue to **Athens** (5hr.), **Sparta** (2hr.), and **Tripoli** (3hr.).

Shuttles: Run between **Geyfra** and the Old Town, stopping at the kiosk before the bridge in the New Town, and outside the main gate of the Old Town (every 15min. 8am-midnight, €1).

Taxis: (☎27320 61 274). A few line up on one side of the bridge near the bus stop.

PELOPENNESE

⊞ ⁊ ORIENTATION AND PRACTICAL INFORMATION

Facing the causeway from the village, the harbor is to the right, and a pebbled beach is to the left. The main street runs inland from the causeway before becoming **Spartis** and splitting off to the right at the fork. Most offices are on this street, while the restaurants and hotels line the water and the smaller roads that turn off from the main stretch.

Tours: Malvasia Travel Agency (☎27320 61 752). Exchanges currency, arranges moped rentals, and sells tickets for ferries and Flying Dolphins. Also houses the bus station. Open daily 8am-3pm and 5-8pm; reduced hours in low season.

Bank: National Bank (☎27320 61 201). **24hr. ATM** and **currency exchange.** Open M-Th 8am-1:30pm, F 8am-1pm.

Police: (☎27320 61 210), on Spartis, 50m to the right of Malvasia Travel. Open 24hr.

Internet Access: Baywatch Cafe, on the left when facing the causeway 25m down the pebble beach. Internet €3 per hr., min. €1.50. Beer €2. Coffee €2-4. Open daily 11am-2am.

Post Office: (☎27320 61 231), next to the National Bank. Open M-F 7:30am-2pm. **Postal Code:** 23070.

⌂ ⌂ ACCOMMODATIONS AND CAMPING

A room in one of the Old Town's traditional hotels will cost more than a room on the mainland (doubles from €80). An abundance of *domatia* options in the New Town keeps prices down (doubles €25-40).

Hotel Belessis (☎27320 61 217), about 250m from the causeway down Spartis to the right at the fork. 20 rooms in 2 picturesque stone buildings. The hard rock exterior belies cozy, comfortable rooms with A/C, TVs, baths, and lots of wood paneling. Rooms in the uphill building feel slightly more modern, though not more comfortable. Singles and doubles €30-50; 4-person apartment with kitchenette and 2 baths €60-80. ❸

Hotel Flower of Monemvassia (☎27320 61 395), immediately to the right when you enter the city. Very hospitable owners. Breakfast included. Singles from €45; doubles from €55. Prices are negotiable. ❹

Camping Paradise (☎27320 61 123), 4km along the water on the mainland beach. ❶

⊡ FOOD

If dining in Old Monemvasia seems attractive, try one of the first *tavernas* off the main road on the right. Bakeries and fast food are to the left off Spartis as the road forks by the harbor. For groceries, **Lekakis Supermarket** is on the left two blocks up off Spartis, across from Malvasia Travel. (☎27320 61 167. Open M-Sa 7am-9pm.)

Restaurant Matoula (☎27320 61 660). The oldest *taverna* in town. The gorgeous views and traditional ambience justify the €8 moussaka. It might be hard to resist a bottle of regional wine (€7-23) and the nut cake with ice cream (€4) for dessert. *Dolmades* €8. Entrees €8-14. Open daily noon-midnight. MC/V. ❸

Korali Grill House (☎27320 61 134). To the left walking away from the causeway, on the water just after the dock landing. Cheap and delicious pitas (souvlaki, gyros, and burgers; €1.70) that threaten to run its more expensive neighbors out of business. It also doubles as **Paros Restaurant,** which serves seafood (€7-30) and nicely rounds out the food groups. Grilled entrees €6.50-12. Open daily 11am-2am. ❷

Akrogiali Tavern (☎27320 61 056). Walk over the bridge into the Old Town and continue 400m; it's on the right with seating to your left. Food and service is so good that locals have their rehearsal wedding dinners here. Since it's tucked away, you can enjoy traditional Greek cuisine without a gaggle of tourists around.

SIGHTS

OLD TOWN MONEMVASIA. The medieval city deserves the constant attention it receives. An undeniable other-worldliness shrouds the city, adding an aura of medieval mystery to every tunnel and turn. The town's name, which means "one way," makes sense once you've passed through the single gate to Old Town Monemvasia, entering a city frozen in time. No cars or bikes are allowed through the gate, so packhorses bearing groceries and cases of beer are led back and forth to restaurants. Upon entering the gate, a cobbled street, lined with the surprisingly charming and whimsical decorations of tourist shops, winds through to the central *plateia*. There, the 1697 church of **Christos Elkomenos** (Christ in Chains) is on the left as you face the ocean, next to the bell tower. Continue on; the Old Town's greatest charm lies in the winding, nameless side streets to the fortified sea wall.

ARCHAEOLOGICAL MUSEUM. An air-conditioned former mosque, the museum chronicles Monemvasia's 13th-century prominence and strong commercial ties to the Western world. *(On the right of the plateia while facing the ocean. ☎27320 61 403. Open M noon-7:30pm, Tu-Su 8:30am-7:30pm. Free.)*

AGIA SOFIA. The 12th-century Agia Sofia is the centerpiece of the Old Town. Though invading Turks defaced its frescoes, its oft-photographed beauty is still breathtaking, as is the dramatic drop to the sea behind the church. It is balanced on the edge of the rock cliffs that also hold the remains of the city's castle. *(Go up the stairs behind the Christos Elkomenos bell tower, to the left off the main road walking toward the plateia and continue uphill until you reach the staircase, about 20min.)*

OTHER SIGHTS. At the top of the staircase where signs point down one short path to Agia Sofia, an arrow points the way to the **cistern** that still provides the town's water. Rain was once Monemvasia's only source of water, and the complex network of cisterns have continued to collect and distribute water since their conception. The hike along it is full of slippery stones and uneven ground, so wear suitable shoes. From Agia Sofia, arrows pointing uphill indicate the path to the **citadel.** The arched ruins nearest to the New Town, a 10min. walk away, are visible from the mainland and offer a magnificent view over Gefyra and the surrounding coast.

TIP **HANDICAPPED INACCESSIBLE.** Old Town Monemvasia's shortage of sidewalks, ramps, and elevators makes it nearly impossible for disabled travelers to explore the small island. The tourist office may be able to help make arrangements for visiting Monemvasia and other challenging areas nearby.

NEAPOLI Νεάπολις ☎27340

The most convenient gateway to Kithera from the Peloponnese, Neapoli is a small seaside destination. The town's pebble and dark-sand beaches are accessible down a flight of steps from the waterfront road, lined by restaurants.

Because travelers (mostly old Europeans) flow through Neapoli on their way to summer vacations in Kithera, hotel prices skyrocket from mid-July to

August. The best overall deal is probably **Hotel Arsenakos ❸**, Akti Voion 198. Rooms have ceiling-to-floor windows opening on to balconies that provide a refreshing sea breeze and views of the beach. Rooms have A/C, private baths, phones, balconies, fridges, and Wi-Fi. (From the port, keep the beach on your left and walk for 10min. ☎27340 22 991. Singles €35-55; doubles €45-60; triples €55-65; 4-person suites €110. MC/V.) **Hotel Vergina ❹** (☎27340 23 443) has higher prices but slightly more comfort. The added cost brings cable TVs and breakfast. (Singles €40-50; doubles €50-70. Cash only.) **Hotel Aivali ❷** (☎27340 22 287), at the corner of the street to the post office next to the bridge, rents large rooms with lots of natural light, air-conditioning, TVs, fridges, and balconies. (Singles €30-40; doubles €35-50.)

As you walk past the pier with the water on your right, there are a clump of restaurants with similar food and prices. **Tzivaeri ❷** serves affordable seafood dishes (€6-14) as well as a variety of other entrees (€5-8.50) to patrons seated outdoors on the walk above the beach. (☎27340 22 545. Stuffed peppers with cheese €4.50. Mixed meat dish €6.50. Open daily 6am-1am.) **Moreas ❷**, two blocks past Aivali with the water on the left, makes delectable meat and fish dishes for a mostly local clientele. Its outside tables are pulled as close to the beach as they can get, so you can watch the waves crash while you choose from the rotating menu. Indoors, the elegantly appointed dining room is set with non-paper tablecloths, a rarity on the *taverna* scene. (☎27340 23 845. Salads €2.50-5. Entrees €5-8. Fish €40-45 per kg. Open daily 12:30-5pm and 8:30pm-midnight.)

For the **ferry** to Kithera (1½hr., 1 per day, €11), purchase tickets at **Vatika Bay,** located about 500m from the port as you walk out of town with the water on your left. (☎27340 29 004. Open 2hr. before a ferry departure.) The **bus station** (☎27340 23 222) is two blocks inland of the main town street, perpendicular to the water. A **KTEL** sign pops out of the office and is visible from the main road. **Buses** only head toward Athens (6hr., 3 per day 8:15am-5pm, €30), often making stops in Gythio, Sparta, and Tripoli. Buses also run to Pounta, the port for Elafonissos (M-F 4 per day 7am-1:45pm, €1.20). The **National Bank,** with a **24hr. ATM,** is on the waterfront across from the pier. (Open M-Th 8am-2:30pm, F 8am-2pm). The **port authority** is one block from the National Bank on a small *plateia* behind the statue. (☎27340 22 228.) The **post office** is one block inland on Dimokratias, to the left of the waterfront as you face inland, past the bridge. (Open M-F 7:30am-2pm.) **Postal Code:** 23053.

KITHERA Κύθηρα   27360

According to myth, Cronus castrated his father Ouranos and threw his genitals into the sea. What washed up onto the shores of Kithera eventually became the goddess Aphrodite. Visitors, fortunately, do not have to make similar sacrifices to see why the island is divine. Beaches and coves stashed away in the island's 52km of coastline and dramatic ravines leading to Byzantine ruins are just a little of what the island has to offer. The island, still protected by its remote location, remains blissfully untouched by mass tourism.

PELOPENNESE

TRANSPORTATION

Public transportation does not exist on the island. If unable to rent a car or bike, bus tours are the best way to get acquainted with the island. Not renting a vehicle will limit your mobility, but Kithera will not disappoint if you choose your base wisely.

Flights: Kithera Island National Airport (☎27360 33 292), about 10km from Diakofti and 4km from Friligianika. **Olympic Airlines** (☎27360 33 362) flies to **Athens** once a day with increasing frequency during July and August (40min., €45).

Ferries: Depart and arrive at Diakofti. Port Authority (☎27360 34 222). Ferries go to **Neapoli** (1½hr., 2 per day, €13). Tickets are available through **Koroneos Travel** (☎27360 31 390). Call for reservations and timetables. Ferries also leave less frequently to **Chania, Crete; Gythio; Kalamata; Piraeus.**

Taxis: Samios (☎69779 91 799) or **Progoulakis** (☎69442 60 571). Fixed rates according to distance. 24hr.

Car Rental: Drakakis Tours, Livadi (☎27360 31 160). Cars from €30 per day, includes tax and insurance. Longer rentals have a reduced daily fee. No drop-off fee. Open M-Su 9am-7pm. MC/V. **Panayotis** (☎6944 263757) and **Cerigo** (☎6944 770161), at the airport.

ORIENTATION AND PRACTICAL INFORMATION

The island has three towns with substantial populations: **Chora** (or **Kithera**) is on the southern tip of the island; Agia Pelagia occupies a stretch of beaches along the northeastern side; and **Potamos** perches on a hill in the northern area about 10km from Agia Pelagia. The island has an interwoven network of hiking trails and unmarked roads leading to the best beaches, ruins, and caves of the island. The tumultuous landscape naturally hides the most spectacular areas.

Bank: National Bank (☎27360 31 209), in Chora on the main square. Branch in Potamos (☎27360 33 209), also off of the main square. Both have **24hr. ATM.** Open M-F 9am-2pm. ATMs are also available in Agia Pelagia, Diakofti, and along the main road in Chora.

Police Station: In Chora (☎27360 31 206); in Potamos (☎27360 33 222). Open 24hr.

Hospital: in Potamos (☎27360 33 203). Open 24hr.

Pharmacy: (☎27360 34 220) in Potamos, in the main square. Open M-Sa 9am-7pm.

Post Office: In Chora (☎27360 31 274); in Potamos (☎27360 33 225). **Postal Code:** 80100.

AGIA PELAGIA Άγια Πελαγία ☎27360

Since the ferries have stopped docking in the port, the town's beaches and atmosphere have improved greatly. The town has relatively well-priced accommodations and food, and it is near some of the island's best beaches on its northern coast. Agia Pelagia has everything you would need in a small stretch of waterfront stores all within walking distance of the towns' many accommodations.

ACCOMMODATIONS

In addition to hotels, rooms to let are available throughout the town. Try **Stella Rooms** (☎27360 33 264), on the main street, or **Panorama Apartments** (☎27360 33 840), off to the left of the port when facing inland. Call ahead to check for availability. These are the cheaper options in low season, but the prices can exceed those of hotels in the summer months. Singles start at €35.

Hotel Venardos (☎27360 34 100), 300m up the road from the main beach. Large rooms with balconies. The hotel has a pool with deck chairs if you want a break from the beach. Breakfast included. Wheelchair-accessible. Singles €45; doubles €60. MC/V. ❹

Hotel Filoxenia (☎27360 33 100), next to Hotel Venardos. Slightly closer to town, this hotel was recently renovated and now includes a snazzy pool-bar. A gregarious and helpful family runs the hotel. Wheelchair-accessible. Rooms from €45. Prices rise significantly July-Aug. MC/V. ❹

FOOD

This small town has the highest concentration of restaurants on the island. The five restaurants lining the beach seem to differ only in the color of their tablecloths, but don't be fooled—the food is not all the same.

Moustakias (☎27360 33 519). The 1st place coming into town from the south, Moustakias makes a mockery of the other *tavernas*. The food at this local favorite might not look like much, but is cheaper and tastes better than anywhere else in town. Appetizers €3-5. Entrees €5-9. Cash only. ❷

Kaleris (☎27360 33 461), at the far end from Moustakias. The reworked menu offers heaping salads with chicken and balsamic dressings. Salads €4-9. Entrees €6-16. Cash only. ❹

Stella (☎27360 33 513), opposite the dock and the beach. A giant selection of food in a quieter area than the tavernas in the center of town. Try the stuffed calamari with feta cheese (€8). Salads and starters €4-7. Entrees €5-12. ❷

BEACHES

Agia Pelagia boasts six beaches, all within a short distance of the town center. Starting from the main beach, continue south toward Potamos with the water on your left to five more beaches; bear left when the road forks. The road is paved as you pass the second beach, **Neo Kosmos,** about 300m from town, and turns to dirt after the Aphrodite Pelagia Hotel. Next is stunning **Fyriamo Beach** (500m from town), with its long stretch of red sand and dramatic cliffs in the background. About 1km farther is **Kalamitzi Beach;** the path there is difficult to find off the main road, so ask for directions at the information office. The gorgeous landscape, however, justifies the circuitous route. From there, the last beaches are easy to find. Isolated **Lorenzo Beach** is in a small cove providing welcome shade from the hot midday sun. **Lagatha** lies at the base of a dramatic ▓canyon at the end of the road, separating the ocean from the deep green waters of Lake Pekelagada.

Agia Pelagia is a convenient base for visiting Kithera's beaches. When you face the port from the center of town, you'll see the town's main beach. Within walking distance of the town, however, there are more than three better options: **Lorentzos, Lagada,** and **Limni.** Walk along the coast keeping the water on your left. Keep walking as pavement turns into a dirt track until you reach the ravine. Limni Beach has a bar and umbrellas as well as the occasional live music performance. At the southern end of the island is **Kaladi Beach,** two kilometers south of Palaiopoli along a dirt road. The eastern coast has more accessible and sandy beaches. In Chora there is **Feloti Beach.** Word on the street is that the un-missable beach is in the neighboring town of **Kapsali.**

KITHERA TOWN Χώρα ☎27360

Kithera (also called "Chora"), the island's southern capital, is most famous for its large **castle** (open 7am-7pm; wheelchair-accessible; free) and whitewashed houses. Though usually a small, low-key community, it's often overwhelmed with visitors in high season.

The few accommodations that cater to visitors offer similar views and amenities, but *domatia* may have kitchens and lower prices. Hotels and *domatia* are mostly clustered around and along the main road. **Castello Apartments ❷**, up a few stairs to the left of the main road as you approach the fork from the *plateia*, offers rooms with A/C, TVs, kitchens, baths, and large balconies. Follow the path leading to the back of the building to find the reception. (☎27360 31 069; www.castelloapts-kythera.gr. Doubles €30-45; triples and studios €45-55. MC/V.) **Margarita Hotel ❸** is tucked in a tight cluster of buildings and has a wonderful porch wrapping around the hotel. Rooms are small but cozy and well-decorated. (☎27360 31 711. Singles €40-50; doubles €50-70. MC/V. Call ahead for reservations.) At family-run **Salonikios ❷**, the only *taverna* in town, diners are invited into the kitchen to choose their meals. Head up the stairs to the right of the post office and turn right. Sit inside or outside on the pleasant patio with a view down to Kapsali below. (☎27360 31 705. Appetizers €2.50-5. Salads €4-5.50. Entrees €5-8.50. Cash only.)

CYCLADES
Κυκλάδες

Sun-drenched white houses, winding stone streets, and trellis-covered *tavernas* define the Cycladic islands as a whole, but each has its own proud culture and not-so-subtle distinctions. Orange and black sands coat the shoreline of Santorini, rocky cliffs shape arid Sifnos, and celebrated archaeological sites testify to the mythical and historical legends surrounding Delos. Naxos and Paros offer travelers peaceful mountains and villages, Milos's coast is spectacularly unusual with its caverns and deeply colored sand, and notorious party spots Ios and Mykonos uncork some of the wildest nightlife on earth. The Little Cyclades are blissfully under-touristed, populated only by locals and a smattering of Greek vacationers. Visitors to any island, however, are sure to encounter large quantities of unadulterated local flavor, surrounded by the ever-present cerulean sea.

HIGHLIGHTS OF THE CYCLADES

PARTY your liver away on **Mykonos** (p. 260), **Ios** (p. 307), and **Santorini** (p. 311).

MUNCH on **Naxos'** famous local cheese and citron liquor (p. 282).

RELAX on the **Little Cyclades'** perfectly calm beaches (p. 289).

MYKONOS Μύκονος

Mykonos is known around the world as the party center of the Greek isles. Having come a long way since ancient times, when it was a mere stopping point on the way to sacred Delos, Mykonos is now one of the most heavily trafficked and lusted-after destinations in Greece. The island's beautiful sand beckons hedonists of every age, and its narrow, whitewashed streets are lined with shops, restaurants, and every travel service imaginable. After sunset, the unparalleled island-wide party revs into high gear. Mykonos's gay scene, which reached its prime in the 1970s, remains alive and kicking as the island continues to be accepting in a way that most of Greece is not.

MYKONOS TOWN   ☎ 22890

Mykonos Town owes its labyrinthine streets, now closed to motor traffic in the afternoon and evening, to Mediterranean pirates. The city's maze was planned expressly to disorient marauders and now has a similar effect on tourists. The massive influx of visitors has brought equally massive changes to the Mykonian way of life, but so far the town has resisted large hotel complexes, allowing historical churches, fishing boats, and friendly pelicans to provide a picturesque backdrop for the happy crowds.

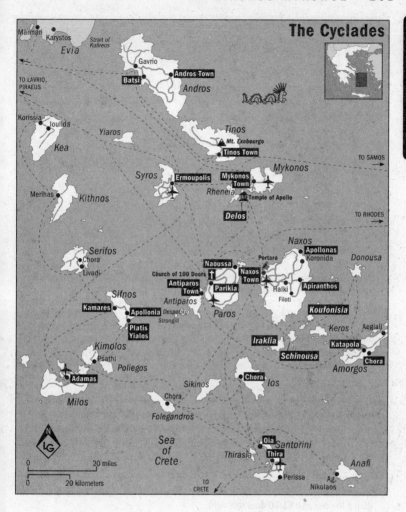

The Cyclades

TRANSPORTATION

Flights: Mykonos Airport (JMK) is accessible by taxi (€6) or bus from Fabrika (11 per day, 9:30am-8:30pm, €1.40). **Olympic Airways** (☎22890 22 490) flies to **Athens** (30min., 4-5 per day, €80-120) and **Thessaloniki** (1hr., 2 per week in peak season, €120-150). **Aegean Airlines** (☎22890 28 720) also goes to **Athens** (30min., 3-4 per day, €90-140) and **Thessaloniki** (1hr., 1 per week, €140-170). **Athens Airways** flies to **Athens** only from **Mykonos** (30min., 2 per day, €60-100).

Ferries: Most boats dock at the New Port near Ag. Stefanos beach, 3km away from Mykonos Town, but some high-speed boats still dock at the Old Port. KTEL buses run between the 2. For information on which boats arrive where, call the **port authority** (☎22890 22

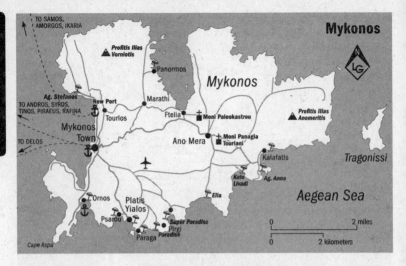

218). Buy tickets at **Sea and Sky Travel Agency** (☎22890 24 582), on the road above Remezzo bus station or on the waterfront at Matogianni, where the latest ferry schedules are posted on its front porch. To: **Andros** (2hr., M-F 2-3 per day, €10.50-11.90); **Naxos** (3hr., F 9:20pm, €7.70); **Paros** (3hr., €6.80); **Rafina** (5hr., 4 per day, €19-22.40); **Piraeus** (6hr., 1-3 per day, €38); **Syros** (2hr., 2-3 per day, €11.50); **Tinos** (35min., 4-5 per day, €4.50-5). To get to **Santorini,** you must connect through **Paros.**

High-Speed Boats: To: **Heraklion, Crete** (1-2 per day, €48); **Ios** (2hr., 5 per week, €26.10); **Naxos** (1hr., 1-2 per day, €21.50); **Paros** (1hr., 2-3 per day, €14-19); **Piraeus** (4hr., 1-2 per day, €51.50); **Santorini** (3hr., 1-2 per day, €28); **Syros** (1hr., 1-2 per day, €16.50); **Tinos** (30min., 3-4 per day, €11).

 ON A FIRST NAME BASIS When you're talking about ferries, knowing the name of the boat is almost as important as knowing the departure time. Dock personnel will want the name of the boat to answer your questions, and looking for the name on the side is the best way to figure out if the ferry pulling into the port is the one that should be carrying you out again.

Buses: KTEL (☎22890 23 360) has 2 main stations. Unless noted, buses are €1.40 during the day and €1.70 after midnight.

Remezzo Station, on the paved road from the ferry dock to the center of town, sends buses to **Agios Stefanos Beach** (every 30min.), **Elia** (5 per day 11am-7:pm, €1.70) via **Ano Mera,** and **Kalafatis** (6 per day 10am-10pm, €1.70) via **Ano Mera.**

Fabrika Station, at the opposite edge of town, near Fast Internet, serves: **Agios Ioannis** and **Ornos Beach** (7:30am, every hr. 9:30am-5:30pm, 2 per hr. 6pm-1:30am); **Paradise Beach** (7:30, 9am, 2 per hr. 10am-9pm, every hr. 8pm-2am); **Paraga** (9am, every hr. 11am-midnight); **Plati Yialos Beach** (7:50, 9am, 2 per hr. 10am-midnight, 1, 2am). Buses also run from Fabrika to the **New Port** (6 per day, 9am-7pm) and to the **airport** (11 per day, 9:30am-8:30pm). Schedules are posted at the stations and change according to season.

Taxis: ☎22890 22 400. Wait at Taxi Sq., along the water. Allow plenty of time; there usually aren't enough taxis to meet demand, especially late at night.

Car and ATV Rental: Agencies, around the bus stops, expect bargaining. Driver's license required. ATVs €20 per day.

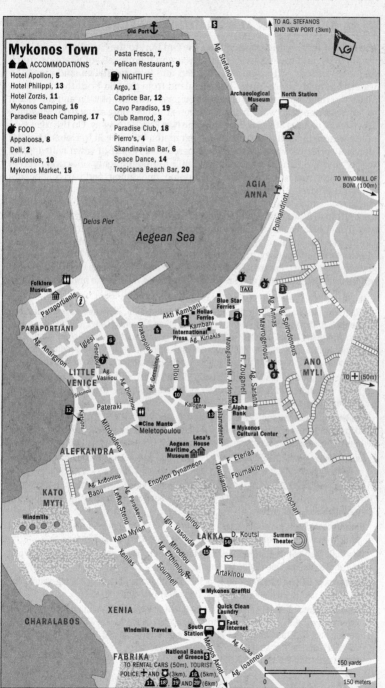

Mykonos Town

Mykonos Town

ACCOMMODATIONS
Hotel Apollon, 5
Hotel Philippi, 13
Hotel Zorzis, 11
Mykonos Camping, 16
Paradise Beach Camping, 17

FOOD
Appaloosa, 8
Deli, 2
Kalidonios, 10
Mykonos Market, 15

Pasta Fresca, 7
Pelican Restaurant, 9

NIGHTLIFE
Argo, 1
Caprice Bar, 12
Cavo Paradiso, 19
Club Ramrod, 3
Paradise Club, 18
Pierro's, 4
Skandinavian Bar, 6
Space Dance, 14
Tropicana Beach Bar, 20

Old Port

TO AG. STEFANOS
AND NEW PORT (3km)

Aegean Sea

Delos Pier

Ag. Stefanou

Archaeological
Museum

North Station

AGIA
ANNA

Pollikandrioti

TO WINDMILL OF
BONI (100m)

Folklore
Museum

Paraportianis

PARAPORTIANI

Ag. Anargyron

Iglesi

Gerogouli

Drakopolou

Ag. Gerasimou

Akti Kambani

Blue Star
Ferries

Hellas
Ferries

Kambani

International
Press

Ag. Kinakis

Matogianni (M. Andronikou)

Fl. Zouganeli

TAXI

Ag. Annas

Ag. Spiridonous

D. Mavrogenous

Ag. Saranta

ANO
MYLI

TO (50m)

LITTLE
VENICE

Ag.
Vasiliou

Ag. Dimitriou

Dilou

Kalogera

Alpha
Bank

Paterakì

Solomou

Karsoni

Mitropoleos

Cine Manto
Meletopoulou

Lena's
House

Aegean
Maritime
Museum

Malamatenias

Mykonos
Cultural Center

ALEFKANDRA

Enoplon Dynameon

F. Eterias

Fournakion

Touliaris

Rochari

KATO
MYTI

Ag. Andoniou

Baou

Lefko Steno

Ag. Paraskevis

Ipirou

Windmills

Kato Mylon

Xenias

Ign. Vasouda

Mirodiou

Ag. Efthimiou R.

LAKKA

D. Koutsi

Summer
Theater

Artakinou

XENIA

Mykonos Graffiti

CHARALABOS

Windmills Travel

Quick Clean
Laundry

Fast
Internet

South
Station

Melpos Axioti

Ag. Louka

FABRIKA

National Bank
of Greece

TO RENTAL CARS (50m), TOURIST
POLICE, AND (3km), 16 (5km),
17, 18, 19 AND 20 (6km)

Ag. Ioannou

0   150 yards

0   150 meters

ORIENTATION AND PRACTICAL INFORMATION

The bulk of ferry service shifted from the Old Port to the New Port in the summer of 2009, and travel service agencies are in the process of adapting. You'll find most offices still around the **Old Port** and **Remezzo Station,** and along the waterfront in Mykonos Town. Facing inland from the Old Port, the road leading to the right along the water takes you past Remezzo Station and the beach to **Taxi Square** and the waterfront. This same road heading away from Mykonos Town leads to **Agios Stefanos Beach** and the **New Port,** 3km away. On the right side of the waterfront is a pier from which excursion boats head to Delos. Past the pier is a series of white-washed churches, a lovely part of town called **"Little Venice,"** and the famous windmill-lined hill. Although plenty of action centers on the waterfront, most of the real shopping, fine dining, and partying occurs among the narrow, winding back streets. Some of the important streets are **Matogianni,** which leads inland from the water, **Enoplon Dynameon,** which catches the bottom of Matogianni, and **Mitropoleos,** which intersects E. Dynameon on its way from Little Venice to Lakka and South Station. The sooner you pick your landmarks the easier it will be to get around, as navigating Mykonos's maze of streets is not an easy task. The road heading uphill from Fabrika Station goes to the airport, campsites, and **Paradise Beach.** The town's essentials—post office, internet, markets, and so forth—mostly lie near **Lakka** and **South Station.**

Tourist Office: Sea and Sky Travel Agency (☎22890 24 582), on the road above Remezzo bus station or on the waterfront at Matogianni. **Mykonos Accommodations Center,** E. Dynameon, above the Aegean Maritime Museum. Offers tips for gay travelers. **Windmills Travel,** Xenias (☎22890 26 555; www.windmillstravel.com), around the corner from South Station. Has maps and can help with last-minute accommodations. Scuba diving (2 dives €110) and snorkeling (€38) excursions. Open daily 9am-9pm.

Banks: Alpha Bank, Matogianni 41 (☎22890 23 909), at the corner of Kalogera. **Currency exchange** and **24hr. ATM.** Open M-Th 8am-2:30pm, F 8am-2pm. Police station also exchanges currency.

Bookstore: International Press, Kambani 5 (☎22890 23 316), in a small *plateia* opposite Pierro's. Follow signs from the waterfront. Sells an eclectic selection of books, magazines, and newspapers in several languages. Open daily noon-1am.

Laundromat: Quick Clean (☎22890 27 323), just below South Station on the right, up 1 flight of stairs. Wash and dry €10. Open daily 10am-11pm.

Police: (☎22890 22 716), by the airport. Open 24hr. **Tourist Police** (☎22890 22 482), also by the airport. Helpful English-speaking staff. Open daily 8am-9pm. For **emergencies,** dial ☎108.

Pharmacies: Look for pharmacies along Matogianni. Ag. Efthimiou 57 (☎22890 24 188), downhill from South Station. Open M-Sa 9am-2pm and 5-11pm.

Hospital: Medical Center (☎22890 23 994), on the higher road leading from the port to Fabrika Station. Open 24hr. for emergencies.

Telephones: OTE (☎22890 22 699), at the left end of the waterfront in a big white building, uphill and to the right of the dock. Open M-F 7am-2:40pm.

Internet Access: Several cafes on the waterfront and by Fabrika station offer Wi-Fi. **Fast Internet** (☎22890 28 842), next to Quick Clean Laundry near South Station. €2.40 per hr., min. €2. Open daily 9am-2am. **Mykonos Internet World,** Ag. Louka 8 (☎22890 79 194), across the street from Fast Internet and up a flight of stairs. International phone calls and laptop connections. €2.50 per hr., min. €2. Open daily 9am-1am.

Post Office: (☎22890 22 238), down the street to the right after South Station, across from Space. Open M-F 7:30am-2pm. **Postal Code:** 84600.

ACCOMMODATIONS AND CAMPING

Mykonos is one of the most expensive of the Greek islands, and rooms are accordingly pricey. Many student travelers find their niche at the island's campgrounds, whose options far surpass the standard plot of grass. The regular bus service to town is cheap and fast. Plus, most of the early (and late) partying happens near Paradise Beach. Information offices by the dock in town are numbered according to accommodation type: 1 for hotels (☎22890 24 540; open 9am-4pm), 2 for rooms to let (☎2289024 860; open 9am-11pm), and 3 for camping (☎2289023 567; open 9am-midnight). Signs on the streets and at the New Port advertise *domatia*, but the rooms farther from town, available through the information office, tend to have better amenities for lower prices. In high season, *domatia* doubles range €40-80. For hotels, calling ahead is a must.

Paradise Beach Camping (☎22890 22 852; www.paradisemykonos.com), on Paradise Beach. Take the bus from South Station (15min., 2 per hr., €1.40). Free pickup at the port or airport. Popular campground has clean showers and bathrooms, bars, and a restaurant—just don't come here (or to Mykonos, for that matter) expecting any peace and quiet. A deal with neighboring Paradise Club means that guests pay only €13 for the clubs' parties, which includes 1 drink. Hotel rooms available with A/C and baths. Breakfast included. Free luggage storage; bring your own lock. Internet €4 per hr. Open Apr.-Oct. €5-10 per person; €3.50-5 per regular tent, €5-8 per large tent; 3-person tent rental with beds €10-22 each; 1- to 2-person cabins €15-56. Singles €30-100; doubles €40-120; triples €60-150. Apartments also available. Cash only. ●

Mykonos Camping (☎22890 25 915; www.mycamp.gr), above Paraga beach. Provides a slightly more subdued camping experience in a picturesque location on the sea cliffs. Free pickup and drop-off at the port and airport. Clean showers and bathrooms, a mini-mart, beachside cafe-bar, and restaurant. Internet €1 per 10min. €4.70-10 per person; €2.60-5 per small tent, €5-8 per large; tent rental with beds €10-25. Dorms €5-20; 2-person bungalows €12.50-30. Cash only. ●

Hotel Zorzis, Kalogera 30 (☎22890 22 167), down the street from Hotel Philippi. 10 rooms, each with TV, A/C, and bath. All rooms are full of carefully selected Art Deco pieces. Owner Jonathan is a great source for information about the "real Mykonos," having lived here for much of his life. Ask him for info over coffee in the hotel's charming breakfast garden. Singles €45-115; doubles €65-145; 2-bedroom suites €95-215. Call ahead for better rates. Cash only. ❺

Hotel Philippi, Kalogera 25 (☎22890 22 294), across from Zorzis. The rooms in this light-blue shuttered hotel have baths, fridges, TVs, phones, and A/C, arrayed around a gorgeous garden courtyard. A lovely spot of color in this stone-and-whitewash town. Open Apr.-Oct. Singles €60-90; doubles €75-120; triples €90-150. AmEx/MC/V. ❺

Hotel Apollon (☎22890 22 223), with a sign on the waterfront. An enchanting antique house. The owner loves to chat with guests, giving the place a hostel-like atmosphere, but rooms are comfortable, clean, and cheaper than others in town during the summer. All have sinks and fridges. Doubles €65-70, with bath €85-95. Cash only. ❹

FOOD

Food is expensive on Mykonos, with no middle ground between gourmet meals and gyros. **Mykonos Market,** between the post office and Fabrika Station, is good for cheap meals. (☎22890 24 897. Open daily 8am-12:30am.) Creperies and souvlaki joints crowd almost every street. Man cannot live on souvlaki alone, but remember that quality and price don't always go hand in hand. Scan menus for the local flavors—capers, oregano, mint, and fresh mussels—and wander outside of the high-traffic areas.

Maria's Rendezvous (☎22890 22 840), just north of Taxi Sq. Look for signs on Agia Anna. Tucked away behind the beach, Maria's simple, modest menu is a welcome relief from the fussy fare you'll find elsewhere in Mykonos Town. Look to this family place for some of the cheapest mussels *saganaki* in town (€9). Rendezvous pizza (with Mykonos sausage and mushrooms) €9. Open noon-1am. Cash only. ❷

Jimmy's Special Souvlaki, E. Dynameon and Mitropoleos. Has no doors and never closes. Stop in after a late night at the clubs for a gyro pita from the friendly staff (€2.50). Open 24hr. Cash only. ❶

Sale e Pepe (☎22890 24 207), in Lakka. If you're looking to splurge, come here for one of the best meals in town. Pasta is made fresh every afternoon. Whereas most of the local *tavernas* serve frozen shellfish, Sale e Pepe's is all fresh. Linguine with mussels, shrimp, and cockles €20. MC/V. ❹

Yialos (☎22890 23 552), on the waterfront next to Hotel Apollon. If you're looking for a snack along the waterfront and don't want to pay big bucks at the *tavernas*, Yialos offers the same harbor views as the big guys and serves tasty food. Mykonian sausage €6. Yogurt with fresh fruit €7. Open daily 6am-3am. Cash only. ❷

Mandarini (☎22890 29 001), next to Maria's, behind Agia Anna beach. Not only does Mandarini sell scrumptious baklava (€3) and other desserts, they also serve Greek specialties from all over the country. Stop in for *hanoumakia* with kiwi (€1.30) and pick up a jar of feta cheese packed in herbed olive oil to take back home with you. Open 10am-1:30am. MC/V. ❶

Deli (☎22890 22 967), on the left side of Taxi Sq. The spaghetti bolognese (€7.50) and pizza (€3) at this self-service joint are better than at other similarly priced restaurants. Open daily 10:30am-2am. Cash only. ❶

◉ SIGHTS

Losing yourself in its whitewashed alleyways can be one of Mykonos Town's cheapest and most wonderful experiences. Walk up to the line of windmills along the waterfront for a fabulous sunset vantage point, but do your main exploring after dark, when the daytime heat has subsided and the lights of town glitter in the harbor. A stroll south along the waterfront will lead you to the *kastro* area and Paraportiani, a cluster of white churches and some of the oldest buildings on Mykonos. This is also a prime spot to encounter one of the island's famed local pelicans, who wait outside the *tavernas* in the square hoping for a tasty treat. They're great fun to see up close—just be careful not to get pecked. From there, wander through **Little Venice,** where the Aegean's sapphire waters lap at the legs of cafe tables and chairs. Stop by ◨**Nikoleta's Shop,** near the waterfront, to watch her at her loom—one of the last on Mykonos—and consider leaving with one of her luxurious scarves woven from Mykonian wool (€70-100). The colorful domes of the town's many churches dot the skyline, but it's another experience entirely to see their doors still open at night and their sanctuaries glowing with candlelight. Just about everything in Mykonos Town stays open until the wee hours of the morning.

FOLKLORE MUSEUM. For a look at Mykonos's past, visit the Folklore Museum, divided among three of the island's most historically significant buildings. The main museum in the **House of Kastro,** just above the Delos pier, has displays of traditional Mykonian household items. **Lena's House,** the third of the Folklore Museum buildings, next to the Aegean Maritime Museum, is an 18th-century home preserved exactly as its last owner (Lena) left it. *(House of Kastro ☎ 22890 22 591. Lena's House ☎ 22890 28 764. House of Kastro open Apr.-Oct. M-Sa 5:30pm-8:30pm, Su 6:30-8:30pm. Lena's House open Apr.-Oct. M-Sa 6:30pm-9:30pm, Su 7-9pm. Each €2, students and seniors €1.)*

WINDMILL OF BONI. Overlooking the harbor and accessible from the road that leads uphill from North Station, the windmill hosts a **wine festival** each September to celebrate the town's agricultural history. *(Open Apr.-Oct. daily 4-8pm.)*

AEGEAN MARITIME MUSEUM. The museum contains models of traditional ships and recovered artifacts from wrecks found in the area. The beautifully manicured back garden contains gigantic nautical instruments, including the largest lighthouse in the Aegean. *(Around the corner from the inland end of Matogianni on E. Dynameon, just past Lena's House. ☎ 22890 22 700. Open Apr.-Oct. daily 10:30am-1pm and 6:30-9pm. €4, students and seniors €1.50, children free.)*

ARCHAEOLOGICAL MUSEUM. This museum displays a large collection of pottery found throughout the island, including a renowned seventh-century BC amphora with scenes depicting the fall of Troy. *(On the paved road between the dock and the center of town. ☎ 22890 22 325. Open Tu-Su 8:30am-3pm. €2, students and seniors €1, EU students and under 19 free.)*

CULTURAL CENTER OF MYKONOS. Check out rotating exhibits that feature the work of up-and-coming Greek artists. *(On Matogianni. ☎ 22890 27 791. Open daily 11am-2pm and 7pm-1am. Free.)*

🎵 🎭 ENTERTAINMENT AND NIGHTLIFE

At night, the gods of pleasure descend upon Mykonos to mingle with mere mortals at cafes, nightclubs, and a handful of pubs. The most popular venues are in Little Venice and near the waterfront. Music pumps into the streets starting around 11pm, but the party doesn't begin in earnest until 2am, when the crowds start to concentrate around a handful of packed dance clubs. Around 3 or 4am, the scene shifts to the world-class nightclubs around **Paradise Beach,** where the dancing continues well past dawn. Mykonos's club scene is one of the most vibrant in Europe, regularly attracting big-name DJs and entertainers, and it's a singular experience that's worth the exorbitant cover fees. If you get tired of crazy parties, head to **Cine Manto,** in Pl. Lymni, which shows English-language films. *(☎ 22890 27 190. Shows 9, 11:30pm. €7.)*

🎵 **Cavo Paradiso** (☎ 22890 27 205; www.cavoparadiso.gr), on the cliff over Paradise Beach. Considered 1 of the world's premier dance clubs. Rumor has it that even internationally renowned DJs will settle for a lower salary to spin at the open-air venue. The debauchery centers on a glowing pool and continues well past sunrise. Check the club's website for opportunities to get onto its text message guest list. Vodka and Red Bull €10. Cover €15-50. Alternates events with Paradise Club in the high season; look at the website or at posters around town and the beach. Open daily 12:30am-9am.

🎵 **Paradise Club** (☎ 22890 28 766, www.paradiseclub-mykonos.com), on Paradise Beach. This open-air venue can accommodate thousands of revelers, who gather to drink and dance to famous guest DJs and performers like Erick Morillo and Boy George. Add the pool, beachside tables, and sea breezes, and Paradise is easily one of the top clubs in Mykonos. Cover €15-40. Open daily 11pm-morning.

🎵 **Caprice Bar,** in Little Venice. Crowds cluster around the candlelit bar, and jump and sing exuberantly with the funky music at this popular post-beach hangout. Gathering steam earlier than most other establishments on the island, its waterfront cafe tables are the perfect vantage point to watch the sun set and kick off the night. Beer €7. Mixed drinks €12. Open daily 6:30pm-4am.

Skandinavian Bar (☎22890 22 669), near the waterfront. This 2-building complex includes 2 bars, a cafe seating area, and a 2nd-floor disco. Drinks are cheaper here than most places in the area, and the massive crowds often pour down the stairs and into the street, making it the perfect place to dance the night away. Beer and shots €4-6. Mixed drinks from €8. Open daily 8pm-late.

Space Dance (☎22890 24 674; www.spacemykonos.com), by the post office. This is the nightclub your mother feared when you told her you were going to Mykonos. Scantily-clad dancers strut on elevated platforms, while spectacular light shows and pounding beats saturate the 2-story complex. When things get too hot, sweaty partiers cool off in the posh outdoor bar and lounge. Beer €6. Mixed drinks €8. Cover €10 for women, €20 for men, €25 for couples; includes 1 drink. Open daily midnight-morning.

Pierro's, in Pl. Kiriaki on Matogianni, upstairs. The oldest gay club in Mykonos is still the place to go for a good time. Spontaneous glitter parties and an annual summer theme event (e.g. jungle) keep the crowd on their toes. The owner also runs a downstairs bar called **Pierro's by Manto,** for those who prefer standing to dancing. Beer €5. Mixed drinks €9-10. Nightly 1:30am drag shows. Open daily 10pm-5am.

Club Ramrod (☎22890 24 301), at the far end of Taxi Sq. from the waterfront, on the 2nd fl. As the not-so-subtle name makes clear, this is 1 of the most popular gay clubs in Mykonos, especially late at night. Lasers and disco balls illuminate the colorful dance floor, while the DJ spins techno-pop. If you would rather just watch the fun, go outside and recline on the balcony's pink cushions. Beer €5. Mixed drinks €9-10. Nightly 2am drag show. Open daily 9pm-5am.

◪ BEACHES

Mykonos has a beach to please everyone. Although all of the island's beaches are nude, the degree of nudity depends on where you go—and has decreased considerably since peaking in the 1970s. Although many of the beaches look close together on the map, the island's rocky coastline and winding streets make traveling between beaches difficult. If you want to beach hop, best to stick to water taxis, which are less expensive than cabs.

The **small beach** in Mykonos Town is nice for a quick swim, but the best beaches are out of town, accessible by bus or water taxi from Ornos or Platis Yialos (€1-3). Chairs and umbrellas (€4) line gorgeous but always crowded **Paradise Beach** in front of the bars and clubs. Widely known as the party beach, it blasts music and serves drinks all day; the revelry kicks into full gear between 5pm and sundown, when bars give away free drinks and T-shirts to get the beachgoers onto the dance floor. **Tropicana Beach Bar,** on Paradise beach, is where international youth go to make spring break last all summer. The most popular place to party your liver away by day, the crowd reaches its peak around late afternoon or early evening, and chugs on into the night. Just don't try to pull any funny business: locals report that the owner, a former heavyweight wrestler, isn't afraid to take discipline into his own hands. (☎22890 26 990. Open daily 8:30am-late.) Water sports (tubing €15, jet-skiing €30-50, water-skiing €30, and wakeboarding €30) are available in the afternoon. Nearby **Paraga Beach** is a quieter version of Paradise, sans water sports. Farther away from Mykonos Town, **Elia** has a slew of water sports (jet-skiing €35, wakeboarding €13, paddle boats €15).

TIP

BREAKING NEW GROUND. Although every beach seems like it's already been claimed by the sun-chair-and-umbrella racketeers out to get your €5, don't hesitate to unroll your towel and plant your own umbrella amid the umbrella jungle and sunbathe for free. The chair rentals don't own the sand, and savvy travelers can put their extra money toward their next souvlaki (or drink) instead.

THE LOCAL STORY

PETROS: PELICAN OF MYSTERY

Every summer, tourist-paparazzi swarm Mykonos, attempting to snap a photo of the island's biggest celebrity in action—perhaps taking a stroll by the windmills or enjoying a seafood dinner in Little Venice.

The town superstar is a pelican—or three—called "Petros." According to legend, in 1958, a Mykonos fisherman found a wounded White Pelican and nursed it back to health. The fisherman then set the pelican free, but instead of taking flight, Petros decided to make Mykonos his home. The pelican was adopted by the locals and eventually became the official mascot of the island, until, on December 2nd, 1985, he was run over by a car. The people of Mykonos were so bereaved by Petros' death that Jackie Kennedy-Onassis gave another pelican, called Irene, to the island. Today, three pelicans live around the main town of Mykonos, including one called Petros. All three receive the royal treatment from residents and visitors alike, and fishermen will often offer the best of the day's catch to these diva pelicans.

The special birds have been sighted all over the northwestern city. In their standard pose, the pink-and-white pelicans can be hard to pick out against the town's white buildings—at least until they blink their beady black eyes and extend their heavy wings and long, slender necks. To catch a glimpse, wander around the whitewashed churches of the Paraportiani and the surrounding *tavernas*, keeping your eyes peeled for a crowd of tourists wielding cameras.

Nearby **Kalo Livadi,** with similar activities, is more family-oriented but is only accessible by private transportation or water taxi. You can also ask the bus to Elia to drop you at the top of the road to Kalo Livadi and walk the 2km down to the beach. **Agios Stefanos** has a magnificent view of the harbor and a small sandy beach perfect for relaxing and working on your tan. Fashionable, trendy **Psarou** stays crowded with vacationing Athenians, as waitresses in bikinis serve drinks from the pricey beachside cafes and restaurants. **Ornos** has a lifeguard on duty, and **Platis Yialos,** one of the busiest beaches on the island, offers a variety of water sports; both are geared toward families. (Chairs and umbrellas are €12 for 2 of each.) **Panormos,** on the northern coast, 15km from town and accessible only by private vehicle, is remote and private, a relief for those trying to escape the crowds. Windsurfing and sailing are also available (€15-40). **Agios Ioannis,** accessible via the bus to Ornos, may not be as remote as Panormos, but is ideal for swimming thanks to its crystal clear water. **Super Paradise,** accessible by water taxi or private vehicle, 8km from town, is the island's most notorious beach, since its situation in an intimate cove once encouraged patrons to sunbathe nude. Fame has tamed the scene a bit, making it a quieter option for those who want the freedom of Paradise with less noise and activity.

DAYTRIP FROM MYKONOS

DELOS Δήλος

Excursion boats leave from the dock (40min., Tu-Su 4 per day 9am-11am, round-trip €15). Buy tickets at either Hellas or Blue Star Ferries on the waterfront. The last boat returns at 3pm. Companies also offers guided tours (€30, including admission). A cheaper option is to buy a guidebook with a map (€5-15) in town, or pick up a free map at the entrance to the site. Tinos, Naxos, Paros, and other islands run joint trips to Mykonos and Delos but allow less time to explore. Open Tu-Su 8:30am-3pm. €5, students and EU seniors €3, EU students free.

With its impressive ruins, continuing excavations, and fascinating museum, Delos—the sacred center of the Cyclades—is a must-see. The tiny island is home to the most important Temple of Apollo, built to commemorate the birthplace of the god and his twin sister, Artemis. A site of religious pilgrimage in the ancient world, today Delos is essentially a giant, island-wide museum.

After **Zeus,** the philandering king of the gods, impregnated the mortal **Leto** with Artemis and Apollo, he sent her away from Olympus in an attempt to shield her from the wrath of his jealous wife, **Hera.** Leto, desperately seeking a place to give birth, wandered the Aegean, but was refused by island after island, each afraid of Hera's fury. At last, exhausted Leto came upon a floating island shrouded in mist, but it too cowered under Hera's threats. Leto swore by the river Styx—the most sacred of all oaths—that if she were allowed to give birth on the island, it would no longer have to float and that her future son Apollo would bring fame and riches to its shores. Upon hearing this vow, the reassured island stopped drifting and welcomed her. Unhappy and vengeful, Hera made the goddess of childbirth, **Eilythia,** prolong Leto's labor for nine days in revenge. When the infants finally arrived, the mist disappeared and the island basked in light. The island's name thus changed from "Adelos" ("invisible") to "Delos" ("visible" or "clear"). True to Leto's vow, Delos soon became the seat of her son's worship. Attracting many pilgrims, Apollo's sanctuary grew to be one of the most important religious and cultural centers in ancient Greece.

Although Delos was colonized by the Ionians in the 10th century BC, its status as a center of worship arose only in the eighth century BC. After it emerged untouched from the **Persian Wars** (p. 40), Delos became the focal point of the **Delian League.** During these years, the Athenians ordered at least two "purifications" of the island in Apollo's honor. The second, in 426 BC, decreed that no one should give birth or die on its grounds—an order worshippers took retroactively, exhuming graves and moving bodies to a "purification pit" on nearby **Rheneia.** (Many of the artifacts from the mass grave at Rheneia are now in Mykonos Town's Archaeological Museum, p. 267.) After Sparta defeated Athens in the **Peloponnesian War,** Delos enjoyed a period of autonomy and wealth. This prosperity soured, however, during the Roman occupation in the second century BC, when Delos became the slave-trading center of Greece. By the end of the AD second century, after successive sackings, the island was left nearly deserted. Today its only residents are legions of lizards and members of the French School of Archaeology, which has been excavating here since 1873.

Occupying almost 2.5 sq. km, the **archaeological site** includes the Temple of Apollo, the agora, Mt. Kythnos, and the theater quarter. While it would take days to explore the ruins completely, you can see the highlights in a few hours. Most visitors follow a similar route when they disembark the ferry; reverse it for a more contemplative experience. There are frequent chances to explore off the beaten path; keep an eye out for footpaths off the main trails. A hat, good shoes, and a water bottle are musts. The cafeteria next to the museum is exorbitantly priced, so it's wise to pack some snacks.

The path beyond the admission booth points toward the **Agora of the Competaliasts,** where Roman guilds built their shop-shrines. Continue in the same direction and turn left onto the **Sacred Road.** Two parallel **stoas,** the more impressive of which (on the left) was built by Phillip of Macedon in 210 BC and dedicated to Apollo, adorn the walk. Bear right and follow this road to the **Sanctuary of Apollo,** a collection of temples built in the god's honor. The sanctuary complex begins when you reach the **Propylaea.** The biggest and most important of the temples is on the right; the famous **Temple of Apollo,** or Temple of the Delians, was completed at the end of the fourth century BC. Its immense, hexagonal pedestal once supported an 8m marble statue of the god. Following the direction of the Sacred Road north, 50m past its end, will lead you to the **Terrace of the Lions,** where replicas of the ancient Naxian Lions overlook the Sacred Lake. Five of the original lions are still whole, protected from the elements inside the museum, along with the partial remains of three others. The body of the ninth, plundered by Venetians, guards the entrance to the Arsenal in Venice. Past the lions, the **House of the Lake,** with a well-preserved mosaic decorating its atrium, and the desecrated **Sacred Lake,** drained in 1925 to protect against malaria, are both at the bottom of a hill populated with Roman houses. Today, the round shape of the former lake appears as a leafy oasis with a palm tree at its center. On the lake's south side is the **Roman agora.**

From the **Archaeological Museum** (free with admission to the site), you can ☐hike to the summit of **Mount Kythnos** (112m). Crumbling ruins are still crumbling ruins from up close, but the layout of the site is much easier to discern from above. Wear sturdy, comfortable shoes; though the trail is not too difficult, it can be steep and some of the rocks dislodge easily. Ascending the mountain from the direction of the Temple of Apollo, you will pass temples dedicated to Egyptian gods. The elegant bust in the perfectly preserved **Temple of Isis** depicts the sun goddess. The building blocks of the nearby **Grotto of Heracles** reflect Mycenaean architecture (though some experts suggest they're knockoffs). Coming down the mountain, bear left to reach the **House of the Dolphins** and **House of the Masks,** which contain intricate mosaics of dolphins, as well as the most famous mosaic on Delos, *Dionysus Riding a Panther.* Continue to the ancient theater, which has an intricate cistern called **"Dexamene,"** with nine arched compartments. As you weave down the rough path back toward the entrance, you'll see the **House of the Trident,** graced by a mosaic of a dolphin twisted around a trident; the **House of Dionysus,** containing another mosaic

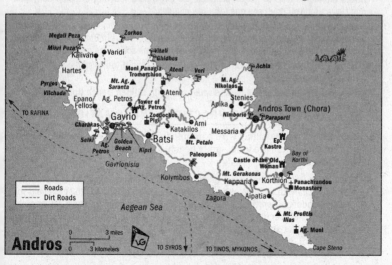

of Dionysus and a panther; and the **House of Cleopatra.** The famous statue of Cleopatra and Dioscourides is sheltered in the site's museum.

ANDROS Άνδρος

The second-largest Cycladic island, Andros is a weekend destination for Greece's wealthy ship captains, many of whose families originated here. In an attempt to keep their hideaway unspoiled, the residents have restricted ferry access to the island. Pockets of civilization are tucked into Andros's mountain ranges, and narrow roads weave around their peaks and valleys down to the coast below. Though Athenians crowd in on the weekends, Andros generally remains a serene escape for international tourists who delight in untrodden ground and quiet nights.

BATSI Μπατσί   22820

Climbing its way up the mountainside above an expansive sandy beach, Batsi is the tourist capital of Andros, with the liveliest nightlife and a wide variety of food and accommodation options. Visitors stroll the waterfront by night, have drinks at a *kafeneion*, and dance away the hours in a club.

TRANSPORTATION

Ferries: Ferries to the island arrive in **Gavrio.** From there, ferries sail to **Mykonos** (2hr., 4-5 per day, €9.50), **Rafina** (2hr., 4-6 per day, €9.10), and **Tinos** (2hr., 4-5 per day, €7.20).

Buses: (☎22820 22 316). Buses pass through Batsi on their way to **Andros Town** (45min.; M-F 7 per day 7:15am-9:45pm, Sa-Su 7 per day 10am-9:15pm; €3) and **Gavrio** (15min.; M-F 7 per day 7:45am-11:15pm, Sa-Su 8 per day 8:30am-11:15pm; €1.50) via **Agios Petros.** Buses also run to **Korthi** (2 per day 10:30am-12:15pm). Buses on Andros tend to get off schedule, so make sure you're at the stop early, and don't give up if you don't see one for a few minutes.

Minibuses: Between Batsi and **Gavrio.** From the ferry, a bus immediately picks up passengers going to Batsi and Andros Town. The bus makes 2 stops in Batsi: by the beach in front of Dino's Bikes and along the wharf, where the bus schedules are posted.

Taxis: (☎22820 41 081), line up on the wharf side. 24hr. If you miss the bus from the ferry, a taxi to Batsi is €6.

Taxi boats: Dock at the end of Batsi's wharf and go to **Golden Beach** (round-trip €13).

ORIENTATION AND PRACTICAL INFORMATION

Batsi is oriented around a bay with a dimple in the middle. As you face inland, to the left of the dimple is a long, sandy beach, and to the right is a wharf where smaller boats are moored.

Tourist Office: Batsi has no tourist office—the "Andros Information" center merely has a list of *domatia* with phone numbers. **Colours Travel** (☎22820 41 252) will help you find accommodations, provides a free tourist info booklet and map, books ferry tickets, rents cars (€25-60 per day), and gives helpful advice about hiking on Andros. Entrance up 1 level; look for stairs to the right from the sign. Open M-Sa 10am-1:30pm and 6-11pm, Su 10:30am-12:30pm and 6pm-8:30pm. **Hellas Ferries,** across from the ferry dock, books tickets, accommodations, and tours. Open daily 8am-11pm.

Bank: National Bank (☎22820 41 400), up the hill past the *plateia*. Has a **24hr. ATM** and offers **currency exchange.** Open M-F 8:30am-1pm.)

Police: ☎22820 41 204.

Pharmacy: (☎22820 41 541), all the way up the hill, past the National Bank. Open M-Sa 9am-1:30pm and 6:30-8:30pm.

Medical Services: Medical Center (☎22820 22 222 or 23 333), in Andros Town. To the left of the beach, behind a playground, is a small **medical office** (☎22820 41 326); follow the signs. Doctor available daily 9am-1pm.

Internet Access: Themelos Art Cafe and Wine Bar (☎22820 41 241; www.themelos. gr). Continue up the stairs near Colours Travel until they create a T with another street, then turn right and walk approximately 50m. Open M-F 6:30pm-midnight, Sa-Su 10:30am-2pm and 6:30pm-midnight. **Apomero Cafe** (☎22820 71 681), a 5min. walk from the port in Gavrio, on an uphill road to the right. €3.50 per hr. Open daily 10am-3pm and 5pm-3am.

Post Office: (☎22820 41 443), between Andros Travel and Dino's Bikes. Open M-F 7:30am-2:30pm. **Postal Code:** 84503.

ACCOMMODATIONS AND CAMPING

Accommodations are easier to find in Batsi than elsewhere on the island, as the plentiful *domatia* here tend to be nicer than similarly-priced hotels. Expect to pay €25-40 per night, lower if you bargain well.

Villa Lyra (☎22820 41 432), at the end of the waterfront with the water on the right. The best value in town. Panayiotis Barous, the friendly owner, will most likely be at the souvenir shop he runs, next to the National Bank. Pleasant rooms include TVs, A/C, fridges, kitchens, baths, and balconies. Singles €25-40; doubles and triples €30-50. MC/V. ❷

Villa Aegeo (☎22820 41 327; www.villa-aegeo.gr), up 4 flights of stairs to the right of Batsi Gold; past the tree, look for the small sign on the side of the building. Airy rooms have TVs, A/C, baths, fridges, kitchenettes, and balconies. Singles may not be available during high season. Call ahead for someone to meet you at the bus stop. Singles €40; doubles €65; triples €80. Cash only. ❸

Hotel Chryssi Akti (☎22820 41 236; www.hotel-chryssiakti.gr), directly across from the beach. Guests relax by the pool or laze around in plush, spotless rooms complete with TVs, fridges, A/C, baths, and waterfront views. Breakfast €4.50. Singles €45-65; doubles €60-80; triples €70-95; family suites for 4-5 €85-120. MC/V. ❹

Andros Camping (☎22820 71 444; www.campingandros.gr), 300m from Gavrio; follow the directional arrows. This remote campground has a pool, clean bathrooms with showers, a communal kitchen, a mini-mart, and laundry. Open Apr.-Oct. €6.50 per person; €3 per tent. Tent rental €6-10. ❶

FOOD

For fresh produce, stop by the **fruit market,** under Capriccio Music Bar on the right side of the harbor facing inland. (☎22820 42 333. Open daily 8am-10:30pm.)

Taverna Stamatis (☎22820 41 283), on the wharf side of the harbor up the stairs near the National Bank. Serving local specialties since 1965. The chef's specialties are Andros chicken cooked in wine (€8), a country lamb wrapped in phyllo with green pepper, onion, and chunks of firm, fresh cheese (€9), and a lamb *kleftiko*, cooked in a clay pot with wine and herbs (W only; €9). Call ahead to reserve your helping. Open M-F 10:30am-4pm and 7pm-midnight, Sa-Su 10:30am-midnight. MC/V. ❷

Villy's Place (☎22820 41 025), across from the wharf-side bus stop. The perfect spot to grab a sandwich (from €2.50) to bring to the beach. Open June-Aug. 24hr. ❶

👁 🏖 SIGHTS AND BEACHES

With its ruins and first-rate beaches, Andros is best explored by moped or car.

TOWER OF AGIOS PETROS. A 1hr. hike or €6 taxi ride north of Gavrio will bring you to this stone tower, which provides superb views of the harbor below. If you crawl inside the bottom of the tower, built in the forth century BC, you can gaze up at its interior where the floors have long since collapsed. The tower's original purpose remains unclear, but most believe that it once served as a *friktoria*—a building used to send torch signals.

OTHER SIGHTS. The bus from Batsi can drop you off at the ancient capital of **Paleopolis**, where you can explore the remains of an ancient theater, stadium, and small stone houses. Another bus from Batsi (€3) runs twice per day to the **Bay of Korthi**, the site of a charming village and Andros's finest swimming. Korthi is also home to the 30 **watermills** that run alongside the Dipotamata (Twin River) as well as the remnants of the impressive **Castle of the Old Woman,** which once protected its inhabitants from attacking forces.

BEACHES. Golden Beach has a popular bar for daytime partying (beer €2.50-4), accessible by water taxi (round-trip €13), taxi (round-trip €8, arrange a pick-up time), or foot (45min.). The beach also offers a number of water sports. **Kipri,** 400m back on the road toward Batsi, is more low-key. Following the road toward Gavrio, you'll find **Agios Petros,** another secluded stretch of sand. You can also access the peaceful beach of **Vitali,** which sits in a small protected cove 26km north of Gavrio, by private vehicle. If you continue along the river bank in the back left corner of the beach for 200m, you'll find a cave with beautiful stalagmites.

🎵 NIGHTLIFE

In the evening, Batsi's wharf becomes the center of activity.

Skala Music Cafe (☎22820 41 656), next to the taxi stand. This indoor bar features a 2-tiered seating area covered in greenery. Mixed drinks €9. Open daily 9am-4am.

Vraxos (☎22820 41 219), on the beach side of the taxi stand. Porch perfect for lounging with a group. Beer €3.20-6. Mixed drinks €9. Open daily 10am-3am. Cash only.

Capriccio Music Bar's (☎22820 41 770), just around the curve of the wharf. The outdoor patio is a great spot to people-watch or gaze at the harbor while sipping your drink. The party moves to the indoor dance floor around midnight. Happy hour 7-9pm. Beer €4. Mixed drinks €9. Open daily 9am-late.

ANDROS TOWN Χώρα   ☎22820

Andros Town, or Chora, is the island's cultural center and one of the most "Greek" towns you're likely to encounter in the Cyclades. A wide, cobbled main street runs along a narrow peninsula, with cafes giving way to colorful homes and rocky outcroppings. Expanses of sandy beach lie directly on either side of the peninsula. Because the accommodations may be prohibitively expensive for budget travelers, Andros Town is also an ideal destination for a daytrip from Batsi.

TRANSPORTATION. The **bus** leaving Andros Town for Gavrio (1hr., M-F 8 per day 7am-10:30pm, €4) via Batsi (45min., €3.50) runs out of a depot near the main *plateia*, accessible via the alleyway at the back left corner of the bus depot, where **taxis** (☎22820 22 171) wait. A schedule is posted in the outdoor waiting area.

ORIENTATION AND PRACTICAL INFORMATION. The pedestrian-only main street, **Georgios Ebirikos,** runs in front of the main *plateia* and continues past cafes, boutiques, and banks, ending in Pl. Kairis. A 5min. walk past the arch at the far end of Pl. Kairis (go left at the dead end) brings you to the outer edge of town, where those in the know ⬛swim among the ruins of a Venetian castle off the easily accessible dock. The **tourist information kiosk** is in the main *plateia*. (☎25 162. Open 8am-11pm.) The **police station,** G. Ebirikos 2, is on the inland end of the main street to the left. (☎22820 22 300. Open 24hr.) One of several **pharmacies** along the main street sits right across from the main *plateia* at G. Ebirikos 29. (☎22820 23 203. Open daily 8am-3pm and 6-11pm.) In **medical emergencies,** dial ☎22820 22 222 or visit the **health center** in the back right corner of the main *plateia* facing away from G. Ebirikos. The **OTE** is across from the *plateia*. (☎22820 22 099. Open M-F 7:30am-2:30pm.) **Alpha Bank,** G. Ebirikos 49, with a **24hr. ATM** and **currency exchange,** is down the street on the right as you turn right and walk toward the water. (☎22820 23 900. Open M-Th 8am-2:30pm, F 8am-2pm.) **Andros Island Travel,** across from the bank, can book tickets, find rooms, and plan excursions. (☎22820 29 220. Open M-Sa 8:30am-9pm, Su 9:30am-9pm.) You can buy **ferry tickets** at the **Blue Star office,** on the left before Pl. Kairis. (☎22820 22 257. Open daily 9am-2pm and 7-9pm.) Take the side street across from Alpha Bank all the way down to the water to find **Riva,** on the left (entrance around the corner on the street parallel), which rents mopeds from €15 per day and boats from €80. (☎22820 24 412. Open daily 8am-10pm.) **Art Cafe,** on the left side of the main street before Pl. Kairis, has **internet access** upstairs in its cafe-bar. (☎22820 29 129. €3 per hr. Open daily 9am-2am.) The **post office,** G. Ebirikos 14, is inland from the *plateia* on the main street. (☎22820 22 260. Open M-F 7:30am-2pm.) **Postal Code:** 84500.

ACCOMMODATIONS AND FOOD. If you visit in high season, be prepared to spend big, though accommodations still aren't cheap during the low months. Domatia are the best options (rooms €35-50, in low season €25-35). The **tourist information kiosk** has a list of names and numbers. To get to **Karaoulanis Rooms ❸,** take the street opposite Alpha Bank and turn right at the arrow, down another set of stairs; it's on the left corner of Nimborio beach facing inland. It rents spacious rooms and studios with kitchens, baths, air-conditioning, and TVs. There is another Karaoulanis further away from the main part of town, in Anemomilous, with five studio apartments and wireless internet. Ask Yannis at Riva for more info. (☎69744 60 330; www.androsrooms.gr. Doubles €30-70; studios €50-120. Cash only.) **Hotel Niki (Nikh) ❺,** on the left just as you enter Pl. Kairis, has six nicely decorated rooms with TVs, A/C, fridges, baths, and balconies. (☎29 155. Doubles €65-90; triples €90-110. Cash only.)

A number of small family-owned cafes and restaurants along the pedestrian main street serve *mezedes*, milkshakes, and pizza. For a delicious traditional meal, try **Parea ❷,** in the corner of Pl. Kairis, overlooking Paraporti beach. (☎23 721. Cover €1. Entrees €6-9. Open daily noon-1am. MC/V.) For savory and sweet crepes, head to **Sofrano Kreperi ❷,** across from Alpha Bank on the left. (☎24 152. Crepes from €2.70. Open daily 7am-3pm and 6pm-2am.) In the afternoon, when

CYCLADES

other cafes and restaurants have closed until dinner, enjoy an *espresso freddo* and some *kataifi* at **Ermis,** on Pl. Kairis. (☎22 233. Open daily 8am-midnight.)

SIGHTS. Andros Town's museums go above and beyond the usual offerings of small island towns. The **Archaeological Museum,** a large white building on the left as you enter Pl. Kairis, displays enormous *pithoi* (storage jars) from the Geometric-era village of Zagora. The collection includes a famed marble **statue of Hermes,** whose discovery prompted King Otto to make a special trip to Andros. (☎22820 23 664. Open Tu-Su 8:30am-3pm. €3, students and seniors €2, EU students free.) Turn down the lane to the left upon exiting, and follow the arrows on the left to find the permanent wing of the **Museum of Contemporary Art.** Its exhibits display selections of modern art by Greek and foreign artists, with one room devoted works by 20th-century Greek sculptor Michael Tombros. The echoing noises emanating from below are part of an electromagnetic art installation, in which a triptych of electromagnets manipulate dangling metal rods to strike plastic strings. The museum's new wing is further down on the right, and houses three levels of rotating contemporary exhibitions. (☎22820 22 444. Open June-Sept. M and W-Sa 10am-2pm and 6-8pm, Tu and Su 10am-2pm; Oct.-May M and Sa-Su 10am-2pm. €6, students €3, seniors and under 12 free.) Follow the main road past Pl. Kairis, turn left at the dead end, and continue almost to the end of the street to reach the **Maritime Museum of Andros.** It houses models, paintings, and photographs of 19th- and 20th-century sailing vessels. (Open daily 8am-10pm. €2, seniors and under 12 free.) Past the museum is a *plateia* where the larger-than-life **Alfanis Nautis Statue,** honoring lost soldiers, gazes out at the Venetian castle's humble ruins.

BEACHES. Facing infland from this *plateia*, you should be able to see **Paraporti Beach** to the left and **Nimborio Beach** to the right. To reach Paraporti's expansive sands, take the steps down from the back right corner of Pl. Kairis. Nimborio, the more popular and more developed beach, is most easily accessed via the street that leads down to the water across from Alpha Bank. **Achla,** north of town, is considered one of Europe's most beautiful beaches, but is accessible

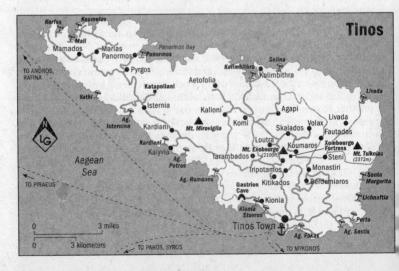

only by moped or fishing boat. Just north of Achla lies **Vori,** where you can swim among shipwrecks; locals warn tourists to be careful of sharp metal in the wreckage. Those yearning to see more secluded spots—the many rivers, waterfalls, and monasteries of the island's interior—should inquire at **Andros Travel** (p. 275). A beautiful hiking trail originates in **Apika,** 6km north of Andros Town, and leads past **Sariza Springs** to the village of **Stenies.** This small town is home to the largest waterwheel in the Balkans and is the site of an old spaghetti factory that was accidentally burned down in 1916 by a Greek priest.

TINOS Τήνος

Marked by towering Mount Exobourgo, Tinos consists of a tourist-oriented harbor town and a number of remote villages that seem untouched by commercialism. Despite a bustling nightlife, Tinos's main attraction remains the Panagia Evangelistria Church, the largest contemporary shrine of the Greek Orthodox religion. The cool, often unruly breezes that envelop the island explain why the ancient Greeks believed Tinos to be the home of Aeolus, the god of wind.

TINOS TOWN Χώρα ☎ 22830

The initial view of Tinos Town—also commonly referred to as Chora or simply "town"—may be intimidating, with its busy harbor, crowded streets, and cars zipping up and down the waterfront road. A quick walk up pedestrian-friendly Evangelistrias or along the harbor-front's cafes and *tavernas*, though, will prove that beneath Tinos Town's frenetic exterior is a calm, friendly community.

▉ TRANSPORTATION

Ferries: Ferry schedules vary, so check at the **port authority booth** (☎22830 22 220) in the central port or at one of the many **Blue Star ticket offices** (☎22830 24 241) along the waterfront. The largest one is directly across from the buses. Ferries run to: **Andros** (2hr., 4-6 per day, €8); **Mykonos** (30min., 5-6 per day, €5.50); **Rafina** (4hr., 4 per day, €19); **Syros** (40min., 3-4 per week, €8.10). The **Hellas Ferries** office, next door to the port authority booth, has schedules and tickets for **highspeed** to: **Mykonos** (20min., 6 per day, €9.50); **Paros** (2hr., 4 per day, €21.50); **Piraeus** (4hr., 3 per day, €44); **Rafina** (1hr., 4 per day, €40); and **Syros** (20min., 3 per day, €9). There are 3 **ferry ports** in Tinos, so ask where you're leaving from when buying tickets.

Buses: Buses depart from the central port and run to: **Agios Fokas** (5min., 5 per day 11am-5:30pm, €1); **Kalloni/Kolimbithra** (30min.; 4 per day 6:45am-4pm, 7:30pm from the new port; €1.30) via **Tripotamos, Chinara, Loutra, Krokos, Komi,** and **Agapi: Kionia** (7min.; every hr. 9:30am-7:30pm, 8:30pm-9:30pm from the new port; €1); **Pirgos/Panormos** (45min., 4 per day 6:30am-6pm, €3) via **Tripotamos, Kampos, Tarampados, Kardiani, Isternia, Pirgos,** and **Marlas; Porto** (10min.; every 2hr. 8am-8pm, 10pm from the new port; €1); **Skalados** (20min.; M 6:45am, 1pm; €1.60); **Steni/ Potamia** (30min.; 7 per day 6:45am-6pm, 10pm from the new port; €1.30) via **Trandaros, Dio Horia, Arnados, Monastiri, Mesi, Falatados, Steni,** and **Mirsini.** A schedule is posted at the **KTEL ticket agency** (☎22830 22 440), across from the central port, next to a Blue Star ticket office. Open daily 8am-9:30pm.

Taxis: (☎22830 22 470), 1 block past the waterfront base of Evangelistrias. Available daily 6am-1:30am.

Car and Moped Rental: Vidalis (☎22830 23 400). Several locations on the waterfront. Also has free maps. Mopeds €20-25 per day. Cars €40-60 per day. Open daily 9am-9pm.

CYCLADES

⊕ 🔃 ORIENTATION AND PRACTICAL INFORMATION

The town's **central port,** across from the bus depot, is the docking point for many ferries. Highspeeds dock at the port to the left, facing inland. The **newest port,** farther to the left around the waterfront, past a playground, is equally trafficked. Activity centers on wide **Megalochares** (you can see the church at the top) and parallel, pedestrian **Evangelistrias** (known as "Bazaar") to the right, facing inland. Among the restaurants near the base of Megalochares, an alley leads away from the central port, through a small *plateia* with a dolphin statue, to a handful of restaurants and Tinos's cafes and clubs. A **map** of Tinos is to the left of the central port, and most ferry offices give out free paper maps of the town and island.

Tourist Office: Windmills Travel, Kionion 2 (☎22830 23 398), on the left side of the playground by the far left port. Arranges accommodations and rental cars (low season €25-30, high season and weekends €45-60). Also offer bus tours of the island (€15) and arrange private boat and scuba diving expeditions for groups. English spoken. Open daily 10am-6pm.

Banks: National Bank (☎22830 22 088), opposite the bus depot along the waterfront. Open M-Th 8am-2pm, F 8am-2pm). **Alpha Bank** (☎22830 23 603), by the post office. Open M-Th 8am-2:30pm, F 8am-2pm. Both have **ATMs** and **currency exchange.**

Police: (☎22830 22 255), 5min. out of town on the road to Kionia. Accessible by phone 24hr. **Tourist police** (☎22830 23 670), in the same building as the police. Open daily 8am-10pm.

Pharmacy: (☎22830 22 272), just to the right of the base of Evangelistrias, next to a Hellas Ferries ticket office. Open M-F 8am-2pm and 6-9:30pm.

Medical Services: (☎22830 22 210), by Tinos Camping.

Telephones: OTE (☎22830 22 139), up Megalochares on the right. Open M-F 7:45am-1:30pm.

Internet Access: Symposion Cafe, Evangelistrias 13 (☎22830 24 368), on the left up the stairs above a photo shop. Internet and Wi-Fi €5 per hr., min. €3. Open daily 8:30am-midnight.

Post office: (☎22830 22 247), on the right end of the waterfront. Sells phone cards. Open M-F 7:30am-2pm. **Postal Code:** 84200.

🏠 🏕 ACCOMMODATIONS AND CAMPING

Tinos has plenty of accommodations, but rooms fill up around Easter and on weekends in July and August. Many *domatia* are off Evangelistrias and Alavanou, on the right of the waterfront.

Nikoleta Rooms to Let, Kapodistriou 11 (☎22830 24 719 or 69374 56 488), on the 2nd right off the traffic circle uphill from the post office. Rooms just 100m from Agios Fokas beach include A/C, TVs, fridges, and balconies. Though only some rooms have baths and kitchenettes, common kitchen and laundry facilities are available. If the rooms are full, Nikoleta will be happy to help you find alternate lodging nearby. Reservations recommended. Singles €20-25; doubles €25-30; triples €35-45; quads €45-50. ❶

Hermes Rooms to Let, Evangelistrias 33 (☎69475 34 225), midway up the road to the left. Look for a sign on the balcony above street level; enter from the alley just before it. Rents cozy rooms with a central kitchen and common baths. Also has **apartments** on Marcos Psaros with more amenities. Doubles €20-45; triples €40-60. ❷

Faros, Foskolou 2 (☎22830 23 530). Walk around the playground near the far-left port, up the set of stairs just before the church, and turn right at the street. The 6 rooms have baths, TVs, and A/C. Common balconies have harbor views. Singles €35-45; doubles €50; triples €70. Call ahead for lower prices. ❸

Tinos Camping (☎22830 22 344). Signs off the traffic circle past the post office. Grounds have a kitchen, laundry, showers, cafe, and bar. Watch out for the chickens and peacocks—and their droppings. Tent rental €7.50. €8 per person; €3-5 per tent; 2- to 5-person bungalows €30-35, with baths €45-50. 10% discount for stays over 4 days, 20% for 15 days or more. ❶

🍴 FOOD

A line of *tavernas* begins at the base of Megalochares and stretches all the way to the new port, each offering nearly identical fare. For the real gems, venture away from the waterfront and into its side streets and alleyways. The **farmer's market,** on the playground, sells local crops—artichokes, capers, and tomatoes—in abundance. (Jarred items typically €5. Open from mid-morning to mid-afternoon.)

🔲 **Palaia Pallada** (☎22830 23 516), in an alley just off the *plateia* with the dolphins, walking away from the main port. This *taverna,* with an attractive vine-shaded seating area, has earned its top-notch reputation by serving authentic favorites like grilled lamb (€7), vegetable dishes (€3-6), and pasta (€5-8). The proprietor has been known to offer complimentary wine and sweets to friendly customers. Open daily noon-midnight. MC/V. ❷

🔲 **Kafeneio Kiriakatiko** (☎22830 22 606), in an alley just to the right of Evangelistrias. Where Tinians go for homemade *loukoumades* (balls of fried dough glazed in honey and cinnamon; €5), and ouzo with *mezes* (€3). The gramophones, old-fashioned sofas, and art nouveau light fixtures will really take you back. Open daily 8am-2am. ❶

Sikoutris (☎22830 24 855), around the corner from Palaia Pallada and down the alley to the right. This souvlaki stand has cheap beer (€1.50-3) and gyros (€1.90) that are a hit with the late night crowd. Open daily 5pm-3am. Cash only. ❶

Agkyra (☎22830 23 016). Look for the blue tables flanked by 2 large trees. Removed from the frenetic *plateia,* this *ouzeri* provides a peaceful haven for locals seeking fresh fish (€40-60 per kg) and traditional grilled meats (€8-12). Open daily 11am-4pm and 8am-midnight. Cash only. ❷

👁️ 📷 SIGHTS AND BEACHES

PANAGIA EVANGELISTRIA. In 1822, a Tiniot nun, Sister Pelagia, had a vision in which the Virgin Mary told her about an icon buried in a field. A year later, the prophesied icon was unearthed, and the imposing Panagia Evangelistria was built to house it. The marble church draws daily visits from those who consider it evidence of the Virgin's divine power. The relic is said to have healing powers and is credited with ridding Tinos of cholera, saving a sinking ship, and giving a blind man sight. Gifts of gold, diamonds, jewels, and countless *tamata* (plaques praising Mary's healing powers) cover the chapel. The famous icon sits up the red-carpeted flight of steps. More devout pilgrims will approach on hands and knees, some beginning at the red carpet at the base of the church, others as soon as they get off the boat at the port, continuing all the way up the hill. The **Well of Sanctification** is a natural spring that appeared when the icon was found. Today it flows from one of many faucets in the church between two sets of marble entrance stairs to the chapel; visitors can scoop up a bottle of it to drink or to carry as a talisman. To the right is the **mausoleum** of the Greek warship Elli, sunk by an Italian torpedo in 1940. *(Open daily 6:30am-8:30pm. Modest dress required. Free.)*

ARCHAEOLOGICAL MUSEUM. This small museum displays an ancient sundial, sculptures from the sanctuary of Poseidon and Amphitrite at Kionia, a fifth-century BC relief from a cemetery at Xombourgo, and a seventh-century BC relief showing Athena bursting from Zeus's head. (*Megalochares 35, uphill from the OTE. ☎ 22830 29 063. Open Tu-Su 8:30am-3pm. €2, students and seniors €1, EU students and children free.*)

OTHER SIGHTS. Tinos is strewn with over 1000 medieval birdhouses called **dovecotes.** They are made of intricate white lattices and are full of nesting birds, and are the island's symbol. The largest and most impressive collection of dovecotes can be found in the village of **Tarambados,** 6km from Tinos Town, accessible by bus. To explore the poorly-preserved ruins of the fourth-century BC **Temple of Poseidon and Amphitrite,** near the beach, drive left along the waterfront road.

BEACHES. Sun-worshippers take a page out of the religious pilgrims' book and prostrate themselves on Tinos's beautiful beaches. Facing inland at the center of town, **Agios Fokas** is on the other side of the peninsula to the right, with pebbly sand lining a shallow bay. Picturesque **Kolimbithra** is in a small cove 12km north of Tinos Town. The stretch of sand on the island's northern coast lies seductively below a few small *tavernas.* In the unlikely event that the beach gets crowded, walk uphill facing the sea to the right and around the peninsula to remote **Selina.** If you find yourself in the Pyrgos or Panormos bay region, continue past the harborside village of **Panormos** and down to the lovely beach. **Kionia,** 3.5km from the center of town, is narrow and pebbly but still attracts a healthy crowd thanks to the frequent buses and multitude of nearby *tavernas.*

█ NIGHTLIFE

The harbor-front closes to traffic at 8pm. Streets that just minutes before were full of cars quickly fill with pedestrians eager to enjoy Tinos Town's many bars and clubs.

- **Koursaros Music Bar** (☎22830 23 963), at the end of the harbor restaurant row. Start your night at this popular bar amid colorful hanging baubles and stashes of pirate booty. Beer €4-6. Mixed drinks €9. Open daily 8am-4am.

- **Sibylla,** Taxiarchon 17. Look for the entrance to an alleyway at the base of Megalochares. Enter it, and pass the string of clothing boutiques. Draws include a marble dance floor and a DJ who mixes Greek and Euro dance music. Beer €4-6. Mixed drinks €7-9. Open daily 10pm-3am.

- **Village Club,** next door to Sibylla. Packs dancers onto its laser-lit floor. Beer €4-6. Mixed drinks €7-9. Open daily 10pm-3am.

- **Kactus Bar,** at the base of a windmill above Tinos Town. Take a taxi (€2). Listen to American and international pop music while savoring the unbeatable view. Beer €5-6. Mixed drinks €8. Open daily 10pm-7am.

- **Paradise.** Take a taxi (€2). A thatched-roof "after-club" for those still raring to go when the bars shut down. Open daily 3am-9am.

█ HIKING

MOUNT EXOBOURGO. This mountain, 14km north of Tinos Town, dominates the terrain of the island's interior. The Venetian Fortress Xombourgo on the northeastern side of the mountain, the island's 13th-century capital, withstood 11 assaults from the Ottomans before finally falling to them in 1715, the conquerors' last territorial gain. For a panoramic view of the entire island, drive up to the foot of the fortress, where sits the **Sacred Heart Monastery,** a site of Catholic pilgrimage. If you're feeling energetic, climb the mountain from the eastern foothill on a trail lined with wildflowers and brilliant orange moss. On a clear day, the peak offers a magnificent view extending as far as Santorini. Cross the Sacred Heart *plateia* to the small gate where the trail to the top starts. At a fork, the road detours around to a church. Proceed straight up to get to the fort. Strong winds buffet Exobourgo, causing the fort to close occasionally; stay low to avoid getting blown off balance.

ADDITIONAL ROUTES. The trip from Tinos Town to Loutra and back takes 3-4hr. and traverses much of the island's interior. Other routes, marked by wooden signposts, are shorter and don't cut through all the villages. Regardless of which trail you choose, remember to bring food, water, comfortable shoes, and a hiking partner. Stick to the trail and be prepared for extremely high winds. Travel agents in Tinos Town (p. 278) can provide more information on the particular trails.

DAYTRIPS FROM TINOS TOWN

PYRGOS Πύργος

Surrounded by arid, intricately terraced mountainsides, Pyrgos gleams white in the midday sun. It is a center for many of the island's renowned marble sculptors. The influence of **marble** seems to crop up everywhere: in streets, monuments—even the bus stop is marble. Pyrgos has evaded the crush of the island's tourists, and an unmistakable small-town charm emanates from its narrow, winding streets. Pyrgos has a variety of ways for visitors to learn more about its central occupation. The two **museums** next to the bus stop are nice introductions, displaying the works of local sculptors. The building closer to the bus stop holds examples of the marble-sculpting process, while the traditional building on the right houses the busts and drawings of **Ylannoulis Halepas** (1851-1938), the town's most famous sculptor. After his first period of productivity was cut short by mental illness, his mother destroyed all his work, believing that his creativity caused him to go mad. Two years after her death, he began to create again, and continued consistently, in both Pyrgos and Athens, until his death. Most of the works on display are plaster, since few of his concepts were ever realized in marble, but the many sketches and artifacts of the great sculptors life make this museum a worth while visit. (Museums open daily 11am-2pm and 5:30-9pm. Each €3.)

Pyrgos has been home to a **School of Fine Arts,** which has taught the marble craft to area youth since 1955. Continue away from the bus stop past the museums, cross the *plateia* to the right, and turn left at Ag. Nikolaos church to find Pyrgos's marble-covered **cemetery;** School of Fine Arts graduates are responsible for many of the monuments on view. Just past the cemetery is a set of stairs, and the end of which is the school itself. Although the school is closed during prime tourism season, a peep into the windows reveals a staggering number of sculptures lining the walls. For a more hands-on experience, the walk from the bus stop to the *plateia* crosses many **marble workshops,** including that of **Michalis Saltamanikas,** who attended the School of Fine Arts. Visitors are welcome in his roomy workshop, and he's happy to demonstrate—and sell—his work. (☎22830 31 554. Open M-Sa during the work day. Sculptures range from €40 to thousands.) Pass the School of Fine Arts and keep an eye out on your left for the banners of the **Museum of Marble Crafts,** which opened in May of 2008. Exhibits take visitors through the entire marble-crafting process, from quarrying to the installation of finished marble carvings. A separate building houses special exhibitions, such as a photo narrative of the Greek-American immigrant experience. (☎22830 31 290. Open M and W-Su 10am-6pm Mar.-Oct., Nov.-Feb. 10am-5pm. €3.)

Throughout the day, locals and tourists gather for casual drinks in the cafes that line the main *plateia*. For an excellent lunch or dinner, try **Ta Muronia❷**, on the left as you enter the *plateia*. It serves spaghetti with local sausage (€4.50) along with traditional favorites. (☎22830 31 229. Entrees €4.50-12. Open daily noon-late.) Indulge your sweet tooth next door at **To Kentrikon ❶** (☎22830 31 670) with sweet and rich *ekmek*, a dessert made with shredded flatbread, honey, and custard. **Taverna Eirinis ❷**, across from the bus stop, makes *furtalia* (an omelette with vegetables and local sausage; €8.50)—the island specialty. (☎22830 31 165. Entrees €5-10. Open daily 10am-2am.)

NAXOS Νάξος

The gleaming marble Portara, the lone remaining arch of a temple to Apollo, has beckoned visitors to Naxos since 522 BC. Centuries later, Venetians safeguarded their profits in Naxos, the capital of their mercantile empire. Today, Naxos celebrates both its ancient and its recent past, as well as its very delicious present. The local produce and linens are some of the best among the Cyclades. Taste and browse at the shops and eateries of Chora, then take a bus or moped to the placid villages of Halki and Apiranthos. Take the winding mountain roads past old Venetian towers and early Christian churches, marble quarries and pristine beaches, expansive vineyards and quiet olive groves.

NAXOS TOWN   ☎22850

A dense collection of labyrinthine streets, bustling *tavernas*, and tiny museums radiates to the sea in Naxos Town, also known as Chora. Despite its claim as the urban center of Naxos, the town retains an old island charm. Among the tightly packed buildings of Old Naxos, stone archways curve over streets, and trellises of flowers drape over the whitewashed buildings and Venetian ruins.

▣ TRANSPORTATION

Flights: Leave from **Naxos Airport (JNX)**. **Olympic Airways** (☎22850 23 292) has a desk in **Naxos Tours** (☎22850 22 095; www.naxostours.gr), on the left end of the waterfront. Flights go to **Athens** (€62).

Ferries: All ferries from Naxos leave from Naxos Town. 2 docks are at the left end of town, 1 for large ferries, the other for smaller ferries and daily cruises. For updated schedules and prices, consult travel agencies. To: **Amorgos** (2-6hr., depending on stops; 1-2 per day; €14); **Astypalea**, (3hr., 1 per week, €23); **Donousa** (1-4hr., 4 per week, €8.50); **Ios** (1½hr., 6 per week F-Su, €9.30); **Koufonisia** (3hr., 1-2 per day, €7.50); **Paros** (1hr., 4 per day, €7.50); **Piraeus** (6hr., 3-4 per day, €30); **Rhodes** (13hr., 2 per week, €32); **Santorini** (2-6hr., 1-3 per day, €15.50); **Schinousa** (2hr., 1-2 per day, €6.50); **Syros** (2hr., 4 per week, €18).

High-Speed Boats: To: **Ios** (45min., 1 per week, €20.50); **Mykonos** (45min., 1 per day, €18.50); **Paros** (30min., 2 per day, €13); **Piraeus** (3½hr., 2 per day, €45); **Santorini** (30min., 1 per day, €27.50).

Buses: (☎22850 22 291). Tickets for all buses €1.40-5.50. Current schedules are available at the station (across from the largest dock) and at tourist offices. Buses to **Apollon** (2 per day 9:30am-1:30pm) and **Filoti-Chalki-Sagri** (6 per day 9:30am-3pm) are often packed. Buses also run to: **Ampram** (Tu and Th 2:30pm); **Apiranthos** (5 per day 7:15am-3pm); **Apollon** (Tu and Th 2:30pm) via the coast; **Engares** (Tu and Th 2:30); **Glynado-Tripodes** (4 per day, 7:30am-3pm); **Kastraki** (3 per day 7:30am-3pm); **Kinidaros** (2 per day, noon-3pm); **Korono-Skado** (2 per day, 9:30am-1:30pm); **Melanes-Miloi** (2 per day noon-3pm); **Mikri Vigla** (3 per day 7:30am-3pm); **Pyrgaki Beach** (3 per day 7:30am-3pm).

Taxis: (☎22850 22 444). On the waterfront, next to the bus depot.

Car Rental: Auto Tour (☎22850 25 480; www.naxosrentacar.com), before Zas Tours on the waterfront. Cars €25-40 per day, including 24hr. roadside assistance. Luggage storage €1.50. Open daily 8:30am-9:30pm.

🖊 🛈 ORIENTATION AND PRACTICAL INFORMATION

The waterfront along **Protopapadakis,** to the right of the harbor, is lined with cafes, *tavernas,* and clubs. After 500m the road forks inland; after another 70m, turn right to find the roundabout of **Plateia Protodikiou,** the central square. The **Old Town** is to the left as you walk toward Protodikiou, accessible via any of the alleyways running inland from the waterfront.

Budget Travel: Zas Travel (☎22850 23 330). 1 location 2 doors down from the tourist center and another 50m away from the port; both are on the waterfront. Sells ferry and plane tickets and offers information about daytrip cruises and tours of the island. Internet access (€4 per hr.) available at the port location. Open daily 8:30am-midnight.

Bank: National Bank (☎22850 23 053) is 1 of many banks on the waterfront offering **currency exchange** and an **ATM.** Open M-Th 8am-2:30pm, F 8am-2pm.

Bookstore: Papyrus (☎22850 23 039), in an alley to the left of the 1st inland street before Vrakas jewelry, with blue signs reading "gold-silver, used books." Open M-Sa 10am-2pm and 6-11pm, Su 6-11pm. **Zoom** (☎22850 23 675), next to the bakery, approximately 50m from the end of the harbor. International magazines, stationery and stamps, photocopying, and internet access (€3 per hr.). Open daily 8:30am-11pm.

Police: (☎22850 22 100 or 23 280), on Amortou, the main road heading toward Ag. Giorgios beach from Pl. Protodikiou, 1km out of town. Open 24hr. **Port Police,** Protopapadakis (☎22850 22 300), across from the small port dock.

Pharmacy: (☎22850 24 946 for on-duty pharmacy), on the waterfront, right before the OTE. Open M-F 8:30am-2:30pm and 6-10pm.

Medical Services: (☎22850 23 333 or 23 550). Turn inland at the fork in the road past the OTE, at the right end of the waterfront; it is 500m farther on the left. Helicopter to Athens available for **emergencies.** Open 24hr.

Telephones: OTE (☎22850 29 110), left of the fork in the road to the right of the waterfront. Open M-F 8am-2pm.

Internet Access: Photo @ Naxos (☎22850 25 008), behind the OTE, just past Waffle House near the waterfront. Photocopies and ID photos. Open daily 9am-2am. **Heavens Cafe Bar** (☎22850 22 747), 20m beyond the police station on the road leading toward Ag. Giorgios Beach. Internet €3 per hr. Free Wi-Fi. Belgian waffles with fresh fruit €5. Open daily 8am-2am. The waterfront cafe of the Vallindras family, **Citron Cafe and Cocktail Bar,** has free Wi-Fi.

Post Office: (☎22850 02 221). Walk down the waterfront with the water on your right and continue beyond the main street that turns left. Keep the playground on the right; the post office is on the left. Open M-F 7:30am-2pm. **Postal Code:** 84300.

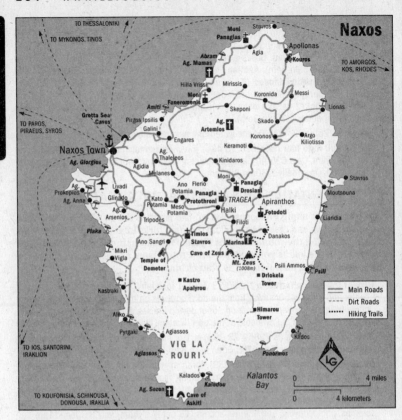

Naxos

TO THESSALONIKI
TO MYKONOS, TINOS
TO AMORGOS, KOS, RHODES
TO PAROS, PIRAEUS, SYROS
TO IOS, SANTORINI, IRAKLION
TO KOUFONISIA, SCHINOUSA, DONOUSA, IRAKLIA

Moni Panagias
Stavros
Apolionas
Abram
Ag. Mamas
Agia
Kouros
Hilia Vrissi
Mirissis
Moni Faneromenis
Koronida
Messi
Amiti
Skeponi
Lionas
Grotta Sea Caves
Pirgos Ipsilis
Ag. Artemios
Skado
Naxos Town
Galini
Koronos
Argo Kiliotissa
Ag. Giorgios
Engares
Keramoti
Agidia
Ag. Thaleleos
Kinidaros
Melanes
Moni
Ano Flerio
Stavros
Livadi
Panagia Drosiani
Ag. Prokopios
Glinado
Potamia
Moutsouna
Ag. Anna
Kato Potamia
Panagia Protothroni
TRAGEA
Apiranthos
Ag. Arsenios
Meso Potamia
Halki
Fotodoti
Tripodes
Filoti
Liaridia
Plaka
Timios Stavros
Danakos
Mikri Vigla
Ano Sangri
Ag. Marina
Temple of Demeter
Cave of Zeus
Mt. Zeus (1008m)
Psili Ammos
Psili
Kastraki
Kastro Apalyrou
Driokela Tower
Aliko
Himarou Tower
Pyrgaki
Agiassos
VIG LA ROURI
Kitlos
Aglassos
Panormos
Kalados
Kalantos Bay
Ag. Sozon
Kaladou
Cave of Askiti

Main Roads
Dirt Roads
Hiking Trails

N
LG

0   4 miles
0   4 kilometers

▮▮ ACCOMMODATIONS AND CAMPING

Naxos has three beach camping options, whose representatives wait eagerly at the dock. All the sites have mini-marts, restaurants, internet access, moped rentals, and laundry facilities. Prices are similar at each campground (€4-8 per person; tent rental €2-3). By far the closest to town (2km away) and the most convenient for bar hoppers, **Naxos Camping ❶** is 150m from Ag. Giorgios beach and has a swimming pool. (☎22850 23 500; www.naxos-camping.gr. 10% discount for *Let's Go* readers. Cash only.) For well-maintained facilities 6km inland from Naxos Town, try **Plaka Camping ❶**, next to Plaka beach. (☎22850 42 700; www.plakacamping.gr. Cabins and rooms €30-85. Cash only.) **Maragas Camping ❶** is on Ag. Anna about 7km from town. (☎22850 42 552 or 42 599; www.maragascamping.gr. Doubles €20-45. Studios and apartments €30-90. Cash only.)

▣ **Panorama** (☎22850 22 330; www.panoramanaxos.gr), near the *kastro* area. Superb location high in the *kastro* affords panoramic views of the harbor, town, and mountains. Tasteful, recently refurbished rooms come with fridges, baths, and TVs; ask about A/C. Breakfast €5. High-season doubles €55-65, depending on A/C and view; triples €78; 4-person suite €110-115. Cash only. ❸

Windmill Studios (☎22850 24 594; www.windmillnaxos.com), near Ag. Giorgios beach. Owner George is among the island's most attentive proprietors, and his place among the most sought after on the island. Book in advance. Aug. 1-week min. stay. High-season singles €50; doubles €55; triples €60. Low season singles €22-35; doubles €26-40; triples €30-45. Cash only. ●

Pension Irene I and II (☎22850 23 169; www.irenepension-naxos.com), near Ag. Giorgios beach. 2 popular options, with laundry and a swimming pool available between the 2. All rooms have kitchenettes and A/C. Laundry €8. Free Wi-Fi. Singles €30-70; doubles €40-85; triples €50-90. Cash only. ●

Pension Sofi (☎22850 26 437; www.pensionsofi.gr) and **Studios Panos** (☎22850 26 078; www.studiospanos.com), near Ag. Giorgios beach. Attached to each other. Free pick-up at the port. Doubles €45. Book online for lower rates. Cash only. ●

Hotel Grotta (☎22850 22 215; www.hotelgrotta.gr), near the *kastro* area. Get the free port shuttle, or take the road across from the bus station along the water to the dirt path at the left; the hotel is at the top of the hill. It might not seem like a bargain, but the airy spaces and amenities at this placid escape will convince you otherwise. Breakfast included. Laundry €8. Singles €35-80; doubles €45-90; triples €55-100. MC/V. ●

🍴 FOOD

Naxos brims with cafes and outdoor *ouzeria*, where chefs cook up fresh seafood and traditional dishes. The *tavernas* along the harbor have some of the best deals in town; many of them offer ample meals, including wine or a Coke, for under €8. Naxos is particularly proud of its local cheeses, wine, preserved fruits, and honey—which you can find at just about any mini-market. And don't leave without tasting the **citron**—Naxos is home to the only two distilleries in the world that still produce this pungent citrus liqueur.

To Elliniko (☎22850 27 050; www.toelliniko.com). Past the main square, along the road to the police station. A 1st-class *taverna* in the middle of the Ag. Giorgios hotel zone. Choose from daily specials behind the counter (such as boiled goat €6), or grilled fare off the menu (veal chop €8.50). Grilled entrees come with potatoes and vegetables. Open daily noon-midnight. Cash only. ●

Taverna To Kastro (☎22850 22 005), before the entrance to the *kastro*. Turn left away from the waterfront after Rendez-Vous Cafe and up to the right, following signs for the castle and museums. At this hilltop *taverna*, the view is as spectacular as the menu. For 31 years, the chef, Sulis, has been serving local specialties such as baked giant beans in tomato sauce (€4) and grilled catch of the day (€9.50). Excellent service with a handshake and a smile. Open daily 6pm-late. Cash only. ●

Labyrinth, (☎22850 22 253), in the Old Town. Follow the signs from the entrance to the Old Market at Captain's Cafe on the waterfront. There's nothing labyrinthine about the intelligent, classic fare at this Old Market spot. Take this opportunity to try one of the Naxian wines from the restaurant's extensive list; they're the least expensive and pretty darn good. Seafood risotto in ouzo sauce €7.50. After dinner, step across the way to Cafe Naxos, which hosts occasional live music and rotating art displays. Open daily noon-midnight. Cafe Naxos open M-Sa 9pm-2am. Cash only. ●

Aktaion, (☎22850 25 112), on the waterfront, about 200m from the bus station. Alice in Wonderland would feel right at home at this charming patisserie, which serves Greek pastries and homemade ice cream on its pastel-and-white patio. Pastries €3-5. Open daily 9am-midnight or later. AmEx/MC/V. ●

Irini's (☎22850 26 780), the 2nd taverna along the waterfront after Zas Travel. A cluster of blue- and white-checked tablecloths under a leaf-covered terrace, nestled in between the waterfront park area and the pedestrian path. The attentive staff serves

ON THE MENU

A DRINK TO REMEMBER

The island of Naxos is one of only three places in the world where fragrant citron trees grow. The citron fruit, introduced to the Mediterranean region in 300 BC by Alexander the Great, was the only citrus fruit grown in Europe until the Christian era.

The raw fruit contains hardly any juice, but in Greece the rind is often preserved in syrup to make a treat known as a "spoon sweet," while the leaves are made into an aperitif liqueur called *kitron*, one of three officially recognized State liqueurs. Collected in October, the leaves are then laid out in a dry room, dampened with water, placed in a boiler with pure alcohol and water, and distilled up to three times, before being flavored with sugar. Natural colors are also added to distinguish different flavors and strengths: the traditional green liqueur is the sweetest and least alcoholic, while the yellow is the strongest, and the clear lies somewhere in between.

The first *kitron* distillery was established in Haiki in 1896 by Markos Vallindras. The liquor was soon exported worldwide, becoming popular in Russia, France, Austria, and the United States. Visitors to the original factory can to see the ancient copper stills in which the kitron is made and sample the different flavors.

The Vallindras distillery (☎22850 31 220) in Halki offers free tours and tastings. Representatives of the Promponas distillery (☎22850 22 258) also provide info and samples at their store in Naxos Town, across from Myroditssa.

flavorful local fare and appetizers including the particularly tasty cheese croquettes (€5.50). Fresh green peppers stuffed with Naxian goat cheese and feta €6. Oven-baked Naxian lamb €9.50. Open Mar.-Oct. daily noon-late. MC/V. ❷

👁 🌊 SIGHTS AND BEACHES

From the waterfront, you can gaze at the chapel of **Myrditiotissa**, floating above the harbor on its manmade islet, and the marble **Portara** archway, on its own peninsula. Climb up to it to view the ambitious beginnings of an unfinished **temple** dedicated to Apollo, begun on the orders of the tyrant Lydamis in the sixth century BC.

◾MITROPOLIS MUSEUM. The museum, sunk into the plateia next to the Orthodox Church, is an enclosed archaeological site, with elevated glass walkways to lead you over the reconstructed buildings of a 13th-century BC settlement. (☎22850 24 151. Open Tu-Su 8:30am-3pm. Free.)

KASTRO. Naxos Town is crowned by the *kastro*, with small museums and churches within. Descendants of the Della Rocca Barozzi family, former Italian aristocrats, still inhabit a section of the castle; they have designated part of it as a **Venetian museum.** In an enchanting courtyard, the dignified and hospitable owner hosts frequent sunset concerts with classical music and traditional Greek dancing. (☎22850 22 387. Open daily 10am-3pm and 7-10pm. 30min. tours in English, French, and German throughout the day. €3, students and seniors €2. Tour €2. Sunset Concert tickets, which often sell out, are available at reception; €18-25. Complimentary soft drinks and local citron M-W and F-Su.)

OTHER SIGHTS. The **Byzantine Museum** museum is a two-room collection of artifacts from the AD eighth-tenth centuries found on Naxos and other Cycladic islands. (Open M-Sa 8am-2pm. Free.) Located in the former Collège Français where Nikos Kazantzakis (p. 56) studied, the **Archaeological Museum** boasts the world's largest exhibit of early Cycladic marble figurines. (Open Tu-Su 8:30am-3pm. €3, students €2.) The impressive **Catholic Church** is just around the corner. (Open daily 10am-7pm. Tours start at 5pm. Free. Modest dress required.)

BEACHES. Beachgoers seeking solitude head away from Naxos Town, but the closest waters are equally beautiful. Buses (€1.40) run regularly from the bus stop to **Agios Prokopios, Agia Anna,** and **Plaka** (a beach popular with nude bathers), while **Agios Giorgios** is a short walk from anywhere in town.

Clear, sparkling water laps up onto the shores of all these pristine spots, where a wide variety of sporting activities are available. **Naxos Surf** (☎22850 29 170), **Flisvos Sport Club** on Ag. Giorgios (☎22850 24 308), and **Plaka Water sports** at Plaka and Ag. Anna (☎22850 41 264) offer windsurfing, kayaking, and mountain biking equipment and lessons. Desert meets sea at the more secluded beaches of **Mikri Vigla, Abram, Aliko, Moutsouna,** and **Pyrgaki,** where scrub pines, prickly pear, and century plants grow on the dunes. All are accessible by bus from Naxos Town. Nude bathers gather on a small portion of the southern protuberance of **Kastraki Beach. Walking tours** of the island (€22) are available. Contact Iris Neubauer for information about a 3hr. horseback tour. (☎69488 09 142. €45.)

ENTERTAINMENT AND NIGHTLIFE

Starting around 11pm, music leads partiers to waterfront clubs, and extended happy hours lure them into lively bars. Try **Diogenes** and the **Captain's Club,** adjacent bars that advertise €4 mixed drinks until 2am. For an alternative to the club scene, try the island's outdoor theater, **Cine Astra.** A 15min. walk from the waterfront on the road to Agia Anna from Pl. Protodikiou, the theater shows English movies with Greek subtitles at 9 and 11pm. (☎22850 25 381. Open May-Oct. daily. €7.) If you're planning a full night out, start at **Prime;** head to **Naxos on the Rocks** and **Jam Bar** later; finally, end your night at the **Ocean Club** in the early hours of the morning.

Naxos On the Rocks (☎22850 29 224; www.naxosontherocks.com), behind the OTE. Delicious mixed drink, many of which use Caribbean rums. The pulsating music delivered by guest DJs will carry you well into the night. Get introduced to the top 40 of Greece, France, and Germany. Hookah available. W karaoke party. Cash only.

Ocean Club (☎22850 26 766), at the right end of the harbor, facing the water. The partier's last stop. Don't bother arriving before 2am, but once you get here, stay all night. Sip a mixed drink under pink crystal chandeliers on the waterfront patio or retreat indoors to join the gyrating crowds on the laser-lit dance floor. Mixed drinks €5-8. Cover €10; includes 1 drink. Open M-Th and Su 11pm-late, F-Sa 11pm-morning.

Prime, (☎22850 23 747; www.primenaxos.com), near the National Bank on the waterfront. Lures daytime crowds with its giant outdoor television screen and a full program of soccer and rugby, and nighttime crowds with its mood lighting. Make this your 1st stop to sip a drink and watch the sun set over the harbor. Mixed drinks €6-7. Daytime menu includes sandwiches (€3-4.50), fruit, and, ice cream. Open 9am-4am. Cash only.

Jam Bar (☎22850 69420 19 426). Take the 1st left after Klik Cafe; it's behind the OTE. Enjoy signature mixed drinks such as the Naxos Butterfly (€7) in the cool, dim interior or in the outdoor area, a small island of seats sectioned off by low pink walls and spherical lights. Shots €2-2.50. Open M-Th and Su 7pm-3:30am, F-Sa 7pm-late.

DAYTRIPS FROM NAXOS TOWN

CENTRAL NAXOS AND THE TRAGEA

A bus runs the 17km from Naxos Town to Halki (30min., 5 per day 9:30am-3pm), from which hikers can access Moni, Filoti, and Panagia Drosiani. Passengers can ask to be let off between stops; the path to Mt. Zeus is on the way.

Ancient ruins, medieval churches, and quaint, untouched towns are scattered within the Tragea, central Naxos's enormous, picturesque olive grove. By far the best way to see the inner island is by private transport; the sights are primarily along one main road but are often several kilometers from the closest

CYCLADES

bus stop. An ambitious but feasible bike ride can take you to the major sights, and an even more ambitious walker can hit a few of the highlights.

Colorful buildings and Venetian towers make up **Halki,** the village east of Naxos Town. The surrounding area is known as "Little Mystras" because of its many sixth- to 14th-century churches. In town, store owners hawk homemade linens, jam, and olive oil, while market vendors and the main *taverna* offer local produce (try the local specialty, pork with mushrooms, red peppers, and red beans; €10). Halki boasts the **Vallindras family's citron distillery,** one of only two in the world. Recently uncovered frescoes from the 11th and 13th centuries are displayed at Halki's **Medieval Panagia Prottheroni.** The church, adjacent to the bus stop, is often closed, but if you can find the Reverend Vasllis Scordas—he'll open the doors. (If you miss him, check out the photos at the Byzantine Museum in Naxos Town, p. 286.)

Panagia Drosiani, a well-preserved, early Christian edifice with a beautiful miniature dome and seventh-century frescoes, is a short drive or very scenic 30min. walk north of Halki on the road to Moni. The road south brings travelers to Filoti, another sleepy cluster of houses, tavernas, and small churches on a lush, steep hill. A 1hr. hike extends from Filoti to the mouth of the **Cave of Zeus,** a damp, dark grotto where an eagle gave the king of the gods his thunderbolts. Forty-five minutes from the cave is **Mount Zeus** (1008m), the tallest peak in Naxos, which usually takes visitors about 2hr. to climb.

The stretch of road leading east from Naxos Town toward **Melanes, Kinidaros,** and **Keramoti** is dotted with intriguing sights. A half-finished but distinguishable sixth-century BC **kouros** lies on its back in a wild garden in Flerio (7km east of Melanes), where narrow dirt paths lead to a modest statue garden and a small cafe. Keep an eye out of your car window or sit near the front of the bus for the best view of the sights on the road back to Naxos Town through Moni, Halki, and Filoti; you will pass the **Timios Stavros** (Holy Cross), a 17th-century nunnery, the **Temple of Demeter,** which experts currently are restoring, and the **Tower of Belogna**.

APIRANTHOS Απείρανθος
Buses run the 32km from Naxos Town (1hr., 5 per day 9:30am-3pm).

Venturing into Apiranthos may feel like a trip back in time. Fig trees overhang the sidewalk, and the townspeople speak a unique dialect—a legacy of the political refugees who fled here from Crete in the late 18th century. Its small size and proximity to Naxos Town make the quiet village an ideal destination for a leisurely half-day trip. Drive in early or take a morning bus. Start the day at cafe **O Tiorgos** with a coffee accompanied by homemade cake (€2.30), then continue down the blue marble road into the modest *plateia* that is Apiranthos's center; beyond the row of tavernas overlooking the valley lie Venetian ruins and 400-year-old homes that are worth a peek. Once the sun starts heating up, visit the town's handful of small museums. The one-room **archaeology museum** exhibits early third-century statues and pottery. (Open daily 8am-3pm. Free.) A €2 ticket grants admission to the **folk art museum** (in the main square; open 10am-1:30pm), the **natural history museum** (to the right of the bus stop; open 10:30am-2:30pm), and the **geological museum** (just beyond the natural history museum; open 10am-1:30pm). For lunch, try **Taverna O Platanos ❷,** a sophisticated terrace restaurant with generous helpings of traditionally prepared local products. (☎22850 61 460. Raki from Apiranthos €5.50. Roasted pork in tomato sauce €8.80. Open daily 10am-midnight.) Once you've fortified yourself, take advantage of the **hiking** trails, which start out near the bus stop. At the start of the main road, steps veer downward and to the right toward marked walking paths. The closest destination is a 25min. hike, the farthest approximately 90min., so bring water, a hat, and a partner.

APOLLONAS AND NORTHERN NAXOS
Buses run from Naxos Town to Apollonas (2hr., 2 per day 9:30am-1:30pm).

Countryside views make the trip to and from Apollonas a peaceful, pleasant way to spend an afternoon. You'll pass the secluded beach at Amiti, down the road from Galini. Farther on is the monastery of Faneromenis. One of the more famous *kouroi* of Naxos is just a short walk from the harbor. This *kouros* is nearly 11m tall. From the Apollonas bus stop, walk back along the main road uphill to the fork in the road. Take a sharp right and walk up until you see the stairs at the sign reading "προς κουρο" ("toward the *kouros*"). A car will make the trip much easier to manage.

LITTLE CYCLADES

Good things come in small packages, and nothing proves it better than the Little Cyclades. These tiny isles bridging Naxos and Amorgos are a tranquil and rustic interlude between their larger, increasingly crowded neighbors. In their towns, goats often outnumber people, and star-studded nights center on a single town cafe, drawing an eclectic mix of alternative campers and Greek tourists seeking the road less traveled.

RELAX, JUST DO IT. To fully appreciate the Little Cyclades, make sure you have at least a week for them. Most of the activities and sights center around walking, which is arduous and often takes the whole day. Give your self the time to slow down, disconnect from a busy schedule, and become part of the pace of these little islands. One or two nights apiece does not do them justice.

KOUFONISIA Κουφονήσια ☎ 22850

The smallest and most popular of the inhabited Little Cyclades, Koufonisia is surrounded by beaches on the southeastern side of the island, called "Ano Koufonisia." The name, meaning "hollow," refers to the caves perforating the island's coastline. Small clothing boutiques, cafes, and a lone ATM line Koufonisia's two main streets, which spring to life in the early evening. Recent spurts in the popularity of Koufonisia's picture-perfect beaches has driven up the price of rooms in the past few years. Despite rising prices, the island's town has preserved a simplicity that continues to lure those in search of total relaxation.

TRANSPORTATION. Ferry tickets are sold at **Prasinos Tours,** on the main road parallel to the beach, a few buildings past the blue-domed church; a schedule is updated on a board outside its door. (☎22850 71 438. Open daily 8am-2pm and 5-10:30pm.) **Ferries** go to: Aegiali, Amorgos (2-3hr.; 3 per week M, Th, Sa; €7.80); Iraklia (1 hr., 1-2 per day, €4.50); Katapola, Amorgos (3-4hr., 1-2 per day, €8) via Donousa (1½hr.; 3 per week M, Th, Sa; €5); Naxos (2hr., 1-2 per day, €7.50) via Schinousa (30min., €4); Paros (2-3hr.; 3 per week M, Th, Sa; €16); Piraeus (7hr., 1-2 per day, €30-40).

⚎ ▨ ORIENTATION AND PRACTICAL INFORMATION.

Head straight off the ferry dock and hug the beach to find accommodations. Koufonisia's commercial center consists of two main streets branching from the square behind the beach. The shorter one runs inland to the left; the longer one is on the right. This right fork heads straight but then veers left and circles back around, leading to Prasinos Tours. Free maps are available at a number of boutiques and markets. The 24hr. **police** (☎22850 71 375) are on the right fork leading inland from the port. Next door is the **medical center.** (☎22850 71 370, doctor ☎69738 18 612. Open M, W, F 9am-2pm and 6-8pm; Tu and Th 9am-2pm. 24hr. emergency service.) The **OTE** is on the main road inland, across from Pension Melissa. (☎22850 22 392. Open 8am-2pm and 5-10pm.) **Internet** access is available at Kalamia Music Cafe (p. 290). The **post office,** up the shorter left fork in a boutique next to the Keros Hotel, has **currency exchange** and a **24hr. ATM.** (☎22850 74 214. Open daily 10:30am-1:30pm and 6-11:30pm.) **Postal Code:** 84300.

⌂ ACCOMMODATIONS.

Many homes with rooms to let sit on the main road and next to the beach, but the rising popularity of Koufonisia's beaches unfortunately means rising prices. Affordable rooms can still be found among the numerous *domatia*, especially if you abandon the sea view and are willing to barter with the *domatia* owners upon arrival at the port. **Helene Despotidi ❷** rents relatively new, spacious and clean rooms, each with bath, A/C, fridge, and hotpot. (☎22850 71 848. Doubles €30-40; triples €40-60. Discounts for extended stays. Cash only.) **Akrogiali Rooms ❸**, along the road past the beach, has brightly decorated rooms with baths, fridges, TVs, air-conditioning, hot pots, stocked dishes, and intimate, blue balconies with unbeatable beach views. (☎22850 71 685. Doubles €40-60; triples €45-75. Cash only.) **Maria Prasinou ❸**, the first hotel on the road past the beach, has a quaint cafe over the water where beachgoers pass their nights. The rooms have baths, balconies, and beautiful harbor views. (☎22850 71 436. Doubles €40-60; triples €45-70. V.)

◳▨ FOOD AND NIGHTLIFE.

For tasty, cheap gyros (€2.50) or souvlaki (€1.50), swing by the enormously popular ▨**Strofi ❶**, behind a green window just around the corner from the church on the main road. (☎22850 11 818. Open 6:30pm-12:30am.) **Kohili ❶**, on the main road past Strofi, has croissants and cakes (€1.30-4), coffee (€1.30-3.50), great views of the harbor, and instrumental tunes wafting from the cafe across the street. (☎22850 74 279. Open daily 9am-midnight.) **Kalamia Music Cafe ❶**, 150m along the inland road, by the public phones, provides frappes (€2.50), sweets (€3-6), casual foods (€4-7), and an eclectic blend of world music for a crowd of chic, hipster customers on a beach-themed patio. (☎22850 71 741. Free Wi-Fi. Mixed drinks €7-8. Open daily 8am-4am.) People crowd into the purple-draped interior of **Emplo** for late-night dancing. Walk uphill to the left of the port and listen for Greek music. (Beer €3. Mixed drinks €6. Open daily 10pm-late.)

◪ BEACHES.

You will find more stunning, white-sand ▨**beaches** on little Koufonisia than on most of the other Cyclades combined. The crystal blue stretches spool out in a continuous ribbon along the southern coast. **Ammos** is closest to Chora, just to the right of the ferry dock facing inland; you can spot nearby fishing boats here while spirited locals play soccer on the fine, white sand. Continuing 10min. down the road behind the sand past clusters of *domatia* leads you to pebbly but pristine **Porta**, followed by the long stretch of fine sand at **Harakopou**. Quieter and smaller **Fanos** waits on the other side of the ridge. The farther you walk, the fewer people (and clothes) you'll see. A 3km walk along the main inland road (turn right after Neo Fanari restaurant and the mini market) takes you to ◪**Pori,** hands down the most gorgeous beach on the island. The brilliant blue, glassy water and fine, white sand are magnificent even by Greek island standards (though blustery winds can whip up the sand to harangue lounging beachgoers). If the sand begins to burn, head for the shaded rocks behind the beach where cave-lined coves and cliffs provide amazing vistas. You can also climb down on the side of the cliffs and swim next to the natural cave formations. Small boats make trips to Pori from the dock at Chora (20min., 4 per day noon-6pm, round-trip €5). A boat can take you on a scenic coastal ride to **Kato Koufonisia,** an oasis removed from commercial bustle. (20min., 4 per day 11am-8pm, round-trip €5)

SCHINOUSA Σχοινούσα ☎22850

Isolated beaches line the coast of untouched, rural Schinousa, all but guaranteeing peaceful communion with nature. The island is best enjoyed on foot; explore its rustic, donkey-patrolled interior and get to know its 220 affable inhabitants.

🖃🛱 TRANSPORTATION AND PRACTICAL INFORMATION. All boats dock at tiny **Mersini,** with the village, **Chora,** a 1km walk uphill. **Ferries** go to: Aegiali, Amorgos (3hr.; 3 per week M, Th, Sa; €8.50); Donousa (1½hr.; 3 per week M, Th, Sa; €7); Iraklia (20min., 1-2 per day, €3.50); Katapola, Amorgos (3hr., 1-2 per day, €10.50) via Koufonisia (40min., €2.60); Naxos (1hr., 1-2 per day, €6.50); Paros (2hr., 2-3 per week W and Th, €10); Piraeus (7hr., 1 per day, €29-35).

Nearly everything you'll need can be found on the main road, a 5min. walk from end to end. On the right coming from the port is **Paralos Travel,** a shop and Greek bookstore that doubles as the **ferry ticket agent** for Blue Star lines and the **post office.** (☎22850 71 160 or 29 349. Open daily 10am-2pm and 7-10:30pm and before the first ferry of the day.) At the end of the main road on the left is **Giorgos Grispos Travel Agency,** where you can access Western Union and buy **ferry tickets** for all other ferry lines. It also has useful maps of the island, a small selection of English books, and odd souvenirs such as handcuffs. (☎22850 71 930. Open Tu, Th, Sa-Su 8am-1pm, 4-4:45pm, and 8-10pm; M, W, F 9am-1pm and 8-10pm.) A **24hr. ATM** is on the main road, on the right after Paralos Travel. Two public **card phones** are down at the port and in Chora's *plateia.* Turning left off the main road at the ATM takes you to the **medical center** (☎22850 71 385), on the right in a clearly marked white building with a red cross; 24hr. emergency care is available (☎69792 21 735). Free **Wi-Fi** is available courtesy of the island, but the signal only reaches a small circumference around the medical center and its patio. **Postal Code:** 84300.

🛏 ACCOMMODATIONS. There are more *domatia* in town than any other type of building, so accommodations should not be too difficult to come by. Most offer free transportation to and from the port. **Meltemi ❷,** at the edge of town before Gripsos Travel, welcomes you with the shade of three large palm trees, friendly staff, and a comfortable restaurant downstairs. The rooms are spacious and clean, each with bath, fridge, TV, air-conditioning, and balcony. The large studios come equipped with kitchenettes. (☎22850 71 947 or 74 037. Doubles €30-40; triples and studios €40-65. Cash only.) **Anesis ❸,** on the right after the ATM, has large, clean rooms with fridges, baths, and panoramic balcony views that look over Tsigouri beach to Iraklia. (☎22850 71 180. Doubles €30-50; triples

CYCLADES

€45-60. Cash only.) **Agnantema ❸**, past the medical center, has rooms with baths, fridges, kitchenettes, air-conditioning, phones, and TVs. (☎22850 71 987. Doubles €30-50; 4-person studios €80. Cash only.) To find **Grispos Villas ❹**, follow the signs in Chora to Tsigouri beach on the main road and proceed 500m down the dirt road. Grispos's rooms, in a pleasant beachside location, include air-conditioning, TVs, fridges, and breakfast. (Doubles €40-70. AmEx/MC/V.)

☐ FOOD. Turning right down a small alley after Paralos Travel reveals **Margarita Restaurant ❷**, run by trendy 20-somethings. The restaurant has great views and serves traditional Greek food and a large selection of wines. (☎22850 71 185. Greek salad €5. Octopus in vinegar sauce €7. Open daily 9:30am-midnight.) **Loza Pizzeria ❷**, filled with traditional music and tasty food, is in the main *plateia*. (☎22850 74 005. Pizza €6-8. Baklava €1.30. Open daily 10am-12:30am.) Soft lighting and a stone facade marks **Deli ❸**, a restaurant and sweet bar that serves pricier seafood dishes accompanied by panoramic views. (☎22850 74 278. Seafood dishes €13-20. Greek salad €5.50. Open noon-midnight.) On the left of the main road you'll find **To Emporio,** a bakery and mini-mart. (☎22850 71 873 or 71 987. Open daily 6:30am-11pm.)

◢ BEACHES. The island's pothole-ridden dirt roads are virtually car-free, making it easy to explore the island on foot. Grab a bottle of water and wander until an alluring cove catches your eye. **Tsigouri,** 450m down the first road on the right heading into town from the port, is easily accessible and more developed than the other beaches, with a view of neighboring Iraklia. **Livadi,** a thin stretch of sand cradled by a small bay, is a 15min. walk down the right fork of the road through Chora. Follow the dusty road 2km past the bakery, across the fields, and through the tiny village of Messaria to **Psili Ammos.** This secluded, rocky beach on the far side of the island is sheltered from the heavy surf.

IRAKLIA Ιράκλια   ☎22850

People come to Iraklia to escape the bustle of modern life, unplug from the rest of the world, and immerse themselves in the friendly, small-town atmosphere of this coastal community. You won't have too much company on its peaceful beaches, and a cave with circuitous underground passages contributes to the hideaway feel of this tiny island.

▤ TRANSPORTATION. Ferries head to: Amorgos (3hr., 1-2 per day, €8.50); Donousa (2hr., 1-2 per day, €6.50); Koufonisia (1hr., 1-2 per day, €5); Naxos (1½hr., 1-2 per day, €8); Paros (4hr., 3-4 per week, €14); Piraeus (6-7hr., 3-4 per week, €29); Schinousa (20min., 1-2 per day, €2.60). Maria Prasinos at Villa Panorama (p. 293) rents **cars** and mopeds. (☎22850 71 991. Cars €45 per day. Mopeds €15 per day.) There are no official buses or taxis on the island, though a free local **mini-bus** runs a few times per day M-Sa from the port to Panagia, with various stops along the way. Check the schedule on the front door of Perigali grocery store (p. 292) for specific times.

▨ ▨ ORIENTATION AND PRACTICAL INFORMATION. Agios Giorgios is the island's port and its largest settlement; turn right off the dock past the beach to reach the center of town. To the right of the beach facing the town, there is a small stone *plateia* with a **24hr. ATM.** The main road splits at multi-story **Perigali,** the local mini-mart and grocery store. (☎22850 71 145. Open daily 9-1pm and 5-9pm.)

A small ravine runs through the center of town; two roads run alongside it and merge at the top. The **medical center** is past Perigali on the right branch. (☎22850 71 388 or 69774 68 649. Open M, W, F 9:30am-1:30pm. 24hr. emergency service.) All-purpose **Melissa**, 50m farther along the right-hand road, is a mini market, ferry ticketer, and **post office**. (☎22850 71 561 or 71 539. Open daily 6am-11pm.) One of the island's three **phones** is just outside Perigali; the second is in Panagia, and the third in restaurant Maistrali up the left fork in the road. **Postal Code:** 84300.

▐ ACCOMMODATIONS. If you call and book ahead, your hosts most likely will pick you up at the port. **Anna's Place ❸** is up the hill on the first left off the left fork of the main road. Friendly Anna greets her guests with orange juice. Her comfortable rooms have fridges, baths, and balconies overlooking the port; the studios are palatial. (☎22850 71 145. Doubles €40-60; 3-person studios €50-70. Cash only.) Turn right on the road after Anna's and then left on the gravel road to find **Villa Panorama ❷**, whose luxurious rooms have fridges, TVs, baths, ceiling fans, and personal patios. Enjoy spectacular and expansive views of Agios Giorgios and Livadi beach. (☎22850 71 991. Doubles €20-40. Cash only.) **Alexandra ❸**, at the top of Agios Giorgios on the left just beyond Anna's, has four small, breezy rooms with baths, A/C, and fridges, a shared kitchen, and an airy common courtyard and veranda. (☎22850 71 482. Doubles €30-50. Cash only.) **Maria's ❸**, across the road, rents homey rooms with large kitchenettes, baths, fans, and a shared balcony. (☎22850 71 485. Doubles €30-50. Cash only.)

▐ FOOD. Ten minutes down the road to Livadi, situated in an isolated spot before the beach along the water, you'll find an enticing variety of creative Greek dishes and international music at alterative **Makuba ❷**. An open veranda right on the water gives top-notch views to lounging diners who sip on mixed drinks well into the night. (☎22850 71 226. Raki-marinated pork with rice and vegetables €8. Open May-Sept. daily 10am-late. Cash only.) **O Pevkos ❷**, up the left fork of the road past Perigali, prepares fresh fish caught by the owner and tasty Greek salads with local feta. You also can buy raw fish (€10-20 per kg) to prepare yourself. (☎22850 72 021. Prepared fish €20-40 per kg. Open daily 8am-11pm or midnight. Cash only.) **Maistrali ❷**, up the hill across from O Pevkos, serves meals all day on a casual deck. It also sells postcards, foreign papers and books, and has Internet (€3 per hr.) and an international telephone. (☎22850 71 807. Omelettes €2-3.50. Appetizers €2-5. Grilled meat €6-9. Open daily 8am-11pm or midnight. MC/V.)

◙▐ SIGHTS AND BEACHES. The shallow, clear waters of **Livadi beach** epitomize Iraklia's appeal: they draw only small crowds, even on hot summer days. If you wade out, you can look at the ruins of the **Venetian Castle** overhead. The water taxi "Anemos" (☎69773 10 427) will take you to **Karvounlakos, Alimia, Schinousa,** or beaches on Iraklia; buy tickets at Perigali and inquire for specific times. To get a sense of what Greece was like 40 years ago, continue past Livadi to the town of **Panagia** (45min. from Ag. Giorgios), where you'll find a church, some cows, and not much else. The *taverna* **To Steki ❷**, with rooftop seating overlooking hills and the sea, also serves as a general store, bakery, and the island's only gas station—fill up from a canister. (☎22850 71 579. Open daily 7am-2am.)

▐ OUTDOOR ACTIVITIES. **▨Agios Ioannis Cave,** with tiny waterways, dramatic depths, and a seemingly endless series of chambers, will fascinate adventurous travelers. Bring a flashlight, candles, matches, and a walking stick if possible, and get ready to get filthy. The steep 1hr. **hike** begins past the church in

Panagia, where the blue sign points away from the village. After 20min. along the stone-walled dirt path, you'll reach a gate at the bottom of a dip in the land. Pass through and follow the stone wall on your right until it meets another one. Begin a descent down **Mount Pappas** until you encounter a small ravine. From here, it should be about a 10min. walk to the tiny, bright-white cave entrance. Crawling through the small entrance brings you into the caves. You'll need your flashlight right away; leave lighted candles along the way à la Hansel and Gretel to mark your path back. An icon of St. John, who is celebrated in an August **festival** at the cave, is to the left as you enter. There are said to be 15 rooms inside the cave; the final chamber is so deep that there is no oxygen inside. Be careful—the rocks are slippery and daylight vanishes quickly.

If crawling through caves sounds claustrophobia-inducing, there are a number of other walks to take in the island's nature and peaceful scenery. From Panagia, it is a 2km walk to **Profitis Ilias** and **Pappas Peak** (418m), the highest point on the island. From here, panoramic views embrace the surrounding islands—Ios, Paros, Antiparos, Naxos, and Koufounissia. Alternatively from Panagia, a 1.5km walk leads to **Agios Athanassios,** an abandoned settlement with street plans of old, traditional Cycladic houses. The ancient footpath crosses a mountain stream and offers an up-close-and-personal interaction with nature.

PAROS Πάρος

Pieces of Paros are sprinkled throughout the Western world in the form of its famed translucent marble. Many of antiquity's most celebrated statues and buildings—the *Venus de Milo*, the *Nike of Samothrace*, and parts of Napoleon's mausoleum in Paris—took their materials from this island. Seemingly bottomless Parian quarries still export regularly. The island comes alive in summer, when the golden beaches and lovely mountains teem with travelers. The main port of Parikia is more relaxed than other Cycladic cities, but parties in the small port of Naoussa stretch into the wee hours of the morning.

PARIKIA Παροικία   ☎22840

Behind Parikia's commercial facade, flower-lined streets wind through archways, past whitewashed houses, and by dozens of ancient, intimate churches. Wander through the agora to find trendy clothing, colorful jewelry, homemade goods, and many outdoor cafes. While the town's small, pebbly beaches are overpowered by souvenir shops and touristy *tavernas*, this transportation hub is a lively and convenient base for reaching more remote island locations.

▐ TRANSPORTATION

Flights: Leave from **Paros Airport (PAS)**. Olympic Airways does not have an office in Paros, but you can find schedules at the **Polos Tours** counter. To **Athens** (M-F 3 per day, Sa 2 per day; €71). From the airport, take the public bus to **Parikia** (20min.) or **Naoussa** (35 min.), or a taxi for €10-12.

Ferries: To: **Amorgos** (3hr., 7 per week to Egiali and Katapola, €12.20-15); **Astypalea** (4hr., 3 per week, €28.50); **Crete** (10hr., 1 per day, €65); **Folegandros** (4 hr., 3 per week, €16.70); **Ikaria** (3hr., 5 per week, €24.50); **Ios** (3hr., 5 per week, €19.90); **Milos** (4hr. 30min., 3 per week, €24.50); **Naxos** (1hr., 3-4 per day, €7); **Piraeus** (5hr., 2-3 per day, €29); **Samos** (5hr., 5 per week, €30); **Santorini** (3hr., 1-2 per day, €16.50); **Sifnos** (2hr., 1 per week, €9); **Sikinos** (4hr., 3 per week, €15.10); **Syros**

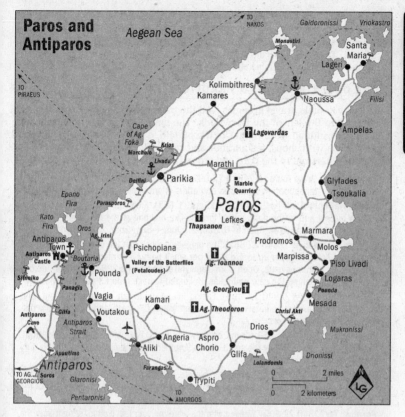

Paros and Antiparos

Aegean Sea

TO NAXOS

Gaidoronissi   Vriokastro

Monastiri

Santa Maria

Lagen

TO PIRAEUS

Kolimbithres

Kamares

Naoussa   Filisi

Ampelas

Cape of Ag. Foka

Krios

Marchelo

Livada

Delfini

Lagovardas

Marathi

Parikia

Marble Quarries

Glyfades

Tsoukalia

Epano Fira

Parasporos

Paros

Kato Fira

Oros

Lefkes

Marmara

Antiparos

Ag. Irini

Thapsanon

Prodromos

Molos

Antiparos Town

Boutaria

Psichopiana

Marpissa

Piso Livadi

Antiparos Castle

Pounda

Valley of the Butterflies (Petaloudes)

Ag. Ioannou

Logaras

Silnaiko

Panagia

Vagia

Ag. Georgiou

Pounda

Mesada

Antiparos Cave

Glifa

Kamari

Ag. Theodoron

Chrisi Akti

Voutakou

Antiparos Strait

Angeria

Aspro Chorio

Drios

Makronissi

Aliki

Glifa

Dnonissi

Apautims

TO AG. GEORGIOS

Soros

Glaronisi

Antiparos

Farangas

Lolandomis

Trypiti

Pentaronisi

TO AMORGOS

0   2 miles

0   2 kilometers

N

(1hr., 4 per week, €7); **Tinos** (2hr., 4 per week, €9). Ferry schedules fluctuate often; for current info, ask at Polos Tours.

High-Speed Boats: To: **Ios** (1hr., 1 per week, €27); **Mykonos** (45min., 4-5 per day, €20); **Santorini** (2hr., 1 per day, €36); **Tinos** (1½hr., 3 per day, €24.50).

Buses: Station (☎22840 21 395) is on the water, to the right of the windmill as you exit the ferry gate. The free local bus (every 30min. 7am-2:30pm) has 8 stops along Parikia's perimeter, including 1 right outside the gate of the bus station. For all other buses, prices range €1.40-2; since times and frequencies change constantly, consult the timetable posted at the bus stop or request a printed schedule at the booth. Tickets are available at the terminal, and at shops displaying the **KTEL** sign. On weekdays, buses run on 5 main routes, 4 of them leaving from Parikia. Bus #1 runs to **Drios** via **Marathi, Kostos, Lefkes, Prodromos, Marmara, Marpissa, Piso Livadi, Logara, Punda Beach,** and **Chrisi Akti** (a.k.a. Golden Beach) (1½hr.; 13 per day 7:30am-11:30pm). Bus #2 leaves for **Naoussa** (15min., 7:40am, every 30min. 9am-noon, every hr. noon-1am). Bus #3 runs to **Aliki** (25min., 10 per day 7:05am-12:10am). Bus #4 runs to the port of **Punta** (45min., 7:05am, every hr. 9:10am-12:10am, with 1 additional at 10:30am). Schedules fluctuate seasonally, so check at the station for the most up-to-date times.

Taxis: (☎22840 21 500). Facing inland, walk to the right of the windmill and take the 1st left; taxis line up at the corner of the *plateia*. Prices range from €8 (to Naoussa) to

€18 (to Agnat). Surcharge of €0.32 per piece of luggage weighing more than 10kg. €1 surcharge after midnight. Available 8am-3am.

Car and Motorcycle Rentals: Rental shops line the waterfront. **Iria Rent-a-Car** (☎22840 22 132). Cars €25-50 per day. Valid driver's license from your home country held for at least 1 year required. +21. Iria also provides maps of the island and major villages.

✦ 🛈 ORIENTATION AND PRACTICAL INFORMATION

Inexpensive hotels, travel agencies, and the town beach lie along the curving waterfront to the left of the ferry dock. The main *plateia* is straight ahead, behind the windmill. To the right of the *plateia*, a whitewashed labyrinth of streets brims with shops, restaurants, and cafes. The island's party district is along the waterfront to the right and around the bend.

Budget Travel: Polos Tours (☎22840 22 092 or 093; www.polostours.gr), to the right of the OTE. Has transportation schedules and offers information about island cruise tours.

Banks: National Bank (☎22840 22 012 or 21 663). From the windmill, head inland to the *plateia* and to the right. In the fortress-like building at the far corner. **Currency exchange** and **24hr. ATM.** Open M-Th 8am-2:30pm, F 8am-2pm.

Luggage Storage: (☎22840 22 861). The luggage deposit just left of the ferry dock facing inland holds bags for up to 1 day. €2 per small bag; €3 per large. Provides info on the island's cultural events. Open 9am-1am. **Hotel Kontes** (☎22840 21 096), across from the port, behind the cafe umbrellas. Unlimited storage time €3 per piece per day.

Laundromat: Top (☎22840 21 491). Facing inland, head left on the waterfront, and right after the ancient cemetery; it's on the left. Wash €7; wash and dry €9. 10% discount for *Let's Go* readers.

Pharmacy: ☎22840 22 223 for the on-duty pharmacy. Walk left along the waterfront, and take the 2nd right past the small church. Another is on the *plateia*, with the on-duty schedule posted in the window.

Police: (☎22840 23 333), across the *plateia* behind the OTE, 1 fl. up. Open 24hr. **Tourist Police** (☎22840 21 673), opposite the entrance stairs, at the other end of the porch. Open M-F 7am-2:30pm.

Hospital: (☎22840 22 500). Walking with the water on your left, it's the 1st right after the small church in the large white building. Open M-F 8am-2:30am, 24hr. for **emergencies.**

Telephones: OTE (☎22840 22 799), 1 block to the right of the windmill (facing inland). Open M-F 8am-3pm.

Internet Access: Many restaurants offer access at no charge; look for the "@" symbol. The city offers "ParosWi-Fi," with slow but free service; the strongest signal is at the windmill. **Marina Internet Cafe** (☎22840 24 885), on the waterfront by the ancient cemetery. €1 per 15min., €3 per hr. Open daily 8am-midnight.

Post Office: (☎22840 21 236), along the left side of the waterfront facing inland, beyond the ancient cemetery. Open M-F 7:30am-2pm. **Postal Code:** 84400.

🏠 🏕 ACCOMMODATIONS AND CAMPING

Hotels, pensions, and *domatia* in Parikia are as numerous as the hucksters who gather at the ferry gates to advertise low prices. Negotiating rates can save you money. Always insist on seeing rooms before handing over cash. Nickel-pinchers and nature lovers find some of the best bargains at campgrounds.

▣ **Hotel Arian** (☎22840 21 490; www.cycladesnet.gr/arian). From the port, walk along the water to the left, turn right at the ancient cemetery, and right again past Rena Rooms, or call ahead for a shuttle. Immaculate rooms overlook a picturesque, lantern-lit garden courtyard. Daily breakfast (€7) includes delicious marmalade made by the owner's mother, homemade cake, and fresh-squeezed OJ. The attentive owner provides flower-adorned beds, Wi-Fi in the courtyard, and a generous dose of hospitality. A/C, TV, fridge, and balcony in each room on the upper floor. Singles €20-40; doubles €30-65. ❷

☒ **Rena Rooms** (☎22840 22 220; www.cycladesnet.gr/rena). Turn left from the dock and take a right after the cemetery, or call ahead for a port shuttle. Owners George and Rena provide detailed information about the island, a comfortable, cottage-like atmosphere, and bright, clean rooms with fridges, ceiling fans, baths, and balconies. Free luggage storage. A/C and TV €5. Singles €25-30; doubles €35-45; triples €55-70. Re-confirm booking 1 day before arrival. 20% discount for *Let's Go* readers. MC/V. ❷

Hotel Anna Platanou (☎22840 21 751; www.annaplatanou.gr), a 15min. walk from the port and 5min. from Parikia's clubs. Turn right from the windmill and walk along the water. Take a left at the church with 2 light blue domes; the hotel is directly behind a parking lot. This peaceful hideaway is well worth the winding trek through the Old Town, thanks to its high-ceilinged rooms and family hospitality. All rooms have A/C, TVs, fridges, and balconies; some balconies are sheltered by apricot trees. Doubles €40-85. 10-30% discount for booking online. ❷

Argonauta Hotel (☎22840 21 440; www.argonauta.gr), across the street from the ferry port, with a prominent sign visible from the *plateia*. Enter through Bakiliko Cafe on the *plateia*, or through the main entrance off the side street just behind. A spacious rooftop terrace, private balconies, soothing pastel walls, and location in the town's center make this pricier option worth it. Free Wi-Fi. Singles €48-65; doubles €58-80; triples €68-95. ❹

Sofia Pension (☎22840 22 085; www.pension-sofia.gr). Turn left from the ferry gate and walk along the main waterfront past the post office; turn inland at the sign for Cine Paros. Proprietors Sofia and Manolis have created an island haven away from home, from the front-yard garden accented with fountains and a swing set to the canary on the front terrace. Upstairs rooms have balconies with views of the Aegean. A/C, TV, and bath in each room. Doubles €65-95; triples €75-100. ❹

Koula Camping (☎22840 22 081; www.campingkoula.gr). Guests receive a 50% discount at Cine Paros. Aqua Cafe next door offers ½L tankards of the Greek beer Alfa for only €2 and ice cream for a steal at €1.50, plus free Wi-Fi. Open Apr-Oct. €6.50-8 per person; €4 per tent. Tent rental €7. Cabins €6-8. MC. ❶

Parasporos Camping (☎22840 21 394), between Parasporos and Delphini Beach. Another thrifty option. €2 per tent. Tent rental €4. ❶

▐ FOOD

Identical (and identically overpriced) restaurants share space with bars along the waterfront. Venture inland for better food at better prices. Wandering through the **Old Market** area yields a selection of old family places and contemporary eateries. If you're looking for a daytime snack, stop by the **fruit market** near the small church to the left of the windmill for local produce, open through the early afternoon for a honey melon, one of the island's specialties.

☒ **Apollon Garden Restaurant** (☎22840 21 875). Dart into the alley behind the National Bank, past Happy Green Cow, and follow the signs. Enjoy traditional dishes such as *dolmadakia* (stuffed vine leaves with ground beef in an egg and lemon sauce; €6) or filet of pork with dried fruits, figs, plums, apricots, and wine (€17.50) amid the garden's lush plant life. And don't skip the bread; it's served with olive oil from the owner's own olive groves in Sparta. Open May-Oct. daily 6pm-1am. AmEx/MC/V. ❸

☒ **Paros Family Taverna** (☎22840 24 397), 100m beyond the Church of Our Lady of 100 Doors; take a left at the parking lot. Locals swear by this family-run spot, where Mama and Papa Bizas serve up a thrifty carnivore's feast: pork souvlaki (€6.50), grilled lamb chops (€8), and beef burgers (€6.50). A grapevine-covered terrace, large portions, and a decent selection of veggie options (stuffed tomatoes; €4.50) add to the appeal. Open June-Sept. daily 1pm-1am. AmEx/MC/V. ❷

Old Baker's, near the *plateia*, on the main market street. Local and regional specialties crowd the counters, tabletops, and refrigerators of this bakery, which has been supplying locals with their daily bread since 1912. Find a bottle of citron liqueur from Naxos, or *chalvatopia* from Syros. Miniature versions of Greek pastries go for €13 per kg and homemade local sweets for €16 per kg, but you can put together a decent selection for under €5. Open 7:30am-11:30pm. Cash only. ❶

CyberCookies (☎22840 21 610). Go down the alley behind the National Bank and turn left; it's on the right. CyberCookies loves students as much as students love CyberCookies. Art school students get 20% off at this creperie and internet cafe, which offers free Wi-Fi for 20min. to patrons. Giant fresh-squeezed juices (they recommend having your camera ready) €5. Crepes €4.50-9. Mixed drinks and coffee also available. Open daily 9:30am-2:30am. Cash only. ❷

Nick's Hamburgers (☎22840 21 434). Walk right from the port; it's tucked away in a small square on the left. Signs boasting "Pure 100% Beef" tempt carnivores to this diner-style burger joint, which features 14 types of burgers. Cheeseburgers and hot dogs €2.90. "Nickfeast" (2 burgers, chips, and salad) €6.50. Open Apr.-Oct. daily 11am-2am. ❶

Happy Green Cow (☎22840 24 691), off the *plateia* in the narrow walkway behind the National Bank. Vegetarian and chicken dishes in an atmosphere that fuses traditional Greek sculpture with the psychedelic 1960s. Colorful walls, hanging lamps, crystal chandeliers, and mellow music make this restaurant a popular venue. The creative dishes have equally creative names, including the "Cow's Orgasm" (pastry with cheese and peppers; €14). Open Apr.-Nov. daily 7pm-midnight. Cash only. ❸

🔘 🄰 SIGHTS AND OUTDOOR ACTIVITIES

Almost every **beach** on Paros can be reached in under an hour's drive. **Livadia** is the town beach, a 10-15min. walk left of the port as you face inland. It starts out pebbly, but keep walking and you'll find sandier areas. **Chrisi Akti** and **Aliki** are accessible by bus, and **Krios,** across the harbor from Parikia, is accessible by water taxi (every 30min. 10am-6pm, round-trip €2.30). Celebrated **Santa Maria** beach is accessible by bus from Naoussa. For a round-the-clock party, try **Punda Beach Club** (☎22840 41 717; www.pundabeach.gr) on the island's eastern shore. Punda is also accessible by bus, but don't confuse it with **Punta,** from which ferries leave for Antiparos.

To explore Paros on horseback, call **Horse Riding Koukou.** (☎22840 51 818. €35 for 1hr., €50 for 2hr.) For water adventures, take a scuba lesson offered by **Eurodivers Club,** based at Punta beach (☎22840 92 071 or 69323 36 464; www.eurodivers.gr. 3hr. of instruction and diving for the uncertified €65; 2hr. dive for the certified €55. 10% discount for booking online), or by **X-tasea-divers,** based at **Kolimbithres,** near Naoussa. (☎22840 51 584 or 69776 89 067; www.paros-diving.gr. Dives €45 for certified divers.) Alternatively, kiteboard with **Paros Kite.** (☎6977 003 855; www.paroskite.gr or www.paroswindsurf.com. 6hr. of lessons €200-230.)

🏛**PANAGIA EKATONTAPILIANI.** According to local legend, the mother of Emperor Constantine stopped to pray at the site in AD 326, vowing to build a church on the spot if her quest for the Holy Cross was successful—apparently, it was. The main structure of the complex is the mammoth **Church of the Assumption,** dating to the sixth century, where Orthodox Christians make pilgrimage every August in honor of The Feast of Panagia, or Ekatontapiliani. The **Church**

of Agios Nikolaos (the oldest of the three) and the baptistry flank this centerpiece to the north and south, respectively. The white cloister at the entrance of the complex was built in the 17th century as a monastery, but now hosts church offices, the **Ecclesiastic Museum**, and housing for the Paros-Naxos High Priest's infrequent visits. In the church's ▓**galleries** are Byzantine religious icons and texts, some dating as far back as the 15th century. *(Church open daily 7am-10pm. Services daily 7am. Museum open daily 9am-10pm. Modest dress required. €1.50.)*

OTHER SIGHTS. The **Archaeological Museum** displays masterpieces alongside curiosities in a courtyard and three small rooms. The museum claims fame for its glorious *amphorae* (commemorative vases), fifth-century wingless Nike, and its archaic sixth century Gorgon, discovered only a few meters away from its display case. A slab of the marble Parian Chronicle, a history of Greece up to 264 BC, is also housed here. *(Heading away from the water, take a left after Panagia Ekatontapiliani; the museum is at the end of the road. ☎ 22840 21 231. Open Tu-Su 8:30am-2:45pm. €2, students €1, EU students free.)* Signs in the Old Town will direct you to the lone remaining wall of the Venetian **Frankish Castle,** where you can see sections of marble and columns removed from the fifth-century BC Ionic Temple of Athena.

🎵 🎦 ENTERTAINMENT AND NIGHTLIFE

For an alternative to club hopping, try **Cine Paros,** across the street from Pension Sofia to the left of the windmill. American films with Greek subtitles begin at 9pm nightly (€8); guests at Koula Camping receive a 50% discount. After dark, most of the activity in town moves to the waterfront. Groups amble lazily on the sidewalk and the beach, relaxing around the many cafes and bars along the waterfront.

Pirate Blues and Jazz (☎22840 21 114), a block inland from the waterfront in the market area to the right of the windmill. An eccentric bubble of New Orleans jazz culture in the sprawl of Old Town Parikia. Black and white photographs of John Coltrane, Ella Fitzgerald, and the Cotton Club dot the walls of this intimate, low-ceilinged establishment. Mixed drinks €8. Open daily 8pm-3:30am.

Saloon d'Or (☎22840 22 176), on the waterfront. Compels loungers off the cushion-clad couches and onto the funky, checkered dance floor. Beer €2-3. Mixed drinks €7. Happy hour 7-11pm; drinks €5. Open Apr.-Oct. daily 8pm-4am.

Karl's (☎69818 72 824), at the harbor's end. Mixed drinks are €4 all night long, and a large beer is €3. W from 8pm "alternative" music. Open M-F 6pm-late, Sa-Su 3pm-late.

Gelato Sulla Luna (☎22840 22 868. www.parosweb.com/sullaluna), on the waterfront, in a nook about 200m to the right of the windmill. No better companion on a moonlit walk than gelato from this little shop, called "gelato under the moon" in Italian. The owner whips up daily batches of exceptionally smooth and creamy gelato just for the nighttime strollers. €2 per scoop. Open from 7pm until the moon goes down. Cash only.

🔆 DAYTRIPS FROM PARIKIA

VALLEY OF THE BUTTERFLIES (PETALOUDES; Πεταλούδες**).** The rare (and tongue-twisting) Panaxi Aquadripunctaria moths return to this place of their birth to breed. June provides only a smattering of the bright black-and-yellow moths, while the height of mating season (from late July to late Aug.) sometimes draws millions in a miraculous display. *(10km south of town. Take bus #3 from Parikia to Aliki (12min., 7 per day, €1.40) and ask to be dropped off at Petaloudes. Follow the signs road for 2km. ☎ 22840 91 211. Open daily June 15-Sept. 20 9am-8pm. €2.)*

MARATHI (Μαράθι). This island is home to Paros's ancient marble quarries. Still considered to be among the finest in the world, Parian marble is translucent up to 3mm thick, with one-third the opacity of most other marble. A visit to the quarries is a serious undertaking; bring a flashlight and strong shoes, and don't go alone. *(5km from Parikia in the center of the island. Take bus #1 from Parikia (10min., €1.40). From the bus stop, signs will direct you to the quarries.)*

LEFKES (Λεύκες). This tiny town 5km from Marathi was the largest village on the island until the 20th century, thanks to the terror of coastal piracy. Quaint, untouristed streets make Lefkes a pleasant place to spend a morning. *(Take bus #1 from Parikia (20min., €1.40).)*

PISO LIVADI. This quiet town includes a handful of cafes and hotels clustered together on a pristine bay. While it feels removed from the hubbub of the two port cities, Piso Livadi is close to some of Paros's nicest beaches, Logaras and Chrisi Akti. *(11km from Lefkes. Take bus #1 from Parikia or Lefkes (30min. or 10min., €1.60).)*

NAOUSSA Νάουσσα ☎ 22840

Naoussa is Paros's second port, a natural harbor cradled by long, sandy beaches in the shape of crab claws. Persian, Greek, Roman, Venetian, Ottoman, and Russian fleets have anchored here over the years, leaving subtle marks on the sophisticated town. Naoussa is colorful and festive, overflowing with unique shops, inviting coffeehouses, and trendy nightclubs, but budget travelers should be wary—the upscale environment is pricey.

◼ TRANSPORTATION. Naoussa can be difficult to navigate, but the central bridge is a useful landmark. Facing inland, one road leads from the bridge steps to the right and out of town toward the beaches of **Kolimbithres** and **Monastiri**. Another road stretches directly in front of the bridge with a stream down the middle. Finally, another road begins at the stairs on the left side of the bridge and leads into Naoussa's winding commercial streets. **Buses** from Parikia typically drop passengers at the bridge, but the main bus stop—a booth where a bus timetable is posted—sits inland approximately 300m along the road with the stream, set back from the street on the left. Naoussa is on two of Paros's bus lines, and buses connect it to Parikia (15 min., every 30min. 9am-noon and every hr. noon-1am, €1.40) and to Drios via Prodromos, Marpissa, Piso Livadi, Logaras, Pounda Beach, and Akti (40min. total, 10 per day 10am-midnight). Buses also go to the nude beach at Lageri. Since departure times change frequently, check the schedule at the bus booth in Parikia and in Naoussa. From Naoussa, **water taxis** also go to the beaches. The white booth with the Greek flag on the waterfront sells round-trip tickets to Kolimbithres (12min., 12 per day, €5), Lageri (20min., 5 per day, €6), and Monastiri (15min., 5 per day, €5). **Taxis** (☎22840 53 490) are available 24hr. by the bridge.

◼ PRACTICAL INFORMATION. Naoussa's **tourist office,** near the taxi stand by the bridge, has info about the town and accommodations. (☎22840 52 158. Open daily June-Sept. 10am-3pm and 6-10:30pm.) On the road without a stream, **Alpha Bank** is on the left. (☎22840 28 233. Open M-Th 8am-2:30pm, F 8am-2pm.) For the 24hr. **police,** call ☎22840 51 202. The **pharmacy** is on the left on the same road. (☎22840 51 550. Open daily 8:30am-2pm and 5-11pm.) A **medical center** is farther along, in the park just before the church. (☎22840 51 216. Doctor available 8:30am-2:30pm.) In **medical emergencies,** call the clinic in Parikia at ☎22840 22 500. Near the tourist office, enjoy a mixed drink (€6-7, well below the town's standard price) while you check e-mail at **Netcafe. gr.** (☎22840 52 203. Wi-Fi €2 per hr.. Laptop rental €1.50 per hr. Open daily 9:30am-late.) The **post office** is 300m up the main street. Go right at the gelateria when the road forks; it's just beyond the Santa Maria turn-off. (☎22840 51 495. Open M-F 7:30am-2pm.) **Postal Code:** 84401.

ACCOMMODATIONS AND CAMPING.

Though Naoussa has many places to sleep, prices skyrocket in summer when package-tour groups book hotels months in advance. **Domatia** cost about €35-55 for doubles and €40-60 for triples. **Pension Anna** ❸ sits around the corner from the taxi stand, the first left off the road out of town. It has spacious rooms with air-conditioning, TVs, fully stocked kitchens, and shared balconies. (☎22840 51 328. Doubles €35-65. 10% discount during the high season for *Let's Go* readers.) Look for the sign to **Irini Rooms to Rent** ❷ on another side street farther along the road out of town, which offers basic doubles and triples with refrigerators for €40-50 during the high season. (☎22840 51 355.) Farther still, situated around a small beach and accessible off the same side road, are a number of upscale hotels and pensions with spectacular views of the harbor. Among these is **Hotel Castello** ❹, a value gem in this very expensive neighborhood. (☎22840 52 600; www.castelloparos.gr. Singles €40-65; doubles €55-75.) Brother hotel **Margarita's House,** with studios and apartments, is another value option for larger groups. (☎22840 51 020; www.margaritashouse.gr.) Book online at either for better rates. **Camping Naoussa** ❶ is on the road to Kolimbithres and sends plenty of representatives to the port in Parikia. You can also call to arrange a pick-up. (☎22840 51 595 or 6937 200 504; www.campingnaoussa.gr. €6 per person. €3-6 tent rental.)

FOOD.

Naoussan kitchens cook famously delicious seafood; the local specialty is the sun-dried mackerel *gouna*—served at surprisingly low prices. All the way on the end of the harbor sits scenic **Barbarossa** ❸, where chic guests dine on octopus with orange and fennel (€12) and grilled swordfish with oil and lemon sauce (€11.50). Behind the church on the commercial road 300m from the bridge, family-run **Diamantis** ❷ features meat-heavy Greek fare. Sit on the tree-studded terrace just below the sidewalk and feast on lamb *diamantis* stuffed with feta, tomatoes, peppers, and onions (€12) and other dishes. (☎22840 52 129. Open daily Apr.-Nov. 7pm-1am. AmEx/MC/V.) Most of Naossa's dining options are on the waterfront, however. **Bitzendaakhe Fish Taverna** ❷ earns praise from the locals for the freshest sole filet (€8.50) and swordfish (€10) in town. (☎22840 51 205. Open daily 7pm-midnight. Cash only.)

ENTERTAINMENT AND NIGHTLIFE.

The **Aqua Paros water park** (☎22840 53 271), at Kolimbithres, is a pricey option for waterslide aficionados. On the first Sunday in July, eat, drink, and be merry as you cruise Naoussa's harbor and watch traditional dancing at the **Wine and Fish Festival;** call the tourist office for details.

Go around the corner at the farthest end of the waterfront to find a complex of clubs and bars, where the young and attractive chat on outdoor sofas or grind to the pulsing club music rolling from the many available dancing floors. The DJ at **Shark** delivers a mix of pop and world rhythms. (☎69792 27 760. Mixed drinks €8. Open daily 9pm-4am.) On the other side of the building, the bartender at **Sanfos** makes a delicious mojito (€10). **Barbarossa** anchors this scene, as well, with a cafe and a dance club. Also try **Del Mar,** where you can enjoy a mixed drink (€11) or bottle service (€100), while waves lap at your feet, and **Te Quiero,** which breaks the techno tyranny with Latin beats. If you're in Naoussa in low season before many of the clubs have opened, check out

CYCLADES

Insomnia, a two-level cafe and bar to the left of the bridge. Atop the balcony overlooking sea and sunset, try the club's trademark mixed drink, "The Insomnia," a blend of peach, strawberry, and rum in a sugar-rimmed glass. (☎22840 53 388. Beer €5. Mixed drinks €8-10. Cafe open from 8am.)

ANTIPAROS Αντίπαρος ☎22840

Literally meaning "opposite Paros," Antiparos is so close to its neighbor that, according to local lore, travelers once signaled the ferryman on Paros by opening the door of a chapel on Antiparos. Most travelers visit the small, undeveloped island as a daytrip to see the caves, while others find it restorative to find a place to stay on the tiny island, which is as peaceful as it is welcoming. Most of the island's 1000 or so inhabitants live in Antiparos, where the ferry docks and most accommodations are found.

TRANSPORTATION. Take a direct **ferry** from Parikia (35min., 6 per day 9:30am-8:30pm, €5) or a **bus** to Punta (15min., every hr. 7:05am-12:10am, €1.40), then take a ferry to Antiparos (10min., every 20-30min. 6:50am-1:30am, €1). The island has two bus routes. One heads for the caves (3 per day 11am-3pm, round-trip €5); another travels to Soros via St. George (3 per day 10am-2pm). During high season, departure frequency may increase, so call Oliaros Tours for up to date information.

PRACTICAL INFORMATION. Waterfront **Oliaros Tours** helps with accommodations and sells maps (€0.50). It also has boat and bus schedules, **internet access** (€2 per hr.), **currency exchange,** and information about cruises and vehicle rentals. (☎22840 61 231 in high season, 61 189 in low season. Open daily 9am-10:30pm.) Many cafes along the main street offer free **Wi-Fi** to patrons. The **National Bank,** on the left up the road to the *plateia,* is open only April to October, so if you're not visiting during these months, you better get cash in Parikia. (☎22840 61 294. Open M-F 8:30am-1pm.) The **laundromat** is behind the windmill, to the left of the port facing inland. (Wash, dry, and soap €8. Open daily 8am-9:30pm.) Reach the 24hr. **police** at ☎22840 61 202. To reach the **medical clinic,** walk 200m inland on the main street and take a left before the post office. The number of the doctor on duty is posted. The **post office** is on the left side of the street leading from the water to the *plateia.* (☎22840 61 223. Open M-F 7:30am-1pm.) **Postal Code:** 84007.

ACCOMMODATIONS AND CAMPING. **Mantalena Hotel ❹,** to the right of the dock when facing inland, offers large rooms with baths, fridges, air-conditioning, TVs, and free Wi-Fi. A family-owned establishment for 39 years, the relaxing, comfortable hotel has a cafe and bar downstairs and two large communal verandas with views of the glittering harbor. (☎22840 61 206. Doubles €35-70; triples €42-80. AmEx/MC/V.) About 150m up the main street into town, turn left to find **Galini Hotel ❷.** Clean, spacious rooms with baths, air-conditioning, fridges, and private patios with sea views sit above a restaurant. (☎22840 61 420. Doubles €35-60.) A few steps beyond Galini Hotel at the end of the same street, take a retreat on **Lilly's Island ❹.** Though this hotel, with well-manicured gardens and a pool, is on the pricey side, sharing a studio or two-bedroom apartment can make it affordable for a group of up to five travelers. (☎22840 61 411; www.lillysisland.com. Breakfast included. Doubles €85.) **Camping Antiparos ❶** is 800m northwest of town, on the way to Ag. Yiannis Theologos beach. Camping areas are separated by bamboo walls. The beachside has its own mini-mart and restaurant. (☎22840 61 221; www.campingantiparos.gr. €4-6 per person; €2-4 per tent. Tent rental €3-4.)

◨◪ FOOD AND ENTERTAINMENT. ▨**Lollo's** dedicates itself to *pinsa*, the hand-pressed oval flatbreads offered to the gods by the ancient Romans. Nowadays, this means pizza, which Lollo's makes both white (*taleggio*, speck, and olive oil; €13) and red (fresh spicy tomato sauce, garlic, and oregano; €9). The restaurant also serves homemade lasagna (€11) and a dessert pizza with apples, marmalade, and cinnamon (€8). (☎22840 61 215. Reservations strongly recommended.) On the main road, **Taverna Klimataria ❷** serves traditional dishes worth much more than their low prices. Look for signs, as the restaurant is sheltered by hanging branches and low yellow walls. (☎22840 61 298. Most entrees under €8. Open June-Aug. 24hr.; Sept.-May daily 4pm-late.) On the waterfront next to the church, **O Statheros ❷** dishes out fresh, hefty portions of seafood under a canopy of hanging octopi. (☎22840 61 172. Grilled swordfish €7. Open daily noon-midnight.)

◪ SIGHTS. The dank stalactite ▨**caves** at the southern end of the island are Antiparos's main attraction. Buses run from the port from morning to early afternoon (20min., return an hour later, €5 round-trip). Unfortunately, some of the stalactites were broken off by Russian naval officers in the 18th century and "borrowed" on behalf of a St. Petersburg museum, while still more were destroyed by the Italians during WWII. Despite this defilement, the caves, which plunge over 100m into the earth, are dramatic and impressive; the stalactites stretch to over 7m in length, and the cavernous interior is a surreal, otherworldly landscape. Names of 250 years' worth of visitors are written on the walls with their years of entry. (Open daily 10am-4pm, last entry at 3:15pm; low season 10am-2pm.) Go through the stone archway to the immediate right of the *plateia* to reach the meager ruins of the 15th-century **Castle of Antiparos,** a village built by the Venetian Loredano to defend his holdings from rampant piracy. Though new buildings exist in place of the first ones, which had 3m thick walls, they retain Loredano's original layout.

◪◪ NIGHTLIFE AND OUTDOOR ACTIVITIES. Bars, clubs, and late-night eateries can be found around the main *plateia*. Follow signs past Taverna Klimataria to find **Cafe Yam,** an outdoor restaurant and cocktail bar. Live Brazilian music and colorful plants fill the large, trendy terrace. (☎22840 61 055. Mixed drinks €6. Most entrees €8-13. Open daily July 11-Sept. 15 8:30pm-3am.) **The Stones** is a spacious bar with a dance floor and a patio for people-watching. (Beer €2-4. Mixed drinks €6-8. Open daily 7pm-late.) **Cafe Margarita,** across from the National Bank, offers a relaxed cafe atmosphere, delicious juices (strawberry spearmint €4.50), and inexpensive mixed drinks (€6.50) that you can afford to sip all night. (☎22840 61 717. Cash only.)

Oliaros Tours has information about daily boat cruises around Antiparos and the nearby Cyclades. **Blue Island Divers** offers dive packages, including hotel stays and multiple dives, from €140 for four dives in the low season to €440 for five nights and 10 dives in the high season. (☎22840 61 493; www.blueislanddivers.gr.) **Psaraliki,** a 5min. walk south of town, is a pleasant beach, as is **Glifa,** a 15min. ride to the east on the bus toward the caves (every hr., €2).

AMORGOS Αμοργός

King Minos of Crete was said to rule a kingdom on Amorgos in ancient times, a legend supported by the 1985 discovery of artifacts atop Mt. Moudoulia. Today, much of Amorgos resembles its most enduring sight, the Hozoviotissa Monastery, which burrows into the cliffs below Chora. The steep, barren cliffs and clear waters were captured 20 years ago in the film *The Big Blue (Le Grand Bleu)*, and Amorgos's stunning natural beauty has not changed much since the movie's filming. Though tourism has boomed recently, Amorgos's small size and tight-knit local community have preserved the tranquility and local feel of its port towns. Ferry connections generally stop at Amorgos's two ports in succession—Aegiali in the northeast and larger Katapola in the southwest.

KATAPOLA Κατάπολα ☎22850

Whitewashed houses with trim, narrow streets climbing up the coastal hillside and an overhanging Venetian castle make up Katapola, Amorgos's central port. Free from the commercial bustle and tourist hoards of many other Cycladic port towns, the town retains a serene, communal atmosphere even as more visitors come to the island. The small streets hardly extend beyond the waterfront, where the town's main activity is centered; a short walk will bring you to deserted beaches and Minoan ruins.

▐ TRANSPORTATION

Ferries and Speedboats: To: **Donousa** (1½hr., 5-6 per week €7); **Iraklia** (2-5hr., 1-2 per day, €8.50-12); **Koufonisia** (1½hr.-4½hr., 1-3 per day, €7.50-11); **Naxos** (1½hr.-5hr., 1-2 per day, €14); **Paros** (4hr., 1-2 per day, €15); **Piraeus** (5-8½hr., 2 per day, €32-55); **Schinousa** (2-4hr., 1-2 per day, €10.50); **Santorini** (1¼hr., 1-2 per day, €21).

Buses: The bus station is to the left of the dock facing inland, 200m past the ferry landings. To: **Aegiali** (45min., 7 per day, €2); **Agia Anna** (25min., 5 per day 10am-6pm, €1.40) via **Hozoviotissa Monastery** (20min., €1.40); **Chora** (15min., 10 per day 9:45am-10pm, €1.40); **Plakes** and **Maltezi** beaches (7 per day, 11am-5pm, €2.50-3).

Taxis: (☎69378 83 838). 24hr.

PORT CHECK. If arriving by ferry, be sure to double check at which Amorgos port your boat will dock. Oftentimes, the boats stop at Aegiali first, then continue to Katapola. There are times, however, when it is only one or the other. If you get stranded at one, there are buses between the two or you can take one of the taxis for a hefty €23.

◆ ▐ ORIENTATION AND PRACTICAL INFORMATION

The town surrounds the ferry dock in a horseshoe, with restaurants, bars, and accommodations on either side. The port is at the center; most tourist services are between the ferry dock and the road to Chora.

Tours: Synodinos Tours (☎22850 71 201 or 71 747. Exchanges currency, has maps, and sells ferry tickets. Open daily May-Oct. 8:30am-2:30pm, 5:30-9:30pm, and 1hr. before all boat departures; Nov.-Apr. 10am-1:30pm and 5-8:30pm and 1hr. before all boat departures.

Bank: Agricultural Bank (☎22850 71 872), opposite the ferries. **24hr. ATM.** Open M-Th 8am-2:30pm, F 8am-2pm.

Laundromat: (☎22850 71 723), past the docks on the way to the beach; take the 1st right after Pension Amorgos. Wash and dry €10. Open M-Sa 9am-9pm, Su 10am-2pm.

Police: (☎22850 71 210), in Chora. **Port police** (☎22850 71 259), across from the ferry dock. Open 24hr.

Pharmacy: Nearest one in Chora.

Medical Services: (☎22850 71 805, emergencies 71 805 or 69772 99 674), at the far left end of the waterfront, in the white building behind the 3 statues. Open M-F 9am-2:30pm.

Internet Access: Minoa Hotel (☎22850 71 480), in the central *plateia*. €5 per hr. Open daily 8am-4pm and 6-10:30pm.

Post Office: (☎22850 71 884), in a small boutique next to the Minoa Hotel, at the back left of the main *plateia*. Open M-Tu, Th, Sa 10am-1pm and 7-10pm; W and F 10am-1pm. **Postal Code:** 84008.

ACCOMMODATIONS

Katapola is a small town with few hotels and many *domatia*.

Big Blue Pension (☎22850 71 094). From the ferry dock, turn right after the *plateia* and follow the signs uphill. Spacious rooms, blue windows and doors, and open patios where guests can enjoy spectacular harbor views. Flower-studded walkways. Rooms have baths, fridges, A/C, and TVs. Doubles €30-50; triples €35-60. Cash only. ❸

Pension Amorgos (☎22850 71 013), across from the small ferry dock. Modern rooms with beguiling white-stucco and purple-shuttered balconies. Light blue sheets and yellow walls make the rooms light and airy. Doubles €35-45; triples and quads €60-70. Cash only. ❸

Titika Rooms (☎22850 25 749), at the far end of the beach from the port. Centered on a flowery, stone-lined garden. Each room has bath, fridge, TV, A/C, mosquito net, hair dryer, and balcony. Doubles €25-45; triples €30-55. Cash only. ❷

FOOD

Aigaion Cafe (☎22850 71 549), in the center of the main *plateia*. Serves fruit juice (€3), crepes (€4-7), omelettes (€2.50-4), and mixed drinks (€6) to locals who lounge and chat into the nights. Inside the funky interior, patrons play board games, listen to pop music, and watch TV. Open daily Apr.-Oct. 8am-3:30am, Nov.-Mar. 9am-midnight. Cash only. ❶

Mourayio (☎22850 71 011), across from the dock. Authentic meals in a simple outdoor seating area. Inside, you can get a sneak preview of your meal in coolers full of fresh fish. Boiled octopus €8. Moussaka €6. Open daily 1pm-late. Cash only. ❷

El Greco (☎22850 74 102), in the middle of the wharf. Pizza €8-11. Open daily noon-midnight. Cash only. ❷

SIGHTS AND BEACHES

HOZOVIOTISSA MONASTERY. A trip to Amorgos is incomplete without a visit to otherworldly Hozoviotissa Monastery. The 11th-century Byzantine edifice was built into a cliff face—one of the most exhilarating spectacles in all of Greece and an inspiration to the great 20th-century Swiss architect Le Corbusier, among others. Legend tells that attempts to build the monastery on the shore were thwarted; when the workers discovered their tools mysteriously hanging from the cliff, they figured it was an omen and started construction in the seemingly impossible location. If you complete the hike (up 350 stone

CYCLADES

steps), the monks will treat you to cold water, a shot of honey *raki* (liquor), and *loukoumi* (a jello). Inside, visitors must lean to the left when climbing the narrow staircase to avoid the cliff face—it protrudes into the building's cave-like interior, which is never more than 5m deep. At the top, a multilingual monk may greet you to provide a short history and answer questions. To see more of the building, come in November when the entire island celebrates the **Feast of Panagia Hozoviotissa** at the monastery. If you miss the bus back, take the stone stairway (10m uphill from the fork in the road leading away from the monastery). A 20min. climb up the stairs will lead you to Chora. The road from the monastery also takes you to the crystal waters of Agia Anna and its two small, rock coves; from the bus stop, one is at the end of the path through the clearing, the other at the bottom of the central steps. *(Catch a bus (20min., 5 per day 10am-6pm, €1.40) from Katapola to the monastery.* ☎ *22850 71 274. Open daily 8am-1pm and 5-7pm. Modest dress required. No trousers, shorts, or mini skirts for women. There are a few extra cover-ups to borrow at the entrance, however be prepared to wait if they are all being used. Free.)*

BEACHES. Agios Pavlos's shallow turquoise lagoon is exquisite and is only a short walk downhill from the bus stop. Adventurous swimmers can make the 150m crossing to **Nikouria Island,** or take a boat, which leaves for the island every hour, for even more seclusion. Take a bus toward Aegiali and ask to be let off at Agios Pavlos (5 per day, €1.40). Various nude beaches provide sand and sun outside of town, opposite the dock. Smooth-stoned **Plakes** and the sandier **Agios Panteleimonas** and **Maltezi** are quiet easily accessible by boat—taxi boats leave from the left of the dock (every hr. 11am-5pm, round-trip €2.50-3.00). Look for the signs along the waterfront advertising the different beaches and boats that will take you there.

AMORGOS TOWN Χώρα   ☎22850

Also known as Chora, the island's small, untouristed capital lies 6km uphill from the harbor at the top of the mountains. An example of Byzantine village planning, Chora's winding streets were constructed to deter and confuse raiding pirates. They now allow visitors to meander along the narrow, cafe-lined walk to **Platela Loza,** at the far end of town. Sights include a 14th-century Venetian fortress, a row of 10 defunct windmills on the mountain ledge above town, numerous Byzantine churches, and the first secondary school in Greece, built in 1821. The remnants of Amorgos's Minoan civilization are visible in the statues and relief carvings at the **Archaeological Museum,** across from Zygos Cafe and downhill from the large church at Pl. Loza. The museum displays unsigned inscriptions and sculptures from Minoa in a small courtyard and indoor area. (☎22850 29 279. Open Tu-Su 8:30am-3pm. Free.)

Rugged mountains and a placid coast run alongside the road from Chora to Aegiali. The clearly marked, sunny 4hr. **hike** begins behind Chora and stretches up the mountains to Potamos. Forty minutes into the hike, you'll find the crumbling Byzantine church of **Christososmas** (The Body of Christ) hewn out of a small cave that was once a hermit dwelling. The trail ascends past a series of monasteries before descending to views of miniature **Nikouria Island.** Deserted **Agios Mammas** church is the last significant marker before Potamos appears. From Potamos, hikers can walk 15min. to catch the bus in Aegiali to return to Chora (€2).

If you decide to spend the night in Chora, you can strike a deal with the *domatia* owners who meet your boat, or look for "rooms to let" signs along side streets. The reception for **Pension Ilias ❷** is along the road from Chora to the monastery, while the rooms are one street uphill. Each room has bath, TV,

A/C, hotpot, fridge, and a common balcony with views of the valley below; the apartments include full kitchens. (☎22850 71 277. Free transportation from the port. Doubles €25-55; apartments €50-80. Cash only.) **Zygos ❶**, on the cafe-lined alley below Pl. Loza, serves coffee (€1.50-3), breakfast from 9-1pm (€4-6), homemade sangria, and mixed drinks (€5) on a vine-roofed patio. The comfy shaded tables are a perfect setting for a leisurely afternoon. (☎22850 71 350. Open daily 8am-3:30am. Free internet for patrons. Cash only.) **Liotrivi ❷**, near the bakery on the road to the monastery, puts delicious twists on Greek standards—*kalogiros* (eggplant with veal, feta, gouda, and tomato; €7.90) and *exohiko* (lamb and vegetables in pastry shell) are the creative house specialties. (☎22850 71 700. Entrees €7-10. Open daily May-Oct. 12:30pm-midnight. MC/V.) The relaxed **cafe** downstairs at Bayoko, by the bus station, caters to people-watchers and music aficionados, with live jazz performances three times a week. Upstairs, at one of Chora's only clubs, nightly DJs spin Greek dance hits over the small dance floor from 9pm until dawn. (Beer €3-5. Ouzo €2. Mixed drinks €7. Cash only.)

The **police** are in the main *plateia* with the big church, by Cafe Loza. (☎22850 71 210. Open daily 8am-2pm.) A **24hr. ATM** is located below the bus stop next to the mini market. The **pharmacy** is opposite the bus stop. (☎22850 73 391. Open M-F 9:30am-2pm and 5:30-9:30pm, Sa 10am-2pm and 6-9:30pm, Su 10:30am-2pm and 6-8:30pm.) The **medical center** sits below the bus stop on the main road into Chora from Katapola. (☎22850 71 207. Open M-F 9am-2:30pm.) Chora is home to the main **post office** (☎22850 71 250; open M-F 7:30am-2pm), in a corner beyond Pl. Loza. Western Union available.

IOS Ίος

This drink-till-you-drop party island is rivaled only by Mykonos when it comes to nocturnal Dionysian rites. Daytime activity centers on the coast, as beachgoers settle down with a drink by the pool or sea to soak up the sun's energy or nap to prepare for the long night ahead. Ios's hoteliers and restaurateurs have been making a successful effort to bring families to enjoy its more peaceful side, which emerges as visitors move farther away from the carousing, hedonistic center. And despite the island's knack for revelry, only three of its 36 beaches have been developed for tourism, so there are plenty of places to stretch out and soothe that hangover, before starting all over again.

IOS TOWN Χώρα   ☎ 22860

If you're not drunk when you arrive, you will be when you leave. In Ios Town, also known as Chora, shots go down and clothes come off faster than you can say "Opa!" Though it is an eerie, unpopulated oasis of calm during the day, the town stirs to life in the evening hours as revelers gear up for another round of drunken festivities. You'll see everything your mother warned you against—wine swilled from the bottle at 3pm, all-day drinking games, partiers dancing in the streets and on bars, people swimming less than 30min. after they've eaten, and so much more. Those in search of quieter pleasures stay in Gialos (the port), while the party animals crowd into Chora and along Mylopotas beach.

TRANSPORTATION

Ferries and Highspeed Boats: The price and time ranges vary according to ferry line and type of boat. Inquire at travel agencies throughout the port, Chora, and Mylopotas beach for specific timetables and prices. To: **Anafi** (3hr., 3-4 per week, €9); **Folegandros** (1½hr., 1-2 per day, €6); **Iraklion, Crete** (2½hr., 3 per week, €37.80); **Mykonos** (2hr., 1-2 per day, €27); **Naxos** (1-1½hr., 1-4 per day, €12-22); **Paros** (1½-2½hr., 1-4 per day, €13-20); **Piraeus** (5½-8 hr., 2-4 per day, €35-50); **Santorini** (45min.-1½hr., 2-4 per day, €9-19); **Sifnos** (4hr., 2 per week, €12); **Sikinos** (30min., 1-3 per day, €5); **Syros** (3½hr., 3-4 per week, €21).

Buses: Frequent buses shuttle between port, village, and beach (every 10-20min. 7:20am-12:05am, €1.40). There are clearly marked stops in all 3 locations: near the square of the port, along the main road in Chora, and all along the beach road in Mylopotas.

Taxis: (☎69787 34 491, 69770 31 708, 69777 60 570, or 69780 96 32). 24hr.

Rentals: Jacob's Moto Rent (☎22860 91 047), by the bus stop at the port and right before entering Mylopotas beach. Motorbikes and ATVs €15-25. Cars €35-80. **Ios Rent-A-Car** (☎22860 92 300), located in Acteon Travel in the port. Cars €35-60. MC/V.

ORIENTATION AND PRACTICAL INFORMATION

Ios Town's action is based in three locations, each 10-20min. apart along the island's paved road. **Gialos,** the port, is at one end; **Chora,** the village, sits above on a hill; frenzied **Mylopotas** beach is 3km farther. During the day in Chora, the winding streets behind the church are filled with boutique clothing shops and postcard pushers. As the sun sets, they become the hub of nighttime activity. During the day, cheap and frequent buses connect the three locales (see **Transportation,** p. 308). After midnight, people generally walk the downhill 2km (25 min.) between Chora and Mylopotas and 15min. downhill path from Chora to Gialos, but for uphill, taxi services are preferable.

Budget Travel: ⊠**Acteon Travel** (☎22860 91 343; www.acteon.gr), at the bottom of the village in Chora. Also has a branch adjacent to the bus stop in the port and another at Mylopotas beach. Sells ferry tickets, offers assistance with accommodations, exchanges currency, has internet access (€1 per 15min.), and rents vehicles. Main port office open daily 8am-11pm; Chora branch open daily 10am-11pm.

Banks: National Bank (☎22860 91 565), by the main church in Chora. **24hr. ATM.** Open M-Th 8am-2:30pm, F 8am-2pm.

Laundromat: Sweet Irish Dream Laundry (☎22860 91 584), by the club with the same name, on the main road from the port. Wash and dry €9. Open daily 10am-9pm.

Police: (☎22860 91 222), on the road to Kolitsani beach, past the OTE. Open 24hr.

Pharmacy: (☎22860 91 562), in Chora, next to Acteon Travel. Open daily 8am-midnight.

Medical Center: (☎22860 91 227), at the port, 100m from the dock. Specializes in drunken mishaps. Open M-F 8:30am-2:30pm and 6-8pm for emergencies only. In

Chora, you can reach a **doctor** (Yiannis) 24hr. at ☎22860 91 137 or 69324 20 200. His office is on the main road next to Fun Pub; open for emergencies 24hr.

Internet Access: All over the port and village. Most charge €4 per hr. **Acteon Travel,** at the port. **Francesco's,** in the village. **Far Out Beach Club,** on Mylopotas beach.

Post Office: (☎22860 91 235). On the main road coming from the port, take a right after Sweet Irish Dream. **Poste Restante.** Open M-F 7:30am-2pm. **Postal Code:** 84001.

ACCOMMODATIONS AND CAMPING

Affordable accommodations exist in the frenetic village and beach and in the quiet port. Each area has its own personality, so weigh your interests before making a choice. A tent, bungalow, or room on Mylopotas beach lets you roll hazily from blanket to beach with a herd of other tanned, recovering partiers, cutting out the daytime bus ride in between. However, a village room enables easy access to clubs and a safer journey home from all-night revelry. Most accommodations provide free shuttles to and from the port.

▨ **Francesco's** (☎22860 91 223; www.francescos.net), in the village. With your back to the bank, take the steps up from the left corner of the *plateia,* then take the 1st left. Owned by friendly Francesco, this hostel is right out of a hip backpacker's dream, with fun people, a patio perfect for catching the stunning sunset, and clean dorms to crash in, most with only 3-4 beds. Every night at 11pm, shots are handed out in the bar off the patio to welcome new guests and begin the night's partying. Reception 9am-2pm and 6-9:30pm. Check-out 11am. Breakfast €2-4.50. Dorms €11-18; 2-4-person rooms €15-28 per person. Cash only. ❶

▨ **Far Out Beach Club and Camping** (☎22860 92 302; www.faroutclub.com), at the end of Mylopotas beach. A non-stop, hopping beachside complex and the hub of activity at Mylopotas beach. Far Out has rooms for every budget, from tents to hotel studios, at rock-bottom prices. Hotel rooms are equipped with A/C, mini bars, TVs, terraces, and phones, while camping involves basic tents and bamboo-covered bungalows. Restaurant, bar, mini-mart, volleyball court, swimming pools, bungee jumping, free new movies (shown every evening), showers, laundry, internet, live music, scuba diving, and nightly Happy Hour. Check-out noon. Open Apr.-Oct. Camping €7 per person; 2-person bungalows €16; rooms €30-50 per person. Cash only. ❶

Ios Resort (☎22860 92 685, www.iosresort.com). With the village on the left, turn right before the supermarket. Walk up the hill, then turn right down the alley. The hotel is down another small street to the left. Look for the name on the building. A new and chic addition to the hotel scene in Ios. Clean rooms with A/C, baths, and fridges located around the central pool and patio. Hotel bar next to the pool. Rooms €25-30 per person. ❷

Purple Pig Stars Camping (☎22860 91 302 and 91 611), off the main road entering Mylopotas beach from Chora. 1 of the original campgrounds on the island of Ios, open since 1983. Outdoor sleeping, camping, dorms, and bungalows, all shaded by large eucalyptus trees. The site also has a pool, weekly barbecues, restaurant, bar, international live music, laundry, currency exchange, film viewings, internet, travel agency, and safe deposit boxes. Tent rental available. Dorms with A/C €12; bungalows €15-20. Cash only. ❶

Hotel George and Irene (☎22860 91 927, www.irene.gr), 3 blocks up from the village's main road. Away from the noise, but still near the action. The clean rooms have balconies, TVs, A/C, baths, and safes. Doubles €45-75; apartments €70-100. AmEx/MC/V. ❸

FOOD

Most eating on Ios coincides with heavy drinking, peaking in the middle of the night at gyro and crepe joints. During the day, fast food is the primary source

CYCLADES

of nourishment. For dinner, better restaurants among the ubiquitous bars and discos, at the port, and on the beach finally open their doors. **Caio Market** is opposite the bus stop in Chora and provides basic goods. (☎22860 91 035. Open 24hr.) There's also a **supermarket** in the main *plateia*.

- **Ali Baba's** (☎22860 91 558), by the Ios gym. Coming down from the main *plateia*, take a right after you reach the fast-food restaurants. Continue down to the bottom of the road and take a left. Sweat through the delicious, spicy, and impressively authentic Thai menu in the enclosed garden and finish your meal with a complementary jello shot. Pad thai €9. Open daily 6pm-1am. Cash only. ❷

- **Pomodoro** (☎22860 91 387), uphill behind Disco 69. As the sister restaurant to Ali Baba's, this sleek addition to Ios's eating scene serves Italian-Mediterranean cuisine from a perch on Chora's central hill. Diners escape the buzz of bars and shops on the rooftop deck, which has panoramic views of the island. Traditional wood-fired pizzas €7.50-10.50. Pasta €8.50-11. Open daily 6:30pm-1:30am. Cash only. ❷

- **Piperri at Old Byron's** (☎69781 92 212). Look for the sign by the pharmacy pointing up 3 blocks. An intimate bistro in a shady side street. Creative tapas and *mezes*, such as Byron's Balls (rolled cheese in bread crumbs and dip; €6). Entrees €9-14. Large *meze* platter €25. Open daily M-Sa 6-11:30pm. Reservations recommended for dinner. MC/V. ❸

- **Polydoros** (☎22860 91 132), on Koumbara beach. Walk 2km or take the bus on the road along the harbor beach. The beloved hangout of many of Ios's residents, who will stand for nothing less than the freshest ingredients. Shrimp *saganaki* (fried cheese dish) with feta €8.50. Open daily 1pm-midnight. Cash only. ❷

👁 ↻ SIGHTS AND BEACHES

An **Open Theater Festival Program** is held every summer above the windmills on the island—inquire at a travel agency for more info.

BEACHES. Lounging on the beaches and sampling different water sports are the most popular daytime activities on the island. **Mylopotas Beach,** a 25min. walk downhill from Chora, has music blasting, and all parties flock to the debaucherous **Far Out Beach Club** to lounge by the pool, try water sports in the bay, and start drinking early. The long, wide stretch of sand also has beach soccer and volleyball areas. **Koumbara,** 1.75km down the road that follows Gialos beach, draws a much smaller crowd to its large cove, which is a popular place for windsurfing. For those who want quiet and beauty of the natural variety, buses (30min.; depart 11am and noon, return 5 and 6pm; €3) go to the more secluded ⬛**Manganari,** the island's nicest stretch of sand. Gialos (the port beach), Mylopotas, and Manganari all offer water sports, from tubing to windsurfing. You can also make a daytrip to **Saint Theodotis Beach,** on the northeast side of the island, with golden sand and even fewer people (bus departs 11:30am, returns 5pm; €2.50). For a more local experience, head to **Kolitsani,** a secluded beach and crystal pool of water at the little bay. On the way to Mylopotas, look for the sign on the right labeled Kolitsani, then follow the road until another sign points downhill to a rocky path. Nude **Psathi,** on the eastern coast, is accessible by moped and car.

OTHER SIGHTS. Away from the sunshine, you can pay a visit to the **Ios Archaeological Museum,** in the town hall across from the bus stop, to view artifacts from Ios's long and rich history, particularly from the ruins of Skarkos. Watch for a tablet that mentions Homerium, an ancient month named in honor of the poet. *(Open Tu-Su 8:30am-3pm. €2, students and under 18 free.)* According to legend, Homer died and was buried on Ios; the supposed site of **Homer's tomb** has been worn to rubble, but the spot in Plakatos, on the island's northern tip, still draws a few dedicated tourists. To repent for the previous night's excess, walk toward the windmills to the path at the top of the hill, which leads to the solitary **monastery.**

NIGHTLIFE

Most of Ios's extraordinary number of bars are packed into the old village, making it easy to hit all the hot spots in one night. The largest and loudest discos line the main road. Many start their night at rooftop and hostel bars, like those at Francesco's and Far Out, swilling liquor from the bottle in the main *plateia* or by the pool at sunset, hitting the village between midnight and 2am, then migrating to the discos before sunrise. Alcohol is cheap, and most places offer specials like "2 cocktails for €5 all night," free shots with all drinks, or "buy 7 shots and get a free t-shirt."

Circus Bar, up a side street off the main *plateia*. The dance floor gets packed, so hop onto a side table, grab the poles on the ceiling, and perform your own circus tricks. The bartender will often juggle with flaming vodka bottles. Open daily 10pm-late.

Disco 69 (☎22860 91 064; www.disco69club.com), on the main bar street on the right. Blares mainstream dance music; when the cavernous dance floor gets too crowded with grinding bodies, people hop onto the bar and carry on. Free shot with all drinks. Open daily 10pm-4am.

Blue Note (☎22860 92 488), off the main *plateia*, past the fast-food joints, and around the corner to the left. A good place to get the night started. Hit this club early in the evening (around 12:30 or 1am), when the dance floor is packed before the crowd heads to other places. The jolly owner Francesco (also the owner of the popular backpackers' hostel) and his staff will give free shots to those staying in the hostel. Open daily 10:30pm-4:30am.

Red Bull (☎22860 91 019), in the main *plateia* in the village. If flashing lights and glitzy club decor aren't your thing, this small, wood-trimmed bar, which plays loud 90s music and pop hits, will give you wings. Happy hour all night long. Open daily 9pm-4:30am.

The Slammer Bar (☎22860 91 019), in the left inland corner of the main *plateia*. If you ask, the bartender will whack your helmeted head with a blunt object before you down a tequila slammer (tequila, Tía María, and Sprite), which gets you equally hammered. Open daily 10pm-4:30am.

Sweet Irish Dream, in a large building on the main road leading from the port. Most save this nighttime Narnia for their last stop, pausing to dance on the tables beneath green neon lazers, then squinting out into the bright, early morning sun. Open daily 11am-late.

SANTORINI Σαντορίνη

Whitewashed towns balanced on plunging cliffs, scorching black-sand beaches, and sharply stratified geological rock formations make Santorini's landscape nearly as dramatic as the volcanic cataclysm that created it. This eruptive past—and stark beauty—has led some to believe that Santorini is the lost continent of Atlantis. The island, also called "Thira," was an outpost of Minoan society from 2000 BC until around the turn of the 17th century BC, when an earthquake destroyed the wealthy maritime settlement of Akrotiri. All hope of recovery vanished when a massive volcanic eruption spread lava and pumice across the island around 1625 BC. The destruction of Santorini heralded the fall of Minoan civilization, and the volcanic eruption may have led to a tidal wave that leveled the ancient Minoan palaces on Crete. Yet the volcanoes greatly enriched the island's soil, bestowing upon Santorini a greener landscape than that of its mostly barren Cycladic neighbors. Beauty this stunning couldn't be kept secret for long, and armies of tourists pour into Santorini from across the world in parades of weddings, honeymoons, and family vacations. Due to its popularity and the cost of importing water and produce, however, the prices on the island are as steep as the cliffs of the caldera.

Santorini

THIRA Φήρα
☎ 22860

Atop a hill and far from the black-sand beaches, Thira's congested assemblage of glitzy shops, whizzing mopeds, and hyperactive crowds can be overwhelming. Tourist traffic has made it easy to find a hamburger or wiener schnitzel, and groups of hotels fearlessly peer over steep cliffs, almost daring the seismically active island to send them tumbling into the sea. Even kitsch and overcrowding, however, can't negate the pleasure of wandering the cobbled streets and arriving at the caldera in time to watch the sunset.

☐ TRANSPORTATION

Boats dock at one of three ports on the island: Athinios, Thira, or Oia. Most **ferries** arrive in Athinios and buses meet every boat to take passengers to Thira (25min., €2). Be aware that even if your ferry ticket says "Thira," you may be landing in the town of Athinios. Thira's port is down a 588-step footpath from the town; you can walk, take a **cable car** (☎22860 22 977; every 20min. 6:30am-11pm; €4, children €2, luggage €2), or hire a **donkey** (€4). All these methods of transportation are fun and scenic. Santorini's buses run frequently and can take you anywhere you want to go, but they're often crowded. Arrive at the station 10min. early to make your bus. Estimated journey lengths are based on ideal circumstances; buses often move much more slowly.

Flights: Santorini National Airport (JTR; ☎22860 28 400). **Olympic Airways** (☎22860 22 493) and **Aegean Airlines** (☎22860 28 500) fly to **Athens** (50min., 3-6 per day, €50-90) and **Thessaloniki** (1hr., 1-2 per day, €85-100). Airline tickets are available at most travel agencies; look for the Olympic Airways and Aegean Airlines banners in the windows.

Ferries and Flying Dolphins: Check the ferry schedules at Pelican Tours or at any travel agency in town. Fast ferries run more often than slow ferries, take half the time, and generally cost twice as much. Slow ferries €7-30; fast ferries €15-60. Destinations include: **Amorgos** (1¼hr., 1 per day); **Anafi** (1½hr., 7 per week); **Folegandros** (1½hr., 1-3 per day); **Ios** (¾-1½hr., 3-6 per day); **Iraklion, Crete** (2-4hr., 2-3 per day); **Mykonos** (3hr., 1 per day); **Naxos** (3hr., 2-4 per day); **Paros** (4hr., 2-5 per day); **Piraeus** (10hr., 4-8 per day); **Rafina** (5hr., 1 per day); **Sifnos** (7hr., 2 per week).

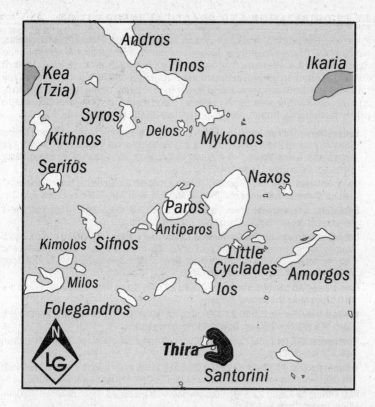

Buses: (☎22860 25 404). To: **Akrotiri** (30min., 7-8 per day, €2); **Athinios** (25min., 7-8 per day, €2); **Kamari** (20min., 30 per day 7:30am-midnight, €1.40); **Monolithos** (30min., 12 per day 7:10am-8pm, €1.40) via the **airport; Oia** (30min., 32 per day 6:50am-11pm, €1.40); **Perissa** (30min., 32 per day 7am-midnight, €2).

Taxis: (☎22860 22 555). In Pl. Theotokopoulou by the bus station. Available 24hr.

Car and Moped Rental: Car, moped, motorbike, and ATV rental companies line the streets in and around the Pl. Theotokopoulou as well as 25 Martiou. Cars €40-60 per day. Mopeds/motorbikes €15-20 per day. ATVs €20-30 per day. Make sure helmets are included. During the summer months, most rental agencies are open from 8 or 9am to 8 or 9pm daily. Off Pl. Theotokopoulou, **Moto Kostas** (☎22860 22 801) has cheaper prices than most and will discount for multiple-day rentals. ATVs €10-15 per day.

 FREEDOM OF THE ROAD. If you're only in Santorini for a day or two and want to see as much as possible, rent an ATV, car, or motorbike. This saves you the hassle of riding in crowded buses, and gives you access to the hidden nooks of the island that the flocks of tourists can't reach. ATVs are simple to operate, and gas is cheap.

⊞ 🔀 ORIENTATION AND PRACTICAL INFORMATION

From the bus station, walk uphill and to the right to **Plateia Theotokopoulou,** which is full of travel agencies, banks, and cafes. At the fork, the street on the right is **25 Martiou,** the main cobblestone road. It leads from the *plateia* toward Oia and is home to several accommodations. Head onto the left branch of the fork and turn onto any westbound street to find many of the best bars, stores, and discos. Farther west is the **caldera** (basin), bordered by **Ypapantis,** where pricey restaurants, hotels, and galleries bask in the stunning vista.

Budget Travel: Pelican Tours (☎22860 22 220), in the *plateia,* next to the port police. Sells ferry tickets and organizes boat trips to the volcano, hot springs, and Thirasia. Also assists with airline tickets, left luggage, helicopter or plane chartering, and currency exchange. Open 8am-11pm. AmEx/MC/V.

Bank: National Bank (☎22860 22 370), on a road off 25 Martiou to the left before the *plateia.* **Currency exchange** and **24hr. ATM.** Open M-Th 8am-2:30pm, F 8am-2pm.

Bookstore: International Press (☎22860 25 301), in the *plateia.* Magazines and a selection of popular books. Open daily 7:30am-11:30pm.

Library: The Greek Cultural Conference Center and Library (☎22860 24 960), off 25 Martiou, on the corner before the post office. Has a few shelves of English books and free internet (for 20min.) in the basement. Open M 9am-3pm and 5-8pm, Tu 9am-3pm, W 9am-3pm and 5-8pm, Th-Su 9am-3pm.

Laundromat: AD Laundry Station (☎22860 23 533), on Ag. Athanassiou. Wash and dry. €10. Open M-Sa 9-2pm and 5-8pm.

Medical Services: (☎22860 23 333). Turn left out of bus station and take another left. Open M-F 8:30am-2:30pm. Open 24hr. for emergencies.

Telephones: OTE (☎22860 22 121). 200m uphill past the *plateia* on 25 Martiou. Open M-F 7:30am-3:10pm.

Internet Access: PC World (☎22860 25 551), in the main *plateia* 2 doors down from the international bookstore. €2.50 per hr. Wi-Fi €4 per hr. Open daily 9am-9pm.

Post Office: (☎22860 22 238). 50m downhill from the *plateia.* Open daily M-F 7:30am-2pm. **Postal Code:** 84700.

▐▘ 🄿 ACCOMMODATIONS AND CAMPING

In summer, pensions and hotels fill up quickly and prices skyrocket. The cheapest options on the island are the youth hostels on Perissa beach and in Oia and camping in Thira. You can find cheaper places in Karterados, 2km south of Thira, or in the small inland towns along the main bus routes—try Messaria, Pyrgos, or Emborio. Hostels and many pensions will pick you up at the port if you reserve ahead.

Hotel Leta (☎22860 22 540; www.leta-santorini.gr), 200m from the *plateia.* Follow signs across from the laundromat on the main road. This colorful building provides a quiet escape from the crowds, as well as a pool and a scenic view of the sea. Clean and homey rooms have A/C, TVs, baths, and fridges; some have balconies with view of the Aegean. Free transport to and from the port. Singles €40; doubles €50-65; triples €60-80. Cash only. ❸

Pension Petros (☎22860 22 573; www.astirthira.com). With International Press to your right, follow the traffic downhill to the right, off the *plateia.* Turn left and then right at the end of the street and continue for 50m. Simply-decorated rooms are cozy and have baths, TVs, fridges, and A/C. Owner Petros provides free transport from the port. Singles €40-50; doubles €45-55; triples €55-85. Cash only. ❸

Santorini Camping (☎22860 22 944; www.santorinicamping.gr). Follow the blue signs away from the *plateia* for 300m. This shady campground is the most festive spot in town and among the most affordable. The grounds have a pool, bar and billiards, cafe, mini-mart, laundry facilities, and an internet room. Free transport to and from the port. 24hr. hot showers. Check-out noon. Quiet hours 11:30pm-7am. Reservations required unless you bring your own tent. Open May.-Oct. Camping €6-10 per person; €4-6 per child; €3-5 per tent; €4 per car. Dorms €10-20; singles €20-50; doubles €30-70; triples €40-80. MC/V. ❶

Costa Marina Villas (☎22860 28 923; www.costamarina.gr), 2 doors down from Pension Petros. In a quiet space away from the road. Traditionally decorated, spacious rooms, each with wrought-iron bed, A/C, fridge, bath, phone, and safe; some have kitchens. Recommended for families and couples. Breakfast included. Singles €55-75; doubles €68-88; triples €84-105; quads €105-122. Under 6 free. MC/V. ❺

🍴 FOOD

Inexpensive restaurants are hard to find in Thira, but the few that exist are crammed between shops on the tiny streets between the caldera and the *plateia*. The caldera is lined with fine dining options that charge hefty prices for their "priceless" views. Generic but convenient snack shops and gyro joints dot the *plateia* as budget-friendly alternatives for the hungry traveler.

■ **NRG Cafe** (☎22860 24 997), on Eth. Stavrou, next to Koo Club. This tiny creperie makes the largest, most delicious sweet and savory crepes on the island with a variety of fresh ingredients. Choose from the extensive menu or craft your own. Bacon, egg, gouda, and feta crepe €5. Apple, rum, and honey crepe €4.40. Open daily 9am-10pm. Cash only. ❶

■ **Mama's House** (☎22860 23 032), on the left on the way to the bus station from Pl. Theotokpoulou. Homemade preserves and syrup round off this eatery's cozy morning feel. Chatty and endearingly loud, Mama makes sure her "babies"—you—are stuffed when they leave. French toast and 2 eggs €5. Open daily 8am-midnight. MC/V. ❶

Nikolas, on Eth. Stavrou (☎22860 24 550), next to the Town Club. In stark contrast to the tourist restaurants overlooking the caldera, Nikolas's atmosphere is undeniably local and down-to-earth. Extensive selection of traditional Greek fare. Come early to avoid the waiting in line with the dinner-time crowds. Moussaka €9. Open M-Sa noon-11pm, Su 5-11pm. ❷

China Restaurant (☎22860 24 760). Turn left past the OTE and walk 50m up the street. This decidedly non-Greek option has a rooftop garden complete with hanging lanterns. Prices are appreciably lower than nearby caldera restaurants. Portions are medium-sized, so order multiple dishes if you plan to share. Chicken chow mein €7.90. Beef with broccoli €9.90. Open daily noon-midnight. MC/V. ❷

📷🏖 SIGHTS AND BEACHES

Most visitors are understandably content wandering the town, lying on the beaches, and gazing on the dramatic cliffs of the caldera. If you're in the mood for some history about the island, however, there are a number of museums scattered near the city center.

THE MUSEUM OF PREHISTORIC THIRA. The sleek collection charts the history of excavation and the geology of Thira, as well as the island's history from the Late Neolithic to the Late Cycladic I Period through fossils, tools, vases, figurines, and other vessels. Of particular interest is Santorini's pre-eruption civilization and the magnificent city of Akrotiri, which has been reconstructed in a three-dimensional model. The partially restored **wall paintings** from Akrotiri are beautifully preserved. One from the House of Ladies depicts large blue papyrus plants and slender women at two-thirds life-size, typical of the Theran scale. The equally impressive wall painting of the Blue Monkeys was done by an avant-garde painter for the city. The gold ibex figurine is a miniature masterpiece discovered in 1999 in a wooden box at the site. Each exhibit has detailed signs in English. *(Across the street from the bus station toward the caldera. ☎ 22860 23 217. Open in summer daily 8:30am-8pm; in winter Tu-Su 8:30am-3pm. €3, students and EU seniors €2, EU students free.)*

MEGARO GYZI MUSEUM. Housed in a 17th-century family mansion, the Megaro Gyzi Museum documents Santorini's history with Venetian maps, engravings, and manuscripts from the 15th to the 19th centuries. A collection of old photographs of scenic Santorini before the earthquake of 1956 provides historical context. An interesting group of paintings by well-known Greek painters, all of Santorini landscapes, explore a variety of stylistic influences and use different media. *(Off Eth. Stavrou below the clock tower. ☎ 22860 23 077; www.megarogyzi.gr. Open May-Oct. M-Sa 10am-4pm. €3, students €1.50, under 11 free.)*

THE PETROS M. NOMIKOS CONFERENCE CENTER. This exhibition center currently displays life-size reproductions of Ancient Thira's and Akrotiri's magnificent wall paintings; the prized originals are in the National Archaeological Museum in Athens (p. 98) and the Museum of Prehistoric Thira. The brightly colored and intricately detailed murals give insight into the history and culture of Santorini's ancient Minoans, as well as the island's former plant and animal life. In a hallway outside the museum, there is a new photographic tour of the excavation site of Akrotiri. Because the site is still closed to visitors, these real-life photos with English captions are a way to explore Akrotiri and the artifacts found there. *(Follow the signs past the cable car station. ☎ 22860 23 016. Open daily May-Oct. 10am-7pm. Conference center €4, students and seniors €2. Audio tour €3. Photograph exhibit free.)*

BEACHES. Santorini has a wealth of beaches, many of which are easily accessible from Thira by bus. **Kamari** is the island's most popular beach, with a large expanse of fine black sand and a proudly waving Blue Flag award. The festive beach towns of **Perivolos** and **Perissa** lie along an endless 9km stretch of black sand on the southeastern coast, welcoming a more casual crowd of beach bums. Bars, restaurants, and laid-back rooms for rent line the beach literally steps from the black sand—it's hot, so bring sandals. Buses leave Thira for Perissa and Perivolos (20min., every 30min., €1.90). Right by the beach, cheery **Youth Hostel Anna ❶** in Perissa greets budget travelers with internet and helpful receptionists, who will find you rentals, ferry tickets, diving and snorkeling trips, and sail boat tours. From the bus stop, take the road along the beach, turning left at the main intersection. The hostel is 500m farther on the right. (☎22860 82 182. Reception 9am-2:30pm and 6-10pm. Dorms €12-15; quads €15.) One of the closest beaches to Thira is **Monolithos,** which has thin, yellow sand and shallow water. You can reach it by bus (€1.40). Some of the best and most peaceful beaches are not directly accessible by bus. If you have your own wheels, be sure to explore **Vlychada,** a fine black-sand beach backed by white pumice rocks that create a moon-like landscape.

> **TIP** **WATER, WATER, EVERYWHERE.** Nor any drop to drink. It is an unfortunate irony that Santorini, though surrounded by the Aegean and the Sea of Crete, suffers from a major water shortage. Santorini's residents are quick to turn off their faucets, flush every other time they use the toilet, and head to the kiosk or mini-mart for bottled water to drink or cook. Travelers should follow suit, conserving water at every opportunity and not drinking from the tap.

ENTERTAINMENT AND NIGHTLIFE

Those who want to catch the summer's latest blockbusters can go to the **open-air cinema** in Kamari, where American films (with Greek subtitles) and live concerts take place twice a week; pick up programs at roadside stands in Thira and Kamari. (☎22860 31 974. www.cinekamari.gr. Shows in summer daily 9:30pm.) **Villaggio Cinema** is an air-conditioned indoor cinema in the Kamari Shopping Center showing American films with Greek subtitles. (☎22860 32 800; www. villaggiocinema.gr.) Thira's nightlife begins late at night and ends early in the morning. Clubs gear up around midnight or 12:30am. Most line **Ethnikis Stavrou,** between the caldera and 25 Martiou. Beer is €3-5; mixed drinks run €8-9. On particuarly hectic evenings, there may be a cover (€5-10).

Tropical Club (☎22860 23 089), high on the caldera, on the road down to the Old Port. The breezy balcony has magnificent views of Thira's nightly lights. If it gets too windy, head inside where a DJ spinning American music transforms the cafe into a choice location to bust a move. Open daily noon-4am. Cash only.

Koo Club (☎22860 22 025; www.kooclub.gr). Duck off Thira's debaucherous streets into Koo's luxurious, palm-tree-lined garden. High-decibel music and flashing neon lights make the dance floor a little intense. Open Apr.-Sept. 10pm-late. Cash only.

Murphy's (☎22860 22 248), next to Enigma. Claims to be the 1st Irish pub in Greece. International flags, outdated license plates, and satellite TVs tuned into international rugby and soccer games surround patrons getting down on the dance floor. Happy hour 3:30-5:30pm and 9:30-10:30pm. Open Mar.-Oct. daily 11:30am-3:30am. Cash only.

Kira Thira Jazz Club (☎22860 22 770), across from Nikolas Taverna. Bar hoppers sip the special house sangria while jazz, blues, and world music set a mellow mood to offset the frenetic pace outside. Periodic live jazz. Open daily 9:30pm-3:30am. Cash only.

BEACHES

Santorini has a wealth of beaches, many of which are easily accessible from Thira by bus. **Kamari** is the island's most popular beach, with a large expanse of fine black sand and a proudly waving Blue Flag award. The festive beach towns of **Perivolos** and **Perissa** lie along an endless 9km stretch of black sand on the southeastern coast, welcoming a more casual crowd of beach bums. Bars, restaurants, and laid-back rooms for rent line the beach literally steps from the black sand—it's hot, so bring sandals. Buses leave Thira for Perissa and Perivolos (20min., every 30min., €1.90). Right by the beach, cheery **Youth Hostel Anna ❶** in Perissa greets budget travelers with internet and helpful receptionists, who will find you rentals, ferry tickets, diving and snorkeling trips, and sail boat tours. From the bus stop, take the road along the beach, turning left at the main intersection. The hostel is 500m farther on the right. (☎22860 82 182. Reception 9am-2:30pm and 6-10pm. Dorms €12-15; quads €15.) One of the closest beaches to Thira is **Monolithos,** which has thin, yellow sand and shallow water. You can reach it by bus (€1.40). Some of the best and most peaceful beaches are not directly accessible by bus. If you have your own wheels, be sure to explore **Vlychada,** a fine black-sand beach backed by white pumice rocks that create a moon-like landscape.

DAYTRIPS FROM THIRA

PYRGOS (Πύργος) AND ANCIENT THIRA (Αρχαία Φήρα). Once a Venetian fortress, the lofty town of Pyrgos is entirely enclosed by medieval walls. The tiny blue-domed churches dotting this hilltop settlement are a visible legacy of Ottoman occupation. If you continue up past Franco's Cafe and the large church, you'll see a small set of steps on the left that leads to rooftop with magnificent, panoramic views. A 45min. hike up the mountain leads to **Profitis Ilias Monastery.** Built in 1711, it graciously shares its site with a radar station installed by the Greek military, who thought that the station would be safe from attack alongside this antique monastery. The original monastery is open only for formal liturgies; visitors must dress modestly and cover their arms and legs. (Check the schedule outside for current opening times. Free.) A small, newer church sits in the shadow of its imposing predecessor's looming bell towers, with a small, well-kept garden and chapel providing shelter from the mountain-tops' gusty breezes. The unmarked entrance can be found by walking along the left side of the final path; a friendly, multilingual monk greets the few visitors upon entry and answers questions. (Open daily 10am-1pm. Free.)

From Profitis Ilias, the ruins of **Ancient Thira** are a 1hr. ▓hike away. (Open Tu-Su 8:30am-2:30pm. €2. EU students free.) This challenging trek gives hikers the opportunity to unleash their inner mountain goat as they scramble over the rocky, exposed face of the mountain that separates Kamari and Perissa, revealing fantastic views of the entire island. The winding mountainside path, discreetly descending to the left of the monastery before the radar station, is made up of slippery gravel and craggy rocks, so wear shoes with good traction. Hikers should also keep their eyes peeled for stacks of rocks, red spots, and views of more well-trodden stretches of the path below to navigate the poorly marked first third of the trail. At the site of Ancient Thira, the ruins of the ancient theater, church, baths, and forum of the island's former capital are still visible, replete with carved dolphins and ruined columns overlooking surrounding islands and sea. *(To reach Pyrgos, take the bus (15min., €1.30) from Thira to Perissa, Athinios, or Akrotiri and ask the driver to let you off at Pyrgos, from where you can hike to the site. To reach Ancient Thira directly, take a bus to Kamari or Perissa (20min., 32 per day, €1.90). Climb the long paths (1hr.) up the mountain beside the water to reach the ruins. Access to the ruins from Kamari is by a paved road, but from Perissa only by footpath. The monastery is also accessible by road from Pyrgos.)*

AKROTIRI (Ακρωτήρι) AND RED BEACH. The volcanic eruption that rocked Santorini in the 17th century BC blanketed Akrotiri with lava. Despite destroying the island, the disaster gave Akrotiri a Pompeii-like immortality, preserving the maritime city more completely than almost any other Minoan site. In 1967, its paved streets were uncovered by Professor Spiridon Marinatos. Only an estimated 3-5% of the massive city has been excavated, but the sprawling remains attest to the sophistication of Minoan society, with multi-storied houses and extensive sanitary, sewage, and drainage systems. Each house had at least one room decorated with wall paintings; the originals are at the National Archaeological Museum in Athens (p. 98) as well as in the Museum of Prehistoric Thira. The wall paintings are the earliest large-scale examples of this art form in Europe, and they provide valuable information about daily Minoan life. Since no skeletons were found in the city, scholars theorize that everyone escaped before the eruption devastated the area. Due to construction and "technical reasons" involving a lawsuit, the area has been shut down until further notice. Check with tourist agencies in Thira to see if the site has reopened and to confirm hours. *(Take the bus from Thira; €1.70.)*

There is not much happening in the village of Akrotiri, 1km from the archaeological site, but there are a few mid-range hotels and restaurants. **Carlos Pension** ❸ offers rooms with baths; some have balconies with views of the southern part of the island and the sea. (☎22860 81 370. Doubles €35-55; triples €45-65.)

To enjoy a meal as the ocean laps at your feet, follow the signs down the road perpendicular to the archaeological site on the way to Red Beach to reach **Dolphins Fish Restaurant ❸**. Diners sit under umbrellas on sun-drenched piers extending onto the water. (☎22860 81 151. Seafood €6.50-€40. Open daily noon-11pm. AmEx/MC/V.) Away from the ancient site, past the Dolphins Fish Restaurant, is the magnificent ■**Red Beach,** a 15min. walk from the Ancient Akrotiri bus stop. Though Santorini is renowned for its black beaches, this stretch's remote location, smooth sand, and brick-red cliffs set it apart. The narrow, red beach is, unfortunately, crammed with umbrellas and beach chairs.

VOLCANO AND THIRASIA (Θηρασία). The little islands along Santorini's caldera rim cater to curious visitors tired of viewing the volcanic strata from afar. The most popular boat excursion goes to the active volcano (€2), with a 30min. guided hike up the black rocks to see the crater. Views from the top of the volcano are spectacular. Most boats make a stop afterward in the nearby waters of Palea Kameni or Nea Kameni, where you can jump off the boat into the green, chilly water, then swim to the orange-colored hot sulfur springs—more luke-warm than hot. A longer excursion goes to the island of Thirasia, stopping for about 2hr. on the island. At the port, there is not much besides *tavernas,* so consider hiking up to explore the towns. Built along Thirasia's upper ridge, the sleepy, whitewashed villages of **Manolas** and **Potamos** have gorgeous views of Santorini's western coast. Tour groups dock at Korfos or Reeva. From Korfos, you'll have to pant up 300 steps to get to the villages; Reeva has a paved road. All travel agencies sell boat tours of the caldera, ranging from 3hr. excursions to the volcano and hot springs (€18-25) to full-day cruises including dinner and sunset views in Oia (€38-42); no single travel agency offers every option. Ask around to find the right tour to suit your interests.

OIA Οία ☎22860

Dazzling sunsets have made the cliffside town of Oia (EE-ah) famous; the little stucco buildings on the cliffs make it breathtaking. In the after-math of the 1956 earthquake that leveled the town and much of the north-western tip of the island, inhabitants carved whitewashed houses into the sheer faces of the cliffside. The budget traveler, however, will not survive long in this spectacular setting. Window-shopping pedestrians and hand-holding honeymooners rule the narrow cobblestone streets at the town's many upscale boutiques, glitzy art galleries, and craft shops. If browsing isn't your bag, hightail it to the cliffs and secure a prime sunset view before camera-armed crowds fill the Western perches of town.

■🛈 **TRANSPORTATION AND PRACTICAL INFORMATION. Buses** run from Thira (25min., 23 per day 6:50am-11pm, €1.40). From the bus stop, face away from the road to Thira, walk to the back left corner of the bus turnaround area, and zigzag to the first alley to the left. Follow it uphill to the main *plateia.*

Karvounis Tours, on the main street near the *plateia,* sells ferry and airline tickets, exchanges currency, and even plans traditional Greek weddings. (☎22860 71 290. Open daily Apr-Oct. 10:30am-2:30pm and 6:30pm-10:30pm.) There is a **24hr. ATM** next to Karvounis Tours. ■**Atlantis Books,** along the main road across from the mayor's office, stocks more than just standard beach reads. Sift through Tolstoy, Shakespeare, and new fiction, creatively displayed on hand-built shelves in a variety of languages; some used books and exchange

CYCLADES

available. Look for book bundles (2 books for a discount price) with creative themes. (☎22860 72 346; www.atlantisbooks.org. Open daily 10am-midnight.)

ACCOMMODATIONS. Most *domatia* proprietors expect extended stays, so prices rise with shorter durations. █Youth Hostel Oia ❶ has a courtyard, impeccable rooms with baths, and a bar open for breakfast and evening drinks. This picturesque white-and-blue hostel makes painfully expensive Oia bearable. Get more bang for your buck during happy hour (7:30-8:30pm) on the roof patio, with cheap drinks and a view of the spectacular sunset. Book online for advance reservations. To get there from the bus station, face the caldera and walk down the top right pathway. Signs will point you to another right turn, and the hostel's daytime back entrance will be on your left. (☎22860 71 465; www. santorinihostel.gr. Breakfast included. Laundry €8 per 5kg. Internet €2 per hr. Check-in 8am-10pm. Open from May to mid-Oct. Single-sex dorms €14-16. Cash only.) After the youth hostel, the prices for accommodations jump drastically. There are a number of boutique hotels in Oia that cater to couples on romantic getaways; doubles start at €80.

FOOD. There aren't as many budget dining options here, and high-priced restaurants with a view are comparable to Thira's. A good, cheap option that goes beyond souvlaki is **Edwin's ❷,** across the street from the Oia parking lot and on the road to Ammoudi beach. There are mouth-watering pizzas (€6.50-15) in small and large sizes, create-your-own pasta dishes (€7.50-9.50), and traditional Greek appetizers. (☎22860 71 971. Tzatziki €2.80. Delivery available. Open daily 1pm-late. Cash only.) Toward the southern end of the town's main road, **Thalami Taverna ❷** serves standard dishes on a patio with views of the ocean and Thira in the distance. (☎22860 71 009. Seafood spaghetti €8. Grilled octopus €10. Open daily noon-midnight. MC/V.) If you can afford to splurge, there is no better place to do it than **1800 ❺,** the town's classiest bistro, with flowering terraces and soft, classical music wafting through the eating area. In a 19th-century mansion, 50m north of the main church and furnished with antique pieces from the original house, this self-titled "slow-food" restaurant has a rotating menu of creative dishes with international influences. (☎22860 71 485; www.1800.gr. Entrees €19-32. Open daily 7pm-midnight. AmEx/MC/V.)

SIGHTS AND BEACHES. Follow the signs from the *plateia* to the **Thira Maritime Museum,** which charts the island's rich nautical tradition with model ships, anchors, cannons, antique navigational equipment, maps, and other sea paraphernalia. (☎22860 71 156. Open M and W-Su 10am-2pm and 5-8pm. €3, students €1.50.) A 20min. trip down the 236 stone stairs at the end of the main road leads to rocky **Ammoudi Beach,** where boats are moored in a startlingly deep lagoon. There is no sand and no obvious beach, but the path to the left leads to swimming holes filled with blue water and volcanic rocks; swimmers should prepare themselves for a refreshing shock when jumping in. In the evening you can hire a donkey (€4) to get back up the steep slope.

MILOS Μήλος

Milos's shoreline curves in and out, stretching into some of the most celebrated beaches in the Cyclades. Shaped over centuries by mineral deposits and volcanoes and accented by pale, cerulean waters, the coast is sublimely dramatic. Venturing past the cavernous rock formations toward the island's center leads to the small towns of Plaka and Trypiti, where travelers can explore winding roads, catacombs, and Orthodox churches.

ADAMAS Αδαμάς ☎22870

You'll find more picturesque towns elsewhere on the island, but you won't regret spending a few nights in Adamas. Inviting eateries, a wide array of accommodations, and the centralized bus system make the buzzing port a decent, if unremarkable, base for exploring the island's outlying beaches and villages.

TRANSPORTATION

Flights: Olympic Airways (☎22870 22 380) flies from **Milos Airport (MLO;** ☎22870 22 381). Take the stairs up to your left after the National Bank. Daily flights to Athens (€35-55) fill up quickly, especially during high season; book far in advance. Open M-F 9am-3pm.

Ferries: From Milos, ferries follow an ever-changing but (luckily) posted schedule. Look for it on the doors of travel agencies. Ferries go to: **Folegandros** (3hr., 3 per week, €8); **Kimolos** (30min., 7 per day, €1); **Kithnos** (4hr., 1-2 per day, €16); **Piraeus** (7hr., 1-2 per day, €30.50); **Rhodes** (20hr., 1 per week, €36); **Santorini** (6hr., 3 per week, €15.50); **Serifos** (3hr., 1-2 per day, €16); **Sifnos** (1hr., 1-2 per day, €13.50). A ferry stopping at **Folegandros, Sikinos, Ios, Naxos, Pyros, Syros**(€8-25) leaves 3 times per week.

High-Speed Boats: 15 per week travel the **Sifnos-Serifos-Kithnos-Piraeus** line (€26-42).

Buses: (☎22870 51 062). Buses leave from the stop in front of ATE Bank on the waterfront. Routes include: **Ahivadolimni-Provatas** (15min., 5 per day 10:15am-6:20pm); **Milos Camping** (30min., 5 per day 10:15am-6:20pm); **Pahena-Filakopi (Papafragas)-Pollonia** (30min., 6 per day 6:45am-7:15pm); **Sarakiniko** (10min., every 2hr. 11am-3pm); **Triovassalos-Plaka-Trypiti** (20min., roughly every hr. 7:30am-11:30pm); **Zefiria-Paliochori** (30min., 5 per day 11:30am-7:15pm). Tickets €1.40-1.60. Schedules change, so check in the bus station and travel offices; the tourist office has English schedules.

Taxis: (☎22870 22 219) in Adamas, 21 306 in Triovassalos. Line up by the waterfront. The chart at the bus station lists prices. 24hr.

Moped and Car Rental: Milos Rent a Car (☎22870 22 120), across from the port. Part of Sophia's Tourist Office. Cars from €50 per day. Bikes from €15 per day. 23+. **Camping Milos** (p. 322) and most hotels also rent vehicles at competitive prices.

ORIENTATION AND PRACTICAL INFORMATION

From the ferry dock, follow the waterfront to the right to reach the center of town.

Tourist Office: (☎22870 22 445; www.milos-island.gr), across from the dock. Has brochures, maps, ferry and bus timetables in English, and a complete list of the island's rooms and hotels. Agents can provide useful information about daytrip excursions including diving, kayaking, and boat trips. Free luggage storage. Open M and Su 8:30am-midnight, Tu-Sa 8:30am-11pm.

Tourist Agencies: Sophia's Tourist Office (☎22870 24 052). Facing inland, to the right along the waterfront next to the blue railing. Friendly and knowledgeable staff. Open nearly 24hrs. **Brau Kat Travel** (☎22870 23 000), about 100m from the port, up 1 fl. The incredibly attentive staff offers advice about island tours and accommodations. Open daily 10am-10pm. Others are located farther down the waterfront. All agencies sell ferry tickets and provide bus schedules.

Banks: National Bank (☎22870 22 332), near the post office along the waterfront. **24hr. ATM. Agricultural Bank** (☎22 330), in the central *plateia*. Both open M-Th 8am-2pm, F 8am-1:30pm. Both banks have currency exchange.

Laundromat: (☎22870 22 228). Take the 1st left after the waterfront up a narrow street. After taking a sharp right at the "Corali" sign, take the next left; it is at the end of the street on the left. €9 per 5kg.

Police: (☎22870 21 378), in Plaka. Open 24hr. **Tourist police:** ☎22870 22 445.

Pharmacy: (☎22870 21 405). On the right on the main road, past the ATE Bank and the supermarket. Open M-Sa 9am-2pm and 6-10pm, Su 11am-2pm.

Medical Services: (☎22870 22 700 or 22 701), in Plaka. Open 24hr.

Telephones: OTE (☎22870 21 214), in Plaka, before the bus station.

Internet Access: Internet Info (☎22870 28 011), on the main road past the Agriculture Bank. €3 per hr. Open daily 10am-midnight.

Post Office: (☎22870 22 345). On your right, past Internet Info, part of a newsstand. Offers **Poste Restante** and express mail services. Open M-F 8am-2pm. Larger post office is in Plaka. **Postal Code:** 84801.

ACCOMMODATIONS AND CAMPING

Rooms fill up quickly at the cushier hotels, but a smattering of inexpensive *domatia*, where availability is often plentiful and bargaining fruitful, lies 200m behind the waterfront. Many establishments also offer well-priced studio apartments, a good option for groups.

Portiana Hotel (☎22870 22 940), at the far end of the ferry port. Butter-colored walls, translucent window swags, and a terrace that overlooks the bay make this conveniently located hotel a good, if pricey, bet. Rooms have A/C, fridges, TVs, and private terraces, some with sea views. Breakfast included. Doubles €85-135; triples €90-140. ❺

Semiramis Hotel (☎22870 22 117; www.hotelsemiramis.gr). Follow the main road to the left of ATE Bank, and bear left at the fork 25m after the supermarket. The exceptionally generous owner offers spacious rooms with A/C and fridges. If he can't provide that, he'll help you find someone else who can. Take breakfast (€4) in the leafy, trellised backyard. Sister hotel **Dionysus,** 50m farther along the main road, has pricier accommodations with a few more amenities. Doubles €30-55; triples €35-70. MC/V. ❷

Anezina and Iliopetra (☎22870 24 009; www.anezinahotel.com), set back from the waterfront about 50m. These sister hotels offer colorful rooms with A/C and fridges, but at prices that climb steeply in the high season. Doubles €40-95; triples €50-120; studio apartments with kitchens €65-140. MC/V. ❹

Camping Milos (☎22870 31 410), located at Hivadolimni beach, 7km from the port. Buses go to and from the port after the public buses stop running. A pristine, turquoise pool and open-air cafeteria, both overlooking Hivadolimni beach from a steep cliff, lend this campground an air of elegance and luxury. At dusk, a poolside bar and dance floor opens. Communal kitchen, laundry, and mini-mart on site. Tent, bike, and car rentals available. €4.50 per person; €5.50 per tent. Bungalow for 2 with fridges and bath €48-90. ❶

FOOD

At dusk, the waterfront *tavernas* on Adamas's shoreline fill with lively diners and the glow of hanging lanterns. Most offer traditional Greek menus. If you want to bring home a taste of Milos, the streets around the waterfront are lined with shops selling local wines, cheeses, and especially preserves; look for *koufeto*, a traditional wedding sweet made of pumpkin, almonds, and honey.

O Kinigos (☎22870 22 349), 50m from the main dock. Incredibly reasonable prices distinguish this traditional eatery from its plainer neighbors. *Soutzoukakia* (spicy meatballs in garlic tomato sauce) €5. Open daily 9am-midnight. ❶

Artemis Bakery, on the corner at the fork in the road across from ATE Bank. Ideal for picnics or breakfast. Exceptionally wide selection of freshly baked goods that stretches from local specialties like watermelon pie (€2 for a big slice) to mini-pigs in a blanket (€1.30). Open daily 11am-6pm. ❶

Navayio (☎22870 23 392). Facing inland, walk along the water to the right of the port about 100m beyond ATE Bank. This outdoor *taverna* serves well-prepared fresh seafood and local favorites with a cheeky grin. Swordfish fillet €11. Open daily 1pm-1am. ❷

Caramella. Homemade spoon sweets line the shelves at this tiny nook near the ferry pier. Taste some served alongside your Greek coffee (€1.80) and then buy a jar of your own. Everything, from *koufeto* to potatoes in syrup with cloves, is €8. Open daily 10am-dark. Cash only. ❷

Pitsounakia (☎22870 21 739), opposite the Agricultural Bank. The souvlaki (€1.80) here is a tasty, fast option; those who want to linger can eat in the garden seating area (€6.50). Tomato baked with egg €4. Open daily 11am-1am. ❶

👁 🌊 SIGHTS AND BEACHES

OTHER SIGHTS. A few meters beyond Adamas's narrow strip of activity is the icon-filled **Ecclesiastical Museum.** *(Open daily 9:15am-1:15pm and 6:15-10:15pm. Free.)* While perusing the exhibit, you might overhear music from the adjacent **Church of the Holy Trinity.** Farther along the harbor toward the airport is the **Milos Mining Museum,** which celebrates the island's igneous mineral deposits and illustrious mining past.

BEACHES. Years of volcanic eruptions, mineral deposits, and aquatic erosion have carved each beach on Milos into a small natural wonder. The island's unique, impressive coast is comprised of dark, multicolored sand, cavernous rock formations, and steep, jutting cliffs. Swimmers wade between the rocks at the canyon of 🏖**Papafragas**, near the Filokipi bus station, and look at years of graffitied engravings. Beachgoers can lie near the enormous orange- and red-striped sedimentary rocks at 🏖**Provatas**, tiptoe across a smooth, glacier-like stretch at **Paleochori**, stake out a spot at crowded **Chivadolimni,** or explore the deep, secluded cave hideouts at a local favorite, **Kleftiko,** known to locals as "pirates'

ON THE MENU

GOLD LEAF

What kind of leaf tastes as good with spinach as it does with honey, is golden all year round and is found more often frozen than fresh? That would be phyllo dough, literally meaning "leaf" in Greek, which you'll find wrapped around everything from spinach to sausage in Greece.

For such a ubiquitous substance, phyllo dough is notoriously difficult to use, and even more notoriously difficult to make. Individual sheets of tissue-thin pastry must be kept moist lest they crack and handled gently lest they tear. Those brave enough to work with phyllo must layer the sheets individually, brushing each with butter ever so delicately lest they damage the stack and ruin the whole batch. Is it any wonder, then, that bakers leapt at the convenience of buying factory-made phyllo when the mass-marketed stuff became available in the 1970s?

For those who value tradition enough for its own sake—there really is no difference between home- and factory-made phyllo—the recipe itself could hardly be simpler: flour, water, oil, and sometimes egg yolks are mixed together to become the basic dough. Time, skill, and patience are all that are added from this point forward. A long table and an even longer roller are used to flatten and stretch the dough beyond what you would think possible. Eventually the dough will be thin enough to see through, with three pounds of dough yielding approximately 4160 sq. in. of pastry!

hideaway." If you're having trouble choosing which beaches to visit, you can check out pictures of each on postcards at every kiosk and tourist office. Boat and kayak excursions will take you to hard-to-reach spots like **Tsigrados,** a glittering beach only accessible by private transport on tricky roads. **Buses** travel to the major shores every one to two hours for €1.40. The tourist office or any tourist agency can help arrange all-day **boat tours,** which usually cost about €20-40 per person and include a lunch stop in Kimolos. **Sea Kayak Milos** (☎22870 21 365; www.seakayakgreece.com) plans **kayak trips** (from €60) and **Milos Diving** (☎22870 41 296; www.milosdiving.gr) provides a range of **diving excursions.**

NIGHTLIFE

Nightlife in Adamas is less than wild, but the few bars that exist are chic, relaxed, and popular.

Aragosta Cafe, above Milos Travel. White chairs, a balcony, and a seaside view give this cafe a magnetic and laid-back sense of cool. Late-night dancing takes place at the upstairs cafe. Mixed drinks €10. Open daily 8pm-3am. MC/V.

Vipera Lebetina, next door to Aragosta Cafe. A dance club draped with sheer, blue curtains and metal decorations. DJs spin mainstream foreign music until they switch to Greek tracks late into the night. Mixed drinks €9. Open daily 9pm-2am. Cash only.

Miuro (☎22870 23 372), beyond Vipera Lebetina along the upper harbor road. The owner and bartender knows his spirits and his jazz, and will be happy to give you an intoxicating introduction to the many flavors of the Cyclades. The more you drink, the less you pay. Beer €4. Mixed drinks €9. Open daily 7pm-late. Cash only.

DAYTRIPS FROM ADAMAS

PLAKA Πλάκα AND TRYPITI Τρυπητή
Buses from Adamas run to Plaka and Trypiti (15min., every hr. on the half-hour, €1.40).

Plaka is the island's capital, 6km from Adamas, where a neat cafe and a stunning vista seem to wait around every corner. For a 360° view of the island, start by climbing upward for 15min. from the bus station to the **Panagia Thalassitra Monastery** at the top of the old castle. If you're willing to sacrifice a little convenience for a spectacular view, **Epano Kastro** (☎22870 21 702 or 69443 22 321), on the way to the monastery, offers studio rentals. Opposite Plaka's police station, follow the signs downhill through twisting streets to the terrace of the **Church of Panagia Korfiatissa,** which opens directly onto the lush countryside and the bordering sea. Next door in a 200-year-old house is the **Folk Museum.** It captures the lives of Miloans from the 17th century to nearly present-day, displaying artifacts and heirlooms donated by local villagers. (☎22870 21 292. Open Tu-Su 10am-1pm and 7-10pm. €3, students and children €1.50.) For a bite to eat, go back in the direction of the bus stop and along the road into town to find **Plakami taverna and snack bar ❷,** where the smiling owners have been serving tasty local cheeses (€3.50) and plates like the "drunkard's snack" (pork with wine sauce, €7.50) for years. Follow the road adjacent to Plakami to the large, yellow **Archaeological Museum.** It houses artifacts unearthed at Fylakopi, including the 14th-century BC painted statuette known as the "Lady of Fylakopi." (☎22870 21 620. Open Tu-Su 8:30am-3pm. €3, seniors and students €2, EU students free.)

A 3min. walk from the Archaeological Museum leads to the tiny town of **Trypiti**. From Trypiti, a paved road winds down past several sights, including the spot where the Venus de Milo, since moved to the Louvre in Paris, once stood, and a well-preserved Roman theater with a riveting ocean view; ask at the tourist office about performances there. If the idea of sleeping in historically important places appeals to you, see if you can book a room at **Machis Guesthouse ❺**, which professes to be where the Venus de Milo was hidden after it was found. (High-season doubles €70; 2- to 4- or 5-person studio €130. Low-season doubles €40-60; 2- to 4- or 5-person studio €60. ☎22870 41 353.) At the end of the road and down a set of stairs, you will see signs for the **catacombs**, an early Christian burial site hewn into the cliff face. Virtually no painting or artifacts remain, but the well-lit cavern is eerily fascinating. Of the five chambers, only one is open to the public. (☎22870 21 625. Open Tu-Su 8am-7pm. M-Sa €2, students €1, Su free.) You also can see part of a **Dorian stone wall** built between 1100 and 800 BC. At the ruins of **Fylakopi**, 3km from the fishing village of Pollonia toward Adamas, British excavations unearthed 3500-year-old frescoes, now displayed in the National Museum in Athens. Other treasures from the site are exhibited in Plaka's archaeological museum (see above).

KIMOLOS Κίμωλος AND POLLONIA

Ferries go from Adamas to Kimolos 3-4 times per week (€2). Another ferry, which also transports cars and mopeds, runs several times per day from Pollonia, on the northeastern shore of Milos (see below for more information). Check at the tourist office for a current schedule.

An island of one village and 80 churches, Kimolos is a lovely place to pass a morning and afternoon. Boats drop visitors off in the sleepy port of **Psathi**, where a few cafes serve frappés on the beach and the family-run *taverna*, **To Kima ❶**, cooks tasty traditional dishes. (☎22870 51 001. Zucchini pie €5. Fava beans €3.50. Chicken souvlaki €8. Open M-Sa noon-midnight.) Look for a paved road leading uphill across from the dock, which connects to most of the island's major sights, including the village Chorio. A bus stops at Psathi a few times a day to take visitors to Chorio and the beaches Aliki, Bonatsa, Kalamitsi, and the settlement at Prassa. There are no hotels on the island, but each beach has its own smattering of *domatia*. Of these, **Sardis ❹** at Aliki beach is the most established; look for signs at the port and along the road. (☎22870 51 458. *Taverna* attached. Doubles and quads with fridges, A/C, and baths €40-70.) If you haven't rented a moped, traveling around the island is difficult, but the island's single **taxi** (☎22870 51 552) is available to take you wherever you please. Water taxis, such as **Delphini Sea Taxi** (☎22870 51 437), are also available to take you back and forth between hard-to-reach beaches.

Chorio, perched on a low hill, is within walking distance of the port and has a terrific view of the harbor. A 16th-century castle dominates the town, and is both a relic of its past and a fixture of its present. The buildings in the interior of the square courtyard now lie in ruins, but the buildings that make up its exterior walls still provide homes to the town's residents. One such home near the *kastro*'s northeast gate was recently converted into the **Folk and Maritime Museum**, displaying artifacts of the daily lives of Kimolans from the 19th through the mid-20th century. Dr. Manolis Christoulakis, the museum's founder, will be happy to give you a thorough tour. Be prepared for a quiz at the end. (☎22870 51 118. Open Tu-Sa 11am-1pm, although will stay open later if there are patrons. €1.) Just outside the *kastro*, near the enormous blue-domed **church of Panagia Ogiditria,** is Kimolos' small **Archaeological Museum,** which opened to the public late in 2008. There, you'll primarily find artifacts from the archaeological site at **Ellinika,** which is itself accessible to visitors with private transport. Highlights of the collection include a glass-floored reconstruction of a burial ground at the site, as well as a headless female statue from the second century BC. After you've explored the *kastro* and meandered through the town's whitewashed streets, stop for traditional cuisine at **Panorama ❶,** east of the *kastro*, with its glassed-in patio and view over the domes of Panagia Ogiditria. (☎22870 51 531. Fried meatballs €5. Seasonal fruit €2.50. Open daily 11:30am-6pm and 8pm-2am. Cash only.)

Although ferries to Kimolos leave from Adamas, your best (and less expensive) bet is to leave from the beach town **Pollonia,** on the island's northeastern shore. If you're hungry again after stepping off the ferry, head the few short meters to **Gialos ❶,** one of the many *tavernas* lining the waterfront. Praised by the locals and less expensive than its peers, Gialos serves up a tasty array of both classic and modern takes on Greek cuisine, making it an ideal stop if moussaka and souvlaki have lost their charms. (☎22870 41 208; www.gialos-pollonia.gr. Fava with roasted onions €3.20. Mrs. Ioanna's octopus stew €6. Open Apr-Oct 11am-midnight. Cash only.) Pollonia is an ideal place to stay for relaxation and rejuvenation. At **Captain Zeppos Sea Studios ❸,** plush, tranquil rooms and a patio overlooking a secluded portion of coastline will relax and revive. (☎22870 41 327 in summer, 69776 90 311 in other seasons; www.captainzeppos.com. Studios €45-80.) After you've rejuvenated, head to **Pigaki cafe ❷,** for an afternoon treat or a evening drink—or the other way around, if you prefer. (☎69425 46 933. Crepes €7-8. Mixed drinks €8. Open daily 7am-2am. Cash only.)

SIFNOS Σίφνος

Ships to Sifnos drop visitors at Kamares, a tiny collection of *tavernas* and pottery shops that overflow with celebrated Sifniot *keramika* (ceramics). Though the port has abundant accommodations and a pleasant strip of beach, most travelers head straight to Apollonia or to the small villages nestled on cove-like shores. Days in Sifnos are quiet, spent either lounging on the beach or hiking one of the island's many trails, but nights often bring lively local festivals; each of the island's 365 churches hosts an annual celebration for the entire community on its patron saint's name day.

KAMARES Καμάρες　　　　　　　　　　☎22840

Kamares is a modest, attractive port. Hovering yachts, sailboats, and ferries almost overwhelm the thin strip of beach, which is surrounded by *tavernas* and information offices. Peaceful and mellow, the town is filled with vacationing families who sun themselves on the shore.

▐ **TRANSPORTATION.** Most **ferries** from Sifnos travel in short routes with multiple stops. To: Folegandros (4 per week, €18); Ios (2 per week, €13.50); Kimolos (1-2 per day, €6); Kithnos (1-2 per day, €13.50); Milos (2-3 per day, €13.10); Piraeus (3-4 per day, €28); Santorini (4 per week, €13.50); Serifos (3-5 per day, €13.50); Sikinos (3 per week, €13.50). **High speed boats** go to Milos (2 per day, €14.50), Piraeus (2-3 per day, €36), and Serifos (4 per week, €13). The main **bus** stop is in front of the tourist office near the ferry landing. **Buses** leave for Artemonas via Apollonia every 1-2hr. (10min., every hr. 7:30am-10:15pm, €2). Change buses in either town to get to Faros, Kastro, Platis Vathy, and Yialos, and in Artemonas to get to Cherronisos; consult the schedule in the tourist office for more details. A number of **taxis** are available 24hr. on the island. Obtain a list of the drivers' cell phones from the tourist office. **Niki Rent a Car**, 200m down the main road from the dock, has some of the best rates. (☎22840 33 993 or 69456 56 147. Cars €25-65. Bikes €15-25. Prices vary with season, increasing from mid-June to Aug. AmEx/MC/V.)

ORIENTATION AND PRACTICAL INFORMATION. Slightly to the left opposite the ferry dock, the extremely helpful English-speaking staff in the **information office** help visitors find rooms, store luggage (€1 per piece, €2 overnight), and decipher boat and bus schedules. (☎22840 31 977. Maps €1.80-6. In high season, the office is typically open M-Th and Sa-Su 9:30am-11:30pm, F 9:30am-2pm and 6-11:30pm; in low season before and after ferry arrivals.) Along the waterfront as you walk from the dock to town, the English-speaking staff at **Aegean Thesaurus Travel Agency** happily provides the same services as the tourist office; they also sell tickets for ferries and Flying Dolphins. Also stop by for information on trekking tours of the island, as well as Greek folk dancing and Sifniot cooking classes (☎22840 33 151. Hours vary by day and season.) **The Bookshop,** a few stores down on the main strip, sells maps with hiking trails (€1.50), international newspapers, magazines, and fiction and also offers a used book exchange. (☎22840 33 521. Open daily 8am-1am.) In an emergency, call the **police** (☎22840 31 210) in Apollonia. The **pharmacy** (☎22840 33 033) is about 200m away from ferry port on the main road. A doctor is on call 24hr. at the **medical clinic.** (☎22840 31 315. Open M, W, F 10am-1pm; Tu and Th 10am-1pm and 5-7pm.) Mailboxes are scattered throughout the town, but the nearest **post office** is in Apollonia. **Postal Code:** 84003.

ACCOMMODATIONS AND CAMPING. During high season, it may be difficult to find a budget hotel room. *Domatia* are good options in terms of availability, price, and quality, and Kamares is full of them (doubles typically €40-60); the tourist office has an exhaustive list. Walk 150m on the main road along the ferry port, turn right at the mini-market, and go up the stairs to find **Podotas Group Hotel and Apartments ❹**. Sizable, simply-adorned studios have TVs, air-conditioning, and balconies. Some have kitchenettes, and all come with stellar service by attentive owners George and Margarita Podotas. There is a sister property with similar prices in Apollonia. (☎22840 32 329. Doubles €45-65; triples €55-70.) Take the first right (non-stairs) uphill from Niki's Car Rental on the main road and look for **Hotel Kiki ❺** on your left. The spotless rooms with baths, TV, air-conditioning, fridges, and balconies overlook Kamares and the harbor. (☎22840 32 329. Doubles €60-75; triples €72-90.) **Meltemi Rooms ❷**, behind Hotel Kiki, has clean rooms with air-conditioning and baths. (☎31 653. Doubles €20-50; triples €30-60; quads with kitchen €50-90. Lower if you bargain; play hardball and they'll play right back.) To re-experience the simple joys of sleep-away camp, look for ⊠**Maki's Camping ❶**, to the left of the port and around the harbor, approximately 200m from Niki Rent a Car along the road descending toward the beach. The conscientious staff enforces and sets the example for the site's "only for friendly people" policy, and happily volunteers information about the island. The campgrounds include a mini-mart, laundry (€5 per load), common kitchen, and showers. Private rooms and Wi-Fi are also available. (☎22840 32 366; www.makiscamping.gr. Camping €6 per person; €17 per tent. Doubles €20-30.) A more secluded campground, **Platis Gialos Camping ❶** is a 30min. bus ride from Kamares then a 10min. walk down a rocky road away from the beach; follow the signs. (☎22840 71 286. €4 per person. Tent rental €3.)

⬛⬛ **FOOD AND NIGHTLIFE.** Chickpeas are a Sifniot specialty. Dishes like the chickpea soup *revithada*, chickpea balls *(revikefthedes)*, and baked chickpeas can be found almost anywhere that serves Greek cuisine. ⊠**Ristorante Italiano de Claudio ❷**, up the main street toward Apollonia, serves memorable pizza (€8-13.50) and *spaghetti alla puttanesca* (with an anchovy, olive, and caper-flavored tomato sauce; €8.50). (Open 6pm-"till I am fed up." AmEx/MC/V.) Across the street, **O Kapetan Andreas ❷** specializes in seafood and has a rotating menu of daily specials (☎22840 32 356. Fish soup €4. Open daily noon-midnight). Its neighbor, **Cafe to Kima ❶**, serves standard cafe fare (☎22840 32 025. Yogurt with fruit €5.50. Open daily 7am-midnight). Both have tables on the beach.

Don't go looking for a wild night out in Kamares, but if a good drink, a comfy chair, and a great sunset vantage point is what you're after, you'll find it at ⊠**The Old Captain Bar**, midway along the waterfront strip. Milkshakes (€5) and signature rum punches (€8), served under thatched umbrellas on the sand, keep everyone happy. (☎22840 31 990. Free Wi-Fi. Open daily 10am-3am. Cash only.)

APOLLONIA Απολλώνια   ☎22840

The streets of Apollonia, the island's capital and heart, meander about the hilltop, but each leads back to the main paved road, from which buses carry beachgoers to nearby shore-side villages. Memorable restaurants and quaint houses carpet the small village, and the narrow lanes contain almost all the island's nightlife.

◪ **TRANSPORTATION.** All the essentials a traveler needs can be found in the main *plateia*, where the bus from Kamares makes its first stop. **Buses** to Artemonas and Kamares (10min., €1.40) wait in front of the post office; those to villages and beaches like Kastro (€1.60) and Platis Yialos (€2.10) stop around the corner on the mountain road next to the Hotel Anthousa. Buses run to these destinations at least once every hour. The schedules by the *plateia* stop outside the travel agency have exact times.

ORIENTATION AND PRACTICAL INFORMATION. Side streets with hotels, restaurants, and nightclubs branch off the main road, which wiggles to the right and left (follow the pavement) before splitting in two at a deep ravine.

Aegean Thesaurus, near the post office, has currency exchange, accommodations assistance, bus and ferry schedules, a **24hr. ATM,** and useful island information packs for €2.50. (☎22840 33 151. Hours vary.) The **post office** is in the main *plateia* (☎22840 31 329; open M-F 7:30am-2pm), and the **pharmacy** is right next door (☎22840 33 541; open daily 9am-2:30pm and 5pm-10pm.) **Alpha Bank** is up the main road from the bus stop, on your left before Hotel Anthousa. It has a **24hr. ATM.** (☎22840 31 317. Open M-Th 8am-2:30pm, F 8am-2pm.) To get to the **police station,** walk up the main road from the *plateia*. Turn left where the road splits at the signposts. A bit farther up, it is the building on the right with the large Greek flag in front. (☎22840 31 210. Open daily 9am-1pm.) The **medical center** (☎22840 31 315) is across from the police station. An **OTE** is 50m down the road back to Kamares on the right (☎22840 31 215. Open daily 7:30am-2:30pm.) **Internet Cafe 8,** on the road out of Apollonia to the right, has Internet access and Wi-Fi. (☎22840 33 734. €3 per hr., min. €1. Open daily 9am-midnight.) **Postal Code:** 84003.

ACCOMMODATIONS. Summer vacancies are rare in Apollonia, and it's best to make reservations far in advance if you're traveling in July or August. **Hotel Anthousa ❸** on the mountain road to Artemonas, is above the pastry shop to the right where the main road splits. From its clean rooms with air-conditioning, TVs, fridges, baths, and phones, you can see both the ravine and the sea. The video arcade is an added perk for those who need their fix of push-button animation. (☎22840 31 431. Laundry €12. Singles €35-50; doubles €40-65. MC/V.) To find the **Sifnos Hotel ❸,** head up the cobbled road adjacent to the Folk Art museum on the *plateia*, then turn right again and look for the attached *taverna*. The hotel's spacious, inviting rooms include air-conditioning, TVs, fridges, baths, and phones. (☎22840 31 624. Singles €30-45; doubles €40-65. MC/V.) **Hotel Sofia ❸** is just off the *plateia;* head up the wide paved road from the *plateia* until you see it on your left, above the supermarket. Rooms have TVs, air-conditioning, and baths. (☎22840 31 238. Doubles €40; triples €60.) **Nikoleta Rooms ❹,** across from the Eko gas station, rents quiet and clean doubles with TVs, air-conditioning, kitchenettes, phones, baths, and balconies, some with a peaceful view of the sea. (☎22840 31 538. Doubles €40-60.)

FOOD AND NIGHTLIFE. On the main street, **I Frai Sifnos ❷** serves fresh traditional Sifnos fare. (☎22840 33 069. Lamb in wine sauce cooked ina clay pot €11. Open daily noon-1am.) The restaurant at the **Sifnos Hotel ❷** serves *revithada* (€5) only on Sundays, but you can get *imam baldi* (eggplant with onions and tomato; €7.50), another local favorite, any day of the week. (☎22840 31 624. Open daily 8am-1am. MC/V.) The strong coffee (€1.50) brewed at **Vegera ❶,** on your left just before the police station and clinic, makes their rich, gooey caramel cake (€3) taste even sweeter by comparison. The expansive balcony that looks over Sifnos's gentle mountains provides a lovely setting in which to savor your dessert. (☎22840 33 385. Open daily 9am-3am.)

Stroll up from the *plateia* past the **Popular Art and Folklore Museum,** and take your first right to find the cafes and clubs that constitute Sifniot nightlife. If you'd rather go outside this concentrated area, try **Aloni**, on the road to the police station before Vegera, about 75m toward Artemonas on the left, where live Greek music plays every night until sunrise.

HIKING. While the beaches are pleasant and diverting, the inland **hiking trails** are the big draw, leading adventurous tourists along scenic mountain paths to villages off the asphalt network. The **tourist office** in Kamares has a map of the main trails (€6), but any travel agency should be able to give you information. The "classic route" from Kastro to Apollonia traverses shady gardens and tiny farm plots, and continues along to the wee village of **Ano Petali**. For more of a challenge, start near Kamares at **Aghios Giorgios** and follow the marked path up the mountain to the **Mavri Spilia cave**, and then continue along the goat path to the **Tsigoura mines**. Sturdy shoes and a big water bottle are recommended, and don't go without a map and a friend.

DAYTRIP FROM APOLLONIA: ARTEMONAS AND KASTRO. Buses travel to enchantingly remote villages throughout the island—maps are available at bookstores and tourist agencies for €2-6. To see fascinating architecture and a slice of history, catch the bus to **Artemonas**, 1.5km from Apollonia, where Greek aristocrats from Alexandria built mansions. In **Kastro**, 2km east of Apollonia, a cluster of whitewashed houses are balanced on a mountain with a sweeping panorama of the steep drop to the sea below. You can take the bus or walk to Kastro along the road from Apollonia; it's mostly downhill. The quiet village has just a few sleepy cafes, but the architectural remains, including remnants of homes from the Geometric period, a wall from the Classical period, and Venetian ruins, give a broad overview of the island's past. The tiny **Archaeological Museum**, at the center of the town, houses a handful of clay figurines of goddesses from the Mycenaean period and the head of an archaic *kouros*. (Open Tu-Su 8am-3pm. Free.) There are no hotels in Kastro, but if you ask around, you will be able to find domatia. Visible from the path around the town's periphery and accessible by a marked footpath, a stone cliff juts into the ocean. On it is the tiny **Epta Martires Church** (Seven Martyrs), as well as a popular spot for those daring enough to go **cliff diving**. Another footpath leads to the sparkling cove at **Poulati**, which is a great place for snorkeling.

DAYTRIP FROM APOLLONIA: PLATIS YIALOS. Families crowd Lavarou beach at **Platis Yialos**, a busy, beautiful town 12km from Apollonia. Hotels and domatia in Platis Yialos are similar in price to those in Kamares, making it a great place to settle in for a few days. For a home-cooked meal, try **To Kamini**, which serves Greek classics, such as its specialty *dolmades* with yogurt or *tzatziki* (€6.50), *moussaka* (€6), and *revithada* (€6; only on Sunday). (☎22840 71 337. Pork souvlaki €8.50. Open 9am-1am. Cash only.) **Faros**, the bus stop before Yialos, is a series of round shores connected by footpaths. Since there is plenty to do in the area and the public transportation is infrequent, you may want to make this stop a full daytrip. Numerous little *tavernas* blend together at the busy Fasolou and Apokofto beaches nearby. A mountainous footpath leads to the striking **Panagia Chrysopigi Monastery**. To reach it, as well as the adjacent Chrysopigi beach, take the 30min. hike from Faros or walk 10min. from Platis Yialos. A bridge connects the 17th-century monastery's rocky islet to the mainland. Forty days after Easter, locals celebrate the two-day **Festival of Analipsos**.

READY. SET.

LET'S GO

www.letsgo.com

THE STUDENT TRAVEL GUIDE

DODECANESE
Δωδεκάνησα

Closer to Turkey than to Athens, the Dodecanese are slightly less touristed than other island clusters, yet they still have the stunning views and beachy fun of more mainstream destinations plus a tumultuous history of piracy and warfare. Home to Hippocrates, father of medicine, and the exile asylum of St. John, author of the Bible's book of Revelation, the Dodecanese are marked by the footsteps of every major invader throughout Greek history. The islanders experienced the cultural flourish of the Hellenistic period, then did as the Romans did during the Pax Romana, and were soon struck with the religious fervor that marked the advent of Byzantine Christianity. During the 14th century, Christian crusaders built medieval fortresses to ward off the Muslim invaders, but despite their best efforts the Ottomans invaded in 1523 and stayed until 1912, leaving a distinct Islamic architectural presence. Mussolini and the Italian fascists took over in 1912 and developed the islands as naval bases during WWII, although islanders pride themselves on being the first of the Greek islands to expel the Italian occupiers. After millennia of foreign conquest, the Dodecanese finally joined the Greek nation in 1948. Eclectic architecture is the most visible legacy of all these comings and goings: Greek and Roman ruins, knight's castles, Ottoman mosques, and stark Italian architecture are sprinkled among the bright blue-and-white homes that characterize the island's traditional look. The islands themselves are just as diverse as their conquerors have been. From Rhodes's imposing Old Town to Symi's charming pastel houses, and Kos's nightlife to Kalymnos's mountains, the Dodecanese offer a thorough mix of traditional villages, stunning beaches, ruined temples, and young metropolises.

HIGHLIGHTS OF THE DODECANESE

JUMP back to medieval times in **Rhodes Town,** built in the 14th century by the Knights of Rhodes (p. 333).

IMMERSE yourself in the small town charm of **Symi,** an island too often overlooked in favor of its busier neighbors (p. 354).

PEER into **Nisyros's** simmering volcano (p. 357).

RHODES Ρόδος

Rhodes is easily the busiest island of the Dodecanese, jam-packed with everything from beaches to ruins to sunburned tourists. Though resort towns cluster in the north, Rhodes's natural wonders dominate other sections of the island, with sandy beaches stretching along the east coast, jagged cliffs skirting the west, and green mountains dotted with villages filling the interior. The island is most famous for a sight that no longer exists: the **Colossus of Rhodes,** one of the Seven Wonders of the Ancient World. This enormous bronze statue of Helios, constructed in the 3rd century BC, once loomed over Mandraki Harbor

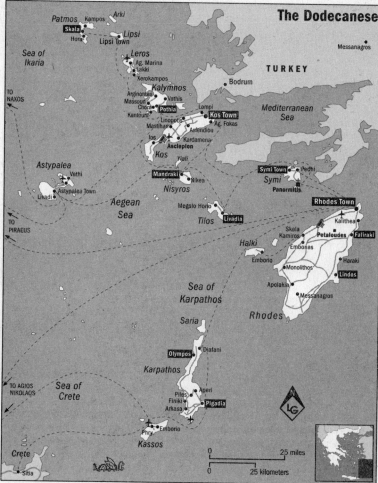

The Dodecanese

as a testament to the island's military power and a monument to the sun god. Sadly, sunset came quickly for the 33m tall Colossus—it stood for just over 50 years before collapsing in an earthquake. Superstitious Rhodians left the statue where it lay, and the pieces were eventually looted by Arab pirates and lost forever. Today, the Colossus exists only in the imagination, though more tangible ruins in Kamiros, Ialyssos, and Lindos reveal Rhodes's bygone days as a Hellenic power, while the medieval fortress towns of Monolithos and Rhodes Town retain their architectural and historical majesty.

RHODES TOWN ☎ 22410

As locals like to say, Rhodes Town has always been a conquered city. First came the Turks, then the Italians, and now the Tourists who annually flood the

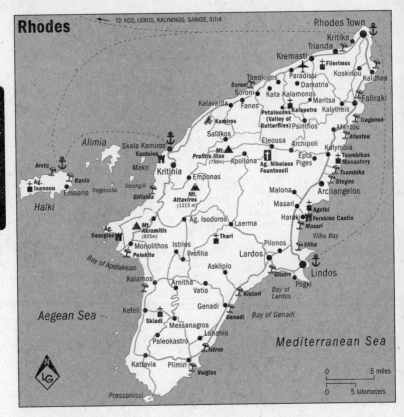

Rhodes

TO KOS, LEROS, KALYMNOS, SAMOS, SITIA

DODECANESE

Aegean Sea

Mediterranean Sea

Rhodes Town
Kritika
Trianda
Kremasti
Flierimos
Theologos
Paradissi
Koskinou
Kalithea
Soroni
Damatria
Faliraki
Soroni
Kata Kalamonos
Kalavarda
Fanes
Maritsa
Kalopetra
Kalytheis
Petaloudes
(Valley of
Butterflies)
Psinthos
Traganon
Kamiros
Afantou
Afantou
Salakos
Eleousa
Archipoli
Skala Kamiros
Mt.
Profitis.Ilias
(798m)
Apollona
Epta
Piges
Kolymbia
Kasteios
Makri
Kritinia
Emponas
Ag. Nikolaos
Fountoucli
Tsambikas
Monastery
Areta
Kania
Strongili
Tragoussa
Glifalda
Mt.
Attaviros
(1215 m)
Malona
Tsambika
Ag.
Ioannou
Emborio
Archangelos
Halki
Masari
Ag. Isodoros
Mt.
Akramitis
(825m)
Laerma
Haraki
Agathi
Ferakios Castle
Ag.
Georgios
Thari
Masari
Monolithos
Istrios
Pilonos
Vilha Bay
Pelekito
Profilia
Lardos
Vilha
Bay of Apolakkias
Asklipio
Kalamos
Glistra
Lindos
Arnitha
Pogki
Vatio
Bay of
Lardos
Genadi
Kiotari
Kefali
Genadi
Bay of Genadi
Skladi
Messanagros
Lahania
Paleokastro
Istros
Kattavia
Plimiri
Vuiglas
Prassonissi

Alimia

0   5 miles
0   5 kilometers

streets from any of the 11 cruise ships accommodated offshore. Sunburned masses crowd into souvenir shops on the main drive of the Old Town; stick to the quieter labyrinth of picturesque backstreets. A walk along the perimeter of the Old Town showcases the simple beauty of the high stone walls and white streets, and a hike to the ancient acropolis at sunset rewards trekkers with a view of a fire-streaked sky over the stadium. The thoroughly modern New Town is neither bustling enough to be exciting nor drowsy enough to be relaxing, but it does offer some mondo nightlife and the town's best beaches.

TRANSPORTATION

Flights: Diagoras International Airport (RHO; ☎22410 88 700), 16km out of town, near Paradisi. Accessible by bus (M-F 4:45am-11:30pm, Sa 5:45am-11:30pm, Su 5:15am-11:30pm; €2.20) from the west bus station. **Olympic Airlines** (www.olympic-airlines.com) flies to **Athens** (5 per day, €89); **Karpathos** (2 per day, €32); **Kos** (2 per day, €150); **Mikonos** (4 per day, €171); **Thessaloniki** (daily, €126) and more (check online for more flights). **Aegean Airlines** (www.aegeanair.com) flies to **Athens** (6 per day, from €48) and **Thessaloniki** (daily, €137). Scattered around town and clustered by the bus and ferry stations are numerous travel agencies.

Buses: Rhodes Town's 2 stations lie 1 block apart behind Pl. Alexandrias, along Averof, across from the Sound and Light show. Schedules at the station kiosks or the EOT (p. 336). Be sure to ask for complete times and listings when you arrive.

East Station is served by **KTEL** (☎22410 24 268). Schedules listed are for M-Sa; contact EOT or ask the station clerk for Su schedules. To: **Afantou** (11 per day 7am-9:15pm, €2); **Archangelos** (10 per day 7am-9:15pm, €2.70); **Genadi** (8 per day 7am-7:30pm, €5.50) via **Kiotari; Kalithea** (7 per day 10am-9:15pm, €2); **Kolymbia beach** (4 per day 2:30-9:15pm, €3); **Laerma** (1 per day, €5.50); **Lardos** (9 per day 7am-7:30pm, €4.60); **Lindos** (12 per day 7am-7:30pm, €4.50); **Malona/Massari** (4 per day 9am-2:30pm, €3.40); **Pefki** (8 per day 7am-7:30pm, €5); **Pilonia** (1 per day, €4.30); **Stegna Beach** (1 per day, €3.50).

West Station is served by **RODA** (☎22410 26 300). To: **Butterfly Valley** (5 per day 9:30am-2:00pm, €5); **Damatria** (4 per day 7:10am-9:30pm, €2.50); **Fanes** (11 per day 4:45-9:45pm); **Ialissos/ Ixia** (multiple per day 4:45am-11:30pm, €2); **Kamiros** (3 per day 9am-2:50pm; €5); **Kremasti** (multiple per day 4:45am-11:30pm, €2); **Paradisi** (6 per day 10:30am-9:10pm, €2.20); **Paradisi Airport** (40 per day 5:45am-11:30pm, €2.20); **Pastida/Maritsa** (10 per day 5:30am-9:30pm, €2); **Salakos** (5 per day 5:45am-3:40pm, €3.50); **Soroni** (14 per day 4:45am-9:45pm, €2.50); **Tholos** (21 per day 4:45am-9:45pm, €2.50).

Ferries: Leave from the eastern docks in Commercial Harbor, across from the Milon Gate into the Old Town. Ferry schedules should be confirmed at a travel agency or the Port Authority upon arrival because they change weekly without notice. **Halki Island** can also be reached by boat from Skala Kamiros on the western side of Rhodes. **Dodikanisos Seaways,** Australias 3 (☎22410 70 590; www.12ne.gr) sends frequent ferries to neighboring islands, as does **Blue Star Ferries** (bluestarferries.com). To: **Agathonisi** (5hr., M 8:30am); **Chalki** (1¼hr., Sa-Su 8:00am); **Kalymnos** (3hr., 1-3 per day); **Kastelorizo** (2½hr., M 8:30am); **Karpathos** (5hr., 2 per week); **Kassos** (7hr., 6 per week); **Kos** (2hr., 3 per day); **Leros** (4hr., daily); **Lipsi** (5hr., M-Tu and Th-Su); **Nisyros** (3hr.; Sa 10:30am, Su 8am); **Patmos** (7hr., daily); **Piraeus** (13hr., daily); **Samos** (10hr., 1 per week); **Santorini** (7hr.; M, W, F 5pm); **Symi** (1hr., daily); **Syros** (8hr.; Tu, Th, Su 5pm); **Tilos** (2hr.; Sa 10:30, Su 8am); **Thessaloniki** (25hr., Th 5pm).

Hydrofoils and Catamarans: Run to all the nearby islands and beaches. Contact any of the travel agencies or inquire on the docks for schedules and ticket information. **Dodekanisos Express**(run by Dodekanisos Seaways, above), a high-speed catamaran, leaves at 8:30am from the western docks of Commercial Harbor and runs to: **Kalymnos** (3hr., daily); **Kos** (2hr., daily); **Leros** (4hr., daily); **Lipsi** (6hr., daily); **Patmos** (5hr., Tu-Su); **Symi** (1hr., W-Su). All trips return at 6:30pm.

Taxis: Pl. Alexandrias (☎22410 69 800). Prices posted across from the kiosk. 24hr. Radio taxis (☎22410 64 734) also are available.

Car Rental: Filimon Rent-a-Car, Diakou 7B (☎22410 31 702), in the New Town. Motos €15 per day. Cars €20 per day; includes insurance. 23+. Open Apr.-Oct. daily 7:30am-9pm.

✈️🏛 ORIENTATION AND PRACTICAL INFORMATION

Rhodes Town is composed of two districts as different as night and day. The modern **New Town** spans the north and west with ritzy hotels, trendy boutiques, and a rowdy club scene. The **Old Town** centers on touristy **Sokratous**—a bustling, cobbled street descending from the castle to the commercial harbor. The Old Town streets are a labyrinth of medieval structures that are still in use as houses, tavernas, and souvenir shops. Keep your eyes open for Byzantine influences, and be prepared to get lost in the maze of narrow streets despite your best efforts to follow a map. Unless you're in the market for an "I love Rhodes" magnet, skip the central plazas and wander the outer streets, many of which still have an Old World charm and ambience.

Ferries depart from the Commercial Harbor outside the Old Town. **Mandraki,** the New Town's waterfront, is where yachts, hydrofoils, and excursion boats dock. Beaches lie to the north, beyond Mandraki and along the city's west coast. The tourist office, bus stations, and a taxi stand are in **Plateia Rimini,** beneath the fortress's turrets, at the junction of the Old and New Towns. From Mandraki, head a block inland with the park on the left. From the Old Town, walk out the D'Amboise Gate in front of the Palace and follow the road as it curves around the park. Or, follow Aristotelous to Ermou until it joins Mandraki. Tourist nightlife in the New Town swarms around **Orfanidou,** dubbed "bar street," while the local scene converges mainly at **Militadou** in the Old Town.

Tourist Office: EOT (☎22410 44 333; www.ando.gr/eot), at the corner of Makariou and Papagou, a few blocks up Papagou from Pl. Rimini. Helpful advice for daytrip planning as well as free maps, brochures in several languages, and complete M-Sa bus schedules. English and Greek information desks. Open M-F 8:30am-2:45pm. State-run tourist office, Averof 3 (☎22410 35 945), next to the New Town taxi stand near Pl. Alexandria. Ferry and bus schedules available. Open daily 8am-11pm.

Budget Travel: Your Travel, Alex. Papagou 4 (☎22410 75 828), in the New Town, across from the Sound and Light Show. Provides money exchange, car rentals, air and ferry bookings. Open M-F 9am-2pm, 5:30-9pm, Sa 9am-2pm.

Banks: Banks and ATMs abound throughout both the New and Old Towns. **Eurochange** (☎22410 31 847), at Pl. Hippocratous in the Old Town, has **currency exchange** and cash advances. Open daily 9am-9pm. **National Bank of Greece,** at Pl. Moussiou, across from the Archeological Museum, has an **ATM.** Open M-Th 8am-2:30pm, F 8am-2pm. The **Commercial Bank of Emporiki,** Ippoton (☎22410 22 123) also has an **ATM.** Open M-Th 8am-2:30pm, F 8am-2pm. **Attica Bank** and **Emporiki Bank,** Averof, have **24hr. ATMs.** Both open M-F 8am-2:30pm, Sa 8am-2pm.

American Express: Rhodos Tours Ltd., Amohostou 23 (☎22410 21 010). Open M-Sa 9am-1:30pm and 5-8:30pm.

Western Union: (☎22410 26 400), behind the central plaza. Open M-F 8:30am-9pm, Sa 8:30am-3pm.

Bookstore: Akademia Bookshop, Amerikis 93 (☎22410 32 690). A small selection of paperbacks in English, including both literary classics and trashy beach reads. Books up to €13. Open M-F 9am-2:30pm and 5-9pm, Sa 9-2:30. MC/V.

Laundromat: Express Laundry, Kosti Palama, 1 block north of the bus stops. €6 wash and dry (2hr.). Open M-Sa 8am-11pm. **Star Laundry,** across the street, offers similar services. **Laundromat,** Platonos 33 (☎22410 76 047), by Pl. Athina in the Old Town. Wash and dry €5. Open M-Sa 8am-8pm.

Police: Dodekanission (☎22410 27 653), 1 block behind the post office. Open 24hr. **Tourist Police** (☎22410 27 423), behind the EOT building and up a flight of stairs. Open daily 8am-2pm.

Hospital: Apostoli (☎22410 80 000). Open 24 hr. for emergencies.

Telephones: OTE, Amerikis 91, at the corner of 25 Martiou in the New Town. Open M-F 7:30am-1:30pm.

Internet Access: Most cafes in the New Town have Wi-Fi, and there is an internet cafe on almost every corner. **Mango Bar** and the **Spot Hotel** (see **Accommodations,** p. 336). In the Old Town, many cafes in the Jewish Quarter offer Wi-Fi, especially those on Pl. Evreon Martiron. **Control Cafe** and **Galileo Cafe** also provide internet access (see **Food,** p. 338).

Post Office: Main branch, on Mandraki (☎22410 30 290), next to the Bank of Greece. Open M-F 7:30am-8pm, Sa 7:30am-2pm. **Postal Code:** 85100.

ACCOMMODATIONS

Most pensions in the Old Town are scattered about the narrow, cobbled paths between **Sokratous** and the outer city walls. Prices vary with the season. You

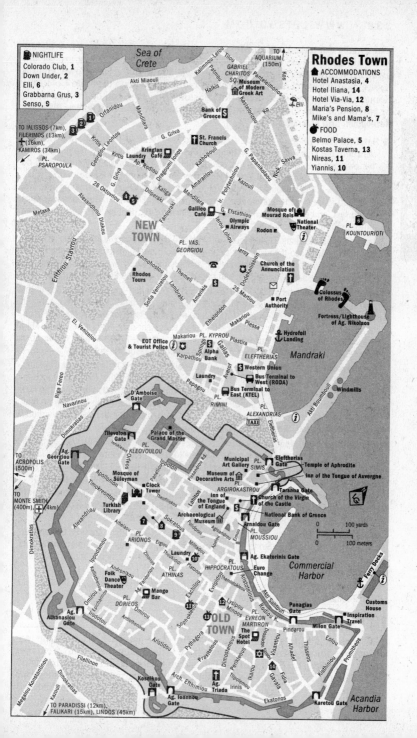

Rhodes Town

Sea of Crete

TO AQUARIUM (150m)

NIGHTLIFE
Colorado Club, 1
Down Under, 2
Elli, 6
Grabbarna Grus, 3
Senso, 9

ACCOMMODATIONS
Hotel Anastasia, 4
Hotel Iliana, 14
Hotel Via-Via, 12
Maria's Pension, 8
Mike's and Mama's, 7

FOOD
Belmo Palace, 5
Kostas Taverna, 13
Nireas, 11
Yiannis, 10

GABRIEL CHARITOS SQ.
Museum of Modern Greek Art

Akti Miaouli
Kalimmou-Lerou
Tilou
Patmou
Peteleimonos
Kos
Elli
Halkis
Kastelorizou
Ko

Bank of Greece

St. Francis Church

TO IALISSOS (7km),
FILERIMOS (13km),
(16km),
KAMIROS (34km)

PL. PSAROPOULA

Orfanidou
Mandilara
Kritis Leontos
Georgiou Kritis
G. Griva
G. Griva
Kritis
28 Oktovriou
Dilperaki
Alexandhrou Diakou
Metaxa
Fanourakik

Kringlan Laundry
Ap. Rodiou Ionos
Dragoumi
Amarantou
Mandilara
Kaliga
Kathopouli
G. Papanikolaou
Nick. Sarva
G. Efstathiou
Ir. polytechniou
Kazouli

Galileo Café
G. Papanikolaou
It. polytechniou

Mosque of Mourad Reis
National Theater

Rodon
Olympic Airways
Jeroy Lohou
Jeroy
Dodecanissou

PL. KOUNTOURIOTI

NEW TOWN

Aammohostou
Themeli
Lambraki
Sofia Venizelou

PL. VAS. GEORGIOU

Rhodes Tours

Church of the Annunciation

Amerikis
Ethelondon
25 Martiou
Dodecanissou
Makariou
Plessa

Port Authority

Colossus of Rhodes

Fortress/Lighthouse of Ag. Nikolaos

El. Venizelou
Erithrou Stavrou
Riga Fereo

Makariou
PL. KYPROU
Springs
Gallas
Karpathou
Plastira

EOT Office & Tourist Police
Alpha Bank

PL. ELEFTHERIAS

Hydrofoil Landing

Mandraki

Laundry
Papagou
Avepof

Western Union
Bus Terminal to West (RODA)
Bus Terminal to East (KTEL)

Windmills

Navarinou
Dimokratias

D'Amboise Gate

RIMINI

PL. ALEXANDRIAS
TAXI

Akti Boumbouli

TO ACROPOLIS (500m)

Tilevofon Gate
Ag. Georgiou Gate

Palace of the Grand Master

PL. KLEOVOULOU

Ippoton

Eleftherias Gate
Temple of Aphrodite
Inn of the Tongue of Auvergne

TO MONTE SMITH (400m), (4km)

Apollonos
Timofonon
Mosque of Süleyman
Clock Tower
Turkish Library
Theofiliskou

Panetiou
Orfeos
Lahtos
Pisanorodou Rd.

Municipal Art Gallery
Museum of Decorative Arts

PL. SIMIS

Inn of the Tongue of England
Archaeological Museum

ARGIROKASTROU

Tarsana Gate
Church of the Virgin of the Castle

National Bank of Greece

Alexandriou
Atheleou

PL. ARIONOS

Sokratous
Miltiadou
Apollon
Agisandrou

Arnaldou Gate
PL. MOUSSIOU

0   100 yards
0   100 meters

Androniki
Ippodamou
Omirou

Folk Dance Theater

PL. DORIEOS

Mango Bar

Laundry
PL. ATHINAS
Platonos

PL. HIPPOCRATOUS
Euro Change

Ag. Ekaterinis Gate

Commercial Harbor

Ag. Athanasiou Gate

Kosnikou Gate

Filellinon

Dimokratias
Antisthenous
Aristidou

Sognrofou
Minoos
Lysipou
EVREON MARTIRON
The Spot Hotel

OLD TOWN

Panagias Gate

Customs House
Inspiration Travel

Milon Gate
Pindarou

Kisthiniou
Fidia
Alinadei
Eofou
Thisseos
Prometheos

Ag. Triada

Pythagora
Praxitelous
Dimostenous
Periklous
Gavala

Ag. Ioannou Gate

TO PARADISSI (12km),
FALIKARI (15km), LINDOS (45km)

Ekatonos
Karetou Gate

Acandia Harbor

Ferry Docks

can usually cut a deal with hostel owners if you plan to stay for a few nights. Even the cheapest accommodations are bright and airy, and most are tucked away in picturesque (if hard to find) medieval alleys. In the New Town, charmless, expensive hotels seem to merge into one sprawling corporate Colossus. Some affordable and even delightful pensions, however, can be found a block or two inland from the waterfront and on the narrow streets of **Rodiou, Dilperaki, Kathopouli,** and **Amarandou.**

Hotel Via-Via, Pythagora 45 and Lisippou 2, Old Town (☎22410 77 027; www.hotel-via-via.com). The chic Belgian owner, Beatrice, designed each individually themed room in her own personal style, helping this colorful hotel live up to its reputation as "Hotel de Charme." The relaxing rooftop terrace looks over the skyline of Old Rhodes, with a spectacular view of the Mosque and Palace of the Old Masters. Clean, bright rooms have TVs, A/C, and fridges; some share bathrooms. Breakfast €5. Free Wi-Fi. Book ahead; rooms fill up fast, and prices vary with the season. Singles €45; doubles €70—ask about the private rooftop double. Cash only. ❸

Domus Rodos, Platonos 31, Old Town (☎22410 25 965; info@domusrodoshotel.gr). Simple hotel near Senso nightclub has clean sheets and towels, tasteful rooms, good water pressure, A/C, TV, and Wi-Fi in an excellent location. The friendly Swedish owner keeps the place spic-and-span. Singles €20, with breakfast €30; doubles €40. Cash only. ❷

Mango Bar, Pl. Dorieos 3 (☎22410 24 877). One of the low-key social hotspots of the Old Town, doing triple duty as an internet cafe, pub, and hotel. Rooms are clean and simple. Popular with English-speaking locals, who come here for the €4 Mango Punch, a pint of alcoholic fruitiness guaranteed to start your night right. Night receptionist Mike has the mullet of a lion but the heart of a lamb. Free Wi-Fi. Computers €4 an hour. Singles €35; doubles €48. Prices negotiable with the season. Cash only. ❸

Hotel Anastasia, 28 Oktovriou 46, New Town (☎22410 28 007; www.anastasia-hotel. com). Just off the street and away from the rowdy hordes, find the peaceful, vine-enclosed garden-bar of this family-run pension, with elegant 1930s tile floors. The New Town location isn't the best, but the friendly owner readily shares the lowdown on Rhodes. 9 bright, airy rooms include at least 2 twin beds, bath, and a large wardrobe. Breakfast included. Singles €35; doubles €50. V. ❸

The Sunlight Hotel, Ipodamou 32 (☎22410 21 435, stavroshotel.com). Walk up Sokratous toward the Mosque, then make a left onto Ipodamou before the Turkish Library; continue for 100m. The rooms are simple but tidy, complete with clean baths, refrigerators, TVs, hot water boilers, and A/C. Singles €30; doubles €40. Cash only. ❷

Maria's Pension, Lisia 147 (☎22410 22 169), off the main drag of Sokratous, toward the Turkish Quarter. This charming, family-run pension has clean, breezy rooms arranged around a courtyard. Singles €20; doubles €25. Cash only. ❶

Hotel Iliana, 1 Desiadou Gevala St., Old Town (☎22410 30 251). From Pl. Evreon Martiron, follow Dossiadou Simiou past the synagogue; it's across the street on the left, up a flight of stairs. Budget's the word at Hotel Iliana with its simple rooms with bath. Singles €10; doubles €25. Cash only. ❶

The Spot Hotel, 21 Perikleous (☎22410 34 737), near Pl. Hippocratous. Wi-Fi €5 per hr. Rooms from €35. Open 8am-11pm. ❸

▲ FOOD

With their quadrilingual menus and matching tree canopies, many of the restaurants in Rhodes Town will seem to have little setting them apart from one another. Traditional Greek fare and fish and chips abound at the more touristed spots along Sokratous, but the real gems are in the hard-to-navigate alleys off the main drag. Some of the best dining options in the Old Town are clustered on **Plateia Sophokleous;** from Pl. Hippocratous, turn onto Pithagora, hang a right on Platanos, then veer left after the mosque to find this hidden street's excellent cuisine. Since street signage is lacking in the Old Town, the best way to find food is to stumble in while wandering the labyrinth of backstreets, or ask a friendly local to point you in the right direction.

Nireas, Sophokleous 22 (☎22410 21 703). Savor delicious fresh seafood, prepared according to recipes from Symi, in a quiet courtyard under a leafy canopy. The mussels *saganaki* (€9) are unbelievable. Chat about books with the gregarious owner Theo, who nicknames the waitresses after famous literary heroines; "Madame Bovary" may serve you your grilled scallops (€10). The family-run restaurant is housed in a centuries-old building that once served as a stable. Try sharing various dishes among a group, including fresh fish (€30-48 per kg). Open daily 5pm-late. AmEx/MC/V. ❷

Kostas Taverna, Pythagora 62 (☎22410 26 217), 2 blocks south of Pl. Hippocratous. Peacefully hidden away from the tourist centers (i.e., hard to find), this cozy taverna is a beacon of light on an otherwise deserted street. Read the effusive praise from satisfied customers tacked out front, then go inside to enjoy some hearty souvlaki (€8.50) or seafood (€9-22.) Check out the vintage jukebox on your right as you enter. Open daily 10am-midnight. MC/V. ❷

Yiannis Taverna, Platonos 41, Old Town (☎22410 36 535). Go down the street next to Senso nightclub for 50m; it's right next to Hotel Domus Rodos. Yiannis offers unparalleled traditional food, all simple and home-made. Try the Greek salad (€4.80) and the *pastitsio* (€8), or treat yourself to the selection of fresh fish (€9-16). Entrees €5.50-8.50. Open daily 9am-11pm. Cash only. ❷

Belmo Palace, 28 Oktovriou and Ionos Dragouni, New Town (☎22410 25 251; www.belmopalace.gr). Takes charming kitsch to the next level, with blue plaster Ionic columns and fake grapes tacked to a tree in the breezy outdoor seating area. Don't be surprised if your national flag pops up at your table; the waiters like to make you feel at home. Hospitable owner Yiannis will probably visit as you munch on unusually affordable Greek salad (€3.50) and fresh fish (€9). The Greek platter (€8) comes piled with *tzatziki*, stuffed tomatoes, *dolmades*, meatballs, and *pastitsio* covered with a tasty red sauce. Open daily 10am-11:30pm. AmEx/MC/V. ❷

Cafe Medieval, 25 Apellou, Old Town (☎22410 30 013). This cafe, in between Sokratous and the Archeological Museum, has the best ice cream in the city. The hand-made gelato (€1.30 per scoop) is created from fresh fruit and carved into kid-friendly animal shapes complete with googly eyes. Also serves delicious cappuccinos (€3.20) and pastries. Open daily 8am-late. Cash only. ❶

Control Cafe, Diakou 44 (☎22410 65 099). Get a coffee (€2) or play pool while you wait for internet access. Computer with internet €2.80 per hr. Open M-Sa 8:30am-midnight, Su 11:30am-midnight. ❶

Galileo Cafe, Polytechniou 13 (☎22410 20 610; www.galileocafe.gr), at the corner of Efstathiou in the New Town. Offers both computers and ethernet cables for laptops. Mixed drinks €5. Internet €1.20 per 30min., €2 per hr. Open daily 9am-3am. ❶

🔎 SIGHTS

Rhodes's tumultuous history provides tourists with many fantastic sights, all of which are contained in the Old Town's medieval labyrinth. Plaques scattered throughout the Old Town mark so many historical sites and museums constructed by the island's various occupants that it's tricky to keep them all straight. The Knights of St. John conquered the Dodecanese (except Astypalea, Karpathos, and Kassos) in 1309, replaced Rhodes's Hellenistic ruins with an imposing Gothic fortress, revived trade with Europe, and made it home in time

DODECANESE

for jousting. The Knights, who originated as an order of medics in the Crusades, built the Hospital of the Knights (now the Archaeological Museum) and the Palace of the Grand Masters, both in the style of medieval castles of the North. But their shining armor and mighty turrets were no match for the Ottomans, who conquered Rhodes in 1523. The old Turkish bazaar is nearly unrecognizable as the busy shopping strip of Sokratous, but the historic mosque, Muslim library, and Turkish baths are more enduring monuments to the city's Islamic ancestry. The ⬛parkland surrounding the fortifications (accessible through any of the tunnels in the fortress wall) has cannonball-strewn pathways in the peaceful region lying between the fortress's inner and outer walls.

⬛PALACE OF THE GRAND MASTERS (MEGALOU MAGISTROU). At the top of the Avenue of the Knights, a tall, square tower marks the entrance to the Palace of the Grand Masters, erected in the 14th century as a testament to the Knights' military power. With moats, drawbridges, watchtowers, and enormous battlements, the castle is worth visiting for its fairy-tale architecture alone—not to mention its impressive history and collections. The palace survived the long Ottoman siege of 1523, and was converted into a prison by the Turks after their victory. After damage from earthquakes and explosions in the 19th century, the citadel was restored at the beginning of the 20th under the watchful eye of Mussolini, who planned to use the palace as a summer home. Just after the Italians imported a collection of exquisite second-century mosaic floorwork from Kos, however, WWII broke out, leaving little time for the dictator to take vacations. The art inside the palace ranges from Hellenistic sculpture to medieval tapestry to Japanese vases, but the real highlight is the accompanying exhibit on Ancient Rhodes, which presents similar content to the Archeological Museum but with a more comprehensive narrative. (☎ 22410 25 500. Open M 12:30-7:10pm, Tu-Su 8am-7:10pm. Exhibit on Ancient Rhodes open Tu-Su 8am-7:10pm. Walk Around the Walls tour, Tu-Su 8:30am-1pm. €2 ticket available at Palace ticket window. €6, students €3, EU students free. Tour €2; buy tickets at Palace ticket window.)

ARCHAEOLOGICAL MUSEUM OF RHODES (PLATEIA ARGIOKASTROU). Dominating one side of Pl. Mouisou with its imposing facade, the former Hospital of the Knights now serves as an Archaeological Museum housing art and architecture from ancient and medieval Rhodes. Enter a sunny central courtyard strewn with welcoming pyramids of deadly cannonballs and featuring a statue of a lion pawing a charmingly half-eaten bull's head. Other treasures include the exquisite "Marine Venus" from the late 4th century BC (whose fluid contours were partly carved by sea erosion), funeral slabs of Knights of various nationalities who died at Rhodes, expressive Hellenistic sculptures, and impressively preserved geometric and archaic vase paintings. Check out the morbid **Archaic Burial Pithoi** exhibit next door to the museum entrance, which displays massive jars where the ancients buried their dead children. If you're in the mood for some prehistoric beads and bones, go around the corner to the **Museum of Prehistoric Rhodes** to see how ancient artifacts were excavated. (☎ 22410 25 500. Open Tu-Su 8am-7:30pm, M 1:30-7:30pm. €3; includes Burial Pithoi and Museum of Prehistoric Rhodes.)

AVENUE OF THE KNIGHTS. Also known as Ippoton, this austere avenue was the city's main boulevard 500 years ago and is one of the few major streets free of souvenir shops. The stark simplicity of this avenue makes it one of the most picturesque streets in the city—uncluttered by shops, restaurants, or even parked cars. During the Knights' reign, each national division—called a "tongue"—maintained its own inn along this street, where members would gather to eat, socialize, and converse without pesky language barriers. Follow the Avenue of the Knights all the way to the top of the hill to reach the back entrance of the Palace of the Grand Masters. *(Directly to the north of the Archeological Museum when standing in the entrance; it's the street on the left.)*

TURKISH QUARTER. The beautiful pink **Mosque of Süleyman** was originally built to commemorate Sultan Süleyman the Magnificent's capture of Rhodes in 1522, and later restored. It's not open to the public, but you can enjoy its impressive dome and minarets from the outside. The 1793 **Hafiz Ahmed Aga Library** (Turkish Library), opposite the mosque, houses 830 volumes of handwritten 15th- and 16th-century Persian and Arabic manuscripts of classic literature. Scrolls and paintings are displayed in the museum off the courtyard. The best way to experience Turkish Rhodes, however, is literally to bathe in it: the ◼**Turkish Hamam** in Pl. Arionos welcomes locals and travelers alike to the 500-year-old baths. Relax in the steamy maze of marble rooms and stone basins under high domed ceilings, or pay an extra €10 for a soapy wipedown and a massage. To get there from the Mosque, turn left on Ipodamou and then left Xenofodos before you hit Stavros Bar. *(Either follow Sokratous all the way to the top of the hill, or exit the Palace of the Grand Masters to Orfeos, then turn left. ☎22410 27 739. Library open M-Sa 9:30am-4pm. Hamam open M-F 10am-5pm, Sa 8am-5pm. €5.)*

GALLERY OF MODERN GREEK ART (PLATEIA SIMIS). The Municipal Art Gallery boasts rotating exhibitions from modern and contemporary Greek artists. Some exhibitions are influenced by ancient crafts, while others are truly unique. You can gaze over the entire *plateia* from its cool, sunny rooms. *(Inside Eleftherias Gate to the right and up a flight of stairs. Open Tu-Sa 8am-2pm and 6-9pm. €3, students €1.)*

JEWISH QUARTER. Sephardic Jews, who arrived on the island after fleeing the Spanish Inquisition in 1492, added their distinctive flair to some of the Old Town's medieval architecture. In 1944, almost 2000 Jews were taken from **Plateia Evreon Martiron** (Jewish Martyrs' Square; in the heart of the old Jewish Quarter) to Auschwitz, and of those only 151 Rhodesian Jews survived the Holocaust. The *plateia* has since been overrun by tourist cafes and shops, though a small, touching memorial in the center pays tribute to the victims of the Holocaust. Down Dossiadou Simiou (off Pl. Evreon Martiron and Simiou) is the **Kahal Shalom Synagogue.** Originally constructed in 1577 and restored by five Greek-Jewish families after WWII, the synagogue is the last of the six that once stood in Rhodes. Inside, intricate stone mosaics cover the floor and a newly opened museum offers visitors information on the heritage of Jews in Rhodes. *(☎22410 22 364; www.jewishrhodes.org. Open M-F 10am-3pm. Services F 5pm. Modest dress required.)*

🎵 ENTERTAINMENT

Before hitting the rowdy bars, check out one of several cultural events in Rhodes Town.

Folk Dance Theater, check with the EOT to see if you can catch a performance here.

National Theater (☎22410 20 265), on Efstathiou Georgiou off Mandraki across from the Church of the Annunciation. Stages productions. Ask for a performance schedule at the EOT.

Rodon. Shows flicks and subtitled classics in an outdoor, vine-covered amphitheater. Every June, it hosts an **Ecocinema film festival,** showing environmentally and anthropologically themed documentaries.

St. Francis Church, Dragoumi Ionos (☎22410 23 605; www.catholicchurchrhodes. com), in the New Town, echoes with sublime organ recitals (every Su 10pm).

DODECANESE

NIGHTLIFE

OLD TOWN

A mellow crowd of locals and tourists gathers in the bars on **Plateia Arionos** in Old Town, around the Turkish Hamam, while more hardcore partiers gather further down **Sokratous**. Flashing lights and packed clubs can be found down the street on **Militadou**, one block behind Sokratous, where bars line the street and music pours out of every door. Quieter bars more suitable for conversation can be found in the *plateias* between Fanouriou and Eschilou, where tourists and locals alike linger over mixed drinks and *mezedes*.

Rogmi tou Hronou (☎22410 25 202). This bar's stone-walled rooms are illuminated by a back-lit drink selection. F live music. Open noon-4am.

Moooi, near Rogmi tou Hronou. A mod lounge with leather couches and €8 cocktails made with fresh juice.

Baduz (☎22410 92 069), near Rogmi tou Hronou. For a more lively atmosphere, check out this dance club with finger food and themed music nights. Tu Greek rock, W night disco, Su live music. Open daily 8:30-dawn.

NEW TOWN

The New Town is the real place to be after 10pm. Popular bars and clubs are scattered all over, but nothing compares to "bar street"—**Orfanidou,** once featured on MTV as an international nightlife hotspot—where the street itself can become a dance floor during the high season.

Colorado Club, Orfanidou 57 (☎22410 75 120; www.coloradoclub.gr). The king of New Town nightlife, this club packs revelers onto 3 floors of perpetually crowded rooms. 1st floor has a live rock band blasting 80s hits, the 2nd offers disco music and an accompanying light show, and the 3rd provides a bump-and-grind venue with a live DJ. Drinks €3-8. €8 cover; includes 1 free drink. Open daily 10:30pm-6am.

Pacha and **Toxic,** Orfanidou 42 and 45. Sister clubs down the street from Colorado. Pacha experiments with mod lighting while Toxic has a darker vibe, but the clubs share DJs and dancers. Pacha features a VIP back room, complete with beds under an open roof. Don't miss the Tu night pub crawl, starting at 9pm at Pacha; €20 buys you a free shot at each bar, and a dousing with a super-soaker filled with alcohol. F 9pm-12:30am Alcohol Night; unlimited drinks €20. Happy hour daily 9pm-midnight at Pacha, midnight-1am at Toxic; 2-for-1 drinks and €1 shot bar wtih exotic flavors (try cappuccino). Pacha open 9pm-4am. Toxic open daily 10pm-5am.

Grabbarna Grus, Orfanidou (☎22410 69 394), just a few doors down from Pacha and Toxic. Has a live DJ and themed Th parties. Open daily Apr.-Sept. 10pm-5am.

Elysium, Orfanidou (☎22410 74 644), next to Grabbarna Grus. This hookah lounge is owned by the same Scandinavian owners as its neighbor and offers a chill vibe as well as a €10 hookah. Open daily Apr.-Sept. 9pm-4am.

OUTDOOR ACTIVITIES

Rhodes doesn't have fluorescent coral or exotic fish, but there are scuba daytrips for beginners who just have plain gill-envy. **Waterhoppers** (☎22410 38 146; www.waterhoppers.com) and **Dive Med College** (☎22410 61 115; www.divemedcollege.com) run a joint beginner excursion to the crystal-clear waters off Kalithea beach, where divers explore the underwater world with a team of certified instructors. Snorkeling is available for those who don't want to dive, and the boat is a perfect place to catch some rays. The beginner package (€52.50) includes one dive with all equipment and insurance, but a second, longer dive costs an extra fee. For already qualified divers, Waterhoppers offers technical diving and cavern diving, while Dive Med College also offers cavern diving, wreck diving, and night diving, as well as an open water course. (Sign up at Mandraki harbor M-Sa at 8:45; the boat leaves at 9:30 and comes back around 5pm. Pack a lunch and sunscreen.)

Excursion boats trace the coast from Rhodes Town to Lindos, providing a great escape to an ancient town less tinged by commercial fever. The boats stop at the beaches of Kalithea, Faliraki, and Tsambika, among others. Ask around for prices and schedules on the docks until you find the right fit. (Most leave the city around 8:30am and return in the early afternoon. Tickets from €11.) Excursion boats also go to nearby islands like Symi and Halki for €25 roundtrip.

Trident Diving School (☎22410 29 160; www.tridentdivingschool.com). This PADI-certified school offers dives to any of the number of coves and wrecks offshore. Pack a lunch. 2-tank dive €70; equipment included.

◪ DAYTRIPS FROM RHODES TOWN

A few kilometers inland from the coast, the Rhodian geography changes drastically. Beaches seamlessly rise into mountains, offering opportunities for scenic hikes or quiet contemplation. These quieter spots are often left out of the party package tours, so you're more likely to encounter families and older couples than young revelers. Sturdy shoes and bug repellant are a must for attempting these often steep and wooded trails.

KALITHEA SPRINGS. Once believed to be a sacred spring of curative waters, Kalithea Springs is close to perfect harmony between beach and architecture. The intimate beach boasts crystal waters and elegant lounge chairs while the 1920s Italian spa rotunda is a refreshing alternative to ancient Doric ruins. The peaceful white building around a central courtyard features beautiful mosaic floors created in the traditional Rhodian style, using whole beach pebbles instead of cut tessarae. To avoid the overpriced snacks sold inside the springs, try the snack cart in the parking lot, where just about everything is €2. If you want to get to the beach without going to the springs, follow the signs for **Jordan's Grill,** on your right as you approach the springs from the bus stop. (Bus (15min., every 30min.) €2. ☎65 691. Open daily 8am-8pm. €2.50, children under 12 free.)

VALLEY OF BUTTERFLIES. For those who crave shade on the Island of the Sun, this cool forested hike is the perfect opportunity to trade in sunscreen for bug spray. In the late summer months, countless Jersey tiger moths migrate to **Petaloudes,** or the Valley of Butterflies, to spend their final days in the shade of fragrant Styrax trees. Although the butterflies are most visible in July and August, the tranquil 1km hike alongside a bubbling stream with cascading waterfalls makes the valley a worthwhile destination any time of year. At the top of the trail is the **Monastery of Kalopetra,** featuring restored mosaics and a panoramic view of the island. Admission also includes entrance to the small **Natural History Museum,** which has exhibits on butterflies and insects. (From Rhodes Town's West Station, the bus (45min., 4 per day 9:30am-1:30pm, €5) drops you off at the main station; visitors can also enter near the monastery atop the mountain or at the museum below. ☎22410 81 801. Open daily Apr.-Oct. 8am-7pm. High season €5, low season €3; under 12 free.)

EPTA PIGES. The aqueduct, built by Italians to bring water to Kolymbia, now quenches its visitors' thirst for excitement. Hurtling down the 150m pitch-black natural waterslide is the fastest way to reach the picturesque fresh water pool below. If the destination sounds nicer than the journey, take the path next to

DODECANESE

the tunnel that is used to return from the pool. A streamside **taverna,** home to a family of peacocks, sits at the mouth of the aqueduct. Continue inland past Epta Piges to visit the 13th- and 15th-century frescoes of the Byzantine **Church of Agios Nikolaos Fountoucli,** 3km past Eleousa. *(Eleven kilometers south of Faliraki, just before Kolymbia, a road to the right leads 3km down an unshaded highway and up a steep incline to Epta Piges. Or get off the Rhodes-Lindos bus at Kolymbia, and follow the sign to Epta Piges, which you'll reach after a 50min. walk. Renting a car or moped is generally a much better way to get there, especially in the midday sun. 12 buses to Lindos per day 7am-7:30pm, €4.50.)*

TSAMBIKAS MONASTERY. A restaurant on the coastal road marks Tsambikas Monastery. A 1km road will lead you to the restaurant; the Byzantine cloister and its panoramic views are 1km farther up a steep, rocky trail. The monastery takes its name from the sparks *(tsambas)* that reportedly were seen coming from atop the hill. Upon climbing up to investigate, locals discovered a Cypriot icon of the Virgin Mary that had mysteriously appeared there, miles from its home. Angry Cypriots ordered that the icon be returned, and the locals obliged—but the icon kept coming back. By its third return, everyone agreed that it belonged in Rhodes. To this day, women ascend the mountain to pray to the Virgin Mary for fertility. If the prayer works it is said that the baby should be named "Tsambikos" or "Tsambika." *(A bus runs to long, sandy Tsambika beach, 1km south of the turn-off for the monastery; ask at the east bus station in Rhodes Town for times. Buses to Archangelos, Faliraki, and other destinations that pass the turn-off will let you off there.)*

KAMIROS. The smallest of Rhodes's three ancient cities, Kamiros surpasses Rhodes Town in intricacy and preservation. This Hellenistic city was built into a hollow and constructed in an impressive chessboard design. The lowest, "public" level slopes up like an amphitheater to the highest level, which contains the acropolis. A visit to the precinct of Athena Kamiras on the acropolis gives a clear sense of the city's well-planned layout. The giant cistern on the north side of the temple (circa fifth or sixth century BC) and the colonnade (second century BC) are other noteworthy archaeological finds. *(Buses (daily 9, 11:15am, 1:30pm; €4) run from Rhodes Town's West Station. ☎ 22410 40 037. Open Tu-Sa 8am-7:10pm. €4, students €2.)*

LINDOS Λίνδος ☎22440

Escape into the undisturbed past of Lindos, only 50km from the hustle and bustle of Rhodes Town. The whitewashed houses clustered at the foot of a castle-capped acropolis make Lindos one of the most picturesque—and most visited—towns on the island. Stroll the winding alleys tiled with cobbled mosaics and shaded by leafy trellises. Tourist shops cater to the daytime crowds on the roads leading up to the acropolis, but other, less traveled streets remain untouched, offering a glimpse of the ancient serenity of this beach village. Lindos has made recent efforts to become more accessible to visitors, offering improved amenities and expanded nightlife while retaining its small-town charm.

▐ TRANSPORTATION

Lindos is a pedestrian-only city—no traffic may pass beyond the town square at the bottom of the hill. Your sole alternative to walking is renting a donkey and guide (€5). It's a traditional way for visitors to ascend the mountain to the acropolis or head down the steep paths to the beach. Pick up a ride at the donkey stand just past the town square. If you do choose to walk, watch out for donkey excrement.

Buses: The main road to Rhodes Town and Pefkos lies at the top of the hill, where you'll find the KTEL bus stop and kiosk. After 3pm, buses also make a stop in the town square. To: **Kalithea** (6 per day 1pm-7:15pm); **Kiotari-Genadi** (10 per day 8am-10pm, €2); **Kolymbia beach** (1:00, 2:30, 3:30pm, €3); **Pefkos-Lardos** (10 per day 8am-10pm, €1.50); **Rhodes Town** (14 per day 6:50am-7:15pm, €4.50). Check at the bus kiosk for changes to the schedule.

Taxis: (☎22440 31 466), in the town square or half-way up the street to the main road. To: **airport** (€48), **Faliraki** (€35), **Kolombia** (€25), **Pefkos** (€7), and **Rhodes Town** (€45).

Shuttles: Free blue-and-yellow shuttles run between the bus station and the Lindos town square down the hill (every 10min. 8am-3pm) and the Lindos beach (approximately every hr. 9am-5pm).

Excursion Boats: Depart at 9am and return at 5pm, hitting **Rhodes Town** (2hr., €10) and other pit stops as they travel along the coast. Boats also take daytrips to **Symi** (€40-45 round-trip) and **Turkey** (€60; passport required).

✚ 🛈 ORIENTATION AND PRACTICAL INFORMATION

Street signs are few and far between, and many streets don't have names at all. From the town plaza, **Acropolis** winds through town and up to the acropolis; signs point to the beach after 50m. **Apostolou Pavlou** crosses Acropolis just past the **Church of the Assumption of Madonna.**

Tourist Information Booth: (☎22440 31 900), in the town *plateia*. Equips you with a free, if vague, map of Lindos town. Provides bus and excursion schedules, general info on Lindos and the acropolis. Doubles as a multilingual newsstand. Open daily 8:30am-10:30pm.

Currency Exchange: Emporiki Bank (☎22440 31 270), right above the donkey stand. Open M-F 8am-2pm. See also **Island of the Sun Travel** (below). A **24hr. ATM** is located to the left of the tourist info booth.

Car and Moto Rental: Island of the Sun Travel (☎22440 31 264), on Acropolis about 100m past the church (20m from Ikon club). Excursion booking, car and moto rental, and **currency exchange.** Open daily from mid-May to Oct. 9am-10pm.

Bookstore: 📖 **Lindos Lending Library** (☎22440 31 443), past the church on the left, take the right fork; it's on the left. Sheila Markiou, an American expat, runs this superb store with her daughter, offering more than 7000 English, French, German, Greek, and Italian books. While it's only a library for permanent residents, visitors can buy a used book for half off, or trade one in for a new read. Sheila also runs a **laundry** service out of the store. Wash and dry €7.50. Open M-Sa 9am-8pm.

Public Toilets: In the *plateia*.

Police: (☎22440 31 223), at the end of the road, 200m past the pharmacy and on the left. Open M-F 8am-3pm; 24hr. for emergencies.

Pharmacy: (☎22440 31 294), just past Yannis Bar, down the right side of Acropolis. Open daily 9am-9pm.

Medical Clinic: (☎22440 31 224), on the right after taking a right facing the church entrance. Open daily 9am-3pm.

Internet Access: Lindos Internet Cafe (☎22440 32 100), 150m up the path to the left of the donkey stand. A comfortable place to check email over a €6 full English breakfast. Internet €4 per hr. Open daily 8:30am-1am.

Post Office: (☎22440 31 314), uphill from the donkey stand, right before the internet cafe. Open M-F 7:30am-2pm. **Postal Code:** 85107.

AN INCONVENIENT TRUTH. The steep, winding streets of Lindos are cluttered with small flights of steps every few meters or so, which makes the town nearly impossible for wheelchair-bound visitors to navigate.

ACCOMMODATIONS

In July and August, room prices rise dramatically as accommodations become scarce, so book early. Some domatia owners meet the buses as they enter the main square; this is usually the best way to find a room in the low season, so you're not trudging the anonymous winding streets with a heavy pack. Don't forget to haggle; it could save you anywhere from €10-15 off the initial price quote, especially if you're there during the low season. If you'd rather not take your chances in the square, follow the stream of donkeys and tourists toward the acropolis. After you pass Village Cafe but before you reach the main ascent, you'll find three comfortable *domatias* on your left.

Pension Katholiki (☎22440 31 445). 4 beautifully decorated rooms with clean, large baths, TVs, and A/C. The decorated stone facade in the courtyard that dates from 1640 and the phenomenal rooftop view are added bonuses. The owners also own a small supermarket right next to the pension, perfect for snacks or a cheap breakfast. Rooms €40. ❸

Pension Electra (☎22440 31 266), across from Pension Katholiki. Spotless, breezy rooms with fridges and shared baths, which open onto a sunny balcony with a terrific sea view. Singles €30; doubles €35. ❷

Stavros (☎22440 31 536), a few doors down from Katholiki and Electra. Rooms, studios and apartments for rent. Simple rooms include A/C and private baths. Excellent mini-kitchens complete with stove, cookware, and utensils are perfect for the budget traveler sick of restaurant prices. Singles €35; doubles negotiable. ❸

FOOD

Many of the tavernas in town serve similar fare at reasonable prices, and some have incredible rooftop views. More restaurants lie along the street on the first left off Acropolis; head farther down the road to the small beach and the number of waterside restaurants at the bottom of the hill.

Elekton (☎22440 31 286), down the street directly across from the Church. Reasonably-priced sandwiches and salads (€3-6) with lots of vegetarian options. Enjoy a delicious iced coffee (€2.50) on quaint blue cushioned benches arranged around a fireplace. Open daily 8:30am-late. MC/V. ❶

Village Cafe (☎22440 31 559). Follow the tourists as they go to the acropolis; it's on the way. Deli and bakery with home-made ice cream (€2 per scoop), pastries (€3-5), and fresh-baked croissants and bagels (€2). Delicious—though pricey—sandwiches and salads. Ask about takeaway packages. Open May-Oct. M-Tu and Th-Su 9am-11pm, W 9am-5pm. Cash only. ❷

Billy's Bar (☎22440 31 655). Look for the blue sign off Acropolis. Enjoy the view from the rooftop terrace. It's cheap (hamburgers €2; beer €2), it's greasy (eggs with bacon €2.50), and it has large projectors showing the latest soccer game. Open daily 8am-3am. Cash only. ❶

Mario's Restaurant, Acropolis. For a bare budget option, try to the left of Yannis bar. Offers similar options to other *tavernas* at slightly lower prices. Munch on Greek salad (€3.20), chicken (€4), or spagetti (€5) in this simply decorated eatery. Open daily 10:30am-midnight. MC/V. ❶

NIGHTLIFE

Yannis Bar, Acropolis (☎22440 31 245). Nightlife action begins at this bar, where €6 mixed drinks are made with fresh fruit. Free Wi-Fi. Drinks €4-7. Sa Latin Night. Open daily 8am-3am.

Four 04, Acropolis, across the street from Yannis Bar. Continue the festivities at Four 04 where indie rock plays till 3am. Free Wi-Fi over drinks (€4.50). Open daily 11am-3am. Cash only.

Ikon Cafe Bar. Head toward the town square on Acropolis to find mixed drinks (€5) and sophisticated conversation.

SIGHTS

CHURCH OF THE ASSUMPTION OF MADONNA. Although Lindos is most famous for its acropolis (see below), this church (100m from the town square) steals the show. The tiny but stunning Byzantine church features exquisite frescoes, hanging chandeliers, silver and gold ikons, and an extravagant throne. The colorful and expressive frescoes are immaculately preserved; check out the massive fire-breathing fish near the door, and lean over the velvet rope to see the enormous Christ fresco looking down from the central dome. *(Modest dress required. Open M-Sa 9am-3pm and 4:30-6pm, Su 9am-3pm. Museum €1.50.)*

ACROPOLIS. Lindos's ancient acropolis is an architectural melting pot; the site includes remains of Neolithic, Doric, Hellenistic, Roman, Byzantine, and Medieval structures erected throughout the city's rich history. The original architectural dig yielded a plaque inscribed by a priest of Athena in 99 BC, listing the dignitaries who supposedly visited Athena's temple—Hercules, Helen of Troy, Menelaus, Alexander the Great, and the King of Persia. This plaque is unfortunately not on display. Just before the final staircase, you'll find a carving of an ancient trireme—or warship with three sets of oars on each side—supposedly built by Pythokreitos (famous for his Nike of Samothrace). Lined with staircases, the daunting 13th-century **crusader castle** marks the site's entrance. The arcade, built around 200 BC at the height of Rhodes's glory, originally consisted of 42 Doric columns laid out in the shape of the Greek letter P. The large stone blocks arranged against the back wall were bases for bronze statues that have long since been melted down. The remains of the fourth century BC Doric-style **Temple of Athena Lindia** come into view at the top of the rocky incline. Today the temple is undergoing renovations, though the spectacular panoramic view still can still be appreciated from its steps. At the foot of the acropolis lie the remains of the ancient amphitheater. Ask for the helpful pamphlet at the acropolis ticket window. *(☎22440 31 258. Open during high season M 1:30-7:40pm, Tu-Su 8am-7:40pm; during low season Tu-Su 8:30am-2:40pm. €6, students €3.)*

MONASTERIES. The Churches of Greece offer a **walking tour** of the monasteries near Lindos. Meet at 10am behind the church, next to the door labeled #99. Walks are personalized for each group and can include swimming or lunch breaks. *(Every M-Sa. Voluntary donation.)*

KARPATHOS Κάρπαθος

Karpathos is one of the most beautiful and friendly islands of the Dodecanese. Although the pale-green coastline and austere mountains have drawn a steady flow of tourists over the past 50 years, Karpathians have resisted the "us vs. them" mentality so pervasive among locals in other popular areas. The mass Karpathian exodus to the United States during the WWII Italian occupation has led many islanders to consider the US a second home and American tourists as long-lost cousins. Karpathos is also known for its revolutionary spirit; islanders pride themselves on being the first of the Dodecanese islands to expel the Italians in 1946, eventually leading to the reunification of the islands with Greece. Ancient cultural traditions have been preserved in the northern villages, where you can still hear strains of Ancient Greek dialects being spoken in the *tavernas*. Its dramatic landscape and remarkable hospitality make Karpathos an ideal stop for beach bums, mountain men, and anyone wanting to kick it with the locals.

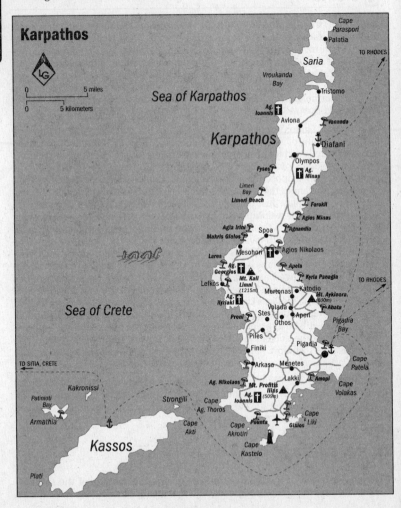

PIGADIA Πηγάδια ☎ 22450

A bustling port, Pigadia is known for outdoor cafes, nightlife hotspots, and spectacular views. In winter, the town lies dormant, reawakening in summer when thousands of Greek-Americans descend to re-open the shops and tavernas for the onslaught of visitors. Many Pigadian families emigrated to America after WWII; in the decades since, these families have slowly trickled back to Karpathos, usually to get married or return to their businesses. As a result, locals are especially friendly to Americans and are eager to share stories about their years living in the States. Many tourists only visit Pigadia on their way to other parts of the island, but don't be surprised if you find yourself lingering in a taverna along the tranquil harbor with some new Karpathian friends.

DODECANESE

⬛ TRANSPORTATION

Flights: Karpathos Airport (AOK). To: **Athens** (1¼hr., daily, €73); **Kassos** (15min., daily, €25); **Rhodes** (30min., 1-3 per day, €28); **Sitia** (1hr., daily).

Ferries: To **Kassos** (1hr., 2 per week, €10), **Piraeus** (16hr., 2 per week, €35), and **Rhodes** (5hr., W and Sa, €25). **Chrisovalandou Lines** runs daily excursions to **Olympos** (2hr.; leaves 8am, returns 6pm; €25, including bus ride into the town) and offers other beach packages (3 beaches in one day; €25 including lunch). Schedules change seasonally, so check with **Possi Travel** (☎22450 22 235) when you arrive.

Buses: Karpathos Station (☎22450 22 338), on the 3rd street parallel to the water, across the street from the supermarket and the minigolf course. Although there is another bus stop across from the taxi stand on Dimokratias, getting on at the origin is a better bet unless you're sure of the schedule. Buses only run on a regular schedule during the high season from mid-May to Oct. Call the main station for the timetable. Buses go to most villages on the southern part of the island (€1-3). Buy tickets on board. No service Su or local holidays. To: **Amopi** (20min., 2 per day); **Aperi** and **Apelia** (1hr.; M, W, F mornings); **Aperi, Volada, Othos,** and **Piles** (40min., 3 per day); **Arkasa, Finiki,** and **Lefkos** (1hr.; M, W, F 3 per day); **Menetes, Arkasa,** and **Finiki** (45min., M-F 2pm).

Taxis: (☎22450 22 705). 24hr., but cabs might not be at the stand between 2-7am. Arrange the night before for an early-morning ride, either by phone or in person. Taxi prices are posted on a tree outside the stand (€8-18 to nearby villages, €16 to the airport).

Car Rental: Circle Rent A Car (☎22450 22 690), close to the waterfront, about 200m west of Hotel Blue Sky. Cars €35-40 per day. 10% discount for rentals over 2 days. Open 8:30am-1pm and 5-8:30pm.

Motorcycle Rental: Moto Carpathos (☎22450 22 382; www.motocarpathos.gr). Facing inland from the bus stand, make a right, walk for two blocks, and it will be on your right. €20 per day, insurance included. 21+. Ask about the 7-day discount. Open daily 8am-1pm and 6-9pm.

⬛ ⬛ ORIENTATION AND PRACTICAL INFORMATION

Three main roads run parallel to each other and the waterfront. The first runs directly along the water and is lined with open-air tavernas and clubs. The second extends above and one block inland from the dock, and features many shops, cafes, and rental locations. The police, post office, main bus station, and some domatia lie along the third. The taxi stand and a bus stop are on **Dimokratias,** a main street which runs perpendicular to the others.

Budget Travel: ⬛ **Possi Travel and Holidays** (☎22450 22 235; fax 22 252), on the waterfront. Sells ferry and plane tickets, books excursions, exchanges currency, and has bus and ferry schedules. The English-speaking staff is ready and willing to help. Flight desk open M-Sa 8am-8pm. Ferry desk open M-Sa 8am-1pm and 5:30-8:00pm.

Banks: National Bank (☎22450 22 409), opposite Possi Travel. **Currency exchange. 24hr. ATM.** Open M-Th 8am-2:30pm, F 8am-2pm. **ATE Bank,** by the police station, 1 block east of the supermarket, also has a **24hr. ATM.** Open M-F 8am-2:30pm.

Police: (☎22450 22 222), on the first left past the hospital, up 1 block and on the left. Open 24hr.

Hospital: (☎22450 22 228), on the 2nd road parallel to the waterfront on your left. English spoken. Open 24hr.

OTE: (☎22450 22 399), past the post office. Open M-F 7:30am-2pm.

Internet Access: Cafe Galileo (☎22450 23 606), on the left past the National Bank. Free Wi-Fi. Open daily 10am-2:30pm and 6pm-late. **Internet Cafe Potpourri** (☎22450 29 073), 1 block west of Galileo, at a 3-way intersection opposite Olympic Airlines. Wi-Fi €5 per hr. Open daily 8am-1am.

Post Office: (☎22450 22 219). Follow the signs to the left from the intersection of Dimokratias and the 2nd street inland. Open M-F 7:30am-2pm. **Postal Code: 85700.**

◤ ACCOMMODATIONS

Most establishments in Pigadia do not accept credit cards, so go to the ATM as soon as you get to town.

Elias Rooms for Rent (☎22450 22 446; www.eliasrooms.com). For clean, affordable accommodations, head 1 block uphill from the taxi stand and take the left fork. Climb stairs until they curve to the right; it's on the left. English-speaking Elias can provide plenty of helpful information about the island as you lounge on the leafy terrace and enjoy both the view of the ocean and Wi-Fi. Rooms and bathrooms are a bit cramped, but spotless. Ask about the traditional *soufa* (lofted) beds. Singles €25; doubles €30. Cash only. ❷

Christina's Rooms (☎22450 22 045). From the water, walk up Dimokratias, take a left, and look for an unsigned pink and yellow house across from the supermarket. Pristine bathrooms and spacious rooms complete with sliding mahogany doors. Rooms include bathtubs, balconies, A/C, TVs, microwaves, and fridges. Several with kitchen. Ask about the top-floor single with exclusive roof access. Singles €20; doubles €25-30; triples €30. Cash only. ❷

Hotel Blue Sky (☎22450 22 356). Head right from Dimokratias on the 2nd major street; it's on the first corner on the left. Apartment-like suites with sitting rooms, kitchens, baths, TVs, fridges, coffee makers, large closets, and wrap-around balconies with sea views. 1970s furniture and the stuffy decorations give off a grandmotherly vibe, and Maria, the owner, might not let you leave the building without a juice box and a pastry. Singles, doubles €25. Cash only. ❷

◖ FOOD

Countless tavernas line the waterfront, each offering some combination of Greek specialties, overwhelming selections of international drinks, and wicker chairs perfect for lounging.

The Life of Angels (☎22450 22 984). 2 blocks past the National Bank on the 2nd road from the water; look for the blue sign in Greek on the right. Owner Zoe and her daughter Angel will welcome you with open arms to this matriarchal family restaurant, started by a great-grandmother 120 years ago. Delicious traditional Greek fare (€5.50-8) with more vegetarian options than other area restaurants (vegetarian platter €9; green been entree €5). Stop by the leafy rooftop terrace to relax with a glass of house wine (€2.50-5) and watch the sun set over the harbor. Wheelchair-accessible. Open daily 10am-2pm and 5pm-midnight. Cash only. ❷

Taverna Orea Karpathos (☎22450 22 501). Sample an unending selection of traditional Karpathian *mezedes* at this taverna located right on the water. Small plates designed for sharing (€3-7) feature local delicacies like *makarounes* (local cheese-and-onion-sprinkled noodles, €7.20) and Karpathian sausages (€4.50). Locals feast on fresh-caught fish priced by the kilo. Wheelchair-accessible. Open daily noon-late. Cash only. ❷

Anemoussa 3 (☎22450 22 164). On the roof, 1 block from Galileo and down some stairs, halfway up the staircase next to **Liquid** (p. 351). Satisfy your craving for Italian, Chinese, or the local fruits of the sea. Nearly endless pasta and tortellini options (€7-10) and delicious calzones (€8.50). Appetizers €2-8. Entrees €7-12. Drinks €2.50-4. Open daily 6pm-midnight. MC/V. ❸

Cafe Hatzantoni Maria (☎22450 22 530), on the corner of Dimokratias across from the ATE bank. Delicious Karpathian-style spinach pies made with bread dough instead of filo (€1.50). Epic selection of fresh-baked Greek pastries like baklava (€1.50). Snacks €1-2. Home-made candies €10-15. Cash only. ❶

Posiden Tavern (☎22450 23 638). Down the harbor from Orea Karpathos, this tavern offers a variety of salads (€3-6) and local seafood delicacies (€10.) Also provides a selection of Chinese (fried rice €10) and Italian food (chicken parmesan €15). Open daily 5pm-late. MC/V. ❸

Five Star Deli (☎22450 23 590), across the street from Galileo. If you're craving a taste of America, look no further. Owned by an American woman and her Greek husband. Try the 100% beef burgers (€2.50) or the ham and cheese sandwich (€2.50). For the ravenous carnivore (or a small family with normal appetites), the Mixed Grill special offers souvlaki, a hamburger, a hot dog, and fries for €11. Open daily 10am-10pm. Cash only. ❶

Beach Club (☎69788 62 226), on Pigadia beach, near the architectural ruins, a few blocks away from the town center. In Minos Beach Hotel, this restaurant has an €11 all-you-can-eat beach barbecue every Th night, complete with live music and fire dancers. Dance a traditional Greek line-dance with the rest of the revelers. Open Th 8 pm-late. Cash only. ❸

▣ NIGHTLIFE

In contrast to the club scenes on islands like Kos and Ios, Karpathos offers a mild take on nightlife. Bars and lounges fill up around 11pm, and revelers mingle until the clubs open at 1am.

Cafe Galileo (☎22450 23 606; www.caffegalileo.gr). Stop by to slip back into the American bar scene, complete with a Jimmy Hendrix poster and classic rock CDs. Come earlier in the day to enjoy the free Wi-Fi in the quiet cafe and nibble on a hard-to-find bagel (€3-4.50). Beer €3-6. Mixed drinks €5-7. Wheelchair-accessible. Open daily 8am-4pm and 6:30pm-late. Cash Only.

Liquid (☎69763 15 529). 1 block from Galileo (p. 339) and down some stairs, next to Anemoussa 3 (p. 351). Wide selection of creative coffee and hot-chocolate themed mixed drinks (€6) in a mod lounge with a balcony overlooking the harbor. Relax on a wicker couch with a beer (€3-5) or get down on the outdoor dance floor. Open 7:30pm-1am. Cash Only.

Anoi (☎23 960), 1 block east of Liquid and up a flight of stairs from the waterfront. The stuccoed mosaic walls and blue cushioned staircase outside provide a chill atmosphere for the conversation-minded traveler. Drinks €2-6. Beer €2.50-4. Open daily 7pm-2am. MC/V.

Enigma Club (☎22450 22 632). 2 doors down at blue-lit club, the DJ plays all night. Drinks €6-7. Don't miss the high-season happy hour 9pm-12:30am where drinks are €4. Open daily 10:30pm-4am.

OLYMPOS Ὄλυμπος ☎22450

Olympos is the epitome of a secluded mountain village, complete with spectacular views, constant gossip, and superb cheese. Perched in the mountains overlooking the ocean, Olympos was inaccessible for centuries, cultivating ancient customs that still fascinate ethnographers and linguists. The brightly colored embroidery worn by many Olympian women is a testament to the village's enduring isolation; the villagers had no colored pigments for thousands of years, so when they finally got dye, they went Technicolor. Visitors weave their way through tightly packed blue and white houses or sit in tavernas and listen to the locals gossip in a dialect closer to the Ancient Greek of Homer and Socrates than anything you'd hear on the streets of Athens. Though outside interest has led older Olympians to preserve and, in some cases, rekindle craft traditions, most of the younger generation has drifted to neighboring islands in search of education and jobs. Those who stay enjoy the windswept beauty of the terraced hills and the staggering coastlines topped by crumbling windmills.

▣ TRANSPORTATION

Ferries: Leave from Diafini to **Pigadia** (2hr.; 4:30pm; €25, includes 10min. **bus** from Olympos to Diafini).

✦ ORIENTATION

In town, navigation is fairly simple: a main pathway snakes uphill and connects to small side streets filled with houses. Many of the town's tavernas and shops can be found on the main road. Meandering through the narrow streets on the crown of the hill provides views of the lines of windmills on the west side of town. The church is located near the **post office,** on the corner where the road ends.

▣ ACCOMMODATIONS

While many visitors only spend the day in Olympos, those who stay overnight are rewarded with peaceful mountain silence and welcoming local tavernas. Colorful local embroidery lines traditional split-level *soufa* beds in most Olympos rooms; it is customary for children to sleep on the raised half of the loft, while dried goods and blankets are stored below.

Hotel Anemous (☎22450 51 314). Family-friendly, colorful rooms with brightly painted and carved *soufa* beds, decorated with traditional water carriers, local pottery, and icons. Each room has a private bath, refrigerator, hot water boiler, table, and sea view from the balcony. Simple restaurant attached. Singles negotiable; doubles €40-50. ❸

Pension Olympos (☎22450 51 009), about 150m up the pathway and down some stairs to your right. Sleep in a hand-carved *soufa* bed, in a room decorated with traditional plates and an Orthodox icons. Clean private bathrooms and peaceful balconies with mountain views. Singles €15; doubles €35. ❶

Hotel Aphrodite (☎22450 51 454), down the stairs to the left of the church. For spotless, spartan rooms, Hotel Aphrodite is your best bet. 4 rooms, outfitted with bath and balcony, command breathtaking views of the coast below. Singles €30; doubles €40; triples €45. ❷

DODECANESE

FOOD

Note that most restaurants don't have set hours; they just serve food until the tourists leave.

Milos Tavern (☎22450 51 333), on the path past Hotel Anemous (p. 352) and down the hill on the left. The kitchen is built around a functional windmill, which grinds the flour for bread baked in traditional ovens. Try the delicious (and hard to find) Karpathian cheese (€4) and zucchini cakes (€4.50) and home-made *pastitsio* (€6) while taking in panoramic views of both sea and mountains. Entrees €5-7. Open daily 7am-10pm. Cash only. ❶

Sinandes, near Milos Taverna to the main road, marked only by a sign advertising fried *loukoumades* (€5). These addictive fried dough balls are covered with honey and sprinkled with cinnamon and ground nuts. Check out the 1974 framed certificate on the wall signed by the Governor of Alabama congratulating the owner on his *zambuna* (goat-skin bagpipe-like traditional instrument) skills. Greek coffee (€1.50). Cash only. ❶

Parthenon Cafe (☎22450 51 307), across from Sinandes. If the crowd at Milos Taverna is too busy, take in the equally spectacular views from this relaxed rooftop where both the homemade lentil soup (€3.50) and the *makarounes* with goat cheese (€5) are definite winners. Open 7:30am-late. Cash only. ❶

Family-run restaurant, attached to Pension Olympos (p. 352). Serves goat with tomato sauce (€8) among other traditional entrees (€4-8), which you can enjoy over a €6 beer. Open 7:30am-late. Cash only. ❷

SIGHTS AND OUTDOOR ACTIVITIES

Olympos's traditional culture and crafts are the region's main draw; tourists marvel at the local women's black-and-white, hand-embroidered garb, and shops selling handmade scarves line the street. Also noteworthy are the locally grown spices, honey, and olive oil.

WINDMILLS. Several working windmills overlook the western cliffs where Olympian women grind the flour that they bake into bread in huge, stone ovens. If you brave the tiny ladder inside one of the windmills, you can watch the whirling from behind the scenes.

KIMISITIS THEOTOKOU. Just past Parthenon Cafe is this lavishly decorated eighth-century church. Gold foil blankets the church's wooden altar and restored 16th-century frescoes of scenes from the life of the Virgin Mary adorn the walls. *(Open every morning and evening for services, and occasionally when daytime tours pass through. Ask Papa Yannis, p. 353, for a tour.)*

PAPA YANNIS'S HOUSE. From the church, follow the stairs down and to the right and ask a local or tour group leader to point you in the direction of Papa Yannis's house. Inside, visitors can chat with Yannis and his wife over juice and see an authentic Olympian *soufa* at its finest, with an overwhelming display of colorful embroidery and ceramic plates covering every inch of wall. *(Free.)*

PINE FORESTS. Try out the footpaths leading both north and south of the town passing through pine forests. Hikes range from 5-16km across an area known for its falcon and eagle populations as well as its spectacular views of the ocean. *(Ask at the post office or at Cafe Parthenon for maps and directions.)*

HIKE. A 2 hr. hike along the valley floor from Pigadia to Olympos is an alternative to the ferry if you have the time, energy, and drinking water—but keep in mind it's a long, hot, uphill trip.

DODECANESE

SYMI Σύμη

Brightly-painted houses bloom like wildflowers on the cliffs overlooking Symi's main port, which has welcomed the incoming boats of sailors, fishermen, and sponge divers for thousands of years. Each of the colonial homes has a unique artistic flourish and individual charm preserved by strict historic conservation laws. While many travelers only stop here for a day between Rhodes and Kos, Symi's beautiful views, delicious cuisine, and friendly townspeople merit a longer visit. The island is tourist-oriented enough to be accessible, but not so much that it overrides the authentic atmosphere, making it the perfect spot to linger with the locals. Panormitis Monastery, on the southern side of the island, remains one of the holiest places in Greek Orthodoxy and an important point of pilgrimage.

SYMI TOWN ☎22460

Symi Town, the heart of the island's activity and where all public boats arrive, is divided into two sections: Yialos, the harbor area, and Chorio, the residential village on the hillside up a flight of 383 steps. Ferries disembark in the main Yialos harbor, and another smaller cove past the clock tower houses the shipyard. An additional small village, Pedhi, sits in the valley below Chorio, south of Yialos. The town was constructed in the Middle Ages as a fortification against pirate raids; trekking your way up to Chorio under the hot Symian sun may give you an appreciation for this defensive tactic—luckily, there's an hourly bus.

▆ TRANSPORTATION

Buses: Symi Bus, Pl. Ikonomou, 2 blocks to the left when facing the pharmacy. Every ½-1hr. 8:10am-11:10pm to **Chorio** (5min., €0.70) and **Pedhi** (10min., €0.70).

Ferries: Tickets can be purchased at any of the travel agencies or at **ANES,** by the waterfront. Open 9am-2pm and 6-8pm. To: **Astypalea** (2 per week, €26); **Kalymnos** (1 per day M-F); **Kos** (1 per day M-F); **Nisyros** (2 per week, €10.60); **Rhodes**(1 per day Tu-Su; €7.50, catamaran €11.50); **Tilos** (2 per week, €8). Schedules vary with the season; check with the travel agencies for the most updated times.

Hydrofoils: To **Rhodes** (1hr., 2-3 per day, €14). **Catamaran Dodekanisos Express** departs W and Su 9:30am to: **Kalymnos** (€28); **Kos** (€20); **Leros** (2 per day, €36); and **Patmos.** Schedules are always subject to change, so check beforehand.

Excursion Boats: The boats **Poseidon** and **Triton** (☎22460 20 215) offer day-long round-trip tours (€35; lunch included) around the island, stopping at **Panormitis Monastery**and a number of coves and beaches. Find them at the docks by the footbridge, on the same side as the pharmacy.

Taxis: Next to the bus stop on the eastern waterfront. The island's taxis must be reached by mobile phone; check the local newspaper for the latest taxi numbers.

Car Rentals: Glaros(☎22460 71 926), to the left of the police station. Cars from €35. Motorbikes €10. Open daily 8:30am-10pm. See also **Symi Tours** (p. 355).

▆ ⓘ ORIENTATION AND PRACTICAL INFORMATION

The steps leading up to Chorio connect to Yialos in two places: behind the pharmacy and next to Kalodoukas Holidays. To reach **Pedhi,** a 30-40min. walk from Yialos, climb up to Chorio and take the main road going down the other side.

DODECANESE

Budget Travel: Kalodoukas Holidays (☎22460 71 077), behind Vapori Bar to the right of the steps to Chorio. Sells hydrofoil tickets, **exchanges currency,** and arranges mountain walks. Open daily 9am-1pm and 5-9pm. **Symi Tours** (☎22460 71 307; www.symitours. com), 1 block inland as the waterfront road curves toward O Meraklis restaurant. Sells tickets for the Dodekanisos Express and rents cars. Open M-Th 9am-1pm and 5:30pm-8pm, F 9am-1pm and 6-8pm, Sa 9am-1 and 5-8pm. **Yialos Travel** (☎22460 71 931; www.yialostours.gr), in the jewelry store on the waterfront, helps find accommodations in Symi and books daytrips to Tilos, Nisyros, and Kos at a group rate.

Banks: National Bank (☎22460 72 249), on the waterfront directly across from the footbridge. **24hr. ATM** and **currency exchange. Alpha Bank** (☎22460 71 085), farther up toward the clock tower. Cashes traveler's checks with a €2 per check fee. Both open M-Th 8am-2:30pm, F 8am-2pm.

Newstand: Sells English and American newspapers and magazines, as well as a small selection of novels. Continue down the waterfront, turn inland (left) at the footbridge instead of crossing it, then make another left before Neraida Restaurant. The newsstand is in the small courtyard.

Laundry: Sunflower Laundry (☎22460 71 785), on the waterfront near the footbridge. Wash and dry €10. Open M-Sa 8:30am-1pm and 4-8pm.

Police: (☎22460 71 111), on the 2nd fl. of the white building near the clock tower. Open 24hr.

Pharmacy: (☎22460 71 888; emergency 69747 29 450), on the waterside one block from the bus stop. Open M-Sa 9am-1:30pm and 5:30-9pm.

Medical Services: (☎22460 71 290), to the back left of the church in Yialos, opposite Hotel Kokona. Open M-F 8:30am-2pm; call 24hr. for emergencies. The **doctor** in Chorio can be reached at ☎71 316. Serious medical concerns are often treated in to Rhodes.

OTE: (☎22460 71 212), inland on the back left side of the town square in Yialos.

Internet Access: Evoi Euav (☎22460 72 525), directly across from the footbridge on the clock-side of the harbor. Free Wi-Fi. Computers €4 per hr. Open daily 8am-late. **Glaros Cafe** (☎69757 86 010), up the hill in Horoi. Computers and high-speed connections €3 per hr. Open daily 8am-6pm. **Vapori Bar** (☎22460 72 082). Free Wi-Fi. Open daily 9am-late. **Roloi** (☎22460 71 597), on the street around the corner from Vapori Bar. Doubles as a recording studio. Computers €2 per hr. Open daily 9am-3am.

Post Office: (☎22460 71 315), in the same building as the police, up the flight of stairs on the left. Open M-F 7:30am-2pm. Also offers **Western Union** services. **Postal Code:** 85600.

ACCOMMODATIONS

Symi is a pricey place to stay: you're unlikely to find anything under €35, though if you haggle at the ferry drop-off you might get lucky. Accommodations get pricier as you head up the hill and the view improves, but you can find some economical pensions in Yialos, one street in from the waterfront. It's better to call ahead for exact prices, since many rates depend on group size and time of the year.

Hotel Albatros (☎22460 71 707), in front of the church. Bright, airy rooms with flowing curtains and tasteful blue and white decorations. Breakfast included. Singles from €40; doubles from €50, depending on season. Prices vary seasonally. ❸

Grace Hotel (☎22460 71 931), on a backstreets in Yialos. Family-run hotel composed of clean rooms with baths and A/C, as well as leafy patios with flowered plants. Longer stays get breakfast included. Inquire at **Yialos Travels** (p. 355) for reservations or directions. Singles from €30; doubles from €45. ❸

Pension Egli (☎22460 71 392), behind the pharmacy and up a flight of stairs in Chorio, only 100m from the Yialos town center. Spacious apartments each with 2 bedrooms, a kitchen, and a bath. Perfect for parties of 2 or more. Apartments €45-55. ❸

Hotel Anastasia (☎22460 71 364), up the white stairs as you approach the Post Office/ Police Station building on the far side of the waterfront. Quiet, well-ventilated, clean rooms with balconies and private baths. Singles €35; doubles €40. Prices vary seasonally. ❸

Hotel Kokona (☎22460 71 451), to the left of the church tower. Simple rooms with bath in an excellent location. Rooms have A/C and TVs, and are arranged around a pleasant shady patio. Breakfast included. Singles €40; doubles €55. ❸

🍴 FOOD

Symi's island waterfront is lined with slightly overpriced cafes catering to day-trippers, but you're unlikely to find any atrocious rip-offs here in either price or quality. More budget options are at the far end of the waterfront past the shipyard, and up in Chorio's heights. Symi's restaurants are renowned throughout the Dodecanese for their seafood, particularly their delightful small shrimp.

O Meraklis Taverna (☎22460 71 003), at the end of the road, inland from Symi Tours. This establishment's friendly owner will likely greet you with a glass of ouzo. Mouthwatering Greek specialties (€5-10) and fish (€8-14) cooked to perfection. Try the hummus (€3.50) and *shrimp saganaki* (€10). Wheelchair-accessible. Open daily 11am-midnight. AmEx/MC/V. ❷

Stanh (☎22460 71 182), next door to O Meraklis. A small bakery with the best baklava (€2-2.50) in Symi—or maybe all of Greece. Handmade ice cream €1.20 per scoop. Open daily 9am-10pm. Cash only. ❶

Manos Fish Restaurant (☎22460 72 429), on the clock tower side of the waterfront. Mouthwatering fish that proves Symi lives up to its culinary reputation. Pricey, but the seafood *mezedes* are worth the splurge. Try the Symi shrimp (€14), octopus *mezedes* (€13), or the fresh fish entrees (€12-35). Open daily for lunch and dinner. MC/V. ❸

Tholos (☎22460 72 033), at the far end of the small harbor on the way to the beach. At this dockside place, try the famed small Symi shrimp (€10) or the stuffed vegetables (€6) while enjoying the sea-breeze. Open daily noon-3:30pm and 7-11:30pm. ❷

Georgios's Taverna (☎22460 71 984). One of the oldest and most respected tavernas in Chorio. Watch your *souvlaki* sizzle on the open grill. Traditional Greek *mezedes* (€3-12) in a boisterous family setting, complete with live music on F nights. Prawns €9. Entrees €6-9. Open daily 9am-4pm and 7pm-midnight. Cash only. ❷

Milos Restaurant (☎22460 71 871). Turn left at the street just before Georgio's when coming up from the stairs; it's 1 block in on the left. A variety of scrumptious *mezedes* (€6.50-9) served on the outdoor terrace of an 18th-century converted windmill. Plenty of hearty vegetarian and vegan options like lentil stew (€5.50) and *briam* (slow cooked mixed Mediterranean vegetables, €6.50). Entrees €5.50-10. Open daily 7:30-11pm. Cash only. ❷

Odyssia Cafe (☎22460 72 642), on the far side of the waterfront, just before Tholos. Perfect if you need to balance your budget after a night at Manos. A small selection of simple, inexpensive dishes, like pizza (€4-6) or the hearty lasagna (€5), made fresh daily. Free Wi-Fi. Open daily 10am-late. Cash only. ❶

🎵 NIGHTLIFE

Symian nightlife keeps it low key as locals and tourists relax with drinks at one of the several cafe-bars in town.

Vapori Bar (☎22460 72 082). Munch on a healthy breakfast (€3-5) and enjoy the free Wi-Fi by day; drink the specialty mojitos (€9) and dance in the street by night. Mixed drinks €6-9. Happy hour 6:30-8:30pm. Open daily 9am-late. AmEx/MC/V.

Harani Bar (☎22460 71 422), across the street from Vapori Bar. Exotic drinks such as the apricot and banana "Yellow Bird" served on a relaxed outdoor terrace. Mixed drinks €7. Happy hour 6:30-8:30pm. Open daily 4pm-late. AmEx/MC/V.

Evoi Euav (☎22460 72 529). A quiet spot for conversation and a selection of over 90 mixed drinks (€5-8). Bask in the breezy blue patio or air-conditioned red interior. Happy hour 5:30-6:30pm. Open daily 8am-late. Cash only.

⚑ DAYTRIP FROM SYMI

⬛PANORMITIS MONASTERY Πανορμίτης
Daily bus service runs between Symi Town and Panormitis. (30min.; departs 8:30am, returns 11:30am and 1:30pm; €2.50.) Weekly tour boats running from Yialos include Panormitis on day-long trips around the island; daily tour boats from Rhodes stop here as well for at least 1hr. on the way to Symi Town. A taxi costs over €20; consider roughing the rigorous 3.2km hike by foot, though ask around about a 2.0km shortcut through the mountains. Modest dress required. ☎72 414. Daily services (7am, 7pm) open to the public. Open daily 7am-2pm and 4-7pm. Entry ticket for both museums €1.50, students and under 12 free. The monastery allows visitors to spend the night in one of the simple rooms in their annexes. Low-season singles €16; high-season 5-bed dorm €32. Reserve ahead.

After the Monastery at St. John in Patmos, Panormitis Monastery is the second most important monastery in the Dodecanese. Dedicated to the Archangel Michael, protectorate of sailors and travelers, Panormitis attracts nearly 4,000 sailors to the islands for the saint's feast day on November 8. Throughout the year, visitors come to the monastery to pay homage, and couples hoping for childbearing luck light votives in the dozens of tiny lamps hanging from the ceiling. Though the monastery's founding date remains a mystery even to the monks, its most recent renovation was in the 1700s. The immense wooden altar screen, carved from a walnut tree over the course of a hundred years, adorns one side of the church, and to the right hangs the main silver icon of Christ, hung with the jewels and watches of the faithful. The walls are decorated with gorgeous Byzantine and Medieval frescoes. The museums contain ecclesiastical relics, a pair of carved ivory tusks over 5ft. tall, and a touching exhibit of prayers to St. John that have been sent out to the sea in bottles and then recovered.

NISYROS Νίσυρος

Nisyros is most famous for its active volcano, which draws wannabe geologists with its sulfur crystals and steaming craters. Daytripping tourists move in predictable, daily cycles from the dock to the volcano to the waterfront *tavernas*, but the rest of the island is a peaceful place to unwind and take in the views. Quiet villages away from the volcano are made up of winding streets and whitewashed, cubic architecture typical of the Dodecanese, though this area is often completely ignored by tourists. Relics dating back to the Classical and Byzantine eras sprinkle the rocky beaches and craggy mountains that make up this rugged but beautiful island.

MANDRAKI Μανδράκι   ☎22420

Mandraki's leisurely rhythm of life seems immune to the bubbling pit of sulfur only 5km away. Although the waterfront establishments mostly cater to

DODECANESE

daytrippers from Kos intrigued by volcanoes, the town is hardly a tourist trap. Beyond the harbor, winding stone streets lead to the cliff-top monastery, the nearby black-stone beach, and gorgeous views of neighboring islands.

TRANSPORTATION

Ferries: Several ferry lines connect Nisyros to neighboring islands on a regular basis. Tickets can be bought at one of the agencies or last minute on the docks. **Blue Star Ferries** has service to: **Astylpalaia** (6hr., 2 per week); **Kalymnos** (3hr., 2 per week); **Kos** (2hr., 2 per week); **Naxos** (6hr., 2 per week); **Paros** (11 hr., 2 per week); **Piraeus** (14hr., 2 per week); **Rhodes** (4hr., 2 per week); **Tilos** (1½hr., 2 per week). **ANES** serves: **Kos** (2 per week), and **Tilos-Symi-Rhodes** (2 per week). Most common ferry departure days are Tu, Th, and Su. Check with Diakomihalis Travel (p. 358) for exact schedules.

Hydrofoils: Tickets are available at Diakomihalis Travel. M-F and Sa to **Kos Town** (1hr., €10). In summer F and Su, in winter F to **Halki** (2hr., €12), **Rhodes** (5hr., €12), and **Tilos** (1hr., €8).

Excursion Boats: Enetikon Travel sends biweekly (M 9:30am, Tu 1pm) commercial boats to **Kardamena** (1hr., €7) and **Kos Town** (2hr., €12.50). Check with Enetikon for updated schedules. Diakomihalis Travel also has boats at 3:30pm to **Kardamena** (1hr., €7.50) and **Kos Town** (daily, €12).

Buses: A municipal bus makes rounds through the villages, leaving from the Mandraki harbor 6 times per day. To: **Emporios** (20min.); **Loutra** (4min.); **Nikea** (25min.); **Pali** (10min.); **White Beach** (10min.). Daily excursion buses also head to the **volcano** when the boats from Kos arrive, usually 10am-noon. €7 round-trip; includes volcano entry. Purchase tickets at the Enetikon dockside stand or in their office.

Taxis: The island's private taxi must be reached by cell phone. **Irini** (☎69799 69 810) is based in Mandraki, and will take you wherever you need to go. To White Beach €5. To the volcano €25 round-trip, with a 25min. stop at the crater.

Rentals: Yannis (☎22420 31 037), across from the bank. Motorbikes from €10 per day. **Manos K.** (☎22420 31 551), on the dockside. Cars €25 for 1 day, but prices shift if you rent for longer. Insurance included. Open M-Sa 9am-2pm and 4pm-9pm, Su 9am-2pm and 5pm-9pm. **Diakomihalis Travel** (see above). Cars €25-35 per day; with minimal insurance included. 21+. 1 year driving experience required.

ORIENTATION AND PRACTICAL INFORMATION

The main road in Mandraki starts at the ferry docks and follows the waterfront (to the right as you face inland) until it forks at the bank. To the right, the road continues along the waterfront, leading down to a small stony beach and ending at the enormous monastery-topped cliff. To get away from the daytrippers, take the left fork at the bank, pass the post office and pharmacy and go up the hill to reach **Plateia Ilikiomeni** (Old Woman Square). You'll find a charming cobbled *plateia* nearly overwhelmed by the ficus tree in its center, filled with cafes and *tavernas*. Cross through the square and take a left to find the poorly signed stairs leading up to the cliff-side monastery.

Budget Travel: Diakominalis Travel (☎22420 31 459), located on the main road to the right of the bank, sells tickets and has schedules. Open daily 9am-1pm and 6pm-9pm. MC/V. **Enetikon Travel** (☎22420 31 180), on the right side of the road leading into town from the docks. Helps with tickets, hotel reservations, book exchange, and bus and boat tours. Friendly, multilingual staff. Walking maps of the island also available. Open daily 9:30am-1:30pm and 6:30-9pm.

Banks: Cooperative Bank of the Dodecanese (☎22420 48 900), the only bank on the island, is on the waterfront road; turn right from the dock. **Currency exchange** available M-F 9am-2pm. A **24hr. ATM** is located right off the ferry docks.

Medical Services: Call ☎22420 31 217 for an ambulance. The surgeon is located right before Pl. Ilikiomeni, down the left fork from the bank. Major medical emergencies are taken to Kos for treatment.

Internet Access: Proveza (☎22420 31 618) is the only internet option, far down the waterfront next to Kleanthis. Several computers with high-speed access and Wi-Fi. €2.50 per hr. Open daily 10am-1am.

Pharmacy: (☎22420 31 745), down the left fork past the bank, next to the post office. Open M-Sa 10am-2pm and 6-9pm.

Police: (☎22420 31 201), in a white building near the dock.

Post Office: (☎22420 31 249), down the left fork past the bank. **Western Union** services available. Open M-F 7:30am-3pm. **Postal Code:** 85303.

ACCOMMODATIONS

Rooms are almost always available, except during the August 15 **Festival of the Panagia,** when reservations are necessary.

Hotel Porfyris (☎22420 31 376; www.porfyris-nisyros.com), in the *plateia,* the more picturesque part of town. Go down the left fork at the bank and past the pharmacy and hardware store. The most bang for your buck, although it's a bit far from the harbor. Clean rooms with baths and balconies overlooking ocean views, a pool in the back, and a sunlit common eating area perfect for enjoying the hearty breakfast included in the price. A/C and TV. Wheelchair-accessible. Singles €27-40; doubles €35-60. Cash only. ❷

Three Brothers Hotel (☎22420 31 344), to the left as you leave the ferry dock. Among Mandraki's most welcoming and convenient establishments. Whitewashed rooms come with baths, fridges, and balconies (as well as some stellar views). The breezy patio overlooking the harbor is a great place to meet other travelers or hang out with the eponymous brothers themselves. Studios with full kitchens, A/C, and TVs also available. Wheelchair-accessible. Singles €25-40; doubles €40-45; studios €35-60. Cash only. ❷

Volcano Studios (☎22420 31 340), on the main road along the waterfront above the Volcano Cafe. Rents tasteful, freshly painted studios with complete kitchens, sitting areas, and ocean views; some have a balconies overlooking the water. Wheelchair-accessible. Singles €25-40; doubles €35-40. Cash only. ❷

Hotel Romantzo (☎22420 31340; www.nisyros-romantzo.gr), behind the Three Brothers. Freshly painted rooms with wooden furniture open onto the upstairs terrace, with an amazing vista. Clean baths and monogrammed sheets. The cafe downstairs serves a €4 yogurt breakfast. Wheelchair-accessible. Singles €20-35; doubles €30-50. Cash only. ❶

FOOD

Restaurants with similar menus and prices line the waterfront, mostly catering to daytrippers. Smaller, more affordable cafes in the *plateia* are more popular with locals.

■ **Restaurant Irini** (☎22420 31 365), in the *plateia*. Draws locals with reasonably-priced dishes made exclusively with ingredients from the island. Pass through the kitchen and take a peek at the grilled special or try delicious fresh cheese, straight from the farm (€3). Irini's newly opened cafe next door offers desserts for €2-2.50. Wheelchair-accessible. Open daily 9am-late. Cash only. ❶

Kalikatsu (☎22420 31 509), on the waterfront, just before Provezo Internet Cafe. Lunch on delicious *pitia* (local specialty chickpea patties, €4) and seafood pasta (€13) at this restaurant formerly known as Tony's Tavern. Don't forget to ask the amiable manager Renata for some travel tips. Wheelchair-accessible. Open daily noon-4pm and 7pm-late. Cash only. ❷

Restaurant Kleanthis (☎22420 31 484), far down along the waterfront. Appetizing *mezedes*, shellfish entrees, and a variety of Nisyrian seafood dishes. Fish soup €6. Wheelchair-accessible. Open daily noon-5pm and 8pm-late. Cash only. ❷

Cafe Alexandros (☎22420 31 031), next door to Volcano Cafe. If you're craving a more substantial breakfast (i.e., not just toast) but don't want to break the bank, hit up this cafe. Delicious eggs and bacon €3. Cappuccinos €2.50. Wheelchair-accessible. Open 9am-late. Cash only. ❶

◢ BEACHES

The black pebble beach of **Hohlaki** is a short walk from the end of the waterfront road along a beautifully striped coastal footpath. **White Beach,** on the road to Pali just past Loutra, is also almost entirely black despite its name. Dust from nearby pumice quarries once gave the pebbly beach a pale top layer, but now that the quarries are inactive, the beach's natural dark color has returned. Sandy, picturesque **Lies,** 3km east of Pali, is the island's optimal tanning spot, just over the hill and within walking distance from the locally favored **Pachy Amos.** If there is sufficient demand, Enetikon Travel runs boats (€8 round-trip) to the beaches of **Yali,** a small island nearby with pumice stone quarries. Otherwise, the best way to reach these beaches is by moto.

◢ DAYTRIPS FROM MANDRAKI

■**MANDRAKI VOLCANO.** Thanks to the pungent sulfur and bright yellow-brown chemical deposits, Mandraki's enormous **Stefanos Crater** looks and smells like a giant fried egg, and a not very appealing one at that. If you're lucky, you'll get to witness some mild volcanic action: steam occasionally hisses from the chalk-white earth, and yellow sulfur crystals grow on the rims of numerous, bubbling pits. Usually, however, the volcano lies dormant. No special safety precautions are necessary, though a bottle of water and a pair of sturdy shoes wouldn't hurt—the ground is boiling hot, the 10min. walk into the crater is steep and rocky, and the snack bar is a long way back up the trail. The volcano has been inactive since its 1872 eruption, though geologists have determined that it is responsible for a number of earthquakes. A 10min. walk along the trail behind the snack bar leads to nearby **Polyvotis and Alexandros craters,** virtually unvisited but no less spectacular because of it. Two different routes lead from the volcano back to Mandraki; ask for a walking map at Enetikon Travel. Both walks afford impressive views of the mountains and sea; neither is difficult, and each takes about 2hr. to complete. *(Municipal bus from Mandraki drops off in the nearby town Emborios, from which the crater is a 4km hike. €2. Excursion (€7, admission included) buses carrying daytrippers to the crater itself leave regularly from the harbor throughout the day.)*

MONASTERY OF OUR LADY SPILLANI. This quaint, whitewashed 17th century church sits atop a massive cliff overlooking Mandraki, with exhilarating views of the sea, mountains, and the town itself. Among the many silver-framed idols and hanging incense-burners lies a portrait of **St. Nikolaos,** recently discovered by an altar boy on the rear face of an icon that had been covered with an old cloth for over two centuries. On your way up to the monastery, you'll pass tiny cells carved into the rock face, once used to house anti-Turkish artillery. To get there, make your way down the waterfront toward the cliff and make a left when the road ends. You'll pass the **Church Museum** on your left; then make a right on the first street. On your right, you'll find a small sign pointing toward the monastery leading up a stone staircase between two houses. *(Monastery open daily 10am-3pm. Donations welcome. Modest dress required. Church Museum open M-F 10am-3pm. €2.)*

KOS Κώς

More relaxed than Rhodes but more exciting than most other islands in the Dodecanese, Kos is famous for its medical history and booming nightlife. Antiquity best knew Kos as the sacred land of Asclepius, god of healing, and the birthplace of Hippocrates, father of Western medicine. Today, Kos attracts young people from across the globe with its endless stretches of beaches and exciting nightlife in places like Kos Town and Kardamena. Don't forget to pray to Asclepius to repair your liver after 2-for-1, all-night Happy hour. Travelers wary of parties or looking for a day off can relax amid the beautiful cliffs and fields dotted by ruins and blue-roofed chapels.

KOS TOWN
☎22420

Radiating from the jumbled ruins at the heart of the city, Kos Town's beaches and pubs remain the city's main attractions. A young crowd arrives each summer to explore the beaches and unkempt ruins by day and hit up the bustling bar scene by night. Visitors can experience Kos Town's cocktail of liquor, lights, and lovin' at the seemingly endless row of bars and clubs that line the beachside streets in the north part of the city or Nafkilrou Street just off the Harbor.

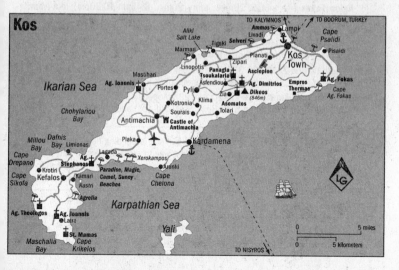

Hippocrates built history's first hospital at the nearby Asclepion; a visit to this tranquil site might cure the hangover developed overnight.

TRANSPORTATION

Flights: Kos International (Hippocrates) Airport (KGS; ☎22420 56000). **Olympic Airways,** Vas. Pavlou 22 (☎22420 51 567 or 22420 28 331). Multiple daily flights to Athens (from €120). Open M-F 8am-2:30pm.

Ferries: Schedules differ among companies and with the season; check at a travel agency. A **Blue Star** office (☎22420 28 914) sits on the waterfront between Ioannidi and Vas. Pavlou. To: **Astypalea** (4hr., 1 per week); **Kalymnos** (1hr., 3 per week); **Katapota** (7hr., 2 per week); **Leros** (3hr., 3 per week); **Nisyros** (2hr., 2 per week); **Patmos** (3hr., 3 per week); **Piraeus** (11-15hr., daily); **Rhodes** (4hr., daily); **Santorini** (4hr., 4 per week); **Syros** (5hr., 3 per week); **Tilos** (3hr., 2 per week). Boats also run to **Bodrum,** Turkey every morning (20min.; round-trip €20, including port tax).

Flying Dolphins: To: **Kalymnos** (40min., daily); **Leros** (1½hr., daily); **Lipsi** (2hr., M-Tu and Th-Su 1 per day); **Patmos** (2hr., Tu-Su 1 per day); **Samos** (5hr., daily, €25). **Dodecanisos Seaways** to: **Halki** (2hr., daily); **Kalymnos** (40min., daily); **Leros** (1½hr., daily); **Lipsi** (2hr., M-Tu and Th-Su 1 per day); **Nisyros** (45min., daily); **Patmos** (2hr., Tu-Su 1 per day); **Rhodes** (2½hr., daily); **Symi** (1hr., Tu-Su 1 per day); **Tilos** (1½ hr., daily).

Trains: Blue mini-trains go from the EOT to **Asclepion** (15min., Tu-Su every hr. 10am-6pm, round-trip €5). Citywide tours on a green mini-train leave every 30min. 10am-5pm from the waterfront train stop (€4).

Intercity Buses: (☎22420 22 292). Leave from the intersection of Kleopatras and Pissandrou. Buses run M-Sa with reduced service Su to: **Antimachia** (40min., 4 per day 9:10am-9pm); **Asfendiou-Zia** (40min., 3 per day 7am-1pm); **Kardamena** (45min., 6 per day 9:10am-9pm); **Kefalos-Paradise** (1hr., 6 per day 9:10am-9pm); **Marmari** (35min., 12 per day 9am-11pm); **Mastihari** (45min., 7 per day 9:10am-9pm); **Pyli** (30min., 4 per day 7am-3pm); **Tigaki** (30min., 12 per day 9am-11pm). Schedules change monthly and are posted by the bus stop and at the EOT; buy tickets on board or get a 20% discount by purchasing beforehand at the bus kiosk.

Local Buses: A. Koundourioti 7 (☎22420 26 276), on the water. Fares run €0.70-1.20. To: **Agios Fokas** (#1 and 5, 20min., every 20min. 6:45am-10:30pm); **Ika-Abavris-Ag. Nektarios** (#6, 11 per day 7:50am-9:15pm); **Lampi** (#2, 10min., every 40min. 6:30am-11pm); **Messaria** (#4, 10min., 15 per day 8am-10pm); **Paradisi-Kako Prinari** (#7, 8 per day 10am-10pm); **Platani** (#6 or 8, 5min., 20 per day 8am-9:30pm); **Therma** (#5, 20min., every 15 min. 6:45am-11pm).

Taxis: Radio Taxi (☎22420 22 333) has a kiosk and 24hr. cabs near the inland end of the Avenue of Palms, just after A. Koundourioti splits. To the airport €25. 24hr. min. €5.

Rentals: Mike's, 20 Amerikis (☎22420 21 729). Mopeds €9-15 per day. Bikes €2-4 per day. Open M-Sa 9am-2pm and 5:30-8pm, Su 10am-1pm and 6-8pm.

 I WANT TO RIDE MY BICYCLE. Kos is building new bike paths all over the city, so the fastest and easiest way to get around is to rent a bike. Perfect for those who crave speed but haven't yet worked up the courage for a scooter, bikes can be found for around €4 in most places that rent *motos*.

ORIENTATION AND PRACTICAL INFORMATION

The coastal roads (Zouroudi in the northwest; Akti Koundourioti curving around the harbor; and both Akti Miaouli and Vasileos Georgiou B' to the southeast, past the castle) are lined with standard theme bars and souvenir

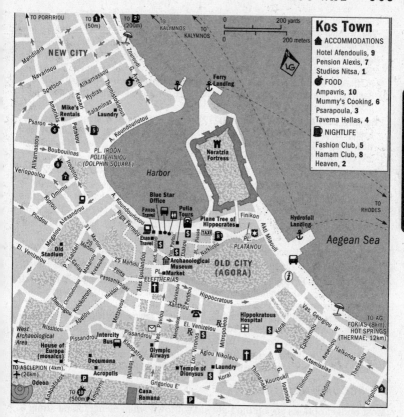

Kos Town

🏠 ACCOMMODATIONS

Hotel Afendoulis, **9**
Pension Alexis, **7**
Studios Nitsa, **1**

🍴 FOOD

Ampavris, **10**
Mummy's Cooking, **6**
Psarapoula, **3**
Taverna Hellas, **4**

🌙 NIGHTLIFE

Fashion Club, **5**
Hamam Club, **8**
Heaven, **2**

stands. On **Vasileos Pavlou,** just off A. Koundourioti, is a practical group of travel agencies, banks, and 24hr. ATMs. The town center is **Plateia Eleftherias,** just a bit farther inland, where you'll find the Archaeological Museum, a large market, and some nondescript cafes. Off the *plateia*, a plethora of pubs pack together on the cobblestone streets branching off **Nafklirou (Bar Street),** where the rollicking night kicks off in Kos Town. Nafklirou borders the ancient agora, and culminates at the gigantic Plane Tree of Hippocrates and the well-preserved Fortress of the Knights of Saint John. Heading south on Vas. Pavlou takes you to **Grigoriou E',** with the Odeon, Altar of Dionysus, and House of Europa. The club scene continues along the beachside bars of **Zouroudi.**

Tourist Office: ◼**EOT,** Vas. Georgiou B' 1 (☎22420 24 460; www.kosinfo.gr). Free maps, hotel review booklets, and info on upcoming events and opportunities on the island. Open M-F 7:30am-3pm.

Budget Travel: Many travel services line the waterfront and side streets, though some do not cover all the ferry lines. **Fanos Travel,** 11 Akti Kountouriotou (☎22420 20 035), on the waterfront, 1 block west of the city bus stop. Sells ferry and air tickets and offers car rental (from €30), motorbike rental, **currency exchange,** excursion booking, and internet. Open 8am-10pm. MC/V. **Exas Travel Service,** 4 Ant. Ioannidi (☎22420 29 900; www.exas.gr) provides schedules for all lines and books tickets for GA Ferries,

Catamaran Dodecanisos Express, and other air and sea lines. Open daily 9am-10pm. MC/V. **Pulia Tours,** Vas. Pavlou 3 (☎/fax 22420 26 388). Offers ferry schedules and can book tickets and arrange excursions to Turkey. Open daily 7am-11pm.

Banks: Banks line A. Koundouriotou between And. Ioannidi and Pl. Plessa, many offering **24hr. ATMs. Alpha Bank,** Koundourioti 5 (☎22420 27 487), between Vas. Pavlou and Al. Diakou. **American Express** and **currency exchange.** Open M-Th 8am-2:30pm, F 8am-2pm. After banking hours, you can exchange currency at virtually any travel agency along the waterfront.

Laundry: Easy Laundry (☎22420 29 172), on Themistokleous. Wash and dry €6. Discounts for those working in Kos Town. Open daily 9am-8pm. **Happy Wash Laundry Service** (☎22420 23 424), on Mitropoleos. Wash and dry €6. Will iron for an additional fee. Open M-F 9am-9pm, Sa 9am-6pm.

Emergency: ☎22420 22 100. For an ambulance, call the hospital at ☎22420 22 300.

Police: A. Miaouli 2 (☎22420 22 100 or 22 222). In the big, white building next to the castle. Some English spoken. **Tourist Police** (☎22420 26 129), upstairs in the same building. Open daily 7am-2pm.

Pharmacy: On almost every major street. 1 is at the corner by the hospital at El. Venizelou 2 (☎22420 26 426). Open M, W, F 8am-1:30pm and 5-9pm.

Medical Services: Hippocratous 34 (☎22420 22 300). Some English spoken. Open 24hr.

Telephones: OTE (☎22420 23 499), at Lor. Vironos and Xanthou. Open M-F 7:30am-3pm.

Internet Access: Expect to pay around €2 per hr. **Factori,** Meg. Alexandrou 36 (☎22420 25 644) offers 24hr. internet and gaming options. Fast connections with special rates for extended periods. €1.50 per hr., €3 per 3hr., €5 per 8hr. Open 24hr. **Jackson's Beach Bar** (☎22420 30 122), on G. Averof. Pool tables and relaxed beach atmosphere. Internet €3 per hr. Open 9am-2am. **De Haven Cafe** (☎22420 26 898), on the waterfront. €3 per hr. Open daily 10am-midnight.

Post Office: Vas. Pavlou (☎22420 22 250). From El. Venizelou, walk 1 block inland. Open M-F 7:30am-2pm. Western Union available. **Postal Code:** 85300.

ACCOMMODATIONS

Most budget options are on the right side of town when facing inland along **G. Averof.** Kos's dock hawks are notoriously aggressive and in most cases should be avoided; if you do choose to haggle, ask for a business card, and insist on seeing the room before you hand over any dough. If possible, try to stay at either Pension Alexis or Hotel Afendoulis; they are run by a brother and sister who seem to have hospitality encoded in their DNA. Those interested in camping should inquire at the EOT for information on open campsites.

▨ **Pension Alexis,** Irodotou 9 (☎22420 28 798). From the port, head inland on Meg. Alexandrou and take the 1st right onto Irodotou. Motherly Sonia knows everybody in town and offers excellent transportation advice, restaurant recommendations, and insiders' tips on Kos. Spacious doubles with funky wallpaper share spotless bathrooms and wrap-around balconies with views. The breezy patio overlooking the scenic garden is the perfect place to swap travel stories. If all rooms are full, Sonia will help arrange other accommodations or finagle a price break at her brother Alexis's elegant Hotel Afendoulis. A/C €3. Breakfast €5. Laundry €5. Singles €25-30; doubles €30-40; triples €45-55; quads €60-65. Cash only. ❷

▨ **Hotel Afendoulis,** Evripilou 1 (☎22420 25 321). From Vas. Georgiou B', take a right on Evripilou. Owner Alexis's mantra is "everybody must be happy," and it is rare that guests leave his hotel any other way. Alexis will pick you up from the port and offer you a tour of the island or join you for a delicious breakfast featuring home-made fig marmalade. Each double has A/C, bath, TV, fridge, and balcony. Fully stocked kitchen and Wi-Fi from a sunny, indoor terrace are bonuses. Breakfast €5. Laundry €5. Singles €20-35; basement €25-30; doubles €25-45; triples €40-55; quads €54-65. MC/V. ❷

Studios Nitsa, Averof 47 (☎22420 25 810). Take Averof inland from A. Koundourioti. Large studios each come loaded with fridge, kitchenette, bath, TV, A/C and balcony overlooking the street. Only 50m from the beach and close to the nightlife, this is a good choice for those planning to paint the town red. Wi-Fi. Singles €20-30; doubles €30-40. Cash only. ❷

🍴 FOOD

The *tavernas* along the waterfront are largely overpriced and variable in quality. For the best value, go at least one block inland to get away from the crowds. A good rule of thumb: if a place has more than 20-30 tables, it's probably best to avoid it.

🏴 **Mummy's Cooking** (☎22420 28 525), 1 block down Bouboulinas from the Dolphin Roundabout. A pleasant mix of locals and tourists stream in to enjoy the delicious homemade food. Plenty of vegetarian options. Mummy's hospitable son Ilias will happily decode Greek menu items and provide suggestions. Appetizers €3-6. Entrees €6-8. Open M-Sa 7am-midnight. Cash only. ❷

Ampavris (☎22420 25 696), a 15min. walk up Ampavris. Homemade Greek dishes are authentic, delicious, and definitely worth the trek down an otherwise deserted street. The menu itself takes a refreshing educational spin, featuring small lessons on Greek language, music, and religion so you can learn while you wait. Grilled salmon with salad, €12. Ask about daily *mezedes* options. Entrees €7-10. Open daily 6pm-midnight. Cash only. ❷

Psarapoula, G. Averof 17 (☎22420 21 909), inland from the far end of the port. Run by matronly Poula and her family, this local favorite serves a wide range of seafood and Greek specialties on a quaint nautical-themed patio. Seafood entrees €7-14. Open daily noon-late. MC/V. ❸

The Village Taverna, 14 Meg. Alexandrou (☎22420 26 538). Reasonable prix-fixe menu options on a pleasant leafy terrace 2 blocks from the harbor. 3-course meal €9.90. Open daily 11am-late. Cash only. ❷

Ouzerie Hellas, Amerikis 13 (☎69960 14 547), down the street from Pension Alexis at Amerikis. This *ouzerie* is a great budget option for a light dinner or aperitif. Special deal on delicious *mezedes:* 4 *meze* for €10. Delicious baked feta €3. Open daily noon-midnight. Cash only. ❷

🔵 SIGHTS

🏛**NERATZIA FORTRESS.** This magnificent fortress, built by the Knights of St. John in the 14th century, greets ships as they glide into the harbor. It is only accessible via a bridge from the Plane Tree of Hippocrates; the bridge once stretched across an outer moat filled with seawater and could draw back to cut the castle off entirely from the mainland. A second construction phase in the late 15th century added the distinctive stout towers and elaborate double walls. Unlike the ruins to the city's south, the fortress remains incredibly well-preserved and is one of the best examples of medieval architecture in all of Greece. Make like the knights and patrol the tops of the exterior walls for unbeatable views from the former lookouts and weaponry holes. Don't forget to poke through the piles of sculpture fragments to find some truly remarkable pieces. (☎22420 27 927. Open M 1:30-8pm, Tu-Su 8am-8pm. Last entry at 7:30pm. €3, students €2, EU students and under 19 free.)

ARCHAEOLOGICAL MUSEUM. Fall head over heels for the collection of headless marble statues at the Archaeological Museum in Pl. Eleftherias. An imposing fourth-century depiction of Hippocrates graces the northwestern room, and a Roman mosaic depicting Asclepius's arrival on Kos can be found in the central courtyard. The beautiful but manageable collection does not overwhelm visitors. (☎ 22420 28 326. *Open M 1:30-8pm, Tu-Su 8am-8pm. Last entry 7:30pm. €3, students €2, EU students and budding archaeologists free.*)

PLANE TREE OF HIPPOCRATES. Off Pl. Platanou, the Plane Tree of Hippocrates, allegedly planted by the great physician 2400 years ago, has grown to an enormous 12m in diameter. While it is alluring to envision Hippocrates teaching and writing beneath its noble foliage, the tree is actually only 500 years old.

RUINS. Along, Grigorio E, the west archaeological area's **House of Europa** contains well-preserved floor mosaics, one depicting Europa's abduction by Zeus in the sneaky guise of a bull. Across the street, wander along the semi-circle of seats at the 3rd-century **odeon** (Roman theater). One block east on the same side of the street, the **Casa Romana villa** is a restored house from the Roman times. Among Kos's Roman ruins stands a desolate pair of Corinthian columns and the scattered remains of what was once a lively agora in the fourth century BC. In the heart of the Old City, the uninspiring field of broken masonry is little more than a jumble of stones amid unruly weeds. Other poorly tended ruins include the **Temple of Dionysus** on Grigoriou E.

🎵 🎭 ENTERTAINMENT AND NIGHTLIFE

On Vas. Georgiou, **Orfeas** (☎ 22420 25 713) is an open-air cinema which shows films during the high season. Ask at the EOT or call the cinema for the schedule. Young crowds are drawn to the exuberant nightlife in Kos Town, which satisfies every taste with its luxurious lounges, disco-pumping nightclubs, and standard pubs. By 11pm, the crowds converge on **Nafklirou** in the Old City and between **Averof** and **Zouroudi** in the New City, and the scene doesn't die down until dawn. Clubs and bars produce an endless supply of live entertainment, themed nights, and half-liter sized drinks to keep up the fun. Expect to pay €3-6 for a beer and €6-8 for mixed drinks.

Heaven (☎ 22420 23 874). Follow Zouroudi north past the end of the string of bars; Heaven is on the left. Guest DJs let loose in the sleek club room, and patrons lounge and dance around the outdoor pool. Luxurious, canopy-covered sofas with an ocean view provide an excellent spot to sip a drink. Beers €4-6. Mixed drinks €8. Open M-Th and Su 10am-4am, F-Sa 10am-6am. Clubs open at midnight. Cash only.

Grabbarna Graus, Dimokritou 6 (☎ 22420 26 435; www.grabbarnagraus-kos.com), on the beach off Averof. Relax with a beer (€3-4) on the beach and chat with the friendly owner or else people-watch. Open daily 11am-midnight. Cash only.

Heart Rock (☎ 69442 11 395; www.heartrock.gr), on Nafklirou. Top 40 tunes keep bodies dancing all night. 2 mixed drinks €7. Free shots all night. Tu ladies' night. Open daily 8pm-5am. Cash only.

Camelot Club (☎ 6977976890) on Nafklirou. The cheapest bar on bar street makes up for what it lacks in fun atmosphere in prices. 3 beers €5. 2-for-1 mixed drinks. 1 beer and 1 tequila €4. Open daily 9pm-dawn. Cash only.

Hamam Club, Nafklirou 1 (☎ 22420 24 938), inland from the Pl. Diagoras taxi station in the Old City. A local crowd lounges outside under the palm trees, listening to covers of popular tunes until the club opens at midnight, when Greek and American hits echo in the former Turkish bath. Happy hour 9pm-midnight; 2-for-1 drinks. 9pm-midnight. Open daily 9pm-late. Cash only.

▶ DAYTRIP FROM KOS TOWN

▨THE ASCLEPION

About 4km southwest of Kos Town. Take a 15min. ride on the blue mini-train to get there in summer (€5, every hr.). By bike or moped, follow the sign west off the main road and go straight. ☎22420 28 763. Open in summer M 1:30pm-8pm, Tu-Su 8am-8pm; in winter Tu-Su 8am-2:30pm. Last entry 7:30pm. €4, students €2.

Nestled in a cyprus forest on the mountainside with a serene view of the island, the Asclepion was an ancient sanctuary devoted to Asclepius, god of healing. In the fifth century BC, Hippocrates founded the world's first medical school and hospital on Kos, forever changing the course of science. Combining early priests' techniques with his own, Hippocrates made the island ancient Greece's leading medical center. Present-day doctors still travel here to take the Hippocratic oath and pay homage, and visitors are rewarded with a sense of serenity outside hectic Kos Town.

Most of the ruins date from the second and third centuries BC. The complex was built on three levels, called *andirons*, which were carved into a hill overlooking Kos Town, the Aegean, and the coast of Turkey. Trees dot each level, providing much-needed shade and creating pleasant areas to gaze at the view. The lowest *andiron* holds a complex of third-century Roman baths, which once had a *natatio* (swimming pool), *tepidarium* (lukewarm pool), and *caldarium* (sauna). It also contained the medical school and the anatomy and pathology museums. Elegant second-century columns remain standing on the second level, which once boasted temples to Asclepius and Apollo. The 60-step climb to the third *andiron* leads to the remnants of the main **Temple of Ascleplus** and an unbelievable view of the site, the town below, and Asia Minor across the sea. Although the temple is remarkably preserved, much of its structure is gone, recycled by the Knights of St. John to build Kos Castle. The spectacular view and what remains of the once-grand layout, however, are still very impressive. Reenactments of the Hippocratic oath are performed once a week in the summer; ask at the EOT for the schedule.

KALYMNOS Κάλυμνος

Kalymnos is most famous for its stunning landscape. Statuesque mountains slope onto purple-tinted meadows, punctuated with cliffs framing serene, blue-green beaches. Most travelers come here for the excellent rock climbing and diving, but even less rugged visitors can appreciate Kalymnos's breathtaking beauty. Arrive at Pothia and get to the Western Coast as soon as you can to avoid the hectic traffic of the main port town. Though more heavily visited than its western neighbor Astypalea, Kalymnos manages to retain its small-island charm alongside all the conveniences of a tourist destination.

POTHIA Πόθια   ☎22430

Visitors pause in Pothia to stop and smell the exhaust fumes, then realize they should have kept going. A bustling port town, Pothia is loud, fast, and dirty. Most travelers can't wait to get to the quieter, more appealing parts of Kalymnos. To its credit, Pothia is an example of a Greek city that caters very little to tourists: locals are proud of their "real" Greek city. Unless you want to get run over by one of the city's many fast-moving garbage trucks, it's best to move on quickly.

▌▀ TRANSPORTATION

Flights: Argos Airport, 3km east of Pothia. To: **Athens** (30min., 8 per week). Inquire at **Magos Tours** (p. 369) for tickets.

Ferries: To: **Agathonisi** (6hr., 4 per week); **Arki** (5hr., 4 per week, €8.50); **Astypalea** (3hr., 4 per week); **Chios** (7hr., 1 per week); **Kos Town** (1hr., 3 per week); **Leros** (1hr., 4 per week); **Lipsi** (2hr., 4 per week); **Patmos** (4hr., 4 per week); **Piraeus** (9 hr., 2 per week); **Rhodes** (5hr., 3 per week); **Samos** (4hr., 4 per week).

Flying Dolphins: Daily to: **Kos** (30min.); **Leros** (40min.); **Lipsi** (1hr.); **Patmos** (1hr.); **Samos** (2hr.). The **Catamaran Dodecanisos Express** runs to: **Kos** (40min., 12 per week); **Leros** (1hr., 10 per week); **Lipsi** (2hr., 6 per week); **Patmos** (1hr., 6 per week); **Rhodes** (3hr., 12 per week); **Symi** (2hr., 10 per week).

Buses: Leave from just past the town hall in the harbor center (€0.60-1.50). M-Sa to: **Argos** (#4, 7:20am and 1:45pm); **Elies** (#2, 15 per day 7:30am-10pm); **Emporios** (50min., 9am and 3pm); **Chora** (#2, 15 per day 7:30am-10pm); **Kantouni** (#2, 20min., 15 per day 7:30am-10pm); **Limani** (#3, 12 per day 7:15am-7:30pm); **Massouri** (#1, 25min., 10 per day 6:50am-9:30pm); **Platy Gialos** (#4, 4 per day 8:45am-7:10pm); **Vlihadia** (#4, 8 per day 6:50am-8pm); **Vathi** (#5, 30min., 4 per day 6:30am-5pm). Check at the kiosk for updated schedules.

Excursion Boats: Round-trip Tu-Sa. Boats to: **Bodrum,** Turkey, via Kos (depart 7:35am; bus tour in Bodrum included); **Kos** (depart 7:35am); **Symi** (depart 9:10am); **Rodos** (depart 10am). Inquire at **Magos Tours** (☎22430 28 777) for more info.

Taxis: (☎22430 50 300), in Pl. Kyprou. 24hr. €7.50 to the airport.

Rentals: Similarly priced options line the waterfront and side streets. **Kostas Moto Rentals** (☎22430 50 110), behind the port authority under the church. €10-12 per day; insurance included. Open daily 9am-1pm and 2-9pm. **Spiros Kipreos** (☎22430 29 104), around Club Miami and upstairs. Cars from €25. Motorbikes €10-12. 21+. Open 9am-8pm. MC/V.

▌▐ ORIENTATION AND PRACTICAL INFORMATION

Ferries arrive at the far left end of the port (facing inland). The road from the dock bends around the waterfront and past the square at the far end, where the large, cream-colored municipal building, church, and Nautical Museum stand. Passing the municipal building to the right, the road continues along the coast to **Vathi.** Turning left just past the municipal building leads inland up the shop-lined Eleftherias to **Plateia Kyprou,** where you'll find the taxi stand and pay phones. Continue on Eleftherias to reach **Chorio, Myrties,** and **Massouri.** Internet is unavailable in most of the villages on the Western Coast, so check your email before you leave.

Tourist Office: Tourist kiosk (☎22430 50 879; www.kalymnos-isl.gr), at the end of the ferry docks. The English-speaking staff provides free maps and info on upcoming events, museums, and island-wide sites. Run by the **Municipal Tourist Organization** (☎22430 59 056), they can also help arrange accommodations and bargain with hostels. Open daily 8:30am-8:30pm.

Budget Travel: ▨**Magos Tours** (☎22430 28 777), on the main road next to Ciao Cafe, before the road curves to the right; look for the Blue Star Ferries sign. Sells airplane, ferry, hydrofoil, catamaran, and excursion tickets for all the islands. Offers 24hr. boat tickets. Open daily 9am-4pm and 5-10pm. **Kapellas Travel** (☎22430 29 265), next to Emporiki Bank, also sells ferry and flight tickets. Open daily 9am-1:30pm and 5:30-9pm.

Banks: Several banks line Patriachou Maximou. **National Bank** (☎22430 51 501) on the waterfront. **24hr. ATM** and **currency exchange.** Open M-Th 8am-2:30pm, F 8am-2pm. **Emporiki Bank** (☎22430 29 475), 1 block inland on the same street. **24hr. ATM** and **currency exchange.** Open M-Th 8am-2:30pm, F 8am-2pm.

Police: (☎22430 22 100). Go up Eleftherias and take the left fork at the taxi stand. In a blue and yellow building on the right.

Pharmacy: (☎22430 28 468), just behind Emporiki Bank. Offers homeopathic and allopathic cures. Open daily 8:30am-2pm and 5:30-9pm. More pharmacies line Eleftherias.

Hospital: (☎22430 23 025), on the main road to Chora, 3km from Pothia. Dial ☎22430 50 499 for an ambulance.

Internet Access: **Neon Internet C@fe** (☎22430 59 120) has 2 locations, though the waterfront one serves more as a late-night hangout. Head 2 blocks up from the bus stop on the street that runs parallel to the coastal road to get to the computer-filled alternative. Pool tables and €3 per hr. internet make this a popular stop for teenagers. Open daily 9am-1am. **Heaven Internet** (☎22430 50 444), closer to the ferry docks. Wi-Fi and high-speed access €3 per hr. Photo printing €2 per photo. Open daily 9am-1am.

Post Office: (☎22430 28 340), up Eleftherias, 200m past the police station on the right. **Western Union.** Open M-F 7:30am-2pm. **Postal Code:** 85200.

▮ ACCOMMODATIONS

Most of Pothia's accommodations are around the waterfront and offer similar prices. Other pensions in neighboring towns and beaches provide more amenities at the same price. Camping, though uncommon, is legal on all the island's beaches.

Hotel Therme (☎22430 29 425), above Cafe Kaiki on the waterfront. Spacious rooms with fridges, TVs, baths, and balconies overlooking the harbor. Singles €25; doubles €35. ❷

Hotel Panorama (☎22430 23 138). Follow the multiple yellow signs through the backstreets. Clean, simple rooms with baths, balconies, fridges, A/C, TVs, and Wi-Fi. The views of the town merit the trek up the hill. Singles €25; doubles €35. ❷

Pension Niki (☎22430 48 135). Niki's daughter Maria waits at the docks; if you don't see her, head inland at the National Bank and follow the road as it curves to the right, then take a slight left at the wedding dress shop. Follow the sign, which points down the side street. Spacious peach-colored rooms with TVs, fridges, A/C, baths, and huge breezy shared terraces. Singles €25. ❷

Greek House (☎22430 29 559), just off the waterfront. Enormous double-decker rooms with kitchenettes; all have tasteful wooden furniture, fridges, A/C, and baths. Though the treehouse-like stairs may be daunting, the view from the terrace at the top is worth the climb. If the Greek House is full, owner Papadi will help you find another room. Singles €25; doubles €30. ❷

■ FOOD

A number of *tavernas* and pizzerias line the waterfront, offering familiar Greek foods at similar prices.

O Stukas (☎69945 93 582), far down the waterfront. Popular with locals and tourists alike for its flavorful Greek dishes. Try the chick pea balls (€3.50). Appetizers €3-5. Entrees €6-8. Open 8am-2pm. Cash only. ❷

Oyzepi (☎22430 24 700), on the waterfront. Traditional Kalymnian oysters (€14) and an excellent deal on octopus balls (8 pieces for €5). Appetizers €3.50-5. Entrees €8-15. Open 6pm-late. Cash only. ❸

Kafenes (☎28 727). Locals admire this dockside eatery for its balls: crab balls, chick-pea balls and aubergine balls (all €5). If you're sick of spherical food, try the kalimari (€7). Appetizers €1.50-3. Fish €4-12. Open noon-midnight. Cash only. ❷

♫ ▣ ENTERTAINMENT AND NIGHTLIFE

Nightlife in Pothia is pretty low key. Locals prefer to sit by the harbor and sip coffee rather than dance until dawn.

Club Miami (☎22430 22 423). This harbor-side club is a young hangout, providing a place for conversation at the tables stretching nearly to the water's edge. Splurge on the Miami Special (€6), a mysterious and intoxicating concoction. Mixed drinks €5. Open daily 7am-2am. Cash only.

Neon Internet C@fe (☎22430 28 343), next door to Club Miami. This cafe is equally popular as its neighbor, though the drinks are slightly less pricey. Beer €2.50. Mixed drinks €3-4. Open daily 9:30am-late. Cash only.

Blue Note (☎22430 50 888), to the left of Hotel Olympiada when facing inland. Locals mingle beneath palm trees bathed in aquamarine light. Outside, the wood and steel tables are just removed enough to allow for cafe conversation. Head inside to try your luck on the dance floor, open only in winter. Mixed drinks €5. Open daily 9am-late. Cash only.

WESTERN COAST OF KALYMNOS

The majestic Western coast is the main draw of Kalymnos, boasting sapphire beaches, quiet mountain roads, and rock formations that look almost like giant natural sculptures. Mountaineers flock here to attempt some of the best climbing in the world, and it's easy to spot tiny climbers hanging off the massive amber cliffs. Cave exploring is also popular, as many mountains have interior caves with stalagmites perfect for climbing. Luckily, climbing is a big enough industry here to have well-marked trails and safe climbing equipment.

The road northwest of Pothia is lined with villages whose boundaries seem to flow into one another. No one village gets enough tourism to stick out more than any other: charming and affordable establishments dot the coastline. Some of the best rock climbing is in the mountains between Masouri and Armeos, where cliff faces are pocked with gargantuan caves. Nearly 20 climbing areas feature over 500 routes of varying levels of difficulty, ranging from level 4C to 9A. Maps of all the caves and detailed books cataloging all the climbs and their relative difficulties can be found in bookstores and supermarkets. (Call ☎22430 59 445 or see the tourist kiosk for more info.) The **Municipal Athletic Organization** (☎22430 51 601; www.kalymnos-isl.gr/climb) also provides useful information. Numerous hiking routes cover the island and its surrounding islets, providing the opportunity to walk through the mountains, along the coast, through gorges and orchards—or all of the above. Ask at the tourist kiosk for routes; maps can be purchased at a supermarket (€5-6).

MASSOURI
☎ 22430

Massouri is one of the more popular destinations for climbers: it's close to the best mountains and has the most active nightlife around to boot. Most visitors are tired from a hard day on the rocks, so you're unlikely to find large dance clubs here; most people prefer to hang out and swap stories at trekker-friendly pubs. The ever-lively Massouri beach stretches down the steep cliff below main street and is well-populated with sunbathers, volleyball players, and watersporting locals.

A number of accommodations hug the cliff above the main street; head 200m south past the bus stop, and make a left up the stairs a little past Igloo Cafe. Take the first left off the stairs and follow the path to its end at **Tina ❷**, where tiled, spacious rooms have kitchenettes, air-conditioning, and enormous balconies with views of Telendos island and the sea. Find friendly American expat owner Kelly at her restaurant on the main street below. (Singles €30; doubles €35-45. Extra bed €5. Rooms for up to 4 available.) For the best gyros on the island, try **Gyro Gyro Oli ❶**, on the first floor of Cristina Hotel. The sign is in Greek, so look out for Christna Hotel, or just follow your nose. (☎22430 48 785. Delivery available. Gyro pita €2. Souvlaki pita €2. Open 1pm-late. Cash only.) Climb up from the beach or down from the street to the tiki-inspired **Stavedo Beach Cafe ❶**, which prides itself on being the only bar that both serves meals and rents watersporting equipment (from €10). Breezes and percussion jazz make for a relaxed atmosphere. (☎22430 47 696; www.stavedo.com. Beer €3. Sandwiches from €2.50. Canoes €7. Windsurf boards €20. Jet ski €25. Open daily 10am-late. Cash only.) Facing the bus stop, walk up the main street to the right to get to **Ambiance Cafe Bar,** whose large circular bar and huge windows overlook the sea. (☎22430 47 882. Mixed drinks €4-5. Open daily 6pm-midnight. Cash only.)

The single paved road houses a line of bars and lounges, as well as places to rent scooters and climbing equipment. In the evening, grab the last bus from Pothia (9:30pm) or a cab (€7.50) to check out the cafe bars and beach scene.

The Chronicle

IN RECENT NEWS

ONE FISH, TWO FISH, RED FISH, STATUE FISH?

It's hard to dig a hole in Greece without coming across some antique ruin—but you don't expect to come across ancient statuary at sea. But for one Greek fisherman, a 2200 year-old bronze statue was the catch of the day. On March 18, 2009, a fisherman in the Aegean Sea thought he had caught a big fish in his net, but instead he brought up a post-Hellenistic statue.

The statue, which dates to the late second century BC, once represented a male horseback rider wearing elaborate breast armor over a short tunic and armed with a sheathed sword. The trunk of the horseman, encrusted in sea creatures, and his raised right arm survived and were found between the Dodecanese islands of Kos and Kalymnos, according to a statement from the Greek Ministry of Culture. The arm would have carried a sword in a scabbard engraved with celebratory scenes and an image of Nike, goddess of victory.

The fisherman turned the corroded metal figure over to authorities, who have begun the cleaning process before passing it on to specialists for further examination. The fisherman, presumably, got a new kind of bait.

DODECANESE

KANTOUNI ☎22430

The village of Kantouni, home to a popular beach south of Panormos, is a 30min. bus ride from Pothia. From the bus stop, follow the beach and clamber over the rocks for about 10min. to reach the relatively empty black sand beach of Plati Yialos, where you can catch the big waves that are absent at more tranquil beaches.

> **PEACE AND QUIET FOR POCKET CHANGE.** Want absolute silence? For €2-3, hop on a boat to vehicle-free, tranquil Telendos, an islet less than 1km away. Pristine pebble and sand beaches with nary a motorbike within earshot will revive even the most traffic-weary traveler. A few pensions and *tavernas* line the waterfront. Boats leave from Myrties every 30min. 6am-midnight. Call ☎69448 79 073 or 69490 28 564 to contact the boat captains.

A number of accommodations dot the cliffs above Plati Yialos. Take the cliffside road up 50m to reach ■**Sanmarkos ❷.** Tasteful but playfully decorated, these spacious suites come with kitchenettes, air-conditioning, baths, and balconies. Ask for the suite with the lofted canopy bed. (☎22430 47 654. Singles €20-35; doubles €35-50. Cash only.) Dine to the reggae beats at the open-air **Domus Restaurant and Bar ❷,** farther up the Kantouni beach. Sun-weary travelers kick back and play pool in this laid-back beach bar. (☎22430 47 760. Mixed drinks €4-5. Restaurant open daily 6:30pm-midnight. Bar open daily 11am-late. Cash only.) Popularly known as Cantena, **Rock & Blues ❷** next door has played just that since 1978. Grab a meal (€6-10) in the evening, and stick around to play darts and listen to international tunes all night. (Mixed drinks €5. Happy hour 8-9pm. Open daily 10am-4am. Cash only.) On the other end of the beach, **Cafe Del Mar,** partners with **Club Loca,** has blue-toned lounge chairs in a breezy spot by the ocean. (☎22430 47 047. Sandwiches €2.50. Crepes €3-4. Open daily 10am-late. Cash only.)

PATMOS Πάτμος

Patmos is unusually serene for the site of the Revelation of the Apocalypse (see St. John the Evangelist's Book of Revelation). The tranquil pebble beaches and simple waterside *tavernas* lend Patmos a sense of contentment, but the fortress-like Monastery of St. John at the top of the hill reminds pilgrims and Patmians alike of the island's unique history. Built in 1088 to house the monks of St. John, the pirate-proof monastery played a central role in Christian theology and Byzantine political history throughout the early part of the second millenium, earning Patmos the nickname, "Jerusalem of the Aegean." Locals claim that Patmos's religious character is most apparent around Easter, but everyone can appreciate the island's rugged beauty and friendly atmosphere any time of year.

SKALA Σκάλα ☎22470

Built along a graceful arc of coastline, the manageable port town of Skala is mirrored by a virtual city of yachts docked in the water; at night, the harbor seems to glitter with lights from land and sea. Town life stretches across the long waterfront strip, where bakeries, *ouzeria*, and *tavernas* lay nestled between night-and-day cafes. With its central location and easy access to most amenities, Skala is the most convenient place to stay on the island, although it's not as charming as medieval Chora. A 10min. bus or moped ride connects you with most major villages and sights, and a short walk brings you to the beach on the other side of the island.

TRANSPORTATION

Ferries: Tickets can be purchased at offices near the *plateia*. Blue Star tickets available at **Apollon Travel.** Check with a few different offices, since there is no central travel agency that carries all the lines. Ferries go to: **Arki** (1hr., 4 per week, €5); **Kalymnos** (3hr., 4 per week, €11.50); **Kos** (4hr., 3 per week, €14); **Leros** (1hr., daily, €8.50); **Lipsi** (1hr., 4 per week, €12.50); **Piraeus** (10-12hr., 3 per week, €33.50); **Rhodes** (8hr., 3 per week, €30); **Samos** (3hr., 4 per week, €8.50).

Catamarans: To: **Kalymnos** (Tu-Su daily); **Kos** (Tu-Su daily); **Leros** (Tu, €16); **Symi** (W-Su daily, €44); **Rhodes** (Tu-Su daily, €46).

Flying Dolphins: Depart at 9:15am and 5pm to: **Kalymnos** (1hr., €26); **Kos** (2hr., €39); **Leros** (50min., €16); **Lipsi** (20min., €15); **Samos** (2hr., €20).

Excursion boats: To **Fourni, Ikaria, Samos, Lipsi, Leros,** and **Psili Ammos,** among several other destinations; some boats offer round-the-island tours of Patmos. Check schedules and prices at the docks or call ☎69767 96 469.

Buses: Next to the Welcome Cafe at the ferry docks. To **Chora** (15min., 8 per day 7:40am-7:30pm, €1.40), **Grikos** (30min., 5 per day 9:15am-5:30pm, €1.30), and **Kampos** (20min., 4 per day 8:15am-6:30pm, €1.30). Purchase tickets on board.

Taxis: (☎22470 31 225). On the waterfront across from the post office. 24hr. €1 surcharge after midnight. €4.50 to Chora.

Rentals: Many car and motorbike rental agencies line the waterfront street. Rates spike July-Aug..; some agencies recommend reserving a car ahead of time for the summer season. Walk down the main street toward the OTE to find **Aris Rent a Car and Moto** (☎22470 32 542), on the left side of the street. Cars from €25 per day. Mopeds €8.50-15 per day. Open daily 8am-8pm. MC/V. **Rent A Car Patmos**(☎22470 32 203), on the 2nd fl. of the building just inland of the post office. Cars €25-35 per day, depending on the season. Open daily 8am-8pm. MC/V. **Motor Rent Express** (☎22470 32 088), next door to Rent a Car Patmos. 1-person motorbikes from €10. Larger mopeds €10-15 per day. Open daily 8am-8pm. MC/V.

ORIENTATION AND PRACTICAL INFORMATION

Skala's amenities are huddled around the **port** and extend along the waterfront road almost all the way to **Meloi Beach.** Excursion boats dock opposite the line of cafes and restaurants, while larger vessels dock near the Welcome Cafe, across from the Orthodox Information Center. The street heading inland from the main *plateia* is lined with cafes and tourist shops and leads to the OTE, ending at rocky **Holhaka Beach.** Facing the ferry docks, head left to **Meloi Beach** (15min. by foot) or right up to the monasteries of **Chora**(4km).

Tourist Office: Across from the taxi stand. Rarely staffed. Instead, head across from the Welcome Cafe to the new ▓**Orthodox Culture and Informational Center** (☎22470 33 316). Provides brochures, timetables, and advice on the island's hidden treasures. Offers interactive multimedia exhibits on Patmos's religious heritage. Open daily 9am-1pm and 5-9pm.

Budget Travel: All over the waterfront, though each only offers info for the ferry lines it works with. **Apollon Travel** (☎22470 31 324) sells hydrofoil, ferry, and airplane tickets, helps with accommodations and rentals, and exchanges currency. Open daily 8am-9pm. **G.A. Ferries** (☎22470 31 217), off the street leading to OTE. Open 9am-1pm and 5-9pm.

Banks: National Bank (☎22470 34 050), in the far end of the *plateia*. **Currency exchange** and **24hr. ATM.** Open M-Th 8am-2:30pm, F 8am-2pm. **Emporiki Bank** (☎22470 34 140), farther down the waterfront toward Meloi. **Currency exchange** and **24hr. ATM.** Also cashes traveler's checks (€6 per transaction; banknotes €3). Open M-Th 8am-2:30pm and F 8am-2pm.

Luggage Storage: Welcome Cafe (☎22470 31 583), next to the dock. Open 24hr. €1 per item.

Laundry: Meltani (☎22470 33 170). Wash and dry €10. Open 8:30am-7pm.

Showers: Internet Place (☎69737 45 253). Soap, shampoo, and towel rental €4. Internet €5 per hr., €3 per 30min. Open 8am-1pm and 5-8pm.

Police: (☎22470 31 303), in the large Italian building on the corner of the main *plateia*. Upstairs from the post office.

Pharmacy: A number of pharmacies surround the *plateia*. 1 can be found a block in from the water north of the *plateia* (☎22470 31 500). Open M-Tu and Th-F 9am-2pm and 5:30-9pm, W and Sa 9am-2pm and 7-9pm, Su 11:30am-1pm and 7-9pm.

Medical Center: (☎22470 31 211), 2km down the main road to Chora, across from Apokalipsi Monastery. Open daily 8am-2pm; 24hr. for emergency care.

Telephones: OTE (☎22470 31 399). Follow the road past Dodoni Internet Place. Open M-F 8am-1pm. The Welcome Cafe at the ferry dock has an international phone.

Internet Access: Igloo Cafe (☎22470 33 188), across from Welcome Cafe. €4.50 per hr.; min. €2. Open 8am-1am. **Dodoni Internet Place** (☎22470 32 202). Facing National Bank, head 1 block inland on the left street. Several computers, 1 with a webcam. Internet €4 per hr., min. €2. Pastries €1.50-2.30. Open 8am-midnight. **Meltemi Cafe** (☎22470 31 839) across from the harbor beach. Free Wi-Fi, even on the beach. Computers available for €4, min. €1. Open daily 9am-late.

Post Office: (☎22470 31 316), in the main *plateia*, across from the bus station. Open M-F 8am-2pm. **Postal Code:** 85500.

📷📷 ACCOMMODATIONS AND CAMPING

Domatia will run approximately €20-30 for singles and €30-35 for doubles. Leaving the docks, head about 400m to the right along the waterfront. A number of pensions and hotels are clustered a couple blocks inland. Stefanos, Katina, and Nikolas Studios all lie on the same plot of land about 700m from the town square; three cousins divided their grandfather's farmland into separate plots and each built a delightful pension. Beachside pensions lie by **Hohlaka Beach,** 200m beyond the OTE, heading inland from the port.

- 🏨 **Stefanos Studios** (☎22470 32 415), directly behind restaurant Remezzo. Spacious studios come with fully stocked kitchenettes, baths, A/C, TVs, and balconies overlooking the harbor, plus tasteful wooden furniture and super-comfortable beds. The lush garden offers zucchini, eggplants, pomegranates, and other seasonal fruits and vegetables which, combined with the kitchen, help minimize food costs. Find Stefanos at the campground; he also will gladly pick you up from the port. Singles €25-35; doubles €25-50. Cash only. ❷

- 🏨 **Stefanos Flower Camping at Meloi** (☎22470 31 821), 1.5km northeast of Skala. Follow the waterfront road along the port and all the way over the hill, taking the left fork to Meloi; or skip the walk and ask Stefanos for a ride. Jungle-like rows of tall grass divide the campground into lots, providing ample privacy and a neighborhood feel to the sprawling maze. On-site restaurant (cheeseburgers €3; grilled platters €6), book exchange, shared kitchen, clean showers, and hospitable managers. Restaurant open daily 9am-12:30am. Parking €1.50. Scooter rental €8-10 per day. Moped rental €1 per day. Open Apr.-Oct. €7 per person; €2 per tent. Cash only. ❶

Katina's Rooms for Rent (☎22470 31 327). Go inland to Argo gas station, continue 100m up and make a right, then continue for 50m. Simple whitewashed rooms have hand-embroidered pillowcases, fresh flowers, kitchens, A/C, and balconies; some have canopy beds. Friendly Katina will offer you snacks and desserts, and even pick you up at the port. Singles €20-25; doubles €25-35. Cash only. ❶

Studios Nikolas (☎22470 31 876), behind Stefanos Studios. Clean white rooms with baths and refrigerators, plus internet in the social common room. Owner Nikolas can show you how to eat a sea urchin, or his wife Theologia will cook you a traditional Greek meal that you can eat with their family. Singles €25-30; doubles €35-50. Cash only. ❷

Pension Sydney's (☎22470 31 689). Take a left 1 block past the electric company and head 150m uphill; it's on the left. Comfortable, whitewashed rooms have tiled baths, A/C, and balconies overlooking the mountains. The gracious owner Dimitrios shares drinking water, house wine, and advice on the island's many restaurants. Rooms €20-45. Cash only. ❷

🔌 FOOD

Patmos seafood is so fresh it's practically still swimming. Local recipes tend to be simple in order to emphasize the flavor of the fish. Side-street *tavernas* with penciled-in prices often offer the freshest seafood at the lowest prices. Don't be daunted by the per kg price for fish: a typical serving is about 250g.

▣ Chiliomodi (☎22470 34 080), past Koukoumavla on the opposite side of the side street; look for the Greek sign. This small restaurant has earned a stellar reputation among locals for its fresh fish lightly cooked in olive oil, lemon juice, and spices. The assorted grilled fish platter (€9) comes heaped with 4 whole fish, pleasing discerning palates and ravenous appetites. The complimentary fruit plate makes for a sweet finish. Open daily 7pm-late. Cash only. ❷

To Kyma (☎22470 31 192), next to Meloi Beach, on Aspiris Bay. The 2km walk from town makes for a pleasant evening stroll. Follow the waterfront road around the port and up the hill; when you start descending, take the right fork at the sign and continue another 200m to the bay. Fresh fish hot off the charcoals (€30-50 per kg) and seating inches from tranquil water. Open daily 6pm-1am. Cash only. ❷

Loukas Taverna (☎22470 32 515), across from the OTE. Serves a variety of standard Greek favorites on a comfortable outdoor terrace. Watch the pig twirl on a spit, and if that doesn't do it for you, try a vegetarian entree (€4-5). Appetizers €4-6. Entrees €5-7. Open daily noon-4:30pm and 6pm-midnight. Cash only. ❶

Remezzo (☎22470 31 553), at the foot of the hill on the road to Meloi. The house specialty, chicken with prunes and orange sauce (€9.50), is a work of art. Complimentary Patmian almond cake from a generations-old recipe will leave you with a sweet taste in your mouth. Open daily noon-2am. Cash only. ❷

🔊 NIGHTLIFE

While Patmos's monastic pilgrims tend to be a high-minded set, the local youth also get their share of earthly pleasures, though nightlife here is tamer than on other islands. Waterside cafes stay open late as locals and travelers linger on the beaches studded with lights, talking and drinking long into the night.

DODECANESE

⊠ **Koukoumavla** (☎22470 32 325; www.patmos-island.com/koukoumavla). Facing inland from the Welcome Cafe, head to the left and take the 1st right up a side street; it is on the left. The free-spirited owner sells the handmade books, purses, and puppets on display in this funky cafe, while her Italian husband whips up flavored coffees (€3-4) and mixed drinks (€4-8) at the hand-finished bar. Patrons can play board games in bohemia or head outside to the shaded garden of colorfully painted furniture and toys. Large pressed sandwiches €2-4.50. Open daily 11am-2am. Cash only.

Alpha Club (☎69753 62 343), down a side street behind the post office. Colorful lights and tealight candelabras cast mysterious shadows on the stone walls and arches of Skala's most popular club. Locals and tourists dance to Greek, Latin, House, and R&B until dawn. Mixed drinks €5-7. Beer €5. Open daily 10pm-late. Cash only.

⊠ DAYTRIPS FROM SKALA

⊠CHORA Χώρα

Chora is 4km from Skala, a trip you can tackle by bus (15min., 8 per day, €1.40), taxi (€4.50), or foot. The hike down along the easily-found foot and donkey paths affords unparalleled views of the entire island. Buses to Grikou also depart from the hilltop bus stop (15min., 5 per day, €1.30).

The serenity of the monastery atop the hill diffuses through the sloped and crooked streets of Chora, while the intricate maze of white houses defies even the most adept cartographers. Built in the 11th century to house the workers who built the monastery, Chora's quiet medieval atmosphere remains unspoiled by the modern tourists who trickle through. Monastery workers enjoyed the first two-day weekends in recorded history on these winding streets, perhaps taking in the unparalleled views of the Patmian coastline.

Even nonreligious visitors can appreciate the **Monastery of Saint John the Theologian** for its breathtaking frescoes, austere architecture, and panoramic views, not to mention the extensive collection of Byzantine artifacts in the ⊠**Treasury Museum.** The monastery's turreted walls and imposing gateway make it look more like a fortress than a place of worship, but the pirate-proof exterior conceals serene chapels and graceful courtyards in the interior. Built in 1088 by St. Christodoulos to commemorate the holiness of the site of the Revelation, the monastery was the first project in history to allow workers a two-day weekend to spend with their families. Around the main courtyard's holy well, the walls are covered with intricate mosaics and 17th-century frescoes, including one portraying St. John's duel of faith with Kinopas, a priest of Apollo. The excellent Treasury Museum preserves 33 original pages from the Gospel of St. Mark, making it the second-largest collection of such original holy written word in the world—though only one page is displayed. Two floors of glass cases with detailed English placards guard 12th-century icons, ornate ceremonial jewels, renowned works of 11th-century Cretan art, and a seventh-century Book of Job. Look for Helkomenos, an icon painted by El Greco, near the end of the exhibit. (☎22470 20 800. Monastery and treasury open M, W, F-Sa 8am-1:30pm; Tu, Th, Su 8am-1:30pm and 4-6pm. Modest dress required; shawls provided. Monastery free. Treasury €6, students €3. Ask at the gift shop about the daily 3pm services.)

The monastery holds 10 chapels within its walls. The **Chapel of the Virgin Mary,** adjacent to the main chapel, is covered with 12th-century frescoes that lay hidden behind the wall until they were exposed by the 1956 earthquake. Up the right side of the hill from the bus stop, follow the white signs to the **Convent of Zoodochos Pege,** where a new museum hosts a number of religious icons and artifacts. The church has a number of beautiful frescoes, including one of the Panagia which, seen from the right, appears to have three eyes. Legend has it that the icon disappeared in 1956 to help cure a sick Patmos woman, returning three days later with an additional eye. (☎22470 31 256. Chapel and museum open M-Sa 10am-noon. Modest dress required. Chapel free. Museum €3.)

A short 2km hike down the road leads to the **Apocalypsis Monastery,** built on the site where St. John stayed while on Patmos from AD 94-97. Head downstairs to the **Sacred Grotto of the Revelation,** adjacent to the **Church of Saint Anne,** where the Apocalypse was revealed to St. John. The power of God is said to have caused the cracks in the walls of the cave as St. John, stricken to the ground in shock, received the book of Revelation. (☎22470 31 234. Open M, W, F-Sa 8am-1:30pm; Tu, Th, Su 8am-1:30pm and 4-6pm. Modest dress required.)

If the monasteries have filled your religious quota but left your stomach empty, try popular (and well-signed) **Vagelis Restaurant ❷,** in the central *plateia*. The cooks whip up a mean eggplant salad (€4) and *rebetiko* (rolled roast pork; €10). Try the Patmos goat (€10). Follow the signs branching off the road to the monastery. (☎22470 31 967. Open daily 11am-2pm and 6pm-late. Cash only)

DODECANESE

NORTHEAST AEGEAN ISLANDS

With limited transportation to even their Dodecanese neighbors, the Northeast Aegean islands go about life at their own pace with their own rules. Sappho, Pythagoras, and Homer hail from these free-thinking islands, which more recently welcomed 15,000 Communist exiles during the Civil War following WWII. Closer to Istanbul than Athens, the Northeast Aegean islands are largely overlooked by major travel companies. This helps the islands retain their original quirks, from chewing gum monopolies to miniature prehistoric cities to lesbian theater festivals. For the more traditional travelers, vast wilderness, local hospitality, and undisturbed beaches reward those who brave the ferry schedules to get here.

HIGHLIGHTS OF THE NORTHEAST AEGEAN ISLANDS

DISCOVER the dazzling beauty hidden in **Limnos's** barren wilderness (p. 405).

ENJOY the enlightened atmosphere in Sappho's hometown of **Skala Eressou** (p. 402).

UNWIND in the storybook village of **Molyvos** (p. 398).

SAMOS Σάμος

Compared to the dry, craggy rock faces of the Dodecanese, Samos is refreshingly green. The lush mountainsides slope gently into crystal seas, making a perfect landscape for quiet walking. Once the home of Pythagoras and Aristarchus (who speculated that the Earth revolved around the sun 1,800 years before Copernicus), Samos retains a proud Greek culture that has remained largely free of Turkish influence despite its proximity to the Turkish mainland.

SAMOS TOWN (VATHY) Βαθύ ☎ 22730

Though larger than Samos's second port Pythagorio, Vathy receives fewer tourists and is generally less concerned with catering to visitors. *Tavernas* unfurl along a graceful parabola of coastline, which leads to narrow streets and stairways stretching up the hillside toward the residential area. Public gardens, a children's playground, hole-in-the-wall restaurants, and excellent bars give Vathy a lived-in quality too often absent from port towns. The entire town is referred to as either "Vathy" or "Samos Town," and both options are correct.

⌐ TRANSPORTATION

Flights: Samos International Airport (**SMI;** ☎22730 87800), near Pythagorio, is only accessible by taxi (€17 from Skala) or infrequent bus service to the airport crossing (4 per day, €1.90). Consider taking a bus to **Pythagorio** (€1.90), followed by a taxi (€3-4). **Olympic Airways** flies to: **Athens** (1hr., 5 per day); **Chios** (20min., 3 per week); **Lesvos** (30min., 3 per week); **Limnos** (25min., 3 per week); **Rhodes** (40min., 2 per week); **Thessaloniki** (1hr., 3 per week). **Aegean Airways** flies to Athens (1hr., 2-3 per day, €30-120); tickets available at travel agencies.

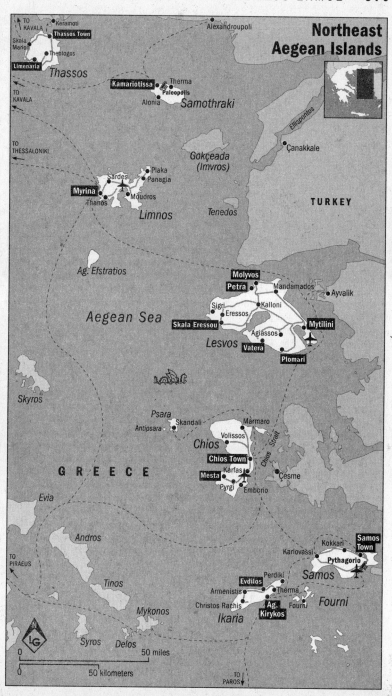

Northeast Aegean Islands

TO KAVALA

Keramoti

Thassos Town

Skala Marion

Limenaria

Theologos

Thassos

TO KAVALA

TO THESSALONIKI

Alexandroupoli

Kamariotissa

Therma

Paleopolis

Alonia

Samothraki

Ellispontos

Çanakkale

Gökçeada (Imvros)

Sardes

Plaka

Panagia

Myrina

Moudros

Thanos

Limnos

Tenedos

TURKEY

Ag. Efstratios

Aegean Sea

Molyvos

Petra

Mandamados

Ayvalik

Sigri

Kalloni

Eressos

Skala Eressou

Agiassos

Mytilini

Lesvos

Vatera

Plomari

Skyros

Psara

Skandali

Marmaro

Antipsara

Volissos

Chios

Chios Town

Karfas

Mesta

Pyrgi

Emborio

Çeşme

Chios Strait

GREECE

Evia

Andros

Tinos

TO PIRAEUS

Kokkari

Samos Town

Karlovassi

Pythagorio

Samos

Evdilos

Perdiki

Armenistis

Therma

Christos Rachis

Ag. Kirykos

Fourni

Fourni

Ikaria

Mykonos

Syros

Delos

0   50 miles

0   50 kilometers

TO PAROS

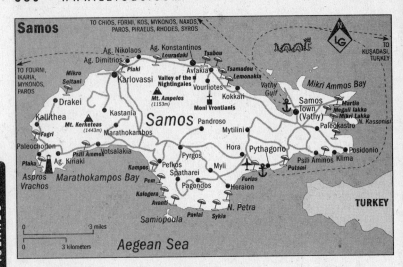

NORTHEAST AEGEAN ISLANDS

Ferries: To: **Chios** (3hr., 2 per week); **Evdilos, Ikaria** (3hr., 9 per week); **Fourni** (1½hr, 3 per week); **Kavala** (1 per week); **Levsos** (5hr., 2 per week);**Limnos** (8hr., 2 per week); **Naxos** (6 per week); **Paros** (8hr., 6 per week); **Piraeus** (16hr., 9 per week). Check at ITSA for updates.

Flying Dolphins: Leave at 8am from the port at Pythagorio, heading daily to: **Kalymnos** (2hr., €33); **Kos** (5hr., €34); **Leros** (1hr., €26); **Lipsi** (1hr., €20); **Patmos** (1hr., €20). Hydrofoils from Vathy service **Fourni** (1hr., 2 per week, €15). Check at ITSA for updates.

Excursion Boats: Daily to **Kusadasi, Turkey** (1½hr.; Tu-Su daily; €50 round-trip, plus €10 Turkish port tax). You can add a bus ride and tour of nearby Ephesus for €25 more, including entrance fees. Turkish entrance visas (US$15) must be purchased at the border by citizens of Australia, Ireland, the UK, and the US planning to stay for over 1 day. Canadians must pay CDN$45 for a visa; euro equivalents accepted.

Buses: KTEL office (☎22730 27 262), 1 block in from the waterfront on Lekati, past Pl. Pythagoras. To: **airport crossing** (25min., 8 per day); **Heraion** (30min., 4 per day); **Chora** (30min., 6 per day); **Karlovassi** (50min., 6 per day); **Kokkari** (20min., 6 per day); **Mytilini** (20min., 4 per day); **Pythagorio** (30min., 11 per day); **Potokaki** (45 min., 4 per day). Most fares €1-3. Reduced service Sa-Su. **Bus tour** around the island stopping at major sights including the **Valley of Nightingales** (Th-F 8:30am, €27). Ask at ITSA for bus timetable to avoid going all the way to the stop.

Car and Motorbike Rental: Autounion (☎22730 27 513), on the waterfront by the docks. Cars from €25 per day. Motorbikes €12 per day. Bikes €7. Open 8:30am-3:30pm and 5:30-9:30pm. MC/V. **Pegasus** (☎22730 24 470), in a kiosk next to ITSA. Cars €30 per day. Motorbikes €12 per day. Open 8am-11pm.

Taxis: (☎22730 28 404), in Pl. Pythagoras. 24hr. €17 to the airport; €12 to Pythagorio.

⚡📍 ORIENTATION AND PRACTICAL INFORMATION

The waterfront is home to most services. **Plateia Pythagoras,** identifiable by its four large palm trees, consists of cafes, a taxi stand, and a giant lion statue. To find pensions, walk toward Pl. Pythagoras from the ferry dock and turn inland before Hotel Aeolis. Signs will point to a number of nearby pensions on the staircases. For nightlife, start up the hill to the left of the port (facing inland); the best bars and clubs are 400m up, though dancing venues are on the far side of the harbor by the post office.

Tourist Office: (☎22730 28 530), on a side street 1 block before Pl. Pythagoras. Open from mid-July to Aug. M-F 10am-1pm.

Budget Travel: ☒ ITSA Travel (☎22730 23 605; www.itsatravelsamos.com), on the waterfront opposite the port. The English-speaking staff helps locate accommodations, has ferry and Flying Dolphin tickets, offers free maps, recommends sights and restaurants, plans excursions to Turkey, and offers free **luggage storage.** Open daily 6am-10pm and when boats arrive. AmEx/MC/V. **Rhenia Tours** (☎22730 88 800), farther along the waterfront. Sells airplane and ferry tickets, offers Western Union services, and rents cars (€41 per day). Open 8am-9:30pm. MC/V for flight reservations. **Ship Travel** (☎22730 25 116), next to ITSA. Excursions, boat schedules, and car rental (€30 per day). All agencies listed have **currency exchange.**

Bank: National Bank, on the waterfront just beyond Pl. Pythagoras. **Emporiki Bank,** just before Pl. Pythagoras. Both banks have **24hr. ATMs.** Both open M-Th 8am-2:30pm, F 8am-2pm.

Police: (☎22730 22 100), after Pl. Pythagoras on the far right of the waterfront when facing inland. The **tourist police** (☎22730 87 344) are in the same office. Open 24hr.

Pharmacy: Numerous pharmacies line the waterfront, and rotate 24hr. schedules. By the dock, there is one open 9am-2pm (☎22730 23 098.)

Hospital: (☎22730 83 100). Facing inland, 10min. to the left of the ferry dock. Open 24hr.

Telephones: OTE (☎22730 22 299), on Kanari behind the church. Open M-F 7:30am-1:30pm.

Internet Access: Nethouse (☎22730 22 986), on the waterfront right before the post office. Offers cheap internet (€2 per hr., min. €1) and a huge DVD selection in English and Greek (€1.50 for 5 days). Open M-Sa 8am-2:30pm and 5-10:30pm. **Pythagoras Hotel** (☎22730 28 601), 600m up the hill from the port, by the hospital. €3 per hr.

Post Office: (☎22730 28 820), on the waterfront, just before the military post and police. Open M-F 7:30am-2pm. Western Union available. **Postal Code:** 83100.

ACCOMMODATIONS

Recent crackdowns on unlicensed pensions have forced many budget accommodations to shut down or operate illegally. Consult **ITSA Travels** for a good deal if you're having trouble finding a room.

☒ **Pythagoras Hotel,** Kalistratou 12 (☎22730 28 601; www.pythagorashotel.com), across from the hospital. Rooms are clean, airy, and the cheapest in town. The location by the beach and several nightlife spots, the snack bar, internet (€3 per hr.), and free Wi-Fi in rooms make this a backpacker's heaven. Friendly owner Stelios helps with ferry schedules and port pickups. The shared terrace overlooking the water is the perfect place to swap travel stories. Rooms with baths, fridges, fans, and flatscreen TVs. Call ahead for reservations. Dorms €15; singles €15-25; doubles €20-45. Cash only. ❶

Medousa Hotel, Sofouli 25 (☎22730 23 501), on the waterfront halfway between the port and Pl. Pythagoras. This is a no-brainer: stellar location, reasonable prices, and excellent quality. An elevator goes up to well-appointed, pristine rooms that have baths, A/C, fridges, and views of the harbor. Singles €25-30; doubles €35-40. Cash only. ❷

Hotel Artemis (☎22730 27 792), on the waterfront next to Pl. Pythagoras. This spartan (not Spartan) option offers spacious doubles with baths, fridges, TVs, and A/C. Smack in the middle of town. The bright indoor sitting room is a popular spot to chat with other guests. A/C €5. Singles with separate bath €20, with ensuite bath €25; doubles €30. Cash only. ❷

Pension Trova, Kalomiris 26 (☎22730 27 759). Head along the waterfront and go inland when you see the sign for Hotel Aeolis; take a left before the stairs and follow the signs. Clean rooms have fans and shared baths with tubs; some with balconies, but the houses for rent are a steal. Maria offers 2 fully equipped houses: 1 adjacent to the pension, 1 near the bus station, usually for longer stays. Each has 3 bedrooms, bath, TV, fan, and fully stocked kitchen. Singles without balcony €20, with balcony €25; doubles €20-25. House near the pension €30 for 2 people, €50 for 4. Slightly fancier house near the bus station €35 for 2, €60 for 4. Cash only. ❶

🍴 FOOD

On side streets just a block inland from the water, a number of hole-in-the-wall *tavernas* serve up unbeatable homemade dishes. As always, follow the "one-block-in" rule; food one block in from the waterfront is usually cheaper and often of better quality. Samian cuisine is notable for its sweet regional wine, the Muscat of Samos, which, depending on your taste, is either sickeningly saccharine or nectar of the gods. A large **supermarket** sits behind the Archaeological Museum.

Taverna Aprovado (☎22730 80 552), 1 block behind the main drag, inland from Hotel Aeolis. Serves up authentic dishes with huge portions at low prices—not to mention the 🍴 **free shot of ouzo** that comes with every meal. Try the house special, minced veal with melted cheese (€8). Entrees €6-9. Open daily 11am-midnight. MC/V. ❷

Gregoris Taverna (☎22730 22 718). From Pl. Pythagoras, make a right at Ireon Cafe, keep going straight for about 300m until you see Gregori's on the right. Try the chickpea balls (€4) and meatballs (€7), prepared according to grandma's Turkish-inspired recipe. Entrees €5-7. Open daily 9am-3pm and 5pm-late. Cash only. ❷

Garden Taverna (☎22730 24 033), on a street off Pl. Nikolaos; follow the signs from Pl. Pythagoras. Well-priced traditional Greek food served in a pleasant garden complete with a fountain and birdcages hanging from the grapevines overhead. Ask about the affordable *prix fixe* menu, which includes an appetizer sampler and choice of entrees (from €12), although prices shift with group size. Try the lamb with lemon and potatoes (€8.50). Also has free Wi-Fi and a very realistic fake donkey. Appetizers €3-5. Open daily 10am-midnight. MC/V. ❷

To Perasma (☎22730 22 763), in Pl. Nikolaos to the left of Pl. Pythagoras facing inland. Traditional Greek meals made with local Samian herbs. Owner Nikos sometimes entertains guests with his *bouzouki*, an instrument similar to a banjo. Try the *stifado* (rabbit with onions; €6.50) or the fresh tuna with lemon sauce (€6.50). Entrees €5-8. Open daily 11:30am-late. Cash only. ❷

Taverna Artemis (☎22730 23 639). Facing inland from the docks, follow the waterfront road to the left. Locals gather to munch on the specialty moussaka (€5.50) and traditional Greek favorites. Appetizers €2-5. Entrees €4-7. Open daily 11am-2am. Cash only. ❷

👁 SIGHTS

TEMPLE OF HERA. This temple was one of the great engineering feats of Polykrates, Samos's tyrannical ruler in the sixth century BC. Unfortunately, fire damage in 525 BC and centuries of wear-and-tear have left mostly rubble at the original site. *(The remains of this temple lie a 30min. bus ride from Skala.)*

ARCHAEOLOGICAL MUSEUM. Skala's excellent and informative **Archaeological Museum** contains proof of the Heraion's bygone splendor. The museum's two buildings house treasures from the ancient Heraion (the temple of Hera) and other local digs, explained in detail by English labels. The first building holds

Laconian ivory carvings and some statues, most notably the colossal 5m *kouroi* from 560 BC. Pieces of this magnificent figure were found built into existing walls and cisterns; its grey-white banded marble was a distinctive regional signature of ancient Samian sculptors, and would have originally been partly painted. The purpose and meaning of the sculptures remains unclear, though the *kouroi* are thought to have been votives to Hera from wealthy families who donated the statues in the image of their oversized demigod ancestors. The same building houses the well-preserved **Genelos group,** a rather ostentatious offering to Hera depicting the aristocratic donors, the Genelos family, themselves. The group once graced the Heraion's Sacred Way, and of the original series of six life-sized sculptures, four have survived. In the second building, an exhibit on Hera worship displays a collection of the various pieces of pottery, jewelry, and small sculptures dedicated to the goddess. The last room, upstairs on the right, includes a case of fascinatingly nightmarish, gryphon-engraved cauldron handles known as **protomes.** *(Behind the Municipal Gardens. ☎ 22730 27 469. Open Tu-Su 8:30am-3pm. €3, students and seniors €2, EU students free.)*

NIGHTLIFE

The nightclub scene centers on two waterfront poles on opposite sides of the harbor. Facing inland from the ferry docks, a number of bars 400m to the left toward the hospital have dance floors and waterfront terraces. Music-blasting discos are 500m in the opposite direction toward the post office, where sound-proof doors keep the neighborhood deceptively quiet. Many clubs don't get busy until July, so some choose to take time off until the high season.

Mble, 400m uphill to the left of the ferry docks. Under blue lighting, sip a mixed drink (€8) on the canopied, mod-furnished balcony overhanging the water, where a spotlight gives the water an eerie glow. Open daily 9:30am-dawn. Cash only.

Stelios Beach Bar (☎22730 87 263), farther up the street past Hotel Pythagoras, to the left and downstairs on the beach. Patrons lounge in this tiki-inspired bar, or dip their feet in the water while drinking a €4 beer. Free sunbeds. Mixed drinks €5. Open daily 9am-late. Cash only.

Escape Music Bar, next to Mble. Outdoor terrace overlooking the green-lit water. The dance floor indoors picks up after 2am, where Greek and American hits keep the young, local crowd on its toes all night. Mixed drinks €7. Happy hour 8-10pm; drinks ½-price. Open daily 7pm-4am. Cash only.

Xantres Club (☎69490 78 611), on the far side of the waterfront by the post office. Soundproof walls conceal the booming Greek pop. Locals gather after 3am to dance in the blacklight to the sounds of the nightly DJ. Mixed drinks €7. Open daily 11:30pm-7am. Cash only.

IKARIA Ικαρία

Ikaria is named after the reckless young Icarus, who plunged to a watery demise after flying too close to the sun (a rock marks the spot of his legendary fall). Ikaria's modern history matches the rebellious attitude of its namesake: the island is a bastion of the Greek Communist Party (KKE), and hammer-and-sickle posters make a jarring addition to the peaceful landscape. During the Civil Wars following WWII, 15,000 Communists were exiled to this island populated by 7,000 villagers, and Ikaria soon became known as "Red Rock." Today, it's safe to assume that most older people on the island participated in the Civil War in some way, giving Ikaria a sense of historical vibrancy. Before the turbulent 20th century, Ikaria was known as one of the most pirate-proof islands in the Northeast Aegean, so locals pride themselves on being more closely related to the Ancient Greeks than other, more heavily raided spots. The coastline is speckled by serene, untouristed beaches, some with natural hot springs, framed by an enormous chain of green alpine mountains. With an agricultural economy and no major tourist industry, the island remains one of the poorest in the region, so transportation around the island is difficult. Visitors patient with the island's often inexplicable schedule, though, are rewarded with an unspoiled slice of Greece.

AGIOS KIRYKOS Ἅγιος Κήρυκος ☎22750

Ikaria's southern port town is little more than a shaded *plateia* stretching along giant steps that lead to the sea. After 6pm, locals begin to hang out by the pier and sip frappés. With the KKE headquarters and a prevalent macho youth culture, the town plays by its own rules and keeps a baffling schedule; even at midnight you'll see small children playing energetically in front of the cafes as their parents chat and gossip, and some clubs don't open until 3am.

 ON YOUR OWN. In Ikaria, buses are unpredictable and often nonexistent. Rent a car or a moped so you don't wait for hours for a phantom bus.

TRANSPORTATION

Flights: Ikaria Island National Airport "Ikaros"(JIK; ☎22750 23 888), on the island's northeastern tip, near Faros Beach. Flights to **Athens** (50min., Tu-Su daily, €44) and **Iraklion, Crete** (2 per week, €100). Contact **Icariada Travel** (☎22750 23 322), in the *plateia*, where the English-speaking staff also provides ferry schedules and free luggage storage. Open daily 8:30am-2:30pm and 6-9pm. Cash only for ticket purchase.

Ferries: Several run to the northern port of **Evdilos**. Plan ahead as bus service between the 2 cities is practically nonexistent and a taxi ride (€27) may be in order. Ferries to: **Fourni** (1hr., daily); **Mykonos** (3hr., 3 per week); **Naxos** (3hr., Tu-Su daily); **Paros** (4hr., Tu-Su daily); **Piraeus** (8hr., daily); **Samos Town** (3hr., daily); **Syros** (3 per week).

Buses: Service on the island is fickle, if it exists at all; buses may run in 1 direction 1 day and the other the next. If you do happen to be relying on public transport, expect to spend the night or call a cab to get home. Buses leave from the waterside parking lot in front of the tourist office for **Evdilos** (1hr.) and continue to **Armenistis** (2hr., 1-2 per day, €6). A fairly regular green bus leaves from in front of Alpha Bank to **Therma** (5min., every hr. 9am-2pm and 5-9pm, €1.20).

Taxis: (☎69726 40 154, 69778 41 327, or 69723 98 568). A queue forms in front of Alpha Bank in the *plateia*. A complete list can be found in the tourist office.

Car Rental: Glaros Car Rental (☎22750 23 637), next to Alpha Bank. Cars from €24 per day. Open 9am-2pm.

ORIENTATION AND PRACTICAL INFORMATION

The town's main pier is marked by a copper sculpture of Icarus plummeting to the ground. Coming off the ferry, walk up the pier onto the main waterfront road, then turn right to reach the town *plateia*, which is the center for all tourist services and most of the town's daily life.

Tourist Office: (☎22750 24 047), the 1st white building on the left walking into the *plateia*. Free maps and island guides, as well as bus and ferry schedules. Open 9am-2pm and 5-9pm.

Banks: Alpha Bank (☎22750 22 264), on the waterfront at the far end from the ferry docks. **Currency exchange** and **24hr. ATM.** Cashes travelers checks with no fee. Open M-Th 8am-2:30pm, F 8am-2pm. **ATE Bank** (☎22750 22 987), up the road inland from the *plateia*, has a **24hr. ATM.** Open M-Th 8am-2:30pm, F 8am-2pm.

Police: (☎22750 22 222), up the stairs to the left of Alpha Bank.

Pharmacy: (☎22750 22 212), 1 block inland on the side street next to Cafe Remezzo. Open 8:30-2:30pm and 5:30-9:30pm.

Hospital: (☎22750 32 330), 2 streets inland from the pier.

Telephones: OTE (☎22750 22 499), about 100m up the street. Open M-F 7:30am-3pm.

Post Office: (☎22750 22 413). Open M-F 7:30am-2pm. **Postal Code:** 83300.

ACCOMMODATIONS

Ikaria does not have a large selection of *domatia*. A few are clustered by the waterfront and above Alpha Bank. Inquire at the tourist office if you are having trouble finding a room.

Akti Hotel (☎22750 23 905; www.pensionakti.gr), climb the stairs on the right side of Alpha Bank and take your 1st right. Guests often sit on the cliffside patio, gazing at the harbor and chatting until late. The friendly Greek-American owner knows the island inside-out and can direct you to the hot springs, nearby sandy beaches, and best places to stop for a drink. Remodeled rooms come with TVs, A/C, hair dryers, well-appointed baths, Wi-Fi, and doors leading onto the patio. Singles €25-35; doubles €40-60. MC/V. ❷

Hotel O'Karras (☎22750 22 494; www.ikariarooms.com), across from Akti Pension. Colorful, well-decorated rooms provide a refuge from the sun. Small rooms come with baths, flatscreen TVs, A/C, shared kitchenettes, Wi-Fi, and balconies directly overhanging the main row of cafes. The rooftop garden is a breezy social space. Singles €25-35; doubles €30-35. Cash only. ❷

Pension Ikaria (☎22750 22 108), 1 block inland from the *plateia* behind Ston Tsouri. Simple, unremarkable rooms with baths, TVs, and A/C. Some with polka-dot curtains. Singles €25; doubles €30. Cash only. ❷

FOOD

Klimataria (☎22750 22 686). Head inland toward the post office and the *taverna* is on the right. Locals enjoy the goat with potatoes (€8) under a trellis of grapevines in the company of local cats. Entrees €5-7. Open daily 10am-midnight. Cash only. ❶

Filoti (☎22750 23 088), 1 block in from the waterfront. Go inland at Alpha Bank, and make the 1st left; it's on the right. Huge portions of hard-to-find pizza with Greek toppings, popular with young locals. Large chicken souvlaki pizza €13. Open daily 10am-late. Cash only. ❷

Ston Tsouri (Ston Tsourh) (☎22750 22 473), in the *plateia*. An Odyssey-length menu rotates what's available daily. Local cheeses and Ikarian wines make watching the stunning sunsets from the tables a multi-sensory experience. Greek entrees €7-8. Open daily noon-late. MC/V. ❷

BEACHES AND NIGHTLIFE

Incredible beaches sprinkled with boulders and white pebbles unfold between the coastal road and the glassy sea. There are two natural hot springs in the

FROM THE ROAD

WEDDING CRASHER

I invited myself to a village wedding while visiting the relatives of a travel acquaintance in Petropouli, on Ikaria. The tiny Orthodox chapel was too full for anyone but relatives, so the villagers sat on the outdoor benches and gossiped until the reception started. As evening fell, attendees sat in a light-strung *plateia* and drank home-made wine out of plastic bottles.

It was a people-watcher's paradise. Even though I knew no guests and no Greek, I could still tell who was who. When I congratulated the bride with a mispronounced *"kronyapola,"* she hugged me as if she knew who I was.

Village boys made their way through the crowd carrying food-laden tabletops. School children played tag between the packed tables. Then, the inevitable happened: someone scampered, someone tripped, and lamb and rice rained down on the one person who hadn't actually been invited to the wedding. For one terrible moment, I expected everyone to turn and look in shocked silence. They'd check the guest list, and after some loud Greek yelling, I'd be hauled away to prison. With pilaf in my hair.

Instead, someone called, "It's a good omen; next time you come to Ikaria, you'll have uncooked rice thrown on you instead!" Everybody laughed. I was escorted to get cleaned up, then dragged onto the dance floor to attempt the local *karyotikos* dance. I was no Zorba the Greek, but, by the end, I was dancing the *hora* that I'd danced at innumerable bar mitzvahs, and it passed for the real thing.

—Charlotte Alter

ocean. You can bathe in the spring water at **Therma** (Q2rma), 2km north of Agios Kirykos on the way to the airport. The green bus runs approximately every hour from 9am-2pm and 5-9pm (€1.20). You also can walk down the path by the police station. Unlike Agios Kirykos, Therma has a number of bathhouses where spring water is piped into private stalls. The water is used to treat ailments from rheumatism to neurological difficulties. The best is a wood building on the far right of the beach when facing the ocean and is open 8am-noon and 5-8pm. Where the bus lets out, another white stucco bathhouse has several stalls but runs €4.50 for a stay. (Open 7am-12:30, 5-7:30pm.) For those without health problems, the natural hot spring off the beach across the street is free and always open. Farther north, by the airport, the small town of **Faros** offers a number of unremarkable but pleasant beaches. Because of the fickle buses, you may need a taxi from Agios Kirykos.

All the town's nightlife is within a 20min. walk along the coastal road heading left from the ferry dock, facing inland. Ikaria's little light pollution leaves the stars strikingly visible, setting the scene for a lovely stroll above the sea.

5 Minutes Til (Para Pente), near the docks. By 2am, young locals gather here for some liquid courage to get them revved up for the evening. Periodic free shots make it a favorite. Mixed drinks €5-7. Open daily 5pm-late. Cash only.

Wha Wha, 500m down the waterfront. Its classic rock tunes spill over the 3 open-air terraces leading down to the pebbly beach. Drinks €2-7. Open daily 11pm-late.

Ftero (☎22750 23 095), near the big church. Offers mixed drinks (€6) on a balcony overlooking the harbor. Open daily 10:30am-late. Cash only.

EVDILOS Εύδηλος ☎22750

The winding, mountainous road to Evdilos passes craggy rock faces under soaring windmills and skirts village-dotted valleys on its way to the northern coast. Confusing side roads branch off to stretches of sandy beach and up into mountaintop villages, but the main road sees little traffic as not many islanders travel between the two ports. The red-roofed houses of Evdilos circle the serene stretch of pebbled harbor, where locals gather in waterfront cafes or take a swim in the crystalline waters. Because the town is a ferry port in a central location, it serves as a convenient base to explore the many beaches and villages on the northern face of the island.

⊏ TRANSPORTATION.
Hellenic Seaways ferries leave daily from Tuesday to Sunday to Naxos, Paros, and Piraeus, and daily from Tuesday to Saturday to Karlovasi and Samos Town. Book tickets at **Rustas Travel,** on the waterfront. **Buses** are difficult to catch and service is spotty, but regularly run to Armenistis and Agios Kirykos. **Taxis** are a pricier but far more reliable option; call an hour in advance, as cabs are in Agios Kirykos. (☎69726 40 154. To Agios Kirykos €27; Armenistis €9.) The best way to get around the island is to rent a **car;** try **Aventura Car Rental,** just inland from the main harbor square. (☎22750 31 140. Cars €20-35; bikes €10-18. Open daily 9am-2pm and 6pm-9pm. AmEx/MC/V.)

✚🚹 ORIENTATION AND PRACTICAL INFORMATION.
The waterfront curves from the ferry dock around to Alpha Bank on the far end, with a small square marked by a statue in the middle; most *tavernas*, cafes, and shops are along this waterfront. A stone pathway leads up and to the right when facing inland at the bakery, heading 150m to the upper *plateia* where a few more *tavernas* and pensions cluster. **Rustas** (☎22750 32 931), the only travel agency in town, helps with ferry bookings. It's on the far left side of the waterfront facing inland, near Alpha Bank. (Open M-Sa 8am-2pm and 7-9pm. Cash only.) There is a **24hr. ATM** at the end of the harbor, outside Alpha Bank. (Open M-Th 8am-2:30pm, F 8am-2pm.) The **pharmacy** (☎22750 31 394) is on the third floor of the building next to the port police; to get there, take a right up the steps near the bakery, then make the first right. To find the **police** (☎22750 31 222), continue up the steep hill past Hotel Atheras, then make a right and follow the road aroung the bend. In an emergency, call the **health center** (☎22750 33 030). The **post office** is just past the police on the same road. (☎22750 31 225. Open M-F 7:30am-1:30pm.) **Postal Code:** 83302.

🛏 ACCOMMODATIONS.
With few options for *domatia* in the area, consider booking in advance. The best and most convenient option is **Hotel Atheras ❷,** 50m in from the main harbor square, well-marked and easy to find. Stylish rooms from €37 come with TVs, air conditioning, refrigerators, baths, and balconies—but there are three cheaper attic rooms from €20, complete with fans and baths (not advisable for taller visitors). The hotel has a pool and free Wi-Fi, and the friendly staff speaks English. (☎22750 31 434; www.atheras-kerame.gr. Reserve ahead for economy rooms. Regular singles €37-70, economy €20-30; doubles €47-70/25-35. AmEx/MC/V.) **Kerame Studios ❷,** a partner to Hotel Atheras, is about 1km away from the town center, down the main road to the left. Although regular studios are more expensive and come with kitchenettes and balconies, there are also four cheaper rooms with TVs, air conditioning, baths, and communal kitchens. The hotel also has a pool, Wi-Fi, and a restaurant. (☎22750 31 434; www.atheras-kerame.gr. Regular singles €37-82, economy €25-50; doubles €47-82/35-50. AmEx/MC/V.) Soaring ceilings and private balconies jutting out over the waves make the rooms at **Apostolos Stenos's Rooms to Rent ❸** a lovely spot to watch the sunset. Rooms come with baths and shared fridges. From the upper *plateia*, make a right at the snack bar, immediately take the left fork, then make another quick left. Follow the road with white painted circles on it for 20m; the pension is on the right just before the road comes to the edge of the coast. (☎22750 31 365. June-Aug. singles €35; doubles €40.)

FOOD AND NIGHTLIFE. Evdilos has limited options for full meals, so most tourists and locals eat in the snack bars and *ouzeria* on the waterfront. **Kemali ❶**, on the harbor next to Art Cafe, offers gyros and souvlaki (€2) on tables just a meter or from the water. For a light dinner, try the greek salad (€5) with an individual chicken skewer (€1.80). (☎22750 31 923. Beer €2.50. Open 7pm-late. Cash only.) **Steki ❶**, just across from Kemali, offers similar fare in adjacent outdoor seating. (☎22750 31 793. Souvlaki in pita €1.80. Fresh fish €6. Open daily 11am-late. Cash only.) **Ta Kimata ❶**, on the waterfront, caters to late-night ferry arrivals with an array of sweets (€2.50) and ice cream (€1.20). (☎22750 31 952. Open 24hr. Cash only.)

The waterfront nightlife centers on the two bars in town. Locals gather in the modern lounge of **Art Cafe** to sip coffee (€2) and drinks (€5). (Open daily 10am-late. Cash only.) A rowdier crowd gathers around the nightly DJ at **Sto Peripou** and dance to international music as late as the landlord allows. (☎22750 31 974. Mixed drinks €4-5. Sangria €4. Cash only.)

CHIOS Χίος

Chios is most famous for *mastic*, a unique evergreen resin used since antiquity in medicines, cosmetics, candy, and chewing gum. Mastic forms the cornerstone of this diverse island's tourist industry, and is also the key to Chios's historical safety and prosperity. Alexander the Great had a taste for the tree, as did the sultans who allowed Chios special privileges during Turkish rule in the 16th and 17th centuries in return for an endless supply of chewing gum. Chios is also reportedly the birthplace of Homer, who recited his poems at Daskalopetra. Today, Chios is home to loud and glitzy Chios town, serene mastic groves, Genoese mansions, and architecturally diverse inland villages like Mesta and Pyrgi.

CHIOS TOWN ☎22710

Chios's port town has an electric pulse that doesn't pause for the wayward tourist or confused pedestrian. The traffic along the main waterfront can drown out conversation at the many hip cafes, although that doesn't stop trendy young locals from lounging all afternoon drinking frappés and watching the ferries come and go. *Tavernas* are scarce and overpriced and most rooms are unremarkable, so Chios Town is often just a stop on the way to the island's inland treasures. Just a few blocks north of the harbor, the quiet residential section slumbers under the shadow of the castle, disturbed only by the occasional blare of a moped.

TRANSPORTATION

Flights: Chios National Airport "Omiros", 94 Enoseos Ave. (JKH; ☎22710 44260). Olympic Airways flies to: **Athens** (1hr., 3 per day); **Limnos** (1hr., 1-2 per week); **Mytilini, Lesvos** (30min., 2 per week); **Rhodes** (1hr., 2 per week); **Samos** (35min., 2 per week); **Thessaloniki** (1-2hr., 3 per week, €60). **Aegean Air** also flies to **Athens** (1hr., 2 per day, €50-84); contact **Travel Shop** (☎22710 20 160) for rates and schedules.

Ferries: To: **Agios Kirykos, Ikaria** (6hr., every Th); **Çesme, Turkey** (45min., daily, round-trip €30); **Kavala** (10hr., 2 per week); **Lesvos** (3hr., 2 per day); **Limnos** (10hr., 4 per week);

NORTHEAST AEGEAN ISLANDS

Piraeus (9hr.; 2 per day Tu, W, Th, Sa, and Su); **Samos** (3hr., 3 per week); **Thessaloniki** (19hr., every F and Sa).

Excursion Boats: Daily trips leave from Chios to **Çesme** and **Izmir, Turkey** (€30-40 round-trip, plus €10 Turkish port tax); ask at **Sunrise Tours** or **Kanaris Tours** (☎22710 42 490). Open daily 6am-10pm. Kanaris offers excursions to Inousses Island on Th and Su (€20, check for exact schedule).

Buses: Service is split between local blue buses and long-distance green buses; both stations are between the harbor and the Municipal Gardens.

Blue bus station (☎22710 22 079), just up from the *plateia* on Dimokratias. Buses travel short distances from Chios Town. Routes connect **Karfas, Kontari, Megas Limionas, Thimiana,** and smaller towns along the way (14 per day 6:35am-8:30pm, €1.15). Tickets available at the station, or on board for a small fee. Reduced service Sa-Su.

Green bus station (☎22710 27 507), on the waterfront near the ferry docks. Offers bathrooms, lockers, bus tickets, and is a popular backgammon-player hangout. Tickets can be bought at the station or onboard to: **Agia Fotia Beach** (5 per day); **Armolia** (5 per day); **Emporios** (3 per day); **Kalamoti** (5 per day); **Kardamila** (6 per day); **Kataraktis** (6 per day); **Komi** (4 per day); **Lagada** (6 per day); **Lithi** (3 per day); **Mesta** (5 per day); **Nagos** (2 per day); **Nenita** (7 per day); **Pyrgi** (7 per day); **Volissos** (3 per day M, W, and F). Tickets from €1.70. Open 24hr.

Taxis: (☎69756 07 513), across Pl. Vounakio from the Municipal Gardens. To: **Emporios Beach** (€27); **Karfas** (€6.5); **Mesta** (€27); **Nea Moni** (€12-15). €1-2 surcharge after midnight. 24hr.

Car Rental: Europcar (☎22710 21 666), 1 block south of Sunrise Tours on the waterfront. Cars around €30 per day. Open daily 8am-1pm and 5-9pm. **Rent a Moto** (☎22710 25 113), just off the waterfront. Scooters €14-20 per day. Open daily 7am-10pm. AmEx/V.

✦ 🛈 ORIENTATION AND PRACTICAL INFORMATION

Facing inland from the ferry docks, a right on Kanari takes you past the tourist office to **Plateia Vounakio**, the social center of town. Many cafes and services, including taxi and bus stands, can be found right before reaching the Municipal Gardens. Left of Vounakio lies **Aplotarias,** the market street, with several grocery stores and bakeries. Between the ferry dock and the Municipal Gardens, fortress walls hug the predominantly residential **Old Town.**

Tourist Office: Kanari 18 (☎22710 44 344). Walk toward the *plateia* on Kanari, and look for the "i" sign on your left. English-speaking staff has maps, brochures, and

NORTHEAST AEGEAN ISLANDS

bus, ferry, and airplane schedules as well as advice on museum and hiking routes. Open M-F May-June and Sept. 7:30am-3pm; July-Aug. 7:30am-3pm and 7-10pm; Oct.-Apr. in the morning. MC/V. **Kanaris Tours,** L. Aegeou 12 (☎22710 42 490; www.kanaristours.gr), on the waterfront. Books air tickets, boat tickets, excursions to Turkey, accommodations, and bus tours around the island (€15-20). Open daily 6am-10pm. MC/V. **Travel Shop,** Aigeou 56 (☎22710 20 160), on the waterfront under the conspicuous Olympic Airways sign. Air and ferry tickets. Open daily 8:30am-8:30pm. MC/V. **NEL Lines,** Aigeou 16 (☎22710 23 971), near where Kanari meets the waterfront road. Open daily 8am-10pm.

Banks: National Bank, Kanari 8 (☎22710 22 831), next to the OTE in the *plateia*. **Currency exchange** and a **24hr. ATM.** Open M-Th 8am-2:30pm and F 8am-2pm. **Emporiki,** on the waterfront, has a **24hr. ATM.** Open M-Th 8am-2:30pm, F 8am-2pm. **Eurobank,** on the waterfront. Open M-Th 8am-2:30pm and F 8am-2pm.

Pharmacy: Several near Pl. Vounakio. One is on Kanari across from the Tourist Office (☎22710 23 131). Open M and W 8am-2pm, Tu and Th-F 8am-2pm and 5:30-8:45pm.

Hospital: El. Venizelou 2 (☎22710 44 306, first aid 44 302), 3km north of the *plateia*.

Telephones: OTE, Tzon Kenety 1 (☎22710 28 999), up the block from the tourist office. Open M-W 7:30am-2pm, Th-F 7:30am-8:30pm, Sa 9am-2pm.

Internet Access: A number of cafes with fast Wi-Fi connections can be found on the waterfront road. **Fantasy,** Aigeou 60 (☎22710 23 896). €2 per hr., min. €1. Open daily 10am-2am. **In Spot** (☎22710 23 438), farther south on the waterfront, has 24hr. access. €2.40 per hr., midnight-8am €1.20 per hr.

Tourist Police: (☎22710 81 539), on Polemidi.

Post Office: Omirou 2 (☎22710 25 668), on the corner of Omirou and Rodokanaki, 1 block inland. Offers **Western Union.** Open M-F 7:30am-2pm. **Postal Code:** 82100.

ACCOMMODATIONS

Most accommodations are on the far end of the waterfront from the ferry dock and tend to be a bit pricey. In high season, a tourist agency can help you find a room, but consider heading to nearby Karfas if Chios Town gets too crowded.

Alex Rooms, Livanou 29 (☎22710 26 054; roomsalex@chi.forthenet.gr), 1 block behind Satva. 6 nautical-themed rooms with fridges, A/C, TVs, and some with baths, that connect to a shared garden terrace. Former ship captian Alex can give you info on transportation and accommodations anywhere on the island, as well as stories from sea. Rooms €30. Cash only. ❷

Chios Rooms, Aigeou 110 (☎22710 20 198; www.chiosrooms.com). Makes up for in decor what it lacks in amenities. The converted mansion boasts somewhat cramped rooms with fans and seperate baths, but the cozy kitchen area is an excellent place to swap stories with fellow travelers. The New Zealand-born owner can give you advice about Chios, beer, and life. Singles €25; doubles €35, with bath €40; triples with bath €45. Cash only. ❷

Hotel Filoxenia 4, Voupalou 8 (☎22710 22 813), just off the waterfront on Voupalou. Guests are just steps away from both bus stations, the main shopping streets, the Municipal Gardens, and the waterfront. Simple rooms come with A/C, fridges, baths, and balconies. Singles €40; doubles €60. Cash only. ❸

Pelinneon 4, Aigeou 54 (☎22710 43 755), on the water where Paraschou goes inland. Rooms come with A/C, TVs, fridges, spacious baths, and views of the ferries entering the harbor. The location couldn't be better, but rooms may get noisy. Inquire at Rent a Car George Psoras. Rooms €25-55. Cash only. ❸

FOOD

Awash with cafes and gyro stands, Chios comes up short on the *taverna* scene. Several can be found around **Plateia Vounakio** and far down the left side of the waterfront when facing inland, although you may have to search for budget menu options.

Ouzeri Paleo Petrino, Aigeou 80 (☎22710 29 797), on the waterfront. Traditional dishes such as the shrimp with onions (€8) and a large selection of local *ouzos*. The stone facade adds a high-class touch to the outdoor tables, and the cavernous interior is a cool alternative to the bustling waterfront. Entrees €5-8. Open daily noon-2am. Cash only. ❷

To Byzantio, 9 Afon Ralli (☎22710 41 035), around the corner from the mosque. Escape the waterfront's fashion parade at this local favorite where they choose their home-made meals from the counter. Entrees from €5. Open M-Sa 7am-9pm. Cash only. ❶

To Tsikoudho (☎22710 40 111), on the waterfront. Delicious seafood and waterfront seating. The tasteful pale green interior is a perfect place to get away from the motor-cyles as you munch on fried octopus croquettes (€5.90) or shrimp in sauce (€9.80). Appetizers €2.50-5. Seafood €7-13. Open 11:30am-midnight. MC/V. ❷

Tzibaepi Ouzerie (☎22710 43 559), to the right of the ferry dock when facing inland. A family-run alternative to the glitzier options on the main stretch of waterfront. Try the pork in wine €6.50 or the delicious Chios cheese (€4). Appetizers €3-5, Seafood €5-9. Open daily 5am-late. Cash only. ❷

SIGHTS

Chios Town has several museums, with the more worthwhile exhibits located in the southern part of town. In July and August, the **Prefecture of Chios** finances free guided tours of the island's monuments. Visitors must provide their own transportation to the various sites, where a guide will wait at a set meeting point. (Open M-F. Tours start 10am and noon.) For more info, contact the tourist office or **Ena Chios Development Corp** (☎22710 44 830; www.enachios.gr).

BYZANTINE KASTRO. To the right facing inland at Pl. Vounakio, follow Tzon Kenenti toward the waterfront to enter the Byzantine kastro, reconstructed by the Genoese. Enclosing the empty, winding streets of the Old Town, the walls make the neighborhood itself seem like a museum.

ARCHAEOLOGICAL MUSEUM. The best collection resides at this sprawling, 1200 sq. m museum where an extensive array of Neolithic, Archaic, and Classical artifacts have detailed English placards. Don't miss the display of golden lily-form wreaths. (*☎22710 44 239. Open Tu-Su 8:30am-3pm; €2, students €1, EU students free.*)

ENTERTAINMENT AND NIGHTLIFE

From mid-July to mid-September, the open-air cinema in the public gardens shows nightly movies. The tourist office carries a booklet with the season's schedule; posters for that week's movies are also on display outside the cinema. Showings are at 7 and 9pm, and tickets (€5) can be bought at the cinema.

Waterfront bars overflow with chic clientele by 10pm and packs of wandering trendsetters take over the sidewalks later on.

Remezzo, 52 Aigeou (☎22710 42 848). Head to the crowds and Heineken umbrellas of this establishment, where the young and beautiful mingle by the bar decorated with American collegiate paraphanalia. Beer €4.50. Mixed drinks €7. Open daily 8am-3:30am.

Satva, Aigeou 110 (☎22710 21 290), across from Chios Rooms. Puff on a hookah and relax on the cushions of the outdoor couches at this Moroccan-themed bar. Mixed drinks €6-8. Hookah €10. Tobacco €5. Th free tobacco. Open daily 8am-4am.

Avenue, Aigeou 70 (☎22710 24 907), down the waterfront from the ferry dock. Red lights mean "go" at the street-themed Avenue, popular with trendy locals. Drinks €6-7. Open daily 8am-3:30am or later.

Fantasy. Head here for billiards (€8 per hr.) and a beer or to check your email on their internet.

🔁 DAYTRIPS FROM CHIOS TOWN

📓PYRGI Πυργί

Take the bus from Chios (7 per day, €2.40). Pyrgi and Mesta are on the same route; ask at the Chios bus station for info on how to time your visits to catch the bus en route.

The villages in the southern half of the island, called Mastichohoria, cultivate the lentisk trees that produce Chios's famous resin. High in the hills, 25km from Chios Town, the village of Pyrgi greets visitors with its buildings' intricate black-and-white geometric facades, which almost resemble the card houses in *Alice In Wonderland.* In the afternoon, old men congregate in the central *plateia* by the church to gossip over ouzo; their wives pass the time chatting in the rustic narrow alleyways that separate their tiny homes. Pyrgi is also home to the 12th-century 📓**Agioi Apostoloi church,** hidden in a small alley off the *plateia.* Sixteenth-century frescoes cover the haunting interior of the Byzantine church, and the structure itself is exquisitely decorated with 12th-century architectural patterns. The cool, dim interior provides some historical gravitas to an otherwise architecturally playful city.

📓MESTA Μεστά

Green buses run from Chios Town to Mesta 5 per day M-F (€3.10). From Mesta, a 40min. hike along the well-marked trail leads to the similarly walled town of Olympi and makes for a pleasant evening stroll.

One of the most fascinating villages in southern Chios, Mesta got its name from the Greek word *mesto,* meaning "a very well-thought-out idea." The town was founded in 1038, when representatives from four neighboring towns put their heads together to solve the perennial pirate problem. Their solution was to build a town where the houses were connected to one another, forming a fortress-village. Each house had a ladder leading to the roof where residents could flee from one house to another, as well as an incomplete staircases leading down from the roof, from which brave village warriors could battle the pirates. In dire situations, the residents could run along the rooftops to the central tower, now incorporated into the church. Today, Mesta looks almost exactly as it might have during the Byzantine era; by archaeological decree, all new houses must be built in the original style with delightful stonework, rounded arches, and painted wooden doors. It's easy to get lost in the narrow, cobbled streets, but most wind up back at the central *plateia,* the nucleus of village life and home to the town's two tavernas.

While its quaint Byzantine design is an attraction in itself, Mesta houses two beautiful churches that are well worth a look. In the main *plateia,* **The Great Taxiarchi,** once termed "The Manger" is the third-largest church in Greece. The impressive pale blue interior is filled with silver votives and chandeliers, all gifts from the devoted. Dating from 1412, this church contains an enormous walnut iconostasis, carved over the course of 35 years in the early 18th century. Repaired in 1833 after a fire, the altar retains its glory; the church keeper can narrate the Biblical scenes depicted in the intricate carvings as well as the symbolism of its many features. Older Taxiarchi is closed for archeological excavation at time of writing. (☎27710 76 044. Great Taxiarchi open daily 11am-3pm and 4-6pm. Modest dress required.)

Pick your meal from the day's fresh selection at family-run ◼Mesalonas Restaurant ❷.The delicious meatballs (€7) and unbelievable eggplant dishes (€5) are best enjoyed with some sour cherry juice (€1.60). (☎27710 76 050. Open daily 6am-late. Cash only.)

LESVOS Λέσβος

Lesvos defies categorization, offering a taste of everything smaller islands have to offer, from nightlife and a rich collection of museums to hiking and castle-crowned cities. On top of the well-rounded tourist offerings, Lesvos also has a distinctive appeal as the origin of girl-power; the seventh century BC poet Sappho lived here, and lesbians from around the world flock to her birthplace of Skala Eressou to honor her free-spirited artistic and cultural legacy. Sexuality aside, Lesvos is unmatched in its diversity of sights and activities. Sand and pebble beaches, fortresses and castles, and *ouzo* and olive groves litter this large and beautiful island, making it the perfect place to island-hop without getting your feet wet.

MYTILINI Μυτιλήνη ☎22510

Each morning, the capital's harbor yawns into a modern, working city marked by glitzy shops, local markets, and waterfront cafes. The ruined castle looks on from the peninsula to the north; the immense walls that once held off pirates now host occasional rock concerts. Most visitors to Mytilini come on business or en route to the rest of Lesvos, leaving the city a playground for trendy students who buzz around the waterfront clubs. The commercial beat only

NORTHEAST AEGEAN ISLANDS

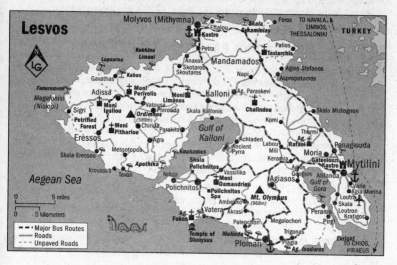

goes so far, though, and exploration farther inland and north reveals calmer, cobblestone streets peppered with old churches and quiet parks.

▚ TRANSPORTATION

Flights: Mytilene International Airport "Odysseas Elytis" (MJT; ☎22510 61 590), 6km south of Mytilini. Take a green bus from the intercity bus station, or a taxi (€5-6). **Olympic Airways,** Kavetsou 44 (☎22510 28 659; open 8am-3pm), has another office at the airport, as does **Aegean Airlines** (☎22510 61 120). Tickets for both Olympic and Aegean flights can be purchased at almost any travel agency in town. To: **Athens** (1hr., at least 6 per day 8am-6:10pm, €50-150); **Chios** (25min., 2 per week, €31); **Limnos** (35min., M-Th and Sa, €41); **Rhodes** (1hr., M-Th and Sa, €58); **Samos** (45min., 2 per week, €41); **Thessaloniki** (daily, €87-98).

Ferries: To: Chios (3hr., daily, €16); **Kavala** (11hr., 2 per week, €32); **Limnos** (5hr., 2 per week, €20); **Piraeus** (12hr., daily, €35-41); **Samos** (7hr., 3 per week, €18); **Thessaloniki** (13hr., 1 per week, €37).

Excursion Boats: Daytrips to **Ayvalik, Turkey** (1hr., daily, €35) and **Dikeli, Turkey** (3 per week, €20).

Buses: Intercity bus station (☎22570 28 873), at the corner of Ilia Iliou and Smyrnis. Buses crisscross the island with Mytilini as the home base. Schedules for the island's buses are available here and at most information or tourist agencies throughout Lesvos. Buses to: **Aglassos** (25min., 6 per day 7am-7:15pm); **Eressos** and **Skala Eressos** (3hr., 3 per day 9am-1:15pm); **Gera** (7 per day 9am-6:30pm); **Mantamados** (1hr., 5 per day 9am-8pm); **Molyvos** (1½hr., 4 per day 9am-6:45pm) via **Kalloni** and **Petra; Plomari** (30min., 5 per day 9am-6:30pm); **Polichnitos** (1hr., 4 per day 9am-6:30pm) via **Vatera; Sigri** (3hr., 2 per day 11am and 1:15pm). Buses run July-Aug. 9am-7pm; Sept.-June 9am-3:30pm. Reduced service Sa-Su. €2-7, depending on distance.

Local Transportation: Local Buses (☎22570 28 873), in Pl. Sappho on the waterfront. Pick up a schedule from the knowledgeable staff in the kiosk. To: **Agia Marina** (45min., every hr. 6:50am-8:40pm) via **Varia** (€1.30), **Agios Rafael** (every 30min. 6am-9:40pm, €1.15) via **Thermi** (€1), and the **airport** (8 per day, 7:10am-7pm).

Taxis: (☎22510 23 500), behind the tourist office and on the corner of Ermou and Vournazon. To the **airport** (€8), **Molyvos** (€45), **Varia** (€3.50), and **Vatera** (€45).

Car Rentals: Payless (☎22510 81 100), in Pl. Sappho €35-45 per day. Open daily 7am-10pm.

▚ ▟ ORIENTATION AND PRACTICAL INFORMATION

Mytilini's harbor opens to the south, and cafes, bars, and hotels line the waterfront street **Pavlou Koundourioti**. On the center of the waterfront, **Plateia Sappho** is home to many tourist amenities and serves as the central day and nighttime hangout. The **old market** stretches along **Ermou**, home to pharmacies, boutiques, and bakeries. Ermou becomes **Kavetsou** at its southern end, where it intersects Vournazon one block inland on the harbor's western side. The south end of the harbor is home to most posh cafe-bars, the north end is littered with standard waterfront seafood joints, and a few blocks inland from Pl. Sappho is where most of the hole-in-the-wall *tavernas* are hidden.

Tourist Office: (☎22510 28 812), in Pl. Sappho. Friendly staff offers free maps, info about the island, accommodations advice, updated listings for nearby concerts and festivals; also showcases an amusing collection of mannequins dressed in traditional Lesvian gear. Open M-F 7:30am-3pm.

Budget Travel: ▮Zoumboulis Travel (☎22510 37 755; www.zoumboulistours.gr.), on the right side of the waterfront facing inland. Provides flight, ferry, and excursion tickets,

NORTHEAST AEGEAN ISLANDS

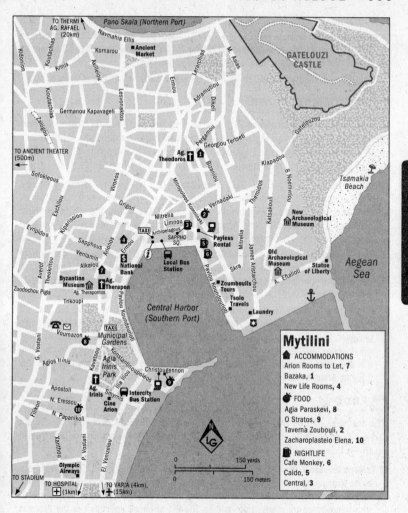

Mytilini

🏠 ACCOMMODATIONS
Arion Rooms to Let, **7**
Bazaka, **1**
New Life Rooms, **4**

🍎 FOOD
Agia Paraskevi, **8**
O Stratos, **9**
Taverna Zoubouli, **2**
Zacharoplasteio Elena, **10**

🍸 NIGHTLIFE
Cafe Monkey, **6**
Caldo, **5**
Central, **3**

plans trips to Turkey, and serves as a de facto tourist office with maps and advice on the island. Open daily 7am-10pm. **Tsolos Travel** (☎22510 48 030), farther down on the north side of the waterfront. Flight and ferry tickets and car rental. Open M-F 8am-9pm, Sa 8am-2pm and 5-9pm, Su 9am-2pm and 5-9pm. AmEx/MC/V.

Bank: National Bank, 28 Kounodourioti, on the left side of the harbor facing inland. **24hr. ATM.** Open M-Th 8am-2:30pm, F 8am-2pm.

Laundromat: (☎22510 27 065), on Aristarchou by the ferry docks. Wash and dry €10. Open M and W 8am-2pm, Tu and Th-F 8am-2pm and 5:30-8pm.

Tourist Police: (☎22510 22 776), across the street from the laundromat.

Hospital: (☎22510 57 700), southwest of town on P. Vostani and Navmachias Elis. 24hr. Ambulance ☎166.

Telephones: OTE, Vournazon 8 (☎22510 27 399). Open M-F 8am-8:30pm.

Internet Access: Sponda (☎22510 41 007), 1 block from Pl. Sappho, on the right side facing inland. €1.80 per hr. **InSpot** (☎22510 45 760), across the harbor. €2.40 per hr. Open 24hr. **Central Cafe,** on the waterfront, has free Wi-Fi.

Post Office: Vournazon 2 (☎22510 28 823). Open M-F 7:30am-2pm. **Postal Code:** 81100.

ACCOMMODATIONS

The hotels on the waterfront are elegant but pricey; head to Ermou to find plentiful *domatia.* If you are met at the ferry, be sure to negotiate, and keep in mind that longer stays often result in lower rates. Doubles run €30-35 before July 15 and €35-55 in late summer.

☒ **Alkaios Rooms** (☎22510 47 737; www.alkaiosrooms.gr), just off Ermou on Alkaioy. Tasteful rooms in a renovated Neoclassical mansion with beautiful wooden doorframes and an elegant facade. Clean rooms come with A/C, TVs, baths, and a light breakfast served on a social outdoor patio. Amiable owner Theofilis can tell you anything you need to know about the city. Singles €30-35; doubles €40-50. Cash only. ❷

Arion Rooms to Let, Alkaiou and Arionos 4 (☎22510 42 650), around the corner from Alkaios Rooms. Gold-toned walls frame beautiful, hand-painted murals. Small rooms with lustrous hardwood floors have TVs, fridges, and baths. Check out the phonograph as you enter. Singles €35; doubles €45. Cash only. ❸

Bazaka (☎22510 26 360), around the corner from Agia Theodoros. Make the 2nd left past Taverna Zoubouli, pass the church and the playground and keep going straight; it's unsigned and on the right. Large, clean rooms with TVs, A/C, fridges, and baths, some with balcony terraces. The inland location allows some relief from buzzing mopeds, while it is still within easy walking distance from both the castle and nightlife scene. Min. stay 2 nights. Doubles €35. Cash only. ❷

FOOD

The far side of the waterfront hosts the waterside fish *tavernas* found on most islands, while more delicious and affordable *tavernas* are scattered on the inland streets.

☒ **Taverna Zoubouli,** Vernardaki 2 (☎22510 21 251). From Ermou, head right on Mitropoleos Komninaki and then left on Vernardaki. Among the oldest *tavernas* in Mytilini. Canaries and hookahs surround the outdoor tables, and the inner walls are cluttered with handwritten messages from guests. The list of house specials like the *tabakas* (veal stewed with tomato, feta, and yogurt; €5.80) and the pork stuffed with orange and cheese makes navigating the large menu easier. Travelers may enjoy one of the 25 available flavors of tobacco with live music. Entrees €4.50-7. Hookah €5 per hr. Open daily noon-2am. Cash only. ❷

O Stratos (☎22510 47 900). Walk to the far left side of the waterfront facing inland. For conflicted travelers this seafood *taverna* doubles as a gyro/souvlaki joint. Octopodes hang to dry in front of the large, shady seafront seating area. Entrees €5-8. Fish €30-40 per kg. Open daily 11am-1am. ❷

Agia Paraskevi (☎22510 46 666), on Vournazon past the intersection with Kavetsou. The best souvlaki in town. Skewers are flavored with delicious sauces and served in platters or pita. Entrees €1.70-8. Open daily noon-2am. Free delivery. Cash only. ❶

NORTHEAST AEGEAN ISLANDS

SIGHTS

ARCHAEOLOGICAL MUSEUMS. Two museums share Mytilini's collection of archaeological relics. Tickets are good for both on the same day. The well-designed **new Archaeological Museum** contains the permanent exhibit "Lesvos from the Hellenistic to Roman Times," displaying finds ranging from second-century BC cooking utensils to AD third-century Roman sculptures and busts. The undisputed highlights are the restored mosaic floors from ancient villas at Ag. Kyriaki, displayed in their original layout under glass tiles, allowing you to walk on top. Most exhibits have English signs and the museum is wheelchair-accessible. *(8 Noemvriou. ☎ 22510 40 223. Open Tu-Su 8:30am-3pm. €3, students €2, EU students and under 18 free.)* The **old Archaeological Museum,** up the hill behind the main port, has a less inspiring roundup of Lesvian artifacts from prehistoric to Roman times. Each exhibit, however, is accompanied signs that use both mythological and historical elements to explain the significance of these fragments of ages past. The collection focuses on earthenware jars and small figurines found during the excavations at Thermi. *(Argiri Eftalioti 7. ☎ 22510 28 032. Open Tu-Su 8:30am-3pm.)*

GATELOUZI CASTLE. The sprawling Gatelouzi Castle extends over a pine-covered hill near the museums, above the northern port. Though the original building was erected in AD 483-565 by Emperor Justinian, the castle bears the name of Franceso Gatelouzi, who received the entire island of Lesvos as a dowry in 1354. Centuries of Genoese, Ottomans, and Greeks have maintained the castle walls and underground crypts that once hid women and children in times of war. The castle, one of the largest in the Mediterranean, was built in several stages by its various captors; the entire lower part was added by the Turks after their 1462 capture of the castle. Because locals took stones from the castle to rebuild fallen structures after WWII, little more than rubble remains of its interior. The path along the walls affords panoramic views of the city and both harbors, and the surrounding pine forest makes for a fragrant walk. *(☎ 22510 27 970. Open Tu-Su 8am-8pm. €2, students €1.)*

RELIGIOUS AND BYZANTINE SIGHTS. The late 19th-century **Church of Agios Therapon,** on the western side of the harbor and one block inland on Ermou, is the largest on the island, boasting a 4½m wide chandelier and elaborate decoration in revivals of Byzantine, Gothic, and Baroque styles.*(☎ 22510 21 549. Open M-F 7am-1pm and 5-9pm, Sa-Su 7am-1pm and 6-9pm. Free. Modest dress suggested.)* Across the square, the **Byzantine Museum,** on Pl. Ag. Therapon, contains Christian iconography from the 13th through 19th centuries along with other ecumenical treasures. *(☎ 22510 28 916. Open M-Sa 9am-1pm. €2, students free.)* Inland and north of the harbor (one block off Ermou) is the **Church of Agios Theodoros,** the oldest in Mytilini, which houses the bones and skull of its patron saint.

OTHER RUINS. The highest point on the northern side of Mytilini is the third-century BC **ancient theater,** from the Hellenistic period, where 15,000 spectators attended performances and enjoyed near-perfect acoustics. The effect was so impressive that it inspired Pompeii to build Rome's first stone theater. The nearby **Roman Aqueduct** also merits a visit.

🎵 📷 ENTERTAINMENT AND NIGHTLIFE

Cine Arion, on Smyrnis across from the intercity bus station, plays mostly American films nightly on the theater's two screens. *(☎ 22510 44 456. Weekly schedules at the ticket window. Showings start 7:30-10:15pm. €6-7.)* Mytilini's nightlife centers on Pl. Sappho, where a number of all-day cafes turn up the lights and music come nightfall.

Cafe Monkey (☎22510 37 717), faces inland on the right. Deliciously creamy coffees (€3.50) and mixed drinks (€7) under outdoor mist fans and distinctive tear-drop lights. Visiting artists occasionally host events here for the sophisticated set. Mixed drinks €6-7. Open daily 7am-3am.

Central (☎22510 47 995), on the corner of the square. International music and a waterfall of mist characterize this establishment. Patrons lounge at the breezy bar, playing backgammon and chatting while enjoying the free Wi-Fi and full menu. Drinks €5-6. Salads €5-7. Open daily 6am-4am.

Caldo (☎22510 28 245). Its funky purple lighting makes it another popular stop on the nightlife circuit. Drinks €6-8. Open daily 7am-3am.

DAYTRIPS FROM MYTILINI

VARIA. Only 4km south of Mytilini along El. Venizelou, the tiny, unassuming village of Varia surprises wayfarers with the ▨**Musée Tériade**. It has an excellent collection of oil paintings, etchings, and Picasso, Miró, Léger, Chagall, and Matisse lithographs with captions in English, French, and Greek. Tériade, a native of Lesvos (born Stratis Eleftheriadis), was a leading 20th-century publisher of graphic art in Paris. (☎22510 23 372. Open Tu-Su 9am-2pm and 5-8pm. €2.) On the same street just before the Musée Tériade, the **Theophilos Museum** exhibits 86 paintings by self-taught Greek folk artist Theophilos Hadzimichali. (☎22510 41 644. Open Tu-Su 10am-4pm. €2, students and under 18 free.) His vivid patriotic works depicting scenes from Modern Greek history are internationally recognized and can be found in homes across the islands. *(Local buses to Varia leave Mytilini every hr. (20min., €1.30). Tell the driver you're going to the museums, as they are a little past Varia town.)*

THE REAL DEAL. Despite an extensive and organized public bus system, many of Lesvos's treasures remain accessible only via taxi or private transportation. Taking out a car is far cheaper than the taxi fare and allows for complete freedom to explore the far-flung villages and monasteries, as well as access to many of the museums and parks only serviced once daily by public transport.

MOLYVOS Μόλυβος   ☎22530

Molyvos (a.k.a. Mithymna) is a quintessential storybook village, winding up from the sea toward a towering mountaintop castle. Shopkeepers lounge in the vine-shaded agora, resting on the medieval stoops that line the steep trek up to the fortress. Down below, the picturesque waterfront is home to glittering boats and relaxed tavernas, while the pebble beach is home to tiki bars and sun worshippers. With an illustrious school of fine arts, a marketplace, and several high-end *tavernas*, the city caters to upscale tourism, but even backpackers can find accommodation, food, and drink to fit their budget.

TRANSPORTATION

Buses: The bus stop is right before town, 10m from the fork that leads to Eftalou. Buses run between **Anaxos** and **Eftalou** (9 per day 10am-10:15pm, €3.20) via **Petra** and

Molyvos. Ask at the tourist office for schedules. The intercity bus runs to **Mytilini** (1½hr., 5 per day 7am-7pm, €6.20).

Taxis: (☎22530 71 480). Stop at the intersection on the main road heading into town from the bus stop. €5 to Eftalou or Petra costs.

Car and Moped Rental: Kosmos Rentals (☎22530 71 710), to the immediate right of the National Bank, near the fork to Eftalou. Mopeds €10-24 per day, varying with duration. Cars from €35. Prices include full insurance, tax, and unlimited mileage. Open daily 8am-1pm and 5:30-9pm.

ORIENTATION AND PRACTICAL INFORMATION

Molyvos has three primary roads that run along different levels of the hill. The main paved road leads from the bus station past the tourist office and runs downhill 600m to the harbor. As you enter town on this main road, a sharp cobbled switchback to the left leads down to the **beach** where a number of bars and restaurants border the shore. 20m from the tourist office, a cobbled road to the right leads through a small tunnel into the old shop-filled **agora,** shaded with leafy canopies. Most practical amenities are in the agora, while most tourist amenities are around the waterfront.

Tourist Office: (☎22530 71 347; www.mithymna.gr), on the main road 30m from the bus stop. The friendly, English-speaking staff provides free maps of the town, updated bus schedules, and sights recommendations. They also can help coordinate where and when to make connections to get around the island by bus, and are very helpful in calling around to accommodations to help you get the best price. Open July-Aug. 10am-3pm and 4-8:30pm, Sept. and May-June 10am-5pm.

Budget Travel: Com Travel(☎22530 71 900; www.comtravel.gr.), on the harbor where the downhill road levels out. English-speaking staff sells flight and ferry tickets and plans excursions. Open daily 9am-9pm; tickets sold 10am-2pm and 5-9pm. Reduced hours in low season. MC/V.

Banks: National Bank (☎22530 71 210), next door to the tourist office. **24hr. ATM.** Open M-Th 8am-2:30pm, F 8am-2pm. **Emporiki Bank,** near the taxi stand, also has a **24hr. ATM,** as does **Pireaus Bank** in the agora.

Bookstore: Estravagario Books (☎22530 71 824), in the agora, past the post office on the right side. Offers English books and Greek-language guides. Open daily 9am-2:30pm and 5-11pm.

Laundromat: (☎22530 71 622). Follow the main road to Eftalou; it is 150m up, at the intersection with the other road leading toward the bus station. Wash and dry €9. Smaller loads €2.60 per kg. Open daily 9am-2:30pm and 5:30-9:30pm.

Tourist Police: (☎22510 71 222). Go up the hill past the post office, down the street across from the bakery, then another 400m.

Pharmacy: (☎22530 71 427), on the main road leading toward the waterfront from the agora; take the left fork after the tunnel. Open M-Sa 9am-2pm and 5:30-10pm, Su 10:30-1:30pm and 7-9:30pm. In an emergency, call ☎6947 66 7868.

Medical Services: (☎22530 71 702), uphill past the post office in the agora. Open daily 9am-1:30pm.

Internet Access: Central Cafe (☎22530 72 255), down the coastal road just before the harbor. €3 per hr., min. €1.50. Open daily 6am-2:30pm and 4pm-midnight. **Conga's Beach Bar** (see **Food,** p. 400) has free Wi-Fi.

Post Office: (☎22530 71 246). Just past the tunnel, follow the right fork 200m up into the agora. **Western Union** and traveler's check exchange (€3 per check). Open M-F 7:30am-2pm. **Postal Code:** 81108.

ACCOMMODATIONS AND CAMPING

Signs for *domatia* dot the road to **Eftalou**, which is lined with more expensive studios and hotels; the tourist office will gladly help you call around to find a bed that meets your budget.

The Schoolmistress With The Golden Eyes (☎22530 71 390), across from the medical center up the right fork after the tunnel, past the post office. A stone's throw from the beach and waterfront. Clean rooms with baths, balconies, and Wi-Fi smack in the heart of the pleasant, vine-shaded agora. Some rooms have sea views. Singles €25-35; doubles €35-45. Cash only. ❷

Nassos Guest House (☎22530 71 432; www.nassosguesthouse.com), on the main road up the hill into town. Head right at the 1st steep switchback and look for the sign. Homey, inviting, and thoughtfully decorated rooms in a converted mansion have a community feel with common kitchens and baths. Your host, Tom, will answer any questions. The book exchange, internet and laundry facilities, and private balconies with views of the water below add to the appeal. Washing machine €3. Open in summer only. Reservations recommended. Singles €25; doubles €30-35; studios €35-40. Cash only. ❷

Sea Melody (☎22530 71 158), farther downhill and across the street from Com Travel. Pretty, peach-colored rooms with shell motifs come with fridges, TVs, baths, A/C, hair dryers, and lovely views of the water—all from an excellent location just minutes from the waterfront, agora, and beach. Inquire at the mini-mart across the street. Singles €25-45; doubles €40-50. Cash only. ❸

Baliaka Mirsini (☎22530 71 414). From the main road, make a right onto the cobbled street across from the Cinema, and continue for 50m. Spacious doubles with baths, TVs, fridges, coffeemakers, kitchenettes, and a shared patio. A/C €5. Singles €30; doubles €40. Cash only. ❷

Camping Mithimna (☎22530 71 169; www.molivos-camping.com), 1.5m out of town on the road to Eftalou; inquire at the tourist office about buses going in that direction. This spacious campground has common picnic areas and sparse foliage separating tent sites. Late arrivals can set up shop and pay rent in the morning, though those without tents should call in advance. €4.50-5.50 per person; €3 per small tent, €3.50 per large tent. Camper rental €5. Cash only. ❶

FOOD

Harbor restaurants line the waterfront but may stretch the pocketbook. Head farther inland for smaller *tavernas* that serve excellent food at better prices.

Taverna Traditional (☎22530 72 250). Follow the road past the tourist office up toward the post office, taking the 2nd steep switchback to the right, just before the tunnel; it's about 100m up. This tiny, family-run *taverna* serves homemade Greek favorites on a rooftop terrace overlooking the town. Entrees €4-7. Open daily 8am-late. Cash only. ❷

Taverna O Gatos (☎22530 71 661; www.gatos-restaurant.gr.), midway up the hill before the post office, just after the tunnel. Has served traditional fare for over 20 years, including lamb with feta and tomatoes (€9.90). The sea breeze and sunset from the rooftop tables garnish the homey dishes. Entrees €6.70-8.50. Open daily 10am-late. MC/V. ❷

The Captain's Table (☎22530 71 241). The fisherman who supplies this Aussie-Greek-owned restaurant is the owner's father, and reputedly among the island's best; if you ask, you can choose your fresh fish in the kitchen. The captain's platter for 1 (€13) or 2 (€25) lets you taste the full range of his talents. Enjoy complimentary olives and peanut brittle. Open daily 5pm-late. MC/V. ❸

Friends Gyros Stand (☎22530 71 567), on the main road. Among delicious standard gyro and souvlaki options, several meatless pitas (€2.30) are stuffed with cucumbers, fries, green peppers, feta, and other tasty ingredients. The gyro skewers have peppers along with meat to add some flavor. Free delivery. Open daily 1pm-late. Cash only. ❶

👁 🏖 SIGHTS AND BEACHES

A narrow, pebbly beach extends to the south toward Petra and is accessible from the first switchback to the left as you enter Molyvos. Beach umbrellas abound, and showers and changing rooms are free. **Fun Club,** under the yellow flag on the grounds of the Olive Press Hotel on the Molyvos beach, offers water sports, lessons, and kayaks. (Parasailing €30 for one, €50 for two; jet ski or water ski lesson €30; water tubing €10 per ride. Open daily noon-6pm.)

EFTALOU. More inviting shores can be found at Eftalou, whose beautiful black-pebble beaches stretch in several coves along the road; the farther ones are more protected from the wind and are frequented by nude bathers. The bus from Molyvos drops off in the middle of the main beach. Walk about 300m to the end of road to the left facing inland and follow the signs to find Eftalou's spa-like **thermal baths,** one of the few with coed pools. The 44-46.5°C, slightly radioactive waters are amazingly relaxing and reportedly effective against an entire host of ailments. The knowledgeable, multilingual staff gives advice on proper soaking procedures and can answer all questions concerning the baths' health benefits. (☎22530 71 245. €4.50 for 45min. in the pool, €7 for 20min. in a private bathtub; includes free locker storage; children 6 and under free. Towel rental €1.)

KASTRO. The dominant feature of Molyvos's skyline is the *kastro*, which affords panoramic views of Molyvos, the beach, and the hills of Lesvos. The castle, once an important transfer point for trade in olives and oil, was repaired by Gatelouzi in 1373 and later buttressed by the Turks. (Open Tu-Su 8am-8pm. €3.)

🎵 📷 ENTERTAINMENT AND NIGHTLIFE

In the summer, spend an evening under the stars at open-air **Cinema Arion,** just past the bus stop heading into town before the tourist office. Posters for that week's English-language showings are outside the cinema. (☎69776 26 976. Showings

ON THE MENU

THE IDIOT'S GUIDE TO DRINKING OUZO

When you go out for your first meal in Greece, don't be surprised, shocked, or flattered if your waiter rushes out before your entree arrives to present you with a shot glass full of opaque liquor and the simple command, "Drink!" He's just assuming that you, like almost every Greek, want to cleanse your palate and ease your mind with some ouzo.

There's an art to enjoying the anise-flavored national drink, which is important to know if you don't want to reveal yourself as a neophyte. First, don't take that shot like a frat boy. Good ouzo is around 40% alcohol by volume, and it just isn't made to be chugged. It's invariably served with a glass of water for the purpose of mixing; that's what turned your shot milky-white. The key is to keep adding water as you drink to avoid dehydration and other ill effects.

Second, snack on some *mezedes* while you take your ouzo. Munching on a salad, some cheese or vegetables will temper the alcohol and prolong the experience. That's the point, after all; Greece's obsession with ouzo is not really focused on getting plastered on something that tastes like licorice. Instead, it's about drinking lazily, relaxing in a *kafeneion*, and chatting with friends for the entire afternoon until the sun sets and dinner begins.

start 9:30pm. €6.50.) Ask at the tourist office about theatrical performances, which occur periodically throughout the summer.

Molyvos keeps a fun and relaxed after-hours atmosphere, with locals dancing until dawn without the frenzied intensity of other island party scenes.

Conga's Beach Club (☎22530 72 181). Begin the night at this tiki-inspired club, accessible from both the beachfront and main roads. Eclectic music and colorful decorations make visitors lounge away entire days in a haze of beach, bongos, and booze. With hammocks, Wi-Fi, and a pool table, Conga's is perfect for a rest from the sun during the day, but the dance floor heats up at night with international music. Beer €3. Mixed drinks €6-7. Cover €5; credited toward the cost of a drink. Happy hour daily 7-11pm. Open July-Aug. daily 10am-3:30am.

Cafe Bazaar, on the right side of the hill heading down to the harbor, has an array of snacks and the best daiquiris (€6.50) on the island, all made from fresh fruit. On summer nights, head across the street to the nightclub of the same name, where soul, funk, and jazz bounce off the blue floor lights in the cave-like hall. Cafe open daily 11am-2:30pm and 4pm-4am. Club open daily midnight-noon.

Club, just down the street from Club Bazaar. Venture into the club with the Greek sign out front; locals gather here to dance traditional Greek dances to live music, so it's a perfect place to observe tourist-free nightlife. Don't try to join in unless you know the steps. Open daily 11pm-late.

SKALA ERESSOU Σκάλα Ερεσού ☎22530

The birthplace of poet Sappho, Skala Eressou welcomes families, archaeologists, and lesbian couples alike to share in its beachy, bohemian atmosphere. The sandy beach, deemed one of the world's best, lies between two mountainous peaks, affording sunset vistas from the cafe-bars on the shore. Visiting artists flock here to honor Sappho's sexuality along with her artistic legacy at the frequent women's arts festivals and performance events. A preponderance of rainbow flags fill storefronts, and many of the town's services are gay-friendly. Still, Skala Eressou's delicious food, laid-back vibe, and diversity of artistic events make this tiny village a paradise for visitors of any sexual orientation.

⌨ TRANSPORTATION

Buses: A bus runs between Skala Eressou and **Mytilini** via **Eressos**(3hr., 4 daily 6:15am-8pm, €8). Reduced service in low season and weekends. The bus stops in a large parking lot on the main road 2 blocks from the waterfront.

Taxis: There are only 2 taxis in the area, and trips must be arranged in advance through **Sappho Travel;** a taxi to Sigri costs about €25, and €70 to the airport.

✈ 🛈 ORIENTATION AND PRACTICAL INFORMATION

Facing inland, the main road hits the waterfront a few meters to the left of a short footbridge (facing inland), which divides the town. Restaurants and cafes line the waterfront to the left, bars cluster to the right, and many accommodations can be found one block inland.

Tourist Office: Joanna and the incredibly helpful, English-speaking team at ▨ **Sappho Travel** (☎22530 52 140; www.sapphotravel.com), 1 block from the bus stop, provide info about the town, book ferry and flight tickets, help with accommodations, and exchange currency. They also arrange boat trips (€32), sunset cruises (€20), and local walks. Open M-Sa 9am-2:30pm and 6-10pm, Su 11am-2pm and 6-9pm.

24hr. ATM: Outside Sappho Travel.

Laundromat: (☎22530 52 255), just in front of a the church. Wash and dry €10. Open M-Sa 10am-1pm.

Police: (☎22530 56 222), in Eressos.

Medical Services: (☎22530 52 132; Eressos 53 221). The medical clinic can be found on a side street; head right when facing Sappho Travel. In case of emergency, call the **health center** (☎22530 56 400, 56 442, or 56 444), in Antissa, 11km from Skala Eressou.

Internet Access: Free Wi-Fi and internet widely available in cafes lining the water; bring your laptop and chill at **Aqua** (☎22530 52 048) over breakfast. Breakfast €4.50-8. Open daily 9am-late. **Internet Eressos** (☎22530 52 082), on the waterfront to the right facing inland, before Zorba the Buddha. €1 per 10min., €5 per hr. Open daily 12:30-2:30pm and 7-10pm.

Post Office: (☎22530 53 227), in Eressos. Open M-F 8am-2pm. **Postal Code:** 81105.

ACCOMMODATIONS

Many options for accommodations can be found close to the waterfront, from pricey hotels to budget, women-only pensions. While most of the town's facilities are gay-friendly, this is not necessarily true across the board. Ask at Sappho Travel if you have trouble finding a room. Unorganized camping is permitted on the beach, though the police have been known to clear out campsites.

Hotel Mascot (☎22530 52 130). Turn right past the bus stop and walk 50m. This women-only accommodation option contains brightly painted rooms with A/C, balconies, baths, and fridges. Breakfast included and served in a common nook that encourages guests to mingle. Reservations are booked through Sappho Travel. Singles negotiable; doubles €35-50. Cash only. ❷

Pension Krinelos (☎22530 53 376). Past Hotel Mascot, make a right and follow the signs. Clean rooms come with bath, A/C, fridges, and Wi-Fi, and open onto the shared social terrace overlooking fruit trees. Singles €20-25; doubles €30-50, with kitchenette €45. Cash only. ❶

Maria Pantermou (☎22530 53 267), on the way to Pension Krinelos. Simple, homestyle, affordable rooms. The husband-wife team provides spartan doubles with A/C, fridges, baths, and access to the wrap-around balcony. Singles €20; doubles €25-35. Cash only. ❶

FOOD

Food in Skala Eressou is generally excellent and affordable. The town is a vegetarian paradise—at least by Greek standards.

Ouzeri Soulatso (☎22530 52 078), to the left of the bridge and on the waterfront when facing inland. The most traditional Greek *taverna* in town. Diners are treated to a deep-sea harvest of fresh fish and a variety of ouzos on an ocean terrace decorated with hanging octopusi; head up to the storefront case to pick your meal. Grilled entrees €7-9. Open daily noon-midnight. Cash only. ❷

Eressos Palace (☎22530 53 858), just past Ouzeri Soulatso off the end of the main waterfront. This family-run place offers huge portions of fresh food at deliciously low prices. The fisherman's souvlaki (€8.50) is made with a variety of skewered and grilled fish, and a number of vegetarian dishes are available as well. Don't miss the delicious *dolmades* (€5.50). Entrees €4-8. Open daily 8am-2am. MC/V. ❷

Samadhi Restaurant(☎69550 54956). Head in the opposite direction on the waterfront. A locally acclaimed *taverna* with pineapple-encrusted chicken bombay (€9) and other international treats. Try the 7 global variations on beef filet (€16.50). Entrees €6.50-9.50. Open daily 7pm-late. MC/V. ❷

To Stenaki (☎22530 53 236), 1 block in from the waterfront just to the right of the bridge. For a deliciously simple budget option, try Stenaki's Greek salad (€3.50), vegetarian pita (€1.50), or souvlaki (€1.20). Open daily 1pm-midnight. Cash only. ❷

🎵 🌴 ENTERTAINMENT AND FESTIVALS

Behind the main *plateia*, open-air **Cine Sappho** has nightly 9:30pm showings of English-language movies in the summer. **Sappho Garden of the Arts,** a cafe, gallery, and women's cultural center, hosts nightly exhibitions and performances by visiting artists in its outdoor garden performance space. It's behind the internet cafe on the far end of the harbor. Check the website for details on who's performing. (☎22530 53 682; www.sapphogarden.net. Open daily 7pm -late.) The first and second weekends in September, Skala Eressou hosts the week-long **Women's Festival.** Around 400 participants come to enjoy the theatrical, artistic, and sporting activities, as well as the series of workshops, massage therapies, and parties all organized by Sappho Travel.

👁 SIGHTS

AGIOS ANDREAS. The fifth-century mosaics once housed in the early-Christian basilica of **Agios Andreas** are now in Mytilini's new Archaeological Museum (p. 397). Though the church was named after the apostle Ag. Andreas, a Cretan archbishop of the same name happened to die nearby a couple centuries later. His grave, the **Tomb of Agios Andreas,** was incorporated into the site, though it only contains half of his remains; the other portion was claimed by Crete. (*3 blocks north of the beach.*)

RIVER. The river is home to many rare and exotic birds. Peak birdwatching season is from April to May. (*Just west of the center.*)

IPSILOU MONASTERY. Heading back toward Sigri 2.5km after the fork, you'll reach the turn-off up to Ipsilou Monastery. Dating back to AD 800, the monastery sits on the Ordymnos volcanic dome and commands an amazing view of northwestern Lesvos's rugged, desolate hills. One of the priests will walk you through the excellent museum, across from the chapel. It houses 17th- and 18th-century artifacts and religious vestments, as well as a number of 16th-century writings and icons. (*Open daily 7:30am-10pm. Modest dress required. Free.*)

🌃 NIGHTLIFE

The nightlife scene, dominated by chill lounges that spill onto the sand, is (unsurprisingly) lesbian-friendly. The close proximity to the water makes for easy swimming access on hot summer evenings. In keeping with town decree, all bars turn off the music at 2am, though patrons are welcome to stay and chat until dawn.

Parasol (☎22530 52 050). Facing inland on the bridge, follow the waterfront to the right. Umbrellas adorn this tropical cocktail bar, where patrons throw back especially delicious mojitos or the patented vodka-and-melon Wooloomooloo Wonders (both €6.50). Mixed drinks €6-7.50. Homemade whole-grain pizzas €9. Open daily 9:30am-late. Cash only.

Zorba the Buddha (☎22530 53 777), on the waterfront away from town past Parasol. Occasional international live music accompanies ouzo and tapas (€3), enjoyed under floaty curtains. Mixed drinks €7. Open 9am-3am.

The Tenth Muse (☎22530 53 287; www.thetenthmusecafe.com), in the main *plateia*. Serves savory pancakes (€5-6) by day and becomes a popular bar by night. Free Wi-Fi.

Beer €2.50-4. Mixed drinks €5.50-6.50. Happy hour daily 6-9pm; drinks €5, food and drink combos from €6. Open daily 9am-late.

LIMNOS Λήμνος

The lively island of Limnos reveals varied treasures, from well-preserved wetlands and prehistoric cities to silent sand dunes and a pack of migrating flamingos. Homer called the prehistoric Myrina a "well-built city," although visitors note that the settlement's tiny scale is almost as impressive as its structural resilience. Peacefully remote and unflinchingly quiet, this far-flung island's majestic sunsets, sparkling beaches, and bustling local communities make it a favorite getaway for Greek families.

MYRINA Μύρινα ☎22540

Fanning out behind the castle-crowned peninsula, the glittering city of Myrina spans two calm beaches that reflect the city's relaxed lifestyle. Residents and visitors windowshop on the cobbled streets, sip frappés on the waterfront until late, or scale the heights of the ancient castle to catch a dazzling sunset behind distant Mt. Athos. Largely untouristed, Myrina's small-town feel has a long history: the prehistoric ruins of ancient Myrina might be the smallest town ever.

TRANSPORTATION

Flights: Limnos Airport (LXS) is 20km out of town and served only by taxis (€20). **Olympic** (☎22540 92 700) and **Aegean** (☎92 720) flights go to: **Athens** (50min., 2 per day, €77-150); **Chios** (2hr., 2 per week, €46); **Lesvos** (35min., 5 per week, €46); **Rhodes** (5 per week, €75); **Thessaloniki** (6 per week, €83-103).

Ferries: Limnos ferry schedules are usually in flux, since different companies serve the island at different times. Ferries dock on either end of the horseshoe-shaped port, so be sure to ask where to wait. Ferries generally run to: **Kavala** (4hr., daily, €16); **Lavrio,** near Athens (10hr., 3 per week, €27.70); **Mytilini, Lesvos** (5hr., 3 per week, €19); **Piraeus** (17hr., 1 per week, €35); **Samos** (13hr., 3 per week, €30); **Samothrace** (2hr., 4 per week, €13); **Thessaloniki** (7hr., 4 per week, €35). **Atzamis Travel** (p. 406) sells flight and ferry tickets for all lines. **Pravlis Travel** sells ferry tickets for GA and NEL. Open M-F 9am-2:30pm and 6-9:30pm, Sa 9am-2pm, Su 6-9:30pm.

Buses: The white, unsigned bus station is in Pl. El. Venizelou, the 2nd *plateia* along Karatza marked by a small park with 4 palm trees. (The buses are a dead giveaway.) **KTEL** (☎22970 22 464) runs to **Kalliopi** (3 per day), **Livadohori** (4 per day), **Plaka** (2 per day), and several other small villages around the island.

Taxis: (☎22540 23 820). Available in the main *plateia*. €25 to the archaeological sights at Poliochni and Hephaestia.

Car Rental: Available at a number of places on the waterfront, including **Holiday Car Rental** (☎22540 23 280), across from Petrides Travel. Cars €30-40 per day.

ORIENTATION AND PRACTICAL INFORMATION

The city has two main waterfronts on opposite sides of the castle. **Turkikos,** facing Turkey, is the active port, with Myrina's best fish *tavernas* and a sandy beach at its far end. **Romeikos,** on the northern side of the castle, is a family-friendly waterfront lined with parks, playgrounds, and hip cafes. To find it, head inland up **Karatza,** the town's commercial artery, and take a left when you can spot the sea in between the buildings. Karatza leads inland from Pl. 8 Oktovriou to the town's central *plateia*, which contains most practical amenities.

Tourist Offices: Atzamis Travel (☎22540 25 936), 1 block behind the harbor, sells flight and ferry tickets for all lines. The friendly staff will help you navigate the seemingly impenetrable tangle of schedules for different ferry lines. Open 8am-3pm, 5:30-11pm. MC/V. Family-run since 1969, **Petrides Travel** (☎22540 22 550; www.petridestravel. gr), on Karatza offers car rental (€25-40 per day), and guided excursions. Buses go to sights and beaches (½-day €15, full day €20), and boats visit Isostatious (€35) and Samothrace (€65). In low season, the agency only sells flight tickets. Open daily 8am-4pm and 6pm-midnight.

Banks: Most banks are in the *plateia,* including **Emporiki Bank, National Bank, Alphabank,** and **Euro Bank.** All banks have **24hr ATMs.** Most open M-Th 8am-2:30pm, F 8am-2pm.

Laundromat: (☎22540 24 392), in the Hotel Paris, just across from the post office. €6.50 per 1-2kg load, €9.20 per 5-6kg. Open daily 8am-2pm and 5-9pm.

Police: (☎22540 22 200), down Garofallidi on the corner of a large intersection.

Pharmacy: (☎22540 22 500). Open 8am-2pm, 6-9pm.

Hospital: (☎22540 82 000). Follow the same street further inland to reach the hospital, near the police station. Open 24hr.

Telephones: OTE (☎22540 29 999), in the *plateia.* Open 7:30am-3pm and 6-9pm.

Internet Access: Turkikos (☎22540 25 525) at the mouth of Karatza at Excite. Internet midnight-8am €1.50, 8am-midnight €2.50.

Post Office: (☎22540 22 462), 1 block inland on Garofallidi. Open M-F 7:30am-2pm. **Postal Code:** 81400.

ACCOMMODATIONS

Catering mostly to Greek families, the hotels in town are scarce and expensive. A few *domatia* can be found in **Turkikos** and a few blocks inland behind the archaeological museum. If you have a phone card and some patience, try calling around to compare prices, though you may end up paying top dollar despite your best efforts.

Hotel Lemnos (☎22540 22 153), near the ferry dock in Turkikos. Rents clean, standard rooms with A/C, TVs, fridges, phones, balconies, elevators, and castle or sea views. Wi-Fi in the lobby. Singles €35; doubles €45. Cash only. ❸

Aithalia, Mitropoleos (☎22540 25 448; www.aithalia.gr). Friendly management offers new doubles with A/C, TVs, kitchenettes, and baths; upstairs rooms have balconies. Doubles €45. Cash only. ❸

FOOD

High-quality, reasonably priced food is easy to find in Myrina. Both Turkikos and Romeikos are lined with quality *tavernas* and cafes. *Psiari* (fish) *tavernas* line the *limanaki* (little port) of Turkiko; facing inland head right, just before the beach begins.

To Limanaki (☎22540 23 744), tucked in the corner of the little port, on the far end. Lets patrons choose whatever fish their hearts desire from the icy vats near the kitchen. Fish €35-45 per kg. Open daily 7pm-late. Cash only. ❷

Ouzerie to "11" (☎22540 22 635), inland near the bus stop. Offers a deliciously wide fish menu. Look in the drink freezer to see the buckets of clams and mussels. Try the sea urchins (€5) or the shrimp souvlaki (€12). Open daily 11:30am-4pm and 8pm-midnight. Cash only. ❷

Taverna Kosmos (☎22540 22 050), along Romeikos to the right on the water, next to the playground. The sea literally crashes up to the tables at this *taverna*. A slew of Greek comfort foods, including moussaka (€6) and garlic mussels (€7), dominate the well-rounded menu. Appetizers €3-6. Open daily 10am-2am. Cash only. ❷

Taverna Oi Tzitzifies (☎22540 23 756), about 50m to the right of the archaeological site facing the water. A popular sand-top lunch spot, featuring delicious stuffed tomatoes and fries (€5.50). Greek salad €5. Open daily 1pm-midnight. Cash only. ❷

Karagiozis. Facing inland at Romeikos, head to the left to join the crowd at this beachfront establishment. Sip frappés and coffee-inspired mixed drinks (€5-6) under lanterns painted to look like moons. Ever caffeinated, it becomes a hopping club by night. Cappuccino €3. Open daily 9am-4am. Cash only. ❶

🔆 🏖 SIGHTS AND BEACHES

Most of Limnos's sandy beaches are near Myrina. The most popular beach on the island is shallow **Riha Nera,** just north of Romeikos. **Avlonas,** on the way to Kaspakas, is large and uncrowded, with two islets of its own. Go along the steep mountain road to find **Agios Yiannis** nearby. On the road to Kontias is **Nevgatis,** an easily accessible beach with 2km of unbroken sands.

◼KASTRO. The *kastro*, piercing the skyline and dividing the waterfronts, is home to several dozen deer. Enjoy the stunning sunset view and the ruins of the seventh-century BC fortress, reworked by Venetians in the 13th century. Signs from the harbor point to the rocky trail leading to the entrance; the hike up is about 10min. The best time to visit is just before sunset, allowing at least an hour of dusk to explore the walls and crumbling buildings. Watch out for deer droppings. *(Always open. Always free.)*

◼PREHISTORIC MYRINA. Catwalk-like paths lead visitors over the well-preserved foundations of a fourth-millennium BC proto-urban settlement that Homer referred to as a "well-built city." Visitors are impressed by the tiny foundations; most houses were the size of modern closets, and the streets of the city are about the width of a small hallway. The stone building that sits at the site's entrance continuously plays an informative video with English subtitles, using computer simulations to show what the village looked like in its heyday. *(100m along the waterfront past the museum. ☎22540 22 257. Open Tu-Su 9am-3pm. Free.)*

THE LOCAL STORY

YO-HO-HO AND A BOTTLE OF OUZO

The islands of the Aegean have a long history of piracy due to their riches and unlucky location on one of the world's major trade routes. While pirates never left any buried treasure (that we know of), they did leave behind an enduring, albeit indirect, architectural legacy. Aegean pirates plundered the crops and food of defenseless islanders, sometimes razing villages and raping women. Many settlements and buildings on the Aegean islands were built specifically in response to these attacks.

Most of the fortresses of the Aegean are situated on mountaintops to give locals an advantageous position against swashbuckling invaders. The fortress monastery at Patmos is a good example of this—Patmians would seek refuge behind its impenetrable walls when they saw the Jolly Roger on the horizon. The houses on Ikaria are carefully nestled into the mountains so they are almost invisible from the sea. Seafaring plunderers would assume the island was deserted and passed on by. The village of Mesta, on Chios, has linked rooftops so villagers could run to safety during a pirate invasion. Locals also constructed half-stairways off their rooftops so they could slash at the pirates from above, but their attackers could not climb up. There's even a theory that the distinctive black-and-white pebble mosaics of the Dodecanese served a defensive purpose in addition to a decorative one—the highly polished stones were meant to be too slippery for clunky pirate boots.

ARCHAEOLOGICAL MUSEUM. The well-curated archaeological museum has a collection of artifacts with informative English and Greek explanations printed on canvas drapes. Finds from the ancient settlements of Hephaestus, Poliochni, and the Kabeiron include a series of terra-cotta siren sculptures and an impressive skeleton of a sacrificed bull calf. Look for the beautiful statue of Eros shooting a bow on the first floor.*(At the far end of Romeikos, to the left when facing inland.* ☎ *22540 22 990. Open Tu-Su 8:30am-3pm. €2, EU students free.)*

◧ DAYTRIPS FROM MYRINA

Though most of the island's attractions are best reached by car or moped, a couple of travel agencies such as Petrides arrange bus excursions around Limnos. Taxis go from Myrina to all sites for €25 each way but will expect to be paid for waiting time; negotiate a total price with the driver before departing.

ARCHAEOLOGICAL SITES

Limnos has a number of notable archaeological sites, all on the opposite side of the island from Myrina.

Poliochni, on the eastern coast, is the oldest proto-urban settlement discovered in all of Europe, dating from the late Neolithic period (5000-4000 BC). One of the most complex fortified cities of its time, it is credited with being the site of Europe's first parliament. (Free admission; ask at the Archeological Museum in Myrina for more details.) **Ancient Hephaestia,** on the northeastern coast of the island, was the location of an eighth-century BC sanctuary to Hephaestus, god of fire and metallurgy, whose divine forge was supposedly on the island. Going on to follow his divine example, ancient Limnians took up the trade and set up their metalworking shops on the island's volcanic soil. Farther up the coast is the **Kaveiron,** an eighth-century BC sanctuary once used by a secret cult to worship the Kaveiroi, Hephaestus's children. Ceremonies were held to honor the birth of humanity and the rebirth of nature. Near the sanctuary is the cave, where Philoctetes, a Greek archer in the Trojan Wars, lived after he was bitten by a snake and abandoned by his companions. During full moons, islanders and visitors still gather on the nearby beach to celebrate with food, drink, guitars, and good spirits.

ECOLOGICAL SIGHTS

Limnos has a number of ecological sights, including the longest sand dunes in Europe (near Gomati beach, on the northern coast), the waterfalls near Kaspakas, and the hot springs at Therma. The baths built over the hot spring offer a variety of massages and facials, with a 20min. soak running €15. If things aren't hot enough, try **Aphrodite's pool** (€35 for 20min.), built for two. (☎ 22540 62 062. Open daily 10am-2pm and 5-9pm.) During winter and spring, the western salt plain of Lake Aliki hosts migrating flamingoes that descend on the island in a blur of pink.

EVIA AND THE SPORADES

Stretching out into the azure depths of the Aegean, Evia and the Sporades contain a mixture of natural, cultural, and archaeological treasures, topped off with a healthy dose of hedonism. Evia, Greece's second-largest island, nudges the coast of Central Greece, stretching from Karystos in the south, through bustling Chalkida, to the therapeutic springs of the northern villages. Beyond Evia, the Sporades arc across the sea to the north. Vibrant Skiathos has the liveliest reputation, flaunting its beach-ringed shores for summer travelers. Skopelos is known as one of the greenest islands in all of Greece, with Byzantine monuments and narrow streets sprinkled among the lush vegetation. Alonnisos harbors pristine wilderness crossed by hiking trails and access to the Marine Park, while Skyros has remained true to its old ways despite the demands of modern-day tourism. These islands have beckoned visitors to bask on their sunlit shores and hike their shaded forests since Greece's earliest days.

HIGHLIGHTS OF EVIA AND THE SPORADES

BE a dancing queen on **Skopelos,** the island made famous by *Mamma Mia* (p. 421).

SETTLE DOWN in a homestay on **Skyros,** the Greekest of the Greek islands (p. 430).

TREK through the gorgeous wilderness of **Alonnisos,** the only inhabited island in Greece's National Marine Park (p. 426).

EVIA Εύβοια

With warm waters, forested highlands, archaeological treasures, charming villages, and therapeutic baths, Evia offers enough variety to satisfy any pleasure-seeker. Its capital, Chalkida, serves as a portal from the mainland into Evia. A new suspension bridge allows visitors to traverse the Channel of Evripos with ease, and ferries connect the island to Aedipsos, Marmari, and Karystos. Because of Evia's proximity to Athens, floods of Greek vacationers arrive during the summer, especially on the weekends, but the island effortlessly absorbs and delights the masses.

CHALKIDA Χαλκίδα   ☎ 22210

Sprawling Chalkida, also known as "Chalkis" or "Halkida," is the capital of Evia as well as its key transportation hub, connecting the island to the mainland. Bustling streets, lively plazas, and packs of young people give the city a vibrant energy in spite of it's somewhat unattractive aesthetic. Its archaeological artifacts, nearby beaches, and urban vibe make Chalkida the natural starting point for exploring the more remote parts of the island.

TRANSPORTATION

Trains: To get to the main part of Chalkida from the train station (☎22210 22 386), walk out to the right, cross the Old Bridge, and take a left along the waterfront; El. Venizelou intersects 5 blocks down. Trains go to **Athens** (1½hr., €6.50), although it's recommended and actually shorter to take the bus.

Buses: Chalkida's hangar-like bus terminal, Stiron 1 (☎22210 22 640), is a 30min. walk from the waterfront's hotels and restaurants. It's easiest to take a taxi (€4) to the waterfront. If you decide to walk, go to the right from the front of the station. At the large intersection, take the middle road, Arethousis. After nearly 20 blocks, take a right on El. Venizelou and follow it until it hits the waterfront. Buses to: **Aedipsos** (3hr., 12:30 and 2:30pm, €10.50); **Athens** (1hr., 2 per hr. 5am-9pm, €6.20); **Karystos** (3½hr.; 6am, 1, 5:40, 7:15pm; €10.50); **Kimi** (1¾hr., 6 per day 9:30am-8:15pm, €7.60); **Limni** (2hr., 12:30 and 5:15pm, €7).

Taxis (☎22210 89 300 or 25 111). Available 24hr. from the Old Bridge, Pl. Agios Niko-laos, El. Venizelou, and just outside the bus station.

ORIENTATION AND PRACTICAL INFORMATION

Chalkida's main thoroughfare is **Eleftheriou Venizelou**, which runs perpendicular to the water and ends just before **Voudouri** (the waterfront promenade), which is lined by hotels, restaurants, and bars. **Agios Goviou** runs off El. Venizelou to the left, behind and parallel to Voudouri and toward the Old Bridge; **Farmakidou** does the same, but to the right. **Avanton**, the primary shopping street, runs behind **Plateia Agios Nikolaos** (a park located midway along Voudouri) parallel to the water. The **Erippon Bridge**, or Old Bridge, connects Chalkida to the mainland at the end of the waterfront. Chalkida also is joined to the mainland via the new **suspension bridge**, the connection for most ground transportation, on the city's southern edge.

Tourist Information: Chalkida has no tourist office, so your best bet is to ask for a map at the hotels on the waterfront. The **port authority** (☎22210 28 888), across the Old

Bridge on Kostantinos Karamanlis, in the white building with blue shutters, dispenses limited info about the city. Open daily 24hr.

Banks: National Bank, El. Venizelou 9, 2 blocks from the water. **Currency exchange** and **24hr. ATM.** Open M-Th 8am-2:30pm, F 8am-2pm. There are also numerous other banks and 24hr. ATMs lining El. Venizelou.

Police: Arethousis 153 (☎22210 77 777), 25min. from the bottom of El. Venizelou. Open M-F 8am-2pm. **Tourist Police** (☎22210 83 333) in the same building.

Pharmacies: Numerous pharmacies are along El. Venizelou; look for the large green crosses on the storefronts.

Hospital: 48 Gazepi (☎22210 21 901). Head up El. Venizelou away from the water and turn left onto Papanastasiou. Take the first right onto Kriezotou, then a left at the butcher shop; the hospital is 400m up the hill on the right. There is also a smaller **emergency building** (☎166) by the museum.

Telephones: OTE (☎22210 22 599), at the intersection of El. Venizelou and Papanastasiou. Phones are directly outside the store, on the Evia side of the Old Bridge.

Internet Access:Surf on Net (☎22210 24 867; www.surfonnet.gr), between Hotel Kentrikon and John's Hotel on Ag. Goviou. €2.50 per hr. Open 24hr.

Post Office: Karamourtzouniis 11 (☎22210 22 211). Walk along El. Venizelou and take the 2nd left from the waterfront. **Poste Restante** and **Western Union** available. Open M-F 7:30am-8pm. **Postal Code:** 34100.

▌ ACCOMMODATIONS

Most hotels are of the €75-per-night variety, catering to business travelers or Athenian families, so you may want to think twice before planning a stop-over in the city. If you bargain, you might be able to get rates as low as €40 for a single without bath, but don't expect anything lower, especially in the summer.

John's Hotel, Ag. Goviou 9 (☎22210 24 996), excellently located near the Old Bridge. Rooms with wall-to-wall carpeting, baths, A/C, phones, balconies, and Wi-Fi. The helpful English-speaking receptionists downstairs will assist you with bus and ferry timetables and give you free maps. Enjoy breakfast (€5) in the attractive dining area. Singles €50; doubles €65; triples €80. AmEx/MC/V. ❹

Hotel Kentrikon, Ag. Goviou 5 (☎22210 22 375), by John's Hotel. 20 rooms with TVs, phones, and shared fridges; some have A/C and private baths. Breakfast included. Singles €50; doubles €60; triples €75. Cash only. ❹

Hotel Hara, Karoni 21 (☎22210 76 305). Bear right after crossing the Old Bridge, then take the stairs across from the fun-park. Simple, unadorned rooms come with A/C, TVs, and tiled baths. Breakfast included. Singles €50; doubles €70; triples €80. MC/V. ❹

▐ FOOD

Several bakeries hide on streets near **Agios Nikolaos,** and fast-food joints are bunched at the base of **Eleftheriou Venizelou** and by the Old Bridge on the waterfront. Small supermarkets, like **Dia Discount,** Favierou 14, cluster around Papanastasiou off of El. Venizelou. (☎22210 78 960. Open M-F 8:30am-9pm, Sa 8am-8pm.)

▨ **Noodle Bar,** Per. Varatasi 5 (☎22210 83 833). Walk down El. Venizelou from the waterfront and make a right before Society Cafe. Large portions of zesty Asian-inspired cuisine. Singapore Noodles (thin rice noodles with chicken, shrimp, cabbage, onion, and a curry sauce) €7.90. Salads €4.50-6.60. Entrees €5.70-10. Delivery available. Open daily 1pm-midnight. MC/V. ❷

Il Posto di Pasta, Voudouri 13 (☎22210 73 841). A smart Italian eatery also offering an impressive selection of pastas from ravioli to gnocchi (€8-12). Elegant waterfront tables. Takeout available. Open daily 1pm-1:30am. MC/V. ❷

Cookie Land, Avanton 59. The shelves of freshly baked cookies, cakes, and confections (€8.50-10.80 per kg) are delicious enough to erase any pangs of calorie remorse. Open daily 10am-10pm. Cash only. ❶

👁 🔽 SIGHTS AND BEACHES

Palm-lined **Voudouri,** Chalkida's waterfront promenade, makes for a splendid evening stroll. Or, if you're in the mood for shopping, the bustle of **Avanton** will get your adrenaline pumping. For a picnic or afternoon stroll, visit **Park Farou,** near the lighthouse, at the northern tip of the city by the beaches.

FORTRESS OF CARABABA. Built by Turks in 1688 to protect Chalkida from Greek and Venetian marauders, the fortress is extremely well-preserved and affords fantastic views of the city, ocean, and surrounding hills. You can picnic, climb on the walls, and check out the lookout posts where Turks once guarded the city. In the summertime, there are also regular **concerts** in the fortress. Flyers and schedules posted outside the walls give info on upcoming events. *(From Chalkida, cross the Old Bridge and head right. Once you reach the now-defunct fun-park, take the stairs on the left, which lead all the way up the hill to the fortress. Open daily 8am-10pm. Free.)*

THE ARCHAEOLOGICAL MUSEUM. Chalkida's Archaeological Museum is full of finds from the Neolithic, Classical, and Roman eras. It has an impressive display of statues, pottery, and shimmering gold laurels—some pieces date as far back as 11,000 BC. *(El. Venizelou 13. ☎22210 76 131. Open Tu-Su 8:30am-3pm. €2, under 18 free.)*

CHURCH OF AGIOS NIKOLAOS. This magnificent church's high vaulted ceilings hover above walls covered in intricate iconography. *(At the far end of Pl. Nikolaos from the waterfront. ☎22210 76 649. Open daily 7am-1pm and 4:30-8pm. Modest dress required.)*

BEACHES. To take a dip or soak in rays, catch the bus to **Eretria,** known for its beautiful beaches. The locals flock to the clean **Souvala, Kourenti,** and **Papathanasiou** beaches, a 15min. walk from the Old Bridge. Walk just past the rocky outcropping at the end of the waterfront to reach Souvala. For Kourenti, follow Avanton four blocks after it becomes G. Chaina, then turn left onto Delagrammatika and walk to the end. Walk across the parking lot and along Eth. Symfiliosis to reach Papathanasiou. For a beach closer to the center of town, head across the Old Bridge and walk to the right on Archien. Makariou until you see the sunbathers on your right; you can see the beach from the waterfront.

🔽 NIGHTLIFE

After dark, follow the glow of cell phones to the waterfront, where you can observe the teenage scene from the safety of one of the many bars that line the boardwalk, where you can buy beer for €4-5.50 and mixed drinks for €6-8.**Cafe Abotis** (☎22210 22 562), just south of the Hotel Paliria, and **Jam,** Voudouri 10 (☎22210 22 156), near the Old Bridge, are two popular venues that blast pop music to their outdoor patios and are packed past midnight. (Both open 8:30am-late.) If you feel like burning off those Cookie Land calories, hop a cab (€5) to the suspension bridge and work it out on the dance floor of **Gaz** (☎6944 520474), a sleek bar, lounge, and club.

KARYSTOS Κάρυστος   ☎ 22240

Unimaginative architecture and a grid-like street plan obscure a city that is vibrant and fun. Located between imposing Mount Ohi and the sparkling waters of Marmari bay, Karystos is best treated as an urban break from the stunning landscape that surrounds the city. Thrills are more likely to come from visiting hole-in-the-wall restaurants than from partying on the beach (although you can do that too); come in with the right expectations and you likely will be pleasantly surprised.

▐ TRANSPORTATION

Buses: The bus station (☎ 22240 22 453) is on I. Kotsika, which runs along the right side of the city hall. Take the bus to **Marmari** (20min.; M-Th 4 per day 5:30am-3:30pm, F 6 per day 5:30am-6:15pm, Sa 3 per day 9am-2:40pm; €1.70), where you can catch the **ferry** to **Rafina** (1hr., daily 5-8, €7). Buses from Karystos also go to **Athens** (4hr.; M-Sa 8am, Su 1:45pm; €9) and **Chalkida** (3½hr.; M-F 5:30am and 1:45pm, Su 1:45pm; €10.50).

Taxis: (☎ 22240 26 500), wait in the *plateia* 6am-2am. If you need after-hours service, get a driver's cell phone number.

▐ PRACTICAL INFORMATION

Travel Agency: ◪**South Evia Tours,** 7 Amalias Square (☎ 22240 26 200), on the left side of the central *plateia* with your back to the sea, through the Kosmos book store. Nikos and his sister Popi can help with everything from car rentals (€30-45 per day) to planning local excursions and booking accommodations. They'll also provide you with a free regional map. Locals often say that if you have a question, Nikos and Popi know the answer—so don't hesitate to ask. Open daily 9am-midnight.

Bans: Alpha Bank (☎ 22240 22 989), off the main *plateia* on Sachtouri. **Currency exchange** and **24hr. ATM.** Open M-Th 8am-2:30pm, F 8am-2pm.

Police: (☎ 22240 22 262). Turn into the small alley just past the bank and climb the stairs at the end of the block on the left. Open 24hr.

Hospital: (☎ 22240 22 257). With the water on the right, turn left 1 block after the Archaeological Museum, and head inland for 8 blocks; the hospital is on the left.

Pharmacy: (☎ 22240 23 505), at the head of the central *plateia*. Open M, Th, Sa 8am-1:30pm; Tu-W, F, Su 8am-1:30pm and 5-8:30pm.

Telephones: OTE, El. Amerikis 73 (☎ 22240 22 399), to the right off I. Kotsika 1 block above the central *plateia* and across from the cathedral. Open M-Th 7:30am-2pm, F 7:30am-1:30pm.

Internet Access: Polychoros (☎ 22240 24 421), just past Hotel Galaxy along the beachfront. €4 per hr. Open daily 11am-late. Wi-Fi is available at Alea (see p. 415).

Post Office: (☎ 22240 22 229), on Th. Kotsika, 1 street over from I. Kotsika, just above El. Amerikis. Open M-F 7:30am-2pm. **Postal Code:** 34001.

▐ ACCOMMODATIONS

Hotels in Karystos start at €35 for singles and €45 for doubles during the summer, but South Evia Tours may help you find cheaper *domatia* (€25-35).

Rooms to Let, Sachtouri 42 (☎ 69726 05 821). Follow the waterfront toward the *bourtzi*, turn left 1 block past the Archaeological Museum, and take the first right. Converted from a charming yellow home, the bright, well-decorated rooms surround a courtyard garden bursting with flowers and statuettes. Each comes with TV, A/C, fridge, bath, and small kitchen. Singles, doubles, and triples €25-40. Cash only. ❷

Hotel Galaxy (☎22240 22 600), opposite the beginning of Kremala beach at the corner of Kriezotou and Odysseos. High-rise rooms, each with smooth earth-colored tiling, TV, A/C, bath, and balcony. Breakfast is included and served in the large, wood-paneled lobby downstairs. Singles €35-40; doubles €45-55; triples €54-66. MC/V. ❸

Hotel Ais (☎22240 22 202), a long-time staple in a central location on the corner of Th. Kotsika and the waterfront. A high-rise with 32 simple rooms that include TV, A/C, and baths; some of the square, concrete balconies have a sea view. Breakfast included. Singles €30-40; doubles €40-50; triples €50-55. Cash only. ❸

⬛ FOOD

The restaurants that line the waterfront have everything from fresh seafood to burgers and fries.

Cavo D'oro (☎22240 22 326), in the alleyway left of the central *plateia* facing inland, just past the back entrance to South Evia Tours. A local favorite. For an appetizer, try the delicious peppers stuffed with mozzarella or the grilled mushrooms. Entrees €5-10. Open daily 9am-4:30pm and 6pm-midnight. Cash only. ❷

Marinos, Kriezotou 98 (☎22240 24 126), on the waterfront to the right as you face the water. Freshly-caught octopus sometimes dries on the racks in front of this seafood bistro. A variety of seafood entrees like octopus with vinegar (€9) and baked sardines (€7). Entrees €7-11. Open daily 11am-midnight. MC/V. ❷

⬛ SIGHTS

The city of Karystos does not boast many sights itself, so you're better taking off into the countryside on day excursions and hikes. That said, there are a few minor attractions.

FORT BOURTZI. The peep-holes in the back of Fort Bourtzi were used to pour boiling oil on attackers in the 11th century. Today patrons invade the fort in August, crowding in to watch student productions; there is a schedule posted on a board outside the fort, or you can inquire at South Evia Tours for more details. *(On the left side of the waterfront.)*

THE ARCHAEOLOGICAL MUSEUM. The modest exhibits include a small collection of marble statues and inscribed tablets, along with artifacts from the ⬛drakospita (dragon houses) of Stira and Mt. Ohi. The entrance hall has some beautiful paintings of the area by local artists. *(Kriezotou 58, in the same building as the public library, just past the bourtzi. ☎22240 25 661. Open Tu-Su 8:30am-3pm. €2, seniors €1, students free. Su free. Library open Tu-F 10am-1:30pm and 5pm-9pm, Sa 10am-1pm.)*

BEACHES. Two beaches, **Kremala** and **Psili,** flank either side of the waterfront and become extremely crowded on the weekends because of their close proximity to the city center.

KARYSTOS ENVIRONMENTAL INFORMATION CENTER. Hands-on exhibits, videos, and informational boards in English and Greek educate visitors about the national environment of the area. It opens occasionally to the general public, but the most reliable way to get inside is to organize a group trip through Nikos at South Evia Tours. *(3km out of town toward Chalkida.)*

MONTOFOLI ESTATE. Rolling vineyards cover this grand estate, built over the ancient site of the church of St. Marcus. The estate also has a wine cellar and occasionally holds concerts. Inquire at South Evia Tours (p. 413) for more info about guided tours and planning a visit. *(North of Karystos in the Old Town and accessible by taxi.)*

NIGHTLIFE

Start your evening at one of the bars that line Karystos's moonlit beaches. The scene especially heats up in the summer, when seasonal bars and clubs open their doors to partygoers. Beers are generally about €3, mixed drinks €6-7.

Kohili Beach Bar (☎22240 24 350), on Psili beach just feet away from the water, past the *bourtzi* and Hotel Karystion. Serves beer and mixed drinks throughout the day and night. Locals rave about its epic F and Sa summer parties. Open daily 10am-late.

Ostria (☎22240 25 678), about 1 block past Hotel Galaxy coming from the *plateia*. Listen to funky instrumental, house, and pop music as you chill in a comfy blue deck chair. Open May-Oct. 24hr.

Aeriko, a few doors before Ostria coming from the *plateia*. The latest addition to the beach bar scene. Its high ceilings, sleek stools, and airy indoor-outdoor design attract a refined crowd. Open daily 10am-late.

Alea, on the right side of the central *plateia* facing inland. Even after the beach has shut down for the night, the party stays in full swing. Still, expect more socializing than dancing. Open daily 9am-late.

DAYTRIPS FROM KARYSTOS

MOUNT OHI AND DIMOSARI GORGE. The widely varied terrain of the Karystos region offers an abundance of spectacular daytrips and hikes for outdoor enthusiasts. The 4hr. hike up Mount Ohi (elev. 1398m) is awe-inspiring, with arresting vistas of southern Evia and the sea. Before hiking, talk to Nikos at South Evia Tours, who can advise you about trails and conditions. It is best to join one of Nikos's inexpensive guided group **hikes** up the mountain (€25 per person; 6-7 times throughout the summer, usually on Sa; leaves at 8:30am, returns at 6pm), however these will not run unless there are enough people to go. If you decide to hike without Nikos, be especially cautious in windy weather and around rocky parts of the trails, and always hike with a partner. To get to the trailhead, take a car or taxi (€6) to the village of Mili, or walk the 3km distance yourself by following Aiolou, one block east of the *plateia*, out of town. A set of mysterious monolithic columns appears on the side of the trail about 45min. into the hike, where they were abandoned at the site of an ancient Roman marble quarry. The haunting ruins of the **Dragon House** *(drakospita)* sit on the summit, which you will reach after another 3-4hr. of walking. Believed to date back to Neolithic times, the ruins represent a major ancient achievement—each stone, weighing several tons, was transported up the mountainside. The building may have served as a temple dedicated to Zeus and Hera, and local legend holds that it was inhabited by a **dragon** who terrorized the region. You can spend the night at the **Mount Ohi Refuge ❶** (elev. 1050m), about 3hr. from the bottom and 1hr. from Profitis Ilias Peak at the top, and catch the heavenly sunrise from the summit the next morning. (Refuge also accessible by 4WD. Contact Nikos at South Evia Tours (p. 413) for access).

Running from the back of Mt. Ohi to Kallianou (41km north of Karystos) and the sea, the Dimosari Gorge is a stunning example of natural architecture. Clear, cold water cascades down its length, shaded by the lush forest. The 3-4hr. trail through the gorge is best accessed by car or taxi. A taxi to Petro Kanolo (a good starting point) and a return trip to Karystos costs around €70. For true mountaineers, a combined Mount Ohi-Dimosari Gorge hike, from Mili to Profitis Ilias Peak and down the northern side of Mt. Ohi through the gorge to Kallianou, can be completed in 8-10hr. It makes more sense, though, to break the trek up into two days, spending the night at the Mt. Ohi Refuge.

CASTELLO ROSSO. On the slopes above Karystos embedded among a number of small Evian towns is the majestic Castello Rosso (a.k.a. Kokkino Kastro; Red Castle), named for the blood spilled there in the many battles for control of it. From Mili, it's a 20min. hike up the hill on the left and across the stone bridge. Other interesting sites in the region include the **Roman aqueduct,** past the Red Castle, and the stone church and cave at **Agia Triada,** accessible by a 2hr. hike from Nikasi (by cab €6).

SPORADES Σποράδες

SKIATHOS Σκιάθος

The most popular tourist destination in the Sporades, Skiathos offers everything from gorgeous beaches and majestic forests to serene boat cruises and vibrant nightlife. The waterfront is a lively mix of *tavernas*, tourist agencies, and rental shops, while side streets reveal an abundance of boutique clothing stores, souvenir shops, and creperies. It's tempting to write off Skiathos as a tourist trap, but don't judge it until you've visited—go with the flow and let the island do what it does best: provide countless ways to have fun.

SKIATHOS TOWN   ☎24270

Skiathos Town is a lively mix of old and new. Arriving at the New Port, hoards of visitors scramble from the ferries to join in the busy waterfront at cafes, ticket offices, souvlaki shops, and rental agencies. *Tavernas* line every street, intermingling with tacky beach shops and expensive boutiques. As soon as you step off the main streets, however, narrow cobblestone alleyways offer charming shops and atmospheric traditional *tavernas*. No matter where you wander, welcoming bars full of talkative travelers, warm *taverna* owners who invite you to dine with them, and an almost palpable spunky spirit quickly draw you into the lively and constant buzz.

⌐ TRANSPORTATION

Flights: Olympic Airways (info ☎24270 22 040; tickets ☎24270 22 200) at the airport (☎24270 22 049). Flights leave for **Athens** (40min.; in summer daily, in winter 3 per week). Taxis (€5) take you from the harbor to the airport.

Ferries and Speedboats: Buy tickets at the **Hellenic Seaways** office, on the corner of Papadiamantis, opposite the ferry landing (☎24270 22 209 and 22 018; open daily 7am-10pm) and at the **GA Ferries** office, along the waterfront to the right from the port, facing inland, 2 doors down from Alpha Bank (open daily 9:30am-10pm). Ferries to: **Agios Konstantinos** (3½hr., 1-2 per day, €27); **Alonnisos** (1hr., daily, €14); **Skopelos** (1hr., 1-2 per day, €9); **Volos** (2hr., 4-5 per week, €18). Speedboats to: **Agios Konstantinos** (1½hr., 1-3 per day, €32.50); **Alonnisos** (50min., 4-6 per day, €16); **Glossa**

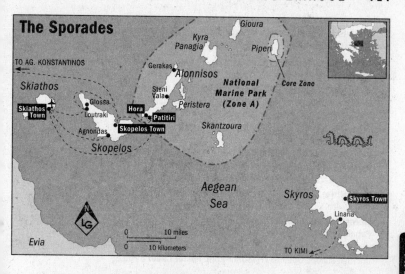

The Sporades

TO AG. KONSTANTINOS

Skiathos

Skiathos Town

Glossa

Loutraki

Agnondas

Hora   Patitiri

Skopelos Town

Skopelos

Gerakas

Steni
Vala

Peristera

Alonnisos

Kyra
Panagia

Gioura

Piperi

Core Zone

National
Marine Park
(Zone A)

Skantzoura

Aegean
Sea

Skyros

Skyros Town

Linaria

Evia

TO KIMI

0   10 miles

0   10 kilometers

(15min., 4 per day, €9.50); **Skopelos** (30min., 5-6 per day, €15.50); **Thessaloniki** (2 hr., daily, €55.50); **Volos** (1hr., 3-4 per day, €30).

Charter Boats: Circuits go around the island and stop at Castro and Lalaria beaches. Boats also run to **Alonnisos, Skopelos,** and **Tsougria** among others. Tours, lengths, and prices vary; browse along the Old Port to find an excursion that best suits your desires.

Buses: Facing inland, turn right and follow the waterfront past the taxi station. The bus stop is on the waterfront just as the road curves to go to the club strip. The bus to **Koukounaries** beach makes 26 stops at southern beaches (30min., every 15-30min. 7am-1:30am, €1.80). Heading outbound, sit on the driver's side for the best view. When returning, stop #4, on the acropolis hill, is at the Old Port near most hotels and *domatia*. Separate buses go to **Evagelistria** (8 per day 7:30am-7:30pm) and **Xanemos** (5 per day 8:10am-7pm). Be sure to check return times before your departure.

Taxis: (☎24270 24 461), along the waterfront. 24hr.

Car and Moped Rental: Numerous rental companies are located along the waterfront to the right from the ferry landing, facing inland. Mopeds and ATVs €15-25 per day. Cars from €35 per day. Prices include insurance. Some have better daily rates, while others have better weekly rates. Decide your desire rental length, then shop around.

✈ 🛈 ORIENTATION AND PRACTICAL INFORMATION

Skiathos's waterfront is more or less an L shape: the **bourtzi**, the small tree-covered peninsula at its corner, divides the Old Port from the New Port. Facing inland in front of the *bourtzi*, the **New Port** runs to the right and is the location of the ferry dock, rental agencies, *tavernas*, cafes, and tourist shops. The **Old Port** is perpendicular to the New Port and to the left of the *bourtzi*. **Papadiamantis**, Skiathos Town's mostly pedestrian thoroughfare, overflows with cafe-bars, souvenir shops, and clothing stores; it intersects the main waterfront across from the ferry dock in the New Port. Farther inland, **Evangelistra** intersects Papadiamantis and connects it to **Polytechniou**, or "Bar Street," which runs parallel to Papadiamantis on the left. On the far right of the waterfront facing inland, the road splits. The branch that continues left passes the bus stop, then follows the island's southern coast to **Koukounaries Beach.** The branch to the right leads to the club strip. Most of the shops and hotels along the waterfront and Papadiamantis give out free maps.

Bank: National Bank (☎24270 22 400), midway up Papadiamantis. **ATM** and **currency exchange.** Open M-Th 8am-2:30pm, F 8am-2pm.

Laundromat: Katerina's Wash and Dry (☎24270 21 9890). From Papadiamantis, turn left onto the diagonal side street before the National Bank; it's on the right after a few blocks. Wash and dry €10. Open daily 9am-midnight.

Police: (☎27270 21 111), upstairs, on the left of Papadiamantis, just past where the road forks around a public water spout. Open 24hr. **Tourist Police** (☎27270 23 172), in a small white building on the right side of Papadiamantis, opposite the police.

Pharmacies: Several pharmacies line Papadiamantis. Look for the green crosses. One (☎24270 24 515) is across from the National Bank. Open daily 9am-2pm and 5pm-midnight.

Hospital: (☎27270 22 040 and 22 222), on the acropolis hill behind Skiathos Town. Open 24hr.

Internet Access: Internet Zone Cafe, Evangelistra 28 (☎24270 22 767), to the right off Papadiamantis. €2 per hr. Open daily 10:30am-1am.

Post Office: (☎24270 22 011), far inland down Papadiamantis, on the left, across from the high school. Open M-F 7:30am-2pm. **Postal Code:** 37002.

ACCOMMODATIONS AND CAMPING

You can bargain for good deals if you let the dock hawks that meet the ferry compete for you. Doubles run €20-30 in spring and fall; €25-50 in summer. The **Rooms to Let Office** in the port's wooden kiosk has lists of available rooms. (☎24270 22 990. Open daily 8:30am-10:30pm.) In August, if you haven't already made reservations, finding a room, much less a cheap one, can be near impossible—forego sleep and party the night away.

Australia Hotel (☎24270 22 488). Turn right onto Evangelistra off Papadiamantis; it's in the 1st alley to the left (look for signs). Right near the center of town, although surprisingly peaceful.22 clean and spacious rooms with A/C, TVs, baths, fridges, and balconies. The friendly owner will help you with directions and make you feel at home. Ring the bell outside for service. Singles €25-45; doubles €30-60; triples €50-70. Cash only. ❷

Pension Argo (☎24270 22 324), on the hill overlooking the Old Port. Walk along the Old Port as it bends to the left, and climb the stairs at the very end. 12 furnished rooms with A/C, fridges, and baths. Some overlook the waterfront from wrought-iron balconies, but the best view is from the rooftop deck. Quiet hours 3-6pm and 11pm-9am. Doubles €40-55; triples €45-65. Cash only. ❸

Aiolus Pension (☎24270 21 402). Turn right off Papadiamantis onto the diagonal street before the tourist police. Go straight past the intersection; it's on the left after the Rent a Moto shop. This slightly out-of-the-way pension's clean, well-furnished rooms have fridges, TVs, A/C, and baths. Some have balconies decorated with a colorful array of flowers. Doubles €30-65; triples €40-75. Cash only. ❸

Camping Koukounaries (☎24270 49 250), on the bus route to Koukounaries, just before stop 23. Close to Koukounaries and Mandraki beach, this shaded campground has showers, toilets, laundry, and a mini market. €8.50 per person; €5 per tent; €3 per car. Tent rental €5.50. Cash only. ❶

FOOD

Skiathan restaurants accommodate a wide range of tastes and budgets. *Tavernas* abound, but Italian restaurants and other ethnic cuisines are also available.

Not surprisingly, exotic food tends to be pricey; souvlaki stands on the main strip feed locals and broke backpackers. While the waterfront restaurants remain popular and always crowded, for charming atmosphere, head behind the Old Port and search for the quieter alleyway tavernas.

▨ **Carnayo** (☎24270 22 868). The 1st restaurant along the waterfront leading to the club strip, past the bus stop. In 1975, this boatyard ("carnayo") was converted into a restaurant with Mediterranean-inspired food served in the lantern-lit waterfront merely feet from the harbor or in the wood and stone interior. While the seafood is pricey, the pastas (€8-12) and meats (€7.50-15.50) are a great value. The spaghetti with chicken fillets, tomato basil, mushrooms, and fresh parmesan (€9.50) is divine. Open daily noon-midnight. MC/V. ❸

Piccolo Grill House (☎24270 21 763). From the Old Port waterfront, take the stairs on the right across from the cannon and flag, walk past the church, and turn right. Set in a romantic *plateia*, Piccolo serves tasty meals in a charming atmosphere, putting a Greek spin on Italian classics. Pastas €7.50-12. Pizzas €8-12. Open daily May-Oct. 6:30pm-midnight. MC/V. ❷

Hellinikon, 25 Martiou 10 (☎24270 23 235), around the corner from Piccolo. Hellinikon, which has been under the same ownership for 17 years, has a menu of meticulously prepared dishes like house specialty lamb *kleftiko* (€9.50). Nightly live *bouzouki* music (8pm-midnight) from a father-son duo enlivens the outdoor seating area. Entrees €8-15. Open daily 6pm-midnight. AmEx/MC/V. ❸

"No Name" Fast Food, on Simionos, 1 block past the left fork on Papadiamantis, down the narrow alleyway; look for the ivy-covered awning. Name or not, this is the best spot for a quick, cheap meal. Gyros, burgers, and chicken pitas €2-4 each. Open daily 11am-midnight. Cash only. ❶

👁 🏖 SIGHTS AND BEACHES

The most notable sights on the island are its many gorgeous beaches. The best of them, along the southern coast, are accessible by bus and are always crowded. Those looking for a more varied experience can consider taking a charter boat from the Old Port for a day-long excursion around the island or to the other Sporades (see **Transportation,** p. 416). The cruise around Skiathos stops at the island's *kastro* and at the small but picturesque **Lalaria** beach, reachable only by boat. A single paved road runs along the southern coast of the island, between Skiathos Town and the most famous beach, **Koukounaries.** The bus makes 26 stops along the road; a list of the stops is available at the bus station in Skiathos and at Koukounaries (stop #26). Soft sand curves between blue waters and the deep pines of the Biotrope, a protected forest area. Koukounaries is the island's most popular and activity-centric beach—in July and August expect crowds that flock to its sandy stretch, backed by pine trees. The full slate of water sports includes **kayaking, water skiing, parasailing, banana boating,** and **wind surfing.** Showers, bathrooms, chairs with umbrellas, and bars pepper the beach.

For the best sunset views on the island, head to **Banana** and **Little Banana** (stop #26) up the hill across from the bus stop through the parking lot; signs lead the way. Banana is popular with young crowds, who enjoy the water sports and loud music from the beach bar. To get to predominately nude Little Banana from Banana, walk down the path to the right just before you reach the main beach. From stop #13 headed toward #14, follow the road on the left to **Vromolimnos,** a sandy beach with water sports and a taverna. The bus also stops at other beaches, including **Megali Ammos** (stop #5), **Kanapitsa** (stop #12), **Kolios** (stop #14) with a trendy beach cafe, and family-friendly **Troulos** (stop

GIVING BACK

DOG'S BEST FRIEND

After a few days traveling in Greece, many tourists begin to treat the abundant stray-dog population as part of the landscape. With a population roaming almost every city's streets, packs of stray-dogs dominate the urban wildlife population. The people of Skiathos, however, decided to take action against this pervasive problem, founding the Skiathos Dog Shelter to benefit both the island and the dogs.

The committed staff at the shelter works year-round to provide medical treatment and housing for strays of all breeds and conditions. They search both in Greece and abroad for permanent owners, and with the help of British, Danish, and German programs, the shelter has been vastly successful. According to shelter manager Helen Bozas, in 2003, staff members were able to find homes for 320 pups. The influx of new strays is constant, however, and in its busiest months the shelter receives up to 14 dogs per day.

Volunteers—both locals and travelers—are welcome to come in and play with the dogs or take them on walks. If you show up with treats from the supermarket, you'll be greeted with affectionate, slobbery kisses (from the pups, of course).

The Skiathos Dog Shelter is about 4km up the hill on the road that intersects the main drag at bus stop #18. ☎24270 49 214; www.skiathosdogshelter.com. Arrive between 9am and 2pm to walk the dogs.

#20), though these beaches tend to be crowded as well. From the later stops, a 30min. walk through a pine forest brings you to the northern beaches, where winds are stronger and beach umbrellas less prominent. **Mandraki,** one of the better options, is up a sandy road from stop #23, and is also popular with nudists. To steer clear of the south coast altogether, a separate bus will take you to past the airport to **Xanemos,** a pebbly beach with good snorkeling.

PAPADIAMANTIS MUSEUM. Author Alexandros Papadiamantis's tiny 140-year-old house, set back off Papadiamantis about one block inland, now serves as the Papadiamantis Museum. The small exhibit honors the 19th-century realist, one of Greece's best-loved prose writers, whose writing dealt with the lives of native inhabitants from Skiathos. Papadiamantis spent his early childhood and then final years of his life on the island, and you can see the bed in the house where he passed away. In the shop downstairs, there are old publications of his novels on display as well as new versions for sale. *(Follow the signs ffrom Papadiamantis street. ☎24270 23 843. Open daily 9:30am-1:30pm and 5:30-8:30pm. €1.)*

MONASTERIES. The **Monastery of Evangelistra** is where the first Greek national flag (a white cross on a blue background) was raised in 1807. Today, most people visit for its Byzantine-style architecture, ancient but still working library, and an exhibition of historical artifacts. *(4km north of Skiathos Town on the slopes of Karaflitzanaka.)* On the northern coast of the island, the **Monastery of the Panagia Eikonistra** or **Kounistra** is accessible by hiking or driving. Panagia Eikonistra marks the spot where an old monk is said to have discovered a miracle-working icon of the Virgin Mary hanging from a tree, emitting light. Today the icon is in the Cathedral of the Three Hierarchs, up the steps from the Old Port, and is escorted back to the monastery every November 20 during the Presentation of the Virgin. People visit the monastery for oil from the church's lamp, which is said to have healing power and to look at the wall frescoes. *(From bus stop #18, they are about 4km along the road, near the top of the large hill. Follow the signs to the monastery.)*

KASTRO. Ten kilometers from Skiathos Town on the northern coast of the island, accessible by private vehicle or by boat, are the unimpressive ruins of the island's *kastro.* The 16th-century walled castle once served as a refuge from marauding pirates.

🎵 🖼 ENTERTAINMENT AND NIGHTLIFE

Open-air **Cinema Attikon,** on Papadiamantis just before the bank and on the right, plays recent Hollywood releases in English with Greek subtitles. (☎24270 22 352. Shows 9pm and 11:15pm. €7.) During the summer, there are concerts at the *bourtzi.* Ask at the information kiosk in the harbor for schedules or read the billboards outside the venue for advertisements.

A row of softly lit, trendy bars lie just above the **Old Port** and at the beginning of Polytechniou. Expect to pay €3-6 for beer and €7-11 for mixed drinks. In general, you'll find a heavy concentration of friendly Scandinavians and Brits, with relatively few Americans. From October to May, Skiathos Town is a ghost town. By July however, it's hard to imagine anything being closed. Partiers stay out until dawn at the disco-bars that line the club strip on the right edge of the harbor, facing inland. While there is no cover, beer costs about €5-6, mixed drinks €8-11, and soft drinks €4.

🎲 **Rock 'n' Roll Bar** (☎24270 22 944), in the Old Port, up the stairs and across from the cannon and flag pole. Pillows and beanbags serve as chairs and patrons enjoy exotic mixed drinks to a variety of music. Come early to secure your beanbag because by nightfall, this place is packed. Happy hour 7-9:30pm; ½-priced drinks. Open May-Oct. 16 daily 7pm-late.

Kentavros (☎24270 22 980), off Papadiamantis to the right beyond the Papadiamantis Museum. This bar everything from British pop to jazz to world soul. Beer €3-4. Mixed drinks €8. Open daily 9:30pm-3:30am.

Kahlua. The big fish in the club strip's large, diverse pond, flaunting multiple red-lit bars and playing a mix of pop music, mostly American. Open daily 10pm-late.

Admiral Benbow Inn (☎24270 22 311; www.admiral-benbow.co.uk.). Run by the wonderful Yorkshire-born Elaine and Mick Lyons, this tiny bar overflows with cozy, quirky personality and also has a free book-borrowing shelf. Take a peek at "Knocking on Heaven's Door," a bathroom door covered with musicians' obituaries. Open daily 8:30pm-3am.

Remezzo (☎24270 24 024), near the start of the strip. In the land of ubiquitous techno syncopation, the hip hop and R&B classics at this white-and-red club are a rare treat. Open daily 9:30pm-late.

SKOPELOS Σκόπελος

Tourist-friendly Skopelos sits between the whirlwind of Skiathos and the largely untouched wilderness of Alonnisos, incorporating the best elements of both. Hikes and moped rides through shady forests lead to numerous monasteries, bright beaches, and white cliffs that drop into a sparkling blue sea. By night, the town's waterfront strip closes to traffic, crowds swarm the streets, and a number of low-key bars and a few quality clubs maintain a party atmosphere. The island's most recent claim to fame as the filming location of the movie *Mamma Mia* has brought the beautiful beaches and towns into the spotlight. The island itself is still starstruck, rebranded as "Mamma Mia's island," a status which will only increase Skopelos's popularity as an up-and-coming tourist destination.

SKOPELOS TOWN   ☎24240

Skopelos Town is built on the steep hills above the harbor; the square white buildings slowly merge into the green hills behind it. The many moped rental

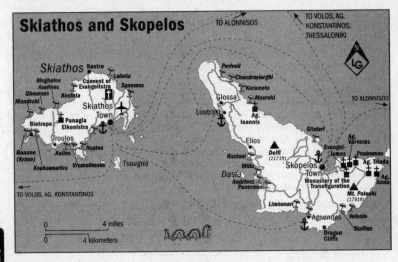

Skiathos and Skopelos

EVIA AND
THE SPORADES

shops, cafes, and *tavernas* near the waterfront contrast with the narrow streets that twist among whitewashed buildings, churches, cafes, and shops inland.

 TRANSPORTATION

In good weather, ferries and speedboats dock at the landing on the left side of the harbor facing inland or at the ferry dock in the center of the waterfront. When it's windy, they dock at Agnondas, 8km south of town. If you find that you have landed in Agnondas, wait for the bus, which will take you to Skopelos Town. In Skopelos Town, buy tickets for ferries and speedboats at the ticket booth next to the central ferry landing, the **Hellenic Seaways** office just across the road on the waterfront (open daily 8:30am-10pm), or **Lemonis Travel** (see **Practical Information**, p. 423).

Ferries: To: **Alonnisos** (30min., 1-2 per day, €4-9); **Glossa** (15min., 1 per week, €7.50); **Skiathos** (1hr., 1-2 per day, €10-13); **Skyros** (3hr., 2 per week, €27) via **Kimi** (2hr., €23).

Speedboats: To: **Agios Konstantinos** (2hr., 2-3 per day, €42); **Alonnisos** (20min., 2-4 per day, €8); **Glossa** (10min., 2-4 per day, €7); **Limnos** (1hr., M 3:25pm, €38); **Skiathos** (45min., 3-5 per day, €15); **Thessaloniki** (2hr.; daily 4:40pm, €56.50); **Volos** (2hr.; 2-3 per day, €36). Tickets for Thessaloniki are only available at the Hellenic Seaways office.

> **TIP**
> **CHECK IT TWICE.** Be sure to visit both the Hellenic Seaways office and Lemonis Travel to obtain all the possible ferry times for your destination on a particular day. Each office deals with a different company and multiple boats per company, so they'll each offer a different set of times and destinations.

Buses: The bus stop is left of the ferry dock facing inland. 15-18 buses per day go to: **Agnondas** (15min, €1.90); **Milia** (30min., €3); **Panormos** (30min., €2,50); **Stafilos** (10min., €1.50). 8 per day to **Glossa** and **Loutraki** (both €3.50). Check the schedules at the Skopelos Town stop and be sure to note return times. Schedules change often, sometimes daily.

Taxis: (☎24240 23 240). Available 7am-2am next to the bus stop, or 24hr. by calling.

Car and Moped Rental: Rental agencies line the waterfront to the left of the port, facing inland. Cars €25-40 per day. Mopeds €15-20 per day. Browse around for the cheapest rates, depending on your desired rental length.

⭐ 🚻 ORIENTATION AND PRACTICAL INFORMATION

Tourist agencies, *tavernas*, and cafes line the **waterfront. Pl. Platanos**, a small square packed with souvlaki and gyro joints, is opposite the dock, with the small monument to the right and playground to the left. **Galatsaniou** darts upward about 200m to the right of the dock facing inland, between Nostos and Aktaion restaurants. Free maps of the town are available at most cafes and shops along the waterfront and in town.

Travel Agency: Lemonis Travel (☎24240 22 363), to the right along the waterfront facing inland. Sells ferry tickets, offers accommodation info, and arranges car and moped rentals. Open daily 8:30am-10pm. **Thalpos Travel Agency** (☎24240 22 947), 5m to the right of Galatsaniou on the waterfront. Open M-Sa 10-2pm and 6-9pm.

Banks: National Bank (☎24240 22 691), on the right side of the waterfront facing inland. **24hr. ATM** and **currency exchange.** Open M-Th 8am-2:30pm, F 8am-2pm. There are also other major banks with ATMs along the waterfront, between the cafes.

Bookstore: The newsstand (☎24240 22 236) across from the bus stop has 1 rack of popular English-language books. Open daily 8:30am-10pm.

Landromat: Blue Star Laundry (☎24240 23 123). Head down the street off the back right corner of Pl. Platanos; it is on the left. From the waterfront, take the alleyway directly to the right of Pension Sotos. Wash and dry up to 6kg €12. Open M-Sa 8:30am-2pm and 5:30-9:30pm.

Police: (☎24240 22 295), above the National Bank. Open 24hr. **Tourist Police** ☎24240 22 235.

Pharmacy: In Pl. Platanos and along the waterfront. Look for the green crosses.

Medical Services: (☎24240 22 222). Follow the left-hand road inland from Pl. Platanos past Ag. Ioannis to the end, then go right at the signs. Open M-F 9am-2pm. Open M-F 24hr. for emergencies. Private clinic with **Doctor Skavetzos Elias:** ☎69999 24 555.

Telephones: OTE (☎24240 22 139), 100m from the water on Galatsaniou. Open M-F 7:30am-2pm.

Internet Access: Orange Internet Cafe (☎24240 23 093) is on the road running through the back of Platanos. Coming from the waterfront, turn left at the back left corner of the *plateia;* it's across from Ammos Club. €4 per hr. Wi-Fi, printing, photocopy, and fax services also available. Beer €2.50. Open daily 9am-midnight.

Post Office: (☎24240 22 203). Look for the yellow post box, 50m past Orange Internet cafe on the same road. Open M-F 7:30am-2pm. **Postal Code:** 37003.

🛏 ACCOMMODATIONS

The **Room Rental Association of Skopelos** can provide a list of *domatia*. It's located in the stone building next to the town hall walking inland from the port. (☎24240 22 712. Open daily 9:30am-2pm.) Dock hawks greeting ferries may offer reasonable rooms (singles €15-30; doubles €20-40), but bargaining is expected; be sure to see the room before making final decisions.

Pension Sotos (☎24240 22 549), inside the inconspicuous door on the corner of Galatsaniou on the waterfront. A fantastic location in the heart of the waterfront bustle. The renovated, 150-year-old house has 12 rooms with exposed beams, fans, coffee makers, and baths; some have A/C, TVs, fridges, and balconies. A common kitchen, quiet courtyard, and roof terrace add to the appeal. Singles €25-30; doubles €30-50; triples €30-55; quads €35-55. Discounts for stays of 2 weeks or more. Cash Only. ❷

Hotel Regina (☎24240 22 138, English-speakers ☎69788 64 092). Take the 2nd alley on the left past the back right corner of Pl. Platanos. Kind owner Viki offers simple, cozy rooms with A/C, TVs, ceiling fans, baths, and fridges; some have sea views. Breakfast included; enjoy it downstairs in the elegant dining room with wood paneling. Singles €30-40; doubles €40-70; triples €85. Cash only. ❷

Hotel Akti (☎24240 23 229), on the edge of the town beach; follow the waterfront to the left (facing inland) past the park. Pretty, tiled rooms have TVs, fridges, baths, and balconies with views. Singles €30-40; doubles €35-50; triples €40-60. Cash only. ❷

🔲 FOOD

Also known as "Souvlaki Square," **Plateia Platanos** abounds with quick bites. For slower-paced dining, head to one of the *tavernas* along the waterfront. **Alpha-Pi Supermarket** has groceries. Take a left from the back left corner of the *plateia;* it's on the right. (☎24240 23 533. Open daily 8am-midnight.)

Nostos Taverna (☎24 497), a few steps before Pension Sotos on the waterfront. Beloved by locals and visitors for its impeccable traditional dishes. Extensive wine list. Lamb *stifado* with Skopelos plums €9.50. Pizza €7-12. Open daily noon-midnight. Cash only. ❷

Ambrosia (☎24240 24 363), 1 block past Nostos along the waterfront. This dessert and coffee cafe is the perfect place to sample the traditional Skopelos cheese pie (€4) or Skopelos plum pie (€2.50), 2 of the island's specialties. Cheesecake €2.50. Honey balls €4. Open daily 9am-12:30am. Cash only. ❶

Cafe Barramares (☎24240 22 960), to the right of the boat dock facing inland. Dishes out delicious, filling *tiropita* (€3), crepes to go (from €3.50), ice cream sundaes (€4-7), and an array of other sweet and savory snacks. The luxurious sofas and flatscreen TVs in the outdoor seating area may dangerously encourage your calorie intake. Open daily 8:30am-2:30am. Cash only. ❶

🔲🔲 SIGHTS AND BEACHES

Traveling Skopelos's road by bus or car gives you access to lovely southern and west-coast beaches. Headed out from Skopelos Town, the first sandy beach is dazzlingly beautiful **Stafilos** on the south coast, only 4km from town. This crowded beach is by the hillside where archaeologists discovered the tomb of the ancient Cretan general of the same name. Nearby **Velanio,** over the hill to the left as you face the sea, is less packed. Named for the trickling spring that was a gushing fountain in Roman times, today Velanio is advertised as the only nude beach on Skopelos. Past the small harbor town of Agnondas, a paved road leads about 1km downhill to the secluded beach of **Limnonari.** The name means "waters of a lake," referring to the calm, wave-less water. If you ask in advance, the bus driver will let you off at the top of the road. Silvery **Milia,** 21km from town and accessible by bus, is the island's longest beach and is often considered the most beautiful, surrounded by a lush pine forest. Closer to Loutraki, dirt paths lead to the northern beaches of **Spilia, Mavraki, Keramoto,** and **Chondroyiorgi.** For any *Mamma Mia* fans, the beaches of **Milia, Kastani, Agios Ioannis,** and **Amarantos** might look familiar; they were all used as filming locations in 2007 for the movie. Full-day excursions run to these "*Mamma Mia* beaches" and other areas seen in the film. Look for signs along the waterfront at smaller travel agencies such as Madro Travel at the far right end of the waterfront, facing the town. (*Mamma Mia* tour €47, children €30.)

CHURCHES. Skopelos Town has an abundance of churches; most do not have regular visiting hours, but a good number probably will be open in the morning from 9 or 10am to about 1pm and then again after dinner from around 7pm to

9pm. Around the harbor to the far right, beautiful white-washed **Panagia ston Pirgo** balances on the rocks. From there, the stairs below the church lead up along the border of the city. The ascent along the water's edge passes **Agios Nikolaos**, tiny **Evangelismos**, and 11th-century **Agios Athanasi**, the town's oldest church, just below the *kastro*. Off to the left is **Genesis tou Christou**, a large, cruciform church with a round cupola and clock tower. Slightly farther into the city lies **Papameletiou**, a basilica built in 1662 with a red-tile roof and small clock tower. **Agios Nikolaou** (not to be confused with Ag. Nikolaos), just up Galatsaniou on the left, exhibits brightly colored icons and a marble statue of the Virgin. In **Mikhail-Sinnadon**, a stone basilica contains a remarkable iconostasis.

FOLKLORE MUSEUM. Occupying three stories of an 18th-century house, this museum displays artifacts donated by townspeople. *(100m past the OTE. ☎24240 23 494. Open M-F 10am-2pm and 7-10pm, F 11am-2pm and 7-10pm, Su 7-10pm only. €3.)*

NIGHTLIFE

Skopelos's dance clubs and modern, trendy outdoor bars cluster midway up the street off the back left corner of **Plateia Platanos**. Many are closed in the summer, when the nightlife moves to the waterfront. Dancing queens, your best bet is to follow the loud music and see where you end up.

Anatoli (☎24240 22 851), a 10min. walk up the stairs on the far right of the waterfront, keeping close to the coast. If you stop by this *ouzeri* for a drink just before midnight, you might catch Giorgos Xintaris—1 of the world's last great *rembetika* singers—singing old songs with a group of friends. Beer €3-5. Mixed drinks €3-7. Open daily 8pm-late.

Platanos Jazz Club (☎24240 23 661), on the far right of the harbor facing inland. Relax with jazz, blues, and a drink under a huge tree. Beer €3-4. Mixed drinks €7-8. Open daily 8:30am-2:30am.

The Blue Bar (☎24240 23 731), 2 blocks up Galatsaniou in an alley on the right. Plays folk, rock, and blues music to accompany its impressive collection of malt whiskey. Beer €3-5. Mixed drinks €6. Open daily 9:30pm-2:30am.

HIKING

Because of Skopelos's predominantly dirt roads, it is best to explore the island on moped or foot. A 35km asphalt road runs from the Skopelos bus station through **Stafilos** (4km), **Agnondas** (8km), **Panormos** (18km), **Elios** (24km), **Loutraki** (30km), and **Glossa** (32km). Numerous souvenir shops carry *Skopelos Trails* (€14), a great guide to the island's hikes.

DRAGON CLIFFS. According to local lore, a fierce ◼dragon once went on a fiery rampage, eating almost everyone on Skopelos, until Ag. Rigine killed it and became the island's protector. The ◼**Dragon Cliffs** *(Drakondoschisma)*, where the creature was hurled to its death, are now a quiet overlook with a sea view and an altar portraying the ◼dragon's grisly demise. The beginning of the 10min. walk is best reached by moped or bus. It's just off the highway between Stafilos and Agnondas; about 2km after Stafilos, follow the small dirt road that disappears into the woods on the left.

OTHER HIKES. Two paved roads leave the town from the bus depot on the left end of the waterfront facing inland. To reach a set of monasteries, follow the road out of the harbor to the left—signs mark the way to **Mount Palouki**. Small **Evangelismos** was built in the 17th century as part of the Monastery of Xiropotamos of Athos, but today is inhabited by three nuns. Take the left-hand fork up the hot, winding mountain road for the 1hr., 2km hike; if you start early in the morning, you can avoid the heat and the bugs. Up the right fork, a 45min. walk leads you to the **Monastery of the Transfiguration** (*Metamorphosis*). Its chapel, set in a flowered courtyard, dates from the 16th century. Another hour up the hill along the road takes you to two monasteries on ridges overlooking the sea. The first, the **Monastery of Agias Varvaras**, was built as a fortress in 1648. Nearby **Prodromou** contains several wall paintings along with icons dating back to the 14th and 15th centuries. Prodromou, whose astounding setting surveys the entire coast, is now a cloister dedicated to St. John the Baptist. The dirt path that begins behind the building leads to the smaller monasteries of **Agia Triada** and **Agia**

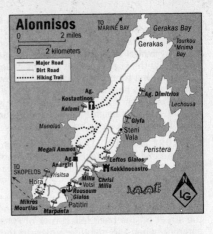

Taxiarches. Farther up the road, a trail leads to beautiful **Agia Anna**. For a 4hr. round-trip hike from Glossa, take the dirt track across the island to the **Monastery of Agios Ioannis**, another *Mamma Mia* filming location. From the main road east of Glossa, turn left on the first dirt road to **Steki Taverna**. At the road's end, a path drops to the sea; stone steps that have been cut in the escarpment lead to the monastery, which clings spectacularly to a boulder above the ocean.

ALONNISOS Αλόννησος

The only inhabited island within Greece's National Marine Park, Alonnisos is a pleasant starting point for those exploring the marine sanctuary and it is refreshing respite after Skiathos. Carpeted with well-marked trails that stretch through the forested hills to the coastal cliffs, it's a paradise for hikers and nature lovers. To the northeast, the small island of Gioura claims to have been the home of Polyphemus, the Cyclops whose eye was gouged out by Odysseus's sizzling lance. Though many islands claim this distinction, Gioura's rocky landscape best fits Homer's description of Polyphemus's cavern, complete with herds of the now-endangered brown goats with black crosses on their backs.

PATITIRI Πατητήρι   ☎24240

All boats dock at Patitiri, the island's main town. Impressive rock formations bookend the small harbor and its waterfront, which is lined by cafes, restaurants, and travel agencies. The town's relaxed atmosphere is conducive to enjoyable evenings by the water, and serves as an excellent home base for exploring the rest of the island.

▐ TRANSPORTATION

Ferries: To **Kimi** (2½hr., Tu and Th, €21) and **Volos** (5hr., 3 per week, €38).

Flying Dolphins: Tickets can be bought just to the left of Ikion Dolophon on the waterfront. To: **Agios Konstantinos** (2hr.; 1 per day; €44); **Skiathos** (1½hr., 2-3 per day,

EVIA AND THE SPORADES

€16) via **Skopelos** (20min., 2-3 per day, €8.50) and **Glossa** (45min., 2-3 per day, €12); **Thessaloniki** (4hr., 1 per day, €56); **Volos** (2hr., 2-3 per day, €50).

Buses: Departures from where Ikion Dolophon hits the waterfront. To **Chora** (also called "Old Village"; 10min., about every ½-1hr. 9am-3:30pm and 5:20pm-12:30am, €1.40) and **Steni Vala** (30min., 3 per day, €1.50). Schedules change often; be sure to check.

Taxis: (☎24240 65 449, 65 425, or 65 573). Available along the waterfront until 2am, or 24hr. by calling.

Water Taxi: (☎69762 09 274). To beaches along the eastern coast and 2 islands of the Marine Park (Peristera and S. Giorgios). Depart from the dock 10:30am, return 5:30pm. Round-trip €30. Sign up at the bulletin board on the dock across from the bus station.

Car and Motorbike Rental: At the numerous shops on Pelasgon and Ikion Dolophon. Cars €20-30 per day. Motorbikes €10-15 per day.

✦ 🛈 ORIENTATION AND PRACTICAL INFORMATION

From the docks and waterfront, two main streets run inland—**Pelasgon** on the left and **Ikion Dolophon** on the right.

Budget Travel: Alonnisos Travel (☎24240 65 188 or 66 000; www.alonnisostravel.gr), on the waterfront. Sells ferry tickets, exchanges currency, and books excursions. Open daily 8am-11pm.

Bank: National Bank, Ikion Dolophon (☎24240 65 777), on the left from the water. **24hr. ATM.** Open M-Th 8am-2:30pm, F 8am-2pm.

Police: (☎24240 65 205), up Ikion Dolophon, past the fire station. Open daily 6am-10pm.

Pharmacy: (☎24240 66 096), near the top of Ikion Dolophon, past Market Pappou on the right. Open daily 9am-10:30pm.

Hospital: (☎24240 65 208), opposite the police. Open daily 9am-1pm, 24hr. for emergencies.

Internet Access: Play Cafe, Ikion Dolophon (☎24240 66 119). €4 per hr., min. €1. Open daily 10am-2pm and 6-11pm.

Post Office: (☎24240 65 560), a short walk up Ikion Dolophon on the right. Open M-F 7:30am-2pm. **Postal Code: 37005.**

🏠 🏕 ACCOMMODATIONS AND CAMPING

The **Rooms to Let Office**, to the right of Ikos Travel, can help find rooms in any of the towns on Alonnisos. (☎24240 66 188. Open daily 10am-midnight.) Most of Patitiri's accommodations offer only doubles, triples, or studios, leaving solo travelers with little choice but to upgrade their digs. *Domatia* hawkers meet the ferry, but beware of prices that seem too good to be true—they often are. Always ask to see the room before finalizing a deal.

Pleiades (☎24240 65 235), up several flights of steps from the 1st alley on the right off Pelasgon, overlooking the harbor (look for signs). The 5 tastefully decorated rooms come with TVs, A/C, fridges, and baths, while the 5 studios also have kitchenettes. Some have balconies. The attached outdoor cafe, which doubles as a restaurant, often serves free coffee for guests. Doubles €30-50; studios €50-60. Cash only. ❸

Panorama (☎24240 65 240). Head down the 1st alley on the left up Ikion Dolophon, walk up the stairs to the top of the hill, and turn into the blue-fenced courtyard. The bright rooms have TVs, A/C, fridges, baths, and a bougainvillea-covered common balconies with port views. The rooms in the front have private balconies. Doubles €30-50; triples €35-60; 2-bedroom suite with kitchen €70-90. Cash only. ❸

Ilias Studios (☎24240 65 451), about 200m down Pelasgon on the left. Lovely rooms with TVs, A/C, baths, balconies, and kitchens. Doubles €25-50; studios €50-60. Cash only. ❷

Camping Rocks (☎24240 65 410 and 65 424), 1km uphill on the first alley on the left of Pelasgon (look for signs). A basic campground almost hidden among the pine trees, only 50m from a beach with flat rocks. Large communal shower and toilet facilities as well as a kitchen area with a grill. €5 per person; €2.50 per tent. Cash only. ❶

🍴 FOOD

Buy fresh produce at **Fruits and Vegetables,** past the first alley on the left off Ikion Dolophon. (☎24240 65 020. Open daily 8am-2pm and 5-9:30pm. Cash only). There are also a number of larger **supermarkets** along Ikion Dolophon.

To Kamaki, Ikion Dolophon, past the National Bank on the left. This little *ouzeri* serves delicious homemade seafood dishes like mussels *saganaki* (€8). Open daily 1pm-1:30am. MC/V. ❷

Tzitziphia (☎24240 65 255), at the corner of Pelasgon on the waterfront. Busily caters to locals and tourists looking for quality Greek fare. Veal *stamnas* with onions €9.50. Moussaka €7. Entrees €7-11. Open daily noon-12:30am. Cash only. ❷

To Steki (☎24240 66 292), near the corner of Pelasgon on the left. Stop by for souvlaki and gyros (€2.50). Open daily 6pm-midnight. Cash only. ❶

👁 🏃 SIGHTS AND OUTDOOR ACTIVITIES

HIKING. Only the southern end of the island is inhabited, leaving mountain wilderness to the north. Trails are marked at regular intervals and range from paved roads to steep, rocky paths. Blue maps, scattered throughout the island, mark trailheads and show routes, indicated by numerical yellow signs. Still, the purchase of a trail map (€6) or *Alonnisos on Foot* (€11-14), a walking and swimming guide, is highly recommended. The numbers below refer to those of the marked trails. The **Megalo Nero-Agii Anargiri-Megali Ammos-Raches-Votsi** trail (#5, 2hr.) takes you along the southeastern side of Alonnisos to the secluded monastery of Ag. Anargiri and the beach of Megali Ammos. The trailhead is on the main road near Votsi. Head out Ikion Dolophon from Patitiri to get to the main road, then follow the signs to Votsi and Steni Vala. From Megali Ammos, two 1hr. trails (#7 and 8) lead north to Megalo Chorafi. East of the main road, Megalo Chorafi is the hub for hikes to **Agalou Laka** beach (#14, 45min.) and the church of **Agios Kostantinos** (#6, 2hr.). From Ag. Kostantinos, the trails lead north to the church of **Agios Georgios** (#12, 1hr.) and **Melegakia** (#13, 1hr.) in the more rugged part of the island. Hikes #12 and 13 both bring you back to the main road. From Steni Vala, hike #10 (1hr.) takes you past Agios Petros beach to **Isomata** and then to the main road. From Isomata, hike #9 (45min.) winds its way down to **Leftos** beach. Far north, past Ag. Georgios, in Kastanorema, a dirt road leads to the #11 trailhead (1hr.), to **Agios Dimitrios** beach.

BEACHES. The closest beach to Patitiri is family-friendly **Rousoum Gialos,** a 5-10min. walk east of the main town. Walk up Ikion Dolophon past the medical center and police station, following the signs. Most of the island's best beaches are accessible from the main road, which runs along the spine of the island from Patitiri to the port of Gherakas in the far north. A 1hr. walk on this road from Patitiri takes you to **Votsi,** the island's other major settlement. Local children dive off the 15-20m cliffs near Votsi beach, just outside the village. The road then passes separate turn-offs for the pine-enclosed beaches of **Milia** and shallower, sandier **Chrisi Milia.** Alonnisos's residents will tell you that **Agiou Dimitriou,** at the end of the coastal road, is the island's most beautiful beach. The

EVIA AND THE SPORADES

clean, pebbled **Marpunta** beach has a strong claim to this title as well; reach it by continuing 1km past Camping Rocks (p. 428) and turning down the path to the left just before you reach the resort entrance. Along the coast from Chrisi Milia is the beach and archaeological site of **Kokkinocastro**, where swimmers occasionally find ancient coins. Nearby **Leftos Gialos** has a sandy beach with two *tavernas*. Buses stop at the tiny fishing village of **Steni Vala**, 12km north of Patitiri (30min., 4 per day, 9:40am, 2:20, 6, 10pm; €1.50). Not surprisingly, the fish *tavernas* here are fantastic. **Glyfa** beach is along the shore, a 5min. walk north of the village.

ALONNISOS MUSEUM. The "Pirate Museum" can be found up the stairs to the far left of the waterfront facing inland. This four-story museum displays a wide variety of cultural artifacts focusing on the weapons and objects used by the pirates of the Aegean Sea. Exhibits include weapons used in the Balkan Wars and WWII, historical maps, and a trade series on everything from wine-making to pack-saddle construction. There are also sculptures and paintings by locals throughout the museum. (☎ 24240 66 250. www.alonissosmuseum.com. Open daily June-Aug. 10am-9pm, Sept. and May 11am-7pm. €4.)

NIGHTLIFE

In the evening, people gather to sip drinks just above the beach and away from the docks at the cafes and bars lining the waterfront.

Enplo, on the far left of the waterfront. Soft lighting by Chinese lanterns, wooden furniture, an outside bar, and a chill atmosphere. Beers €3. Open daily 7pm-3am.

Harmony Club, up Ikion Dolophon on the right. Entertain crowds with loud music and dancing. Open F-Sa midnight-late, Th for special events.

DAYTRIPS FROM PATITIRI

CHORA Χώρα

Buses run from Patitiri (10min., every ½-1hr. 9am-3:30pm and 5:20pm-12:30am, €1.40). Schedules are posted at each bus stop and change often. Round-trip taxi €12.

Set high on a hill to ward off pirates, Chora, also called the "Old Village" or "Paleo Alonnisos," welcomes visitors looking for traditional island charm. When settlers first came to Alonnisos, they performed a goat sacrifice, cutting the animal into pieces, and placed the pieces of meat at potential building locations. Over subsequent days, if the meat had kept, they concluded that the spot was sufficiently sheltered from the sun, pests, and other elements as to be prime for building. With its quiet, crooked alleys that open suddenly onto incredible vistas of the island and wind their way into the dusty hills, Chora is evidence of the success of this system.

To reach the heart of the Old Village from the bus stop, head up the hill and slightly to the right, passing the bakery on the left. You will soon see the tiny 12th-century **Christ Church** across from a large stone *plateia*. The road immediately turns to cobblestone stairs, leading up to the main street lined with cafes, restaurants, and tiny shops bursting with homemade crafts and souvenirs. At the beginning of this street, there is a two-story stone building that has been made to resemble a traditional home, and you're welcome to walk inside and take a look. This museum doubles as a tiny shop that sells postcards, maps, and cheap copies of *Alonnisos on Foot*, the popular island walking guide (€5). If you continue off the main street passing the traditional home museum, you will also find the church of **Agios Georgios** from the 16th century and the remains of the *castro*, the old castle, with beautiful views of the island.

Four easy hiking trails lead from the center of Chora. A short walk along the main road headed toward Patitiri will bring you to the trail to **Vrisitsa** (#3, 1km, 30min.). This miniature beach lies in a secluded cove that seems to smile up at you as you descend to its sandy shore. The trail to **Mikros Mourtias** (#1, 1.5km, 45min.) winds down the hill through the surrounding green trees, offering a fantastic view as it heads to the water. Beginning at the bus stop, walk through town, past the church, and up the stairs to a street lined with cafes; turn left just before the street ends and walk down the steps of a narrow side street to the trailhead. Mikros Mourtias is a small, quiet beach with perfectly shaped skipping stones. A steeper climb to **Kalovoulos** (#2, 1.5km, 45min.) will bring you to one of the highest points on the island. To reach the path, continue on the main road past the bus stop; it will be on the left. As you start back on the main road to Patitiri, the trail Patitiri (#4, 1.5km, 35min.) is a simpler stroll that connects the Old and New Towns.

Chora is also home to a variety of quaint cafes and *tavernas*, many on beautiful overlooks. **To Aloni ❷**, at the base of an old windmill to the right of the bus stop, serves Greek food on tables with stunning views of the island's western coast. (☎24240 65 550. Entrees €7-10. Open daily 6pm-12:30am. Cash only.) **Rocks ❷**, in the upper part of town along the main street, can be reached by climbing the stairs next to Chiliadromia. The cuisine is mostly pizza, with offerings such as the "Inferno" pizza with sausage and hot peppers (€8.50), served in its cobblestone outdoor seating area. (☎24240 65 424. Salads €5-8. Pizzas €7.50-11. Open daily noon-midnight. Cash only.)

NATIONAL MARINE PARK

The park islands are accessible by specially licensed boats. Most trips, sold along the Patitiri harborfront, are all-inclusive daytrips; a typical trip departs from the Patitiri dock around 10am, makes stops on 2 or more islands, stops at the Blue Cave on the east coast of Alonnisos, visits the monastery on Kyra Panagia, and returns around 6pm (€45). Ikos Travel, across from the dock, can assist with arrangements and info. (☎ 24240 65 320. Open daily 9am-1pm and 6-10pm.)

Surrounding Alonnisos are the 22 ecologically protected islets of the National Marine Park as well as the five other larger islands of Peristera, Skantzoura, Piperi, Kyra Panagia, Gioura. Visiting Gioura and Piperi is forbidden in an effort to protect the endangered Mediterranean monk seal, which is one of the rarest mammals in all of Europe. The other rare species include the Eleonore Falcon, the Audouin Gull, and a unique type of goat that grazes the pastures of Gioura. Unless you're a MOm official, forget about seeing the seals, but you can watch a documentary and grab a "Save the Seals" poster from the gallery in MOm's headquarters across from the dock in Patitiri. (☎24240 66 350, www.mom.gr. Open June-Oct. daily 10am-midnight.)

SKYROS Σκύρος

Skyros is dominated by two forces—modern tourism and local tradition—that would seem to be as diametrically opposed as the terrain found on each side of the island. But while the barren landscape of the south and the green hills of the north will always be separate, the two modes of Skyrian life are beginning to coexist. Instead of visitors zooming around the island on ATVs, you will more likely hear walking tours led by a local, and you will smell the aromas of family-run *tavernas* rather than gyro and souvlaki carts.

SKYROS TOWN
Χωριό ☎ 22220

Skyros Town—or Chorio ("the village") to locals—stands out in bright white contrast to the greens, yellows, and browns of the hills that surround it. Beyond the *tavernas*, cafes, and bars are the features that give the island its distinctive, almost otherworldly charm. The characteristically small Skyrian houses were built between the 11th and 12th centuries. They owe their compact size to an effort to build the village so that all the homes would be out of view of marauding pirates. Among this maze of whitewashed houses, old men sew sandals and women embroider patterns by porchlight late into the evening, while the main street bustles with a mix of visitors and locals at restaurants and cafes. During the three-week-long Carnival, just before Lent, the town erupts into a truly wild festival.

▐ TRANSPORTATION

No ferries or hydrofoils run from the other Sporades to Skyros, making it a difficult destination to reach on an island-hopping tour.

Flights: Skiros Airport (SKU; ☎ 22220 91 625), 20km from Skyros Town. To **Athens** (35min., 3 per week, €38) and **Thessaloniki** (45min.; W, Sa, Su; €66).

Ferries: The best way to get to Skyros is to take the ferry from **Kimi, Evia** (2hr., 2 per day, €9), which is accessible by bus from Athens and from other parts of Evia. The ferry to Skyros arrives in **Linaria,** the tiny western port; a bus to Skyros Town (the first stop) picks up when ferries arrive (15min., 4-6 per day, €1.40) and leaves ½-1hr. before ferry departures. Another bus runs from Linaria to **Molos** (10min., 1-2 per day, €1.40). Buy ferry tickets at Skyros Travel (p. 432) or Skyros Shipping Company (☎ 22220 92 164), past the *plateia* on the right. Open daily 9am-1pm and 6:30-10pm.

Buses: The stop in Skyros Town is at the base of Agoras, the town's main road. Schedules change often, so call for times; current schedules are posted at the bus stop.

Taxis: (☎ 22220 91 666), in the central *plateia* and at the bus stop; usually only available in the morning.

Car and Moped Rental: Pegasus Rent A Car runs out of Skyros Travel (p. 432). Cars €40-65 per day. Mopeds €15-25 per day. 24hr. pick-up and delivery.

▐ ORIENTATION AND PRACTICAL INFORMATION

Agoras runs uphill from the bus stop, passing shops, pharmacies, bars, and restaurants along its way through Skyros Town. Maze-like streets extend outward along the hillsides, and buildings are numbered counterintuitively. Few streets are named, so when venturing off Agoras, pick out landmarks. At the far end of town, looking out across the sea, is **Plateia Rupert Brooke,** dedicated to British poet Brooke and to "█immortal poetry." You can reach Pl. Rupert Brooke by walking up Agoras through town until it forks left at Kalypso Bar, then heading left along the wall and walking up until you reach a sign pointing to "Mouseio/Museum." Veer right and follow the stairs built into the narrow street to the *plateia*. At Pl. Rupert Brooke, the stairs to the right pass the Archaeological Museum on a 15min. descent to the beach; another set ahead leads to the Faltaits Museum.

Travel Agency: Skyros Travel (☎22220 91 600; www.skyrostravel.com), past the central *plateia* on the left of Agoras walking away from the bus station. Sells Olympic Airways tickets, rents cars, organizes bus and boat excursions, and helps find rooms. Their port office in Linaria opens when ferries arrive. Open daily 9am-2pm and 7-10pm.

Bank: National Bank (☎22220 91 802), past the central *plateia* on the left. **24hr. ATM.** Open M-Th 8am-2:30pm.

Police: (☎22220 91 274), beyond Nefeli, opposite the gas station. Open 24hr.

Pharmacy: (☎22220 91 817), across the street from the bank. Open daily 9am-2pm and 6pm-midnight.

Hospital: (☎22220 92 222), just out of town, behind Hotel Nefeli.

Internet Access: Planet (☎22220 92 802), on the right past the *plateia* on Agoras. €3 per hr. Open daily 10am-2pm and 6:30-11pm.

Post Office: (☎22220 91 208), on the far side of the *plateia* from Agoras. **Poste Restante.** Open M-F 7:30am-2pm. **Postal Code:** 34007.

ACCOMMODATIONS

Coming to Skyros and staying in a hotel is like coming to Greece to swim in a pool. For the real experience you've got to stay in a *domatia*, such as one of those offered by the old women at the bus stop. Thick-walled, one-room Skyrian houses are treasure troves, brimming with ceramics, Italian linens, icons, embroidery, metalwork, and fine china bought from pirates who looted the Mediterranean. Expect to pay €20-45 for a room; always bargain and look carefully for landmarks and house numbers, as it's easy to lose your way in the maze of streets.

Hotel Elena (☎22220 91 738), on the 1st right off Agoras heading uphill from the bus stop. The clean and comfortable rooms have tiled baths, A/C, TVs, and fridges; some have balconies. Singles €30-40; doubles €35-55; triples €55-70. Cash only. ❷

FOOD

🍴 **To Pappou Kai Ego** (☎22220 93 200), on the right immediately after the sharp bend in Agoras; look for the green chairs. Known in town as "Pappou's," this splendid restaurant serves a delicious "chicken o Pappous" floating in cream sauce over rice (€8) and a tender nanny goat au lemon (€7.50). Entrees €7-12. Open daily 7pm-1am. MC/V. ❷

To Metopo (☎22220 91 995), on the left heading into town from the bus stop. An unassuming hangout for Skyrian men looking for a good meal and conversation. Entrees €6-8. Open daily 1-4:30pm and 7pm-1am. Cash only. ❷

SIGHTS AND BEACHES

Standing in Skyros's pirate-proof streets, it's easy to forget how close you are to the water. An expansive and pleasant sandy beach stretches below the town through the villages of **Magazia** and **Molos** and continues around the point. Head down the stairs after the Archaeological Museum and follow the road leading to the left. The local **nude beach,** ironically named **Tou Papa to Homa** ("The Sands of the Priest"), remains clean and uncrowded, just south of the local beach. Walk 10-12min. to the right along the seaside road at the bottom of the steps to reach a narrow, slippery dirt path lined with spiky plants. It leads downhill along a wire fence—be careful, as the last 4m is especially steep. From here, you'll have a beautiful view of the Southern Mountain. Locals recommend **Pefkos**, tucked into a cove up the coast from Linaria and accessible by taxi. Barren beaches and Rupert Brooke's grave, on the southern portion of the island, are accessible only by dusty paths or boat. Buses from Linaria to Skyros Town will stop at the beaches of **Aherounis**, on the western coast, and small **Mialos**, on the east, if you ask the driver in advance. Boats leaving from Linaria explore the former pirate grottoes at **Spillies**, on the southeastern coast, and **Sarakino Island**, one of the largest pirate centers in the Aegean. For timetables and prices, look for signs labeled "Sea Cave Boats" along Agoras and at the port in Linaria.

FALTAITS MUSEUM. The wonderfully varied private collection of Skyrian ethnologist Manos Faltaits is housed in the frozen-in-time ancestral home of the Faltaits family, one of the first large homes to be built after fears of pirate raids had subsided. The museum collection includes folklore items, book collections, traditional costumes, sculptures, and paintings. The vibrant mix of ancient and modern exhibits, at once respectful and daring, preserves the essence of Skyrian culture. Tours (available in English) take you step-by-step through the collection, offering invaluable insight into the collection and even into the nature of the town itself. *(Just past Pl. Rupert Brooke. ☎ 22220 91 232. Open daily 10am-2pm and 6-9pm. €2, including basic tour. Comprehensive historical tour €5.)*

HILLTOP SIGHTS. At the top of the hill on the way to Pl. Rupert Brooke before descending to the *plateia*, a sign points the way up steps to the **Monastery of Agios Georgios** and the **kastro**. Both are closed, but the climb yields a nice view of Molos and the sea coast.

UPPER VILLAGE. On Agoras after going left at Kalypso, explore the "upper village," a stronghold of island tradition. Jewelry, sandals, and other Skyrian items are crafted and sold in its several shops. The museum shop, **Argo**, can be found here, near Kalypso on the left. *(☎ 22220 92 707. Open daily 9:30am-1:30pm and 6:30-10:30pm.)* The shop's proprietor, Niko Sikkes, also leads 2hr. ◪**walking tours** of the island once or twice a week (€6). He will help make sense of the winding Old Town streets, explain elements of the town's history and mythology, take you into hidden churches, lead you up to the castle and along the coast, and undoubtedly introduce you to neighbors along the way (he seems to know everyone in town).

◪ NIGHTLIFE

The central *plateia* is the heart of nighttime action, surrounded by crowded bars that keep the music loud and the drinks strong.

Iroön, directly across from the *plateia*. Wine €4. Beer €3.50. Open daily 8am-late.

Kalypso Bar (☎22220 92 160), at the top of Agoras past Pappou's. A calmer scene, as people gather to chat and sip a nightcap after a tasty Skyrian meal. Beer €3. Mixed drinks €5-6. Open daily 7pm-late.

IONIAN ISLANDS
Νησιά Του Ιόνιου

Just west of mainland Greece, the Ionian Islands entice travelers with their lush vegetation and shimmering turquoise waters. The region's unusual architecture and distinctive personality are due to a history separate from the rest of Greece—these islands were not conquered by Ottomans, but instead bear the marks of Venetian, British, French, and Russian occupants. Each of these civilizations has left its own cultural trace, which makes visiting the islands all the more enticing. Multicultural for millennia, each of the Ionian Islands maintains a unique identity while sharing an unparalleled beauty.

HIGHLIGHTS OF THE IONIAN ISLANDS

LOUNGE next to **Kefallonia's** sky-blue waters (p. 452).

PUSH past the crowds on **Zakynthos** to find Venetian arches, stunning beaches, and a deep-green forest (p. 459).

EXPLORE the hidden coves of **Paleokastritsa**, on Corfu (p. 446).

CORFU Κέρκυρα

There's a reason why Corfu continues to be desired by so many: from archaeology to debauchery, the island has it all. Budding archaeologists will find ruins galore, those tired of clothes can strip down at a number of nude beaches, and people seeking a laid-back village may stumble upon one without even having to look. Homer first sang Corfu's praise by writing of its "honeyed fig," "unctuous olive," "boisterous waves," and friendly inhabitants, who helped Odysseus in a time of desperate need. From the Franks and Venetians to the British and today's tourist masses, Corfu (KEHR-kee-rah) has captivated all who come to its shores, and its natural and manmade treasures justify the Homeric fuss even today.

CORFU TOWN   ☎ 26610

Trade in *plateias* for *piazze* and ouzo for wine in Corfu Town, which is distinctly Italian. More than just an Italian knock-off, Corfu Town combines big-city glitz with beaches and a multitude of museums and sites that deservedly draw in tourists. English is almost a first language here, where most restaurants and services cater to foreign visitors. As a result, expect to pay more for less. Though budget travel is doable, it's not easy, and you may want to consider loosening the purse strings for a more pleasant stay. Still, Corfu's many attractions make this town a lively center of Mediterranean culture.

⌐ TRANSPORTATION

Flights: Olympic Airways (☎26610 30 180) flies to **I. Kapodistrias (CFU)**, Corfu's international airport. In summer, almost 50 charter flights per day fly through; book 2-3 days

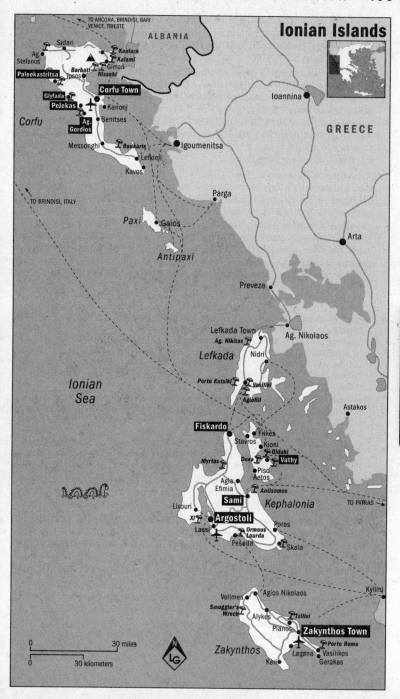

Ionian Islands

ALBANIA

TO ANCONA, BRINDISI, BARI
VENICE, TRIESTE

Sidari
Ag.
Stefanos
Kaulura
Kalami
Barbati
Nissaki
Giman
Ipsos
Paleokastritsa
Corfu Town
Glyfada
Pelekas
Kanoni
Corfu
Ag.
Gordios
Benitses
Messonghi
Baukaris
Igoumenitsa
Lefkimi
Kavos

GREECE

Ioannina

TO BRINDISI, ITALY

Parga

Paxi
Gaios

Antipaxi

Arta

Preveza

Lefkada Town
Ag. Nikitas
Ag. Nikolaos

Lefkada
Nidri

Ionian
Sea

Porto Katsiki
Vasiliki
Agiofili

Astakos

Fiskardo
Frikes
Stavros
Kioni
Myrtos
Gidaki
Dexa
Vathy
Piso
Aetos
Agia
Efimia
Antisamos
Sami
Kephalonia
Lixouri
Xi
Argostoli
Poros
Lassi
Ormous
Lourda
Peseda
Skala

TO PATRAS

Volimes
Agios Nikolaos
Smuggler's
Wreck
Alykes
Tsilivi
Planos
Zakynthos Town
Lagana
Porto Roma
Vasilikos
Keri
Gerakas
Zakynthos

Kyllini

0   30 miles
0   30 kilometers

N

IONIAN ISLANDS

in advance. A 5min. taxi ride (agree on about €10 beforehand) is the quickest way to the airport (☎26610 33 811). You can get dropped off 1km away if you take blue bus #11 to Pelekas (ask the driver). To **Athens** (1hr., 1-2 per day, €32-52) and **Thessaloniki** (1hr.; F 10:55pm, Sa 10:10pm, 4 flights a day via Athens; €65-86).

Ferries: Get tickets at least 1 day in advance during high season; when traveling to Italy, find out if the port tax (€7-10) is included in the cost of a ticket. Prices vary according to season, ferry line, and class. Try **Fragline** or **HML** for Brindisi and **Strindzis Lines** for Venice. **Ionian Travel,** Eth. Antistaseos 1 (☎26610 80 444), close to the New Port. To: **Igoumenitsa** (1hr.; every hr. 7:30am-6:30pm, 8:30, 11:30pm; €8, students €4); **Patra** (8hr., 4 per week, from €36); **Paxi** (1-4 per day, from €15.10); **Bari, Italy** (10hr.; 3 per week M, Th-F 10:30pm; from €23); **Brindisi, Italy** (8hr., Tu-Su 4-5 per day, €38); **Venice, Italy** (24hr., 4 per week, from €51).

Buses: Green KTEL buses (☎26610 28 927) leave from the intersection between I. Theotoki and the New Fortress (accessible from I. Theotoki or Xen. Stratigou). **Blue municipal buses** (☎26610 31 595) leave from San Rocco. For a schedule with return times and prices for both, ask at the white info kiosk at the central San Rocco *plateia*. Most stops have a return schedule posted that can differ from the schedule available at the KTEL in Corfu, always double check to avoid being stranded. Open daily 8am-10pm. The tourist info office in the green kiosk in San Rocco has English timetables for all buses.

Green buses to: **Agios Gordios** (45min.; M-F 6 per day 8:15am-8pm, Sa 5 per day 8:15am-8pm, Su 3 per day 9:30am-5:30pm; €2); **Agios Stefanos** (1½hr.; M-Sa 6 per day 5:30am-4pm, Su 9:30am; €3.70); **Barbati** (45min.; M-Sa 9am and 6:30pm, Su 9:30am; €2); **Cavos** (1hr.; M-F 11 per day 5am-7:30pm, Sa 8 per day 5am-7:30pm, Su 4 per day 5am-7:30pm; €4); **Glyfada** (45min.; M-Sa 8 per day 6:45am-8pm, Su 5 per day 9am-5:30pm; €2); **Ipsos** and **Pirgi** (30-45min.; M-F 10 per day 7am-8pm, Sa 7 per day 9am-6:30pm, Su 9:30am; €1.40); **Kassiopi** (1hr.; M-Sa 6 per day 5:45am-4pm, Su 9:30am; €3.20); **Messonghi** (45min.; M-Sa 5 per day 9am-3:30pm; Su 4 per day 9am-7:30pm; €2); **Paleokastritsa** (45min.; M-Sa 7 per day 8:30am-6pm, Su 5 per day 9am-4pm; €2.10); **Sidari** (1hr.; M-Sa 8 per day 5:30am-7:30pm, Su 9:30am; €3). Buy tickets onboard. **KTEL** also runs to **Athens** (8hr.; 8:45am, 1:45, 7:45pm; €39.50) and **Thessaloniki** (8hr.; 7:45am, 5:45pm; €37.70); prices include ferry. Buy tickets at the green bus station.

Blue buses to: **Achilleon #10** (30min.; M-F 8 per day 7am-8pm, Sa 6 per day 8am-8pm, Su 4 per day 9am-8pm; €1.30); **Agios Ioannis** and **Aqualand #8** (30min.; M-F 13 per day 6:15am-10pm, Sa 9 per day 7:10am-9pm, Su 6 per day 8am-9pm; €1.30); **Benitses** (30min.; M-F 25 per day 6:30am-10:30pm, Sa 22 per day 6:30-10:30, Su 13 per day 6:45am-10pm; €1.30); **Kanoni** and **Mouse Island #2** (30min.; M-F 2 per hr. 6:30am-10pm, Sa 2 per hr. 6:30am-2pm, every hr. 2:30pm-9:30pm, Su every hr. 9:30am-9:30pm; €0.90); **Pelekas #11** (30min.; M-F 8 per day 7am-10pm, Sa 6 per day 7am-8pm, Su 4 per day 10am-8pm; €1.30). Buy tickets at the kiosk.

Taxis: (☎26610 33 811 or 31 595). At the New and Old Ports, the Spianada, Pl. San Rocco, and Pl. G. Theotoki. Ask for the price before you get in—they vary a great deal, especially for short distances. Fares doubled 1-6am. Taxis respond to calls 24hr.

Car Rental: Car rental places line the waterfront. **Europcar,** Venizelou 30 (☎26610 46 931; www.europcar.com.gr), just off the waterfront a few meters from the New Port. Open M-F 8am-9:30pm, Sa-Su 8am-4pm, and 6-9:30pm. **EuroHire,** Theotoki 132 (☎26610 22062), on the corner of the waterfront and the road leading to San Rocco. Small cars from €40; price varies by season. Ask if 20% tax, 3rd-party insurance, and mileage are included. Open daily 8am-10pm.

Moped Rental: Travelers should note that many roads, especially those far from Corfu Town, are not well paved and present serious risks to moped drivers; stick to the main roads, which have fewer potholes. If you decide to rent, there are various places along the waterfront, especially near the New Port. **Scooter Mania,** Eth. Yardikioti (☎6997113 742), a few blocks from the intersection of I. Theotoki and Venizelou on a side street with a sign visible from the main road. Mopeds from €15-20 per day; helmet included.

IONIAN ISLANDS

Rental fee should include 3rd-party liability and property damage insurance. Bikes from €8 per day. Open daily 9am-9pm.

⚡ 🚲 ORIENTATION AND PRACTICAL INFORMATION

Following the waterfront road from the **New Port** to the east will take you past many of the city's museums and popular restaurants. Then the road turns south and leads you to the hub of activity at the large, grassy square **Splanada,** with access to the **Old Fortress,** the souvenir shops, top-notch restaurants in the **Old City,** and more museums. Most visitors arrive in the New Port, which marks the far west of the city—aside from a string of clubs and bars, everything is located to the east of the New Port. From the customs house at the New Port, it's about 1km to the center of town, **Plateia San Rocco;** locals will say and understand "Saroco" for short. To get there from the New Port, cross the intersection at the light, turn left, and walk along Eth. Antistasseos until you hit the intersection in front of the domestic terminal; the waterfront road turns into Xen. Stratigou then El. Venizelou. Turn uphill onto I. Theotoki, from which it is about a 10min. walk. The long driveway of the KTEL (green) bus terminal will be on your left as you pass, and the blue bus terminal is in the *plateia*. The **Old Town** can be reached by walking along the waterfront toward the **Old Port.** If you follow the waterfront with the water on your left past the Old Port square (known as **Spilia**), circling the Old Town, you will see the palace on your left and a long park known as the Spianada, the town's social center, straight in front of you. Two streets encircle the Spianada: **Eleftherias** (which becomes **Kapodistriou**) is farther inland; **Polytechniou** curves around the outside. While picturesque, a walk around the Old Town can confuse even the best navigators. To avoid getting lost, use the prominent and central **National Bank** at the entrance of the Old Town as a reference point; the pedestrian walkway in front of the bank leads to San Rocco's main feeder street, **Georgios Theotoki.**

Tourist Office: Pl. San Rocco (☎26610 20 733), in a green kiosk. Friendly, English-speaking staff helps with any questions. Open daily 9am-2pm and 6-9pm.

Bank: National Bank, Alexandras 30 (☎26610 47 728), on the corner of Alexandras and Rizopaston Voulefton, across from the post office. Open M-Th 8am-2:30pm, F 8:30am-2pm. Banks with **24hr. ATMs** line the larger streets and the waterfront.

Beyond Tourism: The Pink Palace (p. 447) hires hotel and club staff and DJs. Mail a letter of introduction, resume, and photo in advance. Usually a minimum 2-month commitment is required, but friendly owner Dr. George is open to negotiation.

Bookstore: Xenoglosso, Markora 45 (☎26610 23 923). From the police station, walking away from San Rocco, turn left onto Markora. A limited number of classic novels, books about Greece, and language materials in English. Open M 8am-2pm, Tu 8:30am-2pm and 5-8:30pm, W 8am-2pm, Th-F 8:30am-2pm and 5-8:30pm, Sa 8am-2pm.

Laundromat: I. Theotoki 42 (☎26610 35 305). Wash and dry €10. Open M 8:30am-2:30pm, Tu-Th 8:30am-2:30pm and 6-8pm, F 8:30am-2:30pm.

Police: (☎26610 39 294). Heading toward the New Port, turn right off I. Theotoki along Pl. San Rocco onto the short street that intersects Markora. Open 24hr. In an **emergency,** dial ☎100. **Tourist Police** (☎26610 30 265 or 39 503), on the 4th fl. of the police building. Open daily 7am-2pm. **Port Police** ☎26610 32 655.

Hospital: Corfu General Hospital, I. Andreadi (☎26610 88 200 or 45 811). The tourist office or tourist police can help find an English-speaking doctor.

Internet Access: Netoikos Cafe, Kaloheretou 12-14 (☎26610 47 479), behind Ag. Spiridon church. €3 per hr. Open M-Sa 10am-midnight, Su 6pm-midnight. Wi-Fi. **Bits and Bytes** (☎26610 32 812), on the corner of Mantzarou and Voulefton. With your back to the post office, walk straight ahead; it's on your left. €3 per hr. Open 24hr.

Post Office: (☎26610 25 544), on the corner of Alexandras and R. Voulefton. **Poste Restante** and **currency exchange.** Open M-F 7:30am-8pm. **Postal Code:** 49100.

ACCOMMODATIONS

There's no getting around the fact that Corfu Town is expensive; tourist packages drive up prices for the budget traveler. Relatively cheap accommodations do exist, though, especially in low season. If you're traveling in high season, call several weeks in advance to ensure availability. Otherwise, consider staying in towns and campgrounds just outside the city and taking daytrips into Corfu; some cities are accessible through the extensive and frequent green KTEL buses, check prices and times at the station. Prices are flexible and depend on the duration of your stay, the time of year, and the vacancy of the hotel or *domatia*. Since competition is fierce, don't hesitate to ask for a lower rate.

Hotel Astron, Donzelot 15 (☎26610 39 505), past Spilia in the direction of the Old Fortress. Renovated in 2007, the surprisingly stylish and modern baths are a marked contrast to the aged wooden furniture. All room have fridges, TVs, and A/C; some have balconies. Singles €55-70; doubles €65-80; triples €75-90. Cash only. ❹

Hotel Konstantinoupolis, K. Zavitsianou 11 (☎26610 48 716; www.konstantinoupolis. com.gr), in Spilia right across from the Old Port. Perfect location right between the bus stop to the east and the Spianada to the west. This beautiful building has been greeting guests since 1862 with its traditional long Venetian shutters. Spacious rooms, some with balconies and amazing views, are cheery and light. Each room has TV and A/C. Laundry services available. Reception 24hr. Call in advance in high season. Singles €68-98; doubles €78-118; triples €118-140. Cash only. ❺

Hotel Europa, P. Gitsiali 10 (☎26610 39 304), tucked into a residential neighborhood off the waterfront. Walking from the New Port, make a right on the street with Scooter Mania, Eth. Yardikioti, and continue straight. From the KTEL bus station, take the immediate right when you reach the waterfront (forming a V-shape with Eth. Yardikioti) and continue diagonally. Europa is close to the New Port and the bus station, but its perks stop there. As the only budget option in town, it may be many travelers' only choice. Hardly a comfortable stay, the bare rooms have baths and TVs; some have fans. Reception 24hr. Singles €25-30; doubles €40; triples €60. Cash only. ❷

Hotel Hermes, G. Markora 14 (☎26610 39 268; www.hermes-hotel.gr), around the bend from the police station. Right in the heart of the noisy streets off Pl. San Rocco, this hotel boasts a retro style. Spacious, clean rooms with fridges and fans. Reception 24hr. Singles €50; doubles €60; triples €70. MC/V. ❹

Hotel Atlantis, Xen. Sratigou Ave 48 (☎26610 35 560), near the start of I. Theotoki on the waterfront in the direction of the Old Town. Simple rooms with hardwood floors have TVs, A/C, phones, fridges, and baths; some have balconies with views. Reception 24hr. Singles €50; doubles €65; triples €80. AmEx/MC/V. ❹

🔲 FOOD

The main restaurant areas are by the **Spianada** and **Spilia.** Lots of similar *tavernas* are scattered throughout the Old Town's maze of alleyways. Homemade wines and beers are available all over the island: light white *kakotrygis,* richer white *moscato,* dry *petrokorintho* red, and dark *skopelitiko.* Light yellow *tsitsibira* (ginger beer) is another specialty. Liquor made from *kumquats* is sold all over the Old Town and available at some restaurants. An **open-air market** on Dessila along the side of the New Fortress, between the waterfront and San Rocco Square, sells fresh fruit and cheap foods. (Open daily 8am-2pm.) **Supermarkets** are located on I. Theotoki, in Pl. San Rocco, and beyond the bus station on Alexandras. (Open M-F 8am-9pm, Sa 8am-8pm.)

Restaurant Antranik/Pizza Pete, Arseniou 19 (☎26610 22 301), 2min. past Hotel Astron on the waterfront. An Americanized menu—but with a much nicer view. Large pizzas (€7-11) can be finished off with 1 of over 20 ice-cream creations (€6-8). Open in spring and summer daily 9am-midnight. AmEx/MC/V. ❷

To Paradosiakon, Solomou 20 (☎26610 37 578), by Spilia a few steps away from the entrance to the New Fortress, at the corner of Ag. Sofias. Look for the salmon pink walls and bright green chairs. This small restaurant, whose name means "tradition," boasts traditional Greek cuisine that draws tourist and local gourmands alike. Entrees €6-12. Open daily Mar.-Nov. 11am-midnight. Cash only. ❷

Aegli, Kapodistriou 23 (☎26610 31.949). Claims to be the oldest traditional restaurant in town (open for over 4 decades); and its years of experience show in the upscale ambience. Tables either sit on the side of the restaurant in a snug walkway or look out onto the beautiful Spianada. The *lamb à la Aegli* (lamb cooked with potatoes and nuts; €15) is their specialty. Entrees €6-14. Open 10am-11:30pm. AmEx/MC/V. ❸

IONIAN ISLANDS

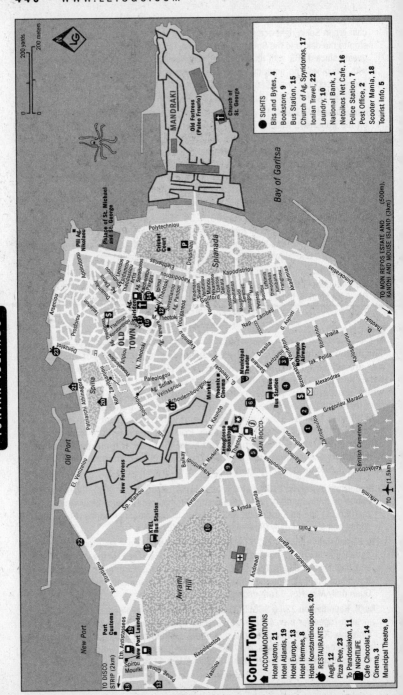

Corfu Town

IONIAN ISLANDS

SIGHTS
Bits and Bytes, 4
Bookstore, 9
Bus Station, 15
Church of Ag. Spyridonos, 17
Ionian Travel, 22
Laundry, 10
National Bank, 1
Netoikos Net Cafe, 16
Police Station, 7
Post Office, 2
Scooter Mania, 18
Tourist Info, 5

ACCOMMODATIONS
Hotel Astron, 21
Hotel Atlantis, 19
Hotel Europa, 13
Hotel Hermes, 8
Hotel Konstantinoupoulis, 20

RESTAURANTS
Aegli, 12
Pizza Pete, 23
To Paradosiakon, 11

NIGHTLIFE
Cafe Chocolat, 14
Cinema, 3
Municipal Theatre, 6

🔄 SIGHTS

After invading Vandals and Goths destroyed ancient Corfu (Paleopolis) in the AD fifth and sixth centuries, residents built a more defensible city between the twin peaks of the Old Fortress. Wary of Ottoman raids, the Venetians strengthened the existing structure, constructed the New Fortress, and built thick walls around the growing city. A series of underground **tunnels,** now closed, connected the Old Fortress to the new one and all parts of Corfu Town. The tunnels later provided refuge for Corfiots after the first WWII air raids in 1940.

OLD FORTRESS (PALEO FROURIO). Linked to the Spianada by a 60m iron bridge that spans the 10th-century moat, the Old Fortress is a symbol of Corfu's history. The Byzantines, Venetians, and British all fortified the two hilltops, and ruins from each period remain. Most visitors find themselves drawn to the red **bell tower** near the summit and the **Church of Saint George,** which for years was closed to the public but is now open most days from 9am-6pm. Amazing panoramic views of the city and the sea await the determined who climb to the top of the tower. In the summer, Greek rock stars perform **concerts** on the vast plateau next to the church (ask at the tourist information kiosk for a concert schedule), and there are small exhibits housed in the first few rooms by the entrance. Explanations in English are sparse, so consider buying a guidebook (€4-6) from the museum. *(Just east of the Spianada.* ☎ *26610 38 313. Open daily 8am-8pm. €4, students and seniors €2, EU students free.)*

NEW FORTRESS. The result of the Venetians' second attempt to protect their city, the 350-year-old walls of the New Fortress were once considered the archetype of military architecture. Less frequented than the Old Fortress, this massive edifice derives its charm from the unrestored rooms that you can explore at your leisure, not to mention a small rotating art exhibit and a cafe (frappuccino €2.50). Concerts and theatrical events also take place here during the summer. *(At the top of Solomou above the steps; look for signs as you walk along Velissariou from the Old Port.* ☎ *26610 27 370. Open daily 9am-9pm. €2, EU students free.)*

CHURCH OF AGIOS SPIRIDON. Housing the embalmed body of the island's patron saint, Ag. Spiridon, this church, built in 1596, is an important Orthodox pilgrimage point. Inside, a silver casket holds the remains of the third-century saint, whose spirit is believed to wander the streets performing good deeds for the island's residents and visitors. In fact, four times per year, the casket is paraded through the city to rid the streets of evil spirits. Rumor has it that if the priest opens the gold cover of Spiridon's casket during your visit, you can catch a glimpse of his blackened face. The biblical scenes on the 18th-century Baroque ceiling and the Renaissance-style icons draw tourists as well. Locals gather here to pray for good fortune, bowing, crossing themselves, and kissing the tomb with fervor. *(Take Ag. Spiridon off the Spianada; it's on the left. Look for the red tower and black clock. Open daily 6am-9pm. Modest dress required.)*

 TICKET TO CULTURE. A combined ticket for the Old Fortress, Byzantine Museum, Archaeological Museum, and Museum of Asian Art is €8, for students and seniors €4; get one at any of the sights.

KANONI AND MOUSE ISLAND. Praised in traditional songs about Corfu, Mouse Island (Pontikonisi) is located near the beautiful bay at Kanoni, the ancient capital of the island. Enjoy the jaw-dropping view at the now-famous Cafe Kanoni, serving patrons since 1864. (Snacks €3.50-8. Open daily in summer

IONIAN ISLANDS

8:30am-12:30am.) Then walk down to the water, where the tiny Vlacherna Monastery of the Virgin Mary juts into the water. Summer tourists can take frequent water taxis to Mouse Island. There, the only building you will find among the rich flora is the one-room 13th-century Byzantine Church of the Pantocrator, surrounded by cypresses. (Take the #2 bus (€0.90) or a taxi to Kanoni, €10-12. Water taxis to Mouse Island 10am-9pm, €2.50.)

🏛 MUSEUMS

🔲MON REPOS ESTATE. In a grandiose effort to please his Corfiot wife, Sir Frederic Adams, the second British High Commissioner of the Ionian Islands, mandated the construction of one of the most elegant and expansive estates in Greece. However, only two years after they moved in, the Adamses relocated to Madras, India. The grounds changed hands many times until they became the summer home of Greece's ex-royal family in 1864. Today, a walk through the estate gives a glimpse of Corfu's gorgeous terrain—including the 2000 trees Adams received as a housewarming gift from the British Empire—and passes by excavation sites. Look for the intriguing **Museum of Paleopolis**, which exhibits an eclectic collection of period rooms from the palace, along with archaeological finds from excavations around Corfu. Each display, including an ancient version of a cosmetics kit and a collection of 510 silver Corinthian and Corycian coins, is labeled with full explanations in English and Greek. Those tired of perusing ancient artifacts can enjoy the air-conditioned multimedia exhibit that gives a thorough summary of local history. (To reach the palace, head up the path to the right just inside the main gate. ☎ 26610 41 369. Estate open daily 8am-7pm. Free. Museum open M 1:30-8pm, Tu-Su 8am-8pm; in winter 8am-5pm. €3, EU students €2.)

When exiting the palace, with the water on your right, follow the overgrown path to your right overlooking the sea to the tiny, pebbly **Kardaki Beach.** Corfiot poet Lorenzos Mavilis wrote that anyone who drinks from its spring will remain on the island forever. To the left of the palace with your back to the museum entrance, a path leads to two Doric temples: the last remains of the **Temple of Hera** (the Heraion), and the more impressive **Kardaki Temple,** thought to have been dedicated to either Poseidon, Apollo, or Asclepius. (Take the #2 bus toward Mouse Island and tell the driver you want to be dropped off at Mon Repos. 10min., €0.90.)

🔲PALACE OF SAINT MICHAEL AND SAINT GEORGE. Forming the northern border of the Spianada, the stunning palace was built by Adams's predecessor, British Lord High Commissioner Sir Thomas Maitland, during the British occupation of the Ionnian Islands (1814-1864). Today, it is better known for housing, of all things, the **Asian Museum.** The delightfully schizophrenic building has an Asian art collection that is punctuated by rooms that recreate the palace's intended purpose. The building originally housed the High Commissioner, the Ionian parliament, and the ceremonies of the orders of St. Michael and St. George. Later used by the ex-royal family as a ceremonial palace, it was renovated to hold the EU summit meeting in 1994. Glance around at the intricate ceilings, heavy mahogany doors, and the impressive Throne Room. The **Museum of Asian Art** within the palace, which has detailed descriptions of the originating countries and religions feels more like an idiot's guide to Asian culture and religion. Over 10,000 artifacts from three formerly private collections are displayed from India, Southeast Asia, Gandhara, Nepal, Tibet, Japan, and China. One of the main highlights is a full suit of Samurai armor. (☎ 26610 30 443. Open M 1:30-8pm, Tu-Su 8:30am-8pm. €3, students and seniors €2, EU students free.)

The **Municipal Modern Art Gallery** (Dimotiko Pinakothiki), beside the palace, has a small display of Corfiot paintings and various rotating exhibits. (☎ 26610 48 690. Open Tu-F 10am-5pm, but hours of special exhibits vary. €1.50, students free.)

BYZANTINE MUSEUM. This impressive collection of religious artifacts is housed in the small, late 15th-century **Church of the Most Holy Virgin Antivouniotissa,** which still operates as a church on the December 26 and August 23 feasts of the Virgin. The church itself is striking enough to merit a visit, if only to observe the painted "wallpaper"—a red floral pattern that adorns much of the church—and wood ceiling carvings. The exhibit has gold communion cups, 15th- through 19th-century priestly vestments, and iron-covered gospel books that form some of the highlights of the permanent exhibit in the room next to the church. The museum displays 90 **Cretan School** icons, including the famed 16th-century icon of Mary Magdalene calling Jesus "Rabouni" ("my teacher"), as described in the Gospel of John. The many different styles and influences in the collection are attributed to the influx of Cretan artists who stopped in Corfu on their way to Venice after the 1646 fall of Rethymno. *(Past the Old Port with the waterfront on your left; there are signs on Arseniou. ☎ 26610 38 313. Open Tu-Su 8:30am-3pm. €2, students and seniors €1, EU students free. Modest dress required.)*

ARCHAEOLOGICAL MUSEUM. Ancient coins, bronze laurel leaves, and detailed statuettes will catch any visitor's attention, but the treasure of this large collection is hands-down the frightening **Gorgon Pediment** (590-580 BC) from Corfu's Doric Temple of Artemis. The oldest surviving pediment in Greece, it shows Medusa with her offspring, Pegasus and Chrysaor. According to myth, the creatures were born at the moment when Perseus cut off their mother's snake-covered head, though in the pediment she appears rather lively. *(Armeni Vraila 1, downhill from the Spianada, past Hotel Corfu Palace, signs point the way. ☎ 26610 30 680. Open Tu-Su 8:30am-3pm. €3, students and seniors €2, children and EU students free.)*

ENTERTAINMENT

The Orpheus Cinema, Aspiotit (☎ 26610 39 768). Take G. Theotoki from San Rocco and take a right onto Dessila, passing the municipal theater; Dessila turns into Aspioti after the intersection. The cinema plays movies in English regularly. Tickets €7.

The Municipal Theater (☎ 26610 33 598), between Dessila and Mantzarou. Has occasional drama, dance, and music performances, publicized on bulletin boards.

STARING CONTEST. Greek men are notorious for casting intense, longing gazes at women in clubs and cafes. The penetrating glares can intimidate those unfamiliar with the culture, but they are usually a harmless—if annoyingly ubiquitous—part of the bar scene. In Greek slang, the men who cast these predatory looks are known as *kamaki,* the Greek word for "harpoon." Unless a woman is looking to be hooked, she should feel free to swim away.

NIGHTLIFE

Less than 2km west of the New Port, the disco strip, known as **Emboriko Center,** is the undisputed center of nightlife in Corfu Town in July and August. The best way to get to the strip, located on Eth. Antistasios, is by taxi (€4-7, more after midnight). Beer is generally €3-5.50, and mixed drinks are €7-10. Crowds of locals and tourists intermingle in the bars and cafes, each of which offers its own take on the ideal evening out. Most clubs here close down for low season and, when they reopen, frequently change names and/or ownership; ask the locals about the status of various clubs before heading out. In the early summer months clubs are only open on the weekends, but beginning in the last week of July they open nightly. Consult locals or the clubs themselves for

IONIAN ISLANDS

exact dates. In Corfu Town itself, the elegant little cafes that line the Spianada are open year-round and usually lively until about 1am.

Au Bar, at the beginning of the strip. The low ceilings and small dance floor mean it fills up quickly, and locals pack the place in the low season, making it a safe option for a decent night out. Drinks €8. Cover €10; includes 1 drink. Open daily midnight-5am.

Villamercedes, Eth. Antistaseos 42 (☎26610 807 80), at the end of the strip. Glitzy, large club where an aqua-colored bar serves drinks to American pop music. Drinks €8. Cover €12. Open daily midnight-6am.

The Island, in the middle of the strip. Pounding American tunes, which lounging locals and tourists listen to amidst palm trees and fountains in the outdoor patio. Drinks €5-7. Cover €10; includes 1 drink. Open daily midnight-5am.

Romeo and Juliet. Walking the fine line between a novelty bar and a romantic night out, the modern take on 70s furniture (complete with heart-shaped tables and floral prints) make this a must for that romantic hook-up you've always wanted. Drinks €8. Cover €12; includes 1 drink. Open daily 11:30pm-5am.

Cascada bar, Eth. Antistaseos 40 (☎6946393 243), on top of a restaurant. Closer to Corfu and a bit removed from the strip, this bar is open all year to tourists and locals, but its main selling point is the unbelievable view of the seaside from the patio. Beer €5. Mixed drinks €8. Open daily 11am-5am.

Cafe au Chokolat, Eleftherias 36 (☎26610 80 019). This young hangout has some fancy hot and cold chocolate drinks as well, including chocolate with rum flavor (€4.50). Sinfully rich frappé €3. Beer €4-7.50. Mixed drinks €6-7. Open daily 9am-1am.

▶️ DAYTRIP FROM CORFU TOWN

ACHILLION PALACE

In Gastouri; take bus #10 from Methodiou, 200m west of Pl. San Rocco (30min.; M-F 8 per day 7am-8pm, Sa 6 per day 8am-8pm, Su 4 per day 9am-8pm; €1.30). Return buses are more frequent in the mornings, ask before leaving. ☎26610 56 210. Open daily 8am-7pm. €7; EU students, ISIC holders, and seniors €5.

From housing an estranged empress to providing the filming location for the 1981 James Bond flick *For Your Eyes Only*, the Achillion Palace has continually intrigued visitors with its exquisite architecture and flourishing gardens. Unfortunately, however, there are few explanations of the rooms and their significance; buying an audio guide (€3) greatly enhances the experience.

Built in 1889, the magnificent property first belonged to the Austrian Empress Elizabeth, whose turbulent familial affairs brought her to this secluded estate. Having developed a penchant for Classical literature, she named her palace after the nearly invincible hero Achilles. The empress spent her summers here until she was assassinated by an Italian anarchist in 1898. The palace then changed hands a number of times. First sold to German Kaiser Wilhelm II, it served as a military hospital for French troops during WWI, then became a Nazi headquarters in WWII. In 1962, it became home to the first Greek casino. Today, the palace houses a **museum** with ornate rooms and beautiful grounds. The most impressive parts of the palace are in its **roof gardens,** including two sculptures of Achilles. The first is a white stone Achilles dying on his side, grabbing the spear that has penetrated his heel. The second Achilles, an imposing statue overlooking the island, stands at the back of the roof garden.

IONIAN ISLANDS

WESTERN CORFU

Western Corfu's diverse beaches range from wide expanses of golden sand in Glyfada and Pelekas to the hidden crystal coves of Paleokastritsa to backpackers' havens at Agios Gordios. Though the picture-perfect cerulean sea sees its share of tour buses, the area doesn't suffer from the same degree of over-development that mars the east and north.

PELEKAS Πέλεκας ☎ 26610

Private beaches are hard to come by in Corfu, but the small ◼beach of Pelekas (about a 30min. walk from the village) may be the next best thing. The village of Pelekas sits at the top of a hill that towers over the island, providing views of breathtaking landscapes and famously beautiful sunsets. The relaxed mentality and proximity to Corfu's nicest beaches make this town a decent (and affordable) base to head to after a long day of tanning. From the bus drop-off, a 10min. walk uphill from the center takes you to the natural "balcony" known as **"Kaiser's throne";** according to locals, Wilhelm II would spend hours on end in silence on this hilltop, staring at the beauty that spread out below him. Indeed, views from this spot, rivaled only by those from Mt. Pantokrator, are arguably the best on the island, letting you admire all of Corfu's glory at once.

Staying in Pelekas can feel jarring—the population consists of a small number of born-and-raised locals, and short- and long-term European tourists. Rooms to let are plentiful since most *tavernas* offer *domatia*, but housing is fairly generic. ◼**Pension Tellis and Brigitte ❷**, down the hill from the bus stop on the left side of the street, has the friendliest hosts in town. "Mrs. Brigette" and her husband Tellis treat each guest like family. The simple rooms (complete with mosquito nets above the bed) are in a little yellow house at the end of the town on the main road to Pelekas. Rooms have common baths and fridges; some come with balconies. Access to communal kitchen and air-conditioning are available by request. (☎26610 94 326. Singles €20; doubles €30-40; triples €40-50. Cash only.) ◼**Jimmy's Pension ❷**, right above Jimmy's restaurant, has spacious rooms with clean white tile, air-conditioning, fridges, and baths. (☎26610 94 284. Reception 8am-midnight. Singles €25-30; doubles €40; triples €50. AmEx/MC/V.) For a long-term stay, consider the rooms at **Pension Paradise ❹**. Walking uphill from the main road take the left fork to Glyfada beach. Each apartment-style room has bath, TV, fridge, and a fully equipped kitchen as well as

IN RECENT NEWS

FRUSTRATED FARMER

As of February 2nd, 2009, police officers at the port of Piraeus have met a new occupational hazard charging tractors. In protests over recent agricultural woes, hundreds of farmers from Crete disembarked from ferries at the port of Athens determined to their demands for government aid to the capital. They quickly found themselves scuffling with police. Not to be deterred the farmers formed up a convoy of some 300 tractors—which they'd brought with them from Crete—along with trucks and other vehicles. Several vehicles attempted to knock aside a police van, while another tractor toppled and injured a female lawmaker. Two of the protesters were arrested for throwing rocks, tomatoes, and potatoes at the police. In return, the officers fired tear gas. Finally, the farmers agreed to stay put, protesting on the harbor docks instead.

Social unrest among farmers has been on the rise all over Greece in recent years, as farmers fed up with falling food prices and harsh winters have demanded government aid. Nationwide protests began January 20, 2009 with thousands of farmers across the country blocking the main roads and obstructing deliveries of food and medicine. Most farmers were pacified by the government's announcement of a new 500 million euro agricultural aid plan, but Cretan protesters said the plan did not do enough to help them. Fortunately, it doesn't look like there'll be a repeat of the tractor episode—according to city authorities, heavy farm vehicles are banned on Athenian roads.

a small living room, perfect for a group of friends. (☎26610 94 530. Reception 9am-10pm. Rooms for up to 6 people €50.)

Pelekas has a disproportionately large number of restaurants and *tavernas* that offer dinner with a spectacular view. Few vantage points match the one provided by **Taverna Pink Panther❷**, a Greek-Italian eatery that sits atop a 300-year-old olive orchard. Don't let the name and cartoon logos throw you off, the upscale ambience and food, not to mention the spectacular view, are hardly those of a gimmicky themed restaurant. Take a left at the fork above the bus station, and continue for 300m downhill. Large pizzas (€9-14) and pasta dishes (€7-12) are served alongside Greek fare (€7-14). (☎26610 94 361. Open daily 1pm-midnight. Cash only.) Though it does not have a view, the food at **Jimmy's ❷**, on the main road uphill to "Kaiser's Throne" has excellent food, serving local Corfiot dishes such as the minestrone soup (€4) and many vegetarian options, including a truly wonderful plate of stuffed peppers and tomatoes (€7). Wooden floors and furniture lend a comfortable feel to the small restaurant. (☎26610 94 284. Entrees €7-10. Open daily 8am-midnight. Cash only.)

Take **bus** #11 from San Rocco in Corfu Town (20min., 7 per day 7am-10pm, €1.30). Pelekas beach is a 20-30min. walk from town. Walk in the direction of Corfu and follow the signs. A free **shuttle bus** (8 per day 10am-7:30pm) connects the town and the nearby beach of Glyfada. The same bus will take you to the more isolated beach of Myrtiotissa (p. 446), but you must ask the driver first. From the drop-off point, it's a 20min. walk to the water. Signs with bus times are on the door of the bakery by the bus stop and at the Pension Tellis and Brigette.

GLYFADA Γλυφάδα ☎26610

With the most famous beaches on Corfu, Glyfada attracts more tourists than Pelekas, but its seemingly endless shore accommodates the throngs admirably. Cliffs bracket both of Glyfada's beaches, where the unbelievably cool water is a welcome respite from the scorching sand. Those not sunbathing can partake in many activities—the beaches have **parasailing** (singles €30; doubles €50), **waterskiing** (€20), and **jet-skiing** (singles €40; doubles €50), and rent motorboats (from €40 per hr.), canoes (€5 per hr.), inner tubes (€15), and paddle boats (€10 per hr.).

Though this is the ultimate laid-back vacation spot, relatively expensive accommodations might persuade you to stay in nearby Pelekas and take daily excursions here. In July and August, tan-centric mornings turn into dance-and-drink-fueled afternoons at **Aloha Bar** on the beach. (Beer €3-5. Mixed drinks €9. Open daily until 9pm. Cash only.) Three kilometers north of Glyfada, accessible only by car via a dirt path off the main road before it forks for Pelekas and Glyfasa, lies **Myrtiotissa Beach.** Extolled by locals and author and Corfu resident Lawrence Durrell as the most beautiful beach in the world, it may also be the smallest: Myrtiotissa's minuscule coast is divided in two by a large rock formation. The south side is an unofficial nude beach while the north is more family-oriented. A short walk up the road is the monastery **Moni Myrtidion,** which takes its name from an icon of the Virgin found in myrtle bushes over 700 years ago. (Open 8am-1pm and 5-9pm. Modest dress required.)

Green KTEL **buses** leave from Corfu Town (30min., 6 per day 9am-5:30pm, €2), and a free **shuttle bus** that leaves from the parking lot by the beach connects Pelekas to Glyfada (10min., 8 per day 10am-7:30pm).

PALEOKASTRITSA Παλαιοκαστρίτσα ☎26610

The crystal clear waters of Paleokastritsa **beach** rest among six small coves and sea caves, and locals claim its waters are Corfu's coldest and most beautiful. It is worthwhile to head up the mountain overlooking Paleokastritsa for great views from lookout points along the road. Hiring or renting a motorboat (€12 per hr., €30 per day), paddle boat (€10 per hr.), or canoe (€7 per hr.) will enable you to reach the caves where many tourists take a dip and **snorkel.** According to legend, Phoenician princess Nausicaä found the shipwrecked Odysseus washed ashore in one of these caves.

Hop on a taxi boat from the main beach (☎69748 09 030 or 694702 51 17; open 9:30am-6pm) to tour the picturesque caves and travel to incredible off-white beaches, only accessible from the water. Organize pick-up time at your leisure. Prices are negotiable, but the standard cave tour (available in English) is €10 per person. Projecting out from a hill over the sea, bright white **Panagia Theotokos Monastery** (open Apr.-Nov. 7am-1pm and 3-8pm; modest dress required), founded in 1228, has a small museum with a collection of Byzantine icons and engraved Bibles. Come as early as possible—by mid-morning it's a mess of tour buses. Green KTEL **buses** arrive from Corfu Town (45min., 7 per day 8:30am-6pm, €2.10).

AGIOS GORDIOS Άγιος Γόρδιος ☎26610

Fourteen kilometers west of Corfu Town, Agios Gordios is highlighted by impressive rock formations and a lovely wide **beach,** as well as stores and restaurants that cater to the college-aged partying crowd. The main road, running perpendicular to the sand, has a short stretch of touristy restaurants and a series of mini-marts and domatia, including the town's infamous **Pink Palace Hotel ❷,** a favorite with American and Canadian backpackers in search of instant (and constant) gratification. Spend your nights at the free nightclub or lounge in the jacuzzi. On Saturday nights, take part in the pink toga parties where the hostel's owner, Dr. George, and volunteers partake in the Greek tradition of breaking plates over willing guests' heads in a drink-fueled Dionysian revel. (☎26610 53 103; www.thepinkpalace.com. Breakfast and dinner included. Laundry service available. Free internet. Check-out 9am. Dorms, open only in high season, from €22-25; rooms with A/C, phones, balconies, and baths €27-30. AmEx/MC/V with surcharge.)

From Corfu Town, take the green KTEL **bus** to Agios Gordios; it leaves from the New Port. (45min.; M-Sa 6 per day 8:15am-8pm, Su 3 per day 9:30am, 1, 5:30pm; €2). Dr. George sends staff to meet incoming ferries at the port, and buses arranged by the Palace run to and from Athens, stopping in Patra, every other night. (€49. Breakfast, dinner, and pick-up/drop-off at the Corfu Town ferry included.)

NORTHERN CORFU ☎26630

Past Pirgi, the road winds below steep cliffs. ◪**Mount Pantokrator,** a bare rock jutting out of the forested hills, towers 1km above, while dramatic vistas of wooded Albania are visible across the straits. Roman emperors Tiberius and Nero both vacationed here, though tourism has erased most traces of the ancient world on the northern coast. This area is not Corfu's most attractive, but the mountain road and lovely small beaches make it worth a short visit.

The wide, sandy beach of **Agios Stefanos** in the northeast (not be to be confused with the smaller Ag. Stefanos in the northwest) are popular enough to merit their own stop on the bus route. With a host of *tavernas* and hotels, there is so much choice that the places pull out all the stops, with theme nights and discounts that have a perpetual spring break vibe. Though this area usually is visited as a daytrip, the few who decide to stay will find hotels and *domatia* for around €15-30; be sure to bargain as there are plenty of options. **Buses** run from

Corfu Town to Sidari-Ag. Stefanos (M-Sa 5 per day 5:30am-5:30pm, Su 9:30am; €3.70). There is no bank or ATM in town, so bring enough cash for your stay.

The sheer slopes of northeastern Corfu cradle several fine **beaches,** including **Barbati,** 10km north of Ipsos, nearby **Nissaki,** and the twin beaches **Kalami** and **Kouloura.** These flat-stoned beaches are very small, but are also less frequented by tourists, giving you more space to grab some rays. The feel of these beaches is also completely different from most of the larger ones on the east coast—nice *domatia* and a few upscale *tavernas* give these beaches a classier touch. It could be because Kalami attracts literature lovers who come to see the home of British author Lawrence Durrell. His childhood abode "set like a dice on a rock" on the southern end of town, away from the main highway, is now the pleasant **Taverna White House ❷,** an upscale restaurant that serves typical Greek fare and overlooks the sea. Try the Durrell Salad (lettuce, onions, walnuts, and crumpets; €7.20). (☎26630 912 51. Entrees €8.50-11.90. Open 9am-midnight. Cash Only.) For classic Greek seafood, the first restaurant you see when entering Kalami, right on the shore, is the nationally recognized **Kalami Beach Taverna ❹,** with vegetarian options, fresh fish, and a nice view of the marina. (Fish dishes €11-28. Cash Only.) Kouloura and Kalami are a brief walk from the main road north of Gimari village. Head down from the bus stop on the main road until you reach a fork with signs for Kouloura and Kalami; turn left down this road for Kouloura, right for Kalami. Blue "To the Beach" signs on the left mark shortcuts down to Kouloura and Kalami.

Mount Pantokrator offers breathtaking views of all of Corfu. To get to the top, start at **Spartillas,** a village 7km north of and inland from Pirgi along the bus route. You can also catch an infrequent bus that takes you right to Spartillas at the foot of the mountain. Follow the road used each summer by villagers on their way to the annual festival at Pantokrator Monastery. There is no footpath, but hikers can embark on a nice 4-5hr. walk to the top by taking the same dirt road as the cars. The windy road leads you through small clusters of houses and green orchards; if you look toward the west in the early evening, you may see one of the famous Corfiot sunsets that paint the entire sky a dazzling gold. As you make your way up to Pantokrator, try to make a stop in a small town called **Strinilas,** on the way if you're starting from Spartillas. Don't pass up the opportunity to eat at 🔪**A La Palala ❷.** With an astonishing view of perfect sunsets, this traditional, family-fun restaurant is as authentic as it gets. All the fruits and vegetables are grown organically in their gardens, and all the meat is raised locally. (☎26630 72 622. Entrees €6-9. Open 11:30am-11pm.) **Buses** run to Spartillas (5am, 12:30, and 2pm) and Pirgi (M-F 10 per day 7am-8pm, Sa 7 per day 9am-6:30pm, Su 9:30am; €1.40.)

ITHAKA Ιθάκη

What Homer called a "wine-dark" sea of legend appears instead a clear and beckoning blue as it meets the steeply rising green hills and white beaches of Ithaka. Panoramic vistas of the Adriatic are as ubiquitous as the motor scooters that transport locals to tiny villages, where the atmosphere is far more relaxed and quiet than that found on nearby Kefallonia or Lefkada. Massive ferries, the island's only physical connection to the outside world, dwarf Ithaka's small port towns. Traverse Odysseus's legendary home to see the pebbled beaches, rocky hillsides, and terraced olive groves that drew him back here through countless obstacles.

IONIAN ISLANDS

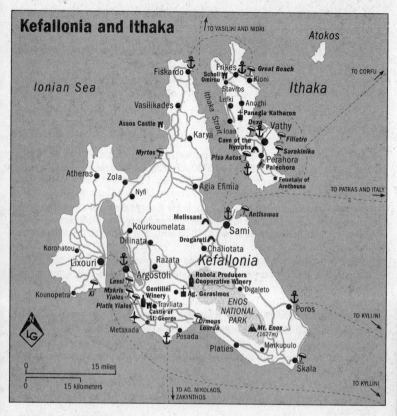

Kefallonia and Ithaka

VATHI Βαθύ ☎ 26740

The clear waters of the bay are the focus of Ithaka's capital, which unfolds along the curving perimeter of the cove. Slightly inland, the red-roofed, pastel-colored houses, separated by narrow streets and stone stairways, compete for views of the sloping Ithakan landscape. The charming stone *plateia* and old-fashioned streetlamps are the deliberate touches of a town aware of the romantic stirrings it evokes in visitors, Greek and foreign alike.

⬛ TRANSPORTATION

Ferries: Vathi's docks are on the far right of the waterfront, about a 4min. walk to the right of the town *plateia*. Ferries leave M-F at 7am to **Patra** (3½hr., €16) and **Sami, Kefallonia** (1hr., €8). From Pisaetos Port on Ithaka daily ferries go to **Patra** (3hr.; M-F 4pm, Sa 7am; €16) and **Sami** (30min.; M-F 4pm, Sa 7am; €8). More information can be found at the **Strintzis** office in Vathi (☎ 26740 33 338).

Taxis: (☎ 26740 33 030). Taxis line up by the water, in front of the *plateia*. Call ahead, as there are not many on the island. Even better to arrange in advance with the drivers in person; find them sitting at outdoor tables in the *plateia* next to their cars. €30 per hr.

Car Rental: AGS Rent a Car (☎26740 32 702), on the waterfront 2 blocks to the right of the *plateia*. Manual and automatic cars, scooters, and bicycles all available. Car rental in summer months from €30 per day, every additional day for less. Prices significantly lower in the winter. Includes insurance. Call ahead to reserve automatic transmission vehicles. Open daily 9am-1:30pm and 5-9pm.

Scooter Rental: Rent a Scooter (☎26740 32 840), on a side street off the waterfront, directly across from the port police and to the right before the *plateia*. From €10 per day. Open daily 9am-2pm and 5-9pm.

🏷 PRACTICAL INFORMATION

Tours: Delas Tours (☎26740 32 104), in the main *plateia*. Open daily 6-7am, 9am-2pm, and 5:30-9:30pm. **Polyctor Tours** (☎26740 33 120), along the far side of the *plateia* as you approach from the port police. Open daily 9am-1:30pm and 5:30-9pm. **Strintzis Ferries** (☎26740 33338), on the *plateia*, has cruises (July-Aug. 3 per week, €35).

Banks: National Bank (☎26740 32 720), in the far right corner of the *plateia*, with Polyctor Tours on your left. **24hr. ATM** and **currency exchange.** Open M-Th 8am-2:30pm, F 8am-2pm. **ATE** and **Alpha Bank** (☎26740 33 690), also located on the *plateia*, have the same services and hours.

Laundry: Polifimos (☎26740 32 032), behind the National Bank, in the far right corner of the *plateia*. Wash and dry €4 per kg. Open M-Sa 8am-1pm and 6-8pm, sometimes closed during winter.

Police: (☎26740 32 205). From the *plateia*, turn right on the 1st street after Drakouli and walk straight uphill for 3 blocks. It's on the right side.

Pharmacy: (☎26740 33 105), to the right of the post office. Open daily 8:30am-2pm and 5-9pm.

Medical Services: (☎26740 32 222). Turn right after Drakouli and walk uphill about 150m past the police station. For more extensive medical care, there are larger hospitals in Patra and Argostoli.

Telephones: OTE (☎26740 32 299), on the waterfront, just before Hotel Mentor when coming from the *plateia* with the water on your left. Open M-F 7:20am-3pm. Hours vary seasonally.

Internet Access: Net Wi-Fi, on the left side of the *plateia* if you're facing inland. €4 per hr. Open daily 8am-2:30pm and 6pm-midnight. **Drakouli** (see **Food,** p. 451) also offers internet.

Post Office: (☎26740 32 386), in the *plateia* near Delas Tours. Open M-Th 8am-2:30pm, F 8am-2pm. **Postal Code:** 28300.

🏠 ACCOMMODATIONS

In July and August, cheap *domatia* are everywhere, a much better option than the pricey hotel rooms. Numerous signs around town advertise homes with rooms to let—no dearth of accommodating hosts.

Aktaion Domatia (☎26740 32 387), on the left wing of the port. Convenient location and comfortable environment. Each room has A/C, TV, and fridge along with a glorious view of the harbor. Singles €30; doubles €40. Prices rise in summer. Cash only. ❷

Hotel Mentor (☎26740 32 433; www.hotelmentor.gr.). Walk from the center of town along the harbor about 100m. The large "HOTEL" sign on the roof will give it away. Each room is spacious and includes bath, balcony, A/C, TV, and Wi-Fi. A few of the pricier rooms have harbor views, but the regular rooms' balconies still provide a sweet view. Breakfast included. Check-out noon. Singles €40-50; doubles €55-105. Prices rise in July and Aug. MC/V. ❸

FOOD

The waterfront is lined with nearly-identical *tavernas* and seafood restaurants. In addition to these, a picnic could easily be concocted with the help of the supermarkets, bakeries, and produce stands located a block behind the waterfront.

O Nikos Restaurant (☎26740 33 039), in the heart of the port, across the street from the National Bank. Countless varieties of meat minced, roasted, and grilled. Don't fret, herbivores—there are plenty of vegetarian options, too. Specialties include traditional moussaka, stuffed calamari, veal *stifado*, and whatever the fishermen catch that day. Try local red and white wines with dinner. Salads €3. Entrees €6-9. Open Apr.-Nov. 7pm-midnight or late. Cash only; MC/V for large groups. ❷

Siren's (☎26740 33 001), across the street and to the right of Trexantiri. Offers an Ithakan omelette and basic Greek fare featuring locally grown vegetables. Menu also includes more exotic entrees cooked in *tserepa* clay pots—a traditional, slow cooking technique. Dishes made with a variety of meats and vegetables. One of the port's more upscale taverns. Entrees €7-18. Open daily 7-11:30pm. MC/V. ❸

Drakouli (☎26740 33 435), on the left end of the waterfront facing the harbor. Outside this ultra trendy mansion-turned-cafe, white cushioned lounge chairs and dark basket woven tables fill the yard and circle the pool in the center. Despite the lack of menu and the ritzy decor, this relaxing cafe keeps prices low and will fix up any snack or sandwich (€3-5). Ice cream and coffee €2-5. Beer and mixed drinks €3-6. Open daily 9am-midnight. ❶

SIGHTS AND OUTDOOR ACTIVITIES

Though small, Ithaka has so much historical tradition that each little village has something worth seeing. In Vathi, most everything is located near the central *plateia*.

ARCHAEOLOGICAL MUSEUM. The tiny collection displays finds from ongoing excavations at the Sanctuary of Apollo at Aetos—a site containing the ruins of a city dating back to 700 BC—as well as ceramics and artifacts from the Dark Ages. Animal-shaped ritual vases from the sixth or seventh century BC and ivory and amber jewelry from the Geometric period are highlights. (*Turn right after Dragoumi cafe and take the first left; it's 2 blocks down on the right.* ☎26740 32 200. *Open Tu-Su 8:30am-3pm. Free.*)

FOLKLORE AND NAUTICAL MUSEUM. This peach-colored museum houses a large collection of nautical memorabilia as well as artifacts from Ithaka's colonial period. Art and literature buffs will appreciate the early 19th-century illustrations of Homer's characters on the second floor. (*Turn right onto the footpath near Alpha Bank.* ☎26740 33 398. *Open M-Sa 10am-2pm. Closed sometimes during the low season; call ahead to make sure it's open. €1.*)

BEACHES. Ithaka has a plethora of coves hidden by ledges of the overhanging steep mountains. Every beach is inviting, with white pebble beaches and vibrant turquoise waters, but keep in mind that the best undiscovered coves are only accessible by water taxi or car. The combination of the sun and the uphill climb will not encourage your trek. If transportation allows, make your way over to **Aghios Ioannis** on the west coast of the island about 10 kilometers from Vathi. Even if you can't get around, Vathi has a brace of wonderful beaches within walking distance. **Filiatro** is a manageable 3km away. (*Walk with the water to your left toward Hotel Mentor. At the hotel, turn right and walk a block; you'll see a sign for the beaches. Bear left. Small tavern with snacks, drinks, and such. Calamari and fish €6. Drinks €2-3. Open Sept.-June daily 10:30am-8pm; July-Aug. open much later.*) If you bear right down the hill instead, you'll get to **Sarakiniko,** more cluttered with boats than people.

IONIAN ISLANDS

The basin's steep dropoff attracts boats with big hulls, luring beautiful classic yachts to anchor here. If neither of these beaches appeal to you, try **Dexa** beach on the other side of town. *(Head in the opposite direction out of town along the road.)*

CAVE OF THE NYMPHS. According to tradition, this is where water naiads (nymphs) were worshipped and where Odysseus hid the treasure the Phoenicians gave him. Archaeologists had been excavating the cave, but the site appears to have been abandoned and remains a bit of a mess. There are rumors of buried treasure in the cave, so bring a shovel. Even if you don't strike it rich, the hike offers unparalled views of Vathi. *(Walk around the harbor with the water on your right on the road to Piso Aetos and Stavros. Follow the signs along the road winding up the mountain for 1.5-2km. Entrance up a flight of steps to the right, just before the paved road ends.)*

🔹 DAYTRIPS FROM VATHI

Trying to get to most of the sights on this small island without a taxi or car may make you feel like Odysseus on his beleaguered journey home. If you plan to see many sights, there isn't any one great, cheap option. Renting a car or motorbike for a day is comparable to hiring a taxi. If you just want to explore Vathi and break a healthy sweat, rent a bicycle for €4 a day (see **Transportation,** p. 453). The island's sole **bus** starts running for tourists in July and travels north from Vathi to **Frikes** (30-40min). Taxis to Frikes cost about €25. The bus goes on to exceptionally beautiful **◪Kioni** (1hr.; taxi €30+), a small village whose crystal blue harbors and white-pebble beaches make it a favorite of locals and tourists. In high season, the bus generally runs twice per day, at 7:30am and 3pm.

STAVROS. This tiny town perches amid the mountains of Ithaka. You'll find road signs with sights in the center of town. The town's **Archaeological Museum,** about a kilometer past the church, exhibits a collection of excavated items from the local archaeological site. *(Open July-Aug., Tu-Su 8am-2pm. Small donations appreciated.)* The supposed site of Odysseus's Palace, **"Scholi Omirou"** ("Homer's School"), is nearby. Until very recently, the location and even the existence of this palace was little more than a rumor. In the last decade, however, after a resurgence of interest in the area, archaeologists have dated Mycenaean ruins, intact architectural structures, Hellenistic towers, and even an untouched Roman grave. *(Down the road from the museum. Signs direct the way from the town square, 5km from Stavros. Taxi from Vathi €20. Free.)*

THE KATHARA MONASTERY. Dedicated to the island's patroness, the Virgin Kathariotissa, the monastery is more than 600m up on Ithaka's highest mountain, **◪Mount Neritos.** This monastery has been a church since the 16th century. The icon of the Virgin Mary, painted by St. Luke, is rumored to work miracles. Women must cover their legs in the sanctuary, and all visitors must observe the monks' rule to close the front door in order to keep wandering goats off the premises. In Anoghi, the island's former capital, the 12th-century church **Agia Panagia** fronts the square. Go inside the church to see what remains of the ancient frescoes. *(Take a car, moped, or taxi (round-trip €25) toward Anoghi and follow the signs. Monastery open dawn-dusk.)*

KEFALLONIA Κεφαλονιά

The biggest of the Ionian Islands, Kefallonia rises high above sea level with grand peaks and plunging cliffs. Mountainous terrain and austere coastlines present logistical problems. Since Kefallonia lacks convenient public transportation, the best way to explore it is by car. The winding roads perched on

IONIAN ISLANDS

cliff edges, along with Greek drivers, can make driving an adrenaline-filled activity, but the pebble beaches, craggy hills, and more than 250km of coastline make it worth the trouble. If you're traveling without a car, you may have to stick closer to the towns, but daily cruises and local beaches are a nice way to get a feel for the island.

ARGOSTOLI Αργοστόλι ☎26710

The capital and largest town on Kefallonia, Argostoli buzzes with energy in typical Greek style, with yellow and orange buildings sprawling far into the horizon. Other areas of the island are undeniably more picturesque, but Argostoli offers urban convenience and access to the rest of Kefallonia.

▐▀ TRANSPORTATION

Flights: Olympic Airways (☎8011 14 444), located on Vergoti St. near the airport. Airport services **Athens, Corfu, Zakynthos,** and **London** (infrequent).

Buses: KTEL, 5 Ant. Tritsi (☎26710 22 281 or 22 276). To: **Ag. Gerasimos** (20min., 10am and 12:30pm, €2.40); **Fiskardo** (1½hr., 11:30am, €8); **Pessada** (30min., 9:30am and 12:30pm, €3); **Poros** (1hr., 11:30am and 2:10pm, €4); **Sami** (1hr.; 7:30, 11:30am, 1, 3:45pm; €4). No bus service Su, reduced service Sa.

Ferries: Kefallonia has multiple ports for different destinations. **Agrostoli Port Authority** (☎26710 22 224) is the best source of information for frequently changing schedules.

Sami Port: To **Corfu** (infrequent; check at Port Authority), **Ithaka** (1hr, 1 per day, €8), and **Patra** (2½hr., 2 per day, €18).

Argostoli Port: To **Lixouri** (20min., every 30min. 7am-10:30pm, €1.60).

Pessada Port: To **Zakynthos** (1½hr., 7:45am and 5:30pm, €7).

Poros Port: To **Killini** (1½hr., 2 per day, €8).

Taxis: ☎26710 28 505. Plenty line up along the port and main square. Any trip within Argostoli €5. Fixed rates to all destinations on island.

Car and Motorbike Rentals: Along the waterfront, **Sunbird,** 127 A. Tritsi Av. (☎26710 23 723), has best rates. €30 per day, additional days less. Open daily 8:30am-2pm and 5-9pm.

▄▌ ▐ ORIENTATION AND PRACTICAL INFORMATION

All of the city's commotion takes place around **Vironos Square** and spreads down along **Lithostrotou Avenue.** From the water, turn left onto Vironos or 21 Maiou and walk two blocks. The large hotel signs and crowded cafes identify the square. Approaching the square from the water, turn left onto the pedestrian plaza, lined with window shops and outdoor lounges. The main museums and galleries sit between the square and Lithostrotou Ave.

Tourist Office: ☎26710 22 248. Beside the Port Authority near the ferry docks. Free maps and information about sights and beaches and some assistance with accommodations and restaurants. Information in English, French, German, Greek, and Italian. Open July.-Aug. M-Sa 9am-2pm.

Bank: National Bank (☎26710 25 191), between Hotel Olga and Hotel Tourist along the harbor. **Currency exchange** and **24hr. ATM.** Open M-Th 8am-2:30pm, F 8am-2pm. Other banks and ATMs line the waterfront.

Laundromat: Laundry Express, Lassis 46b. Walk inland on Vyronos for 9 blocks and turn left onto Lassis. The laundromat is 2 blocks farther on your right. Self-service.

Police: (☎26710 22 200), on I. Metaxa across from the tourist office.

Tourist Police: (☎26710 22 815), in the police station. Open daily 9am-10pm.

Telephones: OTE (☎26710 28 599), on Gerassimou Livada, to the left of the Archaeological Museum walking toward the *plateia*. Open M-Th 7:30am-1:30pm, F 7:30am-1pm.

Internet Access: B.B.'s Club, in the bottom right corner of the *plateia* facing inland. €2.50 per hr., minimum €1. Coffee €2. Open daily 9am-2am.

Post Office: ☎26710 23 173. 2 blocks up from the water on Lithostrotou, at the intersection of Kerkyras. Open M-F 7:30am-4pm. **Postal Code:** 28100.

▛ ACCOMMODATIONS

Rooms in bustling Argostoli are in high demand. In high season, private rooms are often the cheapest option, though many are relatively far from the town center. Bargain, but don't expect to find a room for much less than €35. In low season, the prices of **domatia** and hotels are fairly similar. If you plan to stay in a hotel, call ahead. Otherwise, renting a car or moped allows you to stay in domatia and still have access to the beach. The tourist office maintains a list of available domatia.

St. Gerassimos, 6 Ag. Gerassimou St. (☎26710 28 697). Turn left past Hotel Olga on the waterfront road with the water on your right; the hotel will be on the right. Family-run establishment offers 7 rooms from June-Sept., each with TV, balcony, A/C, and bath. A larger room is available for a family—call ahead to reserve. Rooms €30-50. Cash only. ❸

Hotel Tourist, Ant. Tritsi 109 (☎26710 22 510), along the waterfront across from the harbor police. Each room comfortably equipped with TV, A/C, and fridge. Some pricier rooms have a deck with a great harbor view. Breakfast €5. Wheelchair-accessible. Low season singles €35, high season 45-50; doubles €55/60-80. MC/V. ❸

Hotel Castello (☎26710 23 250 or 251), on the Central Square in the upper right corner from the water. Opens on to the top of the square. Modern decor and low prices. Breakfast €5. Singles €30; doubles €40; triples €50. MC/V. ❸

Hotel Mirabel, Central Square 281 (☎26710 25 381 or 383; www.mirabel.gr), in the lower left of the main square. Cozy rooms cluttered with all the amenities—the balcony provides a little breathing room. Breakfast included. Wi-Fi available but expensive. Singles €40; doubles €50. Prices rise July-Aug. MC/V. ❸

▟ FOOD

Argostoli has a range of dining and wining options, though the Greek cuisine taverns have a strong and unfortunate tourist flavor. Kefallonia's proximity to Italy makes for some surprisingly exquisite Italian dishes; some of the best restaurants on the island serve fresh pastas and many varieties of pizza. Most of the Italian places are located in the streets extending from the main square heading down to the water. The most scenic restaurants are a short walk past the harbormaster along the water. For fresh produce, there are fruit stands and a supermarket a little ways out of town with the water on your left.

Portside Restaurant, 58 Metaxa St. (☎26710 24 130), across from the Coast Guard and tourist office. Escape the main tourist traps and head to the Portside. Local favorite serving scrumptious Greek cuisine and plenty of vegetarian options. Starters €3-5, entrees €5-10. Drinks and desserts €3-6. Cash only. ❷

Kiami Akti (☎26710 26 680). Walk away from the port along the water, across from Coast Guard Academy. The old dark wooden porch and canvas cover create a sort of pirate atmosphere. Dockside dining well worth the extra 5min. hike, landlubber. Cash only. ❷

Kohenoor (☎26710 26 789), at the intersection of Str. Metaxa and Lavraga, 1 block toward the water from the *plateia*. The sign reading "Indian Restaurant" sums it up. Tasty

IONIAN ISLANDS

curries at reasonable prices. Specialties include chicken tikka masala (€9) and vinda-loo lamb (€10). Appetizers €4-5. Open daily 6:30pm-midnight. MC/V. ❸

🔯 SIGHTS

FOCAS-COSMETATOS FOUNDATION. Established on the estate of three Argos-toli-born brothers, this museum was founded in 1984 for the exhibition of their family heirlooms as well as pieces of art focused on Kefallonia. The display includes wonderful paintings and drawings by Joseph Cartwright, Edward Lear, and Henry Cook. Recently, the museum has expanded with the addition of a botanical garden located at the edge of town. *(1 Vallianos St., just off of the main square. ☎ 26710 26 595. Open May-Oct. M 9:30am-1pm, Tu-Sa 9:30am-1pm and 7-10pm. €3, under 14 free. Museum admission also covers botanical gardens.)*

ARCHAEOLOGICAL MUSEUM. Pottery and jewelry from excavations around the island and Melissani Lake are on display in this beautiful museum. Vin-tage photographs of an 1899 excavation at Sami are exhibited, along with some of the third-century BC tombstones found there, complete with well-preserved names of the dead. Make sure to stop by the second-century BC mosaic from the temple of Poseidon. *(A few blocks south of the plateia, across from the Municipal Theater on R. Vergoti. ☎ 26710 28 300. Open Tu-Su 8:30am-3pm. €3, seniors and students €2, children and EU students free.)*

🔯 DAYTRIPS FROM ARGOSTOLI

Renting a moped or car allows you to roam between sights and beaches, unrestrained by inconvenient bus schedules. You can also get to 🔳**Myrtos beach** (p. 458) on the western coast, considered to be one of Europe's most stunning stretches of sand.

THE WINERIES. An excellent break from the beach are Kefallonia's famous wineries, of which two of the most inviting are Gentilini and Robola Produc-ers Cooperative. **Gentilini Winery** is located 8km south of Argostoli, close to the airport. If you're arriving or departing Kefallonia by plane, then a visit to the vineyard for a tour and wine tasting makes a fine introduction or farewell to the island *(☎ 26710 41 618. Open June-Sept. M-Sa 10:30am-2:30pm and 5:30pm-8:30pm.)* **Robola Producers Cooperative Winery** is 13km east of Argostoli, next to the Monas-tery of Agios Gerasimos. The winery has spectacular views and wonderful free wine samplings. *(☎ 26710 86 301. Open Apr.-Oct. 7am-8:30pm.)*

SAMI Σάμη   ☎ 26740

As you stroll through Sami, stunning views in all directions make it difficult to decide which is more lovely: the tempestuous blue waves crashing on the white-sand beach or the lush, village-dotted hills cradling the town. Sami's main advantages are its central location as a small port and its proximity to the natural wonders of Melissani Lake, Drogarati cave, and Antisamos beach. In the late 1990s, Nicolas Cage starred as an Italian military officer occupy-ing Kefallonia during WWII in *Captain Corelli's Mandolin.* The picturesque Venetian buildings seen in the film, however, were actually created by skilled set-makers; in reality, the 1953 earthquake wiped out most of Sami, leaving modern architecture in its wake.

IONIAN ISLANDS

TRANSPORTATION

From Sami, **ferries** sail to **Patra** (2hr.; M-F 8:30am and 5pm, Sa 8:30am; €13) and **Ithaka** (1hr., 2 per day, €8). In July and August, international ferries go to **Brindisi, ITA** (daily, €45). The Port Authority (☎26740 32 909) can answer questions about all ferries. **Buses** leave from the wharf on the inside of the gate. The **KTEL bus** stop on main road next to Strintzis Ferries rarely has bus service. Buses come off ferries and continue to **Argostoli** (1hr., 8am and 3:15pm, €4). The staff at **Blue Sea Travel,** next to the bus station, sells ferry tickets and offers minimal transportation information. (☎26740 23 007; www.samistar.com. Open M-Sa 8am-11pm, Su 9am-9pm.) There are no buses on Sundays. Expensive taxis (☎26740 22 308) line up on the waterfront facing the *plateia*. For car rentals, turn left past Blue Sea Travel and then take a right onto the road just one block inland. **Karavomilos Rentals** (☎26740 23 769) offers great deals and friendly service.

ORIENTATION AND PRACTICAL INFORMATION

Poseidonos, the waterfront street lined with cafes, intersects the main *plateia*. White-pebble beaches lie both to the left and right of the town center. Ferries land on the left side of the *plateia* facing inland. From the bus station, facing the water, turn left to reach the *plateia*. You may be able to see the top of the blue-and-white Hotel Kyma, which sits on **I. Metaxa,** Sami's main road; this road runs parallel to the water one block inland. The *plateia* lies between the road and the waterfront. Following the inland road with the water on your right leads to Argostoli.

Tourist Office: ☎26740 23 280, on the left of the waterfront, in the far left corner facing inland. Free luggage storage during office hours. Open daily 9am-9pm.

Bank: Emporiki Trapeza, on the waterfront to the right of the *plateia* as you face inland, has **currency exchange** and a **24hr. ATM.** Open M-Th 8am-2:30pm, F 8am-2pm.

Police Station: I. Metaxa 14 (☎26740 22 100), on the main road toward Argostoli, near the post office, 3 blocks from the *plateia*.

Pharmacy: I. Metaxa 37. Take a right onto the road from the *plateia* facing inland, and it's on the left. Also along the main road to Argostoli.

Hospital: ☎26740 22 222, on the road toward Argostoli. Also has large pharmacy.

Internet Access: Available at many of the cafes at the far end of the port. Wi-Fi free at most cafes.

Post Office: ☎26740 22 012, on the road to Argostoli, 2 blocks off the right corner of the *plateia* at the fork in the road. (Open M-F 7:30am-2pm.) **Postal Code:** 28080.

ACCOMMODATIONS AND CAMPING

Because Sami is one of the larger ports on Kefallonia, day traffic is heavy at times and restaurants along the wharf easily fill up around lunch. Most people, however, stay overnight on beaches along the neighboring coasts. Consequently, Sami has few hotels in town or even within walking distance of town. Having a car is recommended for exploring.

Hotel Melissani (☎26740 22 464), past the tourist office in sight of the port. A smaller hotel with a more comfortable atmosphere than Kastro and a roof deck patio, run by an old welcoming couple. Breakfast €7. Singles €35-40; doubles €45-50; triples €60-70. Cash only. ●

Kastro Hotel (☎26740 22 656), a short walk beyond the port's main strip. Standard rooms at standard prices. Wheelchair-accessible. Open mid-June-Sept. Singles €40; doubles €50; triples €60-70. MC/V. ●

Karavomilos Beach Camping 1 (☎26740 22 480; www.camping-karavomilos. gr), in a huge field about 2km from town, walking with the water on your right. A campsite with luxury amenities: hot showers, electricity, free Wi-Fi, mini-market, refrigerators, cooking facilities, first aid, and more. Office open 8:30am-noon and 4:30pm-midnight. €7.50 per person; sleeping bag rental €0.50; €4 per small tent, €6 per large tent. Electricity €4. Cash only. ❶

🍴 FOOD

Tavernas clutter the waterfront, and daytrippers do a good job filling the tables. **Super Market "Sami"** ❶ has a wide selection of meat, fruit, vegetables, breads, and sweets. (☎26740 22 803. Open M-Sa 8am-9pm.)

▨ **Adonis** (☎26740 23 101). Some of the best meals on Kefallonia. The servers all speak English and will happily share the inside scoop on the best beaches on the island. Salads and starters €3-6. Entrees €6-8. Cash only. ❷

Pizza Tereza, toward the far right end of the waterfront cafes facing inland. Cheap and quick. A little taste of Italy with vegetarian options. Pizzas €5-8. Cash only. ❷

👁️ 🏖️ SIGHTS AND BEACHES

▨**ANTISAMOS BEACH.** Isolated and alluring, the beach is a must-see if you get to this side of Kefallonia. This white pebbled stretch of sand was the set for *Captain Corelli's Mandolin* and is home to the island's colorful butterflies and many wandering goats. To get to the beach you may want to splurge for a taxi (€6) because the hike up the paved road midday can be quite grueling. (*Follow the road that leads uphill and to the east (left if facing inland). The beach is 2km away, approx. an hr. walking.*)

CAVES. Sami's two popular caves are a short drive from town. Stalactite- and stalagmite-filled **Melissani Cave**, 2km from Sami, is part of the huge, underground **Lake Karavomilos.** Its deep blue waters run deeper than 15m and flow from as far as Argostoli. The boat tour of the cave lasts 10-15min., and the knowledgeable boatmen explain the history and pose for photos. Because the cave has an open roof measuring 50m by 30m, you'll want to go when the sun is high in the sky. (*Walk along the beach with the water to your right until you come to a small ocean-fed pond with a waterwheel on the far side. Turn left after the restaurant by the pond, walk inland to the road about 30m, and turn right; you'll see signs down this street. Boat tours of cave ☎22997. Open 9am-8pm. €8.*)

Drogarati Cave, 4km from Sami, is a large cavern full of spectacular stalactites and stalagmites over 150 million years old. (*Walk inland on the road to Argostoli and follow the signs for 45min. or take the bus to Argostoli and ask to be let off at Drogarati; you'll be dropped off at the fork, a 5min. walk from the caves. ☎26740 22 950. Open daily 9am-8pm. €4.*)

FISKARDO Φισκάρδο   ☎26740

The road north ends at must-see Fiskardo, one of the few Kefallonian villages unaffected by the 1953 earthquake. That stroke of luck has left it a rare example of the island's 18th- and 19th-century architecture. The crescent-shaped waterfront is tinged with the pastel hues of the modest buildings surrounding it. At night a romantic aura pervades the town, which twinkles with the dim lights of boats resting in the water. A splendid walk through the woods or a swim from the rocks takes you to the forested bit of land across the harbor, home to a lighthouse and a ruined 15th-century Venetian fortress. The port, meanwhile, is home to a great number of yachts and boats clustered closely

IONIAN ISLANDS

together on the docks. Fiskardo's white-pebble beach is only 500m from town, on the road to Argostoli, in a quiet cove with flat rocks for sunbathing.

⚏ ▨ TRANSPORTATION AND PRACTICAL INFORMATION. Ferries go to Patra on the Peloponnese (2½hr., 12:30 and 8:30pm, €18); Frikes, Ithaka (1hr., 10:15am, €4); Vasiliki, Lefkada (1hr., 10:15am and 6:15pm, €8); and to Nidri, Lefkada (2hr., 1-5 per day, €7). **Buses** leave from the parking lot next to the church twice a day for **Argostoli** (1hr., €6) and **Sami** (1hr., €5). Usually one bus departs in the morning and the other in the late afternoon or early evening, but make sure to check the exact times ahead of time at **Nautilus Travel Agency** (☎26740 41 440). Walking from the base of the port, the office is in the first building along the right of the pier. **Internet** is also available there. (Open M-Sa 9am-9pm.) **Tours** head out on the water to Ithaka on Thursday at 10am and arrive back at Fiskardo port at about 5pm. (☎26740 41 440. €30 per person.) **Motorboat rentals** are available at **Regina's Rentals** (☎69389 84647), located next to Nicholas' Tavern. Daily rates start at €50; the price does not include fuel. (Open daily July-Aug. 9am-6pm.)

▨ ▢ ACCOMMODATIONS AND FOOD. Few accommodations are located in town, unsurprising given its size. Many visitors stay along the shore outside of town in rented villas and rooms for let. If you're looking for a place in town, the best option is ◪**Panormos: Restaurant & Hotel ❸**, balanced on the cliffs at the very end of the restaurant-lined pier. The environmentally aware hotel exudes character rarely found in popular tourist destintations. Rooms have fans instead of A/C and recycling bins, and the restaurant serves only local produce. There are only six rooms, so book ahead. (☎26740 41 203. Singles and doubles €40-60. Cash only.) Check with Elli's Restaurant on the right side of the harbor for rooms at **Anatoli ❸**. All include A/C and TV. Shared kitchen is a bonus. (☎26740 41 204. Rooms €35-70. Cash only.)

   Lagoudera ❷, right next to the post office on the waterfront, provides outdoor dining illuminated by lanterns under a roof of reeds. Popular and delicious. (☎26740 41 275. Starters €4-6, entrees €6-12.) You can't miss the sign, or billboard, for **Nicholas Taverna ❷**, on the less cluttered-side of the harbor, about 200m inland. Enjoy a romantic dinner on the edge of the water hosted by Nicholas himself. (☎26742 41307. Salads €4-7. Fish €46-70 per kg. Entrees €8-15. Open 9am-1am. MC/V.) For pastries and breakfast, try **Tselentis Cafe ❶**, a block inland from the post office. This cozy bakery cooks up mouthwatering pastries and breads from scratch. Stop by early in the day, because bread tends sell out by 2pm. (☎26740 41 204.)

◔ ◪ SIGHTS AND BEACHES. Venturing away from the waterfront proves quite rewarding. To reach the old-fashioned lighthouse, walk all the way around the waterfront with the sea on your right to Nicholas Taverna. A short and shaded path picks up where the road ends. Ruins of an old fortress are nearby. If you need to cool off and aren't in the mood for a trek, a smaller, though heavily trafficked, pebble beach offers first-rate views of neighboring Ithaka. With the water on your left, head along the waterfront road for about 10min.; the beach is just past the Roman graves. Off the road from Argostoli and Sami to Fiskardo is one of Europe's most breathtaking beaches, ◪**Myrtos.** The snowy white pebbles and clear, blue water are stunning enough, but the beach's location, pressed against the cliffs, makes it divine (4km from main road turn-off). Ten kilometers up the road from the Myrtos turn-off is the equally incredible Venetian **Castle of Assos**, on a steep, wooded peninsula connected to the island by a narrow isthmus. Completed in the early part of the 17th century, much of the castle is well preserved. Fiskardo buses stop at the Assos turn-off; it's a 4km walk to the small, peaceful village (also worth a visit) and another few kilometers to the castle.

ZAKYNTHOS Ζάκυνθος

The varied landscapes of Zakynthos are filled with an exceptional palette of colors—white cliffs rise from aquamarine water, sun-bleached wheat fields wave in the shadow of evergreens, and magenta flowers frame the twisting streets. It is also the only remaining habitat of the endangered loggerhead sea turtles, and as soon as you step on the island, you understand why—the waters' exceptional beauty and clarity would attract any creature. The area surrounding the town of Zakynthos, also called Zante, makes a good base, with many accommodations near the town's center. Public buses travel up and down the island, helping pale visitors escape to the coastal beaches and back again. The northern tip of the island, accessible by boat tours leaving from the port of Zante, is less trafficked. Day cruises are a pleasant way to visit the island's renowned shipwreck and blue grottoes.

ZAKYNTHOS TOWN
☎26950

Beyond the heavily-kiosked sidewalk of the waterfront road, arcaded streets and delicate Old World buildings welcome visitors to Zakynthos Town. After the earthquake of 1953 destroyed the city, locals faithfully rebuilt its traditional Venetian style while making the buildings strong enough to withstand the wrath of the gods. Though throngs of tourists and street vendors make for a hectic midday scene, the evening sees the crowd settle and the temperature drop, creating a pleasant promenade through the streets and along the waterfront. Leave your luggage in one of the town's many hotels and take a boat cruise or a bus to a remote beach to escape the midday crush.

▐ TRANSPORTATION

Flights: The **airport** (☎26950 28 322) is 3km south of town. Flights to: **Athens** (45min., 1-2 per day, €76-10); **Corfu** (3 per week, €52); **Kefallonia** (3 per week, €32); **Thessaloniki** (3 per week, €96). **Olympic Airways**, 16 Al. Roma (☎26950 28 611), recently moved to the airport. You can also purchase plane tickets from tour companies along the waterfront road 9am-2pm.

Buses: Central Bus Station, 42 Filita St. (☎26950 42 656). From the police station, walk 1 block inland on Lomvardou and take a right onto Filita St; it's 3 blocks to the bus station. Schedules change monthly, and Su service is reduced. Check with the tourist office or info window before leaving. To **Athens** (6hr.; 5:30, 8:30, 11am, 2:30, 6:45pm; €23), **Patra** (3hr.; 8:30am, 2:30, 6:45pm; €7), and **Thessaloniki** (10hr., 7:30am, €45).

Ferries: Ferries for **Killini** in the Peloponnese (1hr.; M-Sa 5 per day 6am-7:15pm, Su 4 per day 8am-7:15pm; €8) depart from the southern dock, on the left side of the waterfront as you face inland. Tickets for Killini ferries can be bought at **Ionian Ferries** (☎26950 49 500), next to Hertz on Lomvardou past the police station with the water on your right. Open daily 8:30am-8:30pm. **Agios Nikolaos (Skinari),** about 30km north of Zakynthos Town, has ferries to **Pesada, Kefallonia** (1hr., 1-2 per day, €4). Zakynthian buses do not run to Ag. Nikolaos, and a taxi will run €40. Returning to Kyllini and

IONIAN ISLANDS

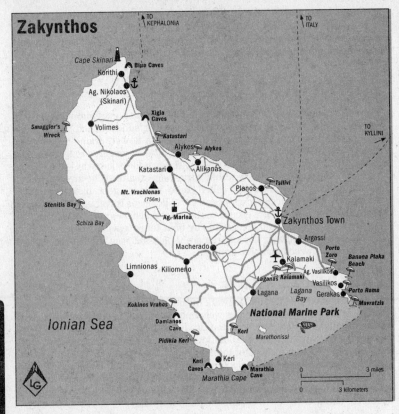

Zakynthos

TO KEPHALONIA

TO ITALY

Cape Skinari

Korithi — Blue Caves

Ag. Nikolaos (Skinari)

Xigia Caves

Smuggler's Wreck

Volimes

Katastari

TO KYLLINI

Alykes — Alykes

Katastari

Alikanas

Mt. Vrachionas (756m)

Planos — Tsilivi

Stenitis Bay

Schiza Bay

Ag. Marina

Zakynthos Town

Argassi

Macherado

Porto Zoro

Kalamaki

Banana Plaka Beach

Limnionas — Kiliomeno

Laganas — Kalamaki

Ag. Vasilikos

Vasilikos

Porto Roma

Kokinos Vrahos

Lagana

Lagana Bay

Gerakas

Mavratzis

Ionian Sea

Damianos Cave

Pidikia Keri

Keri

National Marine Park

Marathonissi

Keri Caves

Keri

Marathia Cape

Marathia Cave

0 ——— 3 miles

0 ——— 3 kilometers

heading to Kefallonia by ferry is another alternative. For more information, call the **port police** (☎26950 28 118).

Local Buses (€1.40-1.50) run to: **Alykes** (M-F 4 buses per day 7am-4:30pm, Sa 3 per day 7:40am-noon); **Argassi** (45min.; M-F 7 per day 6:45am-8:10pm, Sa 4 per day 9:30am-3pm); **Kalamaki** (25min.; M-Sa 10 per day 7:15am-8:10pm, Su 4 per day 7:15am-3:30pm); **Lagana** (25min.; M-Sa 11 per day 7:15am-8:10pm, Su 4 per day 7:15am-3:30pm). From Argassi buses continue on to **Porto Roma, St. Nikolas,** and **Vasilikos** (M-F 6:55am, 10am, and 2:40pm).

Taxis: ☎26950 22280 and 23788. Line up on Venizelou street, a left off the waterfront road just before Pl. Solomou with the water on the right. You also can flag one down on the waterfront road in front of Solomou. Available 24hr. For rides in the early morning, make arrangements the day before.

Car Rentals: Hertz, Lomvardou 38 (☎26950 45 706). Cars from €50 per day; includes unlimited km, insurance, and tax. Open daily 8am-2pm and 5:30-9pm. **EuroSky Rentals,** A. Makri 6 (☎26950 26 278; www.eurosky.gr), 2 blocks inland on A. Makri, by Pl. Solomou. Mopeds €15 per day. Cars from €30. Open daily 9am-2pm and 6-9pm.

Bike Rentals: Rent-a-Bike (☎69471 80928). Try to bargain down a bit. €4 per hr., €10 per day.

⚡ 🛈 ORIENTATION AND PRACTICAL INFORMATION

The waterfront runs between **Plateia Solomou** and **Agios Dionysios church.** Each end has a dock: Kyllini ferries dock at the left end facing inland, by Ag. Dionysios; all other boats, including daily cruises, dock at either end. The waterfront street, **Lomvardou**, is lined with restaurants, gift shops, ferry agencies, and car and moped rentals. The next street inland is **Filita**, with the bus station and fast-food stands; Filita becomes **Klavdianou** toward Pl. Solomou. Behind it are **Foskolou, Alexandrou Roma,** and **Tertseti,** all of which either change names or end between **Martinegou** and Ag. Dionysios. Just inland from Pl. Solomou is **Plateia Agiou Markou,** a major gathering spot for both locals and tourists, separated by a pedestrian-only street called **Dimokratias Square.** Al. Roma becomes a pedestrian shopping area between **Tzoulati** and Pl. Ag. Markou.

Tourist Office: 1 D. Roma St. (☎26950 48 073). Has information on travel and the area.

Bank: National Bank, 1 Dionissiou Salomou Sq. (☎26950 26 737). **Currency exchange** and **24hr. ATM.** Open daily M-F 8am-2:30pm. Many other ATMs and banks in the area. **Alpha Bank** (☎26950 45 357) and **Postal Savings Bank** (☎26950 44 611) are other options.

Police: 62 Lombardou St. (☎26950 22 100). Emergency ☎100. Enter through the door to the side of Fra. Tzoulati. Open daily 7:30am-2:30pm. **Tourist Police** (☎26950 27 367) in the same building.

Hospital: ☎26950 49 111. Uphill and 600m inland from the city center. Walk down Lomvardou to Ag. Eleftheriou. Follow this road inland to Kokkini, where the road goes right, becoming Ag. Spiridona. Follow the signs from the waterfront. Open 24hr.

Internet Access: Home Internet Cafe, L. Ziva 31 (☎26950 28 198). Has Wi-Fi. €2 per hr. Open daily 9am-2am.

Post Office: ☎26950 44 875, at the intersection of Tertseti & S. Kouskou. Open M-F 7:30am-3:30pm. **Postal Code:** 29100.

🏠 ACCOMMODATIONS

Rooms in Zakynthos Town fill up in July and August and tend to be expensive year-round. The larger hotels are the best bet in terms of value. If you're looking for something cheaper, there are rooms to let along the coast to both the north and south of Zante. Convenient information signs on the main road heading out of town have the distance and names of all the rooms to let in the vicinity. If you really want to stay in town, bargaining is worth a shot.

Hotel Yria, Kapodistrou 4 (☎26950 44 682). Located in the heart of Zante. Most rooms come with waterfront views. Staff eager to help with recommendations for restaurants and the latest hot club. Breakfast included. Free internet. Singles €45; doubles €55; extra bed €10. MC/V. ❹

Hotel Bitzaro, 52 Dionisiou Roma (☎26950 45 733), a short walk along the water. All rooms are by the seaside. Breakfast included. Singles €40; doubles €50; triples €60. MC/V. ❸

Hotel Phoenix, Solomou 2 (☎26950 23 514). Prime location on the square. Breakfast buffet includes scrambled eggs and bacon, mmm. Breakfast and other amenities like cable TV are reflected in the price tag. Free Wi-Fi. Wheelchair-accessible. Singles €50; doubles €60. Extra beds available. MC/V. ❹

Athina Marouda Rooms for Rent, Tzoulati and Koutouzi (☎26950 45 194), 3 blocks inland from the police. Narrow, twisting staircases lead to simple, sparsely-furnished rooms. Communal kitchen. Singles €15; doubles €25. Cash only. ❶

🍴 FOOD

Along the waterfront road, restaurants fill up nearly every block. On Al. Roma, toward Pl. Ag. Markou, cafes and fast-food joints line up one after another. The **Veropoulos Supermarket,** on Lomvardou, 50m to the right of the police station facing inland, sells a wide variety of fruit, vegetables, cereal, and snacks. In the sweltering summer, swing by for the freezing-cold air-conditioning even if you're not hungry. (Open M-F 8am-9pm, Sa 8am-8pm.)

> **Green Boat, Fish Tavern & Snack Bar,** Krioneri (☎26950 22 957), 1 km outside the town. Worth the stroll along the water to enjoy your meal on the shore. Fresh and cheap seafood. Dip your toes in as you eat. Entrees €7. Cash only. ❷

> **"O Zoxios",** 9 Psarron (☎26950 27 575), at the corner of Venzelou. A wonderfully antique taverna set in a small green courtyard a block inland from all the portside commotion. The most authentic Greek cuisine of Zante at the lowest prices. Salads and starters €2.50. Entrees €5-7. Cash only. ❷

> **Saffran,** 50 Lomvardou (☎26950 42 034), right next to the police station. The freshest fish in town—don't miss it, lost amid the overpriced tourist joints. How can you refuse fried dandelions? And octopus? Starters and salads €2.50-5. Entrees €6-20. Cash only. ❷

👁 SIGHTS

ECCLESIASTICAL MUSEUM. The Ecclesiastical Museum features beautifully sculpted crosses, Ag. Dionysios's vestments, and his handwritten documents. Engraved Bibles from the 13th through 17th centuries were protected from repeated pirate attacks on the Monastery of Strofades, where the saint lived. Letters written in Latin between late 16th-century religious leaders are remarkably well-preserved, and magnificent paintings line the stairs to the second floor. (Behind the Church of Agios Dionysios. ☎ 26950 44 126. Open daily 8am-10pm. €4, under 18 free.)

CHURCH OF AGIOS DIONYSIOS. The intricate designs throughout the church, named in honor of the island's patron saint, make its colorful frescoes pale in comparison. In a room enclosed by silver walls, a silver chest holds some of the saint's relics. At night, only the iconostasis is lit up, making it visible from the street. (In front of the Ecclesiastical Museum. Open daily 8am-10:30pm. Modest dress required.)

MUSEUM OF DIONYSIOS SOLOMOS. Solomos, born in Zakynthos and buried inside the museum, is Greece's national poet; the first verses of his "Hymn to Liberty" became the Greek National Anthem. The exhibit includes everything from the dust from Solomos's first grave to inkpots used by the poet to handwritten manuscripts of his most famous poetry. It also highlights the lives of other famous Greeks, showcashing curios like the piano of composer Paul Karren. There is little explanation provided, but tours in English and Greek can be arranged with the museum staff for a small donation. (In Pl. Ag. Markou. Open daily 9am-2pm. Info booklet €3. €3, seniors and students €2, under 12 free.)

STRANIS HILL. A small jaunt gets you to Stranis Hill, one kilometer above town. Along with a ruined Venetian castle, Solomos's home, where the famous poem "Free Besieged" was written, stands on this hill. The views of Zakynthos are particularly dazzling at night. (Take Tertseti, which becomes N. Koluva, to the edge of

IONIAN ISLANDS

town, or head inland from Pl. Ag. Markou. Take a right onto Therianou, a left onto Filikon, and follow the signs uphill to Bohalis. Turn left at the junction and go a bit farther.)

🢒 DAYTRIPS FROM ZAKYNTHOS TOWN

You can see all of Zakynthos, including the otherwise inaccessible **western cliffs,** by boat. Shop around for a cruise on Lomvardou. The tours that highlight most of the island's sites usually run €16-25. Tours leave around 9am and return around 5:30 or 6pm. It's best to reserve the day before. Don't buy from hawkers around gift shops—their ticket prices are usually about the same as the agencies', but they do not refund nor do they give ample information about the cruise. Cruises go to many of the island's most spectacular sights and allow for swim stops at picturesque spots like the island's famous **Blue Caves** and Shipwreck Beach on the northeastern shore past Ag. Nikolaos. At the Blue Caves, the azure sea reflects off the ceilings of the stalactite-filled caverns, creating a blue glow throughout. Southwest of the Blue Caves is the ▨**Smuggler's Wreck,** a large boat skeleton that has made the beach one of the most photographed in the world ever since it was accidentally discovered in 1980. Most cruises stop for 30-60min. on the beach. Cruises also stop at **Marathonissi,** which is nicknamed Turtle Island because of its proximity to loggerhead turtle nesting grounds and its turtle-like shape. If you're looking for an alternative to boat tours, then renting a car or motorbike might be a worthwhile investment. Many rental agencies located in all the larger towns, especially Zante, offer reasonable rates. (Motorbikes €10-15 per day. Cars €30-40. Maps €3-5.) If you decide to go solo, buy a road map and ask for directions; the island is developing rapidly, and new roads may not appear on old maps.

PLAY NICELY. Sunbathers should note that they share Zakynthos's beaches with a resident population of **endangered sea turtles;** a simple stroll through the sand could potentially destroy hundreds of turtle eggs. Zakynthos is making efforts to protect the turtles and their nests, encouraging waterfront properties to take certain precautions and indicating which beaches have nests. Gerakas, Kalamaki, and Laganas have turtle populations; ask at tour companies which other beaches are turtle territory.

The bustling beach town of **Argassi** is 2km south of Zakynthos Town. Buses run to the village daily (M-F 10 per day 6:45am-11:30pm, Sa-Su 7 per day 9am-11:30pm; €1.20). Argassi, like nearby Laganas, overflows with tourists kitschy shops. Argassi is filled with restaurants and clubs designed in the typical style-over-substance manner—an artificially appealing show to attract tourist dollars. Bars host nightly parties with themes like Toga Night, and one spot, Avalon, is a re-creation of a medieval castle. Moped and car rental agencies, many restaurants, and a children's go-cart racetrack are just a few of Argassi's amenities.

Instead of going south from Zakynthos town toward Argassi, try heading north keeping the water on your right. The best way to access the northern beaches is by car or motorbike, though a bicycle is another great way to manage the island. Buses heading north are less frequent and unreliable, so stick to your own means of transportation. Head up the coast toward **Alikanas** (15km from Zante); road signs will guide you. When you reach Alikanas, continue through the tiny town and make a right toward **Alykes Bay.** The beaches here are just as pretty but have much smaller crowds. You can even spend the night in the area at **Alykes Camping and Apartments ❶,** a fully stocked site with great prices. (☎26950 83 233. €5 per night.)

Porto Zoro and **Banana Beach** can't be beat for quiet afternoons of sipping piña coladas and lounging under the sun. Buses leave Zakynthos Town for Vasilikos (M-F 4 per day 6:45am-5:30pm, Sa-Su 10am, 3pm; €1.50). Rent a bike in Zakynthos Town and take an early morning ride to Porto Roma. Try **Rent A Bicycle;** make a left at the road just before Pl. Solomou walking with the water on your right; the shop is on the left one block down. (☎69471 80 928. €4 per hr., €10 per day.) There are plenty of domatia by the beaches if you want to lengthen your stay or head back to Zakynthos beach by beach. Travelers should note that some spots on the western coast of the peninsula are protected areas that must be vacated in the evenings when sea turtles come ashore to nest. Soft, white-sand beaches fringe **Alykes,** 8km from Zakynthos Town. Buses run from Zakynthos Town (M-F 4 per day 6:50am-4:45pm, Sa-Su 4 per day 7:40am-4:30pm; €1.50).

CRETE Κρήτη

On an island barely 250km long, palm-tree forests collide with mountain ravines; sheltered, white-sand coves lie alongside slopes of olive groves; and windmill-strewn plains are minutes from limestone caverns. Crete's diversity is as cultural as it is environmental. Isolating mountain ranges have preserved rural lifestyles that seem completely removed from the cities and tourist towns along the coast. Its location as the southernmost point in Europe invited influence from the Egyptians and Phoenicians along with the Turks, Venetians, and Germans, the echoes of which can be seen in everything from ancient ruins to WWII memorials strewn across the island. Fusing together Eastern, African, Mediterranean, and European influences, the laid-back sensibility of this island is distinctly Cretan.

The seeds of civilization (as well as the first olives) were planted in Crete, with records of life on the island dating back to 6000 BC. Its ruins predate Hellenic culture, attesting to the advancement of Minoan society. Disasters—earthquakes, a tidal wave from an enormous volcanic eruption on Santorini, and Mycenaean invasions—plagued third millennium BC Minoan society until the civilization was wiped out entirely. Power struggles ensued for the next 3000 years as empires strove to claim this hotly contested island as their own. Dorians occupied the island in the eighth century BC, followed 1000 years later by Romans. Next, Crete fell under rickety Byzantine rule before Arabs conquered the island in AD 827, only to lose it again to the Byzantines. In 1204, the Byzantines again ceded the island, this time to Frankish crusaders. When it was finally sold to the Venetian Empire, Crete became a thriving commercial hub dominated by Venetian nobles and local merchants. In 1646 the island fell to the Turks, who reigned over the resentful islanders until the Cretans finally won independence in 1898, 70 years after most of Greece. After the Balkan Wars, Crete joined the Greek state. A strong guerrilla resistance combated the German occupation here during WWII, leaving the islanders with a justifiable sense of pride about their indomitable nature.

Though Crete is divided into four prefectures—Chania, Iraklion, Lasithi, and Rethymno—the territorial divisions do not undermine the feeling of unity. According to a Greek saying, a Cretan's first loyalty is to his island, his second to his country. Crete's sense of identity, however, also expresses itself in an overwhelming hospitality, as natives strive to show visitors why their island is so exceptional. Don't be surprised to be invited in to share watermelon or a bottle of *raki* with your pension hosts on a hot day. Locals are eager to share their insider knowledge of secluded beaches and gorgeous hikes with interested visitors. Yet Crete's spirit is almost impossible to capture or define, as its best qualities—the relaxed pace of life, rebellious streak, and seemingly infinite diversity—are only minuscule samples of the island's rich offerings.

HIGHLIGHTS OF CRETE

HOP around the caves of the former hippie mecca of **Matala** (p. 490).

RELAX in the peaceful, waterfront city of **Sitia** (p. 501).

HIKE through the beautiful and lively **Death Gorge** (p. 505).

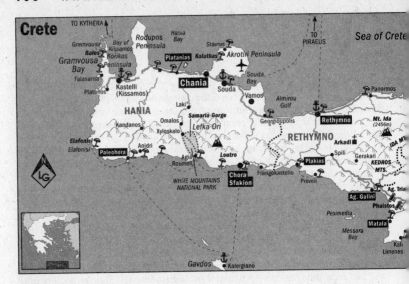

Crete

✈ **GETTING THERE. Olympic Airways** (☎21096 66 666) and **Aegean/ Cronus Airlines** (☎21099 88 300) run frequent, cheap, and fast domestic flights from Athens to Iraklion, Chania, and Sitia. Consult the **Transportation** section of your destination for more information on flights. Many travelers take the 14hr. ferry from Piraeus to Crete, landing in Iraklion, Chania, Sitia, or occasionally Rethymno or Agios Nikolaos. Boats run frequently during the summer, but often on an irregular schedule. All prices listed are for deck-class accommodations; bring a sleeping bag to snooze on the deck or lounge.

CHANIA PREFECTURE

Gorgeous beaches, steep, rocky gorges, and pine-covered hills dot the western tip of Crete. Tourists flock to these natural wonders in droves, yet the buzz of visitors does not overwhelm the beauty of the beaches, the distinct character of the towns, and the friendly faces of the locals. By day, the region's small villages and pristine beaches call nature lovers to experience untapped wilderness and local hospitality. By night, the capital city welcomes party animals seeking hedonistic revelry.

CHANIA Χανιά   ☎28210

The island's second-largest city, Chania takes on its annual surge of summer tourists with a refined ease typical of this port town's open atmosphere. The less picturesque outer streets evolve into the charming pedestrian boulevards of the Old Town as you approach the Old Venetian Harbor—full of stylish shops and cafes. Visitors meander through labyrinthine cobblestone alleys listening to traditional Cretan music and browsing through jewelery, or dine at a

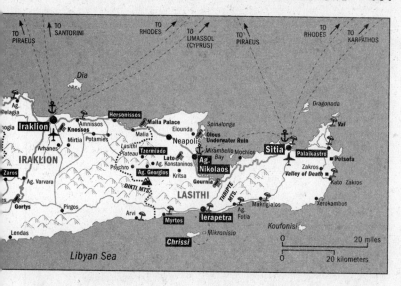

waterside cafe as the sun sets behind the lighthouse and nearby Venetian and Ottoman domes.

TRANSPORTATION

Flights: Chania Airport (CHQ; ☎28210 63 264). Olympic Airlines, Tzanakaki 88 (☎25210 53 760), across from the municipal gardens. Tickets sold daily 8:15am-3:30pm. To **Athens** (4-5 per day, €55-90) and **Thessaloniki** (1hr., 3 per week, €115).

Ferries: Dock in the nearby port of **Souda**. Take the bus from the dock, which stops on Zymvrakakidon by Pl. 1866 (15min., €1). **ANEK**, Pl. Market 2 (☎28210 27 500). Open daily 7:30am-9pm. From Souda, ferries go to **Piraeus** (9hr., approx. 2 per day, €30). Catch the bus to Souda in front of the municipal market where El. Venizelou meets Chatzimichali Giannari (25min., every 20min. 6am-10pm, €1.10). For long-distance ferries to Athens and other islands, check at the ANEK office. Schedules change constantly.

Buses: ☎28210 93 052. The station fills the block of Kidonias, Zymvrakakidon, Smyrnis, and Kelaidi. To: **Elafonisi** (2½hr., 1 per day, €10); **Chora Sfakion** (2hr., 2 per day, €6.50); **Iraklion** (2hr., every 30min. 5:30am-8pm, €10.70); **Kastelli**, also called Kissamos (1hr., 10 per day 6:30am-9pm, €4.20); **Paleohora** (2hr., 4 per day 5am-4pm, €6.80); **Platanias** (20min., every 30min. 6:30am-11pm, €1.70); **Rethymno** (1hr., 20 per day 5:30am-10:30pm, €6); **Samaria Gorge (Omalos)** (1hr., 4 per day 6:15am-2pm, €12.90); **Sougia** (2hr., 1 per day, €6.40); **Stavros** (30min., 3 per day, 6:50am-2:15pm, €2); **Sternes** (20 min., 6 per day 6:50am-8:15pm, €1.90); **Chania Airport** (20 min., 3 per day 6am-6:30pm, €2.40). Many bus routes (with the exception of major destinations such as Rethymno and the Airport) are extremely limited or nonexistent Su.

Taxis: ☎28210 98 700. In Pl. Machis Tis Kritis and on Pl. 1866's eastern side. 24hr. Taxis from the airport to the city center about €20.

Car and Moped Rental: Agencies are on Halidon. Mopeds €18-25 per day. Cars €25-50. Some rentals only allow for 100km; driving more may cost €0.06-0.20 per km.

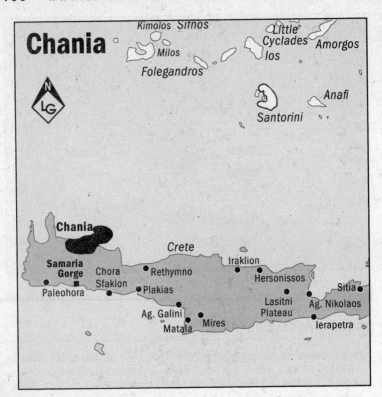

CRETE

TIP

CAR COUNTRY. Though bus service between major hubs in Crete like Chania, Iraklion, and Rethymno is surprisingly prompt, frequent, and cheap, it will only get you as far as the next trampled tourist destination. To really mine the island's gems, consider renting your own wheels.

ORIENTATION AND PRACTICAL INFORMATION

To get to the city center from the bus station, turn right onto **Kidonias,** walk one block, then turn left onto **Zymvrakakidon,** which runs along one side of a long park called **Plateia 1866.** At the far end of Pl. 1866, the road becomes **Halidon** and leads to the **Old Venetian Harbor,** full of outdoor restaurants, pensions, and narrow alleyways. **Skalidi** intersects Zymvrakakidon where it becomes Halidon, just before the Municipal Art Museum, and then to the right, Skalidi becomes **Chatzimichali Giannari.** One hundred meters farther, Chatzimichali Giannari splits into **Tzanakaki** to the right and **Eleftheriou Venizelou** to the left. Chania's **business district** is across from the Municipal Market near the fork in Chatzimichali Giannari. Sunbathers can head west of the harbor along the waterfront to find a popular long, thin stretch of sand at **Nea Hora.** This 1km walk is especially entertaining on Thursdays, when the weekly market bazaar overtakes the waterfront, with wares from bikinis to batteries (Th 8am-1pm). The top of **Promahonas Hill,** on Baladinou just off of Halidon, offers a birds-eye view of the layout of Chania below.

Tourist Office: Kidonias 29 (☎28210 36 155; www.chania.gr), in the city hall. Free maps of the city and info on buses, museums, monasteries, Samaria Gorge hikes, and boats on the southern coast. Open daily 8:30am-2:30pm, self-service 8:30am-8pm.

Bank: National Bank (☎28210 38 934), on the corner of El. Venizelou and Tzanakaki. **24hr. ATM.** Open M-Th 8am-2:30pm, F 8am-2pm. There are a number of other **ATMs,** including Citibank and Alpha Bank along Halidon in the Old Town.

Luggage Storage: Kidonias 73-77 (☎28210 93 052), in the bus station. €1.50 per bag per day. Open daily 6am-9pm.

Bookstores: Mediterraneo Bookstore, Akti Koundourioti 57 (☎28210 86 904), has a number of English novels and books on Crete, as well as handy, miniature-size street maps of Chania, Rethymno, and Iraklion (€3.50). **NewsStand,** Skalidi 8 (☎28210 95 888), sells guidebooks, newspapers, and a large selection of Dutch, English, French, German, and Italian magazines. Open daily 8am-11:30pm. **To Pazari,** Daskalogianni 46, the American and Irish owners of the consignment shop, buys and sells used books in English, French, and German as well as an eclectic mix of second-hand clothes, jewelry, appliances, and music. Open M and W 8:30am-2pm, Tu and Th-F 8:30am-1:30pm and 6-9pm, Sa 8:30am-3pm.

Public Toilets: In Pl. 1866 near the bus stop and at the corner of El. Venizelou and A. Papandreou near the Municipal Market.

Police: (☎28210 25 811), 250m down Apokronou on the left. Open daily 8am-2pm. **Tourist police** (☎28210 25 931), in the tourist office at the Town Hall. Open daily 8am-2:30pm.

Hospital: Chania Hospital (☎28210 22 000), in Mournies, 6km south of Chania. Open 24hr.

Telephones: OTE, Tzanakaki 5 (☎28210 11 888). Open M and W 7:45am-1:45pm, Tu and Th-F 7:45am-8pm.

Internet: Triple W Internet Cafe, Baladinou (☎28210 93 478), just off Halidon. Prints, burns CDs, faxes, scans, has webcams, and uploads digital photos. Internet €2 per hr. Open 24hr. **Cosmos 2,** Pl. Venizelou (☎28210 74 499), at the end of Halidon in the Old Harbor. Full computer services and Wi-Fi €2 per hr. Open daily 9am-2am.

Post Office: Peridou 10 (☎28210 28 445). Open M-F 7:30am-8pm, Sa 7:30am-2pm. **Postal Code:** 73100.

ACCOMMODATIONS AND CAMPING

Rooms in Chania are plentiful, but the prices and quality vary. While many of the waterfront properties offer dazzling views of the harbor, their rates are higher and many neighbor noisy night spots. Reasonable prices, though, can be found in Old Town pensions, where the homey atmosphere more than compensates for slightly smaller quarters. Reception desks are usually open 8-10am, so call ahead if you plan to arrive early.

Hotel Neli, Isodion 21-23 (☎28210 55 533; www.nelistudios.com). This classy pension in the Old Harbor boasts spacious and elegant rooms that are impeccably clean and tastefully decorated, each with kitchenette, fridge, bath, TV, and A/C. Each room also has a private wrought-iron balcony overlooking narrow cobblestone streets or the plaza and Cathedral. Walk down sparkling, mosaic hallways to wooden doors, all labeled with unique Greek names. Singles €30; doubles €40-48; triples €45-55; quads €55-60. ❷

Pension Orio, Zambeliou 77 (☎28210 94 357). Located in the heart of the twisting cobblestone roads that make up the Old Harbor. Four-poster beds and old-fashioned tubs in some of the rooms. The owners are also in charge of the nearby pensions **Ifige-**

nia II and **Ifigenia III,** so if availability is low, they will be able to direct you elsewhere. Breakfast included. Singles €25-30; doubles €35-40; triples €40-45. ❷

Pension Lena, Ritsou 5 (☎28210 86 860; www.lenachania.gr). Turn off Theotokopoulou on the way to the Byzantine Collection to discover a peaceful street lined with multi-colored buildings and potted plants. Hospitable owner Lena welcomes you to the small but cozy rooms, each with a TV, A/C, bathroom, hot pot, and a random assortment of dishes and books. Communal roof deck and tables with chairs lining the alley below. Wheelchair-accessible. Singles €25; doubles €35; triples €45. ❷

Eftihis, Tsouderon 21 (☎28210 46 829), on a street of trendy shops off Skrydlof. The most affordable rooms in the city. Clean rooms with balconies and A/C. Some have shared bathrooms and there is a sink in every room. Singles €15-18; doubles €20; triples €30. ❶

Camping Chania, Apostoli (☎28210 31 138). If you have a car, drive on Skalidi west out of town and continue as it becomes Kisamou; 4km down the road, take a right at the sign. Alternatively, take the bus to Kallimaki (15min., every 15min., €1) from Pl. 1866 and get off once you see the signs. Sequestered within walls among a number of hotels and apartments, this site has a pool, a restaurant, and a mini-mart. Proximity to the beach (450m) is another plus. Laundry €4.50. Tent rental €10. €6 per person; €4 per tent. ❶

> **TIP**
>
> **CASH ME IF YOU CAN.** While all of the accommodations in the Old Town accept credit cards, cash is preferred, especially in cafes, clubs, and pensions. Luckily, Chania has numerous banks and ATMs, so it's easy to have plenty of cash on hand.

FOOD

You can build a fantasy meal from the snacks at the open-air **Municipal Market** between Pl. Market and Pl. Machis Tis Kritis. The smells of cheeses, meats, fish, spices, and baked goods waft from the stalls, which sell everything from sea sponges to sunglasses. (Open M, W, Sa-Su 8am-2:30pm Tu and Th-F 8am-2:30pm and 6-9pm.) Inside, there are a number of cafes with freshly cooked seafood (€4-11) or you can just snack on bags of nuts and jars of olives (€2-4). Many places accept credit cards, but don't worry if you're strapped for cash—there is an ATM in the Market building. For other cheap options, try the well-stocked and convenient **IN.KA. Supermarket,** in Pl. 1866, on the right coming from Halidon. (☎28210 90 558. Open M-F 8am-9pm, Sa 8am-6pm.)

▨ **Tamam,** Zambeliou 49 (☎28210 96 080). Traditional Greek meal options such as Greek salad (€4.50) and moussaka (€7) served in a former Turkish bath complex. Open daily 1pm-12:30am. ❷

▨ **Bougatsa Iorthanis,** Apokronou 24 (☎28210 88 855). This local favorite serves 1 dish and 1 dish only: *bougatsa* (€2.60). The warm and scrumptious ricotta-like cheese pastry is available with or without sugar. Open M-F and Su 6am-2pm, Sa 6am-1pm. ❶

Ababa, on Isodion, down the street from Hotel Neli. Brightly colored tables and green wicker chairs on the alleyway. The perfect spot for an afternoon coffee or early evening drink. The owner is actually an artist who re-paints the walls with floor-to-ceiling murals every few months. Coffee and espressos €2-3. Open daily 10am-late. ❶

Doloma, Kalergon 5 (☎28210 51 166). If you want to escape the touristy waterfront cafes and hunker down for a quiet, traditional Greek meal, sneak behind the Venetian shiphouse to order yogurt with honey (€3.50) or a Greek salad (€4.50) with locals. From the outdoor seating, you can watch the neighbors going about their daily tasks. Open daily noon-11pm. ❷

Apovrado Taverna (☎28210 58 151), on Isodion off the cathedral plaza. Candlelit tables spill out onto Athinagora under fuchsia bougainvilleas and the shadow of the city's cathedral. In this quiet, romantic setting, the menu pictures will get your taste-buds watering for spaghetti carbonara (€6) or an egg omelette with mushrooms and cheese (€4-5.50). The lengthy wine list describes the taste and origin of each type of wine. Open daily 10am-midnight. ❷

🔵 SIGHTS

VENETIAN INNER HARBOR. The **Venetian lighthouse** marks the entrance to Chania's stunning architectural relic, the Venetian Inner Harbor, which retains its original breakwater and arsenal. The Egyptians restored the lighthouse in the style of a minaret during their occupation of Crete in the late 1830s, leaving only the base as part of the Venetian original. On the western side of the main harbor, the **Maritime Museum** describes the tumultuous 6000 years of Crete's naval and merchant history in maps and models, while the second floor houses a large exhibition on Crete's remarkable expulsion of the Nazis in 1941. (☎28210 91 875. Open daily Apr.-Oct. 9am-4pm; Nov.-Mar. 9am-2pm. €3, students €2.) The **Venetian shiphouse,** at the end of the harbor where Arholeon meets Akti Enoseos, provides lasting evidence of Venetian influences in Chania. Turning left on the waterfront from Arholeon you will come to the **Center for Mediterranean Architecture (CMA),** which hosts symposia, conferences, and exhibits open to the public on issues ranging from water management to modern Greek art. (☎28210 27 184. Call for availability and schedule of current exhibit.) At the corner of Kandanoleu and Kanevaro, just north of Kanevaro on **Kastelli Hill,** lie reminders of Chania's Bronze Age prosperity, including the **Late Minoan House** (1450 BC) and other fenced-off and unmarked monuments.

MUNICIPAL ART GALLERY. This gallery shows rotating exhibits of modern Greek art. The exhibits span three floors in an impressive wood-floored building and last one to three months. (Halidon 98, near the intersection with Skalidi. ☎28210 92 294. Open M-F 10am-2pm and 7-10pm, Sa 10am-2pm. Wheelchair-accessible. €2; students €1; seniors, artists with ID, military personnel, under 18, and W free.)

ARCHAEOLOGICAL MUSEUM. This museum is a paradise for history and archaeology buffs, featuring a broad collection of Cretan artifacts from early Minoan to Hellenistic times. The building's high-ceilinged halls are lined with clay shards, gold jewelry, glassware, and other artifacts, but be sure to look for the three-floor mosaics featuring Dionysus and other Greek gods as well as the intricately crafted gold jewelery from the Hellenistic period. A modern room to the right of the entrance displays a bronze cup with a rare inscription in Linear A, the Minoans' mysterious, undeciphered script. The ancient coin collection includes gold tokens once placed in the mouths of the dead to pay Charon, the ferryman of the River Styx, to ferry souls to the underworld. (On Halidon about 40m past the cathedral. ☎28210 90 334. Open M 1:30-8pm, Tu-Su 8am-8pm. €2, students and senior citizens €1, EU students free; if you have an ISIC, you can finagle your way into free admission as well. Joint ticket with Byzantine Collection €3, reduced €2.)

BYZANTINE COLLECTION. Housed within a former Venetian monastery, which later was converted into a mosque during Turkish occupation, the collection charts the history of Chania from early Christian times to Ottoman rule in wall paintings, mosaics, coins, and icons. (Theotokopoulou. ☎28210 96 046. Open Tu-Su 8:30am-3pm. €2, students and seniors €1, EU students free. Joint ticket with the Archaeological museum €3, reduced €2.)

CRETE

MUNICIPAL GARDENS. For a slight change of pace, take a walk and relax on a bench beneath the floral shade of the Municipal Gardens *(Dimotikos Kypos)*, along Tzanakaki in the city center. Once the property of a *muezzin* (Islamic prayer caller), the garden is now home to an open-air movie theater that screens international films, two tiny zoos that house an amusing combination of goats and peacocks, and the city's clock tower. *(Theater ☎ 28210 41 427. Check show times and prices at front desk.)*

NIGHTLIFE

Despite its small-town feel, Chania offers a variety of entertainment options fit for a cosmopolitan metropolis. The Old Town has the best bars and clubs with a mix of Greeks and foreigners. Venture to New Town if you wish, but be prepared to be turned away: some clubs there won't even let you in the door unless you're a local. The nearby town of Platanias has crazy nightlife for beach-party devotees. Platanias is easily accessible from Chania by bus (see **Transportation,** p. 467). To get back to Chania, either take a cab (€11) or party until the 6:30am bus arrives the next morning.

Synagogue, Skoufou 15 (☎28210 96 797.) As its name suggests, this relaxed bar, also known as the Blue Room, is housed in a former synogogue hidden in the alleyways of the Old Town. A favorite of locals and one of the few places that keep their doors open really late, sometimes until dawn. Open 9pm-late.

The Point, Sourmeli 2 (☎28210 57 556; www.pointchania.com), in the corner of Plaza Venizelou on the Old Harbor; take the stairs. An oasis for those maxed out on techno and *bouzouki*. Eclectic music, from 60s hits to hip hop, and balconies with harbor views. Mixed drinks €6. Open daily 9pm-late. AmEx/MC/V.

Kafe Kriti, Kalergon 22 (☎28210 58 6610), on the eastern side of the harbor. Live Greek and Cretan music plays nightly; ask the owner, an instructor of traditional dance, to teach you some moves. Beer €3. Bottle of raki €5. Open daily 8pm-3am.

Elli, Akti Koundourioti, (☎28210 72 130), near the Maritime Museum. This waterfront bar cranks loud music for a club vibe inside, while others enjoy the large patio with candlelit seating outside. Beer €3. Mixed drinks €6-7.

BAR-HOP 'TIL YOU DROP. Many clubs will give you a free shot or mixed drink as a first drink just to get you in the door. Although they are more watered down than a normal drink, it's a good way to save some cash and a great excuse to keep bar-hopping to find the next freebie.

DAYTRIPS FROM CHANIA

AKROTIRI PENINSULA Ακρωτήρι
The Akrotiri Peninsula is best navigated by car, which will allow you to visit all of the sights in 1 day. You will need 2 days using the bus due to erratic schedules.

Just northeast of Chania is the sparsely populated peninsula of Akrotiri, home to herds of goats, rows of olive trees, several monasteries, and sheltered coves. Since WWII, it's also been inhabited by American soldiers who live in the US military base there and coexist, sometimes uneasily, with Chania's natives.

KALATHAS. Kalathas is a small white-sand beach 11km from Chania, where sunbeds with umbrellas go for €4 per day. Enjoy the soothing Mediterranean sun from the shore or swim out to the craggy little island to explore tide pools. *(On the bus route from Chania to Stavros (6 per day 6:45am-8pm, €1.50).)*

STAVROS. Another sheltered inlet with crystal-clear waters and sunbeds for daily rental, Stavros might seem familiar to you as the setting of the movie *Zorba the Greek*. Stavros is also home to a handful of cafes, a calm cove, and a mining hill, as well as **Cristiana's Restaurant ❸**, set under a large wooden roof on stone floors, with a view of the water. *(☎ 28210 39 152. Greek salad €3.50. Shrimp with bacon €12. Open daily 7:30am-11pm.)* Get refreshments under a lush grape arbor 100m inland at **Zorba's Original Tavern ❷**. *(☎ 28210 39 402. Souvlaki €5.20. Open daily 8:30am-midnight. To get to Stavros from Chania, take the bus (1hr., 6 per day 6:45am-8pm, €1.50) and get off at the end of the line, in front of Cristiana's Restaurant.)*

AGIA TRIADA. Built in 1606 near ruins of a Minoan temple, the monastery of Agia Triada has produced traditional olive oil since 1632. Enjoy a peaceful walk through the grounds and small **museum**, with a collection of mostly 19th-century pieces. You can bottle the experience in the form of the famous olive oil. *(Just past the Chania airport, 16.5km from the city, and accessible by bus (30min., 2-3 per day, €2). ☎ 28210 63 310. Open M-Sa 9am-7pm, Su 10am-7pm. €2.)*

GOUVERNETO. Follow the road up into the hills, complete with wild goats, unmarked ruins, and narcissus flowers, 4km to Gouverneto. This austere monastery requires modest dress, so leave your shorts and sleeveless shirts at home. From the monastery, the stone path leading down to the sea passes **St. John's Cave** and numerous Venetian ruins after about 1km. Legend has it that St. John was attacked by a bear while drinking from the cave's fountains. Before any harm was done, a miracle turned the animal to stone, saving the monk and preserving the outline of the beast in the shape of the cave's stalagmite patterns. Following the path about 5km farther leads you through the ruins of a bridge complex and into the rocky gorge below, eventually presenting a spectacular vista from bluffs and Venetian ruins overlooking the Cretan Sea. It's worth the long—around 1hr.—rocky walk, but remember to bring sunblock and a water bottle. *(☎ 28210 63 319. Monastery open M-Tu and Th 9am-noon and 5-7pm, Sa-Su 5-11am and 5-8pm. Free.)*

BALOS

You can reach Balos by car or boat. To drive there, take Skalidi west out of Chania toward Kissamos. You will hit Kissamos after about 40km of beautiful countryside. Pass the town and in about 3km look for a sign for a phone on the side of the road. Make a right at the phone, where you'll also see signs for Kaliviani, and make an immediate left by the sign for the Balos Hotel. After about 1km, you will pass through a tiny town. Just outside of it, make a right at the small sign for Balos. After 5km on this road, you will pass a white chapel; the parking lot lies 3km beyond the church. When you arrive at the parking lot, take the small marked path and hike 30min. to the lagoon.

Nestled away on the northwestern tip of Crete, Balos's heavenly ⬛**blue lagoon** is Crete's uncontested best beach, where sand, sea, and sky melt into one. Almost entirely enclosed by bright-white sand, the lagoon's knee-deep, warm water drifts seamlessly into the deeper waters closer to shore. For those more inclined to hike than lounge on the beach, take one of the **boat cruises** that leave from Kissamos port, 3km outside of town along the main road heading away from Chania. The boat stops at nearby **Gramvousa,** an island with a 16th-century Venetian fortress and a cave that supposedly led the Minoans to Scandinavia in ancient times. The steep walk up to the fortress yields a breathtaking view of the sheer cliffs of Crete and the sparkling water below.

SAMARIA GORGE
Φαράγγι της Σαμαριάς   ☎ 28250

The most popular excursion on Crete is the spectacular 5-6hr. hike down the Samaria Gorge, a formidable 18km pass through the White Mountains National Park. The gorge is the longest in Europe and was sculpted over 14 million years by rainwater. The rocky trail can trip you up, but if you take a look around you'll see epiphytes (plants that don't need soil to grow) peeking out from sheer rock walls, wildflowers bordering the path, and endangered gryphon vultures and golden eagles soaring overhead.

🚌 TRANSPORTATION. Though it's possible to reach the gorge from many tourist towns, Chania is the closest and allows for the most flexibility. **Buses** from Chania go to Omalos and Xyloskalo, the town at the trailhead (1hr., 3 per day, €12.90). Early buses (6:15, 7:30, and 8:30am) can get you to Xyloskalo in time for a day hike. Busing in from Rethymno or Iraklion requires stopping in Chania for a connecting bus to Omalos. To get out of the gorge and back to Chania at the end of a day hike, take the 1hr. ferry from Agia Roumeli to Chora Sfakion (3-4 per day, €8) via Loutro (45min.) From Chora Sfakion, the last bus (direct to Chania; to Rethymno or Iraklion via Virses) leaves at 6:45pm. **Ferries** also run from Agia Roumeli to Paleohora (1hr; €11) via Sougia (45min., €6.50). In Agia Roumeli, buy tickets at the **ferry office** (☎28250 91 251), a tiny white and blue building next to the market on the main road. Call in advance for ferry times.

🏠 ACCOMMODATIONS. If you want to spend the night near the Gorge, you can either stay in Omalos, Chora Sfakion (p. 475), or Agia Roumeli. The town of Agia Roumeli, at the end of the gorge, specifically caters to tired, hungry hikers. Though it has little more than restaurants, souvenir shops, and lodgings, its peaceful beach is a well-deserved reward for a hard day's hike. **Hotel Agia Roumeli ❷** is a good place to crash, with air-conditioning, balconies, and a prime location directly behind the beach. (☎28250 91 241. Singles €30; doubles €40; triples €45.) Though you may be tempted to fall into the first bed you see after the strenuous hike, Chora Sfakion is worth the 1hr. ferry ride for a more picturesque harbor town.

🥾 HIKING. To complete the hike, you'll need to gain entry into **White Mountains National Park** (Open May-Oct. 6am-6pm. €5, under 15 and student groups free. Keep your ticket, as you must return it when you exit.) The trailhead in the town of **Xyloskalo** contains little more than a ticket booth, a cafeteria, a shop, and the last toilets you'll see for hours. From there, follow a noisy but nearly dry river and pass between stunningly steep cliff walls as high as 600m and as narrow as 3.5m. Much of the hike is shaded by clumps of pines and by the walls of the gorge itself. For the first 6km, the trail continues the seemingly never-ending descent into the gorge. After 1km more, hikers reach the former village of **Samaria**, inhabited in prehistoric times and part of the national park since 1962. The trail continues past Samaria on a rocky riverbed through the narrowest part of the gorge. You'll end up in the small beach town of **Agia Roumeli** on the southern coast; from there, experienced hikers can embark on a 10hr. trail to **Chora Sfakion** (p. 475) along one of the most outstanding coastlines in Greece. Another easier option for the gorge is to start at Agia Roumeli, which will allow you to take in the gorge's final, dramatic tail in much less time. This 1hr. climb to the north takes you through the gorge's narrowest

CRETE

Adventure in Europe?
Do it by rail

With a Eurail Global or Select Pass you zoom fast from country to country, from city centre to city centre. So you can soak up hip street scenes. Shop till you drop. Explore the nightlife and meet cool people.
Why wait? Go to www.adventure-europe.com or contact your local travel agent now!

Eurail.com	ACP Rail International	Flight Centre	Gullivers Travel Associates	Rail Europe	STA Travel
www.eurail.com	www.eurail-acprail.com	www.flightcentre.com	www.gta.co.jp (Japan)	Rail Europe Group - North America:	North America:
	+1-866-9-EURAIL	+1-866-WORLD-51	www.gtarail.co.kr (Korea)	www.raileurope.com	www.statravel.com
	(North America only)	(North America only)	www.octopustravel.com.au (Australia)	+1-800-4-EURAIL	+1-800-781-4040
				Rail Europe 4 A - Rest of the World:	Rest of the world
				www.raileurope.fr/wheretobuy/	www.statravelgroup.com

FIRST IN STUDENT DISCOUNTS WORLDWIDE

International Student Exchange Identity Card

INTERNATIONAL IDENTITY CARD

University of Maryland

STUDENT

Ashley Michaels

15 Mar 1989 American

ISEC/SCT / 12 Feb 2011

Control No. 1234567890

Cost: $25 per year

With the ISE Card you will receive discounts on airfare, accommodations, transportation, computer services, phone calls, major attractions, and more. You will also receive airline bankruptcy protection, and basic medical & evacuation benefits when traveling outside your home country and access to 24 hour worldwide emergency assistance.

11043 N Saint Andrew's Way • Scottsdale, Arizona 85254 USA • Tel: 480-951-1177 • Fax: 480-951-1216
Toll Free: **1-800-255-1000** • www.isecard.com • info@isecard.com

Buy your Eurail Pass from ISE
Get your ISE Card FREE

The ISE Card can save you hundreds of dollars at thousands of locations throughout Europe, North America, Egypt, Africa and Australia.

- All Major Credit Cards Accepted
- All Handling Fees Waived
- Free Eurail Timetable
- Free Eurail Guide and Map

CALL TOLL FREE: 800-255-1000

Tel: 480-951-1177 • Fax: 480-951-1216 • http://www.isecard.com

One SimCard
www.onesimcard.com

International Mobile/
Phone Solutions

75-90% Savings on Global Cell Phone Service

OneSimCard.com - Simple, reliable, low-cost mobile phone service for over 170 countries

OneSIMcard

- Single SIM and Phone Number for over 170 countries
- Extra US, Canada or UK phone number
- Free incoming calls in over 60 countries
- Receive Free SMS messages anywhere
- Send Free SMS to OneSimCard phone by email
- No Contract, No monthly chargers
- Internet Access on the mobile phone in over 70 countries

Buy or Rent
ready-to-go Mobile Phone
or buy just a SIM Card

www.onesimcard.com
phone: *1-617-489-5952*
Get additional discount by using coupon LETSGO2010

Hostels🏠.com

Every Hostel, Everywhere!

- Largest Selection of Hostels on the Web
- Over 28,000 Hostels Across the Globe
- No Booking Fees
- Travel Features & Guides
- Hostel Forums, Blogs & More on...

www.hostels.com

www.hostels.com

pass: the **Iron Gates,** an opening 3m across flanked by 300m-high walls. In Agia Roumeli, the path begins behind Hotel Livikon at the rear of the village.

If you get an early start, the soft morning light lends the park a surreal, lunar feel. It's always smart to bring water, trail snacks, and supportive shoes with good treads. One small water bottle will suffice; potable water sources line the trail. There are enforced rules concerning littering, so make sure to dispose of your trash in one of the bins along the trail. The gorge is dry and dusty in summer, and worn stones on the path are very slippery. If you get tired, look for **donkey taxis** that wait to pick up weary travelers at sporadic rest stations. Be sure to bring enough cash to get to the gorge and home again; there are no banks or ATMs on either end.

CHORA SFAKION
Χώρα Σφακίων   ☎ 28250

The tiny port town of Chora Sfakion, often simply called Sfakion, serves as the southern coast's transportation hub. Its quiet streets and arbor-covered tavernas are a common resting spot after the Samaria Gorge hike, and its location makes it a convenient base for daytrips to the area's smaller gorges and lovely beaches.

▣ TRANSPORTATION. From the bus stop and down the hill, the road leads left to the ferry dock and right to the town's single harborfront road. **Buses** (☎28210 91 288) leave for Chania (2hr., 3 per day, €6.80), dropping off passengers bound for Iraklion (3hr., €12) and Rethymno (2hr., €6.50) at Vrises. Buses leave Vrises for Rethymno and Iraklion every hour. After a day of hiking and swimming at Agia Roumeli or Loutro, don't worry if your ferry is late—the buses wait for the boats to arrive. **Ferries** from Chora Sfakion go to Agia Roumeli (1hr., 3-4 per day, €8). From April to October, most routes stop in Loutro. To get to Loutro in the winter, go by foot or boat taxi. **Boats** also run 2-3 days a week to Gavdos, a sparsely populated island that is the southernmost point in Europe (2hr., F and Su 11:30am and 2:30pm, €12.50). At the ferry office, inquire about daily **fishing boats** to Sweetwater beach (€6), between Chora Sfakion and Loutro. Secluded in a cove beneath the mountains, it is named for the spring water that bubbles up through the limestone

FROM THE ROAD

RETURN TO SFAKIA

I first went to the small town o Sfakia on my third day in Greece I fell in love with the beautifu coastline and the way the town had absorbed tourism, but wasn' defined by it. I stayed two days which was too short according to the visitors I encountered—a Bri who had been visiting for three weeks every year for the last 20 years and a South African couple who came every other year.

At first I was confused by what could possibly occupy them for such long periods of time in such a small town surrounded by cliffs and gorges, but soon I realized that they had gotten to know everyone in the town. In fact, everyone in Sfakia knows everyone else, and the locals make an effort to welcome every one, no matter how brief your stay.

I had met some locals there who had been urging me to come back ever since I left, so when I had some extra time before leaving Crete, I made my way back to Sfakia.

My newfound friends and I spent the day exploring the neigh boring town of Loutro, eating unbe lievably fresh seafood, hiking back to Sfakia on the edge of the cliffs and scuba diving. Everywhere we went, they introduced me to thei friends—the hotel and restauran owners—and by the end, I had found my own network of friends in this small town. This type of inter action had surpassed hospitality to a kind of integration; I had found my own group of friends to return to—maybe for the next 20 years.

—Ansley Rubinstein

below. Ferry schedules change often and unpredictably, so you may want to check with the **ticket office** (☎28250 91 221) once you arrive.

⁊ PRACTICAL INFORMATION. The **ATM** is to your right at the beginning of the harbor road. The **police station** (☎91 205) is about 1km up the road away from the harbor in the village. Kenzo Cafe has **internet** (€2 per hr.). The **post office** is to your right when walking down the hill from the bus station. **Postal Code:** 73011.

⁊⁊ ACCOMMODATIONS AND FOOD. Hotel owners in Chora Sfakion know that their town is a convenient rest stop for hikers, and they charge accordingly. Sequestered behind a thick arbor and shaded stone archways, grotto-like **◪Hotel Xenia ❸**, on the harbor road at the far end from the ferry landing, has refreshing, spacious rooms with air-conditioning, fridges, TVs, phones, and balconies on the shoreline. The stairs behind the parking lot lead to private deck chairs overlooking the water. (☎28250 91 490. Breakfast €4. Check-out noon. Doubles €35; triples from €40.) Following the right fork of the harbor road uphill past the bakery leads to **Stavris ❶**, where the friendly owners rent clean rooms, each with bath, balcony, and a great view of the western coastline. (☎28250 91 220. A/C €4. Singles €20-22; doubles €22-25; triples €25-35.) Catch a bite to eat and a charming seaside view at one of the many tavernas which line the harbor road. For snacks, drinks, and other goods, there is a **mini market** on the harbor road and a **bakery** with cookies, breads, and other pastries. **Lefka Ori ❶**, near the end of the harbor road next to Hotel Xenia, serves hearty food and Sfakion specialties. (☎28240 91 209. Stuffed aubergine with onions, tomatoes, and feta €4.50. Open daily 8am-11pm.)

⁊ HIKING. Although the town of Chora Sfakion itself doesn't have much in the way of sights, there's lots of good walking in the area. An 8km hike through the historic footsteps of former British and Cretan evacuees during World War II will bring you to the coastal town of **Komitades,** where you can catch the daily bus back to Chora Sfakion. Ask to be dropped off at Imbros Gorge by one of the buses to Chania. At **Aredana Gorge,** after strapping on your hiking boots, you can cross the vertigo-inducing **Bailey Bridge** to visit the abandoned traditional Cretan village of **Aredana.** Descend the challenging, worn mule track to trek the gorge to its outlet at **Marmara beach** (2hr.), from which you can walk 2km along to the coast to Loutro and catch a ferry (20min., 3 per day, €4) back to Sfakion. For more information about the hikes and bus availability, visit www.westcrete.com. Also, for recommended hikes, inquire at **Lefka Ori** (p. 476) about their book of walks in the area, with corresponding maps, directions, and estimated hours. The book points out nine hikes in all, each of increasing difficulty and taking in the sights to the east or west of Sfakion.

RETHYMNO PREFECTURE

Even though western Crete has struggled for years to maintain its identity amid surging tourism, Rethymno has met success where its neighbor Iraklion has failed. Each town in the area manages to maintain a sense of local authenticity and fill only short sections of the shore with tavernas, leaving long stretches to the birds, waves, and hikers. The melding of Ottoman, Venetian, and Greek architecture complements the blue waters of the southwestern coast and the rich, dark mountains and deep canyons of the interior.

CRETE

CRETE

RETHYMNO Ρέθυμνο ☎ 28310

Rethymno is one of the most picturesque cities on the island of Crete, with an old Venetian Harbor and lighthouse that is slightly smaller than Chania's, farther west down the Cretan coastline. While the New Town sprawls somewhat randomly, the Old Town contains a mix of Venetian, Ottoman, and Greek architecture that gives the city its unique character and skyline. The town also has its own beach, although much of the waterfront is currently being repaved and modernized, as are many other areas and restaurants in town.

⌨ TRANSPORTATION

Flights: Olympic Airlines, Koumoundourou 5 (☎28310 22 257), opposite the public gardens. Open M-F 8am-3:45pm.

Ferries: To **Piraeus** (2-3 per day in the evening, €30-36). Tickets for sale at any travel office.

Buses: Rethymno-Chania Station (☎28310 22 212), overlooking the water off I. Gavriil. To: **Agia Galini** (1½hr., 3-4 per day, €5.60); **Arkadi Monastery** (1hr., 2-3 per day, €2.50); **Chania** (1hr., 17 per day 6:15am-10:30pm, €6); **Iraklion** (1½hr., 18 per day 6:30am-10:15pm, €6.30); **Plakias** (45min., 4-5 per day, €4.10).

Taxis: ☎28310 22 316 or 24 316 or 28 316. Queues form at Pl. Martiron 4, Pl. Iroon, and the Public Gardens. 24hr.

☀ 🔢 ORIENTATION AND PRACTICAL INFORMATION

Plateia Martiron is between the **Old City** to the north and the **New City** to the south. To get to the *plateia* from the bus station, climb the stairs at the back of the station's parking lot onto **Igoumenou Gavriil** and go left; Pl. Martiron is to your left just after the **public gardens.** The **waterfront** lies at the north end of the Old City, with a maze of ancient streets filling the space between the main thoroughfare of I. Gavriil and the water. The **Venetian Fortezza** overlooks the waterfront, and a beach meets the city's eastern edge.

Tourist Office: (☎28310 29 148; www.rethymnon.gr), at the far eastern end of the water-front on El. Venizelou. Pick up free town maps, bus and ferry schedules, and info on rooms, restaurants, and Rethymno Prefecture. Open M-F 8:30am-8:30pm, Sa-Su 9am-8:30pm.

Banks: Numerous banks with **24hr. ATMs** line Koundouriotou to the east of the public gardens.

Luggage Storage: At the bus station. €1.50 per day.

Bookstores: Ilias Spontidaki, Souliou 43 (☎28310 54 307), buys and sells new and used books. Open daily 9am-11pm. **NewsStand** (☎28310 25 110), in Pl. Iroön carries a wide selection of English books, travel guides, and foreign magazines and newspapers. Open daily 9am-midnight.

Laundromat: Tombazi 45 (☎28310 29 722). Wash and dry €10. Open daily 9am-2pm and 6-9pm.

Public Toilets: On the corner of the Public Gardens closest to Pl. Martiron.

Police: ☎100. In Pl. Iroön Polytechniou. Open 24hr. **Tourist police** (☎28310 28 156), in the same building as the tourist office. Open daily 7am-2:30pm.

Pharmacy: Over 35 pharmacies dot the city, each marked by a green cross. Every pharmacy lists the 24hr. pharmacy rotating schedule.

Hospital: Rethymno Hospital, Trandalidou 17 (☎28310 27 491). From I. Gavriil at the bus station, take a right on Kriari and turn left onto Trandalidou. Open 24hr.

Telephones: OTE, Koundouriotou 26 (☎28310 59 500). Open M and W 7:30am-3pm, Tu and Th-F 7:30am-9pm, Sa 9am-3pm.

Internet: Game Net Cafe, Koundouriotou 8, in Pl. Martiron. The best rates in town at €2.50 per hr., €1.50 after midnight. Open 24 hrs. **Cafe Galero** (☎28310 54 345), at the Rimondi Fountain. €3 per hr. Open daily 6am-1am. MC/V. There are also a number of cafes on Pl. Plastira with free Wi-Fi on personal computers with any purchase.

Post Office: Moatsou 19 (☎28310 22 302). From the OTE, walk down G. Hatzidaki into the New City. **Western Union** available M-F 7:30am-8pm. Open M-F 7:30am-7pm. **Postal Code:** 74100.

🏠 ACCOMMODATIONS

Picturesque streets near the fortress and the Venetian port offer ideally located but expensive hotels and domatia. It is difficult to find both low prices and a good location in the Old Town, and there are not nearly as many pension options as in nearby Chania.

🛏 **Olga's Pension,** Souliou 57 (☎28310 53 206), off Antistasis. Navigate through potted plants and knick-knacks to find 9 oddly shaped rooms with earthy decorations and colorful wallpaper. Owners George and Stella immediately feel like old friends. Each room has a ceiling fan, TV, A/C, and fridge; some have bath or balcony. For an additional €5, enjoy Stella's delicious cooking either downstairs at **Stella's Kitchen** or on the rooftop garden. Singles €25-35; doubles €35-45; triples €50. ❷

CRETE

Atelier, Himaras 27 (☎28310 24 440; atelier@ret.forthnet.gr), above the Frosso Bora pottery workshop. Clean and spacious rooms with private bathrooms, kichenettes, and stone walls. Some offer a quiet balcony with great views of the city and a small table and chairs behind an ivy-covered iron railing. Doubles €35-45; triples €45-50. ❷

Youth Hostel, Tombazi 41-43 (☎28310 22 848; www.yhrethymno.com). From the bus station, walk down I. Gavriil and take the 1st left at Pl. Martiron through the Porta Megali; Tombazi is the 2nd right. Basic dorm rooms, gardens, and an outdoor courtyard. Game room with cards and books. Safe at reception. Sheets €1. Blankets free. Wi-Fi €5 per day. Reception July-Aug. 8am-noon and 5-9pm. Check-out 10:30am. Dorms €10 per night, €60 per week. ❶

Hotel Leo, Vafe 2 (☎28310 26 197), off Souliou. Decorated with wood floors, high windows, antique lamps, and white stucco in a 650-year-old building. Rooms with bath and quiet atmosphere. The stone paneling, archways, and fireplaces make every room its own Venetian fortress with A/C, flatscreen TVs, and kitchenettes. Breakfast included. Singles €80; doubles €90; triples €115. MC/V. ❺

🔲 FOOD

An **open-air market** on El. Venizelou by the New Town marina opens Thursdays at 7am and closes around 2:30pm—perfect for creating your own meal of fruits, breads, and olives. A number of restaurants with outdoor seating and great atmosphere line the alleyways of the Old Town, ranging widely in price. Look for restaurants that offer meals for two to get better value. For affordable nighttime eats, tourists and locals head to **Plateia Titou Petichaki.**

Lemonokipos, Antistasis 100 (☎28310 57 087). This atmospheric eatery offers candlelit dining under a lemon tree canopy, in the shadow of a minaret. The friendly waiters are eager to make conversation (and later give you wine on the house). Kleftiko (oven-baked lamb with potatoes and herbs; €11.30) and stuffed tomatoes and peppers (€6.70) are tasty entrees. For smaller bites, try the stuffed vine leaves (€4.70). Complimentary gelato for dessert. Open daily 10am-midnight. MC/V. ❷

Ovelisterio, Arkadiou 70 (☎28310 55 249), on the corner of Arkadiou and Varda Kallergi. Look for the round wooden entrance and a sign that says "O Nikos." Delicious gyro or souvlaki pitas (€2) or gyros plates (€5). Open daily 10am-midnight. ❶

DiPorto, Vafe 7 (☎28310 26 800), across from Hotel Leo. This alleyway nook is a welcome lull from the bustle of shopkeepers and tourists around the corner on Souliou. Romantic candlelit tables, hearty portions, and a bougainvillea trellis. Moussaka €6. Schnitzel €6.50. Open daily 11am-midnight. ❷

Katerina's, Melissinou 34 (☎28310 57 024). Flavored *raki* and bright blue outdoor seating beneath the Fortezza and off the city's main thoroughfares. For good value, consider one of the many 2-person meal combinations, such as moussaka, Greek salad, *tzatziki*, wine, and coffee all for €16. Open daily 10am-11pm. ❷

👁️🔲 SIGHTS AND BEACHES

Options are limited for beach-lovers in Rethymno. For those determined to enjoy prime sunbathing hours, however, avoid the somewhat gritty stretch nearest the Old Town and walk east 10min. past Pl. Iroon to reach **Ikarus Beach,** an unremarkable but well-populated strip of fine sand and gentle waves.

VENETIAN FORTEZZA. The sprawling 🔲**Venetian Fortezza,** a fortress whose foundation was laid in 1573, is the high point of the city and commands magnificent views of the coast and surrounding towns. Exploring the series of caves, churches, and crumbling facades that make up the ruins can entertain visitors for half an hour or half a day. Some choose to bring a picnic and dine overlooking the water and the city. (☎ 28310 23 653. Open daily 8:30am-7pm. Last entry 6:45pm. €4, family €10, ages 65 and over €3, students with ID and those with disabilities free).

ARCHAEOLOGICAL MUSEUM. Rethymno's Archaeological Museum occupies a former Ottoman prison adjacent to the *fortrezza*. In a single, large room, the collection contains an eclectic mix of knives, coins, lamps, sarcophagi, helmets, bone tools, and statues from Neolithic to Classical times. (☎ 28310 54 668. Open Tu-Su 8:30am-3pm. €3, students and seniors €2, EU students and under 12 free.)

HISTORICAL FOLK-ART MUSEUM. The small but creatively displayed Historical Folk-Art Museum, showcases artifacts of Cretan social history and traditional trade workshops such as weaponry, basket weaving, and embroidery. (Vernardou 28-30. ☎ 28310 23 398. Open M-Sa 9:30am-2:15pm. €4, students €2.)

L. KANAKAKIS MUNICIPAL GALLERY OF CONTEMPORARY ART. The L. Kanakakis Municipal Gallery of Contemporary Art displays 19th- and 20th-century Greek art and hosts temporary exhibits in twin galleries across from each other in the Old City. (Himaras 5, at the corner of Salaminos. Open M-F 10am-2pm and 7-10pm, Sa-Su 11am-3pm. €3, students €1.50.)

PUBLIC GARDENS. On the corner of Pl. Martiron, the public gardens are a much-needed oasis of shade in the scorching Greek sun. Tall, exotic trees line shady paths toward the central fountain surrounded by flowers. Spotty but diverse flora is scattered between the walkways. Midday, you will see many people relaxing on benches reading the newspaper or taking a stroll beneath the leafy canopies.

OTHER SIGHTS. Rethymno's Ottoman monuments are unfortunately tattooed with graffiti and in a state of forlorn disarray. The prominent **Neratzes Minaret** on Antistasis, however, is currently being refurbished. Also struggling for space in the modern city's streets are the **Nerdjes Mosque,** a former Franciscan church located a block away on Fragkiskou 1 and called "St. Francis" on many maps; the **Kara Pasha Mosque** on Arkadiou near Pl. Iroön; and the **Valides Minaret,** which presides over the gate called "Porta Megali" at Pl. Martiron (if you're having trouble finding it, look up). Small but impressive, the Corinthian columns and stone lion heads of the **Rimondi Fountain** are accented by soft lights among the alleyways and outdoor restaurants in the Old Town.

▨ ◖ FESTIVALS AND NIGHTLIFE

Rethymno's **Wine Festival** at the end of July is a crowded, all-you-can-drink celebration, with a local dance troupe performance each evening. The city's **Renaissance Festival,** featuring theater, concerts, and exhibitions, is held in the fortezza's theater in July and August. The attractions of Rethymno's **February Carnival** include a parade, a masked ball, and a treasure hunt. Call the tourist office for information.

The bar scene in Rethymno centers on **Ioulias Petichaki, Nearchou,** and **Plateia Plasteira** past the Old Venetian Harbor, with trendy outdoor seating and loud pink and purple accented interiors. Along the beach waterfront **Eleftheriou Venizelou** has a few more low-key bars, also with outdoor seating, scattered among the waterfront restaurants that have closed their doors in the late hours.

Living Room, El. Venizelou 5 (☎ 28310 51 462). Silver metallic "living room" lamps and cozy clusters of couches. Filled with groups of young Greeks and tourists alike. "Angel's Love" (Kahlua, Bailey's, milk, and fresh banana juice) €7.50. Open daily 10:30pm-late.

Karma Cafe, Plastira 2 (☎28310 57 564). Popular mostly with 20-something Greeks. Fills its waterfront lounge seating quickly, leaving later arrivals to peer out from the pop-thumping, trendy interior. Open daily 10am-late.

🔁 DAYTRIPS FROM RETHYMNO

🔳ARKADI MONASTERY (Μονή Αρκαδή). The site of one of the most famous battles in the War of Independence, Arkadi Monastery became an incendiary symbol to accompany the rallying motto "Freedom or Death!" Greeks refer to the event that took place here as the Holocaust of 1866. In November of that year, Greeks and Turks fought a two-day standoff at the monastery, where Greek villagers had gathered to seek refuge from over 2000 Turkish soldiers. When Greek defenses gave way, the monks and guerrilla fighters holding out in the monastery set off their own ammunition supply, obliterating the outer complex and sacrificing themselves to kill hundreds of Turks. A bust commemorates the sole survivor, a young girl who lived to tell the tale. A few monks maintain what is left of the monastery today: the imposing church and the outer complex, a roofless chamber where the ammunition was set off. A small **museum** contains 300-year-old Bibles and a portion of the church's original decoration, including Byzantine paintings and Orthodox vestments. Despite its abandoned state, Arkadi is a stunning example of 15th-century Cretan architecture, and a stroll through the rose-lined gardens and dilapidated rooms gives a powerful sense of the site's historical significance. The small, unmarked building across from the parking lot houses over 60 of the recovered skulls of the freedom fighters—a grisly testament to the monastery's explosive end. *(Take the bus from Rethymno (45min.; 3-4 per day, return trips 30min. after arrival; €2.50). Site open daily 9am-8pm. Modest dress encouraged. €2.50. Ask for a free map at the ticket desk.)*

IRAKLION PREFECTURE

The Iraklion Prefecture has been thinking big ever since the Minoans built their gargantuan palaces here 4000 years ago. You can wander through their hulking ruins at Knossos, Phaistos, and Gortys; or, if you like your heavyweight urban centers alive and kicking, explore Iraklion, Crete's largest city.

IRAKLION Ηράκλειο ☎28102

The fifth-largest city in Greece, Iraklion is Crete's capital and primary port. The city's size is both its greatest attraction and its main drawback. Though urban grit and labyrinthine streets make the scenery less than picturesque, an influx of wealth has produced bustling shopping streets, posh cafes, and a native population with the requisite chic and urban brusqueness. While architectural aficionados will most likely find Iraklion's unplanned jumble offensive to their historical sensibilities—Venetian monuments are sandwiched between Turkish houses and two-story concrete flats—the varied buildings remind travelers of the city's impressive history. Ultimately, Iraklion is a convenient base for beginning your exploration of the island, due to its airport and proximity to well-known Knossos. However, its sprawling metropolis is hardly representative of all that Crete has to offer.

CRETE

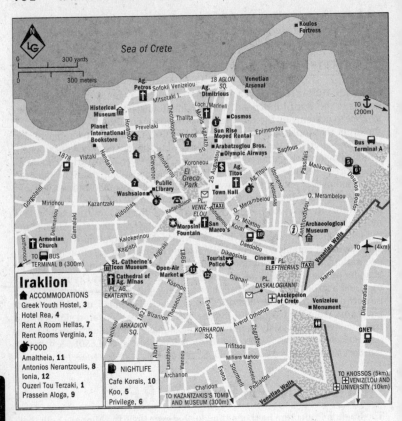

Iraklion

ACCOMMODATIONS
Greek Youth Hostel, **3**
Hotel Rea, **4**
Rent A Room Hellas, **7**
Rent Rooms Verginia, **2**

FOOD
Amaltheia, **11**
Antonios Nerantzoulis, **8**
Ionia, **12**
Ouzeri Tou Terzaki, **1**
Prassein Aloga, **9**

NIGHTLIFE
Cafe Korais, **10**
Koo, **5**
Privilege, **6**

CRETE

TRANSPORTATION

Flights: Nikos Kazantzakis Airport (**HER;** ☎ 28102 45 598). To **Athens** (50min., 5-6 per day, €75-115), **Rhodes** (1hr., 1-2 per week, €100-110), and **Thessaloniki** (1hr., 2 per day, €105-130). To get to the city, take bus #1 from the airport parking lot to Pl. Eleftherias (every 10min., €1.30). Taxis from the airport cost €8-10. Ask about flights at **Olympic Airways,** 25 Augustou 27 (☎28102 44 824; www.olympicairlines.com) and at **Aegean Airlines,** Leoforos Dymokratias 11 (☎28103 44324, www.aegeanair.com).

Ferries and Hydrofoils: The gradual phasing out of slow ferries means shorter journeys to other islands but higher ferry prices. Boat offices and travel agencies line 25 Augustou. Ferries go directly to: **Mykonos** (1 per day, €66.50); **Paros** (1 per day, €65); **Piraeus** (1 per day; around €37); **Santorini** (1-2 per day, €42). Other islands can be reached from Iraklion, but stop-overs at other islands may be required. Inquire specifically about ferry connections at the travel agency where you purchase your tickets.

Buses: Iraklion has 2 **KTEL** bus terminals (www.ktel-heraklio-lassithi.gr).

Terminal A: (☎28102 45 019), between the Old City walls and the harbor near the waterfront. Buy tickets at the ticket counter inside the bus station. Buses to: **Agios Nikolaos** (1hr., 23 per day 6:30am-9:30pm, €6.50); **Arhanes** (40min., 17 per day 6am-9pm, €1.70); **Chania** (3hr., 16 per day 5:30am-9pm, €9.50) via **Rethymno** (1hr., €6.30); **Ierapetra** (2hr., 8 per day 6:45am-7:30pm, €10); **Malia** (1hr., every 30min. 6:30am-10pm, €3.70) via **Hersonissos** (45min., €2.90); **Sitia** (3hr., 5 per day 7am-7pm, €13.80).

Terminal B: (☎28102 55 965), outside the Chania Gate of the Old City walls. Take bus #11 from Terminal A (€0.80) or walk 15min. down Kalokerinou from the town center. Buses to **Agia Galini** (2hr., 8 per day 6:30am-4:30pm, €6.50), **Matala** (2hr., 6 per day 7:30am-4:30pm, €6.20), and **Phaistos** (1hr., 10 per day, €5.10).

Taxis: Tariff Taxi of Iraklion (☎28102 10 102) or **Ikarus Radio Taxi** (☎28102 11 212). Cabs wait in Pl. Venizelou, in Pl. Eleftherias, at bus stations, by the pier, and across the fountain. 24hr.

Car and Moped Rental: Inexpensive rental agencies sit on Handakos, 25 Augustou, and in El Greco Park. Check if quoted price includes the 20% tax and insurance. **Sun Rise Car & Bike Rentals,** 25 Augustou 46 (☎28102 21 609 or 80 891) has some of the cheapest prices. Cars from €14-35 per day. Mopeds from €12-26 per day. Rates reduced for multi-day rental, and the owner is willing to bargain. Open daily 8am-8pm.

ORIENTATION AND PRACTICAL INFORMATION

The maze-like city of Iraklion has two centers. **Plateia Venizelou** (known to tourists as **Lion Fountain** or **Four Lion Square**) is home to **Morosini Fountain,** which features—surprise!—four lions; the *plateia* forms where Handakos meets Daedolou and 25 Augustou in the center of town. **Plateia Eleftherias** sits at the intersection of Doukos Boufor and Dikeosinis on the east side of the Old City and has views of the harbor. Most necessities can be found in or near these two squares. Between the two centers, a web of streets hides a network of trendy, open-air cafes and shops flashing upscale designer labels.

> **TIP** **ABC—EASY AS 123.** Many of Iraklion's street names contain numbers, like the streets 25 Augustou and 1866, for example. *Let's Go* lists the address number after the street name.

Tourist Office: Xanthoudidou 1 (☎28102 46 299), across from the entrance of the Archaeological Museum. The English-speaking staff dispenses free maps and info on both the area and other major destinations in Crete. Open M-F 8:30am-2:30pm.

Travel Agencies: Several agencies line 25 Augustou and offer daytrips and excursions around Crete (€30-50). You can also buy ferry and flight tickets and rent cars.

Banks: Banks on 25 Augustou have **24hr. ATMs** and **currency exchange.**

Bookstore: Planet International Bookstore, Handakos 73 (☎28102 89 605). 3 floors of books in several languages, with a broad selection of classics and travel literature. Open M, W, Sa 8:30am-2pm; T and Th-F 8:30am-2pm and 5:30-9pm.

Laundromat: WashSalon, Handakos 18 (☎28102 80 858). Wash and dry €7. **Luggage storage** €3 per bag per day. Open M-F 9am-9pm, Sa 9am-7pm.

Police: Pl. Venizelou 29, in a blue building among the cafes. Turn away from the fountain with your back to San Marco Church; it will be on your left. 1 station serves the east side of town (☎28102 82 243) and another in the same building serves the west side (☎28102 47 758). Open 24hr. **Tourist Police,** Dikeosinis 10 (☎28102 83 190), 1 block from the intersection with 25 Augustou, between Dikeosinis and Giannari. Open daily 7am-10pm.

Medical Services: University Hospital (☎28103 92 111). Take bus #11 for 20min. from anywhere along Kalokerinou or from Pl. Eleftherias. **Medical Crete,** Pl. Eleftherias 712 (☎28103 42 500), on the 2nd fl. of a large building on the southern side of Pl. Eleftherias. Both open 24hr.

CRETE

Telephones: OTE, Minotavrou 10 (☎28103 95 205), on the far side of El Greco Park as you enter from 25 Augustou. Open M-F 8am-2pm and 5-10pm.

Internet Access: Tunnel Internet Cafe, Ag. Titou and Milatou 1 (☎28103 90 011). €2 per hr. Open 10am-late. **Gallery Games Net,** Korai 14 (☎28102 82 804), around the corner from the cinema at Pl. Eleftherias and down 1 block on Korai. €1.50 per hr., €5 per 7hr. Open daily 10am-4am.

Post Office: The main office, in Pl. Daskalogianni, offers all major services. Open M-F 7:30am-8pm, Sa 7:30am-2pm. The tiny branch in El Greco Park only offers mailing service. Open M-F 9am-9pm. **Postal Code:** 71001.

ACCOMMODATIONS

Most of the cheap hotels and hostels in Iraklion cluster near **Handakos** at the center of town, though good budget options are becoming more and more difficult to find. Below are some of the best deals you will find in the city, geared mostly toward backpackers. If cheap beds are scarce or you're in the mood to upgrade, there are a number of mid-range hotels scattered around the city and closer to the waterfront.

Hellas Rent Rooms, Handakos 24 (☎28102 88 851), 2 blocks from Pl. Venizelou. The best budget option in town. Simple, medium-sized dorm rooms with sinks, ceiling fans, and small balconies. Helpful staff provides city maps and any directions you require. Casual rooftop restaurant with a panoramic view of Iraklion. Breakfast €3.30-5 from 6:30am. Free luggage storage. Check-out 11am. Quiet hours after 11pm. Dorms €12; doubles €29; triples €40. Cash only. ❶

Hotel Rea, Kalimeraki 1 (☎28102 23 638; www.hotelrea.gr). From Sof. Venizelou, turn left on Horatson (right before the Historical Museum) and continue a few blocks until it intersects Kalimeraki on the left. Airy, clean rooms sandwiched between a concrete jungle of local residences. Run by hospitable, English-speaking owners. Rooms with common or private bath, fans, and sinks. Free luggage storage. Reception 7am-midnight. Doubles €28-40; triples €39-50; quads €48-60. Cash only. ❷

Greek Youth Hostel, Vironos 5 (☎28102 86 281), 1 block from El Greco Park, off 25 Augustou. Clean, spare, well-located dorm rooms. Common room with TV and small restaurant area. Breakfast from €3. Luggage storage €3 per day for guests, €5 per day otherwise. Reception 8am-noon. Dorms €10. Cash only. ❶

FOOD

The ritzy cafes around **Morosini Fountain,** near El Greco Park, and in **Plateia Venizelou** cater to lounging tourists and modish locals looking to beat the heat in the presence of the similarly chic. Souvlaki, gyro, crepe, and hamburger joints are scattered along **25 Augustou** and around **Plateia Daskalogianni.** Bargain-seekers should take a left off 1866, one block from the *plateia,* to reach tiny **Theodosaki,** where there are a number of bustling *tavernas.* The best-tasting show in town is the **open-air market** on 1866, starting near Pl. Venizelou. Stalls piled with sweets, spices, produce, cheeses, meat, and Cretan muscle shirts line both sides of the narrow street. (Typically open M-Sa 9am-5pm; hours vary by stall.) In the market, about halfway down 1866 on your right (coming from the fountain), **Amaltheia,** named after the goat that nursed Zeus, has actual cauldrons of yogurt. The store also sells local cheeses including a Cretan gruyère, and the owner will give you samples to help you decide. (Cheese €3-10 per kg.)

Toili, Tsikritzi 4 (☎28102 85 988). Open since 1865, this tiny bakery dishes out mounds of flaky morning sweets and fluffy breads to salivating customers. Cookies, almond bread, and chocolate croissants are all favorites. Pastries around €1.80. Open M-Sa 8am-2pm. Cash only. ❶

▓ **Ouzeri Tou Terzaki,** Loch. Marineli 17 (☎28102 21 444), behind Agios Dimitrios chapel, off Vyronos. A sophisticated, modern *ouzeri* serving organic food at outdoor tables. Do not miss the large portion of moussaka (€7), served steaming and smothered with cheese. Open M-Sa 12:30pm-midnight. MC/V. ❷

Ladadika, Tsikritzi 5 (☎28102 46 135), across from the bakery. A bustling eatery that serves traditional Cretan fare made with local olive oil and vegetables. *Aubergines saganaki* (eggplant with fried cheese) €4.60. Open daily 10am-midnight. MC/V. ❶

Prassein Aloga, Kidonias 21 (☎28102 83 429; www.prassein-aloga.gr), between Wash-Salon and Planet Bookstore. Sample fresh Mediterranean fare in the tree-lined outdoor seating area or the more softly lit interior. *Dakos,* a Cretan appetizer of shredded feta and tomatoes on dark bread (€3.80), is popular. Risotto with seafood €10. Open M-Sa noon-midnight. MC/V. ❷

⊙ SIGHTS

While many people simply use Iraklion as a base to take daytrips and see other parts of the island, if you have some extra time, there are a few sights and museums in the city itself worth exploring.

IRAKLION ARCHAEOLOGICAL MUSEUM. After Knossos, Iraklion's main attraction is its Archaeological Museum. When the full museum is open, it presents a comprehensive, chronologically organized record of the Neolithic and Minoan stages of Crete's history. Even as the museum undergoes renovations, a visit to Knossos or another Minoan palace on the island is incomplete without seeing the museum's inventory of artifacts excavated from the sites, particularly the original Knossos frescoes.

The cryptic **Phaistos disc** is the most celebrated discovery from the palace of Phaistos (p. 491). It has 214 pictographs etched into the solid clay disc, arranged in a spiral running form the circumference to the center. The symbols include human limbs, birds, boats, tools, animals, and vases, and the intricate impressions suggest that they were made with metal stamps, an ancient form of printing. To this day, scholars have been unable to decipher the symbols, but hypothesize that they represent a ritual hymn or astrological chart.

Two **snake goddesses** clad in layered skirts balance cats on their heads and support flailing serpents on each outstretched arm. The **bull-head rhyton,** a kind of libation vase, sports a white moustache and red eyes made of painted rock crystal. Scholars speculate that the sacred liquid used as paint may have been blood from a sacrificial bull. The ivory and gold **bull-leaper figurine** features a contorted acrobat, probably engaging in a Minoan ritual. The gold **bee pendant** from Chryssolakkos at Malia is composed of two bees placing a drop of honey in a honeycomb they hold between their legs; it is a masterpiece of Minoan goldwork, using filigree and granulate decoration of the most intricate detail.

The **Minoan Frescoes** exhibit features the original wall paintings found at Knossos—replicas adorn the reconstructed palace. Depicting ancient Minoan life, the frescoes show ladies offering drinks, blue monkeys frolicking in palatial gardens, and Minoans in procession. The famous **Toreador Fresco,** with images of the gutsy Minoan sport of bull jumping, is a particular gem of the collection. The original excavator of Knossos, Sir Arthur Evans, didn't spare these priceless finds from his revisionist hand; in restoring the frescoes, he added his own ideas about the original compositions. So before you get too excited about the explosive colors and ancient themes, check out the restoration work up close;

CRETE

you will see that the frescoes were reconstructed from very small original pieces, leaving room for Evans's imagination. Subsequent study of the **Prince of Lilies** fresco, for example, has revealed that the fragments actually depicted three figures—a priestess in a lily crown and two boxers flanking her—rather than the visible one. *(The permanent exhibit, Xanthoudidou 1, off Pl. Eleftherias, has been withdrawn since 2006 for renovation of the main building. In the meantime, a temporary exhibit next door (follow the signs) displays a selection of some of the museum's most notable items. ☎ 28102 42 655. Open M 1:30-8pm, Tu-Su 8am-8pm. €4, students and EU seniors €2. Dual ticket for Archaeological Museum and Knossos €10, reduced €5.)*

VENETIAN IRAKLION. As you wander around the city, take in the various Venetian monuments such as **Morosini Fountain,** the centerpiece of Pl. Venizelou, with four lions around the center. The reconstructed **Venetian Loggia** nearby is now a town hall, and the 17th-century **Venetian Arsenal** is off Sofokli Venizelou near the waterfront. Most impressive is the **▓Koules Fortress** guarding the old harbor. The fortress provides Iraklion's only seaside access, so head here if the city's left you itching for some fresh sea air. For another peaceful, calming walk, meander along the olive trees lining the southeastern section of the **Venetian walls,** though the cityscape along the way isn't particularly picturesque.

CHURCHES. Several majestic, ancient churches hide on Iraklion's winding streets. Though some are still places of worship, others have—or have had—an intriguing variety of uses. The impressive **Agios Titos Church,** on 25 Augustou, once served as a mosque, so its architecture combines Islamic geometric designs with Christian regalia. Lit up every night, it glows a surreal green. Built in 1735, the **Cathedral of Agios Minas** graces Pl. Agia Ekaternis. Inside, look up to view impressive multicolored paintings of Gospel scenes and an intricate gold chandelier. **Saint Catherine's Church of Sinai,** located slightly behind the Cathedral of Agios Minas, served as the first Greek university after the fall of Constantinople in 1453 and today houses the **Icon Museum.** The more modest **Metropolitan Church of Agios Minas** stands under the shade in the corner of Pl. Agia Ekaternis, hosting local baptisms and services in its pious, glitzy interior. In Pl. Venizelou, the **Basilica of Saint Marcos,** built in 1239, hosts a rotating exhibition space that displays everything from 14th-century monastery frescoes to modern art as the city's Municipal Gallery. *(Modest dress required. Free.)*

HISTORICAL MUSEUM OF CRETE. The impressive collection at Iraklion's Historical Museum is housed in a modern building with spectacular views over the harbor. The four floors of exhibits and artifacts include a scale model of the city, the only two El Greco paintings in Crete, Byzantine and medieval Cretan artwork, and stone coats of arms from the period of Venetian Rule. There is an extensive exhibit on author Nikos Kazantzakis, including a recreation of his study and library using original furnishings and his personal effects. The **Kazantzakis Exhibit** also uses fascinating interactive media displays and visual art, which can give great insight into the author's life and also pass many hours of your day. Finally, the top floor houses the museum's folk collection. *(Sofokli Venizelou 27/Kalokerinou 7, at Grevenon overlooking the harbor. ☎ 28102 83 219; www.historical-museum.gr. Open M-Sa 9am-5pm. Wheelchair-accessible. €5, students €3, under 12 free.)*

KAZANTZAKIS TOMB. With magnificent views of Iraklion, the sea, and Mt. Ida, the Tomb of Nikos Kazantzakis offers a peaceful break from crowded Iraklion. Though some say that church authorities exiled the author of *Zorba the Greek* and *The Last Temptation of Christ* to this hilltop for his unorthodox views, the literary giant and native Cretan actually picked the spot himself. The stunning view it affords provides the perfect location from which to watch the sun descend spectacularly behind the mountains to the west. Surrounded by magenta bougainvillea, Kazantzakis's grave is marked by a wooden cross and an epitaph drawn from his own work reading, "I hope for nothing, I fear nothing, I am free." *(Walking away from Pl. Venizelou and the Morosini Fountain (the opposite direction of the ocean), head down Evans until you reach the Venetian walls. Do not pass through the walls, but turn right onto Nikolaou Pastira, the street that runs along the inside of the walls. Keep walking until you see a ramp leading up to a stone building on the hill, which is the tomb. There are stairs and an entrance sign to the right of the tomb, after walking up the ramp.)*

◾ NIGHTLIFE

Iraklion boasts trendy, dynamic nightlife. The cafes and bars along Korai abound with a mass of under-30, sunglass-sporting, black-clad clientele. Around 11pm or midnight, the young and the restless overflow onto the small streets between Pl. Venizelou and Pl. Eleftherias. Swarms of young drinking, smoking, and chatting Greeks gather on **Androgenou** and other side-streets. As the night proceeds, these activities merge with the rhythms of techno and pop along the waterfront, which now has many newly renovated clubs and bars at its western edge.

Cafe Korais Club, Korai 3 (☎21803 46 336). Patrons observe the parade of well-dressed bar-hoppers from an expansive deck with low couches and soft lighting. Inside, the loud, undulating ceiling will make you woozy if the drinks haven't already done the trick. Mixed drinks €6-8. Open daily 10pm-late. Cafe open daily 10:30am-10pm.

Desire, Arhepiskopou Makariou 17 (☎28103 46 626). Attracts crowds to its breezy outdoor seating with stunning views of the ocean. Open daily noon-late.

Yacht Club, Doukos Boufor. Closer to the city center than Desire but with equally good views. A winter hotspot for late-night dancing, pricey drinks, and a panorama of the port. Open only in winter.

◾ DAYTRIPS FROM IRAKLION

KNOSSOS Κωσός

From Iraklion, take bus #2 from Terminal A (20min., every 10min.) or catch it at Pl. Venizelou along 25 Augustou. Buy your bus ticket at Terminal A or the news stand between Pl. Venizelou and El Greco Park (blue ticket, B-zone, €1.30). ☎28102 31 940. Open daily 8am-8pm; ticket window open daily 8am-7:35pm. €6; students and seniors €3; Classicists, EU students, fine arts students, and under 18 free. Dual ticket for Knossos and Iraklion Archaeological Museum €10, reduced €5. 1½hr. tour €10, under 12 free. Private tour €150.

Fact and fancy are woven together at Crete's most famous Minoan ruins in Knossos, a testament to ancient Minoan power. Inventor **Daedalus** and his son **Icarus** once built wax and feather wings to carry out their legendary escape from the grounds. Despite his father's warnings, giddy Icarus flew too close to the sun, which melted his wings and caused him to plunge to his death. Today, tourists flock to the palace to relish the evidence of King Minos's former glory. Although Cretans were once ridiculed for claiming Minoan roots, the British archaeologist **Sir Arthur Evans** secured the last laugh for them when his excavations from 1900-1943 confirmed the Minoans' ancient presence on the island. While other archaeological digs have unearthed similar finds at Phaistos (p. 491) and Malia (p. 489), at about 150 sq. m, Knossos is the largest and most intricate of Crete's Minoan palaces. The original palace dates back to 1700 BC, but it was partially destroyed by a fire and leveled by a mysterious cataclysm around 1450 BC. Knossos lay forgotten until Evans excavated the palace over 3000 years later. Ostensibly based on evidence he had recovered, Evans disastrously tried to restore the palace. Walls, window casements, stairways, and

CRETE

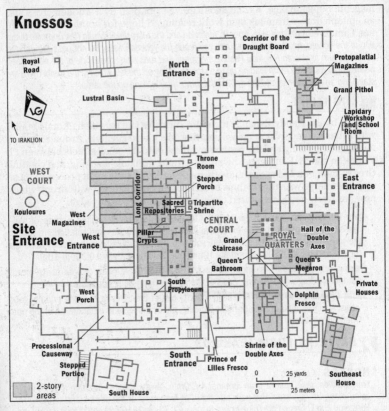

Knossos

Royal Road

TO IRAKLION

North Entrance

Lustral Basin

Corridor of the Draught Board

Protopalatial Magazines

Grand Pithoi

Lapidary Workshop and School Room

WEST COURT

Kouloures

Site Entrance

West Magazines

West Entrance

Long Corridor

Throne Room

Stepped Porch

Sacred Repositories

Tripartite Shrine

Pillar Crypts

CENTRAL COURT

Grand Staircase

ROYAL QUARTERS

Hall of the Double Axes

East Entrance

Queen's Bathroom

Queen's Megaron

Private Houses

West Porch

South Propylaeum

Dolphin Fresco

Processional Causeway

Stepped Portico

South Entrance

Prince of Lilies Fresco

Shrine of the Double Axes

Southeast House

South House

0   25 yards

0   25 meters

2-story areas

CRETE

columns were reconstructed in reinforced concrete, and some of the ruins were painted. Today, Evans's changes are indistinguishable from the original layout, exacerbating the controversy over whether the reconstruction is at all accurate or just a figment of Evans's design. Along with the structural alterations, copies of the magnificent frescoes have replaced the originals, which are now a must-see in the Archaeological Museum's temporary exhibit in Iraklion (p. 485). Visiting throngs and brightly painted walls can make the complex seem like a Disney-esque Minoanland, but the explanatory signs, mysterious history, and renowned frescoes make the palace Iraklion's premier attraction.

As reconstruction work continues, some of the site remains off-limits to visitors, including some of the base floors. The gaping space in the middle of the site is the **Central Court,** which was the heart of the palace and the arena for the traditional bull-leaping. In the back left corner of the court, a colonnade hides the **Throne Room,** where the original, preserved limestone seat still sits in splendor, surrounded by paintings of gryphons. A priestess—not King Minos—probably occupied this famous chair, and today visitors can rest their weary feet by relaxing in a wooden replica. A grand staircase leads down to the **Royal Quarters,** the sturdiest part of the palace. Built into the landscape's rock and situated two stories below the main court, it survived destructive earthquakes better than other quarters. The **Queen's Bathroom** where, over 3000 years ago, she took milk baths while gazing up at elaborate dolphin frescoes, still holds her luxurious bathtub. The king's quarters were in the attached **Hall of the Double Axes.** The tangled maze of the palace's layout and the omnipresent sacred symbol of the double axe, known as a *labrys*, combined to form the present-day word "labyrinth." Walking north from the royal quarters, you'll stumble across the grand **pithoi**—jars so big that, according to legend, Minos's son drowned in one filled with honey. The areas painted red around each window and door originally were made of wood; they cushioned the walls from frequent seismic shock, but ultimately facilitated the palace's destruction by fire after the mysterious disaster of 1450 B.C.

DIKTAIAN CAVE

From Iraklion, take a bus to Lasithi Plateau from Terminal A (2hr., 1 per day, €6.50), and disembark in the small town of Pyschro. From where the bus drops you on the main road, a strenuous 1km walk up winding streets and paths will lead to the cave entrance (follow the signs). Local donkey drivers will offer to taxi you up (€15, round-trip €20). Open daily 8am-7:30pm. €4, students €2. Parking €2.

This massive cave's multiple levels, irregular hanging rock formations, and mythical history as Zeus's birthplace make it the most visited site in Crete's Lasithi Plateau. The cave is hidden amid extensive orchard grounds and the remains of old windmills that once powered the plateau; it is only accessible by a somewhat strenuous uphill walk from the main road. Once inside the cave, wander along narrow staircases and walkways that lead you in a large loop throughout the cave. Some of the upper portion of the cave was destroyed in excavation, but a number of artifacts found at the entrance are now housed in Iraklion's Archeology Museum (p. 485). The lower half of the cave is the most impressive, with floor-to-ceiling stalactites and stalagmites illuminated by eerie green and yellow lights. If the climb and cave stairs exhaust you, recuperate with a glass of freshly-squeezed ▓**orange juice** at one of the *tavernas* near the parking lot, made from oranges of Lasithi's own groves (€2.50).

MALIA Μάλια

Follow the road from Iraklion east along the ocean passing through Hersonissos and turn left toward the sea when you see signs for the palace. Buses from Iraklion (every 30min. 7:15am-11pm, €1.40) via Hersonissos stop at the main road turn-off. If taking the bus to Malia, be sure to specify that you want to go to "Malia Palace" or the bus will drop you in the town of Malia, and you will be stuck walking 3km along the highway to the archaeological site. ☎ 28970 31 597. Open daily 8:30am-3pm. €4, students and seniors free.

Malia's majestic ruins remind visitors of its history as one of the three great cities of Minoan Crete. Although its **palace** lacks the labyrinthine plan of Knossos and Phaistos, it was a long-time center of Minoan power. First built in 1900 BC, the palace was destroyed around 1650 BC, rebuilt on a larger scale, then destroyed again by the mysterious cataclysm that decimated all Minoan civilization around 1450 BC. The **Hall of Pillars,** located on the northern side of the large central courtyard, supports its roof with six enormous columns. The *loggia*, a raised chamber on the western side, was used for state ceremonies; west of it are the palace's living quarters and archives. A small altar can be found in the center of the central courtyard. Northwest of the *loggia* and main site, under a shaded covering, is the **Hypostyle Crypt,** which is thought to have been a social center for Malia's educated citizens. Farther northwest, under another covering, a suspended bridge over the ruins affords visitors a bird's eye view of the portico and light well below. Signs marking the site help visitors locate each structure, although there are no helpful descriptions as at Knossos and Phaistos. Because it's less touristy, most of the palace is open to visitors. The admission fee includes entrance to a small **gallery** with three-dimensional reconstructions of the site and photographs of its excavation.

MATALA Μάταλα ☎ 28920

Free spirits who visited Matala a few decades ago might have only blurry memories—the caves along its seaside cliffs, originally used as Roman cemeteries, more recently were full of psychedelic lovers tripping to folk music. This is where Joni Mitchell admired the "Matala moon" and "met a redneck on a Grecian isle." In the years since, Matala has rapidly developed an impressive beachfront industry of shops and tavernas, exchanging countercultural liberation for beach bars, crafts markets, and hotels. Vestiges of the age of Aquarius survive in the yin-yang and peace carvings found in the regal backdrop of the sharply striated caves over the beach a well as the large graffitied motto by the water that reads, "Today is life. Tomorrow never comes."

TRANSPORTATION AND PRACTICAL INFORMATION. Buses leave Matala for Iraklion (2hrs., 3-4 per day 7am-5:30pm, €7.80), Mires (25min., 2-4 per day 7am-5:30pm, €2), and Phaistos (35min., 2-3 per day 11:30am-5:30pm, €2).

Matala's main street, where the bus stops, provides most necessities. The majority of pensions are off of the main road to the left (follow the signs). Where the main road becomes a pedestrian walk-way, the right fork closer to the water is a covered market with steps leading down to the beach. Both forks lead to a small central square, with restaurants, shops, and a bookstore.

Cretan Travelers, next to the bus stop, rents motorbikes and cars, and exchanges currency. (☎28920 45 732. Motorbikes €20 per day. Cards €30 per day. Open daily 9am-1pm and 5-10pm.) A few **24hr. ATMs** line the main street. The **laundromat** is across the street up the hill from the bus stop. (Wash €7.50. Wash and dry €10. Open M-Sa 10am-2pm.) Free **public toilets** are located at the head of the beach. The closest **police, pharmacy,** and **medical clinic** are in Mires, 17km to the northeast. In an emergency, call ☎51 111 for the Mires police and ☎28920 51 219 for the **medical center.** Hook up to the **internet** in a room labeled **Game Net,** at the fork in the main road; it is a public room with computers and has the best rates in town (€1 per 30min.). The nearest **post office** is in Mires, but you can buy stamps from any *periptero* and use the ubiquitous yellow drop boxes to mail letters. **Postal Code:** 70200.

ACCOMMODATIONS AND CAMPING. Though it may be tempting, sleeping on the beach or in the caves is illegal, and the law is strictly enforced. Instead, you can find reasonable prices in a quieter setting once you leave the main street. The owner at **Matala View Studios ❷,** 20m down the road to Red Beach on the left, rents clean, breezy rooms with bath, fridge, hot pot, and balconies with views of the plateau. (☎2892045 114; www.matala-apartments. com. Some doubles have kitchenette. A/C €5. Singles €20-25; doubles €25-30; triples €30-35. Longer stays may receive discount. Cash only.) Last along the row of flashy pensions lining the road to Red Beach, **Xenos Dias Hotel ❷** distinguishes itself with its subdued, sophisticated hospitality and large, relaxed front patio. The spacious, quiet rooms all have baths and fridges, and some have a balcony that overlooks the sea or the vineyards beneath the mountains. (☎28920 45 116. A/C and breakfast each €5. Free parking. Singles €25;

CRETE

doubles €35; triples €35-40; apartments €40-60. Cash only.) Along the pensi
lined street off the main road, **Eva Marina Hotel ❸** has rooms with balcony vie
onto the pension's colorful, Bougainvillea-filled garden. (☎28920 45 125, ww
evamarina.com. All rooms with baths and telephones. A/C €5. Breakfast €5
Singles €30-35; doubles €40-45; triples €52-58. Cash only.) **Matala Camping ❶** has
the best location in town, behind the beach at the end of the road in a wooded
grove. While this used to be an official campsite, the lot is now free and open
24hr. (No electricity. Public bathrooms and showers available.)

🍴🎵 **FOOD AND NIGHTLIFE.** There is a **supermarket** next to the parking lot
for the beach, which has drinks, foodstuffs, and toiletries. **Waves Restaurant ❷**,
on the western end of the beach, serves traditional Cretan fare at reasonable
prices. Come early to snag a table at the edge of the balcony for a panoramic,
unobstructed view of the beach and caves. (☎28920 45 361. Greek salad
€3. Moussaka €5. Grilled octopus €8. Open daily 9am-11pm. MC/V.) Head to
Notos ❶, between the waterfront and the covered market, for good souvlaki
(€2.50), delicious, greasy gyros (€2-4), and fast food. (☎28920 45 533. Open
daily 10am-midnight. Cash only.) For slightly healthier but equally cheap fare,
the **bakery ❶** next to the *plateia* sells freshly made sandwiches. (☎28920 45
450. Chicken and cheese sandwich €2.75. Coffees €2.20-4. Pastries €1.30-1.50.
Open daily 8am-midnight. Cash only.)

Evening activities tend to be low-key. Cluttered with candles and overlooking the main *plateia*, **Kantari** is a popular place to catch world music. (☎28920
45 404. Beer €3-5. Mixed drinks €6. Open daily 9am-late.) Groups of twenty-
somethings convene at **Zafiria Cafe,** on the main road, with seating indoors or
on the softly lit patio. (☎28920 45 496. Open daily 8am-late.)

📷🏖 **SIGHTS AND BEACHES.** Matala attracts visitors with three tiers of
spectacular ▧**caves** to the right of the main beach. As you sit in the dank interiors, reflect on the caves' previous visitors: Roman corpses, Nazis searching for
British submarines, and songwriter Joni Mitchell. Matala has some of Crete's
best **beaches;** the main one is the rounded cove next to the caves with pebbly
sand and aquamarine water. If you don't mind a strenuous 25min. hike, follow
the pension-lined street until you reach a magnificent strip of sand known as
Red Beach. Follow the fence to the right and go through the goatherd gate to the
shore. Cliffs surround this isolated, picturesque beach with nude bathers. Five
kilometers from Matala stretches long, pebbly **Kommos,** dotted with enclaves of
nude bathers and free from much development. Take the Matala-Iraklion bus,
ask to be let off at Kommos (€1.10), and walk 500m down to the beach. Neither
beach is shaded, leading to speculation that Red Beach may take its name from
the lobster skin tone of unprepared visitors and not from its clay-colored sand.
If you want to avoid this fate, bring plenty of sunscreen and consider renting an
umbrella and chair (€4 per day). Many of Matala's beaches are also spawning
grounds for endangered sea turtles. Environmentalists run a kiosk at the bus
stop, providing info on the turtles and their habitat; if you want to support the
cause, pick up a ▧**Save the Turtles** t-shirt (€12).

PHAISTOS Φαιστός ☎28920

Seated on a plateau with magnificent views of the mountains, the ▧**ruins** of
Phaistos are one of the finest reminders of the grandeur of Minoan palaces.
(☎28920 42 315. Open daily 8am-8pm. €4; students and EU citizens over 65
€2; classics students, EU students, and under 18 free.) The site has undergone

's more famous counterpart, Knossos, and attracts fewer
...ng the first two hours that the site is open to avoid the
...span epochs of Greek history: founded by Minos and named
...Herakles, the settlement at Phaistos contains structures from
... the Hellenistic periods. Four **palaces** have been discovered on
...first, built around 1900 BC, was destroyed by the earthquake
...ound 1700 BC. The second structure was leveled by the mysteri-
...ysm in 1450 BC; traces of two even older palaces were detected by
...vation in 1952. Since only minor reconstructive work has been done
...ghout the palace, visitors have almost unlimited access to the site and
...wander the ruins more freely than at Knossos.

Built according to the standard Minoan blueprint, the complex included
central court surrounded by royal quarters, servant quarters, storerooms,
and rooms for state occasions. Visitors enter Phaistos at the upper court of
the **Early Palace,** and immediately see the **west courtyard** and **theater** area at the
lower level on their right. Particularly impressive is the intact **grand staircase**
that leads to the foot of the regal **propylaea** on the left. The staircase, the
largest of its kind on Crete, has steps built in a slightly convex form to shed
rainwater. The *propylaea*—consisting of a landing, portico, central column,
and well—served as the ceremonial entrance to the palace. Its resemblance
to the *propylaea* of the Acropolis in Athens demonstrates the influence of
Minoan architecture on that of Classical Greece. Walk through the *propylaea*
and take the next left to reach the main hall, containing a central fenced-off
storeroom that housed the massive *pithoi*.

On the perimeter of the central court, columns and boxes mark the place
where sentries used to stand guard. The covered **royal apartments,** with a queen's
megaron, wall paintings, and a lustral basin (covered purifying pool), sit past
the entrance gate. Just beyond, in the **peristyle hall,** the remains of some of the
Minoans' signature cigar-shaped columns can be seen lining the walls. In the
opposite direction, northeast of the central court, are the halls of the **Northeast
Complex** and the seven-compartmented room where the renowned **Phaistos disc,**
now in the Archaeological Museum in Iraklion, was discovered.

Buses from Phaistos leave for Agia Galini (25min., 2-3 per day 11:40am-
3:10pm, €2); Iraklion (2hrs., 5-8 per day 9:45am-5:45pm, €7.40); Matala (20min.,
2-3 per day 9am-4:30pm, €2); Mires (15min., 6 per day 8:30am-5:30pm, €1.70).

HERSONISSOS Χερσόνησος ☎28970

With numerous bars, discos, and nightclubs around its harbor, Hersonissos
(hehr-SON-i-sos) becomes a playground for European teenagers every summer.
Go-carts, water slides, fast-food joints, and fake designer-label shops clutter
the beachfront. At night, lounging sunbathers become energetic club-hoppers
who overrun the town's many sports bars and dance clubs. Amid Hersonissos's
cosmopolitan millieu, it's easy to forget that you're in Greece at all.

TRANSPORTATION

Buses: Station office in the mall at the western perimeter of town. To: **Agios Nikolaos**
(1hr., 16-20 per day 7am-10pm, €3.70); **Ierapetra** (2hr., 8 per day 7am-8pm €7);
Iraklion (45min., every 30min. 6:45am-10pm, €2.90); **Malia** (20min., every 30min.
7am-11:30pm, €1.40); **Sitia** (2hr., 5 per day 7am-7pm, €10.70).
Taxis: (☎28970 23 723 or 28 970), by the bus stop on El. Venizelou. 24hr.

CRETE

Car Rental: Countless rental agencies line El. Venizelou. **Autotravel,** El. Venizelou 20 (☎28970 22 761. www.autotravel.gr). €35-55 per day, full insurance and tax included; reduced for multiple days. Open daily 8:30am-11pm.

Motorcycle Rental: On nearly every street. €10-30 per day.

ORIENTATION AND PRACTICAL INFORMATION

Hersonissos is 26km east of Iraklion on the north coast of Crete. The town's offices, markets, and shops are on the main road, **Eleftheriou Venizelou.** Perpendicular streets lead to either the beach or the hills. There is also a pedestrian-only walkway running along the waterfront parallel to El. Venizelou, where visitors can find numerous waterfront restaurants, bars, and dance clubs.

Travel Agencies: On nearly every block of El. Venizelou. **Serapis Travel,** El. Venizelou 141 (☎28970 24 610). Rents cars, books flights, finds and reserves accommodations, and charters daytrips all over Crete. **Currency exchange.** Open daily 10am-11pm.

Banks: Several on El. Venizelou with **currency exchange** and **24hr. ATMs,** including **Alpha Bank, Citibank,** and the **National Bank of Greece.**

Laundromat: Ilios Wash Saloon, Em. Maragaki 3 (☎28970 22 749). Look for the sign on the lamppost before the turn-off. Wash and dry €7. Open M-Sa 9am-8pm.

Police: Minos 8 (☎28970 22 100 or 22 222). Open 24hr. The **tourist police** (☎28970 21 000) are in the same building; walk toward the beach 2 blocks after the bus stop. Open 8am-2pm.

Medical Services: Cretan Medicare, El. Venizelou 19 (☎28970 25 141 or 25 143), 500m from the bus station on the way to Iraklion. Open 24hr.

Telephones: OTE, Eleftherias 11 (☎28970 22 299). Go in the direction of the mountains just before Jackpot Internet (see below) and look for the sign. Open M-F 7:30am-2:30pm, Sa 9am-3pm.

Internet: Cafes are everywhere, but the cheapest rates are at **Jackpot Internet Cafe,** El. Venizelou 30 (☎28970 22 911), 250m toward Malia past the bus stop. €2 per hr. Open daily 9am-late.

Post Office: (☎28970 22 022) on El. Venizelou, 8 blocks from the bus stop when walking toward Malia. Open M-F 7:30am-2pm. **Postal Code:** 70014.

ACCOMMODATIONS AND CAMPING

The hotels that line El. Venizelou rent rooms for €25-70. During the summer, they are overrun with loud partygoers who tend to blare music from their balconies. Tour companies book most of the rooms in town during high season, so reserve in advance if you're visiting in late July or August.

Hotel Despina, Vitsentzou Kornarou 10 (☎28970 22 966), opposite the post office. A relaxed, bright lobby and bar at the eastern end of the beach. White stucco rooms with wooden furniture include baths and balconies; some have fridges (€2 per day). A/C €5. Check-out noon. Singles €20-25; doubles €35-40; triples €50. ●

Hotel Dimitrion, El Venizelou (☎28970 23 741 or 22 220). An industrial gray hotel in the heart of town. 93 modern rooms with balconies and A/C. Bar and swimming pool downstairs. Breakfast included. Singles €20-25; doubles €30-35; triples €40-45. ●

Camping Caravan (☎28970 22 025), by the port of Hersonissos next to the Star beach water park. Walk 1km from the fork in the road along the beach at the eastern side of town toward Agios Nikolaos. Has its own taverna with billiards, pool, and mini-mart. €7 per person; 2-person bungalow €20-30. ●

❖ FOOD

On the Hersonissos waterfront, "traditional Greek food" is often code for high prices and laminated facsimile menus. Sandwich and fast-food places line the main road by the beach, while a few far calmer eateries can be found on the outskirts of town and in some alleyways off the main road.

Passage to India, Petrakis (☎28970 23 776), just off El. Venizelou, opposite the church. Delicious Indian dishes, boudoir-like drapery, and Hindi music videos. Acclaimed as some of the best Indian food in Crete. Chicken tikka masala €9.40. Open daily 2:30pm-11:30pm. ❷

Pietra Snacks, El Venizelou 98 (☎28970 22 531). Inexpensive snacks include crepes (€3-6) and souvlaki (€4). Breakfast €3.50-4.50. Open daily 8am-late. ❶

Ristorante Vesuvios (☎28970 21 474), just off El. Venizelou across from Tzatziki Grill House. An international clientele dines outdoors in an atmosphere that strives to evoke the Italian countryside. Combination meals of appetizers and entrees for groups of 2 or more. Over 50 kinds of wine. Pizza €7-11. Pasta €6.50-13. Open daily 6pm-2am. ❷

👁 SIGHTS

LYCHNOSTATIS OPEN-AIR MUSEUM A refreshing alternative to Hersonissos's bright beaches and water slides, the open-air museum recreates a thriving traditional Cretan village, complete with a windmill, herbarium, bee-house, chapel, and workshops for weaving, ceramics, and wool-dying. From late August to October, visitors can stomp on grapes, participate in traditional dance, and sample wine and *raki* at the museum's **Grape Feast.** Make sure to finish your visit with a toast with the traditional alcoholic beverage *tsikoudia* and a walk through the garden with native fruit trees, including pomegranate and fig. (*Walk down El. Venizelou toward Malia, then follow the beach road to the left at the fork in the eastern end of town; the entrance is on the left past the water park. ☎28970 23 660 or 22 021; www.lychnostatis.gr. Open Apr.-Oct. Tu-Su 9am-2pm. Excellent tours in English every hr. 10:30am-12:30pm. For info on the Grape Feast, call or pick up the information leaflet at the entrance. Partially wheelchair-accessible. €5, students €3, under 12 €2; discounts for groups.*)

🎵 NIGHTLIFE

Hersonissos's nighttime hubs typically open at dusk and close at dawn, but you'll be lonely at most of them before midnight or 1am. You can't stray a block without encountering a bar or disco; they generally charge no cover and sell beer for €2-4 and mixed drinks for €3.50-6. Many clubs also have "happy hour all night long," meaning that with the purchase of one drink, you get your second free.

Amnesia Club (☎28970 25 490; www.amnesiaclub.gr), at the western end of town; take a right off El. Venizelou onto Ag. Paraskimis. Fancy laser-light displays and thumping music let you forget where and who you are. The best dancers strut their stuff on elevated platforms, while the masses below grind to tunes spun by one of the well-known DJs. Open 10pm-late.

Status, Ag. Paraskevis 47 (☎28970 22 734; www.status-club.gr). Colored laser lights, illuminated floors, and a spiral staircase. Open 8pm-late.

Camelot Dancing Club, across from Amnesia. Shimmy to international rave music under fake torches and elaborate medieval decor. Open daily 10:30pm-late.

LASITHI PREFECTURE

The Lasithi Prefecture doesn't make a great first impression: in the heavily touristed towns on the western side, all local culture seems to be lost in a flurry of summer hedonism. The road east from Iraklion, however, eventually passes over these jam-packed, overpriced resort towns and leads to the quiet, scenic inland region. The smaller villages that line the eastern edge, sustained not by tourism but by thriving local agriculture, are spread out between olive groves and stretches of unblemished coastline. Lasithi's abundance of stunning natural sights— the palm-tree forest at Vai, the Valley of Death near Kato Zakros, and the desert island of Chrissi off the coast of Ierapetra, and more—will make you forget even the tackiest of resort towns.

AGIOS NIKOLAOS Άγιος Νικόλαος ☎28410

On a small peninsula on Crete's northeastern edge, Agios Nikolaos is a harbor resort town where vacationers spill over from Hersonissos and Malia to explore the steep, boutique-lined streets and then relax at harborside cafes. The hills lend magnificent views of the lake and the sea, and restaurants and

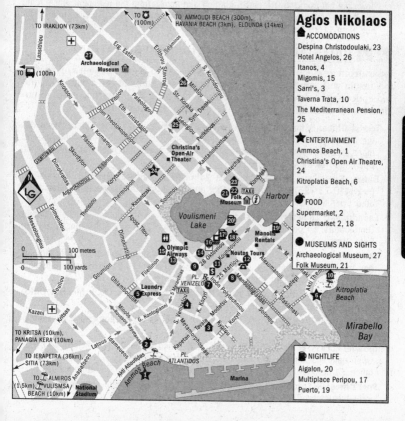

Agios Nikolaos

ACCOMODATIONS
Despina Christodoulaki, 23
Hotel Angelos, 26
Itanos, 4
Migomis, 15
Sarri's, 3
Taverna Trata, 10
The Mediterranean Pension, 25

ENTERTAINMENT
Ammos Beach, 1
Christina's Open Air Theatre, 24
Kitroplatia Beach, 6

FOOD
Supermarket, 2
Supermarket 2, 18

MUSEUMS AND SIGHTS
Archaeological Museum, 27
Folk Museum, 21

NIGHTLIFE
Aigalon, 20
Multiplace Peripou, 17
Puerto, 19

CRETE

modern cafes with outdoor seating occupy prime overlooks and waterfront positions. Although it lacks the Venetian waterfronts and lighthouses of the west-side cities, Agios Nikolaos has the best beaches on the north coast of the island, all of which have been awarded prestigious Blue Flags by the EU.

▐ TRANSPORTATION

Ferries: Since most ferry service from Agios Nikolaos ceased about two years ago, the port is now only used for ferries to the popular island **Spinalonga. Nostos Tours,** R. Koundourou 30 (☎28410 22 819) charters roundtrip excursions to the island (€17).

Buses: The station (☎28410 22 234) is just off Epimendiou, inconveniently northwest of the city center. To: **Ierapetra** (1hr., 9 per day 6:30am-9pm, €3.50); **Iraklion** (2hr., 20 per day 6:15am-8:30pm, €6.50) via **Malia** and **Hersonissos; Kritsa** (15min., 7 per day 7am-8:15pm, €1.40); **Sitia** (1hr., 6 per day 6:15am-8pm, €7.30). Buses to **Elounda** (20min., 7 per day 6am-9pm, €1.50) and **Plaka** (40min., 2 per day 6am-1pm, €1.90) leave from across from the bus station and from clearly marked stops around town.

Taxis: ☎28410 24 000 and 24 100. Wait at Pl. Venizelou and the bridge by the tourist office. 24hr.

Rentals: A number of car rental agencies are on I. Koundourou and S. Koundourou. Most rent cars for about €35-40 per day, including insurance. **Manolis** (☎69457 36 690), down the hill from the OTE on 25 Martiou and across from the telegraph office, rents mopeds (€20-30 per day, including insurance) and bikes (€10-15). Open daily July-Aug. 8am-11pm, Sept.-June 8am-9pm.

▐ ▐ ORIENTATION AND PRACTICAL INFORMATION

Apart from its steep hills, Agios Nikolaos is easy to get around—it's on a small peninsula with services, hotels, restaurants, and clubs in the center. The one exception to the simplicity is that R. Koundourou, I. Koundourou, and S. Koundourou are three different streets—read addresses carefully.

Tourist Office: S. Koundourou 21A (☎28410 22 357; www.aghiosnikolaos.gr), across the bridge at the harbor. Posts accommodations, has transportation schedules and maps, displays car and bike rentals, and offers daytrip info and prices for nearby sights. Open Apr.-Nov. daily 8am-9:30pm.

Banks: Several on 28 Oktovriou have **24hr. ATMs. National Bank,** R. Koundourou (☎28410 23 725), exchanges currency and has 2 24hr. ATMs. **Western Union** available. Open M-Th 8am-2:30pm, F 8am-2pm.

Laundromat: Laundry Express (☎23787 23 349), at the corner of Fillelinon and Dimokratias. €4 per load. Open M-Tu and Th-F 8am-2pm and 5:30-9pm, W and Sa 8am-2pm.

Police: Stavrou 25 (☎28410 22 251). Walk up E. Stavrou off Paleologou from the harbor; it's on the left. Open 24hr. The **Tourist Police** (☎28410 91 418) are in the same building. Open 8am-3pm. There is also **Port Police** (☎28410 90 108).

Medical Services: Hospital of Agios Nikolaos (☎28410 43 000). **Medical Office** (☎28410 41 563), in Elounda.

Telephones: OTE (☎28410 95 333), on the corner of 25 Martiou and K. Sfakianaki. Open daily 8-3pm.

Internet Access: ▓ **Multiplace Peripou,** 28 Oktovriou 25 (☎28410 24 876). €4 per hr. Open daily 9:30am-late. **Du Lac Cafe,** 28 Oktovriou (☎28410 22 711), by the post office. €1 per 20min. Open daily 9:30am-late. Both offer free Wi-Fi with purchase.

Post Office: 28 Oktovriou 9 (☎28410 22 062). Open M-F 7:30am-2pm. Western Union available. **Postal Code:** 72100.

CRETE

ACCOMMODATIONS

Many large hotels in Agios Nikolaos fill up quickly. *Domatia* offer clean, cheap rooms, but they are in great demand, so reservations are recommended in July and August. The tourist office has listings and business cards of many of the city's pensions and their prices. Cheaper accommodations cluster inland near the Archaeological Museum and off I. Koundourou.

Hotel Angelos, S. Koundourou 16 (☎28410 23 501). With a prime waterfront location not too far from town, every room comes with a bath, TV, fridge, A/C, and a view of the sparkling sea. Bright, clean lobby with seating area. Market just downstairs. Singles €30-35; doubles €35-40; triples €50. MC/V. ❷

The Mediterranean Pension, Synt. Davaki 27 (☎28410 23 611). Walk up Paleologou away from the lake, turn right on Synt. Davaki, and look for the sign after 1 block. The kind and helpful owner of this clean and homey pension rents bright, airy rooms in a quiet residential area close to the harbor. Each room comes equipped with fan, fridge, and bath. A/C €5. Singles €25; doubles €25-30; triples €38. Cash only. ❷

Despina Christodoulaki, Stratigou Koraka 7 (☎28410 22 525). From the tourist office, turn away from the water and turn right onto the street behind the taxi stand. Walk up the hill and turn left onto Stratigou Koraka. The pension is unmarked; look for the profusion of plants. The 5 clean and cozy rooms share 2 common bathrooms with temperamental showers and a common kitchen. There is also a balcony with a table, chairs, and view of the ocean. Singles €20; doubles €20-25; triples €30-40. Cash only. ❶

Victoria Hotel, S. Koundourou 34 (☎28410 22 731; www.victoria-hotel.gr), about 1km from the harbor, near Ammoudi Beach. Though removed from the city center, this white stucco hotel has a comfy, 2-fl. lounge area and color-coordinated rooms with baths, phones, A/C, TVs, and fridges. Some rooms with small balconies. Prices vary greatly by view, floor, and season, so be sure to inquire beforehand. Singles €17-40; doubles €25-45; triples €35-55. MC/V ❷

FOOD

Agios Nikolaos's waterfront suffers from the predictable price inflation that accompanies the flooding of the city by summer vacationers. There are tasty and more reasonably priced restaurants without the view, as well as some supermarkets on R. Koundourou near the waterfront, off S. Venizelou near Ammos Beach, and on Paleologou toward the Archaeological Museum.

Taverna Trata, Akti Themistokleous (☎28410 220 28). Escape the main waterfront and head here for a wide range of traditional Greek dishes. The sea breeze coming off Kitroplatia Beach is a serene setting for an evening meal. Greek salad €4. *Stifado* €8. Open daily 11:30am-midnight. V. ❷

Itanos (☎28410 25 340), on Kyprou just off Pl. Venizelou. Tourist-friendly without being touristy. A rotating daily selection of dishes and homemade wine served straight out of the barrel. Kind waiters will invite you to the kitchen to look at the different dishes if you are having trouble choosing. Arrive early to snag the limited outdoor seating. Greek salad €4. Roast lamb with pasta €8. Open daily 10am-10 or 11pm. MC/V. ❷

Sarri's, Kyprou 15 (☎28410 28 059), 2 blocks down the street from Itanos. From the outdoor seating enclave shrouded in vines and white flowers, you can practically see your food being cooked in the kitchen and brought to your table. Check the specials board for great deals and combination meals such as chicken with potatoes, salad, and a glass of wine (€6). Open daily 9am-4pm and 5:30pm-11pm. Cash only. ❶

CRETE

Migomis, Plastira 24 (☎28410 24 353). Epitomizes a "special occasion" restaurant. Tasty food served in the classiest of classy settings—live piano plays every night, and the dining room has a tremendous panorama of the city. Appetizers €6-16. Entrees, including an impressive selection of meat and seafood, €12-30. Open daily 4-10pm. AmEx/MC/V. ❹

⊙ ⌕ SIGHTS AND BEACHES

Of all Crete's north coast cities, Agios Nikolaos boasts the most pristine beaches, with water so blue you'll want to drink it (don't). If you need to cool down after a day at the beach, there are a handful of museums interspersed among Agios Nikolaos's colorful pedestrian streets.

BEACHES. All of Agios Nikolaos's beaches are rated ◙**Blue Flag beaches** by the EU, meaning they're the cleanest of the clean. Constant sunshine and a lack of rain make them perfect tanning spots. Three of the beaches—Ammos, Kitroplatia, and Ammoudi—are a quick walk from the main harbor, but the farther you venture, the better they get. The largest local beach, **Ammos,** is by the National Stadium, and slightly smaller **Kitroplatia** is on Akti Panagou. The marina, **Ammoudi,** farther up S. Koundourou away from town, is a popular spot for families. Those with more lofty aspirations can walk 20min. south along the coast or catch the hourly bus to Ierapetra or Sitia and get off at **Almiros** (1km east of Agios Nikolaos). With an island outcropping flying the Greek flag and a long, uninterrupted stretch of fine sand, Almiros is arguably the area's best beach. Just up the hill lies an EU-protected wildlife reserve. A river runs through the reserve and gushes water into the sea at Almiros; the hot springs mix with the cold jet for a refreshing, spa-quality swim. Sandy **Vulisma Beach,** 10km farther near Kalo Chorio, is equally spectacular and less crowded, bordered by climbable, craggy formations. Tell the bus driver to let you off at the Kavos Taverna. Yet another beautiful, sandy spot with perhaps the clearest water is **Havania,** at the Havania stop on the Elounda bus.

ARCHAEOLOGICAL MUSEUM. Head away from the harbor on Paleologou to reach the museum, up a stone ramp on your right. Its collection includes artifacts from the Neolithic to Roman periods, such as Minoan clay sarcophagi with the original skeletons, a well-documented ancient coin collection, clay tablets with Linear A script, and art from the seventh century BC Daedalic period. The last room contains two of the collection's all-stars: an athlete's skull, adorned with both a gold-leaf wreath and a coin to pay the toll to the afterlife, and a bowl of knuckle bones used by the ancients to divine the future, ward off evil, and even play games. (☎28410 24 943. Open Tu-Su 8:30am-3pm. €3, seniors €2, students €1.50.)

FOLK MUSEUM. Next to the tourist office, this museum displays multi-colored woven goods, tapestries, and embroidery, as well as weapons, swords, icons, and objects from daily life on Crete from the 16th to 19th centuries BC. (☎28410 25 093. Open M-Sa 10:30am-4:30pm and 6-8pm. €3)

▣ ⚘ NIGHTLIFE AND FESTIVALS

Fashionable, young crowds gather at the waterfront clubs around the harbor on I. Koundourou and S. Koundourou. Greek and American movies play at **Christina's open-air theater** on Eth. Antistasis near the lake. Every even year, the last week in June or the first week in July brings **Nautical Week.** Greek seamen race in the waters around Agios Nikolaos during the day, and music and dancing fill the late nights. (☎28410 82 047 for info on cultural events and daily shows.) The **Feast of All Saints,** generally on a weekend in June, gives both tourists and locals the coveted chance to visit the forbidden **Island of All Saints** and attend a service at the island's single church. Due to its ecological value, visitors normally are banned from the uninhabited island and the endangered Kri-Kri goats are granted free rein.

■ **Multiplace Peripou,** 28 Oktovriou 25 (☎28410 24 876). This 1-stop entertainment spot has a cafe, bar, internet (€4 per hr.), and a book and music store for an arts-loving, international crowd. Oct.-May Sa offers a rotating showcase of local artists and live music (Greek traditional to jazz). Open daily 9:30am-late.

Puerto, at the corner of I. Koundourou and Evans. Young crowds fill the bright green couches that line this bar's waterfront seating. If the harbor seats are filled, head inside where you can drink at the bar on plush stools surrounded by low-hanging lamps and amusing posters. Frappés €2.80. Beer €4-5. Mixed drinks €6-7. Open daily 10am-late.

Aigalon (☎28410 22 535), by the bridge. Red paisley armchairs under an oak ceiling and chandeliers. Wine, beer, and an extensive selection of mixed drinks. Prime seating is on the balcony, where peaceful views of the bridge, lake, and harbor contrast with American 80s and 90s dance grooves and the Art Deco lounge. Beer €3-5. Mixed drinks €6.50. Open daily 9am-late.

IERAPETRA Ιεράπετρα ☎28420

Ierapetra (yer-AH-peh-tra) is an ideal blend between a big city and small town, with tree-lined streets and many cafes perfect for retreating to in the hottest hours of the day. Tourists and locals gather at restaurants along the waterfront and sun themselves along the strips of beach. Most visitors to Ierapetra, especially during the busy month of August, use it as a base for venturing out to Chrissi Island, 15km offshore. Arabs, Venetians, and Turks once made this a busy, worldly city, and their influences are preserved in the Archaeological Museum and the city's diverse architecture. Today, a laid-back pace and friendly locals preserve the small-town atmosphere.

▬ TRANSPORTATION

Buses: Station at Lasthenous 41 (☎28410 28 237). To **Iraklion** (2hr., 7 per day 6:30am-5pm, €10) via **Agios Nikolaos** (1hr., €3.50), **Myrtos** (20min., 6 per day 6:15am-8:15pm, €1.90), and **Sitia** (1hr., 2-4 per day 6:15am-6:15pm, €5.70).

Taxis: Radio Taxis (☎28410 26 600). Wait in Pl. Plastira, Pl. Venizelou, and Pl. Kanoupaki. 24hr.

Car Rental: Driver's Club, 7 Em. Lampraki St. (☎28410 25 583 or 69446 86 569), behind Ierapetra Express. Cars €35-50 per day. Open daily 9am-2pm and 4-10pm.

✖ ⁊ ORIENTATION AND PRACTICAL INFORMATION

Ierapetra can be difficult to navigate because of its long, maze-like streets. It has four main *plateias* connected by three roads that run from north to south. With your back to the bus station, **Plateia Plastira** is on the right. Walking straight for a block through Plastira on **Lasthenous** leads you to **Plateia Venizelou.** Here, Lasthenous becomes pedestrian-only **Koundouriotou.** Next is the central square: spacious, triangular **Plateia Eleftherias.** Keep walking in the same direction for about 100m to reach the final *plateia,* **Plateia Kanoupaki.** Beyond it is the **Old Town District** running along the waterfront, where the stone streets are crooked and the houses are nestled cozily together.

C R E T E

Tourist Office: Tourist info and maps are available at the kiosk (☎28410 90 014), located by the parking lot in the harbor behind Pl. Kanoupaki. Open daily 9am-1pm.

Ierapetra Express, Eleftherias 25 (☎28410 28 673). Offers travel services and a Western Union. Open M-F 8am-2pm and 5-9pm, Sa 9am-2pm and 5-8pm, Su 10am-noon.

Bank: National Bank, (☎28410 28 374), next to Ierapetra Express. **Currency exchange** and **24hr. ATM.** Open M-Th 8am-2:30pm, F 8am-2pm.

Police: (☎28410 90 160), between Pl. Eleftherias and Pl. Kanoupaki in the yellow building on the waterfront. Open 24hr. The **Tourist Police** (☎28410 90 176) is in the same building. Open 24hr.

Hospital: Kalimerake 6 (☎28410 90 222 or 90 223), north of the bus station, left off Lasthenous. Open 24hr.

Telephones: OTE, Koraka 25 (☎28410 22 799). Open M-F 7:30am-2:30pm.

Post Office: V. Kornarou (☎28410 24 915), on the west side of the Old Town. Open M-F 7:30am-2pm. **Postal Code:** 72200.

ACCOMMODATIONS AND CAMPING

Ierapetra caters mostly to upscale tourists, who want only the best after a day of sunbathing on Chrissi Island. Bargain-hunters looking for a cheaper scene should avoid the waterfront. Rooms for rent are far less common in Ierapetra than in other coastal towns, so prepare to resign yourself to slightly more expensive, if upscale, digs. After making a sharp right out of the bus station, you'll see signs leading to pensions. For a place in the heart of the city, there are more hotels and pensions nestled in the streets of the Old Town..

Cretan Villa, Lakerda 16 (☎28410 28 522; www.cretan-villa.com). 206-year-old building with white stone and stucco-walled rooms tastefully decorated with traditional crafts. Clean bath and satellite TV in each room. A/C €6 per night. Free Wi-Fi. Singles €30-40; doubles €40-50; triples €50-65. MC/V. ❸

Hotel Coral, Ioanidou 18 (☎28410 22 846). Walk down Kyrva past the taxis to the waterfront and make a right onto Ioanidou after passing the port police; Hotel Coral is to the right. Clean, simple rooms with baths, fridges, A/C, and TVs. Doubles €30-35; triples €40-45. Cash only. ❸

Koutsounari (☎28410 61 213), 7km from Ierapetra on the coastal road to Sitia near the restaurant, bar, and beach. Take the bus to Sitia via Makri Gialo (20min., 2-4 per day, €1.20) and ask to be let off at the campground. €5.50 per person; €4 per tent; €3.20 per car. Cash only. ❶

FOOD

Most of Ierapetra's waterfront restaurants are identically priced and have similar offerings, so make your choice based on which food and restaurant atmosphere looks most appealing. For basic foodstuffs and supplies, there is a **supermarket** on Dimokratias, off Pl. Kanoupaki.

Veterano (☎28410 23 175), on the corner of Pl. Eleftherias. A cafe and dessert bar away from the waterfront with a superior view of the palm-edged main *plateia*. Great people-watching and better pastries. Try the *kalitsounia*, an Ierapetrian sweet cheese tart. Open daily 7:30am-midnight. Cash only. ❶

Babi's Taverna, at the end of the row of waterfront *tavernas*. Prime waterfront position and great views of the city and fortress. The scent of freshly-caught seafood from the outdoor grill wafts throughout the palm frond-shaded waterfront seating. *Stifado* €7.50. Seafood dishes €8-13. Open daily 11:30am-1am. Cash only. ❷

👁 🌸 SIGHTS AND FESTIVALS

Held each summer in July and August, the **Kyrvia Festival** features music, dance, and theater performances at local schools; call tourist information (☎28410 90 014) for details.

ARCHAEOLOGICAL MUSEUM. Among the gems at Ierapetra's Archeological Museum are Minoan artifacts from the southern coast, red figure vases, inscribed tablets of treaties made between Cretan cities and Macedonia, and a worthwhile collection of Greek and Roman statues, all with helpful explanations in English. The sarcophagi in the second room, adorned by hunting scenes, are particularly well-preserved examples of Minoan paintings of daily life. The town's pride and joy, a nearly mint condition **Persephone statue** from the AD second century, sits prominently in the third room. *(At Pl. Kanoupaki across from the taxi stand. ☎ 28410 28 721. Open Tu-Sa 8:30am-3pm. €2, EU students free.)*

OLD TOWN. In the Old Town at Pl. Tzami., just off Nik. Vassarmidi, a 19th-century **mosque** and an **Ottoman fountain** are crumbling, and the patches of graffiti do not make them overly impressive sights, despite their venerability. The 13th-century restored **Venetian Fortress of Kales** at the southern end of the old harbor was reputedly built by the Genoese pirate Pescatore in 1212. While it provides a nice view of the town and sea, it is rather modest compared to some of the other fortresses on Crete. *(Open Tu-Su 8:30am-3pm. Free.)* Finally, you can glance at the facade of Napoleon's house, where he stayed in June 1798 on his way to conquer Egypt.

🏛 DAYTRIP FROM IERAPETRA

CHRISSI ISLAND. Ierapetra's star attraction is uninhabited Chrissi Island, 15km offshore. Twisted, water-starved trees and shrubs grow on windy sand dunes in the interior, while the higher ground to the left of the ferry landing is dotted with multicolored volcanic rocks. Chrissi is home to several endangered species and rare European cedars, and visitors are asked to treat the local fauna and flora with care. Most people come to Chrissi for its **beaches:** two long arcs of sand, one on the sea side by the ferry landing and the other facing Crete called Golden Beach. The beaches draw two boatloads of sunbathers daily to enjoy the sparkling turquoise waters and gusty breezes. If the hefty ferry price has you thinking twice, **camping** on the island is permitted. Throughout the summer months, there are a number of people that set up tents in the small patches of shade inland and take advantage of the island's empty hours before and after the daytrippers come. The dock-side, cafeteria-style **Chrissi Island Beach Bar and Restaurant ❶** serves sandwiches (€3), salads (€4-5), and more from the only significant shade on the island. (☎28103 00 032. Open June-Oct. daily 9am-midnight.) You can also rent an umbrella and sunbed set on the beaches for €5. *(Ferries leave Ierapetra May-Oct. daily 10:30am and 12:30pm and return at 4 and 5pm (€20 round-trip, ages 4-12 €15). Tickets are sold on board and at a number of waterfront agencies.)*

SITIA Σητεία ☎28430

A winding drive on coastal mountain roads from Agios Nikolaos leads to the peaceful port town of Sitia. The tourism industry has barely found its way here, and the town maintains a pace of life all its own: the gaudiness of souvenir stands and gift shops are nowhere to be found here. It may be the only north coast city where shop owners will speak to you in Greek first, English second, and restaurant hosts do not clamor for customers along the waterfront. Travelers blend with locals at the seaside *tavernas*, and beach blankets mix with fishing supplies between butcher shops, bakeries, and trendy clothing stores. Sitia also makes an excellent base for exploring Crete's eastern coast, and is the most convenient port for departures to Rhodes.

▐ TRANSPORTATION

Flights: Sitia Airport (JSH; ☎28430 24 666) connects Sitia to **Athens** (1hr., 4 per week, €75). Buy tickets at any travel agency in town.

Ferries: 2-3 ferries per week go to: **Milos** (10hr., €23.20) and **Piraeus** (15hr., €32.10) via **Iraklion** (2hr., €15.40) and **Santorini** (6hr. €22.20), as well as **Rhodes** (10hr., €26.40) via **Kassos** (2hr., €11.10) and **Karpathos** (4hr., €18). Schedules and routes often change weekly, so inquire upon your arrival into Sitia. **Dikta Travel,** Kornarou 150 (☎28430 25 080). Turn right off of Kapetan Sifi from Pl. Polytechniou. Open M-F 9am-9pm, Sa-Su 9-1pm and 5:30-8pm.

Buses: The station (☎28430 22 272) is out of town off Papandreou, inland from the tourist office. To: **Ierapetra** (1hr., 2-4 per day, €5.70); **Iraklion** (3hr., 7 per day, €13.80) via **Agios Nikolaos** (1hr., €7.30); **Kato Zakros** (1¼hr., 1-2 per day, €4.70); **Vai** (1hr., 2-3 per day, €3.10) via **Palaikastro** (20min., €2.30).

Taxis: (☎28430 22 700), in Pl. Polytechniou. 24hr.

Car Rental: Porto-Belis Travel, Karamanli 34 (☎28430 22 370; www.portobelis-crete. gr), along the waterfront. €30-55 per day, including insurance. Call ahead July-Aug. Open daily July-Sept. 9am-9pm, Oct. Apr.-June 9am-3pm and 5-8:30pm.

▐▐ ORIENTATION AND PRACTICAL INFORMATION

Plateia Iroön Polytechniou, the main square, is on the waterfront. With the back of the bus station on your left and the Archaeological Museum on your right, head down the street to the waterfront. Turn left onto K. Karamanli, which runs parallel to the water, to reach the **tourist office**—a small, clearly marked building on your right. Keep following K. Karamanli past the tourist office to reach **Plateia Polytechniou.**

Tourist Office: (☎28430 28 300), in the white building on the waterfront. Maps and information on accommodations, beaches, and restaurants. Checks bus schedules upon request. Open June-Oct. M-F 9:30am-2:30pm and 5-9pm, Sa 9:30am-2:30pm.

Banks: Emporiki Bank (☎28430 22 291) in Pl. Polytechniou. Open M-Th 8am-2:30pm, F 8am-2pm. **24hr. ATMs** line El. Venizelou, 1 street back from Pl. Polytechniou.

Police: Therissou 31 (☎28430 24 200). Follow Kapetan Sifi 2 blocks to Mysonos; go left and continue until it becomes Therissou. Also serves as **Tourist Police.** Open 24hr.

Hospital: (☎28430 24 311 or 24 312), past the police, off Therissou. Open 24hr.

Internet Access: J@va Cafe, V. Kornarou 113 (☎28430 22 263). Turn right off Kaptean Sifi onto V. Kornarou. Internet €2 per hr. Wi-Fi available. Open daily 9am-1am.

Post Office: Dimokritou 10 (☎28430 22 283). Walk inland on El. Venizelou and go left on Dimokritou; it will be on your right. **Currency exchange** and **Western Union.** Open M-F 7:30am-2pm. **Postal Code:** 72300.

▐ ACCOMMODATIONS

While many of the larger hotels occupy the waterfront on **Karamanli,** there are a number of smaller pensions and hotels behind the waterfront on the quieter streets of **Kornarou** and **Kondilaki.** Reserve ahead in July and August.

CRETE

▨ **Hotel Arhontiko,** Kondilaki 16 (☎28430 28 172). From Kapetan Sifi, take a right on Kondilaki and walk 3 blocks. Owner Alexandra may well be the warmest and most helpful host in Greece. If she's not inviting you for *raki* or apricots on the garden patio, she'll be ushering you into 1 of the bright, impeccably clean rooms, wood floors and private sinks. Singles €22-24; doubles €33-37; triples €38-42. Cash only. ❷

Rooms to Let Apostolis, Kazantzakis 27 (☎28430 22 993). From Pl. Polytechniou, head inland on Kapetan Sifi and turn right onto Fountalidou, then go left onto Kazantzakis after 2 blocks. Bright granite stairs lead to spacious rooms, each with bath, A/C, and fan. Friendly owners, a common fridge area, a covered balcony, and a securely locked front door complete the welcoming atmosphere. Doubles €30-37; triples €42-48. Cash only. ❸

Venus Rooms to Let, Kondilaki 60 (☎28430 24 307). Go uphill on Kapetan Sifi from the main *plateia* and take the 1st right after the OTE. Walk through the owners' living room to reach the 6 rooms with high ceilings and small, bright balconies in a purple flower-lined home. Watch your head on the stairs up to the 3rd fl. Doubles €25-30, with bath €30-33; triples €30/35. Cash only. ❷

▐ FOOD

Il Forno, El. Venizelou (☎28430 23 270), past Pl. Polytechniou toward the fortress. Diners can construct sweet dessert or hearty savory crepes (€2-5) from whatever strikes their fancy. Eat in the pleasant, harborside seating area. Delivery and take-out available. Waffles €4-6. Pizza €6-8. Open daily 6:30pm-late. Cash only. ❶

Cretan House, Karamanli 10 (☎28430 25 133). Turn right off the main *plateia* as you face the water and continue past the tourist office. The intriguing array of Cretan appetizers, such as snails with tomato sauce (€3.90) and cheese pies (€2.90), spices up the traditional menu at this waterfront *taverna*. Entrees €5-12. Open daily 11:30am-midnight. AmEx/MC/V. ❷

Taverna Mixos, V. Kornarou 117 (☎28430 22 416), 1 block up from Pl. Polytechniou. Serves souvlaki (€6-9) and other Greek dishes. The flavorful chicken fried rice with vegetables (€9) is large enough for 2. Sit at the quieter, traditional location on Kornarou or walk down the steps to the waterfront seating on El. Venizelou. Open daily 11:30am-4pm and 7pm-1am. MC/V. ❷

◉ ▐ SIGHTS AND BEACHES

Sitia's long beach extends 3km past the tourist office, and is separated from the main waterfront by the port, which provides a slightly more peaceful beach atmosphere. At some points, the roadway edges the beach, but there are a number of areas with comfortable expanses of undisturbed sand.

FORTRESS OF KAZAMARA. The Venetian fortress of Kazarma presides over the town from a high hill, offering a decent panorama to those who choose to make the short trek. It hosts Sitia's **Kornareia Festival,** which runs through late July and August, with open-air theater (€10-15) and free concerts of Greek music and dancing. The tourist office and small office within the fortress has details. *(Open Tu-Su 8:30am-2:30pm. Free.)*

ARCHAEOLOGICAL MUSEUM. The Archaeological Museum is the low, gray building opposite the bus station. It contains artifacts such as *pithoi* and sarcophagi from the many excavation sites around Sitia, which were once prominent Minoan peak sanctuaries used for worship and villas, or large country estates. It also shows items, such as numerous tablets engraved with Linear A, from the palace complex at Kato Zakros. The Minoan Palaikastro **kouros** at the entrance is a masterpiece made of hippopotamus ivory, with flecks of gold clothing and rock crystals for eyes. *(☎28430 23 917. Open daily 8:30am-3pm. €2, students and seniors €1, children and EU students free.)*

FOLKLORE MUSEUM. Sitia's Folklore Museum exhibits traditional 19th-century items from carvings to coins. *(Walk up Kapetan Sifi from the main plateia; the museum is on the right. ☎28430 22 861. Open M-Sa 10am-2pm. €2.)*

🎤 NIGHTLIFE

Sitia's nightlife is a mix of waterfront clubs and *tavernas* on **Eleftherios Venizelou,** where locals and out-of-towners lounge and drink well into the night.

Nouvelle Boutique, El. Venizelou 161 (☎28430 28 7580). The hottest waterfront bar in town, busy with groups of young Greeks every night. Lounge in the purple armchairs along the waterfront or gather around high wooden tables in the stone-walled, trendy interior. Coffee €2-4. Beer €3-5. Mixed drinks €5-8. Open daily 9:30am-late.

Pulse, El Venizelou (☎69741 94 416), a few doors down from Nouvelle Boutique. The outdoor lounge is identifiable by the psychedelic paintings on the front wall, bright orange chairs, and thumping dance beats. Mixed drinks €7. Open daily noon-late.

🏖 DAYTRIPS FROM SITIA

🏖VAI Βάϊ
Buses from Sitia to Vai (45min., 3 per day, €3.10) via Palaikastro (€2.30) stop in the parking lot in front of the beach. Bathrooms and pay showers (€0.50) are near the parking lot. Showers on the beach free. Chairs on the beach €4.50. Parking €2.

Not long ago, travelers headed to Vai to get off the beaten path. Today, tourists flock to this smooth, sandy beach, where they swim and rest under the shady fronds of Europe's only indigenous **palm-tree forest.** In the 1960s and 70s, Vai became a haven for British bands like Cream and 🎸**Led Zeppelin,** who would camp out, smoke out, and rock out under the palms. Nowadays, both camping and smoking are prohibited, whereas rocking out is merely frowned upon. The palm trees have been fenced off except for a small patch in the area immediately next to the beach. The sand is less crowded over the hill past the restaurant to the right; climb up to the viewpoint, pass through the gate, and follow the path over the hill. Those in search of a still more secluded beach experience should go left from the palm beach along the cliffs.

Although camping is forbidden in the park, many unroll their sleeping bags in this cove to the south of the palm beach. If sandy pajamas and the possibility of arrest don't appeal to you, you can rent a room in quiet Palaikastro, 8km toward Sitia. When you get hungry, try **Vai Restaurant and Cafe Snack Bar ❷.** (Tzatziki €4. Stuffed tomatoes €5.80. Open daily noon-7pm. MC/V.) If you don't want to stray too far from your sunbathing spot, there is a refreshment stand with ice creams, chips, and drinks. Still, you're probably better off packing a picnic. **Natura Water Sports**, on the beach, rents jet skis and other water sport equipment (☎28430 61070. €30 per 15min. for 1, €40 per 15min. for 2).

ZAKROS Ζάκρος
Buses run from Sitia to Zakros (1hr., 1-2 per day, €3.70) and Kato Zakros (1¼hr., 1-2 per day, €4.70) via Palaikastro. Buses stop in Zakros on the main plateia and pick up in Kato Zakros along the main road in front of the harbor, just before Nikos Platanakis Taverna. Follow red arrows, E4, and labeled gorge signs leading away from the Zakros plateia marking

CRETE

the path through the Valley of Death (2hr.). It is a 1.5km walk from the town of Zakros to the official entrance to the Gorge.

Surrounded by cliffs and streams and carpeted in brilliant wildflowers and lush shrubbery, the 6.5km hike through the ▧**Valley of Death** leads from the quiet village of Zakros to the beach enclave Kato Zakros. The ravine, also known as "Death's Gorge," got its morbid name from the beehive of surrounding caves in which the Minoans buried their dead. A fast-flowing stream winds its way between sheer cliffs during the winter and spring. The wildlife includes the usual herds of fearless wild goats, along with a charming selection of snakes and ubiquitous bees sampling the gorge's many flowering plants. Although it's difficult to wander too far astray in any gorge, the path can occasionally be hard to follow; it is frequently but discreetly designated by red paint markings on rocks. In some areas, the vegetation is so overgrown that it will surround you on all sides. Bring water and snacks and wear sturdy shoes to negotiate the occasional rocky climb. Keep an eye out for *phaskomilo*, a sweet-smelling tea plant with small, fuzzy leaves, and onion plants, whose purple flowers are virtually inescapable in the gorge.

At the end of the gorge, turn left and look for the sign pointing past the olive groves to the **Palace of Zakros.** Destroyed in 1450 BC by the mysterious cataclysm of Minoan civilization, the ruins of the palace extend up a hill with views to the sea and farmland below. Although the site is undergoing excavation and currently lacks modern facilities, the stone ruins hint at ancient Crete's opulence. Royalty once bathed in pools near the bottom of the hill, now home to many turtles. There are no signs throughout the palace, however a map and brief explanation is provided upon entrance. (☎28430 26 897. Open daily 8am-3pm. €3, students free.)

Continue along the path away from the palace to the sleepy beach town of **Kato Zakros.** Its waterfront is largely free from clutter, and its beach provides a refreshing, if pebbly, dip after a dusty hike through the gorge. **Nikos Platanakis Taverna ❷,** under shady pine trees with views of the ocean, has friendly, multilingual waiters who serve fresh fish and vegetables from the owner's farm. (☎28430 26 887. Entrees €5-8. Open Apr.-Nov. daily 8am-11:30pm. MC/V.)

CRETE

APPENDIX

CLIMATE

The climate varies significantly between regions of Greece. Southern islands like Crete and Santorini can be exceedingly hot and dry, while the lush Ionians are cooler and receive more rainfall. High-altitude areas (especially in the north) are cooler, and snow lingers on some mountaintops through summer. For the most part, summer is sunny, hot, and dry. In winter, temperatures settle around 50°F, and snow occasionally falls as far south as Athens. The rainy season lasts from October to March.

AVG. TEMP. (LOW/ HIGH), PRECIP.	JANUARY			APRIL			JULY			OCTOBER		
	°C	°F	mm	°C	°F	mm	°C	°F	mm	°C	°F	mm
Athens	6/13	43/55	62	11/20	52/68	23	23/33	73/91	6	15/24	59/75	51
Naxos	10/15	50/59	91	13/20	55/68	14	22/27	72/81	2	18/24	64/75	45
Thessaloniki	2/9	36/48	44	10/20	50/68	41	21/32	70/90	22	13/22	55/72	57
Trikala	0/9	32/48	84	8/21	46/70	80	19/35	66/95	19	12/25	53/77	80

To convert degrees Fahrenheit to degrees Celsius, subtract 32 and multiply by 5/9. To convert Celsius to Fahrenheit, multiply by 9/5 and add 32.

°CELSIUS	-5	0	5	10	15	20	25	30	35	40
°FAHRENHEIT	23	32	41	50	59	68	77	86	95	104

MEASUREMENTS

Like the rest of the rational world, Greece uses the metric system. The basic unit of length is the meter (m), which is divided into 100 centimeters (cm) or 1000 millimeters (mm). One thousand meters make up one kilometer (km). Fluids are measured in liters (L), each divided into 1000 milliliters (mL). A liter of pure water weighs one kilogram (kg), which is divided into 1000 grams (g). One metric ton is 1000kg.

MEASUREMENT CONVERSIONS	
1 inch (in.) = 25.4mm	1 millimeter (mm) = 0.039 in.
1 foot (ft.) = 0.305m	1 meter (m) = 3.28 ft.
1 yard (yd.) = 0.914m	1 meter (m) = 1.094 yd.
1 mile (mi.) = 1.609km	1 kilometer (km) = 0.621 mi.
1 ounce (oz.) = 28.35g	1 gram (g) = 0.035 oz.
1 pound (lb.) = 0.454kg	1 kilogram (kg) = 2.205 lb.
1 fluid ounce (fl. oz.) = 29.57mL	1 milliliter (mL) = 0.034 fl. oz.
1 gallon (gal.) = 3.785L	1 liter (L) = 0.264 gal.

APPENDIX

LANGUAGE AND ALPHABET

The Greek alphabet has 24 letters. In the chart below, the left column gives the name of each letter in Greek, the middle column shows capital and lower case letters, and the right column shows the pronunciation. Greek words often have an accent mark called a *tonos* (τόνος). The *tonos* appears over the vowels of multi-syllabic words and tells you where the stress lies. The stress can change the meaning of the word, so the *tonos* is essential for understanding and communication. The semicolon (;) is the Greek question mark (?).

SYMBOL	NAME	PRONUNCIATION	SYMBOL	NAME	PRONUNCIATION
A α	alpha	*a* as in **f**ather	N ν	nu	*n* as in **n**et
B β	beta	*v* as in **v**elvet	Ξ ξ	xi	*x* as in mi**x**
Γ γ	gamma	*y* or *g* as in **yo**ga	O o	omicron	*o* as in **r**ow
Δ δ	delta	*th* as in **th**ere	Π π	pi	*p* as in **p**eace
E ε	epsilon	*e* as in j**e**t	P ρ	rho	*r* as in **r**oll
Z ζ	zeta	*z* as in **z**ebra	Σ σ/ς	sigma	*s* as in **s**ense
H η	eta	*ee* as in qu**ee**n	T τ	tau	*t* as in **t**ent
Θ θ	theta	*th* as in **th**ree	Y υ	upsilon	*ee* as in gr**ee**n
I ι	iota	*ee* as in tr**ee**	Φ φ	phi	*f* as in **f**og
K κ	kappa	*k* as in **k**ite	X χ	chi	*h* as in **h**orse
Λ λ	lambda	*l* as in **l**and	Ψ ψ	psi	*ps* as in oo**ps**
M μ	mu	*m* as in **m**oose	Ω ω	omega	*o* as in Let's **Go**

Greek has a few sounds that are not intuitive for English speakers. For example, **gh** marks a muted "g" sound produced from the back of your throat. **Dth** denotes a hard "th," as in "thee," as opposed to a soft "th," as in "three." Delta is most often pronounced with a hard "th." Below is a list of challenging double consonants and vowels that do not follow the above pronunciations.

PHONETIC UNIT	PRONUNCIATION	PHONETIC UNIT	PRONUNCIATION
αι	*eh* as in **e**lement	μπ	*b* as in **b**aby
αυ	*ahf/ahv* as in **c**offin/impro**v**	ντ	*d* as in **d**une
γγ	*ng* as in E**ng**lish	ου	*oo* as in s**oo**n
γκ	*g* as in **g**od	οι	*ee* as in b**ee**t
ει	*ee* as in b**ee**t	τζ	*tz* sound or *j* as in **j**ockey
ευ	*ef/ev* as in **ef**fort/**ev**er	υι	*ee* as in b**ee**t

PHRASEBOOK

ENGLISH	GREEK	ENGLISH	GREEK
yes	neh	**no**	oh-hee
okay	en-DAH-kse	**sorry/pardon me**	sig-NO-mee
please/you're welcome	pah-rah-kah-LO	**Thank you (very much).**	Ef-hah-ree-STO (po-LEE).
Help!	vo-EE-thee-ah!	**I am ill.**	EE-meh AH-rose-tose.
I don't understand.	dthen kah-tah-lah-VEH-no.	**I don't speak Greek.**	dthen meel-AOH eh-lee-nee-KAH.
How much does it cost?	PO-so KAH-nee?	**Do you speak English?**	mee-LAH-teh ang-lee-KAH?
FEELINGS			
I love you.	sah-gah-POW.	**I miss you.**	moo LEE-pees.
friend	FEE-los (m)/FEE-lee (f)	**single/free**	eh-LEF-the-ros
happy	ha-ROO-meh-nos	**sad**	lee-pee-MEH-nos

GREETINGS			
Good morning/day.	kah-lee-MEH-rah.	**Good night.**	kah-lee-NEE-htah.
hello/goodbye (polite plural)	yah sahs	**hello/goodbye (familiar)**	yah soo
Mr./Sir	KEE-ree-os	**Ms./Madam**	kee-REE-ah
My name is...	meh LEH-neh...	**What is your name?**	pos seh LEH-neh?

GETTING AROUND			
How much will the trip cost?	PO-so tha KAH-nee tah tax-EE-dee?	**Start the meter.**	ar-HEE-steh to me-tree-TEE.
I am going to...	pee-GHEH-no sto...	**I need a ticket.**	hree-AH-zo-meh ee-see-TEE-ree-o.
I am lost.	HA-thee-kah.	**Where are we going?**	poo pahs?
When do we leave?	tee O-rah FEV-ghoo-meh?	**here/there**	eh-DTHO/eh-KEE
left	ah-rees-teh-RAH	**right**	dthe-KSYAH

TIME			
Monday	dtheh-FTEH-ra	**yesterday**	htehs or ktes
Tuesday	TREE-tee	**tomorrow**	AV-ree-o
Wednesday	TEH-tar-tee	**now**	TO-rah
Thursday	PEM-ptee	**What time is it?**	tee O-rah EE-neh?
Friday	pah-rah-skeh-VEE	**afternoon**	ah-PO-ghev-mah
Saturday	SAH-vah-to	**weekend**	sah-vah-to-RRE-rya-ko
Sunday	kee-ree-ah-KEE	**today**	SEE-mer-a
morning	pro-EE	**daily**	kah-thee-meh-ree-NOS
evening	VRAH-dthee	**year**	HRO-nos or EH-tos

ACCOMMODATIONS AND FOOD			
Can I see a room?	bo-RO nah dtho E-nah dtho-MAH-tee-o?	**Do you have...**	MEE-pose EH-he-teh?
I need...	hree-AH-zo-meh...	**I want...**	THEH-lo...
I will buy this one.	thah ah-gho-RAH-so ahf-TO.	**I would like...**	THAH EE-the-lah...
cheap	ftee-NO	**expensive**	ah-kree-VO
good	kah-LO	**bad**	kah-KOS
Does this have meat?	EH-hee KRAY-auf-TO eh-DTHO?	**I'm allergic to...**	EE-may ah-lehr-ghee-KOS seh...
The bill, please.	oh lo-ghah-ree-yah-SMOS, pah-rah-kah-LOW.	**Cheers!**	yah mahs!

NUMBERS			
zero	mee-DTHEN	**sixteen**	dthe-kah-EH-xee
one	EH-nah	**seventeen**	dthe-kah-ep-TAH
two	DTHEE-o	**eighteen**	dthe-kah-okh-TO
three	TREE-ah	**nineteen**	dthe-kah-en-YAH
four	TES-eh-rah	**twenty**	EE-ko-see
five	PEN-deh	**twenty-one**	EE-ko-see EH-nah
six	EH-xee	**thirty**	tree-AHN-dah
seven	ep-TAH	**forty**	sa-RAHN-dah
eight	okh-TO	**fifty**	peh-NEEN-dah
nine	en-YAH	**sixty**	eh-XEEN-dah
ten	DTHEH-kah	**seventy**	ev-dho-MEEN-dah
eleven	EN-dheh-kah	**eighty**	og-DHON-dah
twelve	DTHO-dheh-kah	**ninety**	eh-neh-NEEN-dah
thirteen	dthe-kah-TREE-ah	**one hundred**	eh-kah-TO
fourteen	dthe-kah-TES-ser-ah	**thousand(s)**	hil-YAH(-dthes)
fifteen	dthe-kah-PEN-deh	**one million**	eh-kah-to-MEE-ree-o

APPENDIX

TRANSPORTATION		
airplane	αεροπλάνο	ah-eh-ro-PLAH-no
bus	λεωφορείο	leh-o-fo-REE-o
car	αυτοκίνητο	af-to-KEE-nee-to
ferry	πλοίο	PLEE-o
international	εξωτερικός	ex-oh-teh-ree-KOS
island capital/main town	χώρα	HO-rah
long-distance	υπεραστικός	ee-peeh-ras-tee-KOS
passport	διαβατήριο	dthaya-vah-TEE-ri-o
port	λιμάνι	lee-MAH-nee
suitcase	βαλίτσα	vah-LEE-tsah
taxi	ταξι	tah-KSEE
ticket	εισιτήριο	ee-see-
train	τραίνο	TREH-no
SIGNS		
bank	τράπεζα	TRAH-peh-zah
church	εκκλησία	eh-klee-SEE-ah
closed	κλειστό	klee-STO
doctor	γιατρός	yah-TROSE
hospital	νοσοκομείο	no-so-ko-MEE-o
hotel	ξενοδοχείο	kse-no-dtho-HEE-o
open	ανοικτό	ah-nee-KTO
pharmacy	φαρμακείο	fahr-mah-KEE-o
police	αστυνομία	as-tee-no-MEE-a
post office	ταχυδρομείο	ta-hee-dthro-MEE-o
room	δωμάτιο	dtho-MAH-tee-o
toilet	τουαλέτα/λουτρό	twa-LE-ta/loo-TRO
FOOD		
baklava	μπακλαβά	bah-klah-VAH
bread	ψωμί	pso-MEE
butter	βούτυρο	VOO-tee-ro
cafe	καφενείο	kah-feh-NEE-o
casual restaurant	ταβέρνα	ta-VEHR-na
cheese	τυρί	ti-REE
chicken	κοτόπουλο	ko-TO-poo-lo
cucumber	αγγούρι	ah-GOU-ree
egg	αβγό	ahv-GHO
egg-lemon soup or sauce	αβγολέμονο	ahv-gho-LEH-mo-no
fish	ψάρι	PSAH-ree
grape leaves stuffed with rice and/or meat (large/small)	δολμάδες/δολμαδάκια	dthol-MAH-dthes/dthol-mah-DTHAH-kya
Greek meatballs	κεφτέδες	kef-TEH-dhes
gyro (meat wrapped in a pita)	γύρο	GHEE-ro
ice cream	παγωτό	pah-gho-TO
lamb	αρνάκι	ar-NA-kee
stew with meat and onions	στιφάδο	stee-FAH-dho
mezedes (assorted appetizers)	μεζέδες/μεζεδάκια	meh-ZEH-dthes/meh-zeh-DTHAH-kya
milk	γάλα	GHAH-lah
moussaka (lasagna-like dish)	μουσακά	moo-sah-KAH
nuts	καρύδια	kah-REE-dthya
pastry-cheese pie	τυρόπιτα	tee-RO-pee-tah

APPENDIX

raki (anise-flavored liqueur)	ρακή	rah-KEE
restaurant	εστιατόριο	es-tee-ah-TO-ree-o
salt	αλάτι	ah-LA-tee
souvlaki (meat on a skewer)	σουβλάκι	soo-VLAH-kee
sweets	γλυκά	ghlee-KAH
water	νερό	ne-RO

GLOSSARY OF USEFUL TERMS

acropolis	fortified high place atop a city	**amphora**	two-handled vessel for oil or wine storage
apse	nook beyond the altar of a church	**architrave**	lintel/lowest part of the entablature resting on columns
atrium	Roman house's open interior courtyard	**basilica**	an especially holy church with a saint's relic
bouzouki	pear-shaped stringed instrument	**capital**	top of a column
catamaran	usually high-speed double-hulled boat	**cella**	inner sanctum of an ancient temple or Byzantine church
Corinthian column	ornate column with engraved acanthus leaves and spirals (volutes)	**Cyclopean walls**	massive, irregularly cut Minoan and Mycenaean stone walls, so called because only a Cyclops could lift such stones
domatia	rooms to rent in private homes	**Doric column**	austere column with wide fluted shafts, cushion top capital, and no base
exedra	curved recess in Classical and Byzantine architecture	**Faneromeni**	term used in Orthodox symbolism to refer to the revealed Virgin Mary
forum	Roman public square or marketplace	**frieze**	decorated middle part of a temple exterior (in particular, the entablature)
heroon	shrine to a demigod	**iconostasis**	screen that displays Byzantine icons
Ionic column	slender column topped with twin scrolling spirals (volutes)	**Katharevusa**	snooty, "pure" Greek literary language, taken from ancient Greek
katholikon	a monastery's main church or chapel	**koini**	"common" Greek used before the Byzantine era
kore	female statue	**kouros**	male nude statue
KTEL	intercity bus service	**malaka**	common obscenity connoting masturbation
megaron	large hall in a house or palace	**meltemi**	unusually strong north wind in the Cyclades and Dodecanese
minaret	a tall, slender tower attached to a mosque, with one or more balconies	**narthex**	vestibule on the west side of a Byzantine church
odeon	semi-circular theater	**OSE**	Hellenic Railways Organization (Greece's national rail)
OTE	Greek national telephone company	**palaestra**	Classical gymnasium
pantheon	the gods of mythology considered collectively	**pediment**	triangular, sculpture-decorated space in an ancient temple's facade
periptero	streetside kiosk selling everything from phone cards to candy bars	**peristyle**	colonnade around a building
plateia	town square	**portico**	colonnade or peristyle
pronaos	outer column-lined temple porch	**propylaion**	sanctuary entrance
prytaneion	public dining room and symbolic heart of a city-state	**stele**	stone slab that marks a tomb or holds an inscription
stoa	public building fronted by rows of columns in ancient marketplaces	**tholos**	earth-covered, beehive-shaped Mycenaean tomb
triglyph	part of a Doric frieze composed of 3 vertical grooves that alternate with metopes	**trireme**	ancient ship with 3 sets of oars

INDEX

INDEX

511

INDEX

INDEX

MAP INDEX

MAP LEGEND

✚ Hospital	✈ Airport	⛪ Monastery	♨ Spring
℞ Pharmacy	🚌 Bus Station	∴ Ancient Site	⌒ Cave
✪ Police	🚆 Train Station	🏛 Museum	♨ Bath
✉ Post Office	Ⓜ Metro Station	🚻 Restrooms	🗼 Lighthouse
ⓘ Tourist Office	💻 Internet Cafe	🏖 Beach	
🏛 Temple	🏨 Hotel/Hostel	Park	
$ Bank	✝ Church	⛺ Camping	
🚩 Embassy/Consulate	✡ Synagogue	🍴 Restaurant	Beach
■ Site or Point of Interest	Mosque	Nightlife	
☎ Telephone Office	Castle	⚓ Ferry Route/Landing	Water
🎭 Theater	▲▲ Mountain	Pedestrian Zone	
📚 Bookstore/Library	⛰ Mountain Range	Stairs	

The Let's Go compass always points NORTH.

HELPING LET'S GO. If you want to share your discoveries, suggestions, or corrections, please drop us a line. We appreciate every piece of correspondence, whether a postcard, a 10-page email, or a coconut. Visit Let's Go at **http://www.letsgo.com,** or send email to:

feedback@letsgo.com, subject: "Let's Go Greece"

Address mail to:

Let's Go Greece, 67 Mount Auburn St., Cambridge, MA 02138 , USA

In addition to the invaluable travel advice our readers share with us, many are kind enough to offer their services as researchers or editors. Unfortunately, our charter enables us to employ only currently enrolled Harvard students.

Maps by Let's Go copyright © 2010 by Let's Go, Inc.

Distributed by Publishers Group West.
Printed in Canada by Friesens Corp.

Let's Go Greece Copyright © 2010 by Let's Go, Inc. All rights reserved. No part of this book may be used or reproduced in any manner whatsoever without written permission except in the case of brief quotations embodied in critical articles or reviews. Let's Go is available for purchase in bulk by institutions and authorized resellers.

ISBN-13: 978-1-59880-302-0
ISBN-10: 1-59880-302-6
Tenth edition
10 9 8 7 6 5 4 3 2 1

Let's Go Greece is written by Let's Go Publications, 67 Mount Auburn St., Cambridge, MA 02138, USA.

Let's Go® and the LG logo are trademarks of Let's Go, Inc.

LEGAL DISCLAIMER. For 50 years, Let's Go has published the world's favorite budget travel guides, written entirely by students and updated periodically based on the personal anecdotes and travel experiences of our student writers. Although every effort was made to ensure that the information was correct at the time of going to press, the author and publisher do not assume and hereby disclaim any liability to any party for any loss or damage caused by errors, omissions, or any potential travel disruption due to labor or financial difficulty, whether such errors or omissions result from negligence, accident, or any other cause.

ADVERTISING DISCLAIMER. All advertisements appearing in Let's Go publications are sold by an independent agency not affiliated with the editorial production of the guides. Advertisers are never given preferential treatment, and the guides are researched, written, and published independent of advertising. Advertisements do not imply endorsement of products or services by Let's Go, and Let's Go does not vouch for the accuracy of information provided in advertisements.

If you are interested in purchasing advertising space in a Let's Go publication, contact: Edman & Company, 1-203-656-1000.